Annotations for the History of the Classical Guitar in Argentina 1822-2000 Vol. IV

Qué impresión tiene uotod de la Argentina?
— preguntan
a Saint-Saëns.

— Es el paraíso terrenal de los músicos...

The composer Saint-Saëns was asked:
"What impression do you have of Argentina?"

He replied:

"It's an earthly paradise of musicians. . ."

This quote is from the weekly magazine *"Caras y caretas"* published in Buenos Aires on December 3, 1932, issue no. 1,783, page 28.

The cover image of Maria Luisa Anido and Miguel Llobet is from *"La Guitarra"* magazine Issue No. 4 of February 1926, drawn by Dr. Samuel Mallo Lopez, his sketches adorn this book.

by Randy Osborne and Héctor García Martínez

Translation and Photo Documentation by Randy Osborne Index by Jan J. de Kloe

Fine Fretted String Instruments
2345 Winchester Blvd. Suite B
Campbell, Ca. USA 95008
First Edition February 2020
www.finefretted.com
M-S 9:00 – 5:30 PM (408) 879-9930

ISBN 978-1-7345294-3-2

The Guitar in Uruguay

This biography of Isaias Savio is translated from Ricardo Muñoz's unpublished book *"Historia Universal de la Guitarra"* Volume VI *"America"* (South America).

The information through 1932 is derived from Domingo Prat's *"Diccionario de Guitarristas"*, all subsequent information is from Ricardo Muñoz's indefatigable research.

"Isaias Savio

His Origin:

He was born in Montevideo, Republic of Uruguay, on the 1st of February of 1902.

His Education:

He began his musical studies at the age of nine years old, with the organist *Don* Carlos Dubar and practiced the piano for a few years, in 1917 he abandoned the instrument for the guitar beginning with the late Conrado P. Koch.

His Virtuosity:

He had the necessary superior technique, to give concerts in Montevideo at the Sociedad *"Jutip-Raimi"* in the year 1929, obtaining a resounding triumph that permitted him to continue his successful performances one after another.

El concertista uruguayo Isaias Savio que dio un recital de guitarra en la reunión ofrecida por la sociedad Yntip-Raymi en el local del citado colega.

This photo of Isaias Savio is from the *"Reuniones Culturales"* section of the *"Caras y Caretas"* magazine of June 30, 1928 issue No. 1552 Año XXXI.

The translation is: "The Uruguayan concert guitarist Isaias Savio who gave a guitar recital at a reunion offered by the *"Yntip-Raymi"* (sic) society in the location of the cited colleague."

For the first time a Uruguayan guitarist showed his instrument with thse praise of the press and the public in the European and American halls, where he amply brought forth, without propaganda, nor Bengal lights, until in 1931 he visited Porto Alegre, Brazil causing a real sensation, the motive of which being invited by the "Instruccion Artistica do Brasil" in Sao Paulo, which contracted him for a series of concerts in the Teatro Municipal. —

He then made a tour for the interior of the country and returned to Sao Paulo; he performed in the same theater on February 11, 1932 with the eminent Brazilian pianist Anthony Rudge and the quarteto Brazil; the 15th of June he gave a concert in Rio de Janeiro in the Teatro San Nicolas, and the press called him the greatest virtuoso of the guitar; the 23rd of July he played in Belo Horizonte, and obtained one the most consecrated triumphs; on the 11th of August a daily of Minas Geraes said:

Portuguese translation by Randy Osborne:

"Yesterday Mr. Isaias Savio gave his first guitar concert in the Teatro Municipal for the Mineiro public, there is no doubt that he is truly an extraordinary artist, a holder of all the secrets of the difficult instrument, for those of us who were able to hear him yesterday the illustrious Uruguayan guitarist demonstrated the great exposition that he can attain with the guitaristic technique.

And some, as a matter of fact, couldn't have been the impression of those that followed, the surprise of an unexpected revelation, that the pieces of the prodigious descriptive suite, through whose interpretation, made with an impulse of the best emotion, with so much clarity, to emphasize the strong characteristics of the high musical vocation that implies the hot temperament of Mr. Savio, the artist.

Beyond this, his other compositions, as well in a deep hardship and the form in the stimulation of the creative emotion, were taken, the guitar under the most lively applause of the audience, as you see for example, the interpretation of the *"Cajita de Música"*, the true filigree of a melody.

Mr. Isaias Savio is an artist who has the capacity to captivate the most educated guitar audience, unless at such a time by a desire to musically express, he will propose melodically rather than use the line of severity and a portion of classic good taste, as he puts in the performance of the sheet music.

— Nevertheless, the folkloric interpreter is full of life and brilliance.

In yesterday's recital, by the applause the audience gave the invited, the Uruguayan maestro had the best demonstration of his great art that had caused true admiration by the audience of Belo Horizonte."

ISAIAS SAVIO

Return to Spanish translation:

The 14th of July of 1951 he performed before a knowledgeable public of the *"Centro Violonistico"* and the 29th of July of 1953 for the *"Associacao Brasileira de Violao"* works by Sor, Beethoven, Mendelssohn, Alba, Waldemar, etc. with true applause of rejoicing.

His Compositions:

For his admirable musical pages he is viewed as one of the most distinguished spirits of the South American guitar, whose magnificent pages of correct writing and construction are considered excellent, such as his *"Preludios"*, especially the one dedicated to Amalita Olave in La menor in 2/4 time, in which the blending of the two melodies, one in the treble and the other in the bass in a consonant form in a delicate arpeggio.

As well he has a group of works formed of *mazurkas, allegros, bourées, pensamientos, pequeña romanzas*, studies, waltzes, *scherzos*, suites, and stylized songs of the Brazilian folklore, that make the delicacies of the performers of the land.

His Pedagogy:

In his capacity as a maestro he attends to a select number of students, he has also spoken relating the life of the great Tárrega in his homage the 15th of January of 1949, the life of Fernando Sor the 19th of February, Mauro Giuliani the 27th of August and Antonio Sinopoli the 26th of November of the same year; he is a Delegate of the Instituto Interamericano de Musicologia and Director of the Departmento de Musica de la Sociedad Panamericana and Professor of the Conservatorio de Sao Paulo.

He has written his book: *"Escuela Superior de Guitarra"* published by D. C. Mangione editan A Melodia, Sao Paulo-Brasil on the 9th of March of 1942, with 49 pages. — When you open the volume you immediately read: Preface, with interesting clarifications, it proceeds with 25 magnificent studies of arpeggios, trills, apoyaturas, legatos, tremolo, chords for three or more fingers, all absolutely his own, nothing foreign with strange pretensions and in this way he surrenders his knowledge and to the public conscience for whom aspire to meditate, play, and feel the exquisite sensibilities of the author.—

Every study he dedicated to a known maestro, to the great Llobet, Pujol, Oyanguren, Prat and other local ones and students; his soul of the human artist and pleasing sense in the family, not forgetting his mother and wife, for whom he dedicated the studies numbers 15 and 25 respectively."

In the 1931 Antigua Casa Nuñez catalog there are 38 compositions by Isaias Savio listed.

Maestro Savio's most well known student is the world-renowned Brazilian guitar virtuoso, Carlos Barbosa-Lima, who recorded his first LP at the age of 13 in 1959.

Below is the dedication to Segundo Contreras from Isaias Savio on the cover of a handwritten manuscript of *"Cajita de Música"*. Translation:

"To the maestro and notable historian Segundo N. Contreras. With all sincerity and profound admiration. Isaias Savio, Sao Paulo January 18, 1947."

Archive: Segundo N. Contreras.

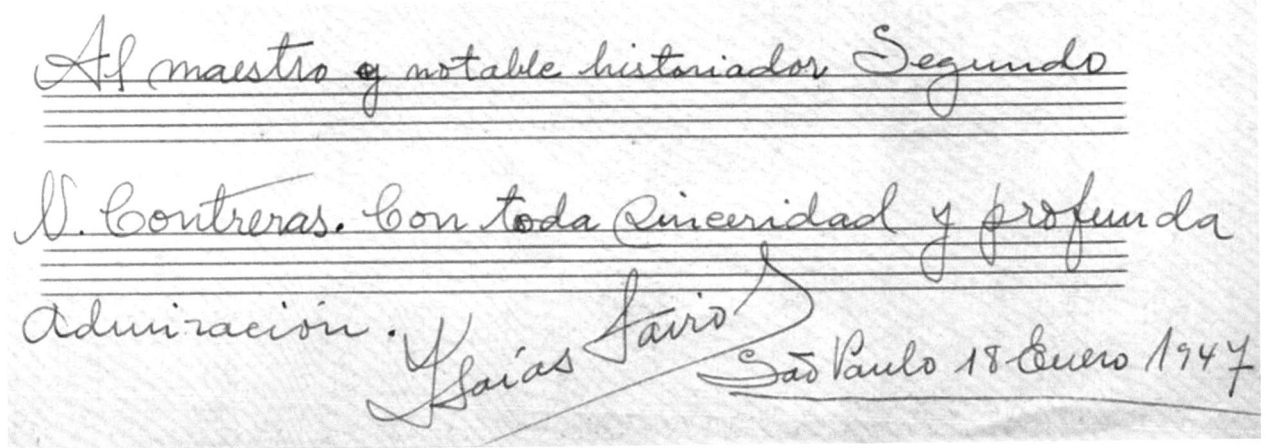

ISAIAS SAVIO

by James M. Leigh (*Brazil and U.S.A.*)

ISAIAS SAVIO was born in Montevideo in 1900. He received his early musical education in that city at the Franz Liszt Conservatory where he studied piano and harmony. Savio was attracted early to the guitar and spent eight years with Professor Konrad Koch, with whom he developed into a concert guitarist.

Savio left Uruguay in 1924 for Argentina where he gave concerts in many cities. He returned to his own country in 1930 where he continued playing in public but in 1931 he moved to Brazil and has been there ever since.

Brazil owes a debt of gratitude and thanks to the Uruguayan maestro who, for the past 27 years has dedicated himself to all aspects of the guitar in that country.

Prior to Savio's arrival in Brazil, the guitar was known chiefly as an instrument to accompany songs and dances, admittedly interesting, of the various regions of the country. The classic guitar, as we call it, practically did not exist. Savio's first important work was his pioneering activities which consisted of giving concerts in the then-remote corners of the Republic (some of those corners are "still-remote") where the inhabitants had never dreamed that such music could be produced by the guitar. These early concerts helped create a new interest in the instrument which, since then, has become more intense yearly.

Savio resided during the first few years in the "Marvellous City" of Rio de Janeiro where he established himself as the outstanding teacher of the instrument. He has lived in Sao Paulo since 1940, where he also quickly established himself as the leading authority on the guitar.

Most of Brazil's first-class teachers of today have felt Savio's influence by having studied with him directly or with one of his disciples. Miss Julieta Correa Antunes, a Director of the São Paulo Guitar School, and Mr. Antonio Rebello of Rio de Janeiro, two of the most important teachers of Brazil, are Savio trained.

Certainly one of the positive steps in introducing the classic guitar in Brazil was the forming in 1947 of the guitar "chair" in the São Paulo conservatory of Dramatics and Music which, of course, was awarded to Professor Savio, who still holds it. Since then, most of the country's conservatories have followed suit and it is now possible to receive one's degree in music with the guitar as the major instrument of study. Savio is also a professor at the Paulista Music Academy and is Supervisor at the São Paulo Guitar School. For four years he was a delegate to the International Institute of Musicology.

Savio began composing for the guitar at an early age and now has well over 100 original works and transcriptions published. Like all busy and active men, he has innumerable not-quite-finished manuscripts "lying around". His friends and students are urging him to put the finishing touches on these

Continued on page 12

This is from the "Guitar News" magazine issue No. 46 of January-February 1959.

GUITARIST IN BRAZIL

Photo by   A. Wiley

ISAIAS SAVIO

This photo is from the "Guitar News" magazine issue No. 46 of January-February 1959.

pieces so they may be published. The writer of these notes has heard parts of some of them and assures the guitar public that there is some wonderful music forthcoming.

Savio's musical tastes are varied and completely without bigotry which is a natural result of his broadmindedness and tolerant attitude toward music and things in general. His transcriptions of the classic musicians are wonderful just as is his transcription of, for example, "Tico-Tico" (which everyone should own). Although he doesn't admit it, one would suspect that Giuliani is his favourite composer. His exceptional music library contains close on 4,000 pieces for the guitar ! ! !

Savio is particularly proud of his student, Master Antonio Carlos Barbosa Lima, who, in spite of being only 13 years of age is considered to be one of the two or three best Brazilian guitarists.

Aside from music and the guitar, Savio's chief interest is photography with the emphasis on the study of lenses, a subject on which he is an expert. He possessed at one time 39 different cameras but now that quantity has been reduced to a mere 12.

Savio is a married man and has one son, Nilo, eleven years old. Both wife and son play the guitar although Nilo's tastes tend, at present, towards sambas which he strums out quite well.

Always enthusiastic, energetic and happy, Savio continues with his work and Brazil says, "Thank you, Maestro".

This is from the "Guitar News" magazine issue No. 46 of January-February 1959. The large music library eventually went into the Ronoel Simões collection.

Brazil. Isaias Savio gave a successful recital at S. Paulo on July 14th, playing the following programme:

Sonata op. 25 (Finale)	Sor
Adagio	Beethoven
Romanza	Mendelssohn
Valse	Brahms
Sueno	Tarrega
Cancao Amazonica	Henrique
Nesta Rua	Savio
Palmeiras do Brasil	Savio
Samba Rural	Savio
Studies Nos. 8 & 22 from op. 2	Savio
Valsa Scherzo	Savio
Preludio Pitoresca No. 3	Savio
Triumph de Arlequin (2nd Movement of Suite)	Savio
Popular Spanish Themes	Arcas-Savio

The guitarists Jane Ferraz Campos and Carlos Carrion shared the thirteenth recital of Associacao Cultural do Violao (Guitar). •Six members took part in the July concert of the Association. During July the famous Argentine guitarist Maria Luisa Anido continued her concert tour of Brazil with recitals at Belem, Maranhao, Recife, Paz and other places.

This is from the "Guitar News" magazine issue No. 3 of October-November 1951.

BRAZILIAN ACTIVITIES

Isaias Savio, Professor of the Guitar at the Conservatory of Sao Paulo, Brazil, gave a recital at Porto Alegre on July 29th the programme of which consisted mostly of his own compositions for guitar.

It opened with his suite—Cenas Brasileiras (Brazilian Scenes) in six movements each based on the folk-lore music of that country. This was followed by Preludio Pintoresco No. 6, Valsa Scherzo, Two Estudos and Suite Descritiva (on the theme of Pierrot and Harlequin). The programme ended with Triste by Luiz Alba, Estilo by Savio and Three Cancoes Amazonicas by Waldmar Henrique arr. Savio.

Professor Savio is a native of Uruguay who made a concert tour of Brazil in 1931. This tour proved so successful and the demands for his services as a teacher of the guitar became so great that he has remained in Brazil ever since, teaching first in Rio de Janiero and then in Sao Paulo where he now lives. He has done an amazing amount of work for the guitar not only as recitalist, teacher and lecturer but as a composer and arranger of music for the instrument.

The Associacao Brasileira de Imprensa presented a Brazilian guitarist, Solon Ayala, in a recital on August 8th in an interesting and varied programme ranging from Bach, Beethoven, Sor and Aguado to Tarrega, Barrios, Albeniz, Granados, Vicente Gomez, etc.

Among the recordings presented in the recent broadcasts of Ronoel Simoes was the 'Concierto de Aranjuez' (Joaquin Rodrigo) with Regino Sainz de la Maza at the guitar and Ataulfo Argenta conducting.

The Cultural Association of the Guitar presented several of its members in its 34th and 35th concerts of guitar music in July and August.

Many articles about the guitar in the Brazilian press have appeared from the pen of Ronoel Simoes and we understand that he will soon commence a series for an important Uruguayan newspaper.

MARIA LUISA ANIDO IN ITALY

IN Milan on October 30th a recital was given by the celebrated Argentine guitarist Maria Luisa Anido at the Conservatorio di Musica. Her programme included Gagliarda (V. Galilei), Pavana (Sanz), Minuetto (Rameau), items by Sor, Minuetto (Mozart arr. Anido), Impromptu and Cancion del Ladron (Llobet), Sueno (Tarrega), Danza No. 7 (Granados), Asturias (Albeniz), Preludio No 1, Choro and Study No. 11 (Villa-Lobos) and concluded with Argentine music by Cassinelli, Guastavino and Anido (Aire Norteno).

SEGOVIA AT BIRMINGHAM TOWN HALL

THE first concert of Segovia's visit to Britain, on October 25th, should have included the Castelnuovo-Tedesco Concerto, but to the disappointment of the large audience, the parts had failed to arrive from Italy. However, Segovia played two groups of solos which included works by Frescobaldi, Bach (Gavotte), Weiss, Moreno Torroba (Sonatina), Granados (Danza No. 10) and Albeniz (Torre Bermeja). The audience clamoured enthusiastically for more but owing to the lateness of the hour an encore could not be granted.

This is from the "Guitar News" magazine issue No. 16 of December 1953-January 1954.

On the next page is the back cover to a sheet music piece by Isaias Savio with its list of over a dozen works published in Brazil by the maestro. There are videos of his works on You Tube.

OBRAS DE ISAIAS SAVIO

Allegro en Re menor.................. $ 1.—
Amalita, Mazurka.................... » 1.—
Andante............................ » 1.—
Andante............................ » 1.—
Bourrée en Mi menor .... » 1.20
Cajita de Música................... » 1.—
Canción de Cuna.................... » 1.—
Danza de los Gnomos .... » 1.—
Estudios N.º 1 y 2................. » 1.—
   »   » 3 » 4............. » 1.—
   »   » 5 » 6............. » 1.—
   »   » 7 » 8............. » 1.—
   »   » 9 » 10............. » 1.—
   »   » 11 » 12............. » 1.—
Fantasía sobre un tema en Do menor ... » 2.—
Mazurka en Do sostenido menor ...... » 1.—
Mazurka en La menor................ » 1.—
Melodía............................ » 1.—
Mis alegrías....................... » 1.—
Murmullos (preludio) .... » 1.20
8 Pensamientos .... » 2.—
Páginas de Album 1 y 2 .... » 1.—
Pequeña Romanza .... » 1.—
Polonesa en La menor .... » 1.50
Preludios N.º 1 y 2 .... » 1.—
   »   » 3 y 4............. » 1.—
   »   » 5 y 6............. » 1.—
   »   » 7 y 8............. » 1.—
   »   » 9 y 10............. » 1.—
   »   » 11 y 12............. » 1.—
Recuerdos.......................... » 1.—
Romanza en La mayor .... » 1.50
Sonatina (Allegretto, Minuet y Rondó)... » 2.—
Vals Estudios...................... » 1.—
Vals............................... » 1.20
Variaciones sobre un mismo tema ...... » 2.—

In the 1920's Isaias Savio's brother was his first distributor. Many of these pieces are from the archive of J. Augusto Marcellino.

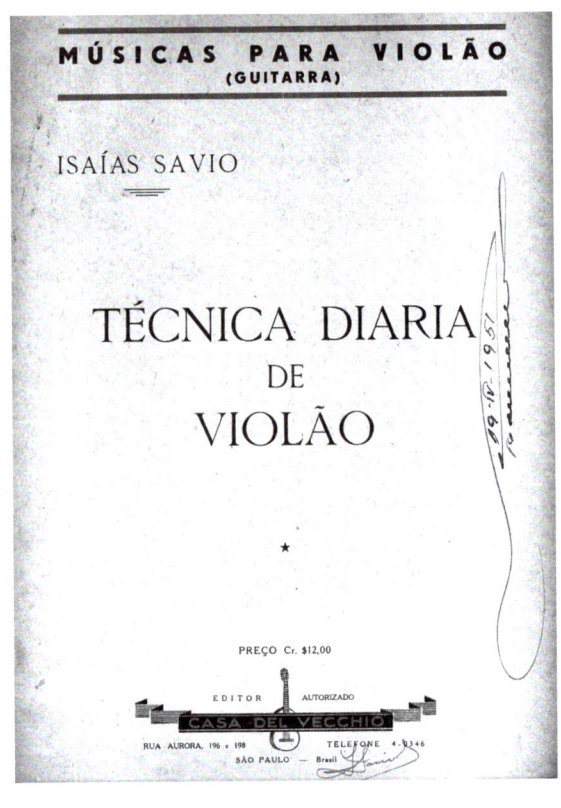

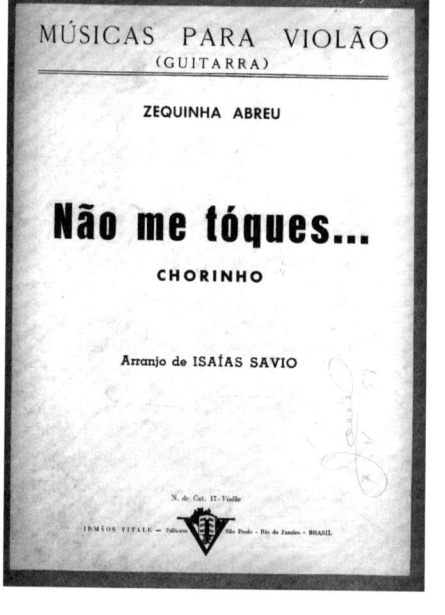

Violão
(Guitarra)

ISAIAS SAVIO

25 ESTUDOS SELETOS, op. 2 — Savio.

MARCHA FÚNEBRE (para dois violões) — Savio.

ANDANTE COM MOTO (para dois violões) — Savio.

COLEÇÃO DE PEÇAS FACEIS (8 peças) — Savio.

COLEÇÃO DE PEÇAS DE PEQUENA DIFICULDADE — (6 peças) - Savio.

COLEÇÃO DE PEÇAS DE MEIA DIFICULDADE — Savio.

QUATRO PEÇAS TÍPICAS DO RIO DA PRATA (Serenata Campera, Estilo, Milonga e Gato) — Savio.

2 PEÇAS FOLCLÓRICAS DO AMAZONAS (Foi Boto Sinhá, Tamba Tajá) — Waldemar Henrique — Savio.

MINUETO DE BOCHERINE — Savio.

MINUET DU BOUEF - Haydn — Savio.

NA SERRA DA MANTIQUEIRA — Ary Kerner.

CHORO N.º 2 — De Isaias Savio.

TANGO BRASILEIRO — Isaias Savio.

CARINHOSO — Samba estilisado — Pixinguinha.

GUACYRA — Heckel Tavares.

FAVELA — Joracy Camargo.

SAUDADES DE OURO PRETO — Do arranjo de Murilo Alvarenga.

ÚLTIMA INSPIRAÇÃO — Peter Pan.

E. S. MANGIONE - *Editor* - Rua Antônio de Godói, 122 - S. Paulo
Impresso no
Estabelecimento Gráfico Mangione - Rua Lavapés, 346 - S. Paulo
Impresso no Brasil — Printed in Brazil

Nº 100

The back cover to Isaias Savio's *"Saudades de Ouro Preto"*, with its list of over a dozen works published in Brazil by the maestro.

Translating from Ricardo Muñoz's unpublished book *"Historia Universal de la Guitarra" Volume VI "America"*. The biographies of guitarists from Uruguay may have contributions by Cedar Viglietti, from his book *"Origen y Historia de la Guitarra"* and will be notated as such.

"Uruguay

Introduction

"I describe it as such that to denote the specific manner prior to the classical guitar in Uruguay that had begun its profile in the second half of the 19th century, initially with those called guitar players, a title that they agree to which those who launched the era to perform passages of plucked accompaniment of songs such as, tristes and estilos.

Then *Don* Carlos García Tolsa and the *"Estudiantina Figaro"* arrived in the country, they were followed by others until our days, such as Manjón, Llobet, Segovia, Sainz de la Maza, Anido, etc. and began the firm evolution in the virtuosity, composition, construction and teaching of the instrument.

We might see the continuation of the developed labor by those of the meritorious sister nation.

Antonio Bachini

Origin:

He is the son of Santiago and *Doña* Emilia Pelayo Benites, and was born in Colonia towards the end of 1859.

His Education:

He was a distinguished journalist, National Senator, candidate for the Presidency of the Republic, Minister of Foreign Relations, and several times a representative of his country to the League of Nations, and Ambassador in Brazil.

His Virtuosity

The Montevideo daily *"Tribuna Popular"* on June 24, 1902 said with as title *Una Notabilidad* — A Notable Person: 'Antonio Bachini isn't only a most notable singer of *Estilos* of an exceptional high range and endowed of an inimitable talent of the satire, he is also an admirable stylist on this instrument, at the same time an Andalucian and National (Uruguayan) as well whose basses have been made for the imitation of the sobbing and his trebles appear to have the convulsive vibrations of a laugh .... Bachini is one of those who knows the secret to make the soul of the guitar speak and it isn't an exaggeration in saying that he plays so well as he writes and as a musician he is so distinguished as a brilliant journalist.'

Julio Sagreras dedicated *"Elisa, mazurka" No.42* to Antonio Bachini, the homage reading: "To the distinguished aficionado Antonio Bachini" (al distinguido aficionado Antonio Bachini), it was published by Francisco Nuñez c. 1903. The two probably met in Montevideo when Julio performed there in 1902.

Luis Alba Tamiozzo

His Origin:

He was born in Villa Colon, Uruguay on May 15, 1886.

His Education:

He made his studies in surveying and is a distinguished sketch artist and painter of quality, who at the age of eleven began his studies of music and harmony with maestro Mateo Garay; two years later he started playing the guitar directed by Candido Silveira.

Luis Alba had 3 pieces listed in the 1931 Antigua Casa Nuñez catalog, this *"Preludio"* by Bach, and a *"Romanza"* by Mendelssohn and his own composition *De mi tierra, "El Uruguay" Estilo*, these pieces being published by Hector N. Pirovano in Buenos Aires.

About 1911 the maestro *Don* Pedro Vittone directed him to study the Aguado method, afterward he studied alone pursuing the courses of Sor and Tárrega until he obtained excellent technique.

His Virtuosity:

He played impeccably in his diverse recitals, which the Montevideo dailies' critics praised his performances.

At times Muñoz drew from Prat's *Diccionario de Guitarristas*. It was listed in the bibliographies of all 8 volumes. More details from the same source are:

'His works until the publication of this (Dictionary of Guitarists) are three, having prepared others for the guitar, and some for orchestra such as *"Evocacion Nativa"*. His taste and musical culture are great.'

This is translated from the book by Cedar Viglietti "Origen y Historia de la Guitarra" published by Editorial Albatros in Buenos Aires in 1973. Translating from pages 197-201:

"From the middle of the last decade of the past century, when a boy walking behind a plough was singing. . . .a *Vidala?*, an *Estilo?* No, it was a song sung, carefully, adjusted, to avoid the slaps of his cheeks with which his maestro would correct his mistakes. This boy was called Luis Alba. He lived an intense life, he loved music passionately. And the guitar, but that was a medium, not an end. and as a medium precisely he spread his guitar transcriptions from a piece by Fabini to one by Bach, of one by Eduardo Caba to one by Ravel, from one by Arturo de Navas to that of Haydn.

Some were respectful adaptations, others were free versions, some being published in Italy and in Brazil; the majority of them, unpublished, he wrote those for his friends, which we value as they correspond, since some of them surpass the most known transcriptions. Some of his works were published for guitar in our book: *"Folklore en el Uruguay"*, an edition from 1947, now out of print; they are twelve compositions over themes of our folkloric pieces, of them which we distinguish a *Cifra*, a *Malambo*, an *Estilo,* a *Polca*, and above all a Triste of an authentic ancient manufacture, that bring reminiscences of Inca like and spontaneous criollismo — In our book *"Folklore Musical del Uruguay"*, an edition from 1968, several of these themes are placed, but in general with only a melodic design.

In respect to the traditional music, we believe that he might have been one of our musicians who knew that theme best, since the beginning and the most genuine source. Quietly, without fuss nor some publicity he knew to collect — not quantity without quality — the best, the purest of our regional songs. He did it spontaneously, without a deliberate purpose and way before that of when the radio would appear — the Argentine source — distorting the Oriental (here he refers to the Republic Oriental of Uruguay). And that is important.

Now to the end of the century that will be hit upon — such as Vicente Rossi, to whom was admired — to bring an *Estilo* to the music staff, a Milonga, heard, or better said, listened to attentively in its long pilgrimage as a surveyor for all this land, living most of the times on the edges of a ranches, in a tent, with his theodolite but also with his inseparable guitar. . . . His measurements, the base of the actual map of the Republic, are employed although by the officials of the staff of our Army, with the name precisely *"cartas Alba"*.

I repeat an idea that this musician had a flower in his mouth, already enunciated by Manjón: the guitarists in general are self-taught, and are limited to the six strings of the guitar, scorned or unknowing the great authors; they suffer from the scarce knowledge and they show evidence of the deficient musical culture, that belittle their horizon or still bring to the commission of errors in the character or interpretation of the works they perform.

Alba transcribed — or wrote — to the requests of his friends: in this way we have succeeded, besides from the cited works, versions of Rameau, Falla, Franck, Debussy, Granados, many of them for two guitars for the recreation of two very musical young boys, E. and J. C. Fernández , some for three or four guitars and up to the reduction of the *"Bolero"* by Ravel for seven guitars.

We distinguish the very well done transcriptions by Alba, for the guitar: *"Preludio"* by Bach, a free version of *"El Carretero"* by Arturo de Navas and the *"Aires indios bolivianos"*, No. 2 and No. 5 by Eduardo Caba (We add that Caba composed directly for the guitar a piece called *"Pastoril"*.) As for the *"Bolero"* by Ravel, after repeated practice sessions and patient direction by Alba — three of the participants played it by ear and the debut was in Minas and then repeated it in the Instituto Verdi in October of 1959.

Commenting on a *"Pericon"* compiled by Alba at the end of the century, we write from a Montevideo daily from twenty five years ago — *"La Tribuna Popular"* of May 23, 1948:

'*Don* Candido Silvera, Vice Mayor in the 17th section of Montevideo, played the guitar by ear and with good taste; he was heard in the pulperia of the Catalan Casella. In 1897 when a young boy who was running stopped behind the grating and listened with recognition from the beginning, attracted by that rare siren that transforms the pulperia then into an enchanted island from a monotone tavern that emerges from those places: after a while he entered, vacillating, the eyes fixed on those strings. Hours later, when he came out, he brought the promise, — a magnificent gift — of which they taught him how to play the *"Pericon"*, "that *"Pericon"*, right, on the guitar.

That year the boy Luis Alba covers his guitar with two other musicians — contemporaries of his maestro — and who are José Riestra and Antolin Amaro. The last one being a judge in the section mentioned of Montevideo, and when he celebrated a marriage of a friend, he brought his instrument and with Riestra and sometimes the boy they played music in the uproar of the wedding. For those people that still loved the native music — close to their heritage — the chords of the *Pericon* had the enchantment of a wedding march: it lacked Mendelssohn and an organ, but it was enough for the dance by *Don* Silvera that he started — and as graphic as this word — of the *criolla* strings that *Don* Amaro presided over by the judicial understanding musician, suddenly on the white band and blue crosses of his guitar.'

So, in this way, Alba began studying with Silvera, then continued with Pedro Vittone. For different reasons they were to be brief lessons — these classes, by that can consider him self-taught, but firmly consecrated to the most serious musical disciplines — the reason of his life —. He dedicated himself to his creative labor, relegating as an interpreter, with the steps of the years, to a second plane.

He didn't miss any important musical happening in the Rio de la Plata, and when the years had already bent his shoulders, he visited Germany to attend the festivals of Bayreuth.

He died in 1967, at eighty years of age, in full dominion of his creative faculties, we had a wake for him in Las Piedras, as a small group of friends, who then accompanied him to the cemetery in La Paz."

Luis Alba was very active for decades with his transcriptions. This *"Romanza"* by Mendelssohn was probably published in the mid 1930's by Hector N. Pirovano in Buenos Aires.

1. Preludio No. 1
2. Mazurka — Chopin
3. Valse — Chopin
4. Preludio No. 2
5. Serenata — Moszkowski
6. Romanza — Rubinstein
7. Romanza — Mendelssohn
8. En la fuente
9. Preludio — Debussy
10. Granada — Albeniz

The *"Suite em La"* was published in Sao Paulo, Brazil in 1958 by Ricordi.

Alais, J. The Washington Post, marcha (Sousa) .... $ 0.80
  — Un momento, valse .... » 0.80
  — Un recuerdo, valse .... » 1.—
  — Un suspiro, schottisch, para dos guitarras .... » 0.60
  — Vita torinesse, polka, para dos guitarras .... » 0.80
  — Zamacueca y Güeya .... » 0.60
Alba, A., Amor naciente, valse .... » 0.80
  — Andante sentimental .... » 0.80
  — Brisas porteñas, schottisch .... » 0.80
  — Caprichosa, polka .... » 0.80
  — Guagiras célebres .... » 0.80
  — Marcha española .... » 0.60
Alba, A., Mi tesoro, polka .... » 0.80
  — ¡Penas!, meditación .... » 1.—
  — Pensando en ti, habanera .... » 0.80
  — Pitios, mazurka .... » 0.80
  — Polka militar .... » 0.80
  — Suspiros del alma, vals .... » 1.—
Alba, Luis, T. Preludio (Bach, J. S.) .... » 1.20
  — Romanza (Mendelssohnn, F.) .... » 0.80
Almirón, B. S., Colección de 4 piezas .... » 2.—
  — Lalita, 2ª. guitarra de la Vidalita María de Alais ... » 0.80
  — La oración, melodía .... » 1.—
Arcas, J., Andante .... » 0.80
  — Andante y estudio de Prudent .... » 0.80
  — Ballo in maschera fantasía, (Verdi, G.) .... » 1.—
  — Barbero de Sevilla, motivos (Rossini, G.) .... » 0.70
  — Batalla, La, fantasía descriptiva .... » 1.20
  — Boleras .... » 0.70
  — Bolero .... » 0.70
  — Colección de 5 tangos .... » 0.80
  — Cubana, danza americana — .... » 0.50
  — Delirio, fantasía .... » 2.—
  — Fantasía sobre motivos heterogéneos .... » 1.80
  — Fantasía sobre el paño, o sea el punto de la Habana ... » 1.20
  — Faust, fantasía (Gounod, Ch.) .... » 1.60
  — Favorita, fantasía (Donizetti, G.) .... » 1.20
  — Gáetana, mazurka (Ketterer) .... » 0.80
  — Guayabito, tango .... » 0.80
  — Guillermo Tell, preludio, y un preludio original (Rossini, G.) ... » 0.80
  — Il Bacio, valse (Arditi, L.) .... » 1.—
  — Incógnito, capricho .... » 1.50
  — Jota aragonesa .... » 1.—
  — Lucía di Lammermoor, escena y aire final (Donizetti, G.) .... » 1.50
  — Madrileño, schottisch .... » 0.50
  — Manuelito, valse .... » 0.70
  — Marcha fúnebre (Thalberg) .... » 1.—
  — Marina, tango, y dos estudios .... » 0.70

Florida 255. — Cangallo 1574. — B. Mitre 947

Here is a listing of two pieces by Luis Alba T., including *"Preludio"* by Bach, and a *"Romanza"* by Mendelssohn. It is from the c. Fall *1928 "Romero & Fernández Catalogo No. 5, Métodos y Musica para Guitarra"* catalog of 34 pages. This shows that Luis Alba's pieces were published in the 1920's.

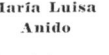

María Luisa Anido

La virtuosa de la guitarra, ha causado admiración en sus conciertos por su estilo artístico.

Irma Haydée Perazzo

Eximia concertista argentina, cuyo temperamento artístico ha sido y es grandemente elogiado.

PUBLICACIONES MUSICALES
Relacionadas con la técnica de la guitarra

	$ m|n.
Aguado Dionisio..Método completo	5.—
„ „ „ „ ed. francesa	6.—
„ „ ..Cincuenta estudios	2.—
Aguado Sinópoli..Método completo	12.—
Amestoy E. .....Escalas y arpegios	2.—
Cano Antonio ....Método completo, 1ª parte (edición española)	6.—
„ „ ....Método completo, 1ª parte. (edición argentina)	4.—
„ „ ....Método completo, 2ª parte. (Tratado de Armonía) ..	4.—
„ „ ...Veinticinco lecciones fáciles.	3.—
„ „ ...Dos estudios de concierto ..	2.—
Carcassi Mateo ..Veinticinco estudios melódicos	2.—
Carulli Fernando.Método completo, 1ª parte .	1.20
„ „ „ 2ª „	1.40
„ „ „ 3ª „	1.50
Coste Napoleón ..Veinticinco estudios de salón	4.—
Damas Tomás ...Método completo	7.—
Gascón L. V. ....Estudios elementales y progresivos	3.—
Iparraguirre Pedro.Escalas y arpegios	3.—
„ Escuela del mecanismo	2.—

	$m n
Leloup Hilarión ..Método elemental	5.—
„ „ ..Escalas, acordes y ejercicios técnicos	5.—
Ortiz Julián......Teoría de las escalas	2.—
Prat Domingo ...Escalas y arpegios.........	2.—
Rizzuti Carmelo..Lecciones elementales	3.—
R. Arenas M. ....Escalas y estudios de autores varios	5.—
„ „ ....Escuela de la guitarra, primera parte	4.—
„ „ ....Escuela de la guitarra, segunda parte	6.—
Roch Pascual.....Gran método I Parte....	7.—
„ „ .... „ „ II „	7.—
„ „ .... „ „ III „	7.—
Sagreras Julio ....Primeras lecciones	2.50
„ „ ....Técnica superior	4.—
Segovia Andrés ..Escalas diatónicas, primer cuaderno	2.50
Sinópoli Antonio..Ejercicios de escalas	2.50
„ „ ..Ejercicios técnicos	2.50
Sors Fernando Gran método completo ...	5.—
(Coste) ....Edición francesa	8.—

MÚSICA DE SALON

	$m/n.
Alais Juan ......Seis piezas fáciles	1.—
„ „ ......Plegaria a Moisés, de Rossini	1.—
„ „ .....Música prohibida, melodía ..	0.60
Alba Luis ......Serenata, de Schubert	0.80
„ „ ......Romanza, de Mendelsshonn	1.—
Anido M. L. ....Preludio, de Bach	1.20
„ „ ....Sarabanda, de Bach.......	1.50
„ „ ....Vals, de Grieg...........	1.20
„ „ ....Le petit Berger, de Debussy	1.50
„ „ ....Rancho abandonado, de Mac Dowell	1.50
Almirón ....Leyenda	1.—
Arcas Julián......El delirio, fantasía	1.30
„ „ ......El sueño de Rosellén	1.—
„ „ ......Jota aragonesa	1.—
„ „ ......Minueto en Sol	1.—
„ „ „ Mi menor	1.—
„ „ ......Mi segunda época, fantasía .	1.—
Brocá José.....Pensamiento español, fantas.	1.—
„ „ .....Mi patria, fantasía	1.—
Cano Antonio....La gallegada, fantasía	1.—
„ „ ....Marcha triunfal	1.—
„ „ ....Ultimo adiós, romanza	0.80
„ „ ....Andante en Do, Haydn	1.—
„ „ ....Tres valses	1.50
„ „ ....Tarantella	1.50
„ „ ....Pomponet, de Durand......	1.50
Cano Federico ..Catania, siciliana	1.—
„ „ ....Carmen, romanza..........	1.—
„ „ ...Bodas de plata, reverie	1.—
„ „ ...Preludio, estudio	1.—
„ „ ...Las montañas de la selva, capricho	2.—
„ „ ....Estudio dedicado a Viñas ..	1.—
„ „ ....Estudio dedicado a Tárrega	1.—

	$m/n
Cimadevilla F. ...Fantasía morisca, serenata .	1.—
„ „ ...Gran jota aragonesa	1.50
Damas Tomás....Trémolo, nocturno	1.50
Del Valle Adela..Seis piezas fáciles	1.50
Ferrer José.......Recuerdos de Montgrí, capricho	2.—
„ „ ....Los encantos de París	2.—
„ „ ....Monuet, op. 49	1.—
„ „ ....Doce minuetos	1.—
„ „ ....Veladas íntimas	1.—
„ „ ....El talismán, vals	1.—
Fontaine F. ......En la sierra	1.—
Galluzzo ....Adiós al piano, de Beethoven	0.80
„ ....Canción húngara (Alma de Dios)	1.—
García Fortea S.Zambra granadina	2.—
„ „ „ Torre bermeja, de Albéniz .	2.—
Gascón L. V. ...Minueto núm. 1	1.—
„ „ „ ...Adiós, Granada (granadinas)	1.50
„ „ „ ...Sonatina en cuatro tiempos	2.—
„ „ „ ...Variaciones sobre una canción	1.—
„ „ „ ...Variaciones de gato a 3 guitarras	2.—
„ „ „ ...Gran jota aragonesa	2.—
Gottschalk J. M.Gran trémolo	1.50
Iparraguirre Pedro El recreo, colección	1.20
„ „ Sueño de un ángel, de Ludovic	1.—
„ „ Plegaria de una virgen, de Badarzewska	1.—
„ „ Serenata, de Toselli	1.—
„ „ Serenata D'Autrefois, de Silvestri	1.—
„ „ Berceuse, de Jocelin de Godard	1.—

Here is a listing of two pieces by Luis Alba T., including *"Serenata"* by Schubert, and a *"Romanza"* by Mendelssohn. It is from the c. 1928 Casa America catalog.

Abelardo Rodríguez

His Origin:

He was born in Florida, Uruguay on August 10, 1898.

His Education:

He studied guitar with Conrado P. Koch.

His Virtuosity:

He gave many concerts in Montevideo and the interior of the country.

His Pedagogy:

He has been dedicated to teaching and is the Chief in charge of a commercial company in Montevideo.

The above Muñoz drew from Prat's *Diccionario de Guitarristas*.

Guillermo José Corcoran

His Origin:

He is the son of Guillermo Corcoran and *Doña* Dominga Odriozola, born in Montevideo on November 25, of 1901.

His Education:

He is devoted to art, especially music, which he has listened to on all instruments, by vocation he resolved to play the guitar, about which he says: 'It is the best interpreter and transparent of the deepest emotions, the most resonant of happiness and sadness and the most bitter anguish, the most passionate, most violent, smoothest, sweetest dreams which hide and move the soul.'

In the middle of 1922, he began his studies of the instrument with maestro Pedro Martin Mascaro y Reissig, until in the year 1926, when he presented him in public, later he received lessons of a high guitaristic level with *Don* Miguel Llobet.

His Virtuosity:

The 11th of August of 1926 he made his debut before the public of Montevideo in the hall of the Instituto Verdi, interpreting *"Minuetto"* by Sor, *"Estudio"* by Aguado, *"Andante"* by Mozart, *"Allegro"* by Coste, *"Tres Preludios"*, *"Dos Estudios"*, *"Pequeña Romanza"*, *"Cajita de Musica"* and *"Bourée"* by Isaias Savio, *"Melodia Catalana"* by Llobet, *"Barcarola"* by Mendelssohn, *"Gavota"* by Barrios and *"Recuerdos de la Alhambra"* by Tárrega with such success that his own maestro said: 'Guillermo Corcoran has been one of the few, maybe the only one of my disciples which since the first studies demonstrated an admirable inclination toward the musical works that are most distinguished by their austerity of the nature, instead not showing a major preference for those others whose suggestive intensity only originates in the most effects, a child of the frivolity.... today he is an artist with certain rebellious aspects of his exquisite temperament.... he doesn't sacrifice the beauty in place of an established rule. His soul on the strings is all art, warmth, youth, and spiritual energy.'

Since then his concerts continued in the "Casa del Arte", "Instituto Verdi", "Conservatorio La Lira", in the social headquarters of the "Centro de Viajantes del Uruguay", "Asociacion Cristiana" and other entities. When he was heard by the great Barrios, he hugged him effusively, and the eminent Llobet qualified him as "Someone Notable", inviting him to organize an artistic tour jointly, which he couldn't do, by having been the victim of a grave accident which weakened him for some time, and was the true cause of his later death.

In 1931 he got married to Miss Delida E. Moreno, and then initiated a tour of the interior of the country, performing in Tacuarembo, Rivera, Treinta y Tres, Durazno, Flores and in Montevideo.

Corcoran in his performances obtained a pure sound winged by the employ of the skin of his fingers and without the use of the nails, when he played the guitar, of his own model, he profoundly listened and said: 'I began to love the guitar alone, without the advice of the maestro, without the protection of my parents, with a desire almost native of truth and beauty.... neither stimulus nor caring helped my fondness.... guarded by the guitar and an expression so deep that I heard in its voice the complaints of the hearts of men.... and in my solace, I felt as the owner of that pain and of mine, which I confided in it, as a docile and blind confidant.'

He also performed admirably on the radio stations *"El Espectador"* and *"Radio Sport"* (*Radio Colon* beforehand).

His Compositions:

We know *"Divagaciones"* and *"Variaciones de Jota"* which he didn't publish.

His Pedagogy:

A refined man of culture, who read and studied a lot, he was named professor of the Conservatorio *"La Lira"*.

His Passing:

He was of a reserved temperament, happy and decided, his friendship overflowed to full hands; he abhorred the use of the underhand and lies; he was a quick genius and knew how to return over his steps renewing his stillness.

He submitted to a difficult surgical intervention, and died on March 4, 1940 in the locality of Colon, and is buried in the Cemeterio del Buces."

El notable guitarrista Guillermo Corcorán y su maestro Pedro Mascaro y Reissig, que compartieron el brillante éxito de anoche

In the Montevideo daily *"La Razon"* on Thursday August 12, 1926 Pedro Mascaro y Reissig's student Guillermo Corcoran's Instituto Verdi concert was reviewed. The translation is:

Archive: Pedro Mascaro y Reissig 1917-1938

"The brilliant revelation of the notable concert guitarist Guillermo Corcoran

And the deserved consecration of the maestro Pedro Mascaro y Reissig

———————————————

The artistic happening celebrated last night in the Instituto Verdi.

Todo un acontecimiento artístico resultó el concierto de guitarra que nos ofreció anoche en el Instituto Verdi el joven guitarrista uruguayo Guillermo J. Corcorán, notable discípulo del maestro Pedro Mascaró y Reissig.

A pesar de que ya esperábamos oír a un buen ejecutante del instrumento que inmortilizó a Sors, dada la escuela que siguen los alumnos

la yema de los dedos, tal cual lo estableció el inmortal Tárrega. Precisamente esto es una de las condiciones que solo habíamos visto en el maestro Mascaró y Reissig, único en nuestro país que sigue los principios de Tárrega, y los inculca en todos sus alumnos.

Infinitas veces hemos oído a muchos guitarristas nacionales, pero lamentablemente, a excepción de

el concertista, como su maestro, quien también se vió obligado a salir al escenario del Verdi en compañia de su discípulo, debido al insistente pedido del público, quien deseaba ovacionarlo por su escuela perfecta.

Las obras que más se destacaron en el recital de anoche fueron: el "Allegro" de Coste, el "Estudio en Si Menor" de Sors (ejecutado fue-

Interesante aspecto de la sala del Instituto Verdi en la que una numerosa concurrencia consagró la velada artística

de Mascaró y Reissig, el recital de anoche ha sido para nosotros y para el público que llenó la sala del Verdi una revelación. En efecto Corcorán es un artista en toda la expresión del vocablo, su dicción es intensamente comunicativa, llega realmente al alma del oyente, conmoviéndolo. Pero lo que más nos ha persuadido de que dicho artista triunfará desde hoy en adelante, como un digno sucesor de su maestro, es la calidad de sonido que saca de la guitarra, empleando únicamente

Mascaró y Reissig, todos nos habían dejado la mala impresión del sonido desagradable producido por el error de pulsación.

Recién anoche, con la impecable ejecución de Corcorán, nos hemos convencido que la verdadera pulsación está en eliminar todo contacto de las uñas con las cuerdas. Y no se crea que esta es solamente nuestra impresión, sino también la del público que oyó anoche al eximio discípulo de Mascaró y Reissig.

Tal vez por eso fué tan aclamado

ra de programa), "Andante de Don Giovanni" de Mozart, "Recuerdos de la Alhambra" de Tárrega y "Cajita de música" de Savio, autor nacional este último cuyas obras formaron la segunda parte del programa y quien también fué ovacionado anoche por el público.

Felicitaciones, pues, para éste, para Corcorán, y sobre todo para el maestro Mascaró y Reissig, único fiel consecuente de la escuela de Tárrega.

Guillermo Corcoran's Instituto Verdi concert photo caption translation is:

"An interesting aspect of the hall of the Instituto Verdi in which the numerous gathering consecrated the artistic evening."

The text translation is:

"The guitar concert last night offered us by the young Uruguayan guitarist Guillermo J. Corcoran, notable disciple of Pedro Mascaro y Reissig turned out to be completely an artistic happening.

In spite of that we already wait to hear a good performer of the instrument that immortalized Sor, given the school which the students follow of Pedro Mascaro y Reissig, the recital of last night had been for us and for the public that filled the hall of the Verdi a revelation. In effect Corcoran is an artist in all the expression of the word, his diction is intensely communicative, it really reaches to the heart of the listener, moving it. But what persuaded us the most of who the said artist triumphed from today onward, as a dignified successor of his maestro, is the quality of sound which he brought from the guitar, employing only the skin of his fingers, just as the immortal Tárrega established. Precisely this is one of the conditions that we have only seen in the maestro Mascaro y Reissig, the only one in our country which follows the principles of Tárrega, and he inculcates in all of his students.

Infinite times we have heard many national guitarists, but lamentably, to the exception of Mascaro y Reissig, all have left us with the bad impression of the unpleasant sound produced by the error of plucking.

Just last night, with the impeccable performance of Corcoran, we have been convinced that the true playing is to eliminate all contact with the fingernails with the strings. And we don't believe that it is only our impression, but also of the public that listened last night to the eminent disciple of Mascaro y Reissig.

Perhaps therefore the concert guitarist was so acclaimed, as his maestro, who we also saw was obligated to leave the stage of the Verdi in the company of his disciple, due to the insistent requests of the public, who desired to give him ovations for his perfect school.

The most distinguished choruses in the recital last night were: the *"Allegro"* by Coste, the *"Estudio en Si menor"* by Sor, (performed as an encore), *"Andante* from *Don Giovanni"* by Mozart, *"Recuerdos de la Alhambra"* by Tárrega and *"Cajita de musica"* by Savio, a national author of this last one whose works formed the second part of the program and who also was given ovations last night by the public.

Congratulations, since, for this, for Corcoran, and overall for the maestro Mascaro y Reissig, the only consistent faithful one of the school of Tárrega.

Translation from the *"Montevideo Musical"* magazine of September, 1926 issue No. 1376 *Año* XLI:

"The Guitarist Corcoran

Guillermo Corcoran, a young guitarist who was just heard in the Hall of the Instituto Verdi provoked true enthusiasm by his vast and difficult program interpreted and by the delicate and elevated school, demonstrating to us to be a praiseworthy student of Mr. Pedro Masscaro y Reissig.

Among the works that Corcoran performed, it deserves to cite the compositions of another compatriot, the young Isaias Savio, who achieved true artistic success.

The only aspect the young Corcoran lacked was a foreign name to elevate him to a greater height, because everything is never given our rightful place for justice."

EL GUITARRISTA CORCORAN

Guillermo Corcoran, joven guitarrista que acaba de hacerse oir en la Sala del Verdi provocó verdadero entusiasmo por el vasto y difícil programa interpretado y por su escuela delicada y elevada, demostrándonos ser un alumno digno de su profesor, el Sr. Pedro Mascaró y Reissig.

Entre las obras que Corcoran ejecutó, merecen citarse las composiciones de otro compatriota, el joven Isaias Savio, que alcanzaron verdadero éxito artístico.

Faltaría sólo al joven Corcoran un nombre extranjero para elevarlo a mayor altura, ya que a todo lo nuestro nunca se le da el lugar que corresponde por justicia.

Translating from Ricardo Muñoz's unpublished book *"Historia Universal de la Guitarra"* Volume VI *"America"*.

"His Origin:

Julio J. Otermin was born to Aureliano Otermin and *Doña* Isabel Gonzalez Miranda on December 3, 1877 in Montevideo.

His Education:

Since he was a child he picked up the guitar, which he also practiced in the Military Academy, where, he entered the Army and later obtained the grade of Comandante; he retired and kept practicing his beloved instrument. Then he entered the Conservatorio *"La Lira"* in Montevideo and studied with Pedro Maza.

His Virtuosity:

He gave many concerts in the capital of his country, in the inner areas as well as outside of Uruguay, of which the honorific distinctions were many: a Gold Medal awarded by the Asociacion Patriotica de Buenos Aires, due to a competition that took place in the Teatro Politeama in the year 1907, for whomever could best perform the Antonio Jiménez Manjón work *"Capricho Andaluz"*. In the same year in Montevideo he was awarded two new Gold Medals in the *"España"* competition, one for his performances and the other for his interpretation of the *"Vals Boston"* called *"Calderon"*. In 1909 the "Circulo Catolico" of Montevideo they gave his third Gold medal for his performance at the institution, winning the First Prize for his transcription of the Vals Boston "Perlas del Uruguay".

His Compositions:

Some of his works for the guitar that are known are:

"Perlas del Uruguay"
"Un Sueño"
"Apasionada" — Gavota
"Olas que Mueren" — Vals
"En el Poncho" — Pericon
"Mi Nena" — Tango
Casa Nuñez Editions
"Una Mas" — Tango
"Te Vas" — Tango
"Las Quejas" — Yaravi

His Pedagogy

He taught the instrument for many years, to around 2,000 students and with great success, which the newspaper *"El Debate"* reported at the completion of 25 years of guitaristic teaching.

His Passing

He died the 15th of October 1943 in the city of Montevideo.

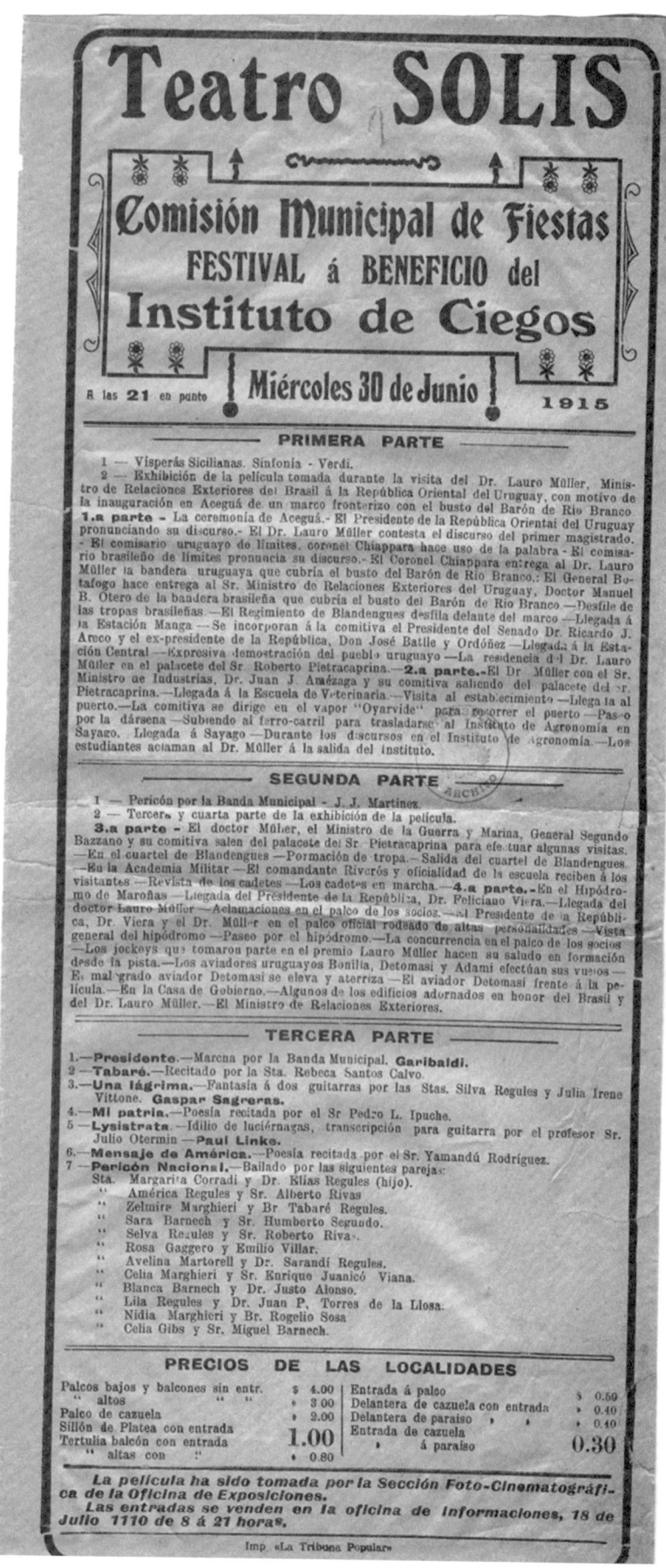

Teatro SOLIS

Comisión Municipal de Fiestas
FESTIVAL á BENEFICIO del
Instituto de Ciegos

A las 21 en punto | Miércoles 30 de Junio | 1915

PRIMERA PARTE

1 — Vísperas Sicilianas. Sinfonía - Verdi.

2 — Exhibición de la película tomada durante la visita del Dr. Lauro Müller, Ministro de Relaciones Exteriores del Brasil á la República Oriental del Uruguay, con motivo de la inauguración en Aceguá de un marco fronterizo con el busto del Barón de Rio Branco **1.a parte** - La ceremonia de Aceguá.- El Presidente de la República Oriental del Uruguay pronunciando su discurso.- El Dr. Lauro Müller contesta el discurso del primer magistrado. - El comisario uruguayo de límites, coronel Chiappara hace uso de la palabra - El comisario brasileño de límites pronuncia su discurso.- El Coronel Chiappara entrega al Dr. Lauro Müller la bandera uruguaya que cubría el busto del Barón de Rio Branco.: El General Botafogo hace entrega al Sr. Ministro de Relaciones Exteriores del Uruguay, Doctor Manuel B. Otero de la bandera brasileña que cubría el busto del Barón de Rio Branco.—Desfile de las tropas brasileñas.—El Regimiento de Blandengues desfila delante del marco —Llegada á la Estación Manga —Se incorporan á la comitiva el Presidente del Senado Dr. Ricardo J. Areco y el ex-presidente de la República, Don José Batlle y Ordóñez —Llegada á la Estación Central—Expresiva demostración del pueblo uruguayo—La residencia del Dr. Lauro Müller en el palacete del Sr. Roberto Pietracaprina.—**2.a parte.**-El Dr. Müller con el Sr. Ministro de Industrias, Dr. Juan J. Amézaga y su comitiva saliendo del palacete del Sr. Pietracaprina.—Llegada á la Escuela de Veterinaria.—Visita al establecimiento —Llega la al puerto.—La comitiva se dirige en el vapor "Oyarvide" para recorrer el puerto—Paso por la dársena—Subiendo al ferro-carril para trasladarse al Instituto de Agronomía en Sayago, Llegada á Sayago —Durante los discursos en el Instituto de Agronomía.—Los estudiantes aclaman al Dr. Müller á la salida del Instituto.

SEGUNDA PARTE

1 — Pericón por la Banda Municipal - J. J. Martínez.

2 — Tercera y cuarta parte de la exhibición de la película.

3.a parte - El doctor Müller, el Ministro de la Guerra y Marina, General Segundo Bazzano y su comitiva salen del palacete del Sr. Pietracaprina para efectuar algunas visitas. —En el cuartel de Blandengues—Formación de tropa.—Salida del cuartel de Blandengues. —En la Academia Militar—El comandante Riverós y oficialidad de la escuela reciben á los visitantes.—Revista de los cadetes—Los cadetes en marcha.—**4.a parte.**—En el Hipódromo de Maroñas—Llegada del Presidente de la República, Dr. Feliciano Viera.—Llegada del doctor Lauro Müller—Aclamaciones en el palco de los socios.—Al Presidente de la República, Dr. Viera y el Dr. Müller en el palco oficial rodeado de altas personalidades—Vista general del hipódromo—Paseo por el hipódromo.—La concurrencia en el palco de los socios —Los jockeys que tomaron parte en el premio Lauro Müller hacen su saludo en formación desde la pista.—Los aviadores uruguayos Bonilla, Detomasi y Adami efectúan sus vuelos— El mal-grado aviador Detomasi se eleva y aterriza—El aviador Detomasi frente á la película.—En la Casa de Gobierno.—Algunos de los edificios adornados en honor del Brasil y del Dr. Lauro Müller.—El Ministro de Relaciones Exteriores.

TERCERA PARTE

1.—**Presidente**.—Marcha por la Banda Municipal. **Garibaldi.**

2.—**Tabaré**.—Recitado por la Sta. Rebeca Santos Calvo.

3.—**Una lágrima.**—Fantasía á dos guitarras por las Stas. Silva Regules y Julia Irene Vittone. **Gaspar Sagreras.**

4.—**Mi patria.**—Poesía recitada por el Sr Pedro L. Ipuche.

5 —**Lysistrata**.—Idilio de luciérnagas, transcripción para guitarra por el profesor Sr. Julio Otermin —**Paul Linke.**

6.—**Mensaje de América.**—Poesía recitada por el Sr. Yamandú Rodríguez.

7 —**Pericón Nacional.**—Bailado por las siguientes parejas:
Sta. Margarita Corradi y Dr. Elías Regules (hijo).
" América Regules y Sr. Alberto Rivas.
" Zelmira Marghieri y Br Tabaré Regules.
" Sara Barnech y Sr. Humberto Segundo.
" Selva Regules y Sr. Roberto Rivas.
" Rosa Gaggero y Emilio Villar.
" Avelina Martorell y Dr. Sarandí Regules.
" Celia Marghieri y Sr. Enrique Juanicó Viana.
" Blanca Barnech y Dr. Justo Alonso.
" Lila Regules y Dr. Juan P. Torres de la Llosa.
" Nidia Marghieri y Br. Rogelio Sosa
" Celia Gibs y Sr. Miguel Barnech.

PRECIOS DE LAS LOCALIDADES

Palcos bajos y balcones sin entr.	$ 4.00	Entrada á palco	» 0.50
" altas " "	» 3.00	Delantera de cazuela con entrada	» 0.40
Palco de cazuela	» 2.00	Delantera de paraíso	» 0.40
Sillón de Platea con entrada	1.00	Entrada de cazuela	
Tertulia balcón con entrada		á paraíso	0.30
" altas con "	» 0.80		

La película ha sido tomada por la Sección Foto-Cinematográfica de la Oficina de Exposiciones.

Las entradas se venden en la oficina de Informaciones, 18 de Julio 1110 de 8 á 21 horas.

Imp. «La Tribuna Popular»

On June 30, 1915 in the Teatro Solis a benefit for the Instituto de Ciegos was given.

On June 30, 1915 in the Teatro Solis a benefit for the Institute for the Blind (Instituto de Ciegos) was given. This performance was a combination of a Motion Picture, Music and Poetry.

The performers were:

Rebeca SANTOS CALVO, Poetry reciter
Silvia REGULES, guitarist
Julia Irene VITTONE, guitarist
Pedro L. IPUCHE, Poetry reciter
Julio OTERMIN, guitarist
Yamandú Rodríguez, Poetry reciter

The titles performed were:

Sinfonía — Verdi
Motion Picture 1st and 2nd part
Pericón
Motion Picture 3rd and 4th part
Marcha
Tabaré
Una lágrima
Mi patria
Lysistrata
Mensaje de América
Pericón Nacional

This is a special courtesy by Centro de Investigacion, Documentacion y Difusion de las Artes Escenicas. (CIDDAE) — Teatro Solis

My colleague, Alfredo Escande, went to the Biblioteca Nacional del Uruguay in Montevideo, at my request, to get the review of the benefit concert that involved Julio. J. Otermin.

Here is the translation from the daily *La Razon,* of the 30th of June of 1915:

The benefit of this night. Remembering the "Institute of the Blind"

How can we explain the success of this evening, without precedent of the program of this evening, for which the seating capacity was sold out for more than a week? Is it because the *Pericon* has awakened the enthusiasm so greatly? Is it because the film of *Aceguá* was so interesting? Perhaps it is the finale of the program, the benefit for the school of the blind directed by Mrs. Carmen Cuestas de Nery?

Julio J. Otermin is a professor and composer of guitar music. He resides in Montevideo, Uruguay. In 1906 he studied with the Spanish guitar professor Pedro Maza, then at the time, also residing in the same capital. He has two works published, *"Un Sueño"* and *"Perlas de Uruguay"*, the latter, which obtained the *"Primer Premio — Certamen España — Celebrado en Montevideo"* (First Prize — Spanish Composition Competition — Celebrated in Montevideo). Both of the compositions are *"Boston"* waltzes, of a well-achieved movement and relative musical value. This short biography is translated from the *"Diccionario de Guitarristas"* by Domingo Prat, published in 1934 by Romero y Fernández .

Both of the musical compositions mentioned by Domingo Prat were listed in the 1931 Antigua Casa Nuñez catalog. They are the only listed pieces for this artist.

In Richard "Rico" Stover's "Six Silver Moonbeams" — The Life and Times of Agustín Barrios Mangoré on page 43, he mentions a concert in the fall (March, April, May) of 1912 organized by Carlos Trapani, where Agustín Barrios as well as Julio Otermin and the Spanish guitarist Francisco Calleja performed. In listening to the original works by Otermin such as *"Nocturno"* it is easy to make note of the concert level compositions of his creative ability.

The members of the Trío de Guitarras del Uruguay were Carlos Maria Quintana, Julio Anastasio Méndez and Alberto Geletti. Carlos Maria Quintana wrote all the pieces for the Trio. Julio J. Otermin was not a member of this Trio despite Spanish language information on the internet saying so.

The earliest of these recordings were made on January 22, 1912 by the *Trío de Guitarras del Uruguay* and Julio J. Otermin's 18 guitar solos on February 1 and 2, 1912.

This information is from: The Encyclopedic Discography of Victor Recordings (EDVR) web site. A team of researchers based at the University of California, Santa Barbara Libraries edits the database.

Julio J. Otermin's 18 guitar solos were recorded some 14 months before the release of the initial recordings by Agustín Barrios on March 31, 1913. This now changes the perception that Barrios was the first Classical guitarist in the Rio de la Plata to extensively record, including Julio's recordings of the *Minuet en Do* from Op. 22 and the *Adagio* and *Allegro* from Op. 25 Second Grand Sonata by Fernando Sor.

This guitar solo *Apasionada-Gavota* by Julio Otermin was published by Carlos Trapani in Montevideo and sold in the Palacio de la Musica store operated by Ricardo and Rodolfo Gioscia in Montevideo.

This was the store where Francisco Simplicio, Domingo Esteso, Hermann Hauser I and Santos Hernández guitars were available for sale. Source: Richard Bruné

This song *Apasionada-Gavota* was the last of 18 guitar solos recorded by Julio on February 2, 1912.for Victor records.

Número			Tamaño Pulg. c/m
65604	(a) Por María—*Pericón y Gato* (Ant. D. Podestá) Banda del Pabellón de las Rosas	(b) Princesa—*Tango* (Carlos M. Quintana) Trío de Guitarras del Uruguay	10 25
65605	(a) Nunca me mordió un Chancho—*Tango criollo* (Cipolla) Orquesta Rodriguez	(b) ¿Cómo está la Situación?—*Tango* (G. Metallo) Banda del Pabellón de las Rosas	10 25
65606	(a) Diana—*Polka Militar* (G. Grasso) Banda del Pabellón de las Rosas	(b) Amina—*Polka* (Aguirre) Orquesta Rodriguez	10 25
65607	(a) Prevención—*Paso Doble* (Carlos M. Quintana) Trío de Guitarras del Uruguay	(b) ¿ Sí o No?—*Habanera* (Otermín) *Solo de Guitarra* Julio J. Otermín	10 25
65608	(a) Ciaguá—*Tango* (Carlos M. Quintana) Trío de Guitarras del Uruguay	(b) Qué Piedra—*Tango* (Otermín) *Solo de Guitarra* Julio J. Otermín	10 25
65609	(a) Nocturno (Otermín) *Solo de Guitarra* Julio J. Otermín	(b) Preludio en Mi Menor (Otermín) *Solo de Guitarra* Julio J. Otermín	10 25
63713	(a) María Adela—*Vals—Selección de Acordeón* (R. A. Alcorta) Rafael A. Alcorta	(b) Fantasía Morisca—*Dúo de Guitarra y Bandurria* (Chapi) Los Alpinos	10 25
63714	(a) Desmemoriado—*Monólogo* (Parravicini) Florencio Parravicini	(b) ¡Qué Barbaridad!—*Tango Solo de Guitarra* Julio J. Otermín	10 25
63722	(a) Sueño Magnífico—*Cómico* (I. Corsini) (Con Guitarra) Ignacio Corsini	(b) El Crack Larrea—*Tango* (G. Espósito) (*Bandonión, Clarinete, Violín, Guitarra*) Orquesta Típica de Gennaro Espósito	10 25
63723	(a) Soleares (Juan Ríos) (Con Guitarra) Juan Ríos	(b) Los Invisibles—*Tango* (Barsanti) Orquesta Típica de Gennaro Espósito	10 25

Número			Tamaño Pulg. c/m
65033	(a) Coquimbo—*Tango* (Carlos M. Quintana) Trío de Guitarras del Uruguay	(b) Olas que mueren—*Vals lento* (J. Otermín) *Solo de Guitarra* Julio J. Otermín	10 25
65034	(a) Pobre Valbuena—*Polka Japonesa* (Torregrossa y Valverde) *Dúo de Guitarra y Bandurria* Los Alpinos	(b) Sevillanas—*Varios Estilos Dúo de Guitarra y Bandurria* Los Alpinos	10 25
65035	(a) De Madrid a Paris—*Terceto de las Cigarreras* (Chueca) *Dúo de Guitarra y Bandurria* Los Alpinos	(b) Machaquito—*Paso doble torero* López *Dúo de Guitarra y Bandurria* Los Alpinos	10 25
65161	(a) Las Bribonas—*Fantasía* (Calleja) *Dúo de Guitarra y Bandurria* Los Alpinos	(b) Reverte—*Paso doble torero* (Arraujo) *Dúo de Guitarra y Bandurria* Los Alpinos	10 25
65162	(a) Maldonado—*Tango* (Carlos M. Quintana) Trío de Guitarras del Uruguay	(b) Voluptuoso—*Vals Boston* (J. Otermín) *Solo de Guitarra* Julio J. Otermín	10 25

Número			Tamaño Pulg. c/m
65384	(a) Nuevo Auxilio—*Tango* (Ant. A. Cipolla) Banda del Pabellón de las Rosas	(b) Cuarto Departamental—*Marcha* (C. M. Quintana) Trío de Guitarras de Uruguay	10 25
65391	(a) El Cosquilloso—*Tango* (C. M. Quintana) Trío de Guitarras de Uruguay	(b) Gato—*Solo de Guitarra* (J. Otermín) Julio J. Otermín	10 25
65392	(a) Mazzantini—*Paso Doble Torero* (Martínez) *Dúo de Guitarra y Bandurria* Los Alpinos	(b) De frente—*Marcha Militar Solo de Guitarra* Julio J. Otermín	10 25

Número			Tamaño Pulg. c/m
63724	(a) Don Samuel—*Tango—Bandonión, Clarinete, Violín, Guitarra* (S. Castrioto) Orq. Típica Gennaro Espósito	(b) El Figaro—*Mazurka—Dúo de Guitarra y Bandurria* (Dionisio Granados) Los Alpinos	10 25
63725	(a) Olimar—*Tango* (Quintana) Trío de Guitarras del Uruguay	(b) Vidalita (Otermín) *Solo de Guitarra* Julio J. Otermín	10 25
63731	(a) Soleares Flamencos (T. Castro) *Solo de Guitarra* Niño de Cádiz	(b) Guajiras Vida Mía (Con Guitarra) Juan Ríos	10 25
63735	(a) Gagancha—*Tango* (Quintana) Trío de Guitarras del Uruguay	(b) En el Rancho—*Pericón* (Otermín) (*Solo de Guitarra*) Julio J. Otermín	10 25
63736	(a) Mi Nena—*Tango* (Otermin) (*Solo de Guitarra*) Julio J. Otermín	(b) El Aeroplano Parra—*Monólogo* (Parravicini) F. Parravicini	10 25
65483	(a) Coquito—*Tango* (P. Aguirre) Banda del Pabellón de las Rosas	(b) Vanguardia—*Vals* (Carlos M. Quintana) Trío de Guitarras del Uruguay	10 25
65484	(a) Taura—*Tango* (A. Podestá) Banda del Pabellón de las Rosas	(b) Mazurka Gaucha (Carlos M. Quintana) Trío de Guitarras del Uruguay	10 25
65485	(a) Muleque—*Tango* (A. Podestá) Banda del Pabellón de las Rosas	(b) La Miliquera—*Marcha* (Carlos M. Quintana) Trío de Guitarras del Uruguay	10 25
65486	(a) Apasionada—*Gavota* (J. Otermín) *Solo de Guitarra* Julio J. Otermín	(b) Zorzano—*Vals* (Zorzano) *Dúo de Guitarra y Bandurria* Los Alpinos	10 25
65487	(a) Viva la Jota—*Marcha* (Marquina) *Dúo de Guitarra y Bandurria* Los Alpinos	(b) Capricho Morisco—*Fantasía* (T. Castro) *Solo de Guitarra* Niño de Cádiz	10 25

These are from a 1915 Uruguay Victor Talking Machine Company catalog.

65486
- (a) Apasionada—*Gavota* (J. Otermín) *Solo de Guitarra* — Julio Otermín
- (b) Zorzano—*Vals* (Zorzano) *Dúo de Guitarra y Bandurria* — Los Alpinos
10 25

65487
- (a) Viva la Jota—*Marcha* (Marquina) *Dúo de Guitarra y Bandurria* — Los Alpinos
- (b) Capricho Morisco—*Fantasía* (T. Castro) *Solo de Guitarra* — Niño de Cádiz
10 25

65607
- (a) Prevención—*Paso doble* (C. M. Quintana) *Trío de Guitarras del Uruguay*
- (b) ¿ Sí o No?—*Habanera* (Otermín) *Solo de Guitarra* — Julio J. Otermín
10 25

65608
- (a) Ciaguá—*Tango* (C. M. Quintana) *Trío de Guitarras del Uruguay*
- (b) Qué Piedra—*Tango* (Otermín) *Solo de Guitarra* — Julio J. Otermín
10 25

65609
- (a) Nocturno (Otermín) *Solo de Guitarra* Julio J. Otermín
- (b) Preludio en Mi menor (Otermín) *Solo de Guitarra* — Julio J. Otermín
10 25

65161
- (a) Las Bribonas—*Fantasía* (Calleja) *Dúo de Guitarra y Bandurria* — Los Alpinos
- (b) Reverte—*Paso doble torero* (Araujo) *Dúo de Guitarra y Bandurria* — Los Alpinos
10 25

65162
- (a) Maldonado—*Tango* (Carlos M. Quintana) *Trío de Guitarras del Uruguay*
- (b) Voluptuoso—*Vals Boston* (J. Otermín)
10 25

63736
- (a) Mi Nena—*Tango* (Otermín) *Solo de Guitarra* Julio J. Otermín
- (b) El Aeroplano Parra—*Monólogo* (Parravicini) F. Parravicini
10 25

63786
- (a) Esperanza—*Polka* *Dúo de guitarras* Yañes-Roldán
- (b) La Mesmerista—*Polka* *Dúo de guitarras* Yañes-Roldán
10 25

63694
- (a) Canción del Vagabundo (Serrano) *Dúo de Guitarra y Bandurria* — Los Alpinos
- (b) Genio y Figura—*Serenata* *Dúo de Guitarra y Bandurria* — Los Alpinos
10 25

63695
- (a) Potpourri de Cantos Flamencos—*Dúo de Guitarra y Bandurria* — Los Alpinos
- (b) Garrotin—*Baile Español* *Dúo de Guitarra y Bandurria* — Los Alpinos
10 25

63711
- (a) Alborada de Montes—*Aire Regional Español* *Solo de Gaita con tambor* — Manuel Dopazo
- (b) Rebeirano de Porriño—*Aire Regional Español* *Solo de Gaita con tambor* — Manuel Dopazo
10 25

63713
- (a) María Adela—*Vals* (R. A. Alcorta) *Selección de Acordeón* — Rafael A. Alcorta
- (b) Fantasía Morisca (Chapí) *Dúo de Guitarra y Bandurria* — Los Alpinos
10 25

63714
- (a) Desmemoriado—*Monólogo* (Parravicini) Florencio Parravicini
- (b) ¡Qué Barbaridad!—*Tango* *Solo de Guitarra* Julio J. Otermín
10 25

63725
- (a) Olimar—*Tango* (Quintana) *Trío de Guitarras de Uruguay*
- (b) Vidalita (Otermín) *Solo de Guitarra* Julio J. Otermín
10 25

63731
- (a) Soleares Flamencos (T. Castro) *Solo de Guitarra* Niño de Cádiz
- (b) Guajiras Vida Mia (con *Guitarra*) Juan Ríos
10 25

65483
- (a) Coquito—*Tango* (P. Aguirre) Banda del Pabellón de las Rosas
- (b) Vanguardia—*Vals* (Carlos M. Quintana) Trío de Guitarras del Uruguay
10 25

65484
- (a) Taura—*Tango* (A. Podestá) Banda del Pabellón de las Rosas
- (b) Mazurka Gaucha (Carlos M. Quintana) Trío de Guitarras del Uruguay
10 25

65485
- (a) Muleque—*Tango* (A. Podestá) Banda del Pabellón de las Rosas
- (b) La Miliquera—*Marcha* (Carlos M. Quintana) Trío de Guitarras del Uruguay
10 25

65486
- (a) Apasionada—*Gavota* (J. Otermín) *Solo de Guitarra* Julio J. Otermín
- (b) Zorzano—*Vals* (Zorzano) *Dúo de Guitarra y Bandurria* Los Alpinos
10 25

65487
- (a) Viva la Jota—*Marcha* (Marquina) *Dúo de Guitarra y Bandurria* Los Alpinos
- (b) Capricho Morisco—*Fantasía* (T. Castro) *Solo de Guitarra* Niño de Cádiz
10 25

62582
- (a) La Paloma (Yradier) *Solo de Bandurria* Ramírez
- (b) Cavalleria Rusticana—*Intermezzo Sinfónico* (Mascagni) *Solo de Bandurria* Ramírez
10 25

62800
- (a) Pamplona—*Vals* *Trío de Bandurrias y Guitarra* Estudiantina Centenario
- (b) Alegría de la Huerta—*Jota* (Chueca) *Trío de Bandurrias y Guitarra* Estudiantina Centenario
10 25

62801
- (a) Árabe—*Paso doble torero* *Trío de Bandurrias y Guitarra* Estudiantina Centenario
- (b) Santiago—*Vals* *Trío de Bandurrias y Guitarra* Estudiantina Centenario
10 25

62802
- (a) El Esquinazo—*Tango* *Trío de Bandurrias y Guitarra* Estudiantina Centenario
- (b) La Castaña del Gitano—*Vals* (García) *Trío de Bandurrias y Guitarra* Estudiantina Centenario
10 25

These are from a 1915 Uruguay Victor Talking Machine Company catalog.

2224

xxx

These are from a 1915 Uruguay Victor Talking Machine Company catalog.

On January 22, 1912 The *Trio de Guitarras del Uruguay* began recording. The members were Carlos Maria Quintana, Julio Anastasio Mendez and Alberto Geletti. The four songs they recorded that day were *Cuarto departamental* Victor 65384 A, *Fogonero* Victor 63909 A, *Coquimbo* Victor 65033 A and *Caiguá* Victor 65608 A. They returned the next day January 23, 1912 to record eleven more pieces. The first song was *Princesa* Victor 65604 B. The "A" side was recorded by the Banda del Pabellon de las Rosas. The song was *Por Maria*. The next piece was *El cosquilloso* Victor 65391 A.

The pressing of the Victor "Batwing" label is a later pressing than the original pressings shown at the bottom of this page and others.

The *Trio Guitarras del Uruguay* recorded *Gagancha-Tango* Victor 63735 A on January 23, 1912. On February 1, 1912 Julio J. Otermin went into the Victor recording studio in Buenos Aires and recorded 14 tracks. The first song was *¡Qué piedra!* Victor 65608 B. Track number 4 was *En el rancho — Pericon*.

The *Trio Guitarras del Uruguay* recorded *El Cosquilloso — Tango* Victor 65391 A on January 23, 1912, and Julio J. Otermin had recorded *Gato* Victor 65391 B on February 1, 1912. The Trio recorded *La miliguera* Victor 65485 A on January 23, 1912 and the "B" side *Muleque* by the *Banda del Pabellón de las Rosas* was recorded on February 15, 1912. The Trio's next release was *El chacarero —Tango* Victor 63715 A recorded on the same day. Julio's *Estilo y Relación*   Victor 63715 B was recorded on February 1, 1912.

The *Trio de Guitarras del Uruguay* piece *Olimar* Victor 63725 A was recorded on January 23, 1912. On February 1, 1912 Julio J. Otermin recorded the guitar solo *Vidalita* Victor 63725 B.

The *Trio de Guitarras del Uruguay* piece *Prevención* Victor 65607 A was recorded on January 23, 1912. On February 1, 1912 Julio J. Otermin recorded the *Habanera Si o no?* Victor 65607B.

The *Trio de Guitarras del Uruguay* piece *Vanguardia* Victor 65483 A was recorded on January 23, 1912, and the *Banda del Pabellón de las Rosas* song *Coquito* was recorded on February 15, 1912.

The *Trio de Guitarras del Uruguay* piece *Guana* Victor 65032A was recorded on January 23, 1912, and the *Banda del Pabellón de las Rosas* song *¿Me gustus, sabes?* was recorded on February 15, 1912.

The *Trio del Guitarras del Uruguay* piece *Mazurka Gaucha* Victor 65484 B was recorded on January 23, 1912, and the *Banda del Pabellón de las Rosas* song *Taura* was recorded on February 15, 1912.

On February 1, 1912 Julio J. Otermin recorded his second and third guitar solos *Mi nena — Tango* Victor 63736 A and *Qué Barbaridad — Tango* Victor 63714 B. The other sides were speeches by Florencio Parravicini recorded on February 23, 1912.

On February 1, 1912 Julio J. Otermin recorded his eighth, ninth and tenth guitar solos *Voluptuoso* Victor 65162 A, *En el prado* Victor 63909 B, *Olas que mueren* Victor 65033 B. Julio's *De frente* Victor 65392 B was coupled with Los Alpinos' *Mazzantini* Victor 65392 A.

Then Julio J. Otermin began to record the first of three pieces by Fernando Sor, two from Op. 25 *Second Grand Sonata. Adagio* Victor 65866 B, this was coupled with the vocal with guitar accompaniment *La novia del payador* sung by Diego Munilla Victor 65866 A. The next Sor piece from Op. 25 was *Allegro* Victor 65867 B and the other side being a different take of *La novia del payador* by vocalist Diego Munilla Victor 65867 A. On February 2, 1912, the last day of Julio's recordings he did Op. 22 *Minuet en do mayor* Victor 65868 B by Fernando Sor and the vocal *Triunfo* by Diego Munilla was recorded on

January 20, 1912.

Next Julio J. Otermin recorded both *Nocturno* Victor 65609 A, and *Preludio en mi menor* Victor 65609 B. The last song he was to record was *Apasionada* Victor 65486 B, coupled with the January 8, 1912 recording of *Zarzano* by the *Bandurria* and Guitar duo *Los Alpinos*.

As Domingo Prat said in his short biography of Julio Otermin in his *"Diccionario de Guitarristas"*, the guitarist had won the *Primer Premio — Certamen España — Celebrado en Montevideo"* (First Prize — Spanish Composition Competition — Celebrated in Montevideo) with his composition *"Perlas de Uruguay"*. There is a stamped date of July 1, 1907 just to the left of the dedication to Francisco Nuñez on the cover of that composition. He became a recording artist less than 5 years later.

These two covers were a part of a multi-volume hardbound edition made for Mario Rodríguez Arenas by his publisher Francisco Nuñez. Volume 6 contains 86 pieces by a dozen composers. The translation of the text on the cover is: "Album of Music for guitar. A gift that is in Honor of the Argentine Centennial made by Casa Nuñez to the Professor and composer Mario Rodríguez Arenas.

Francisco Nuñez
editor
Cuyo 1628 Buenos Aires

Note: The street name Cuyo was changed to Sarmiento after the Centennial in 1910.

Similar commemorative volumes of Juan Alais and Julio S. Sagreras were listed in the 1931 Antigua Casa Nuñez catalog, they were available for 30 and 35 *pesos* respectively having 86 and 110 pieces for each composer respectively.

This *Minuet en DO* from Op. 22 by Fernando Sor was recorded on February 2, 1912, and is one of the earliest recordings of Sor's music.

It predates recordings by Agustín Barrios by at least 9 months.

The tango singer Ignacio Corsini began his recording career on the same day, February 2, 1912 for Victor records as well.

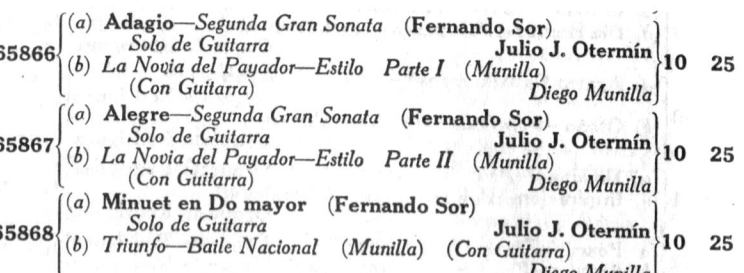

From a 1915 Uruguay Victor Talking Machine Company catalog page 236 are the listings of 3 pieces written by Fernando Sor on three discs recorded by Julio J. Otermin still available to the public in Argentina and Uruguay.

My colleague, Alfredo Escande, went to the Biblioteca Nacional del Uruguay in Montevideo, at my request, to get the funeral notice of Julio. J. Otermin.

Here is my translation from the daily *El Pais* of October 16, 1943.

Retired Capitán, Julio Otermin

Yesterday, the 15th of October of 1943, he passed away in peace of the Lord. His wife, Sara Gomez de Otermin, his daughter, María Julia Otermin, his son, a politician, Juan Pérez Valverde, his grandchildren, Gracielita and Jorgito Pérez Otermin, etc. have given notice that the funeral will be held in the Cementerio Central, of Montevideo.

This is translated from the book by Cedar Viglietti *"Origen y Historia de la Guitarra"* published by Editorial Albatros in Buenos Aires in 1973.

Cedar Viglietti says on page 221: "To Julio Otermin we cite him by 1900 as a duo with José Maria Lopez. We wrote 25 years ago in the book *"Folklore en el Uruguay"* that someone recorded having heard Julio with a brother or two — all young boys — to play on several guitars a Pericon in a small theater on calle Agraciada, between Lima and Asuncion, two centésimos per ticket, the said musicians behind a curtain, while in front of it the puppets danced a gaucha dance. Two of the said brothers, Manuel and Julio, we see much later in *"La Lira"* at an important performance for the Asociacion de la Prensa: among phrases by Chapi, *"La Africana"*, *"Celeste Aida"*, directing the Manuel Pérez Badia orchestra (possibly the symphonic orchestra of the Sociedad Beethoven that had performed since 1897), were heard to the poem by Papini y Zas, a Lieutenant Vicente F. Magallanes in a discourse, and a finale by Juan Zorilla of San Martin. The 1st part of the variety show finished with a *"Fantasia para seis (6) Guitarras"* by the gentlemen José R. Habiaga, Leoncio Marichal, Antonio Piola, Julio and Manuel Otermin and Hilario Garalde, certainly was a very beautiful song and quite applauded." (*"Montevideo Musical"* November 1900.)

The 18th of July of that year, in the club Naval: "by Mattini, *4th Minueto*, quartet of mandocello, mandola, and two mandolins, by Carlos, Elbio, and Horacio Trapani and S. Cetrulo. To that the two Otermin brothers playing a duo of *"Una Lagrima* and *"Manonga"* — a *salon mazurka* — both by Gaspar Sagreras.

We can say that only Julio Otermin dedicated to the discipline in a preferred form: a disciple of Pedro Maza, he studied for a month at a later date with Pujol. Generally, he is remembered giving classes. He played the typical music well, having recorded some tangos with good taste.

He composed and published some pieces: *"Un Sueño"* and *"Perlas de Uruguay"*, *"El Uruguayo"*, etc. We have *"En el rancho"* a manuscript we were given many years ago by Mr. Conti, an adimrer and disciple of his. They are works of discreet worth. Perhaps his best merit would have been to guide the first steps of Conrado P. Koch. Julio was a military man and held the rank of Captain."

Cedar Viglietti says on page 202: "From some unpublished notes by Miguel Herrera Klinger — he synthesizes the following: 'By 1912 Herrera was invited one night to the Trapani music house since two foreign guitarists (Agustín Barrios and Francisco Calleja) awaited him: Julio Otermin who played an eleven string guitar, the novelty that Manjón brought.' This concert has been well documented by Richard "Rico" Stover in his "Six Silver Moonbeams — The Life and Times of Agustín Barrios". The Victor recordings in February 1912 by Julio Otermin were played on a six string guitar.

(Right) The transcription by José Maria Lopez of the *"Himno Nacional de Uruguay"* by Deballi (sic) Debali. It was published by *"Edicion Luis Esteve"* Sarandi 361. Montevideo / Edicion Luis Filardi Bme' Mitre 2288 Buenos Aires. The address of Luis Filardi is a later one than his turn of the century address, dating this to probably c. 1920.

José Maria Lopez's first advertisement in the *"Montevideo Musical"* magazine on August 24, 1892 No. 32 Año VIII. He is listed at the bottom of the list of 25 professors of Voice, Piano, Harp, *Solfeggio,* Harmony, Violin, Oboe, Flute, Mandolin and Guitar.

Below that is a standard advertisement for Luis Esteve.He was initially a piano teacher, then opened his piano store, after which he became a publisher of sheet music. As we see he offered 12 brands of pianos to the wealthy population of 400,000 in Montevideo. These were imported from both Europe and the United States.

His announcement of his intentions and first advertisement were on September 24, 1887 No. 35 Año II.

From the *"Seccion Noticiosa"* (News Section) of the Montevideo Musical" magazine on October 16, 1892 No. 39 Año VIII.

Translation: "The *Estudiantina* of the Rio de la Plata, that is under the direction of professor José M. Lopez, continues their rehearsals and is available to perform their debut in one of our social centers.

It is comprised of guitars and mandolins."

✠

La Estudiantina del Plata que está bajo la direccion del profesor, José M. Lopez, prosigue sus ensayos y se dispone á efectuar su debut en uno de nuestros centros sociales.
Esta ella compuesta de guitarras y mandolines.

✠

Iparraguirre, P., Bailecito "Cuando nada te debía" .... $ 1.—
— Chúcaro, gato clásico (Filiberto, J. de D.) .... » 1.—
— Cuartelera, La., estilo con letra .... » 0.50
— De tierra adentro, zamba N.º 2 de "Auras argentinas" .... » 1.—
— Los rosales se han secao, zamba (Avilés, A.) .... » 1.—
— Pampeano, El, estilo con letra .... » 0.50
— Pobre mi madre querida, estilo con letra (Bettinoti) .... » 0.50
— Queríme, serrana; tonada (Filiberto, J. de D.) .... » 1.—
— Robarla será mejor, zamba (Avilés, A.) .... » 1.—
— Tacuarita, La; zamba (Filiberto, J. de D.) .... » 1.—
— Triste entrerriano .... » 1.—
— Variaciones sobre la vidalita N.º 3 de "Auras argentinas" ..... » 1.—
— » » un triste N.º 1 de » » ...... » 1.—
— Zamba de Vargas .... » 1.—
Juarranz, E., La Giralda, marcha andaluza .... » 1.20
Leloup, H., Aires argentinos, gran poutpourri .... » 1.80
— Himno Nacional Argentino .... » 1.50
— No te olvido, zortzico .... » 1.—
— Pericón Nacional .... » 1.—
Llobet, M., Danza española N.º 5 (Granados) .... » 1.50
— Filla del Marxant, La (La hija del Mercader), melodía popular
catalana .... » 1.—
— Hoja del album y Romanza (Schumann) .... » 1.20
— L'Hereu Riera, melodía popular catalana .... » 1.50
— Mestre, El (El maestro), melodía popular catalana .... » 1.50
— Minueto de la Sinfonía N.º 39 (Mozart), para dos guitarras ..... » 1.50
— Plany, melodía popular catalana .... » 1.50
— Romanza .... » 1.50
— Testament d'Amelia, El; melodía popular catalana .... » 1.50
Lopardo, J., En la selva, estilo con letra .... » 0.60
— Llora, guitarra mía; estilo .... » 0.70
López, J. U., Himno Nacional Uruguayo (Deballi) ......p...... » 0.60
López Villanueva, J., Guajiras .... » 0.80
Luna, A. V., ¡Ay, mi negra!; vidala, armonizada para una y tres guitarras » 0.80
— Chacarera, danza popular .... » 1.—
— Donosita, zamba .... » 0.80
— Flor de tusca; zamba riojana, canto y guitarra .... » 0.80
— Música incásica, álbum de 5 piezas (Manuel José Benavente):
1) Himno al sol; 2) Huaynú; 3) Marcha del inca; 4) Yaraví, y
Danza del sol (Danza de las ñustas) .... » 3.—
— Música nacional, 1er. álbum de 5 piezas (M. Gómez Carrillo):
1) Pobre mi negra; 2) Zamba de Vargas; 3) Gato; 4) Trova, y
5) El Cuando .... » 2.50
— Música nacional, 2.º álbum de 5 piezas (M. Gómez Carrillo):
1) Nocturno; canto de amor, estilo; 2) No me pagues mal, bai-
ecito; 3) Yerba buena, zamba; 4) Chacarera, danza, y 5) Chu-
rito, gato .... » 2.50
— Música nacional, 3er. álbum de 5 piezas, para canto y guitarra

Florida 255. — Cangallo 1574. — B. Mitre 947

The listing of the transcription by José Maria Lopez of the *"Himno Nacional de Uruguay"* by Deballi (sic) Debali in the c. Fall *1928 "Romero & Fernández Catalogo No. 5, Métodos y Musica para Guitarra"* catalog of 34 pages.

2235

Translating from Ricardo Muñoz's unpublished book *"Historia Universal de la Guitarra"* Volume VI *"America"*. The photo below is from the same biography.

"Abel Julio Carlevaro

His Origin:

He is the son of the Doctor *Don* Juan Carlos Carlevaro and of *Doña* Blanca Casal, born in Montevideo the 16th of December of 1918, and baptized with the names Abel Julio Carlevaro Casal.

His Education:

He started on the guitar at the age of 7 with the maestro Pedro Vittone, and later harmony, counterpoint and orchestration in the Conservatorio of Montevideo, with maestro *Don* Pablo Kombos. At the same time, he studied agricultural engineering.

In 1937 he met the great Andrés Segovia, who recognized in the young Carlevaro his exceptional faculties already developed, and he became his adviser for the next 9 years.

His Virtuosity:

The 25th of October of 1940, in honor of the eminent Brazilian musician *Don* Heitor Villa-Lobos at the Centro Guitarristico del Uruguay "Conrado P. Koch", after the opening words by the musicologist *Don* Francisco Curt Lange, he played on his guitar *"Preludio"* by Mujica, *"Confesion"* by Barrios, *"Choro No. 1"* by Villa-Lobos, *"Vals"* by Ponce, *"Nocturno"* by Moreno Torroba, and *"Leyenda"* by Albeniz with great success.

In 1942 *Don* Andrés Segovia presented him before the public at the S. O. D. R. E. in Montevideo, saying among other things: 'This austere young man, whose soul heard the unequivocal call of the Vocation loves the Saint of disciplined Study. He has vigorous wings to advance to the far heavens. I predict a good crossing and happy arrival at the legitimate Success.' This performance gave the guideline about the prophecies of Segovia; the critics of the magazine *"Mundo Uruguayo"* said: '.... the most beautiful affirmation of nobility and of artistic and instrumental capacity.' (November 19, 1942)

The daily *"El Debate"* of the 13th of the same month reported: '.... We are in the presence of an absolute artist, essence and outside spiritual flesh.'

Don Leopold Stokowski who heard him aboard the steamship *"Uruguay"*, en route to the United States of America, made the departure of the ship delayed, in order to continue listening to him in his private cabin.

In 1943 he performed among other works, the *"Concertino"* for guitar and orchestra, which the maestro Santorsola wrote expressly for him; *"El Tiempo"* the 5th of September, said: 'In Abel Carlevaro I had an admirable interpreter, who reveals himself as an artist.'

In 1946, the distinguished musician *Don* Eduardo Fabini, expressed: 'I think that, the State must facilitate the making of an artistic tour which can culminate in North America, of the mode that they will know the admirable endowments of his instrumental skill and fine musicality.'

Similar declarations spill from critics in general of the country and finally, the Government, in that scholarships don't exist for the case, conferred upon him the necessary resources. Then he made an important tour that traveled to Paris, London, Barcelona, Granada, New York, Rio de Janeiro, Porto Alegre, Buenos Aires and Montevideo, consecrated by the best guitaristic capitals of the Americas. 'A new Segovia' said the *"Arte de Paris"*; 'He possesses the talent to enchant the audience' was declared in London; 'A secure and rich range of timbre' was said in Barcelona; 'He is called the Glory of Uruguay, as one of the most serious values of his instrument, technically perfect, clean and pure he unites in it a very pure musicality, for giving the sum of his art which he raises by his warmth and renovated possibilities.'

On Monday the 23rd of July of 1945 he arrived at the Teatro Odeon in Buenos Aires and performed *"Preludio, Allemande, Sarabanda, Bourée, Double* and *Gavota"* by Bach, *"Variaciones sobre la Folia de España"* and *"Fuga"* by Ponce, *"Nocturno"* by Moreno Torroba, *"Rafaga"* by Turina and *"Leyenda"* by Albeniz with a complete success. *"La Prensa"* the following day reported: '.... accredited to be a noble stylist, of a ductile and personal temperament, an instrumentalist which he, has the security of technique that forms an alliance of the variety and amplitude of sonority.'

In Rio de Janeiro, he recorded the *"Concertino"* for guitar and orchestra by the composer Santorsola, and the *"Concierto para guitarra y orquesta"* by the great composer *Don* Mauricio Ohana in Paris in the years 1950-51.

So ends the short biography by Ricardo Muñoz.

In Alfredo Escande's biography of "Abel Carlevaro — Un nuevo mundo en la Guitarra" other details are of interest. Abel had received a scholarship from the government of Uruguay on June 14, 1946 to study in Europe for two years. On September 1, 1947 he gave his farewell concert in the Teatro Solis. At the end of April of 1948 he boarded a ship bound for Barcelona, and arrived just after the middle of May. In August of that year he made a short documentary for Warner Brothers. On August 12, 1948 the Barcelona Teatral made mention of this film, also on the 25th of the same month the daily *El Noticero Universal* praised the completion of such a work. In it he performed *"Asturias"* by Albeniz and *"Las Abejas"* by Agustín Barrios. On the same steamship Abel returned to Montevideo in February of 1951. On February 26, 1951 the Montevideo daily *"La Mañana"* reported that the film had been shown in Canada and North America and had been shown on television some sixty times.

In London in October of 1949 Abel recorded a 12 inch disc of *"Tarantella"* by Castelnuovo-Tedesco, *"Las Abejas"* by Agustín Barrios and *"Estudio No. 1"* by Villa-Lobos for Parlophone-Odeon records.

This is from the *"Revista de la Guitarra"* magazine issue No. 10 *Año* IV of June 1942.
Translation:

"From Abroad

Montevideo (Uruguay)

The guitarist Abel Carlevaro made his presentation to the public of the neighboring edge in the Estudio Auditorio (S. O. D. R. E.) on Thursday the 12th of November with a program on a great scale, by authors such as Alonso de Mudarra, Bach, Sor, Ponce, Castelnuovo-Tedesco, Moreno Torroba, and Albeniz.

He is a student of the great guitarist Andrés Segovia, and it is true that is a sufficient label of heirarchy."

DEL EXTERIOR

MONTEVIDEO (Uruguay) —

El guitarrista Abel Carlevaro hizo su presentación al público de la vecina orilla en el Estudio Auditorio (S. O. D. R. E.) el jueves 12 de noviembre con un programa de gran embargadura, de autores como Alonso de Mudarra, Bach, Sor, Ponce, Castelnuovo Tedesco, Moreno Torroba y Albéniz.

Alumno del gran guitarrista Andrés Segovia, cabe decir que ya eso es sello suficiente de gerarquía.

This review of the award winning 12" LP by Abel Carlevaro in 1958 is from the "The Guitar on Discs" section by Carl Miller from "The Guitar Review" magazine issue No. 23 of June 1959. Abel used a 1933 Santos Hernández guitar in his many concerts and on this LP. His tone and interpretation were very much like his maestro, Andrés Segovia, rather than the approach he used later in his career. In 1972 Abel Carlevaro sold the guitar to American Classical Guitarist Guy Horn, and in 1997 I sold this instrument at my guitar store Fine Fretted String Instruments.

ABEL CARLEVARO, Recital de Guitarra
(Antar-Telefunken ALP 1002) [PONCE: Variaciones sobre "Folia de Espana" y Fuga; TORROBA: Preambulo, Oliveras, Nocturno; ALBENIZ: Torre Bermeja, Asturias.]

This recording from Uruguay by an outstanding guitarist has been awarded a Gran Premio del Disco, 1958. To have a complete version of Ponce's Variations available is a good thing. Carlevaro plays with taste and skill. Ranging from simple, folk-like settings to intensely complicated versions, the variations are a real test for the performer. At times the performance loses energy especially in the more contemplative sections.

It is difficult not to compare the Torroba pieces with Segovia's playing of them. This would be most unfair to do. Suffice to say that there can always be more than one way of performing a musical composition. Carlevaro's way is not the most dynamic. He spins out a quiet line, full of dark colors and mysterious perfumes. His performances of the Albéniz pieces are really the best on this disc.

Abel Carlevaro farewell recital on Monday September 1, 1947 in the Teatro Solis in Montevideo, before his departure fro Europe in April of 1948.

This is a special courtesy by Centro de Investigacion, Documentacion y Difusion de las Artes Escenicas. (CIDDAE) — Teatro Solis.

FUNDAMENTOS DEL

Mensaje del Poder Ejecutivo

a la Asamblea General, solicitando una beca a favor de ABEL CARLEVARO para que se traslade a Europa y a los Estados Unidos de N. América.

Ministerio de Instrucción Pública y Previsión Social.

Ministerio de Hacienda.

A la Asamblea General:

Con fecha 14 de junio de 1946, la Cámara de Representantes elevó al Ministerio de Instrucción Pública y Previsión Social, versión taquigráfica de las palabras pronunciadas en aquel Cuerpo por el señor Diputado doctor José P. Cardozo referente a la gestión planteada ante esta Secretaría de Estado por los críticos musicales, autoridades del S.O.D.R.E. y otras organizaciones culturales tendientes a lograr medios para facilitar el traslado del artista compatriota don Abel Carlevaro a los Estados Unidos de Norte América.

El Poder Ejecutivo, haciéndose eco de tan autorizadas opiniones y considerando que no pueden ser desoídas tan justas aspiraciones, tratándose de un artista de singular valía, ha resuelto elevar a ese alto Cuerpo para su consideración y aprobación el adjunto proyecto de ley.

En razón de no existir un sistema de becas que contemple casos como el presente, el Poder Ejecutivo se ve en la necesidad de hacer conocer al Parlamento la justicia en que funda esta solicitud de recursos para facilitar el traslado a los grandes centros de cultura de un joven músico que ha sido una extraordinaria revelación en el ambiente nacional.

Las opiniones críticas de tres países del Continente: Uruguay, Argentina y Brasil, consignan sus relevantes cualidades, clasificándolas como excepcionales.

Es necesario pues, y así lo estima el Poder Ejecutivo, que Abel Carlevaro ensanche su panorama de actuación en ambientes que como el de Estados Unidos congrega en su seno en la actualidad a los más grandes valores del arte contemporáneo.

El S.O.D.R.E. expresó en su oportunidad ante las palabras del Diputado Cardoso lo siguiente: "Que considera de evidente importancia e interés, tanto para la brillante carrera artística del guitarrista Carlevaro, como para el conocimiento de uno de nuestros más representativos valores musicales, el facilitar el viaje de dicho concertista a la Estados Unidos de América".

Eduardo Fabini, nuestro gran compositor manifestó: "Pienso que el Estado debiera facilitarle la realización de una gira artística que podría culminar en Norte América, de modo que se conocieran sus admirables dotes de instrumentista diestro y su fina musicalidad".

En idénticos términos admirativos se dirigen al Ministerio de Instrucción Pública y Previsión Social, la unanimidad de los críticos musicales de nuestro país.

Cree pues el Poder Ejecutivo recoger en el adjunto proyecto de ley, una aspiración unánime de quienes han juzgado los grandes valores de Abel Carlevaro.

Para el cumplimiento de lo cual, solicita de ese alto Cuerpo la sanción del adjunto proyecto de ley.

Aprovecha la oportunidad para saludar a esa Asamblea General con su mayor consideración. — TOMAS BERRETA. — FRANCISCO FORTEZA. — LEDO ARROYO TORRES.

This page details the scholarship awarded by the Parliament of Uruguay for a tour of Europe and the United States for a period of two years.

2240

Translation of the previous page:

Basics of the Message by the Executive Power

to the General Assembly, soliciting a scholarship for Abel Carlevaro, to move to Europe and The United States of North America.

Minister of Public Instruction and Social Outlook.
To the General Assembly:

With the date of the 14th of June of 1946, the Chamber of Representatives has raised to the Minister of Public Instruction and Social Outlook, a shorthand version of the spoken words in that Body by the Delegate Dr. Jos P. Cardoso referring to the management raised before the Secretary of State by the music critics, authorities of the S.O.D.R.E. and other cultural organizations tending to achieve measures to facilitate the moving of the compatriot artist *Don* Abel Carlevaro, to the United States in North America.

The Executive Power, to be making an echo of such authorized opinions and considering that such just aspirations can't be disregarded, a case of an artist of outstanding worth, has turned out to raise to this high Body for its consideration and approval of the bill.

On account that a system of scholarships doesn't exist that contemplates cases like the present one, the Executive Power sees the necessity to make it known to the Parliament of the justice to which it funds this solicitation of resources to facilitate the move to the great centers of culture by a young musician that has been an extraordinary revelation in the national ambiance.

The critical opinions of three countries of the Continent: Uruguay, Argentina and Brazil, allocate his relevant qualities, classifying them as exceptional.

Since it is necessary, as the Executive Power esteems him, that Abel Carlevaro widens his panorama of performance in an ambiance like that in the United States and gathers in his bosom in the present to the greatest values of the contemporary art.

The S.O.D.R.E. expressed in its opportunity before the words of the Delegate Cardoso the following: "Who considers by evident importance and interest, so much for the brilliant artistic career of the guitarist Carlevaro, as for the knowledge, of one of our most representative musical investments, the facilitation of the move of the mentioned concert guitarist to the United States of America."

Eduardo Fabini, our great composer declared: "I think the State must facilitate the realization of an artistic tour that can culminate in North America, of a manner that they can know his admirable endowments of the skilful instrumentalist and his fine musicality."

In identical admiring terms the unanimity of the music critics of our country directed this to the Minister of Public Instruction and Social Outllook.

It is believed since the Executive Power recognizes in the bill, a unanimous aspiration by who have judged the great values of Abel Carlevaro.

For the completion of which, the solicitation to this high Body sanctioning of the bill in question.

We take the opportunity to give our regards to this General Assembly with its best consideration.
— Tomas Berreta. — Francisco Forteza. — Ledo Arroyo Torres.

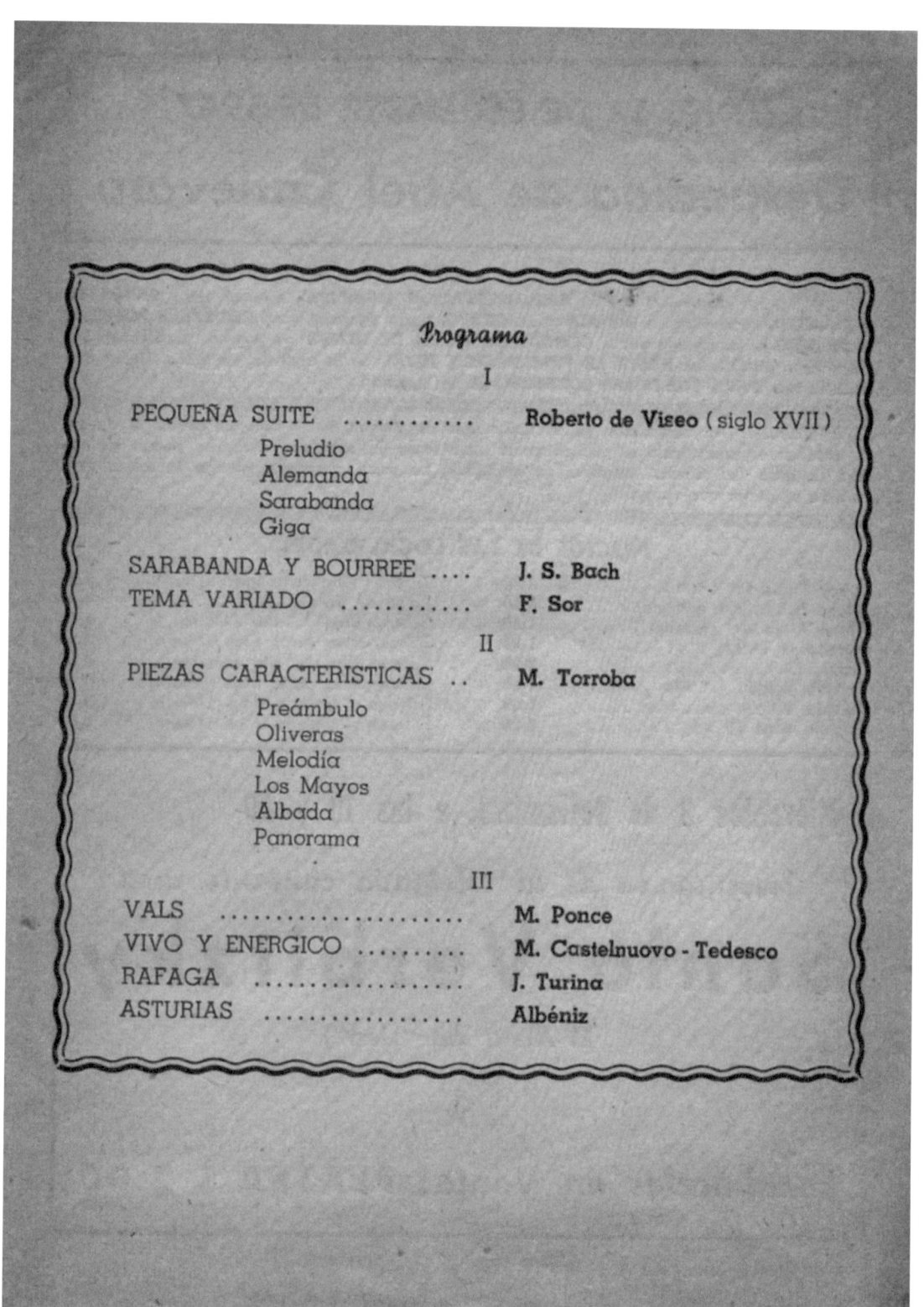

Programa

I

PEQUEÑA SUITE .... Roberto de Viseo (siglo XVII)
    Preludio
    Alemanda
    Sarabanda
    Giga

SARABANDA Y BOURREE .... J. S. Bach
TEMA VARIADO .... F. Sor

II

PIEZAS CARACTERISTICAS .. M. Torroba
    Preámbulo
    Oliveras
    Melodía
    Los Mayos
    Albada
    Panorama

III

VALS .... M. Ponce
VIVO Y ENERGICO .... M. Castelnuovo - Tedesco
RAFAGA .... J. Turina
ASTURIAS .... Albéniz

Abel Carlevaro plays the whole gamut of classical guitar repertoire from the seventeenth century pieces of Robert de Visée to Joaquín Turina's *"Rafaga"*, which in the 1940's was recorded by one of his compatriots: Julio Martínez Oyanguren.

Translating from Ricardo Muñoz's unpublished book *"Historia Universal de la Guitarra" Volume VI "America"*. The photo below is from the same biography.

Ramon Ayestaran

"His Origin:

He was born in the Departamente of Flores, in the present century.

His Education:

He became enthusiastic about the guitar by hearing it played in the hands of his father, he began to play it when he was a child, at 15 years of age he resided in Montevideo, and a relative orientated him in the modern technique and he received lessons from maestro *Don* José Tomas Mujica until 1933 when he met the notable Julio Martínez Oyanguren, who guided him for two years, indicating the road to follow.

Then he began to meet and become friends with the great guitarists of his country, and the foreign ones that visited Montevideo. Abel Carlevaro, Olga Pierri and others, with whom he latently maintained the mechanism of the difficult instrument, adding the knowledgeable musical advice from personalities such as the musicologist *Don* Lauro Ayestaran, a relative of his, *Don* Francisco Curt Lange and others.

His Virtuosity:

In 1940 he initiated his performances in the interior of the country, in 1942 he performed in the S.O.D.R.E. of Montevideo, he visited the city of Porto Alegre, Brazil, where he made a series of concerts for the station *"Radio Farronpilha"*, and in the Teatro de San Pedro, obtaining flattering results.

The 9th of November of 1945 he arrived at the Teatro del Pueblo, in the city of Buenos Aires and the audience heard him play the *"Largo"* and *"Estudio en Sib"* by Sor, *"Estudio No. 12"* by Aguado, *"Allegro en Do mayor"* by Giuliani, *"Preludio, Sarabanda* and *Courante"* by Bach *"Gavota"* by Rameau, *"Sonata"* by Cimarosa, *"Danza Castellana"* and *"Fandanguillo"* by Moreno Torroba, *"Danza Española"* by Granados and *"Leyenda"* by Albeniz; his performance was surprising, being judged by the excellent daily critics.

AMIGOS de la GUITARRA

SECRETARÍA: CASTRO 675

•••

CONCIERTO INAUGURAL

4º. CICLO

AUSPICIADO POR LA

Asociación Argentina de Música de Cámara

POR EL NOTABLE

CONCERTISTA
RAMON AYESTARAN

☆ ✹ ☆

SABADO 20 de ABRIL a las 18 hs.

en el Salón "LA ARGENTINA"

RODRIGUEZ PEÑA 361

ENTRADA GENERAL, $ 1.—

Los socios de la As. Argentina de Música de Cámara, tienen derecho a 2 entradas, presentando el carnet social. Tendrán rebaja del 50 % los socios de la "As. Guitarrística Argentina", "Círculo de la Guitarra" y Alumnos.

This is the concert that was given at the Salon "La Argentina" in Buenos Aires on Saturday April 20, 1946, on behalf of the "Amigos de la Guitarra" and sponsored by the Asociacion Argentina de Musica de Camera.

Saturday the 20th of April of 1946 (above), sponsored by the Asociacion Argentina de Musica de Camara, he performed works by de Visée, Narvaez, Sanz, Ferrandiere, Bach, Haydn, Beethoven, Mussorgsky, Villa-Lobos, Gilardi and Parga, with great success; in 1947 he repeated the visit to Buenos Aires and *"La Prensa"* of the 20th of July reported: 'He is a cultured artist of a fine temperament and instrumentalist for whom the guitar has no secrets, his interpretations attract by the security of the technique, the richness of the sound and the stylistic comprehension and emotion of the integral works of his programs.'

During the years 1949 and 1950 he made a tour of Europe and visited the B.B.C. in London and the Universities of Oxford and Cambridge, getting applause in Italy and arriving in Paris, to be presented in diverse performances before the public and the French critics *"La Semaine de Paris"* said: 'Ayestaran is a great artist who revealed to us all the guitar, an instrument not well known, has the capacity to give, dealing with classical music and of the *folklore*.... he has left in each one of the listeners a desire to hear this great artist again.'

In August of 1952 in Sao Paolo, he performed in the "Asociacao Cultural do Violao", works by Galilei, Bach, Sor, Ferrandiere and in duets with Lola Gonella, pages of Satie, Granados, Sinopoli and Prat. The following month in the Teatro Colombo he ably threshed out a difficult program of classic and modern works.

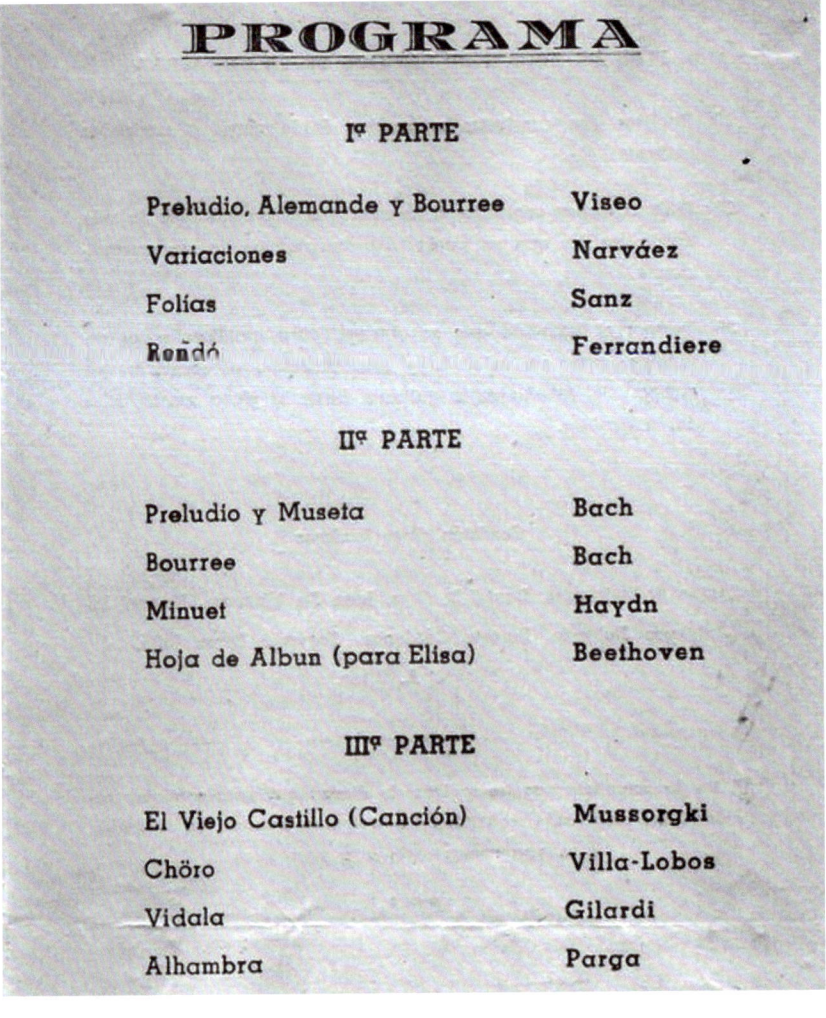

PROGRAMA

Iª PARTE

Preludio, Alemande y Bourree	Viseo
Variaciones	Narváez
Folías	Sanz
Rondó	Ferrandiere

IIª PARTE

Preludio y Museta	Bach
Bourree	Bach
Minuet	Haydn
Hoja de Albun (para Elisa)	Beethoven

IIIª PARTE

El Viejo Castillo (Canción)	Mussorgki
Chöro	Villa-Lobos
Vidala	Gilardi
Alhambra	Parga

His Compositions:

Of his very important compositions we recall his transcriptions of *"Preludio Vasco"* by Padre Donostia, *"El Vals No. 15"* by Brahms, *"El Preludio"* by Bach and others.

His Pedagogy:

In his capacity as a maestro he collaborated in perfection studies, among others, the artistic endowments of his ex-student, Oscar Caceres.

His Passing:

He died in Montevideo the 4th of October of 1957."

This comes from the March 26, 1937 issue of the magazine: Programa oficial de las estaciones uruguayas de radio (Official program of the Uruguayan Radio Stations).

Translation: Ramon Ayesteran of the new program of Radio Carve.

We don't want to make a eulogy just for the sake of it. We only leave a steadfastness of a good impression caused by the presentations to the listeners of this excellent guitarist who has shown to possess an excellent school and who is a disciple of Julio Martínez Oyanguren. And as it's been already said that Martínez Oyanguren is the dignified successor to Andrés Segovia, we can say that it is good to be a student of such a great maestro.

Ramon Ayesteran will continue to be heard on Radio Carve.

Below are two folkloric pieces Ramon Ayestaran recorded in the 1950's.

This from the "Guitar News" magazine issue No. 10 of December 1952 – January 1953.

Translating from Ricardo Muñoz's unpublished book *"Historia Universal de la Guitarra"* Volume VI *"America"*. The photo below is from the same biography.

Olga Pierri

"Her Origin:

She is the daughter of the composer and guitarist *Don* José Pierri and *Doña* Pilar P. de Pierri, and she born in Montevideo on the 3rd of June in 1922.

Her Education:

Since she was a young child, she began to play the guitar and the music, which her father taught to her.

Her Virtuosity:

At 15 years of age she performed in the *"Estudio Auditorio"* (S. O. D. R. E.) of Montevideo, in a very serious and difficult program playing *"Danza Mora"* and *"Recuerdos de la Alhambra"* by Tárrega, *"Estudio en Sib"* by Sor, *"Serenata Española"* by Malats, *"Serenata"* by Borodin, *"Fandanguillo"* by

Turina, *"Preludio"* and *"Sonatina Allegro"* by Moreno Torroba, *"Andante"* and *"Minueto"* by Haydn, *"Courante"* by Bach, *"Canzoneta"* by Mendelssohn, with a great approval by the audience gathered there.

The Centro Guitarristico del Uruguay "Conrado P. Koch" solicited a performance by her on the 6th of November of 1939 and in the program was noted: 'She is the best guitarist of Uruguay of all epochs'.
It turned out to be such a flattering success, that the 25th of July of the following year she repeated a concert in the same Centro, playing works by Sanz, Bach, Handel, Barrios, Sor, and Mendelssohn, in the 1st part. As for the 2nd part, she performed integrating in a trio with Atilio Rapat and P. M. Marin Sanchez: *"Andante"* and *"Momento Musical"* by Schubert, *"Minueto"* by Mozart, *"Recuerdos de la Alhambra"* by Tárrega, being extensively applauded, the same in December of 1941 in which she reiterated her appearance for the cited society.

In 1945 she was presented before the public of the "Club Social" and "Biblioteca Popular", in 1946 in the "Teatro Español" and again in the Centro Guitarristico del Uruguay "Conrado P. Koch". In 1947 she acquired her Ricardo Muñoz Argentine Model guitar, and the 17th of July she offered a recital for the "Asociacion de Empleados del Instituto de Jubliados y Afines", playing works by Fortea, Anido, Aguirre, Aredes, Sapere, Malats, Moreno Torroba, Turina, Tárrega, and Sor, with the most gratifying success.

Her Compositions:

We know her transcription of the *"Estilo"* by Lauro Ayestaran and the following works for her group: *"Vidalita"* by Mortet, *"Huella"* by Aguirre, *"Triste"* (of the poem *"Sinfonico Campo"*) by Eduardo Fabini, *"Triste No. 2"* by the same author, *"Gato"* *"Malambo"* and others.

Her Pedagogy:

In her capacity as a maestro she teaches a good number of students, among which we find in her famous groups: *"Conjunto de niños"* and as well her *"Conjunto de femininos"* formed by Ms. Carmen Torraza, Ms. Margarita and Ms. Matilde Sena, Ms. Margot Prieto, Ms. Teté Ricci and herself.

This group of women, has already performed with the most frank success since the year 1951, in the "Gran Cine Patria", "Asociacion Cristiana Feminina" of Montevideo, in the "Club Banco de Seguros", in the "Facultad de Medicina", in the "Club Progresso", "Teatro Solis", etc., etc. With it Ms. Pierri initiated brilliantly and gallantly an era of hierarchy of national *folklore* which will be difficult to surpass the technical and expressive quality of her legitimate values."

Olga Pierri's *"Conjunto Folklorico Feminino de Guitarras"* that recorded in the 1950's.

Olga Pierri passed away on September 28, 2016 at the age of 102, videos of her are on You Tube.

INDUSTRIA URUGUAYA

SONDOR

MARCA REGISTRADA

EJECUCION PUBLICA Y RADIODIFUSION RESERVADAS
FABRICADO POR SONDOR LTDA. MONTEVIDEO · URUGUAY

Grabado en Uruguay
AGADU

15011 - A

(2612)

MALAMBO

(J. Pierri Sapere)

Conjunto Folklórico Femenino
de Guitarras

Dir.: OLGA PIERRI

INDUSTRIA URUGUAYA

SONDOR

MARCA REGISTRADA

EJECUCION PUBLICA Y RADIODIFUSION RESERVADAS
FABRICADO POR SONDOR LTDA. MONTEVIDEO · URUGUAY

Grabado en Uruguay
AGADU

15011 - B

(2611)

ESTILO No. 4

(J. Pierri Sapere)

Conjunto Folklórico Femenino
de Guitarras

Dir.: OLGA PIERRI

C X 22 — FADA RADIO

Administración: Av. 18 de Julio 110. - Teléf. 1733, Central
Estudio: Larrañaga 2781. - Teléf. 687, Unión
Dirección Artística: Luis Rodríguez Legrand. - Ganaderos 4267

DOMINGO 27

11. Discos por Magaldi, Gardel, etc.
12. Discos por Lily Pons, Sagi Barba, Schipa, Fleta, Tita Ruffo y Caruso.
13. **Suplemento Artístico-Literario-Musical**, a cargo del poeta Sr. L. Rodríguez Legrand.
14.30 **Hora Libanesa.** Al piano el Sr. Bark.
17. **Hora de los Meritorios.**
19.30 **Hora de los Magos.**
20.30 **Ejecución al piano:** por el profesor paraguayo Sr. Eugenio Rojas.
21. Trasmisión de la ópera "**Traviata**".

LUNES 28

11. **Hora del fox trot americano.**
12. **Selección de** música clásica.
13. **Hora del Tango,** por **Orquesta Cen-**

22. Ejecución de: Sinfonía Nº 8 B minor, Sinfonía Nº 4 G mayor.

JUEVES 1º

11. Romanzas por Lily Pons, Enrique Caruso y Tito Schipa.
12. **Hora de la Alegría.**
13. Bailables por orquesta típica.
14.30 **Solos de piano,** prof. E. Rojas.
17. **Una hora para niños,** por Mister Pololito. Los botijas pueden divertirse.
18. **Hora Agrícola-Ganadera,** dirigida por el presbítero Ing. E. Facelli Villar.
19.30 **La Hora Literaria,** a cargo del poeta "Justo Claro".
20.30 **Concierto de guitarra,** a cargo de la Srta. Olga Pierri.
21. Trasmisión de la ópera "**Boheme**".

This comes from the September 27 to October 3, 1931 issue of the magazine: Programa oficial de las estaciones uruguayas de radio (Official program of the Uruguayan Radio Stations). Olga Pierri at the age of sixteen played concert works for guitar on Thursday October 1, 1931 at 8:30 in the evening for 30 minutes on radio station CX 22 in Montevideo.

Translating from Ricardo Muñoz's unpublished book *"Historia Universal de la Guitarra" Volume VI* *"America".*

"Oscar Caceres

His Origin:

He was born in Montevideo in 1928.

His Education:

At 11 years of age he began to play the guitar with the maestros Ramon Ayestaran, P. M. Marin Sanchez and Atilio Rapat; in a parallel manner he attended classes of the cello and South American music in the "Escuela Municipal de Musica", given by the maestros *Don* Oscar Nicastro and Lauro Ayestaran, respectively, and went to classes of "Formas Musicales" entrusted to *Don* Hector Tosar Errecart.

His Virtuosity:

In 1943 his public presentations in the "Victoria Hall" and the "Steneo" of Montevideo, "Sala Verdi" and in the Centro Guitarristico del Uruguay "Conrado P. Koch"; he crossed the Rio de la Plata and arrived in Buenos Aires in 1947, performing for the "Amigos de la Guitarra" and in the "Club Oriental" with satisfactory success.

He returned to his country and performed in the S. O. D. R. E., selected for a tour of the interior of the country, performing for the Centro Guitarristico del Uruguay "Conrado P. Koch" on the 22nd of October of 1949 the following works: *"Folias de España"*, *"Variaciones de Fuga"* by Ponce, *"Preambulo"* and *"Olivares"* by Moreno Torroba, *"Anecdotas"* by Segovia, *"Humorada"* by Madriguera, *"Sevilla"* by Pujol, and *"Tarantella"* by Castelnuovo-Tedesco being applauded resoundingly.

In 1951, in the Teatro Solis, performing a program integrated with pieces by the *vihuelists* of the 16th century, and later in the first performance of the *"Concierto de Aranjuez"* by J. Rodrigo. Finally, he visited Palma de Mallorca, and gave a concert and the critic said: 'He is a guitarist of great sensibility, who has developed a program of total beauty and impeccable diction, clean, without carelessness.... the concert guitarist put the best of his soul, very sensible and open to all the delicacies ....'

In 1955 he arrived in Barcelona at the Peña Guitarristica Tárrega and interpreted works by Purcell, Scarlatti, Rameau, Bach, Fabini, Villa-Lobos, Fleury, Barrios, Tárrega, Rodrigo and Castelnuovo-Tedesco, with agility and satisfaction."

So ends the biography by Ricardo Muñoz.

This biographical material about Conrado P. Koch is translated from Ricardo Muñoz's unpublished book *"Historia Universal de la Guitarra"* Volume VI *"America"*.

"Conrado P. Koch

His Origin:

He is the son of *Don* Francisco Koch and Elodia Rodríguez, and he was born in Montevideo the 29th of June in 1898.

His Education:

He was inclined toward the guitar since a very early age; at 10 years old he attended the practices of a recreative society orchestra, in which he accompanied the pieces with a small tiple.

In 1914, the First World War was declared, his father worked in the home of person of English nationality, being of German descent, he lost his employment. The son saw that he was obliged to play the guitar in public to help, in any way possible, to provide subsistence for the family.

In 1915, the maestro Julio Otermin heard the young Conrado Koch and impartially offered him lessons as a guide on the instrument; then he studied harmony with maestro Felipe Peyrallo, all that at the same time as his studies for High School. His anxious and curious spirit, eager to know, permitted him to acquire a critical sense toward the foreign and personal.

His Virtuosity

In 1917 he gave his first public concert in the Instituto Verdi of Montevideo, performing works by Sor, Tárrega, Albeniz, Granados, Manjón and others; the daily *"Cronica"* said: 'The most flattering success has crowned the efforts of the young performer, the public that hasheard him, has recognized in Koch a good player, refined and exquisite on the guitar.'

'A solid apprenticeship, an uncommon musical temperament and an intimate affection toward the instrument he performs, they are the principle qualities of this new virtuoso. Conrado Koch has demonstrated that he possesses the necessary abilities to be placed on the plane in which figure the best guitarists.'

He offered other performances in Melo, San José, and Tacuarembo; in Montevideo he continued and in the same Instituto Verdi, the 19th of December of 1920, he interpreted *"Minuetto en LA"* and *"Estudio en SIb"* by Sor, *"Variaciones"* by Mozart-Sor, *"Barcarola"* by Mendelssohn, *"2 Mazurkas"*, *"Recuerdos de la Alhambra"*, *"Minuet"*, *"Sonatina"* by Tárrega, *"Serenata"* by Manjón, *"Cancion Catalana"* by Llobet, *"Granada"* by Albeniz, *"Danza Española"* by Granados and *"Estudio"* by Coste. The journalism critic expressed it as such:

'....As a performer he possesses a good technique, in which we notice the careful desire to be clear and to play with good sound; two qualities that many guitarists of great fame do not possess; as an artist he has a good sense. With these abilities the young Koch marvelously directs his temperament, in which the most perfect taste predominates.'

Another critic said: 'He isn't one of many vocational guitarists. He is an erudite musician to which Sor and Tárrega revealed the secret of the interpretive complexity which is encased in the instrument.'

Don Juan C. Badazan wrote: 'The guitar in his hands has life, a life which expresses all the manifestations and states of the soul. His sonority is pure, his timbre mellow and his tone is firm. His diction is admirably penetrating in the profoundest of the works that he interprets and translates, within a simplicity and really seductive spontaneity.'

When Andrés Segovia listened to him, he declared: 'I don't believe in Spain that there is anyone who plays better than you....'

His Compositions:

He composed a few works during his very short life of study and concerts; of those we recall:

"Berceuse Rustica"; it is a well marked rhythm by a succession of chords, whose insistent intervals of 5th communicate a rare taste of rusticity; the movement is harsh and anxious during the whole work, in opposition, it develops themes full of tenderness which make the group a strong originality.

"El Surtidor", is a prelude in which the he efficiently exploits the sonorities and particular effects of the instrument; its descriptive character with profusion of distinct timbres, color the agile and fluid arpeggio, giving the lyrical sensation, rarely found in works of this genre.

His Pedagogy:

He played the eleven string guitar, which he quit to play the six string; with the modern school of Tárrega, achieving an impeccable and ample technique; he dedicated himself to teaching, thriving of his intelligence the great maestros: Manuel Sopena, Muro Rivas, Abelardo Rodríguez, Isaias Savio (beginning in 1911) and others.

His Passing:

At the height of youth, he died in Montevideo on the 27th of December of 1924: the 25th of December of 1934, the Comité Pro-Homenaje a Conrado P. Koch paid tributes of admiration, in the session *Don* Raul Mancebo Rojas, a member of the mentioned Committee, said:

'Few are the spirits which, as that of Koch, have demonstrated to possess qualities of the ambience of his specialization. We can say that to initiate in his artist life, he had the fact after finding his own center, inspired by this vocational force of the choices to amply triumph, with this elevation which distinguishes the great souls.'

'His exquisite spirit marked day by day, the constant rhythm of his perfection; it was as if it might be said, a sublime force that accelerated a personality of unmistakable relief, where the comprehension, the methodic analysis, the clear and serene judgement, the honest and just interpretation, they let be translucent the purist expression of the artist which is emotion and emotion with the art by the art itself.....'

'... as a tribute of his unrestrained anxieties it announced the arrival of the maestro Pujol .... and along with Mascaro y Reissig and Rosendo Barreiro.... they began in the school of the immortal Tárrega, until the unknown epoch of our environment.... Julio Otermin had molded his soul; the great Pujol finished the work chiseling these words in his spirit: 'You already know how to hear and interpret'....'

'Conrado P. Koch was born a musician, he was what is called a modeled spirit for the perfect purification of the expressive manifestations, within the magnificent conception of a very ample expression; he was the logical consequence of his same sensibility; he was the perfect harmony that told in his own soul and which elevated him eternally in the immaterial of a sublime illusion.... His life had the duration of the beautiful things, it was as if it might be said an incommensurate spark of divine transportation, of brilliant light, cut down by the greed of life....'

Much of Ricardo Muñoz's biography of Conrado P. Koch was drawn from Domingo Prat's biography of Conrado P. Koch, as Prat's *Diccionario de Guitarristas* is credited in the bibliographies of all of the Ricardo Muñoz's seven unpublished books of the series *"Historia Universal de la Guitarra"*. But if we look at some other details that are different, we find that Domingo states the birthdate for Conrado as July 29, 1898. In that Muñoz had the parent's names and Prat did not, he may have the correct date of June 29, 1898, maybe not, on that point, and further investigation is needed. Julio Otermin began to teach Conrado for a period of 2 years in 1915. Prat states that Conrado's first concert was given when he was 19 years old at the "Circulo Napolitano" in Montevideo. At times Prat was in Spain and maybe not aware of various events that he tried to document in the 8 years that were spent compiling and writing his *Diccionario de Guitarristas*.

Ten years after Conrado P. Koch died Pedro Mascaro y Reissig paid homage to him on the radio station *C. X. 14 "El Espectador"* in Montevideo. It was Conrado's sister, Maria, that wrote a thank you note on behalf of her mother and herself that was a part of Pedro Mascaro y Reissig's 194-page scrapbook from 1917-1938.

Here's the translation, a copy of the letter is on the next page:

"Montevideo, December 30 of 1934

Mrrs. Mascaro y Reissig and Conti,

Distinguished Gentlemen,

We always (Mama and I) keep alive the emotion that the eloquent and moving homage produced for us, which a group of friends paid tribute to the memory of that unforgettable brother that was Conrado. It has been made transparent in such affection, and so much admiration, through the noblest inspired words of the orators, through the concert program brilliantly completed which shows the delicate sentiments that they were able to put in their selection, which we want to express, not in the form of simple courtesy, but in a lively fashion that our gratitude towards you and towards all of those friends of Conrado, united to him by the intimate bays of friendship and community of ideals, that will be eternal and deep as are the true sentiments.

A cordial salute to all of you very affectionately, in the name of Mama and in my own name,

Maria E. Koch de Martínez.

s/c San Lorenzo 3197"

Montevideo, Diciembre 30 de 1934

Señores Mascaró Reissig y Conti

Distinguidos Señores:

Por siempre mamá y yo guardaremos viva la emoción que nos produjo el elocuente y conmovedor homenaje, que un grupo de amigos acaba de tributar a la memoria de aquel hermano inolvidable que fué Conrado. Se ha transparentado en él tanto afecto, tanta admiración, a través de la forma en que fué organizado, a través de las inspiradas y nobilísimas palabras de los oradores, a través de un programa de concierto cumplido brillantemente y que exteriorizó los delicados sentimientos que presidieron a su selección, que nosotras queremos expresarles, no en forma de simple cortesía, sino vivamente, que nuestra gratitud hacia Uds y hacia todos esos amigos de Conrado, unidos a él por entrañables lazos de amistad y comunidad de ideales, será eterna y honda como son los sentimientos verdaderos.

Saludo a Uds muy atte. en nombre de mamá y en el mío propio

María E. Ihode de Martínez

S/c San Lorenzo 3197

2256

In 1923 *Don* Conrado P. Koch wrote an article entitled *"Algunas consideraciones sobre la guitarra"* ("Some considerations about the guitar") on pages 28 and 29 for issue No. 1 July of 1923 of the *"La Guitarra"* magazine published in Buenos Aires by Juan Carlos Anido.

The translation is:

"A lot has already been written about the historical development of the guitar and the importance that this musical branch genuinely Spanish has acquired in the latest years.

There isn't an instrument that by its harmonic capacity and its variety of timbres unites in it as the guitar, something in this way as an idealization of the quartet or of a miniature orchestra, without counting with the characters that is its own as the illustrious musicologist Felipe Pedrell already pointed out in a beautiful article about Tárrega.

Surely that this instrument is recently in full bloom and we will try to inquire as to the cause of this evolution so late in relation to other expressive agents of the music.

The first revelations that we must observe from the point of view of probabilities and afterwards they had completed, are those of the Spanish writers such as Juan Carlos Amat, Luis Milan, Fuenllana and many other authors of works for the unfortunately little known vihuela and, however that, contain the seed of the future musical manifestations of the complexity that has brought the music in the present time; the use of counterpoint and voices already well differentiated as they appear later in the works of the notable French guitarist Robert de Visée; the scales and arpeggios of Federico Moretti; up to the music of religious character of Padre Basilio, maestro to Aguado; the use of harmonic octaves by Francois de Fossa and the creation of a technique already ample by Aguado in his didactic works as in his own creations; until brought to the truly great and incomparable Fernando Sor, that Mitjana justly called the Beethoven of the guitar.

Effectively, he appears in the evolutionary process of the instrument as a true genius; all of the works that have classical flavor, a logical progression of the voices, the real melodic invention; they denote by the other part the influence of the epoch and an extraordinary musical culture.

After him only one disciple of his shines, Napoleon Coste, who has left a magnificent collection of studies, although somewhat in an ornate style.

Of this epoch so brilliant it is followed by a real decline.

To what can one owe this relapse? Examining the biographies and their own works of Sor and of Aguado we see they unite the genius of the great capacity for the work, to be creating a solid technical preparation that doesn't suffocate the natural expression and which, however, is transparent in their works.

Only in this way, when the genius possesses it makes the name last and honorably contributes to the flowering of such an expressive art.

It is curious to observe the haste, the lack of preparation and of good taste that appear in all of the later works.

In Arcas and in Parga, the two authors most characterized of this epoch of decadence, it can be seen that joined to the light sparkles of originality, appear long periods of the most common aspects that break the unity of the work and completely fog up the small beauties of which they were capable.

As for that in their works; and if we refer to the transcriptions, especially of Arcas we begin by the absolute deficiency of artistic sense that denotes to choose phrases of operas, with which surely they got a lot of success in the public masses, but suffocated atemperament perhaps by the lack of the fine instinct of the artist that has to refocus in his true spirit, without being predominately preoccupied by the tastes that passed.

Of this manner it explains the advent of Tárrega as a true revelation. View a logical technique, rational, he employs combinations of unsuspected blends; he manifests in his works an extraordinary temperament of a composer that now beautiful with the daringly modern and guided by his superior spirit that turns to the great composers, Bach, Beethoven, Schumann, Chopin, etc.; Albeniz and Malats among the modern; he chose many of his good works and creates those again with the resources of the guitar without making them lose the central character of the author and maintaining the idiosyncrasy of his favorite instrument; besides he forms a group of eminent disciples who without losing the tradition and preserved his own personality they continue the labor of the maestro for the glory of the guitar. Among them he of the delicate temperament from Emilio Pujol, and Miguel Llobet endowed with extraordinary musical abilities such as they test his works, his masterful harmonization of popular Catalan themes and his transcriptions, real jewels of the modern flowering of the guitar. All that must be from the genius, to the effort, to the preparation.

We point out that the same lack of culture that has produced such ill-fated results in the composition, that it produces among the performers; in this way today we see the elevation of names that can't be on an artistic plane truly elevated, for the disgrace of the guitar and of them the same. But this can't impede that the reduced number of real and aware interpreters circulates and spreads day to day the innumerable beauties of the guitar, the most popular and at the same time the most aristocratic.'

"

Montevideo, 1923.

This biographical material about Pedro Mascaro y Reissig is translated from Ricardo Muñoz's unpublished book *"Historia Universal de la Guitarra"* Volume VI *"America"*.

"Pedro Mascaro y Reissig

His Origin:

He is the son of a Uruguayan father, the Dr. Pedro Mascaro y Sosa and an Argentine mother of Rosario, *Doña* Luisa Reissig Giles; he was born in Montevideo the 11th of November in 1888, and baptized with the names Pedro Martin.

Pedro Mascaro y Reissig   c. 1934

His Education:

He was inclined by temperament toward music, since a very early age, at age 6 he practiced on a guitar, melodies that he heard on the piano played by an older sister who took note of the excellent predisposition of the child, and him gave lessons of *solfeggio* and the piano.

At 10 years of age, without carelessness to his beloved guitar, his father, a professor of living languages prodded him toward the knowledge of those idioms, achieving to dominate four of them in his youth: French, English, German and Latin.

Being 14 years old, the maestro Eduardo Lenzi (a Carlos García Tolsa student) began his initiation in serious studies of the instrument, interrupted by military service; ending up entering into Public Administration, then into journalism, making a study of the literature and writing his novels: *"El Destino"* in 1910; (Published by *Libreria "Mercurio", Luis y Manuel Pérez*, Montevideo) *"Flores de Araza"* in 1912; and *"El Canalla"* in 1913.

He received a Bachelor of Science and Letters degree, he studied harmony and composition with the organist Felipe Larrimbe, then heard the maestro Antonio Gimenez Manjón and left the literature for the guitar, to which he surrendered completely. He studied Aguado, Sor, Coste, Arcas, Parga, Viñas, Ferrer, Carcassi, etc, until his maestro Mr. Lenzi gave him the diploma of Professor, after his first public presentation.

His Virtuosity:

He only gave concerts in Montevideo and other cities of the interior of his country, with great success; the applause never attracted him, he was a man who built tomorrow, of everlasting benefit, not of the moment by removing vanity and pride, and therefore he was dedicated to composition and teaching.

However I said he gave performances in 1917, which he repeated on the days of the 22nd and 24th of April of 1920, performing, in the Cine Uruguayo of Santa Isabel, the works by Sor, Aguado, Tárrega, Viñas, Schubert, Rovira, Chopin, Llobet, Manjón, García, Alais, Coste, Weber, Mendelssohn, Parga and his own pieces. The success obtained was emphatic, to judge by the journalism; *"Juventud"* of the 24th of the same month said: 'A numerous gathering filled the hall, and the program was completed with proper skill, gathering just applause in all the parts, which put in relief the vast knowledge that Mascaro possesses in the musical art.'

He was presented in other recitals in the same year, in 1921-1925 and on the days of the 13th, 14th, 17th, 18th, 20th and 21st of April of 1926, interpreting in one of them: *"Minuetto en La"* by Sor, *"Ultimo Pensamiento"* by Weber, *"Allegro Moderato"* and *"Recuerdos de la Alhambra"* by Tárrega, *"Cajita de Musica"* by Savio, *"Granada"* by Albeniz, *"Preludio"* by Chopin, *"Andante Largo"* by Sor, *"Capricho Arabe"* by Tárrega and his own works: *"Mazurka"*, *"Vals"*, *"Variaciones sobre un Tema de Jota"*. The daily *"De Colonia Suiza"* of the 14th of April declared:

'The cited artist in the difficult performances which he played last night, fully confirmed the fame of which might come before and the consecration of which he enjoys in Montevideo. Mascaro y Reissig in reality possesses an exquisite artistic temperament. The strings plucked by his fingers are six souls infinitely great, which vibrate emerging indescribable esthetic emotions. Technically he is a maestro, a noble and impartial artist who doesn't vacillate in the choice of the location and the public which must hear him, his work is of beauty and the beauty is for everyone.'

His Compositions:

He has published many works for the guitar and other instruments; of which we recall:

Momento Musical	Casa Nuñez	
Ultimo Pensamiento (Weber)	"	(sic) Hector N. Pirovano No. 682
Bosquejo Sinfonico	"	(sic) Hector N. Pirovano No. 683
Minuetto (Dedicated to Llobet)	Ricordi	
Oracion India	"	Not published by Ricordi despite Muñoz's attribution.
Vespero-Vals	Ricordi	
La Cabalgata	"	"Cabalcata" Hector N. Pirovano
In Memorium	"	
Mazurka en MI	"	

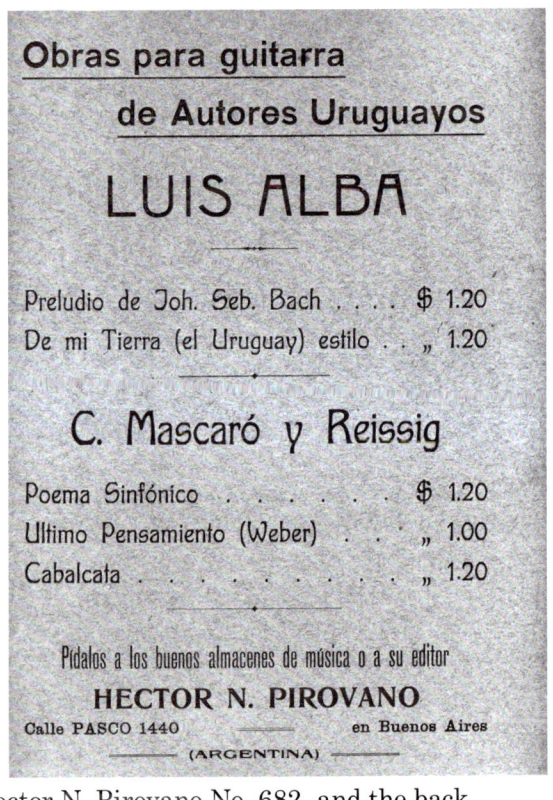

Pedro Mascaro y Reissig's *"Ultimo Pensamiento"* (Weber) Hector N. Pirovano No. 682, and the back cover of Luis Alba's *Preludio* by J. S. Bach. The typographical error of C. Mascaro y Reissig in place of P. Mascaro y Reissig must have been corrected sometime after this. This was published before 1925. *"Bosquejo Sinfonico"* No. 683 was dedicated to Miguel Herrera Klinger and Hector G. Costa. It is not known whether this was published before or after Miguel's criticism of Pedro in September of 1926. — this has to be verified! 9 25 12

This is translated from the book by Cedar Viglietti *"Origen y Historia de la Guitarra"* published by Editorial Albatros in Buenos Aires in 1973.

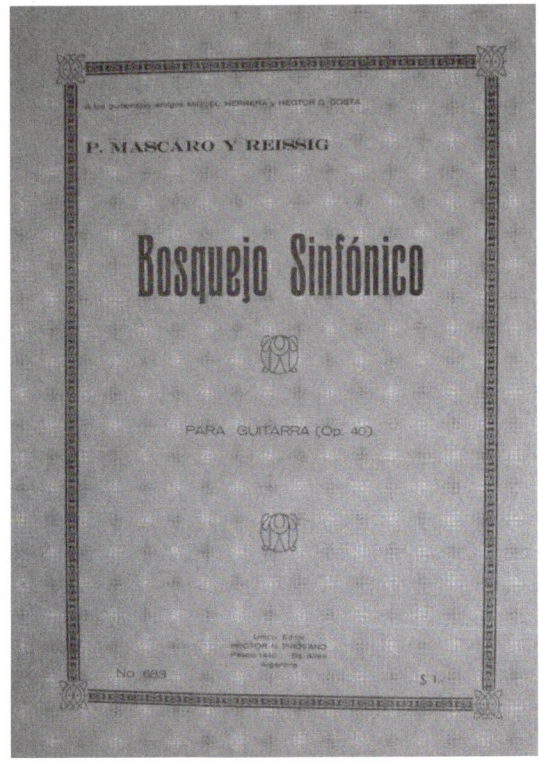

Cedar Viglietti says on page 221: "Pedro Mascaro y Reissig was a cousin of Julio Mascaro y Reissig — who was a student of Lenzi, cultivated the guitar in quite a sporadic form, alternating with the piano, novels, and journalism. He received lessons from Llobet and Pujol, was dedicated to teaching, composing pieces that only his students played, a *Minué, Sonatinas, Bosquejo Sinfonico, Romanza,* etc. and Method with some works of Sor, Tárrega, Coste, where it showed a photo of the author with a guitar of nine strings and which was dedicated to Pujol and Lenzi. He had the merit to be the first President of the Centro Guitarristico."

Mazurka en RE	Ricordi
Scherzo	"
Variaciones sobre un Tema de Jota	"
Danza Gitana	"
Aire Andino	"
Jueguito de Muñecas	"
Reminiscences Criollas	"
Sonatinas en MI y SOL	"
Sueño Eternal	"
Impromptu en RE	"

Romanza, dedicated to the author of this *"Historia Universal de la Guitarra"*, a fine and delicate page of a Cantabile en MI Mayor in 4/4 time, which it best appears as a melodic study without difficult technical consequences, because it is accessible to the beginner's hands, anxieties of delight with musical feeling and pleasant.

Besides, he has written two works for the piano:

Yamandu
Trianon

All of them are pages of musical and technical value, admissible in the purest artistic program; in this way the daily "La Union" understood that, the 15th of January of 1921, it expressed it in the following manner:

'Where Mascaro y Reissig has demonstrated to us all of his naked soul of the consummate artist, is in the composition of his works. The ingenuity of his melody, blended with an impeccable harmony and in many difficult moments, counterpoint of agreement with the necessities of the periods, he arrives to enchant us in ecstasy, whose sensations, are difficult to describe.'

His Pedagogy:

He wrote specialized collaborations in diverse newspapers; founded the "Centro Guitarristico Uruguayo Conrado P. Koch" and the "Instituto Guitarristico Sors", in which he gave his private lessons to many students, of which we recall the notable Guillermo Corcoran, Ciro Castillo, Matilde and Margot Sena, Pedro M. Aguirre, Raul Mancebo Rojas, Beatriz N. Hansen, etc.

He published his *"Método Complementario/ comprendido /Una teoria de los equisonos/ Diez ejercicios diarios/ Cinco sonatinas/ y Cinco estudios célebres de/ diversos autores, digitados de acuerdo con la escuela moderna."* This consists of 22 pages, of a 34cm x 25cm format. (13 3/8" by 9 7/8")

He also wrote a *"Tratado de Armonia Aplicado a la Guitarra"* which he didn't achieve to publish by having been surprised by death in the moments he tried its publication; this book carries the Prologue which has the continuation transcribed by the author of this *"Historia Universal de la Guitarra";*

'..... Today, the maestro Pedro Mascaro y Reissig writes and presents this new *Tratado de Armonia Apropiado para los Guitarristas*, including scales, intervales, sounds, chords and movements of voices, cadences, modulations, composition, counterpoint, fugue and canon, with an interesting appendix — advice and an exercise in A Major employing diverse chords classified individually, one by one, a labor really magnificent and necessary given the guitaristic non-existent of a work about the theme, complete and conscientious as the present.'

'Of this prudent content, a product of unmistakable discipline, patient investigation and very erudite personal ability, three principal points, guitaristically novelties, contributes his most spectacular didactic and historical hierarchy to the work.'

'1st. The inclusion, for the first time, in the didactic methods of the instrument, of the complete definitions and examples practiced of the chords Simplified by *"elision"*. Transformed by *"enharmonics"* and the Modes of Dorian, Phrygian, Lydian, Mixolydian introduced by the Greeks, in the religious music, of the first years of Christianity, equally, the Plagal cadences: Hypodorian, Hypophrygian, Hypolydian, Hypomixolydian, Hypoaeolian and Hypoionian.'

'2nd. That the majority of the practical examples consigned belong to passages of works and original studies or transcriptions, of guitarist authors.'

'3rd. To treat the cadences in all its forms, it synthetically touches one of the most important points of the South American music: The Cadences of the Rio de la Plata. It is a style of *"clarin"* (a call to resistance) directed to the musical historians of our medium, elegant and sincere Invitation to unravel all that exists of beauty in the sonorous panorama of the Rio de la Plata, since its discovery by *Don* Juan Diaz de Solis (1515), to our days. A magnificent triumph, if someone picks up the sponge and produces the gift...'

'....my epistolary friend *Don* Pedro Mascaro y Reissig, possesses the profoundest knowledge of his very noble anxieties; his vast ethical, esthetic and pedagogic preparation, acquiring in the constant study and observation of his students, of his works and performances, they permit him to appreciate the serene authority of his very honest meditations.'

'The present work honors its author, with the following — lending qualified services to the humanity and very particularly to his esteemed country and to all of South America. I, as an integral part, of the same, in the present Prologue paid homage of my most respectful and ardent admiration. Buenos Aires March 7, 1946. (Signed: Ricardo Muñoz).'

Don Miguel Llobet called him 'the distinguished professor'; *Don* Emilio Pujol 'a cultured artist'; Maria Luisa Anido wrote to him: 'Permit me to send this congratulations for your labor which reveals your dedication, study and love to the delicate and beloved instrument'; the great Barrios called him 'the notable professor', the same which the eminent *Don* Andrés Segovia had called him.

He was a corresponding member of the Asociacion Guitarristica Argentina and the Academia Argentina de la Guitarra of Buenos Aires.

His Passing:

He died the 1st of May of 1952 in the city of Montevideo, 18 months after his exemplary companion's death, whose absence he couldn't endure; his remains were deposited in the grave number 396 (nicho) of the 2nd body (cuerpo) of the Cemetario Central de Montevideo, accompanied by his friends, students and family members, at 11:30 of the following day.

The day of *Todos los Santos* (All Saints' Day), 1st of November of the same year, the Centro Guitarristico del Uruguay Conrado P. Koch paid posthumous homage; Mr. *Don* Raul Mancebo Rojas, a member of the Commision Directiva of the same institution and student of the late professor, on the radio station *"El Espectador"* of Montevideo, spoke the following words: 'He left among us an unerasable memory of his sensitive personality; cultured spirit, he was distinguished with indelible reliefs, the possession of elevated virtues, which characterized the infinite bond of his soul, dominated by the suggestive action of the ideal. His life was consecrated to teaching; Mascaro y Reissig had a defined concept of the art of teaching. The maestro made present in the platform of life for conquering in it the ideal, which offered the reason of his existence. He has understood to have been born for the music and the problems of the harmony and the technique that gravitates over his soul, with an acceleration of such emotion, in which the hours appear to lose their rhythm when the maestro was isolated to work in his hall of study...'

Then his students Juan Cerrutti and Ciro Castillo, interpreted some of his works: *Minuetto, Romanza, Cabalgata,* etc. closing the act of homage the President of the institution *Don* Pedro M. Aguirre declared: 'His greatest honor is to have formed in that limited cluster of maestros that introduced the guitaristic teaching of our country, the culture and the love toward the musical pages of the classics of the instrument. Understanding that with other maestros that already passed away, they formed the base of the select guitaristic culture of our medium....' " So ends the entry by Ricardo Muñoz. The next several dozen pages are from the archive scrapbook of *"Guitarrista Pedro Mascaro y Reissig 1917-1938 Su Diario"*, this was acquired in 2004.

Director: LORENZO CARNELLI

Montevideo, Miercoles 19 de Diciembre de 1917

Año II — Núm. 348

"ORACION INDIA" —

Por el profesor Pedro Mascaró y Reyssig. — Hemos tenido oportunidad de oír — ejecutada por su autor, en una íntima reunión de amateurs — esta bella y exquisita producción, que rebela en el señor Mascaró, un verdadero temperamento artístico. Esta obra es, sin duda alguna, una de las mejores producciones de su género; pues si existen en nuestro medio buenos compositores, pocos hay — cosa que es de lamentar — que se dediquen a escribir para guitarra. Quizá sea la causa de ello, el que este instrumento que al decir del poeta "tiene" un alma de mujer enamorada", no se presta para lucirar con él; pero su voz es armoniosa y bella, y es el que mejor se presta para expresar nuestros más íntimos y profundos sentimientos; por eso el poeta lo prefiere. Con él, Mascaró y Reyssig hace filigranas; una prueba de ello es la audición íntima a que nos referimos anteriormente, motivada por la aparición de esta obra, y donde pudimos apreciar el talento de este artista que, a la vez que un inspirado autor, es un exquisito ejecutante. — A. Merea.

On Wednesday December 19, 1917 the daily in Montevideo *"El Pueblo"* covered the publication of "Oracion india" by Pedro Mascaro y Reissig. The release of this new piece for Classical Guitar was also covered by 4 other newspapers of the Uruguayan capital: *"El Siglo"* on Saturday the 22nd, by both *"La Tribuna Popular"* and *"El Dia"* on Saturday the 29th of the same month, and by *"El Plata"* on Monday January 7, 1918. The translations are on the next page:

From *"El Pueblo"* Wednesday December 19, 1917: "Oracion india" by the professor Pedro Mascaro y Reissig. "We had the opportunity to hear — this beautiful and exquisite production — performed by the author, in an intimate reunion of amateurs, which rebels in Mr. Mascaro, a true artistic temperament. This work is, without any doubt, is one of the best productions of its genre; since if good compositions exist in our modium, there are few — a thing to lament — which dedicate to write for the guitar. Perhaps the cause of it might be, that this instrument which the poet says 'has a soul of a woman in love', it isn't lent to make money with it; but its voice is harmonious and beautiful, and it is the best that lends for expressing our most intimate and profound sentiments: therefore the poet prefers it. With it, Mascaro y Reissig makes filigree; a proof of it is the intimate performance to which we referred to beforehand, motivated by the apparition of this work, and where we could appreciate the talent of this artist that, who at the same time is an inspired author, is an exquisite performer. — A. Merea."

From *"El Siglo"* on Saturday December 22, 1917 Año LIII — No. 15.969: *"Arte y Artistas* — Composition for Guitar — The young composer Pedro Mascaro y Reissig just published a new musical work for guitar, which constitutes the Op. 6 of his collection. It has to do with a South American caprice entitled *"Oracion india"*. People who have heard his performance make great eulogies of the new work by the young Mascaro y Reissig."

From *"La Tribuna Popular"* on Saturday December 29, 1917 Año XXXIX — No. 11472: *Noticias Diversas* (Diverse Notices) Arte Musical. "Mr. P. Mascaro y Reissig has composed a caprice for the guitar, which is titled *"Oracion india"*. We have received an example of the said composition, that is a completely inspired musical page."

From *"El Dia"* on Saturday December 29, 1917 No. 10.560 *1.a epoca: Año XXXI. 2.a epoca: XXVIII* General Information — *"Oracion india"* "With this title a South American musical caprice was just printed by the professor of guitar Pedro Mascaro y Reissig. It has to do with an original piece that calls attention among the knowledgeable."

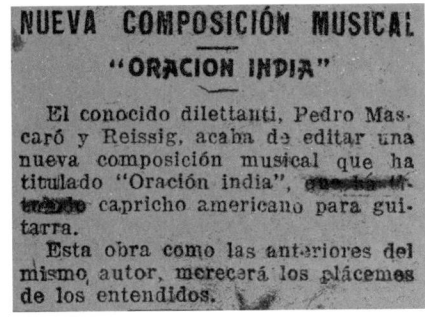

From *"El Plata"* on Monday January 7, 1918 Año V — No. 876 "New Musical Composition *"Oracion india"* The known dilettante, Pedro Mascaro y Reissig, just published a new musical composition which has been titled *"Oracion India"*, a South American musical caprice for the guitar. (Despite the amount of press, the publisher is not named-this song was dedicated to *"A mi Reina Blanca"* — To my Queen Blanca.)

This work as the previous ones by the same author, will deserve to be delighted by the knowledgable."

Buenos Aires 8-5-1919

Sr. D. P. Mascaró Reissig

Distinguido señor. Recibí su cartita la que me ha llenado de satisfacción al ver que se preocupa por nuestro querido instrumento, de muy buen grado puede poner lo que me pide de las "Escalas y arpegios" y le agradeceré muchísimo me mande las novedades musicales que posee y me indica.

Creo que pronto tendré el gusto de conocerlo pues es muy probable que este año venga á esa de Montevideo á dar unos conciertos junto con una discípula mía que es una maravilla, pues es una niña de 12 años y ya ha sido ya juzgada por el público bonaerense. Dentro de unos días estará con Vds. el insigne artista mi amigo Emilio Pujol, pues creo que oyendolo disfrutará en grande.

Mande como guste que esta á sus ordenes

Su afmo

A. Prat

℅ Córdoba 3953

2266

On the previous page is a letter written by Domingo Prat to Pedro Mascaro y Reissig on May 9, 1919. The address at the bottom of the letter indicates that Domingo was living at the home of Juan Carlos Anido, father of his student Maria Luisa Anido. The translation is:

"Buenos Aires May 9, 1919

Mr. *Don* P. Mascaro y Reissig,

Distinguished gentleman. I have received your short letter which fills me with satisfaction to see that you are concerned for our beloved instrument, willingly you can have what you asked of me for the *"Escalas y arpegios"* (Scales and arpeggios) and I can thank you very much that you'll send me the latest music that you possess that you indicate.

I believe that very soon I will have the pleasure of letting you get to know since it is very probable that this year I will come to Montevideo to give a concert with my new disciple who is a marvel, since she is a girl of 12 years of age and has already been judged by the Buenos Aires public. Within a few days the eminent artist my friend Emilio Pujol with be with you, since I believe that when you hear him you will enjoy him immensely.

Send to me as you like, I'm at your service.

Affectionately yours,

D. Prat

Cordoba 3353"

In early 1920 Maria Luisa Anido wrote a reply to a letter from Pedro Mascaro y Reissig. The letter is shown on the next page and the translation is:

"Buenos Aires, March 8, 1920

Mr. P. Mascaro y Reissig

Distinguished gentleman:

I have the pleasure to acknowledge the receipt of your appreciative of the date of the 23rd of January of the current year and, by registered mail, the method that you announced to me in your letter.

I must ask your forgiveness for not having answered earlier, but I just returned to the capital of where I have been absent since the middle of October until the 5th of the current month, in which I returned from Mar del Plata.

With total interest I have reviewed the diverse parts of your method which I have found very interesting, and in it I have found works which are familiar to me as they are in my repertoire.

I thank you for your kind attention of the gift and affectionate thoughts in your letter, allow me to send my congratulations for your labor which reveals your dedication, study and love to the delicate and beloved instrument.

With the security of the best consideration, for you, affectionately yours,

S.S.

Y. Maria L. Anido"

B^s Aires, Marzo 8 de 1920

Sr. P. Mascaró y Reissig

Distinguido Señor:

Tengo el agrado de acusar recibo de su apreciable de fecha 23 de Enero del corriente año y, por paquete certificado, el método que me anuncia en su carta.

Debo pedirle disculpas por no haberle contestado antes, pero recién regreso a la Capital de donde he estado ausente desde mediados de Octubre hasta el 5 del corriente, en que he regresado de Mar del Plata.

Con sumo interés he revisado las diversas partes de su método que he encontrado muy interesante, y en él he encontrado obras que me son familiares por pertenecer a mi repertorio.

Al agradecerle su gentil atención del obsequio y afectuosos conceptos de su carta, permítame que le envíe mis felicitaciones por su labor que revelan su dedicación, estudio y amor al delicado y querido instrumento.

Con las seguridad de la mayor consideración, de Vd. atte y S.S

Y. Maria L. Anido

Above is the letter from Maria Luisa Anido written to Pedro Mascaro y Reissig on March 8, 1920.

In the 1931 Antigua Casa Nuñez catalog there were 3 pieces by Pedro Mascaro y Reissig listed.

CONCIERTO

PRIMERA PARTE

1.0 — *Sinfonía.*

2.0 — **Monólogo**, *por Virtus.*

3.0 — *Piano y Violin* — **A Lei!!** *Mazurca de concierto, por las Stas. Sara Roda y Blanca N. Soldini.*

4.0 — **Baile**, *por las Sras. Aura e Iris Soldini, acompañadas en el piano por la Sta. Blanca N. Soldini.*

SEGUNDA PARTE

5.0 — *Guitarra* por el notable Concertista Pedro Mascaró y Reissig.
a) **Minuet** *en «La» — **Sor.**
b) **Preludio** — «Chopin».
c) **Romanza** — *Mendelssohn.*
6.0 — *Piano* - **Rakoez y March**, *por la Sta Blanca N. Soldini.*
7.0 — *Demostraciones de las piezas de baile para salón por los afamados profesores de baile, Héctor Raul Valentini y Rosario B. de Valentini.*
8.0 — *Transformaciones, por Sanchez — El Espejo, por Sánchez y Lasalle.*

HORA: á las 21

Pedro Mascaro y Reissig performed in a concert that was sponsored by the New Skating Club and took place at the Victoria Hall in Montevideo on Friday July 18, 1919. The Gala had performances of Piano, Violin and Dance, besides the intervention of the Classical Guitar. He played pieces by Sor, Chopin and Mendelssohn. The dress code enforced for this event was to wear a Smoking Jacket.

In late 1919 Pedro Mascaro y Reissig published his guitar method book. This review below is from *"El Dia"* on Saturday January 31, 1920 No. 12.313 *1.a epoca: Año XXXII. 2.a epoca: XXX.*

Un excelente método de guitarra — El señor P. Mascaró y Reissig, renombrado profesor de guitarra, acaba de publicar un método complementario para guitarra de que es autor, que ha llamado jutamente la atención de los profesionales y "amateurs" de la buena música.
El método de la referencia comprende una teoría de los equisonos, diez ejercicios diarios, cinco sonatinas y cinco estudios célebres de diversos autores, digitados de acuerdo con la escuela moderna. Es en fin, todo un estudio racional que se recomienda por sí solo.

The translation is: "An excellent method for guitar — Mr. Pedro Mascaro y Reissig, renowned professor of guitar, has just published a complementary method for guitar, of which he is the author, it has justly called attention of the professionals and "amateurs" of good music.

The referred to method is comprised of a theory of the enharmonics, ten daily studies, five sonatinas and five celebrated studies of diverse authors, fingered in accord with the modern school. At the end, it's a rational study that sells itself."

From the daily *"El Plata — Diario de la tarde"* on Thursday, January 22, 1920 Año VI — No. 2267, translated is:

"The Uruguayan Guitarist Pedro Mascaro y Reissig

The latest production

Correctly published by the house Ortelli Hermanos in Buenos Aires, a complementary method for guitar has just appeared, a work by our compatriot Mr. Pedro Mascaro y Reissig.

It is a meritorious work; since included in it is a theory of the enharmonics, ten daily studies of the concert guitarist, five sonatinas of masterful performance and five celebrated studies of the classics of the guitar, fingered in accordance with the school of the late virtuoso *Don* Francisco Tárrega.

Mr. Mascaro y Reissig, one of the few good cultivators of the guitar, perfected his studies with the Catalan concert guitarist *Don* Emilio Pujol; from there which his latest labor is in agreement with the school of Tárrega, who in his time was the maestro of that concert guitarist.

Persons who have heard Mascaro y Reissig performing the difficult works of the classics, have been persuaded that this artist made real creations on the strings of the guitar. That, in his hands, acquires unsuspected values and marvelous sounds, making them think that it isn't the same instrument that the slow and melancholy playing of the countryman, but a mysterious harp, sweetened with all the tones of emotion."

From the Montevideo daily *"El Telegrafo"* on Sunday, January 25, 1920 Año LXX — No. 24. The translation is:

"Method of Guitar — by the maestro Mascaro y Reissig

A new complementary method for guitar has just been released for sale, of which the author is the known Pedro Mascaro y Reissig. It is a work of true merit of the musical genre of our ambience and which shows a deep knowledge of the music on the part of its cited author. The complementary method for guitar of which we were informed comprises an interesting and well thought out theory of the enharmonics, ten daily studies, five sonatinas and five celebrated studies of diverse celebrated maestros, fingered in accordance with the modern school. As you see, by the transcription summary, the work of Mr. Mascaro y Reissig, will be a real auxiliary to the good performers of the guitar, those which, find in it a medium to perfect their studies. Mr. Mascaro y Reissig has dedicated his method to the concert guitarists Mr. Emilio Pujol and Mr. Eduardo Lenzi, whose lessons he has received."

From the weekly publication published in Paso de los Toros, R. O. del Uruguay *"Juventud-Semanario Independiente-de Literatura, Arte, Cronicas Sociales y Actualidades"* on Saturday April 17, 1920 Año III — No. 84, translated is:

Pròximos conciertos de guitarra

Para el jueves 22 y sàbado 24 del corriente, el aplaudido concertista de guitarra nuestro buen amigo y compañero señor Pedro Mascaró y Reissig, efectuará en el teatro de la Sociedad Italiana, dos interesantisimos conciertos con variadisimos programas.

Mascaró y Reissig, es de aquellos espiritus que se destacan con relieves propios, llegando a desco... fuera de nuestras fronteras.

Varios libros lo acreditan como profundo novelista y psicologo al igual que poeta. Obras suyas son "El Destino" y "El Canalla", que en fácil verba llega a desarrolla tramas de verdadera y concienzuda labor.

Publicamos a continuación el programa del concierto que se efectuará el jueves 22 y que está asi dividido:

Primera parte. 1.º Minuè en "La" —Sor.
2.º Estudio en Arpegios.—Aguado
3.º Lagrima (Preludio)—Tárrega.
4.º Oración India—Mascaró

Segunda parte:
1.º Capricho a imitación del piano.—Viñas.
2.º Momento musical.—Schubert.
3.º Estudio en "Mi"—Rovira.
4.o Sueño Eternal (vals)—Mascaró

Tercera parte:
1.o Preludio N.o 7.—Chopin
1.o Melodia Catalana. —Llovet.
3.o a) Sonatina en "Sol" Mascaró
    b) Impromptu en "Re"
4.o Capricho Andaluz.—Manjón.

Como lo esperamos, el público local prestará su concurso en ambos conciertos, pues se trata de un concertista de reconocidos y saneados meritos.

Se coloca actualmente un abono por los dos recitados al precio de un peso, cuyo nùmero ya colocado es bastante numeroso.

"The upcoming concerts of Guitar

For Thursday the 22nd and Saturday the 24th of the current month, the applauded concert guitarist our good friend and companion Mr. Pedro Mascaro y Reissig will perform in the theater of the Sociedad

Italiana, two very interesting concerts with varied programs.

Mascaro y Reissig is of those spirits that can distinguish with their own reliefs, arriving from parts unknown, outside of our borders.

He is accredited with various books as a profound novelist and psychologist and equally a poet. His works are *"El Destino"* and *"El Canalla",* which in easy verbiage manage to develop plots of true and conscientious labor.

We publish the program, which he will perform on Thursday the 22nd, and it is divided as such:

First part:
1. Minué en "La" — Sor
2. Estudio en Arpegios — Aguado
3. Lagrima (Preludio) — Tárrega
4. Oracion India — Mascaro

Second part:
1. Capricho a imitacion del piano — Viñas
2. Momento Musical — Schubert
3. Estudio en "Mi" — Rovira (Antonio Rubira R. O.)
4. Sueño Eternal (vals) Mascaro

Third part:
1. Preludio No. 7 — Chopin
2. Melodia Catalana — Llobet
3. a) Sonatina de "Sol" — Mascaro
   b) Impromptu en "Re"
4. Capricho Andaluz — Manjón

As we expect, the local public will lend its attendance to both concerts, since it's of a concert guitarist of renown and decent merits.

It is priced in a subscription of the two recitals at a price of one peso, whose numbers have already become sought as very numerous."

This concert took place in a small town about 200 miles north of Montevideo, and about 50 miles north of Durazno, Uruguay.

From the weekly publication published in Paso de los Toros, R. O. del Uruguay *"Juventud"* on Saturday April 24, 1920 Año III — No. 85, translated is:

"Evenings of Art

On Thursday evening, he gave his first announced concert in the hall of the Sociedad Italiana, the concert guitarist, our friend, Mr. Mascaro y Reissig, who came here from Montevideo.

A numerous gathering filled the hall and the program was completed with proper skill, getting in all parts of the theater, just applause, which put in good relief the vast knowledge that Mascaro possesses in the musical art.

And it is clear, already that Mascaro has triumphed in other fields, which he will conquer more laurels in this other. As a prose writer his works are *"El Canalla"* and *"El Destino"* and as a poet his *"Flores de araza";* as a polemic one can read a colossal recompilation of his articles and as an orator, the applause and ovations that the press of the Capitol have consecrated him with.

Our old companion, in this home and with us has stayed long years, occupying, the important position of honorary correspondent in the Metropolis.

For this evening, Mascaro, prepares his last concert with the following program:

First part:
1. Allegro no troppo — Sor
2. Jueguito de muñecas (mazurca) — Mascaro
3. Sonata (célebre) — García
4. Un momento (vals) — Alais

Second part:
1. Romanza — Mendelssohn
2. Estudio (célebre) — Napoleon Coste
3. Recuerdos de la Alhambra — Tárrega
4. Reminiscencias criollas — Mascaro

Third part:
1. Ultimo Pensamiento — Weber
2. Estudio en "La" — Parga
3. a) Sonatina en "Mi" — Mascaro
   b) Danza Americana — Mascaro
4. Capricho Arabe — Tárrega

Again, it is expected the hall of the Sociedad Italiana will be full of the attendees this evening."

In the Santa Isabel weekly *"Tribuna Blanca — periodico semanal, nacionalista"* April 21, 1920 *Año 1*, No. 12 the two guitar concerts of the 22nd and the 24th were announced to be held in *"el salon de actos publicos local"*. In the Paso de los Toros daily *"La tarde — organo independiente"* Thursday April 22, 1920 *Año* II, No. 141 the concert to be held that evening in *"el salon del Cine Uruguayo"* was also hall of the Sociedad Italiana, depending on which newspaper one reads.

Pedro's scrapbook shows a concert poster placed at the train station in the *Estacion Rio Negro (F.C.C. del U.)*. This page shows a poster that was placed in the window of a commercial business of the locality with a "Ramírez" guitar.

The poster reads: *"Guitarra de estudio de la afamada marca mundial — Ramírez, es el mismo tipo de instrumento que empleara en sus conciertos P. Mascaro y Reissig."*

Translated it reads: "A student guitar by the world-famous brand Ramírez, the same type of instrument P. Mascaro y Reissig will use in his concerts."

At the top of both pages is written in ink: Sta. Isabel (1920).

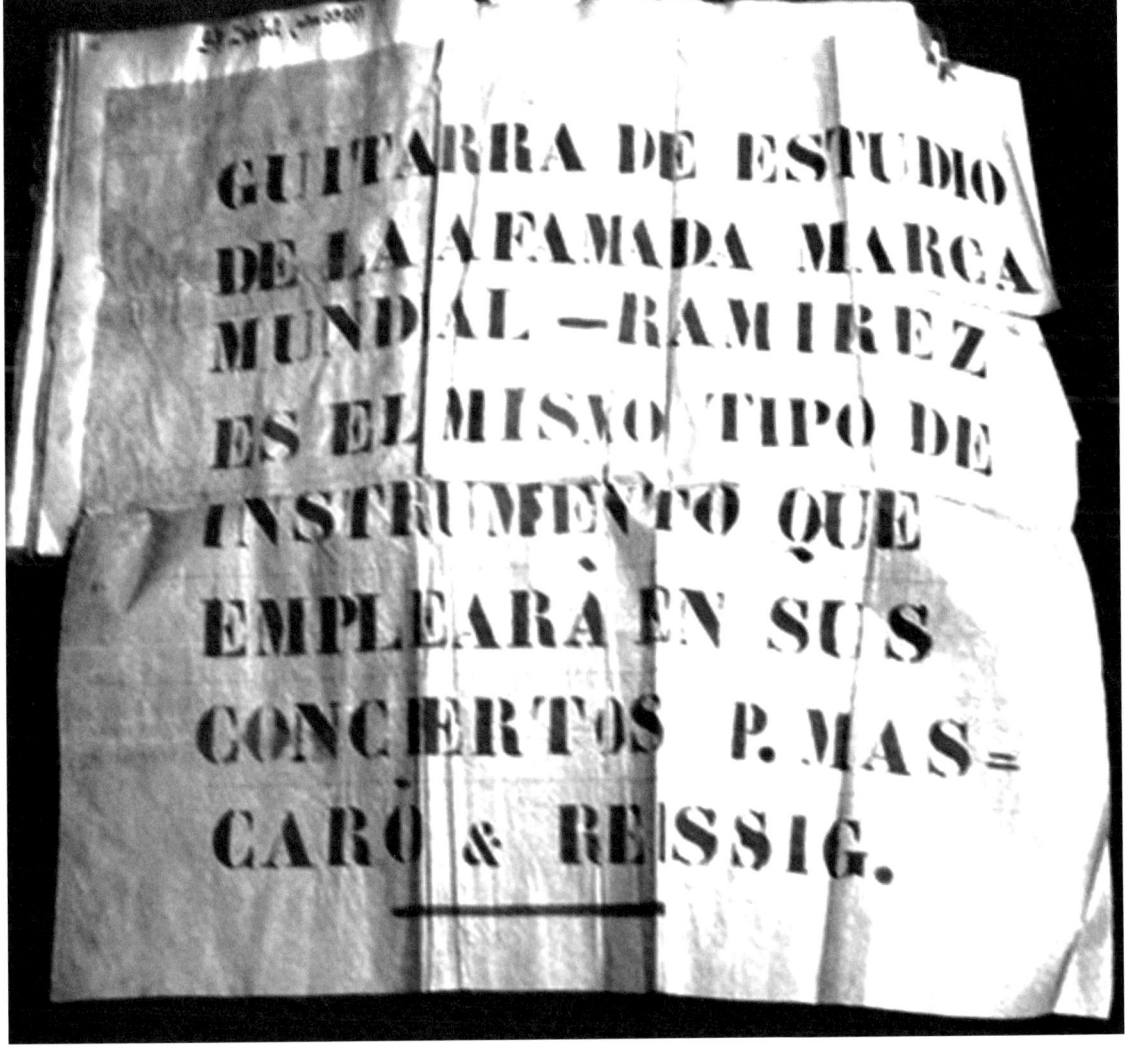

From the tri-monthly publication *"La Union"* published in Montevideo on January 15, 1921 Año III, No. 105. The translation is:

"The guitar and its good cultivators

The eminent Uruguayan guitarist Mr. Pedro Mascaro y Reissig

He just returned to this locality, after a tour of the interior of the country, the celebrated national guitarist with whose name we headed these lines.

It is about a young intellectual which, however has developed in the field of letters, being his novels and books of poetry a faithful exponent of that, has poured out all the potentiality of his psyche and his exquisite artistic temperament, in the cultivation of the instrument that Sor and Tárrega immortalized.

The guitar in the hands of Mascaro y Reissig is transformed completely, it stops being this common instrument which we hear daily strummed at the crossroads or in the home of a friend who is an aficionado; it stops being this guitar of our countrymen, to be placed at the height of the instruments richest in harmony, tone and sonority. This artist treats it with his own subtlety of those that know completely the mysteries that are encased in its fretboard and its six strings. From there which the nocturnes and preludes of Chopin as the compositions of Beethoven, Handel and Mendelssohn, turn out to be on the guitar so emotive and, most of the times, redressed of the best sensationalism of the instrument of Franz Liszt.

The *"Ultimo Pensamiento"* (Weber), the same which *"Granada"* by Albeniz, we can affirm that Mascaro y Reissig not only interprets of an admirable manner, but which both works appear in such moments, born only for the guitar. The same happens to us listening to the *"Momento Musical"* by Schubert, the *"Nocturno No. 2"* and *"Preludio No. 7"* by Chopin, *"Romanza No. 9"* and *"Gondola Veneciana"* by Mendelssohn, *"Minuet en Sol"* by Beethoven and a celebrated choral by Handel, whose chords perfectly transcribed don't stop being an imitation of the mystic magnitude of the organ for which he composed the immortal classic.

If to him we leave expressed, we add all which Mascaro y Reissig interprets of Sor, Tárrega, Arcas, Parga, Aguado, Manjón, and other magicians of the guitar, whose names we don't recall in this moment although we can't give a complete idea of all the worth of this artist, whose temperament and whose technique recalls to us Llobet, Segovia and Pujol who, in their latest concerts, demonstrated with greatness and the marvelous artistic effects encased in this instrument, so less appreciated until today by those that haven't had the chance to hear the guitar in the hands an intelligent cultivator.

Where Mascaro y Reissig has demonstrated to us all of his naked soul, of a consummate artist, is in the composition of his works.

The ingenuity of his melody, blended with an impeccable harmony and, in many difficult moments counterpoint with the necessities of the periods, arrives to enchant us in ecstasy, whose sensations are difficult for us to describe.

We can, now, congratulate ourselves to have the artist among us, who we are concerned with, for the perfection of our aficionados, and the delight of those who live unaware in respect of the marvelous aspects of the classical guitar.

Max."

RAZON

Administración: RINCON 587—Montevideo

Director: EDUARDO FERREIRA

JUEVES 15 de Diciembre de 1921—Año XLIV—Núm. 12.207

Mascaró y Reissig

Caso interesante de renunciación literaria

Rara y sorprendente es la conducta de Pedro Mascaró y Reissig. Su ejemplo es único en nuestro ambiente. Comenzó escribiendo pequeñas páginas en revistas y periódicos lugareños, y concluyó su acervo intelectual con dos novelas: "El destino" y "El canalla", de méritos relativos.

Valieran poco, mucho o nada, sus dos libros, Mascaró y Reissig se hizo un prestigio y una nombradía. Unos los habían leído; otros escribieron sin abrirlos siquiera y los más, los criticaron por referencias...

Con una modestia digna de elogio Mascaró conservó su impavidez e ingenuidad de antes, mostrándose frío a los ditirambos, como a las agresividades de audaces, porque fluían de opiniones sin base ni lectura...

El menos convencido de que realizaba obra meritísima y alta fué el mismo Mascaró, al extremo que se detuvo en mitad de su carrera, auscultando vocación, y cuando pudo lucrar con esa aureola de escritor, conque sueñan obtener pitanzas y lauros tantos intelectuales, buenos, mediocres y malos, en este país de públicos heróicos...!

Hay que ver las perspectivas que ofrece la reputación artística en el Uruguay, para comprender el gesto hermoso de Mascaró y Reissig, iluminado en su voluntad y en su gusto refinado, desdeñoso del falso brillo de las consagraciones repentinas y baladíes...

Por una honda instrospección supo que no era su temple el de los literatos ni su género el de novelador.

No rompió la pluma ni quemó sus libros. Fué grande y magistral su gesto: desdeñó la literatura!!

Sabéis, lectores, lo que significa repudiar las bellas letras?

Sentirse con talento para librar batalla en otro orden de espíritu, ensoñación, belleza y espontánea y cálida tarea!

Mascaró y Reissig, es indudablemente un mozo de inteligencia y lucidez de espíritu, bastante a darle patente de original y sincero.

Tomen nota los mil plumíferos que dicen vaciedades diariamente desde las columnas de la prensa, en libros y revistas, "pour epáter les bourgois"...

Será muy lucrativo ser llamado literato o periodista o dramaturgo, pero es hidalgo y saludable rechazar el remoquete que suena a hueco. Mascaró notó en su alma que había errado el camino y se detuvo para tomar otra senda. Alabado sea!

Yo estoy dispuesto a imitar a Mascaró, el día que me persuada de carecer de ingénita disposición para escribir o que mis colegas prueben la innocuidad o ir apidez de mis lucubraciones.

Admiro la sinceridad en arte y en la vida. Por eso efusivamente elogio a Mascaró por el rasgo de fino paladar que tuvo.

Su caso es típico de los de cambio de vocación, de que nos habla Rodó en sus Motivos.

Ahora Mascaró no escribe: Toca magistralmente la guitarra, talvez mejor que Barrios, al decir de algunos de sus auditores. Ha dado conciertos y cree que descubrió su vocación. A lo menos, si otrora hablaba con indiferencia de la literatura, hogaño se entusiasma por el instrumento aborigen, lo pinta como un predestinado de las cuerdas que cantan, ríen o lloran en las músicas solemnes, clásicas o humildemente terruñeras.

Yo admiro a Mascaró y Reissig.

E. Torres Grané.

On the previous page is the image of the Montevideo daily *"Razon"* of Thursday December 15, 1921 *Año* XLIV No. 12,207. The translation is:

"Mascaro y Reissig

An interesting case of literary renunciation

Strange and surprising is the conduct of Pedro Mascaro y Reissig. His example is unique in our environment. He commenced to writing small pages in magazines and newspapers in our place, and it concludes with his intellectual state with two novels *"El Destino"* and *"El Canalla"*, of relative merits.

They are worth a little, a lot, or nothing at all, his two books, Mascaro y Reissig has made a prestige and a name. They have read one: others write without even opening and the rest, criticize them by reference....

With a modesty worthy to praise Mascaro I preserve his *"iupavidez"* and his ingenuity from before, being cold to the exaggerated flattery, such as the aggressivity of audacity, because they have a difference of opinions without a base nor reading....

The less convinced of which made a meritorious and high work the same Mascaro, to the extreme that he stopped in middle of his career, to listening to vocation, and when he could earn with this aura of a writer, with which they pay to obtain pittances and many intellectual laurels, good, mediocre and bad, in this country of heroic public figures.

You have to take the perspectives that he offers the artistic reputation of Uruguay, to understand the beautiful gesture of Mascaro y Reissig, illuminating in his will and in his refined taste, scornful of the false brilliance of the unexpected and trivial consecrations....

By a deep introspection he found it wasn't his mood that of neither literary ones nor his genre as a novelist.

He didn't break his pen nor burn his books. He was great and masterful in his gesture: scorn the literature!!

Do you know, readers, that he significantly repudiates the beautiful words?

To feel with talent for battle to liberate in another order of *euritmia, ensoñacion,* beauty and spontaneity and a hot chore.

Mascaro y Reissig, is unmistakably a young man of intelligence and a light of spirit, enough to give him an original and sincere patent.

Take note of the thousand free birds that say empty words daily from the columns of the press, in books and magazines, *"pour epater les bourgeoisie"*...(to shock the middle class).

It will be very lucrative to be called a writer, or a journalist or dramatist, but it is noble and healthy to refuse the nickname that sounds hollow. Mascaro notes in his soul that he had taken the wrong road and stopped to take another path. God be praised!

I am disposed to imitate Mascaro, the day that he persuaded me to be in need of a devised disposition to write or what my colleagues test the innocuity and to go apidez of my reflections.

I admire the sincerity in art and in life. Therefore I effusively praise Mascaro by the characteristics of fine palate that he had.

His case isn't typical of those that change vocation, of which Rodo speaks to us in his Motives.

Now Mascaro doesn't write. He plays the guitar masterfully, maybe better than Barrios, as some of his listeners say. He has given concerts and believes that he has discovered his vocation. To at least, if he formerly had spoken with indifference of the literature, in this epoch he is enthused by the aboriginal instrument, he paints it as if he is predestined by the strings that sing, laugh or cry in the solemn music, classical or humbly our native song.

I admire Mascaro y Reissig.

E. Torres Grané."

On the next page is a poster for a Monday October 2, 1922 concert at the Avenida Cine in Montevideo, it also starred the actress Camila Quiroga, who brought Lalyta Almiron to Barcelona a decade later in the spring of 1931. The photo shows Pedro Mascaro y Reissig is using his José Ramírez I guitar.

On January 8, 2011 I sent a copy of the photo to my colleague Richard Bruné to ask as I thought, was it a guitar made by the workshop of José Ramírez I of Madrid? Here's his take:

"I checked it out carefully, seems to be a Jose I instrument, of the largest model he made, probably the 656 mm scale which these usually carried. Fingerboard has the extended portion to carry it to 21 frets. The bridge is definitely of the "pointy arm" version often used by Jose I, but the inlays are different than the ones used in the 1910 Barrios instrument, these are the smaller losanges, the Barrios guitar had the rounded pyramid shapes that echoed the shape of the bridge arms. So, it is definitely a different instrument, but likely from around the same era give or take half a decade. It appears to have been made with machines from the start despite the two barely visible hanging holes in the face of the head. I say this because the ears of the slots are very generous in width and usually when they converted from pegs, the ears had to be a bit thin based on the placement of the 1st and 6th pegs so close to the outside edge of the head. I don't see that here. Also, the machines themselves are of the modern variety with the worms on the head rather than body side of the crown gears, and they look to be butterfly buttons, which in those days usually was a connotation of a very high caliber machine head. The rollers are also the white large size, rather than skinny metal rollers. Rosette looks to be all wood, at least no MOP, as was present in the Barrios Ramírez, another sign the guitar is a high caliber instrument, and the bandings are dark wood rather than white "spats" as were present on the Barrios instrument, suggesting the sides and back are likely dark wood (rosewood?) hence, more expensive, and there are inlays between the banding and the side and back wood, again, a higher level of decoration and hence expense."

AVENIDA CINE CONCERT

El Cine más confortable de la capital

LUNES 2 DE OCTUBRE DE 1922

Extraordinaria función organizada por la

Unión de Operadores Cinematográficos

Y a beneficio de la misma

Primera Parte A LAS 21

APTA PARA MENORES

Sinfonía por la Orquesta "Avenida"
Estreno de la super producción Nacional

"Juan sin Ropa"

- o -

"Nobleza Criolla"

Interpretada por Camila Quiroga

REPARTO

Elena	Camila Quiroga
Juan Ponce	Héctor Quiroga
Aldonata	Julio Escarcela
Alvarado	José de Angel
El Chindo	Alfredo Carrizo
Oscar	Carlos Bonilter
Benitex	Santos Casabal
El Tuerto	A. Cartucci

1.o Palabras por el compañero **José Macías "hijo"**

Platea función entera 0.35

Notable Guitarrista

2.o Recitación de selectas poesías por la precoz niña **Yolanda Parodi**

.o Monólogo cómico «X» por el popular actor **Pedro Martínes**

Segunda Parte

1.o Conferencia cómica por **Aurelio Mastragelo**

2.o Selectas Romanzas por el aplaudido tenor **Raúl López Maccia**

3.o Audición de arte por el notable guitarrista **P. Mascaró y Reyssig**

Quien ejecutará las difíciles partituras:

1.o	Remember «Vals»	Mascaró
2.o	Último pensamiento	Weber
3.o	Capricho Árabe	Tárrega
4.o	Variaciones sobre una Jota de Huerta	Areas

4.o Presentación de la más joven y espiritual tonadillera **Elva Rimbau**

5.o El notable Duo Nacional **Violante - Verdi - Rey** Zambas - Estilos - Tangos

6.o Imitaciones de voces y sonidos, por el excéntrico, **M. Torrini**

P. Mascaró y Reissig

Palcos función entera con 4 entradas $ 1.50

Primera Parte 0.25
Segunda Parte 0.25

Tip. de la F. O. R. U. — Médanos, 1391.

LA UNION

PERIODICO INDEPENDIENTE, INFORMATIVO. APARECE LOS DIAS 5, 15 y 25

Directores: EMILIO F. MASINI y ARMENGOL P. FONT

UNION, Noviembre 5 de 1922

AÑO V — NUM. 168

Apuntes al Carbon

Sobre el último recital de guitarra del celebrado artista Mascaró y Reissig

Todo un acontecimiento artístico resultó el concierto de guitarra que diera el señor Pedro Mascaró y Reissig en el "Avenida Concert" de Montevideo, por cuanto las partituras ejecutadas por el virtuoso concertista, constituyeron una nota culminante en nuestro mundo musical.

Tuvo momentos felices como cuando ejecutó las "Variaciones sobre una jota de Huerta", por Arcas. En ella demostró no tan solo un dominio absoluto en latécnica, sino un alma grande, un alma de artista, por la justa interpretación que diera a la mencionada obra.

Lo mismo podemos decir respecto al "Capricho Arabe" por Francisco Tárrega, partitura de difícil ejecución y que constituyó la nota sobresaliente de la velada, donde Mascaró y Reissig logró conmover hondamente al auditorio con su relevante concepción artística.

El "Ultimo Pensamiento" de Weber, obra que fué transcripta para guitarra por el concertista mencionado, nos impresionó hondamente, así como el vals "Remember", del cual es autor y que demuestra en Mascaró y Reissig condiciones excelentes para triunfar en el vastísimo campo de la armonía.

Pedro Mascaró y Reissig es de esos artistas jóvenes que tienen la virtud de sugerir emociones delicadas a toda alma sensible y ansiosa de ideales amplios en el arte de la música.

Fuera de programa, y a pedido del público que no cesaba en sus ovaciones ejecutó, con la maestría suma que le caracteriza, "La Cabalgata" de Arcas, que es, sin duda alguna, una de las obras de más difícil ejecución y muy poco conocida dentro de nuestro ambiente musical.

R. Mancebo Rojas.

Montevideo, Octubre 23 de 1922.

On the previous page is the image of the review of the performance by Pedro Mascaro y Reissig at the Monday October 2, 1922 Avenida Cine concert. The text underneath *"La Union"* translated says: "Independent newspaper, informative, appears on the days of the 5th, 15th and 25th of the month.

From the tri-monthly publication *"La Union"* published in Montevideo on November 5, 1922 Año V, No. 168. The translation is:

"Apuntes al carbon"

"About the latest guitar recital of the celebrated artist Mascaro y Reissig"

The guitar concert which Pedro Mascaro y Reissig gave in the "Avenida Concert" turned out to be an artistic happening, as for the sheet music performed by the virtuoso, they constitute a culminating note in our musical world.

There were happy moments such as when he performed the *"Variaciones sobre una jota de Huerta"*, by Arcas. In it he demonstrated not only an absolute dominion in the technique, but a great soul, a soul of an artist, by justly interpreting that he gave to the mentioned work.

We can say the same in respect to *"Capricho Arabe"* by Francisco Tárrega, a difficult piece of sheet music to perform and which constitutes the outstanding note of the evening, where Mascaro y Reissig succeeded to deeply move the audience with his relevant artistic conception.

The *"Ultimo Pensamiento"* by Weber, a work that was transcribed for guitar by the mentioned concert guitarist impressed us deeply, in the way the waltz "Remember", of which Mascaro y Reissig is the author and demonstrated the excellent abilities to triumph in the vastest field of the harmony.

Pedro Mascaro y Reissig is of those young artists that have the virtue to prompt delicate emotions to all the sensible and anxious soul of ample ideals in the art of the music.

Outside of the program, and asked for by the public that didn't cease in its ovations he performed, with the total mastery which he characterizes, *"La Cabalgata"* by Arcas, which is, without a single doubt, one of the most difficult works to perform and little known within our musical ambiance.

R. Mancebo Rojas.
Montevideo, October 23, of 1922."

MIERCOLES 3—Desde las 9 a las 11 p. m.—Audición N.o 132

Con el gentil concurso de los guitarristas señores P. Mascaró y Reissig y ñ. Segovia, y tomando parte la soprano lírica señora Josefina Hols de Schusselin, discipula del maestro Pedro Lena Caferatta

PRIMERA PARTE

1 TARREGA — Recuerdos de la Alhambra — Trémolo.
2 MASCARÓ — Remember — Vals.
3 COSTA — Allegro, moderato.
4 SCHUBERT — Momento musical.
5 SEGOVIA — Danza Americana en ía y re.
6 MASCARÓ — Mazurka.
  Los números del 1 al 6 serán ejecutados por los señores Mascaró y Segovia.
7 PERGOLESI — Se tu m'ami — Sra. Schusselin.
8 MASCAGNI — Voi lo sapete o mamma (Cavalleria Rusticana) — Señora Schusselin.

SEGUNDA PARTE

1 PANISIELLO — Chi vuol la zingarella — Sra. Schusselin.
2 PUCCINI — Mi chiamano Mimi (Boheme) — Sra. Schusselin.
3 SEGOVIA — Sueño de Otoño (Trémolo) — Sr. Segovia.
4 TARREGA — Capricho árabe — Sr. Mascaró y Reissig.
5 SOR — Minueto en la — Sr. Mascaró y Reissig.
6 MASCARÓ — In Memoriam — Sr. Mascaró y Reissig.
7 TOSTI — L'avessi tu comprese — Sra. Schusselin.
8 BOITO — L'altra notte in fondo al mare (Mefistófeles) — Señora Schusselin.

In *"Historia de la Guitarra"* published in 1930 by Ricardo Muñoz he says that Andrés Segovia, Miguel Llobet and others played Classical Guitar on the radio in the 1920's. The radio first came to Buenos Aires or the Rio de la Plata itself in the summer of 1920. Here we see Pedro Mascaro y Reissig and his student Alberto Segovia playing on *Radio Sud-America* on Wednesday, October 3, 1923. The performance list shows pieces by, Tárrega, Mascaro, Coste, Schubert, Sor, and Alberto Segovia. This high class music program was from 9PM to 11PM.

Below we see an announcement from the Montevideo daily *"El Dia"* of October 3, 1923 of the performances of Pedro Mascaro y Reissig and Alberto Segovia the lyric soprano Ms. Josefina Schusselin. There are solos and duets of the guitar performed.

Radiotelefonia

The performance of this evening

For the radio performance which they will offer this evening, Radio Station Sud America registers the following:

A Note: By 1935 there were not less than 15 radio stations in Buenos Aires.

Radio Sud-América

(GENERAL ELECTRIC, S. A.)

Longitud de onda: 320 metros

Instalada en el edificio del Instituto Crandon, Colegio Norteamericano para señoritas

Programa de las audiciones que transmitirá la "Estación Radiotelefónica Broadcasting", del 1.° al 6 de Octubre de 1923

Radiotelefonía

La audición de esta noche

Para la audición radiotelefónica que ofrecerá en la noche de hoy la Estación Radio Sud América, regirá el siguiente programa:

Primera parte — Tarega: Recuerdos de la Alhambra, Trémolo; Mascaró: Remember, vals; Costa: Allegro moderato; Schubert: Momento Musical; Segovia: Danza americana en Fa y Re; Mascaró: Mazurca. Los números 1 al 6 serán ejecutados por los señores Mascaró y Segovia. Pergolesi: Se tú m'ami, señora Schusselin; Mascagni: Voi lo sapete, o mamma (Cavalería Rusticana), señora Schusselin. Segunda parte. — Panisiello: Chi vuol la zingarella, señora Schusselin; Puccini: Mi chiamano Mimí, (Boheme), señora Schusselin; Segovia: Sueño de Otoño, (trémolo), señor Segovia; Tarrega: Capricho árabe, señores Mascaró y Reissig; Sor: Minueto en La, señores Mascaró y Reissig; Tosti: L'avessi tu comprese, señora Schusselin; Boito: L'altra notte in fondo al mare (Mefistófeles), señora Schusselin.

CONFERENCIA
POR
CARLOS M. PRANDO
"El carácter de la Música de Albéniz"
TEATRO ZABALA
AVENIDA 18 DE JULIO

Tip. Tall. Don Bosco.

On Tuesday July 15, 1924 in Montevideo at the Conservatorio "Cesar Cortinas" in the Teatro Zabala Dr. Carlos M. Prando gave a lecture on "The character of the music of Isaac Albeniz." The musicians who gave examples of what was discussed were pianist Professor Felipe Larrimbe, cellist Professor Luis B. Amadei, and guitarists Pedro Mascaro y Reissig and his students: Guillermo Corcoran, Alberto Segovia, Mario Mascaro, Raul Dutra and Artigas Rodríguez.

The pieces performed were:

1) El Puerto – Piano
2) Granada – Piano, Cello and Guitars
3) Almeria – Piano
4) Aragon – Piano, Cello and Guitars

Pedro Mascaro y Reissig had studied harmony and composition with Felipe Larrimbe in the decade before this concert or even earlier than that.

From list of members of the Montevideo high society, we see it must have been a well-attended event.

PROGRAMA MUSICAL

Con el concurso del Conservatorio "CESAR CORTINAS"

Intercalando la conferencia sobre «El Carácter de la música de Albéniz» se interpretarán las siguientes obras del autor:

a) EL PUERTO — Piano

b) GRANADA — Piano, Violoncello y Guitarras

c) ALMERIA — Piano

d) ARAGON — Piano, Violoncello y Guitarras

Las interpretaciones de piano estarán a cargo del profesor Felipe Larrimbe, los de violoncello del profesor Luis B. Amadei y los acompañamientos de guitarras a cargo de los señores P. Mascaró Reissig, Guillermo Corcarán, Alberto Segovia, Mario Mascaró, Raúl Dutra y Artigas Rodríguez.

Gran Piano STEINWAY Y SONS de la Casa Mousques

Montevideo Julio de 1924

Distinguido Señor:

La Comisión de Beneficencia que suscribe, tiene el agrado de invitar a Vd. para la conferencia que sobre «El carácter de la música de Albéniz» pronunciará el Dr. Carlos M. Princivalle en el Teatro Zarzuela, el día 15 del corriente a las 18 y 15.

Saluda a Vd. muy atte.

Sras. María Z. de Shaw, M. Elena E. de Casaravilla, Carmen Cuestas de Nery, Plácida S. de Villegas, Elena L. de Castellanos, Bernardina S. de Illa, Carolina Saenz de Zumarán, Matilde R. de Roosen, Zelmira P. G. de Giménez, Carolina Z. de Antuña, Socorro M. de Sosa Díaz, Mercedes F. de Arocena, Adela U. de Guidice, Valentina B. de Fynn, Elvira S. de Vidiella, M. Herminia G. de Mañé, Lola I. de Cortinas, Sara G. L. de Hughes, Asunción R. de Morató, Sara U. de Cuestas, Elisa Z. de Levrero, M. Angélica P. de Wilson, Clotilde I. de Hughes, Rosina A. de García Acevedo, Elisa F. de Biraben, Corina R. de Serró Machovia B. de Comas, Luisa G. de Carve, Valentina F. de Mañé, Amalia F. de Nicolich, M. Luisa G. de Domínguez, Isabel T. de Levrero, Elina E. de Castellanos, María Z. de Montero Bustamante.

Matilde Wilson Platero, Ester Serró Ruchr, Sara Blanco Acevedo, M. Elena y Hortencia Serrato Perey, Carmen y Olga Portillo Díaz, M. Andalia Marquez Vaeza, Plácida Villegas Suárez, Paulina Algorta Camusso, Margarita Cat Alvarez, Mercedes Terra Ilarraz, Susana Cranwell, M. Ester Roosen, M. Elena Marques Castro, Isabel Marie Acevedo, Susana Nery, Elisa Arocena Folle, Sofía Cardoso Sosa Días, M. Elena Taranco, Angélica Iussich Marques, Marieta Morquio Marques, Marta Portillo Urtubey, Sara Cuestas Urtubey, Carola de Soria Gowland, Amelia Mendez Schiaffino, Carlota de Pena, Ana Vasquez Piera, Ofelia Lagos Marmol, Luisa Carve Gurménez, Elvira Serratosa Pringles, Matilde Figari Legrand, Elena Urioste Carve, Josefina Puig Larravide, Marta Hughes Lussich, María Montero Zorrilla, M. Hortencia y Teresa Vilaró Rubio, Elina Castellanos Etchebarne, Margot y Esperanza Durán Rubio, Concepción Zorrilla de San Martín, Susana Howard Tocavent.

Un triunfo Artístico para nuestra localidad.

Tuvo lugar el 15 del corriente, en el teatro «Zabala», la anunciada conferencia que sobre el carácter de la música de «Albéniz» diera el Dr. Prando.

Como para tal fin había necesidad de intercalar números musicales y que éstos estuvieran a cargo de verdaderos artistas, que pudieran interpretar, acabadamente las principales obras del genial compositor español, en sus fieles creaciones, — un artista de nuestra localidad fué llamado á prestar su concurso musical para dicho acto; pues las obras «Granada» y «Aragón», escritas por Albéniz para un conjunto de piano, violoncello y guitarras precisaban de un cultor de este último instrumento, para que el conservatorio musical fuera sintético.

El guitarrista llamado a prestar su concurso fué el profesor Pedro Mascavó y Reissig, a quien nuestro público ha tenido oportunidad de aplaudir más de una vez. — Con él coadyuvaron a dicha labor artística cinco de sus mejores discípulos, casi todos ellos de esta villa, pues sólo uno reside en la ciudad.

Así fué que, en la fecha indicada, y por primera vez en América, «Granada» y «Aragón» estuvieron ejecutadas con su verdadera esencia musical, con un piano, un violoncello y seis guitarras.

Las partes de piano estuvieron a cargo del profesor Felipe Larrimbé, quien ejecutó, también solo, «En el Puerto» y «Alemania», — las partes de violoncello ejecútólas el profesor Luis Amadei, y las de guitarra, como dejamos dicho, estuvieron a cargo del profesor Pedro Mascaró y Reissig y sus discípulos Sres. Guillermo Gorcorán, Alberto Segovia, Mario Mascaró, Artigas Rodríguez y Raúl Dutra.

El público que llenó el teatro Zabala como pocas veces, estaba representado por lo más selecto de la sociedad de Montevideo, — quien premió la labor de los guitarristas pidiendo un bis de «Aragón», última obra en que ellos intervinieron.

Reciban por lo tanto, de nuestra parte, el Profesor Mascaró y Reissig y sus discípulos as felicitaciones más espontáneas, pues sus láuros son nuestros.

From the bimonthly published in Montevideo *"Juventud"* on Wednesday July 30, 1924 Año II — No. 28, translated is:

"An artistic triumph for our locality."

It took place on the 15th of the current month, in the teatro "Zabala", the announced lecture about the character of the music of "Albeniz" given by Dr. Prando.

As for such an end was the necessity in the insertion of musical numbers and those were entrusted to the true artists, which could interpret, completely the principle works of the brilliant Spanish composer, in their faithful creations, an artist of our locality was called to lend his musical expertise for the said act; since the works *"Granada"* and *"Aragon"*, written by Albeniz for the group of the Piano, Cello and Guitars needed a player of this last instrument, for which the music conservatory was out of synthesis.

The guitarist called to lend his expertise Professor Pedro Mascaro y Reissig, who our public has had the opportunity to applaud more than once. With him helping the said artistic labor five of his best students, almost all of them are from this village, only one resides in the city.

In this way it was, on the date indicated, and for the first time in South America, *"Granada"* and *"Aragon"* were performed with his true musical essence, with piano, cello and six guitars.

The piano parts were entrusted to Professor Felipe Larrimbe, who performed, also solo *"En el Puerto"* and *"Almeria"*, the parts of the cello were performed by Professor Luis Amadei, and the guitars, as we have said were entrusted to Pedro Mascaro y Reissig and his students: Guillermo Corcoran, Alberto Segovia, Mario Mascaro, Raul Dutra and Artigas Rodríguez.

The public that filled the Zabala theater as few times, represented the most select of the society of Montevideo, who awarded the labor of the guitarists asking for a repeat of *"Aragon"*, the last work in which they intervened.

Therefore, they receive, of our part, the Professor Pedro Mascaro y Reissig and his students as spontaneous congratulations, since their laurels are ours."

On the next page is the poster of a Pedro Mascaro y Reissig concert held within a variety show at the Montevideo Cine Uruguayo on Tuesday August 26, 1924. This theater was one of dozens managed by the impresario extraordinary Max Glucksmann, also the producer of the record company *Disco Nacional — "Odeon"* in Buenos Aires. According to Juan Pablo Lepra, Max's youngest of 13 brothers, Bernardo, actually ran the chain of theaters in Uruguay.

Dirección **Max Glucksmann** | # Cine Uruguayo | Agraciada 2315 entre Marcelino Sosa y Reducto

HOY MARTES 26 DE AGOSTO DE 1924

1.ª SECCION a las 21 — Apta

Sinfonía por la Orquesta CHAIN

Programá PHILL GOLDSTONE

La Pantera Blanca

Notable cinta de aventuras interpretada por el coloso actor REX (Snowy) BAKER

2.ª SECCION — Apta

Sinfonía por la Orquesta CHAIN

— RECITAL DE GUITARRA —

por el eximio concertista

Pedro Mascaró Reisig

PROGRAMA

Preludio N.o 7	Chopin
Remember (Vals)	Mascaró
Melodía Catalana	Llovet
Capricho Arabe	Tárrega
Granada	Albeniz
Variaciones sobre un tema de jota	Mascaró

"SURCOS" REVISTA de Pedagogía, Ciencias y Literatura de los Estudiantes Normalistas de Montevideo.

Apta

Continuación RECITACION por el señor

Abondio Aron Castillo

Marcha Triunfal	Darío
Cobardía	Nervo
Margarita	Darío
La Giteya	J. Trelles

Les Millans

Notables bailarines Clásicos y característicos Internacionales en sus inimitable Danzas

1	LA ARLESIENE (Farándula)	Bizet
2	ALEGRIAS FLAMENCAS	Valverde
3	RAPSODIA ESLAVA	Volpati

"SURCOS" será la Revista de toda persona de gusto literario y afición científica

3.ª SECCION — Apta

Sinfonía por la Orquesta CHAIN

Subirá a escena la bonita comedia dramática en 2 actos de COLLAZO INSAUSTI

La Barra Provinciana

REPARTO

Chamorro	A. ARON
Marta	Sta. A. Aron
Carmencita	Julio
Dña. María	E. Aron
Leocadio	M. Bracigano
César	A. Larrobia
	A. Veira
	Eduardo
	José Luis
	Lisandro
	M. Aron
	L. Sivori
	A. Sivori
	A. Lloret

SEÑOR PEDRO MASCARÓ REISIG

IMPORTANTE — Al terminar la segunda Sección se sorteará entre los concurrentes la hermosa miniatura escultórica **EL HORCON** gentilmente donada por su autor el celebrado escultor Uruguayo JUAN GAVAGNIN

PRECIOS

F. F. Platea 0.35 ; Tertulia 0.20

By the end of 1924 Pedro Mascaro y Reissig had published a tango as a piano composition entitled *"Yamandu"*. According to the Pedro Mascaro y Reissig biography from the *"Diccionario de Guitarristas"* by Domingo Prat, published in 1934 by Romero y Fernández , this song had gained international recognition. Translating from the end of the biography: "Of all of this production, original for guitar and published

he has for piano *"Trianon"* and *Yamandu"*. This last work was performed on a radio station in New York, as an expression of South American folkmusic, in an hour dedicated to Uruguay, being retransmitted by General Electric of Montevideo. He is a much-illustrated musician figure today among the most distinguished guitarists in the Republic of Uruguay."

On December 30, 1924 the daily *"El Telegrafo"* of Montevideo published this review. The translation is:

"Yamandu"

"Tango for piano by Pedro Mascaro y Reissig

A new tango has just appeared by the national guitarist whose name we have headlined.

Given the success with which the principle orchestras of the capital presently perform, it will be one of the national works called to have great popularity among the lovers of this class of music.

The *tango "Yamandu",* which has been published for piano, its author dedicated it to the musicians of the quartet that take same name, who perform in various theaters here."

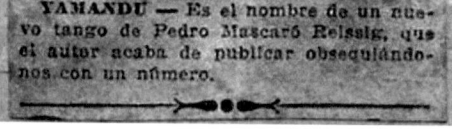

On Friday January 10, 1925 the Montevideo daily *"La Tribuna Popular"* published this note concerning the same piece.

"Yamandu"

"It is the name of a new tango by Pedro Mascaro y Reissig, which the author has just published giving us a copy of this number."

On Saturday April 10, 1926 the Montevideo daily *"El Dia"* published an announcement of the tour of Pedro Mascaro y Reissig, involving back to back concerts in two closely situated towns. The translation is:

"General Information

Tour of the concert guitarist Pedro Mascaro y Reissig.

Next Monday the celebrated concert guitarist Pedro Mascaro y Reissig, who leaves for Colonia Suiza has programmed three concerts of classical music in a recently inaugurated theater in that locality, the first of which will be completed the same Monday.

The 18th and the 20th of the current month he will perform the two remaining, promising all of them to be a flattering success, since besides the select program that will be developed in each one, the appreciated artist will put of his part the exquisite temperament which he possesses and that he has consecrated as a virtuoso in his art.

As well Mr. Mascaro y Reissig will offer three concerts in Rosario on the 14th, 17th, and 21st, for those he has equally arranged select programs of classical music.

In every one of the said concerts the named artist will have known compositions of which he is the author and that they have validated his distinguished triumphs here.

On Saturday April 10, 1926 the Rosario daily *"La Democracia"* published an announcement of the concerts of Pedro Mascaro y Reissig. The translation is:

"Victoria Cinema

For Sunday the following program is announced:

"Transmision del mando Presidencial", presently in 1 act; *"Una enemiga de los hombres"* by Dorothy Revier and the great actor Cullen Landys, a new drama in 6 acts. Ending with a comedy titles: *"Cuidado con resbalarse",* in 2 acts.

A program announcing three concerts to take place in the hall of the Victoria on the 14th, 17th and the 21st of April, entrusted to the celebrated professor Pedro Mascaro y Reissig has been distributed."

The concert programs for both the Colonia Suiza and Rosario performances were the same, he played the same program for 1st, 2nd and 3rd concerts. The only variation in the program shown on the next page was in the name of the town and the dates.

Max Glucksmann produced the Sunday program *"Una enemiga de los hombres".*

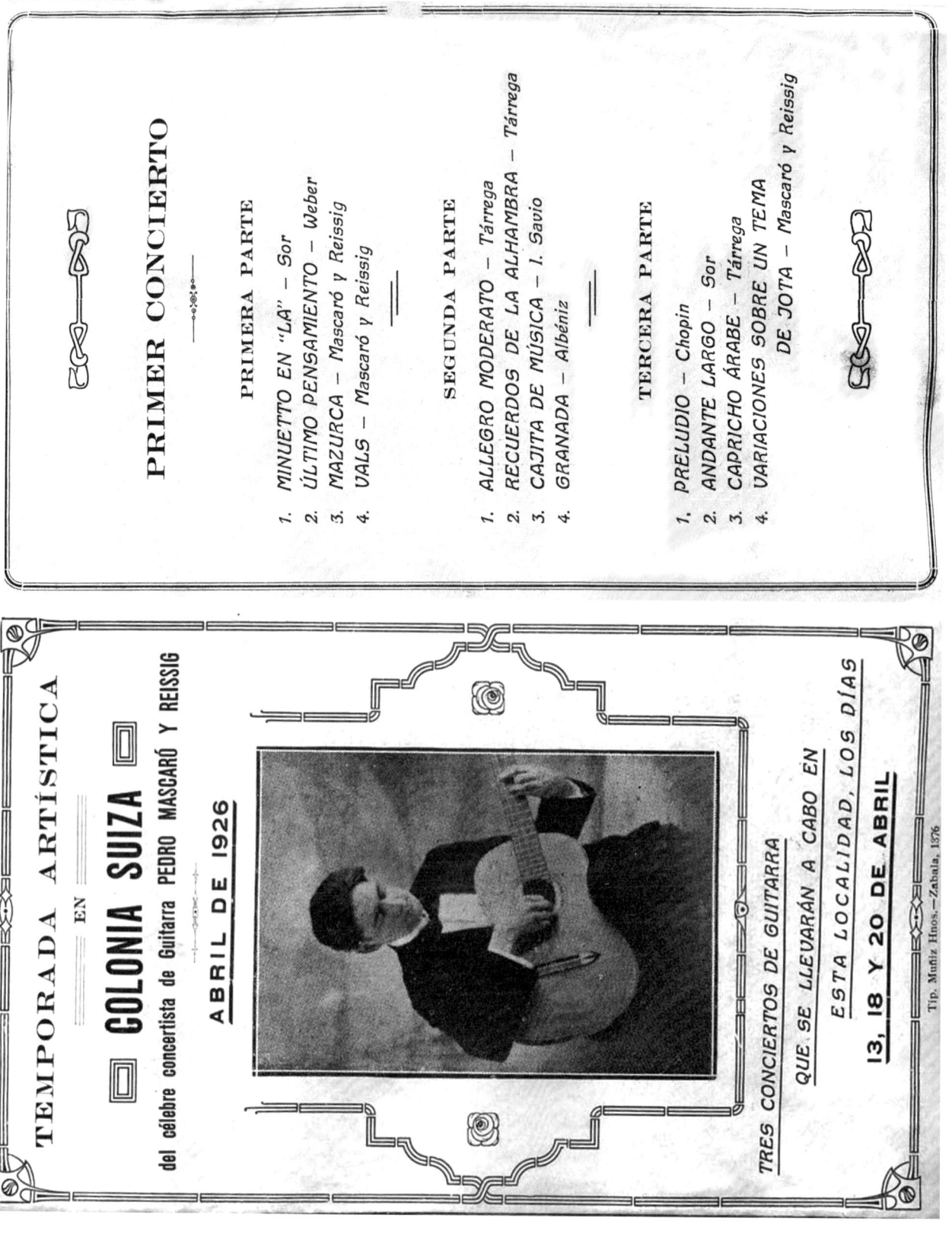

PRIMER CONCIERTO

PRIMERA PARTE

1. MINUETTO EN "LA" – Sor
2. ÚLTIMO PENSAMIENTO – Weber
3. MAZURCA – Mascaró y Reissig
4. VALS – Mascaró y Reissig

SEGUNDA PARTE

1. ALLEGRO MODERATO – Tárrega
2. RECUERDOS DE LA ALHAMBRA – Tárrega
3. CAJITA DE MÚSICA – I. Savio
4. GRANADA – Albéniz

TERCERA PARTE

1. PRELUDIO – Chopin
2. ANDANTE LARGO – Sor
3. CAPRICHO ÁRABE – Tárrega
4. VARIACIONES SOBRE UN TEMA DE JOTA – Mascaró y Reissig

TEMPORADA ARTÍSTICA

EN

COLONIA SUIZA

del célebre concertista de Guitarra PEDRO MASCARÓ Y REISSIG

ABRIL DE 1926

TRES CONCIERTOS DE GUITARRA

QUE SE LLEVARÁN A CABO EN

ESTA LOCALIDAD, LOS DÍAS

13, 18 Y 20 DE ABRIL

Tip. Muñiz Hnos.–Zabala, 1376

According to Victor M. Oxley, Agustín Barrios played at this theater in late January of 1922.

2288

TERCER CONCIERTO

PRIMERA PARTE

1. MINUETTO EN "RE" (Op. 11 N.º 5) – Sor
2. ALLEGRO – Napoleón Coste
3. ROMANZA – Mendelsshon
4. DOS MAZURCAS – Tárrega

SEGUNDA PARTE

1. DOS PRELUDIOS – Tárrega
2. DOS ESTUDIOS – Aguado
3. BOSQUEJO SINFÓNICO – Mascaró y Reissig
4. LA CABALGATA – Mascaró y Reissig

TERCERA PARTE

1. ALLEGRETTO – Cramer
2. LA MARIPOSA – Tárrega
3. CANZONETA – Mendelsshon
4. ADAPCIÓN DE UN AIRE POPULAR AMERI-
   CANO DE J. WELLS – Mascaró y Reissig

SEGUNDO CONCIERTO

PRIMERA PARTE

1. MINUETTO EN "RE" (Op. 11 N.º 4) – Sor
2. ESTUDIO EN SI BEMOL – Sor
3. MINUETTO – Beethoven
4. IN MEMORIAM – Mascaró y Reissig

SEGUNDA PARTE

1. MINUETTO DE LA SINFONÍA N.º 39 – Mozart
2. DANZA N.º 5 – Granados
3. DANZA MORA – Tárrega
4. SUEÑO – Tárrega

TERCERA PARTE

1. MINUETTO EN "MI" – Sor
2. CANCIÓN CATALANA – Llobet
3. MOMENTO MUSICAL – Schubert
4. VARIACIONES SOBRE UN TEMA
   DE MOZART – Sor

INSTITUTO VERDI

DOMINGO 29 DE AGOSTO DE 1926

GRAN VELADA DE ARTE

prestigiada por el Comité de Damas, delegado de la Comisión Organizadora del

1er. Salón Anual de Artistas Libres

PROGRAMA

1ra. PARTE — a las 21 horas

1—ORQUESTA
2—APERTURA DEL ACTO — por el poeta *Carlos Sabat Ercasty*
3—PIANO (Granada de Albéniz) — Srta. *Florencia Catrufo Conti*
4—PARODIAS VOCALES — Sr. *M. Díaz Quijano*
5—POESIAS INÉDITAS — » *Mario Castellanos*
6—ROMANZAS (Canto) — » *Raúl Martínez*
7—RECITAL (varios autores) — Srta. *Ema Avalle*
8—GUITARRA { 1—VALS / 2—MAZURCA / 3—TRÉMOLO } — Sr. *Pedro Mascaró y Reissig*
9—CZARDAS de Monti (Violín) — Srta. *Celia Etchegoyen Xagouapé*
  acompañada al piano por la — » *Gulla Palumbo*
10—WALKIRIA (Wagner. Canto) — Sr. *Nicolás Américola*

INTERVALO

2da. PARTE

1—ORQUESTA
2—RECITAL, (Varios autores) — Sr. *Ricardo Domínguez Alonso*
3—CÁDIZ (Albéniz. Piano) — Srta. *Florencia Catrufo Conti*
4—DANZA de la MARINA — » *Lolita de Selis*
5—ROMANZA (Puccini. Canto) — Sra. *Ana de Colomé*
6—GUITARRA { 1—Minueto [no de Wells / 2—Adaptaciones de un aire america- / 3—Variaciones sobre un tema de jota } — Sr. *Pedro Mascaró y Reissig*
7—RECITAL (varios autores) — Sr. *Santiago Gómez*
8—CANTO { SERENATA de Schubert / LA BRUJA } — » *Dolcey Schenone Puig*
  acompañado al piano por el — » *Félix Carvallo*
9—DIBUJOS RELÁMPAGOS — » *H. Frangella*
10—SCENE DE BALLET (Fantasía. Violín) — Srta. *Haydée Gulla Palumbo*
11—TRAVIATA (Verdi. Dúo. Canto. — Sra. *Ana de Colomé y* Sr. *Nicolás Américola*

NOTA: La Comisión se reserva el derecho de alterar el programa en caso de fuerza mayor

COMITÉ DE DAMAS:—Sras. *Mercedes Pinto, Angela B. de Hernández*, Srtas. Ingeniero *Emilia Loedel Palumbo, Agripina Rodríguez Arasa, Florencia Catrufo Conti, Catalina Rivero, Teresa Marsiglia, Zulema Rivero y Cecilia Catrufo Conti.*

Precio de las Localidades:
Entrada . . . . $ 0.50
Entrada General . . „ 0.15

2290

On the previous page, later in the same month, on Sunday August 29, 1926 we see the intervention of Pedro Mascaro y Reissig in a variety of performances for the evening at the Instituto Verdi.

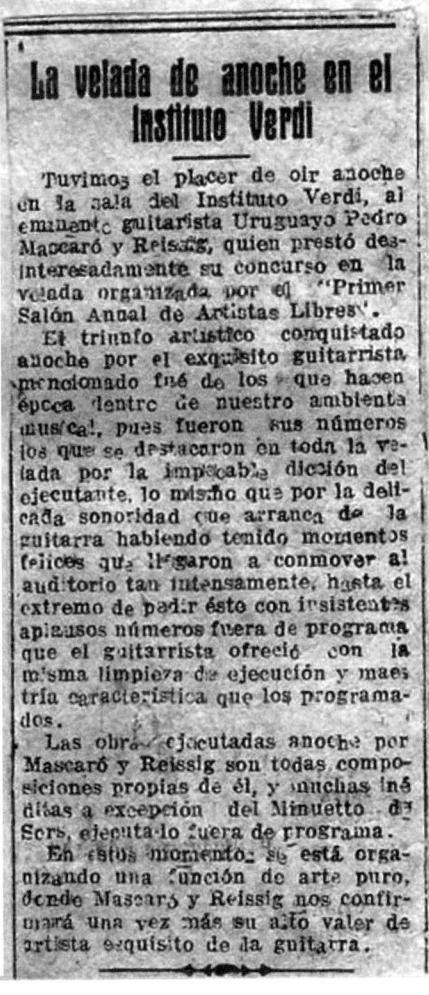

On Monday August 30, 1926 the Montevideo daily *"La Razon"* reviewed the performance of Pedro Mascaro y Reissig at the Instituto Verdi.

"Last night's soirée in the Instituto Verdi.

In the hall of the Instituto Verdi, we had the pleasure last night to listen to the eminent guitarist Pedro Mascaro y Reissig, whose impartial lending of his expertise in the organized evening by the "Primer Salon Anual de Artistas Libres."

The artistic triumph last night conquered by the exquisite mentioned guitarist was of those who make the epoch within our musical ambiance, since they were his numbers that distinguished the whole evening by the impeccable diction of the performer, the same by which the delicate sonority that he extracted from the guitar having had happy moments that reached to move the audience so intensely, to the extreme of asking him with insistent applause encores of the program which the guitarist offered with the same skill of performance and characteristic mastery which he programmed them.

The works performed last night by Mascaro y Reissig were all his own compositions, and many unpublished with the exception of the *Minuetto* by Sor.

In these moments it's organized as a function of pure art, where Mascaro y Reissig would confirm once again for us the exquisite high artistic value of the guitar."

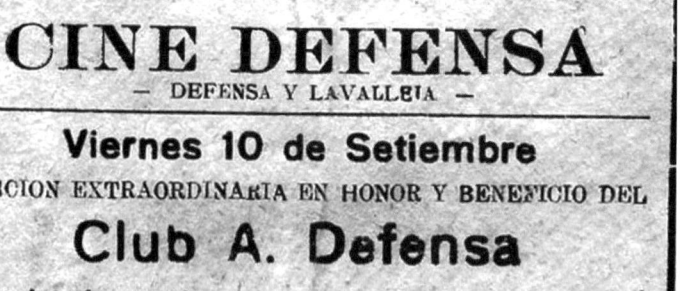

CINE DEFENSA

— DEFENSA Y LAVALLEIA —

Viernes 10 de Setiembre

FUNCION EXTRAORDINARIA EN HONOR Y BENEFICIO DEL

Club A. Defensa

Seleccionado programa cinematográfico y teatral y recital
a dos guitarras por los concertistas

**Pedro Mascaró y Reissig
y Alberto Eugenio Segovia**

quienes harán oir por primera vez en Montevideo, las
siguientes obras armonizadas para dos guitarras

1—ALLEGRO—Napoleón Coste.
2—DOS CORALES Alberto E. Segovia.
3—MOMENTO MUSICAL—Schubert.
4—CAJITA DE MUSICA—I Savio.
5—RECUERDOS DE LA ALHAMBRA—Tárrega.

Localidades en venta

Benedetti Hns. P. Indep'dencia 805.

In the Montevideo daily *"La Razon"* on Friday, September 9, 1926 there was an announcement of the recital of two guitars to take place in the Cine Defensa theater. The translation is:

"The Maestro Mascaro y Reissig — Next Recital of Two Guitars

Next Friday, 10th of the current month, there will take place in the Cine Teatro Defensa, a recital of two guitars that will be entrusted to the professional Pedro Mascaro y Reissig and his disciple Mr. Alberto Eugenio Segovia.

The first we have already heard infinite times in the principle halls of Montevideo, even having the latent impression of his recent recitals in the Instituto Verdi and the Cine Rodo, having gotten in both abundant applause for his exquisite performance.

As for the second, we don't doubt of which his performance will be correct, being that he is a disciple of Mascaro y Reissig.

This recital will have the originality of being the first that will be heard in Montevideo, in it which will be included harmonized works for two guitars and performed by the two Uruguayan interpreters."

¡¡COLOSAL !ACONTECIMIENTO!! Presentación de los reyes de la guitarra

Pedro Mascaró y Reissig y Alberto Eugenio Segovia

QUIENES HARAN OIR POR PRIMERA EN MONTEVIDEO LAS SIGUIENTES OBRAS
ARMONIZADAS PARA DOS GUITARRAS

1—ALLEGRO—Napoleón Coste.
2—DOS CORALES Alberto E. Segovia.
3—MOME TO MUSICAL—Schubert.
4—CAJITA DE MUSICA—I. Savio
5—RECUERDOS DE LA ALHAMBRA—Tárrega.

2292

In the Montevideo daily *"La Razon"* on Saturday September 11, 1926 there was a review of the recital of two guitars in the Cine Defensa theater. The translation is:

"The Maestro Mascaro y Reissig

With his student Alberto E. Segovia, he obtained a brilliant triumph in last night's soirée.

Last night in the Cine Teatro Defensa the recital of two guitars took place entrusted to the maestro Pedro Mascaro y Reissig and his disciple Alberto E. Segovia. Our impression about this recital is that those that missed it, as a consequence of a revelation that was offered to us all of which was the most emotive that could be offered to us of the art of Fernando Sor and Francisco Tárrega.

Above all we must let constancy, that if we gathered at the soirée last night in the Defensa was to hear once again the admirable guitarist Mascaro y Reissig who presented this time in a new variety of his virtuosity and of his undeniable ability of music, in the company of one of his best disciples; in this way which in this chronicle we only make more definite a show of both guitarists, already that the rest of the numbers of the program offered us some interest.

Last night Mascaro y Reissig was in one of his happiest artistic moments, since he shined in three phases which place him at the height of the greatest guitarists today. As a performer he was exquisite; as a musician, impeccable, since the work of the harmonization of the works is profound; such as the *"Allegro"* by Coste and *"Recuerdos de la Alhambra"* by Tárrega only can be done by who possesses the intense musical erudition, and as maestro he put the declaration to present the disciple Segovia, who last night has indicated his perfect school as well in the performance as in the composition, since among the works placed in the recital they played two quite sober chorales of his creation.

Mascaro y Reissig as much as Segovia received a lot of the applause that the public offered them last night, after the performance of *"Momento Musical"* by Schubert this fruit of our admiration, which is a truly sincere applause."

The translation of the image at the bottom of the previous page is: "A colossal happening, presentation of the kings of the guitar: Pedro Mascaro y Reissig and Alberto Eugenio Segovia, who will have us hear for the first time in Montevideo the following works harmonized:"

2293

LA TRIBUNA POPULAR — Montevideo

Domingo 19 de Setiembre de 1926 – página 5

"El arte del Sr. Mascaro y Reissig

Con las reservas del caso, recibimos y publicamos:

Evacuando un pedido de un núcleo de aficionados al clásico instrumento de la guitarra, para que emitiera mi modesta opinión sobre los valores artísticos del señor Mascaró y Reissig como guitarrista, me decido a emitirlo, no sin antes creer que existen otras personas más autorizadas para hacerlo mejor que el que suscribe, que por causas inexplicables han guardado absoluto silencio hasta el presente, dejando propalar con esa actitud algo que conspira contra los prestigios de la buena música y de la guitarra especialmente. Los que conocen al señor Mascaró al través de sus versiones guitarrísticas, se habrán quedado asombrados ante los artículos elogiásticos aparecidos en algunos órganos de la prensa. Los ditirambos, ensalsamientos [sic] y demás zarandajas del elogio se han prodigado con una profusión tal que uno se siente aturdido ante semejantes chaparrones extemporáneos, y digo extemporáneos, por lo absurdo e inmerecidos para quien los recibe. Dice un refrán 'cuando la limosna es pródiga hasta el pobre desconfía'... pero aquí el pobre ... ¡que si quieres! ... Los valores artísticos del buen señor Mascaró son nulos, nulos por los cuatro costados, técnica malísima, interpretación...

¡Pero, señor, si aquello no es música, ni guitarra ni Cristo que lo fundó! aquello es una maraña que sólo la necedad o la necesidad... de no sé qué, puede exponerlo a la pública expectación.

Es sencillamente tomarle el pelo al honorable, lo que está muy mal hecho, pues el honorable, en todos los casos, debe merecer siempre el mayor respeto. Esto que antecede está en la conciencia de todos los aficionados, de los que entienden cuatro notas y de los que no entiendan pero que tengan un adarme de oído para la música, que hayan escuchado al buen señor Mascaró. Este buen señor hace algunos años intentó penetrar en el erizado campo de la literatura, escribiendo algunas novelitas que se caían de raquíticas, olvidando que 'lo que Natura non da Salamanca non presta' y hasta tuvo el coraje de pedirle un prólogo al doctor Schinca que, como es de suponer, eludió la delincuente complicidad. Para mal de nuestros pecados, ahora la emprende nuestro buen señor Mascaró contra el campo musical guitarrístico pretendiendo hacer lo que antaño intentó en el literario. Vamos... buen señor, sosiéguese. Si tanto afán tiene en exhibirse, hay tantos oficios que le darían mejor que el musical, honra y provecho, por lo menos, merecidamente. Por que eso sí, siempre que no atente contra el instrumento de nuestra [sic] predilecciones, cual es la guitarra en su faz artística, le deseamos los mayores éxitos en todo lo que emprenda. Nosotros, socialmente, no la malqueremos, al contrario, pero no podemos tolerar que usted, en desmedro del arte musical, abuse de la paciencia del público y de la benevolencia de la prensa, creándose a su amparo una atmósfera de celebridad mal adquirida como guitarrista eminente. Santo Dios! y pensar que la guitarra ya de por sí desprestigiada por no conocérsela bien o por exigir de quien la escucha una sensibilidad en extremo delicada, para poder valorarla, va a caer en sus manos para soterrarla más de lo que está!

¡Buen señor! en nombre de los manes, Mozart, Bach, Beethoven, dioces [sic] de la música, Sor, Tárrega, dioces [sic] de la guitarra, deje usted en paz este noble instrumento que sostenido por un pequeño y entusiasta grupo de diletantes se transmitirá a las generaciones venideras hasta que ocupe el lugar que le corresponde en el arte musical universal. Y no digo más.

Miguel Herrera
St. 15 de 1926   s/c Industria 55"

I would like to thank my esteemed colleague and published author Alfredo Escande of Montevideo, Uruguay for doing the footwork and typing of this newspaper article from the Montevideo daily *LA TRIBUNA POPULAR* of Sunday September 19, 1926. It was not included in the Pedro Mascaro y Reissig scrapbook of text and images, just the responses to this attack by the guitarist Miguel Herrera Klinger.

"The art of Mr. Mascaro y Reissig

With the reservations of this case, we received it and we publish it:

To take care of a request of a nucleus of friends of the Classical instrument of the Guitar, for which I will emit my modest opinion about the artistic values of Mr. Mascaro y Reissig as a guitarist, I decided to emit it, without believing beforehand that other persons more authorized to do a better job than this writer, which by unexplainable causes have guarded absolute silence, letting be published with this attitude that conspires against the prestige of the good music of the guitar especially. Those who know Mr. Mascaro y Reissig through his guitaristic versions have remained astonished before the articles which praise that have appeared in some organs of the press. The exaggerated eulogies, praises and the rest of the sieves of the eulogy have lavished with such a profusion that one feels dumbfounded before the similar unseasonalable cloudbursts, and I say unseasonalable, by the absurd and undeserved for who receives them. The refrain is said: 'When the alm is lavished until the poor are distrustful'....but here the poor.... if you want!...The artistic values of the good Mr. Mascaro are void, void through and through, the worst technique, interpretation....

But, sir if that isn't music, neither guitar nor Christ that founded it! that is a thicket that only the foolish or the necessity... of I don't know, you can display it to the public expectation.

It is simply pulling the leg of the honorable, what is very wrong, as the honorable, in all cases, always deserves the utmost respect. This above is in the minds of the aficionados, of those who understand four notes and those who do not understand but have an ear formusic, having heard the good Mr. Mascaro. This gentleman a few years ago tried to enter the bristly field of literature, writing a few novels that were unsteadily falling off, forgetting that 'Nature does not speak and does not give a grant to Salamanca' and even had the courage to ask a prologue from the Doctor Schinca that, as expected, avoided the criminal complicity. For the bad for our sins, now our good Mr. Mascaro has undertaken against the guitar music field pretending to do what he once attempted in the literature. Let us ... good lord, calm down. If so much effort has exhibited, there are so many trades that would give honor and profit better than music, at least, deservedly. Why yes, if not undermine the instrument of our preference, which is the guitar in its artistic side, we wish you every success in everything you undertake. We, socially, not wishing to quarrel, on the contrary, but we can not tolerate you, to the detriment of the musical art, abusing the public's patience and benevolence of the press, creating it under an atmosphere of ill-gotten fame as an eminent guitarist. Good God! and to think that the guitar is already discredited for not knowing better or for demanding an extremely delicate sensitivity of the listener, in order to evaluate them it will fall into their hands to bury and what's more!

Good lord! on behalf of those men, Mozart, Bach, Beethoven, the gods of music, Sor, Tárrega, the gods of the guitar, leave this noble instrument in peace held by a small group of enthusiastic amateurs that will transmit to future generations to occupy the rightful place in the universal musical art. I say no more.

Miguel Herrera
St. 15 de 1926

s/c Industria 55"

In the Montevideo daily *"La Tribuna Popular"* on Thursday September 23, 1926 is a mention of an unfavorable critique of Pedro Mascaro y Reissig. For several days this discussion was printed with rebuttals by students of Mascaro y Reissig with quotes from Miguel Herrera Klinger also a student of Eduardo Lenzi — according to Domingo Prat, Miguel was the favorite student of maestro Lenzi. The translation is:

Lío entre artistas

Dias pasados publicamos una crítica de arte acerca de un guitarrista criollo, señor Reissig, donde se emitía un juicio desfavorable, y se le negaba sus condiciones de artista.

Claro está que ese juicio crítico iba abonado por la firma del autor, y que al publicarlo explicamos que lo hacíamos con las reservas del caso.

Prudente y sabia medida fué la nuestra, visto que ayer tuvimos la visita del guitarrista Reissig, quien vino en compañía de un excelente amigo nuestro, y se acreditó ante nosotros exhibiéndonos todos sus títulos.

Como compositor el señor Reissig nos probó que tiene comprometidas con la Casa Editora Pirbano, de Buenos Aires, sus producciones.

Amén de eso es maestro del Instituto Verdi, maestro del Colegio Salesiano y maestro del Conservatorio Larrimbe.

Dejamos, pues, enteramente a cargo del autor de la crítica, la responsabilidad de la misma.

"Fuss between artists"

"Days ago, we published a critique of art about a criollo guitarist, Mr. Reissig, where an unfavorable judgement was emitted, and negated his abilities as an artist.

Clearly that critical judgement that was signed by the author, and that to publish it we explained that we were making reserves in that case.

A prudent and known measure was ours, which saw yesterday we had a visit of Reissig ,the guitarist, who came in the company of an excellent friend of ours, and he vouched before us exhibiting all his titles.

As a composer Mr. Reissig proved to us what he has committed with the Casa Editora Pirbano, of Buenos Aires, his productions.

In addition to that he is maestro of the Instituto Verdi, maestro of the Colegio Salesiano and maestro of the Conservatorio Larrimbe.

We leave, then, the obligation entirely to the author of the critique, the responsibility of the same."

In the Montevideo daily *"El Pais"* on Wednesday October 6, 1926 in the Teatros y Conciertos section a student of Pedro Mascaro y Reissig wrote a rebuttal to the critique by Miguel Herrera Klinger. The translation is:

"Sobre un suelto con pretensiones de critica — (About loose comments with the pretense of being a critique)

Days ago, a friend told me about a pair of loose comments that appeared in a morning daily, in which was put in as a judgement of the artistic personality of Mr. Pedro Mascaro y Reissig. I believed from the start, before I was informed of the subject, that it only would be a negative critique, without imagining not even which I could take the proportions of the incendiary satire, but, there I have what the article writer in question appears unknown in absolute the rules to which must be adjusted to all persons for the power with the due seriousness of a serene judgement, about the positive or negative values that the critiqued, since he doesn't escape any criteria moderately observed which all artistic critics consist of in knowledge and taste.

The first, signifies to know the instrumental technique mechanism, the second is to possess the quality of feeling the beauty which, such as some have said, indicates possession of beauty.

The author of the loose comments titles 'The art of Mr. P. Mascaro y Reissig' who was asked by a group of friends that are aficionados of the classical instrument, obligated to declare the complete nullification of the cited artist, but, he didn't bring any data, nor a judgement across his musical interpretations, nor discussed his works; he only said that he doesn't know how to play and that is a vulgar dealer of the art; but, now I ask: does the author of the loose comments have the sufficient intellectual abilities such to emit a serene judgement in respect?

I believe that he does, already who of a group of friends, has he been, the most indicated to go out to the spotlight imposing his opinion: an opinion I respect but don't share, for the following reason: it lacks logic and reveals venom. Therefore, it's that permit me, to invite Mr. Herrera — who I don't have the pleasure to know and I'm inclined to believe he might be a gentleman — to which if he replies and he finds the capacity to make a formal critique, about the artist that he so mercilessly has pretended to examine closely, over the four phases in which the cited maestro can be judged.

1. As a musician. 2. As a composer and third and fourth, as a performer and as a maestro. If, I only demand as one condition, that rival of me in this emergence might be a critic, that is to say, the indispensable conditions which all critics possess: impartiality, science and liberty, discounting from that, that you only reply to those articles which might put by declaring your version of the theme. Without this, I give up all polemics. — R. (Raul) Mancebo Rojas. —"

In the Montevideo daily *"El Dia — edicion de la tarde"* on Sunday October 17, 1926 in the Vida Social section an article titled *"Callar"* written to the lack of response by Miguel Herrera Klinger. The translation is:

"To be silent when the attack is violent; when it is a child of the excessive passion, of the envy or of the longing of vengeance a long time contained; to be silent when the attack is made on a cultured and respectable person, when it converts him into white virulent diatribes and passionate charges; to be silent when the attack struggles without equal weapons; when it deals, not now as a friend or a brother whose reputation has to be defended, but of the person of the attacked; to be silent when one's own reputation is a thing judged at once by the social conscience, when there are precedents which are to be settled, when the moves of the aggressor aren't mysterious for anyone; to be silent when the attacked can't be mixed with the folks in the gutter, to be silent when all that has happened, the undeserved infringed injuries aren't accepted gently; isn't consented in the damage of their own reputation, the conduct of the adversary nor lick the hand of those that insult isn't approved, neither fear nor cowardice: is to appreciate the things in which they value, is to trample the offenses; to have pity, at least, for the aggressor; is to despise the infamy, is the greatness of the soul, is the protest of the victims; the protest of the truth and of the injustice; the protest of the right; the protest of the gentleman who knows that no is the ultimate that can have reason, but he has it, the protest of the cultured man, the eloquent protest of the silence. That is to be silent."

In the Montevideo daily *"El Pais"* on Saturday October 23, 1926 in the Teatros y Conciertos section a student of Pedro Mascaro y Reissig wrote a second rebuttal to the critique by Miguel Herrera Klinger. The translation is:

"Sobre un suelto con pretensiones de critica — (About loose comments with the pretense of being a critique)

Mr. Miguel Herrera has preferred to remain silent. The loose comments published in a morning daily have left to reveal the ungrateful opinion, of which he is the author, a move by the greatest of bewilderment, had he wanted to throw by land all the good opinion which, some knowledgeable about this topic, we have formed of the maestro Pedro Mascaro y Reissig. It is, that the triumphs that they have consecrated to the maestro Pedro Mascaro y Reissig in the amplest field of music, certainly aren't the ephemeral triumph of a moment, but the compensation of a methodical work, to which brings the consecrated ones almost half of his life.

This has been the motive by which I couldn't have maintained my silence, before the unjust attack by Mr. Miguel Herrera, to whom, by an intermediary of the columns of this hospitable newspaper, I called to sustain a polemic, although beforehand it will bring by taking for granted the triumph; and I say this, because my ex future rival, has left hanging some verbiage in the matter, employing excessive terms, and not bringing to the spotlight any facts which will authorize as an experienced person in the subject in which he has embarked. Between "to hear", and "to know to hear" a great difference exists, and Mr. Miguel Herrera has confessed that the music of the cited maestro *"era una maraña"* (was a thicket) that nothing was understood; possibly, this nothing might refer to the group of aficionados to who the cited mister represents in this emergence.

But exists, another notable difference between to negate and to make a critique; to negate for negating, with knowledge or without it, to whatever artist subtracts his merits, but what is difficult is to bring suitable reasons and support facts which give reason of what is expressed. That has been what Mr. Herrera hasn't known to do and he has spoken a lot, without absolutely nothing specific, leaving to reveal more than nothing, a personal aversion toward Mr. Mascaro y Reissig, who has more than enough merits as for which the critic lends just attention, now which he has in his doing, not only the abilities of an experienced maestro, but as a composer and a concert guitarist.

More than once, the press of the capital or of the exterior or the interior has had the occasion to judge him through his interpretations and his compositions, and to none of the musical critics has it occurred to say to which Mr. Herrera has said. My previous questions remain standing.

R. (Raul) Mancebo Rojas."

In the Montevideo daily *"La Razon"* on Saturday January 15, 1927 in the Teatros y Cines section an interview with Pedro Mascaro y Reissig appeared entitled:

"El Arte Guitarristico en Uruguay — Una Visita al Maestro Mascaro y Reissig"

The translation is: "The Guitaristic Art in Uruguay — A Visit to Maestro Mascaro y Reissig

To finally know about the labor of the admirable technician of the guitar Pedro Mascaro y Reissig, we gathered at his institute on the calle San Salvador. There we spoke to him devoted to the study of the texts by Durant and Goetze, having in front of him a blackboard full of musical examples, which the maestro explained to us were exercises of counterpoint and fugue, developed within the most modern evolutions of the musical art.

"Now you see" — he said to us, indicating to us the mentioned texts, — "I have to resort to the works in French and German, to enlarge my musical knowledge, since the treatises in Spanish aren't sufficient contemporaries for the required ends; but being very familiar with the French and German idioms, I don't lament a lot about their insufficiency."

— We came, maestro, today, to hear about, well, if it is certain as we have already heard it in your guitaristic performances for the public, we want you to also tell us among the congratulations, which they have heard intimately, — it was our insinuation for which the young artist will abandon his illustrative occupation and might put unconditionally at our disposition.

He made us wait a little, to hear his musical phrases, so subtle, so original, so full of emotivity, since, once he extracted his celebrated *"Merialdo"* guitar from the case, he commenced to give a tuning by harmonic notes, a peculiarity of this guitarist, who never has been careless to show that in his performances. Instants after, we heard the enchanted melodious creations of Tárrega in one of his mazurkas. To give an end the performer of this work which its author titled *"Marieta"*, that one remained in front of us, something in this way as to be privileged, and to notice our taste by the character of the said music, he made us hear two more mazurkas of the cited composer, the same that his *"Capricho Arabe"*, *"Danza Mora"*, *"Recuerdos de la Alhambra"*, *"Minuetto"*, various preludes and studies and the celebrated *"Sueño"*.

After a brief interval in our conversation it oscillated about the merits of some Uruguayans, in which Mascaro y Reissig had to declare himself one convinced of the good guitaristic qualities and overall musical pieces of the compatriot Luis Alba, the performer, after a brief demonstration of mechanism, with various studies by Aguado and Napoleon Coste, he let us hear the celebrated compositions of Fernando Sor.

We don't know to say which of them Mascaro was the most admirable; all were performed with the most correct technique; for the Estudio en Sib, as for the Andante largo, it had its instances of emotivity that excited us to the ineffable; in the five minuets which he treated us to, the same which in the Variaciones sobre un tema by Mozart, he put all the musical character that is required in those works, — created in the beginning of the last century, — within a correct mastery.

After a *"Serenata"*, a *"Romanza"* and a *"Capricho Andaluz"* by Manjón, the guitarist made us hear various classical pieces created for piano, violin and orchestra, transcribed for the guitar by the eminent Francisco Tárrega, to be distinguished among them a *Prelude* and a *Nocturne* by Chopin, a fragment of the 7th Symphony by Beethoven, *Granada* by Albeniz, a *Danza* by Granados, the *Preludio de la Gruta de Fingal, Dos Romanzas* and a *Canzoneta* by Mendelssohn, *Serenata* by Malats, an *Estudio de Alard*, and another by Cramer and the *Minuetto de la Sinfonia No. 39* by Mozart.

In spite of which our visit had initiated at nine o'clock in the evening and our watches now said two thirty in the morning, we didn't want to leave without hearing the performer's own creations for us to form a judgement to finish with them.

After a *"La Mariposa"* by Tárrega and a *"La Campanela"* by Arcas, we heard some compositions by Mascaro y Reissig. Although it is certain that his *"Cabalgata"*, his *"Bosquejo Sinfonico"*, his *tremolo "In Memorium"* and his mazurkas let us be convinced of the unmistakable talent of their author, — his *"Minuetto"* and overall his celebrated waltz *"Véspero"* were those which succeeded to bring the profoundest feeling to our hearts. And then, in those moments, we explained to him why that phrase of the poet Abondio Aron Castillo refers to Pedro Mascaro y Reissig: 'The strings plucked by your fingers are six infinitely great souls that vibrate prompting ineffable esthetic emotions.'

"Are you thinking of giving some performances soon?" — we interrogated the maestro.

"For now no" he responded to us; "I have to attend to the course of studies of my disciples, which absorbs a lot of my time; today has been a chance that I might have found in the dominion of my fingers, since days up to entire weeks pass without exercising them; and I repeat, today has been an exception, because they waited for you."

— "Do you presently have some advanced disciple?"

"There are various which are found with these abilities; but, one who I expect much from is a young German descendant, who now shows as a future guitarist, who has powerfully drawn the attention.

We didn't want to bother the distinguished artist anymore and we left in spite of ourselves, nevertheless now the hours were to be nearing the day.

The performance given had begun at nine o'clock in the evening, as we have already said, and in this moment, it is almost four o'clock in the morning, almost seven hours the guitarist had been flattering our ears, without repeating a single piece and playing everything from memory.

To leave that ambiance of the Art, we think once more of the misery of some humans, and, above all of them, the envy which obliges them to negate as far as the light of the sun.

Before the fruit of such poverty, they have been exposed to be victims all of the geniuses of the art, and Mascaro y Reissig has already been. Praised it is. No one concerns himself with that which has no value; in contrast those that are worth something..."

The "celebrated Merialdo guitar" referred to in the first page of the interview was made by the luthier Miguel Merialdo who built on la calle Médanos in Montevideo for over 60 years.
Quote from the internet: "Julio C. Da Rosa: *escritor de memoria* by Lucio Muniz".

On Wednesday November 30, 1927 the Montevideo daily *Imparcial Año* IV No. 1167 had a review of the broadcast of the previous evening on *Radio IMPARCIAL* Estacion General Electric.

The photo below is from that review and was noted in "Last Night's Performance":

"...such as the distinguished professor of guitar Mr. Pedro Mascaro y Reissig and his advanced disciple Ricardo Munz were unsurpassable in their respective numbers, which integrated a real fiesta of native art."

"...and brilliant technique, security of performance and richness of color, ...they contributed to offer moments of healing esthetic relaxation for the thousands of listeners of the *Radio IMPARCIAL*."

Profesor Pedro Mascaró y Reissig su discípulo Ricardo Munz

Professor Pedro Mascaro y Reissig and his disciple Ricardo Munz

On Sunday December 11, 1927 the Montevideo daily *Imparcial Año* IV No. 1178 in it's Escenarios — Conciertos — Artistas section had an article entitled: *"Un Futuro Gran Guitarrista"* (A Future Great Guitarist) Ricardo Adolfo Munz. The translation is:

"An infinity of times, to look over the interesting columns of *IMPARCIAL*, and stop ourselves in the Radio Section we were attacked with the same thought: among the new, varied and numerous group of artistic elements, which parade daily in front of the microphone of the powerful General Electric Radio Station, there must necessarily emerge some appreciable values. This focus of unmistakable artistic culture, which is the *Radio IMPARCIAL*, besides its function such as it, is, it must signal the appearance of promising artists, it must reveal to us the existence of elements that today possess "something" which tomorrow can be converted into something "great".

By exchange of our mind this thought, it made in us an axiom an unmistakable truth....

A few nights ago, gallantly invited by the intelligent Chief of the Radio, we gathered for a performance, and in only that opportunity, we found full confirmation of the thought which always obsessed us, of the truth which always pursues us...

In effect: we had a happy coincidence, of listening to two interesting elements; one, the excellent professor of guitar Mr. Pedro Mascaro y Reissig and the other, his advanced disciple Ricardo Adolfo Munz. Of the first, we won't speak by dealing with an already known value, although we will allow us to speak of the past, of the notable performance, of his impeccable production, which has the suggestive name of "Cabalgata", this production, which to our humble extension, isn't unworthy in any of the known repertoires of the virtuosos of the guitar that visit us, if we insert them in those.

2300

Of the second element, which we heard, and we already named, of this if we will speak by dealing with a new value, which came to confirm, as we have said, our continuing thought.

Ricardo Adolfo Munz has the unmistakable merit, of which "feeling" and know how "to feel" his art. Listening to him play the guitar, I can't sustain two opinions; he is a splendid promise. It pains us to put that phrase, because although the most exact, it has been so used, it has the fact of being so used and abused it can be a compliment, when in reality it is a truth which is sincerely proclaimed.

We hear him play accompanied by his professor, *"Recuerdos de la Alhambra"*, by Tárrega, a known and very beautiful work; the delicate *"Minueto de la sinfonia No. 39"* by Mozart, and *"Vals"* by Mr. Pedro Mascaro y Reissig.

When in one of these works, dominated by an unexplainable nervousness, his fingers didn't respond to what was written on the music staff, a sincere expression of pain was drawn on his face, but he immediately reacted to trying to overcome every time more and more.

He has the pride of his art, and demands of himself, the continuing strength, of which the performances come out the cleanest possible. If this most valuable character persists, soon it would stop being a promise to be a positive value.

He wants to bring, a feeling of imperative mandate to his vocation, the mysterious voice of which we speak of Rodo; therefore, we think that he will arrive at his desired goal.

If it is certain, that a relation exists between the life of a writer and his work, an identical relation must necessarily exist, in a performer although the medium of the realization of the beauty, might be different. And perhaps he here as well, is the secret, the spring, which makes it artistically move, by this way to say, of the young German guitarist, whose pilgrimage of this land, all constitutes a small odyssey, in where the sentiment and the will amply triumph.

Maybe the pains, the sufferings, the varied emotions lived in his path as an immigrant, are those that show and feel, on the strings of his guitar, when he makes them vibrate.

Montevideo, December 10, 1927 — Adolfo de Nava Anatole."

Ricardo Adolfo Munz

His translated dedication is: "To my maestro P. Mascaro y Reissig, R. Munz, January 5, 1928."

In the Montevideo daily *El Plata — diario de la tarde* on Wednesday December 11, 1929 there was a listing of a radio performance on CX 32. It consisted of solos and duets. The translation is:

"Concert of 2 Guitars

The known maestro Mr. Pedro Mascaro y Reissig, with his distinguished disciples Mrrs.Alberto E. Segovia and Luis Oscar Rossano, offer charmingly from our studio an interesting guitar concert, whose program is the following:

Two Guitars: Mrrs. Mascaro y Reissig and Alberto Segovia
1. Coral en Sol — A. Segovia
2. Vals — Mascaro y Reissig
3. Momento Musical — Schubert

Two Guitars: Mrrs. Mascaro y Reissig and Luis Oscar Rossano
1. Recuerdos de la Alhambra — Tárrega
2. Estudio — Napoleon Coste

Guitar Solo Mr. Alberto E. Segovia
1. Aire nacional — A. Segovia
2. Preludio — A. Segovia

Guitar Solo Mr. Luis Oscar Rossano
1. Danza Española No. 5 — Granados
2. Serenata — Malats

Guitar Solo Mr. Mascaro y Reissig
1. Minuet — Paderewski
2. Granada — Albeniz
3. Tremolo — Mascaro y Reissig"

Pedro Mascaro y Reissig writes in his archive that Luis Oscar Rossano had only played guitar for 16 months at the time of the December 11, 1929 radio program.

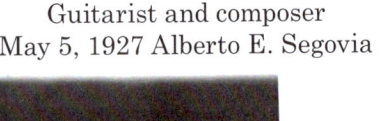

Luis Oscar Rossano

Guitarist and composer
May 5, 1927 Alberto E. Segovia

Another student from the same epoch, Elina Blixen Flores.
The dedication says: "To Pedro and to Blanca (Pedro's wife), Affectionately, Elina."

The following week in the Montevideo daily *"El Plata — diario de la tarde"* on Thursday December 19, 1929 there was a review of a Pedro Mascaro y Reissig concert on radio C. X. 32. The translation is:

C. X. 32 Radio Carve
"Last night's concert

The known professor of guitar Mr. Pedro Mascaro y Reissig, last night offered from our studio a splendid concert, to be distinguished, not only by his technique, but by which the interpretive justice of his performances in the known works of the great Tárrega, culminating in the finalization of the first and second parts of the program with the emotivity and coloring that he gave in the celebrated compositions *"Capricho Arabe"* and *"Sueño"* of this great classic.

The final part of the concert constituted of unpublished works by the distinguished performer, it gave an opportunity, for which we could appreciate not only his abilities as an interpreter, but that as one of the most elevated values of our national composers, outstanding in a special mode in the *Minueto,* which Mr. Pedro Mascaro y Reissig dedicated to the celebrated Catalan concert guitarist Miguel Llobet."

On Tuesday February 11, 1930 the Montevideo daily *Imparcial* had an announcement in the *Escenarios — Conciertos — Artistas* section of the release of the *"Minuetto"* by Pedro Mascaro y Reissig. The translation is:

"Minuetto for guitar by Pedro Mascaro y Reissig —

It has just been published, the new composition for guitar by the known and intelligent professor Mr. Pedro Mascaro y Reissig, a composition which we have had the opportunity to hear, and which constitutes with a doubt, an extremely delicate page, truly valuable, which comes to enrich the literature of that instrument. He tells us, that the great Llobet, in his last tour, heard the *"Minuetto"* which concerns us, and remained so sincerely admired, that besides saying phrases of praise for the labor of the author, he directed to an editor which was found in this opportunity in which he expressed: 'Look. There you have a splendid occasion, for making a production of high value.' This opinion, certainly well concluded, he showed us in an unmistakable form, to which the corresponding category of the work by Mascaro y Reissig that just came out, and which, by that circumstance, carries his dedication for the eminent Llobet."

On the next page is a poetry recital where Pedro Mascaro y Reissig and Mario Mascaro performed background music while poetry and prose were being read. This took place at the S.O.D.R.E. (Estudio Auditorio) on Friday September 18, 1931, the nationally known actor, Santiago Gomez Cou, was the drawing card.

ESTUDIO AUDITORIO

DEL
SERVICIO OFICIAL DE DIFUSION RADIO ELECTRICA
ANDES Esq. MERCEDES

Viernes 18 de Setiembre de 1931

A LA HORA 21 Y 45

RECITAL POETICO

Por el Actor Nacional

Santiago Gómez Cou

Comentarios Musicales ejecutados
por el Profesor PEDRO MASCARÓ Y REISSIG y MARIO MASCARÓ.

Platea $ 0.50.- Galerías $ 0.10

PROGRAMA

Primera Parte

1.—J. Santos Chocano - Nostalgia.
2.—Guillermo Cuadri - Leña e coroniya.
3.—Emilio Carrere - La Musa del Arroyo.
4.—Carlos A. Clulow - La Cita.
5.—Gabriel Dannunzio - Un Sueño.
6.—F. Silva Valdes - Hastío.
7.—Rafael J. Abella - El Aguatero. (Con comentarios de guitarras).

Segunda Parte

8.—Elvio Prunel Alzaibar - Ancestralismo.
9.—Mario Bravo - Canción de las cartas viejas.
10.—Emilio Frugoni - El medio día.
11.—Javier de Viana - Cosas que pasan (Prosa).
12.—Rafael J. Abella - El guacho.
13.—Gustavo A. Becquer - Rimas.
14.—Ovidio Fernández Ríos - Floración suprema.
15.—Atilio Supparo - Mi Ombú.

Tercera Parte

DEDICADA AL POETA
JOSÉ ALONSO TRELLES. (Viejo Pancho).

Canta la noche. Con comentarios de guitarra.
Recordando. id id id
Insomnio. id id id
La Montonera.
Cosas de Viejo. id id id
Del natural. id id id
Mi testamento.

Dirección:
Max Glücksmann.

Cine Stella D'Italia

CALLE MERCEDES
Esq. TRISTAN NARVAJA

VIERNES 23 DE AGOSTO de 1935 Hoy

1.a Sección a las 21 y 10

EL DEBUT DE MICKEY
Dibujos cómicos con Ratón Mickey.

TIENDA DE LOZA
Sinfonía Tonta por Walt Disney.

LA PRESTIGIOSA CORAL DEL
"CENTRO ENCICLOPEDICO"
CANTARA

1.o — GONDOLIERI, Barcarola, de Donizzetti.
2.o — RETRETA, Laurent de Rille.
3.o — PEPITA, Mulei.

Max Glücksmann presenta la producción "Intorgino" Sonora y Hablada en Ruso

EL CAMINO DE LA VIDA

— REPARTO —

Fomka, el cuchillo afilado ..... MICHAEL JAROFF
Loika, la descuidera .... María Gonta
Mustafá, el presumido .... Ivan Kyrla
El Padre .... Vladimir Jaccofarof
La Madre .... Regina Januschkewitsch

HOY ♦ HOY
GRAN VELADA

Conmemorando el 8.o aniversario del asesinato legal de

SACCO y VANZZETI

víctimas de un proceso monstruoso a las ideas que estos hombres sustentaban, por parte de la plutocracia yankee; se realiza este acto de confraternidad proletaria, organizado por la F. O. R. U., a beneficio del Comité pro Presos y de su órgano en la prensa "Solidaridad", con un interesante programa.

2.a Sección

CONCIERTO DE GUITARRA

por el niño Julio César Alonso, de 11 años (alumno del profesor Pedro Martin Mascaró Reissig), el que ejecutara:

1.o — TESTAMENTO DE AMELIA, Melodia, de Llovet.
2.a — PAVANA, de F. Tárrega.
3.o — RECUERDOS DE LA ALHAMBRA, de F. Tárrega.

RECITACION

por la niña URANIA MINOTTI.

CONTINUACION DEL GRAN FILM

EL CAMINO DE LA VIDA

Es el reflejo de la acción pujante de los nuevos forjadores de almas, de los hombres intrépidos que empiezan a modelar en la niñez de hoy, la generación que será fuerte mañana! Dramática, fuertemente dramática, es una nota exótica dentro del cine moderno, y señala la visión genial que los directores rusos tienen del séptimo arte!

PRECIOS: PLATEA 0.30
Cazuela y Paraíso 0.15

HOY - GRAN FESTIVAL DE BENEFICIO - UN NOTABLE PROGRAMA

Es la primera producción parlante del Soviet. Por sus escenas, circula un soplo de realismo asombroso, y la vida desfila a través de su trama, honda, intensa, emocionante!

2306

On the previous page is a variety show where a student of Pedro Mascaro y Reissig performed concert level works. The eleven year old Julio Cesar Alonso performed these pieces on Friday August 23, 1935 at the Cine Stella D'Italia, one ssof the many theaters that was managed by the impresario Max Glucksmann, who also ran the record company *Disco Nacional "Odeon"* in Buenos Aires.

On the back of the photo is a dedication that translates to:

"To my beloved maestro Pedro Mascaro y Reissig, Julio Cesar Alonso, March 2, 1935."

Below is a photo of Pedro Mascaro y Reissig performing for the attendees at the *Legacion de Bolivia* in Montevideo on October 23, 1935. It is from the weekly magazine *"Mundo Uruguayo"* of October 31, 1935. The translation of the photo caption is:

"Mr. Mascaro giving his guitar concert in the hall of festivities of the Legacion."

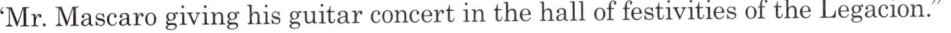

El señor Mascaró dando su concierto de guitarra en el salón de fiestas de la Legación.

P R O G R A M A

PRIMERA PARTE

Concierto de Guitarra, a cargo del
Sr. PEDRO MASCARO REISSIG

Pavana . . . . Tárrega
Minueto en La . . . . Sor
Serenata Española . . . . Malats
Jota . . . . Mascaró Reissig

SEGUNDA PARTE

Srta. MARGOT POU CARDOSO

Chefiero Costume . . . . Legrenzi
Dove? . . . . Schubert
Berceuse . . . . Gretchaminow
Seguidilla Murciana . . . . Falla
Acompaña al piano la señorita
Esther Velasco Lombardini

TERCERA PARTE

Concierto de piano, a cargo de la
Sra. SARA ORLANDI DE LARRAMENDY

CUARTA PARTE

Sra. MARIA L. MORALES DE QUARTINO

Lasciate mi morire . . . . . . Monteverde
Chanson triste . . . . Duparc
Extace . . . . Duparc
Louise . . . . Charpentier
Acompaña al piano la señorita
Esther Velasco Lombardini

Los modelos de las intérpretes son de la
◆◆ Maison A. D. VALIANTE

This is the program for the Pedro Mascaro y Reissig concert at the Legacion de Bolivia in Montevideo on October 23, 1935. This concert was covered by several dailies in Montevideo, those being *"La Mañana"*, *"El Diario"*, *"El Pueblo"*, *"Uruguay – Un Rumbo Cierto Bajo La Cruz del Sur"*, and *"El Plata"*. There were well over a dozen newspapers in this city of 300,000.

EL Diario

DOMINGO 18 DE ABRIL DE 1937

Se acaba de fundar un Centro Guitarrístico

Un grupo de entusiastas cultores del arte de Tárrega, acaba de reunirse, resolviendo fundar una nueva entidad que bajo el nombre de "Centro Guitarrístico del Uruguay Conrado P. Koch", bregará por la difusión y exaltación del noble arte de nuestro ambiente. Nuestro fotógrafo sorprendió ayer durante una de las reuniones preparatorias, a un grupo de los iniciadores que aparecen en la presente nota y son: setado. los señores Alberto Segovia. Pedro Mascaró Reissig, Raúl Mancebo Rojas y Américo L. Castillo; parados: Rivera Castillo, Atilio Rapat, Abel Carlevaro y Arturo Milans. Como es aspiración de los organizadores el de agrupar el mayor número de amigos de ese arte, nos piden hagamos saber que todo quien resee adherir al nuevo centro, puede hacerlo en Comercio 2244.

As was entered in the scrapbook of Pedro Mascaro y Reissig, the founding of the Centro Guitarristico del Uruguay "Conrado P. Koch". The translation is on the next page:

2309

The same text appeared in both the dailies of Montevideo *"El Diario"* on Sunday April 18, 1937 and in *"La Mañana"* Monday April 19, 1937.

"Centro Guitarristico del Uruguay "Conrado P. Koch" was just founded.

A group of enthusiastic cultivators of the art of Tárrega, just united and decided to found,ss a new entity that is under the name of Centro Guitarristico del Uruguay Conrado P. Koch, will struggle for the diffusion and exaltation of the noble art of our ambiance. Our photographer was surprised yesterday during one of the preparatory gatherings, a group of the initiators that appeared present are: seated: Mrrs. Alberto Segovia, Pedro Mascaro y Reissig, Raul Mancebo Rojas and Americo L. Castillo; standing: Rivera Castillo, Atilio Rapat, Abel Carlevaro and Arturo Milans. Such is the aspiration of the organizers to form a group of the most numbers of friends of the art, they asked us to let anyone know that everyone who would like to join at the new center, can do so at Comercio 2244."

In the weekly magazine *"Mundo Uruguayo"* on January 13, 1938 Año XX No. 977 this photo appeared along with its corresponding text. The translation is:

"The components of the Centro Guitarristico del Uruguay Conrado P. Koch, presided over by Mr. Pedro Mascaro y Reissig in an act that took place in memory of the guitarist Conrado P. Koch, the 28th of last December, on the radio station C.X. 14."

Los componentes del Centro Guitarristico del Uruguay, presididos por el señor Pedro M. Mascaró Reissig en el acto realizado en memoria del guitarrista CONRADO KOCK, el 28 de diciembre último, en C X 14.

The last item entered in Pedro Mascaro y Reissig's 1917-1938 scrapbook is this radio program listing from July 5, 1939, from the Montevideo weekly magazine *"Cine Radio Actualidad"* of June 30, 1939. The translation is:

"A debut on *C. X. 32.* Next Wednesday the 5th at 8:45PM on this channel we will present the President of the Centro Guitarristico del Uruguay, Mr. Pedro Mascaro y Reissig, for the continuing Wednesday and Saturday guitar concerts.

Un debut en C. X. 32.— El próximo miércoles 5, a la hora 20 y 45 se presentará en esta onda el presidente del Centro Guitarrista del Uruguay, señor Pedro Mascaró y Reissig, para continuar miércoles y sábados con conciertos de guitarra.

Montevideo, noviembre 28 de 1939
Señor RICARDO F. MUÑOZ
Bucarelli 2887
   Buenos Aires

Distinguido señor:

Tengo el honor de comunicar a Ud. que el Centro Guitarrístico del Uruguay "Conrado P.Koch" que presido, acordó, en sesión de fecha 21 del corriente,- designar a Ud. representante del mismo en la República Argentina.-

La referida decisión, adoptada con la conformidad unánime de esta Directiva, significa incorporar a nuestro Centro, su desinteresado, noble y constante esfuerzo en pro de la guitarra; el acervo invalorable de su profunda versación musical y guitarrística, a la par que la sólida vinculación que une a Ud. con los centros musicales argentinos.-

En la seguridad de que se dignará Ud. aceptar el cargo, tenemos el honor de asegurarle nuestra modesta colaboración para cuanto sea de su interés, ofreciéndole la mas amplia y cordial reciprocidad.-

Saludo a Ud. con la mayor consideración.-

José Piria
Presidente

Secretario

2311

Translation of the previous page from the Archive of Ricardo Muñoz.

"Montevideo, November 28, 1939
Mr. Ricardo F. Muñoz
Bucarelli 2887,
Buenos Aires

Distinguished gentleman,

I have the honor to communicate to you that the Centro Guitarristico del Uruguay "Conrado P. Koch" which presided, agreed, in session the date of the 21st of the current month, to designate to you as a representative of the same in the Argentine Republic.

The referred to decision, adopted with the conformity of this Commission, signifies to involve in our Centro, your impartial, noble and constant effort in favor of the guitar; the invaluable amount of your profound musical and guitaristic verbage, the both of which the solid involvement that you unite with the Argentine musical centers.

In the security of which we designate to you, to accept the office, we have the honor to assure our modest collaboration as might be in your interest, offering the most ample and cordial reciprocity.

Congratulations to you with the best consideration.

José Piria — president
Arturo Milans — secretary"

BAJO EL auspicio del emba-
jador del Uruguay ofreció un
concierto el niño de esa nacio-
nalidad Carlos Méndez Bauer.

Translation of the text of this photo from the daily *"El Mundo"* from December 4, 1942.

"Under the auspices of the Ambassador of Uruguay the child of this nationality Carlos Mendez Bauer offered a concert."

My colleague, Richard Bruné, a friend of Carlos Mendez Bauer (1930-), said the guitar was made by Hermann Hauser I in 1938, and that Carlos began to study with and acquired the guitar from maestro Andrés Segovia in Montevideo in 1939.

Montevideo, 18 de mayo de 1948

Sr. D. Eduardo Bensadón

Estados Unidos 1666

Buenos Aires.-

Muy señor mio:
        Con sigular agrado le dirijo ésta nota - que interpreta los sentimientos de la Directiva del Centro Guitarrístico del Uruguay - como prueba formal de mi agradecimiento por el obsequio que ha hecho a ésta asociación cultural, de un ejemplar de la obra " Tarantela " de la que es usted autor.

        Es para mi motivo de satisfacción, que compositor tan caracterizado, distinga al Centro Guitarrístico con actitudes de naturaleza tan simpática como la que me ocupa.

        Al reiterarle el reconocimiento por su atención me place quedar a sus amables órdenes.

        Suyo afmo.

                                        ALBERTO SENA
                                        Presidente

PEDRO M. AGUIRRE
Secretario ad-hoc

Montevideo May 18, 1948
Mr. *Don* Eduardo Bensadon, Buenos Aires. —

Dear Sir;

With outstanding pleasure I direct this note — that interprets the feelings of the Board of Directors of the Centro Guitarristico del Uruguay — as formal proof of my thankfulness for the gift you have made to this cultural association, of a sample of the work *"Tarantela"* of which you are the author.

As a motive of my satisfaction, that the composer so characterizes, it distinguishes to the Centro Guitarristico with attitudes of a nature so kind such as it concerns me.

To reiterate the recognition of your attention it pleases me to remain at your friendly service.

Sincerely yours,

Alberto Sena — president

Pedro M. Aguirre — Secretary ad-hoc.

2313

Centro Guitarristico
de Uruguay
Standing: E. De Los Santos,
O. Koch, A. Sena, C. F. Freire,
O. Cáceres (Secretary)
Seated: J. L. Blanco,
P. M. Sanchez, O. Rolandi

This photo of some of the members and Board of Directors of the Centro Guitarristico del Uruguay "Conrado P. Koch" is from The Guitar Review magazine issue No. 11 of 1950.

"Julio Martínez Oyanguren-Uruguayan concert guitarist. He was born in the capital of the Durazno province on July 3, 1900. He began his musical studies with the professor of piano, Alfredo Hargain, who also had some knowledge about the guitar. Those being Julio's desires to learn this instrument, his professor began to instruct him in the rudiments of the guitar. In 1919 he moved to Montevideo uniting his knowledge with the modest professor of guitar Leoncio Marichal, who, was enthused by his exceptional gifts, who awakened the interest in him to prepare for a recital. From that moment on he became interested in the foundation of his art; consulting methods, attending performances of guitar, practically without ceasing, and, already oriented, he entered onto a good path that conduced the place where he is admired. His sacrifices weren't small, parallell to his labor of music; he acquired a bachelor's degree and today to be a journeyman mechanical naval engineer of the fleet of his republic. We remember that, by his uncommon intelligence, the government assigned him with a scholarship in 1925 to make studies of perfection in the marine of the Italian war. In July of 1931 he visited Buenos Aires forming a part of an official artistic representation of his country, acting as a guitarist in "La Peña" and on *L.R. 4 Radio Splendid,* always getting a frank success. The Associacion Wagneriana of this capital contracted him and he returned to visit us, giving two recitals: one for the said association and the second for a public performance in the Salon "La Argentina", on the dates respectively of the 18th and 26th of September, the dailies dedicating to him the greatest eulogies '...in this artist the balance of interpreter and performer; sober, elegant and inspired, the first; secure, brilliant or delicate, always just and ample and of colorful sonority, the second.' (*La Prensa,* September 26, 1931).

As for the recordings of discs, he has some works. To the respect of the Victor label, the producer of these discs, says, in a critical paragraph about the concert guitarist that we are concerned with "...His technique, artistic seriousness and temperament, eulogized by the metropolitan press from this artist's concerts, they reflect in those discs. The said discs referred to *"Capricho Arabe"* by Tárrega and *"Gato Polkeado"* by Quijano; *"Un Momento"* by Alais and *"Jota"* by the same Mr. Oyanguren." In these works his pleasant tone can be appreciated; but on the other part, we believe that where he loses his "artistic seriousness", of which the Victor label tells us, is in respect to the work *"Un Momento"* by Alais."

This biography is translated from the *"Diccionario de Guitarristas"* by Domingo Prat, published in 1934 by Romero y Fernández .

JULIO J. MARTÍNEZ OYANGUREN.

This photo is from Ricardo Muñoz's unpublished book *"Historia Universal de la Guitarra"* Volume VI *"America"*.

It is from a Buenos Aires daily. The guitar in Julio's hands is the Sinopoli model, a variant of the double soundhole model by Francisco Simplicio.

This is from Ricardo Muñoz's unpublished book *"Historia Universal de la Guitarra" Volume VI "America"*.

"Julio Martínez Oyanguren was born to Manuel Martínez Sellanes and the pianist Justa Oyanguren in the city of Durazno, Uruguay on July 3, 1901 and baptized with the names Julio Jacinto.

Julio owned guitars made by Ramírez, Simplicio, Sinopoli, Camacho and Interdonatti. The last guitar mentioned was specially made for him and was given after a performance at Columbia University.

In 1932 he was a part of the artistic delegation that was sent from Uruguay to Argentina, and he performed in the salon "La Argentina" and was quite successful. Julio said: 'Already without a doubt, I feel with all evidence that my path is in music.'

On October 12, 1933 he returned to Argentina and gave a concert at the salon Consejo Nacional de Mujeres where he played: *"Minuet"* by Sor, *"Minuet"* and *"Allemande"* by Bach, *"Variaciones"* by Mozart, *"Triste"* by Morales, *"Cordoba"* by Barrios, *"El Poncho"* by Fabini, *"Gato"* and *"Vidalita"* by Sinopoli, *"Zapateado"* by Sirera, *"Rafaga"* by Turina, *"Rumores de la Caleta"* and *"Aragon"* by Albeniz, his own *"Danza Arabe"* with great public satisfaction. The next day *"La Prensa"* said: 'He put his dominion of the instrument to the test, his sense of rhythm, of color and musicality; coming to be applauded by the public which asked for encores.'

Named *"Aggregate"* to the Uruguayan Embassy in the United States, he arrived to the great nation of North America, where he performed at the best concert venue of the world, the Town Hall in New York with great success that accompanied him constantly in all the land; the public powers got to know his art and toasted him with a performance at the White House for Franklin Delano Roosevelt.

He then celebrated a concert with the Philharmonic Orchestra in the Lewisohn Stadium under the direction of F. Weissmann before a public, which exceeded 18,000 spectators; for the first time in the U.S. the famous quartet for Guitar, Flute, Viola and Cello written by Schubert was performed. RCA Victor and the National Broadcasting Company immediately signed him, where he continued performing.

The newspapers said: (New York Herald Tribune) 'At the end of his presentation he was compensated with *"BRAVO"* by the professors of the same Philharmonic.' (New York Times) 'He performed with traditional elegance, smoothness and exquisite taste. He played the passages of the greatest technical difficulty without harming the absolute musicality nor the interpretation.' (New York Daily News) expressed: 'They call him Martínez Oyanguren, the greatest guitarist of the world and by which it concerns us he has the right to the distinction of that title. He has achieved a warmth and expression of music on his instrument which we never thought possible.'

In 1941 he went to Rio de Janeiro and gave concerts and then passed to Montevideo, his homeland, where he was heard for the first time after an absence of eight years, having performed in the most important halls and been the first guitarist to play his instrument on television.

He arrived in Buenos Aires in July of that year and gave concerts with the works of Sor, Bach, Paganini, Gossec, Cimarosa, Turina, Moreno Torroba, Albeniz and Granados. *"La Prensa"* said: 'As an interpreter, his sensibility has been invigorated and acquired a personality and as a performer, his fingering is clearer and secure and his sound is richer in tone color.... his versions deserve the warmest reception of the public which weren't sparing in the applause and he was obliged to play four encores.'

He returned to the United States and a few years later he came back to his motherland, in 1950 he visited Argentina, giving a performance at the Club Oriental, sponsored by the embassy of his country, of the performance *"La Prensa"* said: 'He has already achieved the fullness of his manner of interpretation and performance. He dominates the technical secrets of the guitar, of which he achieves ample sonorities and tone colors.'

His compositions:

Of his interesting works we remember:

"Fantasia Gaucha"; symphonic poem divided in the times: *"Amanacer", Paisaje", "Andar de los caballos" "Partida para la guerra, "La Batalla"* and *"Muerte del Jefe".*

"Oriente": comprised of *"Preludio", Danza"* and *"Leyenda"* of a typical African flavor.

"Aires Andaluces"; is a homage to Antonio Jiménez Manjón.

"Aires Gitanos"; Aires Espanoles" "Preludio y Fuga en DO menor; "Nocturnal"; "Invocacion a la Madre"; "Cronica de la Reja"; "Triste"; "Estilo"; Zamba"; "Cancion de Cuna"; "Jota"; "Arabia"; "3 Canciones" for Voice and Piano; transcriptions of Bach, Handel, Scarlatti, Galilei, Schumann, Schubert, Albeniz and Granados.

"Preludio Triste"; descending melody, very sad in 6/8 time in the key of Bb Major, developing its theme in a simple and eloquent profound sense and with technical access to all players."

The following information is translated from: Julio Martínez Oyanguren: *Una gran guitarra de Uruguay y America (Aportes para su biografia)* 1901-2001 by Oscar Padron Favre, pages 97-98.

"Segovia had his temper and rivalry with Julio Martínez Oyanguren, both respected each other but played pranks on each other. When Martínez was to give a concert in the U.S. Segovia would hand out his own propaganda of his next recital in the seats and Martínez would leave his own propaganda in the concerts of Segovia.

So it was until in 1938 during a concert by Martínez in Columbia University, to which the invited persons were such as Toscanini, Pablo Casals, Lili Pons, Segovia and other famous ones, in the second piece Segovia stood up and left. Martínez left his guitar, and went after him, when he caught up with him, they had a heated discussion, first in English and as it appears that this language didn't allow them to say what they wished they continued tersely in Spanish. They both ended up in the Waldorf Astoria where they spent the night playing the guitar, one would play apiece, then the other the whole evening and so reconciled. The Waldorf had an unexpected concert and the next day the headline of the dailies were: 'Guitaristic Duel of the Century' and related the anecdote."

This was quoted from *"La Guitarra"* in *Boletin de la Biblioteca Artiguista* No. 105 Montevideo, 1999 by Victor y Gonzalez, Fausto Serafino. The story is according to the artist's son Ing. Julio Martínez Arhancet.

Julio Martínez Oyanguren passed away in the Hospital Militar in Montevideo on Saturday, September 14, 1973.

My colleague, Rico Stover, says Julio Martínez Oyanguren was struck by a bus and killed.

Falleció Ayer Julio Martínez Oyanguren

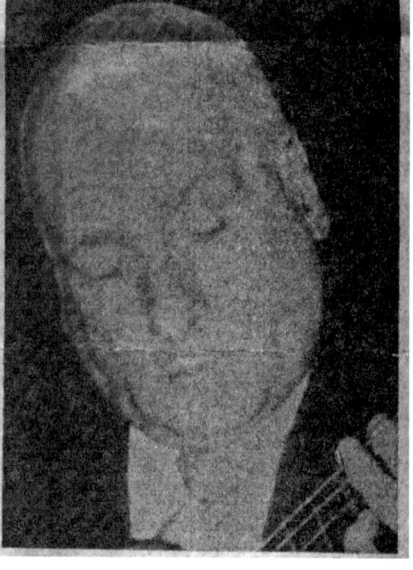

La muerte de Julio Martínez Oyanguren, acaecida ayer en nuestra capital, priva al Uruguay de uno de sus más esclarecidos artistas, cuya trayectoria internacional representó, además de una constante honra para la Patria, el triunfo de las más nobles virtudes humanas.

El extinto, retirado, desde hace muchos años, con el grado de Capitán de Navío, otorgado por nuestra Escuela Naval, había nacido el 3 de julio de 1901 en la ciudad de Durazno. Fue en su pueblo natal donde, quien sería uno de los más grandes guitarristas del mundo, comenzó a dar conciertos, a beneficio de la Escuela Pública de Durazno. Más tarde, también lo hizo en la casa que habitara el General Pablo Galarza. Pese a su irresistible vocación musical (que nunca abandonó), ingresó a la Universidad y a la Escuela Naval, entonces bajo el comando del Capitán de Fragata Ramiro Joan.

Graduado como marino en 1924, vinieron los viajes. Y la guitarra fue, en ellos, su inseparable compañera. Su arte ganó el corazón de sus compañeros. Más tarde, había de extender su radio, a los más grandes públicos.

Su escolaridad le valió, además de las altas calificaciones, becas de perfeccionamiento en los institutos navales europeos. Hacia el año 1931 obtuvo la autorización para realizar conciertos públicos.

Como Agregado Naval a nuestra Embajada, llegó a los Estados Unidos. Le esperaba allí, el primer triunfo internacional. La crítica señaló, con rara unanimidad, las virtudes del guitarrista uruguayo.

Entre los años 1934 y 1941 fue considerado, en aquella nación del Norte, como "el más grande guitarrista del mundo", y como el "más terrible rival de Andrés Segovia".

De su trayectoria como concertista, nuestro pueblo puede dar fe.

Como intérprete, perteneció, netamente, a la clase de los "comunicativos por excelencia". Cada uno de sus recitales estaba signado por el clamor del auditorio; expresado en ovaciones interminables, que obligaban a conceder, como "bis", tantas obras como las que figuraban en cada programa. Desde las galerías, llovían "bravos", voces de aliento y pedidos, que Martínez Oyanguren trataba de complacer en lo posible.

Porque rasgo dominante de su personalidad fue, sin duda, la suma generosidad de artista y de hombre. Estimuló a los compositores, a los incipientes guitarristas y a los simples "sentidores". Como compositor, deja una importante literatura guitarrística y vocal.

Alejado, por razones de salud, de toda actividad pública, Martínez Oyanguren conoció un triste ocaso para la que fuera luminosa y activa vida. Rodeado del cariño y de la admiración de su pueblo, se le tributó, en 1972, un homenaje nacional en el Teatro Solís. El aquejado maestro no quiso asistir personalmente... Era como la rúbrica para su invalidez, diríase un triste refuerzo a su nostalgia.

Siempre inevitable, su arte fue objeto de duras críticas. La "razón de ser" de cada artista, no siempre puede amoldarse a los conceptos de los demás. Lo importante es que obedezca a un real impulso del espíritu, y, —en lo posible— que ese impulso pueda convertirse en mensaje para el mundo. En ese sentido, Martínez Oyanguren fue, desde su primera hora, un legítimo triunfador. Así lo da a entender esta frase de Lauro Ayestarán: "Cuando toca su primera obra, el público es ya cautivo de su arte. Podrá luego tocar bien, o menos bien. Eso es otra cosa. Lo importante es que se comunica de inmediato, con poderosa elocuencia, con el auditorio".

Quien tanto deseó y logró esa comunicación, fue condenado por la naturaleza, a vivir años de amargo retiro; de un verdadero ostracismo en su propia patria. La muerte de Martínez Oyanguren, que a todos nos afecta desde todos los ángulos del sentir —se ha ido el virtuoso, el compositor, el amigo, el estímulo— representa, para él, la liberación total.

Con esta idea intentamos consolarnos, pues, de su irreparable pérdida.

R. E. L.

Julio Martínez Oyanguren, el magistral concertista uruguayo fallecido ayer, era uno de nuestros más grandes ejecutantes de guitarra, excepcional intérprete de los clásicos nacionales y de los maestros españoles, que frecuentó con dedicación

The Montevideo daily *"El Dia"* published this eulogy the next day on Sunday September 15, 1973.

The translation is:

"Julio Martínez Oyanguren Died Yesterday"

(Photo caption) "Julio Martínez Oyanguren, the masterful Uruguayan concert guitarist died yesterday, he was one of our greatest players of the guitar, an exceptional interpreter of the national classics and of the Spanish maestros, who he frequently played with dedication."

"The death of Julio Martínez Oyanguren, occurred yesterday in our capital, depriving Uruguay of one of its most illuminated artists, whose international career represented, besides being a constant honor of the homeland, the triumph of the noblest human virtues.

The defunct, retired, since many years ago, with the grade of Navy Captain, awarded by our Naval School, was born on July 3, 1901 in the city of Durazno. It was in his native town where, who would become one of the most important guitarists of the world, began to give concerts, a benefit for the Public School in Durazno.

Later, he also played in the home of General Pablo Galarza. Weighed down by his irresistible musical vocation (which he never abandoned), he entered the University and the Naval School, then under the command of the Captain of the frigate Ramiro Joan.

He graduated as a seaman in 1924, then came the voyages, and the guitar was, in those, his inseparable companion. His art won the hearts of his companions. Later, they extended to his radio programs to the largest public.

His scholastic ability was valued, besides the highest qualifications, the scholarships of perfection to European Naval institutes. Toward 1931 he received the authorization to make public concert performances.

As a Naval Aggregate of our Embassy, he arrived in the United States. There awaiting him was his first international triumph. The critics pointed out with rare unanimity, the virtues of the Uruguayan guitarist.

Between the years 1934 and 1941 he was considered in that nation of the north, "the greatest guitarist of the world", and as "the greatest rival of Andrés Segovia."

Of his career as a concert guitarist, our public can give faith.

As an interpreter, he belongs, clearly, to a class of those who "communicate by excellence". Every one of his recitals was signaled by the clamor of the audience; expressed in interminable ovations, which obliged him to concede, as encores, many works such as those that were a part of every program. From the balconies, they shouted *"bravo",* voices of breath and request, which Martínez Oyanguren tried to possibly placate.

Because of the dominant characteristics of his personality he was, without a doubt, the total of the generosity of artist and man. He stimulated the composers, the incipient guitarists and to the simple "listeners", as a composer, he left an important guitaristic and vocal literature.

He backed away, because of health reasons, from all the public activity, Martínez Oyanguren knew a sad occasion for which was outside his luminous and active life. Surrounded by the affection and the admiration of the public, that gave tribute, in 1972, a national homage in the Teatro Solis. The distant maestro didn't want to go personally... It was like a symbol of his illness, to be said as a sad reminder of his nostalgia.

Always inevitable, his art was the object of harsh critics. The 'reason to be' of every artist, one can't always be moulded to the concepts of the rest. What was important was to obey a real impulse of his own spirit, and in the possible, which that impulse can be converted in a message for the world. In that sense, Martínez Oyanguren, was, from his first hour a legitimate winner. So Lauro Ayestaran says this phrase of him: 'When he played his first work, the public was already a captive of his art. He could then play well, or less than well. That is another thing. What is important is he communicated the immediate, with powerful eloquence, with the audience.'

Who desired as much and succeeds that communication, was condemned by the nature, to live years of bitter reclusion, of a true ostracism in his own country. The death of Martínez Oyanguren, which to all affects us from all angles of the senses — has been the virtuoso, the composer, the friend, the stimulus — represents, for him, a total liberation.

With that idea we intend to console ourselves, because, of his irreparable loss."

R.E.L.

Archive: Maria Angelica Funes

Julio Martinez Oyanguren

オヤングレンは1905年7月3日ウルグアイの小さな町 Duranzo に生れた。幼少の頃から音楽が好きで、6才の時 Alfred Hargain に師事してギターを学び、11才でモンテビデオにデビューした。それが大成功で、政府は奨学資金を出してヨーロッパ留学をすゝめたが、彼は之を辞退し、自国にとゞまり Hargain 一人を師として更にギターに精進した。

長じてモンテビデオの海軍士官学校に学び、任官してイタリア海軍の麾下に二年間軍務に服し、1929年帰国し、二年後にリサイタルを開いて喝采を博し、1934年には政府のスポンサーでブラジルを演奏旅行し、1935年には時の大統領 Gabriel Terra に選ばれ、ウルグアイの文化使節としてアメリカに渡つた。レビゾンスタジアムに於てニューヨークフイルハーモニーと共演したことは彼にとつてもギター史にとつても記録的な出来事だつた。当時の演奏がデツカ盤に録音された。それが後に Lp にも収録された。

オヤングレンのレパートリーはバツハ、ハイドン、モーツアルト、ソルなどの古典音楽から、中南米諸国の民謡舞踊の類に及び、まことに広く、且つ深いのである。作曲家としてもすぐれてい、「アラビア」外幾多の佳作をものしている。

This is from the September-October 1956 issue of the *"Armonia"* magazine Vol. III No. 5. The magazine was printed in Sen Dai, Miyagiken, a city heavily damaged by the tsunami after the 8.9 magnitude earthquake on March 11, 2011. Japanese translation by Randy Osborne.

"Julio Martínez Oyanguren

Oyanguren was born on July 3, 1905 (sic 1901) in the small town of Durazno, Uruguay. Since his infancy he liked music, at 6 years old he studied guitar under Alfredo Hargain, at 11 years of age he made his debut in Montevideo. That was a big success, the government administration gave him scholarship funding and he was advised to go to Europe to study abroad but, this he declined, he stayed in his own country and studied only under Hargain and improved on the guitar with devotion. (Domingo Prat has different details on this period of his career. R.O.)

When he grew up he entered to study at the Montevideo Naval Academy, he was appointed to be the under the command in Italy in uniform for a length of two years as a naval affairs officer, in the year 1929 he returned to his country, two years later his recitals received great applause, in 1934 the administration sponsored the Brazilian concert tour, in the year 1935 President Gabriel Terra chose him, as an envoy of Uruguayan culture and he was sent to America. At Lewisohn Stadium he costarred with the New York Philharmonic and set a record with his guitar in the history books with this affair. At the time of that performance he was recording for Decca records. That even was an LP record for him.

As for Oyanguren's repertoire it is Bach, Haydn, Mozart, Sor and so forth ranging from old songs to South American folksong dances from several countries, which is quite extensive, truly large and furthermore profound. He is even an excellent composer doing many good works such as *"Arabia"."*

Here we see the publication of the original composition by Julio Martínez Oyanguren *"Arabia"* by Celestino Fernández in Buenos Aires, as well as the New York City productions by Vicente Tatay of Julio Martínez Oyanguren's compositions and transcriptions.

There are videos of him on You Tube.

COMPOSICIONES Y TRANSCRIPCIONES para *Guitarra* por *Julio Martínez Oyanguren*

TRÄUMEREI (Reverie)—Robert Schumann	$ .50
ELEGIE—Jules Massenet	.50
MARCHA INFANTIL (Children's March)—P. I. Tschaikowsky	.50
SWEET LELANI (Canción Hawaiiana)	.50
AY - AY - AY—O. Pérez Freire	.50
CANCIÓN GAUCHA—J. Martínez Oyanguren	.75
VALSE MINIATURA—P. I. Tschaikowsky	.75
LA CUMPARSITA (Tango)—Matos Rodríguez	.75
LA PALOMA (Spanish Serenade)—Yradier	.75
CANCIONES POPULARES UKRANIANAS	.75
MARCHA MILITAR (Military March)—J. Martínez Oyanguren	.75
CANCIÓN DEL ALBA (Serenade)—J. Martínez Oyanguren	.75
ZAPATEADO (Spanish Dance)—J. Martínez Oyanguren	.75
AIRES GITANOS (Gypsy Airs)—J. Martínez Oyanguren	.85
DANZA ARABE (Arabian Dance)—P. I. Tschaikowsky	.85
OJOS NEGROS (Dark Eyes)—Melodía Rusa	.85
DOS GUITARRAS(Two Guitars) Russian Gypsy Song	.85
SERENATA (Serenade)—Franz Schubert	.85
GRAN JOTA (Spanish Dance)—J. Martínez Oyanguren	.85
ANDALUCIA (Spanish Airs)—J. Martínez Oyanguren	.85

Published by
VICENTE TATAY & COMPANY
1318 Fifth Avenue • New York City

This is a list of 20 compositions and transcriptions published by Vicente Tatay in New York of Julio Martínez Oyanguren's works.

These are two of the early Guitar Solo recordings 1931 for Victor records by Julio Martínez Oyanguren, including Juan Alais' *"Un momento"* and the *"Jota"*. This listing is from the *"Catalogo de Discos Victor 1932"* published in Buenos Aires, with a complete list up to January 1, 1932. It shows that the recordings of *"Un momento"* and the *"Jota"* are indeed his debut pieces.

MARTINEZ OYANGUREN, JULIO J., Concertista de Guitarra.	
Jota (Martínez Oyanguren)	37072
Un Momento—Vals (J. Alais-arr. Martínez Oyanguren)	37072

Martínez Oyanguren

Sept. 1931   Un momento
Sept. 1931   Capricho arabe
Sept. 1931   Jota
Sept. 1931   El gato polkeado

This is the recording sequence, thought to be in Buenos Aires but unconfirmed, source: The Encyclopedic Discography of Victor Recordings (EDVR) web site.

Julio Martínez Oyanguren with a Doble Boca Model Guitar. This is from the *"Boletin Latino American de Musica"* of the Instituto de Estudios Superiores del Uruguay, Seccion de Investigaciones Musicales by Professor Francisco Curt Lange and Lauro Ayestaran. *Año* II, Vol. 2 April 1936.

OYANGUREN

By A. P. SHARPE.

JULIO MARTINEZ OYAN-GUREN, whose playing of the Spanish guitar has caused the music critics in the U.S.A. to rank him with Segovia, was born in Durazno, Uruguay, and gave his first concert at the age of eleven. His first public appearance in the U.S.A. was when he gave a concert in the New York Town Hall, in October, 1935. At present he is guest soloist on various national radio programmes and is planning an extensive tour of the United States.

The New York Press says: "Oyanguren plays in the tradition of elegance, suavity and good taste. He can manage brilliant passage work without allowing it to assume undue importance in the musical scheme and

Before visiting the U.S.A., Oyanguren gave concerts in Uruguay, Argentina and Brazil, where audiences and musical critics were equally enthusiastic over his playing. *La Nacion* (Buenos Aires) said: "The concert guitarist, Julio Martinez Oyanguren, revealed outstanding qualities showing his great artistry. The programme was of excellent quality consisting of compositions by Albeniz, Bach, Mozart, Sierra, Sors, Tarrega and Turina, which gave this instrumentalist an opportunity to show his great technique and musicianship to his enthusiastic audience."

We, in England, look forward to hearing Senor Julio Martinez Oyanguren.

JULIO MARTINEZ OYANGUREN

is intent above all in making music on the guitar, not causing music to serve as a medium for the display of his instrument" (*New York Times*). "It happens once in a while that some unusually gifted performer raises the guitar out of its romantic estate as a medium for serenades. This happened last night when Julio Martinez Oyanguren followed in the footsteps of that Spanish wonder, Segovia, and proved his right to stand right up as an equal of the Spanish master" (*New York Journal*). "Martinez Oyanguren plays the guitar with fine skill. There is an elegance and gracefulness in the way he uses his instrument that suggests a charm little known amongst us. Not only is his playing beautiful and delivery fine, but his programme is chosen with taste and care." (*Bridgeport Herald*).

This article is from the B. M. G. magazine No. 375 of July 1936 XXXIII.

JULIO MARTINEZ
OYANGUREN

World Renowned Guitarist

DIRECTION:

RADIO KONCERT BUREAU

HARRY A. CAHILL, Manager

2415 R. K. O. BUILDING

RADIO CITY   •   NEW YORK

2-page promotional flyer circa 1937. Archive: Anna Palmer Coit North (1908-2014)

JULIO MARTINEZ OYANGUREN

whose playing of the Spanish Guitar has brought him the high praise of the music critics of the world, was born in Durazno, Uruguay, and gave his first important recital in Montevideo, at the age of eleven.

With admirably schooled technique, Oyanguren interprets his works with a highly sound musicality which adds a distinguished tone of elegance and flexibility of color in his rendering of Bach, Mozart, Scarlatti, Haydn, and also shows his great ability to advantage in the performance of Spanish music.

INTERNATIONALLY FAMOUS AND RECOGNIZED THROUGHOUT THE WORLD AS A GENUINE ARTIST OF UNUSUAL SIGNIFICANCE

Concert

"It happens once in a while that some unusually gifted performer raises the guitar out of its romantic estate as a medium for serenades. This happened last night when Julio Martinez Oyanguren followed in the footsteps of that Spanish wonder, Segovia, and proved his right to stand right up as an equal of the Spanish master. Vociferous applause and a demand for more marked the evening."
—N. Y. JOURNAL, NEW YORK

"Plays in the tradition of elegance, suavity and good taste. He can manage brilliant passage work without allowing it to assume undue importance in the musical scheme, and is intent above all in making music on the guitar, not causing music to serve as a medium for the display of his instrument."
—N. Y. TIMES, NEW YORK

"Señor Oyanguren gave constant evidence of an amazing virtuosity. Besides the effects of a percussive nature he possesses a singing legato tone of soft-spoken enchantment. Nimble fingers and pliant wrist gave him impish speed."
—N. Y. EVENING POST, NEW YORK

"Mr. Oyanguren, who hails from South America, makes of the guitar a polite rather than virile instrument. His style is one of elegance and finesse, achieved by a fine grained delicacy of expression a meticulous technique, a suavity that the audience found soothing." —DAILY MIRROR, NEW YORK

"He did magical things with his guitar." —WASHINGTON HERALD, WASHINGTON, D.C.

"He is an outstanding instrumentalist, and complete master of the guitar."
—LA PRENSA, BUENOS AIRES

"The master of six strings gave a brilliant performance." —EL MUNDO, BUENOS AIRES

"This great artist symbolizes the true performer by his fine technique and musical virtuosity."
—DIARIO de NOTICIAS, RIO DE JANEIRO

"It appears to be a habit to draw comparisons between any good player of the Spanish guitar and Segovia, which, to my mind, is a foolish thing to do, as is the case with Señor Oyanguren, the spheres of the two artists are entirely different. If one must compare Oyanguren and Segovia, I would be inclined to say they are equally good."
—"B. M. G." MUSICAL MAGAZINE, LONDON

Radio

HEADLINES

"REMARKABLE GUITAR GIVES DISTINCTION TO RADIO BILL"

"There are in the world today very few virtuosos who can play a guitar exactly as though it were a musical instrument, and a distinguished member of that select group is Oyanguren, who, so far as we are concerned, is Uruguay's one legitimate claim to fame."
—AARON STEIN, N. Y. POST, NEW YORK

"OYANGUREN IS A SENSATION." —N. Y. DAILY NEWS, NEW YORK

"OYANGUREN—ACE GUITARIST." —N. Y. JOURNAL, NEW YORK

"Rated among the concert world's outstanding guitarists, Martinez Oyanguren, unveiled his talents to American listeners for the first time as part of the Rudy Vallee—Fleischman bill. He did two numbers and in each his nimble digits blended a telling sense of rhythm with a rich array of tonal variations."
—VARIETY, NEW YORK

COLUMBIA RECORDS

FERDINAND SOR

GRAND SONATE

Op. 22

JULIO MARTINEZ OYANGUREN

(Guitarist)

Set No. X-84

JULIO MARTINEZ OYANGUREN OVER THE AIR

Many were disappointed last month when the broadcasting by the well known guitarist, Julio Martinez Oyanguren was changed from 12:15 Sundays to 9 A. M. of the same day. This artist's program of choice guitar music should not be missed. On that particular Sunday when the hour of broadcasting was changed, he gave a magnificent playing of the last movement of his suite for guitar that was well worthy the inconvenience of leaving a comfortable bed at an unaccustomed hour.

Guitarists, tune in at 12:15 Sundays over the N. B. C. from coast to coast net work.

Oyanguren In Recital

A guitar recital of unusual interest was given last month by Julio Martinez Oyanguren at the Pastorius School of Music, under the direction of George C. Krick.

The program included a Sonata by D. Cimarosa, numbers by Sor. Toroba and Tarrega. Transcriptions from the works of Bach and Granados. It concluded with a "Flamingo Suite" by Oyanguren, Zapateado, Danza Andalucia.

The discs shown on the previous page Ferdinand (sic) Fernando Sor: *Grand Sonata* in C Major, Op. 22. by Julio Martínez Oyanguren, guitar were recorded on July 29 and 30, 1937. Columbia Masterworks set X-84, two discs.

This radio performance announcement and recital review are from the "Fretted Instrument News" magazine issue May-June 1940 Vol. 8 No. 3.

The Cuban guitarists, Rolando and Alberto Valdes-Blain, were page turners for some of the radio programs Julio Martínez Oyanguren did in the late 1930's and early 1940's in New York.

(source: Armando García, Florida)

The *"Flamenco Suite"* played by Julio Martínez Oyanguren in the recital was recorded for RCA on a 12" disc, but it was actually several Guillermo Gomez pieces that had been in print for decades in Mexico and weren't credited to the Spanish born guitarist.

ESTUDIO AUDITORIO

Calle Andes   Teléfono: de Boletería 8 7 2 28
esq. Mercedes   Montevideo

S. O. D. R. E.

JUEVES 4 DE JUNIO DE 1942

A LA HORA 18 Y 15

RECITAL DEL
CONCERTISTA
DE GUITARRA

JULIO MARTINEZ OYANGUREN

PRIMERA PARTE

GIULIANI (1780 - 1840) Sonata Op. 15, original
para guitarra.

     Allegro
     Adagio
     Allegro vivace.

SEGUNDA PARTE

BACH, J. S. Preludio y fuga para laúd.
     Gavota
     Museta
     Polonesa
     Marcha

TERCERA PARTE

VILLA LOBOS	Preludio N° 3.
VILLA LOBOS	Preludio N° 4.
KREISLER	Capricho vienés.
GRANADOS	Danza española N° 10.
ALBENIZ	Leyenda.

NOTA : Las obras que no fueron originalmente escritas para
guitarra son transcripciones de Julio Martínez Oyanguren.

When Julio Martínez Oyanguren returned from the United States in 1942 he played this concert on Thursday June 4, 1942 at the S.O.D.R.E. in Montevideo.

He played works by Giuliani, Bach, Villa-Lobos, Kreisler, Granados and Albeniz.

The note at the bottom of the program says: "The works that were not originally written for the guitar are transcriptions by Julio Martínez Oyanguren."

My colleague, Alfredo Escande, has brought to my attention, the fact that this concert is the earliest known public performance of the *Preludios Nos. 3 and 4* by Villa-Lobos. In Brazil, first public performance of the *Preludios* was by Abel Carlevaro, in Rio de Janeiro — in the presence of Villa-Lobos in December of 1943.

Translating from Ricardo Muñoz's unpublished book *"Historia Universal de la Guitarra"* Volume VI *"America"*.

"Other Guitarists of Uruguay

Ramon Gomez Cruz

He is a student of *Don* Luis Pasquet, founder of the "Academia" that perpetuated his name in the city of Salto, from the years 1935 to 1940, when it closed. In 1949 Gomez Cruz reopened it in homage of his beloved maestro, creating at the same time the "Centro Guitarristico Luis Pasquet", which was founded and exists in that city.

He is a notable resident maestro in the city of Salto, where he directs the "Academia de Guitarra Agustín Barrios", incorporated into the Conservatorio Chopin of the city of Concordia, the professorship at the "Ateneo" of Salto, where he transmits his lessons of the modern school of technical mechanism, to a selected group of students who admire and respect him.

In his numerous artistic tours, he has visited and given concerts in Salto, Montevideo, Paysandu, etc., and in the Argentine cities of Parana, Rosario, Concordia, and others, publishing in 1955 his interesting book "Temas Salteños", well received by the critics.

His distinguished performances have honorably involved the national and foreign, institutions with the following distinctions:

Asesor Musical y Catedratico del "Colegio Liceo Sagrada Familia" in Salto

"Miembro de Honor" del "Archivo General de Musica y Academia Americana de la Historia y la Ciencia de Buenos Aires"

"Miembro Honorario" del Imperial Philo — Bysantine of Constantinople y del Imperio-Romano — Bysantino

"Miembro Honorario" de la Casa Humberto Campos de Matto Grosso en Brasil — Intercambio Cultural Americano

"Miembro de Honor" del "Instituto Tecnico Industrial" de Rio de Janeiro, Brazil

"Miembro Correspondiente de la Asociacion Gente de Arte del Sur

Representante de la Revista Argentina de Artes y Letras — Euterpe

Representante de las guitarras "Santurion"

Socio Correspondiente de A. U. D. E. de Montevideo

He obtained the 2nd prize in the literary competition of the S. O. D. R. E. in Montevideo for his work *"La Guitarra y su Empleo en la Musica Popular Nacional"* in 1955. The Hispanic poet, *Don* Bernardo Martin del Rey, paid homage with his *"Guitarra Gaucha"*, in *"La Vosta del Sol"*, in Almeria, Spain in 1954.

As well, he is known for some interesting musical productions, of which we recall his *"Danza Exotica"* published in Buenos Aires in the year 1949, debuted on Radio Almeria, Spain in the year 1954, by the *rondalla* of *Don* Elias García."

Ramon Gomez Cruz c. 1959, on the right is a piece *"Danza Exotica"* published by Julio Korn. The version by Antigua Casa Nuñez is from 1949.

(Source: Vincenzo Pocci)

Translation: "To the erudite investigator of the guitar, Mr. Ricardo Muñoz, I dedicate this sample, Ramon Gomez Cruz, Uruguayo 828, Salto April 1949 — Uruguay."

Ramon Gomez Cruz's book "Temas Salteños"

Para el gran escrib... [handwritten] Salto, Julio de 1957.
Sr. *José Monegal* [handwritten]
Calle ... *Cordialmente RGC* [handwritten]

**Academia de Guitarra "AGUSTIN BARRIOS" al cumplir su octavo
año de vida artística (2a. Epoca 1949-1957) tiene el agrado de
saludar a Ud. muy cordialmente.**

Prof. Ramón Gómez Cruz
DIRECTOR

Con un especial saludo a los amigos universales en "ZENITH"

Autorizado por la Dirección Gral. de Correos del Uruguay.

Prof. RAMON GOMEZ CRUZ
Audición en C. X. 8 Radio Sarandí de Montevideo. Julio de 1957.
Correspondencia a Rincón No. 72 o Avenida Solari 1250, Teléfono
Salto, Rpca. O. Uruguay.

This is the graduation card used by Ramon Gomez Cruz, with his students: Salto, July of 1957. "For
the great Uruguayan writer Mr. José Monegal, cordially RGC, Academia de Guitarra "Agustín Barrios"
completing his year of performance of artistic life (2nd Epoch 1949-1957) he has the pleasure to give my
regards to you very cordially. Professor Ramon Gomez Cruz, Director."

Prof. RAMON GOMEZ CRUZ

—Director de Academia de Guitarra AGUSTIN BARRIOS incorporada al Conservatorio Chopin de Concordia (E. R.) Catedra en el Ateneo de Salto.
— 1ra. Epoca: — 1935 — 1940
— 2da. Epoca: — 1949 — 1957
Fundada por Luis Pasquet en 1935 y clausurada en 1940. Reabierta por su ex - discípulo Prof. Ramón Gómez Cruz en Julio 1949.

————————

—Asesor Musical y catedrático (Sección Folklore) del Colegio - Liceo Sagrada Familia de Salto, R. O. U.

—Miembro de Honor del Archivo General de Música y Academia Americana de la Historia y la Ciencia con sede en Buenos Aires - Republica Argentina.

Miembro - fundador del Centro Guitarristico LUIS PASQUET de Salto, R. O.

Miembro honorario de la Casa Humberto Campos Matto Groso - Brasil. Intercambio Cultural Americano.

—Miembro Honorario de Imperial Philo - Byzantine Universite Imperial Universiti of Constantinopla S. E. el Príncipe de Grecia y del Imperio Romano Bizantino Duque de Tesalia Theodore Lascaris Comneno Micolaw Madrid España.

Miembro de honor del Instituto Técnico Industrial de Río de Janeiro - Brasil.

Miembro correspondiente de la Liga Mundial por los Derechos del Negro Sección Americana

Segundo y Unico Premio del Concurso Literario - Musical del S. O. D. R. E. , Montevideo sobre el tema: La Guitarra y su Empleo en la Música Popular Nacional. Año 1955.

Miembro correspondiente de la Asociación Argentina GENTE DE ARTE DEL SUR.

Representante para la República Oriental del Uruguay de la revista argentina de artes y letras EUTERPE.

Representante para todo el litoral uruguayo de las afamadas guitarras SANTURION.

CONCERTISTA DE GUITARRA: Capitales visitadas: PARANA (1956); ROSARIO DE SANTA FE (1956); MONTEVIDEO (1953), por intermedio, respectivamente de: Asociación Guitarristica Entrerriana; Asociación Guitarristica de Rosario y Centro Guitarristico del Uruguay. Otros Conciertos: en Concordia Paysandú y Salto.

ACTUACION RADIAL: C. X. 8 Radio Sarandi de Montevideo; L. T. 14 General Urquiza de Paraná; L. T. 15 de Concordia y C. W. 31 de Salto, y en las Ciudades de Concordia y Bella Unión etc. al frente de su conjunto juvenil de 12 guitarristas salteños, formado por sus alumnos aventajados

LIBRO PUBLICADO: - TEMAS SALTEÑOS (edición particular del autor) Año 1955, saludado por la crítica americana con juicios elogiosos.

HOMENAJE AL GUITARRISTA RAMON GOMEZ CRUZ: - Poema GUITARRA GAUCHA por Bernardo Martin del Rey - Poeta de la Costa del Sol, Almería España. (1954).

Obra Musical: - Danza Exotica publicada en Buenos Aires 1949 y estrenada en Radio Almeria España (1954) por la Rondalla de D. Elias García.

Socio correspondiente de A. U. D. E. (Montevideo - Uruguay).

Sobre la plausible labor de Academia Agustin Barrios de Salto (en su 2da. Epoca), se han expedido en forma justiciera y encomiástica el musicólogo Lauro Ayestarán; concertista uruguayo Julio Martinez Oyanguren; eximia guitarrista argentina: Maria Luisa Anido; profesores Apolo Ronchi y Álberto Carbone de Paysandú y Prof. Agustin Satalia de Concordia.

Imp. Sarandi 1515

On this page is a long list of achievements, actually seen in the biography by Ricardo Muñoz, as they were likely taken from the graduation card.

Temas Salteños Ramon Gomez Cruz 1955 Salto Uruguay Dedicado

TEMAS SALTEÑOS, POR RAMON GOMEZ CRUZ

TALLERES GRAFICOS DE IMPRENTA SARANDI – SALTO – 1955

104 PAGINAS – BUEN ESTADO, TAPA CON ALGUNAS ROTURITAS POR CARTON QUEBRADIZO

CON DEDICATORIA DE PUÑO Y LETRA DEL AUTOR

INDICE

Miguel Herrera Klinger

He is the son of Colonel *Don* Miguel Herrera Klinger, born in Salto on the 9th of November 1885; he studied the guitar with maestro *Don* Eduardo Lenzi, and he was his favorite student. He became a fine virtuoso, expressively intelligent, by his emotional endowments and his technical purity he enjoyed great prestige in his country.

Pedro Vittone

He is an Uruguayan guitarist who lived in Montevideo, and taught his instrument with the general approval of the populace.

Juan Valles

He is a professor, a resident of Montevideo, where he performed well.

Manuel Sopena

He studied guitar with the famous *Don* Conrado P. Koch, in Montevideo.

Muro Rivas

An excellent guitarist and classmate of Savio, Rodríguez, etc. who studied with Koch.

Telemaco Morales

He is a good performer, who published some of his works in Montevideo.

Eduardo Pelaez

He lived in Montevideo, held the professorship in the Conservatorio Nacional, in his programs of performances he is distinguished for playing the works of Aguado, Sagreras, Albeniz, Tárrega, etc.

Eduardo Lenzi

He is the son of a patriotic family, who studied guitar with the maestros: Carlos García Tolsa, José M. Lopez and Pedro Bustamante, he was dedicated to teaching, his best student was Miguel Herrera Klinger, who dedicated a homage when he passed away.

Aquiles Ibargoyen

He is a distinguished doctor devoted to the guitar, who played magnificently and studied in his hometown of San José; his production consists of *"Aires Criollos"*, *"Triste No. 20"*, *"Cancion Criolla"*, etc. that were published in the magazine *"O Violao"* in Brazil.

Julián García Rondeau

He is a magnificent exemplary guitarist, a performer of a select and pure repertoire who played on the radio; as such was affirmed by the press of Montevideo in the year 1933.

Rosendo Barreiro

After finishing an artistic tour, he became distinguished in Montevideo, at times playing duets with Martínez Oyanguren, Savio, and others.

Rosendo Barreiro, Contemporary Uruguayan professor and concert guitarist, several years ago he achieved a certain popularity after an intense artistic campaign, where he distinguished himself, in his performances in Montevideo, to that of the level of Isaias Savio, Abel Rodríguez, and Julio Martínez Oyanguren. This is from the Domingo Prat *Diccionario de Guitarristas*.

We now present the archive of Rosendo Barriero 1919-1943:

Rosendo was a student of Miguel Llobet, Andrés Segovia, Emilio Pujol and a colleague of Agustín Barrios, who spoke well of his friend in two daily newspaper interviews.

Guitarist, Hilario Pérez was born on January 22, 1936, it is from his research that this archive comes from.

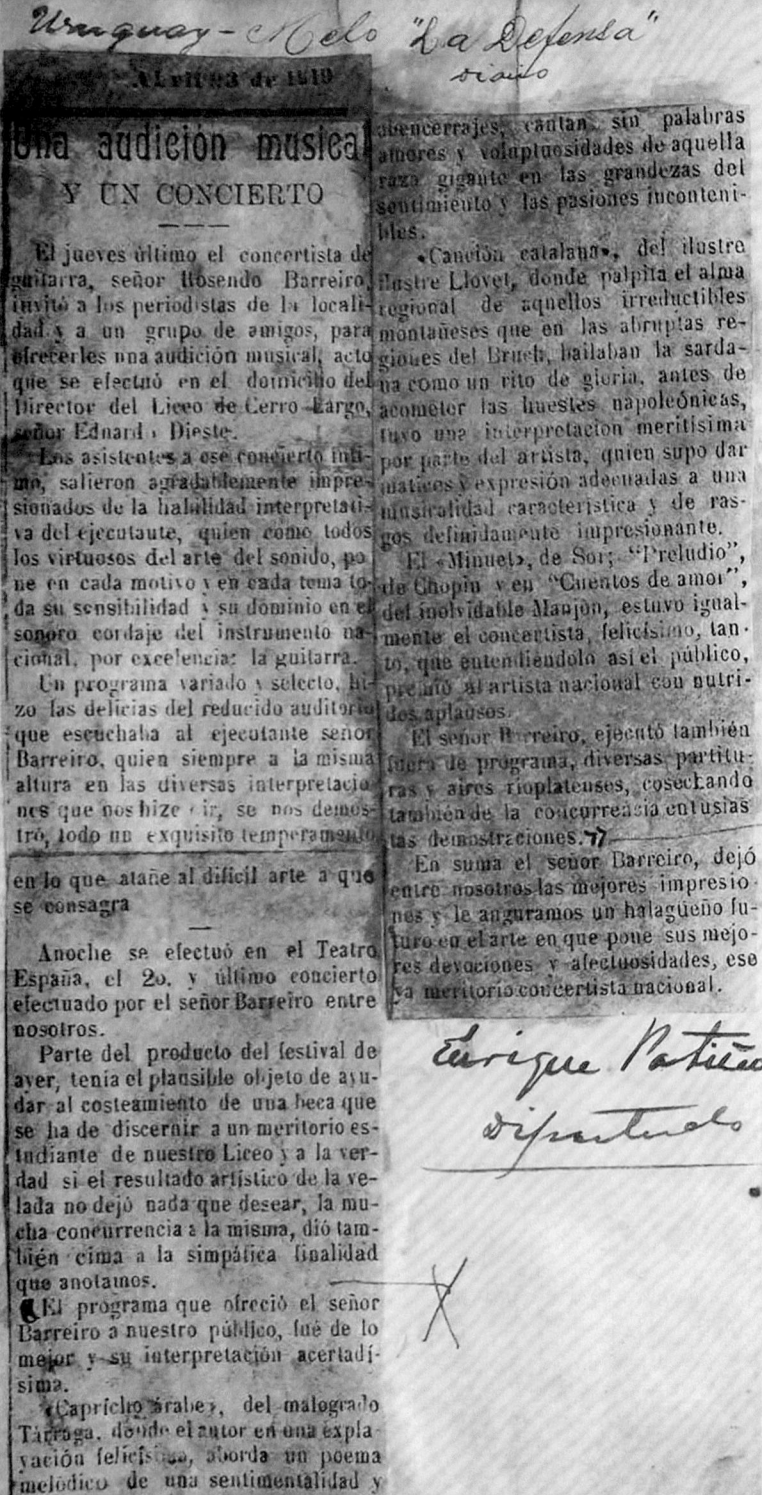

Melo, Uruguay *"La Defensa"* April 23, 1919

"A Musical Audtion and a Concert"

Last Thursday the concert guitarist Rosendo Barreiro invited the newspaper journalists of the city and some friends, to offer them a musical performance, an act that would take place in the home of the Director of the Liceo de Cerro Largo (High school) Eduardo Dieste.

The attendants to this intimate concert left happily impressed by the abilities of the performer, who as, all of the virtuosos of the art of the sound, put in every phrase and every theme all their sensibilities and their control of the chordal sound of the national instrument, by excellence, the guitar.

The varied and select program made the delicacies in the small auditorium that those who heard the performer Mr. Barreiro who always to the same level in the diverse interpretations that we heard demonstrated to us, all in exquisite temperament in which concern the difficult art to which he has consecrated.

Last night in the Teatro España, the 2nd and last concert given by Mr. Barreiro was performed for us.

A part of the product of yesterday's festival, had the plausible object to help the cost of the scholarship that has to discern a meritorious student of our Liceo and to the truth if the artistic result of the evening concert left nothing to desire, the large audience at the hall, It also gave a top to the pleasant finality that we noted.

The program Mr. Barreiro offered to our public, was of the best and his most well-chosen interpretation.

"Capricho arabe", by the late Tárrega, where the composer in a congratulating explanation, mentioned a melodic poem of a sentimentality and the truest finish, the concert artist gave a real relief to the composition, where the dreams and the hot-blooded populace of Granada, sing without amorous and voluptuous words of that gigantic race in the grandness of the sentiment of uncontainable passion.

"Cancion catalana" by the illustrious maestro Llobet, where the beating of the regional soul of the irreducible mountains that in the abrupt regions of the Bruch, dance the Sardana as a rite of glory, before the assault of the Napoleonic hues, had a meritorious interpretation by the artistic part, who knew to give shades and adequate expression to a characteristic musicality and of definite impressionistic aspects.

The *"Minuet"* by Sor; *"Preludio"* by Chopin, *"Cuentos de amor"* by the unforgettable Manjón, were equally the happiest by the concert guitarist, so much, that understanding him so the public awarded the national artist with abundant applause.

Mr. Barreiro also played encores, of diverse sheet music, airs of the Rio de la Plata, drawing the enthusiastic demonstrations as well from the gathering.

The addition of the encores by Mr. Barreiro, left among us the best impressions and he began for us a laudatory future in the art what he does put in his best devotion and affection, is already of merit of the national concert guitarist.

Enrique Patiño

There is a missing review in the archive: May 1919 Buenos Aires *"Critica"*

E. Pujol by photographer Joan Vilatobà. © Isabel Vilatoba Estate.
Dedicated and inscribed:

"To Rosendo Barreiro, my good friend, very beloved and of enthusiastic spirituality. Affectionately,
E. Pujol. Montevideo 1919"

Montevideo - Mayo
La Defensa - 2 - 1919

La actuación simpática de Rosendo Barreiro, en el teatro "España", de Melo—

Es muy reducido el número de uruguayos que conocen artísticamente al inquieto y nervioso compatriota, cultor de la guitarra "Rosendo Barreiro. Eso no nos toma de sorpresa. Sabemos perfectamente de nuestras "nanas" y del zarandeado cantar de las apatías nacionales, para asombrarnos por el hecho de que así no más, de golpe y porrazo, surja toda una personalidad artística de la talla de Barreiro sin que antes se haya hablado nada o casi nada de tal concertista.

Barreiro regresa de un gira doblemente fructífica por los departamentos, en donde cosechó aplausos a granel y la suficiente cantidad de fama para entrar a la metrópoli con la arrogancia de los casi consagrados .

Un diario de la ciudad de Melo comenta las dos audiciones que acaba de dar Barreiro en el teatro España de aquella importante localidad. Una crónica abundante de francos elogios saluda al joven artista, por sus correctas interpretaciones de Schumann, Chopin, Beethoven, Mendelsohn, Sohr, Tárreya, Llobet, Parga, Manjon y otros célebres maestros.

En la segunda de dichas audiciones Barreiro tuvo el bellísimo gesto de destinar cien pesos del producto de boletería, como contribución al costeamiento de una beca a un meritorio estudiante del liceo melense.

Barreiro continuará brevemente su gira y más adelante se presentará al público de la capital.

Alfredo Varzi

Montevideo May 2, 1919

"La Defensa"

"The charming performance of Rosendo Barreiro, in the teatro España, in Melo

It is a small number of Uruguayans who know artistically the brooding and nervous compatriot guitar player Rosendo Barreiro. This isn't a surprising theme. We perfectly know our "lullabies" and of the sway to sing the listless national ones, for surprising us by the fact that so no more, hit and punch, springs up the artistic personality of the frailty of Barreiro without that before nothing might have been said or almost nothing of such a concert guitarist.

Barreiro returns from a tour doubly fruitful in the provinces, where he gathered applause to bulk and the sufficient quantity of fame for entering the metropolis with the arrogance of almost a consecration.

A daily of the city of Melo commented that Barreiro had just given, two performances in the teatro España, in that important locality. A chronicle of frank praises saluted the young artist, for his correct interpretations of Schumann, Chopin, Beethoven, Mendelssohn, Sor, Tárrega, Llobet, Parga, Manjón and other celebrated maestros.

In the second of the said performances Barreiro had the most beautiful gestures by destiny 100 *pesos* of the product of the ticket sales, as a contribution to a scholarship for a deserving student of the High School of Melo.

Barreiro will continue his tour briefly and soon will be presented to the public in the capital.

Alfredo Varzi.

From the daily *"Piedra Alta"* May 28, 1919 Florida, Uruguay

"Rosendo Barreiro His Performance on the 31st

It has been communicated from Montevideo, that the eminent guitarist with whose name we write these lines, will arrive in this city to perform several guitar concerts.

In these interior cities where Barreiro has had the occasion to be put to the test of all the candor of remitting his artistic temperament, he has recognized the prize of his great triumphs.

I have now that which our colleague *"La Defensa"* of Montevideo tells us:
'It is a small number of Uruguayans who know artistically the brooding and nervous compatriot guitar player Rosendo Barreiro. This isn't a surprising theme. We perfectly know our "lullabies" and of the sway to sing the listless national ones, for surprising us by the fact that so no more, hit and punch, springs up the artistic personality of the frailty of Barreiro without that before nothing might have been said or almost nothing of such a concert guitarist.

Barreiro returns from a tour doubly fruitful in the provinces, where he gathered applause to bulk and the sufficient quantity of fame for entering the metropolis with the arrogance of almost a consecration.

A daily of the city of Melo commented that Barreiro had just given, two performances in the teatro España, in that important locality. A chronicle of frank praises saluted the young artist, for his correct interpretations of Schuman, Chopin, Beethoven, Mendelssohn, Sor, Tárrega, Llobet, Parga, Manjón and other celebrated maestros.

In the second of the said performances Barreiro had the most beautiful gestures by destiny 100 *pesos* of the product of the ticket sales, as a contribution to a scholarship for a deserving student of the High School of Melo.

Barreiro will continue his tour briefly and soon will be presented to the public in the capital. ' "

El Concierto Barreiro

UNA NOCHE DE ARTE

delssou. No haremos lo mismo con la *Canción Catalana* del gran Llobet, maravilla de emoción y de arte que, al menos en nosotros, sugiere más de lo que dice.

Barreiro, creemos haberlo dicho ya, no es un maestro. Pero es joven y estudioso, está enamorado de su arte y, sobre todo, tiene alma. Puede llegar muy lejos.

El público de Florida le es deudor a Rosendo Barreiro de una deliciosa noche de arte, de arte maravilloso y puro como lo es la música.

Para nadie es ya una novedad que la guitarra, lo que se ha dado en llamar el instrumento nacional, se ha elevado, por el genio de un Tárrega, de un Llobet, de un Pujol, de un Barrios, a la categoría de un verdadero instrumento de arte, de una «pequeña orquesta», de un instrumento casi tan expresivo, tan humano como el violoncelo.

Barreiro es un discípulo de los maestros nombrados. Pero un discípulo digno que no se cuida solamente de la fidelidad de la ejecución sino que se esfuerza por poner en ella,—y lo consigue—el granito de oro de la emoción personal, ¡el alma! sin lo cual el ejecutante se rebaja a la categoría del simple técnico.

La noche del sábado último, en la que Barreiro se presentó por primera vez a nuestro público, vivirá en el recuerdo de los floridenses.

Con un *Minuet* de Sor se inició el concierto. Al principio el artista vacila, su ejecución no es muy segura ni muy expresiva; lo domina acaso esa impresión inevitable de la presentación. Pero en los *Tres Preludios* y en el alado y sutil *Capricho Arabe* de Tárrega, está ya seguro de su arte, seguro del público que prorrumpe en cálidos aplausos.

Esa seguridad se acentuará en la segunda parte del concierto, más que por los aplausos recibidos, por la inspiración del ejecutante. Los *Preludios* y el *Nocturno núm. 2* de Chopin estuvieron impecablemente interpretados; imposible no sentirse poseído de la melancolía conmovedora, de la delicadeza suma del gran pianista polaco.

La tiranía del espacio nos obliga a pasar muchas cosas por alto entre ellas la deliciosa *Romanza* de Men-

Manuel Benavides

From *"El Heraldo"* June 2, 1919

"A Night of Art

The public of Florida is indebted to Rosendo Barreiro for the delicious night of art, of marvelous and pure art, as the music is.

The guitar is not a novelty for anyone, as it is already called the national instrument, he has elevated it, by the genius of a Tárrega, by a Llobet, by a Pujol, by a Barrios, to a category of an instrument as real art, as a small orchestra, as an instrument so expressive, so human, like a cello.

Barreiro is a disciple of the named maestros. But a dignified disciple that doesn't only care for an instrument of the fidelity of performance but also of the exertion he put in it, the grain of gold of the personal emotion, the soul, without which the performer is knocked down to a simple category as a technician.

Last Saturday evening, in which Barreiro presented for the first time to our public, will live in the memories of the residents of Florida.

With a *"Minuet"* by Sor, he began the concert. At the beginning the artist vacillated, his execution wasn't very steady nor very expressive, perhaps that was an avoidable impression. .

But in the *"Tres Preludios"* and *"Capricho arabe"*, he was sure of his art, sure of the public, that they burst out in hot applause.

This security was accentuated in the second part of the concert, more than by the applause received, but by the inspiration of the performer. The *"Preludios"* and the *"Nocturne No. 2"* by Chopin were impeccably interpreted; it was impossible to not feel the moving melancholy they possessed, of the total delicateness of the Polish pianist.

The tyranny of the space obligated us to miss many things among them the delicious *"Romanza"* by Mendelssohn. We won't say the same with the *"Cancion Catalana"* by the great Llobet, marvelous of emotion and art that, at least in us it suggests more than what it says.

ss

Barreiro, we believe as we have already said, isn't a maestro. But he is young and studious, he is in love with his art, and overall, he has soul. He can go very far."

Signed and inscribed photo by harpist Lea Bach:

"A pleasant memory of the distinguished Mr. Rosendo Barreiro. Lea Bach - Montevideo, June 15, 1919"

San Jose Uruguay Friday September 12, 1919

From *"La Mañana"*

"Teatro"

"The Guitarist Barreiro

As we have announced last night the first and only Rosendo Barreiro performance on the Maccio stage took place.

This young artist undoubtedly possesses meritorious abilities to do the performance. The third prelude of the program was interpreted by Barreiro with justice and sentiment. In the *"Capricho arabe"* it was correctly played, it revealed to us the able performer, not faulting other good artists that have played the beautiful piece.

But where Barreiro, last night reached at expressing his best personality, was in the *"Nocturne"* by Chopin.

In this passage, Barreiro demonstrated his excellent aptitude for interpretation, deserving the repeated salvos of applause.

A numerous amount of people attended this recital, who hotly applauded the guitarist in different parts of the program."

Trio Barcelona Montevideo September 20, 1919

  Photo featuring the Trío Barcelona, hired by "Sociedad Wagneriana" in Buenos Aires.

Signed: "For our colleague and friend R. Barreiro
Affectionately,

Mariano Perelló, Pedro Marés, Ricardo Vives. Montevideo September 20,1919."

"Trio Barcelona, formed by the pianist Ricard Vives, the cellist Joaquim Pedro Marés, and the violinist Mariano Perelló (from left to right in the photograph). The Trio was founded in 1912 and remained active until 1932. From its beginnings, it was valued for its excellence not only in Catalonia but also in Europe, where the group toured Germany, Belgium and France."

This is a historical quote written by: J. Obrador.

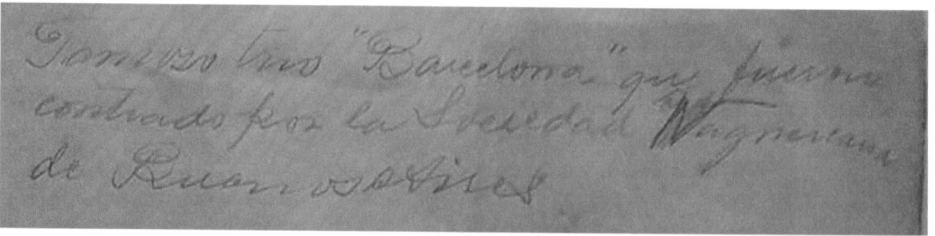

Montevideo *"El Dia"*

"El Guitarrista Barreiro

Next Tour of the guitarist Barreiro

Soon he will leave for Brazil, going to the cities of Sao Paulo, Porto Alegre, Santos, Rio de Janeiro, our compatriot, the guitarist Rosendo Barreiro, in an artistic tour, with the end to make in this concert season with music by Tárrega, Sor, Albeniz, Granados, Beethoven, Schumann, Chopin, Rachmaninoff, Llobet, Aguado, Parga, Manjón, Pujol, García, Segovia, Arcas, Haydn, Mozart, Wagner, Sarasate, Regondi and other great maestros.

It is expected that Mr. Barreiro will renew the successes in this tour that he obtained in Paysandu, Salto, Mercedes and Concordia, cities that have shown appreciation of this concert artist who has studied with eminent maestros Llobet and Pujol whose autographs we have seen."

LA PROVINCIA. Concordia (E. R., noviembre 6 J. 1919

Teatro Odeón

Dió anoche su anunciado concierto el guitarrista uruguayo Rosendo Barreiro, confirmando plenamente todo cuanto en su elogio se había dicho, y demostrando al mismo tiempo lo que puede dar un instrumento como la guitarra en las manos de un buen ejecutante. Los números de Schumann, Chopin, Tárrega, Bach, Beethoven y Mendelssohn tuvieron en la labor del señor Barreiro una excelente interpretación, que premió el auditorio con repetidas e insistentes ovaciones.

La Provincia Concordia, Entre Rios, Argentina November 6,1919

Teatro Odeon

"The announced concert given last night by the Uruguayan guitarist Rosendo Barreiro, fully confirmed the amount of praise we have said about him, and demonstrated at the same time what he can give to his instrument, such as the guitar in the hands of a good performer. The numbers he played by Schumann, Chopin, Tárrega, Bach, Beethoven and Mendelssohn were in the labor of Mr. Barreiro, an excellent interpretation, that the audience awarded with repeated and insistent ovations.

(This concert was performed in Argentina.)

Adolfo Vazquez Gomez (1869-1950)"

"A Rosendo Barreiro el amigo querido y artista de
espíritu hondamente selecto de su affmo.
A. Barrios. Montevideo, 31-VII-920".

"To Rosendo Barreiro the beloved friend and artist of deep select spirit, affectionately, A. Barrios.
Montevideo, July 31, 1920".

My colleague, Rico Stover, said he had never seen this photo in his more than 50 years of tracing the
footsteps of Agustín Barrios.

EL BIEN PUBLICO — Viernes 10 de Septiembre de 1920

El concierto de esta noche en el Instituto Verdi

El eximio guitarrista uruguayo R. Barreiro, visto por nuestro caricaturista, Pedro Zorrilla de San Martin

El Bien Publico Friday September 10, 1920

From the daily: *El Bien Publico* Montevideo

"The concert tonight in the Instituto Verdi

The eminent Uruguayan guitarist R. Barreiro seen by our sketch artist, Pedro Zorilla de San Martin."

Diario Nuevo (Salto) *Teatros* November 7, 1919

"The concert of the ninth

In our Larrañaga next Sunday at 9 PM a great concert will take place by the excellent guitarist, our compatriot, Rosendo Barreiro, who has just conquered a new audience in our near city of Concerdia.

The concert will be a benefit for the Children's asylum, and this fact alone will be enough for the attendance of families to be numerous and those that we already assure will not regret to attend the concert.

There already are many seats that have been taken."

La Noche diario independente Montevideo Sunday December 19, 1920

"Barreiro

Everything was a success obtained last night for this guitarist in the recital that was offered in the Instituto Verdi.

He performed difficult compositions in the program with admirable mastery and receiving unanimous applause by the gathering."

Romeo Negro

Business card Miguel Acosta Hijo (Jr.)

"To the eminent guitarist Rosendo Barreiro that covers the world elevating all the hearts in a moment of emotion and beauty.

Your friend and admirer,"

Miguel Acosta Hijo

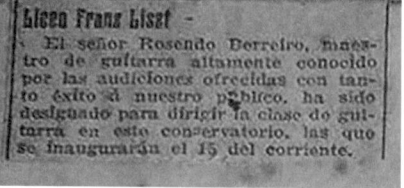

El Plata Diario de la Tarde Saturday

"Liceo Franz Liszt

"Mr. Rosendo Barreiro, the maestro of the guitar, highly known by the audiences of our public that were offered such success, he has been designated to direct classes of the guitar in this conservatory, that will begin on the 15th of the current month."

EL HERALDO

TE PAGADO | TACUAREMBÓ, MAYO 5 DE 1921 | AÑO VII -- NUMF

El Heraldo Tacuarembo Thursday May 5 1921 Año VII

Echos of Society

In the Peixoto home

Ecos de sociedad

En lo de Peixoto

Con motivo de una audición intima ofrecida por el talentoso guitarrista Barreiro, un núcleo numeroso y selecto de familias de nuestra sociedad se congregó el martes en la elegante residencia de los esposos do Amaral Peixoto.

Fué ésta una feliz oportunidad para una reunión que no obstante ser improvisada resultó muy animada e interesante.

Los dueños de casa, secundados por su gentilísima hija Olga, atendieron con fina cortesía a sus visitantes.

Barreiro, inspirado y habilísimo, deleitó al auditorio con sus difíciles y magníficas ejecuciones.

En un ambiente amable y grato las horas se deslizaron fugazmente, retirándose la concurrencia pasadas las 8 de la noche, muy agradecida a las infinitas atenciones de los dueños de casa.

Asistieron entre otras, las señoras de Amaral de Peixoto, Valdez de Nieto y Clavera, Buadas de Ferreira, Rodríguez de Pringles; señoritas de: Peixoto, Ferreira, Nieto y Clavera, Doreste, Nieto Fons, Perdomo, Catalogne, Ovalle, Techera, Peña, Rodríguez, Gómez; señores do Amaral Peixoto, Doctor Ivo Ferreira, Doctor Amadeo Landó Dr. Perdomo, Catalogne, Dr. Pringles, Techera, da Cuaba, etc.

With the motive of an intimate performance offered by the talented guitarist Barreiro a numerous nucleus of the select families of our society gathered on Tuesday at the residence of the Amaral Peixoto couple.

It was a happy opportunity for a reunion nevertheless being improvised it turned out very lively and interesting.

The homeowners, backed up by the kindness of their daughter Olga, who took care of all the visitors with a fine courtesy.

Barreiro, inspired and in his able capacity delighted the audience with his difficult and magnificent performances.

In a friendly and heartwarming environment the hours slipped away fleetingly, the gathering broke up after 8 in the evening, and was very thankful for the infinite attention of the hosting couple.

Among those who attended: Amaral de Peixoto, Valdez de Nieto y Clavera, Buadas de Ferreira, Rodríguez de Pringles; Daughters of: Peixoto, Ferreira, Nieto y Clavera, Doreste, Nieto Fons, Perdomo, Catalogne, Ovalle, Techera, Peña, Rodríguez, Gomez, Mr. and Mrs.: Amaral Peixoto, Dr. Ivo Ferreira, Dr. Amadeo Lando, Dr. Perdomo, Catalogne, Dr. Pringles, Techera, da Cuaba, etc.

Last night's recital   Undated image on the right.

Last night Barreiro got a lot of applause, by his labor as an interpreter of the guitar. The auditorium, that was chosen, spoke so, to the intelligent efforts of the very promising young artist.

We saw him in the Escayola hall, in front of the families: Parisi, Magnone, Rigoli, Tachini, Motta y Esteves, Buadas de Ferreira, Valdez de Nieto Clavera, Daughters of: Buadas, Motta de Tachini, Piguillem, Rios de Paolino, Larrobia, Gravina de Catalina, etc.

El recital de anoche ✕

Muchas ovaciones cosechó anoche Barreiro, por su labor de intérprete de la guitarra. — El auditorio, que era escogido, pronunció así, el esfuerzo inteligente de un joven artista que es toda una promesa.

Vimos en la sala del «Escayola» a las familias de Parisi, Magnone, Rigoli, Tachini, Motta Esteves Amaral Peixoto, Catalogne, Boadas de Ferreira, Valdez de Nieto Clavera, señorita Boadas, Motta de Tachini, Piguillem, Rios de Paolino, Larrobia, Gravina de Catalina, etc.

DE ARTE

EL CONCIERTO DEL MIERCOLES

El joven y prestigioso concertista Barreiro, ha cosechado un nuevo triunfo entre nosotros, haciendo resaltar una vez más, sus excelentes condiciones de guitarrista.

Las difíciles interpretaciones del programa ejecutado por Barreiro, el miércoles, son una prueba concluyente de la clara inteligencia y profundo conocimiento de la literatura musical, de nuestro coterráneo.

La concurrencia selecta que asistió al recital, premió con el homenaje de los aplausos al final de cada interpretación, la labor del artista.

Felicitamos al artista amigo y esperamos que su gira sea una serie minterrumpida de triunfos

---

DE ARTE

Audiciones del miércoles y viernes

Dió el miércoles y viernes sus anunciados conciertos de guitarra, el concertista Rosendo Barreiro, coterráneo nuestro, habiendo obtenido con sus audiciones un verdadero éxito. Barreiro triunfó como triunfan los buenos y valientes; como triunfan los artistas de corazón y de temperamento, poniendo en evidencia grandes condiciones para ejecutar, a la manera de Llobet,

Segovia y Barrios, en la tradicional guitarra, las más difíciles obras clásicas, que hasta hace poco solo se ejecutaran en violin, piano y violoncello. Se reveló una verdadera promesa nacional, como justamente lo han clasificado los mejores críticos de Montevideo, y de él todo lo debemos esperar. Barreiro va ascendiendo, y su ascensión es rápida, lo que evidencia talento y temperamento musical.

No ha nacido ni se ha pasado la vida entre artistas, como otros, en el ambiente de los conservatorios musicales. Se ha hecho solo a fuerza de tesonera voluntad y de estudio, al costo de sacrificios, pues sin poseer la dicha ha abandonado toda otra actividad que le brinda ra una posición desahogada para consagrarse por entero a la guitarra. Así se explica que, relativamente en poco tiempo haya hecho mucho, y figure ya, entre los primeros concertistas de guitarra.

En su primer concierto nos deleitó con obras de más elevado gusto artístico: Capricho andaluz, Capricho árabe, Góndola veneciana y el Andante de Leor, en esta última el concertista hizo derroche de un dominio de la interpretación de la armonía, donde se le puede juzgar un temperamento de músico. En el Capricho árabe del malogrado Tárrega supo interpretar con talento la obra del maestro, dándonos la sensación fiel de los distintos paisajes que en ella se describe.

En su segunda audición nos hizo gustar, a más del capricho árabe de Tárrega, que no puede faltar en ningún programa. «Claro de Luna» de Beethoven, ejecutando con maestría, con fidelidad no superable, los compases del gran músico, dejándonos así la impresión de su temperamento artístico ya consagrado; siempre grande y siempre inspirado. «Nocturno de Chopin», de dificilísima técnica, fué vertido con fidelidad, lo mismo que «Cuentos de amor» de Manjón, la «Gavota de Bach» y «Granada de Albéniz.

2352

Tacuarembo Thursday May 19, 1921 *De Arte*   Previous page image on the left.

About Art

"The Wednesday Concert

The young and prestigious concert guitarist Barreiro, has gained a new triumph among us, making known once again, his excellent abilities on the guitar. The difficult interpretations performed by Barreiro, on Wednesday with a concluding proof of the clear intelligence and profound knowledge of the musical literature, by our compatriot.

The select gathering that attended the recital, awarded with the homage of applause at the end of every interpretation of the artistic labor.

We congratulate the artistic friend and we hope that his tour might be a series of uninterrupted triumphs."

Tacuarembo Thursday May 19 1921   Previous page image on the right.

Of Art

"Wednesday and Thursday Performances

The concert guitarist Rosendo Barreiro gave the announced Wednesday and Thursday concerts, our compatriot, having obtained a real success with his performances. Barreiro triumphed as those good and valiant triumph; as triumph the artists of heart and temperament, making evident the great abilities of the performers, in the manner of Llobet, Segovia and Barrios, on the traditional guitar, the most difficult classical works, that until a while ago were only played on the violin, piano and cello. He revealed a real national promise, as justly classified by the best Montevideo critics, and of all we must expect. Barreiro is going to ascend, and his ascension is rapid, with the evidence of his talent and musical temperament.

He hasn't been born nor hasn't spent his life among the artists, like others, in the environment of the   musical conservatories. It's been done only in the strength and persistent willpower of studying not at the expense of sacrifice, since without possessing a fortune, he has abandoned all his other activities that salute a position that might alleviate to consecrate entirely to the guitar. So it explains what the relatively short time that he might have made a lot, and already places him among, the first rank of concert guitarists.

In his first concert we delighted with works by the most elevated artistic taste: *Capricho arabe, Gondola veneciana* and the *Andante* by Logy, in the last piece the concert guitarist made a dissipation of a .... of the interpretation of the harmony, where one can judge the temperament of music. In the *Capricho arabe,* by the late Tárrega, he knew how to interpret the work of the maestro with talent, giving the faithful sensation of the different countries, in which, it describes.

In his second performance he made us enjoy more of the *Capricho arabe*, by Tárrega, that can't be left out of any program. *"Claro de Luna"* by Beethoven, performing it with mastery, with unsurpassable faithfulness, the measures of the great musician, leaving us as the impression of his artistic temperament already consecrated; always grand and always inspiring. *"Nocturne"* by Chopin, of the most difficult technique, was sprung with faithfulness, the same that *"Cuento de amor"* by Manjón, the *Gavotte* by Bach, and *Granada* by Albeniz."

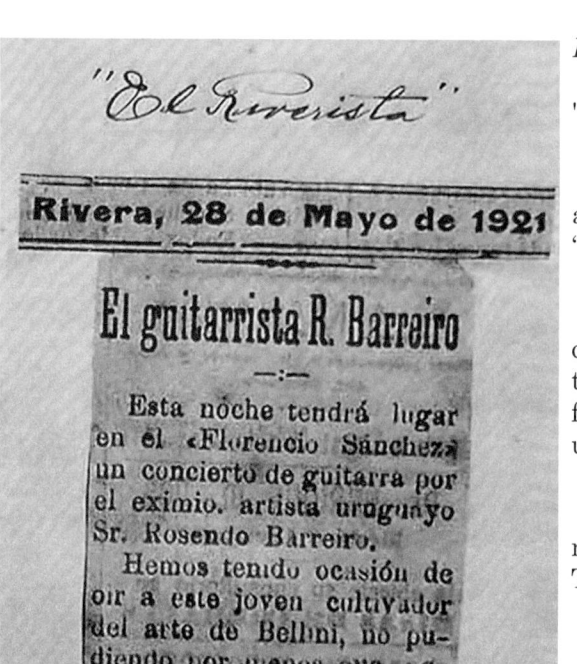

El Riverista Saturday May 28, 1921

"The Guitarist Rosendo Barreiro

Tonight, a guitar concert by the eminent Uruguayan artist Mr. Rosendo Barreiro will take place in the "Florencio Sanchez".

We have had the opportunity to hear this young cultivator of the art of Bellini, we can't help but admire the astonishing delivery and tonalities that he brings forth from the guitar, that he dominates with the unsurpassable mastery of art.

Mr. Barreiro proposes to give another concert next Tuesday to benefit the United League against Tuberculosis."

De arte

BARREIRO

Esta noche disfrutaremos con la guitarra de Barreiro horas de honda emoción. Temperamento flexible, verídico, se amolda a la escuela y modalidades de los grandes maestros de la literatura musical.

Desgrana su guitarra, tan reverenciada en Llovet, Manjón, Barrios, las emotividades de su exquisita concepción. Schumann, Chopin, Beethoven, favoritos de la Armonía, hacen oír sus creaciones eternas por sus bellezas, en la guitarra de Barreiro. El artista este, no es un transeunte en el País del Arte. Acogido a sus manos, lucha y trabaja. Ahonda su temperamento y perfecciona su difícil arte. Ayudarlo con el aplauso es justificar su esfuerzo tan desinteresado. Tacuarembó debe tributar a uno de sus hijos el homenaje de su simpatía. El artista que es modesto, no lo reclama, pero indudablemente, lo necesita como estimulo, y es de justicia no negarlo, a quien desde ya es una promesa para la gloria.

Tacuarembo *El Nacional* Saturday Wednesday May 18 1921

The arts

"Barreiro

   This evening we will enjoy to guitar of Barreiro hours of emotion flexible temperament real-life fashioned to the school and modalities of the great maestros of the musical literature.

   Threshing his guitar, revering so much in Llobet, Manjón, Barrios, the emotive natures of his exquisite concepts. Schumann, Chopin, Beethoven, favorites of the Harmony, make in his eternal creations by their beauty, on the guitar of Barreiro. The artist, he isn't a passer-by in the Country of Art. Taken up in his hands, he struggles and works. He delves into his temperament and perfection of his difficult art. Helping him with the applause is to justify his effort so altruistic. Tacuarembo must tribute to one of its sons the homage of his understanding. The artist who is modest, doesn't demand, but undoubtedly, its necessary as a stimulus, and it is justice to not deny him, to whom, he is already a promise of glory."

El concertista Barreiro

Procedente de Montevideo encuéntrase entre nosotros el eximio guitarrista Uruguayo Rosendo Barreiro. La poca actuación del guitarrista compatriota en el Uruguay, es el motivo de que sean pocos los que conozcan la personalidad artística de Barreiro, el que ha conseguido en su vida ambulatoria los más calurosos elogios de la prensa por haber demostrado que la tradicional vihuela con la que nuestros gauchos exteriorizaban sus sentimientos, también sabe «cuando se ponen en vez de cuerdas delicados nerviss» evocar todo el sentimiento de la música clásica. Discreto ejecutor de las producciones de Bethoven, de Chopin Schuman y otros, el sonoro cordaje de su guitarra, también sabe combinar aires criollos y músicas nativas que por su origen se nos presentará con aspecto afectivo.

Barreiro piensa dar una serie de audiciones en nuestro Coliseo cuyo artista, consagrado ya, sabrá por intermedio del lenguaje indefinido de la música excitar nuestra sensibilidad espiritual

"The concert guitarist Barreiro

Arriving from Montevideo to be found among us the eminent Uruguayan guitarist Rosendo Barreiro.

The small amount of performances of our guitaristic compatriot in Uruguay, is the reason why there might be few who know the artistic personality of Barreiro, who has gotten in his wandering life the hottest eulogies by the press for having demonstrated that the tradition of the *Vihuela* with which our gauchos showed their sentiments, you also know when all the strings at once are played delicately nerves evoke all the sentiment of the classical music. He is a discrete performer of the productions by Beethoven, Chopin, Schumann and others, the sonorous cordage of the guitar, he also knows hot to combine *Criollo* pieces and national music by which the origin he presents us with our affectionate aspect.

Barreiro thinks of giving a series of performances in our Coliseo, whose artists already consecrated, will know by the medium of the undefined language of the music to excite our spiritual sensibilities."

El Dia Montevideo Monday April 10, 1922

El Dia Montevideo Monday April 10, 1922

From the Musical Environment

The Guitarist Barreiro. -

His Integration in the Franz Liszt Conservatory. -

The young and intelligent guitarist Mr. Barreiro, our compatriot already known by our public for various recitals offered in different occasions, has just been named professor of the "Franz Liszt" Conservatorio to direct guitar classes.

Mr. Barreiro enjoys a prestige of having well conquered in the social environment. The idea is truly well-chosen by Camilo Gucci to introduce guitar classes in his institute.

The guitar has taken a position in our environment, gathered great prestige since the extraordinary concerts by the eminent Llobet, and the famous maestro Andrés Segovia, that have left among us unforgettable memories.

Mr. Barreiro possesses an autograph by Llobet where it credits him with merits to occupy this important position. It is his artistic temperament that forcibly with let him triumph. His classes will begin on the 15th of the current month.

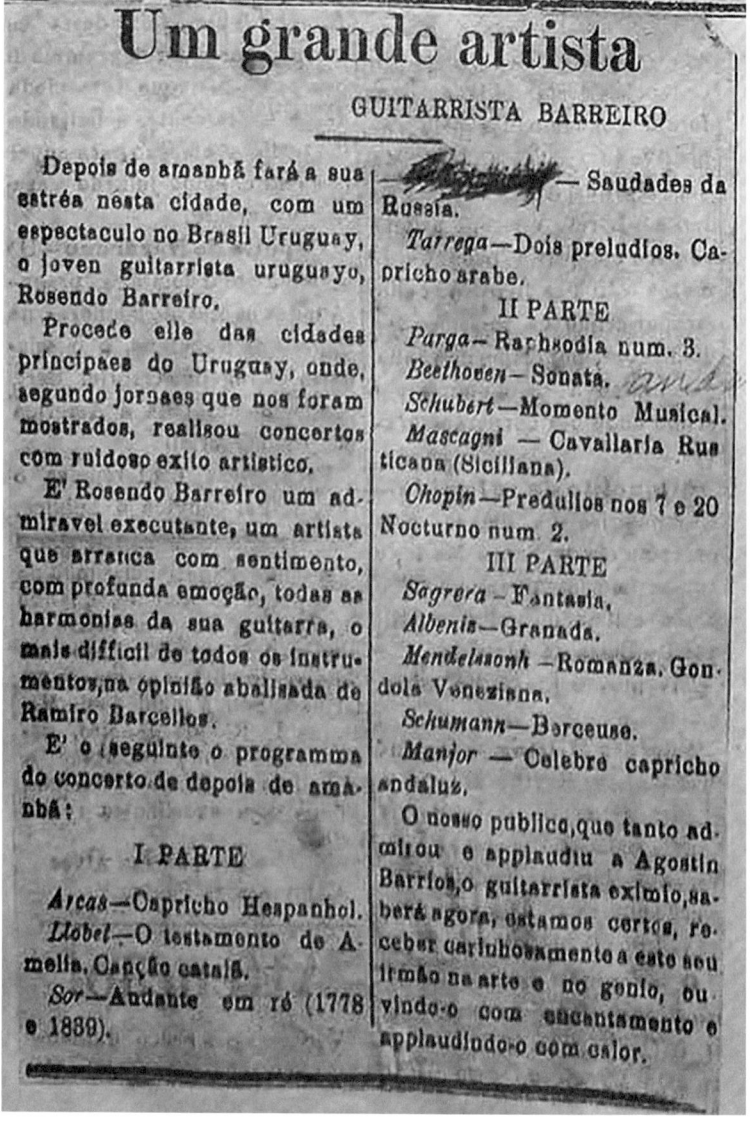

A Tarde Livramento, Brazil Tuesday May 31, 1921

Portuguese Translation by Randy Osborne

A Great Artist

Guitarist: Barreiro

The young Uruguayan guitarist Rosendo Barreiro will make his debut in the city the day after tomorrow.

He's arriving from one of the principal cities in Uruguay, where, in his second tour he is performing for us, giving concerts that draw noisy applause for his artistic success.

Rosendo Barreiro is an admirable performer, an artist who brings with sentiment, with profound emotion, all the harmonies out from his guitar, the most difficult of all instruments, in the opinion of Ramiro Barcellos.

This is the following program for the day after tomorrow:

First Set
Arcas-Capricho Hespanhol
Llobet-O testament de Amelia. Catalan Song.
Sor- Andante in D Major (1778-1839)
Saudades da Russia.
Tárrega-Two Preludes. Capricho arabe

Second Set
Parga-Rhapsodia number 3.
Beethoven-Andante.
Schubert-Momento Musical.
Mascagni-Cavallaria Rusticana (Siciliana).
Chopin-Preludes Numbers 7 and 20. Nocturno No. 2.

Third Set
Sagreras-Fantasia.
Albeniz-Granada.
Mendelssohn-Romanza. Gondola Veneziana.
Schumann-Berceuse.
Manjón-Celebre capricho andaluz.

Our public, that admires and applauds the eminent guitarist Agustín Barrios so much, will know now, we're certain, to affectionately receive his brother in art and in genius, listening with enchantment and applaud him with warmth.

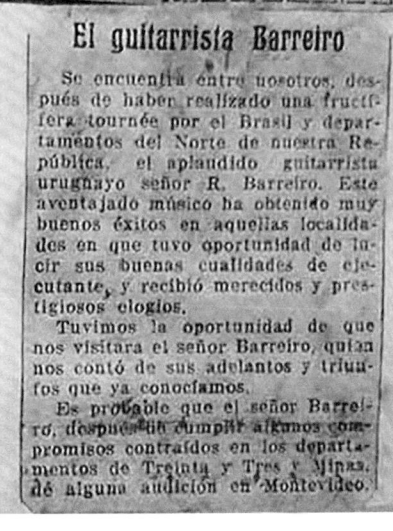

La Defensa Thursday June 30, 1921

The Guitarist Barreiro

The applauded Uruguayan guitarist Mr. Barreiro has been found among us, after having made a fruitful tour of Brazil, and northern provinces of our Republic. This advanced musician has obtained the very good success in those localities in which he took advantage to show his good qualities as a performer, and he received deserved and prestigious praise.

We took the opportunity when Mr. Barreiro visited us, he told us of his progress and triumphs, of which we already knew.

It's likely that Mr. Barreiro after finishing some of his commitments contracted in Treinta y Tres and Minas, will have some performances in Montevideo.

Tribuna Batllista

CONCIERTO DE BARREIRO

Por tercera vez se presentó én el salón del cine Arugas el m a ravilloso de la guitarra, ya mu - conocido en nuestro ambiente y

Si hemos oído a Barreiro con gran agrado en las presentacio- nes anteriores debemos manifes- tar que en el concierto de ano- che ha sobrepasado los anterio- res, estando notable.

Ha sido tanta la aceptación que ha tenido Barreiro ante el prestigioso, que ya nos resulta pe sada la forma en que aplaude el público cuando terminara la eje- cución de una pieza. —Anoche hu bieron momentos en que se inte- rrumpía al guitarrista con los abundantes aplausos.

Concurrieron a presenciar el concierto de guitarra los Sras. de Pomon, Pats, Posada, Leal, Viera, Landó y Suarez; y señori- tas de: Catalogne Caritozo, Mar- tinez, Suarez, Esteves, Peixoto, Seoanes, Posada, Pereira y otras que no recordamos.

Tribuna Batllista

Barriero Concert

For the third time he was presented in the cine Arugas the marvelous player of the guitar, already very well known in our environment.

Yes, we have heard Mr. Barreiro with great pleasure in the previous presentations we must demonstrate that last night's concert surpassed the previous ones, being notable.

He has been so accepted and Mr. Barreiro has had the prestige beforehand, that when he finishes performing a piece it turns out that he appears before us with the heavy applause of the public. Last night there were moments when the guitarist was interrupted by abundant applause.

The gathering present at the guitar concert were Mrs.: Pomon, Pats, Posada, Leal, Viera, Lando, and Suarez, Daughters: Catalogne, Caritozo, Martínez, Suarez, Esteves, Peixoto, Seoanes, Posada, Pereira and other we don't recall.

El Diario Montevideo Thursday November 16, 1923

Barreiro

This virtuoso of the guitar will be presented on the 1st of December in the Cine Teatro Ariel, giving an extraordinary concert of the art he practices.

Mr. Barreiro has combined his chosen sheet music pieces with those that include works by Llobet, Segovia and other admirable maestros.

The artistic endowments of this concert guitarist are already well known since it will be an outright definite success.

La Democracia Montevideo Sunday November 18, 1923

Rosendo Barreiro

This notable artist of the guitar will offer our public an extraordinary concert in the teatro Ariel on Saturday December 1st.

Given the kindness by the notable Barreiro in our artistic environment we guarantee in advance a complete success by our compatriot guitarist.

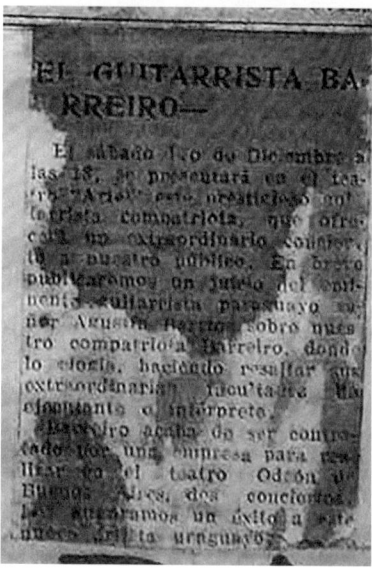

La Razon Independent Daily Montevideo Tuesday November 20, 1923

The Guitarist Barreiro

Saturday the 1st of December at 6PM in the Ariel Theater this prestigious Uruguayan guitarist will be presented in an extraordinary concert that he offers to the public. Soon we will publish a critique by the eminent Paraguayan guitarist Agustín Barrios about our compatriot Barreiro, where the praise, highlights his extraordinary faculties as a performer and interpreter.

Barreiro has just been contracted by a firm to perform two concerts at the Teatro Odeon in Buenos Aires, we expect a success by our Uruguayan guitarist.

El Pais Montevideo Tuesday November 27, 1923

The Guitarist Barreriro

Next Saturday at 6PM he will offer to our public an extraordinary recital of the guitar our compatriot Mr. Barreriro.

Soon we will publish the interesting program and guarantee in advance a complete success since the abilities of the performer Mr. Barreiro with his accredited merits for a triumph as a good aficionado on works like those of Sor.

Diario del Plata Saturday December 1, 1923

Social pages

At 6PM the announced guitar recital that Mr. Barreiro offers will take place. The President of the Republic, *Don* Jose Serrato, the engineer, has been especially invited by Mr. Barreiro.

El Dia Saturday December 1, 1923

Recital Barreiro

    This afternoon at 6PM he will offer in the Hall of the Ariel, an interesting recital by concert guitarist Barreiro, a compatriot of inestimable abilities as an interpreter, that has been making great progress lately consecrating with true love of his art.

    Here we give the combined select program for the performance:

First part:

Three preludes, Tárrega
Cancion Catalana, Llobet
Momento Musical, Schubert
Andante, Haydn
Variaciones sobre una tema de Vidalita, Sinopoli-Barreiro.

Second Part:

Two Preludes, Chopin
Berceuse, Hoja de Album, Traumeri (Ensueño), Schumann
Minuet, Paderewski.

Third Part:

Andante cantabile, Sor
Gondola Veneziana, Mendelssohn
Serenata Española, Malats.
Asturias, Albeniz.

DEL *Ambiente musical*

CONCIERTO DE GUITARRA. — En el teatro Ariel, se realizará esta tarde a la hora 18 un concierto de guitarra a cargo del notable virtuoso señor Barreiro, quien ejecutará el siguiente programa:

1.a parte. — Tres preludios, Tárrega; Canción catalana, Llobet; Memento musical, Schubert; Andante, Haydn; Variaciones sobre un tema de Vidalita, Sinopoli-Barreiro.

2.a parte. — Dos preludios y Berceuse Chopin; Hoja de album y Träumersi (Ensueño), Schumann; Minuet, Paderewski.

3.a parte. — Andante cantábile, Sors; Góndola veneciana, Mendelsson; Serenata española, Malats; Asturia, Albeniz.

El guitarrista Barreiro, que esta tarde ejecutará un interesante concierto en el Teatro Ariel

El Dia Saturday December 1, 1923 Photo Caption below
From the Musical Environment
Guitar Concert

In the teatro Ariel at 6PM this afternoon a guitar concert by the notable virtuoso Mr. Barreiro will take place and he will perform the following program:

First part:
Three preludes, Tárrega
Cancion Catalana, Llobet
Momento Musical, Schubert
Andante, Haydn
Variaciones sobre un tema de Vidalita, Sinopoli-Barreiro
Second Part:
Two Preludes and Berceuse, Chopin
Hoja de Album, Traumeri (Ensueño), Schumann
Minuet, Paderewski.
Third Part:
Andante cantabile, Sor
Gondola Veneziana, Mendelssohn
Serenata Española, Malats.
Asturias, Albeniz.
Photo Caption;
The guitarist Barreiro, who will perform an interesting concert this afternoon in the Teatro Ariel.

El Plata Wednesday May 7, 1924

The Guitarist Barreiro

Our compatriot the concert guitarist Mr. Barreiro of known performances among our public, soon will offer, a series of performances, of music in the towns of Tala, Fray Marcos, and San Ramon.

These recitals have been organized by the social club of the mentioned localities.

Barreiro possesses the Tárrega school and has that as the basis for demonstrating once again his united triumph of his great artistic temperament that is taken for granted.

El Diario Wednesday May 21, 1924

The Guitarist Barreiro

This virtuoso of whose excellent abilities of performing have concerned us on more than one occasion, has just made an interesting tour of some of the interior cities among them Tala, San Ramon, Fray Marcos, Cosura, Cozot and Santa Rosa. Playing in all of them to which they are in debt to his fine artistic sensibilities that he dominates with his technique.

To which his natural qualities give Barreiro a permanency of intelligent studying that gives one an ample ability to triumph in his difficult art.

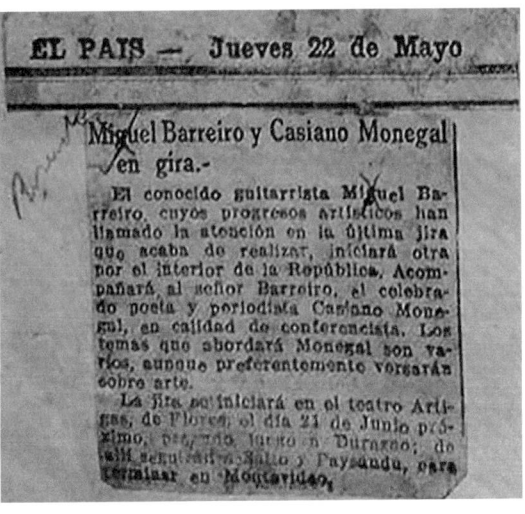

El Pais Thursday May 22, 1924

Rosendo Barreiro and Casiano Monegal on tour.

   The known guitarist Rosendo Barreiro whose artistic progress has called attention in the last tour that he last made, he begins another of the interior of the Republic. He is accompanied by the celebrated poet and journalist, Casiano Monegal, in the capacity as a lecturist. The themes that Monegal touches on vary, but he prefers to talk about art.

   The tour will begin in the teatro Artigas, in Flores, the 21st of June, then on to Durazno, from there to Salto and Paysandu, terminating in Montevideo.

Bebiendo en las fuentes de la emoción

Nuestro "momento musical" con Barreiro

Para EL TELÉGRAFO.

Decididamente, escogimos una ocasión impropia para entrevistarnos con nuestro compatriota el guitarrista Rosendo Barreiro. Triunfaba el carnaval en su día primero. El artista, tenía desde la víspera la intuición comunicativa de que Momo presentaría el aspecto de un farsante viejo, decrépito y desolado. Y por más que su espíritu selecto lo alejara un tanto de esas relaciones banales, no pudo nuestro interlocutor abstenerse de comentar la llegada del regio bufón.

Nosotros, fieles a la tarea impuesta, desviamos desde el principio de la entrevista toda acotación al margen de los días de Momo. Bien era necesario eso para nuestra tranquilidad, ya que tantas veces hemos soportado las consideraciones contrarias a la admiración popular y consagratoria de la locura, que toda filosofía amarga sobre carnaval nos resulta no sólo presente griego, sino también lluvia sobre mojado.

Y sin más preámbulos, despertando en Barreiro la admiración y emulación a Job, interrogamos:

—¿...?

—Nada de reportajes trascendentales, mis amigos. Hablemos mejor como camaradas. Sencillamente. También con un poco de amargura. Esta tiene razón de ser. Porque si yo no fuera un enamorado de mi arte, seguramente, me conocerían mucho más. Daría, como a Vds. les parece mejor, conciertos a granel. La amistad me aseguraría la crítica. Esto por otra parte es tan corriente, que ni siquiera es criticable. Pero...

Y el artista, mientras termina un cigarrillo, trunca allí esa confesión escéptica para continuar seriamente:

—Convendrán Vds. que los conciertos requieren mucha labor de técnica musical y a nadie satisface que por toda compensación reciba un porcentaje que está diciendo a las claras que el beneficiado es el empresario hábil.

Sobre este particular nada nuevo puedo decir; mi camino es el de todos. Por eso, con la libertad que me concede mi situación actual, me dedico a ejecutar por placer propio, y a veces, reuniendo a los amigos predilectos nos permitimos modestas «seratas». En ellas, el bondadoso estímulo de mis camaradas se une muchas veces a mi entusiasmo. Esto es seguramente, lo que hace más amable y llevadera la inactividad a que me he condenado.

—¿...?

—De Llovet no soy el más indicado para agregar nada a todo lo que expuso la crítica mundial. Básteles saber, si mi opinión merece tenerse en cuenta, que estoy entre los que le asignan el primer puesto.

En cuanto a Barrios creo que con la ayuda poderosa de su intuición musical está predestinado a superarse a sí mismo.

Es espléndida la forma como traduce su sensibilidad en las composiciones en que hace entrever un temperamento aún no manifestado totalmente.

Pero su obra es ya personal. De ella emana un soplo vivificador en el que aparece un hondo sentimiento, su aguda cerebración artística, y una comunicativa emotividad. Es un error pensar que Barrios se encuentre actualmente en su cenit consagratorio. Una propensión intuitiva, permanente, lo conducirá a un grado cada vez más alto en su brillante carrera.

Esto, más o menos, nos dijo Barreiro. Que la modestia del artista nos perdone que así lo publiquemos. No es misterio para nosotros que prefiere el comentario amistoso de su refugio artístico a la crónica justa, y por ello mismo, elogiosa. Barreiro es huraño. Quizás no nos perdone que así hayamos hecho conocer sus opiniones di chas sin pretensiones de crítico buena y sinceramente.

Pero la indiscreción es patrimonio de cronistas bien o mal intencionados. Y nosotros somos de los primeros.

Barreiro pulsó la guitarra que tantas veces le ha visto triunfar. No es, quien esto escribe, el más indicado para referirse a lo que el guitarrista amigo sugiere cuando arranca esos sonidos tan puros a su instrumento. Barreiro está lejos de ser un desconocido en Paysandú, donde tantos aplausos conquistara.

Delito sería presentarle.

Pero no lo es decir que al impulso de su arte, el dominio espiritual se acentúa en nosotros vivamente, y que la vida se hace bella y emotiva.

Escenas versallescas de los vals de Chopin, encantadas noches andaluzas, alegría de sol y panderetas, suaves atardeceres de Granada que sugieren Tárrega y Albéniz desfilan por nuestra imaginación que eleva y agudiza el momento musical que nos ofrece el artista.

Afirmemos sin aspavientos; Barreiro es un notable artista. En él se unen la técnica y el sentimiento en una armonía que le valdrá el aplauso unánime y entusiasta de nuestros conterráneos que sepan de algo más que de cosas materiales, en oportunidad próxima.

Cuando salimos, en el ambiente flotaba la fugaz locura colectiva. Locura de sinceridad en medio de la farsa de todo el año. Locura despreocupada y reidora de Colombina, locura amarga de Pierrot... Semblante del mundo en su pasión primitiva y eterna. Superficialidad...

Barreiro nos señaló, con un dejo de decepción, el escenario de la farándula y, apenas hubimos estrechado su diestra amiga, se hundió de nuevo hurañamente en la casa para vivir «su vida»...

Aller.

Montevideo, Marzo—1924.

El Telegrafo Diario de la Manaña July 1 1924

"Drinking from the fountains of emotion"

Our 'Musical Moment' with Mr. Barreiro

For El Telegrafo

Decidedly, we chose an inappropriate time for our interview with our compatriot the guitarist Rosendo Barreiro. He triumphed at the carnival on the first day. The artist had since the eve the communicative intuition of which Momo present him with the aspect of the old trickster, decrepit and desolate. And more than his select spirit he backed off from many of these banal relations, our interviewer couldn't abstain from commenting on the arrival of the regal joker.

We, faithful to the imposed chore, from the outset of the interview we turned away from all stage direction to the edge of the days of Momo. Well it was necessary to for our tranquility, already so many times supporting the contrary considerations, to the popular admiration and consecration of the craziness, that all bitter philosophy about the carnival that turned out not only Greek, but also rain over being drenched.

And without more preambles, awakening in Barreiro the admiration and emulation of Job, we interrogate:

----?....?
"Nothing of the transcendental reports, my friends. We speak better as comrades. Simply. Also of a little of the acerbity. This has the right to be. Because if I wasn't a lover of my art, surely, they would know me more. I would give as you like better bulk concerts. Friendship assured me criticism. This on the other hand is so common, that it isn't even being criticized. But...."

While the artist finished a cigarette, never there that skeptic confession to continue seriously:
"Do you agree?, that the concerts require a lot of musical technique labor and no one is satisfied that by total compensation he who receives a percentage that is saying plainly of who benefits is the able impresario.

About this aspect I can say nothing new; my path is like everyone's. By that, with the liberty that concedes my existing situation, I dedicate to perform for my own pleasure. And at times, reuniting to the favorite friends, permits us modest *"serates"*. In them, the kind stimulus of my colleagues unites many times in my enthusiasm. This is surely, what makes more friendly and will take the inactivity to what I have condemned.

----?....?
For Llobet I am not the best person to add anything to everything that the world critic exposed.

As to Barrios I believe with the powerful help of his musical intuition he is predestined to surpass himself.

The form is splendid how he translates his sensibility in his compositions in what makes you glimpse sight of a temperament not even totally manifested.

But his work is already personal. From it emanates a lively blow in which appears a deep sentiment, his clever artistic mind, and a communicative emotive nature. It's a mistake to think that Barrios is presently found in his consecrated peak. An intuitive propensity, permanent, conduces him to a level every time higher in his brilliant career.

Barreiro more or less told us this. What the modesty of the artist we forgave that so we publish. It isn't a mystery for us that he prefers the friendly commentary of his artistic refuge to a just chronicle, by that itself, praiseworthy. Barreiro is hermit-like. Perhaps he won't forgive us, so that we might make his opinions known said without pretensions of good and sincere criticism.

But the indiscretion is patrimony of chroniclers of good and bad intentions.

Barreiro played the guitar many times that he saw triumph. It isn't who writes this, the best person to refer to what the guitarist friend suggests when he begins those sounds so pure on his instrument. Barreiro is far from being unknown in Paysandu, where he conquered with a lot of applause.

It is a delight to present him.

But it isn't to say that to the imposing of his art, the spiritual dominion lively accented in us and which life makes beautiful and emotive.

Beautiful scenes of the Chopin waltz, enchanted Andalusian nights, *alegria del Sol* (mirth of the Sun), *panderetas* (Tambourines), sweet afternoons of Granada, that suggest Tárrega and Albeniz parading by our imagination that elevate and sharpen the musical moments that the artist offers us.

We affirm without fusses: Barreiro is a notable artist. In him are united the technique and sentiment of a harmony that is worth the unanimous and enthusiastic applause of our local audiences that will know something more of the material things, in the next opportunity.

When leaving we're drifting in the environment of the collective evanescent madness. Madness of sincerity in the middle of the farce of all year. Unconcerned madness and laughing of Columbina, bitter madness of Pierrot... A countenance of the world of primitive and eternal passion. Superficiality...

Barreiro waved to us with a finger of anticlimax, the scene of the showbusiness, and scarcely we could grip his right-handed friend, he sank again sullenly in the sofa to live "his life".

EL TELEGRAFO

OFICINAS: CALLE 18 DE JULIO 300

DIARIO DE LA MAÑANA — martes 22 de Julio de 1924

El guitarrista Barreiro

Un artista de alma

En reunión íntima, familiar, tuvimos noches pasadas el placer de oir a Rosendo Barreiro, el joven y talentoso guitarrista que nos visita.

Lo primero que se nota en Barreiro es un gran amor por su arte; amor de predestinado, de verdadero artista de raza.

Más que mirar, acaricia la guitarra con sus ojos. Cuando habla de Tárrega, de Llovet, de los grandes virtuosos de la guitarra, su alma se enciende en fervorosa admiración.

Luego hay en Barreiro una gran fe. Cree en sí mismo. Acaso esa creencia no reconozca límites, pero sin duda alguna es ella una condición indispensable para el éxito. Sólo creyendo se puede hacer creer a los demás.

—

Barreiro, estamos seguros de ello, va a constituir una grande y grata sorpresa para los que le oyeron hace algunos años en Paysandú. Ha progresado notablemente en todos los sentidos. Es ya todo un concertista, sin necesidad de hacer comparaciones que siempre resultan odiosas.

Su sensibilidad de artista se ha afinado. Siente en toda su intensidad a los grandes maestros de la música. Y como los siente, los comprende e interpreta con fidelidad.

En técnica, se ha superado más de lo que es dable suponer en la labor de pocos años.

Es que Barreiro es un estudioso incansable, además de un artista emotivo y sutil.

Otra novedad debemos anotar: Barreiro se ha aventurado con valentía en el terreno de la composición original.

Oímosle la otra noche un motivo de vidalita que tiene todo el delicioso sabor del terruño y que, sino nos equivocamos, señala la aparición de una obra original y fuerte que el artista está obligado consigo mismo a completar.

Tal es, en síntesis, la impresión que nos ha dejado el guitarrista. Un artista de alma, al que nuestro público tendrá el gusto de aplaudir dentro de muy pocas noches.

M. Benavente

El Telegrafo Tuesday July 22, 1924

The Guitarist Barreiro

An Artist with Soul

In an intimate reunion, of families, of the last several nights we had the pleasure to hear the young and talented guitarist who visits us, Rosendo Barreiro.

The first thing that is noted in Barreiro his great love of his art, love of his destiny, a true artist of the Hispanic race.

More than to look, he caresses his guitar with his eyes. When speaking of Tárrega, of Llobet, of the great virtuosos of the guitar, his soul ignites with fervent admiration.

Then there is in Barreiro a great faith. Because of this belief there are no recognized limits, but without a doubt something in it is an indispensable ability for the success. Only believing can create the rest.

Barreiro, we are sure of it, is going to make a great and free surprise for those who heard him some years ago in Paysandu. He has progressed notably in all the senses. He is already a concert artist, without the necessity of making comparisons that are always turn out hateful.

His sensibility as an artist has become tuned in. He feels so intense toward the great maestros of music. And as he feels, he understands them and interprets them faithfully.

In technique, he has overcome more than should be possible to know in just a few years of labor.

It is that Barreiro is tirelessly studious, besides being an emotive and subtle artist.

Another novelty we need to note is Barreiro has adventured with courage into the world to compose original works.

We heard him the other evening on a motif of a *Vidalita* that has all the delicious flavor of our native land, but if we're mistaken, it signals the appearance of an original work and strength that the artist is obligated to himself to complete.

Such is the synthesis, the impression left to us by the guitarist. An artist of soul, to which our public will enjoy and applaud within just a few nights.

M. Benavente.

EL DIARIO

ño 465   **Paysandú, Miércoles 23 de Julio de 1924**   Admini

El concierto de mañana

Por el guitarrista uruguayo Barreiro

Como se ha venido anunciando, mañana de noche se realizará en el teatro Florencio Sánchez el concierto de guitarra a cargo del jóven Rosendo Barreiro, cuyos éxitos lo consagran como el primer guitarrista del Uruguay y un intérprete extraordinario de Tárrega, según la eminente opinión de Llobet.

He aquí el interesante programa de la velada:

PRIMERA PARTE

1—Presentación del guitarrista por un orador local.

2—«Esquisse» de caricaturas locales, por el señor Héctor Bascans.

3—Minuet de la Sonata Op. 22 Sors.

4—Dos preludios, Tárrega.

5—Capricho Arabe, Tárrega

6—Variaciones sobre un tema de Vidalita, Sinópoli—Barreiro

SEGUNDA PARTE

1—Testamento de Amelia Llobet

2—Gigue, Roberto de Visco

3—Andante en Re (1778-1839) Sors

4—Ensueño, Schumana

5—Recuerdo de la Alhambra, Tárrega.

TERCERA PARTE

1—Andante, Mozart

2—Góndola Veneciana, Mendelssohn

3—Asturias, Albéniz

4—Célebre Capricho Andaluz, Manjón.

Recientemente el joven Barreiro, de paso por la vecina ciudad de Salto, ofreció un recital íntimo, de lo que da cuenta «Tribuna Salteña» en la siguiente forma:

«Anteanoche, en la casa de la señora Adela G. de Errandonea, el guitarrista Rosendo Barreiro dejó oír los acordes de su guitarra ante una selecta concurrencia, pudiéndose apreciar sus buenas cualidades de intérprete que pone sentimiento exquisito en la expresión de la escuela antigua. Después de ejecutar partituras de Mendelshon, y Beethoven, interpretó aires españoles, capricho español, y Estudio en La mayor de Tárrega, así como trozos escogidos de Granados y Albeniz.

Al final tocó algunas composiciones suyas, tales como estilos, vidalitas, y aires argentinos.

Fué en resumen, una selecta velada de sociabilidad y buena música.»

2373

El Diario Paysandu Wednesday July 23, 1924

Tomorrow's Concert

By the Uruguayan Guitarist Barreiro

As it has come to be announced, tomorrow evening the guitar concert by the young Rosendo Barreiro will take place in the Florencio Sanchez theatre, whose success is consecrated as the premier guitarist of Uruguay and extraordinary interpreter of Tárrega, according to the opinion of the eminent Llobet.

I have here the interesting program of the soirée:

First part

1 – Presentation of the guitarist by a local orator.
2 – Display of local sketches, by Mr. Héctor Bascans.
3 – Minuet de la Sonata Op. 22 Sor.
4 – Two Preludes, Tárrega.
5 – Capricho Arabe, Tárrega.
6 – Variaciones sobre una tema de Vidalita, Sinopoli-Barreiro.

Second Part

1 – Testamento de Amelia, Llobet.
2 – Gigue, Robert de Visée.
3 – Andante en Re (1778-1839) Sor.
4 – Ensueño, Schumann.
5 – Recuerdos de la Alhambra, Tárrega.

Third Part

1 – Andante, Mozart.
2 – Gondola Veneciana, Mendelssohn.
4 – Celebre Caprico Andaluz, Manjón.

Recently the young Barreiro, passed through the neighboring city of Salto, offering an intimate recital of which is the account by *"Tribuna Salta"* in the following manner:

The night before last in the home of Adela G. de Erraudonea, the guitarist Rosendo Barreiro let the chords of his guitar be heard, before a select gathering, being able to appreciate his good qualities of interpretation that put the exquisite sentiment in the expression of the old school. After performing the sheet music of Mendelssohn and Beethoven, he interpreted *Aires españoles, Capricho español, Estudio en La mayor* (Alard) by Tárrega, like the chosen pieces by Granados and Albeniz.

At the end he played some of his own compositions, such as *estilos, vidalitas, aires argentinos:*

In summary it was a select soirée of sociability and good music.

EL DIARIO

Año 465   Paysandú, Viernes 25 de Julio de 1924   Admin

El concierto de anoche

Es con honda y legítima satisfacción que, ante todo, queremos destacar el hecho de que el anunciado concierto del jóven guitarrista uruguayo Barreiro, llevó anoche al teatro «Florencio Sànchez» un crecido auditorio. Indudablemente en nuestro público comienza a operarse una reacción altamente plausible, y es así como constatamos que las manifestaciones artísticas no pasan ya en medio de la indiferencia conque años atrás se ahogaba toda cosa del espíritu. Definitiva no es aún la conquista, pero en camino de obtenerla estamos, y día a día los síntomas que los hechos nos proporcionan, robustecen esta profecía, que para enaltecimiento común anhelamos ver cumplida cuanto antes.

Fué la de anoche, digamos ahora, una velada realmente valiosa y coronada por el más hermoso de los éxitos, que ha de haber llevado al espíritu del jóven artista una corriente de optimismo y de aliento. Se le aplaudió con verdadero entusiasmo, sincera y expontáneamente, después de oírsela con hondo recogimiento, con unción religiosa.

Barreiro dió elocuentes pruebas de los extraordinarios progresos que ha experimentado su técnica y de la amplitud de su talento interpretativo. En todo momento, —exceptuando el Minuet de Sors y los dos preludios de Tárrega, ejecutados en una forma que dejaba traslucir cierta nerviosidad, acaso producida por la primera impresión frente al público— el jóven concertista se mantuvo en un plano al que sólo se llega por medios íntimos, personales, y que exigen el cúmulo de la sensibilidad y del talento que atesoran el espíritu y el cerebro del intérprete.

A través de todo el programa, Barreiro admiró por su notable digitación, por el carácter personalísimo de sus interpretaciones y por la limpidez con que supo arrancar los sonidos hasta en las páginas más escabrosas, en la ejecución, como «Recuerdo de la Alhambra» de Tárrega y «Célebre capricho Andaluz» de Manjón, en las cuales culminó en forma realmente magnífica.

La impresión que nos ha causado Barreiro es óptima y decisiva: creemos firmemente que muy pronto ha de llegar a la absoluta perfección de sus medios, ya que talento y voluntad le sobran para ello, y que para él está reservado un sitial en la vanguardia de los grandes artistas.

Sabemos que Barreiro se propone ahora, ofrecer un nuevo concierto en el Ateneo, decisión que aplaudimos.

Veladas de arte como las que puede él ofrecernos, no son, desgraciadamente, en nuestro medio, sino «accidentes» que de tarde en tarde se producen por sorpresa...

2375

El Diario Paysandu Friday July 25, 1924

Last Night's Concert

First of all, it is with the deep and legitimate satisfaction that, we want to highlight the fact that the announced concert of the young Uruguayan guitarist Barreiro, took place last night in the Florencio Sanchez theatre before a grown audience.

Undoubtedly in our public begins to operate in a reaction highly plausible, and it is so as we determine than the artistic demonstrations don't happen in a medium of indifference with what tears ago drowned everything of the spirit. It's definitely not even the conquest, but we are in route to obtain it, and day to day the symptoms that the works proportionate to us, make this prophecy robust, for glorifying the common desire to see completed as soon as possible.

Last night it was, we say now, a very valuable and coronating soirée by the most beautiful of successes, that have taken the spirit of this young artist a current of optimism and encouragement. They applauded him with real enthusiasm, sincere and spontaneously, after hearing him with deep recognition and religious anointing.

Barreiro gave eloquent proof of extraordinary progress, that he has experienced with technique and the magnitude of his interpretive talent. At all times – excepting the *Minuet* by Sor and the two preludes by Tárrega performed in a form that let a certain nervousness be seen, perhaps produced by the first impression in front of the public – the young concert artist maintained a level that only is arrived at in an intimate medium, personal and that demands the total of the sensibilities and of the talent that hoards the spirit and the mind of the player.

Throughout all the program, Barreiro admired for his notable fingering, by the most personal character of his interpretations and by the cleanliness with which he knew how to pull out the sounds of the most daring sheet music pieces, in the performance of *Recuerdos de la Alhambra* by Tárrega, *Celebre capricho Andaluz* by Manjón, in which culminated in a really magnificent form.

The impression that lead us to Barreiro, optimum and decisive, we firmly believe that very soon he has to arrive at the absolute perfection of his medium, already so talented with the will to overcome difficulties for it, which for him there is a reserved seat in the vanguard of great artists.

We know that Barreiro has now proposed to offer a concert in the Ateneo; a decision we applaud.

Soirées of art such as he can offer us aren't wretchedly, in our medium, but rough that from afternoon to afternoon they are produced by surprise.

Diario Moderno

Paysandú, Julio 26 de 1924.

ÓRGANO COLORADO, COMERCIAL, NOTICIOSO, LITERARIO y DE INTERES GENERAL

LAS FIESTAS DE LA MUSICA

EL CONCIERTO DE BARREIRO

Diario Moderno Paysandu Saturday July 26, 1924

The Reunions of Music

The Barreiro Concert

The night before last when Barreiro appeared on the stage of the Florencio Sanchez theatre, one of those great silences; in which appeared to suspend the functions of life, for giving the scene to the free meeting of the souls, prolonging it, smooth, like a shawl of silk, in a weak half-light of the hall.

2377

It had been something substantial, mysterious, that lit up happiness in all the hearts and inundated of kindness of all the looks …..

To tell yourself, of the sublime symbolism of the Rite of *Orpheo*, of embroidering, action and harmony done; like a subterranean gully running coming up suddenly, as a kiss of love and sacrifice, abrogated stones heated by the fever of the sun....

To be purified by the environment. A nervous plaything of fingers pulls out scales as a hug of the soul of the artist to the number of the instrument, they preside, to the austere rite of the Art, officiating the conscience of the artist.

The soul agitates nervously, like an innocent girl, before the fear of the first meeting.

And, when the baptism of the fire of the divinity reaches in the great abstractions of the creative force, to the heart of the artist -- this thrilling and trembling because God also must shake, before the miracle of the light, in the formidable moments of the genesis!

There is silence. And, to move from the nervous pulse and I live scattering with gracious slowness, sweet and gentle; delicate and gallant; like scenes of summer fairs, as a flock of memories that take in their wings the deep romanticism one of our desires, the friendly notes of a minuet.

Then the sparkling grace of some preludes, subtle and caressing, presides over the breathtaking Capricho Arabe by Tárrega.

We expect the deep sensibility of Barreiro offers us its stupendous interpretation. But, there are moments in which, by excess sensibility, that strange harmony ceases between the innervation and the willpower, supporting the imbalance of irksome and unexpected consequences.

But, at times the effect of a shade launched by fatality lays out by contrast the passages of influenced interpretation.to be brighter.

And this happened to Barreiro.

The *vidalita*, this flower of the spiritual life of the countryman, at times melancholic and sad, like dusks in the ….. others, sentimental and at times …. ……………………………(like the lower expectation of the *gaucho*), he ended to first set leaving the spiritual suspense.

And, it's that Barreiro more instinctive than cerebral, sentimental, hermit-like as a *gaucho*, saturated with the life of memories, these variations that perhaps for years of his adolescence, have befuddled his timid spirit in the deep silence of the nights, of the fields....

In the *Testamento de Amelia,* it is felt, a strong creation by Llobet, Barreiro had clear and medium passages. Dealing with a composition essentially subjective, complicated, as the life to which he has spewed out and that breathes and shields illegitimate would wait from a performer, that wasn't its author the revelation of all its mysteries.

All the interpretive capacity of Barreiro manifested, instead with definite and firm character in the *Andante* by Sor.

His execution was impeccable, artistically blended in the changes of its passages, abstract at times, like the clouds of the faraway twilights.

Ensueño is a jewel by Schumann, sweet and serene as a daybreak, fresh and eager as the breeze of the white, like wakening the conscience, didn't have the aptitude ………… In the flight of his music, the joy to be alive…..

I can't explain the scarce success of Barreiro in this composition, in *Recuerdos de la Alhambra*, where the tremolos, muted and opaque notes gave an impression of the undying and miseries.

And I say more above I can't explain by the repeated times we heard, in his intimate performances, masterful demonstrations of this composition which are, casually those of the authors most refined with the musicological morality of Barreiro.

But the public, tht already had vibrated in front of the art of the concert artist, beat their palms and then, the clear and playful notes of a *Jota aragonesa* scattered the jovial and optimistic vibrations.

The miracle had been produced, and until the precise performance of the *Capricho Andaluz* for which Barreiro would reach the background .....

Tribuna Salteña Salto Tuesday August 5, 1924

It was all a artistic soirée – and we're sorry we can't say it was social – because it turned out the public didn't respond in the deserved manner, for the Uruguayan guitarist, Rosendo Barreiro, concert offered us last night.

According to the press, this excellent performer constitutes a real promise for the most selected musical art. And, with all justice, we must say that the commentaries weren't exaggerated, Barreiro, left well seated that he possesses and exquisite temperament, achievable as Agustín Barrios would say, the supreme emotions of the sublime music.

In spite of having begun giving recitals in public just a while ago, he shows that he easily dominates the most difficult classical sheet music and knows how to put the soul of an artist into his interpretations.

In *el testamento de Amelia* by Llobet and in the *Variaciones sobre vidalita*, which he is the author of, he pulled out thunderous applause, because he made the subtle and enrapturing emotions reach the public.

In the *cancion pastoral by de Visee* and the pieces by Tárrega very especially they saw how great his sensibility was.

The *celebre capricho andaluz* by Manjón, ended the concert program like a golden brooch, constituting the best motive for intensely applauding, something that the public did.

In a word, last night Barreiro was eloquent to demonstrate that he awaits great triumphs.

2380

El concierto de anoche

Ante una concurrencia bastante numerosa—si se tiene en cuenta la indiferencia de que siempre ha hecho gala nuestro público cuando de conciertos se trata,—dió anoche su recital el eximio guitarrista compatriota Rosendo Barreiro.

Sin que la admiración que sentimos por este joven y ya consagrado maestro pueda hacer benévolo nuestro juicio, diremos con el crítico musical de nuestro colega «El Plata», «que él posee la escuela de Tárrega y eso basta para que el artista nacional triunfe ante cualquier público por más exigente que sea».

La velada de anoche fué realmente artística, Barreiro desde el principio de la ejecución de su programa demostró tener un gran temperamento musical, que maravilló por la limpidez con que supo arrancar los sonidos en la interpretación de las obras de los grandes maestros, por el alma que puso en todas ellas.

El público que con silencio religioso escuchaba a Barreiro, así lo comprendió ya que al final de cada ejecución lo ovacionó en forma estruendosa. Y cuando el aplauso surge así sincero y expontáneamente de parte de un público selecto como el de anoche, es consagratorio.

Dentro del selecto programa, debemos destacar la culminación de la velada que nos ofreció Barreiro. Ella fué sin duda, en la ejecución de «Recuerdos de la Alhambra» de Tárrega; «Variaciones sobre un tema de Vidalita» de Sinópoli-Barreiro; en la «Góndola Veneciana» de Mendelsohn y en el «Célebre Capricho Andaluz» de Manjón, que hemos de oir seguramente en un próximo concierto, que piensa dar, a pedido de elementos de nuestra sociedad.

N.

El Nacional Salto Tuesday August 5 1924

Last Night's Concert

Before a gathering numerous enough –if you take into account the indifference that is always made when it comes to our public –the eminent guitarist Rosendo Barreiro gave a concert last night.

Without that the admiration we feel for this young and already consecrated maestro can make our judgement charitable, we will say with the music critic of our colleague *"El Plata"* that he possesses the school of Tárrega and that's enough for the national artist to triumph in front of whatever public gathering might exist.

The soirée last night was really artistic, Barreiro from the outset of the performance of his program demonstrated having a great musical temperament, how marvelous was the cleanliness of his playing with how he knew to pull out the sounds in the interpretations of the great masters, and the soul he put in all of them.

The public with its religious silence listened to Barreiro, as they already understood the ending of every piece, they broke out into a thunderous applause. And when the applause surged as such it was sincere and spontaneous on the part of the select public as in the concert last night, it was consecrated.

Within the select program, we can distinguish the culmination of the soirée Barreiro offered. It was without a doubt the rendition of *Recuerdos de la Alhambra* by Tárrega, *Variaciones sobre la tema de Vidalita* by Sinopoli-Barreiro; in the *Gondola Venciana* by Mendelssohn and in the *Celebre Capricho Andaluz* by Manjón, that we surely heard in the next concert, he thinks to give, a request by elements of our society.
N.

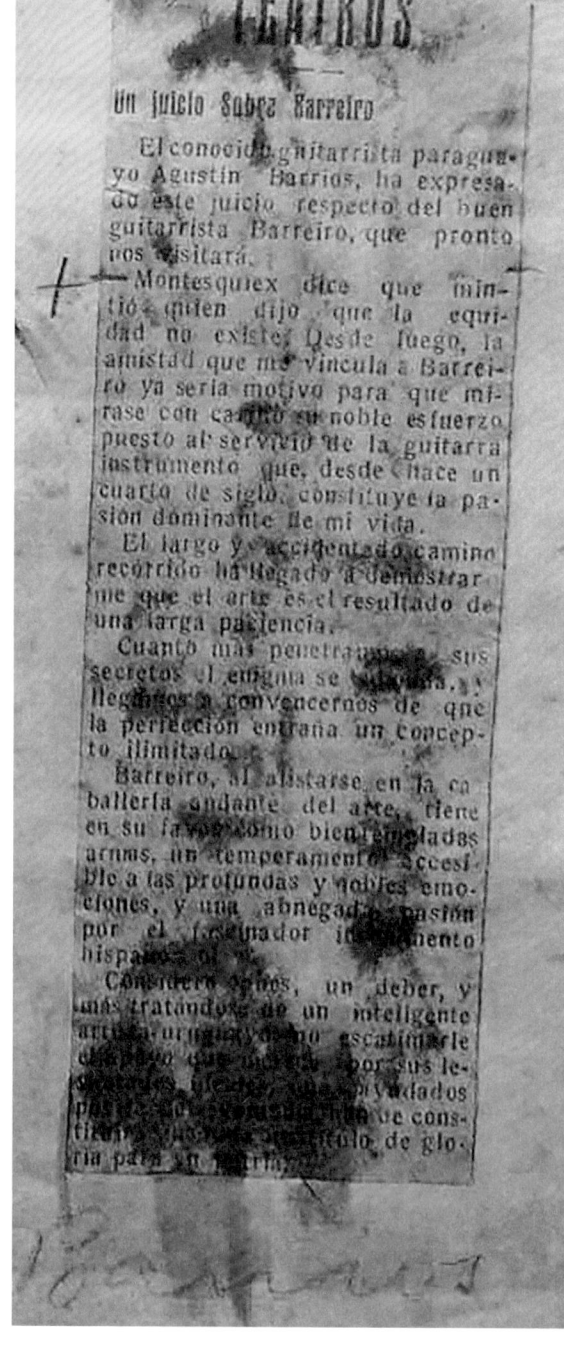

Teatros

A judgement about Barreiro

The known Paraguayan guitarist has expressed a judgement in respect of the good guitarist Barreiro, who will soon visit us.

'Montesquieu says whoever said that the equity doesn't exist had lied, of course the friendship that I link with Barreiro might already be a motive to be seen with affection his noble strength put in service of the guitar, an instrument that, that constitutes the passion for more than a quarter of a century that dominates my life.

The long and rough path has run and reached to demonstrate to me that the art is a result of a long patience.

How much more can its secrets be penetrated? The enigma it deepens. And we come to be convinced that the essence of perfection is a limited concept.

Barreiro, he is enlisted in the cavalry walking of the art, he has in his favor as well restrained arms an attainable temperament to the deep and noble emotions, and a unselfish passion for the fascinating Hispanic instrument.

I consider by reason of, a duty, being treated as an intelligent Uruguayan artist not skimping the support that he deserves by his raised ideals, that helped by his perseverance have constituted without a doubt a title of glory for his nation.'

Organo defensor del Partido Colorado y de los intereses deptales.

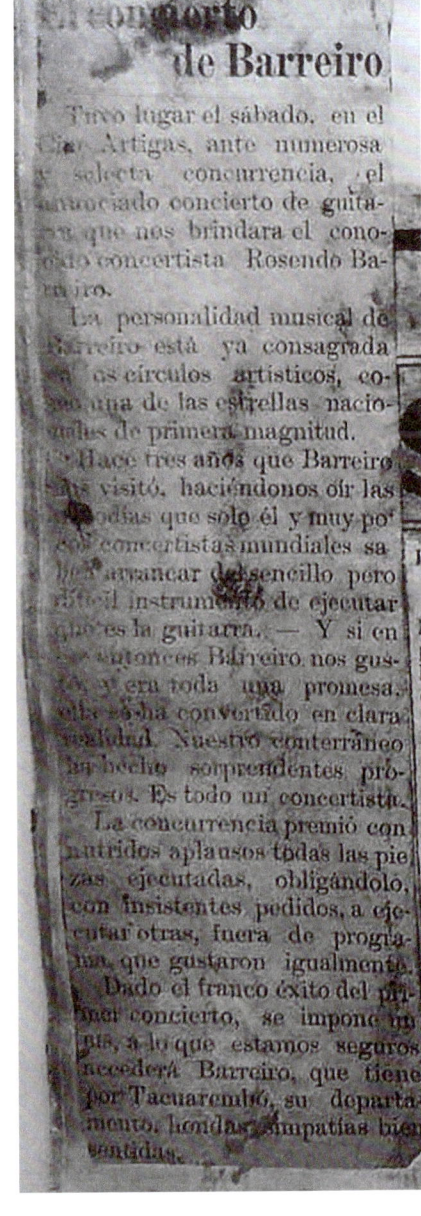

Tribuna Battlista

Barreiro's Concert

   The announced concert of the known concert guitarist Rosendo Barreiro took place on Saturday, in the Cine Artigas, before the numerous select gathering that toasted him.

   The musical personality of Barreiro who is already a consecrated figure in the artistic circles, is one of the national stars of first rank.

   It's been three years since Barreiro visited us, letting us hear the melodies that only he and very few other world-renowned concert artists know how to pull out of the simple but difficult instrument that is the guitar. And if we enjoyed him then, and he was all the promise to be he has converted to a clear reality for us. Our compatriot has made surprising progress. He is a complete concert artist.

   The gathering awarded him with abundant applause for all the pieces performed, obligating him, with insistent requests, to play encores, outside of the program that they enjoyed equally.

   Given the frank success of the first concert, it imposed another, to which we are sure Barreiro will agree to, that has for Tacuarembo, its province, become a deeply held sentiment.

Defensa Popular Salto Friday August 15, 1924

Guitar Concert

Monday the 18th the celebrated concert guitarist Rosendo Barreiro will give a second guitar concert, the meritorious artist who is a true honor to the country by his virtuoso qualities as an interpreter in the difficult art of music.

Barreiro has triumphed with notable success on the national stages with the highest reputation as a concert guitarist.

A week ago the public in Salto had the opportunity to hear his first concert, that there is no doubt it will be a motive to consecrate the success of the next recital he will give on Monday, with which will prove that Salto always reckons and awards the highest demonstrations of superior art.

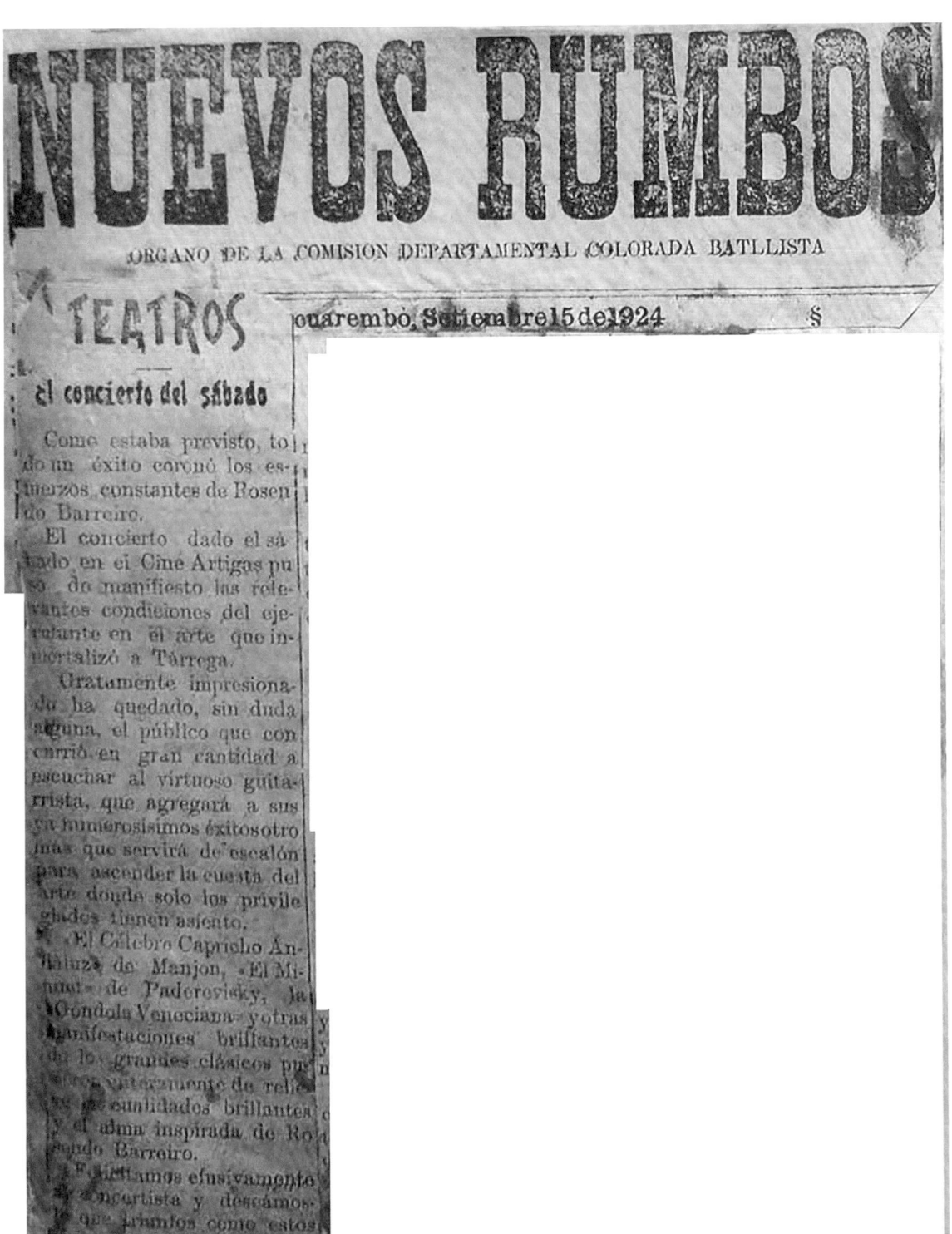

NUEVOS RUMBOS

ORGANO DE LA COMISION DEPARTAMENTAL COLORADA BATLLISTA

Tacuarembó, Setiembre 15 de 1924

TEATROS

el concierto del sábado

Como estaba previsto, todo un éxito coronó los esfuerzos constantes de Rosendo Barreiro.

El concierto dado el sábado en el Cine Artigas puso de manifiesto las relevantes condiciones del ejecutante en el arte que inmortalizó a Tárrega.

Gratamente impresionado ha quedado, sin duda alguna, el público que concurrió en gran cantidad a escuchar al virtuoso guitarrista, que agregará a sus ya numerosísimos éxitos otro más que servirá de escalón para ascender la cuesta del arte donde solo los privilegiados tienen asiento.

El Célebre Capricho Andaluz de Manjón, «El Minuet» de Paderewsky, la «Gondola Veneciana» y otras manifestaciones brillantes de los grandes clásicos pusieron enteramente de relieve las cualidades brillantes y el alma inspirada de Rosendo Barreiro.

Felicitamos efusivamente al concertista y deseámosle que triunfos como estos sigan marcando la estela luminosa de su vocación.

Nuevos Rumbos Tacuarembo Monday September 15, 1924, reporting about the September 13th concert.

From the Saturday concert

As was foreseen, everything was a coronating continuing success of Rosendo Barreiro.

The concert given on Saturday in the Cine Artigas, showed the relevant abilities of the performer in the art immortalized by Tárrega.

Freely impressed he has stayed without a doubt, the public has gathered in large groups to hear the virtuoso guitarist, who adds already to his numerous successes that serve more as a step to ascend the upward slope of the art where only the privileged have seats.

The *Celebre Capricho Andaluza* by Manjón, the *Minuet* by Paderewski, the *Gondola Veneciana* and others brilliant pieces of the great classics put entirely in relief the brilliant qualities of the inspired soul of Rosendo Barreiro.

We exuberantly congratulate the concert guitarist and we wish him that the triumphs such as these continue marking the luminous star of his career.

Tribuna Blanca (probably Tacuarembo)

Rosendo Barreiro

The first performance of Barreiro took place on Saturday in the Artigas, the artist revealed to us.

His masterful interpretations, his exquisite artistic taste, the deep sentiment with which he plays the guitar, attract with all justice the interest and admiration of the audience.

In Barreiro, the young artist that recently began to feel the encouraging impulse of the triumph, he shows without difficulties an excellent memory in the difficult art of the guitar. His artistic personality is distinguished with characteristic of neatness in his performance.

Next Thursday, Barreiro the concert guitarist will offer his second concert in the Cine Artigas, in combination with the film.

Imparcial Thursday September 18, 1924

The Barreiro Concert

As we announced in the salon of the Club Tacuarembo the concert of the celebrated artist Rosendo Barreiro took place, whose many successes he has picked up in his recent visits to the cities of Salto, Paysandu and Tacuarembo. This artistic festival, that was attended by our most distinguished families, took place in an interesting social reunion.

Barreiro performed with an elevated artistic sentiment and a precious cleanliness the chosen works by Tárrega, Paderewski, Chopin, Schumann, Mozart, Albeniz, Barreiro, etc. highlighting once again, his quality of privileged difficult art to which he dedicates himself.

The Concert Artist Barreiro

We have had the occasion to know and appreciate him a lot, of his own personality, and as an artist. It deals with an educated young adult, an engaging and suggesting figure, a modest one is to exaggerate and with an uncommon illustration. That is the man,

Of the artist, it almost doesn't open us to being concerned, as much as by the fear of not being competent to judge him as to offend his modesty with our praise, which, by considering he deserves it, we don't hesitate to make a tribute to him.

We need to conserve our opinion as to his respect, and good or bad we give it.

We have heard him, not only in a public concert, but also in intimate moments where without fear of the critics the artist shows such as, dissipated of inspiration and talent without compromise nor remorse.

To be heard, we could appreciate the true dominion that he has over the guitar whose strings vibrate, with a sweetness, an agility, with a precise technique of admirable performance.

Of his kindness we could hear *Minuetto* by Paderewski, *Asturias* by Albeniz, the *Gavotta* by Lysistrata, the *Andante* from the *Symphony Patetica* by Beethoven, a *prelude "Endecha"* by Tárrega, a precious *Jota* by Arcas, a stupendous Rhapsody and *Aires andaluces*, that he improvised and had the kindness to dedicate the time to play for us.

It wasn't only us who enjoyed the pleasure to hear these pieces by Barreiro in the room at the Hotel Central where he was staying, but also the numerous persons that walked in front of the open balcony who could participate in the unexpected concert.

We're not prodigious in applause but don't throw away the occasion to applaud if there's a reason for that, as an enthusiastic homage to Barreiro, there is the motive of work.

And because of that we did it.

El Diario Montevideo Saturday September 20, 1924

The Guitarist Barreiro

Obtained a Great Success in Tacuarembo

The celebrated guitarist Rosendo Barreiro, whose praiseworthy aptitude as a performer and rare abilities as an educated and delicate interpreter. The high eulogies he has deserved come from the incomparable Miguel Llobet, Two months ago, he made a tour of the capitals of the interior provinces of the country, in which he obtained a just and legitimate success.

Presently he is in Tacuarembo, since he just offered three concerts in the elegant Cine Artigas, where all the aficionados of the good music had gathered.

The program, integrated by works of Tárrega, Albeniz, Paderewski, Granados, and many other renowned composers, Barreiro has deserved the hottest applause by the attendees for his selection as an excellent interpreter.

It gave us pleasure steadfastness for the dreams achieved, by our compatriot, who in more than one opportunity, we have had the satisfaction to applaud.

It won't be difficult, given the enthusiasm that those concerts have awakened among the lovers of good music, and the decided support of the public for the guitarist Barreiro in his upcoming concert in Tacuarembo.

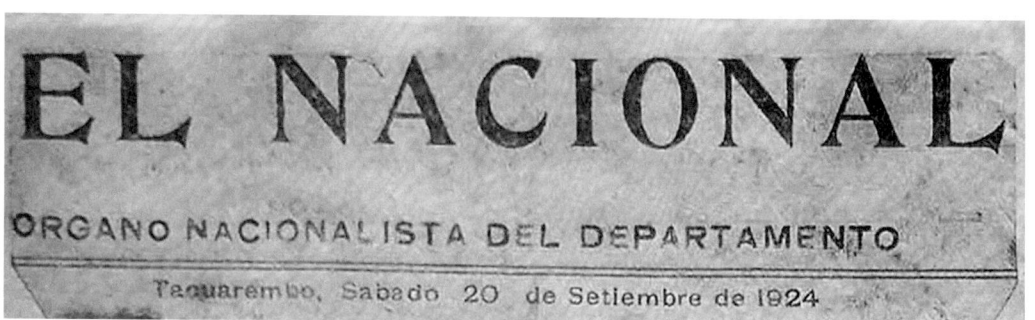

El Nacional Tacuarembo Saturday September 20, 1924

The Concert Guitarist Barreiro

On Thursday the engaging artist Rosendo Barreiro offered his second concert, accenting once again the warranted prestige of one who enjoys it as a real principal of the guitar.

Soon he will offer a performance as a benefit for the Costurero Escolar (School).

Teatros

Rosendo Barreiro

His concert tomorrow

The notable concert guitarist Rosendo Barreiro, with so much ability and captivating admiration of our public in his first musical performance on Saturday, tomorrow he offers us his second concert in the Artigas.

Taken for granted the high artistic personality of Barreiro, which is all consecrated in the difficult art of the guitar, and the awakened interest in our public by the brilliant interpretations performed by the intelligent countryman, we don't doubt that tomorrow we will see in the ample salon of the Artigas one of his best days.

Imparcial Undated Thursday September 25, 1924

Concert apparently on Tuesday September 23, 1924

The Barreiro Concert

On Tuseday the announced concert took place of the guitarist Barreiro, a benefit for the Costurero Escolar held in the Cine Artigas.

The notable artistic abilities of Barreiro who has already revealed himself as a true privileged one of the difficult art, of the guitar, as is the good destiny of the beneficiary, they were a sufficient cause for that the Artigas will be found in his best days.

Imparcial Undated Thursday September 25, 1924

Concert apparently on Tuesday September 23, 1924

With a great success, the young guitarist Rosendo Barreiro offered his first concert in the "Cine Artigas". He will offer a second performance on Thursday.

NUEVOS RUMBOS

ORGANO DE LA COMISION DEPARTAMENTAL COLORADA BATLLISTA

Tacuarembó, Setiembre 25 de 1924

Nuevos Rumbos Tacuarembo Thursday September 25, 1924

El concierto del martes

Por tercera vez Rosendo Barreiro se presentó el martes en la sala del Artigas a dar su último concierto en esta, a beneficio de la benemérita Institución del Costurero Escolar.

Y a la verdad que una vez más el numeroso y selecto público que asistió a la sala del teatrito de la Plaza Colón ha gustado momentos de intensa emoción, ya que Barreiro supo esa noche arrancar de su instrumento las notas más sentidas, ejecutando con precisión admirable y técnica insuperable dificilísimas interpretaciones de los famosos clásicos Paderewsky, Manjón, Schubert, Albeniz, etc. etc.

Triunfos como el del martes son los muchos que conquistará Barreiro en su carrera de artista, que se le presenta brillante por el poder genial de su vocación.

Felicitamos al eximio concertista, que ha sabido, embellecer con ritmos melodiosos, las manifestaciones hermosas del arte musical.

The Tuesday Concert

For the third time Rosendo Barreiro was presented on Tuesday in the Artigas hall to give his last concert, a benefit for the Institution del Costurero Escolar.

And the truth is that once again numerous and select public that attended the hall of the small theatre on the Plaza Colon enjoyed the moments of intense emotion, already that Barreiro knew that evening how to pull out the most heartfelt notes on his instrument, performing the most difficult interpretations of Paderewski, Manjón, Schubert, Albeniz, etc. with admirable precision and unsurpassable technique.

Triumphs like that on Tuesday are many that Barreiro conquered in his artistic career that he brilliantly presents by the genius power of his vocation.

We congratulate the eminent concert guitarist, that has known, how to embellish with melodic rhythms, the beautiful demonstrations of the musical art.

Tribuna Batllista

Found among us is the celebrated countryman concert guitarist Rosendo Barreiro

He will offer several concerts in the Teatro Escayola, that promise to take on brilliant proportions.

An opinion of this son of Tacuarembo by Dr. Emilio Frugoni.

Un excelente guitarrista uruguayo

Debutará el jueves en Paysandú

Se encuentra entre nosotros, procedente de la vecina ciudad del Salto, el señor Rosendo Barreiro, talentoso guitarrista uruguayo a quien nuestro público ha tenido ya oportunidad de oir.

Según hemos leído en diversas crónicas de los más recientes conciertos de Barreiro, éste ha progresado notablemente en su arte al punto de causar verdadera admiración el dominio que de su difícil instrumento tiene.

Pero, con más autoridad que nosotros, hablará del joven ejecutante el celebrado guitarrista paraguayo Agustín Barrios, quien ha vertido a su respecto el siguiente elogioso comentario:

«Montesquieu dice que la equidad no existe. Desde luego, la amistad que me vincula a Barreiro ya sería motivo para que mirase con cariño su noble esfuerzo puesto al servicio de la guitarra, instrumento que, desde hace un cuarto de siglo, constituye la pasión dominante de mi vida.

«El largo y accidentado camino recorrido ha llegado a demostrarme que el arte es el resultado de una larga paciencia.

«Cuanto más penetramos sus secretos el enigma se ahonda, y llegamos a convencernos de que la perfección entraña un concepto ilimitado.

«Barreiro, al alistarse en la caballería andante del arte, tiene en su favor como bien templadas armas, un temperamento accesible a las más profundas y nobles emociones, y una abnegada pasión por el fascinador instrumento hispano.

«Considero pues, un deber, y más tratándose de un inteligente artista uruguayo, no escatimarle el apoyo que merece por sus levantados ideales, que, ayudados por la perseverancia, han de constituir, sin duda, un título de gloria para su patria.»

El señor Barreiro nos ofrecerá, el 24 del corriente, en el «Florencio Sánchez», un concierto en el que podremos apreciar la calidad de su arte.

En este concierto hará la presentación del guitarrista un intelectual sanducero, quien disertará a la vez sobre algún tópico artístico.

Como se vé, múltiples son los motivos que garantizan la bondad de este concierto del guitarrista Barreiro, al que deseamos una feliz estada entre nosotros.

El Telegrafo

An Excellent Uruguayan Guitarist

He will debut in Paysandu on Thursday

We find among us, coming from the neighboring city of Salto, Mr. Rosendo Barreiro, a talented Uruguayan guitarist to whom our public has had the opportunity to hear.

We have read according to several dailies of the most recent concert by Barreiro, he has been progressing notably in his art to the point of causing real admiration for his dominion over the difficult instrument he has.

But, with more authority than us, Agustín Barrios, the celebrated Paraguayan guitarist will speak of the young performer who has sprung up in his respect to the following praiseworthy commentary:

'Montesquiex says that the equity doesn't exist, of course the friendship that I link with Barreiro might already be a motive to be seen with affection his noble strength put in service of the guitar, an instrument that, that constitutes the passion for more than a quarter of a century that dominates my life.

The long and rough path has run and reached to demonstrate to me that the art is a result of a long patience.

How much more can its secrets be penetrated? The enigma it deepens. And we come to be convinced that the essence of perfection is a limited concept.

Barreiro, he is enlisted in the cavalry walking of the art, he has in his favor as well restrained arms an attainable temperament to the deep and noble emotions, and a unselfish passion for the fascinating Hispanic instrument.

I consider by reason of, a duty, being treated as an intelligent Uruguayan artist not skimping the support that he deserves by his raised ideals, that helped by his perseverance have constituted without a doubt a title of glory for his nation.'

Mr. Barreiro offers us on the 24th of the current month, in the Florencio Sanchez theatre, a concert in which we will be able to appreciate the quality of his art.

In this concert will be the presentation of the guitarist, a sanducero intellectual, who will speak at once about some artistic topic.

As you see, many are the motives that guarantee the good nature of this concert of the guitarist Barreiro, to whom we wish a happy stay among us.

El Dia Thursday January 8, 1925

Guitar Concert

Last night in the teatro Artigas, the announced guitar concert by the eminent Uruguayan artist Rosendo Barreiro took place.

This virtuoso of the guitar, performed the select program that had been put together for those of the exquisite cultural art brilliantly.

The public attended, which, sadly didn't respond in the manner we expected to an act so great and few times seen among us, to Barreiro the prodigious magician of the guitar, of a frenzied and justified applause in several performances.

The Guitarist Rosendo Barreiro (From the same newspaper.)

After having mad an advantageous tour of the cities of Brazil and Argentina the excellent Uruguayan guitarist Rosendo Barreiro returned to Montevideo, who has proposed some performances.

El Plata Thursday February 5, 1925

The Guitarist Barreiro

Found among us now is our compatriot and celebrated Uruguayan guitarist Mr. Barreiro, who has just returned from his tour of Argentina, Brazil and Uruguay.

Slated on a date real soon Barreiro will offer a concert in one of our principal halls. He will also offer a recital to those in the prison Carcel Ponotenciaria

Imparcial

In the Liceo

Barreiro Concert.

Organized by the Director of the Liceo Departmental Mr. Jaime Borbonet, and having taken place on Sunday afternoon, in a hall of this cultural institution, an interesting performance of guitar entrusted to the intelligent compatriot concert artist Mr. Rosendo Barreiro, in front of a select and numerous gathering.

The young concert artist had the opportunity to demonstrate again, his relevant abilities as an artist of soul and as a notable performer, that can already offer a lot and who promises yet more, in the difficult art to which he is dedicated.

To an insistent request of the gathering, these men also played besides: Doctor Antonio Urta y Rocca and Captain Americo Castillos, notable educators of this art of the *"Vihuela".*:

All of them were enthusiastically applauded.

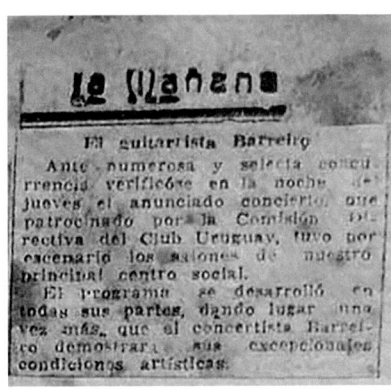

La Mañana

The Guitarist Barreiro

Before a numerous and select gathering verifying on Thursday evening the announced concert that are patronized by the Comision Directiva of the Club Uruguay, had on the stage of the hall of our principal headquarters.

The concert came about completely, showing once again, that the concert guitarist Barreiro demonstrated his characteristic artistic abilities.

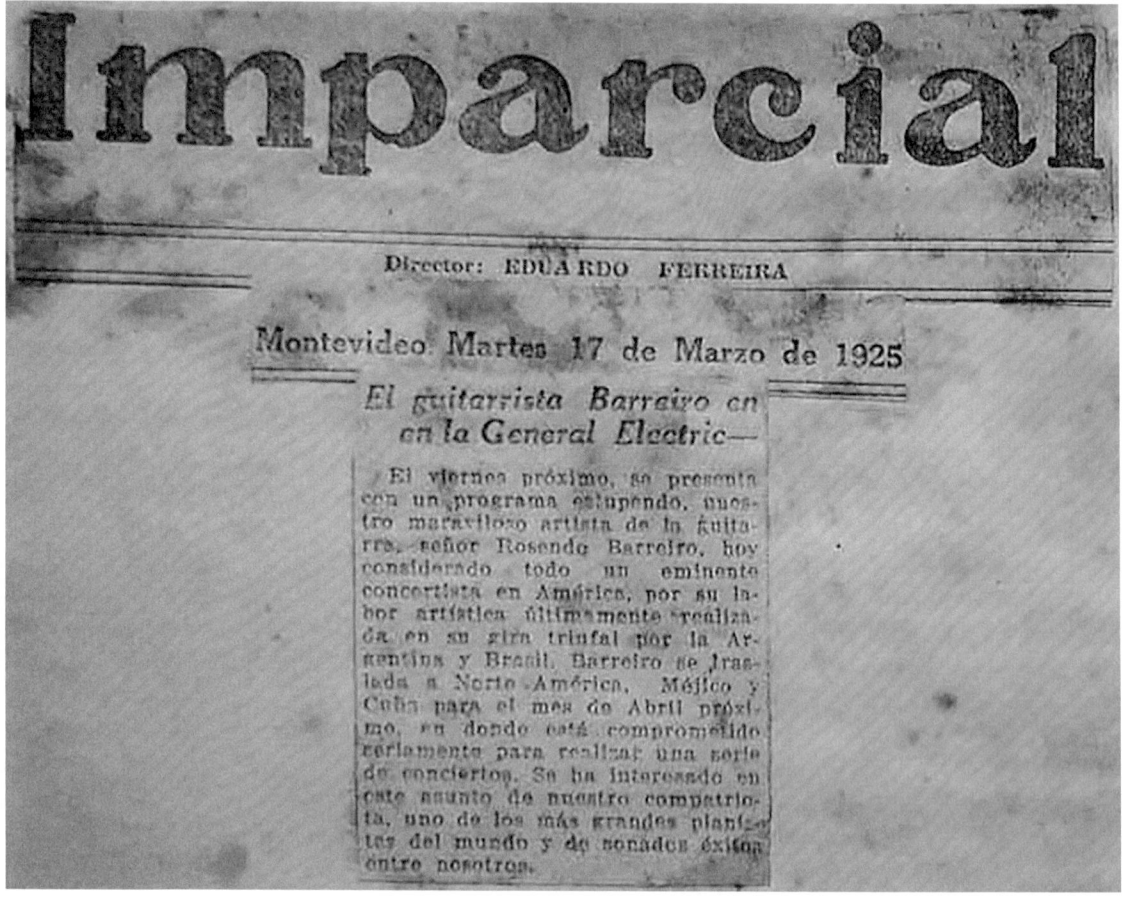

Imparcial Tuesday March 17, 1925

The Guitarist Barreiro at General Electric

Next Friday, a stupendous program with our marvelous artist of the guitar Mr. Rosendo Barreiro, today he is considered an eminent concert artist in South America, by his artistic labor of his latest tour of Argentina and Brazil. Barreiro will travel to Mexico and Cuba in the month of April, where he is contracted to perform a series of concerts there. There has been interest in this affair of our compatriot, one of the greatest pianists (sic) guitarists in the world and a sonorous success among us.

Un celebrado concertista uruguayo
Señor Resende Barreiro

En el vasto y difícil dominio del arte de la guitarra, Barreiro es un previlegiado. Su vocación es genial y estupenda; sus condiciones artísticas, las del reconocido temperamento exquisito; sus aptitudes de intérprete son magistrales y sorprendentes: el sonoro cordaje de la guitarra en manos de Barreiro, revela a un virtuoso del arte que sabe encender en su alma la chispa augusta del arte, a la par que volcar en cada motivo, en cada tema, su sensibilidad arrobadora. Uno de sus críticos,—Emilio Frugoni—dijo:

«No parece que tañera en verdad una guitarra, sino más bien que hiciera vibrar con la acción de sus manos la fibra de su propio corazón: los movimientos interiores del alma parecen comunicarse, por la vía de sus dedos, a las cuerdas, cuyas voces hablan siempre con las voces íntimas, de quien las escucha».

La corriente emotiva se establece y el efluvioso poder del artista subyuga provocando la

preciar el mérito que sella el dolor de parte de sus hijos.

—Recordemos que el muy celebrado concertista mundial Barrios ha indicado a Barreiro como su igual en el manejo del supremo arte sonoro.

¡Guay! que la declaración, en su ingenuidad y sinceridad puede llevar su secreto.

Barreiro lleva en sí la virtualidad de sobreponerse mañana á sus eximias condiciones de artista; y quizás, entonces, Barreiro no llevará cambio para retribuir a Barrios, a menos que peque de sentido real para avalorar su arte.

Barreiro hablará más claro al mundo con sus seguros triunfos cuando lleve su arte allende las fronteras de su patria.—Su puesto—estoy seguro—será debidamente laureado en el concierto universal del Arte.—Debe abandonar el Uruguay, para que éste reconozca con la consagración extranjera el ilustre nombre de un artista, que es su hijo.—Debe abandonar el Uruguay, y recorrer el Mundo con la fé del caballero cruzado del Arte resuelto a salvar todos los sacrificios que importe la consagración de un nombre en el que siempre estará el Uruguay, pero el Uruguay ingrato, que desamparó a un hijo inteligente é ilustre.

Las patrias deberán brindar expontáneamente su apoyo a hijos como Barreiro.

¡Desgraciadamente, todas las patrias resultan, más o menos ingratas, por imperfección del linaje humano!

Un Celebrado concertista uruguayo Señor. Rosendo Barreiro

A Celebrated Uruguayan Concert Artist Mr. Rosendo Barreiro

In the vast and difficult dominion of the art of the guitar, Barreiro is a privileged person. His vocation is brilliant and stupendous; his artistic abilities, those of the recognized temperament are exquisite; his aptitude for interpretation is masterful and surprising; the sonorous chords in the hands of Barreiro, reveal a virtuoso of the art who knows how to set fire to the soul the stately spark of the art, at the same time can overturn in every motif, in every theme, his enrapturing sensibility.

One of his critics, Emilio Frugoni (Uruguayan socialist politician, lawyer, poet, essayist, and journalist) said:

'It doesn't appear that he is really playing a guitar, but rather that he is actually vibrating the fiber of his own heart with the action of his hands; the interior movements of the soul appear to be communicating, by the way of his fingers, to the strings, whose voices always speak with the intimate voices, by whom listens to them.

The established emotive current and the emanation can be by the artist ... provoking.......

......appreciate the merit that seals the pain of the part of his children.

We remember that the very celebrated worldwide renowned concert guitarist Barrios has indicated to Barreiro as his equal in the directing of the supreme sonorous art.

Cool! that the statement, on his ingeniousness and sincerity can take your secret.

Barreiro carries in his potentiality of overcoming tomorrow his blameless abilities as an artist; and maybe then Barreiro will not bring change to give back to Barrios, unless he sticks in a real sense to appreciate his art.

Barreiro will speak clearer to the world with his sure triumphs when they carry his art passed the borders of his country. His position / setting -- I am sure —will be properly honored in the universal concert of the Art. He must abandon Uruguay, for which he might receive recognition with the foreign consecration of his illustrious name as an artist. He must abandon Uruguay and run around the World with the feudal horseman crossed in the Art unfaltering to save all the sacrifices that amount in the consecration of a name in him that will always be in Uruguay, but ungrateful Uruguay, that impoverishes an intelligent and illustrious son.

The countries must spontaneously toast their support to sons such as Barreiro.

Unfortunately, all countries turn out, more or less ungrateful, by the imperfection of the human lineage!

El Diario Montevideo Monday April 20, 1925

The Guitarist Barreiro

He leaves tomorrow for Brazil, in whose principal cities he will offer interesting concerts, our compatriot the guitarist Rosendo Barreiro, virtuoso of excellent abilities well known by our public that has applauded him in several opportunities.

Barreiro puts clear felt music a fine artistic temperament a dominion of the technique that make of him an intelligent conscientious interpreter, a capacity to spring up, with effective esthetic, the most difficult compositions.

In his repertory, a vast collection along with the best great classics the most inspired works of South American musicians.

We wish the esteemed guitarist a complete success in front of the Brazilian public.

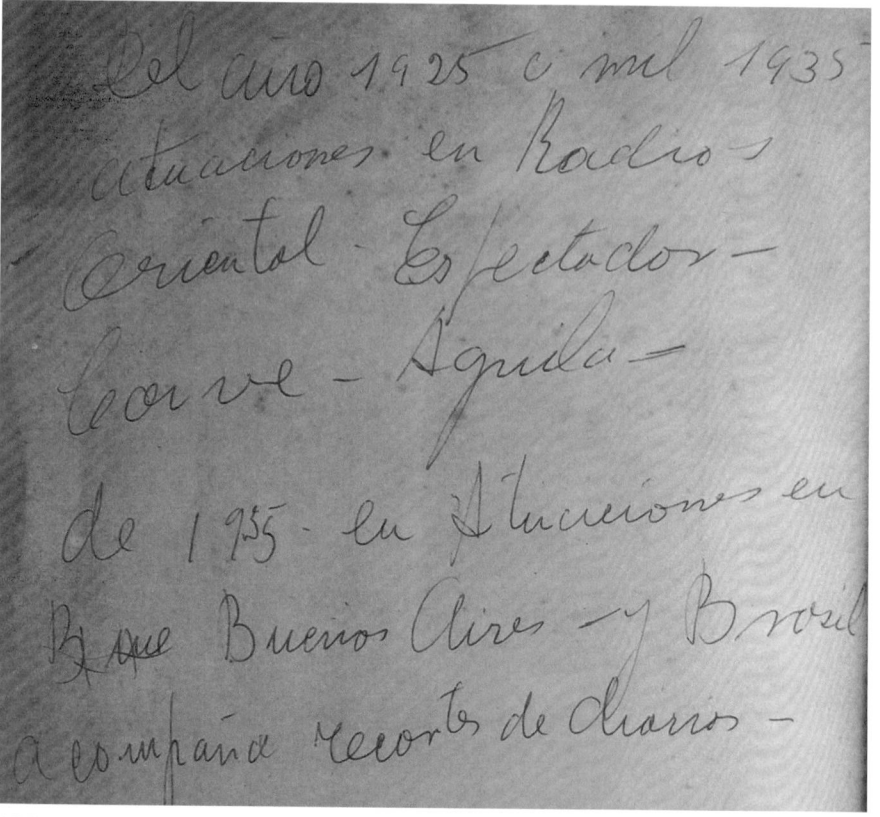

Censor April 22 1925

Barreiro

The known and genius guitarist, within a few days will spend a night of art with us – an evening of good music – in which the guitar will sing its sorrows and laugh its happiness plucked by whom puts his soul on its strings. –It is the spirit of Barreiro – a select and bohemian spirit who can only produce and feel beautiful things. – Tomorrow *"Censor"* will dress up its pages with artistic critiques about our distinguished guest.

1925 to 1935 handwritten

radio performance mentions

"The year 1925 to 1935

Performances on Radio Oriental, Espectador, Carve, Aguila

From 1935 Performances in Buenos Aires and Brazil

accompanied by clippings from Daily Newspapers.

1925 to 1935 handwritten radio performance mentions
"The year 1925 to 1935
Performances on Radio Oriental, Espectador, Carve, Aguila
From 1935 Performances in Buenos Aires and Brazil accompanied by clippings from Daily Newspapers.

Imparcial

y Administración:
ENDENCIA 818 A 824   Director: EDUARDO FERREIRA

El guitarrista Barreiro

Parte a realizar una temporada en la capital paulistana el notable guitarrista compatriota Barreiro, cuya genialidad se impone al alma de los públicos, haciéndola vibrar de emoción al compás de las modulaciones de las cuerdas, acariciadas o sacudidas por sus dedos de mago de la armonía.

Emilio Pujol, guitarrista de fama mundial, en juicio dedicado a nuestro compatriota, afirma que hay en este un artista de alma y corazón. ¿Por qué triunfa Barreiro? –se pregunta; y añade; porque, como artista, posee personalidad y tiene un temperamento muy accesible a las grandes emociones.

Cuando Llobet estuvo en Montevideo por primera vez, tuvo oportunidad de oír al inolvidable Koch, guitarrista de mucha escuela y de impecable ejecución; y también hubo de oír a Barreiro. Sus juicios dejaron un saldo muy favorable a nuestro compatriota. Según Llobet, Koch es un incomparable maestro, conocedor minucioso de la escuela de Tárrega. En cambio, de Barreiro dijo que tiene temperamento artístico y que será, en lo futuro, un concertista de alma.

Barrios, a pesar de ser un revolucionario, se expresó de Barreiro llamándolo un espíritu hondamente selecto, que no sólo impresiona al público, sino también a los más grandes artistas y críticos del arte musical.

Quien como Barreiro ha merecido elogios de Puyol y de Segovia puede confiar en su buen éxito superior ante cualquier público que se presente para lucir sus dotes, que van mucho más allá de la pericia del ejecutante: van al corazón de los auditorios.

Por eso aguardamos las más halagüeñas noticias de sus próximas audiciones en San Pablo.

Imparcial The Guitarist Barreiro

He left to make a season in the capital Sao Paulo the notable guitarist our compatriot Barreiro, whose genius imposes to the soul of the public, making the emotion vibrate to the rhythms of the modulations of the strings, caressed or brought out by the fingers of the magician of the harmony.

Emilio Pujol, the guitarist of worldwide fame, in a critique dedicated to our compatriot, affirms that there is in this artist the soul and heart. Why does Barreiro triumph? – is asked; and added; why as an artist, he possesses personality and has a temperament very attainable to the great emotions.

When Llobet was in Montevideo for the first time, he had the opportunity to hear the unforgettable Koch, a very educated guitarist and impeccable performer and he was also able to hear Barreiro. His critiques left a very favorable tally of our compatriots. According to Llobet, Koch was an incomparable maestro, who knew the Tárrega school to a fine degree. Instead, of Barreiro he said that he has an artistic temperament and who will be in the future, a concert artist of soul.

Barrios, despite being a revolutionary, expressed of Barreiro naming him a deeply select spirit, who not only impressed the public, but also the greatest artists and critics of the musical art.

Who such as Barreiro has received the praise of Pujol and Segovia can entrust in his good superior success before whatever public presented to shine his endowments, which are going to show much more of the skill of the performer there; going to show more of the heart to the audience.

Because of that we are going to wait for the best flattering notices of his upcoming performances in Sao Paulo.

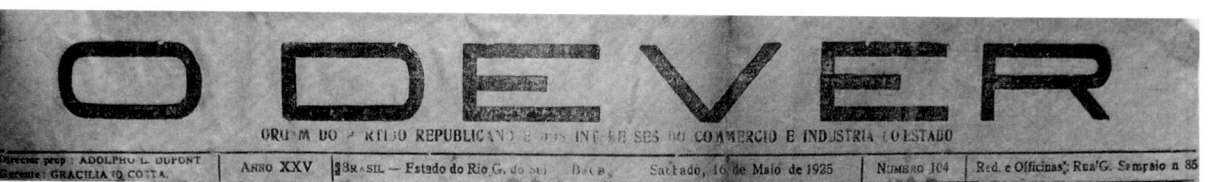

O DEVER

ORGÃM DO PARTIDO REPUBLICANO E DOS INTERESSES DO COMMERCIO E INDUSTRIA DO ESTADO

| Director-prop.: ADOLPHO L. DUPONT — Gerente: GRACILIANO COSTA | ANNO XXV | BRASIL — Estado do Rio G. do Sul — Bagé | Sabbado, 16 de Maio de 1925 | NUMERO 104 | Red. e Officinas: Rua G. Sampaio n. 85 |

GUITARRISTA BARREIRO

Constituiu uma nota do mais apurado valor artístico o concerto que á nossa culta sociedade proporcionou, hontem á noite, o festejado guitarrista uruguayo, sr. Rosendo Barreiro.

O nosso Theatro Avenida estava animado por uma numerosa e selectíssima assistencia, que não regateou os mais calorosos applausos ao brilhante artista que faz do difficilimo instrumento verdadeiros milagres. Um programma da mais alta responsabilidade foi executado com inexcedivel perfeição.

Barreiro é um artista na expressão mais completa do vocabulo. O seu concerto de hontem foi um grande triumpho, que se reproduzirá com maior ruído, em toda a sua tournée pelo nosso paiz.

O Dever Rio Grande do Sul, Brazil Saturday May 16, 1925

Portuguese translation by Randy Osborne

The Guitarist Barreiro

It forms a note to serve pure artistic value a concert that honored our cultured society last night, made by the Uruguayan guitarist Mr. Rosendo Barreiro.

In our Theatro Avenida animated by a numerous and select gathering, that didn't argue over the hottest applause for the brilliant artist who played the most difficult instrument truly miraculously. A program of the highest responsibility was performed in an exceedingly perfect manner.

Barreiro is an artist with the most complete vocabulary, his concert honored him with a great triumph, that produced the noisiest applause, of all his tour in our country.

2404

CORREIO DO SUL

BAGÉ — Estado do Rio Grande do Sul — Brasil ‖ ANNO XI ‖ JORNAL QUOTIDIANO MATUTINO ‖ NUMERO 3.188 ‖ Sabbado, 16 de maio de

ROSENDO BARREIRO, guitarrista uruguayo —

Alcançou um verdadeiro éxito o recital musical do notavel artista da guitarra, sr. Rosendo Barreiro.

Dispondo das qualidades necessarias aos verdadeiros artistas, Barreiro agrada, sensibiliza e arrebata o auditorio desde os primeiros momentos. Por isso conseguindo uma bôa casa e um excellente auditorio, Barreiro impressionou favoravelmente desde os primeiros momentos alcançando franco successo.

Além disso, além das musicas classicas do programma, Barreiro brindou o auditorio com mais uma musica popular ao fim de cada parte, sendo immensamente victoriado.

Sendo adiantada a hora, amanhã, com outros pormenores daremos melhor noticia do bello recital de Barreiro.

Correio Do Sul Rio Grande do Sul Saturday May 16, 1925

Portuguese translation by Randy Osborne

Rosendo Barreiro Uruguayan Guitarist

Mr. Rosendo Barreiro, the notable artist of the guitar has attained a real success of his musical recital.

Displaying the necessary qualities of our true artists, Barreiro pleased, sensitized and grabbed the audience from the first moments. By that, achieving a good house and an excellent audience, Barreiro favorably impressed them from the outset getting a frank success. Besides, the classic music of the program, Barreiro toasted the audience with the most popular music to the end of every set, being immensely victorious.

This being put forth now, tomorrow with other details we will give the best report of the beautiful recital of Barreiro.

Luego de un tiempo de silencio, y después de haber terminado una

Adagio from the Tocata in C major for organ. Bach-Bussoni.
Preludio. Bach-Segovia;
Gigue (1686) Roberto de Visée.
Barcarola. Mendelssohn-Segovia.

Pavana (1535) Luis Milan
Preludio Chopin-Tárrega
Andantino (1780-1839) Sor
Capricho arabe Tárrega
Choros Villa-Lobos

The Uruguayan Guitarist Rosendo Barreiro reinitiates his activities

After a time of silence, and after having finished a brilliant tour of Brazil, the excellent Uruguayan concert guitarist Mr. Barreiro, has dedicated to completing his art in an intensive manner, to the effect of receiving lessons from Llobet and Segovia.

Presently he has finished this cycle of perfecting his technique, and he has programed a series of performances and a concert.

He has already prepared the programs of his first two recitals that will be the following:

As you can see, both programs include works of great encouragement and difficult performance, which undoubtedly will benefit an absolute success for our compatriot, whose reinitiation of these activities have been awaited with outstanding interest by our newspapers.

After a cycle of recitals and his concert, Barreiro expects to make a tour of Brazil again.

Fué Exitosa la Presentación del Guitarrista Barreiro

OFRECIO AYER SU PRIMER CONCIERTO EN EL TEATRO CORRIENTES

Rosendo Barreiro ofreció ayer, en el teatro Corrientes, su anunciado primer concierto programado a base de una calificada selección de autores, la que reveló por sí sola la cultura musical y el depurado gesto del concertista. Inició el programa con la Suite en Re Menor, de Roberto de Visco, escrita en el año 1686, y dedicada a S. M. el rey Luis XIV, discípulo predilecto del autor, alternándose, en el desarrollo de su aplaudido espectáculo musical, composiciones de Mozart, Sor, Chopín, Shuman, Tárrega y García Tolsa. Barreiro impresionó favorablemente por su personal tecnicismo interpretativo y la justeza de sus ejecuciones. Se hizo aplaudir extraordinariamente en "Choros" y en "Mazurka" del maestro Villa Lobos, ésta última escrita especialmente y dedicada al concertista, cuya primera audición tuvo ocasión de conocer ayer nuestra afición musical. Brillante y acertado estuvo Barreiro en sus interpretaciones del Fandanguillo, de Torroba, y la Leyenda, de Albéniz. Finalmente, mención aparte la composición original del propio Rosendo Barreiro, "Capricho español" evocadora y descriptiva que reveló en el cantor una sensibilidad afinada. En fecha próxima Barreiro ofrecerá un segundo concierto.

It was a successful presentation of the Guitarist Rosendo Barreiro

He offered his first concert in the Teatro Corrientes

Yesterday Rosendo Barreiro offered, in the Teatro Corrientes, his first announced concert, programmed with a base of a qualified selection of composers, which revealed by itself the musical culture and the purified gesture of the concert artist.

He began the program with *Suite en Re menor*, Roberto de Visée written in 1686 and dedicated to King Luis XIV, the favorite disciple of the composer, alternating, in the development of his applauded musical spectacular, compositions by Mozart, Sor, Chopin, Schumann, Tárrega and García Tolsa.

Barreiro favorably impressed the audience with his personal interpretive technique and correctness of his performance. He was extraordinarily applauded for both *"Choros"* and *"Mazurka"* by Villa-Lobos, this last piece especially written and dedicated to the concert guitarist, whose debut yesterday gave us the occasion to know it. Brilliant and well-chosen were the interpretations by Barreiro of the *Fandanguillo*, by Torroba, and *Leyenda* by Albeniz. Finally, we mention the original composition by Barreiro of *"Capricho español"* reminiscent and descriptive that revealed the refined sensibility of the singer.

Barreiro will offer a second concert on a date real soon.

SINTONICE

HOY MARTES 12 DE DICIEMBRE DE 1939, A LAS 21 Y 30 HORAS RADIO ZORRILLA DE SAN MARTIN EN EL EXTRAORDINARIO PROGRAMA QUE POR INTERMEDIO DEL CELEBRADO GUITARRISTA ROSENDO BARREIRO, OFRECE A TACUAREMBO, LAS SIGUIENTES FIRMAS COMERCIALES DE ESTA PLAZA:

SASTRERIA LARBANOIS, TIENDA REY, TIENDA «LA CAMPANA», CASA ESTEBAN MARCOS GARCIA, TESTA & Cia., «AGENCIA FORD» de MANUEL R. LUQUE, SASTRERIA FRANCHI, CASA GUTIERREZ «MODAS», PLATERIA CAVALHEIRO, BASTON «SASTRE», CASA ANTUNES, PROVISION CRUZ, PANADERIA «LA ESTRELLA», SOARES NETTO Hnos., CONFITERIA «18 DE JULIO», BAR MODELO, BARRACA DE CEREALES «SEOANE», TIENDA «LOS MAGOS», IGNACIO VIERA «AGENTE COMERCIAL», PERIODICO «LA VOZ DEL PUEBLO», INSTITUTO DE BELLEZA «SUEÑO AZUL».

Tune In Tuesday December 12, 1939

Today Tuesday December 12, 1939 at 9:30PM Radio Zorrilla de San Martin in the extraordinary program that by the medium of the celebrated guitarist Rosendo Barreiro offers to Tacuarembo, the following commercial firms in this plaza: 23 companies announced.

2408

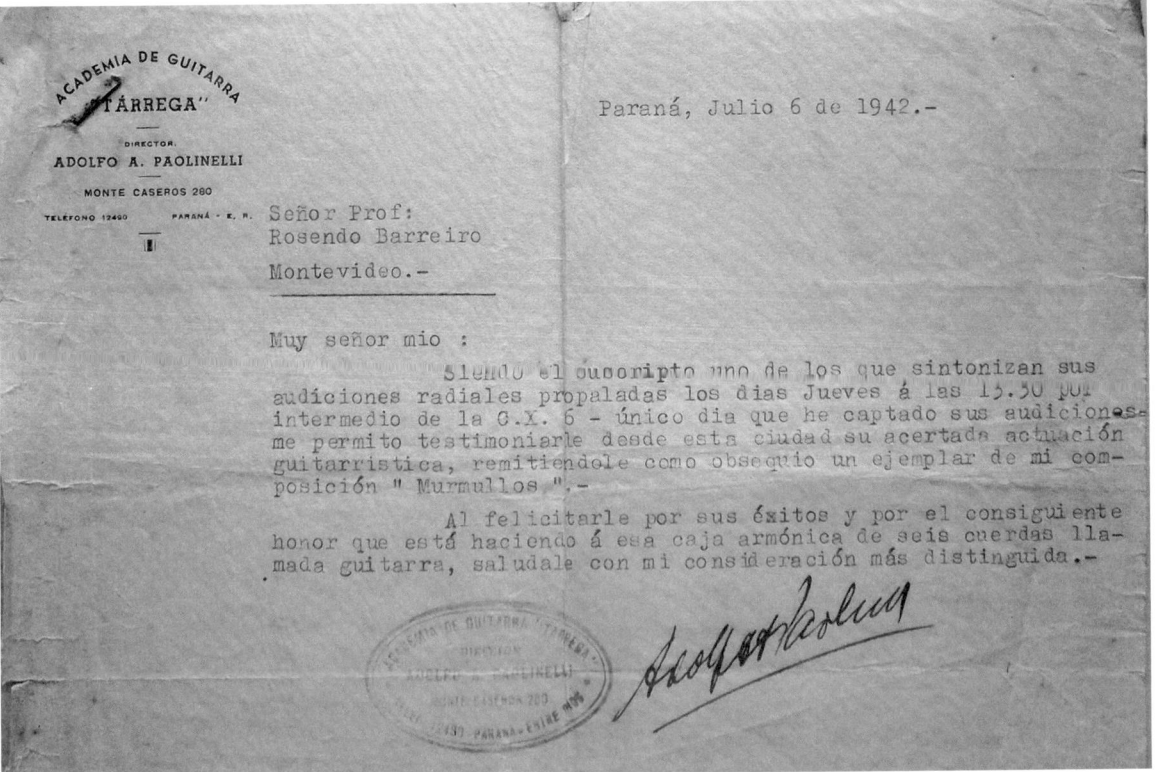

Letter from Adolfo Paolinelli July 6, 1942

Written by Adolfo Paolinelli who was the Director of the Academia de "Tárrega" in Parana, Argentina July 6, 1942

To: Mr. Professor
Rosendo Barreiro
Montevideo

Dear Sir,

Being a subscriber as one of those who tunes in to your radio performances propagated on Thursdays at 1:30PM by Radio C.X. 6 – the only day that I have received your performances to allow me to testify to you from this city of your guitaristic performance, I am sending you a copy of my composition *"Murmullos"* as a gift. –

To congratulate you for your success and by the consequent honor that you are doing to this harmonic box of six strings called the guitar, with my most distinguished consideration I wish you the best of health. –

Adolfo Paolinelli

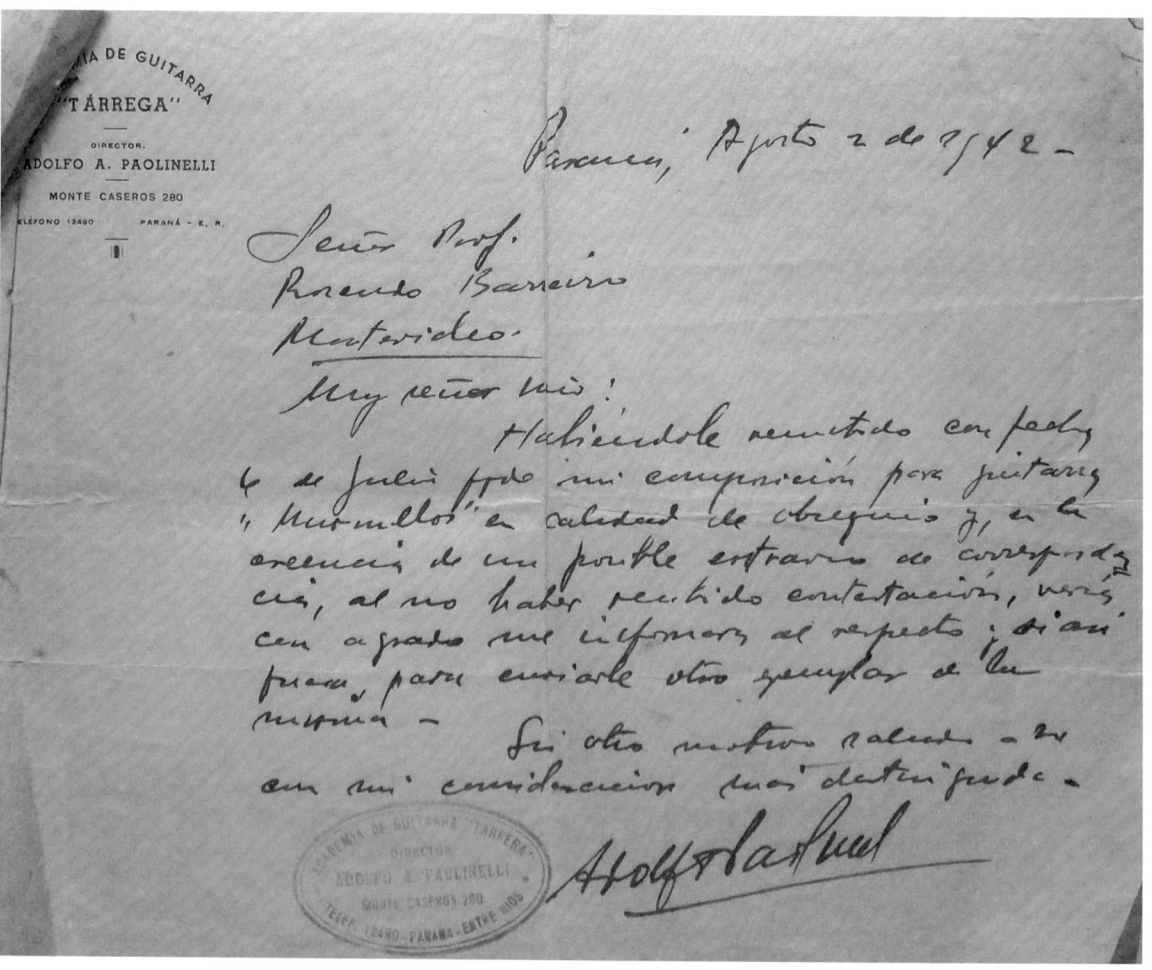

Letter Handwritten from Adolfo Paolinelli August 2 1942

To: Mr. Professor
Rosendo Barreiro
Montevideo

Dear Sir,

Having sent with the date of last July 6th my composition "Murmullos" for the guitar as a gift, and in the belief of a possible loss of correspondence, not having received any response, with pleasure I inform you to the respect if that was the case I plan to send another copy of the same.

Without any other motive best of health to you and with my distinguished consideration,

Adolfo Paolinelli

August 24, 1943 Rosendo Barreiro Concert 9:30 PM

Held in Centro Cultural 1813 Great Literary - Musical Act entrusted to our compatriot Guitarist Rosendo Barreiro and Professor Brenda M. de Rodríguez.

Montevideo, Agosto 15 de 1942.-

Sr. Adolfo A. PAOLINELLI.
Director de la
    ACADEMIA de Guitarra "TARREGA"
Monte Caseros 250.
PARANA E.R. (Reca. Argentina)

Amable y distinguido señor:

                    Deplorando el retraso en contestar
a sus muy amables de Julio 6 y 2 de Agosto del cte. me place
íntimamente agradecerle los conceptos vertidos en su primera
y el obsequio de su obra "Murmullos".-

                    Se debe, en algo, la demora en con-
testarle, el deseo que tuve en preparar en una de mis audiciones subsiguientes al recibo de "Murmullos", su composición.
Pero impedimentos de índole físico y completamente agenos a
mi voluntad no permitieron prosperar ese deseo y esa satisfacción.-

                    Prométole que si Dios quiere, en una
de mis audiciones que ordinariamente efectúo los Jueves en el
SODRE a las 13y45, incluiré su gentil regalo que me honraré en
interpretar ~~~~~~
        en la manera mas fiel posible
                    Sin otro motivo reiterole mi since-
ro agradecimiento por su amable envío y grato testimonio de mi
modesta actuación y a mi vez para agradecerle el honor que me
dispensa en escucharme.

                    Suyo Affmo.

                              Rosendo Barreiro.-

————————
s/c. Avda. 18 de Julio Nº
Montevideo, R.O.U.-

2412

Letter from Rosendo Barreiro to Adolfo Paolinelli August 15, 1942

Montevideo, August 15, 1942

Mr. Adolfo Paolinelli
Director of the
ACADEMIA de Guitarra "Tárrega"
Monte Caseros 280.
 Parana, Entre Rios, Argentina

Gracious and distinguished Mr. Paolinelli

I am deploring my late replies to your very friendly letters of July 6th and August 2nd it pleases me to intimately thank you for the praise in you first letter and the gift of your work *"Murmullos"* in the second letter. –

It is due to something, the delay in answering you, the desire that I had in preparing in one of my upcoming radio broadcasts, having received your composition *"Murmullos"*. But laziness and completely irrelevant impediments to my will didn't permit me to fulfill this desire and that satisfaction.

I promise you that if God wills, in one of my performances that I ordinarily do on SODRE on Thursdays at 1:45 PM, I will include your kind gift that I will honor in the manner most possibly faithful.

Without any other motive I reiterate my sincere thanks for your friendly sent item and heartwarming testimony of my modest performance and to my time to thank you the honor that I am granted to listen to.

Yours affectionately,

Rosendo Barreiro

a/c. Avenida 18 de Julio No.
Montevideo, Republic of Uruguay.

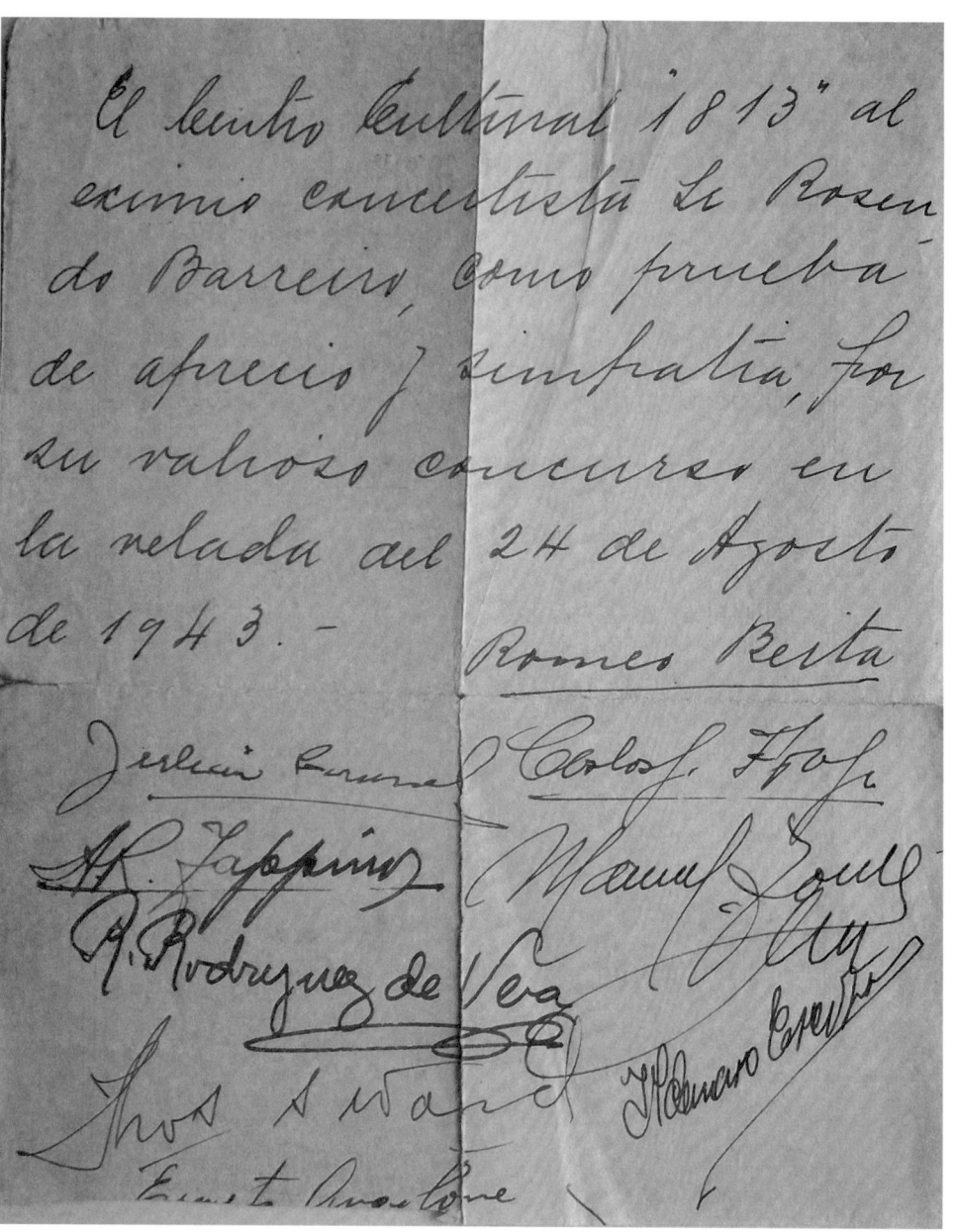

Handwritten with autographs Concert at Centro Cultural 1813 August 24, 1943

The Centro Cultural 1813 to the eminent guitarist Rosendo Barreiro as proof of the offer and kindness, of the valuable program in the soirée on August 24, 1943. --

Romeo Berta

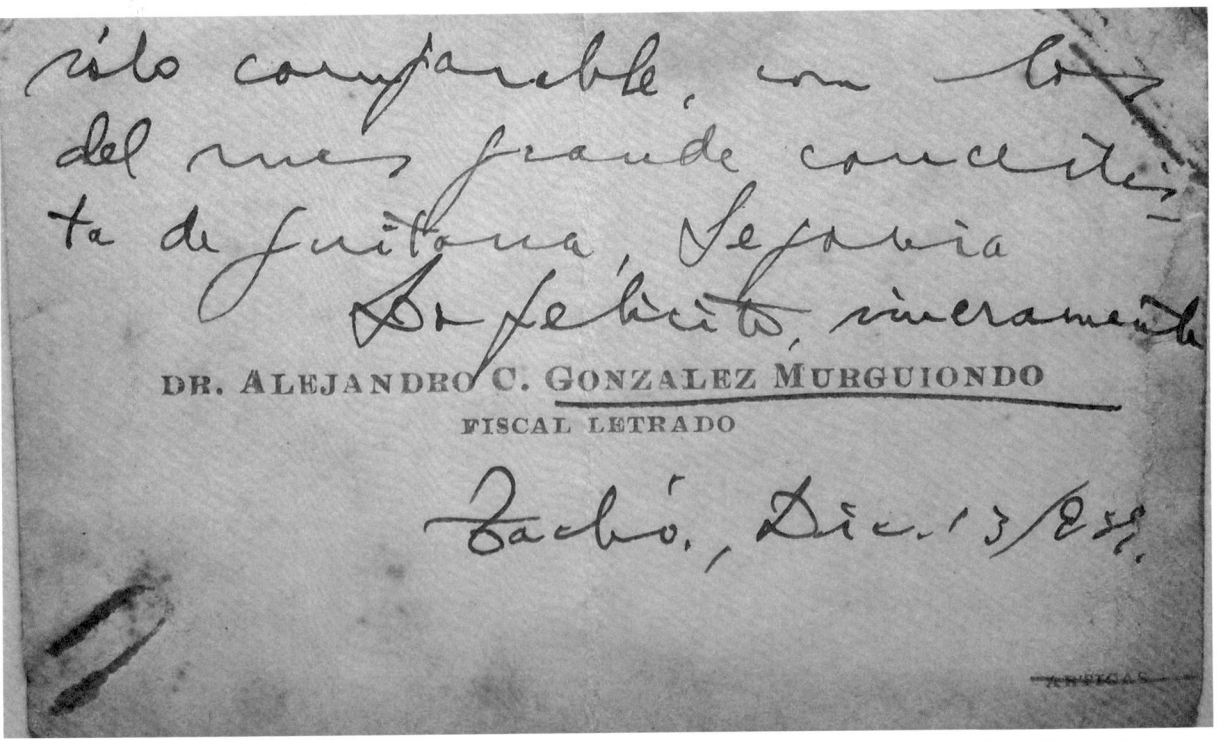

Letter on a back side of a Business card from Dr. Alejandro C. Gonzalez Murguiondo to Rosendo December 13, 1939.

Barreiro, your concert last night, they consecrated it like they toasted it to reach you, and you obtained an extraordinary success only comparable with those ones great concert artists of the guitar, Segovia I congratulate you, sincerely

Zacho, December 13, 1939.

ROSENDO BARREIRO

— Seu concerto, domingo, no Club Commercial —

Não é das que facilmente se desvanecem, a impressão deixada pela hora de arte que o grande guitarrista uruguayo, sr. Rosendo Barreiro, offereceu á sociedade de Cruz Alta, domingo ultimo, no salão nobre do Club Commercial.

Cerca das 21 horas, repleto o salão do que de selecto a nossa sociedade possue, Barreiro, correspondendo á acolhida fidalga que aqui teve, deu inicio á execução de seu programma artistico, dedilhando magistralmente o «Estylo Nacional» de Sinópoli. A escala de Tárrega, elle a domina completamente, o que provou com a interpretação perfeita do «Preludio (Endecha)». Na execução das «Variações sobre um thema de Vidalita», de sua propria creação, Barreiro foi soberbo e revelou todo o seu temperamento de artista apaixonado.

Na segunda parte do programma, foi o «Minueto» de Mozart que agradou sobremaneira, não obstante os demais numeros, e principalmente o «Valzer (Intimo)» de Beethoven, serem calorosamente applaudidos. E tanto agradou ó «Minueto» que no intervallo muitas pessoas solicitaram do artista a repetição desse numero.

A terceira parte do programma foi excellente. Composto de numeros dos mais difficeis, o jovem artista, não obstante, a executou de uma forma impeccavel, arrebatando o auditorio. Fechando o programma com o «Celebre Capricho Andaluz», de Manjon, indiscutivelmente a mais sonora das musicas apresentadas por Barreiro, o

eximio guitarrista viu seus esforços coroados do mais pleno exito.

A pedido de diversas pessoas executou elle ainda o trecho «Siciliana» da «Cavallaria Rusticana», que tanto havia agradado sexta-feira, quando Barreiro deu uma audição a pequeno numero de pessoas.

Os nossos conhecimentos musicaes não estão, por certo, na altura de podermos ousar uma critica de Barreiro. A melhor critica do artista está, como dissemos, no conhecimento perfeito da escala de Tárrega, considerada pelos mais notaveis musicos como uma das grandes difficuldades do violonista. E mais do que isso, Barreiro possue a condição primordial do exito: a confiança em si mesmo. Admirador profundo de Koch, de Llovet e de Tárrega, nelles Barreiro se inspira ecitando-lhes o nome, todos se transmuda.

Dehi tambem a ousadia das suas composições originaes que tão bem executa e que tão bem demonstram que seu espirito selecto, embebido na polychromia, saturado da sonoridade que elle proprio — e o faz com indizivel ternura—arranca de seu instrumento, está sempre propenso á producção e á comprehensão das cousas bellas.

Barreiro é um artista da harmonia. Nas cordas acariciadas por seus dedos, levemente ás vezes e outras vezes sacudidas com vigor, elle vasa toda a emoção que lhe vae nalma bem conformada de artista e de sonhador.

Rosendo Barreiro His Concert Sunday in the Club Commercial –Translation of the Brazilian concert (undated more than likely from the 1920"s.) review on the next page.

Rosendo Barreiro His Concert Sunday in the Club Commercial –

Portuguese translation by Randy Osborne

What easily fades is not given in the impression left in an hour of art by the great Uruguayan guitarist, Mr. Rosendo Barreiro, offered to the society of Cruz Alta, last Sunday, in the noble hall of the Club Commercial.

Around 9PM, the hall that our select society possesses was full Barreiro, corresponding to the reception of the noble welcome here, began to perform his artistic program, masterfully plucking, *Estilo Nacional* by Sinopoli. From the Tárrega school, he dominates it completely, which he proved with the perfect interpretation of *Preludio (Endecha)*. In his performance of *Variaciones sobre un tema de Vidalita*, of his own creation, Barreiro superbly revealed all his passionate artistic temperament.

In the second part of the program, the *Minuet* by Mozart that extensively pleased, however the rest of the pieces, principally *Valzer (Intimo)* by Beethoven, were hotly applauded. The *Minuet* was so pleasing that the audience asked him to play this piece again.

In the third part of the program was excellent. It comprised the two most difficult pieces, the young artist, nonetheless, performed them in an impeccable manner, grabbing the audience. Closing the program with *Celebre Capricho Andaluz*, by Manjón, unquestionably the most sonorous of the music presented by Barreiro, the eminent guitarist saw his efforts crowned in the fullest success.

Due to the request of several persons he performed *Siciliana* from *Cavalleria Rusticana,* that had pleased them so much on Friday, when Barreiro gave a performance to a small number of people.

Our knowledgeable musicians weren't there, certainly, at the high we can challenge a music critic of Barreiro. The best critic of an artist is, as we say, in the perfect knowledge of the Tárrega school, considered among the most notable musicians as one of the most difficult of the guitarist. It is more than that, Barreiro possesses the overriding ability of success; the confidence in himself. He is an admirer of Koch, of Llobet and Tárrega, in them Barreiro is inspired by mentioning their names.

There too the daring given to his original compositions how well he performs them and how well they demonstrate his select spirit, they embody polychromatic settings, saturated of the sonority that is his own, and does so with unspeakable tenderness – he pulls out from his instrument, always the same tendency to produce and understand the beautiful things.

Barreiro is an artist that gives harmony. The chords caressed by his fingers, lightly at times and other times jolting with vigor, he is going to give everything of the emotion that makes him a well-formed artist and dreamer.

La Prensa The Guitarist Rosendo Barreiro will perform in the Teatro Corrientes today

Today, in the Teatro Corrientes the guitarist Rosendo Barreiro will offer a concert at 6:30 PM.

Integrated in the program are:

Minué, Sarabanda and Borrega (sic) Bourée by Roberto de Visée;

Andante, by Mozart;

Minué, by Sor;

Sonata, by García Tolsa;

Dos preludios, by Chopin;

Reverie, by Schumann;

Barcarola, by Mendelssohn;

Capricho arabe, by Tárrega;

Capricho español, by Barreiro;

Mazurka and Choros, by Villa-Lobos;

Fandanguillo, by Torroba,

Leyenda, by Albeniz.

We resume to finish the list of Uruguayan Guitarists by Ricardo Muñoz:

Martin Borda y Pagola

A lover of the guitar, with real passion; he possesses instruments of great artistic worth (Simplicio, etc.), his home is the center of reunions of distinguished guitaristic personalities of the country and those foreigners who arrive to visit him.

Pedro M. Aguirre

An excellent gentleman and performer, a student of the celebrated Pedro Mascaro y Reissig; who integrated at various times in the Comision Directiva of the Centro Guitarristico del Uruguay "Conrado P. Koch", occupying the Presidency of the same institution with great skill and benefit, he is a real social and cultural entity of the instrument in his country.

Beatriz N. Hansen

A distinguished concert guitarist of exquisite sensibilities, she possesses the richest range of technical possibilities on the instrument; which she learned from her eminent maestro Pedro Mascaro y Reissig.

Ciro S. Castillo

He was born in Tucuarembo the 9th of September of 1926, he studied the guitar with Pedro Mascaro y Reissig since the year 1936, he interprets Mozart, Albeniz, Tárrega, Sor, etc.

A. Pereira Arias

A guitarist who interprets Sor, Barrios, and others, who in a duet on the 14th of July of 1949, with the pianist Irma Ametrano, performed works by Couperin, Bach and Mozart, with great skill, in the Centro Guitarristico del Uruguay "Conrado P. Koch".

Ana Maria Verde Ferrero

She has performed works by Aguado, Sor, Tárrega, Brahms and Cimarosa in the Centro Guitarristico del Uruguay "Conrado P. Koch".

Juan Cerrutti

He directed the *"Conjunto Nacional de Guitarras"* integrated by himself and Carlos Pedemonte, Leandro Ibargoyen and Oscar Heguaburo.

Juan J. de Feo

On the 29th of August of 1949 he interpreted works by Roldyn, Bach, Rameau, Diaz, Llobet and Sagreras in the Centro Guitarristico del Uruguay "Conrado P. Koch".

Maria Margarita Sena

She is a student of the celebrated maestro Ms. Olga Pierri, on the 19th of May of 1949, in the Centro Guitarristico del Uruguay "Conrado P. Koch", she interpreted works by Bach, Haydn, San Sebastian, Muro, Beethoven, Llobet, Sirera, de Falla, Tárrega and Pujol; she forms a part of the *"Conjunto Feminino"* of Olga Pierri and is distinguished by her fine esthetic expression.

Ciro S. Castillo Luzardo in 1939.
(Archive: Ricardo Muñoz)

Matilde Sena

She studied with the notable Olga Pierri and forms a part of her *"Conjunto Feminino"*, whose performances were previously referred to.

Margot Pietro Lana

A guitarist of great artistic beauty, who forms a part of the *"Conjunto Feminino"* of the distinguished maestro Olga Pierri.

Pedro M. Marin Sanchez

He is a renowned maestro, very well known in the national guitaristic ambiance of the country, by his students, musical works, and personal performances that take place in his country; he forms a part of the Comision Directiva of the Centro Guitarristico del Uruguay "Conrado P. Koch" and has performed with Conrado P. Koch.

Julio Rapat (probably Atilio Rapat)

He is an interesting and known maestro of the guitar, who has given concerts with success in Montevideo.

Raul Sanchez

In 1952 he gave a performance in Montevideo, and the 30th of April of 1953, in the Centro Guitarristico del Uruguay "Conrado P. Koch", which paid homage to the immortal Tárrega, in the "Sala Verdi" he interpreted the works *"4 Preludios"*, *"Capricho Arabe"*, *"Gavota"*, *"Mazurka"*, *"Pavana"*, and *"Danza Mora"*.

Carlos Ferreiro Freire

In October of 1952 he gave an interesting concert in Montevideo.

Summary

The musicians of this country have favored the best disposition in the guitaristic scene adding through the maturity of time, the very beautiful responsibility that corresponds before the present men and those of the future, in the victorious outcome that the history demands, for which life signifies the full enjoyment of the same.

Many of the eminent maestros, virtuosos and composers that Uruguay has fertilized, continue performing efficiently in the destiny that South America has now designed, with its extraordinary cultural and spiritual potentiality, on the national instrument.

The eminent *Don* Emilio Pujol visited the country and made the modern school of Tárrega known, then Llobet, Segovia, Sainz de la Maza, kept in the technical theme, which the public understood, felt and adopted. The musicians of the country began to work enriching the musical literature of the instrument, the instrumentalists of both sexes sprouted all over, they installed publishers, guitar maker's workshops, imparting their lessons of the guitar in the Conservatorio Nacional and more than a hundred private entities, it has an entity such as the Centro Guitarristico del Uruguay "Conrado P. Koch", which was founded on the 10th of April of 1937, and is of great pride.

This Centro controls the performances of the cultured instrument in the Republic, it gives monthly concerts with artists of the country and foreign artists as well, that make contracts, the culture makes educational in their lectures about technical, historical, musical psychological themes, the instrument develops in a true sea of private and general benefits overall in to regards to its culture.

It is expected in a brief period, its ticket sales will permit the founding of a journalistic organ of education and guitaristic diffusion, with such magnificent results proportionate to the intimate knowledge and international relations of the congregation equally, it is a desire they will want in some moment to constitute competitions, national and international congresses, of virtuosos, students, maestros, constructors, composers of the instrument, for which they can debate the important artistic, technical, economic problems of the great fraternity, a number relegated to the incomprehension of the public and the concepts of the authorities.

Perhaps, the *"Casa de la Guitarra"* was the solution of so many problems . . . ."

So ends the account of the guitarists of Uruguay by Ricardo Muñoz.

On the next page is a photo of many of the members of the Comision Directiva (Board of Directors) of the Centro Guitarristico del Uruguay "Conrado P. Koch". The translation of the dedication is: "To the esteemed friend Ricardo Muñoz in remembrance of the act held in the Ateneo in Montevideo. October 26, 1946."

Idelfonso F. Piñeyro   Pedro M. Aguirre

The members left to right are: unknown gentleman, Idelfonso F. Piñeyro, Pedro M. Aguirre, Ricardo Muñoz, Nelly Zuma Miravelles, Raul Mancebo Rojas, Eduardo R. Gonzalez, Alberto Sena, Pedro M. Marin Sanchez.

I need to thank my colleague, Alfredo Escande, for some help with the identification of the persons in the photo.

The images on the next 11 pages are all from the archive of Ricardo Muñoz.

Al estimado amigo Ricardo Merino en prueba al acto celebrado en el Ateneo de Pontevedra. Octubre 26 de 1946. [firma]

Gulfermo F. Piñeiro

AUDICIONES MUSICALES
:: *Mañana se presentará la guitarrista argentina N'elly Miravalles*

Mañana sábado a las 21 y 45 en el salón de actos del Ateneo, la guitarrista argentina Nelly Miravelles, ofrecerá un recital en el nuevo instrumento, creación del señor Ricardo Muñoz, quien ha logrado mejorar su sonoridad, de manera evidente. Hará uso de la palabra el señor Muñoz lo que unido a la jerarquía de la ejecutante, asegura al recital un gran éxito.

Translation of the text from the Montevideo daily *"El Diario"* of Friday October 25, 1946:

Musical Performances

"Tomorrow the Argentine guitarist Nelly Miravelles will be presented.

   Tomorrow Saturday at 9:45PM in the hall at the Ateneo, the Argentine guitarist Nelly Miravelles will offer a recital on a new instrument, a creation of Mr. Ricardo Muñoz, who has succeeded to improve its sonority, of an evident manner. Mr. Muñoz will speak about that which will unite with the hierarchy of the performer, to assure the recital a great success."

   Translation of the text from the Montevideo daily *"El Pais"* of Saturday October 26, 1946:

"Today the Argentine Guitar will be presented.

   In the hall of the Ateneo, at 9:45PM an act of great interest and undoubtedly transcendental for the guitarristic movement will take place. Mr. Ricardo Muñoz, who in his country, Argentina, has dedicated many years to the study of this instrument, has succeeded to introduce substantial modifications, such as to employ Argentine spruce, to the point of having succeeded which he calls the perfect guitar.

   For demonstrating to us the results of his experiments, he has, organized the act for this evening, which in agreement will continue with the following program:

   Guitarist: Nelly Zuma Miravelles.

   Part I:"1* *Preludio No. 4* by F. Tárrega. This will demonstrate how the instrument responds to chords. 2* *Estudio No. 2* by E. Pujol. This will demonstrate how the instrument responds in the scales. 3* *Scherzo,* by F. Tárrega. This will demonstrate how the instrument responds to arpeggios. 4* *Carrillon,* by V. Terzi. This will demonstrate how the instrument responds in slurs, harmonics and the left hand alone. 5* *Gran Tremolo,* by Gottschalk. This will demonstrate how the instrument responds to tremolo." Part II: *Estilo,* by A. Fleury 2* *Aires de danza,* by R. Muñoz. 3* *Huella.* (Dedicated to the Uruguayan writer Yamandu Rodríguez), by A. Fleury. 4* *Vidalita* (Variations), by J. S. Sagreras. Part III: *Andante,* by F. Sor. 2* *Allegretto,* by N. Coste. 3* +*Allegretto,* (Dedicated to the Uruguayan maestro *Don* Pedro Mascaro y Reissig) by R. Muñoz. 4* *Preludio* by Bach, by R. Ayesteran. 5* +*Preludio (IV Sonata* for Cello by Bach), by R. Muñoz. (+) Debuts of works."

Centro Guitarrístico del Uruguay

CONRADO P. KOCH

Programa

MONTEVIDEO
URUGUAY

La Comisión Directiva del Centro Guitarrístico del Uruguay tiene el alto honor de invitar a usted y familia para los actos a efectuarse los días 26 y 28 del corriente a cargo del conferencista señor RICARDO MUÑOZ y de la concertista señora NELLY ZUMA MIRAVALLES que honran a nuestra entidad con su arte y erudición.

Octubre de 1946.

Translation: "The Board of Directors of the Centro Guitarristico del Uruguay has the high honor of inviting you and your family for the acts to take place on the days 26th and 28th of the current month entrusted to the lecturer Mr. Ricardo Muñoz and the concert guitarist Mrs. Nelly Zuma Miravelles that honor our entity with their art and erudition.

October of 1946."

Apertura del acto por el señor Pedro M. Aguirre.

Presentación de la Guitarra Argentina

por su creador, nuestro Miembro Correspondiente en Buenos Aires señor Ricardo Muñoz.

PROGRAMA

Guitarrista: Nelly Zuma Miravalles

I PARTE

1º PRELUDIO Nº 4, de F. Tárrega.
Demostrará cómo responde el instrumento a los acordes.

2º ESTUDIO Nº 2, de E. Pujol.
Demostrará cómo responde el instrumento en las escalas.

3c SCHERZO, de F. Tárrega.
Demostrará cómo responde el instrumento a los arpegios.

(*) 4º CARRILLON, de V. Terzi.
Demostrará cómo responde el instrumento en los ligados, armónicos y mano izquierda sola.

5º GRAN TREMOLO, de Gottschalk.
Demostrará cómo responde el instrumento al trémolo.

II PARTE

1º ESTILO, de A. Fleury.

2º AIRES DE DANZA, de R. Muñoz.

3º HUELLA (Dedicada al escritor uruguayo Yamandú Rodríguez), de A. Fleury.

4º VIDALITA (Variaciones), de J. S. Sagreras.

III PARTE

1º ANDANTE, de F. Sor.

2º ALLEGRETTO, de N. Coste.

(*) 3º ALLEGRETTO (dedicado al maestro uruguayo don Pedro Mascaró y Reissig), de R. Muñoz.

4º PRELUDIO DE BACH, de R. Ayestarán.

(*) 5º PRELUDIO (IV Sonata para Cello de Bach), de R. Muñoz.

(*) Obras en primera audición.

Presentation of the Ricardo Muñoz model in the Ateneo in Montevideo on Sunday October 26, 1946. After many years of exhaustive research in a lot of different areas, of both botanical and technical inspection of Spanish made guitars, Ricardo Muñoz culminated in the final design of the Argentine Guitar. Nelly Zuma Miravelles performs the pieces, to show the different strengths toward the technical appeal.

Translation of Part 1:

"1* Preludio No. 4 by F. Tárrega
This will demonstrate how the instrument responds to chords.

2* Estudio No. 2 by E. Pujol
This will demonstrate how the instrument responds in the scales.

3* Scherzo, by F. Tárrega
This will demonstrate how the instrument responds to arpeggios.

4* Carrillon, by V. Terzi
This will demonstrate how the instrument responds in slurs, harmonics and the left hand alone.

5* Gran Tremolo, by Gottschalk
This will demonstrate how the instrument responds to tremolo."

In Part III, the 3rd and 5th pieces are public debuts of the pieces written and transcribed by Ricardo Muñoz.

Translation of the typed opening address by Pedro M. Aguirre for the presentation of Mr. Ricardo Muñoz and Nelly Miravelles at the Ateneo in Montevideo on Saturday October 26, 1946.

"Ladies and Gentlemen,

Man has a yearning for knowledge, he lives in incessant search for the truth, his desire to know has no limits, and it dominates the idea to overcome the past. He moves in a world of limited appearance, in a medium whose possibilities to improve appear to be exhausted, but ah!, that is fiction, because this world has a depth of a bottomless abysm, because when there is an intention to embrace it, it is the horizon that widens and makes it intangible. Between these two powers man and world, this brought the fight to wrest nature's secrets and making the disclosure, the welfare of humanity.

The eternal struggle that makes the ancient philosopher say, a measure of the profound knowledge of the universe: he only knows he knows nothing. The culture has succeeded much in the span of the centuries, and of those anxieties, of those longings to know this fact the progress and this desire of self-improvement we owe in the field of the art and of the science, portentous conquests that make the modern life with unsuspected flattery in past centuries.

The progress of the humanity, in constant evolution, is forged by those that have the spirit of the investigation, by those that have gone deeply into things, by those that penetrate in them, those that pass of slow, superficial, those that don't stop in the examination, those that make frivolity a practice, they are the opposite, have done nothing in the self-improvement, and are like pilgrims that don't leave a trace of their voyage of this world. Instead, of those in whose spirits the desire of the perfection breathes, the permanent echo remains in the death of their works, the name of their conquests isn't extinguished, it illuminates successive generations, and their vigorous genius is projected in those times.

Those that we find here reunite, we cultivate the guitar, or we enjoy the subtle message, delicate, full of fragrance that the brilliant interpreter that enchants us obtains from its magic box.

We believe all of the possibilities of the instrument, were in the confines of the unsurpassable, which its little volume only could be altered by the artificial expedients or craftsmen; when I have here a man who has given all to the study of the guitar in the most diverse aspects, a man with the investigative spirit, which is the faithful appearance of this type of whom I have spoken, and insatiable researcher of new forms, which has put his talent, his soul of studiousness, his passionate vocation to the service of the guitar, in a word meritorious of the instrument, he battles, and succeeds until the present to endow of new qualities that improve the result. I'm referring to as you have imagined, the distinguished visitor, Mr. Ricardo Muñoz, to whom the Centro Guitarristico del Uruguay "Conrado P. Koch" has the honor of counting him as a Corresponding Member in the city of Buenos Aires, and in whose name, of our institution, a tribute of the most enthusiastic of welcomes.

Mr. Muñoz by virtue of his knowledge of the material was given a scholarship by the Comision Nacional de Cultura de la Argentina, (National Commission of Culture of Argentina) for constructing the Argentine guitar with woods native to the country. We are at the top of the honor to be among the first to know the fruit of his patient studies that with his great competency, the author will illustrate well with his dissertation that we will hear right away.

Multiple facets adorn the personality of this great visitor. In effect, he has performed with ample dominion in the field of the guitaristic performance, of the composition and in the literary in it. Distinguished maestros forged his personality as an interpreter. He began his musical studies with Professor Justo T. Morales, he continued with the great Hilarion Leloup and finally received classes from Maria Luisa Anido the notable concert guitarist who visited us last year. Not being satisfied to be a notable performer, Ricardo Muñoz, Spanish by origin although South American by heart, penetrated into the sphere of composition to give us works with enthusiastic native flavor. But where his intellectual profile is even more distinguished is in the field of the history and of the didactic.

2427

In the first he has left us with a production of high values, one of them, Historia de la Guitarra, an arranged historical compilation that is the most complete to have been written until now on the material, a factor of unquestionable knowledge to enrich the guitaristic culture. Presently a manner of enlargement of that work in the preparation of the *"Historia Universal de la Guitarra"*, of which he has written two volumes: Antiquity and Middle Ages. In the field of teaching he has delivered to us a beautiful lesson with an accent on teaching *"Psico — Pedagogia de la Guitarra"* adopted as an official text of the Conservatorio de Innsbruck in Austria. He hasn't stopped his literary production there, in this way in 1941 he published his magnificent book *"Identificaciones Vibrometricas"*, an erudite study about woods for the construction of musical instruments, whose conclusions will apply in the creation of his guitar.

His prestige as a man versed in and observant of the worldwide guitaristic movement, which makes the farthest and the most select associations with the guitar, their representative they designate in this part of the hemisphere. He is a Member of Honor of "Le Amis de la Guitare" in Paris, Corresponding Member of "The Philharmonic Guitarist Society" of London and of the "Chicago Classical Guitar Society" of the city of the same name. He is also a Correspondent to the studious Japanese, in all of the cases, an object of appointed distinctions.

A guitarist, composer, lecturer, historian, experimenter, I have condensed, the intellectual profile in a tight synthesis, of the friend that today honors us with his presence in the Centro Guitarristico, this home of the guitar that receives him as a brother of ideals. It isn't strange for us, what happens without moving around, because his personality might be opaque, far from that Ricardo Muñoz, is one of ours, because the common work is consubstancial that unites us, which approaches and identifies us.

Moments ago, I have called him, meritorious of the guitar and it is a just title, because never in a moment has he negated his cooperation, but that he has given the best of his enthusiasm, of his life, of his intelligence. His dedication to study of all that pertains to the instrument will be an example of irrepressible struggle for the studies in the future. As a product of his patient investigations over many years, he leaves his valuable contribution in favor of the improvement of the quality and of the sonorous volume of the guitar. It is that in no moment has the materialistic hard work totally removed from his mind guided him, but as an enthusiastic researcher of the truth and of the perfection.

Along with the distinguished figure of the Argentine guitaristic world, Mrs. Nelly Miravelles de Gonzalez to who I have the honor to salute in name of the institution I represent has her fundamental part entrusted in this act. A disciple of Mr. Muñoz, she has been formed in the manner of the great maestros, of the classics, of those that gave fame and prestige to the instrument, her pending intervention to demonstrate what she can give to the guitar created by our beloved friend, will be to the height of the expectation, I don't doubt that has formed about the programmed acts. Since, by her category, the able performer, will be a distinguished note of this evening.

The Board of Directors of the Centro Guitarristico del Uruguay "Conrado P. Koch", have confided the honorable mission in me to present the visiting friend and the qualified concert guitarist Mrs. Miravelles de Gonzalez and give them the welcome. Interpreting this mandate, which is our entire social nucleus, I desire for us a happy stay among us and I make a sincere vow to you because we have the fruitful results of the intentions that move us. Thank you. (In pen) I dedicate the original text of my words of tribute read on the date and place indicated to my beloved friend Ricardo Muñoz."

El Diario
Montevideo 27-X-1945

LUCIDO ACTO ★ Organizó el Centro Guitarrístico del Uruguay

Se realizó anoche en el Ateneo, organizado por el Centro Guitarrístico del Uruguay, una interesante velada que contó con el concurso del señor Ricardo Muñoz, miembro correspondiente de dicho Centro en Buenos Aires, quien dictó una interesante conferencia y de la Srta. Nelly Zuma Miravalles, quien tuvo a su cargo la ejecución de un extenso concierto de guitarra. En el presente grabado aparecen las nombradas personalidades, en compañía de autoridades del Centro Guitarrístico del Uruguay

Translation of the text from the Montevideo daily *"El Diario"* of Sunday October 27, 1946:

"An Act of Light   Organized by Centro Guitarristico del Uruguay

Last night in the Ateneo, organized by Centro Guitarristico del Uruguay, an interesting evening that counted on the lecture by Mr. Ricardo Muñoz, corresponding member of the said Centro in Buenos Aires, who gave an interesting lecture and Mrs. Nelly Zuma Miravelles, who was entrusted with the performance of the extensive guitar concert. In the photo appear the named personalities, in the company of the authorities of the Centro Guitarristico del Uruguay."

LUNES 28 DE OCTUBRE A LAS 18 y 45
en la
SALA DEL PALACIO DIAZ
18 de Julio 1333

APERTURA DEL ACTO, por el señor Pedro Mascaró y Reissig.

GAUCHOS Y GUITARRAS. - Conferencia por nuestro Miembro Correspondiente en Buenos Aires, señor **Ricardo Muñoz**.
Con ilustraciones musicales a cargo de la guitarrista señora **Nelly Zuma Miravalles.**

PROGRAMA MUSICAL

1° AYACUCHO (Vidala), de R. Muñoz.

2° INSPIRACION (Estilo), de R. Muñoz.

3° MILONGA, de A. Fleury.

4° EL CARRETERO, de R. Muñoz.

5° VIDALITA, de J. S. Sagreras.

On Monday October 28, 1946 at 6:45 PM in the hall of the Palacio Diaz, Ricardo Muñoz gave his lecture on *"Gauchos* and Guitars", the opening address was given by Pedro Mascaro y Reissig, with the musical illustrations being played by Mrs. Nelly Zuma Miravelles.

EL BIEN PUBLICO

Martes 29 de octubre de 1946

MONTEVIDEO

Presentación de la guitarra "Muñoz"

ORGANIZADA por el Centro Guitarrístico, se llevó a cabo en el Ateneo la presentación de la guitarra creada por el Prof. Ricardo Muñoz, en cuya construcción ha aplicado el resultado de pacientes investigaciones.

Empleando nuevas especies de madera e introduciendo innovaciones de carácter técnico en ella, su creador ha obtenido un instrumento con sonoridad más equilibrada y de mayor volumen que el actual.

El Prof. Muñoz ha logrado un magnífico éxito, que su inquieto espíritu de investigador mejorará aún, en breve tiempo.

La parte demostrativa estuvo a cargo de la calificada guitarrista Nelly Miravalles de González. Puso a prueba las virtudes del instrumento frente a las más variadas figuras musicales, sorteando con habilidad las dificultades de un programa escogido especialmente para aquel fin. Intérprete de fino temperamento y formada en la escuela depurada de los clásicos, arrancó entusiastas aplausos de la concurrencia.

Podemos resumir el juicio sobre la presentación de la guitarra, diciendo que abre hermosas perspectivas para el instrumento.

Translation of the article from the daily *"El Bien Publico"* of Tuesday October 29, 1946, published in Montevideo:

"Presentation of the "Muñoz" guitar:

Organized by the Centro Guitarristico, and being carried out in the Ateneo was the presentation of the guitar created by Professor Ricardo Muñoz, in whose construction was applied as the result of patient investigations.

Employing a new species of wood and introducing innovations of technical character in it, its creator has obtained an instrument with a sonority more balanced and, of better volume than the present ones.

Professor Muñoz, he has achieved a magnificent success, which his anxious spirit as an investigator will improve even in a short time.

The demonstrative part was entrusted to the qualified guitarist Nelly Miravelles de Gonzalez. She put to the test the virtues of the instrument facing the most varied musical figures, avoiding with ability the difficulties of a chosen program especially with that end. She interpreted of a fine temperament and formed in the pure school of the classics, she extracted enthusiastic applause of the gathering.

We can summarize the judgement about the presentation of the guitar, saying that it opened beautiful perspectives for the instrument."

Translation of the article from the daily *"La Mañana"* of Wednesday October 30, 1946, published in Montevideo:

"In the Centro Guitarristico del Uruguay

An interesting lecture developed yesterday afternoon, in the hall of the Palacio Diaz, under the sponsorship of the Centro Guitarristico del Uruguay "Conrado P. Koch", an institution that enjoys the prestige within our intellectual medium, by the significance of its efforts in favor of the artistic culture.

A select gathering completely occupied the hall where *Don* Pedro Mascaro y Reissig a member of the board of the Centro presented the lecturer *Don* Ricardo Muñoz, he spoke about *"Gauchos* and Guitars", the Argentine interpreter Mrs. Nelly Zuma Miravelles to whom we already had the opportunity to hear in the Ateneo, illustrated the diverse landscapes of the theme.

Mr. Muñoz, who you already know by his compositions and literary works, had moments we enjoyed in the development of the theme, profoundly interesting with quotations of high historical interest.

The graceful Argentine interpreter who performed the distinct works of national folklore, with skill demonstrated once more the high guitaristic qualities."

DISERTO EL PROF. RICARDO MUÑOZ, SOBRE LA GUITARRA

En la sala del Ateneo, con motivo de la presentación de su guitarra, disertó el profesor argentino Ricardo Muñoz.

Abrió el acto en nombre del Centro Guitarrístico, la institución organizadora, el señor Pedro M. Aguirre destacando la personalidad del distinguido visitante.

Seguidamente el señor Muñoz tomó la palabra para explicar cómo llegó a producir la guitarra de su nombre. Comenzó por decir que luego de prolongadas investigaciones sobre aptitudes de las más variadas maderas a los efectos de la construcción de instrumentos musicales, llegó a la conclusión de que el alerce, árbol conífero muy desarrollado en los Andes del Sur, puede con su madera sustituir a la del abeto, sin desmedro, en la construcción de tapas armónicas.

La forma de la guitarra "Muñoz", que no se aparta en lo fundamental de la clásica, y sus medidas, están basadas en las teorías acústicas y matemáticas de la "forma perfecta" de Pitágoras, constituyendo un instrumento geométricamente correcto.

Una modificación importante, señalada por el autor en el curso de su disertación, es la colocación de la cejuela de hueso, apoyada directamente sobre la de la guitarra a fin de que las vibraciones de las cuerdas se transmitan sin elementos intermediarios a la caja de resonancia para obtener así mayor claridad y volumen sonoro. El equilibrio de los sonidos es una de las cualidades más importantes de la guitarra "Muñoz". Las tapas responden al "la" los fondos responden a la nota "mi" y entre el mi de los fondos y el la de la tapa, hay un intervalo musical de cuarta que es exactamente la distancia de afinación de las cuerdas del instrumento. El Prof. Muñoz se extiende en otras consideraciones para terminar diciendo que entregaba al juicio del público el resultado de sus estudios en la convicción de haber hecho un aporte en pro del mejoramiento del instrumento que ha llenado sus mejores horas de labor.

La guitarrista Nelly Miravalles tuvo a su cargo la parte musical demostrativa. Con alta técnica y fino temperamento, puso a prueba las cualidades del instrumento en acordes, ligados, armónicos y arpegios a los que respondió éste con amplitud. Como resultado de la demostración anotamos un aumento de volumen no despreciable unido a un equilibrio sonoro y a una calidad superior que justifica el esfuerzo realizado por su autor.

Translation of the article from the daily *"La Mañana"* of Thursday October 31, 1946, published in Montevideo:

"Professor Ricardo Muñoz spoke about the guitar.

In the hall of the Ateneo, with the motive of the presentation of his guitar, the Argentine Professor Ricardo Muñoz spoke.

The act was opened in the name of the Centro Guitarrístico, the institution organizer, Pedro M. Aguirre highlighting the personality of the distinguished visitor.

Immediately after Mr. Muñoz began to speak to explain how he came about to produce the guitar of his name. He began by saying after prolonged investigations about aptitudes of the most varied woods to the effects of the construction of musical instruments, he arrived at the conclusion of which alerce, a conifer tree very developed in the Andes of South America, with his wood it can substitute the spruce, without expense, in the construction of the soundboards.

The form of the Muñoz guitar, which doesn't separate from the fundamental of the classical, and its measurements, is based on the acoustic theories and mathematics of the "perfect form" by Pythagoras, constituting a geometrically perfect instrument.

An important modification, pointed out by the author in the course of his dissertation, is the placement of the bone saddle, supported directly above that of the guitar to the end of which the vibrations of the strings transmit without intermediary elements to the resonant body for obtaining in this way better clarity and sonorous volume.

The balance of the sounds is one of the most important qualities of the Muñoz guitar. The soundboards respond to "La", the backs respond to the note "Mi" and between the "Mi" backs and the "La" of the soundboards, there is a musical interval of a fourth that is exactly the distance of the tuning of the strings of the instrument. Professor Muñoz extends it to other considerations to finish saying that he submits the results of his studies to the public's judgement in the conviction to have made a contribution in favor of the improvement of the instrument that has filled his best hours of labor.

Conferencia del Prof. R. Muñoz

En un acto patrocinado por el Centro Guitarrístico, pronunció interesante conferencia sobre el tema "Gauchos y Guitarras", el distinguido autor argentino R. Muñoz.

El conferenciante en estilo ameno, ática la forma, bello el concepto, estableció la íntima relación que ha existido entre el gaucho, hijo de esta tierra, en el que palpitó un ansia incontenible de libertad, y la guitarra que fué el medio con que expresó su pasión erótica o su ideal de ser libre.

La guitarra con su dulce voz, plena de expresión, apuntó el disertante, fué el agente que usó el indio para transmitirnos su mensaje de dolor su pena de raza oprimida, de ser menospreciado.

En ella cantaron el gaucho y el aborigen, su rebeldía, su resistencia a los poderes extranjeros, haciendo de un instrumento foráneo, el suyo, el típico de esta tierra americana.

Acompañó a los guerreros de la epopeya en épicos combates y junto al filo de las lanzas estuyo la voz de bronce de los bordones o el tono melancólico de la prima.

Artigas, Güemes y San Martín Lavalleja y Lamadrid, continuó el conferenciante, la tomaron en sus manos para poner en ella su tristeza, su nostalgia, o un grito de libertad.

De su boca salieron vidalas, estilos y milongas que exhaló un alma enamorada o inspiró el corazón intrépido del guerrillero invicto.

El profesor Muñoz nos fué diciendo con fruición cómo se identificaron gauchos y guitarras, cómo anduvieron juntos los caminos de la emancipación, cómo asistió a la creación de patrias, cómo han sido guitarra y alma criolla una misma cosa.

Intercalando pasajes del conferenciante, la guitarrista Nelly Miravalles de González, hizo oír inspiradas composiciones de exquisito sabor nativo, ofrecidas con alta dignidad.

Una selecta concurrencia premió con cálidos aplausos a los actores.   P. A.

Translation of the article from the daily *"El Bien Publico"* of Thursday October 31, 1946, published in Montevideo:

"Lecture of Professor R. Muñoz

In an act sponsored by the Centro Guitarristico, the distinguished Argentine author R. Muñoz spoke an interesting lecture about *"Gauchos* and Guitars".

The lecturer in a pleasant style, roused the form, the beautiful concept, established the intimate relation that had existed between the *gaucho*, son of this land, in him beat an irrepressible yearning for liberty, and the guitar that was the medium with which he expressed his erotic passion or ideal to be free.

The guitar with its sweet voice, full of expression, the lecturer annotated, was the agent that the Indian used for transmitting his message of pain, his sadness of an oppressed race, to be undervalued.

In it the *gaucho* and aborigine sang, their rebellion, their resistance to the foreign powers, making of a foreign instrument, their own, the typical of this South American land.

It accompanied the soldiers of the epoch of epic combat and along the edge of the spear the voice of bronze of the basses or the melancholy tone of the first string.

Artigas, Güemes, San Martin, Lavalleja and Lamadrid, the lecturer continued, they took in their hands to put on it their sadness, their nostalgia, or a shout of liberty.

From their mouths out came *Vidalas, Estilos* and *Milongas* that exhaled a soul in love or inspired the intrepid heart of the unconquered guerrilla.

Professor Muñoz was telling us with fruition like the gauchos and guitars identified, walked along the paths of emancipation together, as they attended the creation of the countries, like the guitar and *criolla* soul had been the same thing.

Merging landscapes of the lecturer, the guitarist Nelly Miravelles de Gonzalez, made the inspired compositions of exquisite native flavor heard, offered with a high dignity.

A select gathering awarded the performers with enthusiastic applause. P. A."

From the Ricardo Muñoz archive, in his thick volume titled *"Conferencias"* (Lectures) is this gem of thousands of words. It was written in July 1940 and given several times, first on Thursday, July 25, 1940 and the guitar pieces performed by Maria Angelica Funes for the "Circulo Amigos de la Buena Musica" at the "Asociacion Cristiana de Jovenes". Later, once again on Sunday October 1, 1944, in the city of Parana, Ricardo Muñoz gave his lecture *"Gauchos y Guitarras"* with concert guitarist Celia Salomó´ssn de Font musically illustrating the lecture; for the Circulo de la Prensa in Buenos Aires on Saturday May 4, 1946 with Pedro Herrera playing guitar, this time in Montevideo with Nelly Zuma Miravalles on Monday, October 28, 1946, and later at the "Peña Amado Nervo" on Sunday, November 21, 1948 with Elena Beatriz Pereyra. It contains all the original text, including references to Professor *Don* Nicolas Ortega playing the guitar.

"Gauchos y Guitarras" by Ricardo Muñoz

"Musical Program
1. Preludio Indigena by Ricardo Muñoz
2. Nostalgia Triste by Ricardo Muñoz
3. Milonga by Abel Fleury
4. El Carretaro by Ricardo Muñoz
5. Vidalita by Julio Sagreras

Gauchos y Guitarras   (Gauchos and Guitars)

Ladies and Gentlemen:

Before beginning this friendly conversation, I have to intimately thank in name of the artists that accompany me and in my own, the auspices and kind welcome experienced in this house of traditional culture and patria, which permit us to make music, letters, and to use the word to remember that which was the *gaucho* spirit on the guitar, its box of harmony, the inseparable companion that kept in its box, all the South American sentiment in the most diverse aspects of the citizen life.

Thanks to the Director who offers us such a magnificent opportunity, thanks to Mr. (host) by his kind words of affection and stimulus, thanks to the select audience that prepares to listen to us, especially to the Argentine women who arrived to this hall from the four points, impregnating us to the blessed perfume of mother, wife, daughter or sister, and moves us to the most profound of the heart.

Since it is, to be the most possible synthetic without defrauding hopes, within the little I can say on our *gaucho* ancestors; to go back to the origin of the things, to follow them step by step to the cross over the infinite march full of stumbles, successes and doubts, it isn't an erudite display, but, to go directly to the same base of the problem, to scrutinize and understand it, to cerebrally deduce the interesting fundamentals of the future, inherent in every particular case of the same life.

To evoke this historic past of the *gaucho* and his national instrument, it's necessary to make in every moment; next to find the forgotten, especially in the present youth, those that are unconcerned by the past things.

The showy peripheral decoration of the *gaucho*, is undoubtedly, the real cause that has to hide the true profundity, that is to say, is the cause to hide as Pedro Goyena said: 'that beautiful demonstration of the natural human, that kept the germ of the future in the breast of his virgin and potent soul'.

Presently, in fiestas, circuses and theaters the *gaucho* is to be presented in diverse carnival characters, the youth receiving, the most deplorable impression of which really that promising and sensible man was, the same today converted into an easy industry occuring with his song and music.

The product of a native art is listened to daily that no work by inspiration, but interest, the *gaucho* was creating the kind copla and only gained the applause of the populace that admired him profoundly; in the present, (the things have changed), many have dedicated to fabricate gaucho singers with the only interest of gaining money, certainly very legal, but making liars of a pseudo art, prevaricating sentiments that aren't felt and which by that same only arrive at the epidermis of the people.

Sometimes one of these songs fabricated by the mind, brings to the soul of the listeners momentarily, instead, the authentic, always brings, invades and persists in the kindness and the heart of the regions, because its spirit conquers, not only the epidermis, but without some effort, picrces the flesh and intimately takes in the most profound zones of the social roots; the true *gaucho* song, was always an inspiration, admirably felt, expressing the inexpressable, Marquez the poet inspired in the same thoughts, wrote the following:

"They learn our songs
that never cause dishonor,
they are the thread of gold
that adorn the traditions. —

They might have some notions
Of the dressage, shearing, branding,
they discover what is enclosed
in the farmhand's works,
It doesn't appear strange
being in their own land!"

Aprendan nuestras canciones
que nunca causan desdoro,
ellas son el hilo de oro
que bordan las tradiciones.-
Tengan algunas nociones
de la doma, esquila, yerra,
descubran lo que se encierra
en los trabajos camperos,
¡ No parezcan extranjeros
estando en su propia tierra !

And by that the true artist turns out today, at the front of a new wave of a folkloric lie, very difficult to expose his truths in a just measure of his fidelity, as for nothing in the pernicious examples of attested fiction of zapateos that *"patean"* (they stamp their feet), countrymen and *"gauchos"* of a band of street musicians without more *PAMPA* than the audacity; only folkloric falsifications they contemplate of the gaucho and the aboriginal in his simplicity and evident customs, attire and songs; those that worthily concoct with the land of its towns expressing in music exquisite sentiments of mutual understanding among the mankind, whose authentic indigenous treasuries deserve the most sacred respect. –

Lamentably the *gaucho* who leaving dark to light fertile fields has already disappeared, those who wandered in the shade in memoriam of the sons of the pampa; the sad or happy voice, of the beautiful and virile popular romancer, a synthesis of the South American soul, an authentic document of nationality, the blacksmith of a moral physiognomy that set foot in the time and space, of his own accents opening musical routes, who was with his song and his guitar, the polyphonic source of the great modern orchestral conceptions of Latin America.

To examine history of this hero of the Argentine life in society, and classify according to his vocations from Martin Fierro and Santos Vega, the poet, the singer, the *"guitarrero"*, to the *"matrero gaucho"* of shooting, all without exception *payadors* (singers), including herdsman, local guide, pathfinder, tracker, cart driver, soldier, etc. and in these *gaucho* payadors is where we will find the popular instinctive artist, in whose intellectual faculties, without knowing it, the poetry a talent to be a central point where coincides the sensible directions of the multitude of which it formed a part, and as acutely absorbed the sentiment of his collectivity, it converts as says Fernan Silva Valdéz in the *"Termometro de su pueblo"*.
(Thermometer of the populace — literal — Thermometer of his people) –

Gaucho and guitar are the same thing, they are intimately united, forged in the same crucible, one is impossible without the other, even more so than the involvement of man and woman, maybe also of man and his God, and permit me to say this possible sacrilege, from the source of this beautiful poem titled *"PLEGARIS DEL MAZORQUERO A LA VIRGEN DEL LUJAN"* which acutely defines the problem gaucho and guitar with his religion; is one condemned to death that he offered the virgin his life, the spurs, his horses, ultimately the braids of his china and all quantity he had; as to his guitar, he promised to sing with it, but it is the only thing he didn't offer; as says: *Don* Hector Pedro Bloomberg:

Gaucho virgin, my virgin,
Little virgin of Lujan:
Tomorrow at daybreak,
I'm going to shoot Rozas. –

I will bring my Nazarene
of silver to your altar,
and my five parejeros
for your church they will be;

If instead from four bullets
that tomorrow that have to give me,
they only stretch me with stakes
Little virgin of Lujan. –

Issac my poor extremist,
you cry for her in Monserrat,
I will bring you two of your braids
and of blue you will dress.

If in the patio of the retirement,
when I begin to lighten,
only give me a thousand lashes,
Little virgin of Lujan. –

Gaucho virgin, my virgin,
only remains to me a handful
of silver to offer you,
now I don't have any more.
that my criollo guitar
and in it I sing to you
while there remains one string
Little virgin of Lujan. –

/ / / / / / / / / / / / /

Virgen gaucha, Virgen mía,
Virgencita de Luján:
Mañana al clarear el alba,
Rozas me va a fusilar.–

Llevaré mis nazarenas
de plata para tu altar,
y mis cinco parejeros
para tu iglesia serán;
Si en vez de cuatro balas
que mañana me han de dar,
me estaquearan solamente,
Virgencita de Luján.–

I mi pobre mazorquera,
la que llora en Monserrat,
te llevará sus dos trenzas
y de azúl te vestirá.–
Si en el patio del Retiro,
cuando comience a clarear,
solo me dan mil azotes,
Virgencita de Luján

Virgen gaucha, Virgen mía,
solo me queda un puñal
de plata para ofrecerte,
ya no tengo nada mas
que mi guitarra de criollo
y en ella te he de cantar
mientras le quede una cuerda,
Virgencita de Luján.–

/ / / / / / / / / / / / /

The music of the gaucho sprouts on the guitar from the four points, he has already run a great distance; in the supreme idea to involve its art to the most profound arteries of the national music; Boero, Gilardi, Ginastera, Guastavino, Ciacoba, Broqua, Villa-Lobos and many others in the open furrow of the future artistic constructions have overflowed, and significant of the instructed orientations are the seeds of preaching that go on shaping the full work.

The gaucho who is only born, as a natural product of his land, because if he was possibly the sentimental inheritor of the aborigine, primitive and true owner of the land of the continent in the exquisite splendor of his power and civilization, destroyed in the most frightening drama that registers the history of all times, in this way, in the music, which is pure expression, it reveals the predominant ethic of the honesty and loyalty of those cultures, whose moral, was the most exact geometry of his customs.

Today he lives through the lacerated pain that shatters his flesh and permits to contemplate a thousand beautiful things of his spirit, where it shelters the legendary virtues of humility, the most horrifying poverty that consigns it in the secular *"Caballero del Hambre"* (Knight of Hunger). – Those that remain, now cry the sadness of his fainted hopes without tears in music, before the impotence that day to day is gigantic, and impedes to mitigate the desolation of his compressed souls, obliged to a perpetual resignation.

2436

This indigenous music, essentially sorrowful and cadential, humble and sad, tells us of the disaster of a race, legends of the Gods that were, for centuries united in the impenetrable abysm of the night, of religions and rites that never returned, forever fallen in the distant twilight of a fatal dream.

In this way, their songs are, as Musset said in one of his celebrated verses: "the most desperate songs, are the most beautiful songs." We will have to hear professor *Don* Nicolas Ortega in music, we will listen to this sorrow, that agony, that Indian moan that shudders to all South America.

In past centuries, in the coastal, in the forests, in the desert regions, there far away, joined to the tracks born in the strange mountains, where the large rivers that cast down the bottomless in the profundities of the planet began, above the foothills of white peaks among the beauty of the reborn thicket, the man appears harmonized with his song, the murmur of the slopes to climb down from the heights, the whistle of the wind cut by the knives of rock, the placidity of the lagoons and the shining life of a thousand petals born to chance, in the very picturesque and virgin garden of nature.

All this magnificent scenery offered rough places, it contributed to form his spirit besides the mind of the *gaucho* settler, to form a concept of life, tuning in a sacred and intimate communion between his being and his surroundings, about beauty, about the great natural forces of harmony in the Universe; he loved his country as if idolizing it, to God, to the family, and made a cult of friendship.

This settler that was an inventive, energetic, generous, patient, hospitable and haughty man, that was a tamer, a hunter, a shepherd, a fencer, a healer, a saddler, a cook, a veterinarian, meteorologist, he knew music and poetry deeply, all he did was an object to his song, and like the bird, he sang expressions of enjoyment, of impending or satisfied love, of thankfulness and plentifulness; he sang of his own pain and misadventure; as the Indian he sang, that sorrow that is the priest of the experience, that is the anvil forging the character, that knocks down mountains, who appropriates the secret of life and death, who dignifies all, and discovers all; he sang of humble poverty, to that phantasm that liberates us from enemies, that connects the humble virtues of faith, hope and charity, that awards sweet smiles, sincerity, truth and blessed love.

We put a little attention and we hear his sadness and emotion in music, performed on the guitar by the virtuoso hands of maestro Mr. Ortega. . . . . He performs *"Triste"* by Muñoz

The *gaucho payador* (singer) is the bard, the troubadour of the middle ages, who vibrates between life and to be approaching it; he sings to the heroes and in the chronicle of the customs the tears, it is a biography, it is a document to the historian of tomorrow, he is the wandering Jew, without a residence, whose only fortune is his verses and his voice; it is like the poet Marquez says:

A loose piece of the Andes	Un pedazo de Anda desprendido
To sculpt his own monument,	para esculpir su propio monumento,
is a pedestal of glorious Argentina,	es pedestal de glorias argentinas,
a howl of the Pampa, that transports the wind. —	gemido Pampa,,que transporta el viento.-

Every *gaucho payador* (singer) was a lyrical antenna capturing the waves of the terrain that returned extended, perfected or as if they were inside their sentimental measurement; he was an epic poet of the nation, he was a popular genius, he was only one individual creating by mouth the people of that crowd consecrated with his kindness and admiration, because the current of the inspired truth and sincerity, invading the most noble zones of his own strangeness, common to all the hearts, he related equal customs and expressions of the collective sense.

The *gaucho*, he is the same tradition in the plains of the open fields symbolizing the abnegation, the love and the sacrifice of the untamable masses that surrendered life to the magnificent sense of the liberty, constructing titanically the glorious epic of Latin America with the points of his spears.

A symbol of the gaucho spirit, the guitar, hung from his shoulder during the heroic struggles of the emancipation, the enemy's saber cut his strings a thousand times, it splintered its box and injured others a thousand brave as finalized as their guitar, fallen in the fields of glory; later played by chiefs and officials, they sang of the victory, they cried of the defeat, glad for the exile, they shouted independence accompanying the song of the homeland, between the hot coals, ponchos, flukes, penknives and spears.

Delio Panizza, the famous poet, inspired by such tragedy and so much beauty, sculpted the bizarre gaucho epic in letters titled *"Guitarras y Lanzas"*, whose content in the faithful expression of the sentiments of faith and hope, of country and liberty, that sheltered in the breast of the centaur and culminated with the victory. – His verses say so:

The following verse is recited. —

> Guitars and spears, are all of the history;
> all of the epic of my land. . .
> guitars that ring by their performance
> spears that vibrate by their arrogance.
>
> Guitars and spears are the inflamed
> formidable vision of their episodes. . .
> the guitar that marks the faith of its life
> and spears that guide the faith of their hate!
>
> Guitars and spears are the entire poem
> that overturn in the wind of the primitive home. . .
> guitars that sing the supreme desire
> and spears that affirm the native creed!
>
> Guitars and spears translate united
> with all certainty the criollo legend
> guitars that cry over the injuries
> and spears that rise up above the contest!
>
> Guitars and spears give the most profound
> understanding of the soul of our gauchos . . . .
> Guitars that say their life wandering
> And spears that shout their fierce courage!
>
> Guitars and spears lofty stand
> from the same background of the epics . . . .
> guitars that evoke native tragedies
> and spears that put their title in them!
>
> Sonorous guitars, that were going to the shoulder
> of the old gauchos; tigers and improvising poets
> like a hope of an emerald life
> over the ardent ruby of the battles.
>
> Guitars that in the nights of truces, dream
> to the poor fire of sad burners,
> they temper the souls for other days
> awakening brightly in their hearts. –
>
> Issac who some aurora, join to the gate
> of the ranch, lost like a hope,
> they said goodbye to the companion
> that ties the handkerchief, trembling, to a spear!

Guitarras y lanzas, son toda la história;
toda la epopeya de la tierra mía...
guitarras que suenan por su ejecutoria
lanzas que vibran por su altanería.-

Guitarras y lanzas son la enardecida
visión formidable de sus episodios.....
guitarra que marcan la fé de su vida
y lanzas que guian la fé de sus odios !

Guitarras y lanzas son todo el poema
que vuelcan en los vientos del lar primitivo...
guitarras que cantan el ansia suprema
y lanzas que afirman el credo nativo !

Guitarras y lanzas traducen unidas
con toda certeza la criolla leyenda !
guitarras que lloran sobre las heridas
y lanzas que se alzan sobre la contienda !

Guitarras y lanzas dan la mas profunda
comprensión del alma de nuestro gauchaje....
guitarras que dicen su vida errabunda
y lanzas que gritan su fiero coraje !

Guitarras y lanzas se yerguen altivas
desde el fondo mismo de las epopeyas.....
guitarras que evocan tragedias nativas
y lanzas que ponen su rúbrica en ellas !

Guitarras sonoras, que iban a la espalda
de los viejos gauchos; tigres y troveros,
como una esperanza de viva esmeralda
sobre el rubí ardiente de los entreveros !

Guitarras que en noches de tregua, soñadas
a la pobre lumbre de tristes fogones,
templaban las almas para otras jornadas
despertando brios en los corazones.-

I que alguna aurora, junto a la tranquera
del rancho, perdido como una esperanza,
dijeron adioses a la compañera
que atara el pañuelo, temblando, a una lanza !

I lanzas febriles de sangre y denuedo
que fueron amparo, suplicio, tortura,
de aquellos que nunca sintieron el miedo
porque eran probados a ruda bravura !

Lanzas que se alzaban rectas hácia el cielo
sobre la estatuaria fila del gauchaje,
y eran en la plaza del nativo suelo
como admiraciones a tanto coraje !

2439

Issac spears manufacturing of blood and daring
that was shelter, anguish, torture,
of those that never synthesized the fear
because they were tested by a violent ferocity!

Spears that they raised upright toward the heaven
above the statuary row of the gauchos,
and were in the plaza of the native ground
as admiration to such courage!

Issac who some afternoon from mad battles
when the soul acquires a claw of rudeness
to pass a breast with its acute steel
they made pieces, of the poor guitar!

Guitars and spears! or strings and spearheads,
were in my land, dreams and revenges. –
for the battle: spears and guitars!
For the loves: guitars and spears. –

Güemes was a *Gaucho* stopping enemies with spears and guitars; Lamadrid, Paz, Oribe, Quiroga, Urquiza, Artigas, Lavalleja and many others who sang their victories from the fields were *gauchos* from Asencio to Maipo, to the rhythm of the plucked or strummed *milongas* on the strings of their guitars, giving free rein and improvisations that emerged by a thousand triumphs that demanded the independence of the new homelands, great and sovereign over the face of the land. –

We'll listen to our national heroes parading between the masterful fingers of maestro Ortega, in the traditional milonga arranged for the instrument that they loved so; we remember epochs of intense glory and satisfaction:

The *Milonga* by Fleury is performed:

Crossing the immense mass of the Andes, created by God of fire and coronated by snow, of bare granite with the nape of the neck of the condor, of nude peaks and covered by clouds, where time stagnates and the crater buds like the only flower in its maximum dignity or crossing the ardent forests between the clearance limit of the road that sways to the horizon, and while the bushings of the big wheels sigh, slowly the cart slips, an earthen ship tanned by the wind and hugged by the Sun, a relic coated by dust, the legendary grandmother of the railroads masses tufted by smoke devouring distances, that arrives late or problematically.

It leads the festive gaucho or cattleman, to be instinctively knowledgeable of the plains, mountains and forests, that which is the most complete topography, the living map of the regions, capable to announce the enemy from where he approaches; it is that he never erred, on the trail, although in the difficult moments to cut jungles or cross infinite plains under the blue ether of the sky without dimensions or points, in the eternal nights without more light than the stars or in the grays and blackish furies and cruel forces of the crazed nature, sending floods under the trembling thunder that resounds in space, without more resources than the sacrifice.

The wagon proceeds its march rolling between valleys of lighted clouds by flashes of lightning, that visit the landscape of livid colors, sparks that as electric claws seize and splinter the trunks of felled trees and century old *algarrobos,* that fold, twist and stretch out as if they were rubber; distant shouts of quivering ranches that appear as sleepwalking bundles shaking by the impetus of the chilly and occasional violent wind; in this way the march carries on cutting a path through a mountain rim, prairie and epileptic pastures in full din of the torment.

Clad in water over the field the wagon wheel and an illuminated crack of fire for another one; the rain suddenly subsides and the wind relents, the clouds begin to open as if they were immense doors permitting to admire bits of heaven under the rule of the stars; the wagon halts in full desert, in emotional solitude that is a torment born as a negative sign; the gaucho sweeper examines the terrain foreseeing the attacks of the Condor, the serpent, the tiger or puma that always lurks hidden in the thicket, the same that he of the Indians and bandits of those times, that kill and rob the caravans that carry the merchandise of the villages from one extreme to the other of the country.

The *gauchos* crowded together around the improvised burners, frozen stiff, with the hard eyes, the rigid fingers, wrapped in their thick *ponchos* with the guns on their arms and the ears alert; between one and another mate they commented on the day's brave journey, while the wagoner, a *gaucho* of quiet happiness, solemn, a brown figure with a hairy beard, with woodblock reliefs, inspected the vehicles, cargo and animals, convinced of which all is in order and ready for whatever event, takes the guitar that lacks nothing in his hands sound wood that is a fragile thing, docile, familiar; he plucks it slowly and so listening likewise, intoxicates with its vibrations of the basses, whose hesitant melodies, echo of sobs, alternate with clear sounds, tenuous and lacerating of the trebles, with which he accompanies the sacrifice of his life. – The scene is the sonorous expression of human misfortune, smoothed in part, by his song, united to the song of a hundred diverse birds of varied plumage decorating the soul and the courage, now emotional by the fragrance of the thousand rustic petals that candidly, with ingenuity, offer him their color and perfume from the infinite garden of the virgin nature molded by flowers.

His song, is the saddened soul pursuing perpetual distances; it is sorrow, nocturnal, it is the character and the will, it is doubt and firmness, it is sky and land, it is love and a sigh, it is mother, your girlfriend and her puppies which suffer and only God knows, if some day he returns to see.

The good and emotional guitar, that feels, laughs and cries with who plucks it, irradiating the faithful expression of the spirit of man like no other instrument, being adapted to all the sensible kinds, it translates the medullary sense and emotion of the soul of this bronze race in music, whose laments, complaints and tristes, as successive echoes sprinkle the fields of South America.

We'll listen to the sad melodies of his characteristic song, performed by the named artist present:

The song *"El Carretero"* by Muñoz is performed:

In the struggles of South American independence, the guitar was the instrument used along with the spear; San Martin, the *"Santo de la Espada"* (Sword Saint) as he was named by the eminent Ricardo Rojas, was a fairly good performer and among military men of the epoch who most distinguished in such a sense, General *Don* Gregorio Araoz de Lamadrid is found in first place, who organized bands of guitars in his armies. – For Lamadrid, of *gaucho* spirit, civilized and consecrated to liberty, the guitar was an instrument of war and romance; he dominated his troops and entered to slaughter singing *vidalitas;* it is said on a certain occasion his soldiers were starving, living raggedly, wearing worn out shoes almost without food nor pay they murmured unfavorably about him in an ungrateful moment of the campaigns; the General knows confidentially of the silent protest, and to calm it and to obligate his army to confront the enemy, he took a guitar and sang the following phrases of this *vidalita:*

"Constancy, brave men of Rioja!
Vidalita,
Although there isn't anything to eat;
Your friends of Tucuman,
Vidalita,
know to die or to conquer. —

> ¡ Constancia, bravos riojanos !
> Vidalitá,
> aunque no haya que comer;
>   Tus amigos tucumanos,
> Vidalitá,
> sabrán morir o vencer.-

This was sufficient for the army under his command who would search for food where the enemy was found, who strenuously confronted and conquered. —

General *Don* José Maria Paz, also a *gaucho,* left many facts of the intestinal struggles related in his memoirs, in which many times they revealed the shouts of the soldiery, the hunger that consumed them, and also said: "General Lamadrid did more than the Savior when with five pieces of bread he fed five thousand persons, because five pieces of bread, have more substance than two vessels of wine and a *Vidalita.*" —

The thoughts for the guitar by Lamadrid were of a socratical profundity, easy to understand by the following anecdote, from when he was already old and only had to tell his young comrades in arms: "To impose respect and value to the *criollo* soldiers, a good military man needs to dominate three principles: 1st. To know how to command as a father; 2nd. to know how to fight like a tiger; 3rd. to play the guitar, like an angel." —

We'll listen to the famous *Vidalita* of love, of war and sorrow:

The song *"Vidalita"* by Sagreras is performed:

The history that I have now said; after the battle in which Lamadrid and his troops, the field, along with the injuries, the pieces of spears and sabers, the dead horses and spilled blood, remained covered by splintered guitars.

Much later, the *gaucho* seeded his fields with it, loved intensely, constructed the country the most beautiful of the land that our best deposited in our hands, with the hope of the future: we are to be worthy of such a sublime inheritance, tending to progress of which everyone constitutes a happy vocation; only in this way can we avoid to follow being our gaucho, which the poet Ricardo M. Llanes wrote for my *estilo "Inspiracion":*

A laurel of renunciation
in the face of the compatriot,
that cements with his hand
of the progress, the building:
for being the squandering
of the forgotten South American!

> Laurel de renunciación
> en la frente del paisano,
> que cimentó con su mano
> del progreso, el edificio:
> ¡ para ser el desperdicio
> del olvido americano !

Buenos Aires July of 1940
Ricardo Muñoz

I need to thank my colleague, Alfredo Escande, for translating a handful of elusive nouns and adjectives. 1 18 13

This is translated from Ricardo Muñoz's unpublished book *"Historia Universal de la Guitarra" Volume VIII* *"La Escuela de Tárrega en La Argentina"*

"Nelly Zuma Miravalles

Her Origin:

She is the daughter of *Don* Raul Miravalles and *Doña* Margarita Lartigue, born in Buenos Aires, the 16th of June of 1920. —

Her Education:

She studied music in the Conservatorio General Urquiza with the Director *Don* Hector J. Milanese, and at the same time, from the age of 11 years old, with Ricardo Muñoz, the author of this history, the guitar, to be awarded a diploma at the age of 15 years old, then proceeding in a course of perfection, with the same maestro.

Her Virtuosity:

In diverse opportunities she performed as a student in prepared performances in such a quality, achieving to come out very graceful in the responsibilities to which artistically she faced up to in such occasions.

Afterward she gave some concerts with excellent guitaristic results, to be very well applauded by the gathering.— The 26th of July of 1932 she was presented in the Salon Teatro of the Sociedad Española of the town of Marcos Paz, where she lived, performing with her younger sister Elena Judit, who for

household reasons was seen obligated to abandon the instrument, in Part 1. as a soloist: *"Paisano Alegre"* by Schumann, *"Danza Oriental"* by Lubomirsky, and *"Allegro"* by Coste, the 2nd Part entrusted to the named Elena who interpreted *"Minuetto"* by Sor, *"Preludio No. 4"* by Tárrega and *"Sueño"* by Tárrega; in the 3rd Part as a duo, both playing *"Lagrima"* by Tárrega, *"Minuetto"* of *Don Giovanni* by Mozart-Muñoz, *"Vidalita"* by Sinopoli, *"Recuerdos de la Alhambra"* by Tárrega-Sagreras, the clamorous success obtained obligated them to play some encores.

According to their performances and heard by *Don* Domingo Prat, he wrote this in his *"Diccionario de Guitarristas"*: "Although very young the Miravalles sisters will see a frank self-improvement with optimism in the art that they cultivate. — We can appreciate their ponderable present merits.... in the halls of the daily *"La Razon"* and in the *"Direcion Nacional de Bellas Artes"* on the dates December 4, 1932 and July 30, 1933, respectively. — Beautiful acts that illustrated well in documented lectures by their professor Ricardo Muñoz."—

Translation of the photo dedication:

"To our beloved professor Mr. Ricardo Muñoz and family with the most profound gratitude.

Nelly and Elena Miravalles
November 14, 1932."

CABILDO 875

VELADA ARTISTICA

ORGANIZADA POR EL CONJUNTO
DE ARTE NATIVO
"ARIEL"

NOVIEMBRE 10 DE 1931

Nelly and Elena Miravalles take part in an Artistic Evening on Tuesday November 10, 1931. The show opens with a *Laud* and Piano duet. The laud had been popular since the arrival of the Estudiantina Figaro to the Rio de la Plata in 1885. Ensembles of the *Bandurria* and *Laud* existed into the recording age with the *Estudiantina "Centenario" Bandurria* Trio and Guitar for Victor in 1910, *Rondalla Vazquez* for *Disco Atlanta* in 1913, *Rondalla Usandizaga* on Victor during WWI from 1917-1929 and *Rondalla Cauvilla Prim* on *Disco Nacional Odeon* label from1925-1929. This last group played on the *Radio LR2* in Buenos Aires as late as 1937.

Buenos Aires, Noviembre de 1931.

Señor ....

  La Comisión Directiva del Club Colegiales se complace en invitar a Vd. a la velada artística que, organizada por la Agrupación de Arte Nativo "Ariel", se realizará en el local social el Martes 10 del actual a las 21 horas, de acuerdo al programa que se acompaña.

  Saluda a Vd. muy atte.

Lorenzo Sanchez
Secretario

Alberto Garcia Torres
Presidente

"The Board of Directors of the Club Colegiales has the pleasure to invite you to the artistic evening organized by the *Arte Nativo "Ariel"* group, that will take place in the social hall on Tuesday the 10th of the current month, by agreement of the program that accompanies this. Sincerely yours, Lorenzo Sanchez – Secretary, Alberto García Torres – President."

The Miravalles sisters, Nelly and Elena play Tárrega, Sor, Schumann, Mozart, including some transcriptions by their maestro Ricardo Muñoz, and end the evening with a duet of *"Recuerdos de la Alhambra"* by Tárrega-Sagreras, first performed in 1917 by Julio S. Sagreras and his student Adela del Valle.

PROGRAMA

I PARTE:

Presentación del conjunto nativo "ARIEL", que dirije la folklorista: CONCEPCION TRIGUEIRO.

Laud y piano: (Composiciones originales de Concepción Trigueiro ejecutadas por la autora y el PROFESOR ROMAN GONZALEZ:

a) **Vidalita original.**
b) **Zamba pampeana.**
c) **La canción del arriero** (tonada pampeana).
d) **El marucho** (bailecito norteño).

Recitación por JOSE F. RODRIGUEZ DENIS:

1.° **Toque de atención** (soneto), de A. SLIPPARO.
2.° **El facón** (poema), CARLOS A. CASTELLAN.
3.° **(Fragmentos del gaucho Rosendo Flores),** de FLORENCIO IRIARTE.

Con comentarios musicales.

4.° **El camalote**, de RAFAEL OBLIGADO.

Canto, violín y piano, por C. TRIGUEIRO, MIGUEL TAFURI y RAMON GONZALEZ:

e) **La correntina** (chamarrita).
f) **La puestera** (estilo).
g) **Noche serena** (serenata), de C. TRIGUEIRO.
h) **Chi'a perra** (cueca sanjuanina), de C. TRIGUEIRO.

II PARTE:

Guitarra clásica, por las las niñas NELLY y ELENA MIRAVALLES:

ELENA MIRAVALLES { **Preludio N.° 5** — TARREGA.
{ **Minuetto en La** — SORS.

NELLY MIRAVALLES { **Paisano alegre** — SCHUMANN-MUÑOZ.
{ **Danza Oriental** — LUROMIRSKY-MUÑOZ.

ELENA Y NELLY { 1.° **Minuetto** (Don Giovanni) — MOZART-MUÑOZ.
MIRAVALLES { 2.° **Serenata Morisca** — CHAPI-PRAT.
{ 3.° **Recuerdos de la Alhambra** — TARREGA-SAGRERAS.

RECITAL DE POESIA CLASICA IBERO-AMERICANA, por JOSE F. RODRIGUEZ DENIS:

Fugitiva, de PEDRO J. NAON (argentino).
Madrigal romántico, de G. URBINA (mexicano).
La plegaria del lobo, de J. SANTOS CHOCANO (peruano).
Sembrando, de M. R. BLANCO BELMONTE (español).
La vuelta al hogar (fragmentos), de PEREZ BONALDE (venezolano).

Nelly Zuma Miravalles

Translation of the photo dedication on the reverse:

"To my maestro *Don* Ricardo Muñoz with all my affection.
Nelly Miravalles, March 30, 1937."

The 10th of October of 1939, she equally interpreted the lecture of her maestro titled *"La Guitarra Hispano — Japonesa"*, in the hall of the Consejo Nacional de Mujeres, before the presence of the Ambassador of Japan, Dr. Arturo Uchiyama and a gathering of the Japanese community that filled the location. — The 11th of August of 1940 in the Asociacion Guitarristica Argentina interpreting exclusively works of her maestro in a concert that was made in his homage, receiving a lot of applause and congratulations. —

The next year she made a performance in the "Galeria Argentina" de Pintura (Art Gallery), performing works by Sor, Bach, Coste, Terzi, Gottschalk, Muñoz, Fleury and Anido, with full approval of the hall then followed by a long absence for health reasons and a reappearance on the 27th of August of 1946 in front of the Comision Asesora and the Jurado de la Comision Nacional de Cultura, Ministerio de Educacion, to present the "Guitarra Argentina" her maestro *Don* Ricardo Muñoz, in which she performed, demonstrating the sonorous quality of the same on chords, scales, *arpeggios, legatos, tremolos,* national music and of the classics of the piano and the guitar, in the hall of the Museo de Arte Decorativo de la Nacion, the approval was unanimous.

In September of 1946 she gave a concert in the Circulo General Urquiza, being very well received and applauded, then she embarked on a visit to the City of Montevideo, Uruguay, appearing in the "Centro Guitarristico del Uruguay, Conrado P. Koch", presenting to the critics of that nation the Argentine Guitars of her maestro and her personal artistic endowments, to perform on them the 26th of October: *"Preludio"* by Tárrega; *"Estudio No. 2"* by Pujol; *"Scherzo"* by Tárrega; *"Carrillion"* by Terzi; *"Gran Tremolo"* by Gottschalk; *"Estilo"* by Fleury; *"Vidalita"* by Sagreras; *"Andante"* by Sor; *"Allegretto"* by Coste; *"Allegretto"* by Muñoz; *"Preludio"* by Bach-Ayestaran and *"Preludio"* from the 2nd *Sonata* by Bach-Muñoz. —

While it is certain in this case of a student of the author of this present history, for the first time to cross the border of her country, it's impossible for me to praise by my own account this performance of which I was a witness, but neither is it possible for me to remain silent, the performance ended, the great Uruguayan maestro, Pedro Mascaro y Reissig, assistant to the act, with his family, went up all of a sudden to the stage, asked for forgiveness from Mr. Ramon Gonzalez, husband of the artist, evidently emotional he kissed her hands insistently and classified them as *"Divinas"* (Divine).

Two days later she illustrated the lecture of her maestro titled: *"Gauchos y Guitarras"* in the same institution, in which occasion she obtained the same triumph as before.

The following month, the 24th of November, in homage to the Day of the Music, she repeated the concert given in Montevideo and for the same reason, in the Salon "La Argentina", sponsored by the "Asociacion Artistica de Buenos Aires" to which these institutions also lent their support: the "Centro Guitarristico del Uruguay, Conrado P. Koch"; "Les Amis de la Guitare" of Paris, France; "The Philharmonic Society of Guitarists" of London, England; the "Chicago Classic Guitar Society" of Chicago, USA; "Asociacion Tárrega" of Rosario; "Circulo Guitarristico" of La Plata, "Asociacion Guitarristica Entrerriana" of Parana; "Asociacion Guitarristica Argentina" of Buenos Aires; "Sociedad Argentina de Autores y Compositores de Musica", "Asociacion Argentina de Musica de Camara", "Asociacion Cultural El Unisono", "Asociacion Cultural Yaravi".— Her interpretations were insistently applauded.—

The 30th of August of 1947, in the Salon "La Argentina", for the "Amigos de la Guitarra", with the sponsorship of the "Asociacion Argentina de Musica de Camara", she dedicated this performance to the eminent Maria Luisa Anido, and interpreted: *"Corrente"* by Granata; *"Gagliarda"* by Durante; *"Preludio"* by Bach; *"Estudio No. 3"* by Chopin; another *"Preludio"* by Bach; *"Aire Criollo"* by Aguirre-Anido; *"Triste No. 4"* by Aguirre-Anido; *"Gato, Aire Norteño y Evocacion Indigena"* by Anido; dedicated to the performer; *"Carrillion"* by Terzi; *"Estudio No. 2"* by Pujol and *"Capricho Andaluz"* by del Olmo.— In the program of this performance with an etching of the artist, her maestro signed the following presentation: "Since a young girl she began her musical and guitaristic studies, two times interrupted for a long time, a great temperament, fine sensibility and perfect concept of the art she practices, united to a correct willpower and discipline of her norms in the assimilation by the methodical study and patiently serene, it has permitted her to acquire the musical culture and technical capacity and expression that permits me to authorize, maybe to show to the consideration of the knowledgeable listeners and public in general.— In such virtue..... it is worthy in our consideration and artistic respect..... eager for self-improvement, for her consecration she only needs the approval by us....."

The attending public, generally guitarists and musicians, knew how to appreciate the effort made with her magnificent modern technique and her expressive endowments, to applaud incessantly to the new Argentine artist. The 23rd of October of 1954 she performed in the hall of the Damas Catolicas, interpreting works by Milan, Durante, Bach, Sor, Rubinstein, Aguirre, Anido, Williams, Muñoz and her own pieces, the next year she played for the Asociacion Guitarristica de Rosario and in this way she proceeds in her exiting career merging important radio programs, which the Radio Nacional solicited her with insistence.

Her Compositions:

We know various unpublished works of the classic and folkloric styles, of which we recall:

"*Aire Criollo*", "*Cancion de Cuna*", *Pequeña Cancion*", *Preludio No. 1*", "*El Alero*", a very rural style and sense, dedicated to her maestro, therefore we won't give an opinion about it.

Her Pedagogy:

In her private Academia she gives lessons to students, who appreciate and distinguish her."

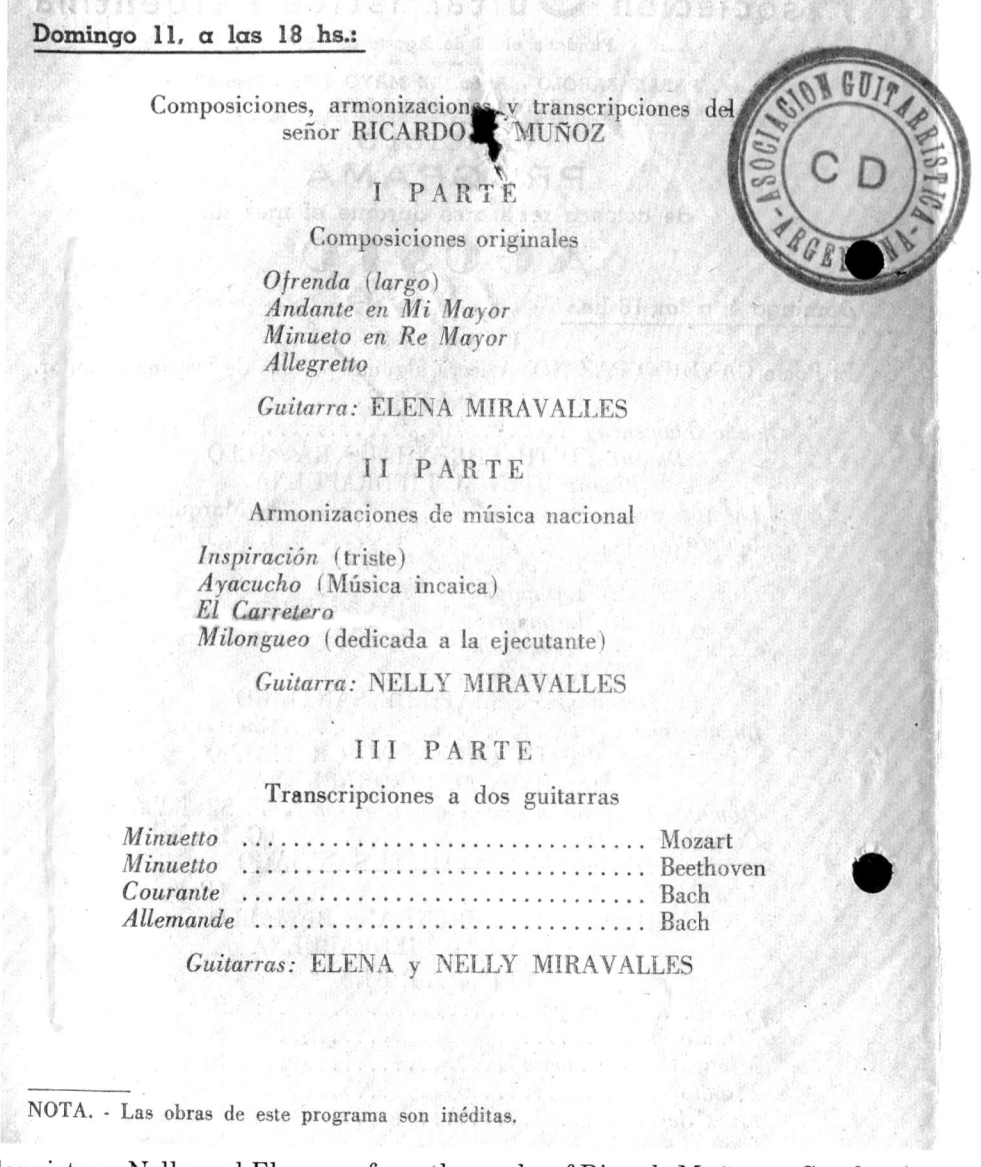

Domingo 11, a las 18 hs.:

Composiciones, armonizaciones y transcripciones del señor RICARDO MUÑOZ

I PARTE

Composiciones originales

Ofrenda (largo)
Andante en Mi Mayor
Minueto en Re Mayor
Allegretto

Guitarra: ELENA MIRAVALLES

II PARTE

Armonizaciones de música nacional

Inspiración (triste)
Ayacucho (Música incaica)
El Carretero
Milongueo (dedicada a la ejecutante)

Guitarra: NELLY MIRAVALLES

III PARTE

Transcripciones a dos guitarras

Minuetto .... Mozart
Minuetto .... Beethoven
Courante .... Bach
Allemande .... Bach

Guitarras: ELENA y NELLY MIRAVALLES

NOTA. - Las obras de este programa son inéditas.

The Miravalles sisters, Nelly and Elena perform the works of Ricardo Muñoz on Sunday August 11, 1940 for the Asociacion Guitarristica Argentina.

ASOCIACIÓN
ARTISTICA DE BUENOS AIRES

SECRETARIA: MUÑIZ 172

Φ

Agosto de 1947

Estimado consocio:

Tenemos el agrado de invitar a Ud. y familia al acto que en adhesión al **97º Aniversario de la Muerte del Gral. Don José de San Martin,** se realizará el próximo Viernes 22 del cte. a las 18.15 horas en los salones del Círculo Militar, Santa Fé 750, cedidos gentilmente a tal efecto.

Saludamos a Ud. atte.

Dr. JORGE M. AGUILAR
Secretario General

Dr. CARLOS FLORIANI
Presidente

PROGRAMA

1º   Apertura del acto por el secretario de la entidad Dr. Jorge M. Aguilar.

2º   LA GUITARRA EN EL ESPIRITU DE SAN MARTIN, disertación a cargo del Maestro Ricardo Muñoz.

3º
a) Inspiración . . . . R. Muñoz
b) Danza Mora . . . . F. Tárrega
c) Jota Aragonesa . . . . . . F. Tárrega
d) Estudio Nº 11 . . . . F. Sor
e) Cádiz . . . . Albéniz
f) Gato . . . . M. L. Anido
g) El Carretero . . . . . . R. Muñoz
h) Minué en mi mayor . . . . . F. Sor
i) Vidalita . . . . A. Fleury
j) Yaraví . . . . D. Prat

Comentarios musicales por la concertista
Nelly Z. Miravalles

INVITACIÓN ESPECIAL

Nelly Zuma Miravalles performs for the Asociacion Artistica de Buenos Aires on Friday August 22, 1947.

AMIGOS DE LA GUITARRA

SECRETARÍA: CASTRO 675

5º. CICLO

9ª. CONCIERTO

AUDICION 69ª

• • •

AUSPICIADO POR LA

Asociación Argentina de Música de Cámara

Dedicado a la eminente María Luisa Anido en el día de
Santa Rosa de Lima, Patrona de América de
Buenos Aires y de la Guitarra.

CONCERTISTA

Nelly Z. Miravalles

Sábado 30 de Agosto a las 18

1947

en el Salón "LA ARGENTINA"

RODRIGUEZ PEÑA 361

ENTRADA GENERAL, $ 1.50.-

Los socios de la As. Argentina de Música de Cámara, tienen derecho a 2 entradas, presentando el carnet social.

Alumnos y Tertulia $ 1.-

PROGRAMA

1ª PARTE

Corrente	*GRANATA*
Gagliarda	*DURANTE*
Preludio	*BACH*
Estudio No. 3	*CHOPIN*
Preludio (IV Sonata)	*BACH*

2ª PARTE

Aire Criollo de Aguirre	
Triste No. 4 de Aguirre	
Gato	*M. L. ANIDO*
Aire Norteño	
Evocación Indígena	
(Dedicado a la Ejecutante)	

3ª PARTE

Carillón	*B. TERZI*
Allegretto	*R. MUÑOZ*
Estudio No 2	*E. PUJOL*
Capricho Andaluz	*M. DEL OLMO*

En 1a. Audición. Las ejecuciones se realizarán en

GUITARRA ARGENTINA

Nelly Zuma Miravalles
performs for the "Amigos
de la Guitarra" on
Saturday August 30, 1947,
using the Ricardo Muñoz
designed model
"Guitarra Argentina".

The concert is dedicated
to Maria Luisa Anido.

2450

De la célebre artista de la guitarra argentina Sta. Maria Luisa Anido; Compositora, Profesora del Conservatorio Nacional de Música de Buenos Aires.—

- - - - - -

Señor Ricardo Muñoz

Estimado amigo:

He tenido la enorme satisfacción de ver y pulsar tres soberbias guitarras construídas de acuerdo a sus teorías, quedando verdaderamente asombrada por la amplitud, generosidad y belleza de su sonido, cuya prolongación, además, responde perfectamente a la vibración y a todos los matices artísticos del intérprete mas exigente, asi como por su diapasón dócil a las dificultades técnicas, condiciones que hacen de dichos instrumentos una magnífica realidad como guitarras de concierto.—

Al manifestárselo me siento orgullosa, como argentina, ya que tan maravillosos instrumentos, construídos con maderas de nuestra patria están llamadas, con seguridad, a tener repercución mundial en el ambiente guitarrístico apenas comprueben sus excepcionales méritos artísticos.—

Al felicitarlo sinceramente le envio un cordial saludo:

(Firmado) Maria Luisa Anido

Buenos Aires, Julio 4 de 1946

Translation: "From the celebrated artist of the Argentine guitar Miss Maria Luisa Anido, Composer, Professor at the Conservatorio Nacional de Musica of Buenos Aires. —

Mr. Ricardo Muñoz
Beloved friend,

I have had the enormous satisfaction to see and play three superb guitars constructed in agreement to your theories, remaining truly amazed at the volume, generosity and beauty of sound, whose prolongation besides, responding perfectly to the vibration and all the artistic blends of the most demanding interpreter, in this way as for its obedient fretboard to the technical difficulties, conditions that make the said instruments a magnificent reality as concert guitars.

To demonstrate them I feel proud, and as Argentine, now that such marvelous instruments, constructed with woods of our country they are called, with security, to have a worldwide repercussion in the guitaristic ambiance to prove their exceptional artistic merits.

To congratulate you I send you a cordial greeting: (Signed) Maria Luisa Anido

Buenos Aires, July 4, 1946"

De la eminente guitarrista y pedagoga de la guitarra argentina Sra.Consuelo Mallo Lopez;Directora de la Academia de su nombre.-

- - - - - - - - - -

He probado las nuevas guitarras construídas por la Casa nuñez,bajo la dirección técnica y sobre teorías acústicas del Profesor Ricardo Muñoz,y puedo afirmar que me han satisfecho plenamente,tanto por su sonoridad generosa y amplia que permiten todos los matices,como por esos detalles tan complejos y diversos que determinan el equilibrio del instrumento y definen su bondad.-

(Firmado) C.Mallo Lopez
Buenos Aires,Agosto de 1946

Translation: "From the eminent guitarist and pedagogue of the Argentine guitar Mrs. Consuelo Mallo Lopez; Director of the academy of her name. —

I have tested the new guitars constructed by Casa Nuñez, under the technical direction and over acoustic theories of Professor Ricardo Muñoz, and I can affirm that they have fully satisfied me, so much by their generous and ample sonority that they allow the full range of tone colors, as by those details so complex and diverse that determine the balance of the instrument and define its goodness.—

(Signed) C. Mallo Lopez
Buenos Aires, August of 1946"

De la notable artista dela guitarra argentina Sta. Irma Haydee Perazzo;Compositora,Profesora del Instituto Nacional de Ciegos.-

- - - - - - - - -

Digna de elogia es la obra realizada por el Profesor Ricardo Muñoz.-

Las guitarras construídas bajo su dirección técnica, poseen bella sonoridad y armoniosa línea.-

Tratandose de instrumentos de reciente construcción, mucho puede esperarse de ellas a travez del tiempo,como así tam - bien la superación de la obra.-

(Firmado) Irma H.Perazzo.-

25-7-1946

Translation: "From the notable artist of the Argentine guitar Miss Irma Haydée Perazzo; Composer, Professor of the Instituto Nacional de Ciegos. — (National Institute for the Blind)

The work done by Professor Ricardo Muñoz is worthy of a eulogy. —

The guitars constructed under his technical direction, possess a beautiful sonority and harmonious line.

These instruments of recent construction, much can be expected of them over the course of time, as well as the improvement of the guitar.

(Signed) Irma H. Perazzo. —
July 25, 1946"

Del decano de los maestros argentinos de guitarra don
Mario Rodriguez Arena; fecundo compositor.-

- - - - - - -

Buenos Aires,Diciembre 16/946

MARIO RODRIGUEZ ARENA saluda muy atentamente a su estima -
do amigo y colega don Ricardo Muñoz y se complace en felicitarlo
sinceramente por el felíz acierto que ha tenido en la selección de
maderas argentinas para la fabricación de guitarras;habiendo podido comprobar que ha conseguido hacer un instrumento "perfecto"tanto por su construcción como por su sonoridad.-

(Firmado) M.Rodriguez Arena

Translation: "From the dean of the Argentine maestros of the guitar *Don* Mario Rodríguez Arenas;
productive composer. —

Buenos Aires, December 16, 1946

Mario Rodríguez Arenas greets his beloved friend and colleague Ricardo Muñoz very attentively and
it pleases me to sincerely to congratulate you for the happy success that I have had in the selection of
Argentine woods for the fabrication of the guitars; having been able to prove that you have gotten to make
the instrument so "perfect" for its construction as well as for its sonority.

(Signed) Mario Rodríguez Arenas"

Del decano de los guitarristas uruguayos,compositor
y eminente pedagogo del instrumento don Pedro Mascaró y Reissig.–

– – – – – – – – – – –

Montevideo Octubre 27 de 1946

Señor don Ricardo Muñoz
Distinguido Profesor:

Me es grato dirigirme a Ud.para expresarle,por
medio de la presente,a las conclusiones que he llegado,despues de
escuchar el recital de guitarra ofrecido anoche en el Ateneo de Montevideo,por la excelente guitarrista Sra.Nelly Zuma Miravalles de
Gonzalez,quien utilizó para ese acto,la guitarra de la que Ud. es
creador y que ha sido construida con maderas argentinas.–

Mi opinión es,al respecto,la siguiente:

Ud. ha logrado,con dicho instrumento,superar
las tres faces primordiales del sonido que,hasta ahora,han podido
producir muchas guitarras célebres.– Esta tres faces primordiales
a que me refiero son: Intensidad,Timbre y Claridad.–

Si ha ello se le añade lo ganado en las rectas
que presentan las cuerdas tercera y cuarta,en lo manuable que le –
resulta el instrumento al ejecutante y en la liviandad de su peso
comparado con otras guitarras,Ud.puede estar satisfecho de haber lo–
grado un triunfo en el terreno de la consecución.–

Si en algo vales ésta,mi modesta opinión,des –
pues de treinta años de pedagogía en la guitarra,que se ella un aci-
cate para sus futuras lucubraciones.–

Afectuosamente suyo:

(Firmado)P.Mascaró y Reissig

Translation: "From the dean of the Uruguayan guitarists, composer, eminent pedagogue of the instrument
Pedro Mascaro y Reissig
Montevideo October 27, 1946

Mr. *Don* Ricardo Muñoz
Distinguished professor:

   It is pleasing to direct this to you to express, by way of the present, the conclusions that I have reached,
after listening to the guitar recital offered last night in the Ateneo of Montevideo, by the excellent
guitarist Mrs. Nelly Zuma Miravelles de Gonzalez, who utilized for this act, the guitar of which you are
the creator and has been constructed by Argentine woods. —

My opinion is, in respect to it, the following:

You have succeeded, with the said instrument, to overcome the three basic facets of the sound which, until now, could have produced many celebrated guitars. — These three basic facets to which I refer are: Intensity, Timbre and Clarity.

If it is added to the gains in the lines that have the third and fourth strings, the instrument turns out to be handy for the performer and in the lightness of its weight compared to other guitars, you can be satisfied by having the degree of triumph in the terrain of construction.

If there is something of value, in my modest opinion, after thirty years of pedagogy on the guitar, it is an incentive for its future lucubration.

Affectionately yours:
(Signed) P. Mascaro y Reissig

Fragmento de una carta de la guitarrista uruguaya Sta. OLGA PIERRI dirigida a su eminente amiga Sta. Maria Luisa Anido:

Sta. Maria Luisa Anido.
Mimita querida:

De la guitarra construída por el Sr. Muñoz te diré que a papá y a mi nos a producido una optima impresión al punto de desear comprarle una, y además las impresiones que hemos recogido han sido todas de admiración.—

El señor Muñoz nos ha sorprendido tambien como autor, las obras que tuve oportunidad de oir son excelentes revelando en él, a un espíritu fino y fuerte personalidad.—

Montevideo 27 -X-de 1946

(Firmado) OLGA PIERRI

Translation: "Fragment of a letter written by the Uruguayan guitarist Miss Olga Pierri directed to her eminent friend Miss Maria Luisa Anido:

Miss Maria Luisa Anido.
Beloved Mimita:

Of the guitar constructed by Mr. Muñoz I will tell you that to Papa and to me to us it produced an optimum impression to the point of desiring to purchase one, and besides the impressions that we have recognized have all been of admiration. —

Mr. Muñoz as well has surprised us as an author, the works that I had an opportunity to hear are excellent revealing in him, a fine spirit and strong personality. —

Montevideo October 27 of 1946

(Signed) Olga Pierri

2456

This translated text and photo are from page 100 of Ricardo Muñoz's unpublished book *"Historia Universal de la Guitarra"* Volume VIII *"La Escuela Tárrega en La Argentina".*

"In 1945 the Comision Nacional de Cultura de la Argentina, (National Commission of Culture of Argentina) awarded Ricardo Muñoz a scholarship for Technical Orientation for constructing the Argentine guitar with woods native to the country."

The Ricardo Muñoz Model *"La Guitarra Argentina-Muñoz"* made by Antigua Casa Nuñez.

El guitarrista Rapat en Radio Uruguay

Un elemento de grandes medios en el dominio del instrumento y a la vez un temperamento emotivo. Sin alardes de virtuosismo, da a la obra una clara sensación de su carácter y la idea del autor, poniendo a la vez de manifiesto una personalidad sobria y definida. Su adquisición por la dirección de Radio Uruguay será un nuevo motivo de alta jerarquía para sus extraordinarios programas.

♦

Translation of the text for *"El Guitarrista Rapat* on *Radio Uruguay"*. This is from an unknown magazine from October 28, 1930, published in Montevideo.

"The Guitarist Atilio Rapat on Radio Uruguay". (C X 26 — Radio Uruguay)

"An element of great measure in the dominion of the instrument and at the same time of an emotional temperament. Without a show of virtuosity, he gives the work a clear sensation of its character and the idea of the author, putting at the same time the demonstration of a sober personality and definition. His acquisition by the directors of Radio Uruguay will be a new motive of high hierarchy for his extraordinary programs."

Atilio Rapat (1905-1988) There are videos of him on You Tube.

Julio Arbelo

CONCERTISTA DE GUITARRA

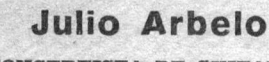

El buen concertista de guitarra Sr. Julio Arbelo reanudó en C X 22 - Fada Radio su interesante labor. Se trata de un verdadero virtuoso de la guitarra, que ha logrado crearse un ambiente de simpatía entre el público radioescucha. Campañas de positivos méritos ha hecho el Sr. Arbelo ante el micrófono de C X 22 - Fada Radio, y en las cuales se reveló como uno de los intérpretes más interesantes del momento en el arte de la guitarra, por la cual siente una gran vocación. En todas las piezas que ejecuta demuestra el temperamento y la técnica, logrando obtener ya un rendimiento que sólo puede hacerlo aquél que demuestre tanta contracción al estudio y que lo haga con entusiasmo y esmero. Este gran concertista puede ser escuchado los lunes y viernes, de las 20 a las 20.30 horas.

Translation of the text for *"Julio Arbelo — concertista de guitarra."*. This is from an unknown magazine from 1937, published in Montevideo. This is possibly from *"Radio Revista — cancionera",* as the border and text font appear the same.

"Julio Arbelo — concert guitarist."

"The good concert guitarist Mr. Julio Arbelo renewed his interesting labor with *CX-22 Fada Radio*. We're speaking of a true virtuoso of the guitar, who has succeeded to create a friendly ambiance among the radio listening public. Mr. Arbelo has made in front of the microphone of *CX-22 Fada Radio* campaigns of positive merits, and in which have revealed him to be one of the most interesting interpreters of the moment in the art of the guitar, for which he feels a great vocation. In all of the pieces he plays he demonstrates the temperament and the technique, succeeding to have already obtained a yield that can only make it that which demonstrates a lot of study and that he might do with enthusiasm and polish. This great concert guitarist can be heard on Monday and Friday from 8PM to 8:30PM."

2458

Julio Arbelo, is listed in this issue of *"Radio Revista — cancionera"* Issue No. 239 Año VI Sunday August 23 – Saturday August 29, 1936, published in Montevideo on August 21, 1936. He played on Friday August 28 from 9:15PM until 9:30 then again from 9:45-10:00 on Radio CX 20 Montecarlo. The listings in bold text are live performances and the listings in plain text are recordings played for the audience.

Also on *CX 20 Montecarlo* another guitarist, Ramon Troche, also played two 15 minute segments on Monday August 24 from 9:30 and 10:30PM.

This is translated from the book by Cedar Viglietti *"Origen y Historia de la Guitarra"* published by Editorial Albatros in Buenos Aires in 1973.

Cedar Viglietti on page 226-227 says: "Raul Mancebo Rojas is a veteran proponent of our guitar, when he wasn't the president of the Centro Guitarristico, he was the Secretary at least.

I transcribe part of a letter of his, in which he synthesizes the Montevideo panorama after 1910:

'In what I refer to as the unfolding of the guitar in that epoch, I know by having lived in those days. I begin by saying that the presence of Josefina Robledo in the Teatro Solis was a revelation. Then we knew some pieces by Alais or Sagreras, approaching Mazurkas, Estilos and Milongas with enthusiasm.'

'In reality, musical disciplines were begun thanks to the good services of Pujol, who oriented and gave classes in an impartial form in the space of a month to the maestros Otermin, Mascaro y Reissig, Koch, Gregorio Rodríguez, Vittone and Rosendo Barreiro."

'When Pujol returned to Europe he sent all of the school of Tárrega — original works and the transcriptions that weren't known here to the Trapani music store — the music house that was at calle Convencion between San José and 18 de Julio.'

'The most highly prized guitars then were the Valenciana guitars and we used gut strings (las cuerdas romanas — the most famous of that epoch). Until the arrival of Agustín Barrios that provoked a revolution: everyone adopted the steel strings.' (Rico Stover wisely discredits this assertion.)

'Then Manjón appeared with his guitar of eight or nine strings: this novelty returned to cause a commotion in the environment: almost all the guitarists named went about reforming their instruments. In the Centro Guitarristico there is a photograph of Otermin and Koch and in the method of Mascaro y Reissig one of those, all of them with similar guitars: but I have here that Llobet arrived and plucked the strings with his fingertips. Then all of them cut their fingernails trying to imitate that beautiful sound. The performances of Sainz de la Maza, Pujol and finally of Segovia plucking with fingernails, calmed down the ambiance, succeeding to define personalities. I believe that in fifty years it has progressed a lot.'

Such is, well, the evocation of my friend Mancebo Rojas"

2459

Translating from Ricardo Muñoz's unpublished book *"Historia Universal de la Guitarra"* Volume VI *"America"*.

"Ronoel Simoes

His Origin:

He is the son Manuel Simões and Maria Srebotuyak de Simoes, born in Araraquara, Sao Paulo, Brazil on the 24th of March of 1919.

His Education:

In 1940 he initiated his guitar studies with maestro Atilio Bernardini, with a passion for the instrument.

His Virtuosity:

With his Del Vecchio guitar and another Valenciana he interpreted the *"Estudio en Si menor" Op. 35 No. 22* by Sor in homage to this great maestro on the 19th of February of 1949, in the following month the *"Adagio"* in C major by Bach in the home of maestro *Don* José Martins Sobrinho.

The 28th of February of 1953, in the "Associacao Cultural do Violao" of Sao Paulo, he performed

"Adagio" by Bach, *"Preludio"* by Chopin, *"Lagrima"* by Tárrega, *"Andante Expressivo"* by Concecao, the following month and in the same institution he played works by Tárrega, Pergolesi and Savio and the 25th of July of the same year in duets with *Don* Diego Piazza, the *"Duettos Nos. 6, 7, 8 and 14"* by Carruli and *"Tre Giorni son che Nina"* by Pergolesi, with great acceptance by the audience.

Ronoel Simoes

His Pedagogy:

He is the owner of one of the most abundant and brilliant record collections, of original works and transcriptions for the guitar, of which he makes known in every special program of national and foreign music, performed by the best virtuosos of the world of the instrument.

He writes about important historical themes of our guitar with skill and exemplary dedication for diverse newspapers in the country and for foreign publications as well."

The above photo accompanied the Spanish language biography of Ronoel Simoes, in the unpublished book. So ends the biography by Ricardo Muñoz.

Ricardo Muñoz had communicated with the guitarists and historical guitar magazine writers of Japan, such as Shun Ogura, as well as the rest of the world since the early 1930's. On the next page we see the source of this photo.

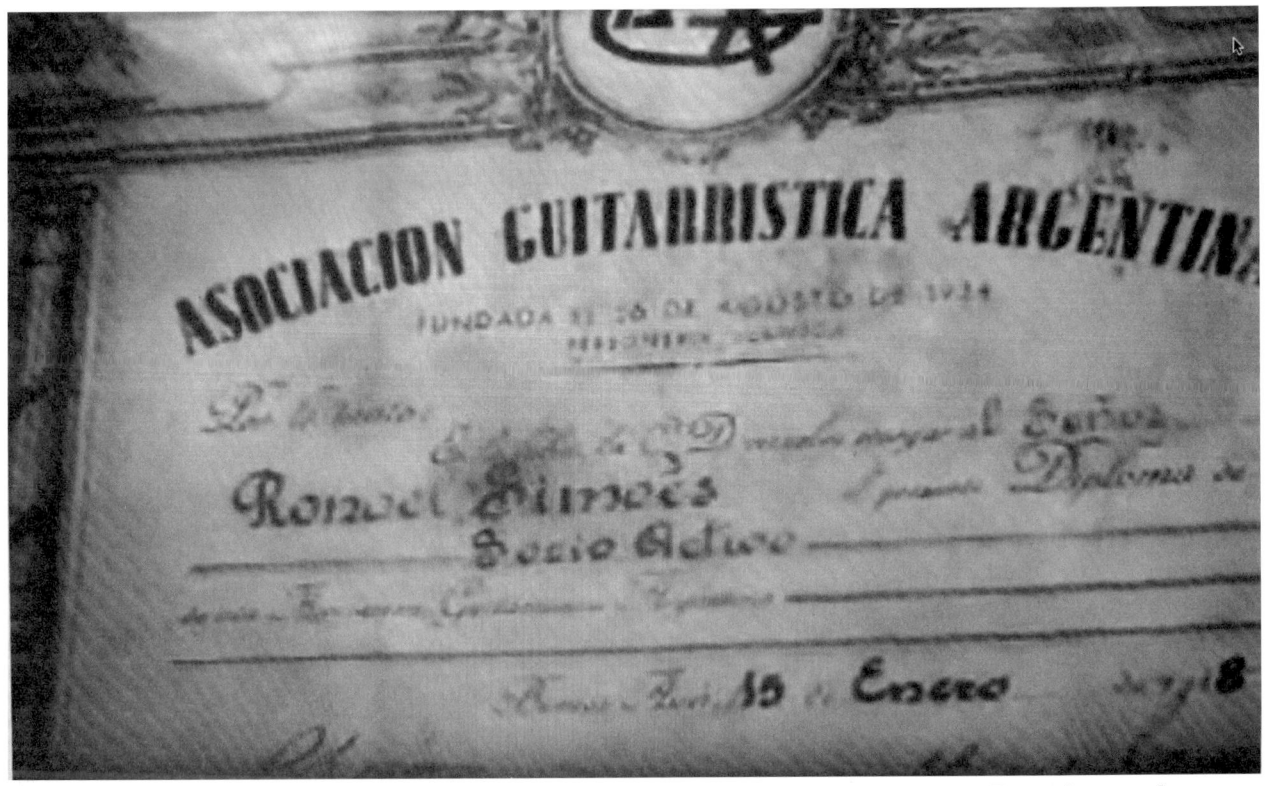

Ronoel Simões joined the Asociacion Guitarristica Argentina on January 15, 1948. Ronoel started collecting Agustín Barrios 78 RPM discs and records in general in 1942.

Ronoel Simoes

ブラジル最大の日刊紙 Gazeta の音楽記者であるロノエル・シモエスは ギターレコードの蒐集家としても世界に冠たる存在である。そのコレクションは独奏だけで 600 種を上廻り、一昨年 9 月までラジオ・サンパウロで行つたシモエスの解説によるギターレコードの放送は 435 回に及び、この番組に用いられた曲は1600といふから驚く外はない。それから今日まで更に二年つゝけているのだから、驚嘆に値する。
　この写真を送つてもらつた時の手紙に、自分はすぐれたギタリストではないから、その旨をことわつてならアルモニア誌上に紹介していたゞいてもいゝと、ことわり書きがしてある。これは謙遜の言葉であらう。サンパウロのギター協会主催のジョイント・リサイタルではカルリの二重奏やソルやタルレガの小品を弾いているからである。独奏家といふほどではないにしても、すぐれた演奏家とは云えよう。演奏家として名が残らなくとも、ギター音楽の愛護者として Ronoel Simoes の名は長く歴史に残るはづである。

This photo and biography of Ronoel Simões is from the September-October 1956 issue of *"Armonia"* Vol. III No. 5. The magazine was printed in Sen Dai, Miyagiken, a city heavily damaged by the tsunami after the 8.9 magnitude earthquake on March 11, 2011. Japanese translation by Randy Osborne.

"The musical writer, for Brazil's largest daily newspaper publication *"Gazeta"*, Ronoel Simoes, has the world's largest guitar record collection without equal that exists. As for that collection it has only classical guitar solos and has reached 600 pieces, according to Simoes' commentary 435 records had been broadcast up until September of last year on Radio Sao Paolo and, besides it is said this show surprisingly had happened to have used 1,600 songs. Therefore, from that time until today the two years that it has been continuing, the value has to be admired.

This photograph was sent at the time of the letter, as for his own it isn't from this excellent guitarist, if it's that principle proverb in an *"Armonia"* magazine to accept the introduction that's alright, he refused to write. As for this humble word it is cleansed. Because of the Sao Paolo Guitar Society's sponsorship of the "Joint Recital" the duets of Carulli, Sor, and the short works of Tárrega were played. Even if it's not the guitar soloist, it's the excellent concert guitarist. If it's not the name of the concert guitarist, the protector of the guitar music, the name Ronoel Simões has to remain in the long history."

In 1953 Peter Sensier began a column in the B.M.G. magazine published in London, called "Guitar News from Overseas". Ronoel Simões was one of the fervent correspondents.

Guitar News from Overseas

Collected by PETER SENSIER

Brazil. Ronoel Simoes, prominent Brazilian guitarist, has recently forwarded me numerous programmes. Most recent recitals, given under the auspices of the " Associacao Cultural do Violao," are No. 38, by Antonio Simalha, on January 28 (including six works composed by the soloist), and No. 39, on February 20, by Sebastiao Galanti, including works by Barrios, Villa-Lobos and Tarrega.

Ronoel Simoes, who is a professor of the guitar in Sao Paulo, is also guitar correspondent to the newspaper " A Gazeta," for which he writes a long and regular column covering all aspects of the guitar, its history and personalities.

June 1954 issue Vol. LI. No. 590

Brazil. " O Violao," Ronoel Simoes' regular column in the Sao Paulo newspaper "A Gazeta," is consistently full of historical and world-wide information about the guitar. His most recent (available) contribution deals, to begin with, with " the golden age " of the guitar; the period when Carulli, Carcassi, Sor, Coste and Mertz were touring Europe and when Carulli alone had 332 guitar pieces published in Paris.

Later Mr. Simoes deals with " Methods " and books of studies by Osvaldo Soares, A. Bernadini, Benedito Moreira and Isaias Savio; the latter producing a new method dealing with the guitar in relation to the modern idea of harmony, etc.

March 1955 Vol. LII. No. 599

Brazil. Sao Paulo is the home of Ronoel Simoes, that indefatigable propagandist for the guitar, who periodically sends me news of the violao, as the Spanish guitar is called in Portuguese. Three programmes were enclosed with his most recent letter, the first being that of Guiomar Santos, the 40th recital given under the auspices of the Associacao Cultural do Violao. It consisted of music by Bach, Beethoven, Sor, Albeniz, Schumann, Gallo, Czibulka, Brahms, Aimoré, Pernamburo and Nazareth.

In Recital No. 41, Othon Salleiro was the soloist, playing pieces by Sor, Aguado, Beethoven, Bach, Barrios, Mendelssohn, Albeniz, Debussy, etc.

The third programme was the First Recital by pupils of the Academia Brasileira de Violao, the Director of which is Atilio Bernardini. Held under the auspices of the Instuto de Educacao, the concert was divided into four sections: (1) 7 soloists. (2) 5 duettists. (3) 3 trios and 4 quartets. (4) three pieces by a group of 10 guitarists.

Ronoel Simoes writes a regular guitar column in the Sao Paulo newspaper " A Gazeta ". Most recently received cuttings included a report of Anido's triumphant tour of Japan.

October 1954 Vol. LI. No. 594

B.M.G.
Guitar News from Overseas

Collected by PETER SENSIER

BRAZIL. Whenever I receive news from Roñoel Simoes I sincerely wish I had both a greater knowledge of Portuguese and more space to give a fuller report on the articles " O Violao " (The Guitar) he writes regularly for the Sao Paulo newspaper A Gazeta.

These articles range through history, news, personalities, biographies, recitals and publications. For instance, this month's batch of six articles of about 1,000 words each includes a discussion of the life and work of Laurindo Almeida; a survey of the " classical " composers for the guitar; the guitar in North America; compositions for the guitar in Spain; and the guitar in Austria.

Last April Sebastiao Galanti gave a recital in Sao Paulo under the auspices of the Associacao do Violao. He included the Weiss " Suite in A," " Asturias " (Albeniz), " Allegretto in A," (Torroba) and " As Abelhas " (Barrios).

August 1955 Vol. LII. No. 605
"As Abelhas" is "Las Abejas" by Agustín Barrios.

Brazil. Two important concerts took place in Sao Paulo towards the end of 1954. The first was given by Prof. Antonio Rebello and his pupils at the Associaçao Atletica Banco do Brasil and was in two parts: the first devoted to solos and duets by the pupils, and the second to group playing and an Anton Diabelli composition for guitar and piano. Almost all the rest of the music performed was by Latin-American composers.

The second recital, under the auspices of the Associaçao cultural du Violao, was given by Guiomar Santos and Jose Alves De Silva (Aimore). Parts 1 and 2 were devoted to solos by these two guitarists and Part 3 to duets. The programme included works by the three " B's," Sor, Barrios, Chopin, Mendelssohn and Savio.

One of Ronoel Simoes regular articles in the Sao Paulo newspaper " A Gazeta " was devoted to " The Guitar in Great Britain." Mention is made of John Williams, Julian Bream, Wilfrid M. Appleby, " B.M.G." and its guitar contributors, and A. P. Sharpe's " Story of the Spanish Guitar."

February 1955 Vol. LI. No. 598

Guitar News from Overseas

Collected by PETER SENSIER

Brazil. A letter and press cuttings from Ronoel Simoes, that indefatigable propagandist of the guitar, are always a pleasure to receive, even though it means that I have to spend an hour or so (accompanied by a Portuguese-English dictionary and a puzzled frown) while I attempt to extricate the salient points of news.

In the present batch one whole article is devoted to the life story of Saint Rosa de Lima who, although she died at the early age of 31, was an excellent guitarist—or, to be more correct, vihuelist.

The suggestion has been made by Domingo Prat, Ricardo Munoz and Adolfo A. Parlinelli of the Argentine, and echoed by Senor Simoes, that the feast day of Saint Rosa de Lima, August 30, should be celebrated as " Guitar Day " in the same way that November 15, is now " Tarrega Day " and November 22, is dedicated to Saint Cecilia—patron saint of all musicians.

Another of Sr. Simoes' articles deals with the recent untimely death of Anibal Augusto, known popularly as " Garoto." Born in Sao Paulo in 1915, " Garoto " had become, by the age of 17, a brilliant instrumentalist. Apart from the Spanish guitar, he mastered many other fretted instruments and before long became an integral part of the artistic and musical life of Brazil. A brilliant exponent of guitar music by modern composers, he also wrote a great deal of music in the Brazilian idiom.

Your Editor tells me that he has quite a number of recordings by this artist and these include solos on the electric plectrum guitar, tenor guitar, mandolin, cavaquinho and, of course, the Spanish guitar.

Laurindo Almeida, another illustrious son of Brazil, also receives considerable mention in Sr. Simoes' newspaper articles.

October 1955 Vol. LIII. No. 606

Brazil. The Teatro Sao Paulo was recently the scene of a joint recital by singer-guitarist Maria Luiza de las Casas Diniz and guitar soloist Maria Livia Sao Marcos. The latter, although only fourteen years of age, played a mature programme that included works by Sanz, Rameau, Sor, Villa-Lobos, Savio, Albeniz and Uhl.

Roñoel Simoes, sends news of the death of a prominent guitarist Rossini Silva, an excellent musician and first-class teacher, who had held many important musical posts in Brazil.

The city of Ceara (Brazil) has throughout the year been visited by many outstanding guitar soloists, such as Maria Luisa Anido, Isaias Savio, Luiz Bonfa and José Menezes and, as a result, local guitarists have developed a high standard of playing the guitar in both classical and popular styles. In November 1952 the Ceara Guitar Club was formed and now boasts a large membership of amateurs and teachers who meet every Sunday morning to talk and play guitar.

May 1956 Vol. LIII. No. 613

Brazil. On August 5th, guitarist Milton Nuñes gave a recital at Santos to commemorate the 14th anniversary of the "Centro Violinistico 'Jose de Patrocinio'." His programme consisted of "Sarabanda" (*Handel*), "Gavota" (*Scarlatti*), "Bourée" (*Bach*), "Minuet" (*Sor*), "Theme and Variations" (*Mozart - Sor*), "Serenata" (*Schubert*), "Vals Op. 70, No. 2" and "Nocturne, Op. 9, No. 2" (*Chopin-Nunes*), "Vals" (*Kreisler-Nunes*), "Petite Valse" (*Ponce*), "Ponteio No. 1" (*Fagnani-Nunes*), "Preludes Nos. 1 & 2" (*Villa-Lobos*) and "Asturias-Leyenda" (*Albeniz*).

Ronoel Simoes, who has a regular record programme of guitar music on Radio Sao Paulo, wishes to feature recordings by John Williams and Dorita y Pepe but is unable to obtain them in Brazil. He would be happy to exchange guitar music not available in Britain with any reader willing to supply the records.

November 1959 Vol. LVII. No. 655
Peter Sensier was "Pepe".

This is from "The Guitar Review" magazine issue No. 7 of 1948. It states Ronoel started his radio program in 1945. This is the oldest evidence I have found on this matter.

Guitar News from Overseas
Collected by Peter Sensier

Brazil. Ronoel Simoes, well-known for his guitar playing, radio programmes and newspaper articles about the guitar, sends news of four recent guitar recitals in Sao Paulo. Two of these were given by the "Sexteto Paulistano de Violoes" (San Paulo Guitar Sextet) led by Prof. Simalha Filho and consisted largely of light music arranged for the sextet, with the exception of two pieces, "Fantazia Hespanhola No. 2" and "Brigada Simalha"—both written by Prof. Simalha.

The two other recitals at the Sao Paulo and Leopoldo Froes theatres, featured 14-years-old Maria Livia Simao Marcos, who played a few transcriptions (Haydn, Rameau, Albeniz, etc.) and a large amount of original music for the guitar—much of it by composers not so well known in Britain, e.g., Isaias, Savio, J. Duarte Costa, Waldemar Henrique and Manuel Sao Marcus.

April 1957 Vol. LIV. No. 624

Brazil. Milton Nunes, professor of guitar at a number of conservatoires, gave two recitals during September: one on the 2nd at the Clure Coronel Barrosa; the other at the Teatro Municipal. On October 6th a further concert was given under the auspices of the Associacao Cultural do Violao.

Sr. Nunes programmes were largely the same for all recitals: "Sarabande" (*Handel*), "Gavotta" (*Scarlatti*), "Bourrée" (*Bach*), "Minuet" (*Sor*), "Theme Varie" (*Mozart-Sor*), "Serenade" (*Schubert*), "Vals Op. 70, No. 2" and "Nocturne Op. 9, No. 2" (*Chopin*), "Vals" (*Kreisler*), "Petita Vals" (*Ponce*), "Ponteio No. 1" (*Fagnani*), "Preludes Nos. 1 & 2" (*Villa-Lobos*), "Asturias" (*Albeniz*) and "Serenata" (*Malats*).

Ronel Simoes recently devoted his article "O Violao" in the weekly Sao Paulo newspaper "A Gazeta" to the work of the 14-years-old Brazilian guitarist Antonio Carlos Barbosa Lima and in particular to his recent LP "O Menino e o Violao" on Chantecler CMG 1004.

January 1960 Vol. LVII. No. 657

Guitar News from Overseas
Collected by Peter Sensier

Brazil. News has just arrived of a brilliant young Brazilian guitarist, Antonio Carlos Barbosa, who is only thirteen years old and who has caused a considerable stir in Brazilian musical circles. At a recent concert in the Teatro Sao Paulo, he played music by Rameau, Bach, Ponce ("Sonata en Homenaje a Sor") Chopin, Mendelssohn, Tarrega, Barios ("As Abelhas"), Lauro

136

("Vals Venezolano"), Villa-Lobos, Savio and Castelnuovo-Tedesco ("Vivo y Energico" and "Tarantela").

This young soloist recently recorded an LP for the new RCA - Victor label "Chantecler" and is under contract to the company for two years, during which time he is to record a minimum of eight discs.

Ronoel Simoes continues to contribute his regular articles "O Violao" (The Guitar) to the Sao Paulo newspaper "A Gazeta." A recent article was devoted to the famous and almost legendary Brazilian popular left-handed guitarist Americo Jacomino, better known by his pseudonym "Canhoto" (lefty)!

February 1959 Vol. LVI. No. 646
"As Abelhas" is "Las Abejas"
by Agustín Barrios.

246

Guitar News from Overseas
Collected by Peter Sensier

Brazil. Towards the end of last year Milton Nunes, who was born in Campinas and studied under the celebrated Alfredo Scupinari, was busy giving recitals around Brazil. His programmes consisted of transcriptions of works by Handel, Scarlatti, Bach, Mozart, Chopin, Kreisler, Malats and Albeniz and originals for the guitar by Ponce, Paganini, Villa-Lobos, Sor and Barrios.

During a recent record programme of guitar music by Ronoel Simoes on P.R.A.6, Radio Gazeta de San Paulo, John Williams was heard playing the Variations on a Catalan Folk Song by Jack Duarte. This was the 569th programme presented by Sr. Simoes during which 164 different guitarists have been heard playing, in all, 2054 pieces.

Ronoel Simoes continues to write regular articles on the guitar for the San Paulo newspaper "A Gazeta." Recent articles have been devoted to Milton Nunes, The Guitar on Record, Jamil Anderaos, The Boccherini Quintet, and the famous popular composer Ernesto Nazareth.

May 1960 Vol. LVII. No. 661

Brazil. Ronoel Simoes, the guitar columnist for the Sao Paulo weekly "*A Gazeta,*" recently devoted a whole article (plus photograph) to the two Délyse recordings of John Williams. "In 'Torre Bermeja' serenade by Albeniz, Williams is magnificent" writes Sr. Simoes—and of his playing of "La Maja de Goya" and "Vals Criollo" he says: "Williams is excellent."

In other issues of "*A Gazeta*" Ronoel Simoes contributes articles on Villa-Lobos; records by guitarists Geraldo Ribeiro and Jesse Silva; and a history of the guitar and the famous guitarist composer and teacher, Isaiis Savio.

Sr. Simoes' radio programmes of guitar on records recently featured an LP by Brazilian guitarist Geraldo Ribeiro, playing solos by Nazareth, Barrios and Ribeiro.

Among guitar recitals in Sao Paulo during recent months was one by José Miranda who played music by Tarrega, Reis, Schubert, Chopin, Cearence and Miranda.

September 1960 Vol. LVIII. No. 665

Brazil. Ronoel Simoes must undoubtedly be one of the world's most active guitar propagandists. Every week he contributes an excellent column "O Violao" (The Guitar) to the Sao Paulo newspaper "A Gazeta" and every week he presents a programme of guitar records on PRA 6, Radio Gazeta de Sao Paulo. In the course of nearly 800 programmes he has presented discs of 275 different guitarists playing some 3,500 solos or duets.

On two recent programmes he played two guitar duets "Guitara Paraguaya" and "Pajaro Campana" by Dorita y Pepe.

When Frank Sinatra recently visited Brazil to sing at a concert in aid of the "Campanha Nacional De Assistencia A Crianca" he was presented with a guitar, specially made for him by the guitar maker Reinaldo Digiorgio.

Early this year a nine-year-old guitar soloist Mara Portela gave a recital in the town of Campinas. Commencing her guitar studies with Prof. Melton Neines in February, 1962 she appeared on the TV programme "Violoes E Mestres" just six months later in August. Her recent recital included works by Bach, Mozart, Beethoven, Chopin, Sois Rovira, Catulo, Neirs, Nazareth, Sario, Tarrega, Lecuona, Ponce and Villa Lobos.

August 1964 Vol. LXI. No. 712

Guitar News from Overseas

Collected by PETER SENSIER

Brazil. A recent communication from the celebrated Brazilian guitarophile Roneol Simoes gives news of his continued radio and press activities concerning the guitar—or as it is called in Brazil, the *violao*. Also included were two recent programmes of guitar concerts given in Sao Paulo.

The first, given under the auspices of the

B.M.G.

"Associacao Cultural do Violao," was by the Sexteto Paulistano de Violoes. This group played "Poema" (*Fibich*), "Minueto" (*Beethoven*), "Serenata" (*Schubert*), "Una Lagrima" (*Sangreras*), "El Relicario" (*Padilla*), "Luar do Sertao" (*Catulo-Scupinari*), "Transdendental" (*Scupinari*), "Odeon" & "Brejeiro" (*Nazareth*), "Inspiracion" (*Paulus*), "Tristeza do Jeca" (*Oliveira*) and "O Maior Espetaculo do Terra" (*Young*).

The other recital, given by Lauro Blandy at the Teatro Leopoldo Froes on Jan. 22nd, included solos by Haydn, Bach, Milan, Villa-Lobos, Tarrega, Chopin, Vicente Gomez and Barrios.

April 1962 Vol. LIX. No. 684

ブラジル：――

サンパウロの有名なギターレコードの蒐集家 Ronoel Simoes のラジオ・ガゼット の放送は昨年 9 月18日で 386 回を数えた。それまでのプログラムにのつた演奏家173、曲目の数は1772曲に及んでいる。週一回の放送だから、すでに七年の長きに亘つているわけで、堀内敬三氏のミ音楽の泉ミより上廻つているのだから驚く外はない。

尚日刊 Gazeta 紙に O Violao と題する記事を定期的に出してい、私の手元に1953年 1 月からその切抜が来ているが、裕に一書を成すギター論であり、シモーエスの博識と努力にはただただ頭が下るばかりである。

(23)

In January of 1963 Ronoel Simões began advertising to expand his collection from discs he could acquire from Europeans. January 1963 Vol. LX. No. 693

This is from the January–February 1956 issue of "*Armonia*" Vol. III No. 1. The magazine was printed in Sen Dai, Miyagiken, a city heavily damaged by the tsunami after the March 11, 2011 8.9 magnitude earthquake. Japanese translation by Randy Osborne.

"Brazil: —

As for Sao Paulo's famous record collector, Ronoel Simoes' Radio Gazeta broadcast last year September 18th was the 386th program. Up until that program 173 guitarists, and the amount of songs has numbered 1,772 pieces. Therefore, he broadcasts once a week, the program has already been running for a length spanning 7 years, according to Mr. Horiuchi Keizo's "Music Fountain" therefore it shouldn't be surprising that it has the best spins.

Furthermore, in the daily "*Gazeta*" and "*O Violao*" to give a title to articles periodically come out, in my usual skill from January 1953 that clipping coming in abundance one letter to become the guitar discussion, Simoes' extensive knowledge and effort — my bowed head is only obliged."

This photo of Ronoel Simões is dedicated to Eduardo Bensadon. "To my friend Eduardo Bensadon, Ronoel Simoes, Sao Paulo, July 1, 1949"

Archive: Eduardo Bensadon

Ronoel Simões passed away on October 5, 2010, and his Classical Guitar record collection, the largest in the world, of over 8,000 discs and estimated 200 scrapbooks of newspaper clippings and photos, as well as thousands of pieces of a very large sheet music collection were purchased from his widow by the Brazilian government.

This from the "Guitar News" magazine issue No. 77 of May-June 1964.

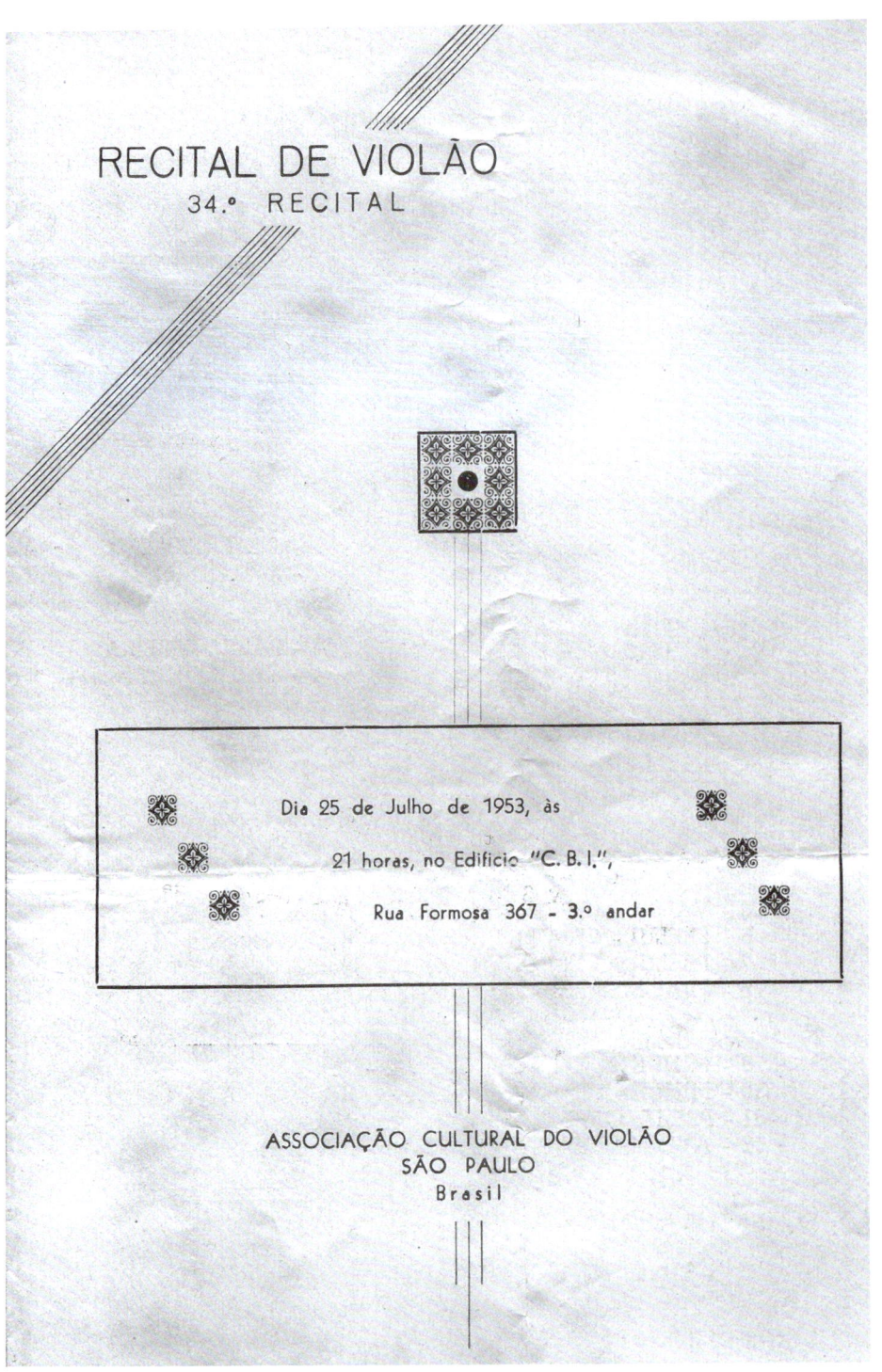

RECITAL DE VIOLÃO
34.º RECITAL

Dia 25 de Julho de 1953, às

21 horas, no Edificio "C. B. I.",

Rua Formosa 367 - 3.º andar

ASSOCIAÇÃO CULTURAL DO VIOLÃO
SÃO PAULO
Brasil

This Ronoel Simões guitar concert in Sao Paulo is from July 25, 1953.

There are videos of him on You Tube.

Archive: Eduardo Bensadon

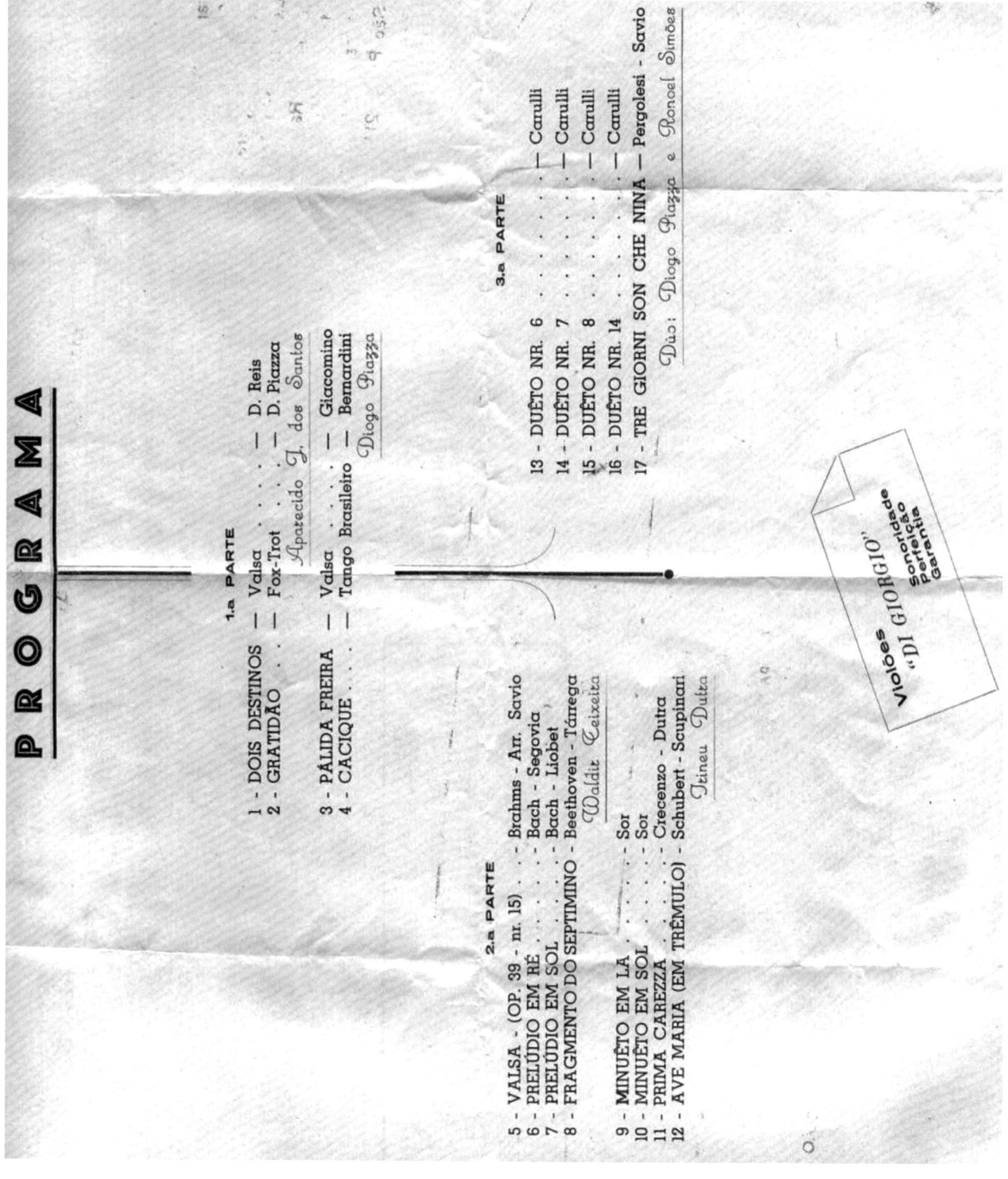

PROGRAMA

1.a PARTE

1 - DOIS DESTINOS .. — Valsa ..... — D. Reis
2 - GRATIDÃO ... — Fox-Trot ... — D. Piazza
Aparecido J. dos Santos

3 - PÁLIDA FREIRA — Valsa ..... — Giacomino
4 - CACIQUE .... — Tango Brasileiro — Bernardini
Diogo Piazza

2.a PARTE

5 - VALSA - (OP. 39 - nr. 15) .. - Brahms - Arr. Savio
6 - PRELÚDIO EM RÉ ...... - Bach - Segovia
7 - PRELÚDIO EM SOL ...... - Bach - Liobet
8 - FRAGMENTO DO SEPTIMINO - Beethoven - Tárrega
Waldir Teixeira

9 - MINUÊTO EM LA ...... - Sor
10 - MINUÊTO EM SOL ...... - Sor
11 - PRIMA CAREZZA .... - Crecenzo - Dutra
12 - AVE MARIA (EM TRÉMULO) - Schubert - Scupinari
Irineu Dutra

3.a PARTE

13 - DUÊTO NR. 6 .... — Carulli
14 - DUÊTO NR. 7 .... — Carulli
15 - DUÊTO NR. 8 .... — Carulli
16 - DUÊTO NR. 14 .... — Carulli
17 - TRE GIORNI SON CHE NINA — Pergolesi - Savio
Duo: Diogo Piazza e Ronoel Simões

Violões
"DI GIORGIO"
sonoridade
perfeição
Garantia

This Ronoel Simões guitar concert in Sao Paulo is from July 25, 1953, the Carulli duets are well thought of repertoire.

2468

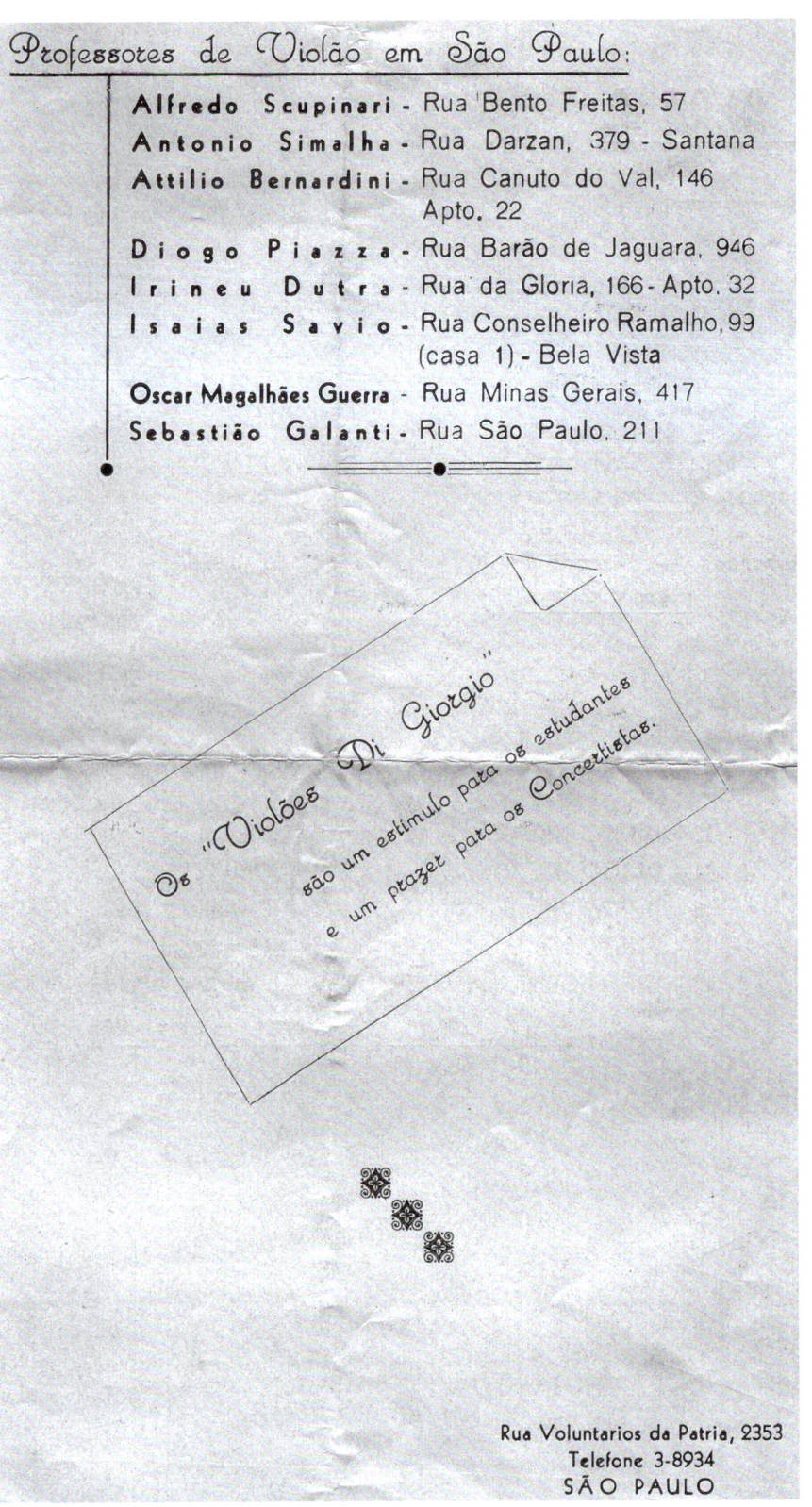

Professores de Violão em São Paulo:

Alfredo Scupinari - Rua Bento Freitas, 57

Antonio Simalha - Rua Darzan, 379 - Santana

Attilio Bernardini - Rua Canuto do Val, 146 Apto. 22

Diogo Piazza - Rua Barão de Jaguara, 946

Irineu Dutra - Rua da Gloria, 166 - Apto. 32

Isaias Savio - Rua Conselheiro Ramalho, 99 (casa 1) - Bela Vista

Oscar Magalhães Guerra - Rua Minas Gerais, 417

Sebastião Galanti - Rua São Paulo, 211

Os "Violões Di Giorgio" são um estímulo para os estudantes e um prazer para os Concertistas.

Rua Voluntarios da Patria, 2353
Telefone 3-8934
SÃO PAULO

This Ronoel Simões guitar concert in Sao Paulo is from July 25, 1953. This back page to the concert program mentions maestros who had been influential for decades, some of those had done transcriptions as well having published their original compositions.

2469

RONOEL SIMOES

BY the end of 1963, Ronoel Simoes of São Paulo, Brazil, had presented 774 radio programmes of classic guitar music, comprising 3,370 items played by 276 guitarists from many different lands.

He also writes a series of articles in the newspaper *A Gazeta* under the heading "The Guitar on Discs" in which he reviews interesting recordings old and new. Geraldo Ribeiro, Jose Rastelli, Dilemando Reis and Barbosa Lima are among the names of guitarists dealt with in recent articles.

In his article on February 27th, Ronoel Simoes reviewed a Caravelle LP disc (CAR 43001) on which Turibio Santos has recorded the complete series of the 12 Villa-Lobos Studies (1929). These Studies were published by Max Eschig of Paris with a foreword by Andres Segovia.

The above is from the "Guitar News" magazine issue No. 78 of July-August 1964, that below is from issue No. 116 of April-June 1972, 3 issues later would be the last issue of "Guitar News".

ABOUT thirty years ago when Ronoel Simoes began to collect records of guitar music the task of making an almost complete collection did not seem impossible—a few hundred, perhaps. He could not have foreseen that guitarists and compositions for the guitar would increase so amazingly during the past three decades.

According to an article in the Brazilian newspaper *Noticias Populares*, his collection now consists of 2,477 discs and 80 special tape

RONOEL SIMOES

recordings of guitar concertos, etc. They range from a disc made by Mario Pinheiros in 1909 to the recordings of 1971 and they are still arriving. Most of this unique collection of recorded guitar music has been broadcast by Ronoel Simoes on Brazilian Radio during the past 24 years in an uninterrupted series which in itself must be a 'record'.

ROSARIO AND JUAN MATEU

SINCE the announcement in *Guitar News* No. 92 of the marriage of Ronoel Simoes and Rosario Mateu in Sãn Paulo, Brazil, some interesting information has been received concerning the charming and talented lady whose portrait is shown.

ROSARIO M. SIMÕES

Rosario Mateu was born in Vall de Uxó, Valencia, Spain, and studied the guitar in Barcelona with Matilde Cuervas (Madame Pujol), Eusebio Gual, Emilio Pujol and Juan Parras del Moral. She was a student at the Escuela Municipal de Barcelona.

Her father, Juan Mateu, made guitars in Barcelona until 1951, but he now lives at Porto Alegre, Brazil, where he occupies himself in making fine guitars and artistic furniture. He owns two splendid guitars made by the great Antonio Torres—but they are not for sale ! Guitars made by Juan Mateu were praised by Daniel Fortea in his publication "Review Biblioteca Fortea" in June 1936. Rosario is shown with a guitar which was made by her father when he lived in Spain.

This is from the "Guitar News" magazine issue No. 94 of June-August 1967.

Juan B. Mateu Palasi

This photo of Juan Mateu is from Ricardo Muñoz's unpublished book "*Historia Universal de la Guitarra*" *Volume VI "America"*. It is dedicated to Ricardo Muñoz from Juan Mateu. "Mr. Señor Ricardo Muñoz jior gratitud Juan Mateu. Buenos Aires November 11, 1956.

Juan Mateu was the father-in-law of Ronoel Simoes.

As the 21st century came about the two Torres guitars belonging to Juan Mateu became for sale, one turning out to be a fake, therefore unsaleable.

THE GUITAR IN BRAZIL

by Ronoel Simoes

S INCE 1917 one of the chief authorities in Sao Paulo on stringed instruments has been Professor Atilio Bernardini, who has been for many years a teacher of music, guitar, violin, piano, etc. Professor Bernardini

received his diploma at the Conservatoire of Sao Paulo, reaching a high place in all subjects, especially in harmony in which he attained the distinction of the highest possible marks.

Many of his guitar pupils became professionals; outstanding among them being Anibal Augusto (Garôto), José Alves da Silva (Aimoré), Oscar Magalhaes Guerra, Guido Moretti and others. As a proof of his enthusiasm Bernardini founded in 1935 a Guitar Club, 'Clube Violonistico', in Sao Paulo, which later had to be dissolved for financial reasons. This club was re-started in 1942 but was again disbanded some time later for the same reason.

In 1934, when the Uruguayan concert guitarist Julio Martinez Oyanguren was in Sao Paulo—where he played with considerable success at the Conservatoire—he was very surprised to find here a centre for the most finished musical and instrumental education, also to find in those days that the guitar was being taught by Bernardini and to hear one of his pupils, Edgard de Mello performing from a well-chosen and scholarly repertoire of guitar music. Senhor Oyanguren is said to have exclaimed admiringly "*Caramba*! they play the guitar well here in Sao Paulo and they learn in a good school".

During the course of this present century the foremost guitarists in Rio de Janeiro have been—Brant Horta, Joaquim dos Santos, Joâo Teixeira Guimarâes, Souza Pombo, Agenor Mascarenhas, Rogerio Guimarâes, Mauricio Gudin, and to these may be added the distinguished composer Mauricio de Medeiros, who also took part in guitarist gatherings, and others. As early as in 1901 Brant Horta was giving guitar concerts before very keen and interested audiences and receiving the plaudits of the newspapers of the time. These concerts of Brant Horta's included works by the most varied composers, such as Bach, Beethoven, Verdi, etc.

In Rio de Janeiro in December, 1928, a review entitled "O Violao" (The Guitar) was founded and edited by Dantas de Souza Pombo, which valiantly championed the instrument in articles written by certain guitarists and composers of the period, chief among them being the famous art critic Bastos Tigre. The singer Olga Praguer Coelho, who is today a distinguished figure in all parts of the world as interpreter of the music of Brazil, was one of the principal figures of the review "O Violao". But this publication too had a short life and did not survive beyond its tenth issue.

In February, 1931 another review entitled "A Voz do Violao", (The Voice of the Guitar) was founded also in Rio de Janeiro and this one got no further than its third issue owing to the lack of unity and lack of standing of the guitarists who were responsible for it.

The peak, however, of all this guitaristic activity was achieved when Villa-Lobos decided to cultivate the guitar. Everyone knows that he had taught the guitar in Sao Paulo and that his first composition "Panquéca" was composed for the guitar. It was actually while studying the method of Dionisio Aguado of Madrid that Villa-Lobos acquired his love of music, which led eventually to his becoming one of the outstanding members of the musical world of our time. . . . . . .

This article appeared in the Brazilian newspaper "A. GAZETA" on February 13th, 1953 and is printed by kind permission of the author. Translation by Mrs. A. Rodziszewska.

This from the "Guitar News" magazine issue No. 14 of August-September 1953. Here is a snapshot of the Brazilian guitar scene, that could literally take up a book the size of this one as well.

12 Interviews:

Buenos Aires October 12, 1980   Translation by Randy Osborne

Interview with **Atahualpa Yupanqui** by Héctor Angel García (Hector García Martínez), when he was a correspondent for the program *"Dialogo"* on *Radio Tabaré* in Salta, Uruguay, owned and operated by German (pronounced Herman) Cincunegui.

H.G.M.: Hello German, good evening everyone, today I have for the audience of *"Dialogo"* the enormous privilege to put us in contact with a unique artist, a person who has let us learn through his teachings, not only what he has investigated, but also about where he has been and by his contact with the customs of the small towns, things he has translated through his unique art that give us the true sense of our nationality and American continental being.

I'm referring to the maestro Atahualpa Yupanqui, that today on *"Dialogo"* we will have a brief conversation with him.

H.G.M.: !!! Good Evening, maestro!!!

A.Y.: Good Evening, Sir, I'm glad to see you and to listen to you......

H.G.M.: I would like more or less, since you've just returned from Europe a little while ago, for you to give me a summary of where you've been, where were the performances you had in Argentina, and what ones you'll have here in the future.......

A.Y.: Well, I can tell you for 12 years now I've been traveling to that old Europe, today in a lot of conflict, so full of rarities and commitments of diverse order. My job is simpler: to play the guitar and make sure the people understand something of our sensibilities and traditions.

Musically, in my capacity I'm a traditionalist, I like the traditions a lot. I like it when people don't ask me for example: what did you bring that's brand-new? But I bring the old. Because I live to delve into old *Vidalitas, Vidalas, Triunfos, Zambas, Estilos* of the *pampas* (grassland). Until where it helps the memory or I'm discovering subject matter of a long time ago. And that makes me happy more than to have composed a *Zamba* last week, which interests me less. Now in Europe, I did many things, I live in Paris but I don't play there much, I play in all of France, in the south of France, in Marseilles, I play in Toulouse, the city where Carlos Gardel was born, I play in Grenoble, in the west near the Pyrenees, in the Alps, I play in Salzburg, in Lyon, Normandy, in Brittany and every year I give 5 or 6 concerts in the city of Paris, no more, 5 or 6 a year, that is to say I don't want to abuse the hospitality of the city that received me, where I live is where I play the least. But instead I have Switzerland, I have Italy, I have quite a bit in Spain, Barcelona, Madrid, Palma de Mallorca, in the Basque country, Santander, Galacia, but every year I make one or two trips, and a lot in Switzerland, as well in Belgium, and from there I go to Mexico, Costa Rica, Columbia, Japan, and I make a trip there, and I return to Paris. But before that, I make a trip to Argentina, I come twice a year to my homeland to see my family, to look at my landscapes, to chat with my compatriots, and to fill myself of that eternal vibration that is to tread on the national land, the land I love and where he was born, and that is all sir....

H.G.M.: Maestro, given your vast activity, your knowledge of the customs and popular traditions of Argentina, there has been a question that I've wanted to ask you for a long time, and when you would come here it had to be thought of. A few months ago, I was with some friends and various aficionados of folklore in a congress that was held in the Casa Museo de Ricardo Rojas there in *calle Charcas 2837* in this city. Casually one theme of discussion was linked with the traditions. Many sustained and others not, assuring to the contrary that, due to the advance of the means of communication, radio, television, the anonymous singers were going to disappear and that it would extinguish our traditions.

What is your opinion in that respect?

A.Y.: That happened a while ago here?

H.G.M.: Exactly seven months ago...

A.Y.:!!Ah!! It's very new, very recently we can say, in all time tradition..... No, no, many years have to pass many moons to be old, right?

Well, those people who have conversed or have been worried over that possibility haven't completely lost their way. I scarcely ascertain pessimism that I see growing, I had thought the same thing as well several years ago. In the measure that people don't study in a manner that could be exact and get heavily involved in the study of anonymous traditions, in the *folklore* that is plural and anonymous. The folklore belongs to nobody and it belongs to all of us, over all to our great-grandfathers and in the proportion that we deserve it belongs to us if we deserve it. To deserve it we can't put leaves of plastic on our tree with the leaves of centuries. We can't put leaves of plastic to our *ombu* (large tree that grows on the *pampas* / grasslands) neither on our algarrobo (typical leguminous tree of the northwest Argentina, very abundant in the Province of Santiago del Estero). It's worth saying we don't incorporate ignoble things lightly or you won't value an old tradition, we can't do it. Then understood, the folklore can disappear when the anonymous singers or an anonymous thing might disappear, it's very possible that it's lost, it wasn't diffused because it didn't even have the diffusion of *folklore* in our country. The aspect of the diffusion of the criolla, of the native criollas, of Argentine compositions with the sufficient *criollo* flavor (*criollo*- originally meaning all the sons of Spain born in the Americas during the colonial period. Later and until the present day it signifies various native generations), with enough flavor, emotion and Comarcano color (relating to the place Comarca). For example they create things very Salteñian (native to those born in the Province of Salta in northwest Argentina), very Tucumanian (native to the Province of Tucuman in northwest Argentina), and very Mendocinian (native to the Province of Mendoza, in west Argentina, pertaining to the zone of Cuyo), and very Entrerrian (natives of the Province of Entre Rios, in the zone of Mesopotamia. But they're not folkloric, folklore is anonymous, that's what Adolfo Salazar said, and it's sustained by Ortega y Gasset, and sustained by Ventura Lynch and as well by maestro Carlos Vega in our land: 'folklore is what the people learn without anyone having taught them.' It is learned because it's worth saying: a lasso, a lasso that is a folkloric effect, it is the prolongation of the yearning of a man that wants to catch a colt, a llama or wild animal. That is a lasso that is the prolongation of the yearning, now the lasso that the Casa Rodríguez and Rodríguez sell, that isn't folklore. It can be a great lasso, very well done, finely woven right? And well-greased, well stretched, and very well done, of 12 braids with 3 at the end of the lasso and a good rope and a good metal ring. It can be famous and prestigious, but it isn't folkloric, it's done with "systematized" knowledge. Instead those lassos that *Don* Leonardo did, for example in the 82 of Tandil (Province of Buenos Aires) it was famous in 8 leagues as it went around and it stretched from tree to tree and they treated it with fresh cow manure. !!That is a folkloric lasso!! Because it was done in the year 2 and in 10 years 6. Because it wasn't dedicated to make lassos, when there was time to make a lasso or a braided whip, it was braided of 4 and of 8 calfskin ropes. And if some day by thanks to the doctor that saved the boy he had to make a small button for the corralera (type of shirt worn by gauchos), he made a button of feathers and it was a jewel, a real gem, he didn't live, to have dedicated himself to make feather buttons of the standard type. He made one faraway there, and then we are facing a work and a spectacular, of a theme, of a producer of *folkloric* artifacts of unsurpassable quality.

Then if that is lost, such as the loss of the feather button, someone will do it, but we don't have news, we don't have news. Giving the impression that the inhabitant had lost it. The popular song, the dance that may have been lost, it's possible that it maybe becoming lost and that it will disappear, that we will call the author "anonymous". Because now all authors have an intention sincerely commercial as we might put it.

All men who compose a *Zamba* would like to gain the author's rights, but in the measure that they composed their *Zambas* and *Chacareras* (traditional Argentine folk dance typical of the Province of Santiago del Estero), *Escondidos, Baguales* (slow sad song that the inhabitants of the Calchaquies valley in Salta and in the *Quebrada* de *Humahuaca* in the Province of Jujuy, northwest Argentina. The song is accompanied by a calfskin drum known as a "caja"), *Vidalas*, right? "*Chayeras*" (*Vidalas Chayeras*-happy song of the Province of La Rioja, principally sung during the days of the carnival) that are called "*Chayeras*". Playing in a rushed manner they are called "*Chayeras*" and it's not such, it's not such, that the *Chayera* doesn't need the hurriedness and I don't know any Riojano (a native of the Province of La Rioja) who rushes it....... (Laughter)

And when they play *Chayeras* they don't have time to breathe, not the drummer on the bombo, neither any guitarist, nor the singer. They believe that is the carnival. !!Lie!!.... it's not certain, nothing is rushed in the provinces, everything is genuine expression, severe, serious.

Our countryman is serious to the point when he will play because a thing is to be played and another is to be clowning around. Our *criollo,* never since our country was born until now, never has been a clown although they had been and so they were considered to be more of one.

Now, the Argentine song, because it didn't occur to us in our youth to take seriously the 80 dances of the province of Buenos Aires and the 2000 *estilos* and *cifras.* Do you know why?.... Because there are very serious musical elements that don't draw frenetic and massive applause. They don't draw it; not any *Cifra* provokes frenetic applause but if it was a *Carnivalito,* the final of a famous *Zamba* or an intended *Chacarera* and lightly stinging and a lot of bombo (bass drum). That can rapidly awaken the consequence of a cordial and sympathetic applause. Instead that of the province of Buenos Aires isn't, because our countryman to the point of his manner of dressing, when he worked in the corrals, through this medium he used clothes that got dirty called *"batarazas"* (typical light gray pants of the farming region), a genre lightly ordinary, easy to wash and put on because it was work clothes. But when they were to *"endomingaba"* (to put on one's Sunday best) they dressed in black-an influence of our "castellania" (inheritance of the zone of Castilla en Spain). It was severe and serious, from the sombrero to the spurs, it was severe and serious...and so it was in their music, their manner of greeting, as in their way of drinking, to never be an alcoholic. Our countryman of the province of Buenos Aires drank his gin and his wine but never was an alcoholic. He was a sober gentleman, some with fortune and others without anything. Although it can't be said that it was without, he who since the horse dominated the *pampas* (grasslands) the landscape of *La Pampa.* He had a lot already. Right?, He had a lot....

Then, to resume what you were communicating to me, the preoccupation of those gentlemen reunited in the Casa de Ricardo Rojas; one can detract in a certain way from the destiny of the national song, it can be debased if it doesn't reach the conscience of the singer, that has more ambition than ability, and looks more to the Society of Authors that is the imperial of its own Argentine conscience. But I don't believe in any way that sometime the song might disappear, the "anonymous" man might disappear, that singer N.N., that silent worker, that minstrel of the *pampas,* of the north, of the littoral, it could disappear by the means of the advance of technology and in the same measure that he will learn to read and write and think. Because generally it was the fruit of the illiterate. The popular song, the literature generally of that time, one didn't have to analyze it, but feel it, receive it, and regard it as such, as popular literature.

I don't believe it will disappear, I hope not, I expect that God won't permit a tremendous happening. The popular song has to follow in spite of the disorientation that many people have, that love the song, that love the guitars, that love the land, but still haven't reached to divide, to establish the borders between their desires to be manifested and the conscience to brake their ambitions.

To that point it appears to me and forgives me if I exceeded.

H.G.M.: !!In no way maestro!!

We continue conversing with maestro Atahualpa Yupanqui.......

Maestro..... giving your knowledgeable words that have left a mountain of teachings and I am tremendously touched by all that you have just told me and the audience of *"Dialogo"* that is going to receive you. There is a question that I think is pointed and is going to serve as an example to many people by what your opinion is. And it deals with declaring the difference that there is between the interpreter of *folklore* and the *folklorist,* what is it to be a *folklorist*? What does it require?

A.Yupanqui: Well, the *folklore* we just said a while ago is all of what the people learn without anyone having taught them, there is no system, there isn't a little book to learn from. The *folklore* isn't learned from a little book, one learns it for example from what is written, of which there is a lot that's important. Reading of our people and of our maestros: Adolfo Salazar.

Adolfo Salazar was a very knowledgeable Spanish gentleman, with a doctorate in musicology, in a time, when he was to live in Mexico. He was a man...who died in Mexico 15 years ago. He was one of those men who traveled the world and knew *folklore,* ethnology, archeology, and popular music, of the working man and minstrels. He knew everything we would have wanted to know, and that we never reach that level of knowledge.

This photo is from *Musica y Musicos de Latinoamerica* by Otto Mayer-Serra published by Editorial Atlante Mexico City in 1947.

Adolfo Salazar

!!How much that Spaniard knew!! !!How much he studied!! He studied as a student not as a maestro, as those maestros say: 'I already know' and they adorn the books, that he lived to consult and consulting others, maybe intellectually inferior to him, but if he could find a small road of interpretation.

Adolfo Salazar, it was he that said: 'Bless that pilgrim of the desert', he wasn't a man of the Saharan desert, but those deserts that are, that you find on the edge of the desert there in Africa, the skeleton of a camel...of a camel...who died of thirst, and fell to the sand and rid himself of or was missing a molar and discovered the first note, in the jawbone of a camel in the desert. It's worth saying that it initiated the first knowledge, the first notice in thousands of years, of what later was to be called the Ocarina (musical instrument). There always will be someone who would make fun of it; claim someone made the hole, it already had two notes. And so they're going to be making the Ocarina, according to him, right? I have studied the ancient music of the Arames, the Egyptians, of the Chaldeans, that is knowledge that comes from quite a distance, with an enormous capacity of assimilation.

Next, Isabel Aretz Thiele, is Argentine, of German ancestry, but is Argentine. Isabel Aretz is married to Felipe Ribera, Felipe Ribera a great *folklorist* of 70 years of age in the INCIBA, Institute of Investigations in Caracas, Venezuela and she got married to Felipe and it joined a pair of *folklorists* .....that is to say expert in *folklore*....

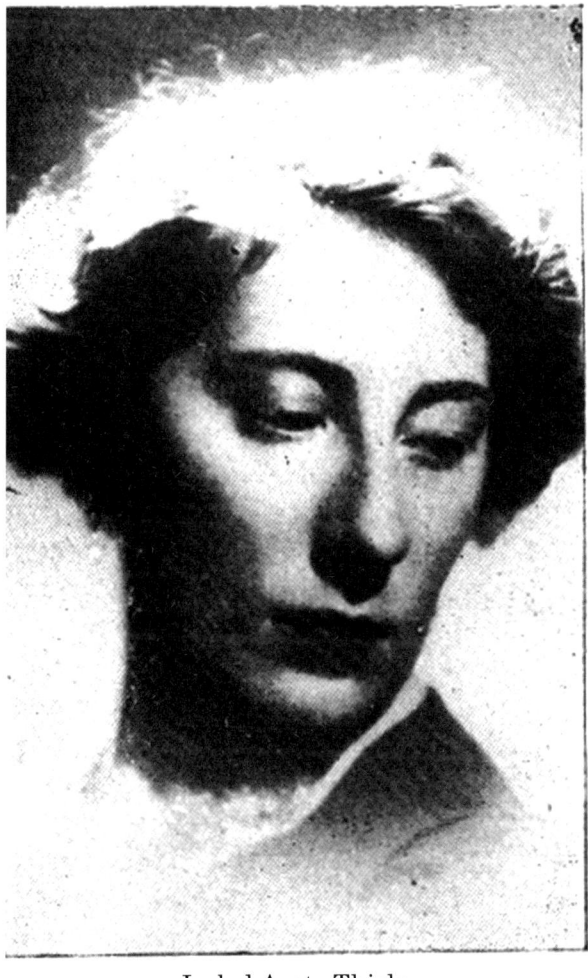

Isabel Aretz-Thiele

This photo is from *Musica y Musicos de Latinoamerica* by Otto Mayer-Serra published by Editorial Atlante Mexico City in 1947.

He......plays the guitar a little and she plays piano, she studied the piano very well, violin, harmony, counterpoint, here in the National Conservatory of Buenos Aires. But her capacity of assimilation and investigation is very vast. She has covered in her travels Europe, Egypt, verifying, annotating, questioning, she is fearless whatever the hour......she is a woman advanced in years and now old. She's over 70 years old, and is heavyset and her body is large, she mustn't be in great health, but she never judged anyone. Before that she aspired to the early morning and the library. Whatever library from Calcutta to Washington and from Caracas to Commodore Rivadavia (in southern Argentina in the zone of Patagonia) to view, to observe, to learn to verify. That is very important.

That famous advice: 'Turn your light out late if you're going to be someone', that is what Isabel Aretz Thiele followed. And in our country: Carlos Vega, *Don* Ventura Lynch, *Don* Domingo Lombardi, Fausto Burgos, Maximiliano Marquez Alurralde in Tucuman, Roberto de la Vega in La Rioja province, Joaquín V. Gonzalez in La Rioja, Ricardo Vera Vallejo in la Rioja, honorable Riojans, Gudiño Kramer in Santa Fe, Draghi Lucero in Mendoza .....

Carlos Vega

This photo is from *Musica y Musicos de Latinoamerica* by Otto Mayer-Serra published by Editorial Atlante Mexico City in 1947.

H.G.M.: Ortiz Oderigo as well?

A.Y.: Yes, Ortiz Oderigo that also dedicated in a special manner to study the music of Africa, of the Negro.

Oderigo began to publish with Arthur Ramos of Brazil, the life of the Negroes.

Arthur Ramos gave us data, which to me resulted in being very important, later when I got involved studying Abyssinian things. For example, that of the 82 different races of Negroes, of Africa 70 are Semitic. Then there's certain tenacity in the maintenance of ancestral rituals; they had some justification because they were rituals. Then that opens for us a road to the curiosities. I am studious as well as curious of those things. I have an infinite curiosity, I stay up late at night, I stayed up late to satisfy my curiosity. Because I don't have a scientific capacity. I am of a temperament to be of service to the things of our nation and even further away.

Why did I study the things that are somewhat universal?....!! To see if I could be at least useful where I was born, where I live, nothing more, right?

Now, what I concretely refer to when I say how it is going as to the Argentine destiny of our knowledge...... is of *folklorists* and *folklore*. One man knows *20 Zambas, 10 Chacareras, 40 Vidalas, 8 Estilos* and *23 Milongas*. He is a singer, a worker, and an artist if he has the artistic insomnia, he is an interesting man, but you can't say *folklorist* if he has ignored *folklore*, if he has ignored that. If he hasn't systematically studied the difference between folklore and popular, between popular and collective. The things of folklore are anonymous, that has a name but are without authorship. *"Caminito de Indio"* isn't *folklore;* it's by Yupanqui.

Now, *"El Condor Pasa"* that Alomias Robles picked up in Cuzco, Peru 60 years ago, *"El Condor Pasa"* comes from a distant epoch, it is a *folkloric* element, a *folkloric* work that he had retrieved. Later, as it was very beautiful, it circuited Europe and that melody passed around there and came out with, not fewer than 72 authors. The whole world seized upon it, as if the prestige had legs. Over there is a Mr. Wismer in Paris that is a co-author and as he brought about a dispute, then they arrived at a settlement of 50% for him and 50% for the descendents of Robles. Another author came out with a film for Paramount and had inserted *"El Condor Pasa"*, a third author, that's going to get 22%. Here in Argentina another wanted to derive a little bit, so he wrote some lyrics, because that isn't a verse as it appears, just a few words, but he'll get 5% or 10%. When the young woman is very pretty suitors come from everywhere. Now there is a thing, that lacks dignity, and of sobriety and of probity in the elements that comes close to notable works and famous South American songs.

The people must feel honored with the playing of *"Zamba de Vargas"*, very honored, but it mustn't ever occur, to add some words, to get close to a little recitation that is to say: 'it'll be good to see if I can get 5% of what can be derived from that'. I believe in whatever language......of the world it can be called!! IMMORALITY!!

H.G.M. We continue conversing on *"Dialogo"* with maestro Atahualpa Yupanqui.... Maestro, if you had to name two poets and two musicians of the Rio de la Plata, who would you be inclined to choose? For example, you knew Abel Fleury?

A.Y.: Abel Fleury, yes, I knew him......

Abel Fleury died more than several years ago, but for me it's like he never died.

He was in my home, Abel, I spent Christmas many times with him, he was a single man, concentrated, very well educated, very studious of the guitar and very intelligent, an active intelligence, active and nervous. Everyday, he was with general literature besides with the guitar, right?

Many times, at Christmas we spent them together, many times. He was a good friend, we played guitar together. And one day his throat became diseased, and it went bad. And it appeared he began to be sick of something, that no one wanted to speak of the bad shade upon humanity!! Cancer!! And it was and it was a few, quite a few years ago in spite of the fact that he lived on *calle Esperanza*.

He was...he was a!! Great Guitarist. !!

The tone Abel had, has still not been surpassed by any of the popular guitarists in Argentina. The tone of Abel was a big sound, ample. The basses, when he played over the basses on his *pampeana* pieces he had kind of a violoncello sound, vibrato like that of a cello, very round and deep, extensive, serious, full of density and with a message, great guy that Abel Fleury.

H.G.M.: Great composer......

A.Y.: Yes, yes, a great composer, everything that he had about *"Los pajaros"* (birds), the *"Sobretarde"*, those *Estilos,* overall his *Estilos*.

H.G.M.: The *Milonga "Ausencia"* ....

A.Y.: Yes, the *Milongas*, he had various *Milongas* .....

H.G.M.: The *Milonga "Del Ayer"*.

A.Y.: Yes, the *Milonga "Del Ayer"*, no, no *"Milongueo del Ayer"*.

!! Ah!!, he had very beautiful things, Abel, very beautiful.

And after among the musicians that I like very much at times it makes me sad when I return here year after year and I see they haven't joined 40 together for a dinner to offer a guitarist and to say to a guitarist: 'We love you very much keep it up'. That thing that stimulates appears to be nonsense, right? But it encourages. For one guy that scores a goal (in soccer) they have 27 banquets, because he scored a goal and for the guy that decently writes Argentine music for 40 years, they say: '!! Hi, how's it going don Carlitos!!' sometime when they see him in the street.

Carlos Guastavino, a musician of serious capacity and intelligent and that had honored popular music, having the abilities or another type of music, that is to say chamber music. He made a serious contribution, intelligent, perfect for the popular music, not seen in many years.

Getting around, I've seen him here, he goes to Santa Fe, then comes here, right? He's completely busy, he's restless, he lives

Abel Fleury with a dedication: "To my friend Segundo Contreras with much affection." (Signed) Abel Fleury, Buenos Aires May 22, 1950

creating, say beautiful things on his piano and in his conducting, and even his neighbors don't hold dinners in his honor, and to me that's a shame. I know that he doesn't live of cheap vanities, no one dignified that loves and treasures dignity lives of cheap vanities.

But the others that they see, those that are, don't move it to that side. It may be because he's not mentioned successively on television, it may be because he's not mentioned successively on the radio stations.

You have to be mentioned on television to be a man worth something?

To me that appears to be even better of course, much better of course.....Because to be named on television and on radio to many people no one can ever see. By so saying, forgive me for speaking *"paisanamente"* (sincerely and spontaneously)....

H.G.M.: !! That's quite fine!!...

A.Y.: It's been a while since I saw Guastavino, some 4 years since I've given him a hug, but I took advantage of the moment and his conversation to tell him that permanently he has the homage of my respect and of my congeniality and of my friendship although I might not see him ever. But in my home, I mention him almost daily.

And I want to thank you for having given me the opportunity to say: "name people", there's one: Abel Fleury that is in silence, that went to the silence and the other who walks in silence in Buenos Aires.

H.G.M.: Maestro, to close and to not abuse anymore of your kindness I would like as a brooch of gold of all of that, this program goes out to all of Uruguay, and as you have composed with the great poet of Uruguay, who is Romildo Risso, I'll ask you to speak a little bit about the poetry of Uruguay.

A.Y.: Well, Romildo Risso is a forgotten one in his land, he died 30 years ago (c.1950) and has been forgotten. To me what they said last night, conversing so with musicians, they told me: 'Look, that in Uruguay, Risso is unknown'.

!!! And I don't miss him!!...!! I don't miss him!! (sarcasm), the people live forgetting their most profound responsibilities. They live to be forgetful. Heroes aren't the only ones who win battles in the heat of battle. Heroes are also those who win battles against ignorance and a lack of culture. Those are truly heroes; those that go on to triumph, illuminating the path of the generations that arrive in a country. Of the new little trees that grow, they are good winds and good suns to develop the plants and to produce noble fruits or of noble shade sometime, right?

And then Risso was one of those people; he was a good wind and good sun to many generations, not only Argentineans, *Rioplatenses* (inhabitants of the Rio de la Plata area) and a little more further away.

Risso was an expert, not only of the *gaucho* subject, but also of the conduct and position of the man confronting misfortune, confronting the contrariness, facing the clouds or the good morning of tomorrow. When a man loves the sun he sincerely says: 'If that isn't beautiful, then I don't know what is'. Well, that was his manner to speak, which was his manner to speak.... He had told me many times: 'do you realize, there are many people that say *"paisana"* (to speak sincerely and spontaneously), that say gaucho, that say *folklorist* and they believe that to write in gaucho with writing in *"guarango"* (stupid, gross and ordinary), that's it'.... And they are...very mistaken, you have to know the Spanish language very well, you have to profoundly know Cervantes, you have to know the grammar to not be mistaken, the prosodic accent to not be mistaken to not err nor to do what's been done by the mistaken lecturers and possible admirers. The word he hated was "admirer". When the people told him: 'I'm an admirer of yours', he turned away and left in a rush. !! No!!, no he didn't like whatever manner of vanity. He was a man of truth, a man with a capital "M".

And among the Uruguayan storytellers there is José Morosoli of the city of Minas, department of Lavalleja, who had published *"El Abañil de los Tapes", "Hombre",* then Javier de Vianna before him, Leandro Ipuche, a mountain of people, *canarios* (natives of the Department of Canelones, Uruguay, whose founders were from the Canary Islands of Spain) and *maragatos* (those born in the locale of San José de Mayo, Uruguay).

Uruguay has given us good poets, among the famous, with the image of fireworks, audacious and beautiful: Yamandu Rodríguez, and some intelligent follower such as Osiris Rodríguez Castillos. It (Uruguay) has given us good poets.

Elderly Silva Valdez, with his good contribution that I don't believe to have been fundamental, the contribution of Silva Valdez. But, yes in his moment, interesting and good. What he lacked was a little bit more of modesty and a little more culture. That is to say information of the universal literature, that many other Uruguayans have.

To that point I believe we can attain.

H.G.M.: Maestro, I don't know how to thank you for this beautiful moment that you have made happen and will be going out to the friends of *"Dialogo"* when they hear your words. I thank you infinitely and the only thing I ask after having listened to you is that I hope we'll have more Atahualpa Yupanquis....

A.Y.: With fewer debts, right? ...!!Thank You!! and until another time.....

H.G.M.: Until the following Sunday German, until the next Sunday family, this has been Héctor Angel García (Héctor García Martínez), exclusive correspondent of "Dialogo" in the city of Buenos Aires that has held this conversation with the maestro Atahualpa Yupanqui.

!!!Thanks, until next Sunday!!!

This interview with Atahualpa Yupanqui was done in his home on the date indicated on *calle San Benito de Palermo 1655-8vo piso "A" (8th floor, Apt. "A")-Buenos Aires-Argentina.*

Interview with **Noemi Toulouse** by Héctor García Martínez on June 10, 2000.

We're in the home of Noemi Toulouse, student of the distinguished Argentine maestro Carmelo Rizzuti. Let's do the interview as a document that will remain of your life with the guitar, the people you knew in the first few decades of the 20th century in Argentina.

Let's start by asking how you began to play the guitar, at what age, and in what form.

N.T. My father was a very good player of the guitar, he had been a student of the Italian maestro who arrived here many years ago, who was called Vicente Caprino.....

H.G.M.!!! Yes, Vicente Caprino!!!....

N.T. Later he was a student of maestro Rizzuti, with whom he did a duo, they had played in concert works such as Miserere del Trovador, and they played those types of things, parts of operas in the years when I still hadn't been born. And that friendship remained very affectionate between them. Well, later when I was 9 years old, they had me study piano, something that never interested me much at all. But one day my father took me to a concert by a distinguished student of maestro Rizzuti that was called Maud Metcalfe. And when I left that concert, I told my father: "Look, dad, it appears I'm going to like to study the guitar more." Immediately they took me to maestro Rizzuti and I began to study with him. And in reality, he was the only real maestro I had and later I studied many things and all because as one gets older you pick up ideas and advice of others. But the truth is, it was this maestro who inculcated the fundamental principles of the guitar, the technique. I remember I studied the Pascual Roch method with him, Aguado and in the end those methods.

H.G.M. How long did you study with maestro Rizzuti?

N.T. I received lessons from him since I was 10 years old, until I stopped when I would have been 14 or 15 years old. There I finished my studies; he gave me a diploma of Superior Professor of the Guitar of his Academia. Because in that time, everything was done in private academies, there wasn't a National Conservatory, it didn't exist for music, I believe.

H.G.M. For guitar?

N.T. For piano, I don't know if it existed, I can't affirm that...But before I had my diploma, I had already been presented in concert before the Academia Rizzuti many times. Because he had as a motive, his birthday, or some anniversary of the Academia, some celebration, and he always had me play. Because I had become his favorite student in those years. So that everytime, he had something doing in the Academia I was always the principal player, and the only one. In many cases I did entire programs of the guitar with him.

H.G.M. Describe for me maestro Rizzuti, his personality, what memories do you have?

N.T. Just once in the magazine of the Circulo Guitarristico Argentino something came out, but that was long ago, in the year 1970 more or less. He was a very pleasant man, a good person, always with an even character, a little weak at times; he never got angry if you didn't study. I liked him a lot, and I have an affectionate friendship with his daughters, overall with his daughter Haydée that is a professor of guitar as well. I had brought my students to take their exam in his Academia, after many years. I can't speak well enough of this maestro, that inclusive you're now going to see a photograph of when he had his 80th birthday and a dinner that was given and I'm at the head of the table along-side him. In ending, I have very good memories of him.

H.G.M. Your first performances in public.....

N.T. My first important concert that I remember took place in a small hall. Once I remember I traveled to the city of "25 de Mayo" (Buenos Aires province) to play in a salon owned by a friend and I gave a concert based on classical music, including, I believe Albeniz, I don't know if I have the program over there. Later in the years 1930-1931, I played in "La Peña", the famous Peña, from there to the Café Tortoni (one of the oldest cafes in Buenos Aires, since the end of the 19th century).

H.G.M. "La Peña" was managed by Quinquela Martin (Benito Quinquela Martin was a famous Argentine painter, who immortalized in his canvases, the scenes of antiquity of the *"La Boca"* — typical neighborhood of the city of Buenos Aires).

N.T. Yes, Quinquela was there in the evening, Alfonsina Storni was there too (famous Argentine poet), I was playing and I saw them seated at the table right in front of me. It was for me, a great presentation, because I was playing for artists, for people who were very cordial with me, they applauded me a lot.

H.G.M. What personalities do you remember were at the "La Peña"?

N.T. I didn't interact with them directly, but I remember they were there that night, I remember exactly, listening to me and applauding me. Here, I have, I'll show you later programs from that night.

Later I had a presentation I did at the Association Guitarristica Argentina in 1935; I had an entire program performed at the Teatro Lassalle. I was at that time 19 years old, ... 19 or 20 years old. It was a program of serious responsibility, and of course I filled the hall. We had that goodwill among us guitarists in that moment, when a guitarist of the group played; we all went to hear them.

H.G.M. Everything contrary to now....

N.T. !! Ah !!, yes, I remember that at that concert there were Maria Angélica Funes, Consuelo Mallo Lopez, Maria Herminia Antola, young women players of the first rank and they were listening to me. When they played, I didn't miss many concerts. It was a commitment of honor to go to listen to them and applaud them. We were friends, we had reunions in one's home and then the other's, and we got together in the evening. I had made a good friendship with Irma Haydée Perazzo, who lived, in the Boedo and Caseros area. And there in the home of Irma Haydée Perazzo we received a guest one night, we had beautiful reunions of the guitar, I heard there for the first time a young man who had come from the interior to make a living and he was looking for someone who could write down music. Do you know who it was?

This photo of Irma Haydée Perazzo is from the *"Galeria de Concertistas y Profesionales"* section of the 1931 Antigua Casa Nuñez catalog.

2486

H.G.M. Who?

N.T. !!! Atahualpa Yupanqui !!! I can tell you he was quite thin...(laughter). That must have been in the year 1935 more or less. Yes, he was looking for someone who could write down his songs.

H.G.M. Atahualpa Yupanqui played there?

N.T. Yes, when he was going to come you had to reverse the strings of a guitar, because.... he was left handed, am I right?

H.G.M. Yes.

N.T. So, when Atahualpa Yupanqui was going to come to the home of Irma Haydée Perazzo, you had to reverse the strings of a guitar. We spent many beautiful nights, there. We never imagined perhaps that this young man would become who he would be later, become known worldwide and appreciated more outside his country, than perhaps inside of it. In spite of all the people who appreciated him here, right? But in Europe he was someone important.

H.G.M. What else do you remember of these reunions, what other figures?

N.T. Not too much, we were pretty much the same people, at the reunions and my father was enchanted the way Irma Perazzo played the guitar, he like to go hear her a lot. In reality, she didn't shine that much in her concerts, because she was a very nervous person and she ran the risk of suddenly making a mistake or balking in a piece. Though in her home, she was quite a bit more tranquil. She had a good tone. And Segovia had given her a few lessons.......

Señorita Noemí Toulouse, que
ejecutó un difícil programa.

This photo of Noemi Toulouse is from the *"Caras y Caretas"* magazine of November 1932, Issue No. 1779. In this performance she was involved in the inauguration of the club "La Choza".

The caption translated say: "Miss Noemi Toulouse, who performed a difficult program."

H.G.M. And Domingo Prat.

N.T. Yes, but after a few voyages that Segovia made here, she played for him and he began directing her quite a bit, right? She didn't have to pay for the classes.

   Is she alive? I don't know if she's alive?

H.G.M. No, she passed away.

N.T. She passed away?.....but not long ago. I know I talked to her by telephone about 10 years ago, she was living at Villa Urquiza or over there near to Devoto (neighborhoods of Buenos Aires) close to San Martin Avenue. and she said to me: 'I'll wait for your visit in my house'.....But those things didn't happen to come about. But we still saw each other a lot, she came to my home many times as well to visit, when I was living in Caballito (neighborhood of Buenos Aires), at that moment.

H.G.M. And of your activities, how long did exercise them?

N.T. No, in reality I....didn't like to teach the guitar.....(laughter)

H.G.M. Why?

N.T. Because as well I was a professor of French, and I liked teaching French much more than teaching the guitar. But however, once maestro Rizzuti called me on the phone and said, I was 14 or 15 years old at the time, 'look, they have called me from the Williams Conservatory annex at Villa del Parque (neighborhood of Buenos Aires), they want me to go give classes twice a week, nothing more, because they have a few students and I don't have the time, but would you like to go?' he said. And I was living in Flores (neighborhood of Buenos Aires) and from there to Villa del Parque wasn't far. So I said, "why not?" and I was in the Williams Conservatory teaching guitar for 1 or 2 years. There were 3 or 4 youngsters and I always went twice a week. And later when I had lots of students was when I got married, not because my husband influenced any part, on the contrary. But I stopped playing the guitar for 20 years, and one day I was with Bianqui Piñero instead of Rizzuti. I had frequented only a few times the Asociacion Guitarristica Argentina, and I ran into Bianqui Piñero. When we were leaving, as we both live near each other, we walked together, I said: "There are days when I have the desire and want to play the guitar again" ...."and I don't even have a guitar".... because the concert guitar I had....I had sold it, my Velasco, I don't have a guitar, I told him. 'Look' he said, 'at least you can play, go shopping to buy a student guitar and try them out until you find one you're content with and stimulated by, and after a little bit of practice you'll start to have a few students again, if you want....in the Asociacion Guitarristica there's always people asking for a professor, if you want, I'll send them to you'...

   And well, I went to the luthier Estrada Gomez and bought a guitar and began to study, and attained the ability almost as well as when I was very young girl and that Bianqui Piñero told me: 'it appears as a lie that after not playing for 20 years that you play so well'. I was practicing 3 hours daily or more and afterward I would practice with the students, with the students a little bit, not more than what I was teaching, because sometimes you have to play as well. After I got married, the music altered me a lot. I had a good student, this young man played quite well. I had another student that gave me great satisfaction, who studied with me many years, who became an architect, and after all those years, he invited me one day to an exposition of art, of works he had painted. He introduced me as a professor of music and said: 'You don't know what happy moments I've had with the guitar since all that you taught me'. Because I had taught him since the beginning, and the things one teaches stay recorded in the minds of those that deserve them .....

H.G.M. So then you were practically; we could say an "amateur of the guitar"......

N.T. Yes, in a certain moment I had my name as a concert guitarist, but then I kind of disappeared a little bit .....

H.G.M. How many years did you give concerts?

N.T. And, I.....How long was I giving concerts?.... What happened is I began giving concerts when I was very young..... Had I started by 15 years old?......and 10 years more or less.

H.G.M. What repertoire did you have?

N.T. Well, the repertoire classic, you're going to see possibly later here, and I'm going to show you programs. And what I played was aimed at the music more or less that was well known in that moment, with a certain preparation I made to give the concerts. I played for example: the *"Variations* by Sor, over the theme by Mozart"*, a series of *minuets* by Mozart, *minuets* by Haydn, Granados, *Sevilla* and *Asturias* of Albeniz, *Recuerdos de la Alhambra* and *Sueño b*y Tárrega, later I would begin with the music that was more modern, The *Suite Castellana* by Moreno-Torroba, the *Canciones Mexicanas* by Manuel Ponce, that I, I don't know now, those things are escaping me, the *Choros* of Villa-Lobos, when they had just come out, they were well applauded by the public.

H.G.M. And the national composers of here?

N.T. National authors, little, in reality the only ones I played were *"tristes"* by Julián Aguirre, when I was a young girl, when I began to play some *"vidalitas"* (lyrical specie of Argentine *folklore*)....I believe it was very much in the mode of a *vidalita* by Justo T. Morales, that I played a lot.

H.G.M. Alais? Didn't you play the waltz *"Un Momento"* by Juan Alais?

N.T. *"Un Momento"*?..... well we did that....do you know what? ...with my maestro, my father and I?
We played *"Un Momento"* by Alais for 3 guitars, because Rizzuti had made I don't know if it was the 3rd guitar part, yes it was the 3rd guitar part, and I played that. Because my father had played *"Un Momento"* a lot with Rizzuti. My father played very good classical pieces, but later gave up the instrument altogether.

H.G.M. Had your father commented something about maestro Vicente Caprino?

N.T. No, he had been his maestro; he was Italian......yes.....because I have seen things, he had some music I still don't know where it went, that he was saying, of Vicente Caprino? I don't know...... I'll have to review and I don't know if I have anything. Things that belonged to my father, were the *Miserere del Trovador,* that I believe was arranged for guitar, I don't know if it was by Vicente Caprino. But it fit the guitar very beautifully, because it was a tremolo piece.

H.G.M. What memories do you have of the maestros of those epochs, tell me of Sagreras, or of all of them.

N.T. I tell you sincerely that the "maestro of maestros" of that epoch was Domingo Prat.

H.G.M. Did you know him?

N.T. I knew him, but he only gave me classes. But I believe I would have gone farther if I'd been a student of Prat. Not that I would want to take anything from Rizzuti that he deserves, perhaps he let things go, if one studied only a little, there was no reprimand. Instead Prat was tougher, he was more demanding with the technique, with some things, by the young women I saw who studied with him. One takes into account certain failings that one had, perhaps the fault of a professor who was not strict enough.

H.G.M. Is it the truth as many have told me, that the students that had become distinguished with Prat, had gone to him with a basis, and that he perfected them?

N.T. I don't know about that, how to know if all that's true, I don't know. I can't exactly tell you the truth. I know people who say: 'I studied with Prat' but I don't know to what point, or if they already knew something, I don't know, I can't answer you.

I know for example that Consuelo Mallo Lopez was a great player with a splendid technique and it was beautiful to listen to her. I heard the best of Consuelo. Because after the Asociacion Guitarristica and everything, after I got married, when I was living on the calle Vidt we had a large house, and I liked receiving people in my home. And in those opportunities Consuelo had come with her husband to eat dinner and pass a pleasant evening listening to good music. Consuelo maintained the technique perfectly in spite of being well along in years. Well, she had been an exemplary maestro she had many students.

H.G.M. That, which you were saying to me about Rizzuti, was that he was a good man, who didn't get mad, he let things go. It appears to me that was an attitude taken by many of the maestros of that epoch. Look, I studied with Adolfo V. Luna, and I tell you the only way he taught me was the place where the notes were. But later after having helped me to perfect my playing, he didn't contribute anything in that sense. The same thing happened with maestro Severo Rodríguez Falcon, later.

N.T. Severo Rodríguez?

H.G.M. Yes, Severo Rodríguez Falcon.

N.T. !!Ah!! But I knew him since he was a boy...a baby....

H.G.M. Of course, yes....

N.T. Student of who?

H.G.M. Of Rizzuti, of Prat, and of Justo T. Morales.

N.T. !!Ah!! Severo Rodríguez?......but he was just a babe when I met Severo Rodríguez.

H.G.M. !!!Very good!!! He was.

N.T. Another boy I met, very young and one day I met in the Guitarristica Argentina (Asociacion Guitarristica Argentina) is a maestro who I believe is still teaching: Torchia.

H.G.M. Yes, yes, a very good friend of mine, and he's still alive.

N.T. One day I heard, 'this gentleman is Torchia', then I got closer to him.... it was when we were, I believe on the calle Mario Bravo, with the Circulo Guitarristica Argentina and I got closer to him and said: "How's it going Mr. Torchia?" ....!!He looked at me!!... and I told him that I was Noemi Toulouse, and the man jumped through the roof and he hugged me, he was younger than I was.

H.G.M. No, there you go I believe....

N.T. I don't know but it appears that he was younger.

H.G.M. Returning again to the beforehand, in general it was that the maestros of that epoch, some of them were disciples of the great European maestros that settled in Argentina, appears that they let things go? ....

N.T. I don't know, I don't know how to tell you how it might have been. But I remember one time, I don't know if he came to my home for a certain reason or if I saw him at Rizzuti's, the maestro Hilarion Leloup. And he began to play guitar that Basque had a technique that was very impressionable, and he was older than I was. But he played with an imposing technique, imposing. I believe he came to my home, I don't know, around the time of the beginning of the old Asociacion Guitarristica Argentina. I don't know why he came. But his technique remained in my mind.

H.G.M. He was a student of Tárrega.......

N.T. It could be, yes......

H.G.M. No, could be no, he was.

N.T. It could be that there he got his great technique, it could be, I don't know. Later he disappeared from the map. I never saw him again; I don't know when he died?

H.G.M. He died in the year 1939, in February during the days of the carnival.

N.T. Well, to have been angry with someone in the Asociacion Guitarristica Argentina .. ....and to not have appeared again.......(laughter) then they went.....(laughter) in that time every session was a boxing match, they fought, no, no they didn't hit anyone, but they got really mad, my father was a secretary for a while, later he got bored and renounced his position. Because every session was a heated discussion, a fight, they got angry over ridiculous things.

H.G.M. Would you tell me about the concert artists of those epochs that you recall, ...
In the majority of times they played for free?

N.T. I believe so, if you didn't have students you couldn't live. Nor could you travel. You see what's happening now with this *"Cuarteto Entre Cuerdas"*. They're young women that enchant me as to how they play; they appear to be people of merit. They appear to me to deserve a tour, to go and play as far as the four walls of our country. If I had money, ... I would support them so they could tour all over.

You were asking me something?

H.G.M. Yes, that the concert artists always had to play for free, in our country.

N.T. I believe that is so, I believe that is so.... the salvation was the ones who could get students. But after concerts did pay....... I believe that now things are the same, it isn't an aspect of fame neither, here in the country the majority of youngsters that win the competition in the Circulo Guitarristico Argentino, all of them fly out of the country. He's not in Italy, he's in France, he's not in France, he's in Spain, and all are out of the country.

H.G.M. You were a co-founder of the Asociacion Guitarristica Argentina?

N.T. Yes, I was a co-founder of the Asociacion Guitarristica Argentina. Because right after it was founded, maestro Rizzuti, came looking for me, and had me play in the hall on Bartolomé Mitre and Rivarola, that was the first location of the Asociacion Guitarristica Argentina, later we were at the Hotel Castelar, and from Castelar to Pasaje Barolo, the Asociacion had rented a beautiful hall in the Barolo. Every Sunday we were there without fail, to the social gathering on the Sunday afternoons. We went, but also the important people that played, Consuelito Mallo Lopez was always there with her mother. We were sure to go as well, and later other people and advanced students of other maestros......there was a young man...what was his name? .... I don't remember right now.....Later when we were at the Pasaje Barolo, I've got a lot of programs from there, there was a monthly program published by the Asociacion Guitarristica Argentina, with all the players who would play every month. Inclusive was that we had acquired a piano and so it wasn't just guitar, but it extended to that instrument as well. I had a close friend who was a professor of piano and a very good student at the National Conservatory and she gave a concert there in the Barolo, she played for the junior high school students. I also played for the blind and their Institute, after which I played a concert monthly, important, at the Salon Teatro Lasalle; I played there, as well all the important young women players. I recognize for example that Consuelo Mallo Lopez was superior to me as a player and in technique. I tell you this, I believe I played.... At least I completed what I had read, I didn't make mistakes with the notes, I didn't play bad notes, I had a technique that was very reasonable, I believe that what I did wasn't very bad. What happened was I didn't dedicate myself to that exclusively.

H.G.M. What methods did you study with Rizzuti?

N.T. I began with the method.....Well I would've started with his book of *"Lecciones Elementales"* that is small, that little book and it was dedicated to me. But later that of Pascual Roch, the 3 volumes of that method. In reality the 3rd volume is dedicated more to works fingered by.... Pascual Roch, who was a Catalan......

H.G.M. That was living in Cuba.

N.T. Yes, I don't know.... later Aguado, the studies of Coste, the things that were serious, right? and then the 30 *Minuets* de Sor (by Domingo Prat), from there, I tell you that I didn't play all 30, but yes, a great majority of them, they served as studies and as well to use in concerts because they were very beautiful. And, well, I don't remember anything else and other things.....later scales, arpeggios, technique. Roch had a lot of technique, it was nothing more than technique.

H.G.M. And it's strange that Rizzuti, being a student of Prat, that he hadn't given you anything out of his books, from the *"Escalas y Arpegios"* or his *"La Nueva Tecnica"*.

N.T. He was a student of Prat?

H.G.M. Yes, he was a disciple of Prat.

N.T. I never picked up a book by Prat, Roch, yes and after I told you Aguado, the famous method of Aguado, yes, very modern, it was different than the one my father had, later I bought the updated edition. And the 20 plus studies of Napoleon Coste that are concert level studies. Well, that's what I know, have I forgotten something, I don't know.

H.G.M. You were telling me about people who would come to your home for dinner; did Julio Sagreras, Abel Fleury, etc. come to these reunions? What can you tell me of Abel Fleury? What memories do you have of him?

N.T. We were close friends with a man that played the guitar, he didn't play well, but instead he arranged things, he was a man called Pablo Santillan. He was, I don't know if he was President, or if secretary of the Asociacion Guitarristica Argentina, he was a tremendous person who had become a good friend of ours. And he was involved in the first commissions of the Asociacion. This man worked a lot but he died too soon, he was a man who had spent much of his life smoking. I believe it was smoking cigarettes that killed him.

Pablo Santillan

Pablo Santillan was President of the Asociacion Guitarristica Argentina before 1939, this photo is taken from an article about the upcoming first anniversary of his death on July 16, 1938. This is from the Boletin de la Asociacion Guitarristica Argentina issue No. 3 of June 1939.

H.G.M. And of Fleury what do you remember?

N.T. Of Fleury I remember an epoch that he came to the Asociacion Guitarristica Argentina and later he came several times to eat in my home and I remember that guest quite a bit, after having dinner he played some guitar, right? He had come.... (laughter). And the things of his that he played were *"Ausencia"* (milonga), *"Te Vas Milonga",* all beautiful things by him, he had a *"Huella"* (traditional Argentine dance) !!! That was precious!!!

H.G.M. *"Pago Largo"* it's called.

N.T. It was *"Pago Largo"* It had some precious things, he played them with a lot of spirit, he had a very beautiful sound that was noticeable when he played. And apart from that, he was an enchanting man, he was very pleasant, a gentleman, very accessible, very honest, as a friend and as a person. He was very agreeable in the relatively short time that he was in my midst. But I won't forget those times he came to my home, I remember them well.

H.G.M. Was he a communicative person or quiet?

N.T. He wasn't a great conversationalist, he was a tranquil man, serene, and he's not the type that would run you over. He never tried to be "him", being that the whole world was enchanted with him. Because he had done the background music a lot for Fernando Ochoa (reciter of verses about the *gaucho) gaucho:* ancient inhabitant of the Argentine *pampas,* the grasslands), they knew that more than anything because of that. When it said: ! Ah!! Abel Fleury!! He was identified as such, because when Ochoa presented his theatrical spectaculars, it was always Fleury who did the background music. All those works of Yamandu Rodríguez (*gaucho* poet, born in Uruguay) that Ochoa recited, not the jokes, the turkeys, but the recitations, they were backed by the playing of a good guitar.

Abel Fleury, who made an enormous impact on the folkmusic of Argentina, and he was a friend to countless musicians.

H.G.M. Did you hear him play classic works?

N.T. No, no I don't remember, if I heard them, I don't know, because what I remember most of all are his works, more than anything, he played them genially of course, very beautifully.

H.G.M. Do you remember some commentary he made about the guitar or about how to study?

N.T. No, no, nothing about that. He was a friend that came to have dinner and converse at the table about a thousand different things. He never delved into things and in those reunions imagine it, I don't know if he had ever made a critique about anyone. But he wasn't the type of person to be in a moment of conversation unless it was about the guitar.

And I remember him as a very friendly guest, no more, I can't tell you anymore and a beautiful player and over all playing his works. I don't remember other things.

H.G.M. In what year more or less did you meet him?

N.T. And it would be around the year 1935, 1936, there, it was the golden year of the Asociacion Guitarristica Argentina, we went a lot, we were there quite a bit, there was an ambiance, when no one came to visit us, we went by ourselves, as I said to you we had reunions, as well in the home of Irma Haydée Perazzo. Or sometimes I went to visit Consuelo Mallo Lopez. And we always went together. After I remember we had a friend who was an old doctor, an aristocratic type who was from Entrerriana (Province of Entre Rios): Dr. Carlos Muniagurria. He had been a military doctor, he was very old, and had an island in the Tigre (Rio Parana delta in the province of Buenos Aires).

For example, as we would go out together on Sunday afternoons, came to my home after and spent the night, afterward we left my home early the next day to go to the Tigre with her. She was a pleasant, young women and very mischievous, as well to make you laugh. There we had a friendship with a young man who I introduced. I knew him from the fiestas, he had nothing to do with the guitar, he then appeared and she partied with him, but nothing ever came of it, it just happened. She was very agreeable, very mischievous......

I don't remember the name of her first husband .....

H.G.M. Caparelli.

N.T. Caparelli? !!! Ah !!! I couldn't remember who, was her husband, I know that he was a professor and guitarist. But I couldn't remember his name .....

H.G.M. What memories do you have of Maria Angélica Funes?

N.T. And, look, the years had passed since I last saw her, and when I saw her again...because they were the ones who quit the Asociacion Guitarristica Argentina, first, it was this group and they were the first socios of the Circulo Guitarristico Argentino....

H.G.M. Yes, after they quit it, they formed the Circulo Guitarristico.

N.T. That they quit it......one year in the Asociacion Guitarristica Argentina they had an election and it was hard fought, with a lot of disgust, in the time when Bianqui Piñero was there, Bianqui was there in the middle of it, but for his input it helped the Asociacion Guitarristica Argentina, because he was a very honest man.

I liked Bianqui very much as a friend, if I needed something Bianqui would run, he made me copies of his music, he loaned me music. Bianqui Piñero was a great friend, I've always said that, and I will say it that, he came to my home many a time to eat, I was already married, he was an adult, and with his wife. We maintained a cordial friendship until he died, and above all we lived very close.

Geronimo Bianqui Piñero, President of the Asociacion Guitarristica Argentina in 1942, 1944 and again in 1947-48. He was President in later years, but these years are the only ones I can document with the various issues of "Revista de la Guitarra". This photo is from the magazine *Revista Opus* of April 1948.

Archive: Ricardo Muñoz

And I don't know what happened to that election, a group formed and left to create the Circulo Guitarristico Argentino. And as I owed much to Bianqui that I started playing guitar again with his advice and everything, then I wasn't so moved as to go. Because I was a friend of everybody, of some and others. But I didn't want to side badly with Bianqui, so I stopped going altogether, it's been a year or two since I went to the Circulo Guitarristico. But one day I told him: "If I knew the Circulo was going to be good as well why then am I not going to go when I have a desire to see and hear them?" And then I played at a reunion in the calle Alsina.

H.G.M. Moreno....

N.T. No, no before Moreno in a hall of....I don't know where it was. I went with a few friends that with that young girl that plays the guitar Norma Canal....I don't know, if you know them? I had been a good friend of hers, and of the family.

H.G.M. Yes, yes.

N.T. I went with them and they saw me enter and after so long a time that I hadn't appeared, it was as a specie of...!!! They were afraid!!! (laughter) and I confessed to Maria Angélica Funes, that I was a spy...... (laughter)!!! God has set me free!!! I told Bianqui afterward: "I'm also going to the Circulo Guitarristico as well"..... and he replied to me: 'Well, do what you want to do, it's not important to me'.

H.G.M. Those that were dissident with Bianqui Piñero separated and formed the Circulo Guitarristico and the Circulo began to grow, after almost automatically the Asociacion Guitarristica Argentina died, why is that?

N.T. I don't know why. Soon the locale brought the misery, very ugly, because it took on humidity, it was an old place, that café on *"la Avenida de Mayo* and *Chacabuco"* (downtown Buenos Aires) and it wasn't maintained, very ugly, the aspect of the walls. After Bianqui Piñero, left the Presidency, and entered Consuelo Mallo Lopez as President. They also wanted to include *folklore* (dance), right? and made at times what was called the *"fiesta del paquetito",* that consisted of everyone bringing some food- the men brought the drinks and the women the food, and they danced exclusively Argentine *folkloric* dances, we had our days (the guitarists) and they theirs, the things weren't mixed. Therefore, there was a little different element, we'd say more *folkloric,* in the Commission as well, but I wasn't on the Commission when those

G. Bianqui Piñero *folklore* pieces published by Litografia Musical Garrot in 1944, as well autographed and dedicated to Blanca Prat and Consuelo Mallo Lopez, from their archives.

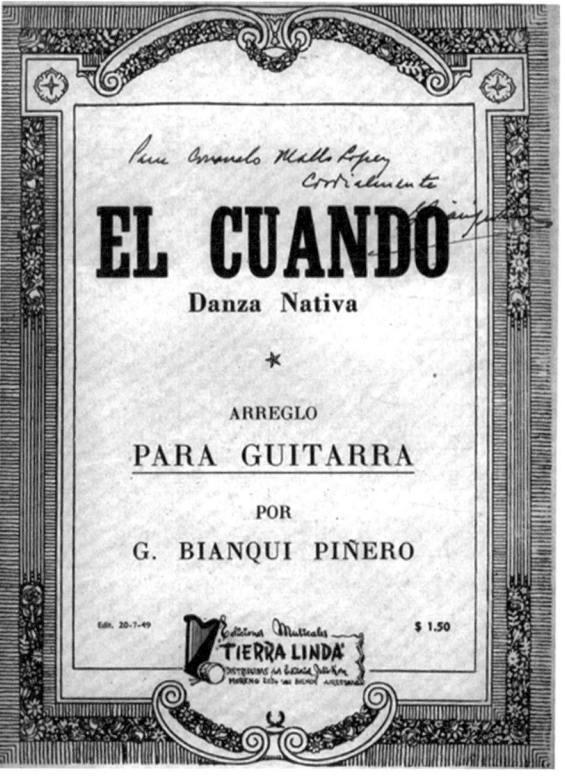

G. Bianqui Piñero *folklore* pieces published by Julio Korn and Antigua Casa Nuñez in 1949, both autographed and dedicated to Consuelo Mallo Lopez.

2496

things were happening, then I don't know why it was dying, I left it...it died from starvation, I believe....(laughter). Many people didn't go anymore, they didn't pay their dues as they had always done and later there was a mass of people with nothing to do, an element not too good in any medium, they knew it was open and they were going to come and take their places, in the afternoon or evening to spend some time and it couldn't be. And well, so the Asociacion was dying, and the Circulo was growing instead.

H.G.M. There is a detail: one analyzes the History of the Guitaristic Movement in Argentina, having begun in the last decades of the 19th century until the first few decades of the 20th century, all that happened was notable: Those European maestros that arrived in Argentina and the disciples that they had, some of them distinguished, such as in the case of Rizzuti, Adolfo V. Luna and others, not only as players, but also as composers, they were the creators of the Argentine repertoire for guitar and after they remain forgotten as composers, why?

N.T. I can't tell you, to the decline of students, for Rizzuti to die, etc., I can't explain why all that is losing its strength.

H.G.M. Why is there an Argentine repertoire of that epoch that is completely ignored...?

N.T. Yes, it could be, but the classical music of Rizzuti isn't of a major size, he made a thing that was called "*Motivo Arabe*", a piece of music of the Middle East, it was fine, it was a pleasant little piece, but he also had made *tangos, valsesitos*, simple things.

H.G.M. But I put to you the case of Sagreras, (Julio) that left a lot of repertoire for guitar, very good, of a national character....

N.T. Sagreras had written very difficult, right? Because the "*Estudio sobre la Huella*", which I didn't want to play. Among the things I played by him was "*El Colibri*", it lasted a minute, unless you made a mistake. !!! Poor you!!! Because it would be the shame of the century, if you made a mistake, because it had to be played perfect. The times that I played it were all-fine.

H.G.M. For example Justo T. Morales is another maestro who left an important work as a composer and now very few play it.

N.T. Yes, and Bianqui had been a student of Morales.....What happened to the guitar library of Bianqui?

H.G.M. I believe it went into the hands of his cousins.

N.T. What cousins? He didn't have any brothers?

H.G.M. Surely it must have been second cousins.....

N.T. Ah yes, it could be second cousins. Because the woman.....well she survived him, but she wasn't interested in those things.

H.G.M. She didn't go to the concerts?

N.T. Yes, sometimes she went, but it was rare. Bianqui, yes, was dedicated to the guitar and as he always had a little bit of money, he was more or less a man who was well off financially. He bought all the music there was and records of everything. He had an extraordinary collection of things.

H.G.M. And guitars as well.......

N.T. And guitars yes, of course?

H.G.M. You told me that the Argentine concert artists in their concerts played for free and as the foreign artists came, they paid them?...

N.T. Ah? You're going to know, why? Because Segovia and Llobet, who are two international figures, came here, but after a while Sainz de la Maza came.... Wasn't there a woman? Robledo?

Regino Sainz de la Maza (1896-1981) in 1923.

Archive: Ricardo Muñoz

H.G.M. Josefina Robledo.

N.T. I didn't know her, but I know a woman came and Regino Sainz de la Maza yes. And well, later Yepes came.

H.G.M. Yes, but he came much later.

N.T. Well, but Yepes is much later. I have a program here of Yepes that I listened to.....!!! What a program!!! Because I was a socio of the Wagneriana (Asociacion) — once he played for the Asociacion Wagneriana. !!! What a concert!!!

H.G.M. In other words they came contracted?

N.T. Of course, of course, they didn't come in thin air they came with.... (pause)

H.G.M. Contracted...

N.T. Ah, of course, not one European came without a contract they were different. But here the young ones no......(pause) look that Consuelito Mallo Lopez was a young girl of merit and the only thing she could do was to give lessons. She formed that group of 20 guitars.... that gave their concerts, but they were all free, I don't know how they did it? The best they charged one time was *2 pesos, 3 pesos* ($2.00, $3.00) and we went to see them. But the guitarists who had fame that when they were to play in a place, and they wouldn't charge *3 pesos*. Now I'm going to tell you poor people of solemnity as were the guitarists I have never seen. Because the element of the pianists is, people with a lot of money that liked the piano. But the guitarists were only poor people in general. And however the European maestros that came to Argentina and Uruguay taught people with money .....

N.T. The concert artists that came?

H.G.M. No, the European maestros that came and settled here taught the people of the upper classes, that had economic means.

N.T. I don't know, but there have been guitarists who never had money to pay their dues to the Circulo Guitarristico Argentino. And the same Circulo is dying now because so many are not paying their dues. And you who've frequented the Circulo Guitarristico lately, see that they have put a small box like a piggy bank, someone put it and it was a personal thing and no one ever verified how much was in it, neither, how it got there. But there have been many youngsters that were going, they played, and they were seated. There if you don't tell them anything they'll play until late in the night, and they haven't paid a dollar. No,.... no it can't be like that neither, there has to be help. It's a place that offers the possibility for one to become known, you can't go neither with an empty wallet. Because lastly the hall costs over 100 dollars.

H.G.M. Was it easy in those times to record?

N.T. No, no, I say to you that long ago many interpreters hadn't recorded.

H.G.M. Why there are many maestros that recorded in that epoch.

N.T. !! Ah!! I don't know but it must have been later......

H.G.M. No, recordings on 78 RPM shellac discs of that epoch.

N.T. !! Ah!! Shellac discs, yes, of course, yes in reality I had discs of Segovia that were of shellac. I had records of Segovia, the first ones that came out of Segovia, he recorded works of Bach that drew one's attention the *"Fandanguillo"* of Turina, I remember, that appeared as an uncommon thing. Aside from the uncommon things that you heard after ..... (laughter) .... it was very accessible music after all.... they were shellac discs, you're right.

H.G.M. Your father, did he comment to you about the guitar of this epoch, the epoch in which he played?

N.T. I don't know, the only thing I can say is he had played but nothing more than in the manner ad-honorem. Other things took place of course. He had played duets in salons with Rizzuti, with another maestro whom he studied with I don't know, but with Rizzuti, yes, they had played duets on guitar though I don't know where.

H.G.M. One of the things that for me that I have as an interrogator, is for example, the history that keeps repeating since the dawn of the Argentine classical guitar. A professor has distinguished students, as in your case you studied with maestro Rizzuti 4 or 5 years, if you had wanted to dedicate yourself to the guitar, would you have had to dedicate yourself to teaching only, that, is it the fault of the institutions of the country? Or is it the fault of the guitarists?

N.T. I don't know, no, because the institutions of the country, after that I passed my epoch and dedicated myself to other things, I got married, at first I was employed, then I resigned my public job, then I stayed at home, after that all the things I did, I believe there are people that have done well with the public job, when the national diplomas first appeared, in the national conservatories.

H.G.M. But all about the level of teaching, I said, "about paid concerts" .....

N.T. !! Ah!! You're referring to that, and I'm not here, I found out no one could have lived doing tours here, within the country, with paid concerts. The guitarist isn't accustomed to pay to go to concerts of guitarists......

H.G.M. Would they pay him, better said?

N.T. What they pay him, and he pays to others...

H.G.M. Neither were they accustomed?

N.T. No, no....

H.G.M. And why must that be so, for you?

N.T. I think also it must be so, for many guitarists are people that don't have sizable economic means. Isn't that certain Maria Theresa? (Here intervenes a friend of both of us: Maria Theresa Cinti Robirosa, who was the one who made contact with Noemi Toulouse for the interview.)

   Maria Theresa: Of course, generally the people, who dedicated themselves to the best of the arts, were generally the people with little money.

N.T. In other instruments I don't know, but in the guitar, it had been a collection of young men that didn't have a cent, but that was in 1935.

H.G.M. But there's something I don't understand, The European maestros that came here to our country to give lessons to the upper classes with economic power that didn't have money?

N.T. You asked me about Antonio Sinopoli, who set up in San Isidro (Gran Buenos Aires- belongs to the province of Buenos Aires) that was a town of the distinguished elite. Because San Isidro was a town of "paqueta" people (aristocracy), of persons with economic possibilities. But Rizzuti had many students; instead Consuelito Mallo Lopez was a very poor girl.

H.G.M. Maestro Domingo Prat, his economic position here made her.

N.T. Yes, but Consuelito was a student of Prat and she was very poor.

H.G.M. For me, I've already said, there was a sector that had little economic means, but on the other hand they didn't know how to get ahead professionally with the guitar, something that happens in the present.

N.T. Maria Angélica Funes was a young girl from a family that was well off socially, but I believe that they had a problem: the father left the mother with two daughters and she was very young when she had to begin, neither was she more or less a fine concert artist, to play a lot the on radio. She had a contract I don't know with Radio Stentor or whatever radio station she was on playing for many years. She promoted the guitar a lot on the radio.

H.G.M. And on the publishing side, how did it go? Did they publish pieces?

N.T. Music?

H.G.M. Yes, for guitar.

N.T. Well, yes, I believe so; of Argentine authors?

H.G.M. Yes.

N.T. I suppose so, Bianqui always published his music, because Bianqui was a young man who always had money. He was of a collectivity of guitarists, but that were of a totally different economic position, he published his music.

H.G.M. What memories do you have of Julio Sagreras?

N.T. And if you conversed with him, he was pleasant, but he appeared to me to be a man of a fierce character. Because I recall that his wife told me one day: "I'm a person of character, but I encountered someone who beat me to it" .... (laughter).... so said his Mrs...... (More laughter).....

   Maria Theresa Cinti Robirosa: She was a fierce little tamed one. (laughter)

N.T. So you see that he was a *"geniazo"* (of very strong character). They were an old-fashioned family, in which he gave the orders and he directed everything within the marriage. From the point of family visits, that the woman couldn't resolve anything, it was very much like that before now. You don't believe I'm speaking of just one example, do you?

H.G.M. Yes, it was very much a macho society.

N.T. Of course, a machismo existed where I haven't told you how it was. I remember my mother had told me one time when she was my father's girlfriend and I don't know what happened, they were going to go to the cinema. I know when it was, I was born in 1915, they were boyfriend and girlfriend since 1912 or 1913, and there was a theater in the neighborhood, which played silent movies. They were going to go to the movies together and with the family as well. It appears that the father became angry and said: 'Tonight no one is going out of the house'. And they couldn't go to the cinema, his son with his girlfriend. And that was what went on in the neighborhood where my mother lived, she knew families that couldn't go to the cine because the father said no one could go out into the street that night.

H.G.M. Of the halls that were used for concerts, there was the Salon "La Argentina", were there others besides"?

N.T. "La Argentina" was the classic, now when important guitarists come, do you know where they gave their concerts? .... in the Teatro Odeon. (Demolished years ago).

H.G.M. And the Teatro Lasalle?

N.T. No, the Teatro Lasalle came after, much later, but in 1920, 1925 it didn't exist. The Lasalle came later, much much later, it was important in its moment...it had been used extensively as a theater for concerts. We gave concerts there because it had beautiful acoustics. But the salon of the opposite was the other, it was the salon where the Asociacion Wagneriana gave their concerts or in other words in the Salon "La Argentina", how's that look to you? An association of the prestige of the Wagneriana gave their concerts there in the Salon "La Argentina". And that association charged the socios *3 pesos* ($3.00) per month and the best maestros of Europe came to the Wagneriana to perform.

H.G.M. And they played in the Salon "La Argentina"?

N.T. !!! And they played in the Salon "La Argentina"!!! And after, it was converted into a *milongueo* (dancehall).

H.G.M. Did you know maestro Francisco Calleja?

RECITAL DE GUITARRA

Por el eminente concertista

FRANCISCO CALLEJA

El Martes 13 de Septiembre de 1938, a las 21.45 horas

en el SALON "LASSALLE"

Cangallo 2263

ORGANIZACION DE ESPECTACULOS "RADIOTOUR'

This Francisco Calleja Tuesday September 13, 1938 concert took place at the Teatro Lassalle. Twenty-five years earlier Francisco played a concert in Montevideo with Julio J. Otermin and Agustín Barrios Mangoré. It was Agustín's first concert in Uruguay.

P R O G R A M A

I

♦ Danza .... **Diego Pisador (1502-1567)**

♦ Preludio .... ⎫
♦ Mazurka .... ⎪
♦ Allemande ⎫   ⎬ **Francisco Calleja**
♦ Pavana   ⎬ De la "Suite Ancienne" ⎪
♦ Courante ⎭   ⎭

II

Andantino .... **Sor**

♦ Minuetto .... ⎫
♦ Gavota .... ⎪
♦ Bourrée .... ⎬ **J. S. Bach**
♦ Preludio .... ⎭

III

Momento Alegre ... . ⎫
Plegaria .... ⎬ **Rebikoff**
♦ El Columpio ... ... ⎭

Nocturno ... . **Moreno Torroba**

Torre Bermeja .... ⎫ **Albéniz**
Leyenda (Preludio Español) .... ⎭

♦ Obras ejecutadas por 1ª. vez en Buenos Aires.

In this September 13, 1938 Francisco Calleja concert, the pieces marked with an asterisk were debuts of those pieces in Buenos Aires.

Noemi Toulouse from the 1930's

Archive: Ricardo Muñoz

N.T. No.

H.G.M. Muñoz?

N.T. Yes, but in the past in the Asociacion Guitarristica Argentina because he was, I believe, Vice-President, when it was founded in 1934.

H.G.M. Segundo N. Contreras?

N.T. I don't remember, I don't remember much of the commissions completely.

COMISION DIRECTIVA

DE LA ASOCIACION GUITARRISTICA ARGENTINA:

Presidente: **Pablo M. Santillán;** Vice-Presidente: **Roberto R. Soriano;** Secretario General: **Alberto Toulouse;** Pro-Secretario: **Ramón A. Zeballos;** Secretario de Actas: **Miguel R. Michelone;** Tesorero: **Francisco Vega Iglesias;** Pro-Tesorero: **Nazareno Sterni;** Vocales Titulares: **Dr. Eleuterio F. Tiscornia,** Carmelo Rizzuti, Gerónimo Bianqui Piñero, **Enrique D. Plater,** León V. Gascón, Juan C. Basavilbaso y **Dr. José María Quevedo (h.);** Vocales Suplentes: Ricardo J. Vergara, **Dr. Juan Carlos Radice,** Abel Fleury y **Ramón Genén;** Comisión Revisora de Cuentas: Tomás Pomilio, Juan M. Seró Mantero y Luis Cisneros.

In the November-December program of 11 performances given in 1937 by guitarists for the Ascociacion Guitarristica Argentina, included was the list of the Board of Directors. In this list are to be found many important figures in the ongoing creation and preservation of the guitaristic environment of the Rio de la Plata. At this time Alberto Toulouse, the father of Noemi Toulouse, was the Secretary General of the Board.

In the May program of 5 performances given in 1938 by guitarists for the Ascociacion Guitarristica Argentina, we see the change of leadership that went on every year. Among this list of Board members are guitarists that owned the best guitars from Spain while brand new. The current President Roberto Soriano owned a very special 1921 Santos Hernández, which has ivory binding. This is now in the Richard Bruné collection. Abel Fleury owned two guitars made by Francisco Simplicio.

Soriano, he was a Spaniard. Soriano that was a maestro, a nice guy, very pleasant, a very good person that attained the presidency of the Asociacion Guitarristica, when we turned over our positions. And later I don't know, I don't remember the commissions apart from the principles: Mr. Santillan, my father, Sagreras and there would be others of course that made them up. Leloup there at the beginning I think, I believe he didn't last long, if that Basque had become angry about something ... (laughter) ......

H.G.M. Thank you very much, until another time.

N.T. You're welcome, when you need to know something else, just knock on the door.

Interview with Maria Herminia Antola by Héctor García Martínez in October 1996.

We're in the home of the maestro Maria Herminia Antola, distinguished maestro of the guitar, and wife of the celebrated composer and guitarist as well: Jorge Gomez Crespo.

H.G.M. Maestro, I would like you to tell me how your vocation for music and the guitar started, how did you approach it, the first contacts you had, and what motivated you.

M.H.A. In reality, the musical part of my life, commenced at 6 years, with the piano, my mother played the piano well, and I was always playing those things that children do, pretending to be the concert artist, to be seated there in front of the keyboard. Then, she decided to try to see if I had some aptitude. I appeared seated, in one of her slips, and she had me play a famous piece of the time: *"El Carnivalito"*, and she saw really right away that I could do a little bit. Another day she took me to a conservatory of a very good professor, and there I commenced to study the piano. I want to say with that, that my musical vocation that I had was when I was very young. And besides, I had the fortune to have musical parents. My mother played the piano well, sang very well, and had studied singing. And my father as aficionado played the piano, he had studied with Juan de Dios Filiberto (author of the famous *porteña* song *"Caminito"*, of world renown). Filiberto had been a student of Alberto Williams (great Argentine musician), something that many people don't know. That is to say that he had seriously studied the piano. So there, those were my beginning approaches to music. But very painfully my mother died when I just turned 8 years old. You have to view the situation of a widower of 39 years old, with 4 children, to see the crumbling of the entire home. This motivated my father, that when I turned 12 years old, he thought seriously to reawaken my musical studies and he himself asked me: Do you like the guitar? Because it is a very beautiful instrument, very simple. Great, I inclined myself towards the guitar. Sadly, the first three years of learning were bad, with a person that didn't implant a school or anything by his style. My father had to hire, due to fortunately finding Justo T. Morales. He came to my house and said all I had been doing was wrong, and that I had to start all over again. I was very obedient, in that moment I was 15 years old, and what I did, had a very good result. He saw my predisposition to study, he demanded much of me, that means to say that in a year, I worked the miracle of getting rid of all of my defects that I had, and not only did I do that, but he created a duo with me. We played as a duo on the radio for months and months. Then the same professor Morales, that was providing my musical education, joined a quartet that can be said as to have made history, because I am speaking of many years ago, that involved logically him, Bianqui Piñero, I, Elsa Molina, who was a great player, sadly whose artistic life was cut short due to the bad luck of an infirmity: arthritis, what made those prodigious fingers that she had, come to a stop. Because, she had a very brilliant execution, the most difficult part of the instrument that she dominated totally, and that, she had to give up. So then in that moment we had a quartet that performed a lot, logically without a great broadcasting, but it was also very positive for me to learn and to share with others. In the end I always think that those little groups make much of the education of the student.

Afterward I studied with Consuelo Mallo Lopez; Consuelo was a great professor. At that moment she was giving concerts, actually concerts that were very important. I remember for example that one dedicated to Bach, something that I never saw another guitarist repeat. And after studying with her extensively, because I studied privately with her 5 years, in one moment she thought about starting a duo with me. We had a great act, including important places such as the Teatro Odeon, Teatro Cervantes, in "El Circulo" in Rosario, (Santa Fe province) that always was of importance to perform there. She was an excellent professor; we studied very conscientiously, thoroughly. That motivated a composer of ours, who is sadly forgotten: Alfonso Galluzzo, who would write many works for us. Possibly the reason why he didn't have extensive fame, was because he wrote in a classical manner and logically there are people who resisted that, which is to say they would write *folkloric* pieces, which was the music of that period of time. But... fine that was his manner to compose and he composed many good works, I must say very difficult, we studied them thoroughly, to the point we gave a concert and used sheet music, we always performed our programs memorized. I remember we did a homage to Sor, with respect to the date of his death. All of Sor's great works were performed; lastly it was a very beautiful season, really. That was during the epoch in which I studied with Consuelo Mallo Lopez. Then my father said: 'You are already giving concerts, the artist has to express the same, and you have to take the determination to do these things yourself.' I must say that in a given moment I had the support of the maestro Gilardo Gilardi (great Argentine musician) with whom I had studied harmony privately. Those contacts are always grateful for the people who study, to be in contact with those who have great knowledge, as in the case of Gilardo Gilardi, who I always had a great admiration for.

Then he said (my father) 'You have to take the determination to be you, you can't follow that course,

GILARDO GILARDI

This photo of Gilardo Gilardi is from the magazine *"Orfeo Revista Musical"* issue No. 39 *Año* IV of July 1921

with the concerts you have given, doing what a professor tells you'. I considered that he was right. He said: 'If you err, you have to be you, if they do your good reviews, they are behind the hand of a professor'. I always said, all my life, with all the professors I have studied, the one I have not named is that who ruined me from the start. We've always stayed in good relations with Consuelo she understood it. That more or less coincides with the epoch in which I met Jorge Gomez Crespo. With him what we had was a relation as colleagues. My father was a friend of everything artistic, he liked having reunions on Saturdays, which drew those restless artists, they could be intellectuals, etc. I remember that there, he made the acquaintance of Malisa Zini, who afterward became a great actress, one of the most highly acclaimed.

Malisa Zini, was a friend of mine, she was named Maria Luisa Zambrini, she was a niece of a great of ear, nose, throat and specialist, the Dr. Zambrini, and she studied in the National Conservatory, as professors she had, Alfonsina Storni (great Argentine poet) and Blanca de la Vega. Malisa was one of the young actresses, perhaps with more culture. Besides, if she wasn't the first, she was one of the firsts to recite García Lorca, and that she did well.

Then when my father held the reunions, she would come, and other personalities, they were reunions without pretensions. Consuelo Mallo Lopez came, Galluzzo, persons who also were in the picture and that helped me besides, to relax while playing, and there I began a cycle of important concerts. There Jorge Gomez Crespo had been coming and ended up giving me the *"Serie Argentina"*, it was the first time the National Commission of Culture (which eventually became the equivalent of the National Foundation of the Arts now) had given a prize to a work for the guitar. It was a great satisfaction because I had given its debut, I should clarify at the time that we were not a romantic couple, I simply liked the work very much. But I believe that when he began to come to my house, he already had come with his intentions, you have to say the truth. (Laughter)

Maria Hermina Antola de Gomez Crespo playing her Velasco guitar, seated across from her is her husband, Jorge Gomez Crespo.

We ended up being a romantic couple, we got married, then they said: ...you, studied with him? no I didn't study with him, I responded, but every time I gave a concert, I said to him: "fine, sit down Jorge, and see how it appears to you". And he would give me his impression. In general, we coincided a lot, and happily in the other part, in the conjugal, besides, well I was married to him for 28 years, and previously two years as his girlfriend, we were very happy, we understood each other. And fine, afterward, our children were born. Next I was named to the *cathedra* of the guitar in the National University of La Plata (province of Buenos Aires), in what was then the Escuela Superior de las Bellas Artes, which later converted to the Faculty of the Arts, which is something that we owe to Buenos Aires because La Plata has always beaten us, and it's been years since they've had the Faculty of the Arts. I commenced to go there, and I had the luck to create many students who are relevant to the music scene today, such as Guillermo De Feo, whom I just received a postcard sent from Zurich, who is performing in Europe. All of the young players then, who are not young now, guys who are 40 years old that are giving classes in the Faculty of the Arts and in the Conservatory Provincial de La Plata, the majority of them began in my cathedra of the guitar. I had at first the basic cycle, afterward I believe the special Bachelor's degree, the first in South America was there in La Plata, a very complete Bachelor's degree because of its university character, like the National College of Buenos Aires (referring to the National College of Buenos Aires, junior high, but with a university character), but with the artistic aspect added. When I believe it was practical and musical, meaning the students studied their Bachelor degree such as they had to study all the added materials.

A few of ceramic arts and others of music, from there they left with an extraordinary formation, because including the students of ceramics who were obligated, at least while I was there, I don't know if there have been any changes in this aspect, to have also materials in league with music, and the musician's materials in league with ceramics. That means that the Bachelor's degree that came from there was very complete in its formation. The sculptor knew who were: Debussy, Beethoven and Bach, and at once the musician knew who were: Manet and Toulouse Lautrec, etc. some of those painters.

I thought that at one time if I lived in La Plata, I would send my children to school there because really it would make a complete preparation for the educating of them. That motivated the work of my obligations to be taken very seriously, because I had the satisfaction, that in an election held at the University, my colleagues in the Department of Music, elected me unanimously. The votes... appeared after I think that a combination had been done, because it was quite something that there wasn't any dissent. From the root of that, I was in that position for almost 8 years, that had me completely occupied and I backed off of my very demanding practice that I had to do to perform concerts and was motivated to dedicate more of my effort towards teaching. And what also happened to us women that have the conscience of a mother, you have to be dedicated to your children, to your husband and to the home. I backed off from that in this aspect, all of us know that to give concerts you have to study a quantity of hours daily that I evidently didn't possess.

H.G.M. And travel?

M.H.A. I traveled during those epochs four times a week to La Plata. But I have a remembrance very extraordinary, I had nothing more than to come upon it, I had the fortune to organize great concerts because the body of professors was mixed with the greatest musicians of our times, there were: Ginastera, Lopez Bouchardo, Gilardo Gilardi, etc.

H.G.M. In the faculty of the Arts in La Plata?

M.H.A. Yes, when I entered I was young, I thought that at one time if I lived in La Plata I would send my children to school there because really I felt a little bit crushed because they were all extraordinary names. There was De Raco, De Raco I called him when I was Dept. Head, Carlos Sufer, Ernesto Epstein, Roberto Castro on the piano, Amicarelli, and they were all such figures. For me it was a very gratifying thing that they elected me as Dept. head and I was there until 1973. Sadly, when the peronismo returned (the government of Peron) they dominated people that included those who weren't peronist. Logically I renounced my position, but he continued as a professor as I had won my position by contest.

H.G.M. Pardon, you renounced the Faculty of the Arts in La Plata?

M.H.A. No, the position as Dept. Head of the Department of Music, it was logical, other authorities came in, sadly there would be reactions that weren't logical. Because that came out well with *peronismo* or without peronismo. It wasn't a question of politics at all, but everyone was very dedicated to do specifically to what they had been dedicated. Afterward, I kept on with my students and I retired from there in 1980.

But previously, when the Juan José Castro Conservatory of La Lucila (province of Buenos Aires) was founded exactly 30 years ago by maestro Tortorella who was the creator, the soul of all that, he maintained that for the duration of 30 years, really in a situation of great importance and artistic dignity. In that sense he was a marvelous director, he told Irma Costanzo he would call me for a professorship, I was there for 23 years. There I also worked very well, forming many students, among them an ex-student, who is a great player that I now admire very much, he is Victor Villadangos, and others that don't have the professional presence he has, but nonetheless are virtuosos in their own right.

H.G.M. Returning to your epoch as a concert artist, I would like that you would tell me when the quartet with Justo T. Morales was formed, what repertoire was used?

M.H.A. When we formed the quartet with Morales, we played some works of the classical guitar, Sor, some things by Carcassi, etc., because there had been a lot of material and Argentine things. Because you can't forget that Morales was composing well within the Argentine style. Afterward with Consuelo we also had the classical repertoire and some transcriptions of contemporary works, we had an extensive repertoire of Alfonso Galluzzo, because he wrote for us and they were really very beautiful works.

When I played solo, at first, I played works that were performed all around the world, I played pieces by Bach, Villa-Lobos, Moreno Torroba. And when I was more in contact with Jorge, he began to provide me with some transcriptions that he had done, others by Gilardo Gilardi and Julián Aguirre, and I began to perform Jorge's pieces around the time when I debuted his *"Serie Argentina"*, one of the numbers is *"La Norteña"*.

This photo of Julián Aguirre, the great Argentine composer, is from the magazine "La Guitarra" issue No. 4 of February 1926 published by Juan Carlos Anido.

I don't know if you want me to tell the story of the history of *"La Norteña"*?

H.G.M. Tell it...

M.H.A. The following occurred; I gave the work its debut for the Asociacion Guitarristica Argentina. The widow of Julián Aguirre had a great affection for Jorge, as he had for her as well. She was a very enchanting woman, very artistic, in her home she received all the great artists from all over the world. I remember even Victor Malcuzynski lived there for a while, and I met Lopez Lagar (great Argentine actor) having tea in her home. She always was telling me an anecdote: when Julián Aguirre died, clearly afterward many people went to see her, including students of Julián Aguirre. And she told us how they played his pieces, but they never reminded her of how Julián played. One nice day when Jorge was young and just a little more than twenty years old, someone who was a friend of hers told her: 'Margarita, I'm going to bring a young man who plays very well, and he has done some very beautiful transcriptions of Aguirre on the guitar'. She told me in a letter I have right here in my house that she sent me when Jorge did a homage and she was in Mendoza and couldn't come. She said 'I had arranged to hear this young man with all my patience, and do you know what happened? But when he was here and played the works of Julián I was crying because it was exactly as Julián had played them....'

Now look at this extraordinary thing, Jorge had only seen Julián Aguirre perform once, and that was when he was accompanying Brigida Frias de Lopez Bouchardo, that means he was doing an accompaniment and nothing more. Now I don't know if it's because the mother of Jorge, my cherished mother-in-law who was an extraordinary woman who had been a student of Alberto Williams, played a few things by Aguirre. It could have been that she also had a friendship with the professor Aguirre, it could have taken place in some way. But it was extraordinary such as it is in this letter I keep right here. *Doña* Margarita as she said to us: 'he made us cry because it was exactly the same as Julián'. Since then she has had a great affection for Jorge, then when she found out we were engaged, she told Jorge 'good: now all those things you have, written them for yourself and nothing more, you're going to send a work to the National Commission of Culture, there is a competition coming up'.

Jorge didn't want to because he always said the same thing: 'But if I write those things, I write them for myself'. But out of a little respect for her and on the other side as well, maybe that it would leave an impression, as we were a romantic couple, it would be nice to see him receive the grand prize.

I made certain he sent the *"Serie Argentina"* and it was the first time a grand prize was awarded to apiece for the guitar at this level. I believe that later Adolfo V. Luna was awarded a grand prize. But until absolutely that moment the guitar had been a little forsaken by the hand of God.

What occurred? Andrés Segovia came here, who had been a friend of my father-in-law, and he had a great affection for Jorge, as soon as he would arrive, he'd dial the phone before he even gotten to his hotel. And also Carlos Vega was (great Argentine musicologist) a good friend of Segovia's and also a good friend of Jorge's as well.

Carlos Vega told Segovia: 'Ah, but you know that they gave the grand prize to Jorge's work'. Segovia responded: 'very well, I'd like to see it.' Jorge wasn't moved to bring it to him, but fine he insisted. (Jorge) 'I had to bring him the work'. He brought the *"Serie Argentina"*, I thought he was going to at least play something. One day we received a letter, I believe from Bolivia, I'm not very sure where the program and the reviews had been done of this concert where he decided to play *"La Norteña"*. It must have been out there for over 40 years. A very special thing happened, I don't know if in some countries it sounded exotic, that work or what it is that happened. But as Segovia played it all over the world, he recorded it on three Long Play records, the first time in London, what happened? It became included in the programs of many players, to the point that we started receiving payments every three months from SADAIC (Society of Argentine Authors and Composers-founded July 9, 1936) at times from Greenland, Scandinavia, Japan, fine we know that in the last country they really like the guitar. Because many guitarists have adopted the song, John Williams recorded it, Lopez Ramos as well, Irma Costanzo recorded it recently very well, she as an Argentine knew how to interpret it. Ediciones Argentinas edition of *"Norteña"* published in Buenos Aires in 1949.

JORGE GOMEZ CRESPO

NORTEÑA

HOMENAJE A JULIAN AGUIRRE

PARA GUITARRA

Ediciones Argentinas
EL ESPECTADOR
Bme. Mitre 544 — T.E. 33 - 5834
Buenos Aires

EJEMPLAR $ 1.50

That was the history of the famous *"Norteña"* that to me continues to be surprising, that it still is interpreted in countries like Turkey. I have come to know Ahmet Kanneci, who is head of the Guitar Department in the National Conservatory in Turkey. He was here a little while ago in the "Guitars of the World" Festival and he said to me that *"La Norteña"* is a required piece in the study program in the National Conservatory in Turkey. He plays it all the time. That's the history of *"Norteña"* that's a very unusual thing.

H.G.M. Let me return to you again, in the conversations we have had you've told me that your guitar has been in many unusual scenes. For example, you acted with great stars of the theatre. The first full-length film in color done in the country, you were the first female guitarist to appear there....

M.H.A. The interesting thing that happened is for the first time a film was done in color.

H.G.M. Short subject?

M.H.A. In reality it was a newsreel, but the director was a man with an artistic sense.

H.G.M. Who was he?

M.H.A. You know that I've forgotten surname but I have it right here, I'm going to remember.
A person very valuable to La Plata (province of Buenos Aires) who wanted to make a short subject with an artistic sense. As the short subject was titled *"El Noticio de Buenos Aires"*.

H.G.M. It was called that?

"El Noticio de Buenos Aires"

M.H.A. Yes, it was a newsreel in reality; he wanted to mold all of Buenos Aires in this film. He had the happy idea to begin the film with a reminiscence of the colonial Buenos Aires, which he filmed in the traditional historic neighborhood of San Telmo. All the women were dressed in the style of the time, how might I say, *"Catita"* (comic personality) from *"mantigua"* (joking deformation of *"manton antigua"*) and the men were logically dressed adequately of the epoch.

To start, the scene took place in a grand living room of the colonial epoch, where the father was, and also the mother doing her embroidery with a stretcher, and the little girl of the home playing the guitar there. Very beautiful scene, very well done, you saw the photographs, I don't know if they did it in *"Lumiton"*, the ambiance of colonial Buenos Aires in a large room of the epoch.

I elected to play a piece by Galilei, a fine old work that could've been played by a girl of that epoch. The whole preamble was to show colonial Buenos Aires, a few scenes were shot in San Telmo (Neighborhood of old Buenos Aires), and the girls and boys were dressed in the clothes that were used at the time, after passing through that scene, then to the living room with the girl playing the guitar. All the preface was visualized with the music I played, whatever was heard was the music of the guitar that I played in the grand living room, even when I wasn't on camera. It was the background music to the film. We finished that scene with an abrupt return to the Buenos Aires of that moment (1941). It was the first color film in Argentina.

H.G.M. And what appeared was a woman guitarist...

M.H.A. Yes, yes in the function as a guitarist, it debuted as all the films did at that time, I believe it was on a Thursday, at the Cine Monumental. Before a full-length film they presented that short subject.

H.G.M. How long did it last?

M.H.A. I don't remember exactly but more or less 20 minutes or so, I really can't say. I remember it had a big repercussion, you saw Héctor, and the critic's reviews I have. It came out in all the magazines; it was what was really happening at that moment. Now I remember, the director was named Candido Moneo Sanz an excellent person that I had met through the friendship with Malisa Zini, because he was also a friend of her's. Afterward Malisa had a brilliant career, but we always had our great friendship. That was a very beautiful experience, clearly for me it gave me great projection because it was a thing that turned out to be a thing that closed concerts.

H.G.M. In that epoch the guitarists had more access to the mediums of mass communication, no?

M.H.A. Look, in respect to that it gives me a lot of sorrow, when I see the great contrast of how well we were received by the press in that epoch, and the reception now of the young players today. It's sad but for example I see that in the daily *"Clarin"* of Buenos Aires they dedicate full pages to rock, I don't oppose it because it's a form of expression, but I don't share in it either, I don't derive any pleasure from listening to rock, I'm not in the popular music field, I think there are many things that don't move me. I think it's a music (rock) that alienates people. Before when there was a Frank Sinatra or a Bing Crosby it didn't occur to anyone to make disasters, something that sadly takes place in the recitals of that genre of music.

But ...you had asked me a question?...

H.G.M. About the possibilities of diffusion that the guitarists had...

M.H.A. In reality many guitarists as young musicians of other types, had the support of the press. You had the opportunity to see the quantity of chronicles that I've had; it was a notable amount. The concert date would arrive and my father that was a fanatic about his daughter...as happens to all us parents, he would get up real early to see what the great dailies were saying, *"La Prensa"*, *"La Nacion"*, etc. As many as there were, it appeared natural to me that 4 or 5 reviews would come out, it's not something I might say for vanity, but that really it was extraordinary, and you could see that.

There were great critics such as Larroque, Gaston L. Talomon and others; I had great reviews from them that really gave me the incentive to really follow through with my career. Now I observe that there is little response, for example I have a nucleus of ex-students that are very excellent guitarists, among them is one who performs frequently that is just the young man I had spoken of before: Villadangos. Really, he plays a lot and very well, I was in the Escuela de San Telmo a few days ago, he gave a magnificent concert, not only for the technique that he has completely overcome, but with that maturity he could do anything. And afterwards there wasn't any clamor, nothing. Because of that I was taken by great surprise and I must mention, that well there was the critic Montero, because he gave an extraordinary review in *"La Nacion"* with a photo of Villadangos, I believe it was the first few days of August.

He gave a debut of a concert of Brouwer, very important, for guitar and orchestra. I told him: "you have an ability that no one will say anything". I don't know if the other dailies reviewed it, for me it was very important to see the enormous importance that the critic Montero gave it in *"La Nacion"*. Including a great big portrait of Victor, pointing out for me, that he is a great guitarist, of the younger generation. Leaving out that I taught him or I didn't teach him, because he has overcome that, because a few years ago he stopped his studies with me in the Conservatory of La Lucila, he had become very secure and he was developing a personality over all the expressive part that a lot of times the great virtuosos forget a little, not him.

H.G.M. We'll return to you again, tell me of your contacts with the artists of the cinema and theater....

M.H.A. Yes, I had quite a bit of contact with them and the painters, because Jorge, my husband, in reality he was connected for many years to the painters and the writers. He was with them almost more than the musicians, because with the painters it gave the situation that for example Larco, Larrañaga, Centurion (Emilio), that made a splendid portrait, Larco as well, they had reunions in their painter's studios, and it was very common that they made music, almost all of those painters liked music. He possibly did it easier with the guitar, I don't know, Jorge played a lot in the painter's studios. When we got married, we had the opportunity to meet a lot of important figures. Including Victor Malcuzynski, I met in the studio of Larco, along with the great orchestra director Older Wolff, Conchita Abadia as well. She sang for us at the bachelorette party we had in the home of Madam Steven, that we now call a sponsor, before we called it a host to the artists. Also, she had studied guitar with Jorge. Well...I got a little away from the theme... you asked me something specifically?

H.G.M. Your relationship with the artists: you shared your guitar with the artists of the theater?

M.H.A. No, I didn't have more than that incursion in the film, and after I met Lydia Lamaison that is a great artist of ours, she was a guitarist.

H.G.M. Lydia Lamaison?

M.H.A. Lydia Lamaison studied guitar with Domingo Prat; it was there that we met. She eventually gave small concerts. I remember when I was 18 years old, her playing in Casa Nuñez, that had in the back a little room for the youngsters that had started. She was precious, a blonde with divine eyes and she played very well.

H.G.M. There was another actress / guitarist, Julia Puigendolas .....

M.H.A. No, but I didn't know her, neither Ana S. de Cabrera (great guitarist and Argentine *folklorist*) because I'm a little old, not real old (laughter). They were from previous epochs.

H.G.M. Didn't you give recitals in shows of the theater?

M.H.A. No, shows in the theater no. What in one opportunity they had used was music that I recorded for something, yes, but did I act? No. In the beginning I acted like everyone that started making a part, and for example I remember the famous chorale of Herman Kumok, that I also acted in with everyone, sharing that yes. After- how would I say-I was connected to the side of the painters, by my husband.... When they gave the grand prize to Jorge for *"Serie Argentina"*, there was a dinner in his homage, that I have the photos of right here. I believe you saw them your last visit, where there was a reunion of the best of the best of the musicians and painters. Also, there was Catulo Castillo (great figure of the Argentine *tango)*, that was a very good friend of his.

H.G.M. If you were to name two of the great maestros of the Argentine Guitar of those epochs, what names come to mind?

M.H.A. One Justo T. Morales, because perhaps he didn't have much fame, but I remember the work he did with me, because you know that it is more difficult to correct than to teach. And he succeeded in correcting me completely, and that I adopted a school. Following I would say Julio S. Sagreras, when

I started to play for the Asociacion Guitarristica Argentina, when I was 16, he told me: 'I'm going to use you for promotion of that which is a good position to hold the guitar'. And I laughed and I told him: "Three years ago you would have used me as an example of how not to hold the guitar", because that was the reality. By that, I can't help but remember Morales, to me, made me very good player. After Consuelo Mallo Lopez was a great professor, very excellent professor. And I know there have been other good professors. I can't forget, Domingo Prat, in reality it was he who brought the school of Tárrega. He was a little rude in his affairs. He wasn't a person with a very extreme sensibility in that sense of the interpretation. But you have to remember that to him, they were all guitarists that played of the old school. Among them Adolfo V. Luna, those that had studied with Manjón, with all those people. And to him they were to be nourished with the new school of the guitar. Because you can't forget that Prat had studied with Llobet and Llobet directly with Tárrega, I believe that Prat had also made some sort of incursion with Tárrega. They were honest professors, developing their labor with a lot of love for the instrument. There were others, for example Leon Vicente Gascon that wasn't my professor, but they tell me he taught very well, Hilarion Leloup and also Antonio Sinopoli in his moment. To have an opinion based on direct contact, I have the great memory of Morales to this very day, I can say his school was purified, very good. And Consuelo Mallo Lopez, they are the ones I had closest to me. Consuelo Mallo Lopez was a student of Domingo Prat, directly, so I can appreciate through her that he had taught well.

H.G.M. The guitarists of that time had access to recording discs?

M.H.A. The guitarists called classical that made us up, not a lot. I had the opportunity to record a disc, a duo with Consuelo. Lamentably they were things of the type that stayed in my father's home when I got married. For example, I had the tape of my film and after these family situations these things became lost. He had brought in a person to take care of my siblings and everything, but it was a service person. It wasn't like having a mother whom would really provide the care of the details of this type. But no, we didn't have a lot of access to recording.

H.G.M. And to the radio?

M.H.A. To the radio, yes, Jorge my husband for example had played quite a bit on the radio.

H.G.M. And you?

M.H.A. I also played on the radio a lot.

H.G.M. On what station?

M.H.A. Look, I started on *Radio Fenix,* I was 15 or 16 and I was very young. My father was saying that I had to play a lot to perfect my ability and after being able to confront larger obligations. Now I'm thinking.... I was afterwards on several other radio stations, on the Radio Stentor just after it began, it was the crest of radio, and I was on Florida 8, there I played a lot, for a long time.

When I played a duo with Morales, we played for 6 months in a row on Radio Nacion that was the radio of Samuel Yankelevich. He had a building where 4 radio stations were housed. By that I possibly met so many people because I was on the radio a lot. At the end I played on *Radio Nacional* or *Radio del Estado.*

H.G.M. That great diffusion that the concert guitar was having compared to the present appears like a fairy tale. Did it serve you for them to call you to give concerts? Were you able to live from the concerts?

M.H.A. No, to live from concerts no, I don't know if I had dedicated to it fulltime. The defect that our country has is its great extension. Here, overall in my epoch, it was a great entity that was "El Circulo" of Rosario, Santa Fe, it was a badge of honor to play there, where I played a very beautiful concert with Consuelo. After I played in the Asociacion Tárrega, I believe you saw something in the albums. But you couldn't live by giving concerts as in other countries.

For example, in the United States there are many states. You can pass from one side to the other, and there are always musical societies that are contracting. But here in this country I played extensively, but for example I gave a concert at the Rivera Indarte theater in Cordoba and I came back to Buenos Aires, afterward I gave a concert in Mendoza and came back to Buenos Aires with prolonged lapses in between them. You couldn't live like that, and then we fell into the professorships, private classes, since the beginning like everyone I had private students, after they gave me a professorship in the Fontava Institute where I had done musical study.

Señorita María Herminia Antola, con-certista de guita-rra que en breve realizará una gira artística por las principales locali-dades de Córdoba.

Maria Herminia Antola from the *"Caras y Caretas"* magazine of March 4, 1939 issue No. 2109 *Año* XLII.

Translation of the caption:

"Miss Maria Herminia Antola, concert guitarist, who will soon make an artistic tour of the principal localities of Cordoba."

H.G.M. The concerts paid well?

M.H.A. The concerts, over all the ones I gave, paid very well, they weren't really. Including when I started, I played a lot for free, because for example I played for the Asociacion Guitarristica Argentina or Amigos de la Guitarra, I didn't charge *one peso,* that I did absolutely free. That's what you had to do in the case of a young girl, as it happened to me, a family, and a father that had to pay all the bills.

H.G.M. As around the time when Segovia came, he performed all over Argentina and charged?

M.H.A. But Segovia was a world-renowned personality, he wasn't like us when we started, that we had to be content that the hall had filled up.

H.G.M. When your name had become known, why didn't the same thing happen to you?

M.H.A. Yes I charged, but in society there wasn't a lot of money. You know that here, the Asociacion Wagneriana, had never called a guitarist. Because of that inconvenience that we guitarists had, the pianists had more possibilities.

H.G.M. And why didn't Segovia have those inconveniences?

M.H.A. No, but when Segovia had already come, including the first time he came, in that epoch I didn't hear him, because it was Jorge who told me, you know we went together a few years...many. The first time that he came, he already came with prestige, I must say he laid the foundation right here.

H.G.M. Interesting, what you say....

M.H.A. To the point that he had a connotation of the intimate type. Segovia was in love with Adelaida, I never met her but Jorge said she was precious.

H.G.M. She was Cuban?

This is a photo of Andrés Segovia and his wife Adelaida, from the early 1920's

Archive: Ricardo Muñoz.

The caption translated is:

"Andrés Segovia, accompanied by his wife in the garden of their home in Berlin."

Andrés Segovia, acompañado de su esposa, en el jardín de su casa de Berlin.

M.H.A. No, no Spanish, His first wife, with whom he had his two oldest children. Adelaida was from the Spanish upper middle class, that you know, that there in that epoch there were great prejudices. I remember my godfather, who was Andalusian, was in my father's business and he was like an uncle to us. He had told me how his sisters there (In Andalucia) were middle class with a priest in the family, in the end the sisters became nuns in a convent. Because you couldn't marry a nobleman and neither with someone from a lower class. Segovia was in love with her and she with him, but she was from the upper middle class, she had almost a romance with a nobleman. At that time, it was terrible. Segovia, they looked at as any guitarist, they looked down on him. They told her: 'How are you going to marry this young man that plays the guitar, and who is this that plays the guitar?' But what happened? He came here, he was such a success and it resounded to the point that the family of Adelaida looked on him with different eyes and allowed the marriage. Look where the love life of Segovia had a connotation.

H.G.M. It is all a documentary you are telling me...

M.H.A. Yes, his success, Jorge told me all that, in that epoch you can imagine I was going with Jorge when I was 16, so I was a child when Segovia came for the first time. In spite of my father, thanks to God, having been very musical, he took me to all the concerts.

I succeeded in seeing Maria Luisa Anido...

Maria Luisa Anido and Miguel Llobet in 1919. This was taken in the Anido home when a series of photos including Maria's father Juan Carlos Anido, Emilio Pujol and Domingo Prat. were taken. This photo is from the book *"Maria Luisa Anido"* by Ercole Remo Rovieri that he published himself in Milan, Italy in 1957.

H.G.M. Let's return to Segovia...

M.H.A. No, I'd like to tell you when I was a child of 6 years old, I saw Maria Luisa Anido playing with Miguel Llobet. Segovia returned with the aura of a great triumphant artist, he was no longer the poor overwhelmed man with nothing, and so it was that the family went forth with the marriage. Segovia when he came the next time, I believe that detail is well known as I remember, his wife was expecting their first child, the first child of Segovia is Argentinean, that is now living in, there in Switzerland I believe, right?

H.G.M. The other one died...

M.H.A. The other died tragically it was terrible what happened....

H.G.M. The daughter also died....

M.H.A. The son was 14 years old, he was in a Swiss college, as he was accustomed, and I believe also that they kept sending the money to keep them in school in Switzerland. He was playing tennis with a friend, the ball went outside, he went out to get it and there was an electric cable, and the youngster was electrocuted. Segovia had very tragic things happen to his family because his daughter committed suicide.

Beatriz, her father Andrés Segovia, and mother Paquita Madriguera, concert pianist c. 1960.

H.G.M. Can it be said that Argentina projected Segovia to world-renown?

M.H.A. I believe so, according to the things Jorge has told me, because I hadn't seen him, you can imagine that in that epoch I was too young, I don't believe I had started to play the guitar. But Jorge was very involved, because my father-in-law was a great admirer of Segovia and when he came here the first time; he invited him over to have lunch. In the end he (Segovia) was a man in a situation economically and educationally to have done those things. And yes, yes, do you know what happened. Argentina had a great prestige. You remember those Spanish dancers that later used the names Rosario and Antonio?

H.G.M. No...

2519

Carmen Amaya en la zambra
gitana. Le "acompañan" su
padre y su hermano.

La
bailarina con
piel de canela

Con el autor de
sus días, en un
garrotín epiléptico.

Lea el texto de esta
nota en la página 4

These two pages of Carmen Amaya's troupe in Buenos Aires in late 1936 are from the *"Caras y Caretas"* magazine of January 2, 1937 issue No. 1996.

El "cantaor"
Chato de Va-
lencia se arran-
ca por pete-
neras.

La extraordinaria danza-
rina disponiéndose a arre-
batar a sus admiradores.

La bailarina "cañí",
en el Fandanguillo
de Almería, "crece
dos palmos", al de-
cir de su proge-
nitor.

Carmen Amaya y
Ascensión Pas-
tor, "cantaora"
del elenco, como
buenas compañe-
ras, se felicitan
mutuamente.

La bailarina no
puede con el ga-
nio, y, como gi-
tana que es, dice
al cronista la
buenaventura.

2521

M.H.A. I was also very young, and my father liked the Spanish theater, Carmen Amaya came here to the Teatro Avenida. I remember well I was very young, I was only 7 or 8 years old and here came *"Los Chavalillos"*. And do you know what happened? There was a great clamor about them in Buenos Aires that from here they went to the United States, and they ended up being Rosario and Antonio. Why when they were growing up, they had been *"Los Chavalillos"*- "The Kids", but they had been the *"Los Chavalillos"* of the Carmen Amaya Company. It was important what happened here in Buenos Aires.

H.G.M. And the same thing happened to Segovia?...

M.H.A. Undoubtedly because Segovia when he came here the first time didn't have worldly fame but much less. Since his performances in Buenos Aires, because this city had the reputation of a cultured public that understood music. It was so, because there was the Asociacion Wagneriana that my father was a founding member of that association. He said: 'I don't understand anything of Wagner, but I would like to understand'. Overall there had been an increase in everything that was French. The French companies came and the French artists and all this was a resounding success. And here there were people who understood it. By that, there was the acceptance of the Argentine public, which wasn't a flock of turkeys. And that's the history, you can verify that *"Los Chavalillos"* left from right here for New York. They were kids that were 14 and 15 years old. When they grew up, they dropped the name of *"Chavalillos"* and became Rosario and Antonio; they were greats of the Spanish music, of the dance Sevillanas. And the repercussion of Carmen Amaya also influenced her (Rosario).

H.G.M. Segovia projected from here to Spain and later to other parts of the world. Can you assure that he bolted to the United States?

M.H.A. I don't know if it was the United States, but Europe yes, very much so. Afterward I was in contact with Segovia a whole lot, because I say as soon as he would

Rosario and Antonio in Buenos Aires in 1948 at the Teatro San Martin, ten years after their debut as "Los Chavalillos de Sevilla". This is from the book "Antonio and Spanish Dancing" by Elsa Brunelleschi published by A. and C. Black, Ltd. in 1958.

arrive the phone would ring in our home: 'Jorge, come, come on over'. He liked that my husband would accompany him, I had the great fortune and pride to see him study with Segovia, Jorge would go in a moment's notice. And so one time Segovia was bathing, and fine he opened the door and said: 'I'm shaving, play for me, you play the guitar'. On a guitar that's action was so stiff that I could never play, Jorge yes, because he had strong hands. Therefore, the tone that I had!, that went to fret that guitar!!, not a chance. From the root of that, I had the luck a morning or two later, the time he was here and he had invited me. We were, for example in the Plaza Hotel (where Segovia stayed in Buenos Aires) and he was seated in the middle, Jorge to his left, and I on the right, seeing him study. You know that it was a marvelous thing, because I in my life saw few scales such as those, with a velocity and a tone and without a doubt, it was marvelous. Without a doubt Segovia was a great guitarist. When he would come, he always would ask us and Jorge told him: "Let's see Andrés tell me ... , which of all of them (Segovia's students) stands out?" He always spoke of "Ion" Williams as he said, he as a good Spaniard, didn't say "John" ... 'You will see, you will see he's going to be a great guitarist'...he was a student of his, he loved him dearly. The other day I saw a video of John Williams and he was with Segovia.

H.G.M. How could it be that Segovia had students if he traveled permanently?... courses that he would have?

M.H.A. Of course, he had in Spain and Italy the 15 to 20 days of courses of perfection. But he also had cases such as John Williams for whom he had a special preference. There were students with which he had affection for, because he was softhearted, as we all are.

H.G.M. John Williams would already have a formation of the basic technique and Segovia would give him his final touch, why didn't he have time to give regular lessons?

M.H.A. Look, it could've taken place as happened to the brother-in-law of Jorge, Celestino Piaggio that was one of the great Argentine musicians, an orchestra director. He even on vacation was being a director...

H.G.M. Traveling the world?

M.H.A. When he was in Europe for example, he was in Romania, because the war had taken a foothold, he had to stay there, and he studied with a great director there and he followed him...

H.G.M. But John Williams followed Segovia to all parts of the world?

M.H.A. No, no, all over the world no, no way. But he must have had a formation perhaps, I don't know. In this video I saw the other day, he wanted to play the guitar since he was very young. He also had a great affection for Segovia, because the maestro was quite occupied by him. Possibly in that epoch when Segovia was making his tours of Europe, it wouldn't have been strange that John Williams would travel to receive lessons from him. Why, I remember that he would always speak to us of John Williams and Julián Bream, who also studied with him. Now I think his perspective of affection was more for John Williams, though he did speak to us of Julián Bream. Did I tell you John Williams recorded *"Norteña"*?

H.G.M. Yes...

M.H.A. He played it a little bit with the ideas Segovia added to it; Segovia always added his touch. Whatever way, John William's version is good it's not a favor that it's in there, but they think that it deserves to be inserted in their discs. In this moment among the great guitarists that there are one finds John Williams the most mentioned, justly Victor Villadangos gave me the data showing he's the most mentioned.

H.G.M. Yes, he is the most often mentioned... The public in those epochs that went to the concerts, were they guitarists or from all of society?

M.H.A. I want to believe that they were an eclectic public, they all couldn't have been guitarists. I played in a hall, if it were filled, I would suppose that it had to be a public dilettante of music and that they liked the guitar.

H.G.M. And why did the majority of the guitarists play in the Salon "La Argentina"? What did that hall have? Why did they play there?

M.H.A. I had my first concert there. Possibly it must have had a good acoustics I think so. Because I was only 18 when I gave my first concert, presented by Consuelo Mallo Lopez. I suspect it must have had good acoustics I really can't say. After I played in the Teatro Lasalle because it had good acoustics and there had been societies such as "Amigos de la Musica" that held concerts there. Then I played in the Teatro Cervantes other locations; I also played with the quartet in different places and in the interior of the country.

H.G.M. Fine... with that I will leave you free, I expect to transcribe this and distribute this through various forms. Thank you very much.

M.H.A. Thanks.

HERMINIA ANTOLA DE GOMEZ CRESPO

This photo of Maria Hermina Antola de Gomez Crespo is from the magazine of the Asociacion Guitarristica Argentina *"Noticero Guitarristico"* of December 1959.

"Jorge F. Gomez Crespo is a contemporary amateur guitarist residing in Buenos Aires. Being occupied with a lot of work, he found out how to apportion his youth with his esteemed instrument: the guitar. He is a player of total delicateness, with accented music criteria, impressing into his versions a refined diction that reminds us of the classics of the instrument. He employs in his plucking, *"un algo de uña"* (a little bit of nail), with tact and mastery, that produces a pleasant sound. He avoids showy variations, exempt at times of musicality, for delivering a pure and continued sentimentalism. His periodic performances on radio are appreciated, you can observe the manner in which he develops his versions, and it is the most apt for the radio transmission. The performances across this medium make worthy of the beautiful instrument, his success and renown."

So ends the entry in the *"Diccionario de Guitarristas"* by Domingo Prat.

JULIÁN AGUIRRE

AIRES NACIONALES ARGENTINOS

Canciones Nos. 1, 2 y 3
(Del op. 36)

Versiones para guitarra
de
JORGE GOMEZ CRESPO

1936
G. RICORDI & C. - EDITORES
BUENOS AIRES

(Right) These Julián Aguirre pieces, transcribed by Jorge Gomez Crespo were published by G. Ricordi in 1936.

March 31, 1941 Buenos Aires, Argentina

"Revista de la Guitarra"— Official organ of the Asociacion Guitarristica Argentina

"Buenos Aires"

"A film documentary that will debut in the next season.

It's auspicious since the whole point of view is for the guitar, to see it reflected on the national cinema and be performed by one of our finest players of the guitaristic art.

For the art its result is extreme flattery, that it is the first Argentine film in color, to have had the occasion for the guitar to be included, and it was represented as it is by one such as Maria Herminia Antola.

It's certainly deserving of praise, the step taken by this film company, to take into account our national instrument, by itself forgotten in other artistic manifestations, where, with a good standard, it would be proper to be dedicated to it as well as a place distinguished by its possibilities.

A scene that evokes of a romantic past, in a mark of an excellent manner, the gentle and gracious melody of a Galliard, that recalls an era, records, with characters of dreaming in the spirit, the grace of its gyrations and arpeggios.

It isn't the historical case here of the grandeur of the guitar, making professorial of erudition, but yes, to record how grand the passion is of its culture, when it is plucked with love, saying in its chords of the divinity of its sweetness, of the fastidiousness of its music, of the richness of its harmonies and the tenderness united that flows in its box to vibrate its strings; that draws in and subdues one.

This is a photo from the magazine article, showing Maria Herminia Antola playing guitar in a 1835 period setting in Buenos Aires, the epoch of Esteban Massini.

The encouraging factor for the Argentine guitar is without a doubt the conquest of the cinema screen by our instrument and moreover, when it has the implicit character as artistic ambassador, that will be accredited before all the public that might see and hear played by the expert hands of Maria Herminia Antola and flattery--I repeat-because it is the first time in a film to see a figure in such a prominent place: that has to be the virtue of encountering in the entertainment world, new horizons, more admirers and better diffusion.

It is a comforting stimulus for the guitarists that see a new stream for the art that they cultivate and that so is Compania Argentine de Peliculas en Color (CAPEC) (Argentine Color Film Company) has known how to value with a high standard, the exquisiteness of its melodies, has to find in other similar ones, the same understanding- without eluding the commercial side-taking the pure art to the seventh art.

Among the Argentine guitarists great values stand that which will honor the filmed material and with those convictions that emanate full of responsibility, that make it a mother Institution of the Argentine guitar, by its elements, expect that, an elevated conception of the cinemagraphic directors, have proportioned a new opportunity for which the traditional instrument might have a place among the many films to produce, with complete security that will result beneficent for the companies producers and if they consider that the guitar being an instrument that doesn't need to be envied by the rest, it is also just to be traditional representative of its musical culture, be it put in front and to the step of many and so varied artistic expressions.

The argumenters have the occasion of presenting works in which the instruments might intervene as an expression of art, since exists in the guitaristic scene genuinely said, composers of talent- the same ones that perform that put well above the beauties of our guitaristic literature, if they prefer the great classics, but the case to make-work and to have the trying to educate delighting which is the best art of teaching. Trying to overcome; a be separate from the common; to teach, demonstrate the unknown, the cult and the good, to make a home; is to demonstrate love for us, is to care for the conquered, in a word; to put in relief all which we are capable to produce; what we value.

Page 14, *Revista de la Guitarra"* (unknown issue number, either No. 7 or No. 8, 1941)

This is from the *"Revista de la Guitarra"* magazine issue No. 10 *Año* IV of December 1942.

Translation:

"Maria Hermina Antola. — The 12th of November the known guitarist, Maria Hermina Antola, was presented in the Salon de la Biblioteca del Consejo de Mujeres. Works by ancient and modern authors comprised the program of Miss Antola. In the second part she offered Argentine compositions by the maestros: Aguirre, Caba, Lopez Buchardo and Gomez Crespo. Once again the performer put into evidence the prestige gained in her artistic career."

MARIA HERMINIA ANTOLA. — El 12 de noviembre se presentó en el Salón de la Biblioteca del Consejo de Mujeres, la conocida guitarrista María Herminia Antola. Obras de autores antiguos y modernos componían el programa de la señorita Antola. En la segunda parte ofreció composiciones argentinas de los maestros: Aguirre, Caba, López Buchardo y Gómez Crespo. Una vez más puso en evidencia la ejecutante los prestigios ganados en su carrera artística.

Blanca Prat Interview
daughter of Domingo Prat (Barcelona 1886-Buenos Aires 1944)
This interview took place on April 26, 2001

H.G.M. We're in the home of Mrs. Blanca Prat, to record anecdotes and little known aspects of her father, the talented maestro Domingo Prat.

Blanca, tell me in this moment the memories that you have of your father, the first things that come to mind....

B.Prat: The truth is you've taken me a little bit by surprise, how to speak, how it can be spoken of quite a bit, to say many things about my father. But if you are interested, for example, how my father arrived in Argentina.

It's a part of his life, he had already dedicated a lot to the guitar, and he had studied very much..... or it influenced a little bit of the idea.... it's an intimidation if you like; I'm going to say it.... he had to enter the militia....

H.G.M. Pardon me, the military service?

B. P. Exactly, it's called the militia; I don't know how it's said in Spain. And that influenced him in that he didn't want to do it, he grasped his guitar, his music and came to Argentina. Knowing that right here the guitar was played a lot, was liked, and had an active environment, where he could work and that was the first time he came right here. The truth is that it resulted, because right here he had become involved with those that were already professors. And he had a success, more than anything the new style of playing the guitar that he brought, the school of Tárrega, right?

H.G.M. When he came here, he came contracted or by his own means?

B. P. Yes, he came of his own means, in this epoch still there wasn't that luxury, he didn't know anyone who would contract him. But after he arrived, they organized intimate concerts, in the beginning. To see how much that the persons here were interested in organizing concerts for him.... He began to light his way working in the field of teaching. So, he was here practically a year, a year and a half I believe it was, I don't have the exact dates and he returned to Spain.

H.G.M. Do you remember the year he came here for the first time?

B.P. It's always been said as 1908, with programs of concerts that testify to it. Some historians have put it as 1907. Such as Mr. Ricardo Muñoz in his *Historia* said that, and he praised him a lot. But I believe there was a mistake, for me it was 1908. When he returned to Spain he was there for a few months, also working, arriving with an aura of having come from a country where he had had a lot of success with the guitar. Then he was very well received, in that moment in Spain, and also began to have students there, a good activity.

He was surrounded by all the best concert artists that were sought after of that moment and had a lot of fame, such as Tárrega with whom he had a friendship, later with Llobet, Pujol, Josefina Robledo. In the end this quantity of people that were very distinguished in the epoch.

And afterward he returned to Argentina, returned to working with his students, as he had done. He made various trips, I don't know...he remained well liked, he passed two or three years here, and two or three years there. In that interim, in 1914 he was taken on as professor for Maria Luisa Anido.... and there he stayed two years. I believe that was the epoch when my father stayed the most in Argentina. Because he had already been contracted by the father of Maria Luisa Anido, to live in the home as professor of the little girl. At that time she was a child.

He had his separate apartment, his valet, and his major domo. They had a great consideration for him and salary. And it stayed that way for two years. And also he had many other students or in other words he was working a lot.

So he was doing and he was working and to be dedicating, internalizing the form of power to teach the classical guitar well...Therefore he made the book of "*Escalas y Arpegios*", and afterward "La Nueva Tecnica", that have to this day endured, they're still for sale.

H.G.M. You told me a little while ago that your father brought here to Argentina the new form of playing the guitar. Or in other words the School of Tárrega but in his *Diccionario de Guitarristas* he denied the existence of that "school" ....

B.P. He had to deny it..... Why I don't know very well how that situation could be, because he always said that it was such a new school that he had brought. Because in Spain, Tárrega and various other guitarists began to play the guitar with the fingernails. Because up until that time they had played the guitar with the flesh directly and they hadn't used the nail. And Tárrega began to play utilizing a little bit of the nail. Since then to utilize the nails the strings of the guitar had a very different sonority. Including the anecdote, I know of how Tárrega had let his thumbnail grow very long on his right hand, to be able to bring out the chords and bass notes of the guitar, and that for example, had an impact on my father. And when he came here, he had begun to play like that.

I don't know why in his *Diccionario* he said he didn't bring the School.

H.G.M. It isn't that he brought it, he said the Tárrega School didn't exist...

B.P. I don't know, it draws my attention, the truth is I don't know how to answer that question.

And if it doesn't exist, well who was the one who said "Tárrega School"? Because the Tárrega school interpreted what he had done and that they had played simply with the flesh and later they began to apply the nail. To see that Tárrega had applied it why I don't know he played simply with the nail. So that I don't know how to tell you. That is a part of my life that I can't answer you. (Laughter)

Now it draws my attention, of course I haven't read the *Diccionario* part by part, because it would be endless. (laughter) It can be read, right? But I didn't read that part, I'm going to read it, I'm going to read..... (Laughter)

And what more would you like to know?

H.G.M. What memories did he have of Tárrega? How did he recall him? What did he tell you about him? and your mother as well...

B.P. My father discussed him, he saw him and looked upon him with a lot of respect, because he was a person who was very integrated with the guitar, he loved the guitar. He dedicated his soul and life. He had a strong personality. According to those that knew him, he was a man very...not harsh...I don't know how to express it... he was tall, with long hair, a beard, always smoking, they say it was terrible, playing with a cigarette in his mouth, that's what they were always saying. I've had that memory, with an image that I tell you very respectfully. And my mother also knew him because she wanted to begin to play the guitar. She began to attend the reunions that Tárrega had, I believe every day. He received people in his home, everyday, every afternoon.

H.G.M. Even the beggars....

B.P. Even the beggars.... yes that could be (Laughter) I don't have that in mind. He was enchanted that they were friends. My father was one of those who attended, and they listened with fascination.... how he interpreted, how he studied, how he was working well with the music. He would put a piece of manuscript paper, and was working, doing and redoing those measures. And of course, in that epoch that was quite a thing, to see that he could dazzle those that in reality wanted to play the guitar well.

And my mother also, she was telling me he was pleasant. My father no, he would tell me that he was aloof, coarse in his manner. I don't know...as my mother was very young, she was only 15 or 16 years old, the man might have had another sense of friendliness even better.... He saw that she was young and that she liked the guitar.... they are memories, beautiful, the truth that is.

H.G.M. We're in the year 1910, that your father was here two years, and afterward he returned to Spain, right? From there, continue the history .....

B.P. (Laughter) I'll continue the history...and my father made at least four voyages here until he came and stayed permanently in 1923. In 1910 he went to Paris, because I believe Miguel Llobet invited him, so he could see the artistic environment that was there. Therefore, when my father saw results less than he expected, he stayed two months with Llobet in Paris, then he returned to Barcelona.

And so successively, the life of my father was to go and return, to leave his students there in Spain, to come right here, he was here a year or two, he returned, and also left his students here. And so he was making a name for himself, because it was a beautiful epoch for the guitar.

H.G.M. We're in the year 1923, he has settled here in Argentina permanently. What was it that made him decide to settle here permanently?

B.P. It was in 1923, when my father married my mother, with the preexisting condition that they go to America, Argentina. (Laughter)

H.G.M. They didn't say Argentina, but America...

B.P. Yes, that thing, he was saying, "to make America mine" (Laughter), and already with that idea on the part of my mother's family there was a negation "and no, how are you going to go and we're not to see you again?" Because they were supposed to be coming at the end of the year, come to Argentina.

But there was this condition to come here and for both of them to work. Because my mother had studied the guitar several years, she studied with him, with Pujol and she knew how to play, she put her everything into playing the guitar, my mother. So that was the preexisting condition.

They got married; they came right here (Buenos Aires) and installed the Academia in the Federal Capital, on Rodríguez Peña at 200.

H.G.M. Rodríguez Peña and Rivadavia? (streets)

B.P. Near the Salon Argentina. There he began to work, to have the Academia, he had a lot of students, and he was beginning to make quite a name for himself. They were living there for a pair of years, then they moved to Rodríguez Peña 119. It's there that I remember because I was born there.

H.G.M. Rodríguez Peña and Rivadavia?

B.P. Yes, at a block down Rivadavia and Bartolomé Mitre, it was on the corner of the house. That is where they installed the Academia Prat, with its years of increasing presence and a lot of success. His students were always filing in and filing out, from 8:00 AM until 6:00 PM at night.

H.G.M. Can you remember names of people, who might have passed by there?

B.P. And of course, someone will come to me I believe. One of those that come to mind is, important; it is musicologist, Carlos Vega.

H.G.M. !!! Grand figure!!!

B.P. Yes, I believe, He came a lot to our home. Among other things I'm remembering, is that one time I gave a concert in the "Consejo de Mujeres", it had already ended and among the people that came to greet me, from the throng a gentleman shouted: "! Blanquita, Blanquita!!!" and it was Carlos Vega, he hugged me and kissed me. Because it had been many years since I'd seen him, he hadn't seen me since I was a little girl (Laughter). I remember those details...We'll continue with his students, one such student who came a lot, and appreciated my father very much was Lydia Lamaison, she came for years...

H.G.M. Actress? Right?

B.P. She is an actress, yes, that I haven't seen in many years, she came to my home when my sister died. She came to greet me and said: "To think how your father, maestro Prat was telling me: 'Why are you going to dedicate yourself to the theatre?... Continue with the guitar that you play so well!'...Because I finally gave concerts. "The things of life", she used to say to me... "I let go of the guitar, and dedicated myself, to being an artist".

And well I don't know, since then of all the notable students were; Consuelo Mallo Lopez, Maria Angélica Funes, Maria Luisa Anido and one of the last Nelly Ezcaray. But Nelly Ezcaray is of the last, of his last students to be distinguished. But he presented very many students.

H.G.M. And of the masculine figures with fame, whom do you remember? Fleury for example...

B.P. Yes, since quite a while ago, I was just a little girl when he came, but I remember him perfectly. I don't know if I have it in mind, he had a student who played very well: Amilcar Verdier.

H.G.M. Right?

B.P. I can't think of it, yes, he gave many concerts, he was a young man in that epoch.

H.G.M. And Adolfo Luna, Atahualpa Yupanqui?

B.P. Yes, that same one Atahualpa Yupanqui I remember, he came to the home not as a student of the Academia, but for classes that were called "cursos libres" (open courses), ...another person who would have come once in a while for the "open courses" in the Academia was folklorist Patrocinia Diaz (a member of Andrés Chazarreta's *Arte Nativo* troupe)

H.G.M.!!! Hmmm...!!!!

B.P. I remember her because after many years we saw one another in a club and when she discovered that "Mrs. Prat" was there she came flying to kiss me and hug me. And she told me: "!!! You are Mrs. Prat!!!" In the end there is a history behind that, all a connection, because I had grown so many years. Yes, Patrocinia Diaz came...

Many good folklorists passed by our home, I don't remember very well, but it could include Rosita Quiroga, yes, yes, yes, she came for perfection studies, it's called. To do "open courses", when they would come to take a class, they would work to perfect the guitar.

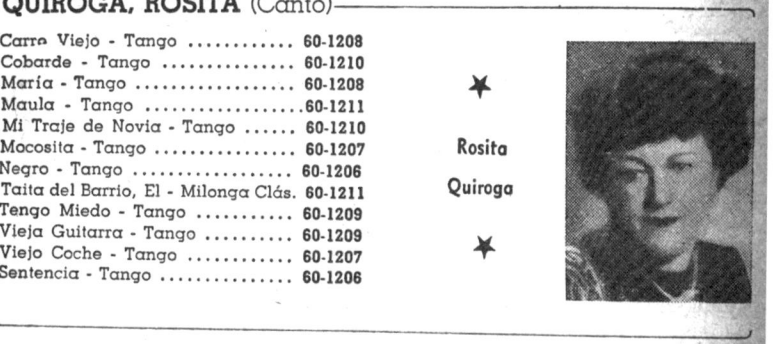

QUIROGA, ROSITA (Canto)

Carro Viejo - Tango	60-1208
Cobarde - Tango	60-1210
María - Tango	60-1208
Maula - Tango	60-1211
Mi Traje de Novia - Tango	60-1210
Mocosita - Tango	60-1207
Negro - Tango	60-1206
Taita del Barrio, El - Milonga Clás.	60-1211
Tengo Miedo - Tango	60-1209
Vieja Guitarra - Tango	60-1209
Viejo Coche - Tango	60-1207
Sentencia - Tango	60-1206

Rosita Quiroga

This listing of the available 78-RPM records of Rosita Quiroga is from the *1949 RCA Argentina Catalogo No. 49* as of August 31, 1949. Her career lasted until the 1970's, when she appeared in the film "El Canto cuenta su Historia" released in 1976.

Singer and guitarist Rosita Quiroga's newest recordings are plentifully listed here. This ad is from the magazine *"Caras y Caretas"* issue No. 1215, *Año* XXVII of January 19, 1922.

H.G.M. How were the classes? Your mother taught in one room and your father in another.

B.P. My father yes, he was in the Academia, he was there in his study-receiving students constantly. But my mother was dedicated more to private classes. Yes, she had a group of students, yes.

Look, in that epoch there were....... always had had..... a distinction of classes that is a shame in this world. But the social part we might say..... played a lot of guitar. There were in the homes, a little girl, a little boy, and they had been studying the guitar, he had to study it..... Generally one would study an instrument, it could be piano, it could be guitar, but he studied the guitar a lot, quite a bit. And he had, in the end this name, his mother was very congenial, a woman of great personality as well. And it was made known that she was Spanish, she was young, very nice. Well, the word got around, the question that had a group of people from the select high society that were saying ...(Laughter). The elite as it is said now, that beforehand that word hadn't been used: "the elite". And he had the best students!!! Man!!! I'll tell you something!!! They came with an automobile and their chauffeur in search of taking a private class. There were several families like these. So, that gave him an idea. What an epoch that was.!!! How he worked!!!

H.G.M. And he had a student that was the wife of an Argentina political personality that is discussed quite a bit. I would like you to tell me how he gave her classes. I'm referring to Mrs. Aurelia Tizon wife of the General Juan Domingo Peron...

B.P. Ah, she was a student of my father. Beautiful time, huh? They came for several years to our home. So that's the truth. I vaguely remember, she was very congenial. And according to my father...because also my father in that sense would see that there hadn't been many conditions, and that he wouldn't lose time and money with his student. He said it very clearly, she wasn't for taking money from the people, he gave her classes, and he could see she had some ability. And Mrs. Aurelia Tizon Peron had conditions, my father would say, and I agree with that. Fine, and him teaching her, she was congenial and pleasant. And there is an anecdote about her that...I don't know if I told it to you?

H.G.M. Why not?

B.P. Total... the years have passed and the two persons that perhaps could be bothered a little bit, they have died, that is her and him, the General.... She had requested of my father, sometimes to borrow money to cover her losses in a card game, poker, which was her perdition.

H.G.M. !! Of her? !!

B.P. Yes,...

H.G.M. !!!! Look you !!!!....

B.P. And I don't want to say anything about Peron because without!!! It's loaded!!!...(Laughter)...it appears.... (More laughter) ....

H.G.M. !!! Hooyyy, very beautiful!!!!... (Laughter)

B.P. So, father was like that, he let her facilitate what she asked of him, and later they would arrange things among themselves. Now how she subscribed to his classes, I don't know those things. It looks like they arranged it well, my father never had a complaint about her, and it looks correct in the sense of money. But as a vice she had, and that her husband was to never know, and her husband was Peron.... (Laughter) And that I remember perfectly, because after that my father decided to move to Haedo (Province of Buenos Aires, locality near Buenos Aires, Capital of Argentina) .... In the year 1935... yes... in the year 35', he closed the Academia and we moved to live in Haedo. Peron with his wife still came to Haedo.

H.G.M. !!!! Ah!!! Yes?...

This is a postcard sent to Domingo Prat's family from Mrs. Aurelia Tizon Peron and her husband Juan Peron.

The text translates to: "For the kind Prat family, affectionately, A. T. de Peron, Juan Peron. On the right: Rembrance of Puente del Tucu" (Tucu Bridge) describing the cover. This was possibly sent with the letter or book.

I need to thank my colleague Matanya Ophee for the willingness to trade the Prat/ Peron memorabilia. The images from this page and 4 pages hence are ex Blanca Prat collection, ex Matanya Ophee collection.

B.P. Yes, yes, ...yes, I remember Peron (three times President of the Republic of Argentina) driving, they came...as there were many cars in that epoch, and he was driving...And within that epoch he gave her classes, Peron walked in the garden..... because it was a house with a very large garden, and big lawn, we had bought a dog from the police to watch, as a guardian. And he was getting big, a puppy; he was just a bit of a beautiful animal. And you have to understand Peron he loved that dog. He would say: 'Prat the dog is very intelligent, why don't you have it trained?' "They can teach this animal" .... "because look" .... And they threw a stick far away and the dog grabbed the stick as if someone had taught it. That's what I remember ... what age I might have been? 10 or 11 years old, 12 and I remember perfectly those details. Of course, after the things in life, they separated, and she died. It appears it was cancer in....the Marin Sanatorium...is it?   It was located on *calle* Santa Fe.

H.G.M. Yes, Marini Sanatorium,

B.P. Yes, she died there, the things of life, right?

H.G.M. And when General Peron was a Military Attaché in the Argentine Embassy in Chile, he wrote a letter sent from there to your father, right? *"Apuntes de Historia Militar"*.

B.P. Exactly, "Annotations of Military History",.... In all I guess it can be said to be a beautiful appreciation, very congenial. After the years passed, look what became of this man, imagine that, right?... (Laughter) A beautiful part...

This is the dedication to Domingo Prat by (Lieutenant Colonel) Teniente Coronel Juan Peron sent on March 1, 1935.

   The dedication translates to: "To the distinguished maestro *Don* Domingo Prat with the testimony of my admiration. Buenos Aires, March 1, 1935

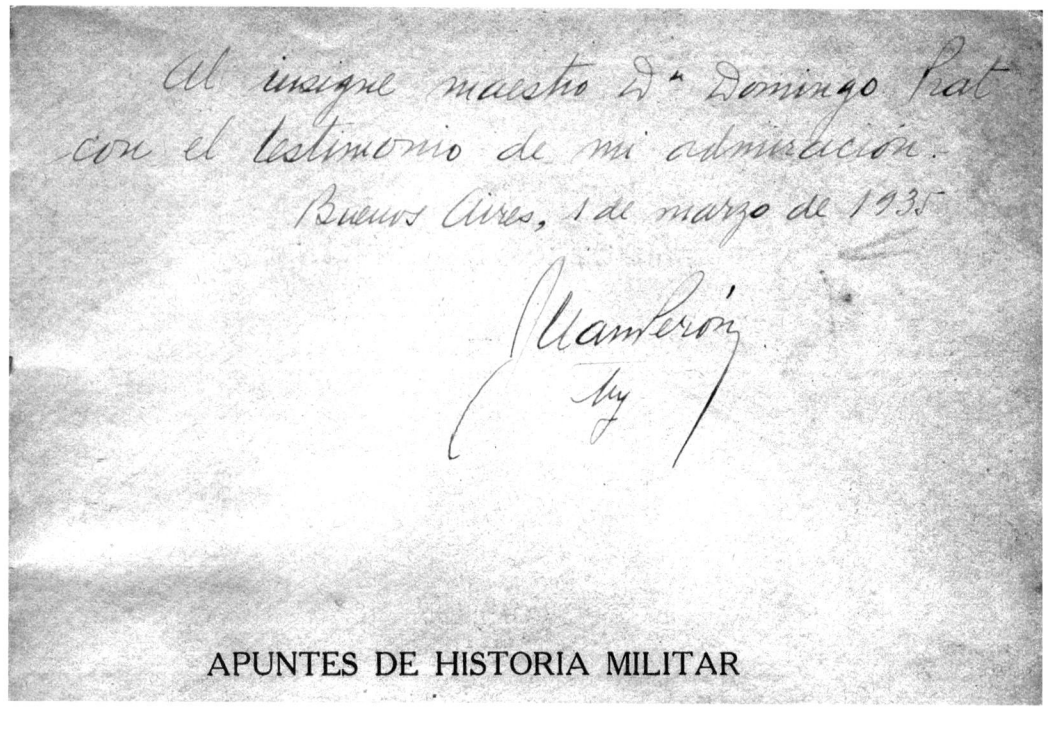

APUNTES DE HISTORIA MILITAR

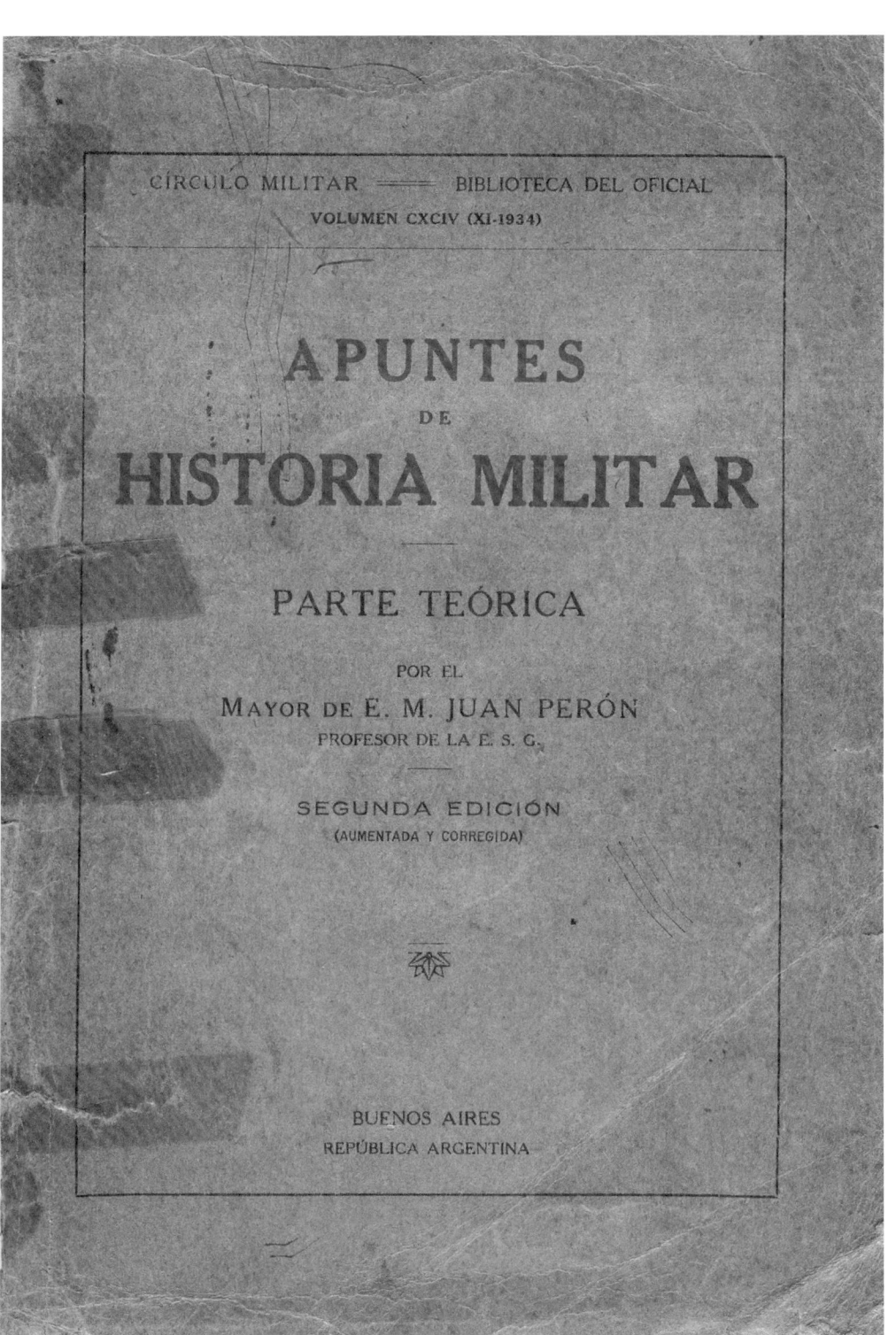

This is the cover of the book *"Apuntes de Historia Militar"* ("Annotations of Military History") written by (Lieutenant Colonel) Teniente Coronel Juan Peron dedicated to Domingo Prat on March 1, 1935. In the packet in the back of this book are a dozen cards of military formations in battles described in the text.

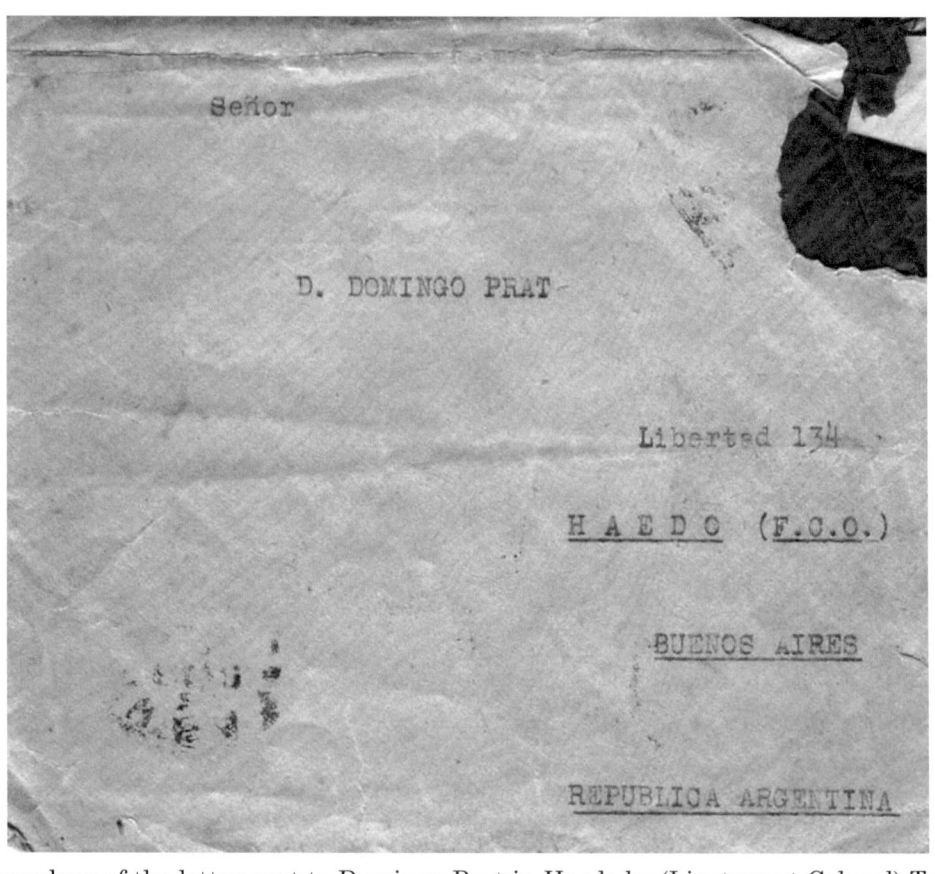

This is the envelope of the letter sent to Domingo Prat in Haedo by (Lieutenant Colonel) Teniente Coronel Juan Peron from Santiago, Chile on January 20, 1937. There was brown colored paper inside the envelope to disguise the contents while en route to its destination. This was Juan Peron's personal stationary.
It appears from the handwritten words that it was answered on February 23, 1937.

Santiago de Chile,16 de enero de 1937

Señor Domingo Prat.

BUENOS AIRES.

Mi querido Maestro:

Recibímos y mucho le agradecemos el gentil saludo de año nuevo,a la par que les deseamos a ustedes toda clase de felicidades y prosperidades para este 1937 que se inicia.-

Siguiendo sus consejos hemos buscado un maestro en Santiago y no le hemos podido encontrar " ni con candil",parece que somos pocos los sudamericanos que hemos heredado de la tierra hispánica la hermosa tradición de la "bihuela".

En cuanto a que nos figuran rosados y salados por los baños de Viña del Mar,aun cuando resulte un anacronismo,en Viña del Mar no hay "viñas ni mar",pues las playas son pequeñitas y las aguas más frias que las del polo. De manera que solo se trata de una demostración de trajes de baño y poca higiene marítima. Hay que confesar sin embargo que son bellos lugares,pero la invasión de turistas de estos tiempos,hace poco menos que imposible el vivir allí. Usted sabe bien que "el turista" es el "bicho" más incómodo que ha producido la tierra.- Nos conformamos en esta época,con atender a los compatriotas que llegan en busca de descanso,que aquí no encuentran,para después,cuando desaparece la nube de paseantes,pasear nosotros tranquilos.-

Creo sinceramente que ustedes disfrutarán de mejor verano en su alegre quinta de Haedo,donde la tranquilidad, que las tareas imponen y el descanso exige,será absoluta y proporcional a las necesidades de un "buen reposo".- Por lo menos así lo deseamos nosotros para nuestros buenos amigos.-

Mi Señora escribe también,pues no ha querido dejar pasar mi carta sin agregar sus saludos especiales para su grande y querido maestro,a quien recuerda a cada instante con el entusiasmo y el calor que solo pueden llegar a inspirar los verdaderos maestros.-

Le ruego quiera presentar mis especiales saludos a la Señora y las niñas,a quienes deseamos la mayor felicidad y bienestar.- Asimismo reciba usted mi gran abrazo.-

The translation of the text of the letter on the previous page:

(Lieutenant Colonel) Teniente Coronel Juan Peron

Santiago, Chile on January 16, 1937.

Mr. Domingo Prat

Buenos Aires

My beloved Maestro:

We received and are very grateful for the charming greeting of the New Year, the pair of us would like to wish you all kinds of happiness and prosperity for the year 1937 which has just begun. —

Following your advice, we have searched for a maestro in Santiago and we have not been able to find one "even with a candle", it appears that we are a few South Americans which have inherited the beautiful tradition of the *"Vihuela"* of the Hispanic land.

In regards that you figure we are tanned and salty to the waters of Viña del Mar, even though it results in an anachronism in Viña del Mar there are no vines nor sea though the beaches are small and the waters are colder than the waters of the poles. Of a manner that only treats it as a demonstration of bathing suits and little maritime hygiene. You have to confess however that they are beautiful places, but the invasion of tourists in these times, makes it less than impossible to live there. You know very well that "the tourist" is the most annoying "bug" which the land has produced. We agree in this epoch, to care for the compatriots that arrive in search of rest, which they don't find here, for after, when the cloud of visitors disappears, we take a walk tranquilly. —

I sincerely believe that you enjoy the best summer in your happy country home in Haedo, where the tranquility, which the chores impose and the rest demands, will be absolute and proportional to the necessities of a "good rest". — At least that way we desire for our best friends. —

My wife writes as well, since she hasn't wanted to let my letter pass without adding her special greeting for her great and beloved maestro, to whom she remembers every instant with enthusiasm and the warmth that can only succeed to inspire the true maestros. —

I wish to present my special greeting to your wife and daughters, to whom we wish the best happiness and well-being. — Likewise, you receive my great embrace. —

Juan Peron

Living in Haedo, my father continued his dedication to teaching he didn't have nearly the students as he did in the Academia in the center of Buenos Aires. Because precisely, what he wanted to do was retire a little bit, or in other words he was already tired ..... He still had some years left.... Poor him, because he died at 58 years of age, he was still young. But you have to think that he began very young with the guitar, and that he gave classes, concerts, working with the guitar always.

And in Haedo he dedicated more time to the music, making transcriptions. He was working on that quite a bit, and I remember in his study and that you weren't to touch anything.... Because well, he could get very angry. 'How could you?!?!!!! They are the writers that have everything, everything is intertwined, because they know where those things are and you're not going to touch one piece of paper because you might die in a fight' (Laughter). It was something he wouldn't put up with. And he worked, but still gave classes.... I now recall Nelly Ezcaray, which was one of the last distinguished students that he had.

H.G.M. Nelly Ezcaray?

B.P. Yes, and she would come...I don't know if it was once or twice a week. That I'll tell you in that epoch she came from the Center of Buenos Aires to Haedo in all that was a long trip. There was the train....

H.G.M. But she had come from farther away in Rosario, Province of Santa Fe..... I believe?

B.P. Yes, she was living in Rosario, her parents were there, but she lived here in the *"Caballito"* (Neighborhood of Buenos Aires) with her aunt and uncle, the Muratorio family, they were like godparents, they were the ones who paid her tuition, everything. Yes, yes, she came many years and eventually played very well. I remember because there, I was a young woman. I remember her perfectly. And he had a good group of students there as well, in that house (in Haedo). Besides my father would go once or twice a week to downtown Buenos Aires, to give very special classes. I don't know if I have him in mind, he was a young boy in that epoch, García Peluffo?

H.G.M. No.

B.P. Yes, this youngster finally gave concerts, I don't know one or two. But my father was giving him private lessons. And to the Dr. Llambias he also gave classes, he was a great surgeon in that epoch. That was in the same epoch that Augusto Marcellino came to our home once or twice.

(Left) J. Augusto Marcellino business card from the Ricardo Muñoz archive.

(Bottom) Listing of a concert by Augusto Marcellino of a composition by Esteban Eitler on November 26, 1943. This is from the *"Revista de la Guitarra"* issue No. 11 of January 1, 1943 to October 31, 1944.

U. T. 37 - 1152   LAVALLE 1378 - PISO 4º

H.G.M. The Brazilian?...

B.P. Yes, the Brazilian, that, among other things courted me.... So, within "parenthesis" ...(Laughter) things of one's youth...(Laughter)...I might have been 16 years old or something like that.

José Augusto Marcellino did the fingering for Esteban Eitler's pieces. Esteban Eitler was an Austrian composer and flautist born in 1913. Marcellino had also invented his *Escuela Ultratecnica de Wiolaum* double pentagram for arranging guitar music with C clef below an ordinary G clef. Below is the debut performance of the Concierto 1944, with José Augusto Marcellino's participation. This was a just part of a concert held on August 13, 1944 at the Instituto Frances.

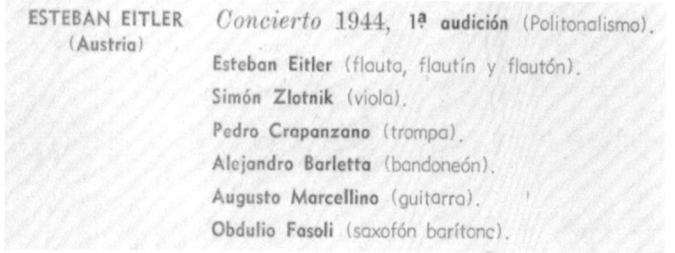

H.G.M. In the works of your father it appears that he was less dedicated as a composer, and was more inclined to be dedicated to teaching and transcriptions, right?

B.P. Yes, in reality that's correct, that is, he made many transcriptions in his life that he had been working on, in the end as well. He was dedicated to ...how would we say... the methods of teaching, the classics, such as ones I've already mentioned *"La Nueva Tecnica"* and *"Escalas y Arpegios"*. But in reality, yes, he dedicated much of his time to making transcriptions.

 But he was always searching to see if a certain work would adapt itself to the guitar, because it's logical that some pieces wouldn't be suitable for the guitar. The guitar is an instrument that is very sweet, it has a sonority but hasn't a great projection. Then he had to look for a transcription, he was always doing that, he worked on it, he searched for the harmony that would bring it to the guitar. His life also was filled with students; it was fantastic what went on in our home.

H.G.M. According to what they have told me, and what I could see in the transcriptions that he made, there appears to be a sense, as well a great devotion to the music of Argentina. Did someone influence him in this aspect? Wasn't it the musicologist Carlos Vega?

Musicologist Carlos Vega studied all the music of the lower part of South America, including the music of Peru. This book *"Escalas con semitonos-Musica de los antiguos peruanos"* (Scales with semitones-Music of the ancient Peruvians) was published by the "Museo Argentino de Ciencias Naturales (Natural Science) in Buenos Aires in 1934, and it was originally included in Vol. 1 of the *"Actas de XXV Congreso Internacional de Americanistas"*. It is autographed and dedicated to Ricardo Muñoz.

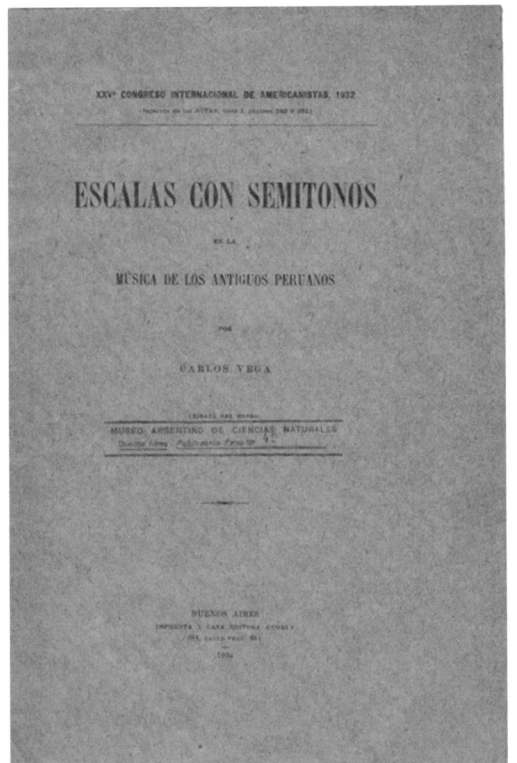

B.P. It could be, yes, because Carlos Vega was dedicated to our music, to Argentine music and they talked a lot, they spoke quite a bit, they spoke quite a bit about these things. No, but it is my father, who always liked the national music as it was known back then.

H.G.M.. The Argentine music...

B.P.. Yes the Argentine music that he always liked and they lived...I say them because my mother as well, it was the epoch of the *"Estilos"* (lyrical specie of Argentine and Uruguayan folkmusic), the *"Vidalitas"* (traditional Argentine song) of this type of music,!!! who didn't play a *"Valsito"* (diminutive of *Vals*) or a *"Vidalitas"*!!!, my father liked all that music.

H.G.M.. Yes, but I have observed another thing, that he dedicated himself as well to the historical music of Argentina. Because there is a transcription of the *"Minué Federal"* (1839) of the epoch of Rosas (Governor of Buenos Aires, political figure also discussed in Argentine political history).

B.P.. Yes, there is a work that he did many years ago, many years before the epoch of which I am speaking. It is certainly, *"El Minué Federal"* ... You know that just recently, sadly enough I wasn't able to attend, the Fernández Blanco Museum of Buenos Aires, they advised me that they were going to have a dissertation and the *"Minué Federal"* was to be played on the guitar. Who played? ...I don't know.

H.G.M.. The transcription of your father?

B.P.. Yes, the transcription of my father, that they were going to name. That was almost 2 years ago. I had the flu and it turned out that it was impossible to go. Interesting, right? I would have liked to be there. It's very beautiful, very well done, very well thought out, and after that (*"Minué Federal"*) they had the famous *"Variaciones sobre la Huella"* (*Huella:* traditional Argentine dance) by 3 guitars.

Afterwards in his last years, he wanted me to learn them; I played them but..... to me.... I didn't like them much; I'm being sincere (laughter). They were by my father.... *"El Escondido"* (traditional Argentine folklore dance), *"La Firmeza"* (traditional Argentine folklore dance), *"El Palito"* (traditional Argentine dance) and they were published by Ricordi.

H.G.M.. And you didn't like them?

B.P.. No,.... ah the *"El Malambo"* (traditional Argentine dance) yes, He made it difficult, the positions here and there and well you had to have very agile fingers (laughter). That is a work he did in his last years. It is not a work he did in the golden epoch, it was from the last years of his life, he dedicated himself to, he was writing, it also inspired the man ....!!! Ufff!!!..... He was working with the guitar, quite a lot, quite a lot.

And I tell you, he wished me to study them, I played them in concert, but not that much. There were certain works of *folklore* that I liked, not only the classics, such as Fleury, I had his *milonga "Pico Blanco"*. I played it with a lot of verve, I felt it. My father always had me include them: 'Always put something of your own country in your concerts'. I was always sure to put 4 or 5 works. He liked what were Argentine and the tango!!! That's why I'm telling you!! (Laughter) You know the quantity of transcriptions he did of the tango, how he took to this work.

Abel Fleury, el mago de la guitarra, deleitando a los radioescuchas patagónicos.

Abel Fleury performing on radio station *L. U. 8*. The caption translated is: "Abel Fleury, the magician of the guitar, delighting his Patagonian radio listeners." This is from *"Argentina Austral"* issue No. 181 of July 1946.

Courtesy of Lucas Agustín de Antoni, Buenos Aires

H.G.M. Now I'd like for you to tell me: about your father that was a historical investigator, how did the idea come about to make the *"Diccionario de Guitarristas"*?

B.P. The truth, I don't know what to tell you, how the idea came about, how it occurred to the man to make a *"Diccionario de Guitarristas"*, I don't know in what moment that might have been? I was a small girl, but, well he began to form the making of it and it took years, it took several years, to inquire, to investigate.... When we were in Spain in 1930, one of the principal motives was that, to inquire over there, he covered half of Spain, verifying dates. He went to the churches, to the monasteries, where the books were, the transcripts of the birth records, to verify dates, names ....!!!! What I know!!!.... He was working like crazy. Now as to when the idea came about exactly, I don't know, the day that it occurred to him: 'it would be interesting to write a *"Diccionario de Guitarristas"*, right?'

Yes, in 1930 he worked a lot on it. No, ... I'm thinking.... because there had been others before him, the one by Ricardo Muñoz is before...

H.G.M. No, but Muñoz didn't write a dictionary....

B.P. And what is the book that he did?

H.G.M. It's a *"Historia de la Guitarra"* in 8 volumes, but they only published 2.

B.P. No, as I know it that it was named by my father, ...but, well...of course, it's different, logically.

Yes, yes, I know that this idea came, and he began to work. I believe that the *Diccionario* was published in 1936 (actually in 1934).... It took 8 to 10 years, to compile everything.

It was a fantastic work, I recognize to this day what he did with that *Diccionario,* with the dates and things that he joined together, to have for placement.

H.G.M. Once the *"Diccionario de Guitarristas"* was published, what kind of repercussion did it have in Argentina?

B.P. It was a huge success, which is the truth of it, all that together, it was such a novelty, as an explosion, a thing that had never been. The format that he gave it was important for the book. I believe the price it had was high for that epoch, it was expensive. Because it had how many pages? 500, right?

H.G.M. 400 and something.

B.P. 400 or 500 yes.... It was very important and later the newspapers, the magazines spoke of the *"Diccionario"* of my father, they were always commenting on this work. He had a big success. But.... it was as I can tell you? .... As a furor, a fast thing...after, it stayed there; of course, it was a large book ...practical? I don't know, the truth is that, it might have influenced sales or not, it was a disgrace that it wasn't done again. It was done in a first edition and no more. I by luck, thanks to God, have the first volume of the *"Diccionario de Guitarristas"*, number 0001.

H.G.M. Listen, did Consuelo Mallo Lopez collaborate with him on the *"Diccionario"*? Is that so?

B.P. Effectively.

H.G.M. Who collaborated in that?

B.P. Consuelo Mallo Lopez and her brother.

H.G.M. Samuel

B.P. Samuel, yes, he was a doctor, and a sketch artist, he collaborated a lot. Imagine Mr. García, in that epoch, well, the medium was to write, and write, you had to write. Because there wasn't even a typewriter in the house ..... That I can assure you .....

H.G.M. !!! There wasn't a typewriter? !!!

B.P. There wasn't a typewriter (Laughter) that I can totally assure you. So that everything was done in writing, filling papers, he needed people that would help him, because he wouldn't have been able to supply enough by himself. And the persons that classified the things and one of them you just mentioned, was Mallo Lopez, the brother Samuel and there was a student that I haven't forgotten as well,.... one such Delbene...his surname.

H.G.M. Ah, yes, Delbene, I believe that it was Ricardo Delbene.

Ricardo Delbene

INAUGURA LA SEMANA DE
FESTEJOS DEL 25° ANIVERSARIO
DE LA A.G.A., QUE CONSTITUYÓ
UNA EFECTIVA MUESTRA
DE CAMARADERIA.

This is a photo of Ricardo Delbene speaking at the inaugural dinner at one of the week-long activities of the 25th annivesary of the Asociacion Guitarristica Argentina. It is part of the cover of the December 1959 edition of the *Noticiero Guitarristico*.

B.P. Yes, that one helped quite a lot, because he lived real close, to our home. He was living over there on calle Rodríguez Peña, or near Rodríguez Peña. Of course, imagine how much help he needed. And my mother, she collaborated quite a bit too. Classify, classify, and proofreading of what had been done, all of the annotations had to be treated in that manner!!! It was fantastic!!! Today I think about it and I tell you!!! My God!!! To think how they did things before computers, the writers now can proof read / edit with great ease. !!! But to think that in that epoch you had to do everything by hand as it is commonly said. Because it was all done in writing and looking up dates and later connecting with the whole world writing to Italy, France and Germany. A brother in law helped in that aspect, my Uncle Angel, it was he who played Flamenco, and enjoyed it all of his life.

H.G.M. Angel?

B.P. Angel Farré, the surname of my mother, my second name. He played the Flamenco style very well, and he liked the classical guitar very much. They wrote to him, he was a contact, a point of contact he had with his brother-in-law, with my Uncle Angel. He would look for him, and from there it was easier to be connected to France and Italy. And he verified 'Look Domingo, Domingo in Catalan is *"Minguet"*, then he would write him *'Minguet* there is this.... Are you interested....?' He would answer: "Fine, look for it", "how much are they offering it for?" 'What will you pay?'!!! Whew...What am I going to tell you of this epoch? Including also my mother would say "!!! Ah, the amount of money you're spending on those things!!!" ......She would say......(Laughter). You had to be connected; there wasn't the computer, no e-mail, there were none of those things (Laughter). And I might say that the epoch of being connected by the airplane had started, right? But only beforehand everything was by ship.

H.G.M. !!! It was by ship!!! (Laughter)

B.P. Yes,!!! It was by ship!!! Therefore, I believe that the trip to Spain...well...there were two good reasons, one was as well for my little sister, who was incapacitated, they did this to have her looked at by the best doctors over there. They took advantage of the trip and I didn't...have anything to do....

H.G.M. How long, in that opportunity, did they stay in Spain?

B.P. And we lived there a year and a half.

H.G.M. Meanwhile he was teaching?

B.P. Yes, yes, not a lot, not a lot, he had a student and another one. Now he was working very well that, imagine this, that my father achieved the acquiring of capital.

H.G.M. Right here?

B.P. No, just a moment.... They acquired the capital in Spain, because with the idea to leave, his brother, Tomas Prat, he's named the same, as my grandfather, their father, was President of the Bank of Barcelona. And my parents sent amounts of money every month for what they were trying to accumulate. And with that amount, they thought they would be able to live perfectly, giving classes and with the capitol, paying the rent. So that when they found out they needed money, they had money. That is what I wanted to comment on to you, see for yourself how he succeeded working with the guitar, giving classes only....

H.G.M. Right here?

B.P. Right here, to maintain a home, make money, sending it to Spain, to put his funds together, that gives you an idea of how it worked. !!! It was fantastic!!!

H.G.M. One has to take into account that he worked with powerful people, with an economic means...

B.P. Yes, yes, in general it had a very good element, very good, although I told you he was disinterested, my father was!!! Thanks to God!!! He wasn't a man of "minding the store".... No, no because he saw conditions where he accepted students who couldn't pay. He has a few students, I remember,.... I don't remember?... that some people came to the house and could play quite a bit, but they couldn't pay him, or they paid him once in a while and to him it wasn't important. And when they named him a professor at the Nicolas Avellaneda...

H.G.M. Of the Nicolas Avellaneda College? ....

B.P. Yes, the Nicolas Avellaneda College all because of the students he had, the two little Alais sisters, I believe an uncle of the Alais sisters...wait a minute? .... wait a minute?... I am...

H.G.M. They were relatives of the guitarist Juan Alais (1844-1914)?

B.P. I don't know that I can't tell you, but if of.... How is it named? .... One such Pueyrredon ... that was Minister of Education at that time, and he was an uncle to these girls, of the Alais sisters. And from there he was sought after in the Nicolas Avellaneda College. Therefore, I tell you there was a sizable group of people, that among other things I believe he was there a year and left because the young men went crazy.... (Laughter) of the college ... (Laughter) he would say: 'Bah, those students don't want to know anything seriously about music'. And he quit, in all, that college has a status today, but in that epoch, it was just a college, it had a status of being crude, to be a professor at the Nicolas Avellaneda College, was an award.

El maestro Domingo Prat,
ha´sido nombrado profesor
del Colegio Nacional.

Con fecha reciente, el Ministerio de Justicia e
Instrucción Pública ha nombrado Profesor de Música del Colegio Nacional Nicolás Avellaneda al distinguido didacta español don Domingo Prat.

Aparte del justo reconocimiento de aptitudes que
importa la designación del excelente maestro, el hecho resulta honroso para el pequeño mundo de la
guitarra, por cuanto uno de sus más destacados es-
pecialistas se incorpora al cuerpo docente de las altas instituciones nacionales de enseñanza.

This announcement is from the *Revista Musical Ilustrada "Tárrega"* magazine issue No. 26 of September 1926. I need to thank the Universidad Catolica Argentina de Buenos Aires for providing me with a copy of the complete issue.

The translation is:

"The maestro Domingo Prat has been named a professor to the Colegio Nacional.

With a recent date, the Minister of Justice and Public Instruction has named the distinguished Spanish didactic don Domingo Prat as a Professor of Music at the Colegio Nacional Nicolas Avellaneda.

Aside from the just recognition of aptitudes that are important of the designation of the excellent maestro, he makes an honorous result for the small world of the guitar, by being one of its most distinguished specialists to be incorporated in the teaching body of the highest national institutions of learning."

H.G.M. How many years exactly did he teach there?

B.P. He wasn't there a very long time, I don't know if he was there two years, that would be a lot. No, no, he couldn't stand it; he didn't have the patience for the adolescents, in that sense, in that sense to teach a group as a professor of music. Now for the guitar, yes, yes, he had a lot of patience and he was very tenacious ....!!! And did I find that out!!!.... (Laughter)

H.G.M. Because you were his student.

B.P. And, I found that out because he was my maestro, very demanding, very demanding, I believe that he was more so with me than with others, more for being his daughter. But he made me understand I knew how to be a student, overall, we left aside the study of the sheet music, the notes, he transmitted the form of how music should be expressed. It was important that a professor should be able to do that.

H.G.M. Another aspect that has been studied or observed very little is that your father was a collector of sheet music....

B.P. Yes, that's certain, my father had a great hobby, I don't know in what moment his interest could have been awakened to acquire sheet music, of antiquity. He was a collector of those things with all his soul, searching for the impossible; he wanted to have it. Over all he had the great ambition to be able to possess, but completely. Of course, his dream was to have had a complete set of Fernando Sor. To him, he was a magnificent composer; he admired him in a fantastic way. And he eventually attained a respectable amount of works by Fernando Sor. With help from all the connections he had around the world, above all in Italy and France. His brother-in-law helped quite a bit, my Uncle Angel, that from Spain he was the interpreter he had, advising him: 'in this place is this piece, are you interested?'

And everything was like that, he sent the money that was requested, he acquired a work and searched for another. And so, over many years, I don't know how many, I don't want to lie, he was acquiring an amount of the works of Fernando Sor. Not only Sor, but other authors of antiquity such as Giuliani, and.... well, in this moment I don't remember, but they were all authors of antiquity. He had this obsession, it's a shame that for poor him, it was cut short. Because he couldn't, end up...I don't know if end up, because it would be a thing that appears to be incalculable (would never end), you could attain everything, but to have had more quantities. Of Sor, I said he had a lot, he wasn't missing much, but fine,...it couldn't be, his desire was never fulfilled. And later a thing that happened, I remember very well because I was a young lady, living in the town of Haedo, they came to visit our home once in a while, let's see.... Wait I might have it in mind..... Eleuterio Tiscornia, Segundo N. Contreras that also were great collectors of musicians of antiquity.

H.G.M. In what year was that?

B.P. It could be 1940, 1942, in his last years, they came!!! Whew....!!! As one left another would come, not together, they arrived separately and would converse with my father, they brought sheet music, they traded pieces, and they bought pieces from each other as well. They sold among themselves because they wanted to attain the acquisition of what they desired to have. One had a piece the other didn't. Because I also know they each had a remarkable collection, above all Eleuterio Tiscornia had an impressionable amount of sheet music. They came, yes, yes, I remember very well, this gentleman conversing and passing the afternoon drinking coffee, and trading sheet music. It was an obsession in their last years, let's say so and to attain a beautiful collection of works of antiquity...that's the truth...

H.G.M. Your father not only dedicated himself to collecting European works of antiquity, but also some old pieces from here in the Rio de la Plata. We know he obtained and had placed it within his collection, a Method for Guitar that belonged to Dr. Fernando Cruz Cordero, Uruguayan-resident of Argentina, functionary of the Government of Juan Manuel de Rosas, there in 1840 approximately. And your father says in his *Diccionario de Guitarristas*, that it was this Uruguayan, who introduced the Spanish school of guitar to the Rio de la Plata... and not the Argentine poet Esteban Echeverria, as he has assured us.

That Method, do you know where it went?

B.P. Look, sincerely I don't know, I know that he had it, it was in our home, but I don't know where it went, and I don't know who acquired it. I can't tell you much about that. Yes, I know he had things that were very interesting in his possession. Logically, in my years in those epochs, you have to take into account I was very young. It wasn't that I wasn't interested, but that, it didn't mean anything to me, I didn't know what he could buy, or do. So, I can't give you this information.

H.G.M. To that you must, how can you explain the attitude of your father for so many years, making a sacrifice to put all this collection of sheet music together? Later when he was at the end of his life, in little parts let's say he divided them among his distinct students, better said to some students. What was that due to?

B.P. No, I can answer you directly. It wasn't my father that divided them up....

H.G.M. !!! Ah!!! It wasn't your father?!!...I had understood that it was .....

B.P. No, it wasn't my father that divided them up; it was my mother at the death of my father. And she didn't divide them up, either. They were divided up because we lived in a house, although many people called it a "little chalet", or "little house", that wasn't so. It was a large house where he had accumulated for a duration of 10 years, with many things referring to the guitar: sheet music, books, my father also had a very important library. I remember 6 bookcases in his study, covering every wall. And my mother, a few months later after his death, let go of the house for us to come to live in the National Capitol (Buenos Aires) with me and my sister.

This is the house in Haedo where Domingo Prat and family moved to in c. 1935. This is from the obituary written by Ricardo Muñoz for the magazine *Mundo Musical* issue No. 76 *Año* VII of January 1945.

My poor mother didn't know what to do with so many things; she didn't know how to place them. Then there is the question you were asking me, dividing up.... because I remember perfectly, I was already 19 years old, in cartons made of good wood and well air-conditioned there held the paper items, many things of my father, sheet music, books and gave them to students to care for, the people in whom she had a lot of confidence. One of those was, Amilcar Verdier, a student of my father, that in one epoch he attained being distinguished, and they appreciated him a lot, and she had a lot of confidence in those persons that she was going to have care for the things. To Consuelo Mallo Lopez she gave many things to hold, they weren't given to her. She divided them up because they had a time, the time that had been necessary. And as well to professor Manuel Paradela, that was a professor of guitar who was perfecting under the direction of my father, without attaining a title from the Academia. But he came a lot to take classes, and we ended up having a great friendship. An excellent person, their marriage, or whereas his wife and him, my father had a lot of esteem for them. And mother, on that basis of confidence also gave them a lot of things to take care of. Sadly, the case of years having passed, we went into a small apartment, there wasn't the capacity to keep all those things there, and sadly passed time, in this course of life I got married and no longer lived with my mother. She moved again and the things stayed in the homes I've been mentioning, with those families. And she never went back to recover them; she didn't ask them, I don't know why? And I can't tell you.

And what happened with my mother? Why didn't she ask for the return of the sheet music? No, there they stay. It's known, for example of Verdier that he positively had them, that someone knows where they went. Because after this youngster Amilcar Verdier died and he was an only child, and the mother remained, and I don't know what she did with that sheet music...these turns of life. And so, it was, that they became scattered things, let's say, by distinct directions. But it wasn't my father; it was my mother at the death of my father divided up all this material. She found herself overwhelmed by so many things. And I..... don't want to be free of fault, I was young, I entered a phase of life I hadn't lived, that was to be in love, to get married and to top it off I left my mother, I had to move to the province of Entre Rios with my husband, then I left and didn't intervene. She had done and undone, it's logical that she was within her right.

H.G.M. Your father, how did he prepare the concerts of himself and of his students? Do you remember?

B.P. Of his I don't know, because when I was born... I don't know if he gave a concert after I was born...of him solo. Now those of his students yes, he gave concerts with a quantity of students, I don't know if it was with 30 students that he had presented.

He made them practice a lot. They came on Sundays to the Academia, my home, they tuned up, and they worked, that's what I recall for the whole morning. He made them study, because it wasn't a joke, right? Suppose yourself it was 30 guitars, all have to be tuned well, as an orchestra without fail, it isn't easy, I believe it was something like that, they tuned up, they worked together. It was Sundays in the morning.

H.G.M. You were a student of his, how did your father aim his plans for your study? How was a class with him? How did it start? How did it end?

Translation of the dedication:

"For the author of the *"Diccionario de Guitarristas"* Prof. Domingo Prat, to whom I owe having me dedicated to study the guitar with the same artistic seriousness that was heard in a concert of students of his very prestigious academy."

Signed Manuel Paradela, Buenos Aires, June 1936.

B.P. Always, always he worked the student, as he did with me, when one starts to give a class you have to begin with a bit of technique. As he would say: 'you have to warm up the fingers'. A few scales, a few *arpeggios*, from there to the *"Nueva Tecnica"*. From there sprang the New Technique. Doing studies from the New Technique (book by Prat) and later when 'you've already done some 5 to 10 minutes although it's only of technique, then begin with what you were studying' -he would say to me: 'and what the professor gave you to study and review'... 'Why the better you know the work very well, but you'll want to have the fingering maintained'. That I remember perfectly, that he said that to me...that was the teaching I had for the morning. Because I also gave a few classes, though not for a very long time. Because this was the epoch in which I got engaged, I got married and I left. But that was his technique. I kept a little surprised because I didn't have any experience in giving classes. But I remembered how he had taught me. Then, to the students that I had, I tried to pass on to them the same things he had given to me. And that was to do technique of a chord that the student knew, until a point, if they knew some work of concert level or not. If you knew easy pieces, then after the technique he would have you play them. And always in that epoch, there was always the lesson notebook, where he wrote in what the student was to do. It was like in school.

You have to annotate, and he annotated what the student brought to class and what he took home with him. And later he would annotate what he had given the student.

H.G.M. How many years did you study with him?

B.P. Well, I began to study the guitar seriously, as it's said, to dedicated myself, at 12 years old. And when he was to die, I was going to complete 19 years. They were years when I picked up the guitar at 6:50 in the morning; he made me get up at 6:00 am. And he was saying to me to make the same effort as he was going to the station...as we lived in Haedo, and he was in route to catch the train to the National Capitol. ...He would take the train at 6:50 am. And I had to be at 6:50 am seated with the guitar 'doing fingers' as it's said. We got up at 6:00 am in the winter and the summer. Even along with the chills in that epoch in Haedo!!! My God!!!. And I studied until 9 am more or less, then had to put it down to have my breakfast, and then I would go out to the park a little bit, I ran a few laps, whatever I felt like. I had an hour and after again until the lunch hour, with the guitar.

H.G.M. How did you begin, with scales, exercises?

B.P. Yes, with the technique that they say, doing scales, the exercises of arpeggios, the thumb, the bar.

H.G.M. How long?

B.P. He said 15 minutes, a half an hour, whatever you would come to like, but to do it. And of course, many exercises to do legatos, bars, he made me do the thumb quite a lot.

H.G.M. And later?

B.P. Later, yes, I dedicated myself to the great studies, we might say serious concert studies, those beautiful studies that there are. After, the work I had to be reviewing, and the pieces I had under my fingers, or the one I was just starting to do or memorize. No, you couldn't always be playing with the music in front of you.

You were given your work, I had only a little bit (laughter) I had only a little bit because with all that, along with the classes of theory and solfeggio that were held twice a week.... I don't know? ...no, no you mustn't have known her, a student of his: Pascual Navas?

H.G.M. I know her by name.

B.P. That young girl knew a lot of music, at that time she was very young, a young woman; she was coming to Haedo twice a week for the music. We had a piano, and with the piano we did the solfeggio. Because don't forget I was 12 years old, and I had to study other things. Because my father asked me when I completed my primary school: 'What would you like to follow?'

Because in that epoch there was a tutor (schoolteacher) or the guitar he told me. And you can see that I told him the guitar, because I got involved in a dance of 'why'... (Laughter) Since I was always listening to the guitar, I said to him the guitar. Then what did he do? I took a professor who also came, I don't know, I believe that it was once a week .....

H.G.M. Professor of guitar?

B.P. No a lady professor of geography, history of ....bla, bla, bla ... of a little bit of everything in life. And later handwriting, he demanded of me the handwriting because it meant something to him.... (Laughter) Yes, he was a maniac about handwriting. And I asked him at that time, if he would agree to give me as a gift a typewriter. And he would say to me: 'I'm not going to give you that gift until you write well, when I like what you do'. And he bought me several notebooks, in which I had to do my writing, writing and writing. And well, so were all of those years, guitar, music, to study the rest, to know something of life, to know something of mathematics, of history, of geography, of life and writing.

H.G.M. You did those studies in parallel with the guitar, and after they gave you an exam?

B.P. With my father no.

H.G.M. No, no, the studies of geography, mathematics, where did they give you the exam?

B.P. By the intervening of Mallo Lopez.... I don't know what brother it was?... he was a Vice-Director of a school...what was the name of that school?

H.G.M. It's not important.

B.P. There I was presented, and they gave me the exams.

H.G.M. And that's how you would have coursed your school years....

B.P. Yes, yes, I was as a "student at liberty". No, no I didn't pass real well, as we would say. You might say I was young, and good I liked, well you could see what I liked. Imagine that I was only 12 years old and at 14 years old I gave my first concert, in 1940.

H.G.M. What do you remember of your first concert?

B.P. !!! Ah, beautiful!!!,!!! Beautiful!!! (Laughter) because at times I thought: "Yes I have a responsibility" but I didn't take it into account, as it appeared to me. Because I was content.... in time to say.... well pardon me..... I played a part of a concert in the Asociacion Guitarristica Argentina there in the *pasaje* Barolo. There I played for the first time, to try myself and see how I looked, to see how I carried myself in front of the public. I, nothing, as if it had rained. And then it was when I had prepared, I did study, study, that would be the certainty, practically every year I did give a concert. In the following year, in 41' I also gave a concert. Later a half a year apart, and five concerts after the death of my father or six, I don't know real well. Yes, I had practiced...I know because I had attained without saying to be given many flowers, and they threw me many things, but I had a great temperament with the public, he told me. But they were demanding and to be demanding I was certain I had studied!!! Hours and hours of the guitar!!! Then with that certainty it gave me tranquility in front of the public.

I was content with the first concert.

H.G.M. What repertoire did you do?

B.P. And, look all very classic, I had formed the first part of my concert with authors of antiquity. I played a lot of Sor, all the works of the other century; logically we're in 2001. Later, as I told you, a part that could have woven in pieces of Argentine authors and after the Spanish classics, always ending the last part with the famous: Granados, Malats, Moreno-Torroba, all those classical authors.

H.G.M. What Argentine authors did your father like, and recommended including in your repertoire?

B.P. At that time this professor played...what was his name? ...of the Conservatory? .....

H.G.M. Williams?

B.P. Yes, Williams, Alberto Williams, also there were others by Fleury, logically I always put something by him, of Prat, and I believe I played an *"estilo"* by Julián Aguirre.

Alberto Williams, from the cover of *Mundo Musical* issue No. 50 from November 1942.

H.G.M. A *"Triste"* (lyrical species of South American *folklore*)?

B.P. Yes, a triste by Aguirre, those classics, right? I don't remember much, but those were the preferred ones. And you always had to have 2 or 3 works; you always had to have something to do, a short work or two, if the public asked for it, according to one's success.

H.G.M. What difference do you find of the epoch of classical guitar of that time compared to the present day?

B.P. "Umm" ... that is difficult.

H.G.M. Tell me what you might think.

B.P. I'm going to be sincere I can't speak well of the guitar of the present day, because I've been estranged lately, to all of that, that appear to be groups, as I see the cultural part of Argentina, that the classical guitar.... There is decadence; sadly, I'll apply that word. I don't know if it will be applied well... there is decadence in the guitar. I'll say again: I've been estranged, the best they've said to me: 'No, madam you're wrong, there are many concerts that are given'...but neither do I live at the end of the world, and I keep up with the notices, But I don't see, I don't see that there is a movement. And I'm also going to give you a detail, I don't know if it's interesting, but I'll base it on the works of my father. Here I am again fitting in my father, but it's the truth. To have works published, such as there are for teaching, of the texts of my father, in an epoch that they were selling as it's said: "like hotcakes". And in these moments, they don't sell as such, that gave a standard that you couldn't teach the guitar as you had done in the years passed. Not here, and not in other parts of the world. Because I have present day requests for the music of my father, from Athens, Greece. I'm speaking of the books of the texts, of the teaching such as *"La Nueva Tecnica"* and *"Escalas y Arpegios",* that they ask for, they come out of Ricordi of Argentina bound for Greece. And that doesn't exist today, I don't know if in Greece they play or no longer play the guitar as was played here. That is my opinion. There appears to me to be decadence, and already in my country. I can't speak of other countries because I don't know. But of here, yes.

H.G.M. How were the relationships between your father and his colleagues, for example with Llobet, with Pujol and with his colleagues from here in Argentina? Let's start with Llobet and Pujol.

B.P. In this sense it was good, the same as with Llobet as with Pujol he had very good relations. Llobet he admired. He had his things, his opinions as every mortal. Perhaps in the form as an interpreter, he liked the way he did things, or he didn't, I don't know. But the relationship was very good. Inclusive I believe I have told you that, in the year 1910, Llobet had him go to Paris and stay where Llobet had been living, with him. It can be said there was a friendship.

H.G.M. And your father brought him to Argentina to give concerts.

B. P. It was he who brought him here, it was he who presented him to Maria Luisa Anido, after that she studied with Llobet. Because for that moment there was an eminence, he was the best to be had.

H.G.M. Can I ask you an indiscreet question?.... (Laughter)

B.P. Well I'll try to answer you.... (Laughter)

H.G.M. If you want to answer, you can answer, both of them are dead, the same as with Llobet as with Maria Luisa Anido. They say there was a romance between them.

B.P. Between Llobet and Anido? Yes, she said so...she said that it was so.... (Laughter) Everything can be.... (More laughter) everything can be....

H.G.M. That's fine, a guitar for everyone. (Laughter).... Free strings.... (Laughter)

B.P. There are moments in daily life; the contact at times brings those things.... For example, now that you say this, as both of them have passed away, they're not going to come back and reprimand us... But, in the very beginning, who was so in love between "quotation marks" with Miss Anido, it was Carlos Vega.

H.G.M. Ah, yes? !!! Look what's come to inform one.

B.P. My mother told me that!! Ah!! He was crazy for her; I tell you that *"Mimita"* (as Maria Luisa Anido was called) didn't give him a chance, speaking finely.

H.G.M. So, she didn't him give her attention.

This photo of Maria Luisa Anido is dedicated to Ricardo Muñoz. The translated dedication is: "For my very esteemed friend Ricardo Muñoz with the greatest affection, Maria Luisa Anido Buenos Aires, January 12, 1924."

The guitar in her hands is the 1864 Antonio de Torres owned by maestro Francisco Tárrega.

B.P. Said in a finer manner, but yes, she liked him.... (Laughter)!! How funny!!. And everything could be with Llobet. The same thing happened to my mother with Pujol. First, she began a courtship with my.... father, because she was his student, from there starts the affair. My mother was only 15 years old when she began to study guitar with Prat, and he was already an adult because he was 15 years older than she was. It didn't seem very important to him. But of course, to her, yes, as a young girl she was in love. But, do you know what happened? Prat went and came back, he was in Barcelona a year or two and he came here and in one of those (voyages) he let her go, my mother wanted to continue her studies and she stayed with Emilio Pujol. There, yes, it was more serious because she was older and a young woman and came to be engaged to Pujol.

H.G.M. !!! Ah!!! I didn't know that, she came to be engaged to Pujol, and later came *Don* Domingo and displaced him?...

B.P. !! He loaded his gun!!...When he saw he had lost her, that she was going to become married to Pujol... but as it looked to my mother, he had shot more times at the other "Catalancito" ...(Laughter)

H.G.M. !! How your mother broke hearts!!

B.P. Yes, she broke up with Pujol who had given her a ring and everything. It was funny because my mother would say: '! Ay, he was very angry with me because my mother broke us up!!'.. 'And, why are you going to return the ring?!!!'. That was my grandmother Ana, because she liked the manner of Pujol a lot. They say he was very refined, quite a gentleman. And he had given my mother a golden ring with diamonds, a real jewel, she gave it back, she didn't keep it. And as I was saying, when my father returned from one of those voyages and saw all that, it was when he decided to marry my mother. But her family didn't like the idea. Therefore, there was a romance he saw, there he told her romantic things.... (Laughter)...

H.G.M. To color the conversation.... (Laughter)...

B.P. Of course, of course, the things in life......

H.G.M. And with colleagues here in Argentina, with whom did he have friendships and who recognized him?

B.P. Look, I remember one friendship, friendship.... I don't remember well, you know how difficult it can be.... How can I explain myself?.... Envy didn't exist, and neither did jealousy but it's very difficult to possess a manner and share with others in the same line of work, in the same profession. And always there are things you like or not. Undoubtedly you must have someone else you would recognize. He always spoke well of Rizzuti. Rizzuti?.... That Carmelo Rizzuti.... one of those names that's going to come that I haven't named in years...professors of that epoch!!! Oh, My God!!! We spoke a while ago of Morales, I remember that he spoke of Morales very well also.

But in a group, I tell you, he was a man, he didn't have too much pride but very... distant.... I'm here and he's there.

H.G.M. He was distant.... He kept his distance....

B.P. Yes, (*parate*) "I stop here and he's there". No, no he didn't want to intervene in their affairs.

H.G.M. And with his contemporaries, with his compatriots, for example: the Basque, Hilarion Leloup. How was that relation?

B.P. Good, good in that sense, I never heard him say anything critical of him. One's own critiques of professors that one has taught are one thing, and the other is of another manner. But no, all was well in that sense, he didn't have any problems, they appreciated him, there was an appreciation of the man's work. In general, he didn't make enemies. I believe in the ambiance of the professors that, they said that Prat was this, that Prat wasn't so, by someone else. The only, it's logical some jealousy.... always there is among professors. But no, no in that respect they got along well. Now he was a reserved man, he wouldn't accept just anyone coming to the home to make a friendship. No, no I don't believe it was easy, no it wasn't easy.

H.G.M. Prat arrived here in Argentina and evidently, he brought something to evolve the ambiance. Because he brought something new, distinct, it can be said that he revolutionized the technique of the guitar and he taught that. That must have brought forth-contrary opinions, critiques, etc. right?

B.P. Yes, by that it was what I wanted to tell you, those critiques, those by them, imagine, he was young when he arrived here, he was a young man, who had success, he began to give classes, he began to amass a quantity of students...And of course why wouldn't he have these students.... We're not going to say enemies, but clearly the jealousy existed, it isn't certain in that sense.

I don't know, you were telling me that in his *Diccionario*, he says he didn't bring forth the "school of Tárrega"?

H.G.M. He says the school doesn't exist.

B.P. Yes, but from somewhere came what is called the "school of Tárrega". The case is very simple; he played the guitar with flesh, later with the nail. That right here they didn't play the guitar with the nails, neither in all of Spain as well. Everyone played with the flesh, you picked up the guitar, and you played using flesh to see what sound would come out, at times they would say to me: 'Play the guitar' and I have short nails now, and they'd break and I'd tell them: "!! I can't!!", not because I couldn't, but when I know I don't like the sound that comes out, I can't play, I need a little bit of nail. And that is the Tárrega School, in the end it is called a "School". Then all of the left hand is to be cut short, but on the right hand to have a little bit of nail, not a lot, because without it won't bring a lot of sound from the string, but you have to have a little bit of nail.

H.G.M. Other opinions that I've heard from people of that epoch logically were not favorable, but it's good what you have declared. Many people say that students who were going to study with your father, many already had a basis, and that he gave them the final touch or in other words he ended up rounding off their technique. There were many students like that, since the beginning he formed very few guitarists.

B.P. Yes, I understand what you're trying to say... and some yes, they came with the teachings of other professors, then he tried to polish them in his manner. Like that yes, a quantity of students came to the Academia, and many that didn't know anything, and he taught them from the beginning, since they picked up the guitar. I can't tell you exactly which one of those or of the others. For example, Mallo Lopez came from other professors, not from one but from various. Well he took her on....! Ah! One, I believe, I'm not sure either, we'll have to look it up in the *Diccionario*.... It was Celia Rodríguez Boqué, which picked it up when she was very small, he made her, and he formed her.

H.G.M. He formed her from the beginning.

B.P. Yes, he formed her from the beginning. Yes, yes, she came many times. All of them more or less had a basis, something they had learned with their professors, but it looks like my father corrected them, he did that for them. And later I did, Yes, I picked it up without knowing anything from any one. He taught me, and that is important as well. What do I owe this to?

H.G.M. Prat had very distinguished students principally women: Irma Haydeé Perazzo, Maria Luisa Anido, Consuelo Mallo Lopez, Maria Angélica Funes, etc. etc. those students before, and after your father had died, they had until the end of their careers generations and generations of disciples and they never told them that their maestro was...Domingo Prat.

B.P. !! Ah!! ! Very mysterious! I don't know why? Sincerely, because it's a shame, firstly, logically it's a shame that for all the work he did with them, they would have had to speak about which their maestro was who their professor was. If they didn't, I don't know why it would be. Sincerely..... I don't know, it's strange for example: I didn't have many students but of those I had, I taught them, and I spoke of my father, and of Prat and from there his methods. Now, they were taught by the method of the Academia, I believe so, that would top it off. The study was based on the study that they had done in the Academia.

You mean that they didn't speak of Prat?

H.G.M. Yes, in their career, which was, important in their contribution, etc., who was in the History of the Rio de la Plata.

B.P. Yes, it's a shame, because some of these people who weren't with us, have let go of this or that student who could have become distinguished, and they don't know, they ignore the procedure of the work of this man, who was my father. !! How he worked with the guitar!! It was his life.

H.G.M. Tell me about your mother, she was born in 1900. You've told me about the teachings of your father, of Pujol and I remember in our talk that you said she knew Tárrega. She was born in 1900 and Tárrega died in 1909, your mother was just a little girl....

B.P. Yes, I don't know in what moment she could've met him, or where it took place. The relationship might have come about such as: Tárrega, had a great protector of the guitar, a great aficionado who was in Barcelona, Léon Farré, the same surname as my mother, but not related. He protected Tárrega a lot, and Tárrega would visit Leon Farré...and how my mother was an aspiring beginner.... But, I don't know she was only nine when Tárrega died.

H.G.M. Of course, she was very small.

B.P. Yes, she was just a child...

H.G.M. She ... What did she comment on about Tárrega?

B.P. She remembered the performances of the guitar, but the performances weren't of Tárrega, they would've been of Leon Farré.

H.G.M. !! Ah!! !! Ah!!...

B.P. And there she would have seen Tárrega, now how many times did she see him?... I know she went with her brothers, because they all liked the guitar very much. She had four brothers, except my Uncle Angel, the others, one played the bandurria another the mandolina, they all played string instruments, there my mother grew to like the guitar. And from there comes, I don't know if it's confusion or that they met Tárrega, and that they saw him there. And it must have stayed in her mind, that memory because she was at that young age. And I'm telling you of things now, of when she was 8 or 9 years old, those that are quite a live in my memory. Then my mother had related to me in the same instance the presence of Tárrega and that of Leon Farré, and of the intimate performances that these men had done. It appears not as copying, but the style of Tárrega's reunions in his home that brought the guitarists that wished to go at specified hours, on specific days to listen to the guitar.

And she also said: I tell you because she told me so, that as well at times and many times in fact, they were attended by great guitarists: Sainz de la Maza, Josefina Robledo, etc..... Segovia came, but not very often, he showed up with a lot of pride, haughty, as we would say here. With her, he was always affectionate, because of the difference of age. When he would see her, he hugged her and would say to her in French: '!! Oh, Mi Petit Carméncita!!' (Little Carmén), that I know, things like that sometimes one can confuse, but that I remember well.

H.G.M. Did your mother form a student that became distinguished?

B.P. No, she had a small group of very beautiful students, because she was named professor to a very aristocratic association, that would have been in that epoch, maybe 1927, 1928, take into account that I was very young...what was it called?... wait a minute.... Association of....Argentina Women's Club, it could be? ...

A sketch of Carmén Farré de Prat by Dr. Samuel Mallo Lopez done in 1929.

Archive: Blanca Prat

H.G.M. Consejo de Mujeres de La Argentina, something like that...

B.P. It could be that, it was very select, all the young girls of the high society, and she had a group that sometimes played in the parties that were held in the same Association, reunions that they had. But to present a student to the public, no.

H.G.M. And of the aspect of your mother as a composer, what can you say about that?

B.P. She had a good moment, it looks, like she was inspired in her youth, and the life always filled with music of the Academia, she made, but always of the simple type, easy pieces, that she sang a lot with the guitar, songs that were stylistic of the country.

H.G.M. What were the song titles?

B.P. "Billiken", "Piniña", there's one *"Cantos Argentinos"* that has lyrics, and others.

H.G.M. You told me the rights of the *Diccionario de Guitarristas* of your father, were sold to England? .....

B.P. Yes, yes, my mother sold the rights. Ricordi had them and by the involvement of this publisher they passed to England, it must be an important publisher there. Yes, it was a shame... it was a shame and not a shame because she did it, not with the idea of wealth, she gave up the rights precisely so that it could be published sometime, it would be known, to continue making this which once it was out of print, it wasn't published again. The years passed, and it wasn't published, due to the cost that would arise, everything had to be together, it would cost an enormous amount to publish a book such as that, it was held up, it wasn't published. Except for the publisher in North America (Matanya Ophee) that did it. Didn't you tell me that you believe it was published in Japan?

Blanca Prat on New Year's Eve 1995, December 31, 1994.

Blanca Prat died in May of 2013.

H.G.M. I have understood that it is I'm not sure.

B.P. I hope, I hope, as a work of the guitar, without speculation of wealth,!! for the guitar!!

H.G.M. In closing this conversation, as a golden brooch, of this beautiful dialogue with you I would like you to define, as the first impression, of the personality of your father.

B.P. As you just have used the word, he had a great personality. He was a man that loved the guitar to death, it was his life, and he dedicated all his hours and his days to form students to be able to bring the best out of the guitar. He was a man very direct, very thorough, with a great character, yes that, I can assure you. For me he was a great maestro and I tell you personally, for me, as he taught me and as I could triumph in only a few years, I owe it all to him.

H.G.M. Thank you very much, I invite you to say goodbye.

B.P. Of course, it's been a pleasure Mr. García Martínez, to converse with you and tell you things that I hadn't thought I was going to say. Sincerely. I have recalled many old times, because I have my best years over with.

!! Many thanks!!

H.G.M. !! Thank you for receiving me!!!.

Interview with **Luisa Camacho**,
daughter of Uruguayan / Argentine luthier Rodolfo Camacho Viera 1887-1973
and his son-in-law **Luis Mendoza**
in José C. Paz, Province of Buenos Aires
on August 8, 2001 by Héctor García Martínez.

We find ourselves in the home of the married couple Mendoza-Camacho. Mrs. Luisa Camacho, daughter of the distinguished Uruguayan-Argentine luthier Rodolfo Camacho Viera with whom we are going to remember works, savory historical anecdotes about her loved one.

H.G.M.: Mrs. Luisa Camacho, where was your father born and secondly when did he begin his artisan work? He began here in Argentina or in Uruguay?

L.C.: My father was born in Uruguay and he began his artisan work here in Argentina. He liked that craft and....well, he dedicated himself to it .....

H.G.M.: Did he begin by building guitars? According to my understanding he began in the National Congress making.... What work did he do in the National Congress?

L.C.: He did cabinetry works, including the railing of a stairway that is still in the Basilica of Lujan (Province of Buenos Aires).

H.G.M.: That fact you gave me is golden .....

L.C.: It's still in the church in Lujan, I believe that it's on the second floor, not on the first floor where the parishioners come through, it's in the upper part. I believe the railing has been kept there. It's a wooden railing.

H.G.M.: Is that the only important work he did in cabinetry?

L.C.: I believe so, because he commented to me about it, he did various jobs.

H.G.M.: For example?

L.C.: Well, various jobs in the beginning he worked in one of the largest furniture manufacturers and later he was to be dedicated to lutherie.

H.G.M.: How did he arrive at making musical instruments? Was he a musician?

L.C.: He played a little guitar, he liked the instrument, and he was practicing its construction, studying the methods to make them. He was enjoying it, and was making them with the help of my mother; she was a good collaborator with him.

H.G.M.: Did he have a maestro in respect to lutherie or did he begin by himself?

Luis Mendoza (son-in-law): No, he always commented to us when the family was together, that he was a profound investigator and very studious. He ended the days of his life investigating, studying. I don't remember in those moments that he might have had a maestro. His uncles were from the Canary Islands, Spain, I believe they were great cabinetmakers and his father as well. His contact with them allowed him to learn the secret of high-grade cabinetry. He worked here in the furniture manufacturing plants where they did artisan works for very wealthy people and he was always inquisitive about lutherie.

I believe, remotely that he had someone in the beginning that guided him but sincerely I don't remember those moments neither can I affirm it. I tell you that he was a constant investigator and had a great passion for the secrets of lutherie.

He had the wood stored for years and years, with an admirable constancy. He would grab the top of a guitar or the back, he held it delicately up in a position and by giving it a little tap made the wood sound and said to the musician "this instrument will give whatever note".... At times the guitarist or violinist continued to doubt. When at times this artist returned from a tour and tried out the instrument and said: 'look maestro it's an amazing thing that it gave the phenomenon that you said here'...

Of course, he worked on various violins, some Stradivarius' he had to open up and repair them. He also worked on some Stradivarius cellos as well. He made notes about everything. The violins he constructed were made with all the technique that had been employed by Stradivari and after a lot of investigation he encountered how to dissolve the varnish that he said was of amber.

When he was finishing a violin, the day before he would remove all the dust from the work area, to clean and wash the area where he would apply the finish, he did this along with his wife, and they would look to see that there wasn't one bit of dust in the workshop, then would he put on the first coat of varnish. After which he would let it carefully dry and put it in a showcase that was a meter tall by a half meter wide and there laid the violin so it wouldn't get dust on it. He would let it sit two, three, four days up to a week and later add a second coat. The he would leave it for various months and when he considered it dry, he gave it a luster with a fine paste, with a material he had. After he would string it up, put on the bridge, the soul, as with the cello, with care trying to get the best result possible to come out.

It was amazing to watch him work.

H.G.M.: How did he derive the making of violins, did he begin making them or was it making guitars initially?

L.C.: No, first he began with guitars.

H.G.M.: And how did he begin making the violins?

L.C.: As my husband said, they brought him violins to fix, and that opened up the desire for investigation and there was born the enthusiasm for constructing those instruments.

H.G.M.: I see here photos of distinguished violinists, that are photos with dedications, do you remember what violinists came to Camacho's workshop?

L.C.: There was Henry Szeryng, we went with my father and a friend of his to one of Henry's concerts. Other violinists I don't remember because ..... So many years have passed.....Andrés Dalmao as well came to the workshop.... though I never met him .....

Luis Mendoza: .... "He had violins made by my father-in-law" ......(Dalmao)

And it had given cases where great guitarists appeared in the workshop of Camacho with great interpreters of the violin, and my father-in-law understood there by their prompting that if the guitarists could have an instrument that would satisfy their necessities, they also desired that he come to grips with the construction of the violin and would discover it's secrets. Because those musicians needed good instruments as well. On the basis of that he read a lot and investigated Stradivari. Therefore, he studied and was passionate for the construction of violins that were convincing for the artists.

H.G.M.: Do you remember the anecdotes he told you about Agustín Barrios? Did he like the Paraguayan very much?

L.M.: Yes, that Paraguayan, he spent a lot of time in the home and stayed till the late hours of the evening. Barrios was an artist, apart from being a musician he was a great poet. And as such my father-in-law had written, he had written poetry and had some very beautiful verses....

H.G.M.: !!! Ah!!!......Yes?

2562

L.M.: My father-in-law had won prizes in poetry contests. So that with Barrios he understood well, he got to know the great poets with him .....

H.G.M.: Don't you remember when he met Barrios?

L.M.: No, no but I believe it must have been around 1920 or 1925, vaguely I remember ....

Now, I'm going to show you clearly of the personality and of the noble heart of Agustín Barrios. In one occasion my father-in-law told me, that he was going through some tough times economically and Agustín Barrios that was totally kind, totally from the heart, completely noble, without saying a word he took off a gold ring that he had and gave it to my father-in-law who didn't want to accept it. Barrios told him: 'No, brother I give it to you from my heart, if it serves as something to help you resolve your problem, here it's yours.' Barrios was a great person apart from being a great artist......

H.G.M.: Did he tell you another anecdote of Barrios? Experiences that they might have had together? ....

L.M.: No, I don't remember so much in detail of that, well yes Barrios told him of his tours and his concerts. They spoke of the goodness of the instrument, that went everywhere with him, it could take on any music, classical music of a high level and that the instrument responded.

Agustín Barrios from the article written by Segundo N. Contreras in the *Revista de la Guitarra* issue No. 14 of September 1946. The sketch of the maestro is by C. P. Dominguez

Through Barrios, Camacho got to know many important people. I believe if I'm not mistaken Martin Gil, the well-known astronomer, and the Paraguayan artist introduced him. Martin Gil had a guitar made by my father-in-law.

H.G.M.: Did he tell you anything in particular about the personality of Martin Gil?

L.M.: Yes, yes, he shared many moments with him. I have right here an opinion, printed on a typewriter by Martin Gil, an opinion about the Camacho guitars.

H.G.M.: Did he tell you something about Segovia?

L.M.: Yes, yes, my father-in-law commented to us about Segovia that he wasn't an easy person to convince, he didn't waste his time, and he was an extremely busy man.

I don't remember who it was that introduced him to Segovia, maybe through one of those great personalities with whom he was associated. Surely someone commented to him that here in Argentina there was a great luthier, one of those persons that made the Camacho guitar known to Segovia.

When Segovia first heard about him, right away he wanted to get to know my father-in-law and then they set up an interview in the Hotel Continental where my father-in-law brought one of his guitars. Later when Segovia came during other tours, I don't know if it was in 1934, that was the first time they got together or if it was the second time when they met. It was when Segovia emitted his favorable opinion about the Camacho guitars.

H.G.M.: Did Segovia visit the Camacho workshop?

L.M.: No, he never was in the workshop; the encounters were in the hotel where Segovia stayed. I believe I've got a photo sitting over there, I don't know where it was taken with Segovia and other personalities with him, but among them, is Camacho Viera.

H.G.M.: In this moment we will read an opinion of Segovia, edited in a label of this luthier, it says among other things, more or less such: "The Camacho Viera guitar is the best instrument to have passed through my hands". That is what Segovia said.

About personalities, works, anecdotes, etc. for example of Martin Gil, didn't he tell you something?

L.M.: Yes, he told us about these personalities that he had known and that they owned instruments made by him. But any anecdote in particular I don't remember.

H.G.M.: And yourself, you might have met distinguished figures that came to the Camacho Viera workshop once you knew your father-in-law? Who do you remember aside from Lucio Nuñez?

L.M.: The Paraguayan Sila Godoy....... the great Sila Godoy. And that other great guitarist of Central America from....

L.C.: Eduardo Falu as well.

L.M.: Yes, yes, but no, I was referring to the great artist .... I don't remember...the great Alirio Diaz.

H.G.M.: You met him?

L.M.: Yes, yes........

H.G.M.: Tell me about him.

L.M.: Yes, I'll tell you about when he came to the workshop.

H.G.M.: What remembrances do you have of Alirio Diaz?

L.M.: !!! Sure!!! I don't know whom he came with, I don't remember. My father-in-law......I laughed.... On one occasion he grabbed a straightedge and he showed Alirio a guitar and another one he was constructing. That man was engrossed with the guitar.....My father-in-law followed by explaining the technique, the development of the construction and Alirio Diaz, told him: 'I hear you, I hear you, but let me play a little bit for you'.

He picked an instrument and it was an extraordinary thing!! Extraordinary!! I lack the words to tell you what he did. And when he finished, he said 'Those works can't be played, without this guitar'.

With Lucio Nuñez we saw him, we saw him, he was a technician, very assured, an amazing unfolding. An extraordinary thing!!! Great artist, Alirio Diaz!!!

Like him others came: Maria Luisa Anido, Irma Haydeé Perrazo, Irma Costanzo and others.

H.G.M.: And what can you tell me about Sila Godoy?

L.M.: He was in the home of Ernesto Castañera with the best guitar my father-in-law could make. That guitar accompanied him all over Europe on a concert tour that Sila Godoy gave. When he came back from the tour, my father-in-law had finished another guitar, and it was already strung up and he was playing it, but he kept the other one. Lucio Nuñez, Ernesto Castañera and Pablo Anapios all said, 'For us, that is the best guitar that Sila Godoy has had'.

Sila frequented our home a lot over many years like he was a part of the family. He was here for hours and hours in our home, he came, he studied, he did everything he had to do, and in our home, he ate, he took coffee, I don't know where he was going... he was attached to my father-in-law. And he played, he played, and later became friends with Lucio Nuñez and Pablo Anapios.

Dr. Alberto also visited our home quite a bit; he would come with Sila Godoy, who was a good friend of his.

H.G.M.: Was Dr. Alberto also Paraguayan?

L.C.: Yes, they were both Paraguayan.

L.M.: I don't know, is Sila Godoy (1921-) is still alive?

H.G.M.: I understand that he's alive, he's about 90 years old if I'm not mistaken, or close to that age. How would you define the personality of Sila Godoy?

(Sila Godoy (December 4, 1919–September 2, 2014 R.O.)

L.M.: I remember Sila as being very focused on what he was doing. He wasn't an outgoing person he was introverted. He opened up eventually he was very measured. But in his art, he was one of the greatest guitarists given to America.

H.G.M.: Do you remember the repertoire he had? Was his repertoire more Paraguayan than classical or the inverse of that?

L.M.: You should know that he played all of the works of Barrios: *Danza Paraguaya, Las Abejas*, etc., he played superbly the music of Villa Lobos as well, he gave it real life, I think because of Sila, Villa Lobos became known in the world.

H.G.M.: Or Agustín Barrios?

L.M.: Villa Lobos and Barrios, for whom he was passionate, he put the music of Agustín Barrios where it belonged. And his music has been played around the world. I believe that Segovia played.......

H.G.M.: It's that I found out that Segovia never played any works of Agustín Barrios .....

Did you personally maintain dialogues with Alirio Diaz? Did you exchange words?

L.M.: Alirio like so many others came to the workshop attracted by the guitars, by the art, by the instruments, etc. When he came to our home, my mother-in-law was a great woman, making some delicious noodles. I don't know if it was mid-day when they came, they stayed to dine and passed many hours. And us, rather than speak with them, we were only listeners to what they conversed about with my father-in-law, about the questions of guitars, the violins, the tours they made. We have known great artists, one would vibrate the string up and down, to see and hear personalities interpreting on the guitar weekly.

When Camacho died, the other day a gentleman came I don't remember his surname, I don't know if, he was the carat of Alirio Diaz. He came from Venezuela as well, because he had seen Alirio Diaz's guitar and he came looking for a guitar, Lucio Nuñez had helped him, he located the workshop through him. He stayed for a long time. There was a guitar that was built for a young lady player in Rosario (Province of Santa Fe) that had already been paid for. And that man had paid some money, some money,.....and because he couldn't take the guitar, this person was in a bad mood. Because he said, 'I had the idea to tour the world, with that guitar'. Then Lucio Nuñez told him, my father-in-law couldn't let that happen, 'suppose that this guitar had been made for you, and the young lady came looking for it, to pay for it, to pay Camacho who wouldn't let it be picked up'. Finally, ... he couldn't do it....And he left without a Camacho guitar, because he learned that the constructor had died.

His guitars took 2 to 3 months to make, but when he had an order, he didn't make another at the same time. Then there were the times when he would repair an instrument brought to him by some musician. There were almost never guitars in the workshop because they were sold, just like the violins.

H.G.M.: Individually to you Luisa and to you Luis, I'm going to ask to define the personality of Rodolfo Camacho Viera.

Luisa: And as his daughter what can I say?...... My father was a great personality, very affectionate, very good, he loved his family. He was a man of strong character although with the family he didn't demonstrate it, but he had a strong character. He also loved his friends very much and was true to them.

Luis Mendoza: About his art?

H.G.M.: No about his personality.

L.M.: Look, if you'll permit me to say the history of my father is very long, I have a blurred image of him. Then, what I received from them, from my in-laws I respectfully would say to them "mom" or "dad". In that great man that was *Don* Rodolfo I found my true father. What he had for me personally was profound advice of a person that had lived a very intense life. He had a defined concept about things. At times I've commented with my family or to someone that this man had learned a whole lot and was a great example. He honored me with his friendship.

How did I meet my wife did you ask?

I was with a singer who came to buy a guitar and well, I left with... marrying his daughter (laughter).

H.G.M.: Who was the singer?

L.M.: Alberto Millan, we went to many luthiers and I told him I couldn't go on, that I didn't want to move, I had bought a guitar and he could continue looking. He had visited all the luthiers, because he knew them and was a friend of theirs. And the last place that we went was there down on calle Oro in the Palermo neighborhood in Buenos Aires.

There are obstinate times in life, because I was insisting, he decide on and buy a guitar. And he, I don't know, had some guitar in his hands and said to me: 'Look, let's go to another shop' and we went to that of Camacho.

H.G.M.: Do you remember the themes that Alirio Diaz played in the Camacho workshop? Were they Venezuelan themes or classical?

L.M.: No, Alirio played the music of all the classical composers and contemporaries but he played the music of Agustín Barrios a whole lot, he was a fervent admirer of that composer.

H.G.M.: I heard that your father-in-law told someone, that Agustín Barrios was blocked in Argentina by a representative and since then to be able to call attention to and earn a little more money he began to give concerts in disguise of an American aborigine. Is that true?

L.M.: Yes, my father-in-law told me that, it is so.

H.G.M.: Do you remember the name of that representative?

L.M.: No, I don't remember.

I also remember that he told me one time, that on one occasion Agustín Barrios was on tour in another country, I believe it was in a nation in Central America, he was traveling with other people in an auto and they were passing over a bridge above a river, a bridge from that epoch, that collapsed as the vehicle tried to pass over it, everything fell into the river with the auto, people, the suitcases, the guitar.... They were able to save their lives and the Camacho guitar that Barrios had brought was in the water more or less 3 hours, it was strung up, until someone came along and could help them get out of that trance. The guitar didn't come apart neither was it broken, they got it out of the river, they let it dry out and Barrios was desperate because he had several engagements, he was able to continue giving concerts with that instrument. That is what he told my father-in-law when he returned. (A similar story is told in Richard "Rico" Stover's "Six Silver Moonbeams — The Life and Times of Agustín Barrios" — on page 227 — The Guitars of Barrios-but the guitar is a 1911 Jose Ramírez in 1915 in Uruguay. It was this guitar that Barrios began his recording career with.)

H.G.M.: That was in Central America, I believe......

L.M.: Yes, in Central America, which all lives were saved. I don't know if the chauffeur drove poorly and the vehicle fell into the river. And they lost things and I believe they suffered injuries, and later someone came to rescue them. They were able to remove the guitar from the water after being in the river many hours. Agustín Barrios was very desperate because he had concerts to give. But he was able to rescue the instrument, to dry it as humanly possible and to continue to play it. Therefore, when he returned he said to Camacho: '!!! Look Rodolfo, how noble your instrument is!!!' He told him of the qualities of the guitar he had constructed.

H.G.M.: As well I've heard an anecdote about Barrios, they say he was very much in love and in one occasion he was here in Buenos Aires was passing through the streets in one of those, old horse-drawn carriages, that here they're called *"Mateos"*. And when the tour was finished, he stepped down and left an album containing the forgotten original manuscripts he had been carrying.

L.M.: (Laughter).... it could happen .... of that, I don't have any knowledge.

H.G.M.: Barrios was a very special man.

L.M.: Yes,....yes *Don* Rodolfo spoke of him a whole lot. They had spent many years together. He told me that when he would arrive for concerts Rodolfo had already been advised of the fact, Barrios had sent him letters and told him: 'I haven't even arrived, and I have to go there'...He was almost always visiting him, or Rodolfo would go to the hotel where Barrios was staying. He would give a concert and leave to go onward to another one. But the relations they had were very fluid and tight.

H.G.M.: In what year did Camacho Viera come to Argentina? Do you remember?

L.M.: No, but he came when he was a child.

H.G.M.: !! Ah!! When he was a child, I had believed that he came when he was grown.

L.M.: In one occasion, after he had been residing here, he went to Uruguay to arrange his immigration papers. And he stayed there; he had to do military service. I'm sure it was in the epoch when they had the draft, the 20 years olds more or less, as was done here. So, he stayed there for a while, surely at least a year.

He told us that he had an accident while standing guard in the sentry box. I don't know how the accident happened, I believe he fell and hurt himself with the tip of the bayonet. And he was ill for a while, in the hospital, he had almost slit his throat........

H.G.M.: He had won prizes, including international distinctions, right?

L.M.: Yes, he was awarded the Grand Prize and Golden Medal in Rome, the Grand Prize of Gold in Barcelona, Spain. And he also received the Grand Prize for a guitar he made here in a competition in Buenos Aires.

H.G.M.: Do you remember anything else?

L.M.: Yes, if you'll permit me to tell you a very rich and passionate anecdote. I don't remember, if it was one of those known personalities, or one of those musicians that we've mentioned that we convinced to take the guitar to Spain for the competition. It appears to be Agustín Barrios, or someone at his level, they were having mate, in one moment of the conversation he said: 'Look Rodolfo, I'm going to give you a great surprise: your guitar in Spain came in 10th, there in the cradle of the construction of guitars'.... My father-in-law couldn't believe it, they continued conversing and a while later he said: 'well I'm going to tell you the truth, your guitar came in 7th'. My father-in-law exclaimed: '!! But you!!.... What a thing!!'... Then he told him again: 'Look, to end this I've got to tell you your guitar came in 3rd place'....and lastly he said the real truth: 'Your guitar took the Grand Prize and Gold Medal.' They say that such emotion grabbed Camacho and it produced a child-like man who couldn't stop laughing. He had to go to a doctor because he believed he was going to die. He was even more confused...

H.G.M.: !! What emotion!!

L.M.: He told me the same thing happened, when he discovered the dissolution of amber varnish (Antonio Stradivari's varnish from his inspection of Stradivarius violins and cellos) that he later applied on the violins. That also caused a great emotion, and equally the prize he won in Rome. The diploma says: 'To Mr. Rodolfo Camacho, in the year (1924) at the International Exposition of Guitar', etc, etc. All those diplomas were in frames, and they were shown in an exposition here.

That's all I can say about that great constructor of guitars and person who was my beloved father-in-law Rodolfo Camacho Viera. Nothing more.

H.G.M.: !!! Many thanks to you and your wife!!!

13

The Concerts of Lalyta Almiron in Barcelona and Madrid, in 1931.

By Josep Maria Mangado y Artigas, translation by Randy Osborne

"According to the investigations made in Barcelona about the guitarist Lalyta Almiron (1914-1997), we have been able to document during her stay in Spain in the year 1931, the concert guitarist gave five performances in Barcelona, recording three records for the house of Odeon, and of her stay in Madrid we only know of one concert. Surely, Lalyta Almiron gave some more concerts, as in Barcelona and in the capital of Spain, but as of this moment, these are the only dates we have found.

On the other hand, as in the case of the available newspapers in Barcelona and Madrid of those years they are very scarce, we haven't been able to exhaustively corroborate her stay in the said city, an investigation being necessary in person, that we will leave for another occasion, centering on and expounding the continuation of the information found in the *Condal* city.

LA CONCERTISTA LALYTA ALMIRON SE EMBARCARA MAÑANA PARA EUROPA

En el "Giulio Cesare" se embarcará mañana para Europa, en compañía de su padre el profesor Almirón, la joven concertista argentina de guitarra Lalyta Almirón, de cuyas brillantes dotes técnicas nos hemos ocupado con elogio repetidas veces.

Lalyta Almirón fué un caso asombroso de precocidad musical; desde muy niña poseía absoluto dominio de la guitarra, tanto o más que afamados concertistas europeos; hoy, a la edad de 16 años, se ha iniciado en ella una saludable evolución: si posee, como siempre, una técnica a prueba de las mayores dificultades, si salva sin esfuerzo los pasajes más intrincados, se nota ya el despertar de una musicalidad que mucho promete; desde luego, algo le falta todavía en ese sentido: la comprensión interior de las obras sólo es posible con los años, con la cultura y con la vida; las confesiones que hicieron los grandes maestros al pentagrama, sólo pueden ser comprendidas y luego traducidas por quienes han vivido y han cultivado su espíritu; es decir, de lo que carecen los que se inician en la carrera artística.

La joven concertista argentina, al emprender esta excursión por Europa, en la que se propone visitar Madrid, Barcelona, París, Berlín y otras grandes ciudades del viejo continente, podrá ponerse en contacto con ambientes de cultura superior que ejercerán beneficiosa influencia sobre su espíritu.

This image of the "La Prensa" article of February 17, 1931 is from the archive of Carlos Guevel, a student of Lalyta Almiron.

Coinciding with the departure toward Europe of Lalyta Almiron the Buenos Aires press referred to the happening, publishing on the 17th of February the following note by *"La Prensa"*, Buenos Aires:

The Concert Guitarist Lalyta Almiron embarks for Europe tomorrow.

Tomorrow aboard the *"Giulio Cesare"* Lalyta Almiron will embark for Europe, in the company of her father the professor Almiron, the young Argentine concert guitarist Lalyta Almiron, whose brilliant technical abilities we have written eulogies about repeatedly.

Lalyta Almiron was a case of surprising precocious musicality; since she was a little girl she has possessed the absolute dominion over the guitar, as much or more so than the famous European concert guitarists; today, at the age of 16 years old, it has initiated in her a healthy evolution; if she possesses, as always, a technique to test the most difficulties, if saving without force the most intricate passages, it is noted that the awakening of the musicality of a lot of promise, of course, something that is still lacking in this sense; the internal comprehension of the works that is only possible with time, with the culture and the life; the confessions the great maestros of the sheet music staff have made, only can be comprehended and then translated by who has lived and cultivated its spirit; that is to say, by which they caress those that initiate in the artistic career.

The young Argentine concert guitarist, to take on this excursion to Europe, in which it was proposed to visit Madrid, Barcelona, Paris, Berlin and other great cities of the old continent, she will be able to be put in contact with environments of superior culture that exercise a beneficial influence over her spirit.

Concerts in Barcelona

The first notice we have of the arrival to the city of Barcelona by the guitarist Lalyta Almiron is found in the newspaper *"El Noticero Universal"*, whose music critic was guitarist Alfredo Romea Catalina. The first recital of Lalyta Almiron was a private concert, as a presentation before the press and a group of chosen guests of the Catalan culture; we don't know where this event was held, but only that the critic who wrote about this concert was Romea, who commented:

"About Music — *De Musica*
Lalyta Almiron

In an intimate recital, we have had the occasion to listen to the young and notable Argentine guitarist, Lalyta Almiron, who is accompanied by her father, who also is a guitarist with quite a bit of prestige in Argentina, and she has come to our city to give some concerts.

Miss Almiron, who is almost a little girl, she is only sixteen possesses a great domination over the guitar and an extensive repertoire.

In the intimate session in which we're referring, it was dedicated to a good number of guitarists and aficionados of the poetic instrument, she interpreted works of Sor, Gottschalk, Chopin, Bach, Schumann, Tárrega, etc., and some pages of very characteristic Argentine music, patenting in all of them an easy and abundant mechanism and a plentiful artistic sensibility. The meritorious concert artist obtained the unanimous praise of many that heard her."

(*El Noticero Universal*. Tuesday March 10, 1931. No. 14.760 *Año* XLIV. Page 11).

The father of Lalyta was Bautista Almiron (1879-1932), is a prestigious guitarist, as the critic commented. The work attributed to one such Golchol, surely must refer to Louis Moreau Gottschalk (1829-1869), just a few days earlier, certainly in the concert on the 13th, Lalyta interpreted the *Gran Trémolo* of the mentioned author.

After that recital, her presentation to the public of Barcelona was by the hand of Camila Quiroga (1891-1948), Argentine artist who acted with her company in the Poliorama theater (still in use today) The theater is situated in the popular Ramblas of Barcelona, where Camila had had quite a bit of success.

With the motive of her presentation in public, the announcements of the artistic engagements appeared in many newspapers of the city, as we can read in *"La Vanguardia"* of Wednesday the 11th, of Thursday the 12th and of Friday the 13th:

"Music and Theaters — *Musica y Teatros*

In the Poliorama this week Camila Quiroga offers two revivals, *"Ejemplo de casadas"* (Example of a married couple) and "Con las alas rotas" (With the broken wings) {...}.

In the function of the following Friday evening, the concert artist Lolita {sic} Almiron will give a guitar recital."

(*La Vanguardia*. Wednesday, March 11, 1931 No. 20.919 *Año* L. Page 21).

"Music and Theaters — *Musica y Teatros*

In the Poliorama, in the function of tomorrow night Camila Quiroga will present the Argentine concert guitarist Lalyta Almiron, after the representation of *"Ejemplo de casadas"* (Example of a married couple), that comes being an uninterrupted success.

Lalyta Almiron, will play a most select program and among other compositions, *"Sevilla"* by Albeniz, whose difficulties for guitar are well known."

(*La Vanguardia*. Thursday, March 12, 1931 No. 20.920 *Año* L. Page 19).

"Music and Theaters — *Musica y Teatros*

In the Poliorama, in the function of tomorrow Camila Quiroga offers the revival of the comedy by Emilio Beriss *"Con las alas rotas"* (With the broken wings) {...}. The art of the great-distinguished Argentine artist in this production will seduce the spectator.

In the function of today, Camila Quiroga presents an Argentine concert guitarist Lalyta Almiron, who will play a program, which includes works by Albeniz and Tárrega."

(*La Vanguardia.* Friday, March 13, 1931 No. 20.921 *Año* L. Page 19).

Another informative note we can read is in *"El Dia Grafico"*, of Thursday the 12th, and Friday the 13th:

"The Theater — *El Teatro*
Informative notes

POLIORAMA — In the function of tomorrow, Friday night, Camila Quiroga will present an Argentine concert guitarist Lalyta Almiron, after the representation of *"Ejemplo de casadas"* (Example of a married couple), that comes being an uninterrupted success since the debut of the company.

Lalyta Almiron, will play a most select program and among other important compositions, *"Sevilla"* by the great Albeniz, whose difficulties for guitar are well known."

(*El Dia Grafico.* Thursday, March 12, 1931 No. 4525 *Año* XX Page 6).

"The Theater — *El Teatro*
Informative notes

POLIORAMA — In the function of today, Friday, Camila Quiroga presents us with an Argentine concert guitarist Lalyta Almiron, who will play a magnificent program which includes works by Albeniz and Tárrega."

(*El Dia Grafico.* Friday, March 13, 1931 No. 4526 *Año* XX Page 7).

Some of the latest informative notes that we can read in *"La Razon"*, of Thursday the 12th, and Friday the 13th:

"THEATERS: POLIORAMA — *Teatrales-Poliorama*

In the function of tomorrow, Friday night, Camila Quiroga will present an Argentine concert guitarist Lalyta Almiron, after the representation of *"Ejemplo de casadas"* (Example of a married couple), that comes being an uninterrupted success since the debut of the company.

Lalyta Almiron, will play a most select program and among other important compositions, *"Sevilla"* by the great Albeniz, whose difficulties for guitar are well known."

(*La Razon.* Friday, March 13, 1931 No. 966 *Año* IV Page 4).

"THEATERS: POLIORAMA — Teatrales-Poliorama

In the function of today, Friday, Camila Quiroga presents us with an Argentine concert guitarist Lalyta Almiron, who will play a magnificent program, which includes works by Albeniz and Tárrega."

(*La Razon.* Friday, March 13, 1931 No. 967 *Año* IV Page 4).

They inserted two announcements in the daily press as well. One the day before her performance (1) and the other the day of the presentation. We reproduce here the announcement, in its actual size, from *"El Noticero Universal"*. (2)

The day after the recital various newspapers published critiques over the performance of the Argentine concert artist, we will look at two of them. The first is something brief but very eloquent, it's not signed but surely it must be the guitarist and music critic Alfredo Romea:

"About Music — De Musica
Lalyta Almiron

In the Poliorama theater and following the representation of *"Ejemplo de casadas"* (Example of a married couple), by the company of Camila Quiroga, was presented to the public by this excellent actress, the notable Argentine concert guitarist Lalyta Almiron, who has visited us recently.

With mastery, performing ostentatiously while possessing an exceptional aptitude for a difficult instrument, Miss Almiron interpreted a few *"Vidalitas"* by Sagreras; the *Gran Trémolo* by Gottschalk, *"Sevilla"* by Albeniz and the *"Jota"* by Tárrega and for an encore to correspond to the expressive applause of public consent, the composition titled *"Dolor"* by Padre San Sebastian.

The young concert artist, who is almost a little girl, she is only sixteen, demonstrates with her exquisite labor as to being one of the most enthusiastic and dignified guitarists of the new and brilliant generation, already plentifully abundant, better said, shows as to being one of the most becoming in artistic qualities."

(El Noticero Universal. Saturday, March 14, 1931. No. 14.764, *Año* XLIV, Page11).

(1)　　(El Noticero Universal. Thursday, March 12, 1931. No. 14.762, *Año* XLIV, Page12).
　　　(La Vanguardia. Thursday, March 12, 1931 No. 20.920 *Año* L. Page 19).
　　　(El Dia Grafico. Thursday, March 12, 1931 No. 4525 *Año* XX Page 6).
　　　(Diario de Barcelona, Thursday, March 12, 1931 No. 61 *Año* 140. Page 40).
(2)　　(El Noticero Universal. Friday, March 13, 1931. No. 14.763, *Año* XLIV, Page 6).
　　　(La Vanguardia. Friday, March 13, 1931 No. 20.921 *Año* L. Page 19).
　　　(El Dia Grafico. Friday, March 13, 1931 No. 4526 *Año* XX Page 7).
　　　(Diario de Barcelona, Friday, March 13, 1931 No. 62 *Año* 140. Page 42).

"Music and Theaters — *Musica y Teatros*
Poliorama
The Guitarist Lalyta Almiron

Following the representation of *"Ejemplo de casadas"* (Example of a married couple), the likeable comedy by Carlos Soldevila, carefully translated by Rivas Cherif, by Camila Quiroga and her excellent collaborators that gave an exquisite interpretation, presented last night in the Poliorama was a young Argentine guitarist, Lalyta Almiron, who quickly conquered the congeniality and applause of the public.

What's appreciated most all in Miss Lalyta Almiron, is to have an extraordinary mechanism, that permits her to easily conquer all of the harmonic difficulties. She still is a sensitive artist, but her sensibility will be undoubtedly most intimate, most profound, when her temperament attains plentiful maturity.

With irreproachable technique, with absolute domination of the guitar, she graciously played a few *"Vidalitas"* by Sagreras, the *"Gran Trémolo"* by Gottschalk, *"Sevilla"* by Albeniz and the *"Jota"* with variations by Tárrega.

The applause received by Lalyta Almiron was very warm, as well; they expected an encore, not announced in the program.

Of the young compatriot, that surely will have an occasion soon to confirm her success last night, Camila Quiroga who made the presentation spoke beautiful and worthy phrases." — Z.

(*La Vanguardia*. Saturday, March 14, 1931 No. 20.922 *Año* L. Page 21).

Beginning Tuesday, the 24th, the newspapers of Barcelona inserted an announcement of the upcoming performance of Lalyta Almiron, this time in the Sala Mozart, the announcement appeared daily until the day of the concert. We reproduce here the announcement from *"El Noticero Universal"*: (4)

Besides, they went on to include informative notes of the performance the first day of the above announcement. (5)

(3)   (El Noticero Universal. Wednesday, March 25, 1931. No. 14.773, *Año* XLIV, Page 12).
        (El Noticero Universal. Thursday, March 26, 1931. No. 14.774, *Año* XLIV, Page 5).
        (El Noticero Universal. Friday, March 27, 1931. No. 14.775, *Año* XLIV, Page 12).
        (La Vanguardia. Tuesday, March 24, 1931 No. 20.930 *Año* L. Page 27).
        (La Vanguardia. Wednesday, March 25, 1931 No. 20.931 *Año* L. Page 21).
        (La Vanguardia. Thursday, March 26, 1931 No. 20.932 *Año* L. Page 17).
        (La Vanguardia. Friday, March 27, 1931 No. 20.933 *Año* L. Page 21).
        (La Vanguardia. Saturday, March 28, 1931 No. 20.934 *Año* L. Page 21).
(4)   (El Noticero Universal. Tuesday, March 24, 1931. No. 14.772, *Año*XLIV, Page 14).
(5)   (El Noticero Universal. Tuesday, March 24, 1931. No. 14.772, *Año* XLIV, Page 11).

"About Music — *De Musica*
Lalyta Almiron

This Saturday there will be a recital by the eminent Argentine guitarist Lalyta Almiron, who attained quite a bit of success in the Poliorama theater recently when presented by Camila Quiroga.

She will interpret a program of chosen works by figures such as Sor, Bach, Coste, Mendelssohn, Albeniz, Turina, Moreno Torroba, Padre San Sebastian, Ponce, Llobet and Tárrega."

(*El Noticero Universal*. Tuesday, March 24, 1931. No. 14.772, *Año* XLIV, Page 11).

"This Saturday there will be a recital by the eminent Argentine guitarist Lalyta Almiron, who attained quite a bit of success in the Poliorama theater recently when presented by Camila Quiroga.

She will interpret a program of chosen works by figures such as Sor, Bach, Coste, Mendelssohn, Albeniz, Turina, Moreno-Torroba, P. San Sebastian, Ponce, Llobet and Tárrega."

(*La Vanguardia*. Tuesday, March 24, 1931 No. 20.930 *Año* L. Page 27).

Tuesday, the 24th, the guitarist performed across the radio waves of *Radio Barcelona* and that same day the newspapers of Barcelona informed of her performance on the radio and published an announcement of the next performance of Lalyta Almiron, Saturday the 26th, in the Sala Mozart.

(3)   (El Noticero Universal. Wednesday, March 25, 1931. No. 14.773, *Año* XLIV, Page 12).
       (El Noticero Universal. Thursday, March 26, 1931. No. 14.774, *Año* XLIV, Page 5).
       (El Noticero Universal. Friday, March 27, 1931. No. 14.775, *Año* XLIV, Page 12).
       (La Vanguardia. Tuesday, March 24, 1931 No. 20.930 *Año* L. Page 27).
       (La Vanguardia. Wednesday, March 25, 1931 No. 20.931 *Año* L. Page 21).
       (La Vanguardia. Thursday, March 24, 1931 No. 20.932 *Año* L. Page 17).
       (La Vanguardia. Friday, March 24, 1931 No. 20.933 *Año* L. Page 21).
       (La Vanguardia. Saturday, March 24, 1931 No. 20.934 *Año* L. Page 21).
(4)   (El Noticero Universal. Tuesday, March 24, 1931. No. 14.772, *Año* XLIV, Page 14).
(5)   (El Noticero Universal. Tuesday, March 24, 1931. No. 14.772, *Año* XLIV, Page 11).

This photo of Rosita Rodes (Left) and Lalyta Almiron (Right) taken on calle Canuda No. 26 in Barcelona on March 10, 1931. Rosita Rodes was a Miguel Llobet student who recorded for Odeon beginning in the late 1920's. In Lalyta's hands is a Francisco Simplico guitar she used for the April 9, 1931 concert.

This photo is courtesy of Carlos Guevel, a student of Lalyta Almiron.

"RADIODIFUSION
Today's programs
Radio Barcelona
{....}.
    10:20 PM Guitar recital by Lalyta Almiron
    10:40 Plectrum instrument concert by Mandolin Orchestra"

        (*Diario de Barcelona,* Tuesday, March 24, 1931 No. 71 Año 140. Page 42).

"CARNET DE T.S.H.
Today's radio programs March 24, 1931

    RADIO BARCELONA, 349m.—
{...} 10:20 Recital by Lalyta Almiron. Dolor, San Sebastian. Cadiz, Albeniz. Estudio, Coste. Sueño,
Tárrega. — 10:40 Concert by Philharmonic Mandolin Orchestra {...}"

        (*La Vanguardia.* Tuesday, March 24, 1931 No. 20.930 *Año* L. Page 13).

    In this epoch, the radio station published a bulletin with details of the weekly programs. We see the announcement of the recital of the Argentine guitarist:

"Programming
Week of March 23-29
Tuesday, 24th {...}

GUITAR
    10:20 Recital by the concert artist Lalyta Almiron. *"Dolor",* (P.A. de San Sebastian); *"Cadiz",* (Albeniz);
"Estudio", (Coste) *"Sueño",* (Tárrega).
    10:40 Concert by Philharmonic Mandolin Orchestra {...}"

        (*Radio Barcelona,* official bulletin, March 21, 1931 *Año* IX Page 21).

    The next notice we find in the press is a note in the *"Diario de Barcelona"* commenting on the next concert of Lalyta Almiron in the Sala Mozart:

"ABOUT MUSIC — *De Musica*
THE GUITARIST LALYTA ALMIRON.

    The young Argentine guitarist Lalyta Almiron, presented with great success by Camila Quiroga, celebrates her only concert in the Sala Mozart tomorrow night at 10:00 PM.

    This celebrated artist is already well appreciated in South America, where she comes from, and her performances have drawn deserved praises from all of the music critics.

    The concert this Saturday will be the only one to be celebrated in our city, to be included in the program are works by authors of antiquity and modern pieces as well."

        (*Diario de Barcelona,* Friday, March 27, 1931 No. 74 *Año* 140. Page 14).

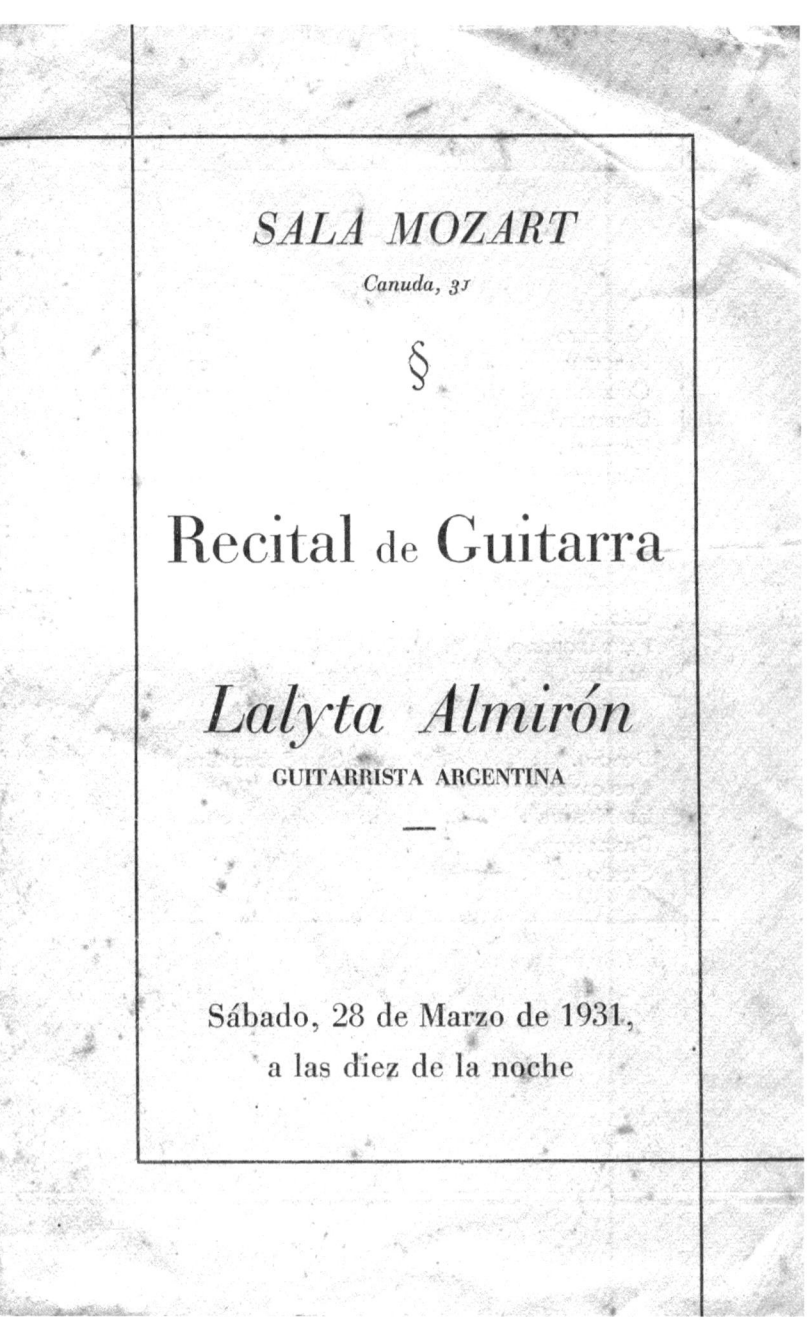

SALA MOZART

Canuda, 31

§

Recital de Guitarra

Lalyta Almirón

GUITARRISTA ARGENTINA

—

Sábado, 28 de Marzo de 1931,
a las diez de la noche

Saturday, March 28, 1931, 10:00 PM concert program by Lalyta Almiron at the Sala Mozart.

This concert program is courtesy of Carlos Guevel, a student of Lalyta Almiron.

We see in the back of the program a fragment of the press clipping published the day before the Argentine guitarist's departure, to which we had translated at the beginning of this article.

PROGRAMA

I

Minuetto	Sor
Preludio	Bach
Courante	»
Bourrée.	»
Estudio	Coste
Variaciones sobre un tema de Mozart . .	Sor

II

Canzoneta	Mendelsshonn
Cádiz	Albéniz
Fandanguillo . . .	Turina
Allegro. . . .	Moreno Torroba

III

Dolor . . . del padre San Sebastián	
Dos cancionces mejicanas . .	Ponce
El Mestre	Llobet
Danza mora . . .	Tárrega
Sueño	»

The only non-European composer she played works by was Manuel Ponce, the debut of his delightful *"Dos Cancionces Mexicanas"*.

This concert program is courtesy of Carlos Guevel, a student of Lalyta Almiron.

Finally, we see some musical critiques appeared in the press commenting on the mentioned concert:

"Latest information from Barcelona — *Ultimas informaciones de Barcelona*
LALYTA ALMIRON

The young Argentine guitarist Lalyta Almiron presented last night in the Sala Mozart a program composed of works by Sor, Bach, Coste, Mendelssohn, Albeniz, Turina, Moreno Torroba, P. San Sebastian, Ponce, Llobet and Tárrega.

The qualities demonstrated by the beginning guitarist, taking into account her very young age, one can foresee a brilliant future for her artistic career with so much of the enterprise already begun.

The facility that she actually possesses, matured by her study and the experience that just puts the final touch on her art, is already notable, and deserves full attention.

The audience awarded the labor of Lalyta Almiron with quite a bit of applause, and as well, she received a gift of a bouquet of flowers." — M.

(*Diario de Barcelona,* Sunday, March 29, 1931 No. 76 Año 140. Page 38).

"Music and Theaters — *Musica y Teatros*
Sala Mozart
LALYTA ALMIRON

Another young artist, whose success isn't elusive, Lalyta Almiron, the Argentine guitarist, applauded only a few nights ago in the Poliorama theater, returned last night to be honored in the Sala Mozart.

Lalyta Almiron dominates the guitar from which she obtains beautiful sonorities, even in the most difficult passages, and when she uses her youthful enthusiasm, that in certain moments draw to the alteration of the movements, her interpretations, already very firm, take on a more intense life.

The art of the guitarist Lalyta Almiron imposed to those in attendance, which applauded and congratulated her cordially."

(*La Vanguardia.* Sunday, March 29, 1931 No. 20.935 Año L. Page 30).

"ABOUT MUSIC — *De Musica*
THE GUITARIST LALYTA ALMIRON.

The young and meritorious Argentine guitarist Lalyta Almiron, whose much applause conquered recently in the Poliorama, has again performed publicly. This time it had been in the Sala Mozart and in front of a not very many of the public, but one devoted to the beautiful instrument that elevated Fernando Sor to his glory and that which means a lot to the very notable cultivators in Barcelona.

Lalyta Almiron offered us a program in which some of the transcriptions were of a good number of works from the guitar's own repertoire, that always bring the best result and let the poetic instrument's emotive sonorities shine.

The young guitarist played them all with great brilliance, playing ostentatiously with an easy mechanism and abundantly thereof.

In Lalyta Almiron exists, without a doubt, the impetus of a great guitarist. She drew a very warm applause and was obligated to amplify the program with a few compositions, among them a "Vidalita" that she interpreted in an exquisite manner with an unsurpassable style."

(*El Noticero Universal.* Monday, March 30, 1931. No. 14.777, Año XLIV, Page 13).

Three months after the performance of Lalyta Almiron in the Sala Mozart, the *Revista Musical Catalana* (Catalan Musical Review / magazine), informs itsss readers of the mentioned concert and others done in this hall in the season 1930-31, let's look at the part that corresponds to Lalyta and another guitarist:

"Musical Movement — *Movimiento Musical*
BARCELONA
SALA MOZART: DIVERSE CONCERTS

In full activity during the present season, this hall has welcomed diverse artists that have been heard by their respective audiences with an attention that demonstrated the interest that their interpretations had awakened.

Two guitarists made themselves felt: *Lolita* (sic) Almiron, Argentine artist, and Francisco Alfonso; that have won among us an excellent reputation. The program of Miss Almiron offered scarcely anything new; they were pieces already well known by Sor, Coste, Moreno Torroba, Llobet and Tárrega and transcriptions of Bach, Mendelssohn, Albeniz, Turina, P. Donostia and in their debut *"Dos Canciones Mexicanas"* by Ponce.

It was impossible attend this recital, I expect on another occasion more favorable to get to know the talent for which in her country the young Argentine guitarist is renowned.

Francisco Alfonso left the audience well satisfied with his excellent demonstration of his refined art. The program was in good taste; one entire part dedicated to Bach; of the modern repertoire he chose compositions by Villa-Lobos, Broqua, Ponce, Turina and Pujol. The ovations that were dedicated to him were vibrant and abundant. {...}". — S.

(*Revista Musical Catalana*. June-1931 No. 330 Año XXVIII Page 222).

Her last documented performance in Barcelona was on the 9th of April 1931 in the *"Salo d' audicions de Ferran Gausente"*. In the said concert she returned to repeat the program she had offered in the Sala Mozart, indicating that she would play a guitar by Barcelona guitar maker: Simplicio.

The Barcelona concert program by Lalyta Almiron on April 9, 1931, 10 PM at the *"Salo d' audicions de Ferran Gausente"*.

This concert program is courtesy of Carlos Guevel, a student of Lalyta Almiron.

Though the text of the cover is in Catalan, the press clipping opposite the titles is in Castellano (Spanish).

LA PRENSA, Buenos Aires
Febrero 17-1931

Lalyta Almirón fué un caso asombroso de precocidad musical; desde muy niña poseía absoluto dominio de la guitarra, tanto o más que afamados concertistas europeos; hoy a la edad de 16 años, se ha iniciado en ella una saludable evolución.

PROGRAMA

I

MINUET	Sor
PRELUDI	Bach
COURANTE	»
BOURRÉE	»
ESTUDI	Coste
VARIACIONS SOBRE UN TEMA DE MOZART	Sor

II

CANÇONETA	Mendelsshonn
CÁDIZ	Albéniz
FANDANGUILLO	Turina
ALLEGRO	Moreno Torroba

III

DOLOR	del pare Sant Sebastià
DUES CANÇONS MEXICANES	Ponce
EL MESTRE	Llobet
DANÇA MORA	Tàrrega
SOMNI	»

This concert was the same program as the success at the Sala Mozart just a couple of weeks earlier.

This concert program is courtesy of Carlos Guevel, a student of Lalyta Almiron.

During her stay in Barcelona of a little more than a month Lalyta took the opportunity to record 6 songs for Odeon. Those discs of 78 RPM, include each one, a work on each side:

Casa Odeon. Guitarra: Lalyta Almiron

203.331 a. Estudio brillante-Tárrega.
       b. Nocturno-Chopin.

183.249 a. Sueño-Tárrega.
       b. Torre Bermeja-Albeniz.

183.338 a. Zambra-Ross. (In most concert programs this is written as Zapateado by Ross. R.O.)
       b. Danza mora-Tárrega.

Of these three discs, a copy of the second one of the above list, is kept, in the *Biblioteca de Catalunya*.

The critic A. Fernández Escobés wrote after the tour of Barcelona and Madrid, in the Revista Blanca, published in the Catalan capital:

"Through Barcelona first, Sala Mozart, Teatro Poliorama, later through Madrid — Ateneo — the magical guitar of the eminent Argentine concert guitarist, pretty as a garnet carnation, is already distinguished in the field of the Llobets and Segovias at just sixteen years of age. The critics have favored her, to the winds the ribbons of fame.

In the hands of LALYTA ALMIRON, animated of an extraordinary mechanism, it ennobles the guitar, it purifies, its sublime..."

As well the famous guitarist Miquel Llobet--Catalan spelling of the well-known Castellano pronunciation of Miguel Llobet (1878-1938) he dedicated a photo with these words:

"To the most notable guitarist LALYTA ALMIRON, with all my kindness and admiration."

These last two items are from the archive of Carlos Guevel, a student of Lalyta Almiron, but without dates attached to them.

This photo of Lalyta Almiron was taken during her stay in Barcelona in March-April of 1931.

This photo is from the archive of Carlos Guevel, a student of Lalyta Almiron,

Concert in Madrid

After her performances in Barcelona the Argentine guitarist Lalyta Almiron set off for Madrid where she gave a concert at the Ateneo of this city on Wednesday April 29, 1931. The daily *A.B.C.* informed its readers the day before of the upcoming concert:

Tomorrow, Wednesday, two recitals are announced, one of piano, in the Circulo de Bellas Artes, by the popular Carmencita Alvarez, who will play a program of works by Scarlatti, Mozart, Debussy, Falla, Usandizaga and Infante, and another, in the Ateneo, in it there will be a presentation of the guitarist Lalyta Almiron, who will interpret a program of works by Sor, Schumann, Moreno Torroba, Granados, Padre San Sebastian, Bach, Burgmüller, Tárrega and Albeniz. — C.

According to Domingo Prat, in his *Diccionario de Guitarristas* (p.22), this concert was favorable that:
....showing the triumph of her art and establishing as a definitive manner with the successes achieved in severe capacities such as the Ateneo where she obtained the most resonant of triumphs according to the critic of the Madrid daily *"A. B. C."* that he dedicated spontaneously full pages....

And effectively, as Prat commented, the daily ABC published the critique of the concert the following day, along with a kind caricature of the Argentina guitarist:

"The guitarist Lalyta Almiron, in the Ateneo"

"In the hall of festivities of the Ateneo yesterday the presentation of the young Lalita Almiron was made, who came from her country, Argentina, with the renown of an excellent guitarist.

In a few years we have attended the interesting recitals of Argentine artists: Berta Singerman, the admirable reciter of poetry; the wife of Cabrera, the most notable interpreter of folkloric songs, *criollas* and pre-Columbian that she herself accompanies with lute or analogous instruments, but of the popular and *pamperos* origin and construction, and this Lalyta, beautiful creature of sixteen years, whose delicate hands make the guitar a clavichord with the fine sonorities of the barren eighteenth century.

To count the chronicles of her triumphs that at the age of nine she gave concerts in the most important cities of Argentina. Recently her guitaristic labor was toasted by the public of Barcelona and she has achieved a complete success. We sincerely believe that this evening the achievement before the grand public of the concerts, that which, free of political preoccupations and of artistic prejudice, attends the musical reunions to be delighted, if it is a recital of guitar, with the art of the Sors, the Tárregas and the Llobets, interpreted by the Segovias, the Forteas, the Sorias, the Sainz de la Mazas.

The impression which the graceful artist gives is that the intuition and temperament make an exquisite performer of her which the exquisiteness of the guitaristic literature appears well formed, which she began with the works of our sublime *vihuelists,* followed with cited maestros and it was stylized and complete with pages of the modern Moreno Torroba and Turina and the adaptations and transcriptions of the great classics and romantics such as Bach and Schumann, that she interpreted yesterday in a program exalted with the signatures of Albeniz and Granados and P. San Sebastian.

The audience was numerous, her notable labor and technique were awarded with fervent applause and even her most notable labor of spirit of the young beautiful Argentine concert guitarist."

A.B.C. Madrid April 30, 1931 No. 8.844, pgs. 48-49.
We thank Ignacio Ramos for facilitating the information from the daily newspaper *A.B.C.*

To the right is a caricature of Lalyta Almiron sketched by Romero Escacena of the *A.B.C.* daily. It was published on April 30, 1931 as well.

LALITA ALMIRON

Another critic, this time very brief, published in the magazine Ritmo, which makes us think surely other magazines and newspapers of the capital of Spain must have published some more critiques:

"Musical Information — *Informaciones Musical*

Madrid
Lalyta Almiron

The young Argentine guitarist Lalyta Almiron was presented to the Madrid public in the Ateneo hall, producing an excellent impression by her artistic qualities, good spirit and secure technique.

The notable artist, being well applauded adorned the works *Gor* (sic-Sor), Granados, Tárrega, Albeniz, Padre San Sebastian and Moreno Torroba.

Ritmo. Madrid May 15, 1931, No. 32, p. 13."

Josep Maria Mangado i Artigas
Sant Feliu de Llobregat (BCN)
7-23-2001
Revised 3-09-2008

I would like to thank Carlos Guevel for his beautiful additions to this work by my esteemed colleague, Josep Mangado i Artigas, they illuminate so much, as this article would have been visually sparse without them. I do not wish to forget Ignacio Ramos, either for his contribution as well.

Randy Osborne
October 29, 2008

Interview with Lalyta Delfina Almiron and her sister Lila.
by Richard "Rico" Stover

Rico: This is an interview with Lalyta Almiron in Rosario, Santa Fe, Argentina on January 10, 1991, and her sister Lila. They both knew Agustín Barrios and his brother Martin. In regard to the dates, they interest me a lot. I know where Barrios was in almost all of the years of his life, but I'm always searching for more details. In what year was the first time Barrios came into your life?

Lalyta: I almost don't remember,

Lila: Lalyta, when he came to our house you were already playing guitar, well, then it would be the year...

Rico: In 1923,

Lila: 1922 or 1923, the year 1922 or 1923.

Rico: I imagine that's logical, because I know Barrios was in Argentina, in 1923, in 1921 and in 1928, I don't know if he came later in 1928, here?

Lalyta: He only came once

Rico: He came once. In 1923. In what month, do you remember?

Lalyta: It was in the winter-(summer in the Northern Hemisphere)

Rico: He came in the winter.

Lalyta: In the winter, it was in the winter, he played a duet with me.

Rico: How?

Lalyta: He played a duet with me, he played a part of a work called *Romanza* for the guitar...

Rico: Which *Romanza* of the Violoncello, of his own?

Lalyta: It was the other one.

Rico: *Confesion?*

Lalyta: Yes, yes.

Rico: (Sings the melody to *Confesion*) And, and he stayed with you for six months?

Lila: He only paid to sleep in a hotel, but my father never let him eat anywhere else. Barrios liked carne asada and empañadas, my mother was a great cook.

Rico: Did he play concerts in Rosario?

Lalyta: He played.

Rico: Did he play several times? More than once?

Lalyta: Three times

Lila: In the Biblioteca Alvarez (Library), that they recently reconstructed, he played, with a group of guitarists.

Lalyta: An intimate reunion, in which they played. My father didn't present just anyone, my father was very proud. If someone came you had to appreciate him, he was right.

Lila: If they weren't of the same school as my father, this boy was... Atahualpa Yupanqui a poet of the guitar, he studied with my father.

Rico: I heard that, his name was Hector...

Lila: Chavero, Hector Roberto Chavero

Lalyta: Horacio Chavero

Rico: Horac..Horacio Chavero

Lila: Horacio Chavero

Rico: Yes, yes, yes.

Lalyta: He lived with his family in calle General Roca, (Buenos Aires Province) where his father was the stationmaster of the train station, and from that was a friendship with my father.

Lila: Studying here, Atahualpa, came on a horse, a little ways to receive a lesson every day. In a concert that he gave here two months ago, in an interval, he spoke quite a bit about my father and Lalyta and said: "Maestro Almiron never wanted to charge me for lessons." He couldn't teach him to play right-handed, because he was left-handed and the truth is that in his specialty there isn't anyone who could surpass him.

Rico: Yes, I know, I have many records of Atahualpa...

Lalyta: I played them a lot and studied them. He was the greatest there is in folklore. Because he is a poet of the guitar, he has many beautiful things. He never wanted to change his style, my father never insisted.

Lila: My father let him study, as he wanted.

Rico: And that was here in Rosario?

Lila: In Junin (province of Buenos Aires) he came with his wife and stayed for many months eating in our home studying with my father.

Rico: In what year was that?

Lila: That took place in 1926 or 1927. (Hector comments that these dates are in error that it was 1928.)

Lalyta: I had already gone to Europe (1931).

Lila: No, no.

Rico: Atahualpa still wasn't famous.

Lila: Yes, he was not really known ...

Rico: Yes, now but, at least since the 40's or 50's..

Lila: I don't know much about *folklore*, but he is a poet who has no equal.

Lalyta: He was authentic, pure art.

Rico: And your father was born in Argentina?

Lila: Yes, he was born in Carmen de Areco a province of Buenos Aires.

Rico: He was Spanish?

Lalyta: He was a descendant of Spaniards.

Rico: The grandson of a Spaniard. Your parents, I mean your grandparents came from Spain?

Lila: No, no, no...they were descendants, my mother was born in Argentina.

Rico: And your father, when was he born?

Lila: The 19th of July. The 19th of July?

Lalyta: No, the 29th of July.

Rico: What year?

Lila: 1879. I remember because my mother in law was born in the same month, in the same year. In 1879.

Rico: Then, he was six years older than Barrios, because Barrios was born in 1885.

Lila: Yes, father was older.

Rico: And how did it become that your father dedicated himself to the guitar?

Lalyta: The guitar was everything to him.

Rico: He studied with a maestro?

Lalyta: No, he studied alone, by himself.

Lila: Alone.

Rico: How did he come to read music?

Lila: He liked the guitar very much, very much. Then began the war. When he was young, he was given a guitar by a distant relative. Then my grandfather found out he liked the guitar, and then he broke it. And you know what my father did? He came home and made a guitar at once from a pumpkin shell. This was his desperation. Until he could convince his father, then little by little he began to study. He had lessons with Prat, my father did. My father studied a lot with Prat.

Rico: With Prat? Then later, he went to Buenos Aires.

Lila: Yes, yes.

Rico: Because Prat arrived in Buenos Aires in 1905 or 07 (January 1, 1908.), I believe. So, your father was going to Buenos Aires to study the guitar?

Lila: My father was married in 1905.

Rico: But he never lived in Buenos Aires

Lila: No, he always lived in Junin.

Lalyta: Where I was born.

Rico, So, with his studies with Prat he was able to perfect his ability.

Lalyta: He also studied with Segovia and Llobet.

Rico: That doesn't surprise me.

Lalyta: Llobet was also a great guitarist

Rico: Of course, very great.

Lila: Do you know Richard, originally that a little while ago almost a couple of years ago, had a photocopy from Tokyo, where figured Andrés Segovia in first place, in second Maria Luisa Anido of Argentina, and in third place was Lalyta Almiron, in Tokyo.

Rico: In Tokyo, an appreciation, right?

Lalyta: I want to go to Japan, there are many guitarists there.

Rico: There are many guitarists there. And you know what, I'm going to do, I'm going to write an article, of this interview we're doing, I'm going speak, I want you to... I don't want you to speak only of Barrios, but of your life as well. I'm going to write an article about both, that will come out in magazines in England and Tokyo.

Lila: How beautiful!

Lalyta: England, They asked me to go there, but a sad situation passed they wanted me I went there to be heard and then I believed they were going to pay me well, but they paid me less.

Lila: Do you know something Richard? I'm going to tell you about her. Lalyta, all her life she was very kind. Kind, in that many concerts were done as benefits, and she has taught a group of blind guitarists for almost four years, without charging anything. She has done many many works of charity. Because, in that manner one doesn't make money, one doesn't make money, she doesn't pity the blind, her emotions....

Lalyta: I'm not the only case.

Lila: She has done many works, many works of charity. So it was and she didn't do it for money, Richard, she didn't make money. I told her many times... (Lalyta crying) Don't get emotional, you'll get sick!!! She could have made a lot of money... and my father, he was also very kind.

Lalyta: We're a family like that, a poor musician who found it difficult to take it home.

Lila: He had great friends here, the best doctors, I tell you, at a gathering they would say: "Maestro Almiron has to be with us, besides his guitar, he loves with a book called Martin Fierro."

Lalyta: That was a cultish book.

Lila: That had quite a cult. They were crazy about it. It seemed there was always an inclusion of a passage from *Martin Fierro* in a conversation, so many opinions it was incredible.

Rico: It doesn't surprise me that your father and Barrios had a friendship.

Lila: An infinite one.

Rico: Because, let's see, in Asuncion, the three favorite books of the young Barrios were: *Martin Fierro, Las mil y una noches* and *El Quijote.*

Lila: *El Quijote.*

Rico: And also Barrios was generous and kind. He didn't make any money from his music in his life, did he?

Lila: She (Lalyta) is a portrait of my father, (it appears that Lalyta is emotional again.) Lila says to her: You're going to grow old if you cry a lot.

Rico: Let's return to the theme. So Barrios was right here for six months?

Lila: Six months

Rico: Simply, just resting?

Lila: Yes.

Rico: Or, he went to Buenos Aires once in a while?

Lila: Yes, Do you know in the home they had a guitar gathering, three, four or five personalities would get together, Lalyta played, dad played, Agustín played and sometimes he would play a duo with her. He had a lot of affection with us, I don't know the reason.

Rico: Because he knew this family was talented, evidently.

Lila: My mother, was a person who hadn't studied a great amount, but she psychologically, she could tell when someone was worth a lot. Bautista said of Barrios "he could steal the heart of anyone". They loved Agustín. He was very kind, very.

Lalyta: Did you spend a lot of time with Barrios?

Rico: No, I was born a year after Barrios died.

Lila: You're very young?

Rico: I was born in '45.

Lila: '45, the year my daughter was born.

Rico: Therefore I never had the pleasure to know Barrios.

Lalyta: Do you have children?

Rico: Yes, I have two, they live in California. A daughter and a son. My son plays the guitar.

Lila: A son.

Rico: Yes.

Lila: They live in California.

Rico: Uh huh.

Lalyta: Have you taught him (the guitar)?

Rico: A little, yes.

Lalyta: Her daughter has a brother in law, that lives on the coast in the northern part.

Rico: Well, then Barrios was here in '23 and one day he left and never came back?

Lila: No, he never came back again to Argentina.

Rico: And when he was here did he leave any manuscripts?

Lalyta: He came with his guitar.

Lila: He brought his guitar.

Rico: So he didn't write anything?

Lila: We don't have any manuscripts of Agustín.

Rico: That would be very valuable, to photograph

Lila: Listen to me. In a scrapbook, there is a manuscript written by Barrios? Don't tell me. Don't tell me. Because I know what is here.

Rico: It might be, it would be very valuable, to photograph that.

Lila: What happened, Richard, is that for many years my sister has lived with me, I've been a widow for almost twelve years.

Rico: Did he leave any photos of himself?

Lila: Richard, no but here's one of my husband.

Lalyta: Do you know the work "Oracion por todos"?

Rico: Yes, yes, I listened to your recording.

Lalyta: It was my best. It is in A minor, I studied composition and harmony. I studied with Teodoro Fuchs as well I studied with maestro Carlos Vega, the musicologist.

Rico: He was famous, I've read books by him about folklore and Argentine music.

Lila: What are you writing about? Is what you were doing of Debussy?

Lila speaking to Rico: You know the guitar is exceedingly...there is very little music of the guitar.

Rico: Yes.

Lila: She has done many transcriptions.

Lalyta: I arranged, The Well-Tempered Clavier by Bach, in E minor and The Death of the Swan by Debussy.

Lila: She has done many beautiful transcriptions.

Lalyta: Tchaikovsky

Rico: Do you know what, you should show me those things because I believe we can put something together to make an album, because you never released anything, I don't know anything of Lalyta Almiron.

Lila: I'll tell you something, our father made some publications of folk music, and he loved folk music. Ricordi edited them, but, three years ago more or less they wrote, the amount of money they wanted, I don't know how they could publish, they charged an enormous amount, Richard.

Rico: How could they charge money?

Lila: To publicize the artist.

Rico: Did they charge you?

Lila: You have to pay a lot.

Rico: That's ridiculous.

Lila: However, that's how ridiculous this country is.

Rico: The artist doesn't have to pay anything.

Lila's son Fredy: They aren't registered.

Rico: Oh, original works? Well, what we can do is to look at everything that is and choose the best, and register the copyright and include it in an edition I can produce in the United States, if you're interested.

Lila and Lalyta: Yes.

Rico: Without charging you anything.

Lila: Ah, with what would we pay?

Rico: Because, I'm in this branch of editing music, such as those things of Barrios I have put out. I'm in that field to make editions. I know the scene, I'm going tell you there is a larger scene more developed in the United States, Europe and in Japan, than right here. There are more sales and more interest than here.

Lila: I would say to you that she would be successful. The music of Lalyta, not because she is my sister. I like to tell the truth, she has beautiful music. You know why? In the past, she lived in another apartment a few blocks from here, And she felt the bells of a church, and she made a beautiful subject on the basis of the bells that she heard.

Rico: When did she do that?

Lalyta: I was grown up.

Rico: When she was an adult.

Lila: Fifteen years old. When she started playing the waltz of Chopin No. 5 she was 15. Her father said: "If you write a second part, it will be an homage to Chopin". It was beautiful. She transcribed the *Vals Brillante* by Chopin.

Lalyta: It is the most difficult of Chopin's works.

Lila: So, she wrote it and to publish the music of Lalyta would be a hit.

Rico: Let's see, what we have to do is look for your papers, to find them, because I can't stay here for a long time. Well, I'm going to stay until tomorrow, then I have to return to Buenos Aires. Then I have to go to Brazil. Therefore, I'm moving around a lot.

Lalyta: In Brazil, are there a lot of good guitarists?

Rico: Yes, there are many.

Lila's son Fredy: Make copies of all the music?

Rico: Making copies is the best.

Lila: Copy all of her music. And when might you be coming back here in Argentina?

Rico: Well, I think I'll be back later this year. Because I have to go to Uruguay, and spend quite a while there as well. Uruguay is the country that is possibly the most interesting in respect to the affairs of Barrios. He lived in Uruguay longer than anywhere else.

Lalyta: Yes, yes.

Rico: With Martin Borda y Pagola they were good friends.

Lila: Yes, he had been a good friend of my father

Rico: It's a very interesting story. Once I'm there, I'll have to stay quite a while to look for all the...

Lalyta: Do you know the Aguirre family, in Montevideo? He's a guitarist whose family is very rich.

Rico: No.

Lalyta: Yes, Aguirre, they are from the Basque region.

Rico: I know an Armando Carrasco, but Aguirre no.

Lalyta: Do you know the heavyset Paraguayan?

Rico: Sila Godoy, yes he still plays well, he's 70 years old.

Lila: He's not very old. Look, Segovia still played at that age.

Rico: Sila's still doing well.

Lalyta: Does he still give concerts?

Rico: He continues giving concerts.

Lila: Listen Richard, I've got something cold to drink if you'd like.

Rico: Of course, thanks very much.

Lila: How does this seem?

Rico: Then, when Barrios was here, you were playing guitar about two years right, two or three years?

Lila: Yes

Lalyta: What year do you have?

Rico: I have '23, September of '23.

Lila: '21. (Referring to Lalyta's first concert at the Savoy Hotel.)

Rico: Then, in your career, later in those years, did you stay here in Rosario, as your base? In Buenos Aires?

Lila: No. No. No.

Rico: Did you play concerts throughout the country?

Lalyta: I was first one to play the *Concierto de Aranjuez* in Buenos Aires..

Rico: That! In what year was that?

Lalyta: There, yes you killed me on that one.

Rico: In the 1940's.

Lila: Were you married?

Lalyta: Yes, I played with the orchestra directed by Bandini.

Lila: You were married, so that would be in 1944, or 45

Rico: How did you come by the sheet music of the *Concierto,* by way of Regino Sainz de la Maza?

Lalyta: No, Though we were close friends, we were close friends.

Lila: How could she get the music?

Rico: Because it was written in '39 in Spain.

Lila: '39.

Lalyta: Do you know why? Because my father was friends with some Spanish priests, because he was an expert in sound, and he was in charge of the sound system in a seminary. Then he said to a priest "I want to buy the *Concierto de Aranjuez* with dollars for my daughter to play it." It was $12.00 I played the *Concierto* with my husband and also maestro Bandini.

Rico: Was it a manuscript or a published edition? Then it was a first edition that Rodrigo came out with in Madrid.

Lalyta: Published.

Rico: Then it was the first edition published.

Lalyta: Yes. I don't know if he is still alive?

Rico: No.

Lalyta: The concierto was to be dedicated to Segovia, but he had a discussion with him.

Rico: It was dedicated to Regino Sainz de la Maza

Lalyta: He had a discussion with Segovia, because Segovia was much more famous than Regino, which was the truth, one thing is glass, and the other is crystal. Because there were things Segovia wanted to change because the *Concierto* wasn't guitaristic.but Rodrigo didn't put the dedication to Segovia.

Rico: Yes, yes, it's difficult.

Lalyta: There are things that aren't guitaristic.

Rico: However, it is a great work.

Lalyta: I recorded it.

Rico: You recorded it?

Lalyta: Yes.

Rico: A commercial recording?

Lalyta: Yes.

Rico: Can we hear it?

Lalyta: The record player doesn't work.

Rico: Oh, the record player doesn't work. How many records has she made?

Lila: Only the ones she recorded in Spain.

Rico: She didn't record anything here with an Argentine record company? Do you have those discs?

Lalyta: With my husband we recorded a tape, nothing more.

Rico: Ah! On a tape you recorded, but not on shellac.?

Lalyta: On shellac (78 RPM), no.

Rico: In what year did you go to Spain?

Lalyta: In 1931

Rico: In '31, so....

Lila: She was 15 years old when she went...

Rico: 15 years old?

Lalyta: I hadn't completed my 15th year, I was just a girl with braids.

Rico: You performed with your father?

Lila: She played in Paris, in the Salle Gaveau...the Ateneo in Madrid. She ended (the tour) playing in Paris.

Lalyta: I played in the Ateneo in Madrid and in the Sala Mozart in Barcelona.

Lila: The reviews that she got were beautiful.

Lalyta: I played on the radio as well.

Lila: Do you know what happened, Richard, when she went to Europe and returned my mother had already died.

Rico: That happened during the trip?

Lila: When she went she was fifteen years old, when she returned they encountered the death of my mother, and my father was without his woman.

Lalyta: I remember when he cried.

Lila: What happened was a lot of sorrow....She was forty one. But when our father died...his health was so poor, he had been very generous with his teaching, why he didn't have a watch to see the hour. But he didn't have a condition for the student to leave, they couldn't steal his time. He was a professor who charged a lot for his classes and had the most distinguished students, the most excellent folks, studied the guitar here with my father. He was a person of quality, a very cultured man. We struggled, Richard, when we both were without a mother and father, she was young, twenty-one years old, almost twenty-one years old. I was going to marry a nice guy, but my father said no when he saw my boyfriend, so I didn't marry him. I had bad luck and didn't find the man who was my husband until I was thirty-five years old. My luck changed, he was a jewel...

Lalyta: Pure gold.

Lila: He had eyes like yours.

Lalyta: He was a beautiful person.

Lila: An extraordinary man. Richard, I was thirty-seven, but he was extraordinary husband. Saturdays he would love to read books. He was a creator.

Lalyta: How long have you been married?

Rico: Me? Eighteen years.

Lila: And you have a son and daughter.

Lalyta: I lost my husband in 1980.

Rico: When did you get married?

Lalyta: Oh, in the year 1933.

Rico: Two years after you returned from Europe. Something like that.

Lalyta: He was a man of many qualities. He was a man of mixed ethnicity, part German, part Irish, Italian and part Spanish.

Rico: After your tour in Europe, you came back right here?

Lalyta: I never left.

Rico: You stayed here all your life?

Lalyta: Yes.

Rico: You never left to play outside the country again?

Lalyta: Yes. In the year 1964 I went to Europe, and was on *radiotelevision*.

Rico: In what country? France?

Lalyta: In Paris, France. I also played on...what's its name...*radio RAI* (Radiotelevisione) in Italy.

Rico: What kind of guitar is that?

Lalyta: It's a (Francisco) Torres.

Rico: Torres? You have one?

Lalyta: A (Francisco) Torres.

Rico: That's a historic guitar.

Lila: She has a guitar with the name (Francisco) Torres.

Lalyta: That's the guitar I used when I stopped playing guitar so much.

Rico: You know, I want to photocopy all that. That begins in '43, is there something earlier?

Lila's son Fredy: Yes.

Lalyta: When are you going to come back?

Rico: We have to do the most we can while I'm here. Because...

Lila: Richard, tell me the truth, seriously, what would you like to eat?

Rico: I don't eat as much meat as they eat here.

Lila: Well, were going to eat.

Lalyta: That's a photo of maestro Bandini.

Rico: And that concierto is yours?

Lalyta: Yes.

Rico: It has three movements.

Lalyta: Yes, yes.

Lila: Well, Richard cheers. (They toast the drinks they are having.) I'm glad to have made your acquaintance. I hope you return soon.

Lalyta: Everyone, cheers.

Rico: Hmm, that's pineapple, it's very smooth, that's nice, very nice. Hmm.

Lalyta: I played solo various times at the SODRE in Montevideo.

2598

Lila: A (Francisco) Torres.

Lalyta: No that's *"La Negrita"*

Lila: Where is the Torres?

Lalyta: It's kept over there.

Fredy: This?

Lila: I don't know, I'm confused about them.

Fredy: Is this the Torres?

Lalyta: No. That's the guitar I use to give classes to my students.

Rico: And the sheet music that you used for *Cordoba,* by Barrios, what was that?

Lalyta: What *Cordoba?*

Rico: I know it came out in '22. *Cordoba,* by Agustín Barrios. (Sings the melody)

Lalyta: What's that?

Rico: *Estilo Cordoba.*

Lalyta: I never played *Cordoba.* (She played it in a concert in 1952, but forgot it due to her age.)

Rico: But, it says here you recorded it. Then what was it? An *Estilo Uruguayo?* Right?

Lalyta: It was Julián Aguirre, *Cordoba Estilo.*

Rico: I see.

Lalyta: Do you know him?

Rico: Yes, I know Julián Aguirre.

Lalyta: A beautiful *Cordoba.*

Rico: But Barrios has one, a piece called *Cordoba.*

Lalyta: I haven't played that one.

Lila's son: The (Francisco) Torres

Lila: It's missing strings.

Rico: Oh, it needs strings.

Lalyta: It has a beautiful quality, Richard.

Rico: It says it was made in 1839 (actually 1859-handwritten number hard to read).

Lalyta: It's extraordinary.

Lila: It's extraordinary., more than a century old.

Photo of Lalyta Almiron and her sister Lila at home, when Rico Stover interviewed them in 1991.

Courtesy: Rico Stover

Rico: It has a special thing about it. Incredible! This was your first guitar?

Lalyta: Yes.

Rico plays the guitar.

Lila: Richard do you use nails?

Rico: Flesh and nails.

Lila: Oh, with flesh and nails.

Rico: It's very beautiful and well preserved. Where did you buy this?

Lalyta: My father bought it in Spain, before I was born.

Rico: In Spain.

Lila: He was single at that time, look at the years that it has.

2600

Lalyta Almiron playing guitar in 1991.

Courtesy: Rico Stover

Rico: It says here: repaired by Don Eduardo Schneider in '73 in Germany. How did that happen?

Lila: What year?

Rico: It says 1973.

Lila"s son: That's when it was repaired.

Rico: By whom? Oh, here in Rosario, by a local luthier and he repaired it, because one can see that it was damaged here.

Lila: It has a divine sound. Richard, listen to the beautiful sound it makes.

Rico: And this is an Antigua Casa Nuñez.

Lila: It has a precious sound.

Lalyta: Did you bring a guitar here with you?

Rico: No, I didn't.

Lalyta: You don't have one here?...

Rico: (As he's tuning the guitar) Perfect pitch. The memory of...

Lalyta: Yes, I understand.

Lila: The guitar has a precious sound.

Rico: He continues to play scales and arpeggios, after tuning, then tunes more.

Lalyta: Do you write your own music?

Rico: Yes, I write.

Lila: Play your music.

Rico: Do you know what I'm going to do?

The tape is shut off and ends.

This Spanish language translation was done from the tape source between April, 27, 2007 and June 1, 2007. All other translations in this book were done from written source material.

In 2010 I asked Hector García Martínez, my co-author to do a transcription, since Spanish is his first language. He provided the readers of this book with corrections and about a page of valuable extra information of names and song titles.

Randy Osborne March 20, 2010.

15 Index

A

B

2613

C

E

H

I

J

K

L

M

O

P

Math B75
Fundamentals of Algebra

Charles P. McKeague

Math B75
Fundamentals of Algebra

Charles P. McKeague

Publisher: XYZ Textbooks

Production and Design:
Katherine Heistand Shields

ISBN-13: 978-1-63098-241-6   /   ISBN-10: 1-63098-241-5

For product information and technology assistance, contact us at
XYZ Textbooks, 1-877-745-3499

For permission to use material from this text or product,
e-mail: **info@xyztextbooks.com**

XYZ Textbooks
1339 Marsh Street
San Luis Obispo, CA 93401

For your course and learning solutions, visit **www.xyztextbooks.com**

Printed in the United States of America

Brief Contents

Contents

5   Factoring   471

6   Functions and Function Notation   525

7   Rational Expressions and Rational Functions   573

Preface

This edition was custom made as directed by the faculty of Bakersfield College to meet the needs of their students studying algebra.

Description

Math B75, Fundamentals of Algebra is an integration of XYZ Textbooks' popular introductory and intermediate algebra textbooks into a concise survey of the subject designed for a one-semester course covering the fundamentals of algebra and its applications. As with all XYZ titles, our emphasis on study skills, and our positive tone toward success, are reflected in the presentation.

You'll find this book to be rooted in the proven teaching methods that you come to expect from an XYZ Textbook, with some innovative features to support your students' success.

The materials for *Math B75, Fundamentals of Algebra* are designed as an activity-based algebra course. The textbook develops the concepts and skills of algebra in the context of modeling and problem solving. Each section includes embedded reading questions for students to check their understanding and exercises that reflect the material presented in the examples. The problem sets consist of two parts: skills practice problems that review prerequisite skills for the section and provide practice with new skills, and applications problems. The applications include a wide range of open-ended problems that emphasize mathematical modeling using tables of values, algebraic expressions, and graphs. Chapter reviews include a glossary and summary, as well as a set of review problems. Encourage your students to make regular use of these features—you'll find that they will gradually build a foundation of successful studying practices that will benefit them in all their future courses.

This textbook is more than just the book itself. We built this book to be the hub of a math "toolbox" of sorts. While most students still prefer to use the printed book in their studies, the eBook extends the reach of the book, giving students and instructors access to a wide array of supporting tools:

- The ebook includes free access to this textbook, plus over 20 other ebooks covering 8 math courses—great for remediation.
- It also includes free access to 10,000 MathTV videos, with 3-4 tutorials for every single example.
- Plus all of the accompanying worksheets and digital supplements for the book.

To Students: A Study Plan For Success

Before Class: Prepare

1. Read the textbook section slowly and carefully. Read one subsection at a time. Don't rush! Work on grasping each concept before going on. You may have to read a difficult passage two or three times before it begins to make sense.
2. Study each example. Read through the example step by step, and make sure you understand the reasoning behind each step. Read with a pencil in hand, and put a question mark beside any explanations that are unclear to you. Jot down in the margins any questions that occur to you.
3. Answer the reading questions and work the exercises as you go along. Check your answers to the exercises when you get to the end of the section.

During Class: Participate

4. Ask questions when you need help. Classtime is the best time to work on understanding new material. Try to get as many of your questions cleared up as possible before you leave class.
5. Look over the homework problems with your group. Exchange e-mail or phone numbers with your group so you can contact each other after class if you get stuck.

After Class: Practice

6. There are two types of homework problems at the end of each section in the textbook, skills practice and applications. Keep your homework problems in a notebook (a three-ring binder is best), so that you can use them to study for tests.

7. Write out the solutions to the skills practice problems neatly and completely, the same way you would write them on a test. If your class uses a computer homework system, you may be asked to enter your answers into the computer for grading.

8. Prepare the solutions to the application problems to hand in at your next class meeting. Follow your instructor's guidelines for written work.

9. Make any corrections necessary in previous Homework assignments. Finally, go back to Step 1 and prepare for the next day's lesson!

What to Do When You Need Help Outside of Class

In college courses it is not unusual for students to need extra help outside of class meetings; it's not possible to learn new ideas in one hour. It is very important that you take advantage of the resources available to you, and seek help as soon as you need it! Do not wait even one day before asking for help; it's very easy to get behind in a math class. Here are some strategies:

1. Go back to the textbook and look for similar examples, or an explanation of the relevant topic.

2. Contact your group members or study buddies and work together.

3. Email your instructor with your question. Try to be specific!

4. Visit your college's Math Lab or tutoring center and ask a tutor for help.

5. Visit your instructor during office hours. Come prepared with your homework notebook and specific questions.

The Secret of Success

In college most of your learning takes place outside the classroom. YOU are responsible for learning the material when it is assigned—don't wait! If you don't understand something, YOU must seek help right away! Practice is the key to learning skills: work problems every night until you have mastered each new topic.

The Basics

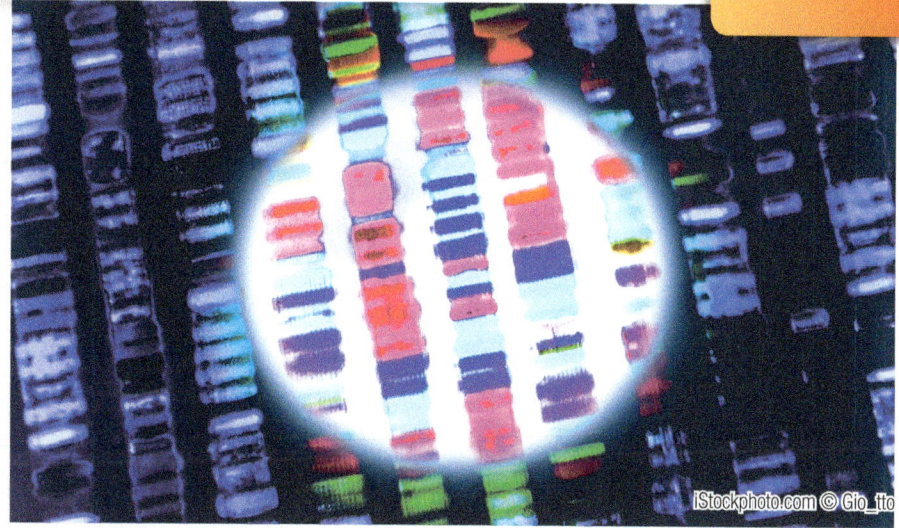

iStockphoto.com © Gio_tto

Much of what we do in mathematics is concerned with recognizing patterns. If you recognize the patterns in the following two sequences, then you can easily extend each sequence.

$$\text{Sequence of odd numbers} = 1, 3, 5, 7, 9, \ldots$$

$$\text{Sequence of squares} = 1, 4, 9, 16, 25, \ldots$$

Once we have classified groups of numbers as to the characteristics they share, we sometimes discover that a relationship exists between the groups. Although it may not be obvious at first, there is a relationship that exists between the two sequences shown. The introduction to *The Book of Squares*, written in 1225 by the mathematician known as Fibonacci, begins this way:

"I thought about the origin of all square numbers and discovered that they arise out of the increasing sequence of odd numbers."

The relationship that Fibonacci refers to is shown visually here.

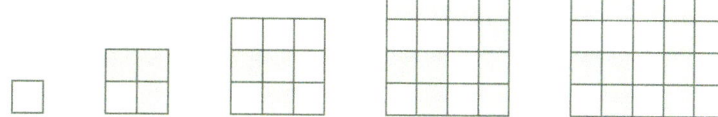

Many times we describe a relationship or pattern in a number of different ways. Here we have a visual description of a relationship. In this chapter we will work on describing relationships numerically and verbally (in writing).

1

Study Skills

Some of the students enrolled in my college algebra classes develop difficulties early in the course. Their difficulties are not associated with their ability to learn mathematics; they all have the potential to pass the course. Students who get off to a poor start do so because they have not developed the study skills necessary to be successful in algebra. Here is a list of things you can do to begin to develop effective study skills.

1. **Put Yourself on a Schedule** The general rule is that you spend 2 hours on homework for every hour you are in class. Make a schedule for yourself in which you set aside 2 hours each day to work on algebra. Once you make the schedule, stick to it. Don't just complete your assignments and stop. Use all the time you have set aside. If you complete an assignment and have time left over, read the next section in the book, and then work more problems.

2. **Find Your Mistakes and Correct Them** There is more to studying algebra than just working problems. You must always check your answers with the answers in the back of the book. When you have made a mistake, find out what it is and correct it. Making mistakes is part of the process of learning mathematics. In the prologue to The Book of Squares, Leonardo Fibonacci (ca. 1170–ca. 1250) had this to say about the content of his book:

> I have come to request indulgence if in any place it contains something more or less than right or necessary; for to remember everything and be mistaken in nothing is divine rather than human . . .

Fibonacci knew, as you know, that human beings make mistakes. You cannot learn algebra without making mistakes.

3. **Gather Information on Available Resources** You need to anticipate that you will need extra help sometime during the course. There is a form to fill out in Appendix A to help you gather information on resources available to you. One resource is your instructor; you need to know your instructor's office hours and where the office is located. Another resource is the math lab or study center, if they are available at your school. It also helps to have the phone numbers of other students in the class, in case you miss class. You want to anticipate that you will need these resources, so now is the time to gather them together.

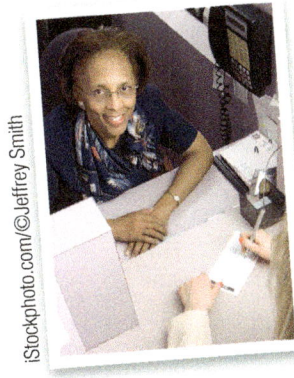

Suppose you have a checking account that costs you $15 a month, plus $0.05 for each check you write. If you write 10 checks in a month, then the monthly charge for your checking account will be

$$15 + 10(0.05)$$

Do you add 15 and 10 first and then multiply by 0.05? Or do you multiply 10 and 0.05 first and then add 15? If you don't know the answer to this question, you will after you have read through this section.

Because much of what we do in algebra involves comparison of quantities, we will begin by listing some symbols used to compare mathematical quantities. The comparison symbols fall into two major groups: equality symbols and inequality symbols.

We will let the letters a and b stand for (represent) any two mathematical quantities. When we use letters to represent numbers, as we are doing here, we call the letters *variables*.

Variables: An Intuitive Look

When you filled out the application for the school you are attending, there was a space to fill in your first name. "First name" is a variable quantity because the value it takes depends on who is filling out the application. For example, if your first name is Manuel, then the value of "First Name" is Manuel. However, if your first name is Christa, then the value of "First Name" is Christa.

If we denote "First Name" as FN, "Last Name" as LN, and "Whole Name" as WN, then we take the concept of a variable further and write the relationship between the names this way:

$$FN + LN = WN$$

(We use the $+$ symbol loosely here to represent writing the names together with a space between them.) This relationship we have written holds for all people who have only a first name and a last name. For those people who have a middle name, the relationship between the names is

$$FN + MN + LN = WN$$

A similar situation exists in algebra when we let a letter stand for a number or a group of numbers. For instance, if we say "let a and b represent numbers," then a and b are called *variables* because the values they take on vary. We use the variables a and b in the following lists so that the relationships shown there are true for all numbers that we will encounter in this book. By using variables, the following statements are general statements about all numbers, rather than specific statements about only a few numbers.

Comparison Symbols

Equality:	$a = b$	a is equal to b
	$a \neq b$	a is not equal to b
Inequality:	$a < b$	a is less than b
	$a > b$	a is greater than b
	$a \geq b$	a is greater than or equal to b
	$a \leq b$	a is less than or equal to b

Note In the past you may have used the notation 3×5 to denote multiplication. In algebra it is best to avoid this notation if possible, because the multiplication symbol $\times$ can be confused with the variable x when written by hand.

The symbols for inequality, $<$ and $>$, always point to the smaller of the two quantities being compared. For example, $3 < x$ means 3 is smaller than x. In this case we can say "3 is less than x" or "x is greater than 3"; both statements are correct. Similarly, the expression $5 > y$ can be read as "5 is greater than y" or as "y is less than 5" because the inequality symbol is pointing to y, meaning y is the smaller of the two quantities.

Next, we consider the symbols used to represent the four basic operations: addition, subtraction, multiplication, and division.

Operation Symbols

Addition:	$a + b$	The *sum* of a and b
Subtraction:	$a - b$	The *difference* of a and b
Multiplication:	$a \cdot b,\ (a)(b),\ (a)(b),\ (a)b,\ ab$	The *product* of a and b
Division:	$a \div b,\ a/b,\ \dfrac{a}{b},\ b\overline{)a}$	The *quotient* of a and b

When we encounter the word **sum**, the implied operation is addition. To find the sum of two numbers, we simply add them. **Difference** implies subtraction, **product** implies multiplication, and **quotient** implies division. Notice also that there is more than one way to write the product or quotient of two numbers.

Grouping Symbols

Parentheses ( ) and brackets [ ] are the symbols used for grouping numbers together. Occasionally, braces { } are also used for grouping, although they are usually reserved for set notation, as we shall see later in this text.

The following table illustrates the relationship between the symbols for comparing, operating, and grouping and the English language.

Mathematical Expression	Written Equivalent
$4 + 1 = 5$	The sum of 4 and 1 is 5.
$8 - 1 < 10$	The difference of 8 and 1 is less than 10.
$2(3 + 4) = 14$	Twice the sum of 3 and 4 is 14.
$3x \geq 15$	The product of 3 and x is greater than or equal to 15.
$\dfrac{y}{2} = y - 2$	The quotient of y and 2 is equal to the difference of y and 2.

The last type of notation we need to discuss is the notation that allows us to write repeated multiplications in a more compact form—*exponents*. In the expression 2^3, the 2 is called the *base* and the 3 is called the *exponent*. The exponent 3 tells us the number of times the base appears in the product; that is,

$$2^3 = 2 \cdot 2 \cdot 2 = 8$$

The expression 2^3 is said to be in exponential form, whereas $2 \cdot 2 \cdot 2$ is said to be in expanded form. Here are some additional examples of expressions involving exponents.

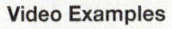

Video Examples

Section 0.1

Example 1 Expand and multiply.

a. 5^2 **b.** 2^5 **c.** 10^3

SOLUTION

a. $5^2 = 5 \cdot 5 = 25$ *Base 5, exponent 2*

b. $2^5 = 2 \cdot 2 \cdot 2 \cdot 2 \cdot 2 = 32$ *Base 2, exponent 5*

c. $10^3 = 10 \cdot 10 \cdot 10 = 1{,}000$ *Base 10, exponent 3*

Notation and Vocabulary Here is how we read expressions containing exponents.

Mathematical Expression	Written Equivalent
5^2	five to the second power
5^3	five to the third power
5^4	five to the fourth power
5^5	five to the fifth power
5^6	five to the sixth power

We have a shorthand vocabulary for second and third powers because the area of a square with a side of 5 is 5^2, and the volume of a cube with a side of 5 is 5^3.

5^2 can be read "five squared." 5^3 can be read "five cubed."

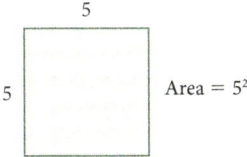

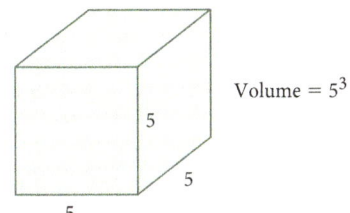

The symbols for comparing, operating, and grouping are to mathematics what punctuation symbols are to English. These symbols are the punctuation symbols for mathematics.

Consider the following sentence:

Paul said John is tall.

It can have two different meanings, depending on how it is punctuated.

  1. "Paul," said John, "is tall."

  2. Paul said, "John is tall."

Let's take a look at a similar situation in mathematics. Consider the following mathematical statement:

$$5 + 2 \cdot 7$$

If we add the 5 and 2 first and then multiply by 7, we get an answer of 49. However, if we multiply the 2 and the 7 first and then add 5, we are left with 19. We have a problem that seems to have two different answers, depending on whether we add first or multiply first. We would like to avoid this type of situation. Every problem like $5 + 2 \cdot 7$ should have only one answer. Therefore, we will use the following rule for the order of operations.

> ### ⟦Δ≠Σ⟧ *Order of Operations*
>
> When evaluating a mathematical expression, we will perform the operations in the following order, beginning with the expression in the innermost parentheses or brackets first and working our way out.
> 1. Simplify all numbers with exponents, working from left to right if more than one of these expressions is present.
> 2. Then do all multiplications and divisions left to right.
> 3. Perform all additions and subtractions left to right.

Example 2   Simplify each expression using the rule for the order of operations.

a. $5 + 8 \cdot 2$

b. $12 \div 4 \cdot 2$

c. $2[5 + 2(6 + 3 \cdot 4)]$

d. $10 + 12 \div 4 + 2 \cdot 3$

e. $2^4 + 3^3 \div 9 - 4^2$

SOLUTION

a. $5 + 8 \cdot 2 = 5 + 16$ Multiply $8 \cdot 2$ first

$\qquad\qquad = 21$

b. $12 \div 4 \cdot 2 = 3 \cdot 2 = 6$ Work left to right

c. $2[5 + 2(6 + 3 \cdot 4)] = 2[5 + 2(6 + 12)]$ Simplify within the innermost parentheses first

$\qquad\qquad\qquad = 2[5 + 2(18)]$

$\qquad\qquad\qquad = 2[5 + 36]$ Next, simplify inside the brackets

$\qquad\qquad\qquad = 2[41]$

$\qquad\qquad\qquad = 82$ Multiply

d. $10 + 12 \div 4 + 2 \cdot 3 = 10 + 3 + 6$ Multiply and divide left to right

$\qquad\qquad\qquad = 19$ Add left to right

e. $2^4 + 3^3 \div 9 - 4^2 = 16 + 27 \div 9 - 16$ Simplify numbers with exponents

$\qquad\qquad\qquad = 16 + 3 - 16$ Then, divide

$\qquad\qquad\qquad = 19 - 16$ Finally, add and subtract left to right

$\qquad\qquad\qquad = 3$

Reading Tables and Bar Charts

The following table shows the average amount of caffeine in a number of beverages. The diagram in Figure 1 is a bar chart. It is a visual presentation of the information in the table. The table gives information in numerical form, whereas the chart gives the same information in a geometric way. In mathematics, it is important to be able to move back and forth between the two forms.

Caffeine Content of Hot Drinks

Drink (6-ounce cup)	Caffeine (milligrams)
Brewed coffee	100
Instant coffee	70
Tea	50
Cocoa	5
Decaffeinated coffee	4

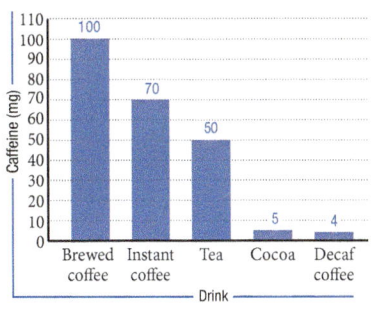

FIGURE 1

Example 3   Referring to the table and Figure 1, suppose you have 3 cups of brewed coffee, 1 cup of tea, and 2 cups of decaf in one day. Write an expression that will give the total amount of caffeine in these six drinks, and then simplify the expression.

SOLUTION   From the table or the bar chart, we find the number of milligrams of caffeine in each drink; then we write an expression for the total amount of caffeine:

$$3(100) + 50 + 2(4)$$

Using the rule for order of operations, we get 358 total milligrams of caffeine.

Number Sequences and Inductive Reasoning

Suppose someone asks you to give the next number in the sequence of numbers below. (The dots mean that the sequence continues in the same pattern forever.)

$$2, 5, 8, 11, \ldots$$

If you notice that each number is 3 more than the number before it, you would say the next number in the sequence is 14 because $11 + 3 = 14$. When we reason in this way, we are using what is called *inductive reasoning*. In mathematics we use inductive reasoning when we notice a pattern to a sequence of numbers and then use the pattern to extend the sequence.

Example 4   Find the next number in each sequence.
a. $3, 8, 13, 18, \ldots$ **b.** $2, 10, 50, 250, \ldots$ **c.** $2, 4, 7, 11, \ldots$

SOLUTION   To find the next number in each sequence, we need to look for a pattern or relationship.

a. For the first sequence, each number is 5 more than the number before it; therefore, the next number will be $18 + 5 = 23$.

b. For the sequence in part **b**, each number is 5 times the number before it; therefore, the next number in the sequence will be $5 \cdot 250 = 1{,}250$.

c. For the sequence in part **c**, there is no number to add or multiply by each time. However, the pattern becomes apparent when we look at the differences between the numbers:

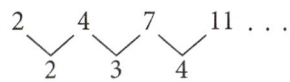

Proceeding in the same manner, we would add 5 to get the next term, giving us $11 + 5 = 16$.

In the introduction to this chapter we mentioned the mathematician known as Fibonacci. There is a special sequence in mathematics named for Fibonacci. Here it is.

$$\text{Fibonacci sequence} = 1, 1, 2, 3, 5, 8, \ldots$$

Can you see the relationship among the numbers in this sequence? Start with two 1s, then add two consecutive members of the sequence to get the next number. Here is a diagram.

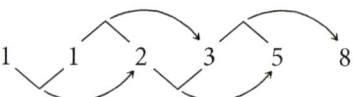

Sometimes we refer to the numbers in a sequence as *terms* of the sequence.

Example 5   Write the first 10 terms of the Fibonacci sequence.

SOLUTION   The first six terms are given above. We extend the sequence by adding 5 and 8 to obtain the seventh term, 13. Then we add 8 and 13 to obtain 21. Continuing in this manner, the first 10 terms in the Fibonacci sequence are

$$1, 1, 2, 3, 5, 8, 13, 21, 34, 55$$

Getting Ready for Class

Each section of the book will end with some problems and questions like the ones below. They are for you to answer after you have read through the section but before you go to class. All of them require that you give written responses in complete sentences. Writing about mathematics is a valuable exercise. If you write with the intention of explaining and communicating what you know to someone else, you will find that you understand the topic you are writing about even better than you did before you started writing. As with all problems in this course, you want to approach these writing exercises with a positive point of view. You will get better at giving written responses to questions as you progress through the course. Even if you never feel comfortable writing about mathematics, just the process of attempting to do so will increase your understanding and ability in mathematics.

After reading through the preceding section, respond in your own words and in complete sentences.

A. What is a variable?
B. Write the first step in the rule for order of operations.
C. What is inductive reasoning?
D. Explain the relationship between an exponent and its base.

Problem Set 0.1

For each sentence below, write an equivalent expression in symbols.

1. The sum of x and 5 is 14.   **2.** The difference of x and 4 is 8.

3. The product of 5 and y is less than 30.

4. The product of 8 and y is greater than 16.

5. The product of 5 and y is greater than or equal to the difference of y and 16.

6. The product of 3 and y is less than or equal to the sum of y and 6.

7. The quotient of x and 3 is equal to the sum of x and 2.

8. The quotient of x and 2 is equal to the difference of x and 4.

Expand and multiply.

9. 3^2 **10.** 4^2 **11.** 7^2 **12.** 9^2 **13.** 2^3 **14.** 3^3

15. 4^3 **16.** 5^3 **17.** 2^4 **18.** 3^4 **19.** 10^2 **20.** 10^4

21. 11^2 **22.** 111^2

Use the rule for order of operations to simplify each expression as much as possible.

23. $2 \cdot 3 + 5$ **24.** $8 \cdot 7 + 1$ **25.** $2(3 + 5)$ **26.** $8(7 + 1)$

27. $5 + 2 \cdot 6$ **28.** $8 + 9 \cdot 4$ **29.** $(5 + 2) \cdot 6$ **30.** $(8 + 9) \cdot 4$

31. $5 \cdot 4 + 5 \cdot 2$ **32.** $6 \cdot 8 + 6 \cdot 3$ **33.** $5(4 + 2)$ **34.** $6(8 + 3)$

35. $8 + 2(5 + 3)$ **36.** $7 + 3(8 - 2)$ **37.** $(8 + 2)(5 + 3)$ **38.** $(7 + 3)(8 - 2)$

39. $20 + 2(8 - 5) + 1$ **40.** $10 + 3(7 + 1) + 2$

41. $5 + 2(3 \cdot 4 - 1) + 8$ **42.** $11 - 2(5 \cdot 3 - 10) + 2$

43. $8 + 10 \div 2$ **44.** $16 - 8 \div 4$

45. $4 + 8 \div 4 - 2$ **46.** $6 + 9 \div 3 + 2$

47. $3 + 12 \div 3 + 6 \cdot 5$ **48.** $18 + 6 \div 2 + 3 \cdot 4$

49. $3 \cdot 8 + 10 \div 2 + 4 \cdot 2$ **50.** $5 \cdot 9 + 10 \div 2 + 3 \cdot 3$

51. $(5 + 3)(5 - 3)$ **52.** $(7 + 2)(7 - 2)$ **53.** $5^2 - 3^2$ **54.** $7^2 - 2^2$

55. $(4 + 5)^2$ **56.** $(6 + 3)^2$ **57.** $4^2 + 5^2$ **58.** $6^2 + 3^2$

59. $3 \cdot 10^2 + 4 \cdot 10 + 5$ **60.** $6 \cdot 10^2 + 5 \cdot 10 + 4$

61. $2 \cdot 10^3 + 3 \cdot 10^2 + 4 \cdot 10 + 5$ **62.** $5 \cdot 10^3 + 6 \cdot 10^2 + 7 \cdot 10 + 8$

63. $10 - 2(4 \cdot 5 - 16)$ **64.** $15 - 5(3 \cdot 2 - 4)$

65. $4[7 + 3(2 \cdot 9 - 8)]$ **66.** $5[10 + 2(3 \cdot 6 - 10)]$

67. $5(7 - 3) + 8(6 - 4)$ **68.** $3(10 - 4) + 6(12 - 10)$

69. $3(4 \cdot 5 - 12) + 6(7 \cdot 6 - 40)$ **70.** $6(8 \cdot 3 - 4) + 5(7 \cdot 3 - 1)$

71. $3^4 + 4^2 \div 2^3 - 5^2$ **72.** $2^5 + 6^2 \div 2^2 - 3^2$

73. $5^2 + 3^4 \div 9^2 + 6^2$ **74.** $6^2 + 2^5 \div 4^2 + 7^2$

Simplify each expression.

75. $20 \div 2 \cdot 10$ **76.** $40 \div 4 \cdot 5$ **77.** $24 \div 8 \cdot 3$ **78.** $24 \div 4 \cdot 6$

79. $36 \div 6 \cdot 3$ **80.** $36 \div 9 \cdot 2$ **81.** $48 \div 12 \cdot 2$ **82.** $48 \div 8 \cdot 3$

83. $16 - 8 + 4$ **84.** $16 - 8 + 8$ **85.** $24 - 14 + 8$ **86.** $24 - 16 + 6$

87. $36 - 6 + 12$ **88.** $36 - 9 + 20$ **89.** $48 - 12 + 17$ **90.** $48 - 13 + 15$

Applying the Concepts

Food Labels In 1993 the government standardized the way in which nutrition information was presented on the labels of most packaged food products. The standardized food label shown here is from a package of cookies that I ate at lunch the day I was writing the problems for this problem set. Use the information on the label to answer the following questions.

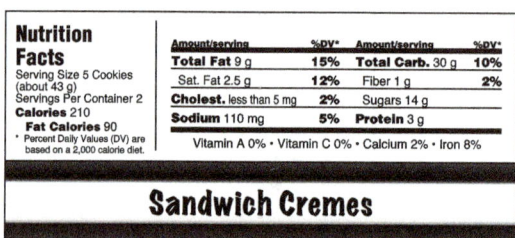

Nutrition Facts
Serving Size 5 Cookies (about 43 g)
Servings Per Container 2
Calories 210
  Fat Calories 90
* Percent Daily Values (DV) are based on a 2,000 calorie diet.

Amount/serving	%DV*	Amount/serving	%DV*
Total Fat 9 g	15%	**Total Carb.** 30 g	10%
Sat. Fat 2.5 g	12%	Fiber 1 g	2%
Cholest. less than 5 mg	2%	Sugars 14 g	
Sodium 110 mg	5%	**Protein** 3 g	

Vitamin A 0% • Vitamin C 0% • Calcium 2% • Iron 8%

Sandwich Cremes

91. How many cookies are in the package?

92. If I paid $0.50 for the package of cookies, how much did each cookie cost?

93. If the "calories" category stands for calories per serving, how many calories did I consume by eating the whole package of cookies?

94. Suppose that, while swimming, I burn 11 calories each minute. If I swim for 20 minutes, will I burn enough calories to cancel out the calories I added by eating 5 cookies?

Food Labels The food label shown here was taken from a bag of corn chips. Use the information to answer the following questions.

95. Approximately how many chips are in the bag?

96. If the bag of chips costs $0.99, approximately how much does one serving of chips cost?

97. The table toward the bottom of the label gives the recommended amount of total fat that should be consumed by a person eating 2,000 calories per day and by a person eating 2,500 calories per day. Use the numbers in the table to estimate the recommended fat intake for a person eating 3,000 calories per day.

98. Deidre burns 256 calories per hour by trotting on her horse at a constant rate. How long must she ride to burn the calories consumed by eating four servings of these chips?

Nutrition Facts
Serving Size 1 oz. (28 g/About 32 chips)
Servings Per Container 7

Amount Per Serving

Calories 160	Calories from Fat 90	

	%?Daily Value*
Total Fat 10 g	15%
Saturated Fat 1.5 g	8%
Cholesterol 0 mg	0%
Sodium 160 mg	7%
Total Carbohydrate 15 g	5%
Dietary Fiber 1 g	4%
Sugars 0 g	
Protein 2 g	

Vitamin A 0%	•	Vitamin C 0%
Calcium 2%	•	Iron 0%

* Percent Daily Values are based on a 2,000 calorie diet. Your daily values may be higher or lower depending on your calorie needs:

		Calories:	2,000	2,500
Total Fat	Less than		65 g	80 g
Sat Fat	Less than		20 g	25 g
Cholesterol	Less than		300 mg	300 mg
Sodium	Less than		2,400 mg	2,400 mg
Total Carbohydrate			300 g	375 g
Dietary Fiber			25 g	30 g

Calories per gram:
Fat 9   •   Carbohydrate 4   •   Protein 4

99. Reading Charts The following table and bar chart give the amount of caffeine in five different soft drinks. How much caffeine is in each of the following?

   a. A 6-pack of Jolt   **b.** 2 Coca-Colas plus 3 Tabs

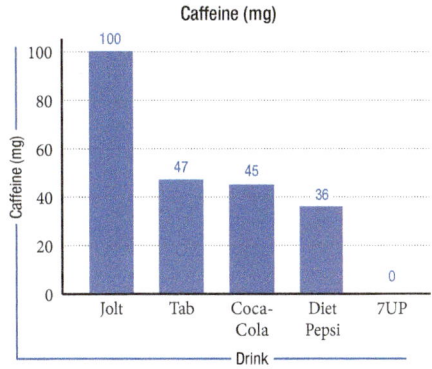

100. Reading Tables and Charts The following table and bar chart give the amount of caffeine in five different nonprescription drugs. How much caffeine is in each of the following?

   a. A box of 12 Excedrin   **b.** 1 Dexatrim plus 4 Excedrin

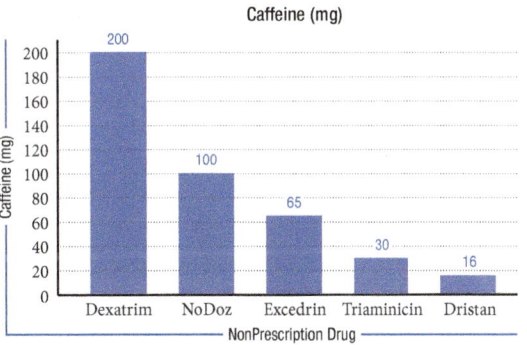

101. Reading Tables and Charts The following bar chart gives the number of calories burned by a 150-pound person during 1 hour of various exercises. The accompanying table should display the same information. Use the bar chart to complete the table.

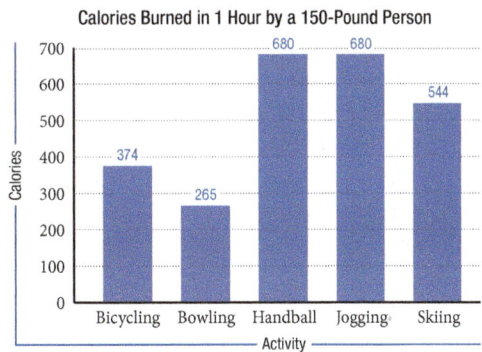

Calories Burned by 150-Pound Person

Activity	Calories Burned in 1 Hour
Bicycling	374
Bowling	
Handball	
Jogging	
Skiing	

102. Reading Tables and Charts The following bar chart gives the number of calories consumed by eating some popular fast foods. The accompanying table should display the same information. Use the bar chart to complete the table.

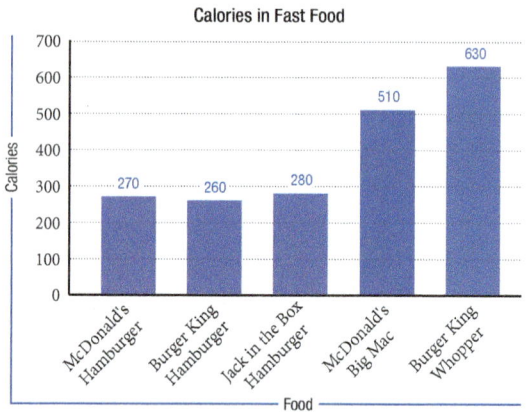

Calories In Fast Food

Food	Calories
McDonald's Hamburger	270
Burger King Hamburger	
Jack in the Box Hamburger	
McDonald's Big Mac	
Burger King Whopper	

Find the next number in each sequence.

103. 1, 2, 3, 4, . . . (The sequence of counting numbers.)

104. 0, 1, 2, 3, . . . (The sequence of whole numbers.)

105. 2, 4, 6, 8, . . . (The sequence of even numbers.)

106. 1, 3, 5, 7, . . . (The sequence of odd numbers.)

107. 1, 4, 9, 16, . . . (The sequence of squares.)

108. 1, 8, 27, 64, . . . (The sequence of cubes.)

109. 2, 2, 4, 6, . . . (A Fibonacci-like sequence.)

110. 5, 5, 10, 15, . . . (A Fibonacci-like sequence.)

Real Numbers

The table and bar chart shown here give the record low temperature, in degrees Fahrenheit, for each month of the year in the city of Jackson, Wyoming. Notice that some of these temperatures are represented by negative numbers.

iStockPhoto.com/
©Nicholas Belton

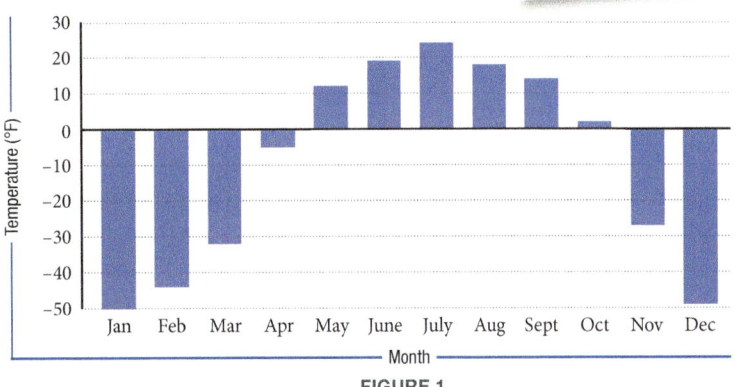

FIGURE 1

In this section we start our work with negative numbers. To represent negative numbers in algebra, we use what is called the **real number line.** Here is how we construct a real number line: We first draw a straight line and label a convenient point on the line with 0. Then we mark off equally spaced distances in both directions from 0. Label the points to the right of 0 with the numbers 1, 2, 3, . . .(the dots mean "and so on"). The points to the left of 0 we label in order, -1, -2, -3, ... Here is what it looks like.

> **Note** If there is no sign ($+$ or $-$) in front of a number, the number is assumed to be positive ($+$).

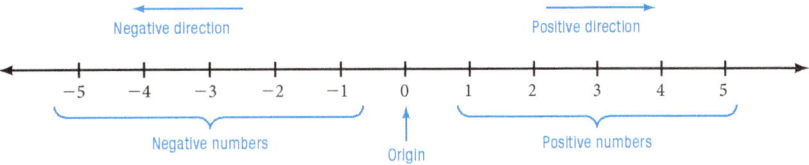

The numbers increase in value going from left to right. If we "move" to the right, we are moving in the positive direction. If we move to the left, we are moving in the negative direction. When we compare two numbers on the number line, the number on the left is always smaller than the number on the right. For instance, -3 is smaller than -1 because it is to the left of -1 on the number line.

Video Examples

Section 0.2

> **Note** There are other numbers on the number line that you may not be as familiar with. They are irrational numbers such as π, $\sqrt{2}$, $\sqrt{3}$. We will introduce these numbers later in the chapter.

Example 1 Locate and label the points on the real number line associated with the numbers -3.5, $-1\frac{1}{4}$, $\frac{1}{2}$, $\frac{3}{4}$, 2.5.

SOLUTION We draw a real number line from -4 to 4 and label the points in question.

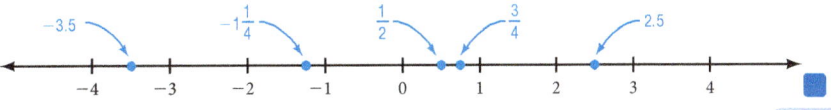

> (dĕf'   *coordinate*
>
> The number associated with a point on the real number line is called the *coordinate* of that point.

In the preceding example, the numbers $\frac{1}{2}$, $\frac{3}{4}$, 2.5, -3.5, and $-1\frac{1}{4}$ are the coordinates of the points they represent.

> (dĕf'   *real numbers*
>
> The numbers that can be represented with points on the real number line are called *real numbers*.

Real numbers include whole numbers, fractions, decimals, and other numbers that are not as familiar to us as these.

Fractions on the Number Line

As we proceed through Chapter 0, from time to time we will review some of the major concepts associated with fractions. To begin, here is the formal definition of a fraction.

> (dĕf'   *fraction*
>
> If *a* and *b* are real numbers, then the expression
> $$\frac{a}{b} \qquad b \neq 0$$
> is called a *fraction*. The top number *a* is called the *numerator*, and the bottom number *b* is called the *denominator*. The restriction $b \neq 0$ keeps us from writing an expression that is undefined. (As you will see, division by zero is not allowed.)

The number line can be used to visualize fractions. Recall that for the fraction $\frac{a}{b}$, *a* is called the numerator and *b* is called the denominator. The denominator indicates the number of equal parts in the interval from 0 to 1 on the number line. The numerator indicates how many of those parts we have. If we take that part of the number line from 0 to 1 and divide it into *three equal parts,* we say that we have divided it into *thirds* (Figure 2). Each of the three segments is $\frac{1}{3}$ (one third) of the whole segment from 0 to 1.

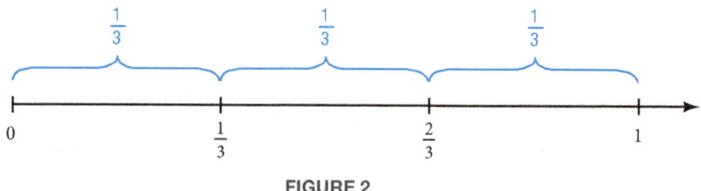

FIGURE 2

Two of these smaller segments together are $\frac{2}{3}$ (two thirds) of the whole segment. And three of them would be $\frac{3}{3}$ (three thirds), or the whole segment.

Let's do the same thing again with six equal divisions of the segment from 0 to 1 (Figure 3). In this case we say each of the smaller segments has a length of $\frac{1}{6}$ (one sixth).

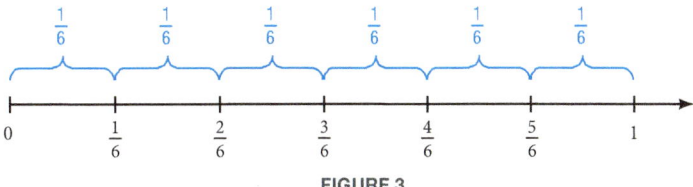

FIGURE 3

The same point we labeled with $\frac{1}{3}$ in Figure 2 is now labeled with $\frac{2}{6}$. Likewise, the point we labeled earlier with $\frac{2}{3}$ is now labeled $\frac{4}{6}$. It must be true then that

$$\frac{2}{6} = \frac{1}{3} \quad \text{and} \quad \frac{4}{6} = \frac{2}{3}$$

Actually, there are many fractions that name the same point as $\frac{1}{3}$. If we were to divide the segment between 0 and 1 into 12 equal parts, 4 of these 12 equal parts $\left(\frac{4}{12}\right)$ would be the same as $\frac{2}{6}$ or $\frac{1}{3}$; that is,

$$\frac{4}{12} = \frac{2}{6} = \frac{1}{3}$$

Even though these three fractions look different, each names the same point on the number line, as shown in Figure 4. All three fractions have the same *value* because they all represent the same number.

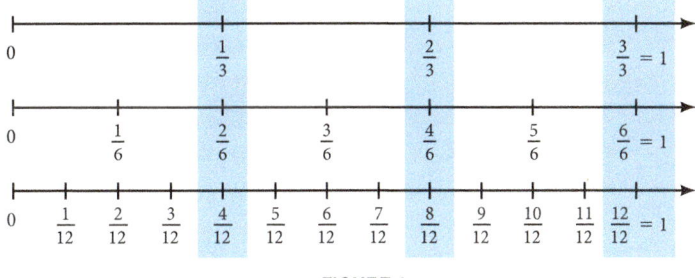

FIGURE 4

(děf *equivalent*

Fractions that represent the same number are said to be **equivalent**. Equivalent fractions may look different, but they must have the same value.

It is apparent that every fraction has many different representations, each of which is equivalent to the original fraction. The next two properties give us a way of changing the terms of a fraction without changing its value.

[Δ≠Σ] *Property 1*

Multiplying the numerator and denominator of a fraction by the same non-zero number never changes the value of the fraction.

⌈Δ≠Σ⌉   *Property 2*

Dividing the numerator and denominator of a fraction by the same nonzero number never changes the value of the fraction.

■ **Example 2**   Write $\frac{3}{4}$ as an equivalent fraction with denominator 20.

SOLUTION   The denominator of the original fraction is 4. The fraction we are trying to find must have a denominator of 20. We know that if we multiply 4 by 5, we get 20. Property 1 indicates that we are free to multiply the denominator by 5 as long as we do the same to the numerator.

$$\frac{3}{4} = \frac{3 \cdot 5}{4 \cdot 5} = \frac{15}{20}$$

The fraction $\frac{15}{20}$ is equivalent to the fraction $\frac{3}{4}$.   ■

Absolute Values and Opposites

Representing numbers on the number line lets us give each number two important properties: a direction from zero and a distance from zero. The direction from zero is represented by the sign in front of the number. (A number without a sign is understood to be positive.) The distance from zero is called the absolute value of the number, as the following definition indicates.

(děf′   *absolute value*

The **absolute value** of a real number is its distance from zero on the number line. If x represents a real number, then the absolute value of x is written $|x|$.

■ **Example 3**   Write each expression without absolute value symbols.

a. $|5|$ **b.** $|-5|$ **c.** $\left|-\frac{1}{2}\right|$

SOLUTION

a. $|5| = 5$ The number 5 is 5 units from zero

b. $|-5| = 5$ The number -5 is 5 units from zero

c. $\left|-\frac{1}{2}\right| = \frac{1}{2}$ The number $-\frac{1}{2}$ is $\frac{1}{2}$ units from zero   ■

The absolute value of a number is **never** negative. It is the distance the number is from zero without regard to which direction it is from zero. When working with the absolute value of sums and differences, we must simplify the expression inside the absolute value symbols first and then find the absolute value of the simplified expression.

■ **Example 4**   Simplify each expression.

a. $|8 - 3|$ **b.** $|3 \cdot 2^3 + 2 \cdot 3^2|$ **c.** $|9 - 2| - |8 - 6|$

SOLUTION

a. $|8 - 3| = |5| = 5$

b. $|3 \cdot 2^3 + 2 \cdot 3^2| = |3 \cdot 8 + 2 \cdot 9| = |24 + 18| = |42| = 42$

c. $|9 - 2| - |8 - 6| = |7| - |2| = 7 - 2 = 5$ ■

Another important concept associated with numbers on the number line is that of opposites. Here is the definition.

> **(dĕf́ *opposites***
>
> Numbers the same distance from zero but in opposite directions from zero are called *opposites*.

Example 5 Give the opposite of each number.

a. 5   **b.** -3 **c.** $\dfrac{1}{4}$ **d.** -2.3

SOLUTION

	Number	Opposite	
a.	5	-5	5 and -5 are opposites
b.	-3	3	-3 and 3 are opposites
c.	$\dfrac{1}{4}$	$-\dfrac{1}{4}$	$\frac{1}{4}$ and $-\frac{1}{4}$ are opposites
d.	-2.3	2.3	-2.3 and 2.3 are opposites

Each negative number is the opposite of some positive number, and each positive number is the opposite of some negative number. The opposite of a negative number is a positive number. In symbols, if *a* represents a positive number, then

$$-(-a) = a$$

Opposites always have the same absolute value. And, when you add any two opposites, the result is always zero:

$$a + (-a) = 0$$

Reciprocals and Multiplication with Fractions

The last concept we want to cover in this section is the concept of reciprocals. Understanding reciprocals requires some knowledge of multiplication with fractions. To multiply two fractions, we simply multiply numerators and multiply denominators.

Example 6 Multiply $\dfrac{3}{4} \cdot \dfrac{5}{7}$.

SOLUTION The product of the numerators is 15, and the product of the denominators is 28:

$$\frac{3}{4} \cdot \frac{5}{7} = \frac{3 \cdot 5}{4 \cdot 7} = \frac{15}{28}$$

Example 7 Multiply $7\left(\dfrac{1}{3}\right)$.

SOLUTION The number 7 can be thought of as the fraction $\dfrac{7}{1}$:

$$7\left(\frac{1}{3}\right) = \frac{7}{1}\left(\frac{1}{3}\right) = \frac{7 \cdot 1}{1 \cdot 3} = \frac{7}{3}$$

■ **Example 8** Expand and multiply $\left(\dfrac{2}{3}\right)^3$.

SOLUTION Using the definition of exponents from the previous section, we have

$$\left(\frac{2}{3}\right)^3 = \frac{2}{3} \cdot \frac{2}{3} \cdot \frac{2}{3} = \frac{8}{27}$$

We are now ready for the definition of reciprocals.

> (dĕf′ *reciprocals*
>
> Two numbers whose product is 1 are called *reciprocals*.

■ **Example 9** Give the reciprocal of each number.

a. 5   **b.** 2   **c.** $\dfrac{1}{3}$ **d.** $\dfrac{3}{4}$

SOLUTION

	Number	Reciprocal	
a.	5	$\dfrac{1}{5}$	*Because* $5\left(\frac{1}{5}\right) \cdot \frac{5}{1}\left(\frac{1}{5}\right) \cdot \frac{5}{5} \cdot 1$
b.	2	$\dfrac{1}{2}$	*Because* $2\left(\frac{1}{2}\right) \cdot \frac{2}{1}\left(\frac{1}{2}\right) \cdot \frac{2}{2} \cdot 1$
c.	$\dfrac{1}{3}$	3	*Because* $\frac{1}{3}(3) \cdot \frac{1}{3}\left(\frac{3}{1}\right) \cdot \frac{3}{3} \cdot 1$
d.	$\dfrac{3}{4}$	$\dfrac{4}{3}$	*Because* $\frac{3}{4}\left(\frac{4}{3}\right) \cdot \frac{12}{12} \cdot 1$

Although we will not develop multiplication with negative numbers until later in the chapter, you should know that the reciprocal of a negative number is also a negative number. For example, the reciprocal of -4 is $-\frac{1}{4}$.

> **Note** The vertical line labeled h in the triangle is its height, or altitude. It extends from the top of the triangle down to the base, meeting the base at an angle of 90°. The altitude of a triangle is always perpendicular to the base. The small square shown where the altitude meets the base is used to indicate that the angle formed is 90°.

Formulas for Area and Perimeter

A square, rectangle, and triangle are shown in the following figures. Note that we have labeled the dimensions of each with variables. The formulas for the perimeter and area of each object are given in terms of its dimensions.

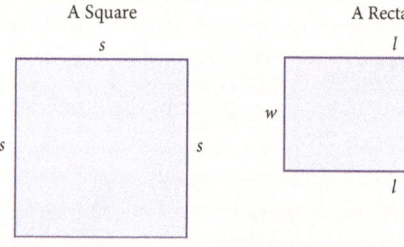

A Square
Perimeter $= 4s$
Area $= s^2$

A Rectangle
Perimeter $= 2l + 2w$
Area $= lw$

A Triangle
Perimeter $= a + b + c$
Area $= \frac{1}{2}bh$

The formula for perimeter gives us the distance around the outside of the object along its sides, whereas the formula for area gives us a measure of the amount of surface the object has.

Example 10   Find the perimeter and area of each figure.

a.

5 ft

b.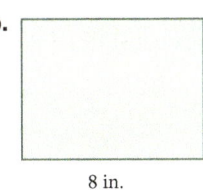

6 in.

8 in.

c.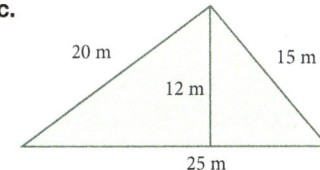

20 m   15 m

12 m

25 m

SOLUTION   We use the preceding formulas to find the perimeter and the area. In each case, the units for perimeter are linear units, whereas the units for area are square units.

a. Perimeter $= 4s = 4 \cdot 5$ feet $= 20$ feet

   Area $= s^2 = (5 \text{ feet})^2 = 25$ square feet

b. Perimeter $= 2l + 2w = 2(8 \text{ inches}) + 2(6 \text{ inches}) = 28$ inches

   Area $= lw = (8 \text{ inches})(6 \text{ inches}) = 48$ square inches

c. Perimeter $= a + b + c = (20 \text{ meters}) + (25 \text{ meters}) + (15 \text{ meters})$

$$= 60 \text{ meters}$$

   Area $= \dfrac{1}{2} bh = \dfrac{1}{2}(25 \text{ meters})(12 \text{ meters}) = 150$ square meters

---

Getting Ready for Class

After reading through the preceding section, respond in your own words and in complete sentences.

A. What is a real number?

B. Explain multiplication with fractions.

C. How do you find the opposite of a number?

D. Explain how you find the perimeter and the area of a rectangle.

Problem Set 0.2

Draw a number line that extends from −5 to +5. Label the points with the following coordinates.

1. 5

2. −2

3. −4

4. −3

5. 1.5

6. −1.5

7. $\dfrac{9}{4}$

8. $\dfrac{8}{3}$

Write each of the following fractions as an equivalent fraction with denominator 24.

9. $\dfrac{3}{4}$ **10.** $\dfrac{5}{6}$ **11.** $\dfrac{1}{2}$ **12.** $\dfrac{1}{8}$ **13.** $\dfrac{5}{8}$ **14.** $\dfrac{7}{12}$

Write each fraction as an equivalent fraction with denominator 60.

15. $\dfrac{3}{5}$ **16.** $\dfrac{5}{12}$ **17.** $\dfrac{11}{30}$ **18.** $\dfrac{9}{10}$

For each of the following numbers, give the opposite, the reciprocal, and the absolute value. (Assume all variables are nonzero.)

19. 10   **20.** 8   **21.** $\dfrac{3}{4}$ **22.** $\dfrac{5}{7}$ **23.** $\dfrac{11}{2}$ **24.** $\dfrac{16}{3}$

25. −3   **26.** −5   **27.** $-\dfrac{2}{5}$ **28.** $-\dfrac{3}{8}$ **29.** x **30.** a

Place one of the symbols < or > between each of the following to make the resulting statement true.

31. −5   −3   **32.** −8   −1   **33.** −3   −7   **34.** −6   5

35. $|-4|$ $-|-4|$ **36.** 3 $-|-3|$ **37.** 7 $-|-7|$ **38.** −7 $|-7|$

39. $-\dfrac{3}{4}$ $-\dfrac{1}{4}$ **40.** $-\dfrac{2}{3}$ $-\dfrac{1}{3}$ **41.** $-\dfrac{3}{2}$ $-\dfrac{3}{4}$ **42.** $-\dfrac{8}{3}$ $-\dfrac{17}{3}$

Simplify each expression.

43. $|8 - 2|$

44. $|6 - 1|$

45. $|5 \cdot 2^3 - 2 \cdot 3^2|$

46. $|2 \cdot 10^2 + 3 \cdot 10|$

47. $|7 - 2| - |4 - 2|$

48. $|10 - 3| - |4 - 1|$

49. $10 - |7 - 2(5 - 3)|$

50. $12 - |9 - 3(7 - 5)|$

51. $15 - |8 - 2(3 \cdot 4 - 9)| - 10$

52. $25 - |9 - 3(4 \cdot 5 - 18)| - 20$

Multiply the following.

53. $\dfrac{2}{3} \cdot \dfrac{4}{5}$ **54.** $\dfrac{1}{4} \cdot \dfrac{3}{5}$ **55.** $\dfrac{1}{2}(3)$ **56.** $\dfrac{1}{3}(2)$

57. $\dfrac{1}{4}(5)$ **58.** $\dfrac{1}{5}(4)$ **59.** $\dfrac{4}{3} \cdot \dfrac{3}{4}$ **60.** $\dfrac{5}{7} \cdot \dfrac{7}{5}$

61. $6\left(\dfrac{1}{6}\right)$ **62.** $8\left(\dfrac{1}{8}\right)$ **63.** $3 \cdot \dfrac{1}{3}$ **64.** $4 \cdot \dfrac{1}{4}$

Expand and multiply.

65. $\left(\dfrac{3}{4}\right)^2$ **66.** $\left(\dfrac{5}{6}\right)^2$ **67.** $\left(\dfrac{2}{3}\right)^3$ **68.** $\left(\dfrac{1}{2}\right)^3$ **69.** $\left(\dfrac{1}{10}\right)^4$ **70.** $\left(\dfrac{1}{10}\right)^5$

Find the next number in each sequence.

71. $1, \dfrac{1}{3}, \dfrac{1}{5}, \dfrac{1}{7}, \ldots$ (Reciprocals of odd numbers.)

72. $\dfrac{1}{2}, \dfrac{1}{4}, \dfrac{1}{6}, \dfrac{1}{8}, \ldots$ (Reciprocals of even numbers.)

73. $1, \dfrac{1}{4}, \dfrac{1}{9}, \dfrac{1}{16}, \ldots$ (Reciprocals of squares.)

74. $1, \dfrac{1}{8}, \dfrac{1}{27}, \dfrac{1}{64}, \ldots$ (Reciprocals of cubes.)

Find the perimeter and area of each figure.

75.

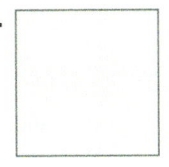

1 in.

1 in.

76.

15 mm

15 mm

77.

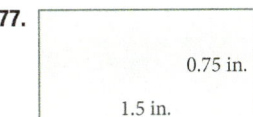

0.75 in.

1.5 in.

78.

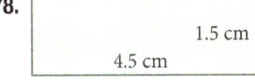

1.5 cm

4.5 cm

79.

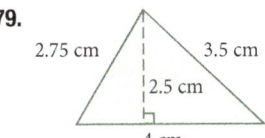

2.75 cm   3.5 cm

2.5 cm

4 cm

80.

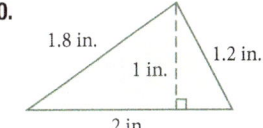

1.8 in.   1.2 in.

1 in.

2 in.

Applying the Concepts

81. Football Yardage A football team gains 6 yards on one play and then loses 8 yards on the next play. To what number on the number line does a loss of 8 yards correspond? The total yards gained or lost on the two plays corresponds to what negative number?

82. Checking Account Balance A woman has a balance of $20 in her checking account. If she writes a check for $30, what negative number can be used to represent the new balance in her checking account?

Temperature In the United States, temperature is measured on the Fahrenheit temperature scale. On this scale, water boils at 212 degrees and freezes at 32 degrees. To denote a temperature of 32 degrees on the Fahrenheit scale, we write

32°F, which is read "32 degrees Fahrenheit"

Use this information for Problems 83 and 84.

83. Temperature and Altitude Marilyn is flying from Seattle to San Francisco on a Boeing 737 jet. When the plane reaches an altitude of 35,000 feet, the temperature outside the plane is 64 degrees below zero Fahrenheit. Represent the temperature with a negative number. If the temperature outside the plane gets warmer by 10 degrees, what will the new temperature be?

84. Temperature Change At 10:00 in the morning in White Bear Lake, Minnesota, John notices the temperature outside is 10 degrees below zero Fahrenheit. Write the temperature as a negative number. An hour later it has warmed up by 6 degrees. What is the temperature at 11:00 that morning?

Wind Chill The table below is a table of wind chill temperatures. The top column gives the air temperature, and the first row is wind speed in miles per hour. The numbers within the table indicate how cold the weather will feel. For example, if the thermometer reads 30°F and the wind is blowing at 15 miles per hour, the wind chill temperature is 9°F. Use Table 1 to answer Problems 85 and 86.

Wind Chill Temperatures

Air Temperature (°F)	Wind Speed (mph)				
	10	15	20	25	30
30°	16°	9°	4°	1°	−2°
25°	10°	2°	−3°	−7°	−10°
20°	3°	−5°	−10°	−15°	−18°
15°	−3°	−11°	−17°	−22°	−25°
10°	−9°	−18°	−24°	−29°	−33°
5°	−15°	−25°	−31°	−36°	−41°
0°	−22°	−31°	−39°	−44°	−49°
−5°	−27°	−38°	−46°	−51°	−56°

85. Reading Tables Find the wind chill temperature if the thermometer reads 20°F and the wind is blowing at 25 miles per hour.

86. Reading Tables Which will feel colder: a day with an air temperature of 10°F with a 25-mile-per-hour wind, or a day with an air temperature of 25° F and a 10-mile-per-hour wind?

87. Scuba Diving Steve is scuba diving near his home in Maui. At one point he is 100 feet below the surface. Represent this number with a negative number. If he descends another 5 feet, what negative number will represent his new position?

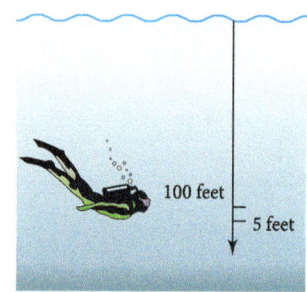

88. Reading a Chart The chart shows yields for certificates of deposit during one week in 2006, write a mathematical statement using one of the symbols < or > to compare the following:

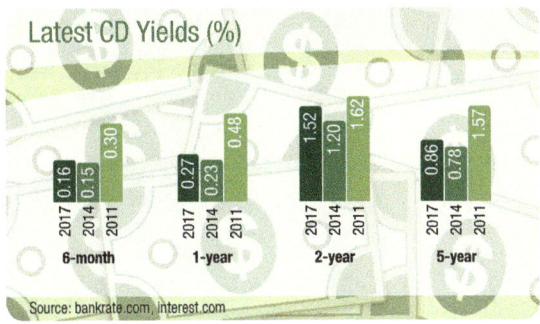

Latest CD Yields (%)

Source: bankrate.com, interest.com

a. 6 month yield in 2014 to 1 year yield in 2017.

b. 2 year yield in 2011 to 5 year yield in 2011.

c. 5 year yield in 2014 to 6 month yield in 2017

89. Geometry Find the area and perimeter of an $8\frac{1}{2}$-by-11-inch piece of notebook paper.

90. Geometry Find the area and perimeter of an $8\frac{1}{2}$-by-$5\frac{1}{2}$-inch piece of paper.

Calories and Exercise The table here gives the amount of energy expended per hour for various activities for a person weighing 120, 150, or 180 pounds. Use the table to answer questions 91–94.

Energy Expended from Exercising

Activity	Calories per Hour		
	120 lb	150 lb	180 lb
Bicycling	299	374	449
Bowling	212	265	318
Handball	544	680	816
Horseback trotting	278	347	416
Jazzercise	272	340	408
Jogging	544	680	816
Skiing (downhill)	435	544	653

91. Suppose you weigh 120 pounds. How many calories will you burn if you play handball for 2 hours and then ride your bicycle for an hour?

92. How many calories are burned by a person weighing 150 pounds who jogs for $\frac{1}{2}$ hour and then goes bicycling for 2 hours?

93. Two people go skiing. One weighs 180 pounds and the other weighs 120 pounds. If they ski for 3 hours, how many more calories are burned by the person weighing 180 pounds?

94. Two people spend 3 hours bowling. If one weighs 120 pounds and the other weighs 150 pounds, how many more calories are burned during the evening by the person weighing 150 pounds?

95. Use the chart shown here to answer the following questions.

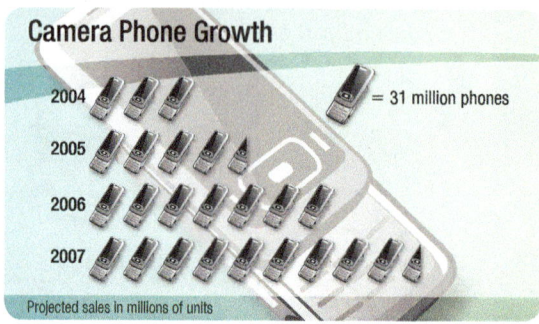

Camera Phone Growth

2004

= 31 million phones

2005

2006

2007

Projected sales in millions of units

  a. How many millions of camera phones were sold in 2004?
  b. True or false? The chart shows sales in 2005 to be more than 155 million camera phones.
  c. True or false? The chart shows sales in 2007 to be less than 310 million camera phones.

96. Improving Your Quantitative Literacy Quantitative literacy is a subject discussed by many people involved in teaching mathematics. The person they are concerned with when they discuss it is you. We are going to work at improving your quantitative literacy, but before we do that we should answer the question, What is quantitative literacy? Lynn Arthur Steen, a noted mathematics educator, has stated that quantitative literacy is "the capacity to deal effectively with the quantitative aspects of life."

  a. Give a definition for the word *quantitative*.
  b. Give a definition for the word *literacy*.
  c. Are there situations that occur in your life that you find distasteful, or that you try to avoid, because they involve numbers and mathematics? If so, list some of them here. (For example, some people find the process of buying a car particularly difficult because they feel that the numbers and details of the financing are beyond them.)

Addition of Real Numbers

Suppose that you are playing a friendly game of poker with some friends, and you lose $3 on the first hand and $4 on the second hand. If you represent winning with positive numbers and losing with negative numbers, how can you translate this situation into symbols? Because you lost $3 and $4 for a total of $7, one way to represent this situation is with addition of negative numbers:

$$(-\$3) + (-\$4) = -\$7$$

From this equation, we see that the sum of two negative numbers is a negative number. To generalize addition with positive and negative numbers, we use the number line.

Because real numbers have both a distance from zero (absolute value) and a direction from zero (sign), we can think of addition of two numbers in terms of distance and direction from zero.

Let's look at a problem for which we know the answer. Suppose we want to add the numbers 3 and 4. The problem is written $3 + 4$. To put it on the number line, we read the problem as follows:

1. The 3 tells us to "start at the origin and move 3 units in the positive direction."

2. The $+$ sign is read "and then move."

3. The 4 means "4 units in the positive direction."

To summarize, $3 + 4$ means to start at the origin, move 3 units in the positive direction, and then move 4 units in the positive direction.

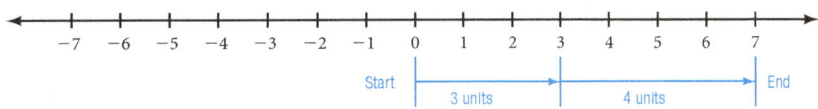

We end up at 7, which is the answer to our problem: $3 + 4 = 7$.

Let's try other combinations of positive and negative 3 and 4 on the number line.

Example 1 Add $3 + (-4)$.

SOLUTION Starting at the origin, move 3 units in the positive direction and then 4 units in the negative direction.

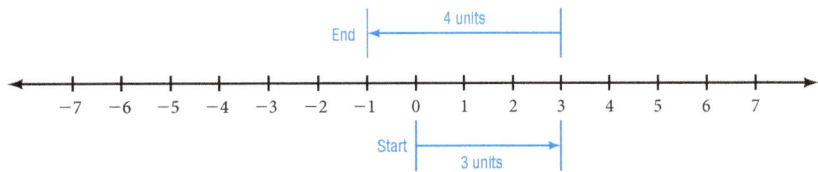

We end up at -1; therefore, $3 + (-4) = -1$.

Example 2   Add $-3 + 4$.

SOLUTION   Starting at the origin, move 3 units in the negative direction and then 4 units in the positive direction.

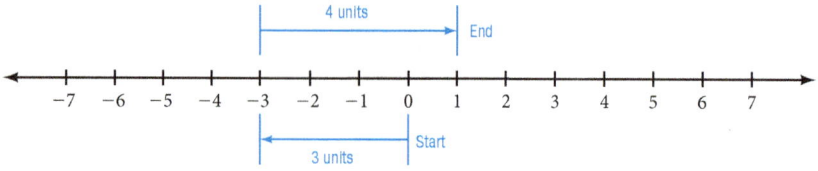

We end up at $+1$; therefore, $-3 + 4 = 1$.

Example 3   Add $-3 + (-4)$.

SOLUTION   Starting at the origin, move 3 units in the negative direction and then 4 units in the negative direction.

We end up at -7; therefore, $-3 + (-4) = -7$. Here is a summary of what we have just completed:

$$3 + 4 = 7$$

$$3 + (-4) = -1$$

$$-3 + 4 = 1$$

$$-3 + (-4) = -7$$

Let's do four more problems on the number line and then summarize our results into a rule we can use to add any two real numbers.

Example 4   Show that $5 + 7 = 12$.

SOLUTION

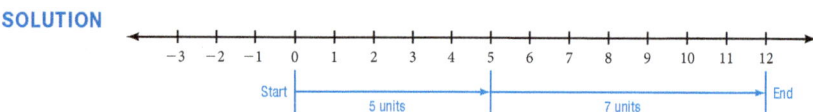

Example 5   Show that $5 + (-7) = -2$.

SOLUTION

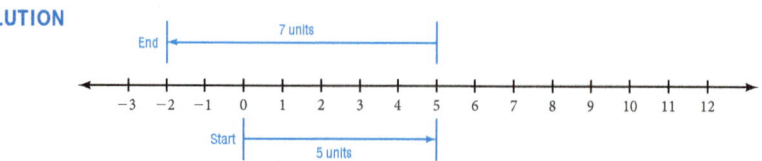

Example 6   Show that $-5 + 7 = 2$.

SOLUTION

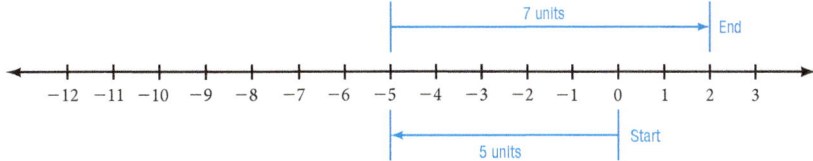

Example 7   Show that $-5 + (-7) = -12$.

SOLUTION

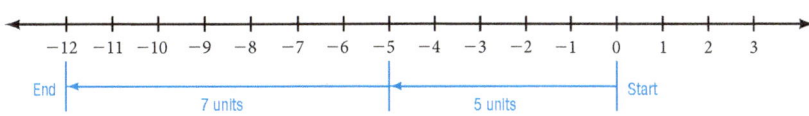

If we look closely at the results of the preceding addition problems, we can see that they support (or justify) the following rule.

> **Rule**
>
> To add two real numbers with
> 1. The *same* sign: Simply add their absolute values and use the common sign. (Both numbers are positive, the answer is positive. Both numbers are negative, the answer is negative.)
> 2. *Different* signs: Subtract the smaller absolute value from the larger. The answer will have the sign of the number with the larger absolute value.

Note This rule is what we have been working towards. The rule is very important. Be sure that you understand it and can use it. The problems we have done up to this point have been done simply to justify this rule. Now that we have the rule, we no longer need to use the number line.

This rule covers all possible combinations of addition with real numbers. You must memorize it. After you have worked a number of problems, it will seem almost automatic.

Example 8   Add all combinations of positive and negative 10 and 13.

SOLUTION   Rather than work these problems on the number line, we use the rule for adding positive and negative numbers to obtain our answers:

$$10 + 13 = 23$$
$$10 + (-13) = -3$$
$$-10 + 13 = 3$$
$$-10 + (-13) = -23$$

Example 9   Add all possible combinations of positive and negative 12 and 17.

SOLUTION   Applying the rule for adding positive and negative numbers, we have

$$12 + 17 = 29$$
$$12 + (-17) = -5$$
$$-12 + 17 = 5$$
$$-12 + (-17) = -29$$

Example 10   Add $-3 + 2 + (-4)$.

SOLUTION   Applying the rule for order of operations, we add left to right:

$$-3 + 2 + (-4) = -1 + (-4)$$
$$= -5$$

Example 11   Add $-8 + [2 + (-5)] + (-1)$.

SOLUTION   Adding inside the brackets first and then left to right, we have

$$-8 + [2 + (-5)] + (-1) = -8 + (-3) + (-1)$$
$$= -11 + (-1)$$
$$= -12$$

Example 12   Simplify $-10 + 2(-8 + 11) + (-4)$.

SOLUTION   First, we simplify inside the parentheses. Then, we multiply. Finally, we add left to right:

$$-10 + 2(-8 + 11) + (-4) = -10 + 2(3) + (-4)$$
$$= -10 + 6 + (-4)$$
$$= -4 + (-4)$$
$$= -8$$

Arithmetic Sequences

The pattern in a sequence of numbers is easy to identify when each number in the sequence comes from the preceding number by adding the same amount each time. This leads us to our next level of classification, in which we classify groups of sequences with a common characteristic.

> (dĕf)   *arithmetic sequence*
>
> An **arithmetic sequence** is a sequence of numbers in which each number (after the first number) comes from adding the same amount to the number before it.

Here is an example of an arithmetic sequence:

$$2, 5, 8, 11, \ldots$$

Each number is obtained by adding 3 to the number before it.

Example 13   Each sequence below is an arithmetic sequence. Find the next two numbers in each sequence.

a. 7, 10, 13, ...   **b.**   9.5, 10, 10.5, ...   **c.** 5, 0, −5, ...

SOLUTION   Because we know that each sequence is arithmetic, we know to look for the number that is added to each term to produce the next consecutive term.

a. 7, 10, 13, ... : Each term is found by adding 3 to the term before it. Therefore, the next two terms will be 16 and 19.

b. 9.5, 10, 10.5, ... : Each term comes from adding 0.5 to the term before it. Therefore, the next two terms will be 11 and 11.5.

c. 5, 0, −5, ... : Each term comes from adding −5 to the term before it. Therefore, the next two terms will be $-5 + (-5) = -10$ and $-10 + (-5) = -15$.

Getting Ready for Class

After reading through the preceding section, respond in your own words and in complete sentences.

A. Explain how you would add 3 and −5 on the number line.
B. How do you add two negative numbers?
C. What is an arithmetic sequence?
D. Why is the sum of a number and its opposite always 0?

Problem Set 0.3

1. Add all combinations of positive and negative 3 and 5. (Look back to Examples 8 and 9.)
2. Add all combinations of positive and negative 6 and 4.
3. Add all combinations of positive and negative 15 and 20.
4. Add all combinations of positive and negative 18 and 12.

Work the following problems. You may want to begin by doing a few on the number line.

5. $6 + (-3)$ 6. $7 + (-8)$ 7. $13 + (-20)$ 8. $15 + (-25)$

9. $18 + (-32)$ 10. $6 + (-9)$ 11. $-6 + 3$ 12. $-8 + 7$

13. $-30 + 5$ 14. $-18 + 6$ 15. $-6 + (-6)$ 16. $-5 + (-5)$

17. $-9 + (-10)$ 18. $-8 + (-6)$ 19. $-10 + (-15)$ 20. $-18 + (-30)$

Work the following problems using the rule for addition of real numbers. You may want to refer back to the rule for order of operations.

21. $5 + (-6) + (-7)$ 22. $6 + (-8) + (-10)$

23. $-7 + 8 + (-5)$ 24. $-6 + 9 + (-3)$

25. $5 + [6 + (-2)] + (-3)$ 26. $10 + [8 + (-5)] + (-20)$

27. $[6 + (-2)] + [3 + (-1)]$ 28. $[18 + (-5)] + [9 + (-10)]$

29. $20 + (-6) + [3 + (-9)]$ 30. $18 + (-2) + [9 + (-13)]$

31. $-3 + (-2) + [5 + (-4)]$ 32. $-6 + (-5) + [-4 + (-1)]$

33. $(-9 + 2) + [5 + (-8)] + (-4)$ 34. $(-7 + 3) + [9 + (-6)] + (-5)$

35. $[-6 + (-4)] + [7 + (-5)] + (-9)$ 36. $[-8 + (-1)] + [8 + (-6)] + (-6)$

37. $(-6 + 9) + (-5) + (-4 + 3) + 7$ 38. $(-10 + 4) + (-3) + (-3 + 8) + 6$

The problems that follow involve some multiplication. Be sure that you work inside the parentheses first, then multiply, and finally, add left to right.

39. $-5 + 2(-3 + 7)$ 40. $-3 + 4(-2 + 7)$

41. $9 + 3(-8 + 10)$ 42. $4 + 5(-2 + 6)$

43. $-10 + 2(-6 + 8) + (-2)$ 44. $-20 + 3(-7 + 10) + (-4)$

45. $2(-4 + 7) + 3(-6 + 8)$ 46. $5(-2 + 5) + 7(-1 + 6)$

Each sequence below is an arithmetic sequence. In each case, find the next two numbers in the sequence.

47. $3, 8, 13, 18, \ldots$ 48. $1, 5, 9, 13, \ldots$ 49. $10, 15, 20, 25, \ldots$

50. $10, 16, 22, 28, \ldots$ 51. $20, 15, 10, 5, \ldots$ 52. $24, 20, 16, 12, \ldots$

53. $6, 0, -6, \ldots$ 54. $1, 0, -1, \ldots$ 55. $8, 4, 0, \ldots$

56. $5, 2, -1, \ldots$

57. Is the sequence of odd numbers an arithmetic sequence?
58. Is the sequence of squares an arithmetic sequence?

Recall that the word sum indicates addition. Write the numerical expression that is equivalent to each of the following phrases and then simplify.

59. The sum of 5 and 9

60. The sum of 6 and -3

61. Four added to the sum of -7 and -5

62. Six added to the sum of -9 and 1

63. The sum of -2 and -3 increased by 10

64. The sum of -4 and -12 increased by 2

Answer the following questions.

65. What number do you add to -8 to get -5?

66. What number do you add to 10 to get 4?

67. The sum of what number and -6 is -9?

68. The sum of what number and -12 is 8?

Applying the Concepts

69. Temperature Change The temperature at noon is 12 degrees below 0 Fahrenheit. By 1:00 it has risen 4 degrees. Write an expression using the numbers -12 and 4 to describe this situation.

70. Stock Value On Monday a certain stock gains 2 points. On Tuesday it loses 3 points. Write an expression using positive and negative numbers with addition to describe this situation and then simplify.

71. Gambling On three consecutive hands of draw poker a gambler wins $10, loses $6, and then loses another $8. Write an expression using positive and negative numbers and addition to describe this situation and then simplify.

72. Number Problem You know from your past experience with numbers that subtracting 5 from 8 results in 3 $(8 - 5 = 3)$. What addition problem that starts with the number 8 gives the same result?

73. Checkbook Balance Suppose that you balance your checkbook and find that you are overdrawn by $30; that is, your balance is $-\$30$. Then you go to the bank and deposit $40. Translate this situation into an addition problem, the answer to which gives the new balance in your checkbook.

74. Checkbook Balance The balance in your checkbook is $-\$25$. If you make a deposit of $75, and then write a check for $18, what is the new balance?

iStockPhoto.com/©Alexander Fairfull

Profit Revenue and Costs In business, the difference of revenue and cost is profit, or $P = R - C$, where P is profit, R is revenue, and C is costs. The bar charts below show the costs and revenue for the Baby Steps Shoe Company for a recent 5-year period. Use this information to answer the questions below.

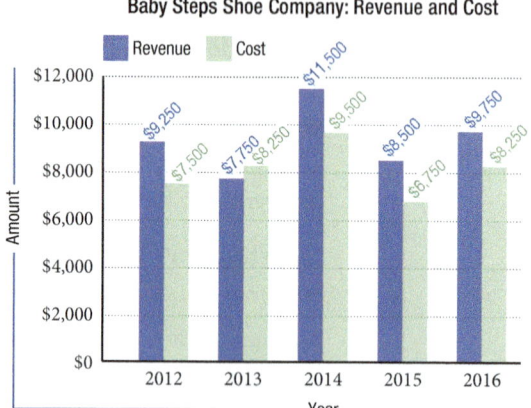

Baby Steps Shoe Company: Revenue and Cost

75. What was the profit for the year 2014?

76. In what year was the largest increase in costs from the previous year? How much was the increase?

77. What was the only year the company had a loss? (Profit is negative.) How much was the loss?

Subtraction of Real Numbers

Suppose that the temperature at noon is 20° Fahrenheit and 12 hours later, at midnight, it has dropped to $-15°$ Fahrenheit. What is the difference between the temperature at noon and the temperature at midnight? Intuitively, we know the difference in the two temperatures is 35°. We also know that the word difference indicates subtraction. The difference between 20 and -15 is written

$$20 - (-15)$$

It must be true that $20 - (-15) = 35$. In this section we will see how our definition for subtraction confirms that this last statement is in fact correct.

In the previous section we spent some time developing the rule for addition of real numbers. Because we want to make as few rules as possible, we can define subtraction in terms of addition. By doing so, we can then use the rule for addition to solve our subtraction problems.

$\lceil \Delta \neq \Sigma$ *Rule*

To subtract one real number from another, simply add its opposite.

Algebraically, the rule is written like this: If a and b represent two real numbers, then it is always true that

$$\underbrace{a - b}_{\text{To subtract } b} = \underbrace{a + (-b)}_{\text{add the opposite of } b}$$

This is how subtraction is defined in algebra. This definition of subtraction will not conflict with what you already know about subtraction, but it will allow you to do subtraction using negative numbers.

Video Examples

Section 0.4

Example 1   Subtract all possible combinations of positive and negative 7 and 2.

SOLUTION

$$
\begin{aligned}
7 - 2 &= 7 + (-2) = 5 \\
-7 - 2 &= -7 + (-2) = -9
\end{aligned}
\right\} \quad \text{Subtracting 2 is the same as adding } -2
$$

$$
\begin{aligned}
7 - (-2) &= 7 + 2 = 9 \\
-7 - (-2) &= -7 + 2 = -5
\end{aligned}
\right\} \quad \text{Subtracting } -2 \text{ is the same as adding 2}
$$

Notice that each subtraction problem is first changed to an addition problem. The rule for addition is then used to arrive at the answer.

We have defined subtraction in terms of addition, and we still obtain answers consistent with the answers we are used to getting with subtraction. Moreover, we now can do subtraction problems involving both positive and negative numbers.

As you proceed through the following examples and the problem set, you will begin to notice shortcuts you can use in working the problems. You will not always have to change subtraction to addition of the opposite to be able to get answers quickly. Use all the shortcuts you wish as long as you consistently get the correct answers.

Example 2   Subtract all combinations of positive and negative 8 and 13.

SOLUTION

$$8 - 13 = 8 + (-13) = -5$$
$$-8 - 13 = -8 + (-13) = -21$$

Subtracting +13 is the same as adding −13

$$8 - (-13) = 8 + 13 = 21$$
$$-8 - (-13) = -8 + 13 = 5$$

Subtracting −13 is the same as adding +13

Example 3   Simplify each expression as much as possible.

a. $7 + (-3) - 5$ **b.** $8 - (-2) - 6$ **c.** $-2 - (-3 + 1) - 5$

SOLUTION

a. $7 + (-3) - 5 = 7 + (-3) + (-5)$
$$= 4 + (-5)$$
$$= -1$$

Begin by changing all subtractions to additions

Then add left to right

b. $8 - (-2) - 6 = 8 + 2 + (-6)$
$$= 10 + (-6)$$
$$= 4$$

Begin by changing all subtractions to additions

Then add left to right

c. $-2 - (-3 + 1) - 5 = -2 - (-2) - 5$
$$= -2 + 2 + (-5)$$
$$= -5$$

Do what is in the parentheses first

The next two examples involve multiplication and exponents as well as subtraction. Remember, according to the rule for order of operations, we evaluate the numbers containing exponents and multiply before we subtract.

Example 4   Simplify $2 \cdot 5 - 3 \cdot 8 - 4 \cdot 9$.

SOLUTION   First, we multiply left to right, and then we subtract:

$$2 \cdot 5 - 3 \cdot 8 - 4 \cdot 9 = 10 - 24 - 36$$
$$= -14 - 36$$
$$= -50$$

Example 5   Simplify $3 \cdot 2^3 - 2 \cdot 4^2$.

SOLUTION   We begin by evaluating each number that contains an exponent. Then we multiply before we subtract:

$$3 \cdot 2^3 - 2 \cdot 4^2 = 3 \cdot 8 - 2 \cdot 16$$
$$= 24 - 32$$
$$= -8$$

Example 6   Subtract 7 from -3.

SOLUTION   First, we write the problem in terms of subtraction. We then change to addition of the opposite:

$$-3 - 7 = -3 + (-7)$$
$$= -10$$

■ **Example 7**   Subtract −5 from 2.

SOLUTION   Subtracting −5 is the same as adding +5:

$$2 - (-5) = 2 + 5$$
$$= 7$$

■

■ **Example 8**   Find the difference of 9 and 2.

SOLUTION   Written in symbols, the problem looks like this:

$$9 - 2 = 7$$

The difference of 9 and 2 is 7.

■

■ **Example 9**   Find the difference of 3 and −5.

SOLUTION   Subtracting −5 from 3 we have

$$3 - (-5) = 3 + 5$$
$$= 8$$

■

⚒) *Complementary and Supplementary Angles*

If you have studied geometry at all, you know that there are 360° in a full rotation—the number of degrees swept out by the radius of a circle as it rotates once around the circle.

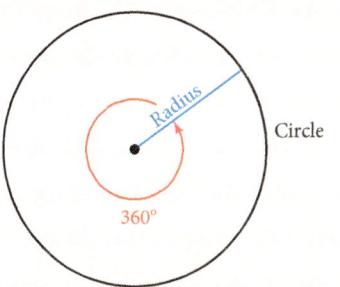

We can apply our knowledge of algebra to help solve some simple geometry problems. Before we do, however, we need to review some of the vocabulary associated with angles.

(dĕf′   *complementary & supplementary angles*

In geometry, two angles that add to 90° are called *complementary angles*. In a similar manner, two angles that add to 180° are called *supplementary angles*. The diagrams below illustrate the relationships between angles that are complementary and between angles that are supplementary.

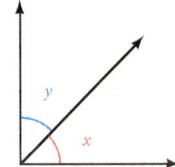

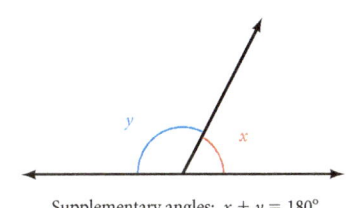

Complementary angles: $x + y = 90°$ Supplementary angles: $x + y = 180°$

Example 10   Find x in each of the following diagrams.

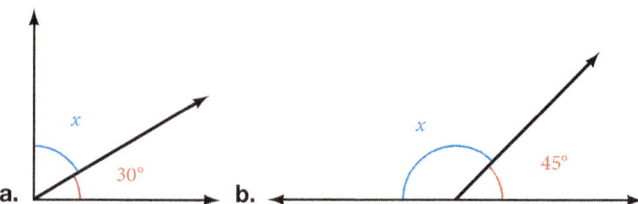

a.   b.

SOLUTION   We use subtraction to find each angle.

a. Because the two angles are complementary, we can find x by subtracting 30° from 90°:

$$x = 90° - 30° = 60°$$

We say 30° and 60° are complementary angles. The complement of 30° is 60°.

b. The two angles in the diagram are supplementary. To find x, we subtract 45° from 180°:

$$x = 180° - 45° = 135°$$

We say 45° and 135° are supplementary angles. The supplement of 45° is 135°.

Subtracting and Taking Away

For some people taking algebra for the first time, subtraction of positive and negative numbers can be a problem. These people may believe that $-5 - 9$ should be -4 or 4, not -14. If this is happening to you, you probably are thinking of subtraction in terms of taking one number away from another. Thinking of subtraction in this way works well with positive numbers if you always subtract the smaller number from the larger. In algebra, however, we encounter many situations other than this. The definition of subtraction, that $a - b = a + (-b)$, clearly indicates the correct way to use subtraction; that is, when working subtraction problems, you should think "addition of the opposite," not "take one number away from another." To be successful in algebra, you need to apply properties and definitions exactly as they are presented here.

Getting Ready for Class

After reading through the preceding section, respond in your own words and in complete sentences.

A. Why do we define subtraction in terms of addition?

B. Write the definition for a − b.

C. Explain in words how you would subtract 3 from −7.

D. What are complementary angles?

Problem Set 0.4

The following problems are intended to give you practice with subtraction of positive and negative numbers. Remember, in algebra subtraction is not taking one number away from another. Instead, subtracting a number is equivalent to adding its opposite.

Subtract.

1. $5 - 8$ **2.** $6 - 7$ **3.** $3 - 9$ **4.** $2 - 7$

5. $5 - 5$ **6.** $8 - 8$ **7.** $-8 - 2$ **8.** $-6 - 3$

9. $-4 - 12$ **10.** $-3 - 15$ **11.** $-6 - 6$ **12.** $-3 - 3$

13. $-8 - (-1)$ **14.** $-6 - (-2)$ **15.** $15 - (-20)$ **16.** $20 - (-5)$

17. $-4 - (-4)$ **18.** $-5 - (-5)$

Simplify each expression by applying the rule for order of operations.

19. $3 - 2 - 5$ **20.** $4 - 8 - 6$ **21.** $9 - 2 - 3$

22. $8 - 7 - 12$ **23.** $-6 - 8 - 10$ **24.** $-5 - 7 - 9$

25. $-22 + 4 - 10$ **26.** $-13 + 6 - 5$ **27.** $10 - (-20) - 5$

28. $15 - (-3) - 20$ **29.** $8 - (2 - 3) - 5$ **30.** $10 - (4 - 6) - 8$

31. $7 - (3 - 9) - 6$ **32.** $4 - (3 - 7) - 8$ **33.** $5 - (-8 - 6) - 2$

34. $4 - (-3 - 2) - 1$ **35.** $-(5 - 7) - (2 - 8)$ **36.** $-(4 - 8) - (2 - 5)$

37. $-(3 - 10) - (6 - 3)$ **38.** $-(3 - 7) - (1 - 2)$ **39.** $16 - [(4 - 5) - 1]$

40. $15 - [(4 - 2) - 3]$ **41.** $5 - [(2 - 3) - 4]$ **42.** $6 - [(4 - 1) - 9]$

43. $21 - [-(3 - 4) - 2] - 5$ **44.** $30 - [-(10 - 5) - 15] - 25$

The following problems involve multiplication and exponents. Use the rule for order of operations to simplify each expression as much as possible.

45. $2 \cdot 8 - 3 \cdot 5$ **46.** $3 \cdot 4 - 6 \cdot 7$ **47.** $3 \cdot 5 - 2 \cdot 7$

48. $6 \cdot 10 - 5 \cdot 20$ **49.** $5 \cdot 9 - 2 \cdot 3 - 6 \cdot 2$ **50.** $4 \cdot 3 - 7 \cdot 1 - 9 \cdot 4$

51. $3 \cdot 8 - 2 \cdot 4 - 6 \cdot 7$ **52.** $5 \cdot 9 - 3 \cdot 8 - 4 \cdot 5$ **53.** $2 \cdot 3^2 - 5 \cdot 2^2$

54. $3 \cdot 7^2 - 2 \cdot 8^2$ **55.** $4 \cdot 3^3 - 5 \cdot 2^3$ **56.** $3 \cdot 6^2 - 2 \cdot 3^2 - 8 \cdot 6^2$

Rewrite each of the following phrases as an equivalent expression in symbols, and then simplify.

57. Subtract 4 from -7.   **58.** Subtract 5 from -19.

59. Subtract -8 from 12.   **60.** Subtract -2 from 10.

61. Subtract -7 from -5.   **62.** Subtract -9 from -3.

63. Subtract 17 from the sum of 4 and -5.

64. Subtract -6 from the sum of 6 and -3.

Recall that the word *difference* indicates subtraction. The difference of *a* and *b* is *a* − *b*, in that order. Write a numerical expression that is equivalent to each of the following phrases, and then simplify.

65. The difference of 8 and 5.

66. The difference of 5 and 8.

67. The difference of −8 and 5.

68. The difference of −5 and 8.

69. The difference of 8 and −5.

70. The difference of 5 and −8.

Answer the following questions.

71. What number do you subtract from 8 to get −2?

72. What number do you subtract from 1 to get −5?

73. What number do you subtract from 8 to get 10?

74. What number do you subtract from 1 to get 5?

Applying the Concepts

75. Savings Account Balance A man with $1,500 in a savings account makes a withdrawal of $730. Write an expression using subtraction that describes this situation.

First Bank
Account No. 12345

Date	Withdrawals	Deposits	Balance
1/1/09			1,500
2/2/09	730		

76. Checkbook Balance Bob has $98 in his checking account when he writes a check for $65 and then another check for $53. Write a subtraction problem that gives the new balance in Bob's checkbook. What is his new balance?

77. Gambling A man who has lost $35 playing roulette in Las Vegas wins $15 playing blackjack. He then loses $20 playing the wheel of fortune. Write an expression using the numbers −35, 15, and 20 to describe this situation and then simplify it.

78. Altitude Change An airplane flying at 10,000 feet lowers its altitude by 1,500 feet to avoid other air traffic. Then it increases its altitude by 3,000 feet to clear a mountain range. Write an expression that describes this situation and then simplify it.

79. Temperature Change The temperature inside a space shuttle is 73°F before reentry. During reentry the temperature inside the craft increases 10°. On landing it drops 8°F. Write an expression using the numbers 73, 10, and 8 to describe this situation. What is the temperature inside the shuttle on landing?

80. Temperature Change The temperature at noon is 23°F. Six hours later it has dropped 19°F, and by midnight it has dropped another 10°F. Write a subtraction problem that gives the temperature at midnight. What is the temperature at midnight?

81. **Depreciation** Stacey buys a used car for $4,500. With each year that passes, the car drops $550 in value. Write a sequence of numbers that gives the value of the car at the beginning of each of the first 5 years she owns it. Can this sequence be considered an arithmetic sequence?

82. **Depreciation** Wade buys a computer system for $6,575. Each year after that he finds that the system is worth $1,250 less than it was the year before. Write a sequence of numbers that gives the value of the computer system at the beginning of each of the first four years he owns it. Can this sequence be considered an arithmetic sequence?

Find x in each of the following diagrams.

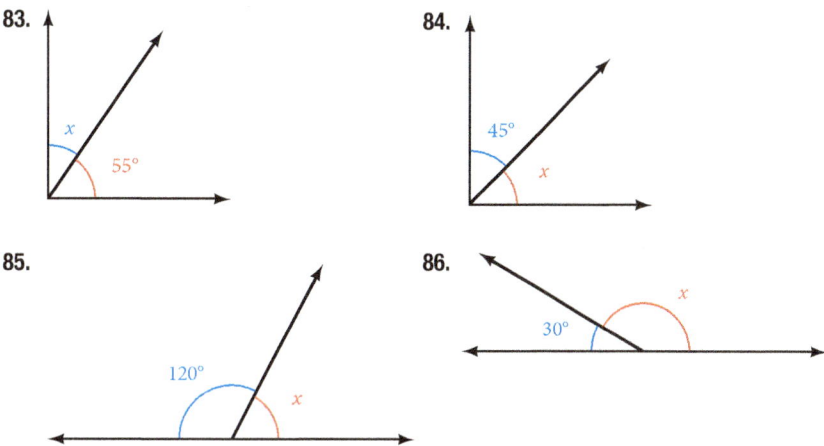

83.   84.

85.   86.

87. **Grass Growth** The bar chart below shows the growth of a certain species of grass over a period of 10 days.

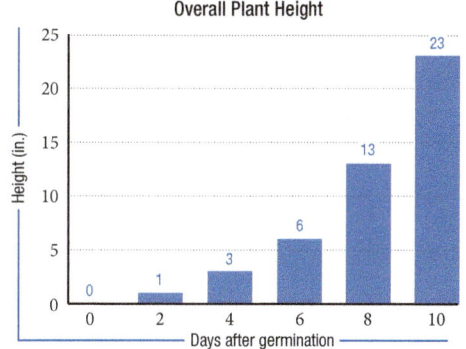

Day	Plant Height (inches)
0	0
2	
4	
6	
	13
10	

a. Use the chart to fill in the missing entries in the table.

b. How much higher is the grass after 8 days than after 2 days?

88. Computer Hard Drive Costs The bar chart below shows the cost of hard drive space in cents per gigabyte.

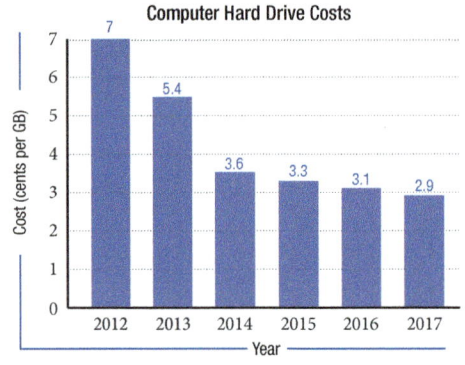

Year	Cents/GB
2012	7
2013	
2014	
	3.3
2016	

a. Use the chart to fill in the missing entries in the table.

b. What is the difference in cost between 2013 and 2014?

89. Triathlon Project Use the chart to answer the following questions.

a. Do you think the numbers in the chart have been rounded? If so, to which place were they rounded?

b. How many more participants were there in 2004 than in 2000?

c. If the trend from 2000 to 2004 continued, how many participants were there in 2008?

Properties of Real Numbers

In this section we will list all the facts (properties) that you know from past experience are true about numbers in general. We will give each property a name so we can refer to it later in this book. Mathematics is very much like a game. The game involves numbers. The rules of the game are the properties and rules we are developing in this chapter. The goal of the game is to extend the basic rules to as many situations as possible.

You know from past experience with numbers that it makes no difference in which order you add two numbers; that is, $3 + 5$ is the same as $5 + 3$. This fact about numbers is called the ***commutative property of addition***. We say addition is a commutative operation. Changing the order of the numbers does not change the answer.

There is one other basic operation that is commutative. Because $3(5)$ is the same as $5(3)$, we say multiplication is a commutative operation. Changing the order of the two numbers you are multiplying does not change the answer.

For all properties listed in this section, a, b, and c represent real numbers.

> **⎡Δ≠Σ⎤ *Commutative Property of Addition***
>
> *In symbols:* $a + b = b + a$
> *In words:*   Changing the *order* of the numbers in a sum will not change
>   the result.

> **⎡Δ≠Σ⎤ *Commutative Property of Multiplication***
>
> *In symbols:* $a \cdot b = b \cdot a$
> *In words:*   Changing the *order* of the numbers in a product will not change
>   the result.

For example, the statement $5 + 8 = 8 + 5$ is an example of the commutative property of addition and the statement $2 \cdot y = y \cdot 2$ is an example of the commutative property of multiplication.

Video Examples

Section 0.5

> *Note* At this point, some students are confused by the expression $x + 8$; they feel that there is more to do, but they don't know what. At this point, there isn't any more that can be done with $x + 8$ unless we know what x is. So $x + 8$ is as far as we can go with this problem.

■ Example 1   Simplify $5 + x + 3$

SOLUTION The expression $5 + x + 3$ can be simplified using the commutative property of addition:

$$5 + x + 3 = x + 5 + 3 \qquad \text{Commutative property of addition}$$
$$= x + 8 \qquad \text{Addition}$$

The other two basic operations, subtraction and division, are not commutative. The order in which we subtract or divide two numbers makes a difference in the answer.

Another property of numbers that you have used many times has to do with grouping. You know that when we add three numbers it makes no difference which two we add first. When adding $3 + 5 + 7$, we can add the 3 and 5 first and then the 7, or we can add the 5 and 7 first and then the 3. Mathematically, it looks like this: $(3 + 5) + 7 = 3 + (5 + 7)$. This property is true of multiplication as well. Operations that behave in this manner are called ***associative*** operations.

The answer will not change when we change the association (or grouping) of the numbers.

> **Associative Property of Addition**
>
> *In symbols:* $a + (b + c) = (a + b) + c$
> *In words:*   Changing the *grouping* of the numbers in a sum will not change the result.

> **Associative Property of Multiplication**
>
> *In symbols:* $a(bc) = (ab)c$
> *In words:*   Changing the *grouping* of the numbers in a product will not change the result.

The following examples illustrate how the associative properties can be used to simplify expressions that involve both numbers and variables.

Example 2   Simplify.

a. $4 + (5 + x)$ **b.** $5(2x)$

SOLUTION

a. $4 + (5 + x) = (4 + 5) + x$ Associative property of addition

$= 9 + x$ Addition

b. $5(2x) = (5 \cdot 2)x$ Associative property of multiplication

$= 10x$ Multiplication

Example 3   Simplify.

a. $\frac{1}{5}(5x)$ **b.** $3\left(\frac{1}{3}x\right)$ **c.** $12\left(\frac{2}{3}x\right)$

SOLUTION

a. $\frac{1}{5}(5x) = \left(\frac{1}{5} \cdot 5\right)x$ Associative property of multiplication

$= 1x$ Multiplication

$= x$

b. $3\left(\frac{1}{3}x\right) = \left(3 \cdot \frac{1}{3}\right)x$ Associative property of multiplication

$= 1x$ Multiplication

$= x$

c. $12\left(\frac{2}{3}x\right) = \left(12 \cdot \frac{2}{3}\right)x$ Associative property of multiplication

$= 8x$ Multiplication

> *Note* Because subtraction is defined in terms of addition, it is also true that the distributive property applies to subtraction as well as addition; that is, $a(b - c) = ab - ac$ for any three real numbers a, b, and c.

The associative and commutative properties apply to problems that are either all multiplication or all addition. There is a third basic property that involves both addition and multiplication. It is called the ***distributive property*** and looks like this.

> **⌈Δ≠Σ⌉   *Distributive Property***
>
> *In symbols:* $a(b + c) = ab + ac$
> *In words:* Multiplication *distributes* over addition.

You will see as we progress through the book that the distributive property is used very frequently in algebra. We can give a visual justification to the distributive property by finding the areas of rectangles. Figure 1 shows a large rectangle that is made up of two smaller rectangles. We can find the area of the large rectangle two different ways.

Method 1

We can calculate the area of the large rectangle directly by finding its length and width. The width is 5 inches, and the length is $(3 + 4)$ inches.

$$\text{Area of large rectangle} = 5(3 + 4)$$
$$= 5(7)$$
$$= 35 \text{ square inches}$$

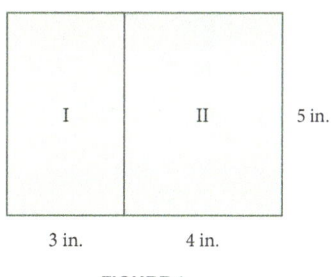

3 in.   4 in.

FIGURE 1

Method 2

Because the area of the large rectangle is the sum of the areas of the two smaller rectangles, we find the area of each small rectangle and then add to find the area of the large rectangle.

$$\text{Area of large rectangle} = \text{Area of rectangle I} + \text{Area of rectangle II}$$
$$= 5(3) + 5(4)$$
$$= 15 + 20$$
$$= 35 \text{ square inches}$$

In both cases the result is 35 square inches. Because the results are the same, the two original expressions must be equal. Stated mathematically, $5(3 + 4) = 5(3) + 5(4)$. We can either add the 3 and 4 first and then multiply that sum by 5, or we can multiply the 3 and the 4 separately by 5 and then add the products. In either case we get the same answer.

Here are some examples that illustrate how we use the distributive property.

Example 4   Apply the distributive property to each expression, and then simplify the result.

a. $2(x + 3)$ **b.** $5(2x - 8)$ **c.** $5(2x + 4y)$ **d.** $4(2a + 3) + 8$

SOLUTION

a. $2(x + 3) = 2(x) + 2(3)$ Distributive property

$\qquad\qquad\quad = 2x + 6$ Multiplication

b. $5(2x - 8) = 5(2x) - 5(8)$ Distributive property

$\qquad\qquad\quad\; = 10x - 40$ Multiplication

Notice in part **b.** that multiplication distributes over subtraction as well as addition.

c. $5(2x + 4y) = 5(2x) + 5(4y)$ Distributive property

$\qquad\qquad\qquad = 10x + 20y$ Multiplication

d. $4(2a + 3) + 8 = 4(2a) + 4(3) + 8$ Distributive property

$\qquad\qquad\qquad\quad = 8a + 12 + 8$ Multiplication

$\qquad\qquad\qquad\quad = 8a + 20$ Addition

Next we have some expressions to simplify that involve fractions.

Example 5   Apply the distributive property to each expression, and then simplify the result.

a. $\dfrac{1}{2}(3x + 6)$ **b.** $3\left(\dfrac{1}{3}x + 5\right)$ **c.** $a\left(1 + \dfrac{1}{a}\right)$ **d.** $12\left(\dfrac{2}{3}x + \dfrac{1}{2}y\right)$

SOLUTION

a. $\dfrac{1}{2}(3x + 6) = \dfrac{1}{2}(3x) + \dfrac{1}{2}(6)$ Distributive property

$\qquad\qquad\quad = \dfrac{3}{2}x + 3$ Multiplication

b. $3\left(\dfrac{1}{3}x + 5\right) = 3 \cdot \dfrac{1}{3}x + 3 \cdot 5$ Distributive property

$\qquad\qquad\qquad = x + 15$ Multiplication

c. $a\left(1 + \dfrac{1}{a}\right) = a \cdot 1 + a \cdot \dfrac{1}{a}$ Distributive property

$\qquad\qquad\qquad = a + 1$ Multiplication

d. $12\left(\dfrac{2}{3}x + \dfrac{1}{2}y\right) = 12 \cdot \dfrac{2}{3}x + 12 \cdot \dfrac{1}{2}y$ Distributive property

$\qquad\qquad\qquad\quad = 8x + 6y$ Multiplication

Special Numbers

In addition to the three properties mentioned so far, we want to include in our list two special numbers that have unique properties. They are the numbers zero and one.

> ### $\triangle \neq \Sigma$ *Additive Identity Property*
>
> There exists a unique number 0 such that $a + 0 = a$ and $0 + a = a$

> ### $\triangle \neq \Sigma$ *Multiplicative Identity Property*
>
> There exists a unique number 1 such that $a(1) = a$ and $(1)a = a$

> ### $\triangle \neq \Sigma$ *Additive Inverse Property*
>
> *In symbols:* $a + -a = 0$
> *In words:*   The sum of opposites is always 0.

> ### $\triangle \neq \Sigma$ *Multiplicative Inverse Property*
>
> *For every real number a, except 0, there exists a unique real number $\frac{1}{a}$ such that*
> *In symbols:* $a\left(\frac{1}{a}\right) = 1$
> *In words:*   The product of reciprocals is always 1.

Of all the basic properties listed, the commutative, associative, and distributive properties are the ones we will use most often. They are important because they will be used as justifications or reasons for many of the things we will do.

The following example illustrates how we use the preceding properties. Each sub-example contains an algebraic expression that has been changed in some way. The property that justifies the change is written to the right.

Example 6   State the property that justifies the given statement.

a. $x + 5 = 5 + x$ Commutative property of addition

b. $(2 + x) + y = 2 + (x + y)$ Associative property of addition

c. $6(x + 3) = 6x + 18$ Distributive property

d. $2 + (-2) = 0$ Additive inverse property

e. $3\left(\frac{1}{3}\right) = 1$ Multiplicative inverse property

f. $(2 + 0) + 3 = 2 + 3$ 0 is the identity element for addition

g. $(2 + 3) + 4 = 3 + (2 + 4)$ Commutative and associative properties of addition

h. $(x + 2) + y = (x + y) + 2$ Commutative and associative properties of addition

As a final note on the properties of real numbers, we should mention that although some of the properties are stated for only two or three real numbers, they hold for as many numbers as needed. For example, the distributive property holds for expressions like $3(x + y + z + 5 + 2)$; that is,

$$3(x + y + z + 5 + 2) = 3x + 3y + 3z + 15 + 6$$

It is not important how many numbers are contained in the sum, only that it is a sum. Multiplication, you see, distributes over addition, whether there are two numbers in the sum or 200.

Getting Ready for Class

After reading through the preceding section, respond in your own words and in complete sentences.

A. What is the commutative property of addition?

B. Do you know from your experience with numbers that the commutative property of addition is true? Explain why.

C. Write the commutative property of multiplication in symbols and words.

D. How do you rewrite expressions using the distributive property?

Problem Set 0.5

State the property or properties that justify the following.

1. $3 + 2 = 2 + 3$ **2.** $5 + 0 = 5$ **3.** $4\left(\dfrac{1}{4}\right) = 1$

4. $10(0.1) = 1$ **5.** $4 + x = x + 4$ **6.** $3(x - 10) = 3x - 30$

7. $2(y + 8) = 2y + 16$ **8.** $3 + (4 + 5) = (3 + 4) + 5$

9. $(3 + 1) + 2 = 1 + (3 + 2)$ **10.** $(5 + 2) + 9 = (2 + 5) + 9$

11. $(8 + 9) + 10 = (8 + 10) + 9$ **12.** $(7 + 6) + 5 = (5 + 6) + 7$

13. $3(x + 2) = 3(2 + x)$ **14.** $2(7y) = (7 \cdot 2)y$ **15.** $x(3y) = 3(xy)$

16. $a(5b) = 5(ab)$ **17.** $4(xy) = 4(yx)$ **18.** $3[2 + (-2)] = 3(0)$

19. $8[7 + (-7)] = 8(0)$ **20.** $7(1) = 7$

Each of the following problems has a mistake in it. Correct the right-hand side.

21. $3(x + 2) = 3x + 2$ **22.** $5(4 + x) = 4 + 5x$ **23.** $9(a + b) = 9a + b$

24. $2(y + 1) = 2y + 1$ **25.** $3(0) = 3$ **26.** $5\left(\dfrac{1}{5}\right) = 5$

27. $3 + (-3) = 1$ **28.** $8(0) = 8$ **29.** $10(1) = 0$

30. $3 \cdot \dfrac{1}{3} = 0$

Use the associative property to rewrite each of the following expressions, and then simplify the result. (See Examples 2 and 3.)

31. $4 + (2 + x)$ **32.** $5 + (6 + x)$ **33.** $(x + 2) + 7$ **34.** $(x + 8) + 2$

35. $3(5x)$ **36.** $5(3x)$ **37.** $9(6y)$ **38.** $6(9y)$

39. $\dfrac{1}{2}(3a)$ **40.** $\dfrac{1}{3}(2a)$ **41.** $\dfrac{1}{3}(3x)$ **42.** $\dfrac{1}{4}(4x)$

43. $\dfrac{1}{2}(2y)$ **44.** $\dfrac{1}{7}(7y)$ **45.** $\dfrac{3}{4}\left(\dfrac{4}{3}x\right)$ **46.** $\dfrac{3}{2}\left(\dfrac{2}{3}x\right)$

47. $\dfrac{6}{5}\left(\dfrac{5}{6}a\right)$ **48.** $\dfrac{2}{5}\left(\dfrac{5}{2}a\right)$

Apply the distributive property to each of the following expressions. Simplify when possible.

49. $8(x + 2)$ **50.** $5(x + 3)$ **51.** $8(x - 2)$ **52.** $5(x - 3)$
53. $4(y + 1)$ **54.** $4(y - 1)$ **55.** $3(6x + 5)$ **56.** $3(5x + 6)$
57. $2(3a + 7)$ **58.** $5(3a + 2)$ **59.** $9(6y - 8)$ **60.** $2(7y - 4)$

Apply the distributive property to each of the following expressions. Simplify when possible.

61. $\dfrac{1}{3}(3x + 6)$ **62.** $\dfrac{1}{2}(2x + 4)$ **63.** $6(2x + 3y)$ **64.** $8(3x + 2y)$

65. $4(3a - 2b)$ **66.** $5(4a - 8b)$ **67.** $\dfrac{1}{2}(6x + 4y)$ **68.** $\dfrac{1}{3}(6x + 9y)$

69. $4(a + 4) + 9$ **70.** $6(a + 2) + 8$ **71.** $2(3x + 5) + 2$ **72.** $7(2x + 1) + 3$

73. $7(2x + 4) + 10$ **74.** $3(5x + 6) + 20$

Here are some problems you will see later in the book. Apply the distributive property and simplify, if possible.

75. $\frac{1}{2}(4x + 2)$

76. $\frac{1}{3}(6x + 3)$

77. $\frac{3}{4}(8x - 4)$

78. $\frac{2}{5}(5x + 10)$

79. $\frac{5}{6}(6x + 12)$

80. $\frac{2}{3}(9x - 3)$

81. $10\left(\frac{3}{5}x + \frac{1}{2}\right)$

82. $8\left(\frac{1}{4}x - \frac{5}{8}\right)$

83. $15\left(\frac{1}{3}x + \frac{2}{5}\right)$

84. $12\left(\frac{1}{12}m + \frac{1}{6}\right)$

85. $12\left(\frac{1}{2}m - \frac{5}{12}\right)$

86. $8\left(\frac{1}{8} + \frac{1}{2}m\right)$

87. $21\left(\frac{1}{3} + \frac{1}{7}x\right)$

88. $6\left(\frac{3}{2}y + \frac{1}{3}\right)$

89. $6\left(\frac{1}{2}x - \frac{1}{3}y\right)$

90. $12\left(\frac{1}{4}x + \frac{2}{3}y\right)$

91. $0.09(x + 2{,}000)$

92. $0.04(x + 7{,}000)$

93. $0.12(x + 500)$

94. $0.06(x + 800)$

95. $a\left(1 + \frac{1}{a}\right)$

96. $a\left(1 - \frac{1}{a}\right)$

97. $a\left(\frac{1}{a} - 1\right)$

98. $a\left(\frac{1}{a} + 1\right)$

Applying the Concepts

99. Getting Dressed While getting dressed for work, a man puts on his socks and puts on his shoes. Are the two statements "put on your socks" and "put on your shoes" commutative? That is, will changing the order of the events always produce the same result?

100. Skydiving A skydiver flying over the jump area is about to do two things: jump out of the plane and pull the rip cord. Are the two events "jump out of the plane" and "pull the rip cord" commutative?

101. Division Give an example that shows that division is not a commutative operation; that is, find two numbers for which changing the order of division gives two different answers.

102. Subtraction Simplify the expression $10 - (5 - 2)$ and the expression $(10 - 5) - 2$ to show that subtraction is not an associative operation.

103. Hours Worked Carlo works as a waiter. He works double shifts 4 days a week. The lunch shift is 2 hours and the dinner shift is 3 hours. Find the total number of hours he works per week using the numbers 2, 3, and 4. Do the calculation two different ways so that the results give further justification for the distributive property.

Multiplication of Real Numbers

Suppose that you own 5 shares of a stock and the price per share drops \$3. How much money have you lost? Intuitively, we know the loss is \$15. Because it is a loss, we can express it as $-\$15$. To describe this situation with numbers, we would write

5 shares   each lose \$3   for a total of \$15

$$5(-3) = -15$$

Reasoning in this manner, we conclude that the product of a positive number with a negative number is a negative number. Let's look at multiplication in more detail.

From our experience with counting numbers, we know that multiplication is simply repeated addition; that is, $3(5) = 5 + 5 + 5$. We will use this fact, along with our knowledge of negative numbers, to develop the rule for multiplication of any two real numbers. The following example illustrates multiplication with all of the possible combinations of positive and negative numbers.

Video Examples

Section 0.6

Example 1   Multiply.

a. $3(5)$ **b.** $3(-5)$ **c.** $-3(5)$ **d.** $-3(-5)$

SOLUTION

a. Two positives: $3(5) = 5 + 5 + 5$

                               $= 15$ *Positive answer*

b. One positive: $3(-5) = -5 + (-5) + (-5)$

                                 $= -15$ *Negative answer*

c. One negative: $-3(5) = 5(-3)$ *Commutative property*

                                 $= -3 + (-3) + (-3) + (-3)$

                                 $= -15$ *Negative answer*

d. Two negatives: $-3(-5) = ?$

Note   You may have to read the explanation for Example 1(d) several times before you understand it completely. The purpose of the explanation in Example 1(d) is simply to justify the fact that the product of two negative numbers is a positive number. If you have no trouble believing that, then it is not so important that you understand everything in the explanation.

With two negatives, $-3(-5)$, it is not possible to work the problem in terms of repeated addition. (It doesn't "make sense" to write -5 down a -3 number of times.) The answer is probably $+15$ (that's just a guess), but we need some justification for saying so. We will solve a different problem and in doing so get the answer to the problem $(-3)(-5)$.

Here is a problem to which we know the answer. We will work it two different ways.

$$-3[5 + (-5)] = -3(0) = 0$$

The answer is zero. We also can work the problem using the distributive property.

$$-3[5 + (-5)] = -3(5) + (-3)(-5) \quad \text{\textit{Distributive property}}$$
$$= -15 + ?$$

Because the answer to the problem is 0, our ? must be $+15$. (What else could we add to -15 to get 0? Only $+15$.)

Here is a summary of the results we have obtained from the first example:

Original Numbers Have		The Answer is
the same sign	$3(5) = 15$	positive
different signs	$3(-5) = -15$	negative
different signs	$-3(5) = -15$	negative
the same sign	$-3(-5) = 15$	positive

By examining Example 1 and the preceding table, we can use the information there to write the following rule. This rule tells us how to multiply any two real numbers.

⎧Δ≠Σ⎫ *Rule*

To multiply any two real numbers, simply multiply their absolute values. The sign of the answer is

1. *Positive* if both numbers have the same sign (both + or both −).

2. *Negative* if the numbers have opposite signs (one +, the other −).

The following example illustrates how we use the preceding rule to multiply real numbers.

Example 2   Multiply.

a. $-8(-3) = 24$

b. $-10(-5) = 50$ If the two numbers in the product have the same sign, the answer is positive

c. $-4(-7) = 28$

d. $5(-7) = -35$

e. $-4(8) = -32$ If the two numbers in the product have different signs, the answer is negative

f. $-6(10) = -60$

Note: Students have trouble with the expression $-8(-3)$ because they want to subtract rather than multiply. Because we are very precise with the notation we use in algebra, the expression $-8(-3)$ has only one meaning—multiplication. A subtraction problem that uses the same numbers is $-8 - 3$. Compare the two following lists.

All Multiplication	No Multiplication
$5(4)$	$5 + 4$
$-5(4)$	$-5 + 4$
$5(-4)$	$5 - 4$
$-5(-4)$	$-5 - 4$

In the following example, we combine the rule for order of operations with the rule for multiplication to simplify expressions. Remember, the rule for order of operations specifies that we are to work inside the parentheses first and then simplify numbers containing exponents. After this, we multiply and divide, left to right. The last step is to add and subtract, left to right.

Example 3   Simplify as much as possible.

a. $-5(-3)(-4)$ **b.** $4(-3) + 6(-5) - 10$

c. $(-2)^3$ **d.** $-3(-2)^3 - 5(-4)^2$

e. $6 - 4(7 - 2)$

SOLUTION

a. $-5(-3)(-4) = 15(-4)$

$= -60$

b. $4(-3) + 6(-5) - 10 = -12 + (-30) - 10$ Multiply

$= -42 - 10$ Add

$= -52$ Subtract

c. $(-2)^3 = (-2)(-2)(-2)$ Definition of exponents

$= -8$ Multiply, left to right

d. $-3(-2)^3 - 5(-4)^2 = -3(-8) - 5(16)$ Exponents first

$= 24 - 80$ Multiply

$= -56$ Subtract

e. $6 - 4(7 - 2) = 6 - 4(5)$ Inside parentheses first

$= 6 - 20$ Multiply

$= -14$ Subtract

Multiplying Fractions

Previously, we mentioned that to multiply two fractions we multiply numerators and multiply denominators. We can apply the rule for multiplication of positive and negative numbers to fractions in the same way we apply it to other numbers. We multiply absolute values: The product is positive if both fractions have the same sign and negative if they have different signs. Here is an example.

Example 4   Multiply.

a. $-\dfrac{3}{4}\left(\dfrac{5}{7}\right)$ **b.** $-6\left(\dfrac{1}{2}\right)$ **c.** $-\dfrac{2}{3}\left(-\dfrac{3}{2}\right)$

SOLUTION

a. $-\dfrac{3}{4}\left(\dfrac{5}{7}\right) = -\dfrac{3 \cdot 5}{4 \cdot 7}$ Different signs give a negative answer

$= -\dfrac{15}{28}$

b. $-6\left(\dfrac{1}{2}\right) = -\dfrac{6}{1}\left(\dfrac{1}{2}\right)$ Different signs give a negative answer

$= -\dfrac{6}{2}$

$= -3$

c. $-\dfrac{2}{3}\left(-\dfrac{3}{2}\right) = \dfrac{2 \cdot 3}{3 \cdot 2}$ Same signs give a positive answer

$= \dfrac{6}{6}$

$= 1$

Example 5   Figure 1 gives the calories that are burned in 1 hour for a variety of exercise by a person weighing 150 pounds. Figure 2 gives the calories that are consumed by eating some popular fast foods. Find the net change in calories for a 150-pound person playing handball for 2 hours and then eating a Whopper.

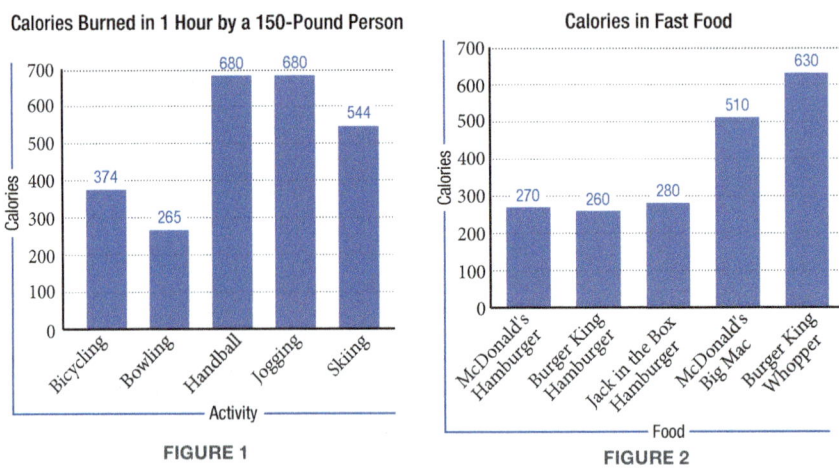

FIGURE 1

FIGURE 2

SOLUTION   The net change in calories will be the difference of the calories gained from eating and the calories lost from exercise.

$$\text{Net change in calories} = 630 - 2(680) = -730 \text{ calories}$$

We can use the rule for multiplication of real numbers, along with the associative property, to multiply expressions that contain numbers and variables.

Example 6   Apply the associative property, and then multiply.

a. $-3(2x)$ **b.** $6(-5y)$ **c.** $-2\left(-\dfrac{1}{2}x\right)$

SOLUTION

a. $-3(2x) = (-3 \cdot 2)x$ Associative property

    $\qquad\quad = -6x$ Multiplication

b. $6(-5y) = [6(-5)]y$ Associative property

    $\qquad\quad = -30y$ Multiplication

c. $-2\left(-\dfrac{1}{2}x\right) = \left[(-2)\left(-\dfrac{1}{2}\right)\right]x$ Associative property

    $\qquad\qquad\quad = 1x$ Multiplication

    $\qquad\qquad\quad = x$ Multiplication

The following example shows how we can use both the distributive property and multiplication with real numbers.

> **Example 7**   Apply the distributive property to each expression.

a. $-3(2x + 1)$ **b.** $-\dfrac{1}{3}(2x - 6)$ **c.** $-4(3x - 5) - 8$

SOLUTION

a.
$$
\begin{aligned}
-3(2x + 1) &= -3(2x) + (-3)(1) &&\text{Distributive property}\\
&= -6x + (-3) &&\text{Multiplication}\\
&= -6x - 3
\end{aligned}
$$

b.
$$
\begin{aligned}
-\frac{1}{3}(2x - 6) &= -\frac{1}{3}(2x) - \left(-\frac{1}{3}\right)(6) &&\text{Distributive property}\\
&= -\frac{2}{3}x - (-2) &&\text{Multiplication}\\
&= -\frac{2}{3}x + 2
\end{aligned}
$$

c.
$$
\begin{aligned}
-4(3x - 5) - 8 &= -4(3x) - (-4)(5) - 8 &&\text{Distributive property}\\
&= -12x - (-20) - 8 &&\text{Multiplication}\\
&= -12x + 20 - 8 &&\text{Definition of subtraction}\\
&= -12x + 12 &&\text{Subtraction}
\end{aligned}
$$

Geometric Sequences

A *geometric sequence* is a sequence of numbers in which each number (after the first number) comes from the number before it by multiplying by the same amount each time. For example, the sequence

$$2, 6, 18, 54, \ldots$$

is a geometric sequence because each number is obtained by multiplying the number before it by 3.

> **Example 8**   Each sequence below is a geometric sequence. Find the next number in each sequence.

a. $5, 10, 20, \ldots$ **b.** $3, -15, 75, \ldots$ **c.** $\dfrac{1}{8}, \dfrac{1}{4}, \dfrac{1}{2}, \ldots$

SOLUTION   Because each sequence is a geometric sequence, we know that each term is obtained from the previous term by multiplying by the same number each time.

a. $5, 10, 20, \ldots$: Starting with 5, each number is obtained from the previous number by multiplying by 2 each time. The next number will be $20 \cdot 2 = 40$.

b. $3, -15, 75, \ldots$: The sequence starts with 3. After that, each number is obtained by multiplying by -5 each time. The next number will be $75(-5) = -375$.

c. $\dfrac{1}{8}, \dfrac{1}{4}, \dfrac{1}{2}, \ldots$: This sequence starts with $\frac{1}{8}$. Multiplying each number in the sequence by 2 produces the next number in the sequence. To extend the sequence, we multiply $\frac{1}{2}$ by 2: $\frac{1}{2} \cdot 2 = 1$. The next number in the sequence is 1.

Getting Ready for Class

After reading through the preceding section, respond in your own words and in complete sentences.

A. How do you multiply two negative numbers?

B. How do you multiply two numbers with different signs?

C. Explain how some multiplication problems can be thought of as repeated addition.

D. What is a geometric sequence?

Problem Set 0.6

Use the rule for multiplying two real numbers to find each of the following products.

1. $7(-6)$ **2.** $8(-4)$ **3.** $-8(2)$ **4.** $-16(3)$

5. $-3(-1)$ **6.** $-7(-1)$ **7.** $-11(-11)$ **8.** $-12(-12)$

Use the rule for order of operations to simplify each expression as much as possible.

9. $-3(2)(-1)$ **10.** $-2(3)(-4)$ **11.** $-3(-4)(-5)$ **12.** $-5(-6)(-7)$

13. $-2(-4)(-3)(-1)$ **14.** $-1(-3)(-2)(-1)$

15. $(-7)^2$ **16.** $(-8)^2$ **17.** $(-3)^3$ **18.** $(-2)^4$

19. $-2(2-5)$ **20.** $-3(3-7)$ **21.** $-5(8-10)$ **22.** $-4(6-12)$

23. $(4-7)(6-9)$ **24.** $(3-10)(2-6)$

25. $(-3-2)(-5-4)$ **26.** $(-3-6)(-2-8)$

27. $-3(-6)+4(-1)$ **28.** $-4(-5)+8(-2)$

29. $2(3)-3(-4)+4(-5)$ **30.** $5(4)-2(-1)+5(6)$

31. $4(-3)^2+5(-6)^2$ **32.** $2(-5)^2+4(-3)^2$

33. $7(-2)^3-2(-3)^3$ **34.** $10(-2)^3-5(-2)^4$

35. $6-4(8-2)$ **36.** $7-2(6-3)$ **37.** $9-4(3-8)$ **38.** $8-5(2-7)$

39. $-4(3-8)-6(2-5)$ **40.** $-8(2-7)-9(3-5)$

41. $7-2[-6-4(-3)]$ **42.** $6-3[-5-3(-1)]$

43. $7-3[2(-4-4)-3(-1-1)]$ **44.** $5-3[7(-2-2)-3(-3+1)]$

45. $8-6[-2(-3-1)+4(-2-3)]$ **46.** $4-2[-3(-1+8)+5(-5+7)]$

Multiply the following fractions.

47. $-\dfrac{2}{3}\cdot\dfrac{5}{7}$ **48.** $-\dfrac{6}{5}\cdot\dfrac{2}{7}$ **49.** $-8\left(\dfrac{1}{2}\right)$ **50.** $-12\left(\dfrac{1}{3}\right)$

51. $-\dfrac{3}{4}\left(-\dfrac{4}{3}\right)$ **52.** $-\dfrac{5}{8}\left(-\dfrac{8}{5}\right)$ **53.** $\left(-\dfrac{3}{4}\right)^2$ **54.** $\left(-\dfrac{2}{5}\right)^2$

Find the following products.

55. $-2(4x)$ **56.** $-8(7x)$ **57.** $-7(-6x)$ **58.** $-8(-9x)$

59. $-\dfrac{1}{3}(-3x)$ **60.** $-\dfrac{1}{5}(-5x)$

Apply the distributive property to each expression, and then simplify the result.

61. $-4(a+2)$ **62.** $-7(a+6)$ **63.** $-\dfrac{1}{2}(3x-6)$

64. $-\dfrac{1}{4}(2x-4)$ **65.** $-3(2x-5)-7$ **66.** $-4(3x-1)-8$

67. $-5(3x+4)-10$ **68.** $-3(4x+5)-20$

69. Five added to the product of 3 and -10 is what number?

70. If the product of -8 and -2 is decreased by 4, what number results?

71. Write an expression for twice the product of -4 and x, and then simplify it.

72. Write an expression for twice the product of -2 and $3x$, and then simplify it.

73. What number results if 8 is subtracted from the product of -9 and 2?

74. What number results if -8 is subtracted from the product of -9 and 2?

Each of the following is a geometric sequence. In each case, find the next number in the sequence.

75. $1, 2, 4, \ldots$ **76.** $1, 5, 25, \ldots$ **77.** $10, -20, 40, \ldots$ **78.** $10, -30, 90, \ldots$

79. $1, \dfrac{1}{2}, \dfrac{1}{4}, \ldots$ **80.** $1, \dfrac{1}{3}, \dfrac{1}{9}, \ldots$ **81.** $3, -6, 12, \ldots$ **82.** $-3, 6, -12, \ldots$

Here are some problems you will see later in the book. Simplify.

83. $3(x - 5) + 4$ **84.** $5(x - 3) + 2$ **85.** $2(3) - 4 - 3(-4)$

86. $2(3) + 4(5) - 5(2)$ **87.** $\left(\dfrac{1}{2} \cdot 18\right)^2$ **88.** $\left[\dfrac{1}{2}(-10)\right]^2$

89. $\left(\dfrac{1}{2} \cdot 3\right)^2$ **90.** $\left(\dfrac{1}{2} \cdot 5\right)^2$ **91.** $-\dfrac{1}{3}(-2x + 6)$

92. $-\dfrac{1}{2}(-2x + 6)$ **93.** $8\left(-\dfrac{1}{4}x + \dfrac{1}{8}y\right)$ **94.** $9\left(-\dfrac{1}{9}x + \dfrac{1}{3}y\right)$

Applying the Concepts

95. Temperature Change The temperature is 25°F at 5:00 in the afternoon. If the temperature drops 6°F every hour after that, what is the temperature at 9:00 in the evening?

96. Investment Value Suppose you purchase $500 worth of a mutual fund and find that the value of your purchase doubles every 2 years. Write a sequence of numbers that gives the value of your purchase every 2 years for the first 10 years you own it. Is this sequence a geometric sequence?

97. Reading Charts Refer to the bar charts below to find the net change in calories for a 150-pound person who bowls for 3 hours and then eats 2 Whoppers.

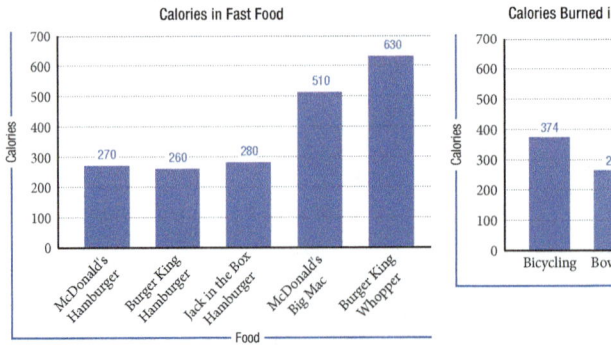

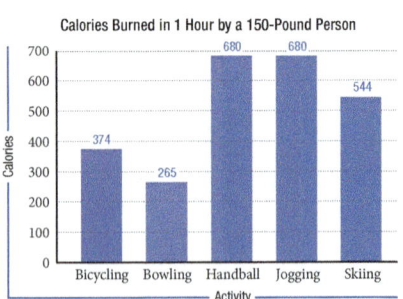

Division of Real Numbers

0.7

Suppose you and four friends bought equal shares of an investment for a total of $15,000 and then sold it later for only $13,000. How much did each person lose? Because the total amount of money lost can be represented by $-\$2,000$, and there are 5 people with equal shares, we can represent each person's loss with division:

$$\frac{-\$2,000}{5} = -\$400$$

From this discussion it seems reasonable to say that a negative number divided by a positive number is a negative number. Here is a more detailed discussion of division with positive and negative numbers.

The last of the four basic operations is division. We will use the same approach to define division as we used for subtraction; that is, we will define division in terms of rules we already know.

Recall that we developed the rule for subtraction of real numbers by defining subtraction in terms of addition. We changed our subtraction problems to addition problems and then added to get our answers. Because we already have a rule for multiplication of real numbers, and division is the inverse operation of multiplication, we will simply define division in terms of multiplication.

We know that division by the number 2 is the same as multiplication by $\frac{1}{2}$; that is, 6 divided by 2 is 3, which is the same as 6 times $\frac{1}{2}$. Similarly, dividing a number by 5 gives the same result as multiplying by $\frac{1}{5}$. We can extend this idea to all real numbers with the following rule.

Note We are defining division this way so we can use what we already know about multiplication to do division problems. We actually want as few rules as possible. Defining division in terms of multiplication allows us to avoid writing a separate rule for division.

> **⌈Δ≠Σ⌉ Rule**
>
> If a and b represent any two real numbers (b cannot be 0), then it is always true that
>
> $$a \div b = \frac{a}{b} = a\left(\frac{1}{b}\right)$$

Division by a number is the same as multiplication by its reciprocal. Because every division problem can be written as a multiplication problem and because we already know the rule for multiplication of two real numbers, we do not have to write a new rule for division of real numbers. We will simply replace our division problem with multiplication and use the rule we already have.

Video Examples

Section 0.7

Example 1 Write each division problem as an equivalent multiplication problem, and then multiply.

a. $\dfrac{6}{2}$ **b.** $\dfrac{6}{-2}$ **c.** $\dfrac{-6}{2}$ **d.** $\dfrac{-6}{-2}$

SOLUTION

a. $\dfrac{6}{2} = 6\left(\dfrac{1}{2}\right) = 3$ *The product of two positives is positive*

b. $\dfrac{6}{-2} = 6\left(-\dfrac{1}{2}\right) = -3$

c. $\dfrac{-6}{2} = -6\left(\dfrac{1}{2}\right) = -3$ *The product of a positive and a negative is a negative*

d. $\dfrac{-6}{-2} = -6\left(-\dfrac{1}{2}\right) = 3$ *The product of two negatives is positive*

The second step in these examples is used only to show that we *can* write division in terms of multiplication. [In actual practice we wouldn't write $\frac{6}{2}$ as $6\left(\frac{1}{2}\right)$.] The answers, therefore, follow from the rule for multiplication; that is, like signs produce a positive answer, and unlike signs produce a negative answer.

Here are some examples. This time we will not show division as multiplication by the reciprocal. If the original numbers have the same signs, the answer will be positive. If the original numbers have different signs, the answer will be negative.

Example 2   Divide.

a. $\dfrac{12}{6} = 2$ Like signs give a positive answer

b. $\dfrac{12}{-6} = -2$ Unlike signs give a negative answer

c. $\dfrac{-12}{6} = -2$ Unlike signs give a negative answer

d. $\dfrac{-12}{-6} = 2$ Like signs give a positive answer

e. $\dfrac{15}{-3} = -5$ Unlike signs give a negative answer

f. $\dfrac{-40}{-5} = 8$ Like signs give a positive answer

g. $\dfrac{-14}{2} = -7$ Unlike signs give a negative answer

Division with Fractions

We can apply the definition of division to fractions. Because dividing by a fraction is equivalent to multiplying by its reciprocal, we can divide a number by the fraction $\frac{3}{4}$ by multiplying it by the reciprocal of $\frac{3}{4}$, which is $\frac{4}{3}$. For example,

$$\frac{2}{5} \div \frac{3}{4} = \frac{2}{5} \cdot \frac{4}{3} = \frac{8}{15}$$

You may have learned this rule in previous math classes. In some math classes, multiplication by the reciprocal is referred to as "inverting the divisor and multiplying." No matter how you say it, division by any number (except 0) is always equivalent to multiplication by its reciprocal. Here are additional examples that involve division by fractions.

Example 3   Divide.

a. $\dfrac{2}{3} \div \dfrac{5}{7}$ **b.** $-\dfrac{3}{4} \div \dfrac{7}{9}$ **c.** $8 \div \left(-\dfrac{4}{5}\right)$

SOLUTION

a. $\dfrac{2}{3} \div \dfrac{5}{7} = \dfrac{2}{3} \cdot \dfrac{7}{5}$ Rewrite as multiplication by the reciprocal

$\qquad\quad = \dfrac{14}{15}$ Multiply

b. $-\dfrac{3}{4} \div \dfrac{7}{9} = -\dfrac{3}{4} \cdot \dfrac{9}{7}$ Rewrite as multiplication by the reciprocal

$\qquad\qquad = -\dfrac{27}{28}$ Multiply

c. $8 \div \left(-\frac{4}{5}\right) = \frac{8}{1}\left(-\frac{5}{4}\right)$ Rewrite as multiplication by the reciprocal

$\qquad\qquad = -\frac{40}{4}$ Multiply

$\qquad\qquad = -10$ Divide 40 by 4

The last step in each of the following examples involves reducing a fraction to lowest terms. To reduce a fraction to lowest terms, we divide the numerator and denominator by the largest number that divides each of them exactly. For example, to reduce $\frac{15}{20}$ to lowest terms, we divide 15 and 20 by 5 to get $\frac{3}{4}$.

Example 4   Simplify as much as possible.

a. $\dfrac{-4(5)}{6}$ **b.** $\dfrac{30}{-4-5}$

SOLUTION

a. $\dfrac{-4(5)}{6} = \dfrac{-20}{6}$ Simplify numerator

$\qquad\quad = -\dfrac{10}{3}$ Reduce to lowest terms by dividing numerator and denominator by 2

b. $\dfrac{30}{-4-5} = \dfrac{30}{-9}$ Simplify denominator

$\qquad\qquad = -\dfrac{10}{3}$ Reduce to lowest terms by dividing numerator and denominator by 3

In the examples that follow, the numerators and denominators contain expressions that are somewhat more complicated than those we have seen thus far. To apply the rule for order of operations to these examples, we treat fraction bars the same way we treat grouping symbols; that is, fraction bars separate numerators and denominators so that each will be simplified separately.

Example 5   Simplify.

a. $\dfrac{2(-3)+4}{12}$ **b.** $\dfrac{5(-4)+6(-1)}{2(3)-4(1)}$

SOLUTION

a. $\dfrac{2(-3)+4}{12} = \dfrac{-6+4}{12}$ In the numerator, we multiply before we add

$\qquad\qquad = \dfrac{-2}{12}$ Addition

$\qquad\qquad = -\dfrac{1}{6}$ Reduce to lowest terms by dividing the numerator and the denominator by 2

b. $\dfrac{5(-4)+6(-1)}{2(3)-4(1)} = \dfrac{-20+(-6)}{6-4}$ Multiplication before addition

$\qquad\qquad\quad = \dfrac{-26}{2}$ Simplify numerator and denominator

$\qquad\qquad\quad = -13$ Divide -26 by 2

We must be careful when we are working with expressions such as $(-5)^2$ and -5^2 that we include the negative sign with the base only when parentheses indicate we are to do so.

Unless there are parentheses to indicate otherwise, we consider the base to be only the number directly below and to the left of the exponent. If we want to include a negative sign with the base, we must use parentheses.

To simplify a more complicated expression, we follow the same rule. For example,

$$7^2 - 3^2 = 49 - 9$$

The bases are 7 and 3; the sign between the two terms is a subtraction sign

For another example,

$$5^3 - 3^4 = 125 - 81$$

We simplify exponents first, then subtract

Example 6   Simplify.

a. $\dfrac{5^2 - 3^2}{-5 + 3}$ **b.** $\dfrac{(3 + 2)^2}{-3^2 - 2^2}$

SOLUTION

a. $\dfrac{5^2 - 3^2}{-5 + 3} = \dfrac{25 - 9}{-2}$ *Simplify numerator and denominator separately*

$$= \dfrac{16}{-2}$$

$$= -8$$

b. $\dfrac{(3 + 2)^2}{-3^2 - 2^2} = \dfrac{5^2}{-9 - 4}$ *Simplify numerator and denominator separately*

$$= \dfrac{25}{-13}$$

$$= -\dfrac{25}{13}$$

Example 7   Simplify each expression.

a. $10\left(\dfrac{x}{2}\right)$ **b.** $a\left(\dfrac{3}{a} - 4\right)$

SOLUTION

a. $10\left(\dfrac{x}{2}\right) = 10\left(\dfrac{1}{2}x\right)$

$$= \left(10 \cdot \dfrac{1}{2}\right)x$$

$$= 5x$$

b. $a\left(\dfrac{3}{a} - 4\right) = a \cdot \dfrac{3}{a} - a \cdot 4$

$$= 3 - 4a$$

Division with the Number 0

For every division problem there is an associated multiplication problem involving the same numbers. For example, the following two problems say the same thing about the numbers 2, 3, and 6:

Division	Multiplication
$\dfrac{6}{3} = 2$	$6 = 2(3)$

We can use this relationship between division and multiplication to clarify division involving the number 0.

First, dividing 0 by a number other than 0 is allowed and always results in 0. To see this, consider dividing 0 by 5. We know the answer is 0 because of the relationship between multiplication and division. This is how we write it:

$$\frac{0}{5} = 0 \qquad \text{because} \qquad 0 = 0(5)$$

However, dividing a nonzero number by 0 is not allowed in the real numbers. Suppose we were attempting to divide 5 by 0. We don't know if there is an answer to this problem, but if there is, let's say the answer is a number that we can represent with the letter n. If 5 divided by 0 is a number n, then

$$\frac{5}{0} = n \qquad \text{and} \qquad 5 = n(0)$$

This is impossible, because no matter what number n is, when we multiply it by 0 the answer must be 0. It can never be 5. In algebra, we say expressions like $\frac{5}{0}$ are undefined because there is no answer to them; that is, division by 0 is not allowed in the real numbers.

The only other possibility for division involving the number 0 is 0 divided by 0. We will treat problems like $\frac{0}{0}$ as if they were undefined also.

Getting Ready for Class

After reading through the preceding section, respond in your own words and in complete sentences.

A. Why do we define division in terms of multiplication?
B. What is the reciprocal of a number?
C. How do we divide fractions?
D. Why is division by 0 not allowed with real numbers?

Problem Set 0.7

Find the following quotients (divide).

1. $\dfrac{8}{-4}$ **2.** $\dfrac{10}{-5}$ **3.** $\dfrac{-48}{16}$ **4.** $\dfrac{-32}{4}$

5. $\dfrac{-7}{21}$ **6.** $\dfrac{-25}{100}$ **7.** $\dfrac{-39}{-13}$ **8.** $\dfrac{-18}{-6}$

9. $\dfrac{-6}{-42}$ **10.** $\dfrac{-4}{-28}$ **11.** $\dfrac{0}{-32}$ **12.** $\dfrac{0}{17}$

The following problems review all four operations with positive and negative numbers. Perform the indicated operations.

13. $-3 + 12$ **14.** $5 + (-10)$ **15.** $-3 - 12$ **16.** $5 - (-10)$

17. $-3(12)$ **18.** $5(-10)$ **19.** $-3 \div 12$ **20.** $5 \div (-10)$

Divide and reduce all answers to lowest terms.

21. $\dfrac{4}{5} \div \dfrac{3}{4}$ **22.** $\dfrac{6}{8} \div \dfrac{3}{4}$ **23.** $-\dfrac{5}{6} \div \left(-\dfrac{5}{8}\right)$ **24.** $-\dfrac{7}{9} \div \left(-\dfrac{1}{6}\right)$

25. $\dfrac{10}{13} \div \left(-\dfrac{5}{4}\right)$ **26.** $\dfrac{5}{12} \div \left(-\dfrac{10}{3}\right)$ **27.** $-\dfrac{5}{6} \div \dfrac{5}{6}$ **28.** $-\dfrac{8}{9} \div \dfrac{8}{9}$

29. $-\dfrac{3}{4} \div \left(-\dfrac{3}{4}\right)$ **30.** $-\dfrac{6}{7} \div \left(-\dfrac{6}{7}\right)$

The following problems involve more than one operation. Simplify as much as possible.

31. $\dfrac{3(-2)}{-10}$ **32.** $\dfrac{4(-3)}{24}$ **33.** $\dfrac{-5(-5)}{-15}$ **34.** $\dfrac{-7(-3)}{-35}$

35. $\dfrac{-8(-7)}{-28}$ **36.** $\dfrac{-3(-9)}{-6}$ **37.** $\dfrac{27}{4 - 13}$ **38.** $\dfrac{27}{13 - 4}$

39. $\dfrac{20 - 6}{5 - 5}$ **40.** $\dfrac{10 - 12}{3 - 3}$ **41.** $\dfrac{-3 + 9}{2 \cdot 5 - 10}$ **42.** $\dfrac{2 + 8}{2 \cdot 4 - 8}$

43. $\dfrac{15(-5) - 25}{2(-10)}$ **44.** $\dfrac{10(-3) - 20}{5(-2)}$ **45.** $\dfrac{27 - 2(-4)}{-3(5)}$ **46.** $\dfrac{20 - 5(-3)}{10(-3)}$

47. $\dfrac{12 - 6(-2)}{12(-2)}$ **48.** $\dfrac{3(-4) + 5(-6)}{10 - 6}$

49. $\dfrac{5^2 - 2^2}{-5 + 2}$ **50.** $\dfrac{7^2 - 4^2}{-7 + 4}$ **51.** $\dfrac{8^2 - 2^2}{8^2 + 2^2}$ **52.** $\dfrac{4^2 - 6^2}{4^2 + 6^2}$

53. $\dfrac{(5 + 3)^2}{-5^2 - 3^2}$ **54.** $\dfrac{(7 + 2)^2}{-7^2 - 2^2}$ **55.** $\dfrac{(8 - 4)^2}{8^2 - 4^2}$ **56.** $\dfrac{(6 - 2)^2}{6^2 - 2^2}$

57. $\dfrac{-4 \cdot 3^2 - 5 \cdot 2^2}{-8(7)}$ **58.** $\dfrac{-2 \cdot 5^2 + 3 \cdot 2^3}{-3(13)}$

59. $\dfrac{3 \cdot 10^2 + 4 \cdot 10 + 5}{345}$ **60.** $\dfrac{5 \cdot 10^2 + 6 \cdot 10 + 7}{567}$

61. $\dfrac{7 - [(2 - 3) - 4]}{-1 - 2 - 3}$ **62.** $\dfrac{2 - [(3 - 5) - 8]}{-3 - 4 - 5}$

63. $\dfrac{6(-4) - 2(5 - 8)}{-6 - 3 - 5}$ **64.** $\dfrac{3(-4) - 5(9 - 11)}{-9 - 2 - 3}$

65. $\dfrac{3(-5 - 3) + 4(7 - 9)}{5(-2) + 3(-4)}$ **66.** $\dfrac{-2(6 - 10) - 3(8 - 5)}{6(-3) - 6(-2)}$

67. $\dfrac{|3 - 9|}{3 - 9}$ **68.** $\dfrac{|4 - 7|}{4 - 7}$

69. Simplify each expression.

    a. $20 \div 4 \cdot 5$ **b.** $-20 \div 4 \cdot 5$ **c.** $20 \div (-4) \cdot 5$ **d.** $20 \div 4(-5)$

    e. $-20 \div 4(-5)$

70. Simplify each expression.

    a. $32 \div 8 \cdot 4$ **b.** $-32 \div 8 \cdot 4$ **c.** $32 \div (-8) \cdot 4$ **d.** $32 \div 8(-4)$

    e. $-32 \div 8(-4)$

71. Simplify each expression.

    a. $8 \div \dfrac{4}{5}$ **b.** $8 \div \dfrac{4}{5} - 10$ **c.** $8 \div \dfrac{4}{5}(-10)$ **d.** $8 \div \left(-\dfrac{4}{5}\right) - 10$

72. Simplify each expression.

    a. $10 \div \dfrac{5}{6}$ **b.** $10 \div \dfrac{5}{6} - 12$ **c.** $10 \div \dfrac{5}{6}(-12)$ **d.** $10 \div \left(-\dfrac{5}{6}\right) - 12$

Apply the distributive property.

73. $10\left(\dfrac{x}{2} + \dfrac{3}{5}\right)$ **74.** $6\left(\dfrac{x}{3} + \dfrac{5}{2}\right)$ **75.** $15\left(\dfrac{x}{5} + \dfrac{4}{3}\right)$ **76.** $6\left(\dfrac{x}{3} + \dfrac{1}{2}\right)$

77. $x\left(\dfrac{3}{x} + 1\right)$ **78.** $x\left(\dfrac{4}{x} + 3\right)$ **79.** $21\left(\dfrac{x}{7} - \dfrac{y}{3}\right)$ **80.** $36\left(\dfrac{x}{4} - \dfrac{y}{9}\right)$

81. $a\left(\dfrac{3}{a} - \dfrac{2}{a}\right)$ **82.** $a\left(\dfrac{7}{a} + \dfrac{1}{a}\right)$

Answer the following questions.

83. What is the quotient of -12 and -4?

84. The quotient of -4 and -12 is what number?

85. What number do we divide by -5 to get 2?

86. What number do we divide by -3 to get 4?

87. Twenty-seven divided by what number is -9?

88. Fifteen divided by what number is -3?

89. If the quotient of -20 and 4 is decreased by 3, what number results?

90. If -4 is added to the quotient of 24 and -8, what number results?

Applying the Concepts

91. **Investment** Suppose that you and 3 friends bought equal shares of an investment for a total of $15,000 and then sold it later for only $13,600. How much did each person lose?

92. **Investment** If 8 people invest $500 each in a stamp collection and after a year the collection is worth $3,800, how much did each person lose?

93. **Temperature Change** Suppose that the temperature outside is dropping at a constant rate. If the temperature is 75°F at noon and drops to 61°F by 4:00 in the afternoon, by how much did the temperature change each hour?

94. **Temperature Change** In a chemistry class, a thermometer is placed in a beaker of hot water. The initial temperature of the water is 165°F. After 10 minutes the water has cooled to 72°F. If the water temperature drops at a constant rate, by how much does the water temperature change each minute?

95. **Sewing** If $\frac{6}{7}$ yard of material is needed to make a blanket, how many blankets can be made from 12 yards of material?

96. **Manufacturing** A clothing manufacturer is making scarves that require $\frac{3}{8}$ yard for material each. How many can be made from 27 yards of material?

97. **Capacity** Suppose a bag of candy holds exactly $\frac{1}{4}$ pound of candy. How many of these bags can be filled from 12 pounds of candy?

98. **Capacity** A certain size bottle holds exactly $\frac{4}{5}$ pint of liquid. How many of these bottles can be filled from a 20-pint container?

99. **Cooking** A man is making cookies from a recipe that calls for $\frac{3}{4}$ teaspoon of oil. If the only measuring spoon he can find is a $\frac{1}{8}$ teaspoon, how many of these will he have to fill with oil in order to have a total of $\frac{3}{4}$ teaspoon of oil?

100. **Cooking** A cake recipe calls for $\frac{1}{2}$ cup of sugar. If the only measuring cup available is a $\frac{1}{8}$ cup, how many of these will have to be filled with sugar to make a total of $\frac{1}{2}$ cup of sugar?

101. **Cartons of Milk** If a small carton of milk holds exactly $\frac{1}{2}$ pint, how many of the $\frac{1}{2}$-pint cartons can be filled from a 14-pint container?

102. **Pieces of Pipe** How many pieces of pipe that are $\frac{2}{3}$ foot long must be laid together to make a pipe 16 feet long?

103. **Internet Mailing Lists** A company sells products on the Internet through an email list. They predict that they sell one $50 product for every 25 people on their mailing list.
    a. What is their projected revenue if their list contains 10,000 email addresses?
    b. What is their projected revenue if their list contains 25,000 email addresses?
    c. They can purchase a list of 5,000 email addresses for $5,000. Is this a wise purchase?

104. **Facebook Ads** A new band has a following on Facebook. They sell their albums by posting Facebook ads and they predict that they sell one $15 album for every 100 people who see one of their ads.
    a. What is their projected revenue if 5,000 people see their ad?
    b. What is their projected revenue if 20,000 people see their ad?
    c. If they need to make $45,000, how many people do they need to see their ad?

0.8

In Section 0.2 we introduced the real numbers and defined them as the numbers associated with points on the real number line. At that time, we said the real numbers include whole numbers, fractions, and decimals, as well as other numbers that are not as familiar to us as these numbers. In this section we take a more detailed look at the kinds of numbers that make up the set of real numbers.

The numbers that make up the set of real numbers can be classified as *counting numbers, whole numbers, integers, rational numbers*, and *irrational numbers*; each is said to be a *subset* of the real numbers.

> **(dĕf) subset**
>
> Set A is called a *subset* of set B if set A is contained in set B; that is, if each and every element in set A is also a member of set B.

Here is a detailed description of the major subsets of the real numbers.

The *counting numbers* are the numbers with which we count. They are the numbers 1, 2, 3, and so on. The notation we use to specify a group of numbers like this is *set notation*. We use the symbols { and } to enclose the members of the set.

Counting numbers = {1, 2, 3, . . . }

Video Examples

Section 0.8

Example 1 Which of the numbers in the following set are not counting numbers?

$$\left\{ -3, 0, \frac{1}{2}, 1, 1.5, 3 \right\}$$

SOLUTION The numbers $-3, 0, \frac{1}{2}$, and 1.5 are not counting numbers.

The *whole numbers* include the counting numbers and the number 0.

Whole numbers = {0, 1, 2, . . . }

The set of *integers* includes the whole numbers and the opposites of all the counting numbers.

Integers = { . . . , $-3, -2, -1, 0, 1, 2, 3, . . .$ }

When we refer to positive integers, we are referring to the numbers 1, 2, 3, ... Likewise, the negative integers are $-1, -2, -3, ...$ The number 0 is neither positive nor negative.

Example 2 Which of the numbers in the following set are not integers?

$$\left\{ -5, -1.75, 0, \frac{2}{3}, 1, \pi, 3 \right\}$$

SOLUTION The only numbers in the set that are not integers are $-1.75, \frac{2}{3}$, and π.

The set of *rational numbers* is the set of numbers commonly called "fractions" together with the integers. The set of rational numbers is difficult to list in the same way we have listed the other sets, so we will use a different kind of notation:

$$\textbf{Rational numbers} = \left\{ \frac{a}{b} \mid a \text{ and } b \text{ are integers } (b \neq 0) \right\}$$

This notation is read "The set of elements $\frac{a}{b}$ such that a and b are integers (and b is not 0)." If a number can be put in the form $\frac{a}{b}$, where a and b are both from the set of integers, then it is called a rational number.

Rational numbers include any number that can be written as the ratio of two integers; that is, rational numbers are numbers that can be put in the form

$$\frac{\text{integer}}{\text{integer}}$$

Example 3　Show why each of the numbers in the following set is a rational number.

$$\left\{ -3, -\frac{2}{3}, 0, 0.333\ldots, 0.75 \right\}$$

SOLUTION　The number -3 is a rational number because it can be written as the ratio of -3 to 1; that is,

$$-3 = \frac{-3}{1}$$

Similarly, the number $-\frac{2}{3}$ can be thought of as the ratio of -2 to 3, whereas the number 0 can be thought of as the ratio of 0 to 1.

Any repeating decimal, such as $0.333\ldots$ (the dots indicate that the 3s repeat forever), can be written as the ratio of two integers. In this case $0.333\ldots$ is the same as the fraction $\frac{1}{3}$.

Finally, any decimal that terminates after a certain number of digits can be written as the ratio of two integers. The number 0.75 is equal to the fraction $\frac{3}{4}$ and is therefore a rational number.

Still other numbers exist, each of which is associated with a point on the real number line, that cannot be written as the ratio of two integers. In decimal form they never terminate and never repeat a sequence of digits indefinitely. They are called *irrational numbers* (because they are not rational):

$$\textbf{Irrational numbers} = \{\text{nonrational numbers; nonrepeating,}$$
$$\text{nonterminating decimals}\}$$

We cannot write any irrational number in a form that is familiar to us because they are all nonterminating, nonrepeating decimals. Because they are not rational, they cannot be written as the ratio of two integers. They have to be represented in other ways. One irrational number you have probably seen before is π. It is not 3.14. Rather, 3.14 is an approximation to π. It cannot be written as a terminating decimal number. Other representations for irrational numbers are $\sqrt{2}, \sqrt{3}, \sqrt{5}, \sqrt{6}$, and, in general, the square root of any number that is not itself a perfect square. (If you are not familiar with square roots, you will be after Chapter 8.) Right now it is enough to know that some numbers on the number line cannot be written as the ratio of two integers or in decimal form. We call them irrational numbers.

The set of real numbers is the set of numbers that are either rational or irrational; that is, a real number is either rational or irrational.

$$\textbf{Real numbers} = \{\text{all rational numbers and all irrational numbers}\}$$

Prime Numbers and Factoring

The following diagram shows the relationship between multiplication and factoring:

Multiplication

$$\text{Factors} \rightarrow 3 \cdot 4 = 12 \leftarrow \text{Product}$$

Factoring

When we read the problem from left to right, we say the product of 3 and 4 is 12. Or we multiply 3 and 4 to get 12. When we read the problem in the other direction, from right to left, we say we have *factored* 12 into 3 times 4, or 3 and 4 are *factors* of 12.

The number 12 can be factored still further:

$$12 = 4 \cdot 3$$
$$= 2 \cdot 2 \cdot 3$$
$$= 2^2 \cdot 3$$

The numbers 2 and 3 are called *prime factors* of 12 because neither of them can be factored any further.

(dĕf′   *factor*

If *a* and *b* represent integers, then *a* is said to be a *factor* (or divisor) of *b* if *a* divides *b* evenly; that is, if *a* divides *b* with no remainder.

(dĕf′   *prime number*

A *prime number* is any positive integer larger than 1 whose only positive factors (divisors) are itself and 1.

> **Note** The number 15 is not a prime number because it has factors of 3 and 5; that is, $15 = 3 \cdot 5$. When a whole number larger than 1 is not prime, it is said to be *composite*.

Here is a list of the first few prime numbers.

Prime numbers $= \{2, 3, 5, 7, 11, 13, 17, 19, 23, 29, 31, 37, 41, \dots\}$

When a number is not prime, we can factor it into the product of prime numbers. To factor a number into the product of primes, we simply factor it until it cannot be factored further.

Example 4 Factor the number 60 into the product of prime numbers.

SOLUTION We begin by writing 60 as the product of any two positive integers whose product is 60, like 6 and 10:

$$60 = 6 \cdot 10$$

We then factor these numbers:

$$60 = 6 \cdot 10$$
$$= (2 \cdot 3) \cdot (2 \cdot 5)$$
$$= 2 \cdot 2 \cdot 3 \cdot 5$$
$$= 2^2 \cdot 3 \cdot 5$$

> **Note** It is customary to write the prime factors in order from smallest to largest.

Example 5   Factor the number 630 into the product of primes.

SOLUTION   Let's begin by writing 630 as the product of 63 and 10:

$$630 = 63 \cdot 10$$
$$= (7 \cdot 9) \cdot (2 \cdot 5)$$
$$= 7 \cdot 3 \cdot 3 \cdot 2 \cdot 5$$
$$= 2 \cdot 3^2 \cdot 5 \cdot 7$$

It makes no difference which two numbers we start with, as long as their product is 630. We will always get the same result because a number has only one set of prime factors.

$$630 = 18 \cdot 35$$
$$= 3 \cdot 6 \cdot 5 \cdot 7$$
$$= 3 \cdot 2 \cdot 3 \cdot 5 \cdot 7$$
$$= 2 \cdot 3^2 \cdot 5 \cdot 7$$

> **Note**   There are some "tricks" to finding the divisors of a number. For instance, if a number ends in 0 or 5, then it is divisible by 5. If a number ends in an even number (0, 2, 4, 6, or 8), then it is divisible by 2. A number is divisible by 3 if the sum of its digits is divisible by 3. For example, 921 is divisible by 3 because the sum of its digits is $9 + 2 + 1 = 12$, which is divisible by 3.

When we have factored a number into the product of its prime factors, we not only know what prime numbers divide the original number, but we also know all of the other numbers that divide it as well. For instance, if we were to factor 210 into its prime factors, we would have $210 = 2 \cdot 3 \cdot 5 \cdot 7$, which means that 2, 3, 5, and 7 divide 210, as well as any combination of products of 2, 3, 5, and 7. That is, because 3 and 7 divide 210, then so does their product 21. Because 3, 5, and 7 each divide 210, then so does their product 105

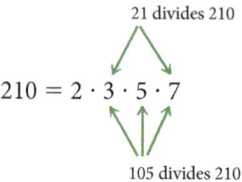

21 divides 210

$$210 = 2 \cdot 3 \cdot 5 \cdot 7$$

105 divides 210

Although there are many ways in which factoring is used in arithmetic and algebra, one simple application is in reducing fractions to lowest terms.

Recall that we reduce fractions to lowest terms by dividing the numerator and denominator by the same number. We can use the prime factorization of numbers to help us reduce fractions with large numerators and denominators.

Example 6   Reduce $\dfrac{210}{231}$ to lowest terms.

SOLUTION   First we factor 210 and 231 into the product of prime factors. Then we reduce to lowest terms by dividing the numerator and denominator by any factors they have in common.

$$\frac{210}{231} = \frac{2 \cdot 3 \cdot 5 \cdot 7}{3 \cdot 7 \cdot 11} \qquad \textit{Factor the numerator and denominator completely}$$

$$= \frac{2 \cdot \cancel{3} \cdot 5 \cdot \cancel{7}}{\cancel{3} \cdot \cancel{7} \cdot 11} \qquad \textit{Divide the numerator and denominator by } 3 \cdot 7$$

$$= \frac{2 \cdot 5}{11}$$

$$= \frac{10}{11}$$

> *Note*   The small lines we have drawn through the factors that are common to the numerator and denominator are used to indicate that we have divided the numerator and denominator by those factors.

Getting Ready for Class

After reading through the preceding section, respond in your own words and in complete sentences.

A. What is a whole number?

B. How are factoring and multiplication related?

C. Is every integer also a rational number? Explain.

D. What is a prime number?

Problem Set 0.8

Given the numbers in the set $\left\{-3, -2.5, 0, 1, \frac{3}{2}, \sqrt{15}\right\}$:

1. List all the whole numbers.   **2.** List all the integers.

3. List all the rational numbers.   **4.** List all the irrational numbers.

5. List all the real numbers.

Given the numbers in the set $\left\{-10, -8, -0.333\ldots, -2, 9, \frac{25}{3}, \pi\right\}$:

6. List all the whole numbers.   **7.** List all the integers.

8. List all the rational numbers.   **9.** List all the irrational numbers.

10. List all the real numbers.

Identify the following statements as either true or false.

11. Every whole number is also an integer.

12. The set of whole numbers is a subset of the set of integers.

13. A number can be both rational and irrational.

14. The set of rational numbers and the set of irrational numbers have some elements in common.

15. Some whole numbers are also negative integers.

16. Every rational number is also a real number.

17. All integers are also rational numbers.

18. The set of integers is a subset of the set of rational numbers.

Label each of the following numbers as prime or composite. If a number is composite, then factor it completely.

19. 48   **20.** 72   **21.** 37   **22.** 23

23. 1,023   **24.** 543

Factor the following into the product of primes. When the number has been factored completely, write its prime factors from smallest to largest.

25. 144   **26.** 288   **27.** 38   **28.** 63

29. 105   **30.** 210   **31.** 180   **32.** 900

33. 385   **34.** 1,925   **35.** 121   **36.** 546

37. 420   **38.** 598   **39.** 620   **40.** 2,310

Reduce each fraction to lowest terms by first factoring the numerator and denominator into the product of prime factors and then dividing out any factors they have in common.

41. $\dfrac{105}{165}$ **42.** $\dfrac{165}{385}$ **43.** $\dfrac{525}{735}$ **44.** $\dfrac{550}{735}$ **45.** $\dfrac{385}{455}$ **46.** $\dfrac{385}{735}$

47. $\dfrac{322}{345}$ **48.** $\dfrac{266}{285}$ **49.** $\dfrac{205}{369}$ **50.** $\dfrac{111}{185}$ **51.** $\dfrac{215}{344}$ **52.** $\dfrac{279}{310}$

53. Factor 6^3 into the product of prime factors by first factoring 6 and then raising each of its factors to the third power.

54. Factor 12^2 into the product of prime factors by first factoring 12 and then raising each of its factors to the second power.

55. Factor $9^4 \cdot 16^2$ into the product of prime factors by first factoring 9 and 16 completely and then raising each of its factors to the indicated power.

56. Factor $10^2 \cdot 12^3$ into the product of prime factors by first factoring 10 and 12 completely and then raising each of its factors to the indicated power.

57. Simplify the expression $3 \cdot 8 + 3 \cdot 7 + 3 \cdot 5$, and then factor the result into the product of primes. (Notice one of the factors of the answer is 3.)

58. Simplify the expression $5 \cdot 4 + 5 \cdot 9 + 5 \cdot 3$, and then factor the result into the product of primes.

Recall the Fibonacci sequence we introduced earlier in this chapter.

Fibonacci sequence = 1, 1, 2, 3, 5, 8, . . .

Any number in the Fibonacci sequence is a *Fibonacci number.*

59. The Fibonacci numbers are not a subset of which of the following sets: real numbers, rational numbers, irrational numbers, whole numbers?

60. Name three Fibonacci numbers that are prime numbers.

61. Name three Fibonacci numbers that are composite numbers.

62. Is the sequence of odd numbers a subset of the Fibonacci numbers?

You may recall from previous math classes that to add two fractions with the same denominator, you simply add their numerators and put the result over the common denominator:

$$\frac{3}{4} + \frac{2}{4} = \frac{3+2}{4} = \frac{5}{4}$$

The reason we add numerators but do not add denominators is that we must follow the distributive property. To see this, you first have to recall that $\frac{3}{4}$ can be written as $3 \cdot \frac{1}{4}$, and $\frac{2}{4}$ can be written as $2 \cdot \frac{1}{4}$ (dividing by 4 is equivalent to multiplying by $\frac{1}{4}$). Here is the addition problem again, this time showing the use of the distributive property:

$$\frac{3}{4} + \frac{2}{4} = 3 \cdot \frac{1}{4} + 2 \cdot \frac{1}{4}$$

$$= (3 + 2) \cdot \frac{1}{4} \qquad \text{Distributive property}$$

$$= 5 \cdot \frac{1}{4}$$

$$= \frac{5}{4}$$

What we have here is the sum of the numerators placed over the **common denominator**. In symbols we have the following.

> **△≠Σ Addition and Subtraction with Fractions**
>
> If a, b, and c are integers and c is not equal to 0, then
>
> $$\frac{a}{c} + \frac{b}{c} = \frac{a+b}{c}$$
>
> This rule holds for subtraction as well; that is,
>
> $$\frac{a}{c} - \frac{b}{c} = \frac{a-b}{c}$$

In Example 1, find the sum or difference. (Add or subtract as indicated.) Reduce all answers to lowest terms. (Assume all variables represent nonzero numbers.)

Note Most people who have done any work with adding fractions know that you add fractions that have the same denominator by adding their numerators but not their denominators. However, most people don't know why this works. The reason why we add numerators but not denominators is because of the distributive property. That is what the discussion at the right is all about. If you really want to understand addition of fractions, pay close attention to this discussion.

Video Examples

Section 0.9

Example 1

a. $\frac{3}{8} + \frac{1}{8}$ **b.** $\frac{a+5}{8} - \frac{3}{8}$ **c.** $\frac{9}{x} - \frac{3}{x}$ **d.** $\frac{3}{7} + \frac{2}{7} - \frac{9}{7}$

SOLUTION

a. $\dfrac{3}{8} + \dfrac{1}{8} = \dfrac{3+1}{8}$ Add numerators; keep the same denominator

$\qquad\quad = \dfrac{4}{8}$ The sum of 3 and 1 is 4

$\qquad\quad = \dfrac{1}{2}$ Reduce to lowest terms

b. $\dfrac{a+5}{8} - \dfrac{3}{8} = \dfrac{a+5-3}{8}$ Combine numerators; keep the same denominator

$\qquad\qquad = \dfrac{a+2}{8}$

c. $\dfrac{9}{x} - \dfrac{3}{x} = \dfrac{9-3}{x}$ *Subtract numerators; keep the same denominator*

$\phantom{\dfrac{9}{x} - \dfrac{3}{x}} = \dfrac{6}{x}$ *The difference of 9 and 3 is 6*

d. $\dfrac{3}{7} + \dfrac{2}{7} - \dfrac{9}{7} = \dfrac{3+2-9}{7}$

$\phantom{\dfrac{3}{7} + \dfrac{2}{7} - \dfrac{9}{7}} = \dfrac{-4}{7}$

$\phantom{\dfrac{3}{7} + \dfrac{2}{7} - \dfrac{9}{7}} = -\dfrac{4}{7}$ *Unlike signs give a negative answer* ■

As Example 1 indicates, addition and subtraction are simple, straightforward processes when all the fractions have the same denominator. We will now turn our attention to the process of adding fractions that have different denominators. To get started, we need the following definition.

> **(dĕf´)   *least common denominator (LCD)***
>
> The *least common denominator (LCD)* for a set of denominators is the smallest number that is exactly divisible by each denominator. (Note that in some books the least common denominator is also called the least common multiple.)
>
> In other words, all the denominators of the fractions involved in a problem must divide into the least common denominator exactly; that is, they divide it without giving a remainder.

■ **Example 2**   Find the LCD for the fractions $\dfrac{5}{12}$ and $\dfrac{7}{18}$.

> *Note* The ability to find least common denominators is very important in mathematics. The discussion here is a detailed explanation of how to do it.

SOLUTION   The least common denominator for the denominators 12 and 18 must be the smallest number divisible by both 12 and 18. We can factor 12 and 18 completely and then build the LCD from these factors. Factoring 12 and 18 completely gives us

$$12 = 2 \cdot 2 \cdot 3 \qquad\qquad 18 = 2 \cdot 3 \cdot 3$$

Now, if 12 is going to divide the LCD exactly, then the LCD must have factors of $2 \cdot 2 \cdot 3$. If 18 is to divide it exactly, it must have factors of $2 \cdot 3 \cdot 3$. We don't need to repeat the factors that 12 and 18 have in common:

12 divides the LCD

$12 = 2 \cdot 2 \cdot 3$
$18 = 2 \cdot 3 \cdot 3$ $\text{LCD} = 2 \cdot 2 \cdot 3 \cdot 3$

18 divides the LCD

■

In other words, first we write down the factors of 12, then we attach the factors of 18 that do not already appear as factors of 12. We start with $2 \cdot 2 \cdot 3$ because those are the factors of 12. Then we look at the first factor of 18. It is 2. Because 2 already appears in the expression $2 \cdot 2 \cdot 3$, we don't need to attach another one. Next, we look at the factors $3 \cdot 3$. The expression $2 \cdot 2 \cdot 3$ has one 3. For it to contain the expression $3 \cdot 3$, we attach another 3. The final expression, our LCD, is $2 \cdot 2 \cdot 3 \cdot 3$.

The LCD for 12 and 18 is 36. It is the smallest number that is divisible by both 12 and 18; 12 divides it exactly three times, and 18 divides it exactly two times.

We can use the results of Example 2 to find the sum of the fractions $\frac{5}{12}$ and $\frac{7}{18}$.

Example 3   Add $\frac{5}{12} + \frac{7}{18}$.

SOLUTION   We can add fractions only when they have the same denominators. In Example 2 we found the LCD for $\frac{5}{12}$ and $\frac{7}{18}$ to be 36. We change $\frac{5}{12}$ and $\frac{7}{18}$ to equivalent fractions that each have 36 for a denominator by applying Property 1, on page 15, for fractions:

$$\frac{5}{12} = \frac{5 \cdot 3}{12 \cdot 3} = \frac{15}{36}$$

$$\frac{7}{18} = \frac{7 \cdot 2}{18 \cdot 2} = \frac{14}{36}$$

The fraction $\frac{15}{36}$ is equivalent to $\frac{5}{12}$, because it was obtained by multiplying both the numerator and denominator by 3. Likewise, $\frac{14}{36}$ is equivalent to $\frac{7}{18}$ because it was obtained by multiplying the numerator and denominator by 2. All we have left to do is to add numerators:

$$\frac{15}{36} + \frac{14}{36} = \frac{29}{36}$$

The sum of $\frac{5}{12}$ and $\frac{7}{18}$ is the fraction $\frac{29}{36}$. Let's write the complete problem again step-by-step.

$$\frac{5}{12} + \frac{7}{18} = \frac{5 \cdot 3}{12 \cdot 3} + \frac{7 \cdot 2}{18 \cdot 2} \qquad \textit{Rewrite each fraction as an equivalent}$$
$$\textit{fraction with denominator 36}$$

$$= \frac{15}{36} + \frac{14}{36}$$

$$= \frac{29}{36} \qquad \textit{Add numerators; keep the common}$$
$$\textit{denominator}$$

Example 4   Find the LCD for $\frac{3}{4}$ and $\frac{1}{6}$.

SOLUTION   We factor 4 and 6 into products of prime factors and build the LCD from these factors:

$$\left. \begin{array}{l} 4 = 2 \cdot 2 \\ 6 = 2 \cdot 3 \end{array} \right\} \quad \text{LCD} = 2 \cdot 2 \cdot 3 = 12$$

The LCD is 12. Both denominators divide it exactly; 4 divides 12 exactly three times, and 6 divides 12 exactly two times.

Example 5   Add $\frac{3}{4} + \frac{1}{6}$.

SOLUTION   In Example 4 we found that the LCD for these two fractions is 12. We begin by changing $\frac{3}{4}$ and $\frac{1}{6}$ to equivalent fractions with denominator 12:

$$\frac{3}{4} = \frac{3 \cdot 3}{4 \cdot 3} = \frac{9}{12}$$

$$\frac{1}{6} = \frac{1 \cdot 2}{6 \cdot 2} = \frac{2}{12}$$

The fraction $\frac{9}{12}$ is equal to the fraction $\frac{3}{4}$ because it was obtained by multiplying the numerator and denominator of $\frac{3}{4}$ by 3. Likewise, $\frac{2}{12}$ is equivalent to $\frac{1}{6}$ because it was obtained by multiplying the numerator and denominator of $\frac{1}{6}$ by 2. To complete the problem, we add numerators:

$$\frac{9}{12} + \frac{2}{12} = \frac{11}{12}$$

The sum of $\frac{3}{4}$ and $\frac{1}{6}$ is $\frac{11}{12}$. Here is how the complete problem looks:

$$\frac{3}{4} + \frac{1}{6} = \frac{3 \cdot 3}{4 \cdot 3} + \frac{1 \cdot 2}{6 \cdot 2}$$ *Rewrite each fraction as an equivalent fraction with denominator 12*

$$= \frac{9}{12} + \frac{2}{12}$$

$$= \frac{11}{12}$$ *Add numerators; keep the same denominator*

Example 6   Subtract $\frac{7}{15} - \frac{3}{10}$.

SOLUTION   Let's factor 15 and 10 completely and use these factors to build the LCD:

15 divides the LCD

$$\left.\begin{array}{l} 15 = 3 \cdot 5 \\ 10 = 2 \cdot 5 \end{array}\right\} \quad \text{LCD} = 2 \cdot 3 \cdot 5 = 30$$

10 divides the LCD

Changing to equivalent fractions and subtracting, we have

$$\frac{7}{15} - \frac{3}{10} = \frac{7 \cdot 2}{15 \cdot 2} - \frac{3 \cdot 3}{10 \cdot 3}$$ *Rewrite as equivalent fractions with the LCD for denominator*

$$= \frac{14}{30} - \frac{9}{30}$$

$$= \frac{5}{30}$$ *Subtract numerators; keep the LCD*

$$= \frac{1}{6}$$ *Reduce to lowest terms*

As a summary of what we have done so far and as a guide to working other problems, we will now list the steps involved in adding and subtracting fractions with different denominators.

⟮Δ≠Σ⟯   **How to Add or Subtract Any Two Fractions**

Step 1: Factor each denominator completely and use the factors to build the LCD. (Remember, the LCD is the smallest number divisible by each of the denominators in the problem.)

Step 2: Rewrite each fraction as an equivalent fraction that has the LCD for its denominator. This is done by multiplying both the numerator and denominator of the fraction in question by the appropriate whole number.

Step 3: Add or subtract the numerators of the fractions produced in step 2. This is the numerator of the sum or difference. The denominator of the sum or difference is the LCD.

Step 4: Reduce the fraction produced in step 3 to lowest terms if it is not already in lowest terms.

The idea behind adding or subtracting fractions is really very simple. We can add or subtract only fractions that have the same denominators. If the fractions we are trying to add or subtract do not have the same denominators, we rewrite each of them as an equivalent fraction with the LCD for a denominator.

Here are some further examples of sums and differences of fractions.

Example 7   Add $\frac{1}{6} + \frac{1}{8} + \frac{1}{4}$.

SOLUTION   We begin by factoring the denominators completely and building the LCD from the factors that result:

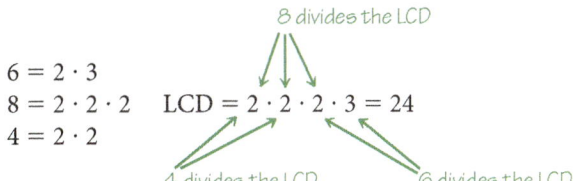

$$6 = 2 \cdot 3$$
$$8 = 2 \cdot 2 \cdot 2 \qquad \text{LCD} = 2 \cdot 2 \cdot 2 \cdot 3 = 24$$
$$4 = 2 \cdot 2$$

8 divides the LCD
4 divides the LCD
6 divides the LCD

We then change to equivalent fractions and add as usual:

$$\frac{1}{6} + \frac{1}{8} + \frac{1}{4} = \frac{1 \cdot 4}{6 \cdot 4} + \frac{1 \cdot 3}{8 \cdot 3} + \frac{1 \cdot 6}{4 \cdot 6}$$

$$= \frac{4}{24} + \frac{3}{24} + \frac{6}{24}$$

$$= \frac{13}{24}$$

■ **Example 8**   Subtract $3 - \dfrac{5}{6}$.

SOLUTION   The denominators are 1 $\left(\text{because } 3 = \dfrac{3}{1}\right)$ and 6. The smallest number divisible by both 1 and 6 is 6.

$$3 - \frac{5}{6} = \frac{3}{1} - \frac{5}{6}$$

$$= \frac{3 \cdot 6}{1 \cdot 6} - \frac{5}{6}$$

$$= \frac{18}{6} - \frac{5}{6}$$

$$= \frac{13}{6}$$

■

■ **Example 9**   Find the next number in each sequence.

a. $\dfrac{1}{2}, 0, -\dfrac{1}{2}, \ldots$ **b.** $\dfrac{1}{2}, 1, \dfrac{3}{2}, \ldots$ **c.** $\dfrac{1}{2}, \dfrac{1}{4}, \dfrac{1}{8}, \ldots$

SOLUTION

a. $\dfrac{1}{2}, 0, -\dfrac{1}{2}, \ldots$: Adding $-\dfrac{1}{2}$ to each term produces the next term. The fourth term will be $-\dfrac{1}{2} + \left(-\dfrac{1}{2}\right) = -1$. This is an arithmetic sequence.

b. $\dfrac{1}{2}, 1, \dfrac{3}{2}, \ldots$: Each term comes from the term before it by adding $\dfrac{1}{2}$. The fourth term will be $\dfrac{3}{2} + \dfrac{1}{2} = 2$. This sequence is also an arithmetic sequence.

c. $\dfrac{1}{2}, \dfrac{1}{4}, \dfrac{1}{8}, \ldots$: This is a geometric sequence in which each term comes from the term before it by multiplying by $\dfrac{1}{2}$ each time. The next term will be $\dfrac{1}{8} \cdot \dfrac{1}{2} = \dfrac{1}{16}$.

■

Getting Ready for Class

After reading through the preceding section, respond in your own words and in complete sentences.

A. How do we add two fractions that have the same denominators?

B. What is a least common denominator?

C. What is the first step in adding two fractions that have different denominators?

D. What is the last thing you do when adding two fractions?

Find the following sums and differences, and reduce to lowest terms. Assume all variables represent nonzero numbers.

1. $\dfrac{3}{6} + \dfrac{1}{6}$ **2.** $\dfrac{2}{5} + \dfrac{3}{5}$ **3.** $\dfrac{3}{8} - \dfrac{5}{8}$ **4.** $\dfrac{1}{7} - \dfrac{6}{7}$

5. $-\dfrac{1}{4} + \dfrac{3}{4}$ **6.** $-\dfrac{4}{9} + \dfrac{7}{9}$ **7.** $\dfrac{x}{3} - \dfrac{1}{3}$ **8.** $\dfrac{x}{8} - \dfrac{1}{8}$

9. $\dfrac{1}{4} + \dfrac{2}{4} + \dfrac{3}{4}$ **10.** $\dfrac{2}{5} + \dfrac{3}{5} + \dfrac{4}{5}$ **11.** $\dfrac{x+7}{2} - \dfrac{1}{2}$ **12.** $\dfrac{x+5}{4} - \dfrac{3}{4}$

13. $\dfrac{1}{10} - \dfrac{3}{10} - \dfrac{4}{10}$ **14.** $\dfrac{3}{20} - \dfrac{1}{20} - \dfrac{4}{20}$ **15.** $\dfrac{1}{a} + \dfrac{4}{a} + \dfrac{5}{a}$ **16.** $\dfrac{5}{a} + \dfrac{4}{a} + \dfrac{3}{a}$

17.

First Number a	Second Number b	The Sum of a and b $a + b$
$\dfrac{1}{2}$	$\dfrac{1}{3}$	
$\dfrac{1}{3}$	$\dfrac{1}{4}$	
$\dfrac{1}{4}$	$\dfrac{1}{5}$	
$\dfrac{1}{5}$	$\dfrac{1}{6}$	

18.

First Number a	Second Number b	The Sum of a and b $a + b$
1	$\dfrac{1}{2}$	
1	$\dfrac{1}{3}$	
1	$\dfrac{1}{4}$	
1	$\dfrac{1}{5}$	

19.

First Number a	Second Number b	The Sum of a and b $a + b$
$\dfrac{1}{12}$	$\dfrac{1}{2}$	
$\dfrac{1}{12}$	$\dfrac{1}{3}$	
$\dfrac{1}{12}$	$\dfrac{1}{4}$	
$\dfrac{1}{12}$	$\dfrac{1}{6}$	

20.

First Number a	Second Number b	The Sum of a and b $a + b$
$\dfrac{1}{8}$	$\dfrac{1}{2}$	
$\dfrac{1}{8}$	$\dfrac{1}{4}$	
$\dfrac{1}{8}$	$\dfrac{1}{16}$	
$\dfrac{1}{8}$	$\dfrac{1}{24}$	

Find the LCD for each of the following; then use the methods developed in this section to add and subtract as indicated.

21. $\dfrac{4}{9} + \dfrac{1}{3}$ **22.** $\dfrac{1}{2} + \dfrac{1}{4}$ **23.** $2 + \dfrac{1}{3}$ **24.** $3 + \dfrac{1}{2}$

25. $-\dfrac{3}{4} + 1$ **26.** $-\dfrac{3}{4} + 2$ **27.** $\dfrac{1}{2} + \dfrac{2}{3}$ **28.** $\dfrac{2}{3} + \dfrac{1}{4}$

29. $\dfrac{5}{12} - \left(-\dfrac{3}{8}\right)$ **30.** $\dfrac{9}{16} - \left(-\dfrac{7}{12}\right)$ **31.** $-\dfrac{1}{20} + \dfrac{8}{30}$ **32.** $-\dfrac{1}{30} + \dfrac{9}{40}$

33. $\dfrac{17}{30} + \dfrac{11}{42}$ **34.** $\dfrac{19}{42} + \dfrac{13}{70}$ **35.** $\dfrac{25}{84} + \dfrac{41}{90}$ **36.** $\dfrac{23}{70} + \dfrac{29}{84}$

37. $\dfrac{13}{126} - \dfrac{13}{180}$ **38.** $\dfrac{17}{84} - \dfrac{17}{90}$ **39.** $\dfrac{3}{4} + \dfrac{1}{8} + \dfrac{5}{6}$ **40.** $\dfrac{3}{8} + \dfrac{2}{5} + \dfrac{1}{4}$

41. $\dfrac{1}{2} + \dfrac{1}{3} + \dfrac{1}{4} + \dfrac{1}{6}$

42. $\dfrac{1}{8} + \dfrac{1}{4} + \dfrac{1}{5} + \dfrac{1}{10}$

43. $1 - \dfrac{5}{2}$

44. $1 - \dfrac{5}{3}$

45. $1 + \dfrac{1}{2}$

46. $1 + \dfrac{2}{3}$

47. Find the sum of $\dfrac{3}{7}$, 2, and $\dfrac{1}{9}$.

48. Find the sum of 6, $\dfrac{6}{11}$, and 11.

49. Give the difference of $\dfrac{7}{8}$ and $\dfrac{1}{4}$.

50. Give the difference of $\dfrac{9}{10}$ and $\dfrac{1}{100}$.

Find the fourth term in each sequence.

51. $\dfrac{1}{3}, 0, -\dfrac{1}{3}, \ldots$

52. $\dfrac{2}{3}, 0, -\dfrac{2}{3}, \ldots$

53. $\dfrac{1}{3}, 1, \dfrac{5}{3}, \ldots$

54. $1, \dfrac{3}{2}, 2, \ldots$

55. $1, \dfrac{1}{5}, \dfrac{1}{25}, \ldots$

56. $1, -\dfrac{1}{2}, \dfrac{1}{4}, \ldots$

Find the perimeter of each figure.

57.

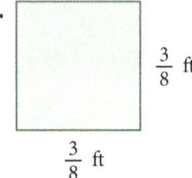

$\dfrac{3}{8}$ ft

$\dfrac{3}{8}$ ft

58.

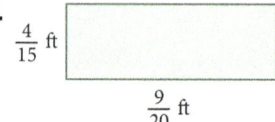

$\dfrac{4}{15}$ ft

$\dfrac{9}{20}$ ft

59.

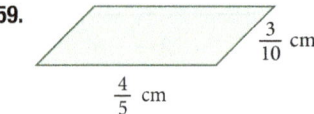

$\dfrac{3}{10}$ cm

$\dfrac{4}{5}$ cm

60.

$\dfrac{2}{3}$ m $\dfrac{2}{3}$ m

$\dfrac{7}{8}$ m

Applying the Concepts

Some of the application problems below involve multiplication and division, while the others involve addition and subtraction.

61. Capacity One carton of milk contains $\dfrac{1}{2}$ pint while another contains 4 pints. How much milk is contained in both cartons?

62. Baking A recipe calls for $\dfrac{2}{3}$ cup of flour and $\dfrac{3}{4}$ cup of sugar. What is the total amount of flour and sugar called for in the recipe?

63. Budget A family decides that they can spend $\dfrac{5}{8}$ of their monthly income on house payments. If their monthly income is \$2,120, how much can they spend for house payments?

64. Savings A family saves $\dfrac{3}{16}$ of their income each month. If their monthly income is \$1,264, how much do they save each month?

Reading a Pie Chart The pie chart below shows how the students at one of the universities in California are distributed among the different schools at the university. Use the information in the pie chart to answer questions 65 and 66.

Cal Poly Enrollment

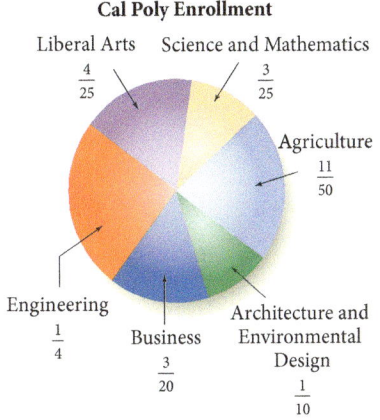

65. If the students in the Schools of Engineering and Business are combined, what fraction results?

66. What fraction of the university's students are enrolled in the Schools of Agriculture, Engineering, and Business combined?

67. **Final Exam Grades** The table below gives the fraction of students in a class of 40 that received grades of A, B, or C on the final exam. Fill in all the missing parts of the table.

Grade	Number of Students	Fraction of Students
A		$\frac{1}{8}$
B		$\frac{1}{5}$
C		$\frac{1}{2}$
below C		
Total	40	1

68. **Flu** During a flu epidemic a company with 200 employees has $\frac{1}{10}$ of their employees call in sick on Monday and another $\frac{3}{10}$ call in sick on Tuesday. What is the total number of employees calling in sick during this 2-day period?

69. **Subdivision** A 6-acre piece of land is subdivided into $\frac{3}{5}$-acre lots. How many lots are there?

70. **Cutting Wood** A 12-foot piece of wood is cut into shelves. If each is $\frac{3}{4}$ foot in length, how many shelves are there?

SPOTLIGHT ON SUCCESS   *Napa Valley College*

You may think that all your mathematics instructors started their college math sequence with precalculus or calculus, but that is not always the case. Diane Van Deusen, a full time mathematics instructor at Napa Valley College in Napa, California, started her career in mathematics in the same class you are taking. Here is part of her story from her website:

Dear Student,

Welcome to elementary algebra! Since we will be spending a significant amount of time together this semester, I thought I should introduce myself to you, and tell you how I ended up with a career in education.

I was not encouraged to attend college after high school, and in fact, had no interest in "more school". Consequently, I didn't end up taking a college class until I was 31 years old! Before returning to and while attending college, I worked locally in the restaurant business as a waitress and bartender and in catering. In fact, I sometimes wait tables a few nights a week during my summer breaks. When I first came back to school, at Napa Valley College (NVC), I thought I might like to enter the nursing program but soon found out nursing was not for me. As I started working on general education requirements, I took elementary algebra and was surprised to learn that I really loved mathematics, even though I had failed 8th grade algebra! As I continued to appreciate and value my own education, I decided to become a teacher so that I could support other people seeking education goals. After earning my AA degree from NVC, I transferred to Sonoma State where I earned my bachelors degree in mathematics with a concentration in statistics. Finally, I attended Cal State Hayward to earn my master's degree in applied statistics. It took me ten years in all to do this.

I feel that having been a returning student while a single, working parent, also an EOPS and Financial Aid recipient, I fully understand the complexity of the life of a community college student. If at any time you have questions about the college, the class or just need someone to talk to, my door is open.

I sincerely hope that my classroom will provide a positive and satisfying learning experience for you.

Diane Van Deusen

Elementary algebra is a great place to start you journey into college mathematics. You can start here and go as far as you want in mathematics. Who knows, you may end up teaching mathematics one day, just like Diane Van Deusen.

Percents, Decimals, and Fractions

If you manage your own money, you probably know the importance of a household budget. The following pie chart shows possible percentages for the various categories to which your money may go. The whole pie chart is represented by 100%. In general, 100% of something is the whole thing.

A Household Budget

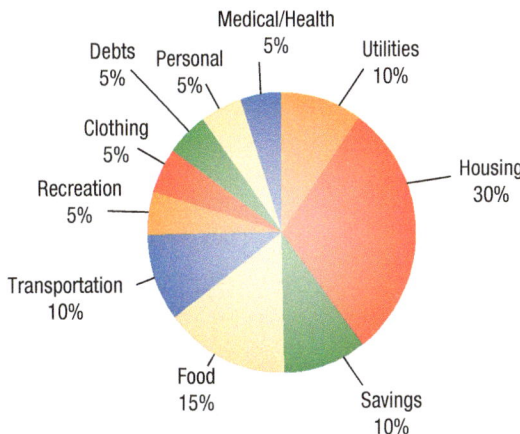

In this section, we will look at the meaning of percent. To begin, we learn to change decimals to percents and percents to decimals.

A The Meaning of Percent

Percent means "per hundred." Writing a number as a percent is a way of comparing the number with the number 100. For example, the number 42% (the % symbol is read "percent") is 42 per 100, or

$$42\% = \frac{42}{100}$$

Percents are really fractions (or ratios) with denominator 100.

Video Examples

Section 0.10

Example 1   Write each percent as a fraction with a denominator of 100.

a. 33%   **b.** 6%   **c.** 160%

SOLUTION

a. $33\% = \dfrac{33}{100}$

b. $6\% = \dfrac{6}{100}$

c. $160\% = \dfrac{160}{100}$

If you are wondering if we could reduce some of these fractions further, the answer is yes. We have not done so because the point of this example is that every percent can be written as a fraction with denominator 100.

B Converting Between Percents and Decimals

To change a percent to a decimal number, we use the meaning of percent.

Example 2 Change 35.2% to a decimal.

SOLUTION We drop the % symbol and write 35.2 over 100.

$$35.2\% = \frac{35.2}{100}$$ *Use the meaning of percent to convert to a fraction with denominator 100.*

$$= 0.352$$ *Divide 35.2 by 100.*

We see from Example 2 that 35.2% is the same as the decimal 0.352. The result is that the % symbol has been dropped and the decimal point has been moved two places to the *left*. Because % always means "per hundred," we will always end up moving the decimal point two places to the left when we change percents to decimals. Because of this, we can write the following rule:

Percent to Decimal

To change a percent to a decimal, drop the % symbol and move the decimal point two places to the *left*.

Example 3 Write each percent as a decimal.

a. 37%   **b.** 68%   **c.** 120%   **d.** 0.8%

SOLUTION We drop the % symbol and move the decimal point to the left two places

a. 37% = 0.37

b. 68% = 0.68

Decimal point originally here

c. 120% = 1.20

Decimal point moved to here

d. 0.8% = 0.008

Example 4 Suppose a cortisone cream is 0.5% hydrocortisone. Writing this number as a decimal, we have

$$0.5\% = 0.005$$

Now we want to do the opposite of what we just did in Examples 2–4. We want to change decimals to percents. We know that 42% written as a decimal is 0.42, which means that in order to change 0.42 back to a percent, we must move the decimal point two places to the *right* and use the % symbol.

$$0.42 = 42\%$$ *Notice that we don't show the new decimal point if it is at the end of the number.*

⌈Δ≠Σ⌉ *Decimal to Percent*

To change a decimal to a percent, we move the decimal point two places to the *right* and use the % symbol.

Example 5   Write each decimal as a percent.

a. 0.27   **b.** 4.89   **c.** 0.5   **d.** 0.09   **e.** 3

SOLUTION

a. $0.27 = 27\%$

b. $4.89 = 489\%$

c. $0.5 = 0.50 = 50\%$ *Notice here that we put a 0 after the 5 so we can move the decimal point two places to the right.*

d. $0.09 = 09\% = 9\%$ *Notice that we can drop the 0 at the left without changing the value of the number.*

e. $3 = 3.00 = 300\%$ *Notice here that we have added the decimal point and two zeros so that we can move the decimal point two places to the right.*

Example 6   A softball player has a batting average of 0.650. Convert this decimal to a percent.

SOLUTION   Moving the decimal two places to the right, we have 65.0%.

As you can see from these examples, percent is just a way of comparing numbers to 100. To multiply decimals by 100, we move the decimal point two places to the right. To divide by 100, we move the decimal point two places to the left.

C Converting between Percents and Fractions

We will now convert a percent to a fraction.

⌈Δ≠Σ⌉ *Percent to Fraction*

To change a percent to a fraction, drop the % symbol and write the original number over 100. Then, if possible, write the fraction in lowest terms with integers in the numerator and denominator.

Example 7   The pie chart shows who pays for college expenses. Change each percent to a fraction in lowest terms.

Who Pays College Expenses

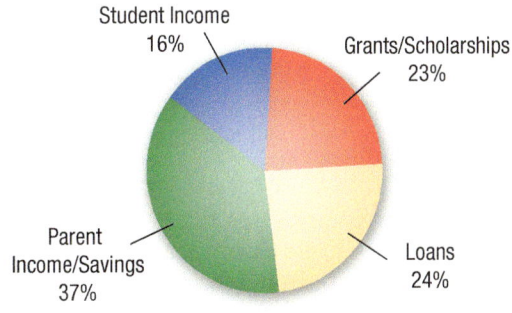

Student Income 16%

Grants/Scholarships 23%

Parent Income/Savings 37%

Loans 24%

SOLUTION   In each case, we drop the percent symbol and write the number over 100. Then we reduce to lowest terms if possible.

$$16\% = \frac{16}{100} = \frac{4}{25} \qquad 23\% = \frac{23}{100} \qquad 24\% = \frac{24}{100} = \frac{6}{25} \qquad 37\% = \frac{37}{100}$$

Example 8   Change 4.5% to a fraction in lowest terms.

SOLUTION   We begin by writing 4.5 over 100.

$$4.5\% = \frac{4.5}{100}$$

We now multiply the numerator and the denominator by 10 so the numerator will be a whole number.

$$\frac{4.5}{100} = \frac{4.5 \times 10}{100 \times 10} \qquad \textit{Multiply the numerator and the denominator by 10.}$$

$$= \frac{45}{1,000}$$

$$= \frac{9}{200} \qquad \textit{Reduce to lowest terms.}$$

Example 9   Change $32\frac{1}{2}\%$ to a fraction in lowest terms.

SOLUTION   Writing $32\frac{1}{2}$ over 100 produces a complex fraction. We change $32\frac{1}{2}$ to an improper fraction and simplify.

$$32\frac{1}{2}\% = \frac{32\frac{1}{2}}{100}$$

$$= \frac{\frac{65}{2}}{100} \qquad \textit{Change } 32\frac{1}{2} \textit{ to the improper fraction } \frac{65}{2}.$$

$$= \frac{65}{2} \div 100 \qquad \textit{Rewrite as division.}$$

$$= \frac{65}{2} \cdot \frac{1}{100} \qquad \textit{Dividing by 100 is the same as multiplying by } \frac{1}{100}.$$

$$= \frac{5 \cdot 13 \cdot 1}{2 \cdot 5 \cdot 20} \qquad \textit{Cancel common factors and multiply.}$$

$$= \frac{13}{40} \qquad \textit{Reduce to lowest terms.}$$

Note that we could have changed our original mixed number to a decimal first and then changed to a fraction:

$$32\frac{1}{2}\% = 32.5\% = \frac{32.5}{100} = \frac{32.5 \times 10}{100 \times 10} = \frac{325}{1000} = \frac{5 \cdot 5 \cdot 13}{5 \cdot 5 \cdot 40}$$

$$= \frac{13}{40}$$

The result is the same in both cases.

To change a fraction to a percent, we can change the fraction to a decimal and then change the decimal to a percent.

Example 10 Suppose the price your bookstore pays for your textbook is $\frac{7}{10}$ of the price you pay for your textbook. Write $\frac{7}{10}$ as a percent.

SOLUTION We can change $\frac{7}{10}$ to a decimal by dividing 7 by 10.

$$
\begin{array}{r}
0.7 \\
10\overline{)7.0} \\
-7\,0 \\
\hline
0
\end{array}
$$

We then change the decimal 0.7 to a percent by moving the decimal point two places to the *right* and using the % symbol.

$$0.7 = 70\%$$

You may have noticed that we could have saved some time by simply writing $\frac{7}{10}$ as an equivalent fraction with denominator 100; that is,

$$\frac{7}{10} = \frac{7 \cdot 10}{10 \cdot 10} = \frac{70}{100} = 70\%$$

This is a good way to convert fractions like $\frac{7}{10}$ to percents. It works well for fractions with denominators of 2, 4, 5, 10, 20, 25, and 50, because these numbers are compatible with 100.

Example 11 Change $\frac{3}{8}$ to a percent.

SOLUTION We begin by dividing 3 by 8.

$$
\begin{array}{r}
.375 \\
8\overline{)3.000} \\
-2\,4 \\
\hline
60 \\
-56 \\
\hline
40 \\
-40 \\
\hline
0
\end{array}
$$

We then change the decimal to a percent by moving the decimal point two places to the right and using the % symbol.

$$\frac{3}{8} = 0.375 = 37.5\%$$

Example 12 Change $\frac{5}{12}$ to a percent.

SOLUTION We begin by dividing 5 by 12.

$$
\begin{array}{r}
.4166 \\
12\overline{)5.0000} \\
-48 \\
\hline
20 \\
-12 \\
\hline
80 \\
-72 \\
\hline
80 \\
-72 \\
\hline
8
\end{array}
$$

Note When rounding off, let's agree to round off to the nearest thousandth and then move the decimal point. Our answers in percent form will then be accurate to the nearest tenth of a percent, as in Example 12.

Because the 6s repeat indefinitely, we can use mixed number notation to write

$$\frac{5}{12} = 0.41\overline{6}$$

We will now round to the thousandths place and convert to a percent.

$$\frac{5}{12} = 0.417 = 41.7\%$$

Example 13 Change $2\frac{1}{2}$ to a percent.

SOLUTION We first change to a decimal and then to a percent.

$$2\frac{1}{2} = 2.5 = 250\%$$

⌈Δ≠Σ⌉ _Fraction to Percent_

To change a fraction to a percent, either write the fraction as a decimal and then change the decimal to a percent, or write the fraction as an equivalent fraction with denominator 100, drop the 100, and use the % symbol.

Table 1 lists some of the most commonly used fractions and decimals and their equivalent percents.

Table 1

Fraction	Decimal	Percent	Fraction	Decimal	Percent
$\frac{1}{2}$	0.5	50%	$\frac{1}{5}$	0.2	20%
$\frac{1}{4}$	0.25	25%	$\frac{2}{5}$	0.4	40%
$\frac{3}{4}$	0.75	75%	$\frac{3}{5}$	0.6	60%
$\frac{1}{3}$	$0.\overline{3}$	$33\frac{1}{3}\%$	$\frac{4}{5}$	0.8	80%
$\frac{2}{3}$	$0.\overline{6}$	$66\frac{2}{3}\%$	$\frac{1}{1}$	1.0	100%

Getting Ready for Class

After reading through the preceding section, respond in your own words and in complete sentences.

A. What is the relationship between the word **_percent_** and the number 100?
B. Explain in words how you would change 25% to a decimal.
C. Explain in words how you would change 25% to a fraction.
D. After reading this section you know that $\frac{1}{2}$, 0.5, and 50% are equivalent. Show mathematically why this is true.

Keep steadily before you the fact that all true success depends at last upon yourself. ~ **Theodore T. Hunger**

Math has always come fairly easily for me and is the academic subject I have enjoyed most. I knew I wanted to attend Cal Poly San Luis Obispo for its high job placement and prestige, but I had no idea what I wanted to study. I decided to major in Mathematics because it is so universal but not so specialized or concentrated that I would get stuck in a field that I did not enjoy. I felt that if I kept studying math and its related fields, I would set myself up to be successful later in life, as math is the foundation for engineering, physics, and other science-related fields. I have not looked back on my decision. I know it will be a degree that I am proud to have achieved.

   I appreciate the consistency that math offers in its problems and in its solutions. I like that math can be simplified into smaller easier-to-understand parts, and its answers are almost always definite. It provides challenges that I enjoy solving, like completing a puzzle piece by piece. In the end, I am able to enjoy the success I have put together for myself.

Problem Set 0.10

Vocabulary Review

Choose the correct words to fill in the blanks below.

ratio   % symbol   percent
left   decimal   right

1. The word _____ means "per hundred."

2. A percent is a _____ with a denominator of 100.

3. To change a percent to a decimal, drop the % symbol and move the decimal point two places to the _____ .

4. To change a decimal to a percent, move the decimal point two places to the _____ and use the % symbol.

5. To change a percent to a fraction, drop the _____ and write the original number over 100.

6. To change a fraction to a percent, we can change the fraction to a _____ and then change the decimal to a percent.

Problems

A Write each percent as a fraction with denominator 100.

1. 20%   **2.** 40%   **3.** 60%   **4.** 80%

5. 24%   **6.** 48%   **7.** 65%   **8.** 35%

Change each percent to a decimal.

9. 23%   **10.** 34%   **11.** 192%   **12.** 387%

13. 9%   **14.** 7%   **15.** 3.4%   **16.** 5.8%

17. 0.087%   **18.** 0.09%   **19.** 0.9%   **20.** 0.6%

B Change each decimal to a percent.

21. 0.23   **22.** 0.34   **23.** 0.923   **24.** 0.874

25. 0.45   **26.** 0.54   **27.** 0.03   **28.** 0.04

29. 0.6

30. 0.9

31. 0.008

32. 0.005

33. 27

34. 6

35. 1.23

36. 2.34

C Change each percent to a fraction in lowest terms.

37. 60%

38. 40%

39. 75%

40. 25%

41. 4%

42. 2%

43. 265%

44. 342%

45. 71.87%

46. 63.6%

47. 0.75%

48. 0.45%

49. $6\frac{1}{4}\%$

50. $5\frac{1}{4}\%$

51. $33\frac{1}{3}\%$

52. $66\frac{2}{3}\%$

D Change each fraction or mixed number to a percent.

53. $\frac{1}{2}$

54. $\frac{1}{4}$

55. $\frac{3}{4}$

56. $\frac{2}{3}$

57. $\frac{1}{3}$

58. $\frac{1}{5}$

59. $\frac{4}{5}$

60. $\frac{1}{6}$

61. $\frac{7}{8}$

62. $\frac{1}{8}$

63. $\frac{7}{50}$

64. $\frac{9}{25}$

65. $3\frac{1}{4}$

66. $2\frac{1}{8}$

67. $\frac{3}{2}$

68. $\frac{7}{4}$

69. Change $\frac{21}{43}$ to a percent. Round to the nearest tenth of a percent

70. Change $\frac{36}{49}$ to a percent. Round to the nearest tenth of a percent

Applying the Concepts

71. Physiology The human body is between 50% and 75% water. Write each of these percents as a decimal.

72. Alcohol Consumption In the United States, 2.7% of those over 15 years of age drink more than 6.3 ounces of alcohol per day. In France, the same figure is 9%. Write each of these percents as a decimal.

73. iPhone The snapshot below shows what users had before their new iPhone. Use the information to answer the following questions.

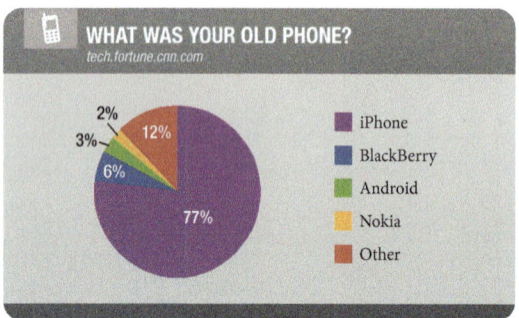

74. Foreign Language The chart shows the extent to which Americans say they know a foreign language. Change each percent to a fraction in lowest terms.

a. Convert each percent to a fraction.

b. Convert each percent to a decimal.

c. About how many times more likely are the respondents to have owned a Blackberry than an Android phone?

75. Nutrition Although, nutritionally, breakfast is the most important meal of the day, only about $\frac{1}{5}$ of the people in the United States consistently eat breakfast. What percent of the population is this?

76. Children in School In Belgium, 96% of all children between 3 and 6 years of age go to school. In Sweden, the number is only 25%. In the United States, it is 60%. Write each of these percents as a fraction in lowest terms.

77. Student Enrollment The pie chart shows enrollment by college for a university. Change each fraction to a percent. Round to the nearest hundredth.

Student Enrollment

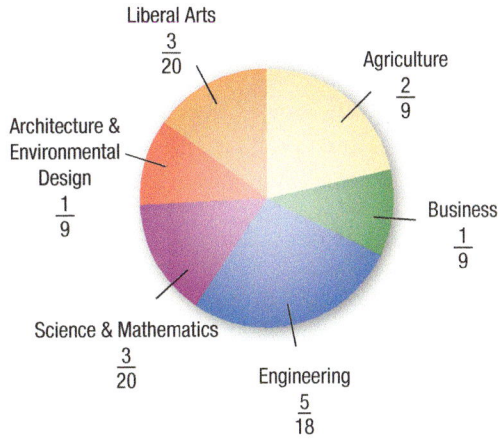

78. Video Games The chart shows the percentage of total Nintendo revenue by region in 2017. Use the information to convert from the percentage to a decimal for the following regions.

a. Europe   b. The Americas   c. Japan

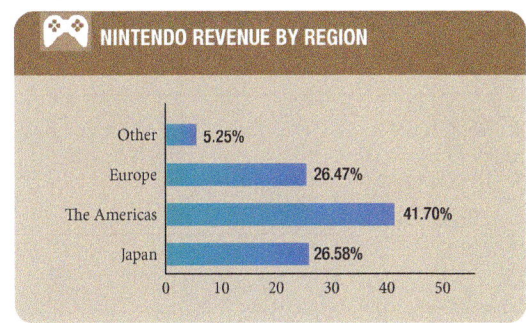

Calculator Problems

Use a calculator to write each fraction as a decimal, and then change the decimal to a percent. Round all answers to the nearest tenth of a percent.

79. $\dfrac{29}{37}$ **80.** $\dfrac{18}{83}$ **81.** $\dfrac{6}{51}$ **82.** $\dfrac{8}{95}$ **83.** $\dfrac{236}{327}$ **84.** $\dfrac{568}{732}$

85. Women in the Military During World War II, $\frac{1}{12}$ of the Soviet armed forces were women. At one time only $\frac{1}{450}$ of the Russian armed forces are women. Change both fractions to percents (to the nearest tenth of a percent).

86. Number of Teachers The ratio of the number of teachers to the number of students in secondary schools in Japan is 1 to 17. In the United States, the ratio is 1 to 19. Write each of these ratios as a fraction and then as a percent. Round to the nearest tenth of a percent.

Getting Ready for the Next Section

Multiply.

87. 0.25(74)   **88.** 0.15(63)   **89.** 0.435(25)   **90.** 0.635(45)

Divide. Round the answers to the nearest thousandth, if necessary.

91. $\dfrac{21}{42}$ **92.** $\dfrac{21}{84}$ **93.** $\dfrac{25}{0.4}$ **94.** $\dfrac{31.9}{78}$

Solve for n. Write the solution using a decimal.

95. $42n = 21$ **96.** $945 = 100n$ **97.** $25 = 0.40n$ **98.** $78n = 31.9$

Find the Mistake

Each sentence below contains a mistake. Circle the mistake and write the correct word(s) or numbers(s) on the line provided.

1. Writing 0.4% as a decimal gives us 0.4.   _____

2. To write 3.21 as a percent, divide the number by 100; that is, move the decimal two places to the left.
   _____

3. Writing 25% as a fraction in lowest terms gives us $\frac{25}{100}$.   _____

4. To change $\frac{5}{8}$ to a percent, we change $\frac{5}{8}$ to 0.625 and then move the decimal two places to the left to get 0.00625%.   _____

Percent Problems

Scientists have discovered a toxin in the spit of a sea snail that works as a pain-killer with greater effectiveness but in smaller dosages and without the addictive risk of the painkiller morphine. The marine cone snail dwells on the ocean floor. The snail shoots its harpoon-like teeth coated in toxic saliva into its prey to poison it. Researchers have discovered how to isolate the saliva's toxin and put it into a pill for humans in pain to ingest. A patient will feel the same pain-reducing effects with 1% of a dose of a popular neuropathic painkiller prescribed in hospitals. If the prescription for an adult of the popular painkiller is 300 milligrams, how many milligrams of the sea snail drug would be dosed as an alternative? In this section, we will work some other percent problems, similar to this one.

A Solving Percent Problems Using Equations

This section is concerned with three kinds of word problems that are associated with percents. Here is an example of each type:

Type A: What number is 15% of 63?

Type B: What percent of 42 is 21?

Type C: 25 is 40% of what number?

The first method we use to solve all three types of problems involves translating the sentences into equations and then solving the equations. The following translations are used to write the sentences as equations:

English	Mathematics
is	=
of	· (multiply)
a number	n
what number	n
what percent	n

The word *is* always translates to an = sign, the word *of* almost always means multiply, and *the number we are looking for* can be represented with a variable, such as n or x.

Video Examples

Section 0.11

Example 1   What number is 15% of 63?

SOLUTION   Using the translations above and converting 15% to a decimal, we have

What number is 15% of 63?

$$n = 0.15 \cdot 63$$

To perform arithmetic with percents, we have to change to decimals. Solving the equation, we have

$$n = 0.15 \cdot 63$$

$$n = 9.45 \qquad \text{Multiply.}$$

Therefore, 15% of 63 is 9.45.

■ **Example 2**   What percent of 42 is 21?

SOLUTION   We translate the sentence as follows:

What percent of 42 is 21?

$$n \cdot 42 = 21$$

We solve for n by dividing both sides by 42.

$$\frac{n \cdot 42}{42} = \frac{21}{42} \qquad \textcolor{green}{\text{Divide 21 by 42.}}$$

$$n = \frac{21}{42}$$

$$n = 0.50$$

Because the original problem asked for a percent, we change 0.50 to a percent.

$$n = 50\%$$

Therefore, 21 is 50% of 42.   ■

■ **Example 3**   25 is 40% of what number?

SOLUTION   Following the procedure from the first two examples, we have

25 is 40% of what number?

$$25 = 0.40 \cdot n$$

We will now solve the remaining equation.

$$\frac{25}{0.40} = \frac{0.40 \cdot n}{0.40} \qquad \textcolor{green}{\text{Divide both sides by 0.40.}}$$

$$\frac{25}{0.40} = n$$

$$62.5 = n \qquad \textcolor{green}{\text{Simplify: } 25 \div 0.40 = 62.5}$$

Therefore, 25 is 40% of 62.5.   ■

As you can see, all three types of percent problems are solved in a similar manner. We write *is* as =, *of* as ·, and *what number* as n. The resulting equation is then solved to obtain the answer to the original question. Here are some more examples:

■ **Example 4**   What number is 43.5% of 25?

SOLUTION   We translate to an equation and solve for n.

$$n = 0.435 \cdot 25$$

$$n = 10.9 \qquad \textcolor{green}{\text{Multiply and round to the nearest tenth.}}$$

Therefore, 10.9 is 43.5% of 25.   ■

Example 5   What percent of 78 is 31.9?

SOLUTION   We will convert to an equation and solve for n.

$$n \cdot 78 = 31.9$$

$$\frac{n \cdot 78}{78} = \frac{31.9}{78} \qquad \text{Divide both sides by 78.}$$

$$n = \frac{31.9}{78}$$

$$n = 0.409 \qquad \text{Divide and round to the nearest thousandth.}$$

$$n = 40.9\% \qquad \text{Convert to a percent.}$$

Therefore, 40.9% of 78 is 31.9.

Example 6   34 is 29% of what number?

SOLUTION $34 = 0.29 \cdot n$

$$\frac{34}{0.29} = \frac{0.29 \cdot n}{0.29} \qquad \text{Divide both sides by 0.29.}$$

$$\frac{34}{0.29} = n$$

$$117.2 = n \qquad \text{Divide and round to the nearest tenth.}$$

Therefore, 34 is 29% of 117.2.

Now we will look at one application of percent problems before exploring an alternative method for solving these types of problems. As you will see, these methods use different approaches but result in the same solution.

Example 7   The American Dietetic [Association recommends a diet] in which the number of calories from fat is less than 30% of the total number of calories. According to the nutrition label, what percent of the total number of calories are fat calories?

SOLUTION   To solve this problem, we must write the question in the form of one of the three basic percent problems shown in Examples 1–6. Because there are 93 calories from fat and a total of 155 calories, we can write the question this way: 93 is what percent of 155?

Now that we have written the question in the form of one of the basic percent problems, we simply translate it into an equation. Then we solve the equation.

Nutrition Facts		
Serving Size 1 oz		
Servings Per Container About 4		
Amount Per Serving		
Calories 155		Calories from fat 93
		% Daily Value*
Total Fat 11g		16%
Saturated Fat 3g		15%
Trans Fat 0g		0%
Cholesterol 0mg		0%
Sodium 148mg		6%
Total Carbohydrate 14g		5%
Dietary Fiber 1g		5%
Sugars 1g		
Protein 2g		
Vitamin A 0%	●	Vitamin C 9%
Calcium 1%	●	Iron 3%
*Percent Daily Values are based on a 2,000 calorie diet		

FIGURE 1

93 is what percent of 155?

$$93 = n \cdot 155$$

$$\frac{93}{155} = n$$

$$n = 0.60 = 60\%$$

The number of calories from fat in this food is 60% of the total number of calories. Thus the ADA would not consider this to be a healthy food.

B   Solving Percent Problems Using Proportions

We can look at percent problems in terms of proportions also. For example, we know that 24% is the same as $\frac{24}{100}$, which reduces to $\frac{6}{25}$. That is,

$$\frac{24}{100} = \frac{6}{25}$$

24 is to 100   as   6 is to 25

We can illustrate this visually with boxes of proportional lengths.

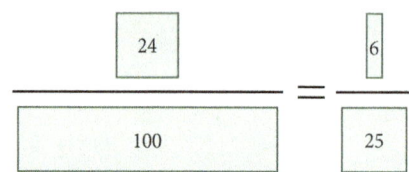

In general, we say

$$\frac{\text{Percent}}{100} = \frac{\text{Amount}}{\text{Base}}$$

Percent is to 100   as   amount is to base.

Example 8   What number is 15% of 63?

SOLUTION   This is the same problem we worked in Example 1. We let n be the number in question. We reason that n will be smaller than 63 because it is only 15% of 63. The base is 63 and the amount is n. We compare n to 63 as we compare 15 to 100. Our proportion sets up as follows:

15 is to 100   as n is to 63

$$\frac{15}{100} = \frac{n}{63}$$

Solving the proportion, we have

$$15 \cdot 63 = 100n \qquad \text{Fundamental property of proportions}$$

$$945 = 100n \qquad \text{Simplify the left side.}$$

$$9.45 = n \qquad \text{Divide each side by 100.}$$

This gives us the same result we obtained in Example 1.

Example 9   What percent of 42 is 21?

SOLUTION   This is the same problem we worked in Example 2. We let n be the percent in question. The amount is 21 and the base is 42. Here is our reasoning and proportion:

n is to 100   as   21 is to 42

$$\frac{n}{100} = \frac{21}{42}$$

Solving the proportion, we have

$42n = 21 \cdot 100$	Fundamental property of proportions
$42n = 2{,}100$	Simplify the right side.
$n = 50$	Divide each side by 42.

Since n is a percent, our answer is 50%, giving us the same result we obtained in Example 2.

Example 10   25 is 40% of what number?

SOLUTION   This is the same problem we worked in Example 3. We let n be the number in question. The base is n and the amount is 25. We compare 25 to n as we compare 40 to 100. Our proportion sets up as follows:

40 is to 100   as   25 is to n

$$\frac{40}{100} = \frac{25}{n}$$

Solving the proportion, we have

$40 \cdot n = 25 \cdot 100$	Fundamental property of proportions
$40n = 2{,}500$	Simplify the right side.
$n = 62.5$	Divide each side by 40.

So 25 is 40% of 62.5, which is the same result we obtained in Example 3.

Note   When you work the problems in the problem set, use whichever method you like, unless your instructor indicates that you are to use one method instead of the other.

Getting Ready for Class

After reading through the preceding section, respond in your own words and in complete sentences.

A. When we translate a sentence such as "What number is 15% of 63?" into symbols, what does each of the following translate to?

  a. is   **b.** of   **c.** what number

B. Using Example 1 in your text as a guide, answer the question below.

The number 9.45 is what percent of 63?

C. Show that the answer to the question below is the same as the answer to the question in Example 2 of your text.

The number 21 is what percent of 42?

D. If 21 is 50% of 42, then 21 is what percent of 84?

Problem Set 0.11

Vocabulary Review

Choose the correct words to fill in the blanks below.

multiply   fraction   decimal   variable   equals sign

1. In a mathematical sentence, the word *is* translates to an _____.

2. In a mathematical sentence, the word *of* almost always means _____.

3. When translating a sentence to an equation, the number we are looking for can be represented with a _____.

4. When performing arithmetic with a percent, change the percent to a _____.

5. Change a percent to a _____ to help solve a percent problem using a proportion.

Problems

A, B Solve each of the following problems.

1. What number is 25% of 32?

2. What number is 15% of 75?

3. What number is 20% of 120?

4. What number is 10% of 80?

5. What number is 54% of 38?

6. What number is 72% of 200?

7. What number is 11% of 67?

8. What number is 2% of 49?

9. What percent of 24 is 12?

10. What percent of 80 is 20?

11. What percent of 50 is 5?

12. What percent of 20 is 4?

13. What percent of 36 is 9?

14. What percent of 70 is 14?

15. What percent of 8 is 6?

16. What percent of 15 is 9?

17. 32 is 50% of what number?

18. 16 is 20% of what number?

19. 10 is 20% of what number?

20. 11 is 25% of what number?

21. 37 is 4% of what number?

22. 46 is 8% of what number?

23. 8 is 2% of what number?

24. 6 is 3% of what number?

The following problems can be solved by the same method you used in Problems 1–24.

25. What is 20% of 87?

26. What is 10% of 102?

27. 25% of what number is 30?

28. 10% of what number is 22?

29. 28% of 49 is what number?

30. 97% of 28 is what number?

31. 27 is 120% of what number?

32. 24 is 150% of what number?

33. 65 is what percent of 130?

34. 26 is what percent of 104?

35. What is 0.4% of 235,671?

36. What is 0.8% of 721,423?

37. 4.89% of 2,000 is what number?

38. 3.75% of 4,000 is what number?

39. Write a basic percent problem, the solution to which can be found by solving the equation $n = 0.25(350)$.

40. Write a basic percent problem, the solution to which can be found by solving the equation $n = 0.35(250)$.

41. Write a basic percent problem, the solution to which can be found by solving the equation $n \cdot 24 = 16$.

42. Write a basic percent problem, the solution to which can be found by solving the equation $n \cdot 16 = 24$.

43. Write a basic percent problem, the solution to which can be found by solving the equation $46 = 0.75 \cdot n$.

44. Write a basic percent problem, the solution to which can be found by solving the equation $75 = 0.46 \cdot n$.

Applying the Concepts

Nutrition For each nutrition label in Problems 45–48, find what percent of the total number of calories comes from fat calories. Then refer to Example 7 and indicate whether the label is from a food considered healthy by the American Dietetic Association. Round to the nearest tenth of a percent if necessary.

45. Pizza Dough

46. Crackers

Nutrition Facts	
Serving Size 1/6 of package (65g)	
Servings Per Container: 6	
Amount Per Serving	
Calories 160	Calories from fat 18
	% Daily Value*
Total Fat 2g	**3%**
Saturated Fat 0.5g	**3%**
Poly unsaturated Fat 0g	
Monounsaturated Fat 0g	
Cholesterol 0mg	**0%**
Sodium 470mg	**20%**
Total Carbohydrate 31g	**10%**
Dietary Fiber 1g	**4%**
Sugars 4g	
Protein 5g	
Vitamin A 0% • Vitamin C 0%	
Calcium 0% • Iron 10%	
*Percent Daily Values are based on a 2,000 calorie diet	

Nutrition Facts	
Serving Size 30 g. (About 27 crackers)	
Servings Per Container: 9	
Amount Per Serving	
Calories 150	Calories from fat 70
	% Daily Value*
Total Fat 8g	**12%**
Saturated Fat 2g	**10%**

47. Shredded Mozzarella Cheese

Nutrition Facts

Serving Size 1 oz (28.3g)
Servings Per Container: 12

Amount Per Serving

Calories 72	Calories from fat 41

	% Daily Value*
Total Fat 4.5g	7%
Saturated Fat 2.9g	14%
Cholesterol 18mg	6%
Sodium 175mg	7%
Total Carbohydrate 0.8g	0%
Fiber 0g	0%
Sugars 0.3g	
Protein 6.9g	

Vitamin A 3%	●	Vitamin C 0%
Calcium 22%	●	Iron 0%

*Percent Daily Values (DV) are based on a 2,000 calorie diet

48. Canned Corn

Nutrition Facts

Serving Size 1 cup
Servings Per Container About 2 ½

Amount Per Serving

Calories 133	Calories from fat 15

	% Daily Value*
Total Fat 3g	3%
Saturated Fat 1g	1%
Cholesterol 0mg	0%
Sodium 530mg	22%
Total Carbohydrate 30g	10%
Dietary Fiber 3g	13%
Sugars 4g	
Protein 4g	

Vitamin A 0%	●	Vitamin C 23%
Calcium 1%	●	Iron 8%

*Percent Daily Values are based on a 2,000 calorie diet

Getting Ready for the Next Section

Solve each equation.

49. $96 = n \cdot 120$

50. $2,400 = 0.48 \cdot n$

51. $114 = 150n$

52. $3,360 = 0.42n$

53. What number is 80% of 60?

54. What number is 25% of 300?

Improving Your Quantitative Literacy

55. Survival Rates for Sea Gulls Here is part of a report concerning the survival rates of Western Gulls that appeared on the website of Cornell University:

Survival of eggs to hatching is 70%–80%; of hatched chicks to fledgling 50%–70%; of fledglings to age of first breeding <50%.

Based on this information, give an estimate of the number of gulls of breeding age that would be produced by 1,000 Western Gull eggs.

Find the Mistake

Each sentence below contains a mistake. Circle the mistake and write the correct word(s) or numbers(s) on the line provided.

1. The question, "What number is 28.5% of 30?" translates to $n \cdot 0.285 = 30$. _____

2. Asking "75 is 30% of what number?" gives us 0.004. _____

3. To answer the question, "What number is 45% of 90?", we can solve the proportion $\frac{90}{x} = \frac{40}{100}$.

   _____

4. Using a proportion to answer the question, "What percent of 65 is 26?" will give us $n = 250\%$. _____

LANDMARK REVIEW: CHECKING YOUR PROGRESS

Write each percent as a fraction with denominator 100.

1. 15%
2. 27%
3. 14%
4. 89%

Change each percent to a decimal.

5. 17%
6. 28%
7. 5%
8. 6.37%

Change each decimal to a percent.

9. 0.38
10. 0.98
11. 0.09
12. 4.87

Change each fraction or mixed number to a percent. Round to the nearest tenth of a percent if necessary

13. $\frac{1}{10}$
14. $\frac{1}{3}$
15. $\frac{1}{7}$
16. $3\frac{1}{5}$

Solve each of the following problems. Round to the nearest hundredth if necessary.

17. What number is 35% of 15?
18. What percent of 85 is 53?
19. 88 is 37% of what number?

In the 1920s the Woolly Adelgid, a female bug about one millimeter long with a two-month lifespan, was first discovered in the United States. When the Adelgid infests a hemlock tree between Georgia and Maine, the tree overreacts, weakens, and then dies within approximately four years. As these stands of hemlock die, animals lose their habitat, carbon cycles are impacted, and the soil composition is altered. The effects of the Adelgid are apparent when visiting the Great Smoky Mountain National Park, often the most visited national park with over 11 million visitors each year. Visitors to the highest point in the park, Clingman's Dome, see dead hemlocks in the wake of an Adelgid infestation. The national park is taking steps to rid the area of the tiny bug. Natural pesticides are sprayed in accessible areas and injected directly into infected trees. More recently, the park has released a predator beetle. Because this is a non-native species that they are introducing, this approach has been criticized. The predator beetle is expected to reduce the Woolly Adelgid population by 47 to 87%, a considerable amount considering that 1 in 5 trees in the national park are hemlocks.

In this section, we continue our study of percent, allowing us to better understand data like that on the Woolly Adelgid infestation and its impact on the Great Smoky Mountains National Park.

A Applications of Percent

Video Examples

Section 0.12

Example 1   On a 120-question test, a student answered 96 correctly. What percent of the problems did the student work correctly?

SOLUTION   We have 96 correct answers out of a possible 120. The problem can be restated as

96 is what percent of 120?

$$96 = n \cdot 120$$

$$\frac{96}{120} = \frac{n \cdot 120}{120} \qquad \text{Divide both sides by 120.}$$

$$\frac{96}{120} = n$$

$$0.80 = n \qquad \text{Divide 96 by 120.}$$

Converting 0.80 to a percent, we see that the student answered 80% of the problems correctly. As a percent, we are comparing the original score to an equivalent score on a 100-question test. That is, 96 correct out of 120 is the same as 80 correct out of 100.

Example 2   How much hydrochloric acid, HCl, is in a 60-milliliter bottle that is marked 80% HCl?

SOLUTION   If the bottle is marked 80% HCl, that means 80% of the solution is HCl and the rest is water. Because the bottle contains 60 milliliters, we can restate the question as

What is 80% of 60?

$$n = 0.80 \cdot 60 \qquad \textcolor{green}{\textit{Convert to an equation.}}$$

$$n = 48 \qquad \textcolor{green}{\textit{Multiply.}}$$

There are 48 milliliters of HCl in 60 milliliters of 80% HCl solution.

Example 3   If 48% of the students in a certain college are female and there are 2,400 female students, what is the total number of students in the college?

SOLUTION   We restate the problem as

2,400 is 48% of what number?

$$2{,}400 = 0.48 \cdot n \qquad \textcolor{green}{\textit{Convert to an equation.}}$$

$$\frac{2{,}400}{0.48} = \frac{0.48 \cdot n}{0.48} \qquad \textcolor{green}{\textit{Divide both sides by 0.48.}}$$

$$5{,}000 = n \qquad \textcolor{green}{\textit{Divide.}}$$

There are 5,000 students.

Example 4   If 25% of the students in elementary algebra courses receive a grade of A, and there are 300 students enrolled in elementary algebra this year, how many students will receive A's?

SOLUTION   We can see that this problem is asking us to find:

What number is 25% of 300?

$$n = 0.25 \cdot 300 \qquad \textcolor{green}{\textit{Convert to an equation.}}$$

$$n = 75 \qquad \textcolor{green}{\textit{Multiply.}}$$

Thus, 75 students will receive A's in elementary algebra.

Getting Ready for Class

After reading through the preceding section, respond in your own words and in complete sentences.

A. On the test mentioned in Example 1, how many questions would the student have answered correctly if she had earned a grade of 40%?

B. If the bottle in Example 2 contained 30 milliliters instead of 60, what would the answer be?

C. In Example 3, how many of the students were male?

D. How many of the students mentioned in Example 4 received a grade lower than an A?

Problem Set 0.12

Vocabulary Review

On the lines below, write the three types of problems found in applications that involve percents. (Hint: We first learned of the three types in the previous section, and then put them to use in this section.)

1. Type A: _____

2. Type B: _____

3. Type C: _____

Problems

A Solve each of the following problems by first restating it as one of the three basic percent problems from the previous section. In each case, be sure to show the equation.

1. Test Scores On a 120-question test a student answered 84 correctly. What percent of the problems did the student work correctly?

2. Test Scores An engineering student answered 81 questions correctly on a 90-question trigonometry test. What percent of the questions did she answer correctly? What percent were answered incorrectly?

3. Mixture Problem A solution of alcohol and water is 80% alcohol. The solution is found to contain 32 milliliters of alcohol. How many milliliters total (both alcohol and water) are in the solution?

4. Family Budget A family spends $720 every month on food. If the family's income each month is $6,000, what percent of the family's income is spent on food?

5. Chemistry How much HCl (hydrochloric acid) is in a 60-milliliter bottle that is marked 75% HCl?

6. Chemistry How much acetic acid is in a 5-liter container of acetic acid and water that is marked 80% acetic acid? How much is water?

7. Farming A farmer owns 28 acres of land. Of the 28 acres, only 65% can be farmed. How many acres are available for farming? How many are not available for farming?

8. Number of Students Of the 420 students enrolled in a basic math class, only 30% are first-year students. How many are first-year students? How many are not?

9. Number of Students If 48% of the students in a certain college are female and there are 1,440 female students, what is the total number of students in the college?

10. Basketball A basketball player made 63 out of 75 free throws. What percent is this?

11. Number of Graduates Suppose 60% of the graduating class in a certain high school goes on to college. If 240 students from this graduating class are going on to college, how many students are there in the graduating class?

12. Defective Parts In a shipment of airplane parts, 3% are known to be defective. If 15 parts are found to be defective, how many parts are in the shipment?

13. Number of Students Suppose there are 3,200 students at our school. If 52% of them are female, how many female students are there at our school?

14. Number of Students In a certain school, 75% of the students in first-year chemistry have had algebra. If there are 300 students in first-year chemistry, how many of them have had algebra?

15. Population In a city of 32,000 people, there are 10,000 people under 25 years of age. What percent of the population is under 25 years of age?

16. Number of Students If 45 people enrolled in a psychology course but only 35 completed it, what percent of the students completed the course? (Round to the nearest tenth of a percent.)

Calculator Problems

The following problems are similar to Problems 1–16. They should be set up the same way. Then the actual calculations should be done on a calculator.

17. Number of People Of 7,892 people attending an outdoor concert in Los Angeles, 3,972 are over 18 years of age. What percent is this? (Round to the nearest whole number percent.)

18. Manufacturing A car manufacturer estimates that 25% of the new cars sold in one city have defective engine mounts. If 2,136 new cars are sold in that city, how many will have defective engine mounts?

19. Laptops The chart shows the most popular laptops among college students surveyed. If 5,280 students were surveyed, how many preferred a Dell?

20. Video Games The chart shows the results of a survey of popular video games. If 12,257 people were surveyed, how many people listed Until Dawn as their favorite?

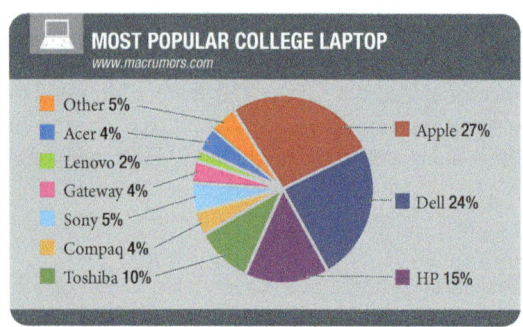

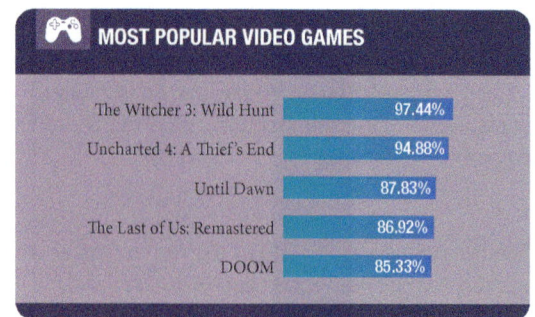

Getting Ready for the Next Section

Multiply.

21. $0.06(550)$

22. $0.06(625)$

23. $0.03 \cdot 289{,}500$

24. $0.03 \cdot 115{,}900$

Divide. Write your answers as decimals.

25. $5.44 \div 0.04$

26. $4.35 \div 0.03$

27. $19.80 \div 396$

28. $11.82 \div 197$

29. $\dfrac{1{,}836}{0.12}$

30. $\dfrac{115}{0.1}$

31. $\dfrac{90}{600}$

32. $\dfrac{105}{750}$

One Step Further: Batting Averages

Batting averages in baseball are given as decimal numbers, rounded to the nearest thousandth. For example, a player had 197 hits in 572 times at bat, for a batting average of .344. This average is found by dividing the number of hits by the number of times he was at bat and then rounding to the nearest thousandth.

$$\text{Batting average} = \frac{\text{Number of hits}}{\text{Number of times at bat}} = \frac{197}{572} = 0.344$$

Because we can write any decimal number as a percent, we can convert batting averages to percents and use our knowledge of percent to solve problems. Looking at the batting average as a percent, we can say that the player will get a hit 34.4% of the times he is at bat.

Each of the following problems can be solved by converting batting averages to percents and translating the problem into one of our three basic percent problems.

33. Ty Cobb has one of the best batting averages of all time. If he has 4,191 career hits in 11,429 times at bat, what percent of the time Cobb was at bat could we expect him to get a hit?

34. Ted Williams has one of the best batting averages of all time. If he has 2,654 career hits in 7,706 times at bat, what percent of the time Cobb was at bat could we expect him to get a hit?

35. Miguel Cabrera had a batting average of .316 in 2016. If his batting average remains the same and he has 500 at-bats in the 2017 season, how many hits will he have?

36. Ichiro Suzuki had a batting average of .291 in 2016. If his batting average remains the same and he has 500 at-bats in the 2017 season, how many hits will he have? Round to the nearest hit.

37. How many hits must Miguel Cabrera have in his first 60 at-bats in 2017 to maintain his average of .316? Round to the nearest hit.

38. How many hits must Ichiro Suzuki have in his first 65 at-bats in 2017 to maintain his average of .291? Round to the nearest hit.

Sales Tax and Commission

0.13

Have an appetite for bugs? A candy company in Pismo Beach, California produces and sells lollipops and other sugary treats with real insects trapped inside! Choose from a wide selection of worms, crickets, scorpions, ants, or butterflies to satisfy that creepy-crawly craving. Suppose you purchase a box of 36 Scorpion Suckers for $81. If sales tax in Pismo Beach at the time of your purchase is 8.75%, how much sales tax will you have to pay in addition to the $81? To solve problems similar to this one, we will first restate them in terms of the problems we have already learned how to solve.

A Application Problems with Sales Tax

Video Examples

Section 0.13

Example 1   Suppose the sales tax rate in Mississippi is 6% of the purchase price. If the price of a used refrigerator is $550, how much sales tax must be paid?

SOLUTION   Because the sales tax is 6% of the purchase price, and the purchase price is $550, the problem can be restated as

What is 6% of $550?

We solve this problem, as we did previously, by translating it into an equation.

$$n = 0.06 \cdot 550$$

$$n = 33 \qquad \text{Multiply.}$$

The sales tax is $33. The total price of the refrigerator would be

Purchase price		Sales tax		Total price
↓		↓		↓
$550	+	$33	=	$583

> *Note*   In Example 1, the *sales tax rate* is 6%, and the *sales tax* is $33. In most everyday communications, people say "The sales tax is 6%," which is incorrect. The 6% is the tax *rate*, and the $33 is the actual tax.

Example 2   Suppose the sales tax rate is 4%. If the sales tax on a 10-speed bicycle is $5.44, what is the purchase price, and what is the total price of the bicycle?

SOLUTION   We know that 4% of the purchase price is $5.44. We find the purchase price first by restating the problem as

$5.44 is 4% of what number?

$$5.44 = 0.04 \cdot n \qquad \text{Convert to an equation.}$$

We solve the equation by dividing both sides by 0.04.

$$\frac{5.44}{0.04} = \frac{0.04 \cdot n}{0.04} \qquad \text{Divide both sides by 0.04.}$$

$$\frac{5.44}{0.04} = n$$

$$n = 136 \qquad \text{Divide.}$$

The purchase price is $136. The total price is the sum of the purchase price and the sales tax.

$$
\begin{array}{lll}
\text{Purchase price} & = \$136.00 \\
\underline{\text{Sales tax}} & \underline{= \;+\; 5.44} \\
\text{Total price} & = \$141.44
\end{array}
$$

■

Example 3   Suppose the purchase price of a stereo system is $396 and the sales tax is $19.80. What is the sales tax rate?

SOLUTION   We restate the problem as

$19.80 is what percent of $396?

$$19.80 = n \cdot 396 \qquad \textit{Convert to an equation.}$$

To solve this equation, we divide both sides by 396.

$$\frac{19.80}{396} = \frac{n \cdot 396}{396} \qquad \textit{Divide both sides by 396.}$$

$$\frac{19.80}{396} = n$$

$$n = 0.05 \qquad \textit{Divide.}$$

$$n = 5\% \qquad \textit{Convert to a percent.}$$

The sales tax rate is 5%.

■

B Application Problems Involving Commission

Many salespeople work on a **commission** basis. That is, their earnings are a percentage of the amount they sell. The **commission rate** is a percent, and the actual commission they receive is a dollar amount.

Example 4   A real estate agent gets 3% of the price of each house she sells. If she sells a house for $289,500, how much money does she earn?

SOLUTION   The commission is 3% of the price of the house, which is $289,500. We restate the problem as

What is 3% of $289,500?

$$n = 0.03 \cdot 289,500 \qquad \textit{Convert to an equation.}$$

$$n = 8,685 \qquad \textit{Multiply.}$$

The commission is $8,685.

■

Example 5   Suppose a car salesperson's commission rate is 12%. If the commission on one of the cars is $1,836, what is the purchase price of the car?

SOLUTION   12% of the sales price is $1,836. The problem can be restated as

12% of what number is $1,836?

$$0.12 \cdot n = 1,836 \qquad \textit{Convert to an equation.}$$

$$\frac{0.12 \cdot n}{0.12} = \frac{1,836}{0.12} \qquad \textit{Divide both sides by 0.12.}$$

$$n = 15,300$$

The car sells for $15,300.

Example 6   If the commission on a $600 dining room set is $90, what is the commission rate?

SOLUTION   The commission rate is a percentage of the selling price. That is,

$90 is what percent of $600?

$$90 = n \cdot 600 \qquad \textit{Convert to an equation.}$$

$$\frac{90}{600} = \frac{n \cdot 600}{600} \qquad \textit{Divide both sides by 600.}$$

$$n = 0.15 \qquad \textit{Divide.}$$

$$n = 15\% \qquad \textit{Change to a percent.}$$

The commission rate is 15%.

Getting Ready for Class

After reading through the preceding section, respond in your own words and in complete sentences.

A. Explain the difference between the sales tax and the sales tax rate.

B. Rework Example 1 using a sales tax rate of 7% instead of 6%.

C. Suppose the bicycle in Example 2 was purchased in California, where the sales tax rate at the time was 8.25%. How much more would the bicycle have cost?

D. Explain the difference between commission and the commission rate.

Problem Set 0.13

Vocabulary Review

Label the following vocabulary terms below as a dollar amount paid/received (D) or a percent (P).

1. Sales tax _____

2. Sales tax rate _____

3. Commission rate _____

4. Commission _____

Problems

A These problems should be solved by the methods shown in this section. In each case, show the equation needed to solve the problem. Write neatly, and show your work.

1. Sales Tax Suppose the sales tax rate in Mississippi is 7% of the purchase price. If a new food processor sells for $750, how much is the sales tax?

2. Sales Tax If the sales tax rate is 5% of the purchase price, how much sales tax is paid on a television that sells for $980?

3. Sales Tax and Purchase Price Suppose the sales tax rate in Michigan is 6%. How much is the sales tax on a $45 concert ticket? What is the total price?

4. Sales Tax and Purchase Price Suppose the sales tax rate in Hawaii is 4%. How much sales tax is charged on a new car if the purchase price is $16,400? What is the total price?

5. Total Price The sales tax rate is 4%. If the sales tax on a 10-speed bicycle is $6, what is the purchase price? What is the total price?

6. Total Price The sales tax on a new microwave oven is $30. If the sales tax rate is 5%, what is the purchase price? What is the total price?

7. Tax Rate Suppose the purchase price of a dining room set is $450. If the sales tax is $22.50, what is the sales tax rate?

8. Tax Rate If the purchase price of a bottle of California wine is $24 and the sales tax is $1.50, what is the sales tax rate?

B Solve the following problems involving commission.

9. Commission A real estate agent has a commission rate of 3%. If a piece of property sells for $94,000, what is her commission?

10. Commission A tire salesperson has a 12% commission rate. If he sells a set of radial tires for $400, what is his commission?

11. Commission and Purchase Price Suppose a salesperson gets a commission rate of 12% on the lawnmowers she sells. If the commission on one of the mowers is $24, what is the purchase price of the lawnmower?

12. Commission and Purchase Price If an appliance salesperson gets 9% commission on all the appliances she sells, what is the price of a refrigerator if her commission is $67.50?

13. Commission Rate If the commission on an $800 washing machine is $112, what is the commission rate?

14. Commission Rate A realtor makes a commission of $3,600 on a $90,000 house he sells. What is his commission rate?

Calculator Problems

The following problems are similar to Problems 1–14. Set them up in the same way, but use a calculator for the calculations.

15. Sales Tax The sales tax rate on a certain item is 5.5%. If the purchase price is $216.95, how much is the sales tax? (Round to the nearest cent.)

16. Purchase Price If the sales tax rate is 4.75% and the sales tax is $18.95, what is the purchase price? What is the total price? (Both answers should be rounded to the nearest cent.)

17. Tax Rate The purchase price for a new suit is $229.50. If the sales tax is $10.33, what is the sales tax rate? (Round to the nearest tenth of a percent.)

18. Commission If the commission rate for a mobile home salesperson is 11%, what is the commission on the sale of a $15,794 mobile home?

19. Selling Price Suppose the commission rate on the sale of used cars is 13%. If the commission on one of the cars is $519.35, what did the car sell for?

20. Commission Rate If the commission on the sale of $79.40 worth of clothes is $14.29, what is the commission rate? (Round to the nearest percent.)

Getting Ready for the Next Section

Perform the indicated operation.

21. $0.05(22,000)$

22. $0.176(1,793,000)$

23. $0.25 \cdot 300$

24. $0.12 \cdot 450$

25. $4 \div 25$

26. $7 \div 35$

27. $25 - 21$

28. $1,793,000 - 315,568$

29. $450 - 54$

30. $300 - 75$

31. $396 + 19.8$

32. $22,000 + 1,100$

One Step Further: Luxury Taxes

Suppose a luxury tax requires an additional tax of 10% on a portion of the purchase price of certain luxury items. For expensive cars, it must be paid on the part of the purchase price that exceeded $30,000. For example, if you purchased a Jaguar XJ-S for $53,000, you would pay sales tax on $53,000 and a luxury tax of 10% of $23,000, because the purchase price, $53,000, is $23,000 above $30,000.

33. If you purchased a Jaguar XJ-S for $53,000 in California, where the sales tax rate was 6%, how much would you pay in luxury tax and how much would you pay in sales tax?

34. If you purchased a Mercedes 300E for $43,500 in California, where the sales tax rate was 6%, how much more would you pay in sales tax than luxury tax?

35. How much would you have saved if you had purchased the Jaguar mentioned in Problem 33 in Alaska, which has no sales tax?

36. How much would you have saved if you bought a car in California with a purchase price of $45,000 without the luxury tax?

37. How much would you save in California on taxes (sales and luxury) and the sticker price on a car with a price of $31,500, if you persuaded the car dealer to reduce the price to $29,900?

38. Suppose one of the cars you were interested in had a sticker price of $35,500, while another had a sticker price of $28,500. If you expected to pay full price in California for either car, how much did you save on the sticker price and taxes (sales and luxury) if you bought the less expensive car?

Find the Mistake

Each sentence below contains a mistake. Circle the mistake and write the correct word(s) or numbers(s) on the line provided.

1. Suppose the sales tax rate on a new computer is 8%. If the computer cost $650, then the total price of purchase would be $52. _____

2. If a new shirt that costs $32 has sales tax equal to $1.92, then the sales tax rate is 8%. _____

3. A car salesman's commission rate is 7%. To find his commission on a $15,000 sale of a Ford truck, we would solve $15,000 = 7n$. _____

4. A saleswoman makes a commission of $6.80 on a sale of $85 worth of clothing. To find the woman's commission rate, solve the equation $6.80n = 85$ _____

Percent Increase or Decrease, and Discount

0.14

Many colleges have programs for students with common interests. For example, your college might have certificates or designators that you can earn in addition to your degree. Assume you are enrolled at a college with two campuses. Recently an honors program was formed, allowing highly motivated students the opportunity to take courses that provide alternative approaches to learning. Faculty and advisors have been actively recruiting students for this program. Below are the enrollment trends for each campus over the last two years.

Number of Students Enrolled in Honors Program

	Year 1	Year 2
Campus A	102	153
Campus B	41	94

Each campus recruited approximately 50 students in the last year. Which campus was more successful in recruiting students? Campus B was arguably more successful because they were able to double the enrollment of honors students on their campus. Percent increase and decrease, the topic of this section, are helpful concepts in understanding problems like this.

A Percent Increases and Decreases

Many times it is more effective to state increases or decreases in terms of percents, rather than the actual number, because with percent we are comparing everything to 100. We saw one example of this in the introduction to this section. By using a percent instead of the number of students recruited, Campus B's recruitment initiatives appear to be more successful. In this section, we will look at several other scenarios in which using a percent is more effective than stating the number.

Video Examples

Section 0.14

Example 1   If a person earns $22,000 a year and gets a 5% increase in salary, what is the new salary?

SOLUTION   We can find the dollar amount of the salary increase by finding 5% of $22,000.

$$0.05 \cdot 22{,}000 = 1{,}100$$

The increase in salary is $1,100. The new salary is the old salary plus the raise.

$22,000	*Old salary*
+ 1,100	*Raise (5% of $22,000)*
$23,100	*New salary*

Example 2   In 1997, there were approximately 1,477,000 arrests for driving under the influence of alcohol or drugs (DUI) in the United States. By 2007, the number of arrests for DUI had decreased 3.4% from the 1997 number. How many people were arrested for DUI in 2007? Round the answer to the nearest thousand.

SOLUTION   The decrease in the number of arrests is 3.4% of 1,477,000, or

$$0.034 \cdot 1{,}477{,}000 = 50{,}218$$

Subtracting this number from 1,477,000, we have the number of DUI arrests in 2007.

1,477,000	*Number of arrests in 1997*
− 50,218	*Decrease of 3.4%*
1,426,782	*Number of arrests in 2007*

To the nearest thousand, there were approximately 1,427,000 arrests for DUI in 2007.

Example 3   Shoes that usually sell for $25 are on sale for $21. What is the percent decrease in price?

SOLUTION   We must first find the decrease in price. Subtracting the sale price from the original price, we have

$$\$25 - \$21 = \$4$$

The decrease is $4. To find the percent decrease (from the original price), we have

$4 is what percent of $25?

$4 = n \cdot 25$	*Convert to an equation.*
$\dfrac{4}{25} = \dfrac{n \cdot 25}{25}$	*Divide both sides by 25.*
$n = 0.16$	*Divide.*
$n = 16\%$	*Change to a percent.*

The shoes that sold for $25 have been reduced by 16% to $21. In a problem like this, $25 is the *original* (or *marked*) price, $21 is the *sale price*, $4 is the *discount*, and 16% is the *rate of discount*.

B Discount

In Example 3, $4 was the discount amount for the shoes on sale. Now we will work some examples that deal directly with **discount.**

Example 4   During a clearance sale, a suit that usually sells for $300 is marked "25% off." What is the discount? What is the sale price?

SOLUTION   To find the discount, we restate the problem as

What is 25% of 300?

$n = 0.25 \cdot 300$	*Convert to an equation.*
$n = 75$	*Multiply.*

The discount is $75. The sale price is the original price less the discount.

$$
\begin{array}{ll}
\$300 & \textit{Original price} \\
-\ \ 75 & \textit{Less the discount (25\% of \$300)} \\
\hline
\$225 & \textit{Sale price}
\end{array}
$$

Example 5   A man buys a washing machine on sale. The machine usually sells for $450, but it is on sale at 12% off. If the sales tax rate is 5%, how much is the total bill for the washer?

SOLUTION First, we have to find the sale price of the washing machine, and we begin by finding the discount.

What is 12% of $450?

$$n = 0.12 \cdot 450$$

$$n = 54$$

The washing machine is marked down $54. The sale price is

$$
\begin{array}{ll}
\$450 & \textit{Original price} \\
-\ \ 54 & \textit{Discount (12\% of \$450)} \\
\hline
\$396 & \textit{Sale price}
\end{array}
$$

Because the sales tax rate is 5%, we find the sales tax as follows:

What is 5% of 396?

$$n = 0.05 \cdot 396$$

$$n = 19.80$$

The sales tax is $19.80. The total price the man pays for the washing machine is

$$
\begin{array}{ll}
\$396.00 & \textit{Sale price} \\
+\ \ 19.80 & \textit{Sales tax} \\
\hline
\$415.80 & \textit{Total price}
\end{array}
$$

> **Note** It is customary to find the discounted price and then find the sales tax for that amount.

Getting Ready for Class

After reading through the preceding section, respond in your own words and in complete sentences.

A. Suppose the person mentioned in Example 1 was earning $32,000 per year and received the same percent increase in salary. How much more would the raise have been?

B. Suppose the shoes mentioned in Example 3 were on sale for $20, instead of $21. Calculate the new percent decrease in price.

C. Suppose a store owner pays $225 for a suit, and then marks it up $75, to $300. Find the percent increase in price.

D. What is discount?

Problem Set 0.14

Vocabulary Review

Read the following description of a television on sale.

An LCD HD television that usually sells for $400 is on sale for $340. The television's price has been reduced $60, which is a 15% percent decrease.

Now match the following quantities mentioned in the above description with their correct labels.

1. $400   a. Discount
2. $340   b. Original price
3. $60   c. Rate of discount
4. 15%   d. Sale price

Problems

A, B Solve each of these problems using the method developed in this section.

1. **Salary Increase** If a person earns $23,000 a year and gets a 7% increase in salary, what is the new salary?

2. **Salary Increase** A computer programmer's yearly income of $57,000 is increased by 8%. What is the dollar amount of the increase, and what is her new salary?

3. **Tuition Increase** The yearly tuition at a college is presently $3,000. Next year it is expected to increase by 17%. What will the tuition at this school be next year?

4. **Price Increase** A supermarket increased the price of cheese that sold for $1.98 per pound by 3%. What is the new price for a pound of this cheese? (Round to the nearest cent.)

5. **Car Value** In one year, a new car decreased in value by 20%. If it sold for $16,500 when it was new, what was it worth after 1 year?

6. **Calorie Content** A certain light beer has 20% fewer calories than the regular beer. If the regular beer has 120 calories per bottle, how many calories are in the same-sized bottle of the light beer?

7. **Salary Increase** A person earning $3,500 a month gets a raise of $350 per month. What is the percent increase in salary?

8. **Rate Increase** A student reader is making $6.50 per hour and gets a $0.70 raise. What is the percent increase? (Round to the nearest tenth of a percent.)

9. **Shoe Sale** Shoes that usually sell for $25 are on sale for $20. What is the percent decrease in price?

10. **Enrollment Decrease** The enrollment in a certain elementary school was 410. The next year, the enrollment in the same school was 328. Find the percent decrease in enrollment from one year to the next.

11. **Soda Consumption** The chart shows the consumption of soda in gallons per person per year in different countries. What is the increase in percent of consumption in the United States as compared to Norway? Round to the nearest percent.

12. **Farmers' Markets** The chart shows the rise in farmers' markets throughout the country. What is the percent increase in farmers' markets from Year 1 to Year 10? Round to the nearest tenth of a percent.

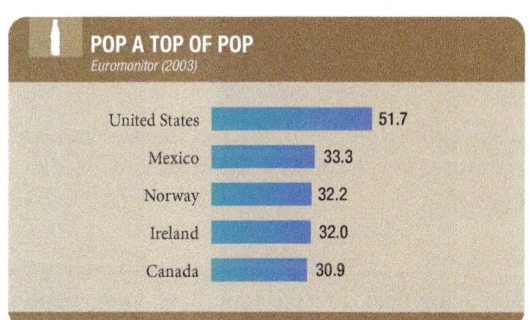

POP A TOP OF POP
Euromonitor (2003)

United States	51.7
Mexico	33.3
Norway	32.2
Ireland	32.0
Canada	30.9

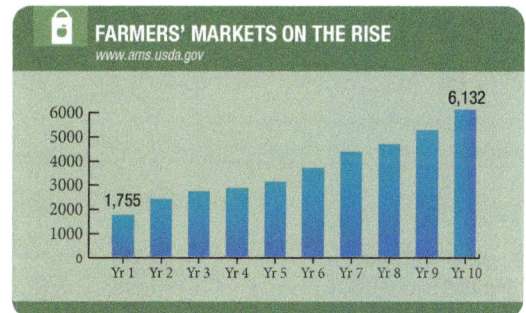

FARMERS' MARKETS ON THE RISE
www.ams.usda.gov

6,132

1,755

13. **Discount** During a clearance sale, a three-piece suit that usually sells for $300 is marked "15% off." What is the discount? What is the sale price?

14. **Sale Price** On opening day, a new music store offers a 12% discount on all electric guitars. If the regular price on a guitar is $550, what is the sale price?

15. **Total Price** A man buys a washing machine that is on sale. The washing machine usually sells for $450 but is on sale at 20% off. If the sales tax rate in his state is 6%, how much is the total bill for the washer?

16. **Total Price** A bedroom set that normally sells for $1,450 is on sale for 10% off. If the sales tax rate is 5%, what is the total price of the bedroom set if it is bought while on sale?

Calculator Problems

Set up the following problems the same way you set up Problems 1–16. Then use a calculator to do the calculations.

17. Salary Increase A teacher making $43,752 per year gets a 6.5% raise. What is the new salary?

18. Utility Increase A homeowner had a $15.90 electric bill in December. In January, the bill was $17.81. Find the percent increase in the electric bill from December to January. (Round to the nearest whole number.)   12%

19. Soccer The rules for soccer state that the playing field must be from 100 to 120 yards long and 55 to 75 yards wide. The 1999 Women's World Cup was played at the Rose Bowl on a playing field 116 yards long and 72 yards wide. The diagram below shows the smallest possible soccer field, the largest possible soccer field, and the soccer field at the Rose Bowl.

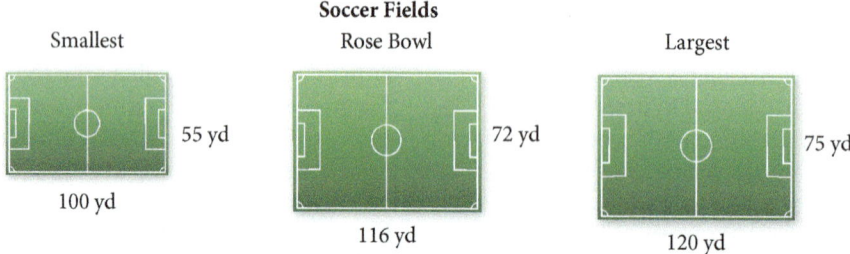

Soccer Fields

Smallest — 100 yd × 55 yd
Rose Bowl — 116 yd × 72 yd
Largest — 120 yd × 75 yd

a. **Percent Increase** A team plays on the smallest field, then plays in the Rose Bowl. What is the percent increase in the area of the playing field from the smallest field to the Rose Bowl? Round to the nearest tenth of a percent.

b. **Percent Increase** A team plays a soccer game in the Rose Bowl. The next game is on a field with the largest dimensions. What is the percent increase in the area of the playing field from the Rose Bowl to the largest field? Round to the nearest tenth of a percent.

20. Football The diagrams below show the dimensions of playing fields for the National Football League (NFL), the Canadian Football League (CFL), and Arena Football.

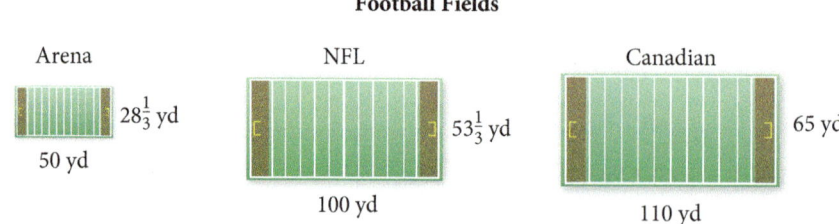

Football Fields

Arena — 50 yd × $28\frac{1}{3}$ yd
NFL — 100 yd × $53\frac{1}{3}$ yd
Canadian — 110 yd × 65 yd

a. **Percent Increase** Kurt Warner made a successful transition from Arena Football to the NFL, winning the Most Valuable Player award. What was the percent increase in the area of the fields he played on in moving from Arena Football to the NFL? Round to the nearest percent.

b. **Percent Decrease** Doug Flutie played in the Canadian Football League before moving to the NFL. What was the percent decrease in the area of the fields he played on in moving from the CFL to the NFL? Round to the nearest tenth of a percent.

Getting Ready for the Next Section

Multiply. Round to nearest hundredth if necessary.

21. $0.07(2,000)$

22. $0.12(8,000)$

23. $600(0.04)\left(\dfrac{1}{6}\right)$

24. $900(0.06)\left(\dfrac{1}{4}\right)$

25. $10,150(0.06)\left(\dfrac{1}{4}\right)$

26. $10,302.25(0.06)\left(\dfrac{1}{4}\right)$

Add.

27. $3,210 + 224.7$

28. $900 + 13.50$

29. $10,000 + 150$

30. $10,150 + 152.25$

31. $10,302.25 + 154.53$

32. $10,456.78 + 156.85$

Simplify.

33. $2,000 + 0.07(2,000)$

34. $8,000 + 0.12(8,000)$

35. $3,000 + 0.07(3,000)$

36. $9,000 + 0.12(9,000)$

Find the Mistake

Each sentence below contains a mistake. Circle the mistake and write the correct word(s) or numbers(s) on the line provided.

1. If a new model of a car increases 12% from and old model's price of $24,000, then the new selling price is $2,880. _____

2. A lawnmower goes on sale from $98 to $63.70. The percent decrease of the lawnmower's price is 65%. _____

3. A backpack that normally sells for $75 is on sale. The new price of $45 shows a percent increase of 40% _____

4. A designer pair of sunglasses is on sale from $125 for 20% off. If the sales tax is 6% of the sale price, then the total bill for the glasses would be $107.50. _____

The number(s) in brackets next to each heading indicates the section(s) in which that topic is discussed.

Symbols [0.1]

$a = b$ a is equal to b.
$a \neq b$ a is not equal to b.
$a < b$ a is less than b.
$a \not< b$ a is not less than b.
$a > b$ a is greater than b.
$a \not> b$ a is not greater than b.
$a \geq b$ a is greater than or equal to b.
$a \leq b$ a is less than or equal to b.

EXAMPLES

1. $2^5 = 2 \cdot 2 \cdot 2 \cdot 2 \cdot 2 = 32$
   $5^2 = 5 \cdot 5 = 25$
   $10^3 = 10 \cdot 10 \cdot 10 = 1{,}000$
   $1^4 = 1 \cdot 1 \cdot 1 \cdot 1 = 1$

Exponents [0.1]

Exponents are notation used to indicate repeated multiplication. In the expression 3^4, 3 is the *base* and 4 is the *exponent*.

$$3^4 = 3 \cdot 3 \cdot 3 \cdot 3 = 81$$

Order of Operations [0.1]

2. $10 + (2 \cdot 3^2 - 4 \cdot 2)$
   $= 10 + (2 \cdot 9 - 4 \cdot 2)$
   $= 10 + (18 - 8)$
   $= 10 + 10$
   $= 20$

When evaluating a mathematical expression, we will perform the operations in the following order, beginning with the expression in the innermost parentheses or brackets and working our way out.

1. Simplify all numbers with exponents, working from left to right if more than one of these numbers is present.

2. Then do all multiplications and divisions left to right.

3. Finally, perform all additions and subtractions left to right.

Absolute Value [0.2]

3. $|5| = 5$
   $|-5| = 5$

The *absolute value* of a real number is its distance from zero on the real number line. Absolute value is never negative.

Opposites [0.2]

4. The numbers 3 and -3 are opposites; their sum is 0:
   $3 + (-3) = 0$

Any two real numbers the same distance from zero on the number line but in opposite directions from zero are called *opposites*. Opposites always add to zero.

Reciprocals [0.2]

5. The numbers 2 and $\frac{1}{2}$ are reciprocals; their product is 1:

$$2\left(\tfrac{1}{2}\right) = 1$$

Any two real numbers whose product is 1 are called *reciprocals*. Every real number has a reciprocal except 0.

Addition of Real Numbers [0.3]

6. Add all combinations of positive and negative 10 and 13.

$$10 + 13 = 23$$
$$10 + (-13) = -3$$
$$-10 + 13 = 3$$
$$-10 + (-13) = -23$$

To add two real numbers with

1. The same sign: Simply add their absolute values and use the common sign.

2. Different signs: Subtract the smaller absolute value from the larger absolute value. The answer has the same sign as the number with the larger absolute value.

Subtraction of Real Numbers [0.4]

7. Subtracting 2 is the same as adding -2:

$$7 - 2 = 7 + (-2) = 5$$

To subtract one number from another, simply add the opposite of the number you are subtracting; that is, if a and b represent real numbers, then

$$a - b = a + (-b)$$

Properties of Real Numbers [0.5]

	For Addition	*For Multiplication*
Commutative:	$a + b = b + a$	$a \cdot b = b \cdot a$
Associative:	$a + (b + c) = (a + b) + c$	$a \cdot (b \cdot c) = (a \cdot b) \cdot c$
Identity:	$a + 0 = a$	$a \cdot 1 = a$
Inverse:	$a + (-a) = 0$	$a\left(\frac{1}{a}\right) = 1$
Distributive:	$a(b + c) = ab + ac$	

Multiplication of Real Numbers [0.6]

8.
$$3(5) = 15$$
$$3(-5) = -15$$
$$-3(5) = -15$$
$$-3(-5) = 15$$

To multiply two real numbers, simply multiply their absolute values. Like signs give a positive answer. Unlike signs give a negative answer.

Division of Real Numbers [0.7]

9. $-\frac{6}{2} = -6\left(\frac{1}{2}\right) = -3$

$\frac{-6}{-2} = -6\left(-\frac{1}{2}\right) = 3$

Division by a number is the same as multiplication by its reciprocal. Like signs give a positive answer. Unlike signs give a negative answer.

10. a. 7 and 100 are counting numbers, but 0 and -2 are not.

b. 0 and 241 are whole numbers, but -4 and $\frac{1}{2}$ are not.

c. -15, 0, and 20 are integers.

d. -4, $-\frac{1}{2}$, 0.75, and 0.666... are rational numbers.

e. $-\pi$, $\sqrt{3}$, and π are irrational numbers.

f. All the numbers listed above are real numbers.

Subsets of the Real Numbers [0.8]

Counting numbers: $\{1, 2, 3, \ldots\}$
Whole numbers: $\{0, 1, 2, 3, \ldots\}$
Integers: $\{\ldots, -3, -2, -1, 0, 1, 2, 3, \ldots\}$
Rational numbers: {all numbers that can be expressed as the ratio of two integers}
Irrational numbers: {all numbers on the number line that cannot be expressed as the ratio of two integers}
Real numbers: {all numbers that are either rational or irrational}

Factoring [0.8]

11. The number 150 can be factored into the product of prime numbers:
$$150 = 15 \cdot 10$$
$$= (3 \cdot 5)(2 \cdot 5)$$
$$= 2 \cdot 3 \cdot 5^2$$

Factoring is the reverse of multiplication.

$$\text{Factors} \rightarrow 3 \cdot 5 = 15 \leftarrow \text{Product}$$

Multiplication

Factoring

Least Common Denominator (LCD) [0.9]

12. The LCD for $\frac{5}{12}$ and $\frac{7}{18}$ is 36.

The *least common denominator* (LCD) for a set of denominators is the smallest number that is exactly divisible by each denominator.

Addition and Subtraction of Fractions [0.9]

13. $\frac{5}{12} + \frac{7}{18} = \frac{5}{12} \cdot \frac{3}{3} + \frac{7}{18} \cdot \frac{2}{2}$

$$= \frac{15}{36} + \frac{14}{36}$$

$$= \frac{29}{36}$$

To add (or subtract) two fractions with a common denominator, add (or subtract) numerators and use the common denominator.

$$\frac{a}{c} + \frac{b}{c} = \frac{a + b}{c} \qquad \text{and} \qquad \frac{a}{c} - \frac{b}{c} = \frac{a - b}{c}$$

The Meaning of Percent [7.1]

1. 42% means 42 per hundred or $\frac{42}{100}$.

Percent means "per hundred." It is a way of comparing numbers to the number 100.

> ⚠️ **Common Mistake**
>
> **1.** Interpreting absolute value as changing the sign of the number inside the absolute value symbols. $|-5| = +5$, $|+5| = -5$. (The first expression is correct; the second one is not.) To avoid this mistake, remember: Absolute value is a distance and distance is always measured in positive units.
>
> **2.** Using the phrase "two negatives make a positive." This works only with multiplication and division. With addition, two negative numbers produce a negative answer. It is best not to use the phrase "two negatives make a positive" at all.

Changing Percents to Decimals [0.10]

2. $75\% = 0.75$

To change a percent to a decimal, drop the % symbol and move the decimal point two places to the *left*.

Changing Decimals to Percents [0.10]

3. $0.25 = 25\%$

To change a decimal to a percent, move the decimal point two places to the *right*, and use the % symbol.

Changing Percents to Fractions [0.10]

4. $6\% = \dfrac{6}{100} = \dfrac{3}{50}$

To change a percent to a fraction, drop the % symbol, and use a denominator of 100. Reduce the resulting fraction to lowest terms, if necessary.

Changing Fractions to Percents [0.10]

5. $\dfrac{3}{4} = 0.75 = 75\%$

or

$\dfrac{9}{10} = \dfrac{90}{100} = 90\%$

To change a fraction to a percent, either write the fraction as a decimal and then change the decimal to a percent, or write the fraction as an equivalent fraction with denominator 100, drop the 100, and use the % symbol.

Basic Word Problems Involving Percents [0.11]

6. Translating to equations, we have:

Type A: $n = 0.14 \cdot 68$; $n = 9.52$

Type B: $75 \cdot n = 25$; $n = 0.33$

Type C: $25 = 0.40 \cdot n$; $n = 62.5$

There are three basic types of word problems:

Type A: What number is 14% of 68?

Type B: What percent of 75 is 25?

Type C: 25 is 40% of what number?

Applications of Percent [0.12, 0.13, 0.14]

To solve application problems, we write *is* as =, *of* as · (multiply), and *what number* or *what percent* as *n*. We then solve the resulting equation to find the answer to the original question.

There are many different kinds of application problems involving percent. They include problems on income tax, sales tax, commission, discount, percent increase and decrease, and interest. Generally, to solve these problems, we restate them as an equivalent problem of Type A, B, or C above. Problems involving simple interest can be solved using the formula

$$I = P \cdot R \cdot T$$

where *I* is the interest, *P* is the principal, *R* is the interest rate, and *T* is the time in years. It is standard procedure with simple interest problems to use 360 days = 1 year.

> **Common Mistake**
>
> **3.** A common mistake is forgetting to change a percent to a decimal when working problems that involve percents in the calculations. We always change percents to decimals before doing any calculations.
> **4.** Moving the decimal point in the wrong direction when converting percents to decimals or decimals to percents is another common mistake. Remember, *percent* means "per hundred." Rewriting a number expressed as a percent as a decimal will make the numerical part smaller.
>
> $$25\% = 0.2$$

Chapter 0 Test

Translate into symbols. [0.1]

1. The difference of 15 and x is 12.

2. The product of 6 and a is 30.

Simplify according to the rule for order of operations. [0.1, 0.3, 0.4, 0.6, 0.7]

3. $10 + 2(7 - 3) - 4^2$

4. $15 + 24 \div 6 - 3^2$

Match each expression below with the letter of the property that justifies it. [0.5]

5. $4(2y) = (4 \cdot 2)y$

6. $5(x - 3) = 5x - 15$

7. $4 + x = x + 4$

8. $(a + 5) - 2 = a + (5 - 2)$

   a. Commutative property of addition
   b. Commutative property of multiplication
   c. Associative property of addition
   d. Associative property of multiplication
   e. Distributive property

Simplify the following: [0.5, 0.6]

9. $-2(3) - 7$

10. $2(3)^3 - 4(-2)^4$

11. $9 + 4(2 - 6)$

12. $5 - 3[-2(1 + 4) + 3(-3)]$

13. $\dfrac{-4(3) + 5(-2)}{-5 - 6}$

14. $\dfrac{4(3 - 5) - 2(-6 + 8)}{4(-2) + 10}$

Apply the associative property, and then simplify. [0.5, 0.6]

15. $5 + (7 + 3x)$

16. $3(-5y)$

Multiply by applying the distributive property. [0.5, 0.6]

17. $-5(2x - 3)$

18. $\dfrac{1}{3}(6x + 12)$

From the set of numbers $\left\{ -3, -\dfrac{1}{2}, 2, \sqrt{5}, \pi \right\}$ list all the elements that are in the following sets. [0.8]

19. Integers

20. Rational numbers

Factor into the product of primes. [0.8]

21. 660

22. 4,725

Combine. [0.9]

23. $\dfrac{5}{24} + \dfrac{9}{36}$

24. $\dfrac{5}{y} + \dfrac{6}{y}$

Write an expression in symbols that is equivalent to each English phrase, and then simplify it.

25. The sum of 6 and -9 [0.1, 0.3]

26. The difference of -5 and -12 [0.1, 0.4]

27. The product of 6 and -7 [0.1, 0.6]

28. The quotient of 32 and -8 [0.1, 0.7]

Find the next number in each sequence. [0.1, 0.2, 0.3, 0.6, 0.9]

29. $-3, 1, 5, 9, \ldots$ **30.** $81, -27, 9, -3, \ldots$

Write each percent as a decimal. [7.1]

31. 27% **32.** 6% **33.** 0.9%

Write each decimal as a percent. [7.1]

34. 0.64 **35.** 0.3 **36.** 1.49

Write each percent as a fraction or a mixed number in lowest terms. [7.1]

37. 45% **38.** 136% **39.** 7.2%

Write each number as a percent. [7.1]

40. $\dfrac{13}{20}$ **41.** $\dfrac{7}{8}$ **42.** $2\dfrac{1}{4}$

Solve each of the following problems.

43. What number is 25% of 48? [7.2]

44. What percent of 80 is 28? [7.2]

45. 30 is 40% of what number? [7.2]

46. Driver's Test On a 25-question driver's test, a student answered 24 questions correctly. What percent of the questions did the student answer correctly? [7.3]

47. Commission A salesperson gets a 6% commission rate on all computers she sells. If she sells $15,000 in computers in one day, what is her commission? [7.4]

48. Discount A dishwasher that usually sells for $725 is marked down to $580. What is the discount? What is the discount rate? [7.5]

49. Total Price A tennis racket that normally sells for $179 is on sale for 30% off. If the sales tax rate is 8%, what is the total price of the tennis racket if it is purchased during the sale? Round to the nearest cent. [7.5]

50. Percent Increase A driver gets into a car accident and his insurance increases by 14%. If he paid $760 before the accident, how much is he paying now? [7.5]

Linear Equations and Inequalities

1

iStockphoto.com © 06photo

Just before starting work on this edition of your text, I flew to Europe for vacation. From time to time the television screens on the plane displayed statistics about the flight. At one point during the flight the temperature outside the plane was −60°F. When I returned home, I did some research and found that the relationship between temperature T and altitude A can be described with the formula

$$T = -0.0035A + 70$$

when the temperature on the ground is 70°F. The table and the line graph also describe this relationship.

Air Temperature and Altitude

Altitude (feet)	Temperature (°F)
0	70
10,000	35
20,000	0
30,000	−35
40,000	−70

In this chapter we will start our work with formulas, and you will see how we use formulas to produce tables and line graphs like the ones above.

Study Skills

If you have successfully completed Chapter R, then you have made a good start at developing the study skills necessary to succeed in all math classes. Some of the study skills for this chapter are a continuation of the skills from Chapter 1, while others are new to this chapter.

1. **Continue to Set and Keep a Schedule** Sometimes I find students do well in Chapter 1 and then become overconfident. They will begin to put in less time with their homework. Don't do it. Keep to the same schedule.

2. **Increase Effectiveness** You want to become more and more effective with the time you spend on your homework. Increase those activities that are the most beneficial and decrease those that have not given you the results you want.

3. **List Difficult Problems** Begin to make lists of problems that give you the most difficulty. These are the problems in which you are repeatedly making mistakes.

4. **Begin to Develop Confidence With Word Problems** It seems that the main difference between people who are good at working word problems and those who are not is confidence. People with confidence know that no matter how long it takes them, they will eventually be able to solve the problem. Those without confidence begin by saying to themselves, "I'll never be able to work this problem." If you are in this second category, then instead of telling yourself that you can't do word problems, decide to do whatever it takes to master them. The more word problems you work, the better you will become at them.

    Many of my students keep a notebook that contains everything that they need for the course: class notes, homework, quizzes, tests, and research projects. A three-ring binder with tabs is ideal. Organize your notebook so that you can easily get to any item you want to look at.

Simplifying Expressions

If a cellular phone company charges $35 per month plus $5 for each gigabyte of data, or fraction of a gigabyte, that you use one of their cellular phones, then the amount of your monthly bill is given by the expression $35 + 5d$. To find the amount you will pay for transferring 12 gigabytes of data, you substitute 12 for d and simplify the resulting expression. This process is one of the topics we will study in this section.

As you will see in the next few sections, the first step in solving an equation is to simplify both sides as much as possible. In the first part of this section, we will practice simplifying expressions by combining what are called *similar* (or like) terms.

For our immediate purposes, a *term* is a number or a number and one or more variables multiplied together. For example, the number 5 is a term, as are the expressions $3x$, $-7y$, and $15xy$.

> **(dĕf′   similar terms**
>
> Two or more terms with the same variable part are called *similar (or like) terms.*

The terms $3x$ and $4x$ are similar because their variable parts are identical. Likewise, the terms $18y$, $-10y$, and $6y$ are similar terms.

To simplify an algebraic expression, we simply reduce the number of terms in the expression. We accomplish this by applying the distributive property along with our knowledge of addition and subtraction of positive and negative real numbers. The following examples illustrate the procedure.

Video Examples

Section 1.1

Example 1   Simplify by combining similar terms.

a. $3x + 4x$ **b.** $7a - 10a$ **c.** $18y - 10y + 6y$

SOLUTION   We combine similar terms by applying the distributive property.

a. $3x + 4x = (3 + 4)x$ *Distributive property*

$\qquad\qquad = 7x$ *Addition of 3 and 4*

b. $7a - 10a = (7 - 10)a$ *Distributive property*

$\qquad\qquad = -3a$ *Addition of 7 and −10*

c. $18y - 10y + 6y = (18 - 10 + 6)y$ *Distributive property*

$\qquad\qquad\qquad = 14y$ *Addition of 18, −10, and 6*

When the expression we intend to simplify is more complicated, we use the commutative and associative properties first.

Example 2   Simplify each expression.

a. $3x + 5 + 2x - 3$ **b.** $4a - 7 - 2a + 3$ **c.** $5x + 8 - x - 6$

SOLUTION   We combine similar terms by applying the distributive property.

a. $3x + 5 + 2x - 3 = 3x + 2x + 5 - 3$ Commutative property

$= (3x + 2x) + (5 - 3)$ Associative property

$= (3 + 2)x + (5 - 3)$ Distributive property

$= 5x + 2$ Addition

b. $4a - 7 - 2a + 3 = (4a - 2a) + (-7 + 3)$ Commutative and associative properties

$= (4 - 2)a + (-7 + 3)$ Distributive property

$= 2a - 4$ Addition

c. $5x + 8 - x - 6 = (5x - x) + (8 - 6)$ Commutative and associative properties

$= (5 - 1)x + (8 - 6)$ Distributive property

$= 4x + 2$ Addition

Notice that in each case the result has fewer terms than the original expression. Because there are fewer terms, the resulting expression is said to be simpler than the original expression.

Simplifying Expressions Containing Parentheses

If an expression contains parentheses, it is often necessary to apply the distributive property to remove the parentheses before combining similar terms.

Example 3   Simplify the expression $5(2x - 8) - 3$.

SOLUTION   We begin by distributing the 5 across $2x - 8$. We then combine similar terms:

$$5(2x - 8) - 3 = 10x - 40 - 3 \quad \text{Distributive property}$$
$$= 10x - 43$$

Example 4   Simplify $7 - 3(2y + 1)$.

SOLUTION   By the rule for order of operations, we must multiply before we add or subtract. For that reason, it would be incorrect to subtract 3 from 7 first. Instead, we multiply -3 and $2y + 1$ to remove the parentheses and then combine similar terms:

$$7 - 3(2y + 1) = 7 - 6y - 3 \quad \text{Distributive property}$$
$$= -6y + 4$$

Example 5   Simplify $5(x - 2) - (3x + 4)$.

SOLUTION   We begin by applying the distributive property to remove the parentheses. The expression $-(3x + 4)$ can be thought of as $-1(3x + 4)$. Thinking of it in this way allows us to apply the distributive property:

$$-1(3x + 4) = -1(3x) + (-1)(4)$$
$$= -3x - 4$$

The complete solution looks like this:

$$5(x - 2) - (3x + 4) = 5x - 10 - 3x - 4 \qquad \text{Distributive property}$$
$$= 2x - 14 \qquad \text{Combine similar terms}$$

As you can see from the explanation in Example 5, we use the distributive property to simplify expressions in which parentheses are preceded by a negative sign. In general we can write

$$-(a + b) = -1(a + b)$$
$$= -a + (-b)$$
$$= -a - b$$

The negative sign outside the parentheses ends up changing the sign of each term within the parentheses. In words, we say "the opposite of a sum is the sum of the opposites."

The Value of an Expression

An expression like $3x + 2$ has a certain value depending on what number we assign to x. For instance, when x is 4, $3x + 2$ becomes $3(4) + 2$, or 14. When x is -8, $3x + 2$ becomes $3(-8) + 2$, or -22. The value of an expression is found by replacing the variable with a given number.

Example 6   Find the value of the following expressions by replacing the variable with the given number.

Expression	The Variable	Value of the Expression
a. $3x - 1$	$x = 2$	$3(2) - 1 = 6 - 1 = 5$
b. $7a + 4$	$a = -3$	$7(-3) + 4 = -21 + 4 = -17$
c. $2x - 3 + 4x$	$x = -1$	$2(-1) - 3 + 4(-1) = -2 - 3 + (-4)$ $= -9$
d. $2x - 5 - 8x$	$x = 5$	$2(5) - 5 - 8(5) = 10 - 5 - 40$ $= -35$
e. $y^2 - 6y + 9$	$y = 4$	$4^2 - 6(4) + 9 = 16 - 24 + 9 = 1$

Simplifying an expression should not change its value; that is, if an expression has a certain value when x is 5, then it will always have that value no matter how much it has been simplified as long as x is 5. If we were to simplify the expression in Example 6d first, it would look like

$$2x - 5 - 8x = -6x - 5$$

When x is 5, the simplified expression $-6x - 5$ is

$$-6(5) - 5 = -30 - 5 = -35$$

It has the same value as the original expression when x is 5.

   We also can find the value of an expression that contains two variables if we know the values for both variables.

Example 7   Find the value of the expression $2x - 3y + 4$ when x is -5 and y is 6.

SOLUTION   Substituting -5 for x and 6 for y, the expression becomes

$$2(-5) - 3(6) + 4 = -10 - 18 + 4$$
$$= -28 + 4$$
$$= -24$$

Example 8   Find the value of the expression $x^2 - 2xy + y^2$ when x is 3 and y is -4.

SOLUTION   Replacing each x in the expression with the number 3 and each y in the expression with the number -4 gives us

$$3^2 - 2(3)(-4) + (-4)^2 = 9 - 2(3)(-4) + 16$$
$$= 9 - (-24) + 16$$
$$= 33 + 16$$
$$= 49$$

More About Sequences

As the next example indicates, when we substitute the counting numbers, in order, into algebraic expressions, we form some of the sequences of numbers that we studied in Chapter 1. To review, recall that the sequence of counting numbers (also called the sequence of positive integers) is

$$\text{Counting numbers} = 1, 2, 3, \ldots$$

Example 9   Substitute 1, 2, 3, and 4 for n in the expression $2n - 1$.

SOLUTION   Substituting as indicated, we have

When $n = 1, 2n - 1 = 2 \cdot 1 - 1 = 1$

When $n = 2, 2n - 1 = 2 \cdot 2 - 1 = 3$

When $n = 3, 2n - 1 = 2 \cdot 3 - 1 = 5$

When $n = 4, 2n - 1 = 2 \cdot 4 - 1 = 7$

As you can see, substituting the first four counting numbers into the formula $2n - 1$ produces the first four numbers in the sequence of odd numbers.

The next example is similar to Example 9 but uses tables to display the information.

Example 10 Fill in the tables below to find the sequences formed by substituting the first four counting numbers into the expressions $2n$ and n^2.

a.

n	1	2	3	4
$2n$				

b.

n	1	2	3	4
n^2				

SOLUTION Proceeding as we did in the previous example, we substitute the numbers 1, 2, 3, and 4 into the given expressions.

a. When $n = 1$, $2n = 2 \cdot 1 = 2$

When $n = 2$, $2n = 2 \cdot 2 = 4$

When $n = 3$, $2n = 2 \cdot 3 = 6$

When $n = 4$, $2n = 2 \cdot 4 = 8$

As you can see, the expression $2n$ produces the sequence of even numbers when n is replaced by the counting numbers. Placing these results into our first table gives us

n	1	2	3	4
$2n$	2	4	6	8

b. The expression n^2 produces the sequence of squares when n is replaced by 1, 2, 3, and 4. In table form we have

n	1	2	3	4
n^2	1	4	9	16

Getting Ready for Class

After reading through the preceding section, respond in your own words and in complete sentences.

A. What are similar terms?

B. Explain how the distributive property is used to combine similar terms.

C. What is wrong with writing $3x + 4x = 7x^2$?

D. Explain how you would find the value of $5x + 3$ when x is 6.

Simplify the following expressions.

1. $3x - 6x$ **2.** $7x - 5x$ **3.** $-2a + a$

4. $3a - a$ **5.** $7x + 3x + 2x$ **6.** $8x - 2x - x$

7. $3a - 2a + 5a$ **8.** $7a - a + 2a$ **9.** $4x - 3 + 2x$

10. $5x + 6 - 3x$ **11.** $3a + 4a + 5$ **12.** $6a + 7a + 8$

13. $2x - 3 + 3x - 2$ **14.** $6x + 5 - 2x + 3$ **15.** $3a - 1 + a + 3$

16. $-a + 2 + 8a - 7$ **17.** $-4x + 8 - 5x - 10$ **18.** $-9x - 1 + x - 4$

19. $7a + 3 + 2a + 3a$ **20.** $8a - 2 + a + 5a$ **21.** $5(2x - 1) + 4$

22. $2(4x - 3) + 2$ **23.** $7(3y + 2) - 8$ **24.** $6(4y + 2) - 7$

25. $-3(2x - 1) + 5$ **26.** $-4(3x - 2) - 6$ **27.** $5 - 2(a + 1)$

28. $7 - 8(2a + 3)$ **29.** $6 - 4(x - 5)$ **30.** $12 - 3(4x - 2)$

31. $-9 - 4(2 - y) + 1$ **32.** $-10 - 3(2 - y) + 3$ **33.** $-6 + 2(2 - 3x) + 1$

34. $-7 - 4(3 - x) + 1$ **35.** $(4x - 7) - (2x + 5)$ **36.** $(7x - 3) - (4x + 2)$

37. $8(2a + 4) - (6a - 1)$ **38.** $9(3a + 5) - (8a - 7)$ **39.** $3(x - 2) + (x - 3)$

40. $2(2x + 1) - (x + 4)$ **41.** $4(2y - 8) - (y + 7)$ **42.** $5(y - 3) - (y - 4)$

43. $-9(2x + 1) - (x + 5)$ **44.** $-3(3x - 2) - (2x + 3)$

Evaluate the following expressions when x is 2. (Find the value of the expressions if x is 2.)

45. $3x - 1$ **46.** $4x + 3$ **47.** $-2x - 5$ **48.** $-3x + 6$

49. $x^2 - 8x + 16$ **50.** $x^2 - 10x + 25$ **51.** $(x - 4)^2$ **52.** $(x - 5)^2$

Evaluate the following expressions when x is -5. Then simplify the expression, and check to see that it has the same value for $x = -5$.

53. $7x - 4 - x - 3$ **54.** $3x + 4 + 7x - 6$

55. $5(2x + 1) + 4$ **56.** $2(3x - 10) + 5$

Evaluate the following expressions when x is -3 and y is 5.

57. $x^2 - 2xy + y^2$ **58.** $x^2 + 2xy + y^2$ **59.** $(x - y)^2$

60. $(x + y)^2$ **61.** $x^2 + 6xy + 9y^2$ **62.** $x^2 + 10xy + 25y^2$

63. $(x + 3y)^2$ **64.** $(x + 5y)^2$

Find the value of $12x - 3$ for each of the following values of x.

65. $\dfrac{1}{2}$ **66.** $\dfrac{1}{3}$ **67.** $\dfrac{1}{4}$ **68.** $\dfrac{1}{6}$

69. $\dfrac{3}{2}$ **70.** $\dfrac{2}{3}$ **71.** $\dfrac{3}{4}$ **72.** $\dfrac{5}{6}$

73. Fill in the tables below to find the sequences formed by substituting the first four counting numbers into the expressions $3n$ and n^3.

a.

n	1	2	3	4
$3n$				

b.

n	1	2	3	4
n^3				

74. Fill in the tables below to find the sequences formed by substituting the first four counting numbers into the expressions $2n - 1$ and $2n + 1$.

a.

n	1	2	3	4
$2n - 1$				

b.

n	1	2	3	4
$2n + 1$				

Find the sequences formed by substituting the first four counting numbers, in order, into the following expressions.

75. $3n - 2$ **76.** $2n - 3$ **77.** $n^2 - 2n + 1$ **78.** $(n - 1)^2$

Here are some problems you will see later in the book. Simplify.

79. $7 - 3(2y + 1)$ **80.** $4(3x - 2) - (6x - 5)$

81. $0.08x + 0.09x$ **82.** $0.04x + 0.05x$

83. $(x + y) + (x - y)$ **84.** $(-12x - 20y) + (25x + 20y)$

85. $3x + 2(x - 2)$ **86.** $2(x - 2) + 3(5x)$

87. $4(x + 1) + 3(x - 3)$ **88.** $5(x + 1) + 3(x - 1)$

89. $x + (x + 3)(-3)$ **90.** $x - 2(x + 2)$

91. $3(4x - 2) - (5x - 8)$ **92.** $2(5x - 3) - (2x - 4)$

93. $-(3x + 1) - (4x - 7)$ **94.** $-(6x + 2) - (8x - 3)$

95. $(x + 3y) + 3(2x - y)$ **96.** $(2x - y) - 2(x + 3y)$

97. $3(2x + 3y) - 2(3x + 5y)$ **98.** $5(2x + 3y) - 3(3x + 5y)$

99. $-6\left(\frac{1}{2}x - \frac{1}{3}y\right) + 12\left(\frac{1}{4}x + \frac{2}{3}y\right)$ **100.** $6\left(\frac{1}{3}x + \frac{1}{2}y\right) - 4\left(x + \frac{3}{4}y\right)$

101. $0.08x + 0.09(x + 2{,}000)$ **102.** $0.06x + 0.04(x + 7{,}000)$

103. $0.10x + 0.12(x + 500)$ **104.** $0.08x + 0.06(x + 800)$

Find the value of $b^2 - 4ac$ for the given values of a, b, and c. (You will see these problems later in the book.)

105. $a = 1, b = -5, c = -6$ **106.** $a = 1, b = -6, c = 7$

107. $a = 2, b = 4, c = -3$ **108.** $a = 3, b = 4, c = -2$

Applying the Concepts

109. Temperature and Altitude If the temperature on the ground is 70°F, then the temperature at A feet above the ground can be found from the expression $-0.0035A + 70$. Find the temperature at the following altitudes.

a. 8,000 feet **b.** 12,000 feet **c.** 24,000 feet

110. Perimeter of a Rectangle The expression $2l + 2w$ gives the perimeter of a rectangle with length l and width w. Find the perimeter of the rectangles with the following lengths and widths.

a. Length = 8 meters
  Width = 5 meters

b. Length = 10 feet
  Width = 3 feet

5 m

8 m

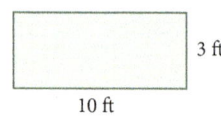

3 ft

10 ft

111. Cellular Data Rates A cellular phone company charges $35 per month plus $5 for each gigabyte, or fraction of a gigabyte, that transfer using one of their cellular phones. The expression $35 + 5d$ gives the amount of money you will pay for using one of their phones for d gigabytes of data a month. Find the monthly bill for using one of their phones.

a. 2 GB in a month
b. 4 GB in a month
c. 8 GB in a month

112. Cost of Bottled Water A water bottling company charges $7.00 per month for their water dispenser and $1.10 for each gallon of water delivered. If you have g gallons of water delivered in a month, then the expression $7 + 1.1g$ gives the amount of your bill for that month. Find the monthly bill for each of the following deliveries.

a. 10 gallons
b. 20 gallons
c. 30 gallons

Getting Ready for the Next Section

These are problems that you must be able to work in order to understand the material in the next section. The problems below are exactly the type of problems you will see in the explanations and examples in the next section.

Simplify.

113. $17 - 5$

114. $12 + (-2)$

115. $2 - 5$

116. $25 - 20$

117. $-2.4 + (-7.3)$

118. $8.1 + 2.7$

119. $-\dfrac{1}{2} + \left(-\dfrac{3}{4}\right)$

120. $-\dfrac{1}{6} + \left(-\dfrac{2}{3}\right)$

121. $4(2 \cdot 9 - 3) - 7$

122. $5(3 \cdot 45 - 4) - 14 \cdot 45$

123. $4(2a - 3) - 7a$

124. $5(3a - 4) - 14a$

125. Find the value of $2x - 3$ when x is 5

126. Find the value of $3x + 4$ when x is -2

Addition Property of Equality

When light comes into contact with any object, it is reflected, absorbed, and transmitted, as shown below.

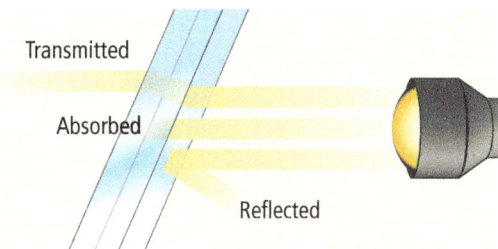

For a certain type of glass, 88% of the light hitting the glass is transmitted through to the other side, whereas 6% of the light is absorbed into the glass. To find the percent of light that is reflected by the glass, we can solve the equation

$$88 + R + 6 = 100$$

Solving equations of this type is what we study in this section. To solve an equation we must find all replacements for the variable that make the equation a true statement.

> **(děf** **solution set**
>
> The **solution set** for an equation is the set of all numbers that when used in place of the variable make the equation a true statement

For example, the equation $x + 2 = 5$ has the solution set $\{3\}$ because when x is 3 the equation becomes the true statement $3 + 2 = 5$, or $5 = 5$.

Video Examples

Section 1.2

Note We can use a question mark over the equal signs to show that we don't know yet whether the two sides of the equation are equal.

Example 1 Is 5 a solution to $2x - 3 = 7$?

SOLUTION We substitute 5 for x in the equation, and then simplify to see if a true statement results. A true statement means we have a solution; a false statement indicates the number we are using is not a solution.

When	$x = 5$
the equation	$2x - 3 = 7$
becomes	$2(5) - 3 \overset{?}{=} 7$
	$10 - 3 \overset{?}{=} 7$
	$7 = 7$ *A true statement*

Because $x = 5$ turns the equation into the true statement $7 = 7$, we know 5 is a solution to the equation.

■ **Example 2**   Is -2 a solution to $8 = 3x + 4$?

SOLUTION   Substituting -2 for x in the equation, we have

$$8 \overset{?}{=} 3(-2) + 4$$

$$8 \overset{?}{=} -6 + 4$$

$$8 = -2 \qquad\qquad \textit{A false statement}$$

$$8 \neq -2$$

Substituting -2 for x in the equation produces a false statement. Therefore, $x = -2$ is not a solution to the equation. ■

The important thing about an equation is its solution set. We therefore make the following definition to classify together all equations with the same solution set.

> **(dĕf   *equivalent equation*)**
>
> Two or more equations with the same solution set are said to be *equivalent equations*.

Equivalent equations may look different but must have the same solution set.

■ **Example 3**

a. $x + 2 = 5$ and $x = 3$ are equivalent equations because both have solution set $\{3\}$.

b. $a - 4 = 3$, $a - 2 = 5$, and $a = 7$ are equivalent equations because they all have solution set $\{7\}$.

c. $y + 3 = 4$, $y - 8 = -7$, and $y = 1$ are equivalent equations because they all have solution set $\{1\}$. ■

If two numbers are equal and we increase (or decrease) both of them by the same amount, the resulting quantities are also equal. We can apply this concept to equations. Adding the same amount to both sides of an equation always produces an equivalent equation—one with the same solution set. This fact about equations is called the ***addition property of equality*** and can be stated more formally as follows.

Note We will use this property many times in the future. Be sure you understand it completely by the time you finish this section.

> **[Δ≠Σ   *Addition Property of Equality*]**
>
> For any three algebraic expressions A, B, and C,
>
> if $\qquad\qquad A = B$
>
> then $\qquad A + C = B + C$
>
> *In words*:   Adding the same quantity to both sides of an equation will not change the solution set.

This property is just as simple as it seems. We can add any amount to both sides of an equation and always be sure we have not changed the solution set.

Consider the equation $x + 6 = 5$. We want to solve this equation for the value of x that makes it a true statement. We want to end up with x on one side of the equal sign and a number on the other side. Because we want x by itself, we will add -6 to both sides:

$$x + 6 + (-6) = 5 + (-6) \qquad \text{\textit{\textcolor{green}{Addition property of equality}}}$$

$$x + 0 = -1 \qquad \text{\textit{\textcolor{green}{Addition}}}$$

$$x = -1$$

All three equations say that x is -1. and, therefore, are equivalent.

Here are some further examples of how the addition property of equality can be used to solve equations.

Example 4   Solve the equation $x - 5 = 12$ for x.

SOLUTION   Because we want x alone on the left side, we choose to add 5 to both sides:

$$x - 5 + 5 = 12 + 5 \qquad \text{\textit{Addition property of equality}}$$

$$x + 0 = 17$$

$$x = 17$$

To check our solution to Example 4, we substitute 17 for x in the original equation:

When	$x = 17$
the equation	$x - 5 = 12$
becomes	$17 - 5 \overset{?}{=} 12$
	$12 = 12$ *A true statement*

As you can see, our solution checks. The purpose for checking a solution to an equation is to catch any mistakes we may have made in the process of solving the equation.

Example 5   Solve for a: $a + \dfrac{3}{4} = -\dfrac{1}{2}$.

SOLUTION   Because we want a by itself on the left side of the equal sign, we add the opposite of $\frac{3}{4}$ to each side of the equation.

$$a + \frac{3}{4} + \left(-\frac{3}{4}\right) = -\frac{1}{2} + \left(-\frac{3}{4}\right) \qquad \text{\textit{Addition property of equality}}$$

$$a + 0 = -\frac{1}{2} \cdot \frac{2}{2} + \left(-\frac{3}{4}\right) \qquad \text{\textit{LCD on the right side is 4}}$$

$$a = -\frac{2}{4} + \left(-\frac{3}{4}\right) \qquad \text{\textit{$\frac{2}{4}$ is equivalent to $\frac{1}{2}$}}$$

$$a = -\frac{5}{4} \qquad \text{\textit{Add fractions}}$$

The solution is $a = -\frac{5}{4}$. To check our result, we replace a with $-\frac{5}{4}$ in the original equation. The left side then becomes $-\frac{5}{4} + \frac{3}{4}$, which reduces to $-\frac{1}{2}$, so our solution checks.

Example 6   Solve for x: $7.3 + x = -2.4$.

SOLUTION   Again, we want to isolate x, so we add the opposite of 7.3 to both sides:

$$7.3 + (-7.3) + x = -2.4 + (-7.3) \qquad \text{Addition property of equality}$$
$$0 + x = -9.7$$
$$x = -9.7$$

Sometimes it is necessary to simplify each side of an equation before using the addition property of equality. The reason we simplify both sides first is that we want as few terms as possible on each side of the equation before we use the addition property of equality. The following examples illustrate this procedure.

Example 7   Solve for x: $-x + 2 + 2x = 7 + 5$.

SOLUTION   We begin by combining similar terms on each side of the equation. Then we use the addition property to solve the simplified equation.

$$x + 2 = 12 \qquad \text{Simplify both sides first}$$
$$x + 2 + (-2) = 12 + (-2) \qquad \text{Addition property of equality}$$
$$x + 0 = 10$$
$$x = 10$$

Example 8   Solve $4(2a - 3) - 7a = 2 - 5$.

SOLUTION   We must begin by applying the distributive property to separate terms on the left side of the equation. Following that, we combine similar terms and then apply the addition property of equality.

$$4(2a - 3) - 7a = 2 - 5 \qquad \text{Original equation}$$
$$8a - 12 - 7a = 2 - 5 \qquad \text{Distributive property}$$
$$a - 12 = -3 \qquad \text{Simplify each side}$$
$$a - 12 + 12 = -3 + 12 \qquad \text{Add 12 to each side}$$
$$a = 9 \qquad \text{Addition}$$

To check our solution, we replace a with 9 in the original equation.

$$4(2 \cdot 9 - 3) - 7 \cdot 9 \overset{?}{=} 2 - 5$$
$$4(15) - 63 \overset{?}{=} -3$$
$$60 - 63 \overset{?}{=} -3$$
$$-3 = -3 \qquad \text{A true statement}$$

> *Note*   Again, we place a question mark over the equal sign because we don't know yet whether the expressions on the left and right side of the equal sign will be equal.

We can also add a term involving a variable to both sides of an equation.

Example 9 Solve $3x - 5 = 2x + 7$.

SOLUTION We can solve this equation in two steps. First, we add $-2x$ to both sides of the equation. When this has been done, x appears on the left side only. Second, we add 5 to both sides:

$$3x + (-2x) - 5 = 2x + (-2x) + 7 \qquad \text{Add } -2x \text{ to both sides}$$
$$x - 5 = 7 \qquad \text{Simplify each side}$$
$$x - 5 + 5 = 7 + 5 \qquad \text{Add 5 to both sides}$$
$$x = 12 \qquad \text{Simplify each side}$$

Note In my experience teaching algebra, I find that students make fewer mistakes if they think in terms of addition rather than subtraction. So, you are probably better off if you continue to use the addition property just the way we have used it in the examples in this section. But, if you are curious as to whether you can subtract the same number from both sides of an equation, the answer is yes.

⟨Δ≠Σ A Note on Subtraction

Although the addition property of equality is stated for addition only, we can subtract the same number from both sides of an equation as well. Because subtraction is defined as addition of the opposite, subtracting the same quantity from both sides of an equation does not change the solution.

$$x + 2 = 12 \qquad \text{Original equation}$$
$$x + 2 - 2 = 12 - 2 \qquad \text{Subtract 2 from each side}$$
$$x = 10 \qquad \text{Subtraction}$$

Getting Ready for Class

After reading through the preceding section, respond in your own words and in complete sentences.

A. What is a solution to an equation?
B. What are equivalent equations?
C. Explain in words the addition property of equality.
D. How do you check a solution to an equation?

Problem Set 1.2

Solve the following equations.

1. $x - 3 = 8$ **2.** $x - 2 = 7$ **3.** $x + 2 = 6$

4. $x + 5 = 4$ **5.** $a + \dfrac{1}{2} = -\dfrac{1}{4}$ **6.** $a + \dfrac{1}{3} = -\dfrac{5}{6}$

7. $x + 2.3 = -3.5$ **8.** $x + 7.9 = 23.4$ **9.** $y + 11 = -6$

10. $y - 3 = -1$ **11.** $x - \dfrac{5}{8} = -\dfrac{3}{4}$ **12.** $x - \dfrac{2}{5} = -\dfrac{1}{10}$

13. $m - 6 = -10$ **14.** $m - 10 = -6$ **15.** $6.9 + x = 3.3$

16. $7.5 + x = 2.2$ **17.** $5 = a + 4$ **18.** $12 = a - 3$

19. $-\dfrac{5}{9} = x - \dfrac{2}{5}$ **20.** $-\dfrac{7}{8} = x - \dfrac{4}{5}$

Simplify both sides of the following equations as much as possible, and then solve.

21. $4x + 2 - 3x = 4 + 1$ **22.** $5x + 2 - 4x = 7 - 3$

23. $8a - \dfrac{1}{2} - 7a = \dfrac{3}{4} + \dfrac{1}{8}$ **24.** $9a - \dfrac{4}{5} - 8a = \dfrac{3}{10} - \dfrac{1}{5}$

25. $-3 - 4x + 5x = 18$ **26.** $10 - 3x + 4x = 20$

27. $-11x + 2 + 10x + 2x = 9$ **28.** $-10x + 5 - 4x + 15x = 0$

29. $-2.5 + 4.8 = 8x - 1.2 - 7x$ **30.** $-4.8 + 6.3 = 7x - 2.7 - 6x$

31. $2y - 10 + 3y - 4y = 18 - 6$ **32.** $15 - 21 = 8x + 3x - 10x$

The following equations contain parentheses. Apply the distributive property to remove the parentheses, then simplify each side before using the addition property of equality.

33. $2(x + 3) - x = 4$ **34.** $5(x + 1) - 4x = 2$

35. $-3(x - 4) + 4x = 3 - 7$ **36.** $-2(x - 5) + 3x = 4 - 9$

37. $5(2a + 1) - 9a = 8 - 6$ **38.** $4(2a - 1) - 7a = 9 - 5$

39. $-(x + 3) + 2x - 1 = 6$ **40.** $-(x - 7) + 2x - 8 = 4$

41. $4y - 3(y - 6) + 2 = 8$ **42.** $7y - 6(y - 1) + 3 = 9$

43. $-3(2m - 9) + 7(m - 4) = 12 - 9$ **44.** $-5(m - 3) + 2(3m + 1) = 15 - 8$

Solve the following equations by the method used in Example 9 in this section. Check each solution in the original equation.

45. $4x = 3x + 2$ **46.** $6x = 5x - 4$ **47.** $8a = 7a - 5$

48. $9a = 8a - 3$ **49.** $2x = 3x + 1$ **50.** $4x = 3x + 5$

51. $3y + 4 = 2y + 1$ **52.** $5y + 6 = 4y + 2$ **53.** $2m - 3 = m + 5$

54. $8m - 1 = 7m - 3$ **55.** $4x - 7 = 5x + 1$ **56.** $3x - 7 = 4x - 6$

57. $5x - \dfrac{2}{3} = 4x + \dfrac{4}{3}$ **58.** $3x - \dfrac{5}{4} = 2x + \dfrac{1}{4}$ **59.** $8a - 7.1 = 7a + 3.9$

60. $10a - 4.3 = 9a + 4.7$ **61.** $11y - 2.9 = 12y + 2.9$ **62.** $20y + 9.9 = 21y - 9.9$

Applying the Concepts

63. Light When light comes into contact with any object, it is reflected, absorbed, and transmitted, as shown in the following figure. If T represents the percent of light transmitted, R the percent of light reflected, and A the percent of light absorbed by a surface, then the equation $T + R + A = 100$ shows one way these quantities are related.

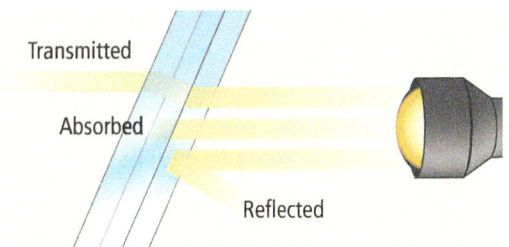

Transmitted

Absorbed

Reflected

a. For glass, $T = 88$ and $A = 6$, meaning that 88% of the light hitting the glass is transmitted and 6% is absorbed. Substitute $T = 88$ and $A = 6$ into the equation $T + R + A = 100$ and solve for R to find the percent of light that is reflected.

b. For flat black paint, $A = 95$ and no light is transmitted, meaning that $T = 0$. What percent of light is reflected by flat black paint?

c. A pure white surface can reflect 98% of light, so $R = 98$. If no light is transmitted, what percent of light is absorbed by the pure white surface?

d. Typically, shiny gray metals reflect 70–80% of light. Suppose a thick sheet of aluminum absorbs 25% of light. What percent of light is reflected by this shiny gray metal? (Assume no light is transmitted.)

64. Geometry The three angles shown in the triangle at the front of the tent in the following figure add up to 180°. Use this fact to write an equation containing x, and then solve the equation to find the number of degrees in the angle at the top of the triangle.

Getting Ready for the Next Section

To understand all of the explanations and examples in the next section you must be able to work the problems below.

Simplify.

65. $\dfrac{3}{2}\left(\dfrac{2}{3}y\right)$ **66.** $\dfrac{5}{2}\left(-\dfrac{2}{5}y\right)$ **67.** $\dfrac{1}{5}(5x)$ **68.** $-\dfrac{1}{4}(-4a)$

69. $\dfrac{1}{5}(30)$ **70.** $-\dfrac{1}{4}(24)$ **71.** $\dfrac{3}{2}(4)$ **72.** $\dfrac{1}{26}(13)$

73. $12\left(-\dfrac{3}{4}\right)$ **74.** $12\left(\dfrac{1}{2}\right)$ **75.** $\dfrac{3}{2}\left(-\dfrac{5}{4}\right)$ **76.** $\dfrac{5}{3}\left(-\dfrac{6}{5}\right)$

77. $13 + (-5)$ **78.** $-13 + (-5)$ **79.** $-\dfrac{3}{4} + \left(-\dfrac{1}{2}\right)$ **80.** $-\dfrac{7}{10} + \left(-\dfrac{1}{2}\right)$

81. $7x + (-4x)$ **82.** $5x + (-2x)$

Multiplication Property of Equality   **1.3**

As we have mentioned before, we all have to pay taxes. According to Figure 1, people have been paying taxes for quite a long time.

FIGURE 1   *Collection of taxes, ca. 3000 b.c. Clerks and scribes appear at the right, with pen and papyrus, and officials and taxpayers appear at the left.*

Suppose 21% of your monthly pay is withheld for federal income taxes and another 8% is withheld for Social Security, state income tax, and other miscellaneous items, leaving you with $987.50 a month in take-home pay. The amount you earned before the deductions were removed from your check, your gross income G, is given by the equation

$$G - 0.21G - 0.08G = 987.5$$

In this section we will learn how to solve equations of this type.

In the previous section, we found that adding the same number to both sides of an equation never changed the solution set. The same idea holds for multiplication by numbers other than zero. We can multiply both sides of an equation by the same nonzero number and always be sure we have not changed the solution set. (The reason we cannot multiply both sides by zero will become apparent later.) This fact about equations is called the *multiplication property of equality*, which can be stated formally as follows.

> **[Δ≠Σ]**   *Multiplication Property of Equality*
>
> For any three algebraic expressions A, B, and C, where $C \neq 0$,
>
> | if | $A = B$ |
> |---|---|
> | then | $AC = BC$ |
>
> *In words:*   Multiplying both sides of an equation by the same nonzero number will not change the solution set.

Note   This property is also used many times throughout the book. Make every effort to understand it completely.

Suppose we want to solve the equation $5x = 30$. We have $5x$ on the left side but would like to have just x. We choose to multiply both sides by $\frac{1}{5}$ because $\left(\frac{1}{5}\right)(5) = 1$. Here is the solution:

$$5x = 30$$

$$\frac{1}{5}(5x) = \frac{1}{5}(30) \qquad \text{Multiplication property of equality}$$

$$\left(\frac{1}{5} \cdot 5\right)x = \frac{1}{5}(30) \qquad \text{Associative property of multiplication}$$

$$1x = 6$$

$$x = 6$$

We chose to multiply by $\frac{1}{5}$ because it is the reciprocal of 5. We can see that multiplication by any number except zero will not change the solution set. If, however, we were to multiply both sides by zero, the result would always be $0 = 0$ because multiplication by zero always results in zero. Although the statement $0 = 0$ is true, we have lost our variable and cannot solve the equation. This is the only restriction of the multiplication property of equality. We are free to multiply both sides of an equation by any number except zero.

Here are some more examples that use the multiplication property of equality.

Video Examples

Section 1.3

Example 1   Solve for a: $-4a = 24$.

SOLUTION   Because we want a alone on the left side, we choose to multiply both sides by $-\frac{1}{4}$:

$$-\frac{1}{4}(-4a) = -\frac{1}{4}(24) \qquad \textit{Multiplication property of equality}$$

$$\left[-\frac{1}{4}(-4)\right]a = -\frac{1}{4}(24) \qquad \textit{Associative property}$$

$$a = -6$$

Example 2   Solve for t: $-\frac{t}{3} = 5$.

SOLUTION   Because division by 3 is the same as multiplication by $\frac{1}{3}$, we can write $-\frac{t}{3}$ as $-\frac{1}{3}t$. To solve the equation, we multiply each side by the reciprocal of $-\frac{1}{3}$, which is -3.

$$-\frac{t}{3} = 5 \qquad \textit{Original equation}$$

$$-\frac{1}{3}t = 5 \qquad \textit{Dividing by 3 is equivalent to multiplying by } \frac{1}{3}$$

$$-3\left(-\frac{1}{3}t\right) = -3(5) \qquad \textit{Multiply each side by } -3$$

$$t = -15 \qquad \textit{Multiplication}$$

Example 3   Solve $\frac{2}{3}y = 4$.

SOLUTION   We can multiply both sides by $\frac{3}{2}$ and have $1y$ on the left side:

$$\frac{3}{2}\left(\frac{2}{3}y\right) = \frac{3}{2}(4) \qquad \textit{Multiplication property of equality}$$

$$\left(\frac{3}{2}\cdot\frac{2}{3}\right)y = \frac{3}{2}(4) \qquad \textit{Associative property}$$

$$y = 6 \qquad \textit{Simplify } \frac{3}{2}(4) = \frac{3}{2}\left(\frac{4}{1}\right) = \frac{12}{2} = 6$$

Note   Notice in Examples 1 through 3 that if the variable is being multiplied by a number like -4 or $\frac{2}{3}$, we always multiply by the number's reciprocal, $-\frac{1}{4}$ or $\frac{3}{2}$, to end up with just the variable on one side of the equation.

Example 4   Solve $5 + 8 = 10x + 20x - 4x$.

SOLUTION   Our first step will be to simplify each side of the equation:

$$13 = 26x \qquad \textit{Simplify both sides first}$$

$$\frac{1}{26}(13) = \frac{1}{26}(26x) \qquad \textit{Multiplication property of equality}$$

$$\frac{13}{26} = x \qquad \textit{Multiplication}$$

$$\frac{1}{2} = x \qquad \textit{Reduce to lowest terms}$$

In the next three examples, we will use both the addition property of equality and the multiplication property of equality.

Example 5 Solve for x: $6x + 5 = -13$.

SOLUTION We begin by adding -5 to both sides of the equation:

$$6x + 5 + (-5) = -13 + (-5) \qquad \text{Add} -5 \text{ to both sides}$$

$$6x = -18 \qquad \text{Simplify}$$

$$\frac{1}{6}(6x) = \frac{1}{6}(-18) \qquad \text{Multiply both sides by } \tfrac{1}{6}$$

$$x = -3$$

Example 6 Solve for x: $5x = 2x + 12$.

SOLUTION We begin by adding $-2x$ to both sides of the equation:

$$5x + (-2x) = 2x + (-2x) + 12 \qquad \text{Add} -2x \text{ to both sides}$$

$$3x = 12 \qquad \text{Simplify}$$

$$\frac{1}{3}(3x) = \frac{1}{3}(12) \qquad \text{Multiply both sides by } \tfrac{1}{3}$$

$$x = 4 \qquad \text{Simplify}$$

> **Note** Notice that in Example 6 we used the addition property of equality first to combine all the terms containing x on the left side of the equation. Once this had been done, we used the multiplication property to isolate x on the left side.

Example 7 Solve for x: $3x - 4 = -2x + 6$.

SOLUTION We begin by adding $2x$ to both sides:

$$3x + 2x - 4 = -2x + 2x + 6 \qquad \text{Add } 2x \text{ to both sides}$$

$$5x - 4 = 6 \qquad \text{Simplify}$$

Now we add 4 to both sides:

$$5x - 4 + 4 = 6 + 4 \qquad \text{Add 4 to both sides}$$

$$5x = 10 \qquad \text{Simplify}$$

$$\frac{1}{5}(5x) = \frac{1}{5}(10) \qquad \text{Multiply by } \tfrac{1}{5}$$

$$x = 2 \qquad \text{Simplify}$$

The next example involves fractions. You will see that the properties we use to solve equations containing fractions are the same as the properties we used to solve the previous equations. Also, the LCD that we used previously to add fractions can be used with the multiplication property of equality to simplify equations containing fractions.

Example 8 Solve $\dfrac{2}{3}x + \dfrac{1}{2} = -\dfrac{3}{4}$.

SOLUTION We can solve this equation by applying our properties and working with the fractions, or we can begin by eliminating the fractions.

Method 1

Working with the fractions.

$$\frac{2}{3}x + \frac{1}{2} + \left(-\frac{1}{2}\right) = -\frac{3}{4} + \left(-\frac{1}{2}\right) \qquad \text{Add } -\frac{1}{2} \text{ to each side}$$

$$\frac{2}{3}x = -\frac{5}{4} \qquad \text{Note that } -\frac{3}{4} + \left(-\frac{1}{2}\right) = -\frac{3}{4} + \left(-\frac{2}{4}\right)$$

$$\frac{3}{2}\left(\frac{2}{3}x\right) = \frac{3}{2}\left(-\frac{5}{4}\right) \qquad \text{Multiply each side by } \frac{3}{2}$$

$$x = -\frac{15}{8}$$

Note Our original equation has denominators of 3, 2, and 4. The LCD for these three denominators is 12, and it has the property that all three denominators will divide it evenly. Therefore, if we multiply both sides of our equation by 12, each denominator will divide into 12 and we will be left with an equation that does not contain any denominators other than 1.

Method 2

Eliminating the fractions in the beginning.

$$12\left(\frac{2}{3}x + \frac{1}{2}\right) = 12\left(-\frac{3}{4}\right) \qquad \text{Multiply each side by the LCD 12}$$

$$12\left(\frac{2}{3}x\right) + 12\left(\frac{1}{2}\right) = 12\left(-\frac{3}{4}\right) \qquad \text{Distributive property on the left side}$$

$$8x + 6 = -9 \qquad \text{Multiply}$$

$$8x = -15 \qquad \text{Add } -6 \text{ to each side}$$

$$x = -\frac{15}{8} \qquad \text{Multiply each side by } \frac{1}{8}$$

As the third line in Method 2 indicates, multiplying each side of the equation by the LCD eliminates all the fractions from the equation.

As you can see, both methods yield the same solution.

$\lceil\Delta\neq\Sigma$ A Note on Division

Because **division** is defined as multiplication by the reciprocal, multiplying both sides of an equation by the same number is equivalent to dividing both sides of the equation by the reciprocal of that number; that is, multiplying each side of an equation by $\frac{1}{3}$ and dividing each side of the equation by 3 are equivalent operations. If we were to solve the equation $3x = 18$ using division instead of multiplication, the steps would look like this:

$$3x = 18 \qquad \text{Original equation}$$

$$\frac{3x}{3} = \frac{18}{3} \qquad \text{Divide each side by 3}$$

$$x = 6 \qquad \text{Division}$$

Using division instead of multiplication on a problem like this may save you some writing. However, with multiplication, it is easier to explain "why" we end up with just one x on the left side of the equation. (The "why" has to do with the associative property of multiplication.) My suggestion is that you continue to use multiplication to solve equations like this one until you understand the process completely. Then, if you find it more convenient, you can use division instead of multiplication.

Getting Ready for Class

After reading through the preceding section, respond in your own words and in complete sentences.

A. Explain in words the multiplication property of equality.
B. If an equation contains fractions, how do you use the multiplication property of equality to clear the equation of fractions?
C. Why is it okay to divide both sides of an equation by the same nonzero number?
D. Explain in words how you would solve the equation $3x = 7$ using the multiplication property of equality.

Problem Set 1.3

Solve the following equations. Be sure to show your work.

1. $5x = 10$ **2.** $6x = 12$ **3.** $7a = 28$ **4.** $4a = 36$

5. $-8x = 4$ **6.** $-6x = 2$ **7.** $8m = -16$ **8.** $5m = -25$

9. $-3x = -9$ **10.** $-9x = -36$ **11.** $-7y = -28$ **12.** $-15y = -30$

13. $2x = 0$ **14.** $7x = 0$ **15.** $-5x = 0$ **16.** $-3x = 0$

17. $\dfrac{x}{3} = 2$ **18.** $\dfrac{x}{4} = 3$ **19.** $-\dfrac{m}{5} = 10$ **20.** $-\dfrac{m}{7} = 1$

21. $-\dfrac{x}{2} = -\dfrac{3}{4}$ **22.** $-\dfrac{x}{3} = \dfrac{5}{6}$ **23.** $\dfrac{2}{3}a = 8$ **24.** $\dfrac{3}{4}a = 6$

25. $-\dfrac{3}{5}x = \dfrac{9}{5}$ **26.** $-\dfrac{2}{5}x = \dfrac{6}{15}$ **27.** $-\dfrac{5}{8}y = -20$ **28.** $-\dfrac{7}{2}y = -14$

Simplify both sides as much as possible, and then solve.

29. $-4x - 2x + 3x = 24$ **30.** $7x - 5x + 8x = 20$

31. $4x + 8x - 2x = 15 - 10$ **32.** $5x + 4x + 3x = 4 + 8$

33. $-3 - 5 = 3x + 5x - 10x$ **34.** $10 - 16 = 12x - 6x - 3x$

35. $18 - 13 = \dfrac{1}{2}a + \dfrac{3}{4}a - \dfrac{5}{8}a$ **36.** $20 - 14 = \dfrac{1}{3}a + \dfrac{5}{6}a - \dfrac{2}{3}a$

Solve the following equations by multiplying both sides by -1.

37. $-x = 4$ **38.** $-x = -3$ **39.** $-x = -4$ **40.** $-x = 3$

41. $15 = -a$ **42.** $-15 = -a$ **43.** $-y = \dfrac{1}{2}$ **44.** $-y = -\dfrac{3}{4}$

Solve each of the following equations using the method shown in Examples 5–8 in this section.

45. $3x - 2 = 7$ **46.** $2x - 3 = 9$ **47.** $2a + 1 = 3$ **48.** $5a - 3 = 7$

49. $\dfrac{1}{8} + \dfrac{1}{2}x = \dfrac{1}{4}$ **50.** $\dfrac{1}{3} + \dfrac{1}{7}x = -\dfrac{8}{21}$

51. $6x = 2x - 12$ **52.** $8x = 3x - 10$

53. $2y = -4y + 18$ **54.** $3y = -2y - 15$ **55.** $-7x = -3x - 8$

56. $-5x = -2x - 12$ **57.** $8x + 4 = 2x - 5$ **58.** $5x + 6 = 3x - 6$

59. $x + \dfrac{1}{2} = \dfrac{1}{4}x - \dfrac{5}{8}$ **60.** $\dfrac{1}{3}x + \dfrac{2}{5} = \dfrac{1}{5}x - \dfrac{2}{5}$

61. $6m - 3 = m + 2$ **62.** $6m - 5 = m + 5$

63. $\dfrac{1}{2}m - \dfrac{1}{4} = \dfrac{1}{12}m + \dfrac{1}{6}$ **64.** $\dfrac{1}{2}m - \dfrac{5}{12} = \dfrac{1}{12}m + \dfrac{5}{12}$

65. $9y + 2 = 6y - 4$ **66.** $6y + 14 = 2y - 2$

67. Solve each equation.

    a. $2x = 3$ **b.** $2 + x = 3$

    c. $2x + 3 = 0$ **d.** $2x + 3 = -5$

    e. $2x + 3 = 7x - 5$

68. Solve each equation.

    a. $5t = 10$ **b.** $5 + t = 10$

    c. $5t + 10 = 0$ **d.** $5t + 10 = 12$

    e. $5t + 10 = 8t + 12$

Applying the Concepts

69. Break-Even Point Movie theaters pay a certain price for the movies that you and I see. Suppose a theater pays $1,500 for each showing of a popular movie. If they charge $7.50 for each ticket they sell, then the equation $7.5x = 1,500$ gives the number of tickets they must sell to equal the $1,500 cost of showing the movie. This number is called the break-even point. Solve the equation for x to find the break-even point.

70. Basketball Laura plays basketball for her community college. In one game she scored 13 points total, with a combination of free throws, field goals, and three-pointers. Each free throw is worth 1 point, each field goal is 2 points, and each three-pointer is worth 3 points. If she made 1 free throw and 3 field goals, then solving the equation

$$1 + 3(2) + 3x = 13$$

will give us the number of three-pointers she made. Solve the equation to find the number of three-point shots Laura made.

71. Taxes Suppose 21% of your monthly pay is withheld for federal income taxes and another 8% is withheld for Social Security, state income tax, and other miscellaneous items. If you are left with $987.50 a month in take-home pay, then the amount you earned before the deductions were removed from your check is given by the equation

$$G - 0.21G - 0.08G = 987.5$$

Solve this equation to find your gross income.

72. Rhind Papyrus The *Rhind Papyrus* is an ancient document that contains mathematical riddles. One problem asks the reader to find a quantity such that when it is added to one-fourth of itself the sum is 15. The equation that describes this situation is

$$x + \frac{1}{4}x = 15$$

Solve this equation.

Getting Ready for the Next Section

To understand all of the explanations and examples in the next section you must be able to work the problems below.

Solve each equation.

73. $2x = 4$ **74.** $3x = 24$ **75.** $30 = 5x$ **76.** $0 = 5x$

77. $0.17x = 510$ **78.** $0.1x = 400$

Apply the distributive property and then simplify if possible.

79. $3(x - 5) + 4$ **80.** $5(x - 3) + 2$ **81.** $0.09(x + 2,000)$

82. $0.04(x + 7,000)$ **83.** $7 - 3(2y + 1)$ **84.** $4 - 2(3y + 1)$

85. $3(2x - 5) - (2x - 4)$ **86.** $4(3x - 2) - (6x - 5)$

Simplify.

87. $10x + (-5x)$ **88.** $12x + (-7x)$ **89.** $0.08x + 0.09x$ **90.** $0.06x + 0.04x$

Solving Linear Equations

We will now use the material we have developed in the first three sections of this chapter to build a method for solving any linear equation.

> **(dĕf′) linear equation**
>
> A *linear equation* in one variable is any equation that can be put in the form $ax + b = 0$, where a and b are real numbers and a is not zero.

Each of the equations we will solve in this section is a linear equation in one variable. The steps we use to solve a linear equation in one variable are listed here.

> **∖Δ≠Σ Strategy for Solving Linear Equations in One Variable**
>
> **Step 1a:** Use the distributive property to separate terms, if necessary.
> **1b:** If fractions are present, consider multiplying both sides by the LCD to eliminate the fractions. If decimals are present, consider multiplying both sides by a power of 10 to clear the equation of decimals.
> **1c:** Combine similar terms on each side of the equation.
> **Step 2:** Use the addition property of equality to get all variable terms on one side of the equation and all constant terms on the other side. A variable term is a term that contains the variable (for example, $5x$). A constant term is a term that does not contain the variable (the number 3, for example).
> **Step 3:** Use the multiplication property of equality to get x (that is, $1x$) by itself on one side of the equation.
> **Step 4:** Check your solution in the original equation to be sure that you have not made a mistake in the solution process.

Note You may have some previous experience solving equations. Even so, you should solve the equations in this section using the method developed here. Your work should look like the examples in the text. If you have learned shortcuts or a different method of solving equations somewhere else, you can always go back to them later. What is important now is that you are able to solve equations by the methods shown here.

As you will see as you work through the examples in this section, it is not always necessary to use all four steps when solving equations. The number of steps used depends on the equation. In Example 1 there are no fractions or decimals in the original equation, so step 1b will not be used. Likewise, after applying the distributive property to the left side of the equation in Example 1, there are no similar terms to combine on either side of the equation, making step 1c also unnecessary.

Video Examples

Section 1.4

Example 1 Solve $2(x + 3) = 10$.

SOLUTION To begin, we apply the distributive property to the left side of the equation to separate terms:

Step 1a: $\qquad\qquad 2x + 6 = 10$ *Distributive property*

Step 2: $\begin{cases} 2x + 6 + (-6) = 10 + (-6) & \text{\textit{Addition property of equality}} \\ \qquad\qquad 2x = 4 \end{cases}$

Step 3: $\begin{cases} \dfrac{1}{2}(2x) = \dfrac{1}{2}(4) & \text{\textit{Multiply each side by }} \dfrac{1}{2} \\ \qquad\quad x = 2 & \text{\textit{The solution is 2}} \end{cases}$

The solution to our equation is 2. We check our work (to be sure we have not made either a mistake in applying the properties or an arithmetic mistake) by substituting 2 into our original equation and simplifying each side of the result separately.

Check:	When	$x = 2$	
	the equation	$2(x + 3) = 10$	
Step 4:	becomes	$2(2 + 3) \overset{?}{=} 10$	
		$2(5) \overset{?}{=} 10$	
		$10 = 10$	*A true statement*

Our solution checks.

The general method of solving linear equations is actually very simple. It is based on the properties we developed in Chapter 0 and on two very simple new properties. We can add any number to both sides of the equation and multiply both sides by any nonzero number. The equation may change in form, but the solution set will not. If we look back to Example 1, each equation looks a little different from each preceding equation. What is interesting and useful is that each equation says the same thing about x. They all say x is 2. The last equation, of course, is the easiest to read, and that is why our goal is to end up with x by itself.

The examples that follow show a variety of equations and their solutions. When you have finished this section and worked the problems in the problem set, the steps in the solution process should be a description of how you operate when solving equations. That is, you want to work enough problems so that the Strategy for Solving Linear Equations is second nature to you.

Example 2   Solve for $x : 3(x - 5) + 4 = 13$.

SOLUTION   Our first step will be to apply the distributive property to the left side of the equation:

Step 1a:	$3x - 15 + 4 = 13$	*Distributive property*
Step 1c:	$3x - 11 = 13$	*Simplify the left side*
Step 2:	$3x - 11 + 11 = 13 + 11$	*Add 11 to both sides*
	$3x = 24$	
Step 3:	$\frac{1}{3}(3x) = \frac{1}{3}(24)$	*Multiply both sides by $\frac{1}{3}$*
	$x = 8$	*The solution is 8*

Check:	When	$x = 8$	
	the equation	$3(x - 5) + 4 = 13$	
	becomes	$3(8 - 5) + 4 \overset{?}{=} 13$	
Step 4:		$3(3) + 4 \overset{?}{=} 13$	
		$9 + 4 \overset{?}{=} 13$	
		$13 = 13$	*A true statement*

Example 3 Solve $5(x - 3) + 2 = 5(2x - 8) - 3$.

SOLUTION In this case we apply the distributive property on each side of the equation:

Step 1a: $5x - 15 + 2 = 10x - 40 - 3$ Distributive property

Step 1c: $5x - 13 = 10x - 43$ Simplify each side

Step 2:
$$5x + (-5x) - 13 = 10x + (-5x) - 43$$ Add $-5x$ to both sides
$$-13 = 5x - 43$$
$$-13 + 43 = 5x - 43 + 43$$ Add 43 to both sides
$$30 = 5x$$

Step 3:
$$\frac{1}{5}(30) = \frac{1}{5}(5x)$$ Multiply both sides by $\frac{1}{5}$
$$6 = x$$ The solution is 6

Check: Replacing x with 6 in the original equation, we have

$$5(6 - 3) + 2 \overset{?}{=} 5(2 \cdot 6 - 8) - 3$$
$$5(3) + 2 \overset{?}{=} 5(12 - 8) - 3$$

Step 4:
$$5(3) + 2 \overset{?}{=} 5(4) - 3$$
$$15 + 2 \overset{?}{=} 20 - 3$$
$$17 = 17$$ A true statement

> *Note* It makes no difference on which side of the equal sign x ends up. Most people prefer to have x on the left side because we read from left to right, and it seems to sound better to say x is 6 rather than 6 is x. Both expressions, however, have exactly the same meaning.

Example 4 Solve the equation $0.08x + 0.09(x + 2,000) = 690$.

SOLUTION We can solve the equation in its original form by working with the decimals, or we can eliminate the decimals first by using the multiplication property of equality and solving the resulting equation. Both methods follow.

Method 1
Working with the decimals.

$$0.08x + 0.09(x + 2,000) = 690$$ Original equation

Step 1a: $0.08x + 0.09x + 0.09(2,000) = 690$ Distributive property

Step 1c: $0.17x + 180 = 690$ Simplify the left side

Step 2:
$$0.17x + 180 + (-180) = 690 + (-180)$$ Add -180 to each side
$$0.17x = 510$$

Step 3:
$$\frac{0.17x}{0.17} = \frac{510}{0.17}$$ Divide each side by 0.17
$$x = 3,000$$

Note that we divided each side of the equation by 0.17 to obtain the solution. This is still an application of the multiplication property of equality because dividing by 0.17 is equivalent to multiplying by $\frac{1}{0.17}$.

Method 2

Eliminating the decimals in the beginning.

$$0.08x + 0.09(x + 2{,}000) = 690 \qquad \text{\small\textit{Original equation}}$$

Step 1a: $\qquad 0.08x + 0.09x + 180 = 690 \qquad$ *Distributive property*

Step 1b:
$$\begin{cases} 100(0.08x + 0.09x + 180) = 100(690) & \text{\small\textit{Multiply both sides by 100}} \\ 8x + 9x + 18{,}000 = 69{,}000 \end{cases}$$

Step 1c: $\qquad 17x + 18{,}000 = 69{,}000 \qquad$ *Simplify the left side*

Step 2: $\qquad\qquad 17x = 51{,}000 \qquad$ *Add $-18{,}000$ to each side*

Step 3:
$$\begin{cases} \dfrac{17x}{17} = \dfrac{51{,}000}{17} & \text{\small\textit{Divide each side by 17}} \\ x = 3{,}000 \end{cases}$$

Substituting 3,000 for x in the original equation, we have

Step 4:
$$\begin{cases} 0.08(3{,}000) + 0.09(3{,}000 + 2{,}000) \overset{?}{=} 690 \\ 0.08(3{,}000) + 0.09(5{,}000) \overset{?}{=} 690 \end{cases}$$
$$240 + 450 \overset{?}{=} 690$$
$$690 = 690 \qquad \text{\small\textit{A true statement}} \quad \blacksquare$$

Example 5   Solve $7 - 3(2y + 1) = 16$.

SOLUTION   We begin by multiplying -3 times the sum of $2y$ and 1:

Step 1a: $\qquad 7 - 6y - 3 = 16 \qquad$ *Distributive property*

Step 1c: $\qquad -6y + 4 = 16 \qquad$ *Simplify the left side*

Step 2:
$$\begin{cases} -6y + 4 + (-4) = 16 + (-4) & \text{\small\textit{Add -4 to both sides}} \\ -6y = 12 \end{cases}$$

Step 3:
$$\begin{cases} -\dfrac{1}{6}(-6y) = -\dfrac{1}{6}(12) & \text{\small\textit{Multiply both sides by $-\dfrac{1}{6}$}} \\ y = -2 \end{cases}$$
$\blacksquare$

There are two things to notice about the example that follows: first, the distributive property is used to remove parentheses that are preceded by a negative sign, and, second, the addition property and the multiplication property are not shown in as much detail as in the previous examples.

Example 6   Solve $3(2x - 5) - (2x - 4) = 6 - (4x + 5)$.

SOLUTION   When we apply the distributive property to remove the grouping symbols and separate terms, we have to be careful with the signs. Remember, we can think of $-(2x - 4)$ as $-1(2x - 4)$, so that

$$-(2x - 4) = -1(2x - 4) = -2x + 4$$

It is not uncommon for students to make a mistake with this type of simplification and write the result as $-2x - 4$, which is incorrect. Here is the complete solution to our equation:

$$3(2x - 5) - (2x - 4) = 6 - (4x + 5) \qquad \text{\small\textit{Original equation}}$$

$$6x - 15 - 2x + 4 = 6 - 4x - 5 \qquad \textcolor{green}{\textit{Distributive property}}$$
$$4x - 11 = -4x + 1 \qquad \textcolor{green}{\textit{Simplify each side}}$$
$$8x - 11 = 1 \qquad \textcolor{green}{\textit{Add 4x to each side}}$$
$$8x = 12 \qquad \textcolor{green}{\textit{Add 11 to each side}}$$
$$x = \frac{12}{8} \qquad \textcolor{green}{\textit{Multiply each side by } \frac{1}{8}}$$
$$x = \frac{3}{2} \qquad \textcolor{green}{\textit{Reduce to lowest terms}}$$

The solution, $\frac{3}{2}$, checks when replacing x in the original equation. ◼

Identities and Equations With No Solution

There are two special cases associated with solving linear equations in one variable, which are illustrated in the following examples.

Example 7   Solve for x: $2(3x - 4) = 3 + 6x$

SOLUTION   Applying the distributive property to the left side gives us

$$6x - 8 = 3 + 6x \qquad \textcolor{green}{\textit{Distributive property}}$$

Now, if we add $-6x$ to each side, we are left with

$$-8 = 3$$

which is a false statement. This means that there is no solution to our equation. Any number we substitute for x in the original equation will lead to a similar false statement. ◼

Example 8   Solve for x: $-15 + 3x = 3(x - 5)$

SOLUTION   We start by applying the distributive property to the right side.

$$-15 + 3x = 3x - 15 \qquad \textcolor{green}{\textit{Distributive property}}$$

If we add $-3x$ to each side, we are left with the true statement

$$-15 = -15$$

In this case, our result tells us that any number we use in place of x in the original equation will lead to a true statement. Therefore, all real numbers are solutions to our equation. We say the original equation is an *identity* because the left side is always identically equal to the right side. ◼

Getting Ready for Class

After reading through the preceding section, respond in your own words and in complete sentences.

A. What is the first step in solving a linear equation containing parentheses?

B. What is the last step in solving a linear equation?

C. Explain in words how you would solve the equation $2x - 3 = 8$.

D. If an equation contains decimals, what can you do to eliminate the decimals?

Problem Set 1.4

Solve each of the following equations using the four steps shown in this section.

1. $2(x + 3) = 12$ **2.** $3(x - 2) = 6$ **3.** $6(x - 1) = -18$

4. $4(x + 5) = 16$ **5.** $2(4a + 1) = -6$ **6.** $3(2a - 4) = 12$

7. $14 = 2(5x - 3)$ **8.** $-25 = 5(3x + 4)$ **9.** $-2(3y + 5) = 14$

10. $-3(2y - 4) = -6$ **11.** $-5(2a + 4) = 0$ **12.** $-3(3a - 6) = 0$

13. $1 = \frac{1}{2}(4x + 2)$ **14.** $1 = \frac{1}{3}(6x + 3)$ **15.** $3(t - 4) + 5 = -4$

16. $5(t - 1) + 6 = -9$

Solve each equation.

17. $4(2x + 1) - 7 = 1$ **18.** $6(3y + 2) - 8 = -2$

19. $\frac{1}{2}(x - 3) = \frac{1}{4}(x + 1)$ **20.** $\frac{1}{3}(x - 4) = \frac{1}{2}(x - 6)$

21. $-0.7(2x - 7) = 0.3(11 - 4x)$ **22.** $-0.3(2x - 5) = 0.7(3 - x)$

23. $-2(3y + 1) = 3(1 - 6y) - 9$ **24.** $-5(4y - 3) = 2(1 - 8y) + 11$

25. $\frac{3}{4}(8x - 4) + 3 = \frac{2}{5}(5x + 10) - 1$ **26.** $\frac{5}{6}(6x + 12) + 1 = \frac{2}{3}(9x - 3) + 5$

27. $0.06x + 0.08(100 - x) = 6.5$ **28.** $0.05x + 0.07(100 - x) = 6.2$

29. $6 - 5(2a - 3) = 1$ **30.** $-8 - 2(3 - a) = 0$

31. $0.2x - 0.5 = 0.5 - 0.2(2x - 13)$ **32.** $0.4x - 0.1 = 0.7 - 0.3(6 - 2x)$

33. $2(t - 3) + 3(t - 2) = 28$ **34.** $-3(t - 5) - 2(2t + 1) = -8$

35. $5(x - 2) - (3x + 4) = 3(6x - 8) + 10$

36. $3(x - 1) - (4x - 5) = 2(5x - 1) - 7$

37. $2(5x - 3) - (2x - 4) = 5 - (6x + 1)$

38. $3(4x - 2) - (5x - 8) = 8 - (2x + 3)$

39. $-(3x + 1) - (4x - 7) = 4 - (3x + 2)$

40. $-(6x + 2) - (8x - 3) = 8 - (5x + 1)$

41. $x + (2x - 1) = 2$ **42.** $x + (5x + 2) = 20$

43. $x - (3x + 5) = -3$ **44.** $x - (4x - 1) = 7$

45. $15 = 3(x - 1)$ **46.** $12 = 4(x - 5)$

47. $4x - (-4x + 1) = 5$ **48.** $-2x - (4x - 8) = -1$

49. $5x - 8(2x - 5) = 7$ **50.** $3x + 4(8x - 15) = 10$

51. $7(2y - 1) - 6y = -1$ **52.** $4(4y - 3) + 2y = 3$

53. $0.2x + 0.5(12 - x) = 3.6$ **54.** $0.3x + 0.6(25 - x) = 12$

55. $0.5x + 0.2(18 - x) = 5.4$ **56.** $0.1x + 0.5(40 - x) = 32$

57. $x + (x + 3)(-3) = x - 3$ **58.** $x - 2(x + 2) = x - 2$

59. $5(x + 2) + 3(x - 1) = -9$ **60.** $4(x + 1) + 3(x - 3) = 2$

61. $3(x - 3) + 2(2x) = 5$ **62.** $2(x - 2) + 3(5x) = 30$

63. $5(y + 2) = 4(y + 1)$ **64.** $3(y - 3) = 2(y - 2)$

65. $3x + 2(x - 2) = 6$ **66.** $5x - (x - 5) = 25$

67. $50(x - 5) = 30(x + 5)$ **68.** $34(x - 2) = 26(x + 2)$

69. $0.08x + 0.09(x + 2{,}000) = 860$ **70.** $0.11x + 0.12(x + 4{,}000) = 940$

71. $0.10x + 0.12(x + 500) = 214$ **72.** $0.08x + 0.06(x + 800) = 104$

73. $5x + 10(x + 8) = 245$ **74.** $5x + 10(x + 7) = 175$

75. $5x + 10(x + 3) + 25(x + 5) = 435$ **76.** $5(x + 3) + 10x + 25(x + 7) = 390$

Solve each equation, if possible.

77. $3x - 6 = 3(x + 4)$ **78.** $4y + 2 - 3y + 5 = 3 + y + 4$

79. $2(4t - 1) + 3 = 5t + 4 + 3t$ **80.** $7x - 3(x - 2) = -4(5 - x)$

The next two problems are intended to give you practice reading, and paying attention to, the instructions that accompany the problems you are working. Working these problems is an excellent way to get ready for a test or a quiz.

81. Paying Attention to Instructions Work each problem according to the instructions given.

   a. Solve: $4x - 5 = 0$
   b. Solve: $4x - 5 = 25$
   c. Add: $(4x - 5) + (2x + 25)$
   d. Solve: $4x - 5 = 2x + 25$
   e. Multiply: $4(x - 5)$
   f. Solve: $4(x - 5) = 2x + 25$

82. Paying Attention to Instructions Work each problem according to the instructions given.

   a. Solve: $3x + 6 = 0$
   b. Solve: $3x + 6 = 4$
   c. Add: $(3x + 6) + (7x + 4)$
   d. Solve: $3x + 6 = 7x + 4$
   e. Multiply: $3(x + 6)$
   f. Solve: $3(x + 6) = 7x + 4$

Getting Ready for the Next Section

To understand all of the explanations and examples in the next section you must be able to work the problems below.

Solve each equation.

83. $40 = 2x + 12$ **84.** $80 = 2x + 12$ **85.** $12 + 2y = 6$ **86.** $3x + 18 = 6$

87. $24x = 6$ **88.** $45 = 0.75x$ **89.** $70 = x \cdot 210$ **90.** $15 = x \cdot 80$

Apply the distributive property.

91. $\frac{1}{2}(-3x + 6)$

92. $-\frac{1}{4}(-5x + 20)$

Formulas

In this section we continue solving equations by working with formulas. To begin, here is the definition of a formula.

> ⟮dĕf′⟯ **formula**
>
> In mathematics, a **formula** is an equation that contains more than one variable.

The equation $P = 2l + 2w$, which tells us how to find the perimeter of a rectangle, is an example of a formula.

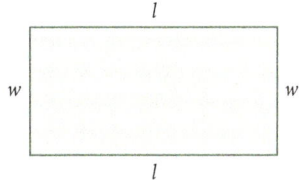

To begin our work with formulas, we will consider some examples in which we are given numerical replacements for all but one of the variables.

Video Examples

Section 1.5

Example 1   The perimeter P of a rectangular livestock pen is 40 feet. If the width w is 6 feet, find the length.

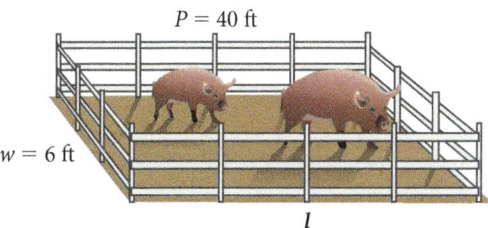

SOLUTION   First we substitute 40 for P and 6 for w in the formula $P = 2l + 2w$. Then we solve for l:

When $P = 40$ and $w = 6$

the formula $P = 2l + 2w$

becomes $40 = 2l + 2(6)$

or $40 = 2l + 12$ Multiply 2 and 6

                        $28 = 2l$ Add -12 to each side

                        $14 = l$ Multiply each side by $\frac{1}{2}$

To summarize our results, if a rectangular pen has a perimeter of 40 feet and a width of 6 feet, then the length must be 14 feet. ■

Example 2   Find y when $x = 4$ in the formula $3x + 2y = 6$.

SOLUTION   We substitute 4 for x in the formula and then solve for y:

When	$x = 4$	
the formula	$3x + 2y = 6$	
becomes	$3(4) + 2y = 6$	
or	$12 + 2y = 6$	Multiply 3 and 4
	$2y = -6$	Add -12 to each side
	$y = -3$	Multiply each side by $\frac{1}{2}$

In the next examples we will solve a formula for one of its variables without being given numerical replacements for the other variables.

   Consider the formula for the area of a triangle:

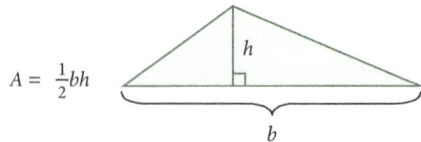

$A = \frac{1}{2}bh$

where A = area, b = length of the base, and h = height of the triangle.

   Suppose we want to solve this formula for h. What we must do is isolate the variable h on one side of the equal sign. We begin by multiplying both sides by 2, because it is the reciprocal of $\frac{1}{2}$:

$$2 \cdot A = 2 \cdot \frac{1}{2}bh$$

$$2A = bh$$

Then we divide both sides by b:

$$\frac{2A}{b} = \frac{bh}{b}$$

$$h = \frac{2A}{b}$$

The original formula $A = \frac{1}{2}bh$ and the final formula $h = \frac{2A}{b}$ both give the same relationship among A, b, and h. The first one has been solved for A and the second one has been solved for h.

⎡Δ≠Σ   Rule

To solve a formula for one of its **variables**, we must isolate that variable on one side of the equal sign. All other variables and constants will appear on the other side.

Example 3   Solve $3x + 2y = 6$ for y.

SOLUTION   To solve for y, we must isolate y on the left side of the equation. To begin, we use the addition property of equality to add $-3x$ to each side:

$$3x + 2y = 6 \qquad \text{\textit{Original formula}}$$

$$3x + (-3x) + 2y = (-3x) + 6 \qquad \text{\textit{Add} } -3x \text{ \textit{to each side}}$$

$$2y = -3x + 6 \qquad \text{\textit{Simplify the left side}}$$

$$\frac{1}{2}(2y) = \frac{1}{2}(-3x + 6) \qquad \text{\textit{Multiply each side by} } \frac{1}{2}$$

$$y = -\frac{3}{2}x + 3 \qquad \text{\textit{Multiplication}}$$

Example 4   Solve $h = vt - 16t^2$ for v.

SOLUTION   Let's begin by interchanging the left and right sides of the equation. That way, the variable we are solving for, v, will be on the left side.

$$vt - 16t^2 = h \qquad \text{\textit{Exchange sides}}$$

$$vt - 16t^2 + 16t^2 = h + 16t^2 \qquad \text{\textit{Add} } 16t^2 \text{ \textit{to each side}}$$

$$vt = h + 16t^2$$

$$\frac{vt}{t} = \frac{h + 16t^2}{t} \qquad \text{\textit{Divide each side by} } t$$

$$v = \frac{h + 16t^2}{t}$$

We know we are finished because we have isolated the variable we are solving for on the left side of the equation and it does not appear on the other side.

Example 5   Solve for y: $\dfrac{y - 1}{x} = \dfrac{3}{2}$.

SOLUTION   Although we will do more extensive work with formulas of this form later in the book, we need to know how to solve this particular formula for y in order to understand some things in the next chapter. We begin by multiplying each side of the formula by x. Doing so will simplify the left side of the equation, and make the rest of the solution process simple.

$$\frac{y - 1}{x} = \frac{3}{2} \qquad \text{\textit{Original formula}}$$

$$x \cdot \frac{y - 1}{x} = \frac{3}{2} \cdot x \qquad \text{\textit{Multiply each side by} } x$$

$$y - 1 = \frac{3}{2}x \qquad \text{\textit{Simplify each side}}$$

$$y = \frac{3}{2}x + 1 \qquad \text{\textit{Add 1 to each side}}$$

This is our solution. If we look back to the first step, we can justify our result on the left side of the equation this way: Dividing by x is equivalent to multiplying by its reciprocal $\frac{1}{x}$. Here is what it looks like when written out completely:

$$x \cdot \frac{y - 1}{x} = x \frac{1}{x}(y - 1) = 1(y - 1) = (y - 1)$$

> ### More on Complementary and Supplementary Angles
>
> In Chapter 1 we defined complementary angles as angles that add to 90°; that is, if x and y are complementary angles, then
>
> $$x + y = 90°$$
>
> If we solve this formula for y, we obtain a formula equivalent to our original formula:
>
> $$y = 90° - x$$
>
> Because y is the complement of x, we can generalize by saying that the complement of angle x is the angle $90° - x$. By a similar reasoning process, we can say that the supplement of angle x is the angle $180° - x$. To summarize, if x is an angle, then
>
> > The complement of x is $90° - x$, and
> >
> > The supplement of x is $180° - x$
>
> If you go on to take a trigonometry class, you will see this formula again.

Example 6   Find the complement and the supplement of 25°.

SOLUTION   We can use the formulas $90° - x$ and $180° - x$.

The complement of 25° is $90° - 25° = 65°$.

The supplement of 25° is $180° - 25° = 155°$.

Basic Percent Problems

The next examples in this section show how basic percent problems can be translated directly into equations. To understand these examples, you must recall that *percent* means "per hundred" that is, 75% is the same as $\frac{75}{100}$, 0.75, and, in reduced fraction form, $\frac{3}{4}$. Likewise, the decimal 0.25 is equivalent to 25%. To change a decimal to a percent, we move the decimal point two places to the right and write the % symbol. To change from a percent to a decimal, we drop the % symbol and move the decimal point two places to the left. The table that follows gives some of the most commonly used fractions and decimals and their equivalent percents.

Fraction	Decimal	Percent
$\frac{1}{2}$	0.5	50%
$\frac{1}{4}$	0.25	25%
$\frac{3}{4}$	0.75	75%
$\frac{1}{3}$	$0.33\frac{1}{3}$	$33\frac{1}{3}\%$
$\frac{2}{3}$	$0.66\frac{2}{3}$	$66\frac{2}{3}\%$
$\frac{1}{5}$	0.2	20%
$\frac{2}{5}$	0.4	40%

■ **Example 7** What number is 25% of 60?

SOLUTION To solve a problem like this, we let x = the number in question (that is, the number we are looking for). Then, we translate the sentence directly into an equation by using an equal sign for the word "is" and multiplication for the word "of." Here is how it is done:

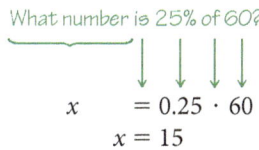

$$x = 0.25 \cdot 60$$
$$x = 15$$

Notice that we must write 25% as a decimal in order to do the arithmetic in the problem.

The number 15 is 25% of 60.

■

■ **Example 8** What percent of 24 is 6?

SOLUTION Translating this sentence into an equation, as we did in Example 7, we have:

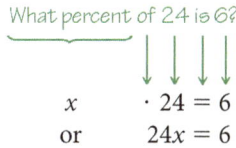

$$x \qquad \cdot 24 = 6$$
$$\text{or} \qquad 24x = 6$$

Next, we multiply each side by $\frac{1}{24}$. (This is the same as dividing each side by 24.)

$$\frac{1}{24}(24x) = \frac{1}{24}(6)$$

$$x = \frac{6}{24}$$

$$= \frac{1}{4}$$

$$= 0.25, \text{ or } 25\%$$

25% of 24 is 6, or in other words, the number 6 is 25% of 24.

■

■ **Example 9** 45 is 75% of what number?

SOLUTION Again, we translate the sentence directly:

$$45 = 0.75 \cdot \qquad x$$

Next, we multiply each side by $\frac{1}{0.75}$ (which is the same as dividing each side by 0.75):

$$\frac{1}{0.75}(45) = \frac{1}{0.75}(0.75x)$$

$$\frac{45}{0.75} = x$$

$$60 = x$$

The number 45 is 75% of 60.

■

Example 10   The American Dietetic Association (ADA) recommends eating foods in which the calories from fat are less than 30% of the total calories. The nutrition labels from two kinds of granola bars are shown in Figure 1. For each bar, what percent of the total calories come from fat?

BAR I

Nutrition Facts
Serving Size 2 bars (47g)
Servings Per Container 6

Amount Per Serving

Calories 210	
Calories from Fat	70

% Daily Value*

Total Fat 8g	**12%**
Saturated Fat 1g	**5%**
Cholesterol 0mg	**0%**
Sodium 150mg	**6%**
Total Carbohydrate 32g	**11%**
Dietary Fiber 2g	**10%**
Sugars 12g	
Protein 4g	

* Percent Daily Values are based on a 2,000 calorie diet. Your daily values may be higher or lower depending on your calorie needs.

BAR II

Nutrition Facts
Serving Size 1 bar (21g)
Servings Per Container 8

Amount Per Serving

Calories 80	
Calories from Fat	15

% Daily Value*

Total Fat 1.5g	**2%**
Saturated Fat 0g	**0%**
Cholesterol 0mg	**0%**
Sodium 60mg	**3%**
Total Carbohydrate 16g	**5%**
Dietary Fiber 1g	**4%**
Sugars 5g	
Protein 2g	

* Percent Daily Values are based on a 2,000 calorie diet. Your daily values may be higher or lower depending on your calorie needs.

FIGURE 1

SOLUTION   The information needed to solve this problem is located towards the top of each label. Each serving of Bar I contains 210 calories, of which 70 calories come from fat. To find the percent of total calories that come from fat, we must answer this question:

70 is what percent of 210?

For Bar II, one serving contains 80 calories, of which 15 calories come from fat. To find the percent of total calories that come from fat, we must answer this question:

15 is what percent of 80?

Translating each equation into symbols, we have

70 is what percent of 210	15 is what percent of 80
$70 = x \cdot 210$	$15 = x \cdot 80$
$x = \dfrac{70}{210}$	$x = \dfrac{15}{80}$
$x = 0.33$ to the nearest hundredth	$x = 0.19$ to the nearest hundredth
$x = 33\%$	$x = 19\%$

Comparing the two bars, 33% of the calories in Bar I are fat calories, whereas 19% of the calories in Bar II are fat calories. According to the ADA, Bar II is the healthier choice.

Applying the Concepts

As we mentioned before, in the U.S. system, temperature is measured on the Fahrenheit scale. In the metric system, temperature is measured on the Celsius scale. On the Celsius scale, water boils at 100 degrees and freezes at 0 degrees. To denote a temperature of 100 degrees on the Celsius scale, we write

100°C, which is read "100 degrees Celsius"

Table 1 is intended to give you an intuitive idea of the relationship between the two temperature scales. Table 2 gives the formulas, in both symbols and words, that are used to convert between the two scales.

Table 1

Situation	Temperature	
	Fahrenheit	Celsius
Water freezes	32°F	0°C
Room temperature	68°F	20°C
Normal body temperature	98.6°F	37°C
Water boils	212°F	100°C

Table 2

To Convert from	Formula in Symbols	Formula in Words
Fahrenheit to Celsius	$C = \dfrac{5}{9}(F - 32)$	Subtract 32, multiply by 5, then divide by 9
Celsius to Fahrenheit	$F = \dfrac{9}{5}C + 32$	Multiply by $\dfrac{9}{5}$, then add 32

Example 11   Mr. McKeague traveled to Buenos Aires with a group of friends. It was a hot day when they arrived. One of the bank kiosks indicated the temperature was 25°C. Someone asked what that would be on the Fahrenheit scale (the scale they were familiar with), and Budd, one of his friends said, "just multiply by 2 and add 30."

©Nikada/iStockPhoto.com

a. What was the temperature in °F according to Budd's approximation?

b. What is the actual temperature in °F?

c. Why does Budd's estimate work?

d. Write a formula for Budd's estimate.

SOLUTION

a. According to Budd, we multiply by 2 and add 30, so

$$2 \cdot 25 + 30 = 50 + 30 = 80°F$$

b. Using the formula $F = \dfrac{9}{5}C + 32$, with C = 25, we have

$$F = \dfrac{9}{5}(25) + 32 = 45 + 32 = 77°F$$

c. Budd's estimate works because $\dfrac{9}{5}$ is approximately 2 and 30 is close to 32.

d. In symbols, Budd's estimate is $F = 2 \cdot C + 30$.

Getting Ready for Class

After reading through the preceding section, respond in your own words and in complete sentences.

A. What is a formula?

B. How do you solve a formula for one of its variables?

C. What are complementary angles?

D. What does percent mean?

Use the formula $P = 2l + 2w$ to find the length l of a rectangular lot if

1. The width w is 50 feet and the perimeter P is 300 feet.
2. The width w is 75 feet and the perimeter P is 300 feet.

Use the formula $2x + 3y = 6$ to find y when

3. x is 3	**4.** x is -2	**5.** x is 0	**6.** x is -3

Use the formula $2x - 5y = 20$ to find x when

7. y is 2	**8.** y is -4	**9.** y is 0	**10.** y is -6

Use the equation $y = (x + 1)^2 - 3$ to find the value of y when

11. $x = -2$	**12.** $x = -1$	**13.** $x = 1$	**14.** $x = 2$

15. Use the formula $y = \dfrac{20}{x}$ to find y when

    a. $x = 10$ **b.** $x = 5$

16. Use the formula $y = 2x^2$ to find y when

    a. $x = 5$ **b.** $x = -6$

17. Use the formula $y = Kx$ to find K when

    a. $y = 15$ and $x = 3$ **b.** $y = 72$ and $x = 4$

18. Use the formula $y = Kx^2$ to find K when

    a. $y = 32$ and $x = 4$ **b.** $y = 45$ and $x = 3$

Solve each of the following for the indicated variable.

19. $A = lw$ for l	**20.** $d = rt$ for r
21. $V = lwh$ for h	**22.** $PV = nRT$ for P
23. $P = a + b + c$ for a	**24.** $P = a + b + c$ for b
25. $x - 3y = -1$ for x	**26.** $x + 3y = 2$ for x
27. $-3x + y = 6$ for y	**28.** $2x + y = -17$ for y
29. $2x + 3y = 6$ for y	**30.** $4x + 5y = 20$ for y
31. $y - 3 = -2(x + 4)$ for y	**32.** $y + 5 = 2(x + 2)$ for y
33. $y - 3 = -\dfrac{2}{3}(x + 3)$ for y	**34.** $y - 1 = -\dfrac{1}{2}(x + 4)$ for y
35. $P = 2l + 2w$ for w	**36.** $P = 2l + 2w$ for l
37. $h = vt + 16t^2$ for v	**38.** $h = vt - 16t^2$ for v
39. $A = \pi r^2 + 2\pi rh$ for h	**40.** $A = 2\pi r^2 + 2\pi rh$ for h

41. Solve for y.

    a. $\dfrac{y - 1}{x} = \dfrac{3}{5}$ **b.** $\dfrac{y - 2}{x} = \dfrac{1}{2}$ **c.** $\dfrac{y - 3}{x} = 4$

42. Solve for y.

a. $\dfrac{y+1}{x} = -\dfrac{3}{5}$ 　　　 b. $\dfrac{y+2}{x} = -\dfrac{1}{2}$ 　　　 c. $\dfrac{y+3}{x} = -4$

Solve each formula for y.

43. $\dfrac{x}{7} - \dfrac{y}{3} = 1$ 　　　　　　 **44.** $\dfrac{x}{5} - \dfrac{y}{9} = 1$

45. $-\dfrac{1}{4}x + \dfrac{1}{8}y = 1$ 　　　　　 **46.** $-\dfrac{1}{9}x + \dfrac{1}{3}y = 1$

Find the complement and the supplement of each angle.

47. $30°$ 　　　　 **48.** $60°$ 　　　　 **49.** $45°$ 　　　　 **50.** $15°$

Translate each of the following into an equation, and then solve that equation.

51. What number is 25% of 40?

52. What number is 75% of 40?

53. What number is 12% of 2,000?

54. What number is 9% of 3,000?

55. What percent of 28 is 7?

56. What percent of 28 is 21?

57. What percent of 40 is 14?

58. What percent of 20 is 14?

59. 32 is 50% of what number?

60. 16 is 50% of what number?

61. 240 is 12% of what number?

62. 360 is 12% of what number?

63. Let F = 212 in the formula C = $\frac{5}{9}$(F − 32), and solve for C. Does the value of C agree with the information in Table 1?

64. Let C = 100 in the formula F = $\frac{9}{5}$C + 32, and solve for F. Does the value of F agree with the information in Table 1?

65. Let F = 68 in the formula C = $\frac{5}{9}$(F − 32), and solve for C. Does the value of C agree with the information in Table 1?

66. Let C = 37 in the formula F = $\frac{9}{5}$C + 32, and solve for F. Does the value of F agree with the information in Table 1?

67. Solve the formula F = $\frac{9}{5}$C + 32 for C.

68. Solve the formula C = $\frac{5}{9}$(F − 32) for F.

69. How far off is Budd's estimate when the temperature is 30°C? (See Example 11)

70. How far off is Budd's estimate when the temperature is 0°C? (See Example 11)

Circumference The circumference of a circle is given by the formula $C = 2\pi r$. Find r if

71. The circumference C is 44 meters and π is $\frac{22}{7}$

72. The circumference C is 176 meters and π is $\frac{22}{7}$

73. The circumference is 9.42 inches and π is 3.14

74. The circumference is 12.56 inches and π is 3.14

Volume The volume of a cylinder is given by the formula $V = \pi r^2 h$. Find the height h if

75. The volume V is 42 cubic feet, the radius is $\frac{7}{22}$ feet, and π is $\frac{22}{7}$

76. The volume V is 84 cubic inches, the radius is $\frac{7}{11}$ inches, and π is $\frac{22}{7}$

77. The volume is 6.28 cubic centimeters, the radius is 3 centimeters, and π is 3.14.

78. The volume is 12.56 cubic centimeters, the radius is 2 centimeters, and π is 3.14.

Nutrition Labels The nutrition label in Figure 2 is from a quart of vanilla ice cream. The label in Figure 3 is from a pint of vanilla frozen yogurt. Use the information on these labels for problems 79–82. Round your answers to the nearest tenth of a percent.

Nutrition Facts	
Serving Size 1/2 cup (65g)	
Servings 8	
Amount/Serving	
Calories 150	Calories from Fat 90
	% Daily Value*
Total Fat 10g	**16%**
Saturated Fat 6g	**32%**
Cholesterol 35mg	**12%**
Sodium 30mg	**1%**
Total Carbohydrate 14g	**5%**
Dietary Fiber 0g	**0%**
Sugars 11g	
Protein 2g	
Vitamin A 6% • Vitamin C 0%	
Calcium 6% • Iron 0%	
* Percent Daily Values are based on a 2,000 calorie diet.	

FIGURE 2   *Vanilla ice cream*

Nutrition Facts	
Serving Size 1/2 cup (98g)	
Servings Per Container 4	
Amount Per Serving	
Calories 160	Calories from Fat 25
	% Daily Value*
Total Fat 2.5g	**4%**
Saturated Fat 1.5g	**7%**
Cholesterol 45mg	**15%**
Sodium 55mg	**2%**
Total Carbohydrate 26g	**9%**
Dietary Fiber 0g	**0%**
Sugars 19g	
Protein 8g	
Vitamin A 0% • Vitamin C 0%	
Calcium 25% • Iron 0%	
* Percent Daily Values are based on a 2,000 calorie diet.	

FIGURE 3   *Vanilla frozen yogurt*

79. What percent of the calories in one serving of the vanilla ice cream are fat calories?

80. What percent of the calories in one serving of the frozen yogurt are fat calories?

81. One serving of frozen yogurt is 98 grams, of which 26 grams are carbohydrates. What percent of one serving are carbohydrates?

82. One serving of vanilla ice cream is 65 grams. What percent of one serving is sugar?

Getting Ready for the Next Section

To understand all of the explanations and examples in the next section you must be able to work the problems below.

Write an equivalent expression in English. Include the words *sum* and *difference* when possible.

83. $4 + 1 = 5$ **84.** $7 + 3 = 10$ **85.** $6 - 2 = 4$ **86.** $8 - 1 = 7$

87. $x - 15 = -12$ **88.** $2x + 3 = 7$

89. $x + 3 = 4(x - 3)$ **90.** $2(2x - 5) = 2x - 34$

For each of the following expressions, write an equivalent equation.

91. Twice the sum of 6 and 3 is 18.

92. Four added to the product of 5 and -1 is -1.

93. The sum of twice 5 and 3 is 13.

94. Twice the difference of 8 and 2 is 12.

95. The sum of a number and five is thirteen.

96. The difference of ten and a number is negative eight.

97. Five times the sum of a number and seven is thirty.

98. Five times the difference of twice a number and six is negative twenty.

Applications

As you begin reading through the examples in this section, you may find yourself asking why some of these problems seem so contrived. The title of the section is "Applications," but many of the problems here don't seem to have much to do with "real life." Example 3 is what we refer to as an "age problem." But imagine a conversation in which you ask someone how old her children are and she replies, "Bill is 6 years older than Tom. Three years ago the sum of their ages was 21. You figure it out." Although many of the "application" problems in this section are unrealistic, they are also good for practicing the strategy we will use to solve all application problems.

To begin this section, we list the steps used in solving application problems. We call this strategy the *Blueprint for Problem Solving*. It is an outline that will overlay the solution process we use on all application problems.

BLUEPRINT FOR PROBLEM SOLVING

Step 1: *Read* the problem, and then mentally *list* the items that are known and the items that are unknown.

Step 2: *Assign a variable* to one of the unknown items. (In most cases this will amount to letting x = the item that is asked for in the problem.) Then *translate* the other *information* in the problem to expressions involving the variable.

Step 3: *Reread* the problem, and then *write an equation*, using the items and variables listed in steps 1 and 2, that describes the situation.

Step 4: *Solve the equation* found in step 3.

Step 5: *Write* your *answer* using a complete sentence.

Step 6: *Reread* the problem, and *check* your solution with the original words in the problem.

There are a number of substeps within each of the steps in our blueprint. For instance, with steps 1 and 2 it is always a good idea to draw a diagram or picture if it helps visualize the relationship between the items in the problem. In other cases a table helps organize the information. As you gain more experience using the blueprint to solve application problems, you will find additional techniques that expand the blueprint.

To help with problems of the type shown next in Example 1, here are some common English words and phrases and their mathematical translations.

English	Algebra
The sum of a and b	$a + b$
The difference of a and b	$a - b$
The product of a and b	$a \cdot b$
The quotient of a and b	$\frac{a}{b}$
of	$\cdot$ (multiply)
is	= (equals)
A number	x
4 more than x	$x + 4$
4 times x	$4x$
4 less than x	$x - 4$

Number Problems

Video Examples

Section 1.6

Example 1   The sum of twice a number and three is seven. Find the number.

SOLUTION   Using the Blueprint for Problem Solving as an outline, we solve the problem as follows:

Step 1:   **Read** the problem, and then mentally **list** the items that are known and the items that are unknown.

Known items: The numbers 3 and 7

Unknown items: The number in question

Step 2:   **Assign a variable** to one of the unknown items. Then **translate** the other **information** in the problem to expressions involving the variable.

Let x = the number asked for in the problem, then "The sum of twice a number and three" translates to $2x + 3$.

Step 3:   **Reread** the problem, and then **write an equation,** using the items and variables listed in steps 1 and 2, that describes the situation.
With all word problems, the word *is* translates to $=$.

The sum of twice x and 3 is 7

$$2x + 3 \qquad = 7$$

Step 4:   **Solve the equation** found in step 3.

$$2x + 3 = 7$$
$$2x + 3 + (-3) = 7 + (-3)$$
$$2x = 4$$
$$\frac{1}{2}(2x) = \frac{1}{2}(4)$$
$$x = 2$$

Step 5:   **Write** your **answer** using a complete sentence.

The number is 2.

Step 6:   **Reread** the problem, and **check** your solution with the original words in the problem.

The sum of twice 2 and 3 is 7; a true statement.

You may find some examples and problems in this section that you can solve without using algebra or our blueprint. It is very important that you solve these problems using the methods we are showing here. The purpose behind these problems is to give you experience using the blueprint as a guide to solving problems written in words. Your answers are much less important than the work that you show to obtain your answer. You will be able to condense the steps in the blueprint later in the course. For now, though, you need to show your work in the same detail that we are showing in the examples in this section.

Example 2   One number is three more than twice another; their sum is eighteen. Find the numbers.

SOLUTION

Step 1: Read and list.

Known items: Two numbers that add to 18. One is 3 more than twice the other.

Unknown items: The numbers in question.

Step 2: Assign a variable, and translate information.
Let x = the first number. The other is $2x + 3$.

Step 3: Reread, and write an equation.

Their sum   is 18

$x + (2x + 3) = 18$

Step 4: Solve the equation.

$$x + (2x + 3) = 18$$
$$3x + 3 = 18$$
$$3x + 3 + (-3) = 18 + (-3)$$
$$3x = 15$$
$$x = 5$$

Step 5: Write the answer.
The first number is 5. The other is $2 \cdot 5 + 3 = 13$.

Step 6: Reread, and check.
The sum of 5 and 13 is 18, and 13 is 3 more than twice 5.

Age Problem

Remember as you read through the steps in the solutions to the examples in this section that Step 1 is done mentally. Read the problem, and then mentally list the items that you know and the items that you don't know. The purpose of step 1 is to give you direction as you begin to work application problems. Finding the solution to an application problem is a process; it doesn't happen all at once. The first step is to read the problem with a purpose in mind. That purpose is to mentally note the items that are known and the items that are unknown.

Example 3   Bill is 6 years older than Tom. Three years ago Bill's age was four times Tom's age. Find the age of each boy now.

SOLUTION   Applying the Blueprint for Problem Solving, we have

Step 1: Read and list.

Known items: Bill is 6 years older than Tom. Three years ago Bill's age was four times Tom's age.

Unknown items: Bill's age and Tom's age

Step 2: **Assign a variable, and translate information.**

Let x = Tom's age now. That makes Bill $x + 6$ years old now. A table like the one shown here can help organize the information in an age problem. Notice how we placed the x in the box that corresponds to Tom's age now.

	Three Years Ago	Now
Bill		$x + 6$
Tom		x

If Tom is x years old now, 3 years ago he was $x - 3$ years old. If Bill is $x + 6$ years old now, 3 years ago he was $x + 6 - 3 = x + 3$ years old. We use this information to fill in the remaining squares in the table.

	Three Years Ago	Now
Bill	$x + 3$	$x + 6$
Tom	$x - 3$	x

Step 3: **Reread, and write an equation.**

Reading the problem again, we see that 3 years ago Bill's age was four times Tom's age. Writing this as an equation, we have Bill's age 3 years ago = $4 \cdot$ (Tom's age 3 years ago):

$$x + 3 = 4(x - 3)$$

Step 4: **Solve the equation.**

$$x + 3 = 4(x - 3)$$
$$x + 3 = 4x - 12$$
$$x + (-x) + 3 = 4x + (-x) - 12$$
$$3 = 3x - 12$$
$$3 + 12 = 3x - 12 + 12$$
$$15 = 3x$$
$$x = 5$$

Step 5: **Write the answer.**

Tom is 5 years old. Bill is 11 years old.

Step 6: **Reread, and check.**

If Tom is 5 and Bill is 11, then Bill is 6 years older than Tom. Three years ago Tom was 2 and Bill was 8. At that time, Bill's age was four times Tom's age. As you can see, the answers check with the original problem.

Geometry Problem

To understand Example 4 completely, you need to recall from Chapter 1 that the perimeter of a rectangle is the sum of the lengths of the sides. The formula for the perimeter is $P = 2l + 2w$.

Example 4 The length of a rectangle is 5 inches more than twice the width. The perimeter is 34 inches. Find the length and width.

SOLUTION When working problems that involve geometric figures, a sketch of the figure helps organize and visualize the problem.

Step 1: Read and list.

  Known items: The figure is a rectangle. The length is 5 inches more than twice the width. The perimeter is 34 inches.

  Unknown items: The length and the width

Step 2: Assign a variable, and translate information.

  Because the length is given in terms of the width (the length is 5 more than twice the width), we let $x =$ the width of the rectangle. The length is 5 more than twice the width, so it must be $2x + 5$. The diagram below is a visual description of the relationships we have listed so far.

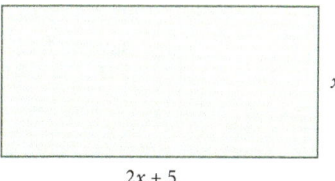

$$2x + 5$$

Step 3: Reread, and write an equation.

  The equation that describes the situation is

   Twice the length + twice the width is the perimeter

$$2(2x + 5) \quad + \quad 2x \quad = \quad 34$$

Step 4: Solve the equation.

$$2(2x + 5) + 2x = 34 \qquad \textit{Original equation}$$

$$4x + 10 + 2x = 34 \qquad \textit{Distributive property}$$

$$6x + 10 = 34 \qquad \textit{Add 4x and 2x}$$

$$6x = 24 \qquad \textit{Add} -10 \textit{ to each side}$$

$$x = 4 \qquad \textit{Divide each side by 6}$$

Step 5: Write the answer.

  The width x is 4 inches. The length is $2x + 5 = 2(4) + 5 = 13$ inches.

Step 6: Reread, and check.

  If the length is 13 and the width is 4, then the perimeter must be $2(13) + 2(4) = 26 + 8 = 34$, which checks with the original problem.

Coin Problem

■ **Example 5**   Jennifer has $2.45 in dimes and nickels. If she has 8 more dimes than nickels, how many of each coin does she have?

SOLUTION

Step 1: Read and list.
   Known items: The type of coins, the total value of the coins, and that there are 8 more dimes than nickels.
   Unknown items: The number of nickels and the number of dimes

Step 2: Assign a variable, and translate information.
   If we let x = the number of nickels, then $x + 8$ = the number of dimes. Because the value of each nickel is 5 cents, the amount of money in nickels is $5x$. Similarly, because each dime is worth 10 cents, the amount of money in dimes is $10(x + 8)$. Here is a table that summarizes the information we have so far:

	Nickels	Dimes
Number	x	$x + 8$
Value (in cents)	$5x$	$10(x + 8)$

Step 3: Reread, and write an equation.
   Because the total value of all the coins is 245 cents, the equation that describes this situation is

Amount of money in nickels		Amount of money in dimes		Total amount of money
$5x$	$+$	$10(x + 8)$	$=$	245

Step 4: Solve the equation.
   To solve the equation, we apply the distributive property first.

$$5x + 10x + 80 = 245 \qquad \text{Distributive property}$$
$$15x + 80 = 245 \qquad \text{Add } 5x \text{ and } 10x$$
$$15x = 165 \qquad \text{Add } -80 \text{ to each side}$$
$$x = 11 \qquad \text{Divide each side by } 15$$

Step 5: Write the answer.
   The number of nickels is $x = 11$.
   The number of dimes is $x + 8 = 11 + 8 = 19$.

Step 6: Reread, and check.
   To check our results

   11 nickels are worth $5(11) = $ 55 cents
   19 dimes are worth $10(19) = $ 190 cents
   The total value is 245 cents = $2.45

When you begin working the problems in the problem set that follows, there are a few things to remember. The first is that you may have to read the problems a number of times before you begin to see how to solve them. The second thing to remember is that word problems are not always solved correctly the first time you try them. Sometimes it takes a few attempts and some wrong answers before you can set up and solve these problems correctly.

Getting Ready for Class

After reading through the preceding section, respond in your own words and in complete sentences.

A. What is the first step in the Blueprint for Problem Solving?
B. What is the last thing you do when solving an application problem?
C. What good does it do you to solve application problems even when they don't have much to do with real life?
D. Write an application problem whose solution depends on solving the equation $2x + 3 = 7$.

SPOTLIGHT ON SUCCESS | *Student Instructor Cynthia*

Each time we face our fear, we gain strength, courage, and confidence in the doing.
—Unknown

I must admit, when it comes to math, it takes me longer to learn the material compared to other students. Because of that, I was afraid to ask questions, especially when it seemed like everyone else understood what was going on. Because I wasn't getting my questions answered, my quiz and exam scores were only getting worse. I realized that I was already paying a lot to go to college and that I couldn't afford to keep doing poorly on my exams. I learned how to overcome my fear of asking questions by studying the material before class, and working on extra problem sets until I was confident enough that at least I understood the main concepts. By preparing myself beforehand, I would often end up answering the question myself. Even when that wasn't the case, the professor knew that I tried to answer the question on my own. If you want to be successful, but you are afraid to ask a question, try putting in a little extra time working on problems before you ask your instructor for help. I think you will find, like I did, that it's not as bad as you imagined it, and you will have overcome an obstacle that was in the way of your success.

Solve the following word problems. Follow the steps given in the Blueprint for Problem Solving.

Number Problems

1. The sum of a number and five is thirteen. Find the number.

2. The difference of ten and a number is negative eight. Find the number.

3. The sum of twice a number and four is fourteen. Find the number.

4. The difference of four times a number and eight is sixteen. Find the number.

5. Five times the sum of a number and seven is thirty. Find the number.

6. Five times the difference of twice a number and six is negative twenty. Find the number.

7. One number is two more than another. Their sum is eight. Find both numbers.

8. One number is three less than another. Their sum is fifteen. Find the numbers.

9. One number is four less than three times another. If their sum is increased by five, the result is twenty-five. Find the numbers.

10. One number is five more than twice another. If their sum is decreased by ten, the result is twenty-two. Find the numbers.

Age Problems

11. Shelly is 3 years older than Michele. Four years ago the sum of their ages was 67. Find the age of each person now.

	Four Years Ago	Now
Shelly	$x - 1$	$x + 3$
Michele	$x - 4$	x

12. Cary is 9 years older than Dan. In 7 years the sum of their ages will be 93. Find the age of each man now. (Begin by filling in the table.)

	Now	In Seven Years
Cary	$x + 9$	
Dan	x	$x + 7$

13. Cody is twice as old as Evan. Three years ago the sum of their ages was 27. Find the age of each boy now.

	Three Years Ago	Now
Cody		
Evan	$x - 3$	x

14. Justin is 2 years older than Ethan. In 9 years the sum of their ages will be 30. Find the age of each boy now.

	Now	In Nine Years
Justin		
Ethan	x	

15. Fred is 4 years older than Barney. Five years ago the sum of their ages was 48. How old are they now?

	Five Years Ago	Now
Fred		
Barney		x

16. Tim is 5 years older than JoAnn. Six years from now the sum of their ages will be 79. How old are they now?

	Now	Six Years From Now
Tim		
JoAnn	x	

17. Jack is twice as old as Lacy. In 3 years the sum of their ages will be 54. How old are they now?

18. John is 4 times as old as Martha. Five years ago the sum of their ages was 50. How old are they now?

19. Pat is 20 years older than his son Patrick. In 2 years Pat will be twice as old as Patrick. How old are they now?

20. Diane is 23 years older than her daughter Amy. In 6 years Diane will be twice as old as Amy. How old are they now?

Geometry Problems

21. The perimeter of a square is 36 inches. Find the length of one side.

22. The perimeter of a square is 44 centimeters. Find the length of one side.

23. The perimeter of a square is 60 feet. Find the length of one side.

24. The perimeter of a square is 84 meters. Find the length of one side.

25. One side of a triangle is three times the shortest side. The third side is 7 feet more than the shortest side. The perimeter is 62 feet. Find all three sides.

26. One side of a triangle is half the longest side. The third side is 10 meters less than the longest side. The perimeter is 45 meters. Find all three sides.

27. One side of a triangle is half the longest side. The third side is 12 feet less than the longest side. The perimeter is 53 feet. Find all three sides.

28. One side of a triangle is 6 meters more than twice the shortest side. The third side is 9 meters more than the shortest side. The perimeter is 75 meters. Find all three sides.

29. The length of a rectangle is 5 inches more than the width. The perimeter is 34 inches. Find the length and width.

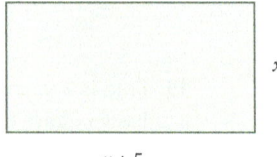

x

$x + 5$

30. The width of a rectangle is 3 feet less than the length. The perimeter is 10 feet. Find the length and width.

31. The length of a rectangle is 7 inches more than twice the width. The perimeter is 68 inches. Find the length and width.

32. The length of a rectangle is 4 inches more than three times the width. The perimeter is 72 inches. Find the length and width.

33. The length of a rectangle is 6 feet more than three times the width. The perimeter is 36 feet. Find the length and width.

34. The length of a rectangle is 3 feet less than twice the width. The perimeter is 54 feet. Find the length and width.

Coin Problems

35. Marissa has $4.40 in quarters and dimes. If she has 5 more quarters than dimes, how many of each coin does she have?

	Dimes	Quarters
Number	x	$x + 5$
Value (in cents)	$10(x)$	$25(x + 5)$

36. Kendra has $2.75 in dimes and nickels. If she has twice as many dimes as nickels, how many of each coin does she have?

	Nickels	Dimes
Number	x	$2x$
Value (in cents)	$5(x)$	

37. Tanner has $4.35 in nickels and quarters. If he has 15 more nickels than quarters, how many of each coin does he have?

	Nickels	Quarters
Number	$x + 15$	x
Value (in cents)		

38. Connor has $9.00 in dimes and quarters. If he has twice as many quarters as dimes, how many of each coin does he have?

	Dimes	Quarters
Number	x	$2x$
Value (in cents)		

39. Sue has $2.10 in dimes and nickels. If she has 9 more dimes than nickels, how many of each coin does she have? (Completing the table may help you get started.)

40. Mike has $1.55 in dimes and nickels. If he has 7 more nickels than dimes, how many of each coin does he have?

41. Katie has a collection of nickels, dimes, and quarters with a total value of $4.35. There are 3 more dimes than nickels and 5 more quarters than nickels. How many of each coin is in her collection? (*Hint:* Let x = the number of nickels.)

	Nickels	Dimes	Quarters
Number	x		
Value			

42. Mary Jo has $3.90 worth of nickels, dimes, and quarters. The number of nickels is 3 more than the number of dimes. The number of quarters is 7 more than the number of dimes. How many of each coin does she have? (*Hint:* Let x = the number of dimes.)

	Nickels	Dimes	Quarters
Number			
Value			

43. Cory has a collection of nickels, dimes, and quarters with a total value of $2.55. There are 6 more dimes than nickels and twice as many quarters as nickels. How many of each coin is in her collection?

	Nickels	Dimes	Quarters
Number	x		
Value			

44. Kelly has a collection of nickels, dimes, and quarters with a total value of $7.40. There are four more nickels than dimes and twice as many quarters as nickels. How many of each coin is in her collection?

	Nickels	Dimes	Quarters
Number			
Value			

Getting Ready for the Next Section

To understand all of the explanations and examples in the next section you must be able to work the problems below.

Simplify the following expressions.

45. $x + 2x + 2x$ **46.** $x + 2x + 3x$ **47.** $x + 0.075x$ **48.** $x + 0.065x$

49. $0.09(x + 2{,}000)$ **50.** $0.06(x + 1{,}500)$

51. $0.02x + 0.06(x + 1{,}500) = 570$ **52.** $0.08x + 0.09(x + 2{,}000) = 690$

53. $x + 2x + 3x = 180$ **54.** $2x + 3x + 5x = 180$

More Applications

Now that you have worked through a number of application problems using our blueprint, you probably have noticed that step 3, in which we write an equation that describes the situation, is the key step. Anyone with experience solving application problems will tell you that there will be times when your first attempt at step 3 results in the wrong equation. Remember, mistakes are part of the process of learning to do things correctly. Many times the correct equation will become obvious after you have written an equation that is partially wrong. In any case it is better to write an equation that is partially wrong and be actively involved with the problem than to write nothing at all. Application problems, like other problems in algebra, are not always solved correctly the first time.

Consecutive Integers

Our first example involves consecutive integers. When we ask for consecutive integers, we mean integers that are next to each other on the number line, like 5 and 6, or 13 and 14, or -4 and -3. In the dictionary, consecutive is defined as following one another in uninterrupted order. If we ask for consecutive odd integers, then we mean odd integers that follow one another on the number line. For example, 3 and 5, 11 and 13, and -9 and -7 are consecutive odd integers. As you can see, to get from one odd integer to the next consecutive odd integer we add 2.

If we are asked to find two consecutive integers and we let x equal the first integer, the next one must be $x + 1$, because consecutive integers always differ by 1. Likewise, if we are asked to find two consecutive odd or even integers, and we let x equal the first integer, then the next one will be $x + 2$ because consecutive even or odd integers always differ by 2. Here is a table that summarizes this information.

In Words	Using Algebra	Example
Two consecutive integers	$x, x + 1$	The sum of two consecutive integers is 15. $x + (x + 1) = 15$ or $7 + 8 = 15$
Three consecutive integers	$x, x + 1, x + 2$	The sum of three consecutive integers is 24. $x + (x + 1) + (x + 2) = 24$ or $7 + 8 + 9 = 24$
Two consecutive odd integers	$x, x + 2$	The sum of two consecutive odd integers is 16. $x + (x + 2) = 16$ or $7 + 9 = 16$
Two consecutive even integers	$x, x + 2$	The sum of two consecutive even integers is 18. $x + (x + 2) = 18$ or $8 + 10 = 18$

Video Examples

Section 1.7

Example 1 The sum of two consecutive odd integers is 28. Find the two integers.

SOLUTION

Step 1: Read and list.

Known items: Two consecutive odd integers. Their sum is equal to 28.
Unknown items: The numbers in question.

Step 2: **Assign a variable, and translate information.**
If we let x = the first of the two consecutive odd integers, then $x + 2$ is the next consecutive one.

Step 3: **Reread, and write an equation.**
Their sum is 28.

$$x + (x + 2) = 28$$

Step 4: **Solve the equation.**

$$2x + 2 = 28 \qquad \text{Simplify the left side}$$
$$2x = 26 \qquad \text{Add } -2 \text{ to each side}$$
$$x = 13 \qquad \text{Multiply each side by } \tfrac{1}{2}$$

Step 5: **Write the answer.**
The first of the two integers is 13. The second of the two integers will be two more than the first, which is 15.

Step 6: **Reread, and check.**
Suppose the first integer is 13. The next consecutive odd integer is 15. The sum of 15 and 13 is 28. ■

Interest

Example 2   Suppose you invest a certain amount of money in an account that earns 8% in annual interest. At the same time, you invest $2,000 more than that in an account that pays 9% in annual interest. If the total interest from both accounts at the end of the year is $690, how much is invested in each account?

SOLUTION

Step 1: **Read and list.**
Known items: The interest rates, the total interest earned, and how much more is invested at 9%
Unknown items: The amounts invested in each account

Step 2: **Assign a variable, and translate information.**
Let x = the amount of money invested at 8%. From this, $x + 2{,}000$ = the amount of money invested at 9%. The interest earned on x dollars invested at 8% is $0.08x$. The interest earned on $x + 2{,}000$ dollars invested at 9% is $0.09(x + 2{,}000)$.
Here is a table that summarizes this information:

	Dollars Invested at 8%	Dollars Invested at 9%
Number of	x	$x + 2{,}000$
Interest on	$0.08x$	$0.09(x + 2{,}000)$

Step 3: **Reread, and write an equation.**
Because the total amount of interest earned from both accounts is $690, the equation that describes the situation is

Interest earned at 8%	+	Interest earned at 9%	=	Total interest earned
$0.08x$	+	$0.09(x + 2{,}000)$	=	690

Step 4: Solve the equation.

$$0.08x + 0.09(x + 2,000) = 690$$

$$0.08x + 0.09x + 180 = 690 \qquad \textcolor{green}{\textit{Distributive property}}$$

$$0.17x + 180 = 690 \qquad \textcolor{green}{\textit{Add } 0.08x \textit{ and } 0.09x}$$

$$0.17x = 510 \qquad \textcolor{green}{\textit{Add } -180 \textit{ to each side}}$$

$$x = 3,000 \qquad \textcolor{green}{\textit{Divide each side by } 0.17}$$

Step 5: Write the answer:
The amount of money invested at 8% is $3,000, whereas the amount of money invested at 9% is $x + 2,000 = 3,000 + 2,000 = \$5,000$.

Step 6: Reread, and check.

The interest at 8% is 8% of 3,000 = 0.08(3,000) = $240
The interest at 9% is 9% of 5,000 = 0.09(5,000) = $450
The total interest is $690

Labeling Triangles and the Sum of the Angles in a Triangle

One way to label the important parts of a triangle is to label the vertices with capital letters and the sides with small letters, as shown in Figure 1.

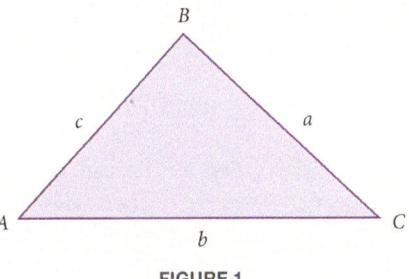

FIGURE 1

In Figure 1, notice that side a is opposite vertex A, side b is opposite vertex B, and side c is opposite vertex C. Also, because each vertex is the vertex of one of the angles of the triangle, we refer to the three interior angles as A, B, and C.

In any triangle, the sum of the interior angles is 180°. For the triangle shown in Figure 1, the relationship is written

$$A + B + C = 180°$$

Example 3 The angles in a triangle are such that one angle is twice the smallest angle, whereas the third angle is three times as large as the smallest angle. Find the measure of all three angles.

SOLUTION

Step 1: Read and list.
Known items: The sum of all three angles is 180°, one angle is twice the smallest angle, the largest angle is three times the smallest angle.
Unknown items: The measure of each angle

Step 2: Assign a variable, and translate information.
Let x be the smallest angle, then $2x$ will be the measure of another angle and $3x$ will be the measure of the largest angle.

Step 3: **Reread, and write an equation.**

When working with geometric objects, drawing a generic diagram sometimes will help us visualize what it is that we are asked to find. In Figure 2, we draw a triangle with angles A, B, and C.

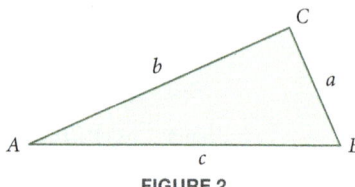

FIGURE 2

We can let the value of $A = x$, the value of $B = 2x$, and the value of $C = 3x$. We know that the sum of angles A, B, and C will be 180°, so our equation becomes

$$x + 2x + 3x = 180°$$

Step 4: **Solve the equation.**

$$x + 2x + 3x = 180°$$
$$6x = 180°$$
$$x = 30°$$

Step 5: **Write the answer.**

The smallest angle A measures 30°
Angle B measures $2x$, or $2(30°) = 60°$
Angle C measures $3x$, or $3(30°) = 90°$

Step 6: **Reread, and check.**

The angles must add to 180°:

$$A + B + C = 180°$$
$$30° + 60° + 90° \overset{?}{=} 180°$$
$$180° = 180° \qquad \textit{Our answers check}$$

Getting Ready for Class

After reading through the preceding section, respond in your own words and in complete sentences.

A. How do we label triangles?

B. What rule is always true about the three angles in a triangle?

C. Write an application problem whose solution depends on solving the equation $x + 0.075x = 500$.

D. Write an application problem whose solution depends on solving the equation $0.05x + 0.06(x + 200) = 67$.

Problem Set 1.7

Consecutive Integer Problems

1. The sum of two consecutive integers is 11. Find the numbers.
2. The sum of two consecutive integers is 15. Find the numbers.
3. The sum of two consecutive integers is −9. Find the numbers.
4. The sum of two consecutive integers is −21. Find the numbers.
5. The sum of two consecutive odd integers is 28. Find the numbers.
6. The sum of two consecutive odd integers is 44. Find the numbers.
7. The sum of two consecutive even integers is 106. Find the numbers.
8. The sum of two consecutive even integers is 66. Find the numbers.
9. The sum of two consecutive even integers is −30. Find the numbers.
10. The sum of two consecutive odd integers is −76. Find the numbers.
11. The sum of three consecutive odd integers is 57. Find the numbers.
12. The sum of three consecutive odd integers is −51. Find the numbers.
13. The sum of three consecutive even integers is 132. Find the numbers.
14. The sum of three consecutive even integers is −108. Find the numbers.

Interest Problems

15. Suppose you invest money in two accounts. One of the accounts pays 8% annual interest, whereas the other pays 9% annual interest. If you have $2,000 more invested at 9% than you have invested at 8%, how much do you have invested in each account if the total amount of interest you earn in a year is $860? (Begin by completing the following table.)

	Dollars Invested at 8%	Dollars Invested at 9%
Number of	x	
Interest on		

16. Suppose you invest a certain amount of money in an account that pays 11% interest annually, and $4,000 more than that in an account that pays 12% annually. How much money do you have in each account if the total interest for a year is $940?

	Dollars Invested at 11%	Dollars Invested at 12%
Number of	x	
Interest on		

17. Tyler has two savings accounts that his grandparents opened for him. The two accounts pay 10% and 12% in annual interest; there is $500 more in the account that pays 12% than there is in the other account. If the total interest for a year is $214, how much money does he have in each account?

18. Travis has a savings account that his parents opened for him. It pays 6% annual interest. His uncle also opened an account for him, but it pays 8% annual interest. If there is $800 more in the account that pays 6%, and the total interest from both accounts is $104, how much money is in each of the accounts?

19. A stockbroker has money in three accounts. The interest rates on the three accounts are 8%, 9%, and 10%. If she has twice as much money invested at 9% as she has invested at 8%, three times as much at 10% as she has at 8%, and the total interest for the year is $280, how much is invested at each rate? (*Hint:* Let x = the amount invested at 8%.)

20. An accountant has money in three accounts that pay 9%, 10%, and 11% in annual interest. He has twice as much invested at 9% as he does at 10% and three times as much invested at 11% as he does at 10%. If the total interest from the three accounts is $610 for the year, how much is invested at each rate? (*Hint:* Let x = the amount invested at 10%.)

Triangle Problems

21. Two angles in a triangle are equal and their sum is equal to the third angle in the triangle. What are the measures of each of the three interior angles?

22. One angle in a triangle measures twice the smallest angle, whereas the largest angle is six times the smallest angle. Find the measures of all three angles.

23. The smallest angle in a triangle is $\frac{1}{5}$ as large as the largest angle. The third angle is twice the smallest angle. Find the three angles.

24. One angle in a triangle is half the largest angle but three times the smallest. Find all three angles.

25. A right triangle has one 37° angle. Find the other two angles.

26. In a right triangle, one of the acute angles is twice as large as the other acute angle. Find the measure of the two acute angles.

27. One angle of a triangle measures 20° more than the smallest, while a third angle is twice the smallest. Find the measure of each angle.

28. One angle of a triangle measures 50° more than the smallest, while a third angle is three times the smallest. Find the measure of each angle.

Miscellaneous Problems

29. **Ticket Prices** Miguel is selling tickets to a barbecue. Adult tickets cost $6.00 and children's tickets cost $4.00. He sells six more children's tickets than adult tickets. The total amount of money he collects is $184. How many adult tickets and how many children's tickets did he sell?

	Adult	Child
Number	x	$x + 6$
Income	$6(x)$	$4(x + 6)$

30. **Working Two Jobs** Maggie has a job working in an office for $10 an hour and another job driving a tractor for $12 an hour. One week she works in the office twice as long as she drives the tractor. Her total income for that week is $416. How many hours did she spend at each job?

Job	Office	Tractor
Hours Worked	$2x$	x
Wages Earned	$10(2x)$	$12x$

31. **Phone Bill** The cost of a long-distance phone call is $0.41 for the first minute and $0.32 for each additional minute. If the total charge for a long-distance call is $5.21, how many minutes was the call?

32. **Phone Bill** Danny, who is 1 year old, is playing with the telephone when he accidentally presses one of the buttons his mother has programmed to dial her friend Sue's number. Sue answers the phone and realizes Danny is on the other end. She talks to Danny, trying to get him to hang up. The cost for a call is $0.23 for the first minute and $0.14 for every minute after that. If the total charge for the call is $3.73, how long did it take Sue to convince Danny to hang up the phone?

33. **Hourly Wages** JoAnn works in the publicity office at the state university. She is paid $12 an hour for the first 35 hours she works each week and $18 an hour for every hour after that. If she makes $492 one week, how many hours did she work?

34. **Hourly Wages** Diane has a part-time job that pays her $6.50 an hour. During one week she works 26 hours and is paid $178.10. She realizes when she sees her check that she has been given a raise. How much per hour is that raise?

35. **Office Numbers** Professors Wong and Gil have offices in the mathematics building at Miami Dade College. Their office numbers are consecutive odd integers with a sum of 14,660. What are the office numbers of these two professors?

36. **Cell Phone Numbers** Diana and Tom buy two cell phones. The phone numbers assigned to each are consecutive integers with a sum of 11,109,295. If the smaller number is Diana's, what are their phone numbers?

37. **Age** Marissa and Kendra are 2 years apart in age. Their ages are two consecutive even integers. Kendra is the younger of the two. If Marissa's age is added to twice Kendra's age, the result is 26. How old is each girl?

38. **Age** Justin's and Ethan's ages form two consecutive odd integers. What is the difference of their ages?

39. **Arrival Time** Jeff and Carla Cole are driving separately from San Luis Obispo, California, to the north shore of Lake Tahoe, a distance of 425 miles. Jeff leaves San Luis Obispo at 11:00 AM and averages 55 miles per hour on the drive, Carla leaves later, at 1:00 PM but averages 65 miles per hour. Which person arrives in Lake Tahoe first?

40. **Piano Lessons** Tyler is taking piano lessons. Because he doesn't practice as often as his parents would like him to, he has to pay for part of the lessons himself. His parents pay him $0.50 to do the laundry and $1.25 to mow the lawn. In one month, he does the laundry 6 more times than he mows the lawn. If his parents pay him $13.50 that month, how many times did he mow the lawn?

At one time, the Texas Junior College Teachers Association annual conference was held in Austin. At that time a taxi ride in Austin was $1.25 for the first $\frac{1}{5}$ of a mile and $0.25 for each additional $\frac{1}{5}$ of a mile. Use this information for Problems 41 and 42.

41. Cost of a Taxi Ride If the distance from one of the convention hotels to the airport is 7.5 miles, how much will it cost to take a taxi from that hotel to the airport?

42. Cost of a Taxi Ride Suppose the distance from one of the hotels to one of the western dance clubs in Austin is 12.4 miles. If the fare meter in the taxi gives the charge for that trip as $16.50, is the meter working correctly?

43. Geometry The length and width of a rectangle are consecutive even integers. The perimeter is 44 meters. Find the length and width

44. Geometry The length and width of a rectangle are consecutive odd integers. The perimeter is 128 meters. Find the length and width.

45. Geometry The angles of a triangle are three consecutive integers. Find the measure of each angle.

46. Geometry The angles of a triangle are three consecutive even integers. Find the measure of each angle.

Ike and Nancy Lara give western dance lessons at the Elk's Lodge on Sunday nights. The lessons cost $3.00 for members of the lodge and $5.00 for nonmembers. Half of the money collected for the lesson is paid to Ike and Nancy. The Elk's Lodge keeps the other half. One Sunday night Ike counts 36 people in the dance lesson. Use this information to work Problems 47 through 50.

47. Dance Lessons What is the least amount of money Ike and Nancy will make?

48. Dance Lessons What is the largest amount of money Ike and Nancy will make?

49. Dance Lessons At the end of the evening, the Elk's Lodge gives Ike and Nancy a check for $80 to cover half of the receipts. Can this amount be correct?

50. Dance Lessons Besides the number of people in the dance lesson, what additional information does Ike need to know to always be sure he is being paid the correct amount?

Getting Ready for the Next Section

To understand all the explanations and examples in the next section you must be able to work the problems below.

Solve the following equations.

51.   **a.** $x - 3 = 6$ **b.** $x + 3 = 6$ **c.** $-x - 3 = 6$ **d.** $-x + 3 = 6$

52.   **a.** $x - 7 = 16$ **b.** $x + 7 = 16$ **c.** $-x - 7 = 16$ **d.** $-x + 7 = 16$

53.   **a.** $\frac{x}{4} = -2$ **b.** $-\frac{x}{4} = -2$ **c.** $\frac{x}{4} = 2$ **d.** $-\frac{x}{4} = 2$

54.   **a.** $3a = 15$ **b.** $3a = -15$ **c.** $-3a = 15$ **d.** $-3a = -15$

55. $2.5x - 3.48 = 4.9x + 2.07$ **56.** $2(1 - 3x) + 4 = 4x - 14$

57. $3(x - 4) = -2$ **58.** Solve for y: $2x - 3y = 6$

Linear Inequalities

Linear inequalities are solved by a method similar to the one used in solving linear equations. The only real differences between the methods are in the multiplication property for inequalities and in graphing the solution set.

An inequality differs from an equation only with respect to the comparison symbol between the two quantities being compared. In place of the equal sign, we use < (less than), ≤ (less than or equal to), > (greater than), or ≥ (greater than or equal to). The addition property for inequalities is almost identical to the addition property for equality.

> **⟦Δ≠Σ⟧ Addition Property for Inequalities**
>
> For any three algebraic expressions A, B, and C,
> $$\text{if} \qquad A < B$$
> $$\text{then} \qquad A + C < B + C$$
>
> *In words*:   Adding the same quantity to both sides of an inequality will not change the solution set.

It makes no difference which inequality symbol we use to state the property. Adding the same amount to both sides always produces an inequality equivalent to the original inequality. Also, because subtraction can be thought of as addition of the opposite, this property holds for subtraction as well as addition.

Video Examples

Section 1.8

Example 1   Solve the inequality $x + 5 < 7$.

SOLUTION   To isolate x, we add -5 to both sides of the inequality:

$$x + 5 < 7$$
$$x + 5 + (-5) < 7 + (-5) \qquad \text{Addition property for inequalities}$$
$$x < 2$$

We can go one step further here and graph the solution set. The solution set is all real numbers less than 2. To graph this set, we simply draw a straight line and label the center 0 (zero) for reference. Then we label the 2 on the right side of zero and extend an arrow beginning at 2 and pointing to the left. We use an open circle at 2 because it is not included in the solution set. Here is the graph.

Example 2   Solve $x - 6 \leq -3$.

SOLUTION   Adding 6 to each side will isolate x on the left side:

$$x - 6 \leq -3$$
$$x - 6 + 6 \leq -3 + 6 \qquad \text{Add 6 to both sides}$$
$$x \leq 3$$

The graph of the solution set is

Notice that the dot at the 3 is darkened because 3 is included in the solution set. We always will use open circles on the graphs of solution sets with $<$ or $>$ and closed (darkened) circles on the graphs of solution sets with $\leq$ or $\geq$.

To see the idea behind the multiplication property for inequalities, we will consider three true inequality statements and explore what happens when we multiply both sides by a positive number and then what happens when we multiply by a negative number.

Consider the following three true statements:

$$3 < 5 \qquad -3 < 5 \qquad -5 < -3$$

Now multiply both sides by the positive number 4:

$$4(3) < 4(5) \qquad 4(-3) < 4(5) \qquad 4(-5) < 4(-3)$$
$$12 < 20 \qquad -12 < 20 \qquad -20 < -12$$

In each case, the inequality symbol in the result points in the same direction it did in the original inequality. We say the "sense" of the inequality doesn't change when we multiply both sides by a positive quantity.

Notice what happens when we go through the same process but multiply both sides by -4 instead of 4:

$$3 < 5 \qquad\qquad -3 < 5 \qquad\qquad -5 < -3$$

$$-4(3) > -4(5) \qquad -4(-3) > -4(5) \qquad -4(-5) > -4(-3)$$
$$-12 > -20 \qquad\qquad 12 > -20 \qquad\qquad 20 > 12$$

In each case, we have to change the direction in which the inequality symbol points to keep each statement true. Multiplying both sides of an inequality by a negative quantity always reverses the sense of the inequality. Our results are summarized in the multiplication property for inequalities.

> **⌈Δ≠Σ⌉ Multiplication Property for Inequalities**
>
> For any three algebraic expressions A, B, and C,
>
> | if | $A < B$ | |
> |----|---------|---|
> | then | $AC < BC$ | when C is positive |
> | and | $AC > BC$ | when C is negative |
>
> *In words:* Multiplying both sides of an inequality by a positive number does not change the solution set. When multiplying both sides of an inequality by a negative number, it is necessary to reverse the inequality symbol to produce an equivalent inequality.

We can multiply both sides of an inequality by any nonzero number we choose. If that number happens to be **negative**, we must also reverse the sense of the inequality.

▌Example 3   Solve $3a < 15$ and graph the solution.

SOLUTION We begin by multiplying each side by $\frac{1}{3}$. Because $\frac{1}{3}$ is a positive number, we do not reverse the direction of the inequality symbol:

Note This discussion is intended to show why the multiplication property for inequalities is written the way it is. You may want to look ahead to the property itself and then come back to this discussion if you are having trouble making sense out of it.

Note Because division is defined in terms of multiplication, this property is also true for division. We can divide both sides of an inequality by any nonzero number we choose. If that number happens to be negative, we must also reverse the direction of the inequality symbol.

$$3a < 15$$

$$\frac{1}{3}(3a) < \frac{1}{3}(15) \qquad \text{Multiply each side by } \tfrac{1}{3}$$

$$a < 5$$

Example 4 Solve $-3a \le 18$, and graph the solution.

SOLUTION We begin by multiplying both sides by $-\frac{1}{3}$. Because $-\frac{1}{3}$ is a negative number, we must reverse the direction of the inequality symbol at the same time that we multiply by $-\frac{1}{3}$.

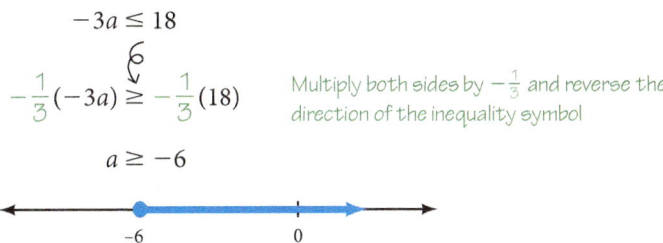

$$-3a \le 18$$

$$-\frac{1}{3}(-3a) \ge -\frac{1}{3}(18) \qquad \text{Multiply both sides by } -\tfrac{1}{3} \text{ and reverse the direction of the inequality symbol}$$

$$a \ge -6$$

Example 5 Solve $-\dfrac{x}{4} > 2$ and graph the solution.

SOLUTION To isolate x, we multiply each side by -4. Because -4 is a negative number, we also must reverse the direction of the inequality symbol:

$$-\frac{x}{4} > 2$$

$$-4\left(-\frac{x}{4}\right) < -4(2) \qquad \text{Multiply each side by } -4, \text{ and reverse the direction of the inequality symbol}$$

$$x < -8$$

To solve more complicated inequalities, we use the following steps.

[Δ≠Σ] *How To Solve Linear Inequalities in One Variable*

Step 1a: Use the distributive property to separate terms, if necessary.

  1b: If fractions are present, consider multiplying both sides by the LCD to eliminate the fractions. If decimals are present, consider multiplying both sides by a power of 10 to clear the inequality of decimals.

  1c: Combine similar terms on each side of the inequality.

Step 2: Use the addition property for inequalities to get all variable terms on one side of the inequality and all constant terms on the other side.

Step 3: Use the multiplication property for inequalities to get x by itself on one side of the inequality.

Step 4: Graph the solution set.

Example 6   Solve $2.5x - 3.48 < -4.9x + 2.07$.

SOLUTION   We have two methods we can use to solve this inequality. We can simply apply our properties to the inequality the way it is currently written and work with the decimal numbers, or we can eliminate the decimals to begin with and solve the resulting inequality.

Method 1 Working with the decimals.

$$2.5x - 3.48 < -4.9x + 2.07 \qquad \text{Original inequality}$$

$$2.5x + 4.9x - 3.48 < -4.9x + 4.9x + 2.07 \qquad \text{Add } 4.9x \text{ to each side}$$

$$7.4x - 3.48 < 2.07$$

$$7.4x - 3.48 + 3.48 < 2.07 + 3.48 \qquad \text{Add } 3.48 \text{ to each side}$$

$$7.4x < 5.55$$

$$\frac{7.4x}{7.4} < \frac{5.55}{7.4} \qquad \text{Divide each side by } 7.4$$

$$x < 0.75$$

Method 2 Eliminating the decimals in the beginning.

Because the greatest number of places to the right of the decimal point in any of the numbers is 2, we can multiply each side of the inequality by 100 and we will be left with an equivalent inequality that contains only whole numbers.

$$2.5x - 3.48 < -4.9x + 2.07 \qquad \text{Original inequality}$$

$$100(2.5x - 3.48) < 100(-4.9x + 2.07) \qquad \text{Multiply each side by } 100$$

$$100(2.5x) - 100(3.48) < 100(-4.9x) + 100(2.07) \qquad \text{Distributive property}$$

$$250x - 348 < -490x + 207 \qquad \text{Multiplication}$$

$$740x - 348 < 207 \qquad \text{Add } 490x \text{ to each side}$$

$$740x < 555 \qquad \text{Add } 348 \text{ to each side}$$

$$\frac{740x}{740} < \frac{555}{740} \qquad \text{Divide each side by } 740$$

$$x < 0.75$$

The solution by either method is $x < 0.75$. Here is the graph:

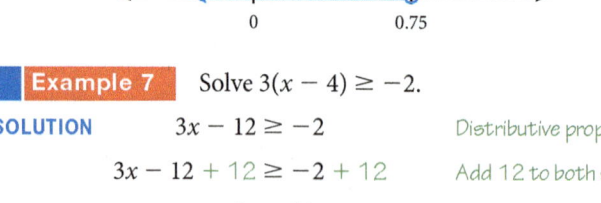

Example 7   Solve $3(x - 4) \geq -2$.

SOLUTION

$$3x - 12 \geq -2 \qquad \text{Distributive property}$$

$$3x - 12 + 12 \geq -2 + 12 \qquad \text{Add } 12 \text{ to both sides}$$

$$3x \geq 10$$

$$\frac{1}{3}(3x) \geq \frac{1}{3}(10) \qquad \text{Multiply both sides by } \frac{1}{3}$$

$$x \geq \frac{10}{3}$$

Example 8 Solve and graph $2(1 - 3x) + 4 < 4x - 14$.

SOLUTION
$$2 - 6x + 4 < 4x - 14 \qquad \text{Distributive property}$$
$$-6x + 6 < 4x - 14 \qquad \text{Simplify}$$
$$-6x + 6 + (-6) < 4x - 14 + (-6) \qquad \text{Add } -6 \text{ to both sides}$$
$$-6x < 4x - 20$$
$$-6x + (-4x) < 4x + (-4x) - 20 \qquad \text{Add } -4x \text{ to both sides}$$
$$-10x < -20$$
$$\left(-\frac{1}{10}\right)(-10x) > \left(-\frac{1}{10}\right)(-20) \qquad \text{Multiply by } -\frac{1}{10}, \text{ reverse the direction of the inequality}$$
$$x > 2$$

Example 9 Solve $2x - 3y < 6$ for y.

SOLUTION We can solve this formula for y by first adding $-2x$ to each side and then multiplying each side by $-\frac{1}{3}$. When we multiply by $-\frac{1}{3}$ we must reverse the direction of the inequality symbol. Because this is a formula, we will not graph the solution.

$$2x - 3y < 6 \qquad \text{Original formula}$$
$$2x + (-2x) - 3y < (-2x) + 6 \qquad \text{Add } -2x \text{ to each side}$$
$$-3y < -2x + 6$$
$$-\frac{1}{3}(-3y) > -\frac{1}{3}(-2x + 6) \qquad \text{Multiply each side by } -\frac{1}{3}$$
$$y > \frac{2}{3}x - 2 \qquad \text{Distributive property}$$

When working application problems that involve inequalities, the phrases "at least" and "at most" translate as follows:

In Words	In Symbols
x is at least 30	$x \geq 30$
x is at most 20	$x \leq 20$

Our next example is similar to an example done earlier in this chapter. This time it involves an inequality instead of an equation.

We can modify our Blueprint for Problem Solving to solve application problems whose solutions depend on writing and then solving inequalities.

Example 10   The sum of two consecutive odd integers is at most 28. What are the possibilities for the first of the two integers?

SOLUTION   When we use the phrase "their sum is at most 28," we mean that their sum is less than or equal to 28.

Step 1:   Read and list.
Known items: Two consecutive odd integers. Their sum is less than or equal to 28.
Unknown items: The numbers in question.

Step 2:   Assign a variable, and translate information.
If we let $x =$ the first of the two consecutive odd integers, then $x + 2$ is the next consecutive one.

Step 3:   Reread, and write an inequality.
Their sum is at most 28.

$$x + (x + 2) \leq 28$$

Step 4:   Solve the inequality.

$$2x + 2 \leq 28 \qquad \text{\textit{Simplify the left side}}$$

$$2x \leq 26 \qquad \text{\textit{Add} } -2 \text{ \textit{to each side}}$$

$$x \leq 13 \qquad \text{\textit{Multiply each side by} } \tfrac{1}{2}$$

Step 5:   Write the answer.
The first of the two integers must be an odd integer that is less than or equal to 13. The second of the two integers will be two more than whatever the first one is.

Step 6:   Reread, and check.
Suppose the first integer is 13. The next consecutive odd integer is 15. The sum of 15 and 13 is 28. If the first odd integer is less than 13, the sum of it and the next consecutive odd integer will be less than 28. ■

Getting Ready for Class

After reading through the preceding section, respond in your own words and in complete sentences.

A. State the addition property for inequalities.
B. How is the multiplication property for inequalities different from the multiplication property of equality?
C. When do we reverse the direction of an inequality symbol?
D. Under what conditions do we not change the direction of the inequality symbol when we multiply both sides of an inequality by a number?

Problem Set 1.8

Solve the following inequalities using the addition property of inequalities. Graph each solution set.

1. $x - 5 < 7$ **2.** $x + 3 < -5$ **3.** $a - 4 \leq 8$ **4.** $a + 3 \leq 10$

5. $x - 4.3 > 8.7$ **6.** $x - 2.6 > 10.4$ **7.** $y + 6 \geq 10$ **8.** $y + 3 \geq 12$

9. $2 < x - 7$ **10.** $3 < x + 8$

Solve the following inequalities using the multiplication property of inequalities. If you multiply both sides by a negative number, be sure to reverse the direction of the inequality symbol. Graph the solution set.

11. $3x < 6$ **12.** $2x < 14$ **13.** $5a \leq 25$ **14.** $4a \leq 16$

15. $\frac{x}{3} > 5$ **16.** $\frac{x}{7} > 1$ **17.** $-2x > 6$ **18.** $-3x \geq 9$

19. $-3x \geq -18$ **20.** $-8x \geq -24$ **21.** $-\frac{x}{5} \leq 10$ **22.** $-\frac{x}{9} \geq -1$

23. $-\frac{2}{3}y > 4$ **24.** $-\frac{3}{4}y > 6$

Solve the following inequalities. Graph the solution set in each case.

25. $2x - 3 < 9$ **26.** $3x - 4 < 17$ **27.** $-\frac{1}{5}y - \frac{1}{3} \leq \frac{2}{3}$

28. $-\frac{1}{6}y - \frac{1}{2} \leq \frac{2}{3}$ **29.** $-7.2x + 1.8 > -19.8$ **30.** $-7.8x - 1.3 > 22.1$

31. $\frac{2}{3}x - 5 \leq 7$ **32.** $\frac{3}{4}x - 8 \leq 1$ **33.** $-\frac{2}{5}a - 3 > 5$

34. $-\frac{4}{5}a - 2 > 10$ **35.** $5 - \frac{3}{5}y > -10$ **36.** $4 - \frac{5}{6}y > -11$

37. $0.3(a + 1) \leq 1.2$ **38.** $0.4(a - 2) \leq 0.4$ **39.** $2(5 - 2x) \leq -20$

40. $7(8 - 2x) > 28$ **41.** $3x - 5 > 8x$ **42.** $8x - 4 > 6x$

43. $\frac{1}{3}y - \frac{1}{2} \leq \frac{5}{6}y + \frac{1}{2}$ **44.** $\frac{7}{6}y + \frac{4}{3} \leq \frac{11}{6}y - \frac{7}{6}$

45. $-2.8x + 8.4 < -14x - 2.8$

46. $-7.2x - 2.4 < -2.4x + 12$

47. $3(m - 2) - 4 \geq 7m + 14$

48. $2(3m - 1) + 5 \geq 8m - 7$

49. $3 - 4(x - 2) \leq -5x + 6$

50. $8 - 6(x - 3) \leq -4x + 12$

Solve each of the following formulas for y.

51. $3x + 2y < 6$ **52.** $-3x + 2y < 6$ **53.** $2x - 5y > 10$

54. $-2x - 5y > 5$ **55.** $-3x + 7y \leq 21$ **56.** $-7x + 3y \leq 21$

57. $2x - 4y \geq -4$ **58.** $4x - 2y \geq -8$

The next two problems are intended to give you practice reading, and paying attention to, the instructions that accompany the problems you are working.

59. Paying Attention to Instructions Work each problem according to the instructions given.

    a. Evaluate when $x = 0$: $-5x + 3$ **b.** Solve: $-5x + 3 = -7$

    c. Is 0 a solution to $-5x + 3 < -7$ **d.** Solve: $-5x + 3 < -7$

60. Paying Attention to Instructions Work each problem according to the instructions given.

    a. Evaluate when $x = 0$: $-2x - 5$ **b.** Solve: $-2x - 5 = 1$

    c. Is 0 a solution to $-2x - 5 > 1$ **d.** Solve: $-2x - 5 > 1$

For each graph below, write an inequality whose solution is the graph.

61.

62.

63.

64.

Applying the Concepts

65. Consecutive Integers The sum of two consecutive integers is at least 583. What are the possibilities for the first of the two integers?

66. Consecutive Integers The sum of two consecutive integers is at most 583. What are the possibilities for the first of the two integers?

67. Number Problems The sum of twice a number and six is less than ten. Find all solutions.

68. Number Problems Twice the difference of a number and three is greater than or equal to the number increased by five. Find all solutions.

69. Number Problems The product of a number and four is greater than the number minus eight. Find the solution set.

70. Number Problems The quotient of a number and five is less than the sum of seven and two. Find the solution set.

71. Geometry Problems The length of a rectangle is 3 times the width. If the perimeter is to be at least 48 meters, what are the possible values for the width? (If the perimeter is at least 48 meters, then it is greater than or equal to 48 meters.)

72. Geometry Problems The length of a rectangle is 3 more than twice the width. If the perimeter is to be at least 51 meters, what are the possible values for the width? (If the perimeter is at least 51 meters, then it is greater than or equal to 51 meters.)

73. Geometry Problems The numerical values of the three sides of a triangle are given by three consecutive even integers. If the perimeter is greater than 24 inches, what are the possibilities for the shortest side?

74. Geometry Problems The numerical values of the three sides of a triangle are given by three consecutive odd integers. If the perimeter is greater than 27 inches, what are the possibilities for the shortest side?

Getting Ready for the Next Section

Solve each inequality. Do not graph.

75. $2x - 1 \geq 3$ **76.** $3x + 1 \geq 7$ **77.** $-2x > -8$ **78.** $-3x > -12$

79. $-3 > 4x + 1$ **80.** $4x + 1 \leq 9$

Compound Inequalities

The instrument panel on most cars includes a temperature gauge. The one shown below indicates that the normal operating temperature for the engine is from 50°F to 270°F.

We can represent the same situation with an inequality by writing $50 \leq F \leq 270$, where F is the temperature in degrees Fahrenheit. This inequality is a *compound inequality*. In this section we present the notation and definitions associated with compound inequalities.

The *union* of two sets A and B is the set of all elements that are in A or in B. The word *or* is the key word in the definition. The *intersection* of two sets A and B is the set of elements contained in both A and B. The key word in this definition is *and*. We can put the words *and* and *or* together with our methods of graphing inequalities to find the solution sets for compound inequalities.

> **(dĕf´ compound inequality**
>
> A *compound inequality* is two or more inequalities connected by the word *and* or *or*.

Video Examples

Section 1.9

Example 1 Graph the solution set for the compound inequality

$$x < -1 \qquad \text{or} \qquad x \geq 3$$

SOLUTION Graphing each inequality separately, we have

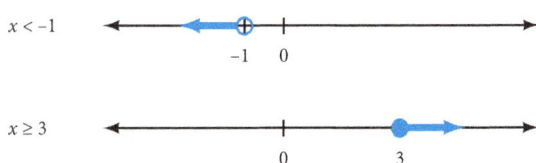

Because the two inequalities are connected by *or*, we want to graph their union; that is, we graph all points that are on either the first graph or the second graph. Essentially, we put the two graphs together on the same number line.

$$x < -1 \qquad \text{or} \qquad x \geq 3$$

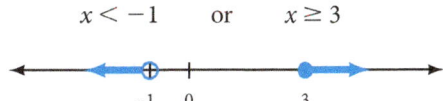

Example 2 Graph the solution set for the compound inequality

$$x > -2 \quad \text{and} \quad x < 3$$

SOLUTION Graphing each inequality separately, we have

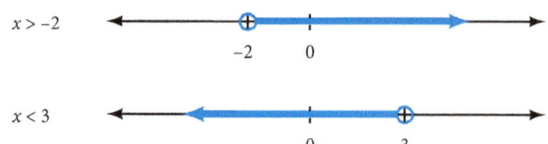

$x > -2$

$x < 3$

Because the two inequalities are connected by the word *and,* we will graph their intersection, which consists of all points that are common to both graphs; that is, we graph the region where the two graphs overlap.

Example 3 Solve and graph the solution set for

$$2x - 1 \geq 3 \quad \text{and} \quad -3x > -12$$

SOLUTION Solving the two inequalities separately, we have

$$2x - 1 \geq 3 \qquad \text{and} \qquad -3x > -12$$

$$2x \geq 4 \qquad\qquad -\frac{1}{3}(-3x) < -\frac{1}{3}(-12)$$

$$x \geq 2 \qquad \text{and} \qquad x < 4$$

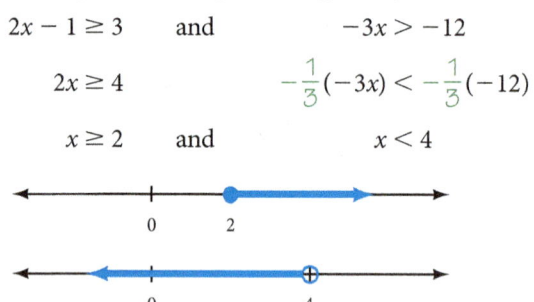

Because the word *and* connects the two graphs, we will graph their intersection— the points they have in common:

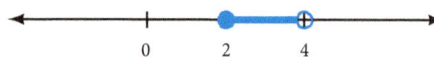

Notation Sometimes compound inequalities that use the word *and* can be written in a shorter form. For example, the compound inequality $-2 < x$ and $x < 3$ can be written as $-2 < x < 3$. The word *and* does not appear when an inequality is written in this form; it is implied. The solution set for $-2 < x$ and $x < 3$ is

It is all the numbers between -2 and 3 on the number line. It seems reasonable then, that this graph should be the graph of

$$-2 < x < 3$$

In both the graph and the inequality, x is said to be between -2 and 3.

Example 4   Solve and graph $-3 \leq 2x - 1 \leq 9$.

SOLUTION   To solve for x, we must add 1 to the center expression and then divide the result by 2. Whatever we do to the center expression, we also must do to the two expressions on the ends. In this way we can be sure we are producing equivalent inequalities. The solution set will not be affected.

$$-3 \leq 2x - 1 \leq 9$$

$$-2 \leq 2x \quad\ \leq 10 \qquad \textit{Add 1 to each expression}$$

$$-1 \leq\ x \quad\ \leq 5 \qquad \textit{Multiply each expression by } \tfrac{1}{2}$$

Getting Ready for Class

After reading through the preceding section, respond in your own words and in complete sentences.

A. What is a compound inequality?

B. Explain the shorthand notation that can be used to write two inequalities connected by the word and.

C. Write two inequalities connected by the word and that together are equivalent to $-1 < x < 2$.

D. Explain in words how you would graph the compound inequality $x < 2$ or $x > -3$.

Graph the following compound inequalities.

1. $x < -1$ or $x > 5$ **2.** $x \le -2$ or $x \ge -1$ **3.** $x < -3$ or $x \ge 0$

4. $x < 5$ and $x > 1$ **5.** $x \le 6$ and $x > -1$ **6.** $x \le 7$ and $x > 0$

7. $x > 2$ and $x < 4$ **8.** $x < 2$ or $x > 4$ **9.** $x \ge -2$ and $x \le 4$

10. $x \le 2$ or $x \ge 4$ **11.** $x < 5$ and $x > -1$ **12.** $x > 5$ or $x < -1$

13. $-1 < x < 3$ **14.** $-1 \le x \le 3$ **15.** $-3 < x \le -2$

16. $-5 \le x \le 0$

Solve the following compound inequalities. Graph the solution set in each case.

17. $3x - 1 < 5$ or $5x - 5 > 10$ **18.** $x + 1 < -3$ or $x - 2 > 6$

19. $x - 2 > -5$ and $x + 7 < 13$ **20.** $3x + 2 \le 11$ and $2x + 2 \ge 0$

21. $11x < 22$ or $12x > 36$ **22.** $-5x < 25$ and $-2x \ge -12$

23. $3x - 5 < 10$ and $2x + 1 > -5$ **24.** $5x + 8 < -7$ or $3x - 8 > 10$

25. $2x - 3 < 8$ and $3x + 1 > -10$ **26.** $11x - 8 > 3$ or $12x + 7 < -5$

27. $2x - 1 < 3$ and $3x - 2 > 1$ **28.** $3x + 9 < 7$ or $2x - 7 > 11$

29. $-1 \le x - 5 \le 2$ **30.** $0 \le x + 2 \le 3$

31. $-4 \le 2x \le 6$ **32.** $-5 < 5x < 10$

33. $-3 < 2x + 1 < 5$ **34.** $-7 \le 2x - 3 \le 7$

35. $0 \le 3x + 2 \le 7$ **36.** $2 \le 5x - 3 \le 12$

37. $-7 < 2x + 3 < 11$ **38.** $-5 < 6x - 2 < 8$

39. $-1 \le 4x + 5 \le 9$ **40.** $-8 \le 7x - 1 \le 13$

For each graph below, write an inequality whose solution is the graph.

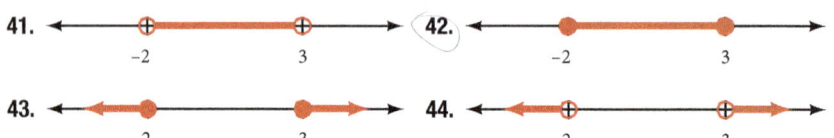

41. (−2, 3)   **42.** (−2, 3)

43. (−2, 3)   **44.** (−2, 3)

Applying the Concepts

Triangle Inequality The triangle inequality states that the sum of any two sides of a triangle must be greater than the third side.

45. The following triangle *RST* has sides of length x, $2x$, and 10 as shown.

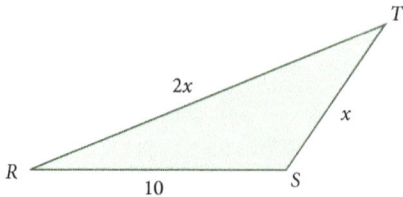

a. Find the three inequalities, which must be true based on the sides of the triangle.

b. Write a compound inequality based on your results above.

46. The following triangle ABC has sides of length x, $3x$, and 16 as shown.

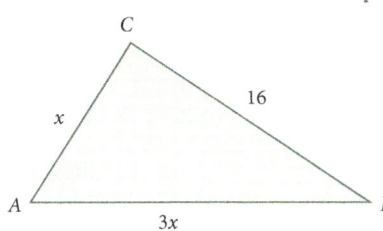

a. Find the three inequalities, which must be true based on the sides of the triangle.

b. Write a compound inequality based on your results above.

47. Engine Temperature The engine in a car gives off a lot of heat due to the combustion in the cylinders. The water used to cool the engine keeps the temperature within the range $50 \leq F \leq 266$ where F is in degrees Fahrenheit. Graph this inequality on the number line.

48. Engine Temperature To find the engine temperature range from Problem 47 in degrees Celsius, we use the fact that $F = \frac{9}{5}C + 32$ to rewrite the inequality as

$$50 \leq \frac{9}{5}C + 32 \leq 266$$

Solve this inequality and graph the solution set.

49. Number Problem The difference of twice a number and 3 is between 5 and 7. Find the number.

50. Number Problem The sum of twice a number and 5 is between 7 and 13. Find the number.

51. Perimeter The length of a rectangle is 4 inches longer than the width. The perimeter is between 20 inches and 30 inches.

a. Write the perimeter as a compound inequality.   ____ $< P <$ ____

b. Write the width as a compound inequality.   ____ $< w <$ ____

c. Write the length as a compound inequality.   ____ $< l <$ ____

52. Perimeter The length of a rectangle is 6 feet longer than the width. The perimeter is between 24 feet and 36 feet.

a. Write the perimeter as a compound inequality.   ____ $< P <$ ____

b. Write the width as a compound inequality.   ____ $< w <$ ____

c. Write the length as a compound inequality.   ____ $< l <$ ____

Maintaining Your Skills

The problems that follow review some of the more important skills you have learned in previous sections and chapters. You can consider the time you spend working these problems as time spent studying for exams.

Answer the following percent problems.

53. What number is 25% of 32?

54. What number is 15% of 75?

55. What number is 20% of 120?

56. What number is 125% of 300?

57. What percent of 36 is 9

58. What percent of 16 is 9?

59. What percent of 50 is 5?

60. What percent of 140 is 35?

61. 16 is 20% of what number?

62. 6 is 3% of what number?

63. 8 is 2% of what number?

64. 70 is 175% of what number?

Simplify each expression.

65. $-|-5|$

66. $\left(-\dfrac{2}{3}\right)^3$

67. $-3 - 4(-2)$

68. $2^4 + 3^3 \div 9 - 4^2$

69. $5|3 - 8| - 6|2 - 5|$

70. $7 - 3(2 - 6)$

71. $5 - 2[-3(5 - 7) - 8]$

72. $\dfrac{5 + 3(7 - 2)}{2(-3) - 4}$

73. Find the difference of -3 and -9.

74. If you add -4 to the product of -3 and 5, what number results?

75. Apply the distributive property to $\dfrac{1}{2}(4x - 6)$.

76. Use the associative property to simplify $-6\left(\dfrac{1}{3}x\right)$.

For the set $\left\{-3, -\dfrac{4}{5}, 0, \dfrac{5}{8}, 2, \sqrt{5}\right\}$, which numbers are

77. Integers

78. Rational numbers

Chapter 1 Summary

Similar Terms [1.1]

1. The terms $2x$, $5x$, and $-7x$ are all similar because their variable parts are the same.

A *term* is a number or a number and one or more variables multiplied together. *Similar terms* are terms with the same variable part.

Simplifying Expressions [1.1]

2. Simplify $3x + 4x$.
$$3x + 4x = (3 + 4)x$$
$$= 7x$$

In this chapter we simplified expressions that contained variables by using the distributive property to combine similar terms.

Solution Set [1.2]

3. The solution set for the equation $x + 2 = 5$ is $\{3\}$ because when x is 3 the equation is $3 + 2 = 5$, or $5 = 5$.

The *solution set* for an equation (or inequality) is all the numbers that, when used in place of the variable, make the equation (or inequality) a true statement.

Equivalent Equations [1.2]

4. The equation $a - 4 = 3$ and $a - 2 = 5$ are equivalent because both have solution set $\{7\}$.

Two equations are called *equivalent* if they have the same solution set.

Addition Property of Equality [1.2]

5. Solve $x - 5 = 12$.
$$x - 5 (+ 5) = 12 (+ 5)$$
$$x + 0 = 17$$
$$x = 17$$

When the same quantity is added to both sides of an equation, the solution set for the equation is unchanged. Adding the same amount to both sides of an equation produces an equivalent equation.

Multiplication Property of Equality [1.3]

6. Solve $3x = 18$.
$$\tfrac{1}{3}(3x) = \tfrac{1}{3}(18)$$
$$x = 6$$

If both sides of an equation are multiplied by the same nonzero number, the solution set is unchanged. Multiplying both sides of an equation by a nonzero quantity produces an equivalent equation.

Strategy for Solving Linear Equations in One Variable [1.4]

7. Solve $2(x + 3) = 10$.
$$2x + 6 = 10$$
$$2x + 6 + (-6) = 10 + (-6)$$
$$2x = 4$$
$$\tfrac{1}{2}(2x) = \tfrac{1}{2}(4)$$
$$x = 2$$

Step 1a: Use the distributive property to separate terms, if necessary.

1b: If fractions are present, consider multiplying both sides by the LCD to eliminate the fractions. If decimals are present, consider multiplying both sides by a power of 10 to clear the equation of decimals.

1c: Combine similar terms on each side of the equation.

Step 2: Use the addition property of equality to get all variable terms on one side of the equation and all constant terms on the other side. A variable term is a term that contains the variable (for example, $5x$). A constant term is a term that does not contain the variable (the number 3, for example).

Step 3: Use the multiplication property of equality to get x (that is, $1x$) by itself on one side of the equation.

Step 4: Check your solution in the original equation to be sure that you have not made a mistake in the solution process.

Formulas [1.5]

8. Solving $P = 2l + 2w$ for l, we have
$$P - 2w = 2l$$

$$\frac{P - 2w}{2} = l$$

A formula is an equation with more than one variable. To solve a formula for one of its variables, we use the addition and multiplication properties of equality to move everything except the variable in question to one side of the equal sign so the variable in question is alone on the other side.

Blueprint for Problem Solving [1.6, 1.7]

Step 1: *Read* the problem, and then mentally *list* the items that are known and the items that are unknown.

Step 2: *Assign a variable* to one of the unknown items. (In most cases this will amount to letting $x =$ the item that is asked for in the problem.) Then *translate* the other *information* in the problem to expressions involving the variable.

Step 3: *Reread* the problem, and then *write an equation,* using the items and variables listed in steps 1 and 2, that describes the situation.

Step 4: *Solve the equation* found in step 3.

Step 5: *Write* your *answer* using a complete sentence.

Step 6: *Reread* the problem, and *check* your solution with the original words in the problem.

Addition Property for Inequalities [1.8]

9. Solve $x + 5 < 7$.
$$x + 5 + (-5) < 7 + (-5)$$
$$x < 2$$

Adding the same quantity to both sides of an inequality produces an equivalent inequality, one with the same solution set.

Multiplication Property for Inequalities [1.8]

10. Solve $-3a \leq 18$.
$$-\frac{1}{3}(-3a) \geq -\frac{1}{3}(18)$$

$$a \geq -6$$

Multiplying both sides of an inequality by a positive number never changes the solution set. If both sides are multiplied by a negative number, the sign of the inequality must be reversed to produce an equivalent inequality.

11. Solve $3(x - 4) \geq -2$.
$$3x - 12 \geq -2$$
$$3x - 12 + 12 \geq -2 + 12$$
$$3x \geq 10$$
$$\frac{1}{3}(3x) \geq \frac{1}{3}(10)$$
$$x \geq \frac{10}{3}$$

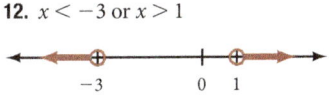

Strategy for Solving Linear Inequalities in One Variable [1.8]

Step 1a: Use the distributive property to separate terms, if necessary.

Step 1b: If fractions are present, consider multiplying both sides by the LCD to eliminate the fractions. If decimals are present, consider multiplying both sides by a power of 10 to clear the inequality of decimals.

Step 1c: Combine similar terms on each side of the inequality.

Step 2: Use the addition property for inequalities to get all variable terms on one side of the inequality and all constant terms on the other side.

Step 3: Use the multiplication property for inequalities to get x by itself on one side of the inequality.

Step 4: Graph the solution set.

Compound Inequalities [1.9]

12. $x < -3$ or $x > 1$

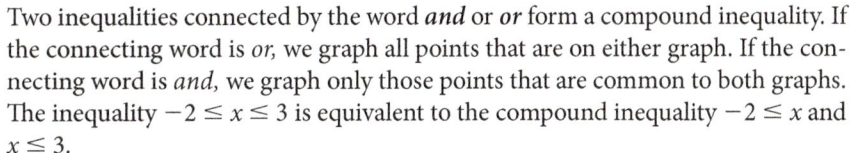

$-2 \leq x \leq 3$

Two inequalities connected by the word *and* or *or* form a compound inequality. If the connecting word is *or,* we graph all points that are on either graph. If the connecting word is *and,* we graph only those points that are common to both graphs. The inequality $-2 \leq x \leq 3$ is equivalent to the compound inequality $-2 \leq x$ and $x \leq 3$.

Chapter 1 Test

Simplify each of the following expressions. [1.1]

1. $5y - 3 - 6y + 4$

2. $3x - 4 + x + 3$

3. $4 - 2(y - 3) - 6$

4. $3(3x - 4) - 2(4x + 5)$

5. Find the value of $3x + 12 + 2x$ when $x = -3$. [1.1]

6. Find the value of $x^2 - 3xy + y^2$ when $x = -2$ and $y = -4$. [1.1]

7. Fill in the tables below to find the sequences formed by substituting the first four counting numbers into the expressions $(n + 2)^2$ and $n^2 + 2$. [1.1]

a.

n	$(n + 2)^2$
1	
2	
3	
4	

b.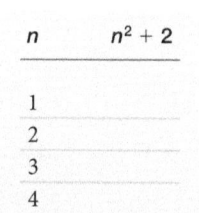

n	$n^2 + 2$
1	
2	
3	
4	

Solve the following equations. [1.2, 1.3, 1.4]

8. $3x - 2 = 7$

9. $4y + 15 = y$

10. $\dfrac{1}{4}x - \dfrac{1}{12} = \dfrac{1}{3}x - \dfrac{1}{6}$

11. $-3(3 - 2x) - 7 = 8$

12. $3x - 9 = -6$

13. $0.05 + 0.07(100 - x) = 3.2$

14. $4(t - 3) + 2(t + 4) = 2t - 16$

15. $4x - 2(3x - 1) = 2x - 8$

For each of the following expressions, write an equivalent equation. [1.5]

16. What number is 40% of 56?

17. 720 is 24% of what number?

Solve each formula for the appropriate variable. [1.5]

18. If $3x - 4y = 16$, find y when $x = 4$.

19. If $3x - 4y = 16$, find x when $y = 2$.

20. Solve $2x + 6y = 12$ for y.

21. Solve $x^2 = v^2 + 2ad$ for a.

Solve each word problem. [1.6, 1.7]

22. Age Problem Paul is twice as old as Becca. Five years ago the sum of their ages was 44. How old are they now?

23. Geometry The length of a rectangle is 5 less than 3 times the width. The perimeter is 150 centimeters. What are the length and width?

24. Coin Problem A man has a collection of dimes and nickels with a total value of $1.70. If he has 8 more dimes than nickels, how many of each coin does he have?

25. Investing A woman has money in two accounts. One account pays 6% annual interest, whereas the other pays 12% annual interest. If she has $500 more invested at 12% than she does at 6% and her total interest for a year is $186, how much does she have in each account?

Solve each inequality, and graph the solution. [1.8]

26. $\dfrac{1}{2}x - 2 > 3$

27. $-6y \le 24$

28. $0.3 - 0.2x < 1.1$

29. $3 - 2(n - 1) \ge 9$

Solve each inequality, and graph the solution. [1.9]

30. $5x - 3 < 2x$ or $2x > 6$

31. $-3 \le 2x - 7 \le 9$

Linear Equations and Inequalities in Two Variables

2

iStockphoto.com © Sierralara

When light comes into contact with a surface that does not transmit light, then all the light that contacts the surface is either reflected off the surface or absorbed into the surface. If we let R represent the percentage of light reflected and A represent the percentage of light absorbed, then the relationship between these two variables can be written as

$$R + A = 100$$

which is a linear equation in two variables. The following table and graph show the same relationship as that described by the equation. The table is a numerical description; the graph is a visual description.

In this chapter we learn how to build tables and draw graphs from linear equations in two variables.

Reflected and Absorbed Light	
Percent Reflected	Percent Absorbed
0	100
20	80
40	60
60	40
80	20
100	0

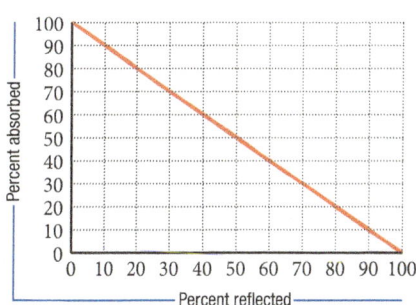

Study Skills

The study skills for this chapter are about attitude. They are points of view that point toward success.

1. **Be Focused, Not Distracted** I have students who begin their assignments by asking themselves, "Why am I taking this class?" If you are asking yourself similar questions, you are distracting yourself from doing the things that will produce the results you want in this course. Don't dwell on questions and evaluations of the class that can be used as excuses for not doing well. If you want to succeed in this course, focus your energy and efforts toward success, rather than distracting yourself from your goals.

2. **Be Resilient** Don't let setbacks keep you from your goals. You want to put yourself on the road to becoming a person who can succeed in this class, or any class in college. Failing a test or quiz, or having a difficult time on some topics, is normal. No one goes through college without some setbacks. Don't let a temporary disappointment keep you from succeeding in this course. A low grade on a test or quiz is simply a signal that you need to reevaluate your study habits.

3. **Intend to Succeed** I have a few students who simply go through the motions of studying without intending to master the material. It is more important to them to look like they are studying than to actually study. You need to study with the intention of being successful in the course. Intend to master the material, no matter what it takes.

Paired Data and Graphing Ordered Pairs

This table and figure show the relationship between the table of values for the speed of a race car and the corresponding bar chart. In Figure 1, the horizontal line that shows the elapsed time in seconds is called the *horizontal axis*, and the vertical line that shows the speed in miles per hour is called the *vertical axis*.

The data in the table are called *paired data* because the information is organized so that each number in the first column is paired with a specific number in the second column. Each pair of numbers is associated with one of the solid bars in Figure 1. For example, the third bar in the bar chart is associated with the pair of numbers 3 seconds and 162.8 miles per hour. The first number, 3 seconds, is associated with the horizontal axis, and the second number, 162.8 miles per hour, is associated with the vertical axis.

Speed of a Race Car	
Time in Seconds	Speed in Miles per Hour
0	0
1	72.7
2	129.9
3	162.8
4	192.2
5	212.4
6	228.1

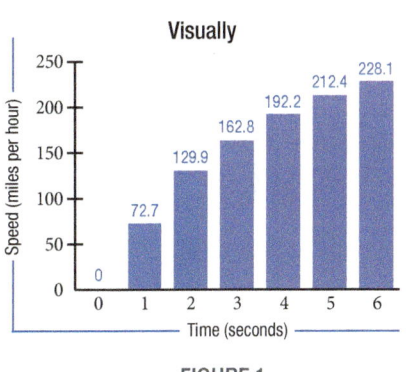

FIGURE 1

Scatter Diagrams and Line Graphs

The information in the table can be visualized with a *scatter diagram* and *line graph* as well. Figure 2 is a scatter diagram of the information in the table above. We use dots instead of the bars shown in Figure 1 to show the speed of the race car at each second during the race. Figure 3 is called a *line graph*. It is constructed by taking the dots in Figure 2 and connecting each one to the next with a straight line. Notice that we have labeled the axes in these two figures a little differently than we did with the bar chart by making the axes intersect at the number 0.

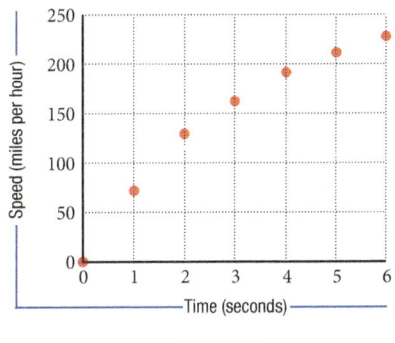

FIGURE 2

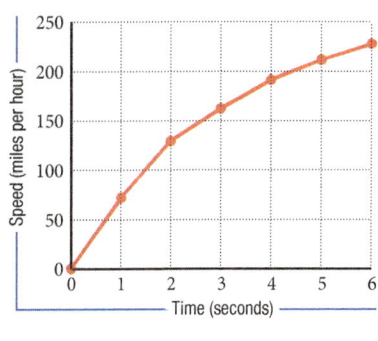

FIGURE 3

The number sequences we have worked with in the past can also be written as paired data by associating each number in the sequence with its position in the sequence. For instance, in the sequence of odd numbers

$$1, 3, 5, 7, 9, \ldots$$

the number 7 is the fourth number in the sequence. Its position is 4, and its value is 7. Here is the sequence of odd numbers written so that the position of each term is noted:

| Position | 1, 2, 3, 4, 5, . . . |
| Value | 1, 3, 5, 7, 9, . . . |

Video Examples

Section 2.1

Example 1   The tables below give the first five terms of the sequence of odd numbers and the sequence of squares as paired data. In each case construct a scatter diagram.

Odd Numbers		Squares	
Position	Value	Position	Value
1	1	1	1
2	3	2	4
3	5	3	9
4	7	4	16
5	9	5	25

SOLUTION   The two scatter diagrams are based on the data from these tables shown here. Notice how the dots in Figure 4 seem to line up in a straight line, whereas the dots in Figure 5 give the impression of a curve. We say the points in Figure 4 suggest a linear relationship between the two sets of data, whereas the points in Figure 5 suggest a nonlinear relationship.

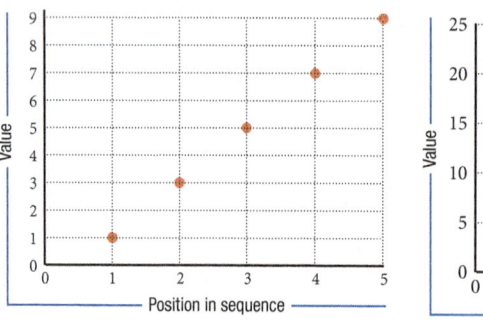

FIGURE 4

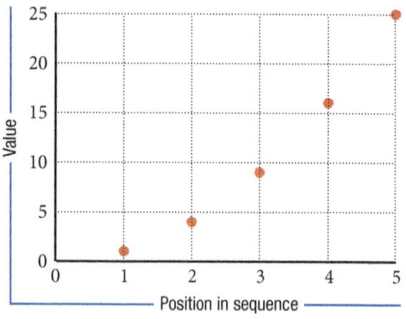

FIGURE 5

As you know, each dot in Figures 4 and 5 corresponds to a pair of numbers, one of which is associated with the horizontal axis and the other with the vertical axis. Paired data play a very important role in the equations we will solve in the next section. To prepare ourselves for those equations, we need to expand the concept of paired data to include negative numbers. At the same time, we want to standardize the position of the axes in the diagrams that we use to visualize paired data.

x-coordinate, y-coordinate

A pair of numbers enclosed in parentheses and separated by a comma, such as $(-2, 1)$, is called an *ordered pair* of numbers. The first number in the pair is called the *x-coordinate* of the ordered pair; the second number is called the *y-coordinate*. For the ordered pair $(-2, 1)$, the x-coordinate is -2 and the y-coordinate is 1.

Ordered pairs of numbers are important in the study of mathematics because they give us a way to visualize solutions to equations. To see the visual component of ordered pairs, we need the diagram shown in Figure 6. It is called the *rectangular coordinate system*.

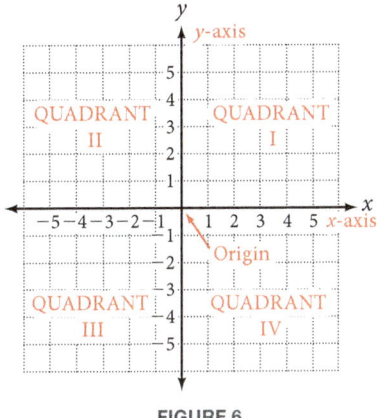

FIGURE 6

The rectangular coordinate system is built from two number lines oriented perpendicular to each other. The horizontal number line is exactly the same as our real number line and is called the *x-axis*. The vertical number line is also the same as our real number line with the positive direction up and the negative direction down. It is called the *y-axis*. The point where the two axes intersect is called the *origin*. As you can see from Figure 6, the axes divide the plane into four *quadrants*, which are numbered I through IV in a counterclockwise direction.

Graphing Ordered Pairs

To graph the ordered pair (a, b), we start at the origin and move a units forward or back (forward if a is positive and back if a is negative). Then we move b units up or down (up if b is positive, down if b is negative). The point where we end up is the graph of the ordered pair (a, b). To graph the ordered pair $(5, 2)$, we start at the origin and move 5 units to the right. Then, from that position, we move 2 units up.

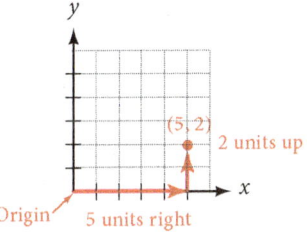

Example 2   Graph the ordered pairs $(3, 4)$, $(3, -4)$, $(-3, 4)$, and $(-3, -4)$.

SOLUTION

> *Note* It is very important that you graph ordered pairs quickly and accurately. Remember, the first coordinate goes with the horizontal axis and the second coordinate goes with the vertical axis.

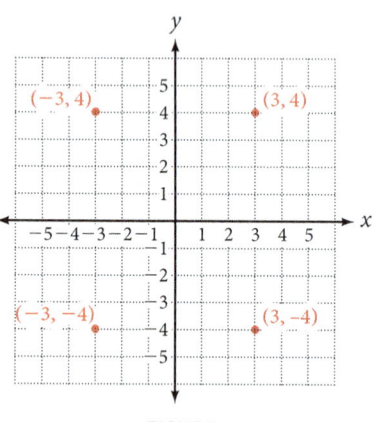

FIGURE 7

We can see in Figure 7 that when we graph ordered pairs, the x-coordinate corresponds to movement parallel to the x-axis (horizontal) and the y-coordinate corresponds to movement parallel to the y-axis (vertical).

Example 3   Graph the ordered pairs $(-1, 3)$, $(2, 5)$, $(0, 0)$, $(0, -3)$, and $(4, 0)$.

SOLUTION   See Figure 8.

> *Note* If we do not label the axes of a coordinate system, we assume that each square is one unit long and one unit wide.

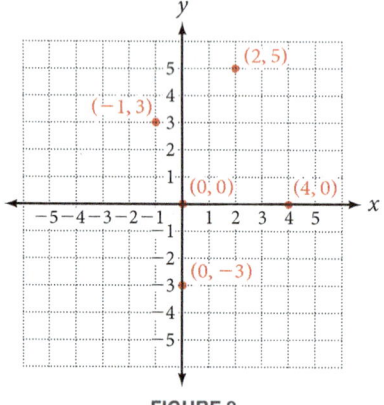

FIGURE 8

Getting Ready for Class

After reading through the preceding section, respond in your own words and in complete sentences.

A. What is an ordered pair of numbers?

B. Explain in words how you would graph the ordered pair $(3, 4)$.

C. How do you construct a rectangular coordinate system?

D. Where is the origin on a rectangular coordinate system?

Graph the following ordered pairs.

1. $(3, 2)$ **2.** $(3, -2)$ **3.** $(-3, 2)$ **4.** $(-3, -2)$

5. $(5, 1)$ **6.** $(5, -1)$ **7.** $(1, 5)$ **8.** $(1, -5)$

9. $(-1, 5)$ **10.** $(-1, -5)$ **11.** $\left(2, \dfrac{1}{2}\right)$ **12.** $\left(3, \dfrac{3}{2}\right)$

13. $\left(-4, -\dfrac{5}{2}\right)$ **14.** $\left(-5, -\dfrac{3}{2}\right)$ **15.** $(3, 0)$ **16.** $(-2, 0)$

17. $(0, 5)$ **18.** $(0, 0)$

Give the coordinates of each numbered point in the figure.

19–28.

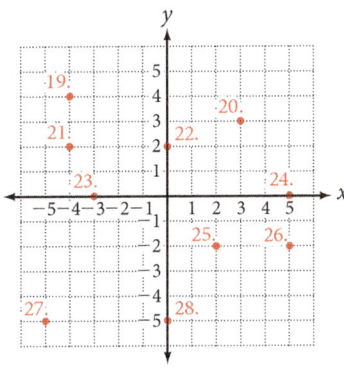

Graph the points $(4, 3)$ and $(-4, -1)$, and draw a straight line that passes through both of them. Then answer the following questions.

29. Does the graph of $(2, 2)$ lie on the line?

30. Does the graph of $(-2, 0)$ lie on the line?

31. Does the graph of $(0, -2)$ lie on the line?

32. Does the graph of $(-6, 2)$ lie on the line?

Graph the points $(-2, 4)$ and $(2, -4)$, and draw a straight line that passes through both of them. Then answer the following questions.

33. Does the graph of $(0, 0)$ lie on the line?

34. Does the graph of $(-1, 2)$ lie on the line?

35. Does the graph of $(2, -1)$ lie on the line?

36. Does the graph of $(1, -2)$ lie on the line?

Draw a straight line that passes through the points $(3, 4)$ and $(3, -4)$. Then answer the following questions.

37. Is the graph of $(3, 0)$ on this line?

38. Is the graph of $(0, 3)$ on this line?

39. Is there any point on this line with an x-coordinate other than 3?

40. If you extended the line, would it pass through a point with a y-coordinate of 10?

Draw a straight line that passes through the points (3, 4) and (−3, 4). Then answer the following questions.

41. Is the graph of (4, 0) on this line?

42. Is the graph of (0, 4) on this line?

43. Is there any point on this line with a *y*-coordinate other than 4?

44. If you extended the line, would it pass through a point with an *x*-coordinate of 10?

Applying the Concepts

45. Hourly Wages Jane takes a job at the local Marcy's department store. Her job pays $8.00 per hour. The graph shows how much Jane earns for working from 0 to 40 hours in a week.

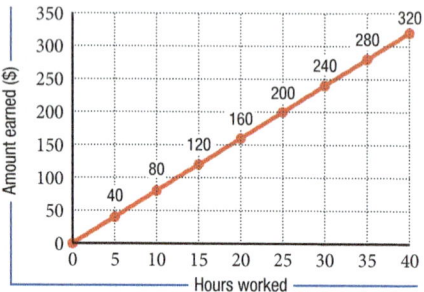

a. List three ordered pairs that lie on the line graph.
b. How much will she earn for working 40 hours?
c. If her check for one week is $240, how many hours did she work?
d. She works 35 hours one week, but her paycheck before deductions are subtracted out is for $260. Is this correct? Explain.

46. Hourly Wages Judy takes a job at Gigi's boutique. Her job pays $6.00 per hour plus $50 per week in commission. The graph shows how much Judy earns for working from 0 to 40 hours in a week.

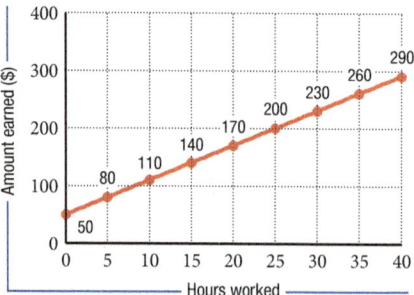

a. List three ordered pairs that lie on the line graph.
b. How much will she earn for working 40 hours?
c. If her check for one week is $230, how many hours did she work?
d. She works 35 hours one week, but her paycheck before deductions are subtracted out is for $260. Is this correct? Explain.

47. **Non-Camera Phone Sales** The table and bar chart shown here show what are the projected sales of non-camera phones for the years 2006–2010. Use the information from the table and chart to construct a line graph.

Year	Sales (in Millions)
2006	300
2007	250
2008	175
2009	150
2010	125

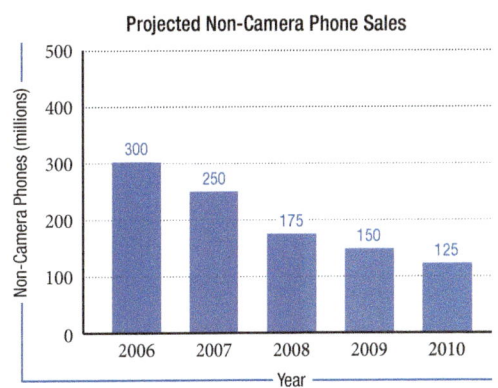

48. **Camera Phone Sales** The table and bar chart shown here show the projected sales of camera phones from 2006 to 2010. Use the information from the table and chart to construct a line graph.

Year	Sales (in Millions)
2006	500
2007	650
2008	750
2009	875
2010	900

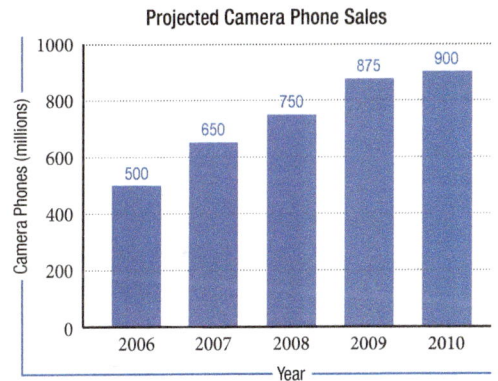

49. **Kentucky Derby** The line graph gives the monetary bets placed at the Kentucky Derby for specific years. If x represents the year in question and y represents the total wagering for that year, write five ordered pairs that describe the information in the table.

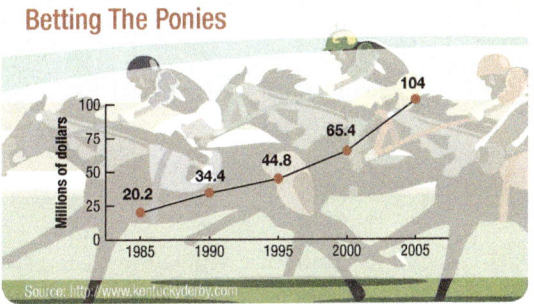

Betting The Ponies

50. Health Care Costs Write 5 ordered pairs that lie on the curve shown below.

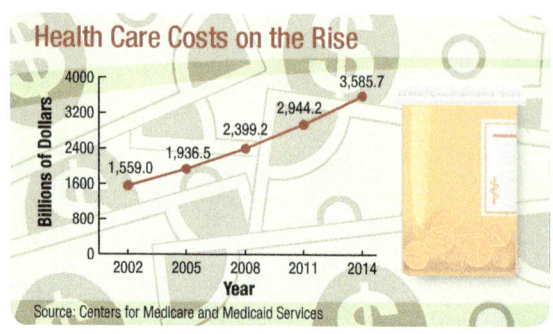

51. Right triangle ABC (Figure 9) has legs of length 5. Point C is the ordered pair (6, 2). Find the coordinates of A and B.

52. Right triangle ABC (Figure 10) has legs of length 7. Point C is the ordered pair $(-8, -3)$. Find the coordinates of A and B.

53. Rectangle $ABCD$ (Figure 11) has a length of 5 and a width of 3. Point D is the ordered pair (7, 2). Find points A, B, and C.

54. Rectangle $ABCD$ (Figure 12) has a length of 5 and a width of 3. Point D is the ordered pair $(-1, 1)$. Find points A, B, and C.

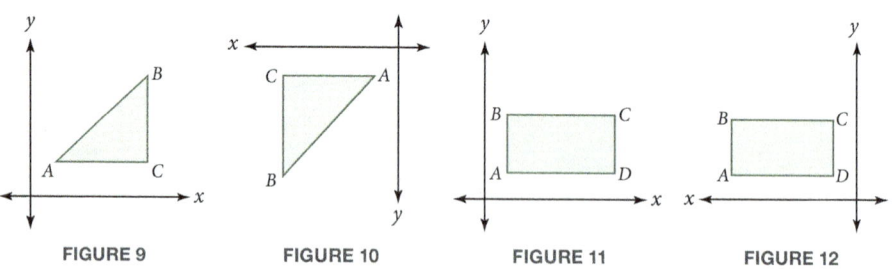

FIGURE 9   FIGURE 10   FIGURE 11   FIGURE 12

Getting Ready for the Next Section

55. Let $2x + 3y = 6$

   a. Find x if $y = 4$ **b.** Find x if $y = -2$

   c. Find y if $x = 3$ **d.** Find y if $x = 9$

56. Let $2x - 5y = 20$

   a. Find x if $y = 0$ **b.** Find x if $y = -6$

   c. Find y if $x = 0$ **d.** Find y if $x = 5$

57. Let $y = 2x - 1$

   a. Find x if $y = 7$ **b.** Find x if $y = 3$

   c. Find y if $x = 0$ **d.** Find y if $x = 5$

58. Let $y = 3x - 2$

   a. Find x if $y = 4$ **b.** Find x if $y = 3$

   c. Find y if $x = 2$ **d.** Find y if $x = -3$

Solutions to Linear Equations in Two Variables

In this section we will begin to investigate equations in two variables. As you will see, equations in two variables have pairs of numbers for solutions. Because we know how to use paired data to construct tables, histograms, and other charts, we can take our work with paired data further by using equations in two variables to construct tables of paired data. Let's begin this section by reviewing the relationship between equations in one variable and their solutions.

If we solve the equation $3x - 2 = 10$, the solution is $x = 4$. If we graph this solution, we simply draw the real number line and place a dot at the point whose coordinate is 4. The relationship between linear equations in one variable, their solutions, and the graphs of those solutions look like this:

Equation	Solution	Graph of Solution Set
$3x - 2 = 10$	$x = 4$	
$x + 5 = 7$	$x = 2$	
$2x = -6$	$x = -3$	

Note If this discussion seems a little long and confusing, you may want to look over some of the examples first and then come back and read this. Remember, it isn't always easy to read material in mathematics. What is important is that you understand what you are doing when you work problems. The reading is intended to assist you in understanding what you are doing. It is important to read everything in the book, but you don't always have to read it in the order it is written.

When the equation has one variable, the solution is a single number whose graph is a point on a line.

Now, consider the equation $2x + y = 3$. The first thing we notice is that there are two variables instead of one. Therefore, a solution to the equation $2x + y = 3$ will be not a single number but a pair of numbers, one for x and one for y, that makes the equation a true statement. One pair of numbers that works is $x = 2$, $y = -1$ because when we substitute them for x and y in the equation, we get a true statement.

$$2(2) + (-1) \stackrel{?}{=} 3$$
$$4 - 1 = 3$$
$$3 = 3 \qquad \text{A true statement}$$

The pair of numbers $x = 2$, $y = -1$ is written as $(2, -1)$. As you know from Section 3.1, $(2, -1)$ is called an *ordered pair* because it is a pair of numbers written in a specific order. The first number is always associated with the variable x, and the second number is always associated with the variable y. We call the first number in the ordered pair the *x-coordinate* (or x component) and the second number the *y-coordinate* (or y component) of the ordered pair.

Let's look back to the equation $2x + y = 3$. The ordered pair $(2, -1)$ is not the only solution. Another solution is $(0, 3)$ because when we substitute 0 for x and 3 for y we get

$$2(0) + 3 \stackrel{?}{=} 3$$
$$0 + 3 = 3$$
$$3 = 3 \qquad \text{A true statement}$$

Still another solution is the ordered pair $(5, -7)$ because

$$2(5) + (-7) \stackrel{?}{=} 3$$
$$10 - 7 = 3$$
$$3 = 3 \qquad \text{A true statement}$$

As a matter of fact, for any number we want to use for x, there is another number we can use for y that will make the equation a true statement. There is an infinite number of ordered pairs that satisfy (are solutions to) the equation $2x + y = 3$; we have listed just a few of them.

Video Examples

Section 2.2

Example 1   Given the equation $2x + 3y = 6$, complete the following ordered pairs so they will be solutions to the equation: $(0, \ ), (\ , 1), (3, \ )$.

SOLUTION   To complete the ordered pair $(0, \ )$, we substitute 0 for x in the equation and then solve for y:

$$2(0) + 3y = 6$$
$$3y = 6$$
$$y = 2$$

The ordered pair is $(0, 2)$.

To complete the ordered pair $(\ , 1)$, we substitute 1 for y in the equation and solve for x:

$$2x + 3(1) = 6$$
$$2x + 3 = 6$$
$$2x = 3$$
$$x = \frac{3}{2}$$

The ordered pair is $\left(\frac{3}{2}, 1\right)$.

To complete the ordered pair $(3, \ )$, we substitute 3 for x in the equation and solve for y:

$$2(3) + 3y = 6$$
$$6 + 3y = 6$$
$$3y = 0$$
$$y = 0$$

The ordered pair is $(3, 0)$.

Notice in each case that once we have used a number in place of one of the variables, the equation becomes a linear equation in one variable. We then use the method explained in Chapter 2 to solve for that variable.

Example 2   Complete the following table for the equation $2x - 5y = 20$.

x	y
0	
	2
	0
−5	

SOLUTION   Filling in the table is equivalent to completing the following ordered pairs: $(0, \ ), (\ , 2), (\ , 0), (-5, \ )$. So we proceed as in Example 1.

When $x = 0$, we have $\qquad$ When $y = 2$, we have

$$2(0) - 5y = 20 \qquad\qquad 2x - 5(2) = 20$$
$$0 - 5y = 20 \qquad\qquad 2x - 10 = 20$$
$$-5y = 20 \qquad\qquad 2x = 30$$
$$y = -4 \qquad\qquad x = 15$$

When $y = 0$, we have $\qquad$ When $x = -5$, we have

$$2x - 5(0) = 20 \qquad\qquad 2(-5) - 5y = 20$$
$$2x - 0 = 20 \qquad\qquad -10 - 5y = 20$$
$$2x = 20 \qquad\qquad -5y = 30$$
$$x = 10 \qquad\qquad y = -6$$

The completed table looks like this:

x	y
0	-4
15	2
10	0
-5	-6

which is equivalent to the ordered pairs $(0, -4)$, $(15, 2)$, $(10, 0)$, and $(-5, -6)$. ◼

Example 3   Complete the following table for the equation $y = 2x - 1$.

x	y
0	
5	
	7
	3

SOLUTION   When $x = 0$, we have $\qquad$ When $x = 5$, we have

$$y = 2(0) - 1 \qquad\qquad y = 2(5) - 1$$
$$y = 0 - 1 \qquad\qquad y = 10 - 1$$
$$y = -1 \qquad\qquad y = 9$$

When $y = 7$, we have $\qquad$ When $y = 3$, we have

$$7 = 2x - 1 \qquad\qquad 3 = 2x - 1$$
$$8 = 2x \qquad\qquad 4 = 2x$$
$$4 = x \qquad\qquad 2 = x$$

The completed table is

x	y
0	−1
5	9
4	7
2	3

which means the ordered pairs $(0, -1)$, $(5, 9)$, $(4, 7)$, and $(2, 3)$ are among the solutions to the equation $y = 2x - 1$.

Example 4   Which of the ordered pairs $(2, 3)$, $(1, 5)$, and $(-2, -4)$ are solutions to the equation $y = 3x + 2$?

SOLUTION   If an ordered pair is a solution to the equation, then it must satisfy the equation; that is, when the coordinates are used in place of the variables in the equation, the equation becomes a true statement.

Try $(2, 3)$ in $y = 3x + 2$:

$$3 \overset{?}{=} 3(2) + 2$$

$$3 = 6 + 2$$

$$3 = 8 \qquad\qquad \text{A false statement}$$

Try $(1, 5)$ in $y = 3x + 2$:

$$5 \overset{?}{=} 3(1) + 2$$

$$5 = 3 + 2$$

$$5 = 5 \qquad\qquad \text{A true statement}$$

Try $(-2, -4)$ in $y = 3x + 2$:

$$-4 \overset{?}{=} 3(-2) + 2$$

$$-4 = -6 + 2$$

$$-4 = -4 \qquad\qquad \text{A true statement}$$

The ordered pairs $(1, 5)$ and $(-2, -4)$ are solutions to the equation $y = 3x + 2$, and $(2, 3)$ is not.

Getting Ready for Class

After reading through the preceding section, respond in your own words and in complete sentences.

A. How can you tell if an ordered pair is a solution to an equation?
B. How would you find a solution to $y = 3x - 5$?
C. Why is $(3, 2)$ not a solution to $y = 3x - 5$?
D. How many solutions are there to an equation that contains two variables?

Problem Set 2.2

For each equation, complete the given ordered pairs.

1. $2x + y = 6$ $(0, \ ), (\ , 0), (\ , -6)$ **2.** $3x - y = 5$ $(0, \ ), (1, \ ), (\ , 5)$

3. $3x + 4y = 12$ $(0, \ ), (\ , 0), (-4, \ )$ **4.** $5x - 5y = 20$ $(0, \ ), (\ , -2), (1, \ )$

5. $y = 4x - 3$ $(1, \ ), (\ , 0), (5, \ )$ **6.** $y = 3x - 5$ $(\ , 13), (0, \ ), (-2, \ )$

7. $y = 7x - 1$ $(2, \ ), (\ , 6), (0, \ )$ **8.** $y = 8x + 2$ $(3, \ ), (\ , 0), (\ , -6)$

9. $x = -5$ $(\ , 4), (\ , -3), (\ , 0)$ **10.** $y = 2$ $(5, \ ), (-8, \ ), \left(\frac{1}{2}, \ \right)$

For each of the following equations, complete the given table.

11. $y = 3x$

x	y
1	3
-3	
	12
	18

12. $y = -2x$

x	y
-4	
0	
	10
	12

13. $y = 4x$

x	y
0	
	-2
-3	
	12

14. $y = -5x$

x	y
3	
	0
-2	
	-20

15. $x + y = 5$

x	y
2	
3	
	0
	-4

16. $x - y = 8$

x	y
0	
4	
	-3
	-2

17. $2x - y = 4$

x	y
	0
	2
1	
-3	

18. $3x - y = 9$

x	y
	0
	-9
5	
-4	

19. $y = 6x - 1$

x	y
0	
	-7
-3	
	8

20. $y = 5x + 7$

x	y
0	
-2	
-4	
	-8

For the following equations, tell which of the given ordered pairs are solutions.

21. $2x - 5y = 10$ $(2, 3), (0, -2), \left(\frac{5}{2}, 1\right)$

22. $3x + 7y = 21$ $(0, 3), (7, 0), (1, 2)$

23. $y = 7x - 2$ $(1, 5), (0, -2), (-2, -16)$

24. $y = 8x - 3$ $(0, 3), (5, 16), (1, 5)$

25. $y = 6x$ $(1, 6), (-2, 12), (0, 0)$ **26.** $y = -4x$ $(0, 0), (2, 4), (-3, 12)$

27. $x + y = 0$ $(1, 1), (2, -2), (3, 3)$ **28.** $x - y = 1$ $(0, 1), (0, -1), (1, 2)$

29. $x = 3$ $(3, 0), (3, -3), (5, 3)$ **30.** $y = -4$ $(3, -4), (-4, 4), (0, -4)$

Applying the Concepts

31. Perimeter If the perimeter of a rectangle is 30 inches, then the relationship between the length l and the width w is given by the equation

$$2l + 2w = 30$$

What is the length when the width is 3 inches?

32. Perimeter The relationship between the perimeter P of a square and the length of its side s is given by the formula $P = 4s$. If each side of a square is 5 inches, what is the perimeter? If the perimeter of a square is 28 inches, how long is a side?

33. Hourly Wages Janai earns $12 per hour working as a math tutor. We can express the amount she earns each week, y, for working x hours with the equation $y = 12x$. Indicate with a yes or no, which of the following could be one of Janai's paychecks. If you answer no, explain your answer.

a. $60 for working five hours. **b.** $100 for working nine hours.

c. $80 for working seven hours. **d.** $168 for working 14 hours.

34. Hourly Wages Erin earns $15 per hour working as a graphic designer. We can express the amount she earns each week, y, for working x hours with the equation $y = 15x$. Indicate with a yes or no which of the following could be one of Erin's paychecks. If you answer no, explain your answer.

a. $75 for working five hours. **b.** $125 for working nine hours.
c. $90 for working six hours. **d.** $500 for working 35 hours.

35. Depreciation The equation $V = -45{,}000t + 600{,}000$, can be used to find the value, V, of a small crane at the end of t years.

a. What is the value of the crane at the end of five years?
b. When is the crane worth $330,000?
c. Is it true that the crane with be worth $150,000 after nine years?
d. How much did the crane cost?

36. Depreciation The equation $P = -400t + 2{,}500$, can be used to find the price, P, of a notebook computer at the end of t years.

a. What is the value of the notebook computer at the end of four years?
b. When is the notebook computer worth $1,700?
c. Is it true that the notebook computer with be worth $100 after five years?
d. How much did the notebook computer cost?

Getting Ready for the Next Section

37. Find y when x is 4 in the formula $3x + 2y = 6$.

38. Find y when x is 0 in the formula $3x + 2y = 6$.

39. Find y when x is 0 in $y = -\dfrac{1}{3}x + 2$. **40.** Find y when x is 3 in $y = -\dfrac{1}{3}x + 2$.

41. Find y when x is 2 in $y = \dfrac{3}{2}x - 3$. **42.** Find y when x is 4 in $y = \dfrac{3}{2}x - 3$.

43. Solve $5x + y = 4$ for y. **44.** Solve $-3x + y = 5$ for y.

45. Solve $3x - 2y = 6$ for y. **46.** Solve $2x - 3y = 6$ for y.

Graphing Linear Equations in Two Variables

In this section we will use the rectangular coordinate system introduced in Section 3.1 to obtain a visual picture of *all* solutions to a linear equation in two variables. The process we use to obtain a visual picture of all solutions to an equation is called *graphing*. The picture itself is called the *graph* of the equation.

Video Examples

Section 2.3

Example 1   Graph the solution set for $x + y = 5$.

SOLUTION   We know from the previous section that an infinite number of ordered pairs are solutions to the equation $x + y = 5$. We can't possibly list them all. What we can do is list a few of them and see if there is any pattern to their graphs.

Some ordered pairs that are solutions to $x + y = 5$ are (0, 5), (2, 3), (3, 2), (5, 0). The graph of each is shown in Figure 1.

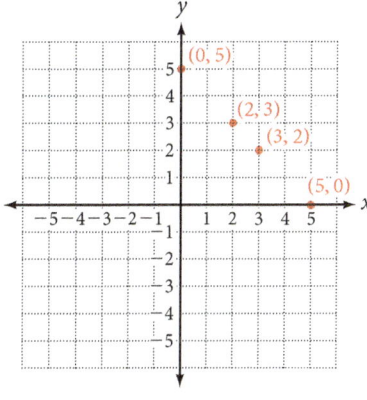

FIGURE 1

Now, by passing a straight line through these points we can graph the solution set for the equation $x + y = 5$. Linear equations in two variables always have graphs that are straight lines. The graph of the solution set for $x + y = 5$ is shown in Figure 2.

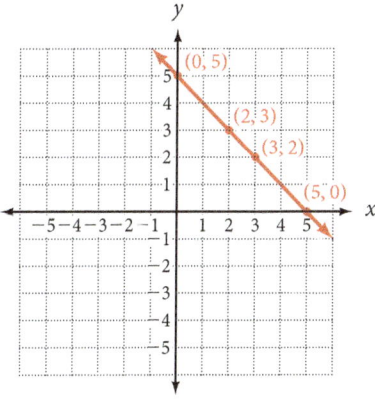

FIGURE 2

Every ordered pair that satisfies $x + y = 5$ has its graph on the line, and any point on the line has coordinates that satisfy the equation. So, there is a one-to-one correspondence between points on the line and solutions to the equation. ∎

Our ability to graph an equation as we have done in Example 1 is due to the invention of the rectangular coordinate system. The French philosopher René Descartes (1595–1650) is the person usually credited with the invention of the rectangular coordinate system. As a philosopher, Descartes is responsible for the statement "I think, therefore I am." Until Descartes invented his coordinate system in 1637, algebra and geometry were treated as separate subjects. The rectangular coordinate system allows us to connect algebra and geometry by associating geometric shapes with algebraic equations.

Here is the precise definition for a linear equation in two variables.

> **(dĕf**   *Linear Equation in Two Variables, Standard Form*
>
> Any equation that can be put in the form $ax + by = c$, where a, b, and c are real numbers and a and b are not both 0, is called a ***linear equation in two variables***. The graph of any equation of this form is a straight line (that is why these equations are called "linear"). The form $ax + by = c$ is called ***standard form***.

To graph a linear equation in two variables, we simply graph its solution set; that is, we draw a line through all the points whose coordinates satisfy the equation. Here are the steps to follow.

> **[Δ≠Σ**   *How to Graph a Linear Equation in Two Variables*
>
> **Step 1:** Find any three ordered pairs that satisfy the equation. This can be done by using a convenient number for one variable and solving for the other variable.
> **Step 2:** Graph the three ordered pairs found in step 1. Actually, we need only two points to graph a straight line. The third point serves as a check. If all three points do not line up, there is a mistake in our work.
> **Step 3:** Draw a straight line through the three points graphed in step 2.

Note   The meaning of the convenient numbers referred to in step 1 will become clear as you read the next two examples.

Example 2   Graph the equation $y = 3x - 1$.

SOLUTION   Because $y = 3x - 1$ can be put in the form $ax + by = c$, it is a linear equation in two variables. Hence, the graph of its solution set is a straight line. We can find some specific solutions by substituting numbers for x and then solving for the corresponding values of y. We are free to choose any numbers for x, so let's use 0, 2, and -1.

> **Note** It may seem that we have simply picked the numbers 0, 2, and −1 out of the air and used them for x. In fact we have done just that. Could we have used numbers other than these? The answer is yes, we can substitute any number for x; there will always be a value of y to go with it.

Let $x = 0$: $\quad y = 3(0) - 1$
$$y = 0 - 1$$
$$y = -1$$

The ordered pair $(0, -1)$ is one solution.

Let $x = 2$: $\quad y = 3(2) - 1$
$$y = 6 - 1$$
$$y = 5$$

The ordered pair $(2, 5)$ is a second solution.

Let $x = -1$: $\quad y = 3(-1) - 1$
$$y = -3 - 1$$
$$y = -4$$

The ordered pair $(-1, -4)$ is a third solution.

In table form

x	y
0	−1
2	5
−1	−4

Next, we graph the ordered pairs $(0, -1)$, $(2, 5)$, $(-1, -4)$ and draw a straight line through them.

The line we have drawn in Figure 3 is the graph of $y = 3x - 1$.

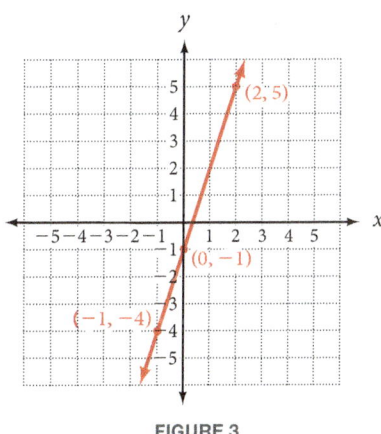

FIGURE 3

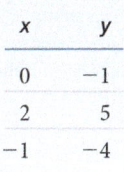

Example 2 again illustrates the connection between algebra and geometry that we mentioned previously. Descartes' rectangular coordinate system allows us to associate the equation $y = 3x - 1$ (an algebraic concept) with a specific straight line (a geometric concept). The study of the relationship between equations in algebra and their associated geometric figures is called *analytic geometry*. The rectangular coordinate system often is referred to as the *Cartesian coordinate system* in honor of Descartes.

Example 3 Graph the equation $y = -\frac{1}{3}x + 2$.

SOLUTION We need to find three ordered pairs that satisfy the equation. To do so, we can let x equal any numbers we choose and find corresponding values of y. But, every value of x we substitute into the equation is going to be multiplied by $-\frac{1}{3}$. Let's use numbers for x that are divisible by 3, like -3, 0, and 3. That way, when we multiply them by $-\frac{1}{3}$, the result will be an integer.

Note   In Example 3 the values of *x* we used, -3, 0, and 3, are referred to as convenient values of *x* because they are easier to work with than some other numbers. For instance, if we let $x = 2$ in our original equation, we would have to add $-\frac{2}{3}$ and 2 to find the corresponding value of *y*. Not only would the arithmetic be more difficult but also the ordered pair we obtained would have a fraction for its *y*-coordinate, making it more difficult to graph accurately.

Let $x = -3$: $y = -\frac{1}{3}(-3) + 2$

$$y = 1 + 2$$

$$y = 3$$

The ordered pair $(-3, 3)$ is one solution.

Let $x = 0$: $y = -\frac{1}{3}(0) + 2$

$$y = 0 + 2$$

$$y = 2$$

The ordered pair $(0, 2)$ is a second solution.

Let $x = 3$: $y = -\frac{1}{3}(3) + 2$

$$y = -1 + 2$$

$$y = 1$$

The ordered pair $(3, 1)$ is a third solution.

In table form

x	y
-3	3
0	2
3	1

Graphing the ordered pairs $(-3, 3)$, $(0, 2)$, and $(3, 1)$ and drawing a straight line through their graphs, we have the graph of the equation $y = -\frac{1}{3}x + 2$, as shown in Figure 4.

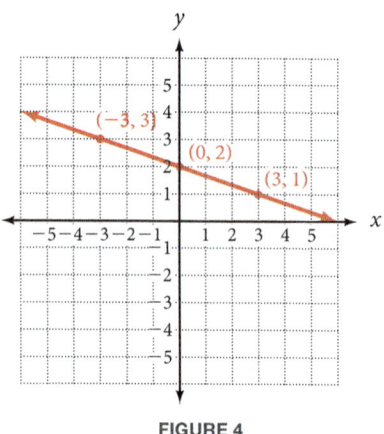

FIGURE 4

Example 4   Graph the solution set for $3x - 2y = 6$.

SOLUTION   It will be easier to find convenient values of *x* to use in the equation if we first solve the equation for *y*. To do so, we add $-3x$ to each side, and then we multiply each side by $-\frac{1}{2}$.

$3x - 2y = 6$	*Original equation*
$-2y = -3x + 6$	*Add $-3x$ to each side*
$-\frac{1}{2}(-2y) = -\frac{1}{2}(-3x + 6)$	*Multiply each side by $-\frac{1}{2}$*
$y = \frac{3}{2}x - 3$	*Simplify each side*

Now, because each value of *x* will be multiplied by $\frac{3}{2}$, it will be to our advantage to choose values of *x* that are divisible by 2. That way, we will obtain values of *y* that do not contain fractions. This time, let's use 0, 2, and 4 for *x*.

When $x = 0$: $y = \dfrac{3}{2}(0) - 3$

$$y = 0 - 3$$

$$y = -3$$

The ordered pair $(0, -3)$ is one solution.

When $x = 2$: $y = \dfrac{3}{2}(2) - 3$

$$y = 3 - 3$$

$$y = 0$$

The ordered pair $(2, 0)$ is a second solution.

When $x = 4$: $y = \dfrac{3}{2}(4) - 3$

$$y = 6 - 3$$

$$y = 3$$

The ordered pair $(4, 3)$ is a third solution

Graphing the ordered pairs $(0, -3)$, $(2, 0)$, and $(4, 3)$ and drawing a line through them, we have the graph shown in Figure 5.

Note   After reading through Example 4, many students ask why we didn't use -2 for x when we were finding ordered pairs that were solutions to the original equation. The answer is, we could have. If we were to let $x = -2$, the corresponding value of y would have been -6. As you can see by looking at the graph in Figure 5, the ordered pair $(-2, -6)$ is on the graph.

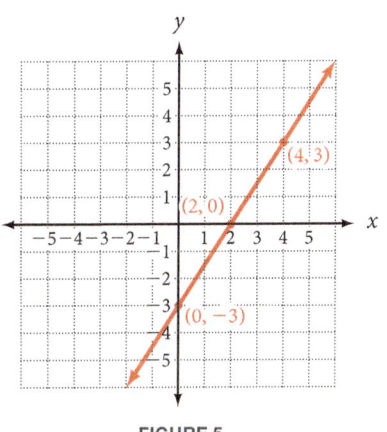

FIGURE 5

Example 5   Graph each of the following lines.

a. $y = \dfrac{1}{2}x$ **b.** $x = 3$ **c.** $y = -2$

SOLUTION

a. The line $y = \frac{1}{2}x$ passes through the origin because $(0, 0)$ satisfies the equation. To sketch the graph we need at least one more point on the line. When x is 2, we obtain the point $(2, 1)$, and when x is -4, we obtain the point $(-4, -2)$. The graph of $y = \frac{1}{2}x$ is shown in Figure 6A.

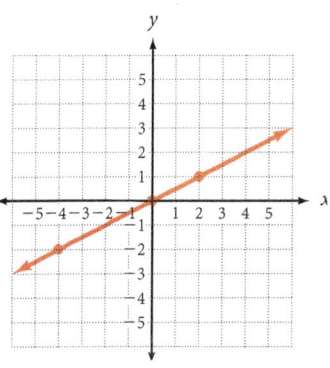

FIGURE 6A

b. The line $x = 3$ is the set of all points whose does not appear in the equation, so the y-coordinate can be any number. Note that we can write our equation as a linear equation in two variables by writing it as $x + 0y = 3$. Because the product of 0 and y will always be 0, y can be any number. The graph of $x = 3$ is the vertical line shown in Figure 6B.

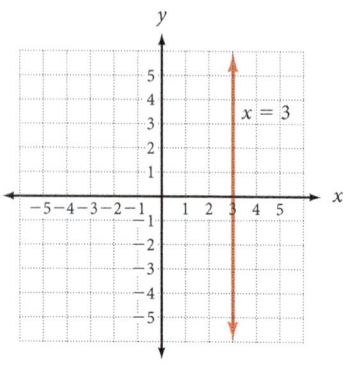

FIGURE 6B

c. The line $y = -2$ is the set of all points whose y-coordinate is -2. The variable x does not appear in the equation, so the x-coordinate can be any number. Again, we can write our equation as a linear equation in two variables by writing it as $0x + y = -2$. Because the product of 0 and x will always be 0, x can be any number. The graph of $y = -2$ is the horizontal line shown in Figure 6C.

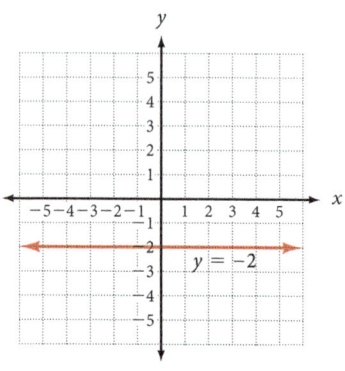

FIGURE 6C

Special Equations and Their Graphs

For the equations below, m, a, and b are real numbers.

Through the Origin

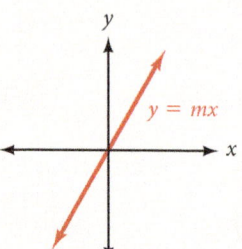

FIGURE 7A Any equation of the form $y = mx$ has a graph that passes through the origin.

Vertical Line

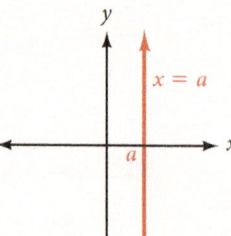

FIGURE 7B Any equation of the form $x = a$ has a vertical line for its graph.

Horizontal Line

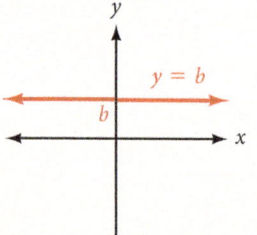

FIGURE 7C Any equation of the form $y = b$ has a horizontal line for its graph.

Getting Ready for Class

After reading through the preceding section, respond in your own words and in complete sentences.

A. Explain how you would go about graphing the line $x + y = 5$.

B. When graphing straight lines, why is it a good idea to find three points, when every straight line is determined by only two points?

C. What kind of equations have vertical lines for graphs?

D. What kind of equations have horizontal lines for graphs?

*Pride is a personal commitment.
It is an attitude which separates excellence from mediocrity.*
—William Blake

The University of Northern Alabama places its Pride Rock, a 60-pound granite stone engraved with a lion's paw print, behind the north end zone at all home football games. The rock reminds current Lion players of the proud athletic traditions that has been established at the school, and to take pride in their efforts on the field.

Photo courtesy UNA

The same idea holds true for your work in your math class. Take pride in it. When you turn in an assignment, it should be accurate and easy for the instructor to read. It shows that you care about your progress in the course and that you take pride in your work. The work that you turn in to your instructor is a reflection of you. As the quote from William Blake indicates, pride is a personal commitment; a decision that you make, yourself. And once you make that commitment to take pride in the work you do in your math class, you have directed yourself toward excellence, and away from mediocrity.

Problem Set 2.3

For the following equations, complete the given ordered pairs, and use the results to graph the solution set for the equation.

1. $x + y = 4$ $\quad (0, \ ), (2, \ ), (\ , 0)$ **2.** $x - y = 3$ $\quad (0, \ ), (2, \ ), (\ , 0)$

3. $x + y = 3$ $\quad (0, \ ), (2, \ ), (\ , -1)$ **4.** $x - y = 4$ $\quad (1, \ ), (-1, \ ), (\ , 0)$

5. $y = 2x$ $\quad (0, \ ), (-2, \ ), (2, \ )$ **6.** $y = \frac{1}{2}x$ $\quad (0, \ ), (-2, \ ), (2, \ )$

7. $y = \frac{1}{3}x$ $\quad (-3, \ ), (0, \ ), (3, \ )$ **8.** $y = 3x$ $\quad (-2, \ ), (0, \ ), (2, \ )$

9. $y = 2x + 1$ $\quad (0, \ ), (-1, \ ), (1, \ )$ **10.** $y = -2x + 1$ $\quad (0, \ ), (-1, \ ), (1, \ )$

11. $y = 4$ $\quad (0, \ ), (-1, \ ), (2, \ )$ **12.** $x = 3$ $\quad (\ , -2), (\ , 0), (\ , 5)$

13. $y = \frac{1}{2}x + 3$ $\quad (-2, \ ), (0, \ ), (2, \ )$ **14.** $y = \frac{1}{2}x - 3$ $\quad (-2, \ ), (0, \ ), (2, \ )$

15. $y = -\frac{2}{3}x + 1$ $\quad (-3, \ ), (0, \ ), (3, \ )$ **16.** $y = -\frac{2}{3}x - 1$ $\quad (-3, \ ), (0, \ ), (3, \ )$

Solve each equation for y. Then, complete the given ordered pairs, and use them to draw the graph.

17. $2x + y = 3$ $\quad (-1, \ ), (0, \ ), (1, \ )$ **18.** $3x + y = 2$ $\quad (-1, \ ), (0, \ ), (1, \ )$

19. $3x + 2y = 6$ $\quad (0, \ ), (2, \ ), (4, \ )$ **20.** $2x + 3y = 6$ $\quad (0, \ ), (3, \ ), (6, \ )$

21. $-x + 2y = 6$ $\quad (-2, \ ), (0, \ ), (2, \ )$ **22.** $-x + 3y = 6$ $\quad (-3, \ ), (0, \ ), (3, \ )$

Find three solutions to each of the following equations, and then graph the solution set.

23. $y = -\frac{1}{2}x$ **24.** $y = -2x$ **25.** $y = 3x - 1$ **26.** $y = -3x - 1$

27. $-2x + y = 1$ **28.** $-3x + y = 1$ **29.** $3x + 4y = 8$ **30.** $3x - 4y = 8$

31. $x = -2$ **32.** $y = 3$ **33.** $y = 2$ **34.** $x = -3$

Graph each equation.

35. $y = \frac{3}{4}x + 1$ **36.** $y = \frac{2}{3}x + 1$ **37.** $y = \frac{1}{3}x + \frac{2}{3}$ **38.** $y = \frac{1}{2}x + \frac{1}{2}$.

39. $y = \frac{2}{3}x + \frac{2}{3}$ **40.** $y = -\frac{3}{4}x + \frac{3}{2}$

For each equation in each table below, indicate whether the graph is horizontal (H), or vertical (V), or whether it passes through the origin (O).

41.

Equation	H, V, and/or O
$x = 3$	
$y = 3$	
$y = 3x$	
$y = 0$	

42.

Equation	H, V, and/or O
$x = \frac{1}{2}$	
$y = \frac{1}{2}$	
$y = \frac{1}{2}x$	
$x = 0$	

43.

Equation	H, V, and/or O
$x = -\frac{3}{5}$	
$y = -\frac{3}{5}$	
$y = -\frac{3}{5}x$	
$x = 0$	

44.

Equation	H, V, and/or O
$x = -4$	
$y = -4$	
$y = -4x$	
$y = 0$	

45. Use the graph at the right to complete the table.

x	y
	-3
-2	
0	
	0
6	

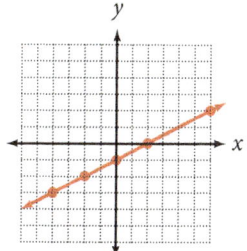

46. Use the graph at the right to complete the table. (*Hint:* Some parts have two answers.)

x	y
-3	6
	4
0	3
	1
6	

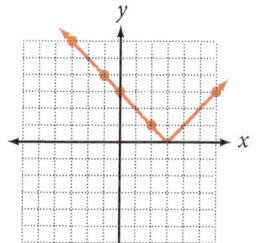

47. Paying Attention to Instructions Work each problem according to the instructions given..

   a. Solve: $2x + 5 = 10$

   b. Find x when y is 0: $2x + 5y = 10$

   c. Find y when x is 0: $2x + 5y = 10$

   d. Graph: $2x + 5y = 10$

   e. Solve for y: $2x + 5y = 10$

48. Paying Attention to Instructions Work each problem according to the instructions given..

   a. Solve: $x - 2 = 6$

   b. Find x when y is 0: $x - 2y = 6$

   c. Find y when x is 0: $x - 2y = 6$

   d. Graph: $x - 2y = 6$

   e. Solve for y: $x - 2y = 6$

Getting Ready for the Next Section

49. Let $3x + 2y = 6$

    a. Find x when $y = 0$ **b.** Find y when $x = 0$

50. Let $2x - 5y = 10$

    a. Find x when $y = 0$ **b.** Find y when $x = 0$

51. Let $-x + 2y = 4$

    a. Find x when $y = 0$ **b.** Find y when $x = 0$

52. Let $3x - y = 6$

    a. Find x when $y = 0$ **b.** Find y when $x = 0$

53. Let $y = -\dfrac{1}{3}x + 2$

    a. Find x when $y = 0$ **b.** Find y when $x = 0$

54. Let $y = \dfrac{3}{2}x - 3$

    a. Find x when $y = 0$ **b.** Find y when $x = 0$

More on Graphing: Intercepts

In this section we continue our work with graphing lines by finding the points where a line crosses the axes of our coordinate system. To do so, we use the fact that any point on the x-axis has a y-coordinate of 0 and any point on the y-axis has an x-coordinate of 0. We begin with the following definition.

> **(dĕf**   *x-intercept, y-intercept*
>
> The *x-intercept* of a straight line is the x-coordinate of the point where the graph crosses the x-axis. The *y-intercept* is defined similarly. It is the y-coordinate of the point where the graph crosses the y-axis.

If the x-intercept is a, then the point $(a, 0)$ lies on the graph. (This is true because any point on the x-axis has a y-coordinate of 0.)

If the y-intercept is b, then the point $(0, b)$ lies on the graph. (This is true because any point on the y-axis has an x-coordinate of 0.)

Graphically, the relationship is shown in Figure 1.

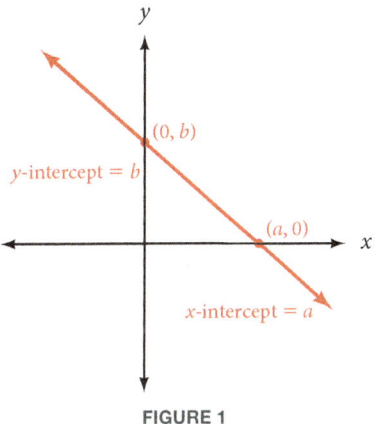

FIGURE 1

Video Examples

Section 2.4

Example 1   Find the x- and y-intercepts for $3x - 2y = 6$, and then use them to draw the graph.

SOLUTION   To find where the graph crosses the x-axis, we let $y = 0$. (The y-coordinate of any point on the x-axis is 0.)

x-intercept:

$$\text{When} \qquad\qquad y = 0$$
$$\text{the equation} \qquad 3x - 2y = 6$$
$$\text{becomes} \qquad\quad 3x - 2(0) = 6$$
$$3x - 0 = 6$$
$$x = 2 \qquad \text{Multiply each side by } \tfrac{1}{3}$$

The graph crosses the x-axis at $(2, 0)$, which means the x-intercept is 2.

***y*-intercept:**

$$\text{When} \qquad\qquad x = 0$$

$$\text{the equation} \qquad 3x - 2y = 6$$

$$\text{becomes} \qquad 3(0) - 2y = 6$$

$$0 - 2y = 6$$

$$-2y = 6$$

$$y = -3 \qquad \text{Multiply each side by } -\tfrac{1}{2}$$

The graph crosses the *y*-axis at $(0, -3)$, which means the *y*-intercept is -3.

Plotting the *x*- and *y*-intercepts and then drawing a line through them, we have the graph of $3x - 2y = 6$, as shown in Figure 2.

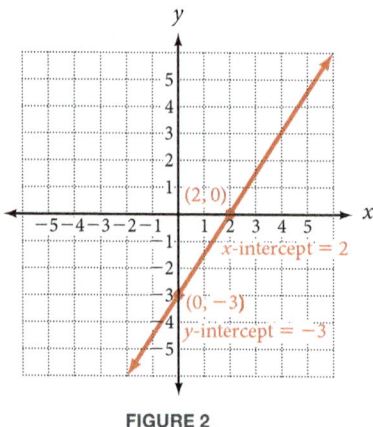

FIGURE 2

Example 2 Graph $-x + 2y = 4$ by finding the intercepts and using them to draw the graph.

SOLUTION Again, we find the *x*-intercept by letting $y = 0$ in the equation and solving for *x*. Similarly, we find the *y*-intercept by letting $x = 0$ and solving for *y*.

***x*-intercept:**

$$\text{When} \qquad\qquad y = 0$$

$$\text{the equation} \qquad -x + 2y = 4$$

$$\text{becomes} \qquad -x + 2(0) = 4$$

$$-x + 0 = 4$$

$$-x = 4$$

$$x = -4 \qquad \text{Multiply each side by } -1$$

The *x*-intercept is -4, indicating that the point $(-4, 0)$, is on the graph of $-x + 2y = 4$.

y-intercept:

When	$x = 0$
the equation	$-x + 2y = 4$
becomes	$-0 + 2y = 4$
	$2y = 4$
	$y = 2$ Multiply each side by $\frac{1}{2}$

The y-intercept is 2, indicating that the point $(0, 2)$ is on the graph of $-x + 2y = 4$.

Plotting the intercepts and drawing a line through them, we have the graph of $-x + 2y = 4$, as shown in Figure 3.

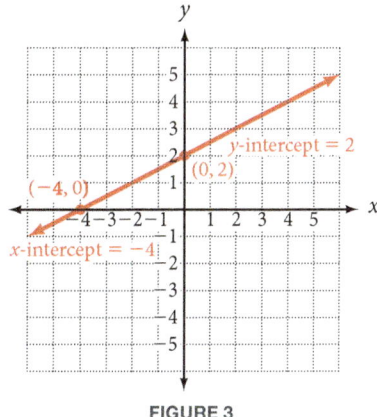

FIGURE 3

Graphing a line by finding the intercepts, as we have done in Examples 1 and 2, is an easy method of graphing if the equation has the form $ax + by = c$ and both the numbers a and b divide the number c evenly.

In our next example we use the intercepts to graph a line in which y is given in terms of x.

Example 3   Use the intercepts for $y = -\frac{1}{3}x + 2$ to draw its graph.

SOLUTION   We graphed this line previously in Example 3 of Section 3.3 by substituting three different values of x into the equation and solving for y. This time we will graph the line by finding the intercepts.

x-intercept:

When $y = 0$

the equation $y = -\dfrac{1}{3}x + 2$

becomes $0 = -\dfrac{1}{3}x + 2$

$-2 = -\dfrac{1}{3}x$ Add -2 to each side

$6 = x$ Multiply each side by -3

The x-intercept is 6, which means the graph passes through the point $(6, 0)$.

y-intercept:

When $x = 0$

the equation $y = -\dfrac{1}{3}x + 2$

becomes $y = -\dfrac{1}{3}(0) + 2$

                  $y = 2$

The y-intercept is 2, which means the graph passes through the point (0, 2).

The graph of $y = -\dfrac{1}{3}x + 2$ is shown in Figure 4. Compare this graph, and the method used to obtain it, with Example 3 in Section 2.3.

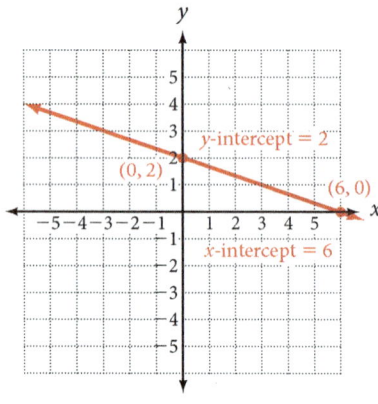

FIGURE 4

Getting Ready for Class

After reading through the preceding section, respond in your own words and in complete sentences.

A. What is the x-intercept for a graph?
B. What is the y-intercept for a graph?
C. How do we find the y-intercept for a line from the equation?
D. How do we graph a line using its intercepts?

Problem Set 2.4

Find the x- and y-intercepts for the following equations. Then use the intercepts to graph each equation.

1. $2x + y = 4$ **2.** $2x + y = 2$ **3.** $-x + y = 3$ **4.** $-x + y = 4$

5. $-x + 2y = 2$ **6.** $-x + 2y = 4$ **7.** $5x + 2y = 10$ **8.** $2x + 5y = 10$

9. $4x - 2y = 8$ **10.** $2x - 4y = 8$ **11.** $-4x + 5y = 20$ **12.** $-5x + 4y = 20$

13. $y = 2x - 6$ **14.** $y = 2x + 6$ **15.** $y = 2x + 2$ **16.** $y = -2x + 2$

17. $y = 2x - 1$ **18.** $y = -2x - 1$ **19.** $y = \frac{1}{2}x + 3$ **20.** $y = \frac{1}{2}x - 3$

21. $y = -\frac{1}{3}x - 2$ **22.** $y = -\frac{1}{3}x + 2$

For each of the following lines the x-intercept and the y-intercept are both 0, which means the graph of each will go through the origin, (0, 0). Graph each line by finding a point on each, other than the origin, and then drawing a line through that point and the origin.

23. $y = -2x$ **24.** $y = \frac{1}{2}x$ **25.** $y = -\frac{1}{3}x$ **26.** $y = -3x$

27. $y = \frac{2}{3}x$ **28.** $y = \frac{3}{2}x$

Complete each table.

29.

Equation	x-intercept	y-intercept
$3x + 4y = 12$		
$3x + 4y = 4$		
$3x + 4y = 3$		
$3x + 4y = 2$		

30.

Equation	x-intercept	y-intercept
$-2x + 3y = 6$		
$-2x + 3y = 3$		
$-2x + 3y = 2$		
$-2x + 3y = 1$		

31.

Equation	x-intercept	y-intercept
$x - 3y = 2$		
$y = \frac{1}{3}x - \frac{2}{3}$		
$x - 3y = 0$		
$y = \frac{1}{3}x$		

32.

Equation	x-intercept	y-intercept
$x - 2y = 1$		
$y = \frac{1}{2}x - \frac{1}{2}$		
$x - 2y = 0$		
$y = \frac{1}{2}x$		

33. Paying Attention to Instructions Work each problem according to the instructions given.

a. Solve: $2x - 3 = -3$

b. Find the x-intercept:
$2x - 3y = -3$

c. Find y when x is 0: $2x - 3y = -3$

d. Graph: $2x - 3y = -3$

e. Solve for y: $2x - 3y = -3$

34. Paying Attention to Instructions Work each problem according to the instructions given.

a. Solve: $3x - 4 = -4$

b. Find the y-intercept:
$3x - 4y = -4$

c. Find x when y is 0: $3x - 4y = -4$

d. Graph: $3x - 4y = -4$

e. Solve for y: $3x - 4y = -4$

From the graphs below, find the x- and y-intercepts for each line.

35.

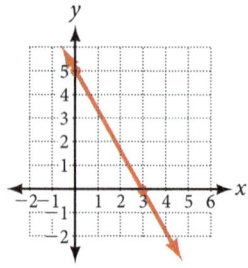

36.

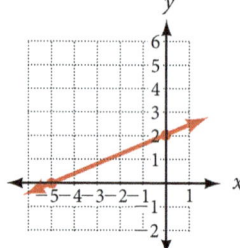

37.

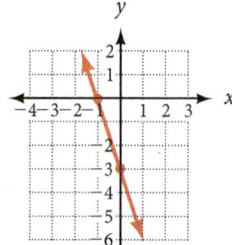

38.

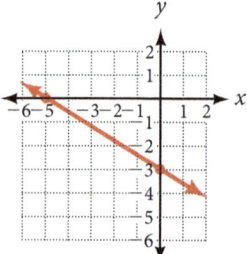

39. Graph the line that passes through the point $(-4, 4)$ and has an x-intercept of -2. What is the y-intercept of this line?

40. Graph the line that passes through the point $(-3, 4)$ and has a y-intercept of 3. What is the x-intercept of this line?

41. A line passes through the point $(1, 4)$ and has a y-intercept of 3. Graph the line and name its x-intercept.

42. A line passes through the point $(3, 4)$ and has an x-intercept of 1. Graph the line and name its y-intercept.

43. Graph the line that passes through the points $(-2, 5)$ and $(5, -2)$. What are the x- and y-intercepts for this line?

44. Graph the line that passes through the points $(5, 3)$ and $(-3, -5)$. What are the x- and y-intercepts for this line?

45. Use the graph at the right to complete the following table.

x	y
-2	
0	
	0
	-2

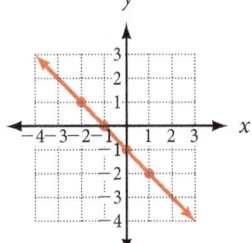

46. Use the graph at the right to complete the following table.

x	y
-2	
	0
	6

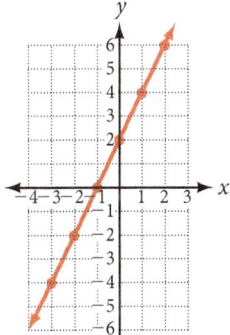

47. The vertical line $x = 3$ has only one intercept. Graph $x = 3$, and name its intercept. [Remember, ordered pairs (x, y) that are solutions to the equation $x = 3$ are ordered pairs with an x-coordinate of 3 and any y-coordinate.]

48. Graph the vertical line $x = -2$. Then name its intercept.

49. The horizontal line $y = 4$ has only one intercept. Graph $y = 4$, and name its intercept. [Ordered pairs (x, y) that are solutions to the equation $y = 4$ are ordered pairs with a y-coordinate of 4 and any x-coordinate.]

50. Graph the horizontal line $y = -3$. Then name its intercept.

Applying the Concepts

51. Complementary Angles The following diagram shows sunlight hitting the ground. Angle α (*alpha*) is called the angle of inclination, and angle θ (*theta*) is called the angle of incidence. As the sun moves across the sky, the values of these angles change. Assume that $\alpha + \theta = 90$, where both α and θ are in degrees measure. Graph this equation on a coordinate system where the horizontal axis is the α-axis and the vertical axis is the θ-axis. Find the intercepts first, and limit your graph to the first quadrant only.

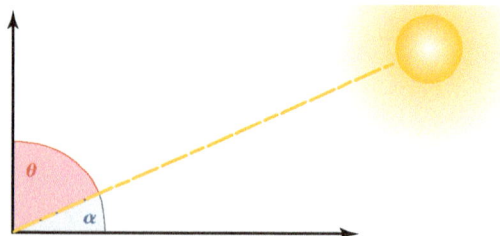

52. Light When light comes into contact with an impenetrable object, such as a thick piece of wood or metal, it is reflected or absorbed, but not transmitted, as shown in the following diagram. If we let R represent the percentage of light reflected and A the percentage of light absorbed by a surface, then the relationship between R and A is $R + A = 100$. Graph this equation on a coordinate system where the horizontal axis is the A-axis and the vertical axis is the R-axis. Find the intercepts first, and limit your graph to the first quadrant.

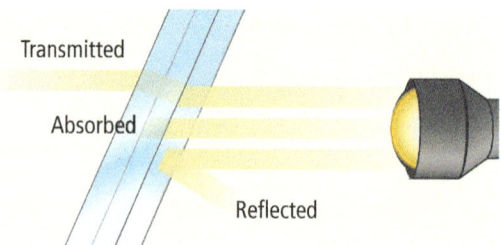

Getting Ready for the Next Section

53. Evaluate.

    a. $\dfrac{5-2}{3-1}$
    b. $\dfrac{2-5}{1-3}$

54. Evaluate.

    a. $\dfrac{-4-1}{5-(-2)}$
    b. $\dfrac{1+4}{-2-5}$

55. Evaluate the following expressions when $x = 3$, and $y = 5$.

    a. $\dfrac{y-2}{x-1}$
    b. $\dfrac{2-y}{1-x}$

56. Evaluate the following expressions when $x = 4$, and $y = -1$.

    a. $\dfrac{-4-y}{5-x}$
    b. $\dfrac{y+4}{x-5}$

The Slope of a Line

In defining the slope of a straight line, we are looking for a number to associate with a straight line that does two things. First of all, we want the slope of a line to measure the "steepness" of the line; that is, in comparing two lines, the slope of the steeper line should have the larger numerical value. Second, we want a line that *rises* going from left to right to have a *positive* slope. We want a line that *falls* going from left to right to have a *negative* slope. (A line that neither rises nor falls going from left to right must, therefore, have 0 slope.) These are illustrated in Figure 1.

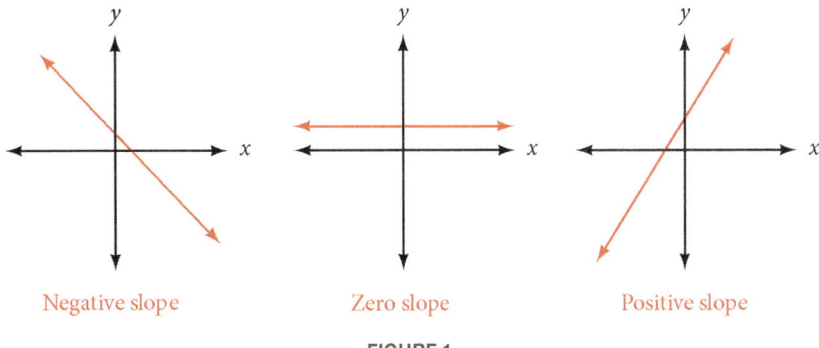

Negative slope   Zero slope   Positive slope

FIGURE 1

Suppose we know the coordinates of two points on a line. Because we are trying to develop a general formula for the slope of a line, we will use general points—call the two points $P_1(x_1, y_1)$ and $P_2(x_2, y_2)$. They represent the coordinates of any two different points on our line. We define the **slope** of our line to be the ratio of the vertical change to the horizontal change as we move from point (x_1, y_1) to point (x_2, y_2) on the line. (See Figure 2.)

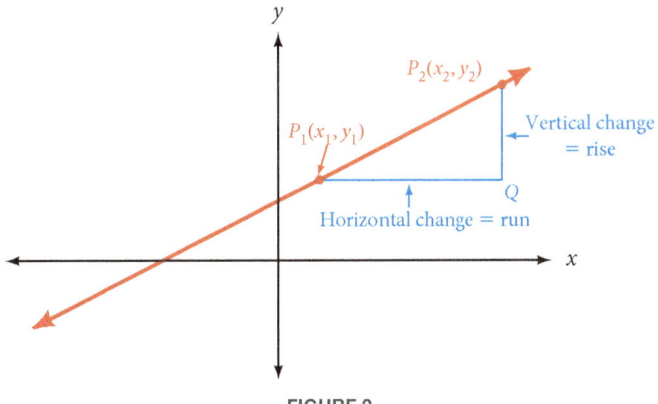

FIGURE 2

We call the vertical change the *rise* in the graph and the horizontal change the *run* in the graph. The slope, then, is

$$\text{Slope} = \frac{\text{vertical change}}{\text{horizontal change}} = \frac{\text{rise}}{\text{run}}$$

We would like to have a numerical value to associate with the rise in the graph and a numerical value to associate with the run in the graph. A quick study of Figure 2 shows that the coordinates of point Q must be (x_2, y_1), because Q is directly below point P_2 and right across from point P_1. We can draw our diagram again in the manner shown in Figure 3. It is apparent from this graph that the rise can be expressed as $(y_2 - y_1)$ and the run as $(x_2 - x_1)$. We usually denote the slope of a line by the letter m. The complete definition of slope follows along with a diagram (Figure 3) that illustrates the definition.

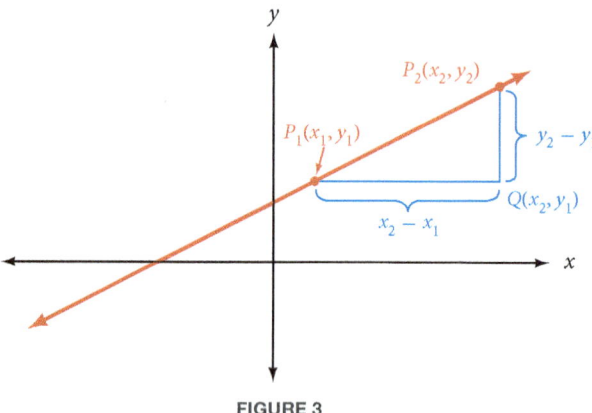

FIGURE 3

(dĕf′   *slope*

If points (x_1, y_1) and (x_2, y_2) are any two different points, then the *slope* of the line on which they lie is

$$\text{Slope} = m = \frac{\text{rise}}{\text{run}} = \frac{y_2 - y_1}{x_2 - x_1}$$

This definition of the *slope* of a line does just what we want it to do. If the line rises going from left to right, the slope will be positive. If the line falls from left to right, the slope will be negative. Also, the steeper the line, the larger numerical value the slope will have.

Video Examples

Section 2.5

Example 1   Find the slope of the line between the points $(1, 2)$ and $(3, 5)$.

SOLUTION   We can let

$$(x_1, y_1) = (1, 2)$$

and

$$(x_2, y_2) = (3, 5)$$

then

$$m = \frac{y_2 - y_1}{x_2 - x_1} = \frac{5 - 2}{3 - 1} = \frac{3}{2}$$

The slope is $\frac{3}{2}$. For every vertical change of 3 units, there will be a corresponding horizontal change of 2 units. (See Figure 4.)

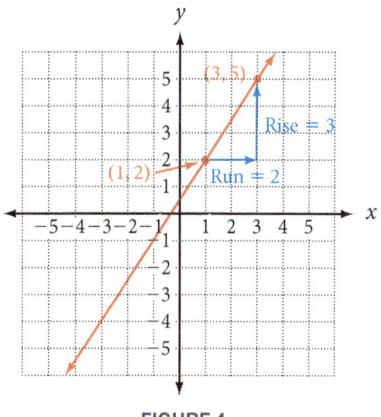

FIGURE 4

Example 2   Find the slope of the line through $(-2, 1)$ and $(5, -4)$.

SOLUTION   It makes no difference which ordered pair we call (x_1, y_1) and which we call (x_2, y_2).

$$\text{Slope} = m = \frac{y_2 - y_1}{x_2 - x_1} = \frac{-4 - 1}{5 - (-2)} = -\frac{5}{7}$$

The slope is $-\frac{5}{7}$. Every vertical change of -5 units (down 5 units) is accompanied by a horizontal change of 7 units (to the right 7 units). (See Figure 5.)

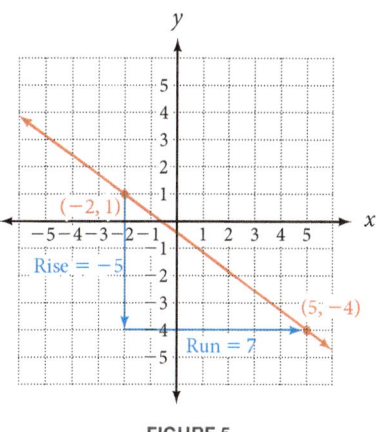

FIGURE 5

Example 3   Graph the line with slope $\frac{3}{2}$ and y-intercept 1.

SOLUTION   Because the y-intercept is 1, we know that one point on the line is $(0, 1)$. So, we begin by plotting the point $(0, 1)$, as shown in Figure 6.

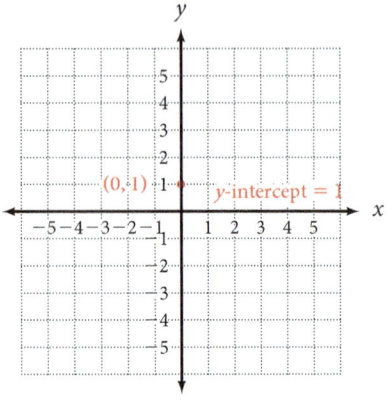

FIGURE 6

There are many lines that pass through the point shown in Figure 6, but only one of those lines has a slope of $\frac{3}{2}$. The slope, $\frac{3}{2}$, can be thought of as the rise in the graph divided by the run in the graph. Therefore, if we start at the point $(0, 1)$ and move 3 units up (that's a rise of 3) and then 2 units to the right (a run of 2), we will be at another point on the graph. Figure 7 shows that the point we reach by doing so is the point $(2, 4)$.

$$\text{Slope} = m = \frac{\text{rise}}{\text{run}} = \frac{3}{2}$$

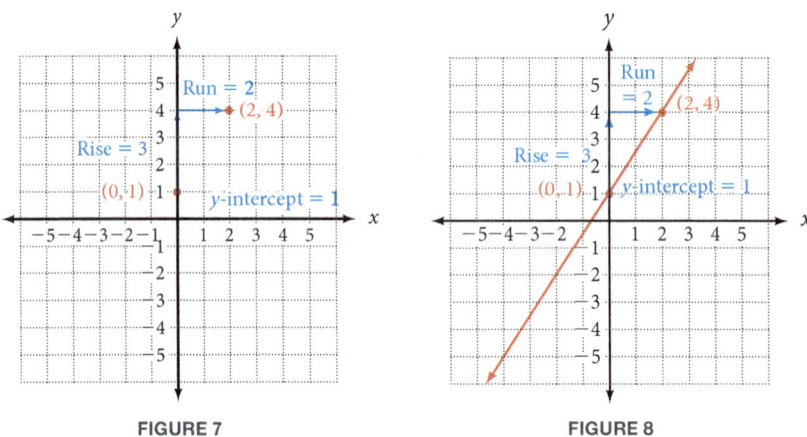

FIGURE 7   **FIGURE 8**

To graph the line with slope $\frac{3}{2}$ and y-intercept 1, we simply draw a line through the two points in Figure 7 to obtain the graph shown in Figure 8.

Example 4   Find the slope of the line containing $(3, -1)$ and $(3, 4)$.

SOLUTION   Using the definition for slope, we have

$$m = \frac{y_2 - y_1}{x_2 - x_1} = \frac{4 - (-1)}{3 - 3} = \frac{5}{0}$$

The expression $\frac{5}{0}$ is undefined; that is, there is no real number to associate with it. In this case, we say the line has *undefined slope*.

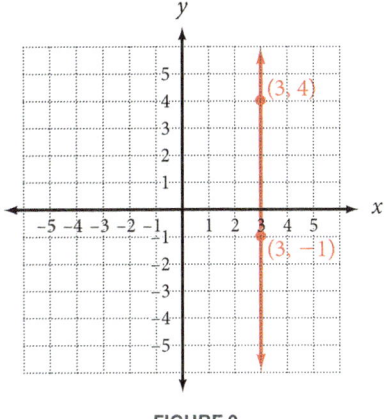

FIGURE 9

The graph of our line is shown in Figure 9. Our line with undefined slope is a vertical line. All vertical lines have an undefined slope. (And all horizontal lines, as we mentioned earlier, have 0 slope.)

As a final note, the summary reminds us that all horizontal lines have equations of the form $y = b$ and slopes of 0. Because they cross the y-axis at b, the y-intercept is b; there is no x-intercept. Vertical lines have no slope and equations of the form $x = a$. Each will have an x-intercept at a and no y-intercept. Finally, equations of the form $y = mx$ have graphs that pass through the origin. The slope is always m and both the x-intercept and the y-intercept are 0.

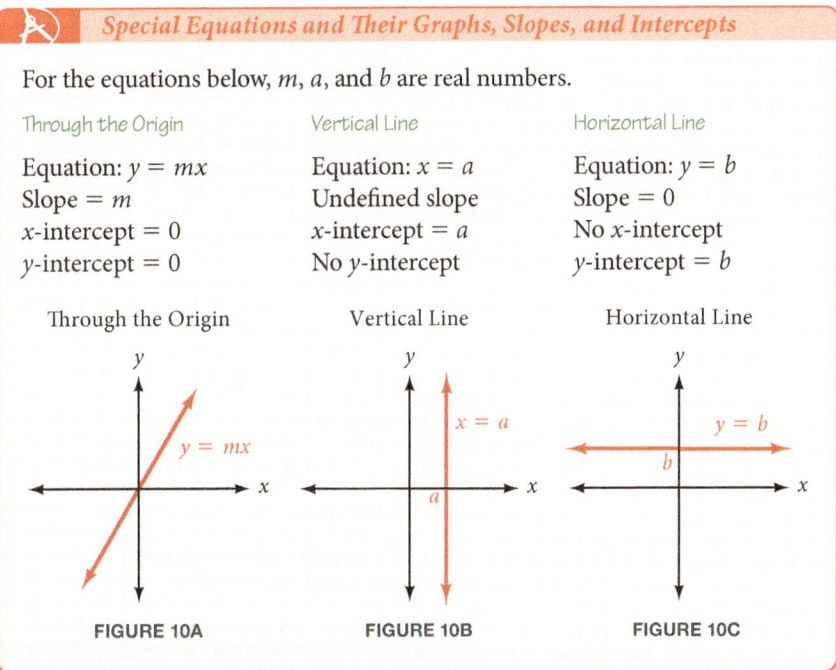

Special Equations and Their Graphs, Slopes, and Intercepts

For the equations below, m, a, and b are real numbers.

Through the Origin	Vertical Line	Horizontal Line
Equation: $y = mx$	Equation: $x = a$	Equation: $y = b$
Slope $= m$	Undefined slope	Slope $= 0$
x-intercept $= 0$	x-intercept $= a$	No x-intercept
y-intercept $= 0$	No y-intercept	y-intercept $= b$

Through the Origin   Vertical Line   Horizontal Line

FIGURE 10A   **FIGURE 10B**   **FIGURE 10C**

Next, we are going to expand our work with slopes and lines to include parallel and perpendicular lines. Once we have done the introductory work we will apply what we have to equations of lines.

Slopes of Parallel and Perpendicular Lines

In geometry, we call lines in the same plane that never intersect parallel. For two lines to be nonintersecting, they must rise or fall at the same rate. In other words, two lines are *parallel* if and only if they have the *same slope.*

Although it is not as obvious, it is also true that two nonvertical lines are *perpendicular* if and only if the *product of their slopes is* -1. This is the same as saying their slopes are negative reciprocals.

We can state these facts with symbols as follows: If line l_1 has slope m_1 and line l_2 has slope m_2, then

$$l_1 \text{ is parallel to } l_2 \Leftrightarrow m_1 = m_2$$

and

$$l_1 \text{ is perpendicular to } l_2 \Leftrightarrow m_1 \cdot m_2 = -1 \text{ or } \left(m_1 = \frac{-1}{m_2} \right)$$

For example, if a line has a slope of $\frac{2}{3}$, then any line parallel to it has a slope of $\frac{2}{3}$. Any line perpendicular to it has a slope of $-\frac{3}{2}$ (the negative reciprocal of $\frac{2}{3}$).

Although we cannot give a formal proof of the relationship between the slopes of perpendicular lines at this level of mathematics, we can offer some justification for the relationship. Figure 4 shows the graphs of two lines. One of the lines has a slope of $\frac{2}{3}$; the other has a slope of $-\frac{3}{2}$. As you can see, the lines are perpendicular.

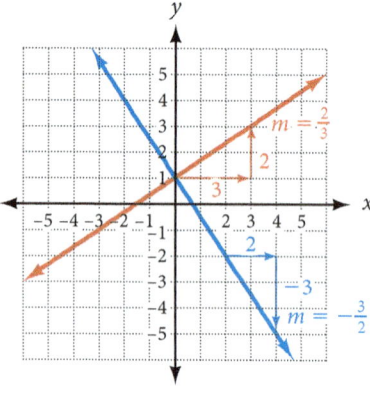

FIGURE 4

Getting Ready for Class

After reading through the preceding section, respond in your own words and in complete sentences.

A. What is the slope of a line?

B. Would you rather climb a hill with a slope of 1 or a slope of 3? Explain why.

C. Describe how to obtain the slope of a line if you know the coordinates of two points on the line.

D. Describe how you would graph a line from its slope and *y*-intercept.

Find the slope of the line through the following pairs of points. Then plot each pair of points, draw a line through them, and indicate the rise and run in the graph in the same manner shown in Examples 1 and 2.

1. $(2, 1), (4, 4)$ **2.** $(3, 1), (5, 4)$ **3.** $(1, 4), (5, 2)$

4. $(1, 3), (5, 2)$ **5.** $(1, -3), (4, 2)$ **6.** $(2, -3), (5, 2)$

7. $(-3, -2), (1, 3)$ **8.** $(-3, -1), (1, 4)$ **9.** $(-3, 2), (3, -2)$

10. $(-3, 3), (3, -1)$ **11.** $(2, -5), (3, -2)$ **12.** $(2, -4), (3, -1)$

In each of the following problems, graph the line with the given slope and y-intercept b.

13. $m = \dfrac{2}{3}, b = 1$ **14.** $m = \dfrac{3}{4}, b = -2$ **15.** $m = \dfrac{3}{2}, b = -3$

16. $m = \dfrac{4}{3}, b = 2$ **17.** $m = -\dfrac{4}{3}, b = 5$ **18.** $m = -\dfrac{3}{5}, b = 4$

19. $m = 2, b = 1$ **20.** $m = -2, b = 4$ **21.** $m = 3, b = -1$

22. $m = 3, b = -2$

Find the slope and y-intercept for each line.

23.

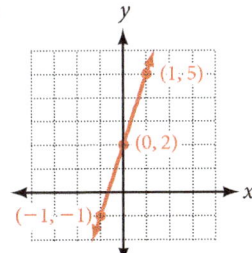

24.

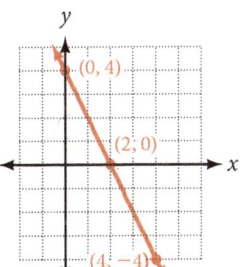

25.

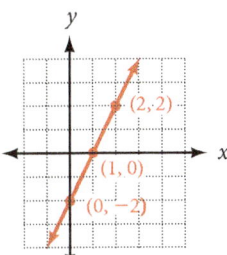

26.

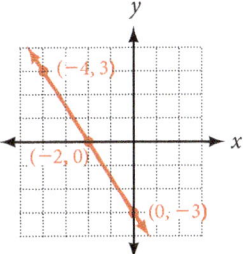

27. Graph the line that has an x-intercept of 3 and a y-intercept of -2. What is the slope of this line?

28. Graph the line that has an x-intercept of 2 and a y-intercept of -3. What is the slope of this line?

29. Graph the line with x-intercept 4 and y-intercept 2. What is the slope of this line?

30. Graph the line with x-intercept -4 and y-intercept -2. What is the slope of this line?

31. Graph the line $y = 2x - 3$, then name the slope and y-intercept by looking at the graph.

32. Graph the line $y = -2x + 3$, then name the slope and y-intercept by looking at the graph.

33. Graph the line $y = \frac{1}{2}x + 1$, then name the slope and y-intercept by looking at the graph.

34. Graph the line $y = -\frac{1}{2}x - 2$, then name the slope and y-intercept by looking at the graph.

35. Find y if the line through $(4, 2)$ and $(6, y)$ has a slope of 2.

36. Find y if the line through $(1, y)$ and $(7, 3)$ has a slope of 6.

For each equation in each table, give the slope of the graph.

37.

Equation	Slope
$x = 3$	
$y = 3$	
$y = 3x$	

38.

Equation	Slope
$y = \frac{3}{2}$	
$x = \frac{3}{2}$	
$y = \frac{3}{2}x$	

39.

Equation	Slope
$y = -\frac{2}{3}$	
$x = -\frac{2}{3}$	
$y = -\frac{2}{3}x$	

40.

Equation	Slope
$x = -2$	
$y = -2$	
$y = -2x$	

41. Parallel Lines Find the slope of any line parallel to the line through $(2, 3)$ and $(-8, 1)$.

42. Parallel Lines Find the slope of any line parallel to the line through $(2, 5)$ and $(5, -3)$.

43. Perpendicular Lines Line l contains the points $(5, -6)$ and $(5, 2)$. Give the slope of any line perpendicular to l.

44. Perpendicular Lines Line l contains the points $(3, 4)$ and $(-3, 1)$. Give the slope of any line perpendicular to l.

45. Parallel Lines Line l contains the points $(-2, 1)$ and $(4, -5)$. Find the slope of any line parallel to l.

46. Parallel Lines Line l contains the points $(3, -4)$ and $(-2, -6)$. Find the slope of any line parallel to l.

47. Perpendicular Lines Line l contains the points $(-2, -5)$ and $(1, -3)$. Find the slope of any line perpendicular to l.

48. Perpendicular Lines Line l contains the points $(6, -3)$ and $(-2, 7)$. Find the slope of any line perpendicular to l.

Applying the Concepts

49. Garbage Production The table and completed line graph gives the annual production of garbage in the United States for some specific years. Find the slope of each of the four line segments, *A*, *B*, *C*, and *D*.

Year	Garbage (millions of tons)
1960	88
1970	121
1980	152
1990	205
2000	224

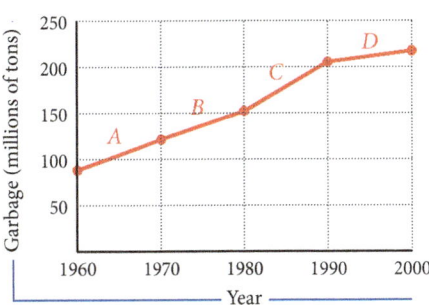

50. Grass Height The table and completed line graph gives the growth of a certain plant species over time. Find the slopes of the line segments labeled *A*, *B*, and *C*.

Day	Plant Height
0	0
2	1
4	3
6	6
8	13
10	23

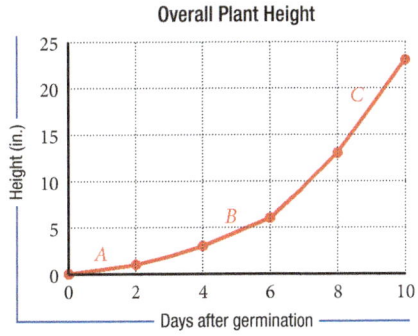

51. Non-Camera Phone Sales The table and line graph here each show the projected non-camera phone sales each year through 2010. Find the slope of each of the three line segments, *A*, *B*, and *C*.

Year	Sales (in millions)
2006	300
2007	250
2008	175
2009	150
2010	125

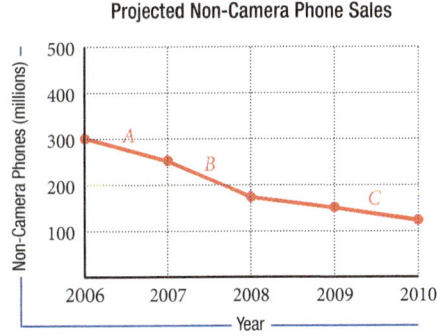

52. Camera Phone Sales The table from Problem 48 in Problem Set 3.1 and a line graph are shown here. Each shows the projected sales of camera phones from 2006 to 2010. Find the slopes of line segments *A*, *B*, and *C*.

Year	Sales (in millions)
2006	500
2007	650
2008	750
2009	875
2010	900

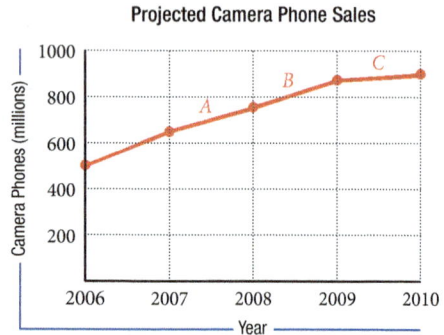

Getting Ready for the Next Section

Solve each equation for *y*.

53. $-2x + y = 4$ **54.** $-4x + y = -2$ **55.** $2x + y = 3$

56. $3x + 2y = 6$ **57.** $4x - 5y = 20$ **58.** $-2x - 5y = 10$

59. $-y - 3 = -2(x + 4)$ **60.** $-y + 5 = 2(x + 2)$ **61.** $-y - 3 = -\dfrac{2}{3}(x + 3)$

62. $-y - 1 = -\dfrac{1}{2}(x + 4)$ **63.** $-\dfrac{y - 1}{x} = \dfrac{3}{2}$ **64.** $-\dfrac{y + 1}{x} = \dfrac{3}{2}$

Finding the Equation of a Line

To this point in the chapter, most of the problems we have worked have used the equation of a line to find different types of information about the line. For instance, given the equation of a line, we can find points on the line, the graph of the line, the intercepts, and the slope of the line. In this section we reverse things somewhat and move in the other direction; we will use information about a line, such as its slope and y-intercept, to find the equation of a line.

There are three main types of problems to solve in this section.

1. Find the equation of a line from the slope and y-intercept.

2. Find the equation of a line given one point on the line and the slope of the line.

3. Find the equation of a line given two points on the line.

Examples 1 and 2 illustrate the first type of problem. Example 5 solves the second type of problem. The third type of problem is solved in Example 6.

The Slope-Intercept Form of an Equation of a Straight Line

Example 1   Find the equation of the line with slope $\frac{3}{2}$ and y-intercept 1.

SOLUTION   We graphed the line with slope $\frac{3}{2}$ and y-intercept 1 in Example 3 of the previous section. Figure 1 shows that graph.

Video Examples

Section 2.6

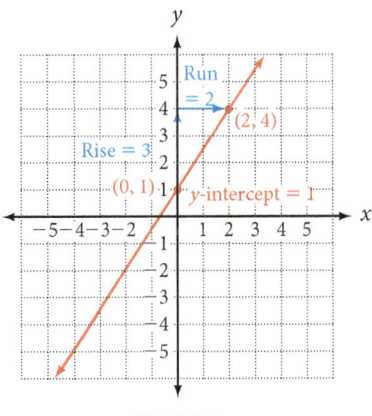

FIGURE 1

What we want to do now is find the equation of the line shown in Figure 1. To do so, we take any other point (x, y) on the line and apply our slope formula to that point and the point $(0, 1)$. We set that result equal to $\frac{3}{2}$, because $\frac{3}{2}$ is the slope of our line and a diagram of the situation follows.

$$\frac{y - 1}{x - 0} = \frac{3}{2} \qquad \text{Slope} = \frac{\text{vertical change}}{\text{horizontal change}}$$

$$\frac{y - 1}{x} = \frac{3}{2} \qquad x - 0 = x$$

$$y - 1 = \frac{3}{2}x \qquad \text{Multiply each side by } x$$

$$y = \frac{3}{2}x + 1 \qquad \text{Add 1 to each side}$$

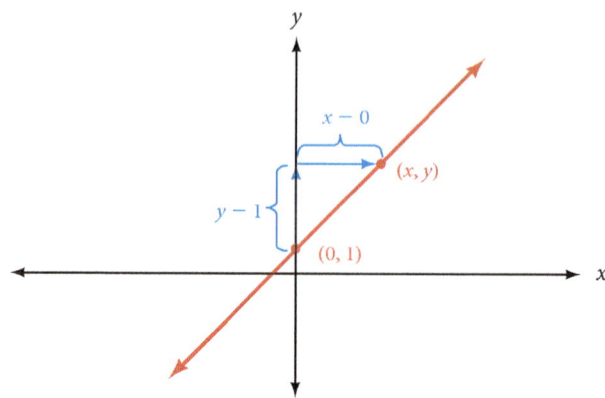

What is interesting and useful about the equation we have just found is that the number in front of x is the slope of the line and the constant term is the y-intercept. It is no coincidence that it turned out this way. Whenever an equation has the form $y = mx + b$, the graph is always a straight line with slope m and y-intercept b. To see that this is true in general, suppose we want the equation of a line with slope m and y-intercept b. Because the y-intercept is b, then the point $(0, b)$ is on the line. If (x, y) is any other point on the line, then we apply our slope formula to get

$$\frac{y - b}{x - 0} = m \qquad \text{Slope} = \frac{\text{vertical change}}{\text{horizontal change}}$$

$$\frac{y - b}{x} = m \qquad x - 0 = x$$

$$y - b = mx \qquad \text{Multiply each side by } x$$

$$y = mx + b \qquad \text{Add } b \text{ to each side}$$

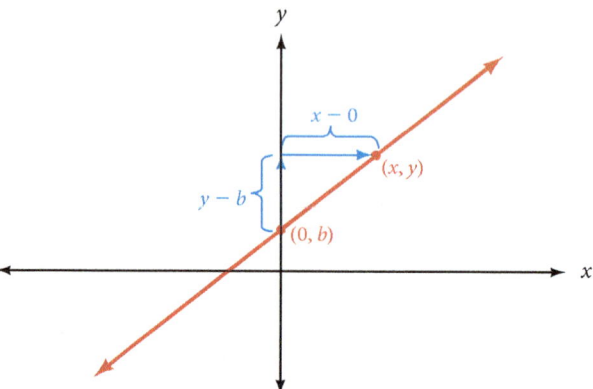

Here is a summary of what we have just found.

> **$\lceil \Delta \neq \Sigma \rceil$ *Slope-Intercept Form of the Equation of a Line***
>
> The equation of the line with slope m and y-intercept b is always given by
>
> $$y = mx + b$$

Example 2 Find the equation of the line with slope $-\frac{4}{3}$ and y-intercept 5. Then, graph the line.

SOLUTION Substituting $m = -\frac{4}{3}$ and $b = 5$ into the equation $y = mx + b$, we have

$$y = -\frac{4}{3}x + 5$$

Finding the equation from the slope and y-intercept is just that easy. If the slope is m and the y-intercept is b, then the equation is always $y = mx + b$.

Because the y-intercept is 5, the graph goes through the point $(0, 5)$. To find a second point on the graph, we start at $(0, 5)$ and move 4 units down (that's a rise of -4) and 3 units to the right (a run of 3). The point we reach is $(3, 1)$. Drawing a line that passes through $(0, 5)$ and $(3, 1)$, we have the graph of our equation. (Note that we could also let the rise $= 4$ and the run $= -3$ and obtain the same graph.) The graph is shown in Figure 2.

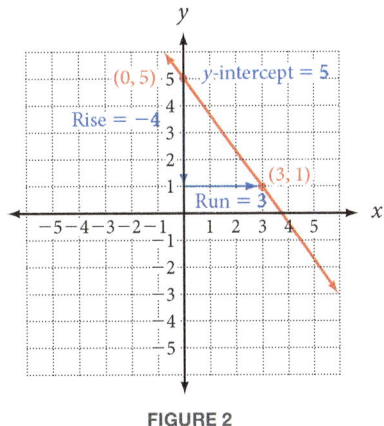

FIGURE 2

Example 3   Find the slope and y-intercept for $-2x + y = -4$. Then, use them to draw the graph.

SOLUTION   To identify the slope and y-intercept from the equation, the equation must be in the form $y = mx + b$ (slope-intercept form). To write our equation in this form, we must solve the equation for y. To do so, we simply add $2x$ to each side of the equation.

$$-2x + y = -4 \qquad \text{\color{green}Original equation}$$
$$y = 2x - 4 \qquad \text{\color{green}Add } 2x \text{ to each side}$$

The equation is now in slope-intercept form, so the slope must be 2 and the y-intercept must be -4. The graph, therefore, crosses the y-axis at $(0, -4)$. Because the slope is 2, we can let the rise $= 2$ and the run $= 1$ and find a second point on the graph. The graph is shown in Figure 3.

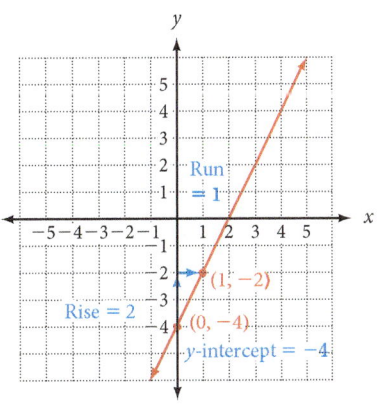

FIGURE 3

Example 4   Find the slope and y-intercept for $3x - 2y = 6$.

SOLUTION   To find the slope and y-intercept from the equation, we must write the equation in the form $y = mx + b$. This means we must solve the equation $3x - 2y = 6$ for y.

$$3x - 2y = 6 \qquad \text{\color{green}Original equation}$$

$$-2y = -3x + 6 \qquad \text{\color{green}Add } -3x \text{ to each side}$$

$$-\frac{1}{2}(-2y) = -\frac{1}{2}(-3x + 6) \qquad \text{\color{green}Multiply each side by } -\frac{1}{2}$$

$$y = \frac{3}{2}x - 3 \qquad \text{\color{green}Simplify each side}$$

Now that the equation is written in slope-intercept form, we can identify the slope as $\frac{3}{2}$ and the y-intercept as -3. The graph is shown in Figure 4.

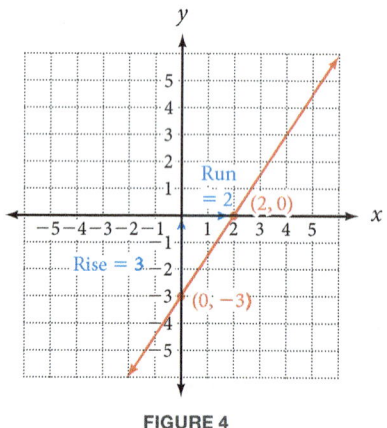

FIGURE 4

The Point-Slope Form of an Equation of a Straight Line

A second useful form of the equation of a straight line is the point-slope form.

Let line l contain the point (x_1, y_1) and have slope m. If (x, y) is any other point on l, then by the definition of slope we have

$$\frac{y - y_1}{x - x_1} = m$$

Multiplying both sides by $(x - x_1)$ gives us

$$(x - x_1) \cdot \frac{y - y_1}{x - x_1} = m(x - x_1)$$

$$y - y_1 = m(x - x_1)$$

This last equation is known as the **point-slope form** of the equation of a straight line.

> **Point-Slope Form of the Equation of a Line**
>
> The equation of the line through (x_1, y_1) with slope m is given by
> $$y - y_1 = m(x - x_1)$$

This form is used to find the equation of a line, either given one point on the line and the slope, or given two points on the line.

Example 5   Find the equation of the line with slope -2 that contains the point $(-4, 3)$. Write the answer in slope-intercept form.

SOLUTION Using $\qquad (x_1, y_1) = (-4, 3)$ and $m = -2$

in $\qquad\qquad y - y_1 = m(x - x_1)$ $\qquad$ *Point-slope form*

gives us $\qquad\quad y - 3 = -2(x + 4)$ $\qquad$ *Note: $x - (-4) = x + 4$*

$\qquad\qquad\qquad y - 3 = -2x - 8$ $\qquad$ *Multiply out right side*

$\qquad\qquad\qquad\quad y = -2x - 5$ $\qquad$ *Add 3 to each side*

Figure 5 is the graph of the line that contains $(-4, 3)$ and has a slope of -2. Notice that the y-intercept on the graph matches that of the equation we found.

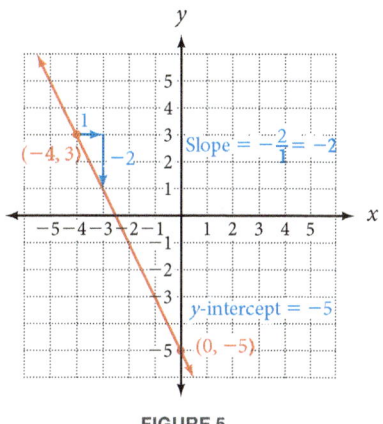

FIGURE 5

Example 6   Find the equation of the line that passes through the points $(-3, 3)$ and $(3, -1)$.

SOLUTION We begin by finding the slope of the line:

$$m = \frac{3 - (-1)}{-3 - 3} = \frac{4}{-6} = -\frac{2}{3}$$

Using $(x_1, y_1) = (3, -1)$ and $m = -\frac{2}{3}$ in $y - y_1 = m(x - x_1)$ yields

$$y + 1 = -\frac{2}{3}(x - 3)$$

$$y + 1 = -\frac{2}{3}x + 2 \qquad \text{\textit{Multiply out right side}}$$

$$y = -\frac{2}{3}x + 1 \qquad \text{\textit{Add} -1 \textit{to each side}}$$

Figure 6 shows the graph of the line that passes through the points $(-3, 3)$ and $(3, -1)$. As you can see, the slope and y-intercept are $-\frac{2}{3}$ and 1, respectively.

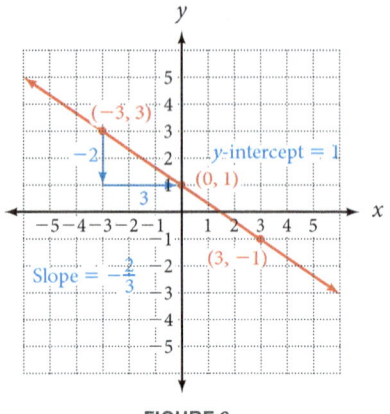

FIGURE 6

Note In Example 6 we could have used the point $(-3, 3)$ instead of $(3, -1)$ and obtained the same equation; that is, using $(x_1, y_1) = (-3, 3)$ and $m = -\frac{2}{3}$ in $y - y_1 = m(x - x_1)$ gives us

$$y - 3 = -\frac{2}{3}(x + 3)$$

$$y - 3 = -\frac{2}{3}x - 2$$

$$y = -\frac{2}{3}x + 1$$

which is the same result we obtained using $(3, -1)$.

Methods of Graphing Lines

1. Substitute convenient values of x into the equation, and find the corresponding values of y. We used this method first for equations like $y = 2x - 3$. To use this method for equations that looked like $2x - 3y = 6$, we first solved them for y.

2. Find the x- and y-intercepts. This method works best for equations of the form $3x + 2y = 6$ where the numbers in front of x and y divide the constant term evenly.

3. Find the slope and y-intercept. This method works best when the equation has the form $y = mx + b$ and b is an integer.

The last form of the equation of a line that we will consider is called the *standard form*. It is used mainly to write equations in a form that is free of fractions and is easy to compare with other equations.

> **⎰Δ≠Σ⎱** ***Standard Form for the Equation of a Line***
>
> If a, b, and c are integers, then the equation of a line is in standard form when it has the form
>
> $$ax + by = c$$

If we were to write the equation

$$y = -\frac{2}{3}x + 1$$

in standard form, we would first multiply both sides by 3 to obtain

$$3y = -2x + 3$$

Then we would add $2x$ to each side, yielding

$$2x + 3y = 3$$

which is a linear equation in standard form.

Example 7   Give the equation of the line through $(-1, 4)$ whose graph is perpendicular to the graph of $2x - y = -3$. Write the answer in standard form.

SOLUTION   To find the slope of $2x - y = -3$, we solve for y:

$$2x - y = -3$$
$$y = 2x + 3$$

The slope of this line is 2. The line we are interested in is perpendicular to the line with slope 2 and must, therefore, have a slope of $-\frac{1}{2}$.

Using $(x_1, y_1) = (-1, 4)$ and $m = -\frac{1}{2}$, we have

$$y - y_1 = m(x - x_1)$$
$$y - 4 = -\frac{1}{2}(x + 1)$$

Because we want our answer in standard form, we multiply each side by 2.

$$2y - 8 = -1(x + 1)$$
$$2y - 8 = -x - 1$$

$$x + 2y - 8 = -1$$
$$x + 2y = 7$$

The last equation is in standard form.

Getting Ready for Class

After reading through the preceding section, respond in your own words and in complete sentences.

A. What are m and b in the equation $y = mx + b$?

B. How would you find the slope and y-intercept for the line
$3x - 2y = 6$?

C. What is the point-slope form of the equation of a line?

D. How would you find the equation of a line from two points on the line?

In each of the following problems, give the equation of the line with the given slope and y-intercept.

1. $m = \frac{2}{3}, b = 1$ **2.** $m = \frac{3}{4}, b = -2$ **3.** $m = \frac{3}{2}, b = -1$ **4.** $m = \frac{4}{3}, b = 2$

5. $m = -\frac{2}{3}, b = 3$ **6.** $m = -\frac{3}{5}, b = 4$ **7.** $m = 2, b = -4$ **8.** $m = -2, b = 4$

Find the slope and y-intercept for each of the following equations by writing them in the form $y = mx + b$. Then, graph each equation.

9. $-2x + y = 4$ **10.** $-2x + y = 2$ **11.** $3x + y = 3$ **12.** $3x + y = 6$

13. $3x + 2y = 6$ **14.** $2x + 3y = 6$ **15.** $4x - 5y = 20$ **16.** $2x - 5y = 10$

17. $-2x - 5y = 10$ **18.** $-4x + 5y = 20$

For each of the following problems, the slope and one point on a line are given. In each case use the point-slope form to find the equation of that line. (Write your answers in slope-intercept form.)

19. $(-2, -5), m = 2$ **20.** $(-1, -5), m = 2$ **21.** $(-4, 1), m = -\frac{1}{2}$

22. $(-2, 1), m = -\frac{1}{2}$ **23.** $(2, -3), m = \frac{3}{2}$ **24.** $(3, -4), m = \frac{4}{3}$

25. $(-1, 4), m = -3$ **26.** $(-2, 5), m = -3$

Find the equation of the line that passes through each pair of points. Write your answers in slope-intercept form.

27. $(-2, -4), (1, -1)$ **28.** $(2, 4), (-3, -1)$ **29.** $(-1, -5), (2, 1)$

30. $(-1, 6), (1, 2)$ **31.** $(-3, -2), (3, 6)$ **32.** $(-3, 6), (3, -2)$

33. $(-3, -1), (3, -5)$ **34.** $(-3, -5), (3, 1)$

Find the slope and y-intercept for each line. Then write the equation of each line in slope-intercept form.

35.

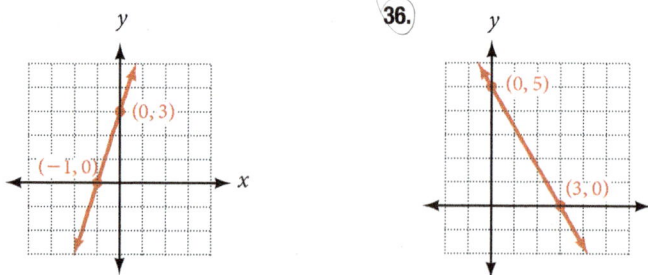

36.

37.

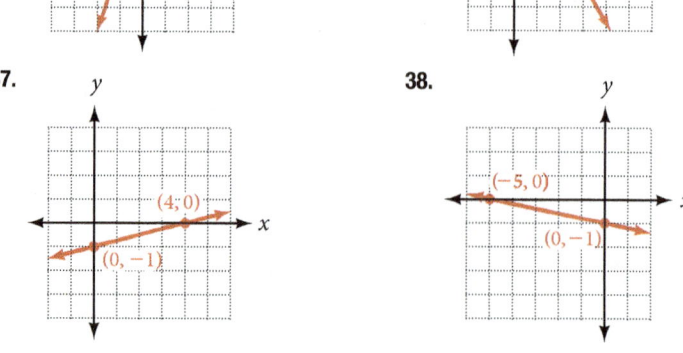

38.

39. Paying Attention to Instructions Work each problem according to the instructions given.

   a. Solve: $-2x + 1 = 6$

   b. Write in slope-intercept form: $-2x + y = 6$

   c. Find the y-intercept: $-2x + y = 6$

   d. Find the slope: $-2x + y = 6$

   e. Graph: $-2x + y = 6$

40. Paying Attention to Instructions Work each problem according to the instructions given.

   a. Solve: $x + 3 = -6$

   b. Write in slope-intercept form: $x + 3y = -6$

   c. Find the y-intercept: $x + 3y = -6$

   d. Find the slope: $x + 3y = -6$

   e. Graph: $x + 3y = -6$

41. Find the equation of the line with x-intercept 3 and y-intercept 2.

42. Find the equation of the line with x-intercept 2 and y-intercept 3.

43. Find the equation of the line with x-intercept -2 and y-intercept -5.

44. Find the equation of the line with x-intercept -3 and y-intercept -5.

45. The equation of the vertical line that passes through the points $(3, -2)$ and $(3, 4)$ is either $x = 3$ or $y = 3$. Which one is it?

46. The equation of the horizontal line that passes through the points $(2, 3)$ and $(-1, 3)$ is either $x = 3$ or $y = 3$. Which one is it?

Finding the Equation of a Line

47. Find the equation of the line parallel to the graph of $3x - y = 5$ that contains the point $(-1, 4)$.

48. Find the equation of the line parallel to the graph of $2x - 4y = 5$ that contains the point $(0, 3)$.

49. Line l is perpendicular to the graph of the equation $2x - 5y = 10$ and contains the point $(-4, -3)$. Find the equation for l.

50. Line l is perpendicular to the graph of the equation $-3x - 5y = 2$ and contains the point $(2, -6)$. Find the equation for l.

51. Give the equation of the line perpendicular to the graph of $y = -4x + 2$ that has an x intercept of   1.

52. Write the equation of the line parallel to the graph of $7x - 2y = 14$ that has an x-intercept of 5.

Applying the Concepts

53. Value of a Copy Machine Cassandra buys a new color copier for her small business. It will cost $21,000 and will decrease in value each year. The graph below shows the value of the copier after the first 5 years of ownership.

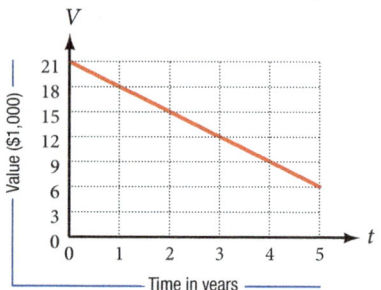

a. How much is the copier worth after 5 years?

b. After how many years is the copier worth $12,000?

c. Find the slope of this line.

d. By how many dollars per year is the copier decreasing in value?

e. Find the equation of this line where V is the value after t years.

54. Salesperson's Income Kevin starts a new job in sales next month. He will earn $1,000 per month plus a certain amount for each shirt he sells. The graph below shows the amount Kevin will earn per month based on how many shirts he sells.

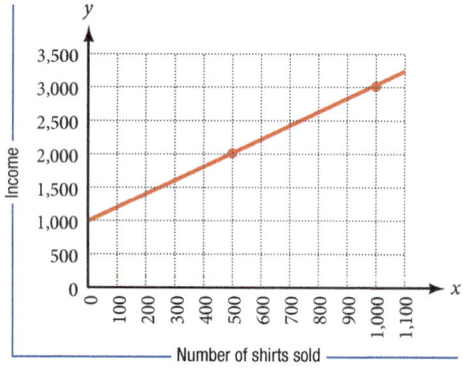

FIGURE 2

a. How much will he earn for selling 1,000 shirts?

b. How many shirts must he sell to earn $2,000 for a month?

c. Find the slope of this line.

d. How much money does Kevin earn for each shirt he sells?

e. Find the equation of this line where y is the amount he earns for selling x number of shirts.

Getting Ready for the Next Section

Graph each of the following lines.

55. $x + y = 4$ **56.** $x - y = -2$ **57.** $y = 2x - 3$ **58.** $y = 2x + 3$

59. $y = 2x$ **60.** $y = -2x$

Statistics: Mean, Median, and Mode, Variance and Standard Deviation

In the 2010 Winter Olympics Games, the United States four-man bobsleigh team of Steve Holcomb, Steve Mesler, Curtis Tomasevicz, and Justin Olsen took the gold medal for their event. The team competed on a 1450-meter-long track at the Whistler Sliding Centre near Vancouver, Canada. During four runs, the team logged a total time of 3:24.46 (read "3 minutes, 24 seconds, and 46 one hundredths of a second"). The following table shows the team's individual run times.

Run	Time
Run 1	50.89 seconds
Run 2	50.86 seconds
Run 3	51.19 seconds
Run 4	51.52 seconds

In this section, we will be discussing averages, which will give us the tools to further evaluate the bobsleigh team's times. For instance, we can calculate their mean run time as 51.12 seconds. We will discuss means and averages in greater depth in just a moment. For now, let's discuss set notation.

A *set* is defined as a collection of objects or things, with the objects in the set called elements or members of the set. More formally, we say:

$$x \in A \text{ is read "}x\text{ is an element (member) of set } A\text{"}$$

If we let n represent the number of elements in a set, then we can use subscripts to write set A as follows:

$$A = \{x_1, x_2, x_3, ..., x_n\}$$

Many times we want to reduce the set to a single value called an *average*. Here is the definition from an online dictionary:

> **av · er · age** *noun* 1 a : a single value (as a mean, mode, or median) that summarizes or represents the general significance of a set of unequal values . . .

A *statistic* is a quantity that is calculated from a sample of data. In this chapter we will use statistics as estimators calculated from samples rather than from entire populations. You will see that some of the formulas and symbols used are different for a sample statistic than they are for a population statistic. In statistics we refer to the mean and median as *measures of central tendency.* In everyday language the word *average* can refer to the mean, the median, or the mode.

A Mean

The *mean* is probably the most common measure of central tendency and it refers to the arithmetic average for a set of numbers. It is typically used to describe data such as test scores, salary, and various averages having to do with sports.

> **dĕf′ *mean***
>
> The ***mean*** ($\bar{x}$) for a set of values is the sum of the values divided by the number of values.
>
> $$\bar{x} = \frac{\{x_1 + x_2 + x_3 + ... + x_n\}}{n} = \frac{1}{n} \sum_{i=1}^{n} x_i$$

Example 1   Enrollment in college over a five-year period is shown by the following numbers. Find the mean enrollment over the five-year period.

16,911,000   17,272,000   17,487,000   17,759,000   18,248,000

SOLUTION   We add the five enrollments and then divide by 5, the number of values in the set.

$$\text{Mean} = \frac{16,911,000 + 17,272,000 + 17,487,000 + 17,759,000 + 18,248,000}{5}$$

$$= \frac{87,677,000}{5} = 17,535,400$$

The mean enrollment in college over the last five years is 17,535,400 students.

The symbol used here, an *x* with a bar over it, read as "*x* bar" represents the sample mean. When we calculate or refer to a population mean we use the Greek letter mu, μ.

Population: Mean = μ
Sample: Mean = $\bar{x}$

B Median

The ***median*** for a set of numbers is the number in the middle of the data, meaning half the numbers in the set have a value less than the median, and half the numbers in the set have a value greater than the median. Housing prices are frequently described by using a median.

> **dĕf′ *median***
>
> The ***median*** of a set of numbers is the number in the middle when the set is written from least to greatest. If the set contains an even number of elements, the median is the mean of the two middle numbers.

Example 2   Find the median enrollment from the numbers in Example 1.

SOLUTION   The numbers in Example 1 are already written from smallest to largest. Because there are an odd number of numbers in the set, the median is the middle number.

16,911,000   17,272,000   17,487,000   17,759,000   18,248,000
↑
Median

The median enrollment for the five years is 17,487,000.

Example 3   These selling prices of four hybrid cars were listed on hybrid-cars.com.

$23,063 $31,700 $28,600 $24,650

Find the mean and the median for the four prices. Round to the nearest cent if necessary.

SOLUTION   To find the mean, we add the four numbers and then divide by 4:

$$\frac{23{,}063 + 31{,}700 + 28{,}600 + 24{,}650}{4} = \frac{108{,}013}{4} = 27{,}003.25$$

To find the median, we write the numbers in order from smallest to largest. Then, because there is an even number of numbers, we average the middle two numbers to obtain the median.

$23,063 $\underline{24{,}650}$ $\underline{28{,}600}$ $31,700

Median

$$\frac{24{,}650 + 28{,}600}{2} = 26{,}625$$

The mean is $27,003.25, and the median is $26,625.

C Mode

The *mode* is best used when we are looking for the most common eye color in a group of people, the most popular breed of dog in the United States, or the movie that was seen the most often. When we have a set of numbers in which one number occurs more often than the rest, that number is the mode. For example, consider the following set of golf caps:

Given the set of caps, the most popular color is green. We call this the mode.

> (dĕf')   *mode*
>
> The *mode* for a set of numbers is the value that occurs most frequently. If all the numbers in the set occur the same number of times, there is no mode.

Example 4   A math class with 18 students had the grades shown below on their first test. Find the mean, the median, and the mode.

77   87   100   65   79   87

79   85   87   95   56   87

56   75   79   93   97   92

SOLUTION   To find the mean, we add all the numbers and divide by 18.

$$\text{Mean} = \frac{77+87+100+65+79+87+79+85+87+95+56+87+56+75+79+93+97+92}{18}$$

$$= \frac{1,476}{18} = 82$$

To find the median, we must put the test scores in order from smallest to largest; then, because there are an even number of test scores, we must find the mean of the middle two scores.

56 56 65 75 77 79 79 79 85 87 87 87 87 92 93 95 9
7 100

$$\text{Median} = \frac{85 + 87}{2} = 86$$

The mode is the most frequently occurring score. Because 87 occurs 4 times, and no other scores occur that many times, 87 is the mode.

The mean is 82, the median is 86, and the mode is 87. ■

More Vocabulary

When we used the word average in the beginning of this section, we used it as a noun. It can also be used as an adjective and a verb. The following is the definition from an online dictionary of the word average when it is used as a verb.

> **av · er · age** *verb* . . . 2 : to find the arithmetic mean of (a series of unequal quantities) . . .

If you are asked for the average of a set of numbers, the word average can represent the mean, the median, or the mode. When used in this way, the word average is a noun. However, if you are asked to average a set of numbers, then the word average is a verb, and you are being asked to find the mean of the numbers.

D Range

The *range* of a set of data is the difference between the least and greatest. For example, the following table shows some of the highest and lowest minimum wages a   c   r   o   s   s the country.

State	Minimum Wage
Arkansas	$6.25
California	$8.00
Connecticut	$8.25
Minnesota	$5.25
Oklahoma	$2.00
Washington	$8.67

Source: U.S. Department of Labor

From the information in the table, we see that the lowest minimum wage is found in Oklahoma at $2.00 per hour for some businesses and the highest minimum wage is found in Washington at $8.67. The range for this set of data is the difference between these two numbers.

$$\$8.67 - \$2.00 = \$6.67$$

We say that the minimum wage in the United States has a range of $6.67.

> (děf   *range*
>
> The **range** for a set of numbers is the difference between the largest number and the smallest number in the sample.

Example 5   Find the range of the test scores given in Example 4.

SOLUTION   The highest score is 100, and the lowest score is 56. The range is $100 - 56 = 44$. ▪

E Variance and Standard Deviation

The variance, denoted as s^2, is the average of the square of the distance between each number and the mean of a set of data. A small variance indicates the values are close together, while a large variance indicates the values are more spread out. The standard deviation denoted as s, is the square root of the variance.

> [Δ≠Σ] *Formula: Sample Variance*
>
> $$s^2 = \frac{(x_1 - \bar{x})^2 + (x_2 - \bar{x})^2 + (x_3 - \bar{x})^2 + ... + (x_n - \bar{x})^2}{n - 1} = \frac{1}{n - 1} \sum_{i}^{n} (x_i - \bar{x})^2$$

> [Δ≠Σ] *Formula: Sample Standard Deviation*
>
> $$s = \sqrt{\frac{(x_1 - \bar{x})^2 + (x_2 - \bar{x})^2 + (x_3 - \bar{x})^2 + ... + (x_n - \bar{x})^2}{n - 1}}$$

Example 6   For the test score data used previously in this section, find the variance and the standard deviation.

SOLUTION   The table shows the set of data for the first example in this section, along with the distance each score is from the mean, along with the square of that distance, and the cumulative sum of these squares.

Score	Mean	Difference	Square
56	82	$82 - 56 = 26$	676
56	82	$82 - 56 = 26$	676
65	82	$82 - 65 = 17$	289
75	82	$82 - 75 = 7$	49
77	82	$82 - 77 = 5$	25
79	82	$82 - 79 = 3$	9
79	82	$82 - 79 = 3$	9
79	82	$82 - 79 = 3$	9
85	82	$82 - 85 = -3$	9
87	82	$82 - 87 = -5$	25
87	82	$82 - 87 = -5$	25
87	82	$82 - 87 = -5$	25
87	82	$82 - 87 = -5$	25
92	82	$82 - 92 = -10$	100
93	82	$82 - 93 = -11$	121
95	82	$82 - 95 = -13$	169
97	82	$82 - 97 = -15$	225
100	82	$82 - 100 = -18$	324
Total Square			**2,790**

To find the variance we divide the total of the squares by one less than the number of test scores . In this case there are 18 test scores.

$$s^2 = \frac{2{,}790}{18 - 1} = \frac{2{,}790}{17} \approx 164.1$$

To find the standard deviation we take the square root of 164

$$s = \sqrt{164.1} \approx 12.8.$$

The formulas above represent the sample variation and sample standard deviation. For a population variance, we use the symbol σ^2 (the lower case Greek letter sigma) which is calculated by dividing the average of the squared deviations by the entire population, N, rather than $n - 1$ for the sample variance. Likewise the population standard deviation is the square root of the population variance, $\sqrt{\sigma^2} = \sigma$.

Getting Ready for Class

After reading through the preceding section, respond in your own words and in complete sentences.

A. The word average can refer to what three mathematical concepts?

B. What is the difference between the median and the mode for a set of numbers?

C. What number must we use for x, if the average of 6, 8, and x is to be 8?

D. How would you find the variance for a set of data? How would you find the standard deviation?

Problem Set 2.7

Vocabulary Review

Choose the correct words to fill in the blanks below.

mode   range   median   standard deviation

variance   average   mean

61. An _____ can refer to the mean, the median, or the mode for a set of values.

62. The _____ for a set of numbers is the sum of the numbers divided by the number of values.

63. The _____ for a set of numbers is the number in the middle of the data.

64. The _____ for a set of numbers is the number that occurs most frequently.

65. The _____ for a set of numbers is the difference between the largest number and the smallest number.

66. The _____ is the average of the square of distance between each number and the mean of a set of data.

67. The _____ is the square root of the variance.

Problems

A Find the mean for each set of numbers.

1. 1, 2, 3, 4, 5

2. 2, 4, 6, 8, 10

3. 1, 3, 9, 11

4. 5, 7, 9, 12, 12

5. 29,500, 10,650, 8,900, 15,120, 16,800

6. 8,040, 5,505, 4,121, 9,910

7. 12.5, 8.2, 1.8

8. 4.1, 6.9, 2.2, 3.6

B Find the median for each set of numbers.

9. 5, 9, 11, 13, 15

10. 42, 48, 50, 64

11. 10, 20, 50, 90, 100

12. 500, 800, 1200, 1300

13. 900, 700, 1100

14. 850, 100, 225, 480

15. 1.0, 6.5, 3.2, 1.7, 2.1, 4.6, 3.9

16. 2.7, 3.4, 1.8, 1.1, 2.3, 3.0

C Find the mode for each set of numbers.

17. 14, 18, 27, 36, 18, 73

18. 11, 27, 18, 11, 72, 11

19. 98, 87, 65, 73, 82, 87, 65, 97, 87, 77

20. 3.0, 3.2, 2.5, 4.0, 3.1, 3.1, 2.6, 1.9, 1.8, 3.4, 3.1, 2.0

21. 1, 1, 2, 3, 1, 3, 3, 2, 1, 2, 2, 3, 1

22. 5, 8, 9, 9, 6, 6, 7, 7, 5, 8, 6, 8, 9, 5, 8, 8, 9

D Determine the range of the given data.

23. 15, 34, 12, 25, 27

24. 2.6, 4.1, 5.4, 3.9, 0.6

25. 1.0, 3.9, 2.1, 3.6, 2.9, 3.8

26. 12,000, 13,500, 10,120, 14,250, 11,490

27. 52, 69, 84, 81, 79, 46, 81, 73, 68

28. 4080, 2900, 1650, 1800, 1925, 690

Determine the variance of the given data.

29. 14, 12, 16, 20, 10, 18 **30.** 32, 58, 43, 40, 32   **31.** 12, 16, 32, 14, 19, 27 **32.** 23, 21, 34, 30, 27

Determine the standard deviation of the given data.

33. 36, 27, 30   **34.** 57, 53, 49, 54, 47   **35.** 4, 3, 5, 9, 13, 7, 15   **36.** 11, 14, 17, 16, 21, 10, 9

Applying the Concepts

37. Test Average A student's scores for four exams in a basic math class were 79, 62, 87, and 90. What is the student's mean and median test score?

38. Test Scores A first-year math student had grades of 79, 64, 78, and 95 on the first four tests. What is the student's mean and median test grade?

39. Average Salary Over a 3-year period a woman's annual salaries were $28,000, $31,000, and $34,000. What was her mean annual salary and median annual salary for this 3-year period?

40. Bowling If a person has scores of 205, 222, 174, 236, 185, and 215 for six games of bowling, what is the median score for the six games?

41. Average Suppose a basketball team has scores of 64, 76, 98, 55, 76, and 102 in their first six games.

  a. Find the mean score.

  b. Find the median score.

  c. Find the mode of the scores.

42. Home Sales Below are listed the prices paid for 10 homes that sold during the month of February in a city in Texas.

  $210,000 $139,000 $122,000 $145,000

  $120,000 $540,000 $167,000 $125,000

  $125,000 $950,000

  a. Find the mean housing price for the month.

  b. Find the median housing price for the month.

  c. Find the mode of the housing prices for the month.

  d. Which measure of "average" best describes the average housing price for the month? Explain your answer.

43. Cost of College The average cost of tuition for a 4-year public college varies by region. Suppose the cost of tuition for different regions of the United States is $8,602, $7,785, $7,565, $6,421, $5,428, and $5,412. What is the mean and median national cost to attend college? Round to the nearest cent.

44. Cost of College The net cost of tuition is the cost that students actually pay when financial aid is taken into account. If the net cost for a 4-year public college for four different years was $2,260, $2,210, $2,130, and $2,850, what was the mean and median net cost? Round to the nearest cent.

45. Financial Aid The following are the amounts of federal grants (in millions) that were given out from 2004 to 2008: $19,788, $20,304, $19,416, $19, 472, $20,946. What was the mean and median amount given out in federal grants? Round to the nearest dollar.

46. Financial Aid The following are the amounts of all financial aid distributed including all grants, loans, and scholarships, from 2004 to 2008: $132,839, $143,694, $149,668, $154,044, $162,501. What was the mean and median amount of financial aid from 2004 to 2008. Round to the nearest cent.

47. Basketball Find the range of the basketball game scores given in Problem 33.

48. Bowling Find the range of the bowling scores given in Problem 32.

49. Cost of College Find the range of the average costs of tuition given in Problem 35.

50. Cost of College Find the range of the net costs of tuition given in Problem 36.

51. Financial Aid Find the range of the amounts of federal grants given in Problem 37.

52. Financial Aid Find the range of the amounts of financial aid given in Problem 38.

Getting Ready for the Next Section

53. An internet company wants to sell ad space on their web site to generate revenue, but they need to average 5,000 visitors each day for a week. Here is the data for the first six days of the week:

Day	Visitors
Monday	4,432
Tuesday	5,340
Wednesday	5,895
Thursday	6,003
Friday	5,486
Saturday	4,789

  a. How many visitors do they need on Sunday?

  b. What type of average is this; a mean, a median, or a mode?

54. Luke's test scores are 84, 65, 91, 75, and 92 points out of 100. He has one more test in the semester.

  a. What score does he need on the last test to average an 83 on all six tests?

  b. If the teacher drops the lowest score, is it possible for Luke to average 90?

55. The mean of a set of numbers is 234, and the sum of the numbers in the set is 1,638. How many numbers are in the set?

56. The mean of a set of numbers is 0.68, and the sum of the numbers in the set is 5.44. How many numbers are in the set?

Find the Mistake

Each problem below contains a mistake. Circle the mistake and write the correct number(s) or word(s) on the line provided.

1. The following is a list of lunch prices at a school cafeteria. Based on the list, the mean cost of lunch is $20.10.

 $3.23 $1.50 $5.27 $4.30 $3.68 $2.12 _____

2. Suppose you collect 10 different leaves and measure their lengths. The following is a list of those measurements in inches.

 1.2 2.5 4.6 1.7 2.4 3.9 3.0 2.7 3.1 4.3

You would find the median by adding 2.4 and 3.9, and then dividing by 2 to get 3.15 inches.

_____

3. The mode for the following list of numbers is 808.

 808 12 32 7 91 808 64 7 12 91 64 32 12 _____

4. Suppose a basketball team scored 80 points during their highest scoring game, and 42 points during their lowest scoring game. The range of points scored is 80 + 42 = 122. _____

Regression Analysis and the Coefficient of Correlation

In 1929, the astronomer Edwin Hubble (shown in the picture) announced his discovery that the other galaxies in the universe are moving away from us at velocities that increase with distance.

Figure 1 shows a plot of velocity versus distance where each dot represents a galaxy. The fact that the dots all lie approximately on a straight line is the basis of "Hubble's law".

The line in Figure 1 was found using the least-squares method of curve fitting, which we will examine later in this section.

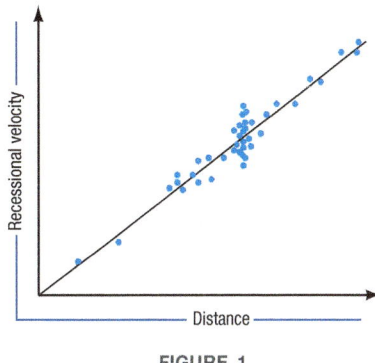

FIGURE 1

Finding a straight line that approximates data that suggests a linear relationship is called *linear regression*, and it is what we will study in this section.

Lines of Best Fit

In most cases, a mathematical model is not a perfect description of reality. Many factors can affect empirical data, including measurement error, environmental conditions, and the influence of related variables. Nonetheless, we can often find an equation that approximates the data in a useful way. The graphs of these equations are called *lines of best fit*, or *regression lines*.

For our first example, we'll find a line of best fit that approximates all the data in the given graph.

Video Examples

Section 2.8

Example 1 The graph below shows the annual average price for gasoline in 5-year increments from 1955 to 2010.

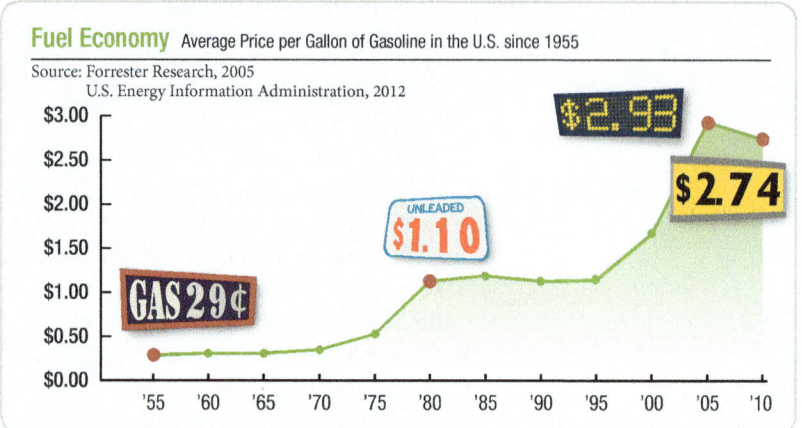

a. Form a line of best fit by connecting the point associated with the year 1980 with the last point on the graph.

b. Find the equation of the line of best fit.

c. Use the line of best fit to predict the average price of gasoline in the year 2015.

SOLUTION We start by drawing our line of best fit by connecting the point at the year 1980 and the last point on the graph.

a.

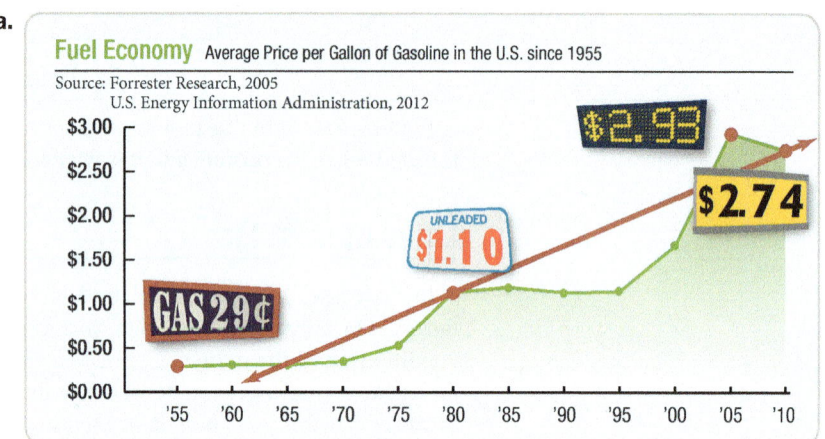

b. If we let x represent the year and y represent the price of gasoline, then the coordinates of our first point are $(1980, 1.10)$ and the coordinates of our last point are $(2010, 2.74)$. First we find the slope, then we use the point slope form of the equation of a line to find the equation of our line of best fit.

$$\text{Slope} = m = \frac{2.74 - 1.10}{2010 - 1980} = \frac{1.64}{30} \approx 0.055$$

Using $(2010, 2.74)$ in

$$y - y_1 = m(x - x_1)$$

we have

$$y - 2.74 = 0.055(x - 2010)$$

$$y - 2.74 = 0.055x - 110.55$$

$$y = 0.055x - 107.81$$

c. To estimate the average price of gasoline in the year 2015, we substitute 2015 for x in our equation.

In the year 2015:

$$y = 0.055(2015) - 107.81$$

$$= 110.825 - 107.81$$

$$= \$3.015$$

Using our line of best fit, we predict the price of gasoline will be approximately $3.02 per gallon in the year 2015.

Note The most important thing to remember with working with lines of best fit is that they are approximations of the data. If we ask you to choose the points through which you'll draw a regression line, your answers may differ than those of your classmates. That's okay as long as you've chosen a line that appropriately represents the data.

Drawing a line of best fit may be done in a variety of ways for the same set of data. In the case of Example 1, we could have drawn a line through two different points than those given, as long as we have about the same number of points below the line as we do above it. On the other hand, the line we chose for Example 1 has a few more points below it than it does above it, but it still fits the collective values because we have minimized the distance between the points and the line itself. Let's try another example that uses a *scatter plot* to illustrate the given data. A scatter plot is a graph of points plotted to show the relationship between two variables. Generally, you will find a nonlinear connection between the points on a scatter plot, unless you suggest a linear relationship using a regression line.

Example 2 Kilauea, on the island of Hawaii, is the world's most active volcano. It sits on top of what geologists call a hot spot. All of the volcanoes on the other Hawaiian Islands have come from this same hot spot. The table shows the ages of some Hawaiian volcanoes compared to their distance from the Kilauea hot spot. (Source: Hawaii Center for Volcanology)

Volcano	Distance from Kilauea (in km)	Approximate Age (in millions of years)
Kilauea	0	0
West Maui	221	1.32
Kauai	519	5.1
Necker	1058	10.3
Midway	2432	27.7
Colohan	3128	38.6
Jingu	4175	55.4
Suiko (central)	4860	64.7

a. Plot the data. Let the *x*-axis represent the distance in kilometers from Kilauea, and the *y*-axis represent age. Is the data linear?

b. Draw a line of best fit for this data. Determine the slope of this line and give an equation that could represent the line.

SOLUTION

a. Kilauea is our origin (0,0). When we plot the rest of the points, we get a graph in the form of a *scatter plot*. We see that the points lie close to but not exactly in a straight line. We can confirm this if we were to find the slopes between two pairs of points. These slopes would not match. Therefore, the data are not linear.

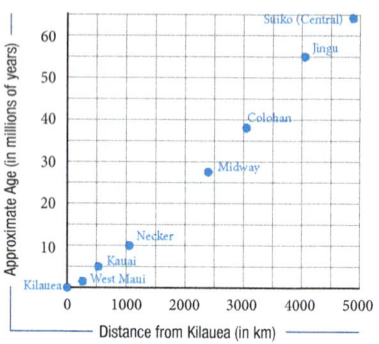

FIGURE 2

b. A line of best fit for our data would be a line with about the same number of points above it as there are below it. One possible regression line is shown in Figure 3, which passes through West Maui at (221, 1.32) and Suiko at (4860, 64.7). The slope of the regression line is

$$m = \frac{64.7 - 1.32}{4860 - 221} = \frac{63.38}{4639} = 0.0137$$

Then we plug our value for m into the point-slope formula to get the following equation for our line:

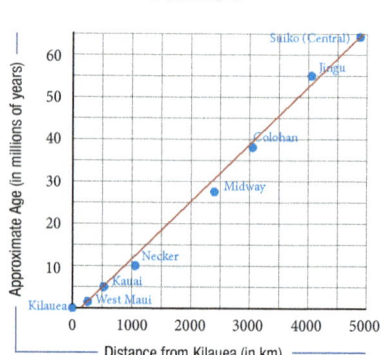

FIGURE 3

$$y - 1.32 = 0.0137(x - 221)$$

$$y - 1.32 = 0.0137x - 3.0277$$

$$y = 0.0137x - 1.7077$$

Remember, the regression line we chose to draw in the above example is just one possible solution. Later in this section, we'll use a graphing calculator to find the most accurate line of best fit. For now, let's try another example by hand.

Example 3   Geologists in Costa Rica have been counting the number of leatherback turtles that nest in Playa Grande each year. The results from 1988 to 1996 are displayed in the table.

Years from 1988	0	1	2	3	4	5	6	7	8
Nestings	1367	1340	665	770	909	180	506	421	125

a. Use the data in the table to construct a scatter plot. Are the data linear?
b. Draw a regression line for the data.
c. What does the slope of the line tell us about the data?

SOLUTION

a. In Figure 4a, we see that the points are not linear.

b. In Figure 4b, we have chosen to draw a line of best fit with a negative slope through points (0, 1367) and (8, 125).

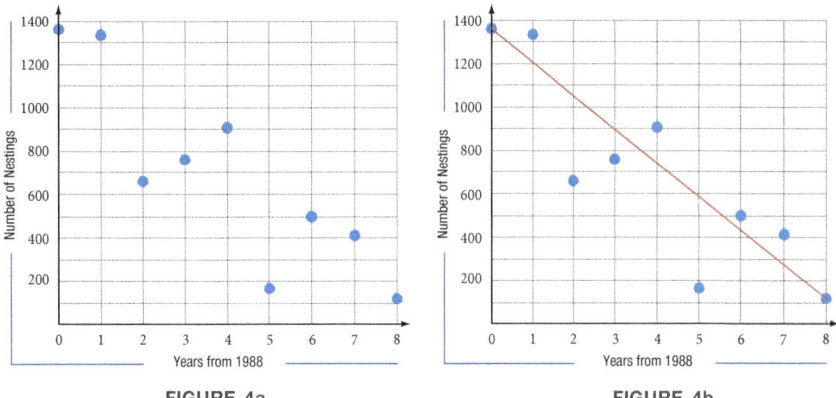

FIGURE 4a   **FIGURE 4b**

c. Let's find the slope by using (0, 1367) and (8, 125).

$$m = \frac{125 - 1367}{8 - 0} = \frac{-1242}{8} = -155.25$$

Our negative calculation for slope tells us that the leatherback turtle nestings are declining at a rate of 155.25 nestings per year. ■

Interpolation and Extrapolation

Now that we are familiar with how to draw regression lines, we can use these lines to learn more about the given data. We can even use the lines to predict values not given in the original data set. Analyzing and making predictions within a data set is called *interpolating*; whereas, making predictions outside a data set is called *extrapolating*.

For instance, revisit the data in Example 3 and consider estimating the number of leatherback turtle nestings halfway through the third year. We would use the process of *interpolation* to estimate the data point that lies between the given points (3, 770) and (4, 909). Suppose we wanted to predict the number of nestings for 1998. We would use the process of *extrapolation* to find that value since 1998 is outside the given data set. You already have some experience with extrapolating data. In Example 1, when you predicted the price of gasoline in the year 2015, you used extrapolation to find your answer.

© Kathy Kifer/BigStockPhoto.com

Example 4   The table below shows the national air pollutant emissions for carbon monoxide from 1970 to 2008.

Years (Since 1970)	Emissions (in thousands of tons)
0	204042
10	185408
20	154188
30	114465
34	99041
35	93034
36	87915
37	82801
38	77685

a. Plot the data and draw a linear regression line.

b. Use your scatter plot to find the coordinates of the regression line in 1980 and in 2005.

c. Use the coordinates from part b to find an equation for the regression line.

d. Use your equation to predict the emissions in 1995, and in 2035.

SOLUTION

a. The scatter plot and a regression line are shown in Figure 5.

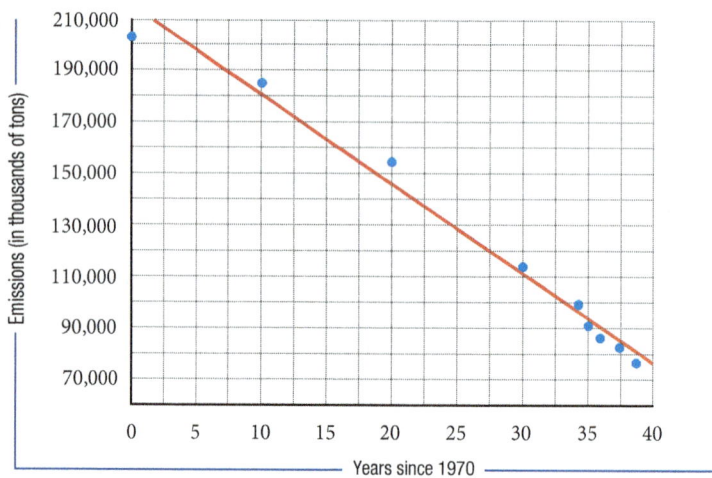

FIGURE 5

The regression line need not pass through any of the data points, but it should be as close as possible. We try to draw the regression line so that there are an equal number of data points above and below the line.

b. In 1980, the regression line appears to pass through the point (10, 180,000). In 2005, the line passes through (35, 95,000). These values are estimates based on our line of best fit. They are not part of the original data set, but they are close enough to provide an accurate approximation.

c. First we use the points from part b, (10, 180,000) and (35, 95,000), to compute the slope.

$$m = \frac{95{,}000 - 180{,}000}{35 - 10} = \frac{-85{,}000}{25} = -3{,}400$$

Now use the point (10, 180,000) in the point-slope formula.

$$y - 180{,}000 = -3{,}400(x - 10)$$

$$y - 180{,}000 = -3{,}400x + 34{,}000$$

$$y = -3{,}400x - 214{,}000$$

d. When the year is 1995, $x = 25$,

$$y = -3{,}400(25) + 214{,}000 = 129{,}000 \qquad \text{Remember, this value is in thousands of tons}$$

We predict that the emissions in 1995 was 129,000,000 tons.

In the year 2035, $x = 65$,

$$y = -3{,}400(65) + 214{,}000 = -7{,}000 \qquad \text{This value is also in thousands of tons.}$$

Because the carbon monoxide emissions cannot be $-7{,}000$ (a negative value), this prediction is not useful.

In Example 4, our interpolated data regarding emissions in 1995 is useful and fairly accurate even though it was not part of the original data set. However, our extrapolated data for emissions in 2035 gave us an unuseful negative value. We must be careful when predicting values too far outside our data. Other factors may influence the results, making our estimates unreliable.

Least Squares Regression Line

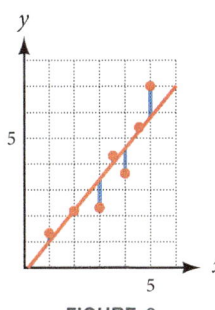

FIGURE 6

Up to now, we have chosen our regression lines by approximating their locations based on the number of data points above and below each line. We can approximate more accurately by finding what is a called a *least squares regression line*. This line is located with respect to the sum of the squares of the distance between each data point and the line. See Figure 6 for an illustration of this concept. Most graphing calculators are equipped to calculate a least squares regression line for you. But first, let's discuss how your calculator finds such a line, or rather how you would do so by hand.

We are familiar with the standard equation for a line $y = mx + b$. We can find the values for m (the slope) and b (the y-intercept) by using a set of data and the following formulas:

$$m = \frac{n(\Sigma xy) - (\Sigma x)(\Sigma y)}{n(\Sigma x^2) - (\Sigma x)^2}$$

$$b = \frac{(\Sigma y) - m(\Sigma x)}{n}$$

In words, the symbol Σ means "the sum of." Here is how we translate the expressions in the above formulas:

Σx Sum of the x-coordinates
Σy Sum of the y-coordinates
Σxy Sum of the products of x- and y-coordinates
Σx^2 Sum of the squares of x-coordinates
n Total number of data points

Suppose we need to find the least squares regression line for the following ordered pairs:

$$(1, 2), (2, 1), (3, 3), (4, 5), (5, 6)$$

First, let's create a table using these coordinates to help us find the expressions in the slope and y-intercept formulas.

x	y $\longrightarrow$	xy	x^2	
1	2	2	1	*First coordinate*
2	1	2	4	*Second coordinate*
3	3	9	9	*Third coordinate*
4	5	20	16	*Fourth coordinate*
+ 5	6	30	25	*Fifth coordinate*
15	17	63	55	*Find the sum of each column.*
$\downarrow$	$\downarrow$	$\downarrow$	$\downarrow$	
Σx	Σy	Σxy	Σx^2	

We have found the sum of each column. Now let's plug in our sums:

To find m, use the formula

$$m = \frac{n(\Sigma xy) - (\Sigma x)(\Sigma y)}{n(\Sigma x^2) - (\Sigma x)^2}$$

$$= \frac{5(63) - (15)(17)}{5(55) - (15)^2} \qquad \textit{n = 5 because we had 5 data points.}$$

$$= \frac{315 - 255}{275 - 225}$$

$$= \frac{60}{50} = 1.2$$

To find b, use the value we found for m.

$$b = \frac{(\Sigma y) - m(\Sigma x)}{n}$$

$$b = \frac{(17) - 1.2(15)}{5}$$

$$= -0.2$$

If $m = 1.2$ and $b = -0.2$, then the equation for our regression line is

$$y = 1.2x - 0.2$$

Let's graph this line and see how it fits with our original data.

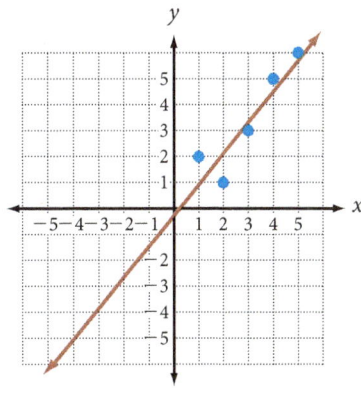

FIGURE 7

Figure 7 shows the least squares regression line fitting the data very well. Let's try another example.

Example 5   Without a calculator, calculate the least squares regression line for the following data points:

$$(2, 4), (3, 2), (5, 5), (6, 9), (8, 7), (9, 10)$$

SOLUTION Here's a table of values to help us find m and b.

x	$\overline{y}$ $\longrightarrow$	xy	x^2
2	4	8	4
3	2	6	9
5	5	25	25
6	9	54	36
8	7	56	64
+ 9	10	90	81
33	37	239	219

Find the sum of each column.

Now let's use the sum from each column in our formulas for slope and y-intercept.

$$m = \frac{n(\Sigma xy) - (\Sigma x)(\Sigma y)}{n(\Sigma x^2) - (\Sigma x)^2} = \frac{6(239) - (33)(37)}{6(219) - (33)^2}$$

$$= \frac{1434 - 1221}{1314 - 1089}$$

$$= \frac{213}{225} \approx 0.9467$$

To find b, use the value we found above for m.

$$b = \frac{(\Sigma y) - m(\Sigma x)}{n} = \frac{(37) - 0.9467(33)}{6} \approx 0.96$$

Therefore, the equation for our least squares regression line is

$$y = 0.9467x + 0.96$$

As mentioned, most graphing calculators will calculate a least squares regression line based on a set of data you enter. The next example shows us how.

Example 6   The table shows the total patents issued by the United States Patent Office for inventions (including individuals, corporations, and the government) from 1990 to 2010 (Source: 2012 Statistical Abstract). The numbers in the first row represent the number of years since 1990.

Years (Since 1990)	Number of Patents Issued (in thousand)
0	90.4
5	101.4
10	157.5
15	143.8
16	173.8
17	157.3
18	157.8
19	167.3
20	219.6

Use your graphing calculator to find the equation of the least squares regression line for the data in the table. Then plot the data points and the least squares regression line on the same axes.

Then plot the data points and the least squares regression line on the same axes.

SOLUTION

***Step* 1:**   Enter data by pressing $\boxed{\text{STAT}}$ $\boxed{\text{ENTER}}$ to select 1:Edit....

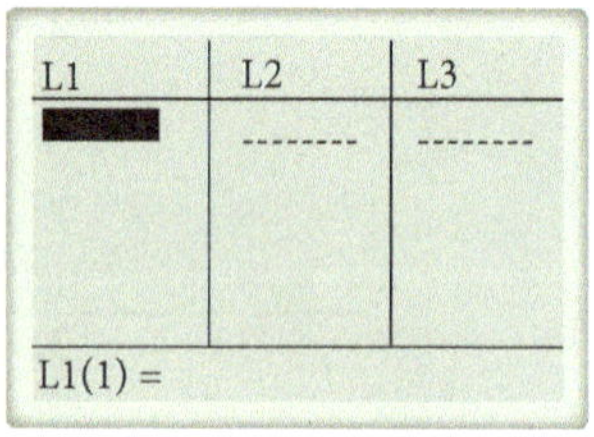

FIGURE 8a

***Step* 2:**   Clear any old data in column L1 or L2.

***Step* 3:**   In the L1 column, enter the x-coordinates. In the L2 column, enter the y-coordinates.

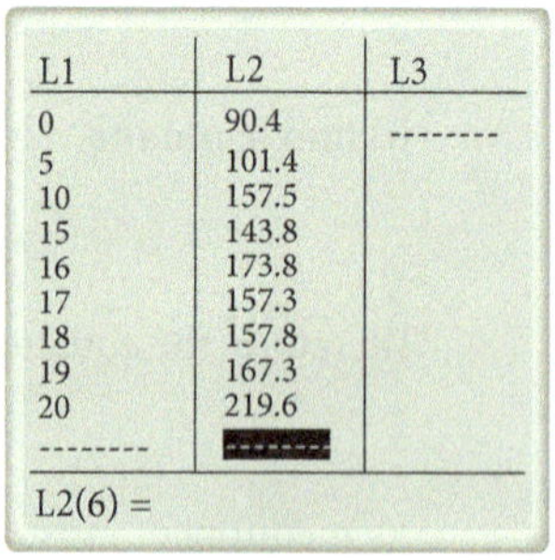

FIGURE 8b

Step 4: Press [STAT] and the right arrow once, then press 4 to select linear regression, or 4: LinReg($ax + b$). On the LinReg($ax + b$) screen, select Calculate and press [ENTER]. You should see a screen similar to that of Figure 8c. Here your regression line should be displayed as approximately $y = 4.88x + 87.08$.

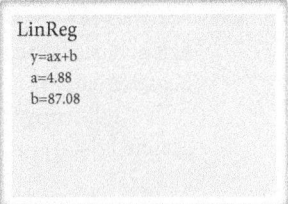

LinReg
y=ax+b
a=4.88
b=87.08

FIGURE 8c

Now let's plot our points and line.

Step 5: Press [Y =], place your cursor after Y1 = and press [CLEAR] to clear any old definitions.

Step 6: Press [VARS] 5 to select 5: Statistics, then press the right arrow twice to display the EQ menu. Finally, press 1 or [ENTER] to select 1: RegEQ, which will have copied your regression line equation.

And finally, we'll draw a scatterplot.

Step 7: Press [2nd][Y =][1] to select Plot 1. Make sure your Plot 1 menu matches that shown in Figure 8d.

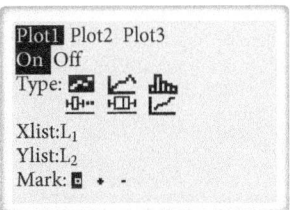

Plot1 Plot2 Plot3
On Off
Type:
Xlist:L₁
Ylist:L₂
Mark:

FIGURE 8d

Step 8: Press [ZOOM] 9 to select ZoomStat and see the scatterplot of the data and the regression line.

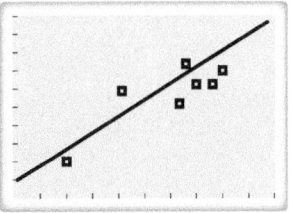

FIGURE 8e

We can see from our least squares regression line that the US Patent office has issued an increasing number of patents for inventions each year since 1990.

Correlation and Cause

> *Note*   Remember that a line with a positive slope has *y* values that increase as the *x* values increase. A line with a negative slope has *y* values that increase and the *x* values decrease.

You may have noticed a couple other numbers listed on your graphing calculator's Linear Regression screen. These values are for *r*, which we call a *correlation coefficient*. A correlation coefficient is a real number *r*, where -1 < *r* < 1. For a certain data set, the data points will correlate with each other in different ways. For a regression line to truly be that of best fit, it should have a correlation coefficient *r* near or equal to 1 (if the line has a positive slope) or −1 (if the line has a negative slope).

The following table shows how we use correlation coefficients to interpret graphed data:

r value	Meaning	Example Graph
$r = 1$	Line with a positive slope passes through all points.	
$r = -1$	Line with a negative slope passes through all points.	
+, near 1	Approximately same number of points above line as below it; *x* values *increase* as *y* values *increase*; positive correlation.	
−, near −1	Approximately same number of points above line as below it; *x* values *decrease* as *y* values *increase*; negative correlation.	
$r = 0$	Points do not display in a linear shape, no correlation.	

It is important to know that correlation does not imply causation; although one variable may correlate with another, it does not always cause the other. In 2012, the *New England Journal of Medicine* published the article, "Chocolate Consumption, Cognitive Function, and Nobel Laureates." The article presented a positive correlation between the number of Nobel prizes won by a country (per capita) and the country's consumption of chocolate. In other words, the study found the more chocolate a country ate, the more Nobel prize recipients they were likely to have.

This scenario is a great example of why correlation does not mean causation. The number of Nobel prize winners may correlate with the amount of chocolate consumed, but the amount of chocolate consumed does not cause the number of Nobel prizes won.

Getting Ready for Class

After reading through the preceding section, respond in your own words and in complete sentences.

A. What is a line of best fit?
B. What is the difference between interpolation and extrapolation?
C. What is the difference between a regression line and a least squares regression line?
D. What is a correlation coefficient?

1. Solar photovoltaics, such as solar panels, convert sunlight directly to electricity. The following graph shows the number of solar photovoltaics installed in residences, non-residences, and utility facilities from 2010 to the third quarter of 2012. Draw a regression line that best fits the data.(Source: Solar Energy Industries Association)

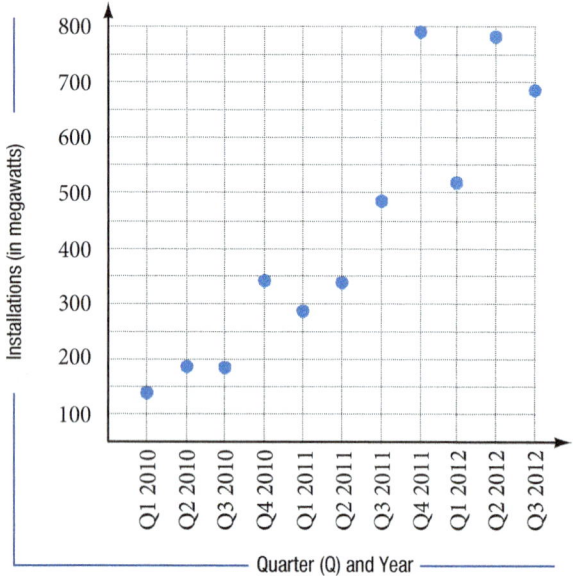

2. The following graph shows the average salaries for Major League Baseball players from 1990 to 2010. Draw a regression line that best fits the data. (Source: 2012 Statistical Abstract, United States Census Bureau)

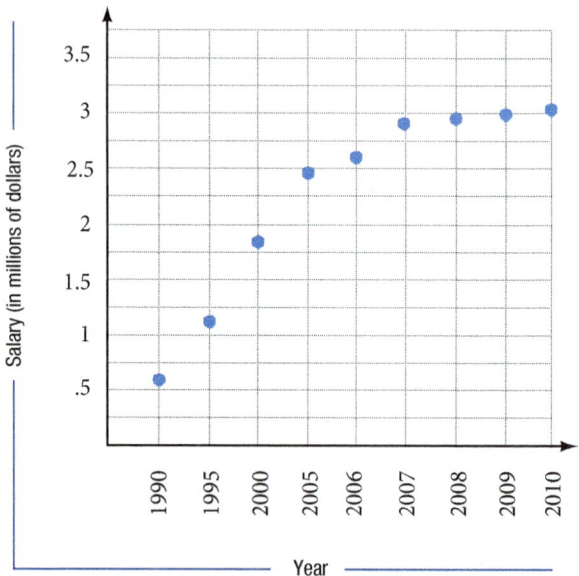

3. The table below shows the consumption of bottled water per person the United States. (Source: Beverage Marketing Corporation)

Year	Gallons Consumed (per person)
2001	18.2
2002	20.1
2003	21.6
2004	23.2
2005	25.4
2006	27.6
2007	29
2008	28.5
2009	27.6
2010	28.3
2011	29.2

a. Plot the data. Let the x-axis represent the years since 2001, and the y-axis represent the gallons consumed per person. Is the data linear?

b. Draw a line of best fit for this data. Determine the slope of this line and give an equation that could represent the line.

4. The following table shows the funds available for the National Endowment for the Arts.

Year	Funds Available (in millions of dollars)
2000	85.2
2004	105.5
2005	108.8
2006	112.8
2007	111.7
2008	129.3
2009	186.8*
2010	152.7
2011	142.4
2012	125.5

*Additional one-time funding from the American Recovery and Reinvestment Act of 2009
 (Source: National Endowment for the Arts)

a. Plot the data. Let the x-axis represent the number of years since 2000, and the y-axis represent the fund available (in millions of dollars). Is the data linear?

b. Draw a line of best fit for this data. Determine the slope of this line and give an equation that could represent the line.

c. How did the American Recovery and Reinvestment Act in 2009 affect our data and the line of best fit? Should you consider this data point when drawing your regression line?

5. Suppose you were a volleyball coach analyzing your team's hitting percentage over the last ten games of the season.

Game Number	Hitting Ratio (per game)
1	0.138
2	0.198
3	0.223
4	0.249
5	0.267
6	0.256
7	0.289
8	0.294
9	0.302
10	0.315

a. Use the data in the table to construct a scatter plot. Are the data linear?

b. Draw a regression line for the data.

c. What does the slope of the line tell us about the data?

6. In 2011, the United States Bureau of Labor Statistics released a report on the number of establishments using green technologies and practices. The following table shows their findings:

Number of Green Practices Reported	Number of Establishments
1	1,646,700
2	1,721,800
3	976,100
4	421,600
5	136,400
6	30,900

a. Use the data in the table to construct a scatter plot. Are the data linear?

b. Draw a regression line for the data.

c. What does the slope of the line tell us about the data?

7. The following table shows the average annual salaries for a job in the field of computer and mathematics. (Source: United States Bureau of Labor Statistics)

Years (Since 2000)	Mean Annual Salary (in dollars)
0	58,050
1	60,350
2	61,630
3	63,240
4	65,510
5	67,100
6	69,240
7	72,190
8	74,500
9	76,290
10	77,230

a. Plot the data and draw a linear regression line.

b. Use your scatter plot to find the coordinates of the regression line in 2002 and in 2010.

c. Use the coordinates from part b to find an equation for the regression line.

d. Use your equation to predict the salaries in 2015, and in 2030.

8. The table below shows the percentage of plastic (PET) bottles that are not recycled in the United States per year since 2003. (Source: NAPCOR)

Years (Since 2003)	Non-Recycle Rate of PET Bottles (%)
0	80.4
1	78.4
2	76.9
3	76.5
4	75.4
5	73.0
6	72.0
7	70.9

a. Plot the data and draw a linear regression line.

b. Use your scatter plot to find the coordinates of the regression line in 2004 and in 2009.

c. Use the coordinates from part b to find an equation for the regression line.

d. Use your equation to predict the non-recycling rate of PET bottles in 2000, and in 2016.

Without a calculator, calculate the equation for the least squares regression line for the following sets of data. Round answers to the nearest ten thousandth.

9.

x	y
1	4
3	3
5	6
8	7
10	8

10.

x	y
1	7
2	4
3	5
5	5
6	3
8	3
9	4
10	2

11.

x	y
$\frac{1}{2}$	1
1	3
$\frac{7}{4}$	3
2	5
$\frac{9}{4}$	7
$\frac{5}{2}$	7
3	8

12.

x	y
0.6	2
1.2	4
2	3
2.9	6.1
4	5.8
4.7	8

13. In 2012, a graphic designer could expect to earn a mean hourly wage of $23.43. The following table shows the mean hourly wages for a job in graphic design every two years since 1999. (Source: U.S. Bureau of Labor Statistics)

Years (Since 1999)	Mean Hourly Wage (in dollars)
0	17.41
2	19.07
4	19.85
6	20.45
8	21.80
10	22.99
12	23.41

a. Using your graphing calculator, find the equation of the least squares regression line.

b. Plot the data points and the least squares regression line on the same axes.

c. Interpolate the mean hourly wage for 2008 based on your data.

d. Extrapolate the mean hourly wage for 2020 based on your data.

e. Find the correlation coefficient.

14. The table lists some of the world record times for the men's 100-meter sprint over the last century. (Sources: IAAF, ESPN)

Year	Years (since 1912)	Time (in seconds)
1912	0	10.6
1930	18	10.3
1956	44	10.1
1968	56	9.95
1988	76	9.92
1991	79	9.86
1996	84	9.84
2002	90	9.78

a. Using your graphing calculator, find the equation of the least squares regression line.

b. Plot the data points and the least squares regression line on the same axes. (Hint: use the values in the Years since 1912 column as your x-values.)

c. In 1960, Armin Hary set a world record for the 100-meter sprint with a time of 10.0 seconds. Use your regression line to interpolate the number of seconds in 1960. How does your calculation compare to the actual time?

d. Use your regression line to extrapolate the number of seconds for a world record time in 2020.

e. Find the correlation coefficient.

Maintaining Your Skills

The problems that follow review some of the more important skills you have learned in previous sections and chapters.

Solve the following equations.

15. $x - 5 = 7$ **16.** $3y = -4$ **17.** $5 - \frac{4}{7}a = -11$

18. $\frac{1}{5}x - \frac{1}{2} - \frac{1}{10}x + \frac{2}{5} = \frac{3}{10}x + \frac{1}{2}$

19. $5(x - 1) - 2(2x + 3) = 5x - 4$

20. $0.07 - 0.02(3x + 1) = -0.04x + 0.01$

Solve for the indicated variable.

21. $P = 2l + 2w$ for w

22. $A = \dfrac{1}{2}h(b + B)$ for B

Solve the following inequalities. Write the solution set using interval notation, then graph the solution set.

23. $-5t \le 30$

24. $5 - \dfrac{3}{2}x > -1$

25. $1.6x - 2 < 0.8x + 2.8$

26. $3(2y + 4) \ge 5(y - 8)$

Solve the following equations.

27. $\left|\dfrac{1}{4}x - 1\right| = \dfrac{1}{2}$

28. $\left|\dfrac{2}{3}a + 4\right| = 6$

29. $|3 - 2x| + 5 = 2$

30. $5 = |3y + 6| - 4$

Linear Inequalities in Two Variables

A linear inequality in two variables is any expression that can be put in the form

$$ax + by < c$$

where a, b, and c are real numbers (a and b not both 0). The inequality symbol can be any of the following four: $<, \leq, >, \geq$.

Some examples of linear inequalities are

$$2x + 3y < 6 \qquad y \geq 2x + 1 \qquad x - y \leq 0$$

Although not all of these inequalities have the form $ax + by < c$, each one can be put in that form.

The solution set for a linear inequality is a section of the coordinate plane. The boundary for the section is found by replacing the inequality symbol with an equal sign and graphing the resulting equation. The boundary is included in the solution set (and represented with a solid line) if the inequality symbol used originally is $\leq$ or $\geq$. The boundary is not included (and is represented with a broken line) if the original symbol is $<$ or $>$.

Let's look at some examples.

Video Examples

Section 2.9

Example 1 Graph the solution set for $x + y \leq 4$.

SOLUTION The boundary for the graph is the graph of $x + y = 4$. The boundary is included in the solution set because the inequality symbol is $\leq$.

The graph of the boundary is shown in Figure 1.

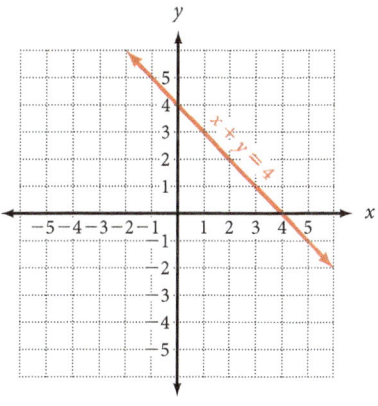

FIGURE 1

The boundary separates the coordinate plane into two sections, or regions: the region above the boundary and the region below the boundary. The solution set for $x + y \leq 4$ is one of these two regions along with the boundary. To find the correct region, we simply choose any convenient point that is *not* on the boundary. We then substitute the coordinates of the point into the original inequality $x + y \leq 4$. If the point we choose satisfies the inequality, then it is a member of the solution set, and we can assume that all points on the same side of the boundary as the chosen point are also in the solution set. If the coordinates of our point do not satisfy the original inequality, then the solution set lies on the other side of the boundary.

In this example a convenient point not on the boundary is the origin. Substituting $(0, 0)$ into $x + y \leq 4$ gives us

$$0 + 0 \overset{?}{\leq} 4$$

$$0 \leq 4 \qquad \textcolor{green}{\textit{A true statement}}$$

Because the origin is a solution to the inequality $x + y \leq 4$, and the origin is below the boundary, all other points below the boundary are also solutions.

The graph of $x + y \leq 4$ is shown in Figure 2.

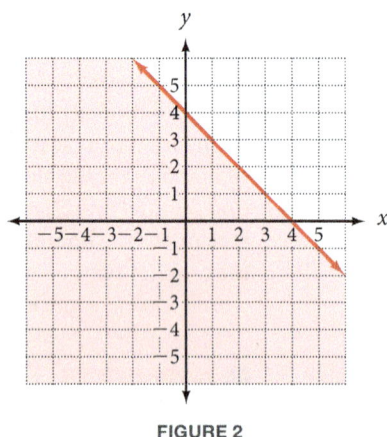

FIGURE 2

The region above the boundary is described by the inequality $x + y > 4$.

Here is a list of steps to follow when graphing the solution set for linear inequalities in two variables.

∆≠Σ   How to Graph the Solution Set for Linear Inequalities in Two Variables

Step 1: Replace the inequality symbol with an equal sign. The resulting equation represents the boundary for the solution set.

Step 2: Graph the boundary found in Step 1 using a *solid line* if the boundary is included in the solution set (that is, if the original inequality symbol was either $\leq$ or $\geq$). Use a *broken line* to graph the boundary if it is *not* included in the solution set. (It is not included if the original inequality was either $<$ or $>$).

Step 3: Choose any convenient point not on the boundary and substitute the coordinates into the *original* inequality. If the resulting statement is *true*, the graph lies on the *same* side of the boundary as the chosen point. If the resulting statement is *false*, the solution set lies on the *opposite* side of the boundary.

Example 2   Graph the solution set for $y < 2x - 3$.

SOLUTION The boundary is the graph of $y = 2x - 3$. The boundary is not included because the original inequality symbol is $<$. We therefore use a broken line to represent the boundary, as shown in Figure 3.

A convenient test point is again the origin. Using $(0, 0)$ in $y < 2x - 3$, we have

$$0 \overset{?}{<} 2(0) - 3$$

$$0 < -3 \qquad \text{A false statement}$$

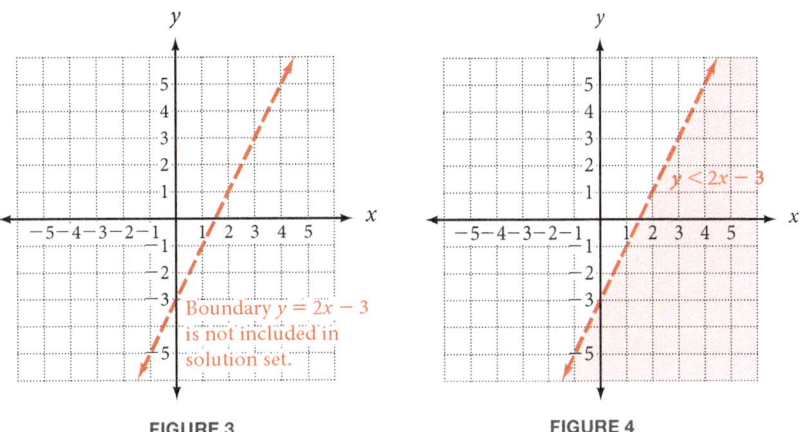

FIGURE 3

FIGURE 4

Because our test point gives us a false statement and it lies above the boundary, the solution set must lie on the other side of the boundary, as shown in Figure 4.

Example 3 Graph the inequality $2x + 3y \leq 6$.

SOLUTION We begin by graphing the boundary $2x + 3y = 6$. The boundary is included in the solution because the inequality symbol is $\leq$.

If we use $(0, 0)$ as our test point, we see that it yields a true statement when its coordinates are substituted into $2x + 3y \leq 6$. The graph, therefore, lies below the boundary, as shown in Figure 5.

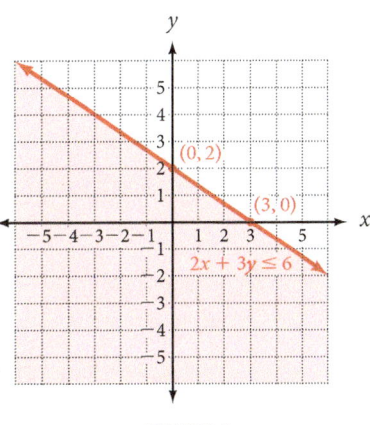

FIGURE 5

The ordered pair $(0, 0)$ is a solution to $2x + 3y \leq 6$; all points on the same side of the boundary as $(0, 0)$ also must be solutions to the inequality $2x + 3y \leq 6$.

Example 4   Graph the solution set for $x \leq 5$.

SOLUTION   The boundary is $x = 5$, which is a vertical line. All points to the left have x-coordinates less than 5, and all points to the right have x-coordinates greater than 5, as shown in Figure 6.

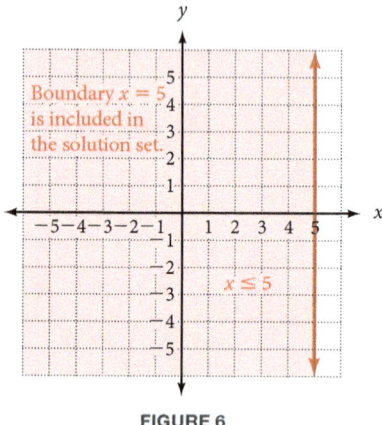

FIGURE 6

Getting Ready for Class

After reading through the preceding section, respond in your own words and in complete sentences.

A. When graphing a linear inequality in two variables, how do you find the equation of the boundary line?

B. What is the significance of a broken line in the graph of an inequality?

C. When graphing a linear inequality in two variables, how do you know which side of the boundary line to shade?

D. Describe the set of ordered pairs that are solutions to $x + y < 6$.

Graph the following linear inequalities.

1. $2x - 3y < 6$ **2.** $3x + 2y \geq 6$ **3.** $x - 2y \leq 4$ **4.** $2x + y > 4$

5. $x - y \leq 2$ **6.** $x - y \leq 1$ **7.** $3x - 4y \geq 12$ **8.** $4x + 3y < 12$

9. $5x - y \leq 5$ **10.** $4x + y > 4$ **11.** $2x + 6y \leq 12$ **12.** $x - 5y > 5$

13. $x \geq 1$ **14.** $x < 5$ **15.** $x \geq -3$ **16.** $y \leq -4$

17. $y < 2$ **18.** $3x - y > 1$ **19.** $2x + y > 3$ **20.** $5x + 2y < 2$

21. $y \leq 3x - 1$ **22.** $y \geq 3x + 2$ **23.** $y \leq -\dfrac{1}{2}x + 2$ **24.** $y < \dfrac{1}{3}x + 3$

25. Paying Attention to Instructions Work each problem according to the instructions given..

  a. Solve: $4 + 3y < 12$ **b.** Solve: $4 - 3y < 12$

  c. Solve for y: $4x + 3y = 12$ **d.** Graph: $y < -\dfrac{4}{3}x + 4$

26. Paying Attention to Instructions Work each problem according to the instructions given..

  a. Solve: $3x + 2 \geq 6$ **b.** Solve: $-3x + 2 \geq 6$

  c. Solve for y: $3x + 2y = 6$ **d.** Graph: $y \geq -\dfrac{3}{2}x + 3$

27. Find the equation of the line in part a, then use this information to find the inequalities for the graphs on parts b and c.

a. 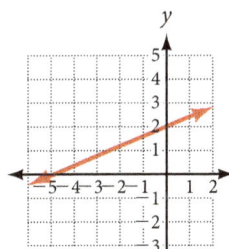 **b.** 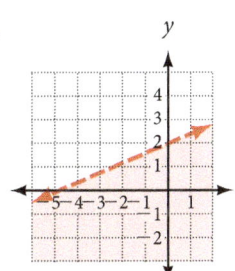 **c.**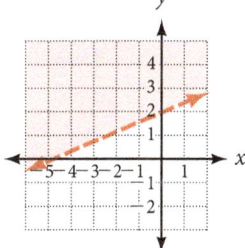

28. Find the equation of the line in part a, then use this information to find the inequalities for the graphs on parts b and c.

a. 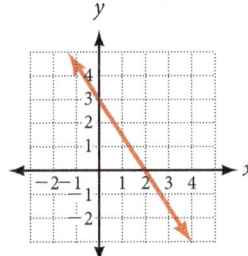 **b.** 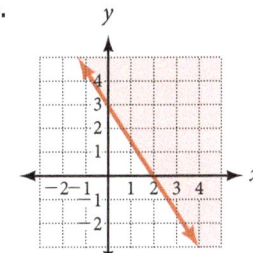 **c.**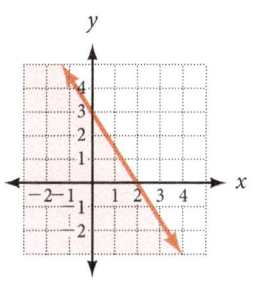

Maintaining Your Skills

29. Simplify the expression $7 - 3(2x - 4) - 8$.

30. Find the value of $x^2 - 2xy + y^2$ when $x = 3$ and $y = -4$.

Solve each equation.

31. $-\dfrac{3}{2}x = 12$ **32.** $2x - 4 = 5x + 2$ **33.** $8 - 2(x + 7) = 2$

34. $3(2x - 5) - (2x - 4) = 6 - (4x + 5)$

35. Solve the formula $P = 2l + 2w$ for w.

Solve each inequality, and graph the solution.

36. $-4x < 20$ **37.** $3 - 2x > 5$

38. $3 - 4(x - 2) \geq -5x + 6$

39. Solve the formula $3x - 2y \leq 12$ for y.

40. What number is 12% of 2,000?

41. **Geometry** The length of a rectangle is 5 inches more than 3 times the width. If the perimeter is 26 inches, find the length and width.

SPOTLIGHT ON SUCCESS   *Student Instructor Lauren*

There are a lot of word problems in algebra and many of them involve topics that I don't know much about. I am better off solving these problems if I know something about the subject. So, I try to find something I can relate to. For instance, an example may involve the amount of fuel used by a pilot in a jet airplane engine. In my mind, I'd change the subject to something more familiar, like the mileage I'd be getting in my car and the amount spent on fuel, driving from my hometown to my college. Changing these problems to more familiar topics makes math much more interesting and gives me a better chance of getting the problem right. It also helps me to understand how greatly math affects and influences me in my everyday life. We really do use math more than we would like to admit—budgeting our income, purchasing gasoline, planning a day of shopping with friends—almost everything we do is related to math. So the best advice I can give with word problems is to learn how to associate the problem with something familiar to you.

You should know that I have always enjoyed math. I like working out problems and love the challenges of solving equations like individual puzzles. Although there are more interesting subjects to me, and I don't plan on pursuing a career in math or teaching, I do think it's an important subject that will help you in any profession.

Linear Equation in Two Variables [2.3]

EXAMPLES

1. The equation $3x + 2y = 6$ is an example of a linear equation in two variables.

A linear equation in two variables is any equation that can be put in the form $ax + by = c$. The graph of every linear equation is a straight line.

2. The graph of $y = -\frac{2}{3}x - 1$ is shown below.

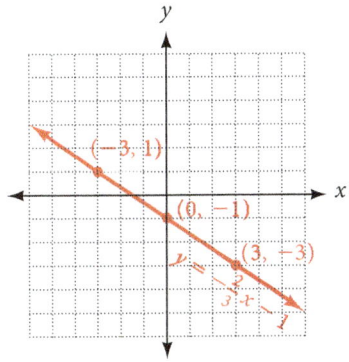

Strategy for Graphing Linear Equations in Two Variables [2.3]

Step 1 Find any three ordered pairs that satisfy the equation. This can be done by using a convenient number for one variable and solving for the other variable.

Step 2: Graph the three ordered pairs found in step 1. Actually, we need only two points to graph a straight line. The third point serves as a check. If all three points do not line up, there is a mistake in our work.

Step 3: Draw a straight line through the three points graphed in step 2.

Intercepts [2.4]

3. To find the x-intercept for $3x + 2y = 6$, we let $y = 0$ and get

$$3x = 6$$
$$x = 2$$

In this case the x-intercept is 2, and the graph crosses the x-axis at $(2, 0)$.

The x-intercept of an equation is the x-coordinate of the point where the graph crosses the x-axis. The y-intercept is the y-coordinate of the point where the graph crosses the y-axis. We find the y-intercept by substituting $x = 0$ into the equation and solving for y. The x-intercept is found by letting $y = 0$ and solving for x.

Slope of a Line [2.5]

4. The slope of the line through $(3, -5)$ and $(-2, 1)$ is

$$m = \frac{-5 - 1}{3 - (-2)} = \frac{-6}{5} = -\frac{6}{5}$$

The *slope* of the line containing the points (x_1, y_1) and (x_2, y_2) is given by

$$\text{Slope} = m = \frac{y_2 - y_1}{x_2 - x_1} = \frac{\text{rise}}{\text{run}}$$

Slope-Intercept Form of a Straight Line [2.6]

5. The equation of the line with a slope of 2 and a y-intercept of 5 is

$$y = 2x + 5$$

The equation of the line with a slope of m and a y-intercept of b is

$$y = mx + b$$

Point-Slope Form of a Straight Line [2.6]

6. The equation of the line through (1, 2) with a slope of 3 is
$$y - 2 = 3(x - 1)$$
$$y - 2 = 3x - 3$$
$$y = 3x - 1$$

If a line has a slope of m and contains the point (x_1, y_1), the equation can be written as

$$y - y_1 = m(x - x_1)$$

EXAMPLES

1. Find the mean for test scores of 74, 63, 74, 80, 83, 88.
We add the numbers and divide by 6:

$$\frac{74 + 63 + 74 + 80 + 83 + 88}{6}$$
$$= \frac{462}{6} = 77$$

Mean [2.1]

To find the *mean* $\bar{x}$ for a set of numbers, we add all the numbers and then divide the sum by the number of values in the set. The mean is sometimes called the *arithmetic mean*.

$$\bar{x} = \frac{\{x_1 + x_2 + x_3 + ... + x_n\}}{n} = \frac{1}{n} \sum_{i=1}^{n} x_i$$

Median [2.1]

2. The median for the test scores in Example 1 will be halfway between 74 and 80.

$$\text{Median} = \frac{74 + 80}{2} = 77$$

To find the *median* for a set of numbers, we write the numbers in order from smallest to largest. If there is an odd number of values, the median is the middle number. If there is an even number of values, then the median is the mean of the two numbers in the middle.

Mode [2.1]

3. The mode for the test scores in Example 1 will be the most frequently occurring score, which is 74.

The *mode* for a set of numbers is the value that occurs most frequently. If all the numbers in the set occur the same number of times, there is no mode.

Range [2.1]

4. The range for the test scores in Example 1 will be the difference between 88 and 63.
$$\text{Range} = 88 - 63 = 25$$

The *range* for a set of numbers is the difference between the largest number and the smallest number in the sample.

Variance [2.1]

5. The variance of the test scores from Example 1 is 76.

The variance s^2 is the average of the square of the distance between each number and the mean of a set of data. A small variance indicates the values are close together, while a large variance indicates the values are more spread out. .

$$s^2 = \frac{(x_1 - \bar{x})^2 + (x_2 - \bar{x})^2 + (x_3 - \bar{x})^2 + ... + (x_n - \bar{x})^2}{n - 1} = \frac{1}{n - 1} \sum_{i}^{n} (x_i - \bar{x})^2$$

Standard Deviation [2.1]

6. The standard deviation of the test scores will be the square root of the variance.

$$\sqrt{76} \approx 8.72$$

The standard deviation s is the square root of the variance

$$s = \sqrt{\frac{(x_1 - \bar{x})^2 + (x_2 - \bar{x})^2 + (x_3 - \bar{x})^2 + \ldots + (x_n - \bar{x})^2}{n - 1}}$$

To Graph a Linear Inequality in Two Variables [2.7]

7. Graph $x - y \geq 3$.

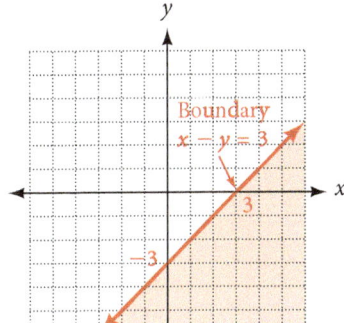

Step 1: Replace the inequality symbol with an equal sign. The resulting equation represents the boundary for the solution set.

Step 2: Graph the boundary found in step 1, using a *solid line* if the original inequality symbol was either $\leq$, or $\geq$. Use a *broken line* otherwise.

Step 3: Choose any convenient point not on the boundary and substitute the coordinates into the *original* inequality. If the resulting statement is *true*, the graph lies on the *same* side of the boundary as the chosen point. If the resulting statement is *false*, the solution set lies on the *opposite* side of the boundary.

Linear Regression [2.5]

4.

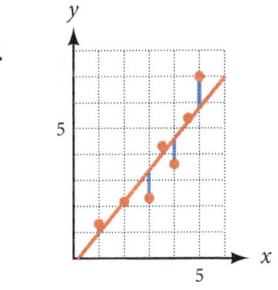

When we approximate a linear pattern with a straight line, that line is called the *line of best fit* or *regression line*. If we use that line to predict values that lie within our original data, we are using *interpolation*. If we use the regression line to make predictions that lie outside our original data we are using *extrapolation*. We can use our graphing calculators to find regression lines that are found using the *least squares* method.

⚠️ *Common Mistake*

1. When graphing ordered pairs, the most common mistake is to associate the first coordinate with the *y*-axis and the second with the *x*-axis. If you make this mistake you would graph (3, 1) by going up 3 and to the right 1, which is just the reverse of what you should do. Remember, the first coordinate is always associated with the horizontal axis, and the second coordinate is always associated with the vertical axis.

2. The two most common mistakes students make when first working with the formula for the slope of a line are the following:
   a. Putting the difference of the *x*-coordinates over the difference of the *y*-coordinates.
   b. Subtracting in one order in the numerator and then subtracting in the opposite order in the denominator.

3. When graphing linear inequalities in two variables, remember to graph the boundary with a broken line when the inequality symbol is $<$ or $>$. The only time you use a solid line for the boundary is when the inequality symbol is $\leq$ or $\geq$.

Chapter 2 Test

Graph the ordered pairs. [2.1]

1. $(2, -1)$ **2.** $(-4, 3)$ **3.** $(-3, -2)$ **4.** $(0, -4)$

5. Fill in the following ordered pairs for the equation $3x - 2y = 6$. [2.2]

$$(0, \ ) \ (\ , 0) \ (4, \ ) \ (\ , -6)$$

6. Which of the following ordered pairs are solutions to $y = -3x + 7$? [2.2]

$$(0, 7) \ (2, -1) \ (4, -5) \ (-5, -3)$$

Graph each line. [2.3]

7. $y = -\dfrac{1}{2}x + 4$ **8.** $x = -3$

Find the x- and y-intercepts. [2.4]

9. $8x - 4y = 16$ **10.** $y = \dfrac{3}{2}x + 6$

11. $y = 3$

Find the slope of the line through each pair of points. [2.5]

12. $(3, 2), (-5, 6)$ **13.** $(0, 9), (7, 1)$

Find the slope of each line. [2.5]

14.
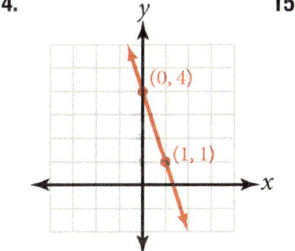

15.
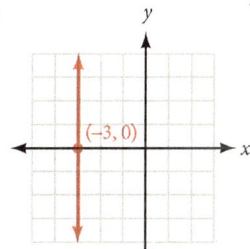

16.
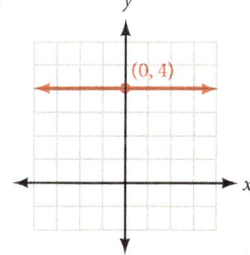

17. Find the equation of the line through $(4, 1)$ with a slope of $-\dfrac{1}{2}$. [2.6]

18. Find the equation of the line with a slope of 3 and y-intercept -5. [2.6]

19. Find the equation of the line passing through the points $(3, -4)$ and $(-6, 2)$ [2.6]

20. A straight line has an x-intercept 3 and contains the point $(-2, 6)$. Find its equation. [2.6]

Find the mean, median, mode, and range. [2.7]

21. 14, 26, 28, 26, 21   **22.** 18, 16, 11, 12, 15, 6

Find the mean, variance, and standard deviation. [2.7]

23. 24, 36, 30, 18

24. 16, 24, 31, 18, 21

© Irina Kozhemyakina/iStockphoto

25. Turtle Population Decline Zoologists in Costa Rica have been counting the number of leatherback turtles that nest in Playa Grande each year. The results are displayed in the table and scatter plot below. [2.8]

Year	Nestings
1988	1,367
1989	1,340
1990	665
1991	770
1992	909
1993	180
1994	506
1995	421
1996	125
1997	195
1998	117
1999	110
2000	88

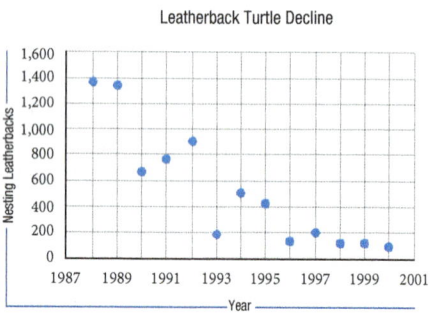

a. Draw a line that connects the first point and last point on your scatter diagram.
b. Find the slope of this line.
c. Find the equation of this line. Let $x = 0$ for 1987.
d. Do you think this line gives a good representation of the trend shown in the data?
e. Draw a line on your scatter diagram that gives a better representation of the data in your scatter diagram.

Graph each linear inequality in two variables. [2.9]

26. $y > x - 6$

27. $6x - 9y \leq 18$

Systems of Linear Equations

3

Chapter Outline

iStockphoto.com © Rawpixel

Two companies offer Internet access to their customers. Company A charges $10 a month plus $3 for every hour of Internet connection. Company B charges $18 a month plus $1 for every hour of Internet connection. To compare the monthly charges of the two companies we form what is called a system of equations. Here is that system.

$$y = 3x + 10$$
$$y = x + 18$$

The top equation gives us information on company A; the bottom equation gives us information on company B. Tables 1 and 2 and the graphs in Figure 1 give us additional information about this system of equations.

TABLE 1	
Company A	
Hours	Cost
0	$10
1	$13
2	$16
3	$19
4	$22
5	$25
6	$28
7	$31
8	$34
9	$37
10	$40

TABLE 2	
Company B	
Hours	Cost
0	$18
1	$19
2	$20
3	$21
4	$22
5	$23
6	$24
7	$25
8	$26
9	$27
10	$28

FIGURE 1

As you can see from looking at the tables and at the graphs in Figure 1, the monthly charges for the two companies will be equal if Internet use is exactly 4 hours. In this chapter we work with systems of linear equations.

The study skills for this chapter are concerned with getting ready to take an exam.

1. **Getting Ready to Take an Exam** Try to arrange your daily study habits so you have little studying to do the night before your next exam. The next two goals will help you achieve goal number 1.

2. **Review With the Exam in Mind** You should review material that will be covered on the next exam every day. Your review should consist of working problems. Preferably, the problems you work should be problems from your list of difficult problems.

3. **Continue to List Difficult Problems** You should continue to list and rework the problems that give you the most difficulty. It is this list that you will use to study for the next exam. Your goal is to go into the next exam knowing you can successfully work any problem from your list of hard problems.

4. **Pay Attention to Instructions** Taking a test is different from doing homework. When you take a test, the problems will be mixed up. When you do your homework, you usually work a number of similar problems. Sometimes students who do well on their homework become confused when they see the same problems on a test, because they have not paid attention to the instructions on their homework. For example, suppose you see the equation $y = 3x - 2$ on your next test. By itself, the equation is simply a statement. There isn't anything to do unless the equation is accompanied by instructions. Each of the following is a valid instruction with respect to the equation $y = 3x - 2$ and the result of applying the instructions will be different in each case:

   Find x when y is 10.
   Solve for x.
   Graph the equation.
   Find the intercepts.
   Find the slope.

There are many things to do with the equation If you train yourself to pay attention to the instructions that accompany a problem as you work through the assigned problems, you will not find yourself confused about what to do with a problem when you see it on a test.

Solving Linear Systems by Graphing

Two linear equations considered at the same time make up what is called a *system of linear equations*. Both equations contain two variables and, of course, have graphs that are straight lines. The following are systems of linear equations:

$$x + y = 3 \qquad\qquad y = 2x + 1 \qquad\qquad 2x - y = 1$$
$$3x + 4y = 2 \qquad\qquad y = 3x + 2 \qquad\qquad 3x - 2y = 6$$

The solution set for a system of linear equations is all ordered pairs that are solutions to both equations. Because each linear equation has a graph that is a straight line, we can expect the intersection of the graphs to be a point whose coordinates are solutions to the system; that is, if we graph both equations on the same coordinate system, we can read the coordinates of the point of intersection and have the solution to our system. Here is an example.

Video Examples

Section 3.1

Example 1   Solve the following system by graphing.

$$x + y = 4$$
$$x - y = -2$$

SOLUTION   On the same set of coordinate axes we graph each equation separately. Figure 1 shows both graphs, without showing the work necessary to get them. We can see from the graphs that they intersect at the point (1, 3). The point (1, 3) therefore must be the solution to our system because it is the only ordered pair whose graph lies on both lines. Its coordinates satisfy both equations.

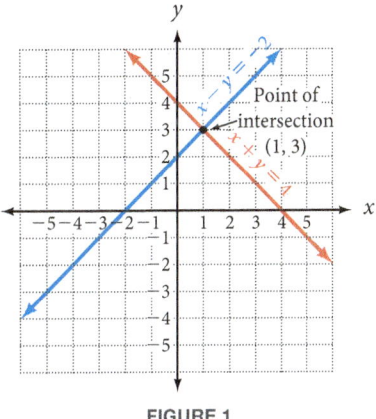

FIGURE 1

We can check our results by substituting the coordinates $x = 1$, $y = 3$ into both equations to see if they work.

When	$x = 1$	When	$x = 1$
and	$y = 3$	and	$y = 3$
the equation	$x + y = 4$	the equation	$x - y = -2$
becomes	$1 + 3 \overset{?}{=} 4$	becomes	$1 - 3 \overset{?}{=} -2$
	$4 = 4$		$-2 = -2$

The point (1, 3) satisfies both equations.

Here are some steps to follow in solving linear systems by graphing.

> **⌈Δ≠Σ⌉ How To Solve a Linear System by Graphing**
>
> **Step 1:** Graph the first equation by the methods described in Section 3.3 or 3.4.
>
> **Step 2:** Graph the second equation on the same set of axes used for the first equation.
>
> **Step 3:** Read the coordinates of the point of intersection of the two graphs.

Example 2   Solve the following system by graphing.

$$x + 2y = 8$$
$$2x - 3y = 2$$

SOLUTION   Graphing each equation on the same coordinate system, we have the lines shown in Figure 2.

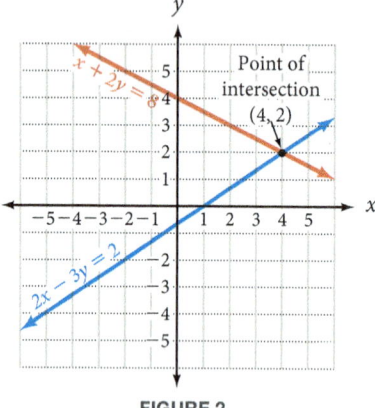

FIGURE 2

From Figure 2, we can see the solution for our system is (4, 2). We check this solution as follows.

When	$x = 4$	When	$x = 4$
and	$y = 2$	and	$y = 2$
the equation	$x + 2y = 8$	the equation	$2x - 3y = 2$
becomes	$4 + 2(2) \overset{?}{=} 8$	becomes	$2(4) - 3(2) \overset{?}{=} 2$
	$4 + 4 = 8$		$8 - 6 = 2$
	$8 = 8$		$2 = 2$

The point (4, 2) satisfies both equations and, therefore, must be the solution to our system.

Example 3   Solve this system by graphing.

$$y = 2x - 3$$
$$x = 3$$

SOLUTION   Graphing both equations on the same set of axes, we have Figure 3.

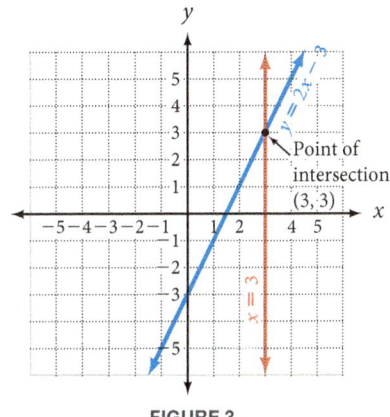

FIGURE 3

The solution to the system is the point $(3, 3)$.

Example 4   Solve by graphing.

$$y = x - 2$$
$$y = x + 1$$

SOLUTION   Graphing both equations produces the lines shown in Figure 4. We can see in Figure 4 that the lines are parallel and therefore do not intersect. Our system has no ordered pair as a solution because there is no ordered pair that satisfies both equations. We say the solution set is the empty set and write $\varnothing$.

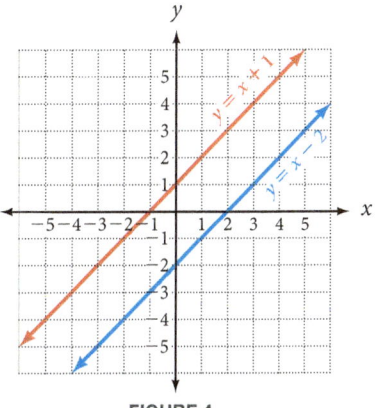

FIGURE 4

Example 5   Graph the system.

$$2x + y = 4$$
$$4x + 2y = 8$$

SOLUTION   Both graphs are shown in Figure 5. The two graphs coincide. The reason becomes apparent when we multiply both sides of the first equation by 2:

$$2x + y = 4$$
$$2(2x + y) = 2(4) \qquad \text{Multiply both sides by 2}$$
$$4x + 2y = 8$$

The equations have the same solution set. Any ordered pair that is a solution to one is a solution to the system. The system has an infinite number of solutions. (Any point on the line is a solution to the system.)

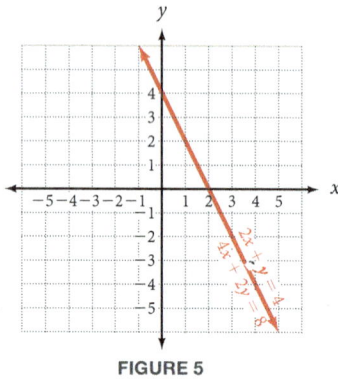

FIGURE 5

We sometimes use special vocabulary to describe the special cases shown in Examples 4 and 5. When a system of equations has no solution because the lines are parallel (as in Example 4), we say the system is *inconsistent*. When the lines coincide (as in Example 5), we say the equations are *dependent*.

The two special cases illustrated in the previous two examples do not happen often. Usually, a system has a single ordered pair as a solution. Solving a system of linear equations by graphing is useful only when the ordered pair in the solution set has integers for coordinates. Two other solution methods work well in all cases. We will develop the other two methods in the next two sections.

Here is a summary of three possible types of solutions to a system of equations in two variables.

One Solution
Lines intersect at a
single point

No Solution
Lines are parallel and
never cross

Infinite Solutions
Lines coincide

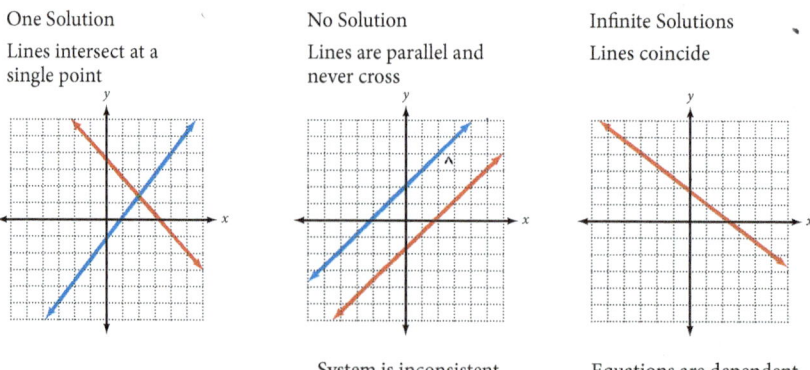

System is inconsistent   Equations are dependent

Getting Ready for Class

After reading through the preceding section, respond in your own words and in complete sentences.

A. What is a system of two linear equations in two variables?

B. What is a solution to a system of linear equations?

C. How do we solve a system of linear equations by graphing?

D. Under what conditions will a system of linear equations not have a solution?

SPOTLIGHT ON SUCCESS *Student Instructor Gordon*

Math takes time. This fact holds true in the smallest of math problems as much as it does in the most math intensive careers. I see proof in each video I make. My videos get progressively better with each take, though I still make mistakes and find aspects I can improve on with each new video. In order to keep trying to improve in spite of any failures or lack of improvement, something else is needed. For me it is the sense of a specific goal in sight, to help me maintain the desire to put in continued time and effort.

When I decided on the number one university I wanted to attend, I wrote the name of that school in bold block letters on my door, written to remind myself daily of my ultimate goal. Stuck in the back of my head, this end result pushed me little by little to succeed and meet all of the requirements for the university I had in mind. And now I can say I'm at my dream school bringing with me that skill.

I recognize that others may have much more difficult circumstances than my own to endure, with the goal of improving or escaping those circumstances, and I deeply respect that. But that fact demonstrates to me how easy but effective it is, in comparison, to "stay with the problems longer" with a goal in mind of something much more easily realized, like a good grade on a test. I've learned to set goals, small or big, and to stick with them until they are realized.

Problem Set 3.1

Solve the following systems of linear equations by graphing.

1. $x + y = 3$
$x - y = 1$

2. $x + y = 2$
$x - y = 4$

3. $x + y = 1$
$-x + y = 3$

4. $x + y = 1$
$x - y = -5$

5. $x + y = 8$
$-x + y = 2$

6. $x + y = 6$
$-x + y = -2$

7. $3x - 2y = 6$
$x - y = 1$

8. $5x - 2y = 10$
$x - y = -1$

9. $6x - 2y = 12$
$3x + y = -6$

10. $4x - 2y = 8$
$2x + y = -4$

11. $4x + y = 4$
$3x - y = 3$

12. $5x - y = 10$
$2x + y = 4$

13. $x + 2y = 0$
$2x - y = 0$

14. $3x + y = 0$
$5x - y = 0$

15. $3x - 5y = 15$
$-2x + y = 4$

16. $2x - 4y = 8$
$2x - y = -1$

17. $y = 2x + 1$
$y = -2x - 3$

18. $y = 3x - 4$
$y = -2x + 1$

19. $x + 3y = 3$
$y = x + 5$

20. $2x + y = -2$
$y = x + 4$

21. $x + y = 2$
$x = -3$

22. $x + y = 6$
$y = 2$

23. $x = -4$
$y = 6$

24. $x = 5$
$y = -1$

25. $x + y = 4$
$2x + 2y = -6$

26. $x - y = 3$
$2x - 2y = 6$

27. $4x - 2y = 8$
$2x - y = 4$

28. $3x - 6y = 6$
$x - 2y = 4$

29. As you probably have guessed by now, it can be difficult to solve a system of equations by graphing if the solution to the system contains a fraction. The solution to the following system is $\left(\frac{1}{2}, 1\right)$. Solve the system by graphing.

$$y = -2x + 2$$
$$y = 4x - 1$$

30. The solution to the following system is $\left(\frac{1}{3}, -2\right)$. Solve the system by graphing.

$$y = 3x - 3$$
$$y = -3x - 1$$

31. A second difficulty can arise in solving a system of equations by graphing if one or both of the equations is difficult to graph. The solution to the following system is $(2, 1)$. Solve the system by graphing.

$$3x - 8y = -2$$
$$x - y = 1$$

32. The solution to the following system is $(-3, 2)$. Solve the system by graphing.

$$2x + 5y = 4$$
$$x - y = -5$$

Applying the Concepts

33. Job Comparison Jane is deciding between two sales positions. She can work for Marcy's and receive $8.00 per hour, or she can work for Gigi's, where she earns $6.00 per hour but also receives a $50 commission per week. The two lines in the following figure represent the money Jane will make for working at each of the jobs.

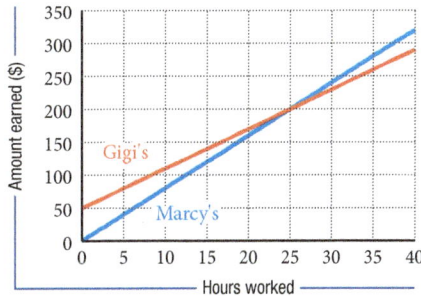

a. From the figure, how many hours would Jane have to work to earn the same amount at each of the positions?

b. If Jane expects to work less than 20 hours a week, which job should she choose?

c. If Jane expects to work more than 30 hours a week, which job should she choose?

34. Truck Rental You need to rent a moving truck for two days. Rider Moving Trucks charges $50 per day and $0.50 per mile. UMove Trucks charges $45 per day and $0.75 per mile. The following figure represents the cost of renting each of the trucks for two days.

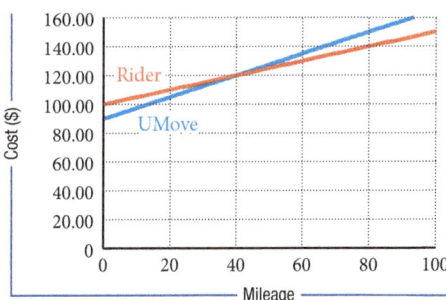

a. From the figure, after how many miles would the trucks cost the same?

b. Which company will give you a better deal if you drive less than 30 miles?

c. Which company will give you a better deal if you drive more than 60 miles?

Getting Ready For the Next Section

Simplify each of the following.

35. $(x + y) + (x - y)$

36. $(x + 2y) + (-x + y)$

37. $3(2x - y) + (x + 3y)$

38. $3(2x + 3y) - 2(3x + 5y)$

39. $-4(3x + 5y) + 5(5x + 4y)$

40. $(3x + 8y) - (3x - 2y)$

41. $6\left(\dfrac{1}{2}x - \dfrac{1}{3}y\right)$

42. $12\left(\dfrac{1}{4}x + \dfrac{2}{3}y\right)$

43. Let $x + y = 4$. If $x = 3$, find y.

44. Let $x + 2y = 4$. If $x = 3$, find y.

45. Let $x + 3y = 3$. If $x = 3$, find y.

46. Let $2x + 3y = -1$. If $y = -1$, find x.

47. Let $3x + 5y = -7$. If $x = 6$, find y.

48. Let $3x - 2y = 12$. If $y = 6$, find x.

The Elimination Method 3.2

The addition property states that if equal quantities are added to both sides of an equation, the solution set is unchanged. In the past we have used this property to help solve equations in one variable. We will now use it to solve systems of linear equations. Here is another way to state the addition property of equality.

Let A, B, C, and D represent algebraic expressions.

$$\begin{aligned} \text{If} \quad & A = B \\ \text{and} \quad & C = D \\ \text{then} \quad & A + C = B + D \end{aligned}$$

Because C and D are equal (that is, they represent the same number), what we have done is added the same amount to both sides of the equation $A = B$. Let's see how we can use this form of the addition property of equality to solve a system of linear equations.

Note The graphs shown in our first three examples are not part of the solution shown in each example. The graphs are there simply to show you that the results we obtain by the elimination method are consistent with the results we would obtain by graphing.

Example 1 Solve the following system.

$$\begin{aligned} x + y &= 4 \\ x - y &= 2 \end{aligned}$$

SOLUTION The system is written in the form of the addition property of equality as written in this section. It looks like this:

$$\begin{aligned} A &= B \\ C &= D \end{aligned}$$

where A is $x + y$, B is 4, C is $x - y$, and D is 2.

We use the addition property of equality to add the left sides together and the right sides together.

$$\begin{array}{r} x + y = 4 \\ \underline{x - y = 2} \\ 2x + 0 = 6 \end{array}$$

We now solve the resulting equation for x.

$$\begin{aligned} 2x + 0 &= 6 \\ 2x &= 6 \\ x &= 3 \end{aligned}$$

The value we get for x is the value of the x-coordinate of the point of intersection of the two lines $x + y = 4$ and $x - y = 2$. To find the y-coordinate, we simply substitute $x = 3$ into either of the two original equations. Using the first equation, we get

$$\begin{aligned} 3 + y &= 4 \\ y &= 1 \end{aligned}$$

The solution to our system is the ordered pair (3, 1). It satisfies both equations.

When	$x = 3$	When	$x = 3$
and	$y = 1$	and	$y = 1$
the equation	$x + y = 4$	the equation	$x - y = 2$
becomes	$3 + 1 \overset{?}{=} 4$	becomes	$3 - 1 \overset{?}{=} 2$
	$4 = 4$		$2 = 2$

Figure 1 is visual evidence that the solution to our system is (3, 1).

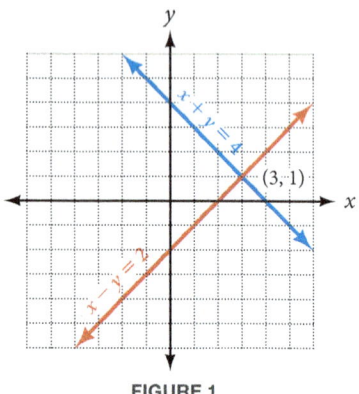

FIGURE 1

The most important part of this method of solving linear systems is eliminating one of the variables when we add the left and right sides together. In our first example, the equations were written so that the y variable was eliminated when we added the left and right sides together. If the equations are not set up this way to begin with, we have to work on one or both of them separately before we can add them together to eliminate one variable.

Example 2   Solve the following system.

$$x + 2y = 4$$
$$x - y = -5$$

SOLUTION   Notice that if we were to add the equations together as they are, the resulting equation would have terms in both x and y. Let's eliminate the variable x by multiplying both sides of the second equation by -1 before we add the equations together. (As you will see, we can choose to eliminate either the x or the y variable.) Multiplying both sides of the second equation by -1 will not change its solution, so we do not need to be concerned that we have altered the system.

$$
\begin{array}{lll}
x + 2y = 4 & \xrightarrow{\text{No change}} & x + 2y = 4 \\
x - y = -5 & \xrightarrow[\text{Multiply by } -1]{} & -x + y = 5 \\
& & \overline{0 + 3y = 9} \qquad \text{Add left and right sides to get} \\
& & 3y = 9 \\
& & y = 3 \quad \left\{ \begin{array}{l} y\text{-Coordinate of the} \\ \text{point of intersection} \end{array} \right.
\end{array}
$$

Substituting $y = 3$ into either of the two original equations, we get $x = -2$. The solution to the system is $(-2, 3)$. It satisfies both equations. Figure 2 shows the solution to the system as the point where the two lines cross.

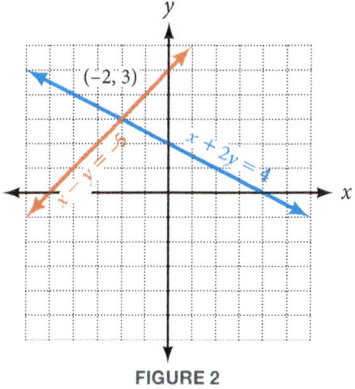

FIGURE 2

Example 3   Solve the following system.

$$2x - y = 6$$
$$x + 3y = 3$$

SOLUTION   Let's eliminate the y variable from the two equations. We can do this by multiplying the first equation by 3 and leaving the second equation unchanged.

$$2x - y = 6 \xrightarrow{\text{3 times both sides}} 6x - 3y = 18$$
$$x + 3y = 3 \xrightarrow{\text{No change}} x + 3y = 3$$

The important thing about our system now is that the coefficients (the numbers in front) of the y variables are opposites. When we add the terms on each side of the equal sign, then the terms in y will add to zero and be eliminated.

$$
\begin{array}{r}
6x - 3y = 18 \\
x + 3y = 3 \\
\hline
7x \quad\quad = 21
\end{array}
$$ Add corresponding terms

This gives us $x = 3$. Using this value of x in the second equation of our original system, we have

$$3 + 3y = 3$$
$$3y = 0$$
$$y = 0$$

We could substitute $x = 3$ into either equation and would still get $y = 0$. The solution to our system is the ordered pair $(3, 0)$. Figure 3 is a picture of the system of equations showing the solution $(3, 0)$.

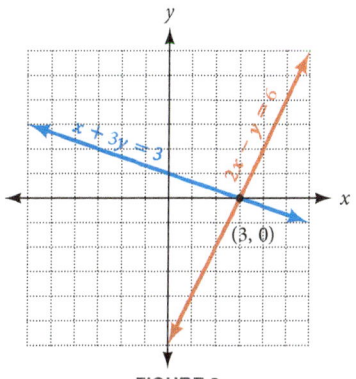

FIGURE 3

Example 4 Solve the system.

$$2x + 3y = -1$$
$$3x + 5y = -2$$

SOLUTION Let's eliminate x from the two equations. If we multiply the first equation by 3 and the second by -2, the coefficients of x will be 6 and -6, respectively. The x terms in the two equations will then add to zero.

$$2x + 3y = -1 \xrightarrow{\text{Multiply by 3}} 6x + 9y = -3$$
$$3x + 5y = -2 \xrightarrow{\text{Multiply by } -2} -6x - 10y = 4$$

We now add the left and right sides of our new system together.

$$
\begin{array}{r}
6x + 9y = -3 \\
-6x - 10y = 4 \\
\hline
-y = 1 \\
y = -1
\end{array}
$$

Note If you are having trouble understanding this method of solution, it is probably because you can't see why we chose to multiply by 3 and -2 in the first step of Example 4. Look at the result of doing so: the $6x$ and $-6x$ will add to 0. We chose to multiply by 3 and -2 because they produce $6x$ and $-6x$, which will add to 0.

Substituting $y = -1$ into the first equation in our original system, we have

$$2x + 3(-1) = -1$$
$$2x - 3 = -1$$
$$2x = 2$$
$$x = 1$$

The solution to our system is $(1, -1)$. It is the only ordered pair that satisfies both equations. ■

Example 5 Solve the system.

$$3x + 5y = -7$$
$$5x + 4y = 10$$

SOLUTION Let's eliminate y by multiplying the first equation by -4 and the second equation by 5.

$$3x + 5y = -7 \xrightarrow{\text{Multiply by } -4} -12x - 20y = 28$$
$$5x + 4y = 10 \xrightarrow{\text{Multiply by 5}} 25x + 20y = 50$$
$$
\begin{array}{r}
\hline
13x = 78 \\
x = 6
\end{array}
$$

Substitute $x = 6$ into either equation in our original system, and the result will be $y = -5$. The solution is therefore $(6, -5)$. ■

Example 6 Solve the system.

$$\frac{1}{2}x - \frac{1}{3}y = 2$$

$$\frac{1}{4}x + \frac{2}{3}y = 6$$

SOLUTION Although we could solve this system without clearing the equations of fractions, there is probably less chance for error if we have only integer coefficients to work with. So let's begin by multiplying both sides of the top equation by 6 and both sides of the bottom equation by 12, to clear each equation of fractions.

$$\frac{1}{2}x - \frac{1}{3}y = 2 \xrightarrow{\text{Multiply by 6}} 3x - 2y = 12$$

$$\frac{1}{4}x + \frac{2}{3}y = 6 \xrightarrow{\text{Multiply by 12}} 3x + 8y = 72$$

Now we can eliminate x by multiplying the top equation by -1 and leaving the bottom equation unchanged.

$$3x - 2y = 12 \xrightarrow{\text{Multiply by } -1} -3x + 2y = -12$$

$$3x + 8y = 72 \xrightarrow{\text{No change}} \underline{3x + 8y = 72}$$

$$10y = 60$$

$$y = 6$$

We can substitute $y = 6$ into any equation that contains both x and y. Let's use $3x - 2y = 12$.

$$3x - 2(6) = 12$$

$$3x - 12 = 12$$

$$3x = 24$$

$$x = 8$$

The solution to the system is $(8, 6)$.

Our next two examples will show what happens when we apply the elimination method to a system of equations consisting of parallel lines and to a system in which the lines coincide.

Example 7   Solve the system.

$$2x - y = 2$$
$$4x - 2y = 12$$

SOLUTION   Let us choose to eliminate y from the system. We can do this by multiplying the first equation by -2 and leaving the second equation unchanged.

$$2x - y = 2 \xrightarrow{\text{Multiply by } -2} -4x + 2y = -4$$

$$4x - 2y = 12 \xrightarrow{\text{No change}} 4x - 2y = 12$$

If we add both sides of the resulting system, we have

$$-4x + 2y = -4$$

$$\underline{4x - 2y = 12}$$

$$0 + 0 = 8$$

$$0 = 8 \qquad \text{A false statement}$$

Both variables have been eliminated and we end up with the false statement $0 = 8$. We have tried to solve a system that consists of two parallel lines. There is no solution, and that is the reason we end up with a false statement. Figure 4 is a visual representation of the situation and is conclusive evidence that there is no solution to our system.

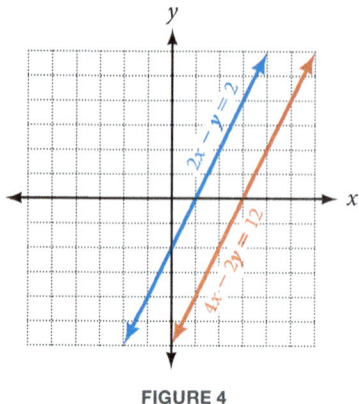

FIGURE 4

Example 8   Solve the system.

$$4x - 3y = 2$$
$$8x - 6y = 4$$

SOLUTION   Multiplying the top equation by -2 and adding, we can eliminate the variable x.

$$4x - 3y = 2 \xrightarrow{\text{Multiply by } -2} -8x + 6y = -4$$

$$8x - 6y = 4 \xrightarrow{\text{No change}} \underline{8x - 6y = 4}$$

$$0 = 0$$

Both variables have been eliminated, and the resulting statement $0 = 0$ is true. In this case the lines coincide because the equations are equivalent. The solution set consists of all ordered pairs that satisfy either equation.

The preceding two examples illustrate the two special cases in which the graphs of the equations in the system either coincide or are parallel.

Here is a summary of our results from these two examples:

Both variables are eliminated and the resulting statement is false.	↔	The lines are parallel and there is no solution to the system.
Both variables are eliminated and the resulting statement is true.	↔	The lines coincide and there is an infinite number of solutions to the system.

The main idea in solving a system of linear equations by the elimination method is to use the multiplication property of equality on one or both of the original equations, if necessary, to make the coefficients of either variable opposites. The following box shows some steps to follow when solving a system of linear equations by the elimination method.

$[\Delta \neq \sum$ *How to Solve a System of Linear Equations by the Elimination Method*

Step 1: Decide which variable to eliminate. (In some cases one variable will be easier to eliminate than the other. With some practice you will notice which one it is.)

Step 2: Use the multiplication property of equality on each equation separately to make the coefficients of the variable that is to be eliminated opposites.

Step 3: Add the respective left and right sides of the system together.

Step 4: Solve for the variable remaining.

Step 5: Substitute the value of the variable from step 4 into an equation containing both variables and solve for the other variable.

Step 6: Check your solution in both equations, if necessary.

Getting Ready for Class

After reading through the preceding section, respond in your own words and in complete sentences.

A. How is the addition property of equality used in the elimination method of solving a system of linear equations?

B. What happens when we use the elimination method to solve a system of linear equations consisting of two parallel lines?

C. What does it mean when we solve a system of linear equations by the elimination method and we end up with the statement $0 = 8$?

D. What is the first step in solving a system of linear equations that contains fractions?

Problem Set 3.2

Solve the following systems of linear equations by elimination.

1. $x + y = 3$
$\quad x - y = 1$

2. $x + y = -2$
$\quad x - y = 6$

3. $\quad x + y = 10$
$\quad -x + y = 4$

4. $\quad x - y = 1$
$\quad -x - y = -7$

5. $\quad x - y = 7$
$\quad -x - y = 3$

6. $\quad x - y = 4$
$\quad 2x + y = 8$

7. $\quad x + y = -1$
$\quad 3x - y = -3$

8. $\quad 2x - y = -2$
$\quad -2x - y = 2$

9. $\quad 3x + 2y = 1$
$\quad -3x - 2y = -1$

10. $-2x - 4y = 1$
$\quad 2x + 4y = -1$

Solve each of the following systems by eliminating the y variable.

11. $3x - \quad y = 4$
$\quad 2x + 2y = 24$

12. $2x + \quad y = 3$
$\quad 3x + 2y = 1$

13. $5x - 3y = -2$
$\quad 10x - \quad y = 1$

14. $4x - \quad y = -1$
$\quad 2x + 4y = 13$

15. $11x - 4y = 11$
$\quad 5x + y = 5$

16. $\quad 3x - \quad y = 7$
$\quad 10x - 5y = 25$

Solve each of the following systems by eliminating the x variable.

17. $3x - 5y = 7$
$\quad -x + y = -1$

18. $4x + 2y = 32$
$\quad x + \quad y = -2$

19. $\quad -x - 8y = -1$
$\quad -2x + 4y = 13$

20. $\quad -x + 10y = 1$
$\quad -5x + 15y = -9$

21. $-3x - \quad y = 7$
$\quad 6x + 7y = 11$

22. $-5x + 2y = -6$
$\quad 10x + 7y = 34$

Solve each of the following systems of linear equations by the elimination method.

23. $6x - y = -8$
$\quad 2x + y = -16$

24. $5x - 3y = -3$
$\quad 3x + 3y = -21$

25. $\quad x + 3y = 9$
$\quad 2x - \quad y = 4$

26. $\quad x + 2y = 0$
$\quad 2x - \quad y = 0$

27. $\quad x - 6y = 3$
$\quad 4x + 3y = 21$

28. $8x + \quad y = -1$
$\quad 4x - 5y = 16$

29. $2x + 9y = 2$
$\quad 5x + 3y = -8$

30. $5x + 2y = 11$
$\quad 7x + 8y = 7$

31. $\dfrac{1}{3}x + \dfrac{1}{4}y = \dfrac{7}{6}$
$\quad \dfrac{3}{2}x - \dfrac{1}{3}y = \dfrac{7}{3}$

32. $\dfrac{7}{12}x - \dfrac{1}{2}y = \dfrac{1}{6}$
$\quad \dfrac{2}{5}x - \dfrac{1}{3}y = \dfrac{11}{15}$

33. $3x + 2y = -1$
$\quad 6x + 4y = 0$

34. $8x - 2y = 2$
$\quad 4x - \quad y = 2$

35. $11x + 6y = 17$
$\quad 5x - 4y = 1$

36. $\quad 3x - 8y = 7$
$\quad 10x - 5y = 45$

37. $\dfrac{1}{2}x + \dfrac{1}{6}y = \dfrac{1}{3}$
$\quad -x - \dfrac{1}{3}y = -\dfrac{1}{6}$

38. $-\dfrac{1}{3}x - \dfrac{1}{2}y = -\dfrac{2}{3}$
$\quad -\dfrac{2}{3}x - \quad y = -\dfrac{4}{3}$

39. Multiply both sides of the second equation in the following system by 100, and then solve as usual.

$$x + y = 22$$

$$0.05x + 0.10y = 1.70$$

40. Multiply both sides of the second equation in the following system by 100, and then solve as usual.

$$x + y = 15{,}000$$

$$0.06x + 0.07y = 980$$

Getting Ready for the Next Section

Solve.

41. $x + (2x - 1) = 2$

42. $2x - 3(2x - 8) = 12$

43. $2(3y - 1) - 3y = 4$

44. $-2x + 4(3x + 6) = 14$

45. $4x + 2(-2x + 4) = 8$

46. $1.5x + 15 = 0.75x + 24.95$

Solve each equation for the indicated variable.

47. $x - 3y = -1$ for x

48. $-3x + y = 6$ for y

49. Let $y = 2x - 1$. If $x = 1$, find y.

50. Let $y = 2x - 8$. If $x = 5$, find y.

51. Let $x = 3y - 1$. If $y = 2$, find x.

52. Let $y = 3x + 6$. If $y = -6$, find x.

Let $y = 1.5x + 15$

53. If $x = 13$, find y.

54. If $x = 14$, find y.

Let $y = 0.75x + 24.95$

55. If $x = 12$, find y.

56. If $x = 16$, find y.

HOWARD
COLLEGE

The motto at Howard College in Texas is "Education, for learning, for earning, for life."

The school's website, www.earnmydegree.com poses the question: "Does a college degree pay off?"

You can make much more money by earning a college degree.

The data shows that a college degree correlates directly to your salary range—and the relationship between compensation and education level is becoming even more prominent.

Employers have increasingly use diplomas and degrees as a way to screen applicants. And once you've landed the job you want, your salary will reflect your credentials. On average, a person with a master's degree earns $31,900 more per year than a high school graduate—a difference of as much as 105%!

Average Annual Earnings by Education Level

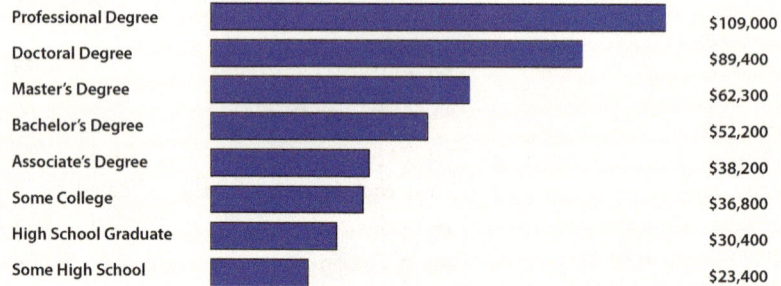

Education Level	Earnings
Professional Degree	$109,000
Doctoral Degree	$89,400
Master's Degree	$62,300
Bachelor's Degree	$52,200
Associate's Degree	$38,200
Some College	$36,800
High School Graduate	$30,400
Some High School	$23,400

Average Annual Earnings — Different Levels of Education
Source: U.S. Census Bureau, Current Population Surveys, March 1998, 1999, and 2000

The Substitution Method **3.3**

There is a third method of solving systems of equations. It is the substitution method, and, like the elimination method, it can be used on any system of linear equations. Some systems, however, lend themselves more to the substitution method than others do.

Example 1   Solve the following system.

$$x + y = 2$$
$$y = 2x - 1$$

SOLUTION   If we were to solve this system by the methods used in the previous section, we would have to rearrange the terms of the second equation so that similar terms would be in the same column. There is no need to do this, however, because the second equation tells us that y is $2x - 1$. We can replace the y variable in the first equation with the expression $2x - 1$ from the second equation; that is, we *substitute* $2x - 1$ from the second equation for y in the first equation. Here is what it looks like:

$$x + (2x - 1) = 2$$

The equation we end up with contains only the variable x. The y variable has been eliminated by substitution.

Solving the resulting equation, we have

$$x + (2x - 1) = 2$$
$$3x - 1 = 2$$
$$3x = 3$$
$$x = 1$$

Note   Sometimes this method of solving systems of equations is confusing the first time you see it. If you are confused, you may want to read through this first example more than once.

This is the x-coordinate of the solution to our system. To find the y-coordinate, we substitute $x = 1$ into the second equation of our system. (We could substitute $x = 1$ into the first equation also and have the same result.)

$$y = 2(1) - 1$$
$$y = 2 - 1$$
$$y = 1$$

The solution to our system is the ordered pair $(1, 1)$. It satisfies both of the original equations. Figure 1 provides visual evidence that the substitution method yields the correct solution.

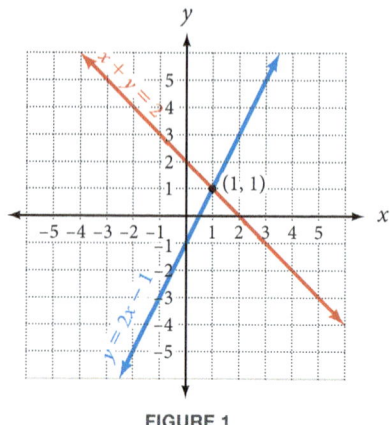

FIGURE 1

Example 2   Solve the following system by the substitution method.

$$2x - 3y = 12$$
$$y = 2x - 8$$

SOLUTION   Again, the second equation says y is $2x - 8$. Because we are looking for the ordered pair that satisfies both equations, the y in the first equation must also be $2x - 8$. Substituting $2x - 8$ from the second equation for y in the first equation, we have

$$2x - 3(2x - 8) = 12$$

This equation can still be read as $2x - 3y = 12$ because $2x - 8$ is the same as y. Solving the equation, we have

$$2x - 3(2x - 8) = 12$$
$$2x - 6x + 24 = 12$$
$$-4x + 24 = 12$$
$$-4x = -12$$
$$x = 3$$

To find the y-coordinate of our solution, we substitute $x = 3$ into the second equation in the original system.

When $x = 3$

the equation $y = 2x - 8$

becomes $y = 2(3) - 8$

$$y = 6 - 8 = -2$$

The solution to our system is $(3, -2)$.

Example 3   Solve the following system by solving the first equation for x and then using the substitution method:

$$x - 3y = -1$$
$$2x - 3y = 4$$

SOLUTION We solve the first equation for x by adding $3y$ to both sides to get

$$x = 3y - 1$$

Using this value of x in the second equation, we have

$$2(3y - 1) - 3y = 4$$
$$6y - 2 - 3y = 4$$
$$3y - 2 = 4$$
$$3y = 6$$
$$y = 2$$

Next, we find x.

When $\qquad\qquad y = 2$

the equation $\qquad x = 3y - 1$

becomes $\qquad\quad x = 3(2) - 1$

$$x = 6 - 1$$
$$x = 5$$

The solution to our system is $(5, 2)$

Here are the steps to use in solving a system of equations by the substitution method.

> **⌈Δ≠Σ⌉** *How to Solve a System of Linear Equations by the Substitution Method*
>
> **Step 1:** Solve either one of the equations for x or y. (This step is not necessary if one of the equations is already in the correct form, as in Examples 1 and 2.)
>
> **Step 2:** Substitute the expression for the variable obtained in step 1 into the other equation and solve it.
>
> **Step 3:** Substitute the solution from step 2 into any equation in the system that contains both variables and solve it.
>
> **Step 4:** Check your results, if necessary.

Example 4 Solve by substitution.

$$-2x + 4y = 14$$
$$-3x + y = 6$$

SOLUTION We can solve either equation for either variable. If we look at the system closely, it becomes apparent that solving the second equation for y is the easiest way to go. If we add $3x$ to both sides of the second equation, we have

$$y = 3x + 6$$

Substituting the expression $3x + 6$ back into the first equation in place of y yields the following result.

$$-2x + 4(3x + 6) = 14$$
$$-2x + 12x + 24 = 14$$
$$10x + 24 = 14$$
$$10x = -10$$
$$x = -1$$

Substituting $x = -1$ into the equation $y = 3x + 6$ leaves us with

$$y = 3(-1) + 6$$
$$y = -3 + 6$$
$$y = 3$$

The solution to our system is $(-1, 3)$.

Example 5   Solve by substitution.

$$4x + 2y = 8$$
$$y = -2x + 4$$

SOLUTION   Substituting the expression $-2x + 4$ for y from the second equation into the first equation, we have

$$4x + 2(-2x + 4) = 8$$
$$4x - 4x + 8 = 8$$
$$8 = 8 \qquad \text{A true statement}$$

Both variables have been eliminated, and we are left with a true statement. Recall from the last section that a true statement in this situation tells us the lines coincide; that is, the equations $4x + 2y = 8$ and $y = -2x + 4$ have exactly the same graph. Any point on that graph has coordinates that satisfy both equations and is a solution to the system.

Example 6   The following table shows two contract rates charged by a prepaid cellular provider for 4G data use. At how many gigabytes of data will the two rates cost the same amount?

	Flat Rate	Plus	Per GB Charge
Plan 1	$15		$1.50
Plan 2	$24.95		$0.75

SOLUTION   If we let y = the monthly charge for x gigabytes of data use, then the equations for each plan are

Plan 1: $y = 1.5x + 15$

Plan 2: $y = 0.75x + 24.95$

We can solve this system by substitution by replacing the variable y in Plan 2 with the expression $1.5x + 15$ from Plan 1. If we do so, we have

$$1.5x + 15 = 0.75x + 24.95$$

$$0.75x + 15 = 24.95$$

$$0.75x = 9.95$$

$$x = 13.27 \qquad \text{to the nearest hundredth}$$

The monthly bill is based on the number of gigabytes of data your phone uses. If you use 13 gigabytes, you are billed for 13 gigabytes. If you use 13.7 gigabytes, you are billed for 14 gigabytes. You are always billed by the gigbyte, with unused data being wasted. So, to calculate the cost of 13.27 GB, we would replace x with 14 and find y. Let's compare the two plans at $x = 13$ GB and at $x = 14$ GB.

Plan 1: $y = 1.5x + 15$ Plan 2: $y = 0.75x + 24.95$

When $x = 13, y = \$34.50$ When $x = 13, y = \$34.70$

When $x = 14, y = \$36.00$ When $x = 14, y = \$35.45$

The two plans will never give the same cost for using x gigabytes. If you use 13 or less gigabytes, Plan 1 will cost less. If you use more than 13 gigabytes, you will be billed for 14 gigabytes, and Plan 2 will cost less than Plan 1.

Getting Ready for Class

After reading through the preceding section, respond in your own words and in complete sentences.

A. What is the first step in solving a system of linear equations by substitution?

B. When would substitution be more efficient than the elimination method in solving two linear equations?

C. What does it mean when we solve a system of linear equations by the substitution method and we end up with the statement $8 = 8$?

D. How would you begin solving the following system using the substitution method?

$$x + y = 2$$
$$y = 2x - 1$$

Problem Set 3.3

Solve the following systems by substitution. Substitute the expression in the second equation into the first equation and solve.

1. $x + y = 11$
$\quad y = 2x - 1$

2. $x - y = -3$
$\quad y = 3x + 5$

3. $x + y = 20$
$\quad y = 5x + 2$

4. $3x - y = -1$
$\quad x = 2y - 7$

5. $-2x + y = -1$
$\quad y = -4x + 8$

6. $4x - y = 5$
$\quad y = -4x + 1$

7. $3x - 2y = -2$
$\quad x = -y + 6$

8. $2x - 3y = 17$
$\quad x = -y + 6$

9. $5x - 4y = -16$
$\quad y = 4$

10. $6x + 2y = 18$
$\quad x = 3$

11. $5x + 4y = 7$
$\quad y = -3x$

12. $10x + 2y = -6$
$\quad y = -5x$

Solve the following systems by solving one of the equations for x or y and then using the substitution method.

13. $x + 3y = 4$
$\quad x - 2y = -1$

14. $x - y = 5$
$\quad x + 2y = -1$

15. $2x + y = 1$
$\quad x - 5y = 17$

16. $2x - 2y = 2$
$\quad x - 3y = -7$

17. $3x + 5y = -3$
$\quad x - 5y = -5$

18. $2x - 4y = -4$
$\quad x + 2y = 8$

19. $5x + 3y = 0$
$\quad x - 3y = -18$

20. $x - 3y = -5$
$\quad x - 2y = 0$

21. $-3x - 9y = 7$
$\quad x + 3y = 12$

22. $2x + 6y = -18$
$\quad x + 3y = -9$

Solve the following systems using the substitution method.

23. $5x - 8y = 7$
$\quad y = 2x - 5$

24. $3x + 4y = 10$
$\quad y = 8x - 15$

25. $7x - 6y = -1$
$\quad x = 2y - 1$

26. $4x + 2y = 3$
$\quad x = 4y - 3$

27. $-3x + 2y = 6$
$\quad y = 3x$

28. $-2x - y = -3$
$\quad y = -3x$

29. $5x - 6y = -4$
$\quad x = y$

30. $2x - 4y = 0$
$\quad y = x$

31. $3x + 3y = 9$
$\quad y = 2x - 12$

32. $7x + 6y = -9$
$\quad y = -2x + 1$

33. $7x - 11y = 16$
$\quad y = 10$

34. $9x - 7y = -14$
$\quad x = 7$

35. $-4x + 4y = -8$
$\quad y = x - 2$

36. $-4x + 2y = -10$
$\quad y = 2x - 5$

Solve each system by substitution. You can eliminate the decimals if you like, but you don't have to. The solution will be the same in either case.

37. $0.05x + 0.10y = 1.70$
$\quad y = 22 - x$

38. $0.20x + 0.50y = 3.60$
$\quad y = 12 - x$

Applying the Concepts

39. Gas Mileage Daniel is trying to decide whether to buy a car or a truck. The truck he is considering will cost him $150 a month in loan payments, and it gets 20 miles per gallon in gas mileage. The car will cost $180 a month in loan payments, but it gets 35 miles per gallon in gas mileage. Daniel estimates that he will pay $1.40 per gallon for gas. This means that the monthly cost to drive the truck x miles will be $y = \frac{1.40}{20}x + 150$. The total monthly cost to drive the car x miles will be $y = \frac{1.40}{35}x + 180$. The following figure shows the graph of each equation.

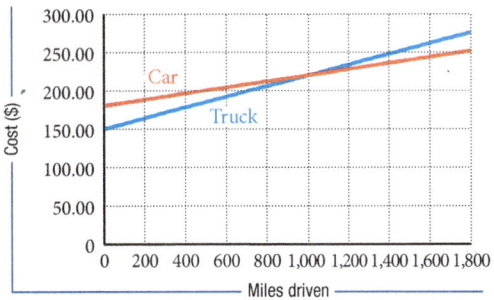

a. At how many miles do the car and the truck cost the same to operate?

b. If Daniel drives more than 1,200 miles, which will be cheaper?

c. If Daniel drives fewer than 800 miles, which will be cheaper?

d. Why do the graphs appear in the first quadrant only?

40. Video Production Pat runs a small company that produces custom Blu-ray video discs. The daily cost and daily revenue for a company producing the Blu-ray discs are shown in the following figure. The daily cost for duplicating x discs is $y = \frac{6}{5}x + 20$; the daily revenue (the amount of money he brings in each day) for duplicating x discs is $y = 1.7x$. The graphs of the two lines are shown in the following figure.

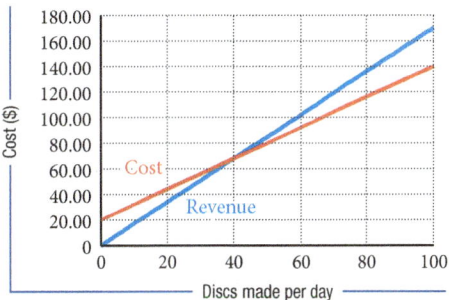

a. Pat will "break even" when his cost and his revenue are equal. How many discs does he need to produce to break even?

b. Pat will incur a loss when his revenue is less than his cost. If he produces 30 discs in one day, will he incur a loss?

c. Pat will make a profit when his revenue is larger than his costs. For what values of x will Pat make a profit?

d. Why does the graph appear in the first quadrant only?

Getting Ready for the Next Section

41. One number is eight more than five times another; their sum is 26. Find the numbers.

42. One number is three less than four times another; their sum is 27. Find the numbers.

43. The difference of two positive numbers is nine. The larger number is six less than twice the smaller number. Find the numbers.

44. The difference of two positive numbers is 17. The larger number is one more than twice the smaller number. Find the numbers.

45. The length of a rectangle is five inches more than three times the width. The perimeter is 58 inches. Find the length and width.

46. The length of a rectangle is three inches less than twice the width. The perimeter is 36 inches. Find the length and width.

47. John has $1.70 in nickels and dimes in his pocket. He has four more nickels than he does dimes. How many of each does he have?

48. Jamie has $2.65 in dimes and quarters in his pocket. He has two more dimes than she does quarters. How many of each does she have?

Systems of Equations in Three Variables

©iStockphoto/fotostorm

After reading through this section, you will be able to assign three linear equations and solve for the three variables in this problem.

Solving Systems in Three Variables

A solution to an equation in three variables such as

$$2x + y - 3z = 6$$

is an ordered triple of numbers (x, y, z). For example, the ordered triples $(0, 0, -2)$, $(2, 2, 0)$, and $(0, 9, 1)$ are solutions to the equation $2x + y - 3z = 6$, because they produce a true statement when their coordinates are substituted for x, y, and z in the equation.

Video Examples

Section 3.4

> (dĕf) **solution set**
>
> The **solution set** for a system of three linear equations in three variables is the set of ordered triples that satisfies all three equations.

Note Solving a system in three variables can be overwhelming at first. Don't get discouraged. Remember to read the solution's explanation slowly, and you may need to read it more than once to fully grasp each step.

Example 1 Solve the system.

$$x + y + z = 6 \qquad \text{Equation (1)}$$
$$2x - y + z = 3 \qquad \text{Equation (2)}$$
$$x + 2y - 3z = -4 \qquad \text{Equation (3)}$$

SOLUTION We want to find the ordered triple (x, y, z) that satisfies all three equations. We have numbered the equations so it will be easier to keep track of where they are and what we are doing.

There are many ways to proceed. The main idea is to take two different pairs of equations and eliminate the same variable from each pair. We begin by adding equations (1) and (2) to eliminate the y-variable. The resulting equation is numbered (4).

$$x + y + z = 6 \qquad (1)$$
$$2x - y + z = 3 \qquad (2)$$
$$\overline{ 3x + 2z = 9} \qquad \text{Equation (4)}$$

Adding twice equation (2) to equation (3) will also eliminate the variable y. The resulting equation is numbered (5):

$$
\begin{array}{ll}
4x - 2y + 2z = -6 & \text{Twice (2)} \\
\underline{x + 2y - 3z = -4} & \text{(3)} \\
5x \quad\ \ - \ z = -2 & \text{Equation (5)}
\end{array}
$$

Equations (4) and (5) form a linear system in two variables. By multiplying equation (5) by 2 and adding the result to equation (4), we succeed in eliminating the variable z from the new pair of equations.

$$
\begin{array}{ll}
3x + 2z = 9 & \text{(4)} \\
\underline{10x - 2z = 4} & \text{Twice (5)} \\
13x \qquad = 13 & \\
x \qquad\ \ = 1 &
\end{array}
$$

Substituting $x = 1$ into equation (4), we have

$$
\begin{aligned}
3(1) + 2z &= 9 \\
2z &= 6 \\
z &= 3
\end{aligned}
$$

Using $x = 1$ and $z = 3$ in equation (1) gives us

$$
\begin{aligned}
1 + y + 3 &= 6 \\
y + 4 &= 6 \\
y &= 2
\end{aligned}
$$

The solution is the ordered triple $(1, 2, 3)$. ∎

Example 2   Solve the system.

$$
\begin{array}{ll}
2x + y - z = 3 & \text{(1)} \\
3x + 4y + z = 6 & \text{(2)} \\
2x - 3y + z = 1 & \text{(3)}
\end{array}
$$

SOLUTION   It is easiest to eliminate z from the equations using the elimination method. The equation produced by adding (1) and (2) is

$$5x + 5y = 9 \qquad \text{(4)}$$

The equation that results from adding (1) and (3) is

$$4x - 2y = 4 \qquad \text{(5)}$$

Equations (4) and (5) form a linear system in two variables. We can eliminate the variable y from this system as follows:

$$
\begin{array}{lcl}
5x + 5y = 9 & \xrightarrow{\ \text{Multiply by 2}\ } & 10x + 10y = 18 \\
4x - 2y = 4 & \xrightarrow[\text{Multiply by 5}]{} & \underline{20x - 10y = 20} \\
& & 30x \qquad = 38 \\
& & x = \dfrac{38}{30} \\
& & \ \ = \dfrac{19}{15}
\end{array}
$$

Substituting $x = \frac{19}{15}$ into equation (5) or equation (4) and solving for y gives

$$y = \frac{8}{15}$$

Using $x = \frac{19}{15}$ and $y = \frac{8}{15}$ in equation (1), (2), or (3) and solving for z results in

$$z = \frac{1}{15}$$

The ordered triple that satisfies all three equations is $\left(\frac{19}{15}, \frac{8}{15}, \frac{1}{15} \right)$.

Example 3   Solve the system.

$$
\begin{aligned}
2x + 3y - z &= 5 &\quad (1)\\
4x + 6y - 2z &= 10 &\quad (2)\\
x - 4y + 3z &= 5 &\quad (3)
\end{aligned}
$$

SOLUTION   Multiplying equation (1) by -2 and adding the result to equation (2) looks like this:

$$
\begin{array}{ll}
-4x - 6y + 2z = -10 & \text{-2 times (1)}\\
\underline{4x + 6y - 2z = 10} & \text{(2)}\\
 0 = 0 &
\end{array}
$$

All three variables have been eliminated, and we are left with a true statement. This implies that the two equations are dependent. With a system of three equations in three variables, however, a dependent system can have no solution or an infinite number of solutions. After we have concluded the examples in this section, we will discuss the geometry behind these systems. Doing so will give you some additional insight into dependent systems.

Example 4   Solve the system.

$$
\begin{aligned}
x - 5y + 4z &= 8 &\quad (1)\\
3x + y - 2z &= 7 &\quad (2)\\
-9x - 3y + 6z &= 5 &\quad (3)
\end{aligned}
$$

SOLUTION   Multiplying equation (2) by 3 and adding the result to equation (3) produces

$$
\begin{array}{ll}
9x + 3y - 6z = 21 & \text{3 times (2)}\\
\underline{-9x - 3y + 6z = 5} & \text{(3)}\\
 0 = 26 &
\end{array}
$$

In this case, all three variables have been eliminated, and we are left with a false statement. The two equations are inconsistent; there are no ordered triples that satisfy both equations. There is no solution to the system. If equations (2) and (3) have no ordered triples in common, then certainly (1), (2), and (3) do not either.

Example 5   Solve the system.

$$
\begin{aligned}
x + 3y &= 5 &\quad (1)\\
6y + z &= 12 &\quad (2)\\
x - 2z &= -10 &\quad (3)
\end{aligned}
$$

SOLUTION   It may be helpful to rewrite the system as

$$
\begin{array}{lll}
x + 3y & & = 5 &\quad (1)\\
6y + & z & = 12 &\quad (2)\\
x & - 2z & = -10 &\quad (3)
\end{array}
$$

Equation (2) does not contain the variable x. If we multiply equation (3) by -1 and add the result to equation (1), we will be left with another equation that does not contain the variable x.

$$\begin{array}{ll} x + 3y \quad\quad = 5 & (1) \\ -x \quad\quad + 2z = 10 & -1 \text{ times } (3) \\ \hline 3y + 2z = 15 & (4) \end{array}$$

Equations (2) and (4) form a linear system in two variables. Multiplying equation (2) by -2 and adding the result to equation (4) eliminates the variable z.

$$\begin{array}{l} 6y + \ z = 12 \quad \xrightarrow{\text{Multiply by } -2} \quad -12y - 2z = -24 \\ 3y + 2z = 15 \quad \xrightarrow[\text{No Change}]{} \quad \underline{-13y + 2z = 15} \\ \qquad\qquad\qquad\qquad\qquad\qquad\qquad -9y \qquad = -9 \\ \qquad\qquad\qquad\qquad\qquad\qquad\qquad\quad y = 1 \end{array}$$

Using $y = 1$ in equation (4) and solving for z, we have

$$z = 6$$

Substituting $y = 1$ into equation (1) gives

$$x = 2$$

The ordered triple that satisfies all three equations is $(2, 1, 6)$. ◼

The Geometry Behind Linear Equations in Three Variables

We can graph an ordered triple on a coordinate system with three axes. The graph will be a point in space. The coordinate system is drawn in perspective; you have to imagine that the x-axis comes out of the paper and is perpendicular to both the y-axis and the z-axis. To graph the point $(3, 4, 5)$, we move 3 units in the x-direction, 4 units in the y-direction, and then 5 units in the z-direction, as shown in Figure 1.

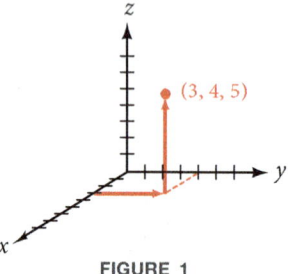

FIGURE 1

Although in actual practice it is sometimes difficult to graph equations in three variables, if we were to graph a linear equation in three variables, we would find that the graph was a plane in space. A system of three equations in three variables is represented by three planes in space.

There are a number of possible ways in which these three planes can intersect, some of which are shown below.

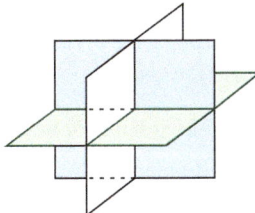

CASE 1: ONE SOLUTION
The three planes have exactly one point in common. In this case we get one solution to our system, as in Examples 1, 2, and 5.

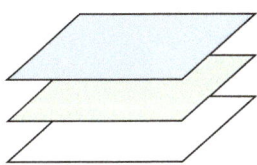

CASE 2: INCONSISTENT SYSTEM, THREE PARALLEL PLANES
The three planes have no points in common because they are all parallel to one another. The system they represent is an inconsistent system.

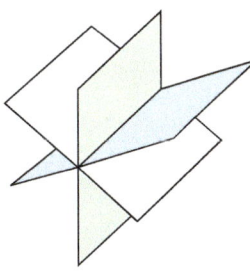

CASE 3: DEPENDENT SYSTEM
The three planes intersect in a line. Any point on the line is a solution to the system of equations represented by the planes, so there is an infinite number of solutions to the system. This is an example of a dependent system.

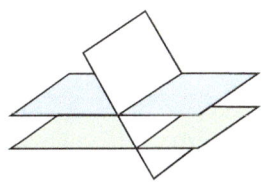

CASE 4: INCONSISTENT SYSTEM, TWO PARALLEL LINES
Two of the planes are parallel; the third plane intersects each of the parallel planes. In this case, the three planes have no points in common. There is no solution to the system; it is an inconsistent system.

In Example 3, we found that equations (1) and (2) were dependent equations. They represent the same plane. That is, they have all their points in common. But the system of equations that they came from has either no solution or an infinite number of solutions. It all depends on the third plane. If the third plane coincides with the first two, then the solution to the system is a plane. If the third plane is parallel to the first two, then there is no solution to the system. Finally, if the third plane intersects the first two but does not coincide with them, then the solution to the system is that line of intersection.

In Example 4, we found that trying to eliminate a variable from the second and third equations resulted in a false statement. This means that the two planes represented by these equations are parallel. It makes no difference where the third plane is; there is no solution to the system in Example 4. (If we were to graph the three planes from Example 4, we would obtain a diagram similar to Case 2 or Case 4 above.)

If, in the process of solving a system of linear equations in three variables, we eliminate all the variables from a pair of equations and are left with a false statement, we will say the system is inconsistent. If we eliminate all the variables and are left with a true statement, then we will say the system is a dependent one.

Getting Ready for Class

After reading through the preceding section, respond in your own words and in complete sentences.

A. What is an ordered triple of numbers?

B. Explain what it means for (1, 2, 3) to be a solution to a system of liner equations in three variables.

C. Explain in a general way the procedure you would use to solve a system of three linear equations in three variables.

D. How do you know when a system of linear equations in three variables has no solution?

Problem Set 3.4

Solve the following systems.

1. $x + y + z = 4$
$x - y + 2z = 1$
$x - y - 3z = -4$

2. $x - y - 2z = -1$
$x + y + z = 6$
$x + y - z = 4$

3. $x + y + z = 6$
$x - y + 2z = 7$
$2x - y - 4z = -9$

4. $x + y + z = 0$
$x + y - z = 6$
$x - y + 2z = -7$

5. $x + 2y + z = 3$
$2x - y + 2z = 6$
$3x + y - z = 5$

6. $2x + y - 3z = -14$
$x - 3y + 4z = 22$
$3x + 2y + z = 0$

7. $2x + 3y - 2z = 4$
$x + 3y - 3z = 4$
$3x - 6y + z = -3$

8. $4x + y - 2z = 0$
$2x - 3y + 3z = 9$
$-6x - 2y + z = 0$

9. $-x + 4y - 3z = 2$
$2x - 8y + 6z = 1$
$3x - y + z = 0$

10. $4x + 6y - 8z = 1$
$-6x - 9y + 12z = 0$
$x - 2y - 2z = 3$

11. $\frac{1}{2}x - y + z = 0$
$2x + \frac{1}{3}y + z = 2$
$x + y + z = -4$

12. $\frac{1}{3}x + \frac{1}{2}y + z = -1$
$x - y + \frac{1}{5}z = -1$
$x + y + z = -5$

13. $2x - y - 3z = 1$
$x + 2y + 4z = 3$
$4x - 2y - 6z = 2$

14. $3x + 2y + z = 3$
$x - 3y + z = 4$
$-6x - 4y - 2z = 1$

15. $2x - y + 3z = 4$
$x + 2y - z = -3$
$4x + 3y + 2z = -5$

349

16. $6x - 2y + z = 5$
$3x + y + 3z = 7$
$x + 4y - z = 4$

17. $x + y = 9$
$y + z = 7$
$x - z = 2$

18. $x - y = -3$
$x + z = 2$
$y - z = 7$

19. $2x + y = 2$
$y + z = 3$
$4x - z = 0$

20. $2x + y = 6$
$3y - 2z = -8$
$x + z = 5$

21. $2x - 3y = 0$
$6y - 4z = 1$
$x + 2z = 1$

22. $3x + 2y = 3$
$y + 2z = 2$
$6x - 4z = 1$

23. $x + y - z = 2$
$2x + y + 3z = 4$
$x - 2y + 2z = 6$

24. $x + 2y - 2z = 4$
$3x + 4y - z = -2$
$2x + 3y - 3z = -5$

25. $2x + 3y = -\dfrac{1}{2}$
$4x + 8z = 2$
$3y + 2z = -\dfrac{3}{4}$

26. $3x - 5y = 2$
$4x + 6z = \dfrac{1}{3}$
$5y - 7z = \dfrac{1}{6}$

27. $\dfrac{1}{3}x + \dfrac{1}{2}y - \dfrac{1}{6}z = 4$
$\dfrac{1}{4}x - \dfrac{3}{4}y + \dfrac{1}{2}z = \dfrac{3}{2}$
$\dfrac{1}{2}x - \dfrac{2}{3}y - \dfrac{1}{4}z = -\dfrac{16}{3}$

28. $-\dfrac{1}{4}x + \dfrac{3}{8}y + \dfrac{1}{6}z = -1$
$\dfrac{2}{3}x - \dfrac{1}{6}y - \dfrac{1}{2}z = 2$
$\dfrac{3}{4}x - \dfrac{1}{2}y - \dfrac{1}{8}z = 1$

29. $x - \dfrac{1}{2}y - \dfrac{1}{3}z = -\dfrac{4}{3}$
$\dfrac{1}{3}x - \dfrac{1}{2}z = 5$
$-\dfrac{1}{4}x + \dfrac{2}{3}y - z = -\dfrac{3}{4}$

30. $x + \dfrac{1}{3}y - \dfrac{1}{2}z = -\dfrac{3}{2}$
$\dfrac{1}{2}x - y + \dfrac{1}{3}z = 8$
$\dfrac{1}{3}x - \dfrac{1}{4}y - z = -\dfrac{5}{6}$

Applying the Concepts

31. **Electric Current** In the following diagram of an electrical circuit, x, y, and z represent the amount of current (in amperes) flowing across the 5-ohm, 20-ohm, and 10-ohm resistors, respectively. (In circuit diagrams, resistors are represented by —W— and cells that provide electrical energy are —||—.)

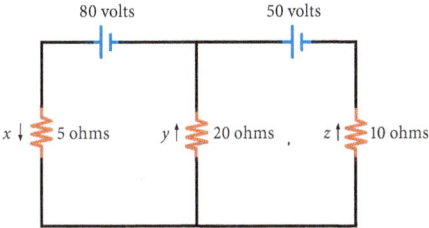

The system of equations used to find the three currents x, y, and z is

$$x - y - z = 0$$
$$5x + 20y = 80$$
$$20y - 10z = 50$$

Solve the system for all variables.

32. **Cost of a Rental Car** If a car rental company charges $10 a day and 8¢ a mile to rent one of its cars, then the cost z, in dollars, to rent a car for x, days and drive y miles can be found from the equation

$$z = 10x + 0.08y$$

a. How much does it cost to rent a car for 2 days and drive it 200 miles under these conditions?

b. A second company charges $12 a day and 6¢ a mile for the same car. Write an equation that gives the cost z, in dollars, to rent a car from this company for x days and drive it y miles.

c. A car is rented from each of the companies mentioned in a. and b. for 2 days. To find the mileage at which the cost of renting the cars from each of the two companies will be equal, solve the following system for y:

$$z = 10x + 0.08y$$
$$z = 12x + 0.06y$$
$$x = 2$$

Getting Ready for the Next Section

Translate into symbols.

33. Two more than 3 times a number   **34.** One less than twice a number

Apply the distributive property, then simplify.

35. $10(0.2x + 0.5y)$ **36.** $100(0.09x + 0.08y)$

Solve.

37. $x + (3x + 2) = 26$ **38.** $5x = 2{,}500$

Solve each system.

39. $-2y - 4z = -18$ **40.** $-x + 2y = 200$
$\,\,-7y + 4z = 27$ $\,\,4x - 2y = 1{,}300$

41. The sum of three numbers is 20. The largest number equals the sum of the two smaller numbers, and the middle number is one more than twice the smaller number. Find these numbers.

42. The sum of three numbers is 34. The largest number is six more than the sum of the two smaller numbers, and the middle number is one less than twice the smaller number. Find the three numbers.

43. A 20 foot board is cut into three pieces. The longest piece is 2 ft. more than the sum of the two smaller pieces, and the middle piece is twice the length of the shortest piece. Find the length of each piece.

44. A 10 foot board is cut into three pieces. The longest piece is the sum of the lengths of the two smaller pieces, and the middle piece is one foot longer than the shortest piece. Find the length of each piece.

© iStockphoto/laughingmango

Suppose you decide to sell homegrown zucchini and artichokes at two local farmer's market. For the first market, you price the zucchini at $0.75 each and the artichokes at $1.50 each, and you make a total of $21. For the second market, you increase your prices by a quarter each and end up selling the same quantity of each vegetables as you did at the first market. You make a total of $26 at the second market. The following system of equations shows how many of each vegetable you sold at the markets.

$$0.75x + 1.5y = 21$$
$$x + 1.75y = 26$$

We can use a matrix to display a system of equations. For example, the above system can be written as a ***rectangular array*** of $m \times n$ real numbers with m rows and n columns. The coefficients of the variables are called the elements of the matrix and are enclosed by brackets.

$$\text{Matrix } A = \begin{bmatrix} -0.75 & 1.5 & -21 \\ 1 & 1.75 & 26 \end{bmatrix} \quad m \text{ rows}$$

$$n \text{ columns}$$

Matrix A above has 2 rows and 3 columns, with elements from the coefficients of the equations in the given system. The dimension of matrix A is written 2×3 and read "two by three."

Matrix Dimensions

In this section, we will learn how to solve a system of equations using a matrix.

Example 1   Give the dimensions of each of the following matrices.

a. $\begin{bmatrix} -2 & 1 \\ 5 & 3 \end{bmatrix}$ **b.** $\begin{bmatrix} 1 & -0 \\ -4 & -2 \\ -3 & -7 \end{bmatrix}$ **c.** $\begin{bmatrix} 5 \\ -2 \\ 1 \end{bmatrix}$ **d.** $[4 \ -2]$

SOLUTIONS

a. $A = \begin{bmatrix} -2 & 1 \\ 5 & 3 \end{bmatrix}$ Matrix A is a 2×2 matrix and is called a square matrix because $m = n$.

b. $B = \begin{bmatrix} 1 & -0 \\ 4 & -2 \\ -3 & -7 \end{bmatrix}$ Matrix B is a 3×2 matrix as there are thee rows and two columns.

c. $C = \begin{bmatrix} 5 \\ -2 \\ 1 \end{bmatrix}$ Matrix C is a 3×1 matrix as there are three rows but one column.

d. $D = \begin{bmatrix} 4 & -2 \end{bmatrix}$ Matrix D is a 1×2 matrix as there is one row and two columns.

Augmented Matrices

Matrices are used to solve systems of equations. When a system of equations is written so that the variables appear in the same order in each equation, the matrix of coefficients if the variables is called the coefficient matrix. The constant terms on the right side of the equations form what is constant matrix. The combination of the coefficients and constants written in one matrix is called the augmented matrix of the system.

Example 2   Find the coefficient matrix, constant matrix and augmented matrix of the system

$$x + 5y - 3z = 4$$
$$-x + 2y = -4$$

SOLUTION   The coefficient matrix comes from the coefficients of the variables written in the same order. The constant matrix comes from the terms on the right side of each equation. Finally the augmented matrix combines these two. They are each written as

Coefficient Matrix	Constant Matrix	Augmented Matrix
$\begin{bmatrix} 1 & 5 & -3 \\ -1 & 2 & -0 \end{bmatrix}$	$\begin{bmatrix} 4 \\ -4 \end{bmatrix}$	$\left[\begin{array}{ccc|c} 1 & 5 & -3 & 4 \\ -1 & 2 & 0 & -4 \end{array}\right]$

Row Operations

Now that we know how a matrix can represent a system of equations, we will now see that operations on that matrix can be used to find solutions to the system. As you will see, these matrix methods are similar to the elimination method used to solve systems of equations. We will apply these methods to rows, columns, and elements rather than equations, variables, and coefficients.

We can use the following row operations to transform an augmented matrix into an equivalent system:

1. We can interchange any two rows of a matrix.
2. We can multiply any row by a nonzero constant.
3. We can add to any row a constant multiple of another row.

The three row operations are simply a list of the properties we use to solve systems of linear equations, translated to fit an augmented matrix. For instance, the second operation in our list is actually just another way to state the multiplication property of equality.

We solve a system of linear equations by first transforming the augmented matrix into a matrix that has 1's down the diagonal of the coefficient matrix, and 0's below it. For instance, we will solve the system

$$2x + 5y = -4$$
$$x - 3y = 9$$

by transforming the matrix

$$\begin{bmatrix} 2 & 5 & | & -4 \\ 1 & -3 & | & 9 \end{bmatrix}$$

using the row operations listed earlier to get a matrix of the form

$$\begin{bmatrix} 1 & \square & | & \square \\ 0 & 1 & | & \square \end{bmatrix}$$

To accomplish this, we begin with the first column and try to produce a 1 in the first position and a 0 below it. Interchanging rows 1 and 2 gives us a 1 in the top position of the first column:

$$\begin{bmatrix} 1 & -3 & | & 9 \\ 2 & 5 & | & -4 \end{bmatrix} \quad \text{Interchange rows 1 and 2.}$$

Multiplying row 1 by −2 and adding the result to row 2 gives us a 0 where we want it.

$$\begin{bmatrix} 1 & -3 & | & 9 \\ 0 & 11 & | & -22 \end{bmatrix} \quad \text{Multiply row 1 by } -2 \text{ and add the result to row 2.}$$

Continue to produce 1's down the diagonal by multiplying row 2 by $\frac{1}{11}$.

$$\begin{bmatrix} 1 & -3 & | & 9 \\ 0 & 1 & | & -2 \end{bmatrix} \quad \text{Multiply row 2 by } \frac{1}{11}.$$

Taking this last matrix and writing the system of equations it represents, we have

$$x - 3y = 9$$
$$y = -2$$

Substituting −2 for y in the top equation gives us

$$x = 3$$

The solution to our system is (3,−2).

Example 3 Solve the following system using an augmented matrix.
$$x + y - z = 2$$
$$2x + 3y - z = 7$$
$$3x - 2y + z = 9$$

SOLUTION We begin by writing the system as an augmented matrix.

$$\begin{bmatrix} 1 & 1 & -1 & | & 2 \\ 2 & 3 & -1 & | & 7 \\ 3 & -2 & 1 & | & 9 \end{bmatrix}$$

Next, we want to produce 0's in the second two positions of column 1.

$$\begin{bmatrix} 1 & 1 & -1 & | & 2 \\ 0 & 1 & 1 & | & 3 \\ 3 & -2 & 1 & | & 9 \end{bmatrix} \quad \text{Multiply row 1 by } -2 \text{ and add the result to row 2.}$$

$$\begin{bmatrix} 1 & 1 & -1 & | & 2 \\ 0 & 1 & 1 & | & 3 \\ 0 & -5 & 4 & | & 3 \end{bmatrix} \quad \text{Multiply row 1 by } -3 \text{ and add the result to row 3.}$$

Note that we could have done these two steps in one single step. As you become more familiar with this method of solving systems of equations, you will do just that.

$$\begin{bmatrix} 1 & 1 & -1 & | & 2 \\ 0 & 1 & 1 & | & 3 \\ 0 & 0 & 9 & | & 18 \end{bmatrix}$$ *Multiply row 2 by 5 and add the result to row 3.*

$$\begin{bmatrix} 1 & 1 & -1 & | & 2 \\ 0 & 1 & 1 & | & 3 \\ 0 & 0 & 1 & | & 2 \end{bmatrix}$$ *Multiply row 3 by $\frac{1}{9}$.*

Converting back to a system of equations, we have

$$x + y - z = 2$$
$$y + z = 3$$
$$z = 2$$

This system is equivalent to our first one, but much easier to solve. Substituting $z = 2$ into the second equation, we have

$$y = 1$$

Substituting $z = 2$ and $y = 1$ into the first equation, we have

$$x = 3$$

The solution to our original system is $(3, 1, 2)$. It satisfies each of our original equations. You can check this, if you want.   ■

Getting Ready for Class

After reading through the preceding section, respond in your own words and in complete sentences.

A. What are the dimensions of a matrix?

B. What are the row operations that can be applied to an augmented matrix?

C. The form for an augmented matrix that solves systems is called upper triangular. Why do you think this term is used?

Problem Set 3.5

Solve the following systems of equations by using matrices.

1. $x + y = 5$
   $3x - y = 3$

2. $x + y = -2$
   $2x - y = -10$

3. $3x - 5y = 7$
   $-x + y = -1$

4. $2x - y = 4$
   $x + 3y = 9$

5. $2x - 8y = 6$
   $3x - 8y = 13$

6. $3x - 6y = 3$
   $-2x + 3y = -4$

7. $2x - y = -10$
   $4x + 3y = 0$

8. $3x - 7y = 36$
   $5x - 4y = 14$

9. $5x - 3y = 27$
   $6x + 2y = -18$

10. $3x + 4y = 2$
    $5x + 3y = 29$

11. $5x + 2y = -14$
    $y = 2x + 11$

12. $3x + 5y = 3$
    $x = 4y + 1$

13. $2x + 3y = 11$
    $-x - y = -2$

14. $5x + 2y = -25$
    $-3x + 2y = -1$

15. $3x - 2y = 16$
    $4x + 3y = -24$

16. $6x + y = 3$
    $x = 4y + 13$

17. $3x - 2y = 16$
    $y = 2x - 12$

18. $4x - 3y = 28$
    $y = -x - 7$

19. $x + y + z = 4$
    $x - y + 2z = 1$
    $x - y - z = -2$

20. $x - y - 2z = -1$
    $x + y + z = 6$
    $x + y - z = 4$

21. $x + 2y + z = 3$
    $2x - y + 2z = 6$
    $3x + y - z = 5$

22. $x - 3y + 4z = -4$
    $2x + y - 3z = 14$
    $3x + 2y + z = 10$

23. $x - 2y + z = -4$
    $2x + y - 3z = 7$
    $5x - 3y + z = -5$

24. $3x - 2y + 3z = -3$
    $x + y + z = 4$
    $x - 4y + 2z = -9$

25. $5x - 3y + z = 10$
    $x - 2y - z = 0$
    $3x - y + 2z = 10$

26. $2x - y - z = 1$
    $x + 3y + 2z = 13$
    $4x + y - z = 7$

27. $2x - 5y + 3z = 2$
    $3x - 7y + z = 0$
    $x + y + 2z = 5$

28. $3x - 4y + 2z = -2$
    $2x + y + 3z = 13$
    $x - 3y + 2z = -3$

29. $x + 2y = 3$
    $y + z = 3$
    $4x - z = 2$

30. $x + y = 2$
    $3y - 2z = -8$
    $x + z = 5$

31. $x + 3y = 7$
    $3x - 4z = -8$
    $5y - 2z = -5$

32. $x + 4y = 13$
    $2x - 5z = -3$
    $4y - 3z = 9$

33. $x + 4y = 13$
    $2x - 5z = -3$
    $4y - 3z = 9$

34. $x - 2y = 5$
    $4x + 3z = 11$
    $5y + 4z = -12$

35. $x - 2y + z = -5$
    $2x + 3y - 2z = -9$
    $2x - y + 2z = -1$

36. $-4x - 3y - z = -7$
    $3x + 2y + 2z = 7$
    $-x - y + 2z = 2$

37. $4x - 2y - z = -5$
    $x + 3y - 4z = 13$
    $3x - y - 3z = 0$

38. $3x - 5y + z = 15$
    $2x + 6y - 4z = 10$
    $x - 5y - 3z = -5$

39. $5y + z = 11$
    $7x - 2y = 1$
    $5x + 2z = -3$

40. $x - 2y - z = 1$
    $3x - 2y + 3z = 3$
    $2x + y + 4z = 5$

Solve each system using matrices. Remember, multiplying a row by a nonzero constant will not change the solution to a system.

41. $\frac{1}{3}x + \frac{1}{5}y = 2$

$\frac{1}{3}x - \frac{1}{2}y = -\frac{1}{3}$

42. $\frac{1}{2}x + \frac{1}{3}y = 13$

$\frac{1}{5}x + \frac{1}{8}y = 5$

43. $\frac{1}{3}x - \frac{1}{4}y = 1$

$\frac{1}{3}x + \frac{1}{4}y = 3$

44. $\frac{1}{3}x - \frac{5}{6}y = 16$

$-\frac{1}{2}x + \frac{3}{4}y = -18$

The systems that follow are inconsistent systems. In both cases, the lines are parallel. Try solving each system using matrices and see what happens.

45. $2x - 3y = 4$
$4x + 6y = 4$

46. $10x - 15y = 5$
$-4x + 6y = -4$

The systems that follow are dependent systems. In each case, the lines coincide. Try solving each system using matrices and see what happens.

47. $-6x + 4y = 8$
$-3x + 2y = 4$

48. $x + 2y = 5$
$-x - 2y = -5$

Getting Ready for the Next Section

Graph the following equations.

49. $y = 3x - 5$

50. $y = -\frac{3}{4}x$

51. $x = -3$

© iStockphoto/Marcco73

In 1714, Daniel Gabriel Fahrenheit invented the first mercury thermometer. Ten years later, he introduced the scale to measure temperature that we use today. He based this scale on the temperature of the human body, which at the time was measured to be 100°F, although has since been adjusted to 98.6°F. In 1742, Anders Celsius invented the centigrade scale based on the freezing point of water at 0°C and the boiling point at 100°C. Since there were now two prominent scales to measure temperature, the linear formula $F = \frac{9}{5}C + 32$ was derived to convert Celsius temperatures to Fahrenheit temperatures. In this section, you will learn how a linear formula can also be written as a determinant equation. For example, $F = \frac{9}{5}C + 32$ is equivalent to the following determinant:

$$\begin{vmatrix} C & F & 1 \\ 5 & 41 & 1 \\ 810 & 14 & 1 \end{vmatrix} = 0$$

But first, let's learn how to expand and evaluate determinants. The purpose of this section is simply to be able to find the value of a given determinant. As we will see, determinants are very useful in solving systems of linear equations. Before we apply determinants to systems of linear equations; however, we must practice calculating the value of some determinants.

2 × 2 Determinants

The value of the **2 × 2** (read as "2 by 2") **determinant** is given by

$$\begin{vmatrix} a & c \\ b & d \end{vmatrix} = ad - bc.$$

From the preceding definition we see that a determinant is simply a square array of numbers with two vertical lines enclosing it. The value of a 2 × 2 determinant is found by cross-multiplying on the diagonals and then subtracting, a diagram that looks like

$$\begin{vmatrix} a & c \\ b & d \end{vmatrix} = ad - bc$$

Example 1   Find the value of the following 2×2 determinants.

a. $\begin{vmatrix} 1 & 2 \\ 3 & 4 \end{vmatrix} = 1(4) - 3(2) = 4 - 6 = -2$

b. $\begin{vmatrix} 3 & -2 \\ 5 & 7 \end{vmatrix} = 3(7) - 5(-2) = 21 + 10 = 31$

Example 2   Solve for x if $\begin{vmatrix} x & 2 \\ x & 4 \end{vmatrix} = 8$

SOLUTION   We expand the determinant on the left side to get

$$x(4) - x(2) = 8$$
$$4x - 2x = 8$$
$$2x = 8$$
$$x = 4$$

We can now look at how determinants can be used to solve a system of linear equations in two variables. We will use Cramer's rule to do so, but first we state it here as a theorem without proof.

Solving Two-Variable Systems with Cramer's Rule

(dĕf′)   *Cramer's Rule I*

The solution to the system
$$a_1 x + b_1 y = c_1$$
$$a_2 x + b_2 y = c_2$$

is given by

$$x = \frac{D_x}{D}, \quad y = \frac{D_y}{D}$$

where

$$D = \begin{vmatrix} a_1 & b_1 \\ a_2 & b_2 \end{vmatrix} \qquad D_x = \begin{vmatrix} c_1 & b_1 \\ c_2 & b_2 \end{vmatrix} \qquad D_y = \begin{vmatrix} a_1 & c_1 \\ a_2 & c_2 \end{vmatrix} \qquad (D \neq 0)$$

The determinant D is made up of the coefficients of x and y in the original system. The determinants D_x and D_y are found by replacing the coefficients of x or y by the constant terms in the original system. Notice also that Cramer's rule does not apply if $D = 0$. In this case the equations are dependent, or the system is inconsistent.

Example 3   Use Cramer's rule to solve
$$2x - 3y = 4$$
$$4x + 5y = 3$$

SOLUTION   We begin by calculating the determinants D, D_x, and D_y.

$$D = \begin{vmatrix} 2 & -3 \\ 4 & 5 \end{vmatrix} = 2(5) - 4(-3) = 22$$

$$D_x = \begin{vmatrix} 4 & -3 \\ 3 & 5 \end{vmatrix} = 4(5) - 3(-3) = 29$$

$$D_y = \begin{vmatrix} 2 & 4 \\ 4 & 3 \end{vmatrix} = 2(3) - 4(4) = -10$$

$$x = \frac{D_x}{D} = \frac{29}{22} \quad \text{and} \quad y = \frac{D_y}{D} = \frac{-10}{22} = -\frac{5}{11}$$

The solution set for the system is $\left\{ \left(\dfrac{29}{22}, -\dfrac{5}{11} \right) \right\}$.

3 × 3 Determinants

We now turn our attention to 3 × 3 determinants. A 3 × 3 determinant is also a square array of numbers enclosed by a vertical line, the value of which is given by the following definition.

> **(dĕf´   3 × 3 Determinant**
>
> The value of the **3 × 3 determinant** is given by
>
> $$\begin{vmatrix} a_1 & b_1 & c_1 \\ a_2 & b_2 & c_2 \\ a_3 & b_3 & c_3 \end{vmatrix} = a_1 b_2 c_3 + a_3 b_1 c_2 + a_2 b_3 c_1 - a_3 b_2 c_1 - a_1 b_3 c_2 - a_2 b_1 c_3$$

At first glance, the expansion of a 3 × 3 determinant looks a little complicated. There are actually two different methods used to find the six products in the preceding definition, which simplifies matters somewhat.

Method 1 We begin by writing the determinant with the first two columns repeated on the right.

$$\begin{vmatrix} a_1 & b_1 & c_1 \\ a_2 & b_2 & c_2 \\ a_3 & b_3 & c_3 \end{vmatrix} \begin{matrix} a_1 & b_1 \\ a_2 & b_2 \\ a_3 & b_3 \end{matrix}$$

The positive products in the definition come from multiplying down the three full diagonals:

The negative products come from multiplying up the three full diagonals.

Note Check the products found by multiplying up and down the diagonals given here with the products given in the definition of a 3 × 3 determinant to see that they match.

Example 4   Find the value of

$$\begin{vmatrix} 1 & 3 & -2 \\ 2 & 0 & 1 \\ 4 & -1 & 1 \end{vmatrix}$$

SOLUTION   Repeating the first two columns and then finding the products down the diagonals and the products up the diagonals as given in Method 1, we have

$$= 1(0)(1) + 3(1)(4) + (-2)(2)(-1) - 4(0)(-2) - (-1)(1)(1) - 1(2)(3)$$
$$= 0 + 12 + 4 - 0 + 1 - 6$$
$$= 11$$

Method 2   The second method of evaluating a 3×3 determinant is called expansion of minors.

(děf) Expansion of Minors

The *minor* for an element in a 3×3 determinant is the determinant consisting of the elements remaining when the row and column to which the element belongs are deleted. For example, in the determinant

$$\begin{vmatrix} a_1 & b_1 & c_1 \\ a_2 & b_2 & c_2 \\ a_3 & b_3 & c_3 \end{vmatrix}$$

Minor for element $a_1 = \begin{vmatrix} b_2 & c_2 \\ b_3 & c_3 \end{vmatrix}$

Minor for element $b_2 = \begin{vmatrix} a_1 & c_1 \\ a_3 & c_3 \end{vmatrix}$

Minor for element $c_3 = \begin{vmatrix} a_1 & b_1 \\ a_2 & b_2 \end{vmatrix}$

Note   If you have read this far and are confused, hang on. After you have done a couple of examples you will find expansion by minors to be a fairly simple process. It just takes a lot of writing to explain it.

Before we can evaluate a 3×3 determinant by Method 2, we must first define what is known as the sign array for a 3×3 determinant.

(děf) Sign Array

The *sign array* for a 3×3 determinant is a 3×3 array of signs in this pattern:

$$\begin{vmatrix} + & - & + \\ - & + & - \\ + & - & + \end{vmatrix}$$

The sign array begins with a plus sign in the upper left-hand corner. The signs then alternate between plus and minus across every row and down every column.

To Evaluate a 3×3 Determinant by Expansion of Minors

> ⌈Δ≠Σ   *How To Evaluate a 3 × 3 Determinant by Expansion of Minors*
>
> We can evaluate a 3×3 determinant by expanding across any row or down any column as follows:
>
> **Step 1:** Choose a row or column to expand.
>
> **Step 2:** Write the product of each element in the row or column chosen in Step 1 with its minor.
>
> **Step 3:** Connect the three products in Step 2 with the signs in the corresponding row or column in the sign array.

To illustrate the procedure, we will use the same determinant we used in Example 3.

■ **Example 5**   Expand across the first row.

$$\begin{vmatrix} 1 & 3 & -2 \\ 2 & 0 & 1 \\ 4 & -1 & 1 \end{vmatrix}$$

SOLUTION   The products of the three elements in row 1 with their minors are

$$1 \begin{vmatrix} 0 & 1 \\ -1 & 1 \end{vmatrix} \qquad 3 \begin{vmatrix} 2 & 1 \\ 4 & 1 \end{vmatrix} \qquad (-2) \begin{vmatrix} 2 & 0 \\ 4 & -1 \end{vmatrix}$$

Connecting these three products with the signs from the first row of the sign array, we have

$$+1 \begin{vmatrix} 0 & 1 \\ -1 & 1 \end{vmatrix} \qquad -3 \begin{vmatrix} 2 & 1 \\ 4 & 1 \end{vmatrix} \qquad +(-2) \begin{vmatrix} 2 & 0 \\ 4 & -1 \end{vmatrix}$$

Note This method of evaluating a determinant is actually more valuable than our first method because it works with any size determinant from 3×3 to 4×4 to any higher order determinant. Method 1 works only on 3×3 determinants. It cannot be used on a 4×4 determinant, which you may see in later math classes.

We complete the problem by evaluating each of the three 2×2 determinants and then simplifying the resulting expression.

$$+1[0 - (-1)] - 3(2 - 4) + (-2)(-2 - 0)$$
$$= 1(1) - 3(-2) + (-2)(-2)$$
$$= 1 + 6 + 4$$
$$= 11$$ ■

The results of Examples 3 and 4 match. It makes no difference which method we use; the value of a 3×3 determinant is unique.

■ **Example 6**   Expand down column 2.

$$\begin{vmatrix} 2 & 3 & -2 \\ 1 & 4 & 1 \\ 1 & 5 & -1 \end{vmatrix}$$

SOLUTION   We connect the products of elements in column 2 and their minors with the signs from the second column in the sign array.

$$\begin{vmatrix} 2 & 3 & -2 \\ 1 & 4 & 1 \\ 1 & 5 & -1 \end{vmatrix} = -3 \begin{vmatrix} 1 & 1 \\ 1 & -1 \end{vmatrix} + 4 \begin{vmatrix} 2 & -2 \\ 1 & -1 \end{vmatrix} - 5 \begin{vmatrix} 2 & -2 \\ 1 & 1 \end{vmatrix}$$

$$= -3(-1 - 1) + 4[-2 - (-2)] - 5[2 - (-2)]$$
$$= -3(-2) + 4(0) - 5(4)$$
$$= 6 + 0 - 20$$
$$= -14$$

Solving Three-Variable Systems with Cramer's Rule

Cramer's rule can also be used to solve systems of linear equations in three variables.

(děf' Cramer's Rule II

The solution set to the system

$$a_1 x + b_1 y + c_1 z = d_1$$
$$a_2 x + b_2 y + c_2 z = d_2$$
$$a_3 x + b_3 y + c_3 z = d_3$$

is given by

$$x = \frac{D_x}{D}, \quad y = \frac{D_y}{D}, \quad \text{and} \quad z = \frac{D_z}{D},$$

where

$$D = \begin{vmatrix} a_1 & b_1 & c_1 \\ a_2 & b_2 & c_2 \\ a_3 & b_3 & c_3 \end{vmatrix} \quad D_x = \begin{vmatrix} d_1 & b_1 & c_1 \\ d_2 & b_2 & c_2 \\ d_3 & b_3 & c_3 \end{vmatrix} \quad (D \neq 0)$$

$$D_y = \begin{vmatrix} a_1 & d_1 & c_1 \\ a_2 & d_2 & c_2 \\ a_3 & d_3 & c_3 \end{vmatrix} \quad D_z = \begin{vmatrix} a_1 & b_1 & d_1 \\ a_2 & b_2 & d_2 \\ a_3 & b_3 & d_3 \end{vmatrix}$$

Again, the determinant D consists of the coefficients of x, y, and z in the original system. The determinants D_x, D_y, and D_z are found by replacing the coefficients of x, y, and z, respectively, with the constant terms from the original system. If $D = 0$, there is no unique solution to the system.

Example 7   Use Cramer's rule to solve.

$$x + y + z = 6$$
$$2x - y + z = 3$$
$$x + 2y - 3z = -4$$

SOLUTION   We begin by setting up and evaluating D, D_x, D_y, and D_z. (Recall that there are a number of ways to evaluate a 3×3 determinant. Since we have four of these determinants, we can use both Methods 1 and 2 from earlier in the section.) We evaluate D using Method 1.

> **Note** When we are solving a system of linear equations by Cramer's rule, it is best to find the determinant D first. If $D = 0$, then there is no unique solution to the system and we may not want to go further.

$$D = \begin{vmatrix} 1 & 1 & 1 \\ 2 & -1 & 1 \\ 1 & 2 & -3 \end{vmatrix} \begin{matrix} 1 & 1 \\ 2 & -1 \\ 1 & 2 \end{matrix}$$

$$= 3 + 1 + 4 - (-1) - (2) - (-6)$$
$$= 13$$

We evaluate D_x using Method 2 from this section and expanding across row 1.

$$D_x = \begin{vmatrix} 6 & 1 & 1 \\ 3 & -1 & 1 \\ -4 & 2 & -3 \end{vmatrix}$$

$$= 6 \begin{vmatrix} -1 & 1 \\ 2 & -3 \end{vmatrix} - 1 \begin{vmatrix} 3 & 1 \\ -4 & -3 \end{vmatrix} + 1 \begin{vmatrix} 3 & -1 \\ -4 & 2 \end{vmatrix}$$

$$= 6(1) - 1(-5) + 1(2)$$
$$= 13$$

Find D_y by expanding across row 2.

$$D_y = \begin{vmatrix} 1 & 6 & 1 \\ 2 & 3 & 1 \\ 1 & -4 & -3 \end{vmatrix}$$

$$= -2 \begin{vmatrix} 6 & 1 \\ -4 & -3 \end{vmatrix} + 3 \begin{vmatrix} 1 & 1 \\ 1 & -3 \end{vmatrix} - 1 \begin{vmatrix} 1 & 6 \\ 1 & -4 \end{vmatrix}$$

$$= -2(-14) + 3(-4) - 1(-10)$$
$$= 26$$

Find D_z by expanding down column 1.

$$D_z = \begin{vmatrix} 1 & 1 & 6 \\ 2 & -1 & 3 \\ 1 & 2 & -4 \end{vmatrix}$$

$$= 1 \begin{vmatrix} -1 & 3 \\ 2 & -4 \end{vmatrix} - 2 \begin{vmatrix} 1 & 6 \\ 2 & -4 \end{vmatrix} + 1 \begin{vmatrix} 1 & 6 \\ -1 & 3 \end{vmatrix}$$

$$= 1(-2) - 2(-16) + 1(9)$$
$$= 39$$

Now find x, y, and z.

$$x = \frac{D_x}{D} = \frac{13}{13} = 1 \qquad y = \frac{D_y}{D} = \frac{26}{13} = 2 \qquad z = \frac{D_z}{D} = \frac{39}{13} = 3$$

The solution set is $\{(1, 2, 3)\}$.

> *Note* We are finding each of these determinants by expanding about different rows or columns just to show the different ways these determinants can be evaluated.

Example 8   Use Cramer's rule to solve.

$$x + y = -1$$
$$2x - z = 3$$
$$y + 2z = -1$$

SOLUTION It is helpful to rewrite the system using zeros for the coefficients of those variables not shown.

$$x + y + 0z = -1$$
$$2x + 0y - z = 3$$
$$0x + y + 2z = -1$$

The four determinants used in Cramer's rule are

$$D = \begin{vmatrix} 1 & 1 & 0 \\ 2 & 0 & -1 \\ 0 & 1 & 2 \end{vmatrix} = -3$$

$$D_x = \begin{vmatrix} -1 & 1 & 0 \\ 3 & 0 & -1 \\ -1 & 1 & 2 \end{vmatrix} = -6$$

$$D_y = \begin{vmatrix} 1 & -1 & 0 \\ 2 & 3 & -1 \\ 0 & -1 & 2 \end{vmatrix} = 9$$

$$D_z = \begin{vmatrix} 1 & 1 & -1 \\ 2 & 0 & 3 \\ 0 & 1 & -1 \end{vmatrix} = -3$$

$$x = \frac{D_x}{D} = \frac{-6}{-3} = 2 \qquad y = \frac{D_y}{D} = \frac{9}{-3} = -3 \qquad z = \frac{D_z}{D} = \frac{-3}{-3} = 1$$

The solution set is $\{(2, -3, 1)\}$.

Finally, we should mention the possible situations that can occur when the determinant D is 0 and we are using Cramer's rule. If $D = 0$ and at least one of the other determinants, D_x or D_y (or D_z), is not 0, then the system is inconsistent. In this case, there is no solution to the system.

However, if $D = 0$ and both D_x and D_y (and D_z in a system of three equations in three variables) are 0, then the equations are dependent.

Getting Ready for Class

After reading through the preceding section, respond in your own words and in complete sentences.

A. Why is Method 2 (Expansion of Minors) a better method for finding determinants than Method 1?

B. What happens if $D = 0$ while using Cramer's rule?

C. If you are solving a 3 × 3 system of equations, how many determinants will you need to find?

D. What is the advantage of using Cramer's rule over either substitution or elimination methods?

Find the value of the following 2×2 determinants.

1. $\begin{vmatrix} 1 & 0 \\ 2 & 3 \end{vmatrix}$

2. $\begin{vmatrix} 5 & 3 \\ 3 & 2 \end{vmatrix}$

3. $\begin{vmatrix} 1 & 2 \\ 3 & 4 \end{vmatrix}$

4. $\begin{vmatrix} 4 & 1 \\ 5 & 2 \end{vmatrix}$

5. $\begin{vmatrix} 5 & 4 \\ 3 & 2 \end{vmatrix}$

6. $\begin{vmatrix} 2 & 1 \\ 3 & 4 \end{vmatrix}$

7. $\begin{vmatrix} 0 & 1 \\ 1 & 0 \end{vmatrix}$

8. $\begin{vmatrix} 1 & 0 \\ 0 & 1 \end{vmatrix}$

9. $\begin{vmatrix} -3 & 2 \\ 6 & -4 \end{vmatrix}$

10. $\begin{vmatrix} 8 & -3 \\ -2 & -5 \end{vmatrix}$

11. $\begin{vmatrix} -3 & -1 \\ 4 & -2 \end{vmatrix}$

12. $\begin{vmatrix} 5 & 3 \\ 7 & -6 \end{vmatrix}$

Solve each of the following for x.

13. $\begin{vmatrix} 2x & 1 \\ x & 3 \end{vmatrix} = 10$

14. $\begin{vmatrix} 3x & -2 \\ 2x & 3 \end{vmatrix} = 26$

15. $\begin{vmatrix} 1 & 2x \\ 2 & -3x \end{vmatrix} = 21$

16. $\begin{vmatrix} -5 & 4x \\ 1 & -x \end{vmatrix} = 27$

17. $\begin{vmatrix} 2x & -4 \\ x & 2 \end{vmatrix} = -16$

18. $\begin{vmatrix} 3x & -2 \\ x & 4 \end{vmatrix} = 21$

19. $\begin{vmatrix} 11x & -7x \\ 3 & -2 \end{vmatrix} = 3$

20. $\begin{vmatrix} -3x & -5x \\ 4 & 6 \end{vmatrix} = -14$

21. $\begin{vmatrix} 2x & -4 \\ 2 & x \end{vmatrix} = -8x$

22. $\begin{vmatrix} 3x & 2 \\ 2 & x \end{vmatrix} = -11x$

23. $\begin{vmatrix} x^2 & 3 \\ x & 1 \end{vmatrix} = 10$

24. $\begin{vmatrix} x^2 & -2 \\ x & 1 \end{vmatrix} = 35$

25. $\begin{vmatrix} x^2 & -4 \\ x & 1 \end{vmatrix} = 32$

26. $\begin{vmatrix} x^2 & 6 \\ x & 1 \end{vmatrix} = 72$

27. $\begin{vmatrix} x & 5 \\ 1 & x \end{vmatrix} = 4$

28. $\begin{vmatrix} 3x & 4 \\ 2 & x \end{vmatrix} = 10x$

Solve each of the following systems using Cramer's rule.

29. $2x - 3y = 3$
$4x - 2y = 10$

30. $3x + y = -2$
$-3x + 2y = -4$

31. $5x - 2y = 4$
$-10x + 4y = 1$

32. $-4x + 3y = -11$
$5x + 4y = 6$

33. $4x - 7y = 3$
$5x + 2y = -3$

34. $3x - 4y = 7$
$6x - 2y = 5$

35. $9x - 8y = 4$
$2x + 3y = 6$

36. $4x - 7y = 10$
$-3x + 2y = -9$

37. $3x + 2y = 6$
$4x - 5y = 8$

38. $-4x + 3y = 12$
$6x - 7y = 14$

39. $12x - 13y = 16$
$11x + 15y = 18$

40. $-13x + 15y = 17$
$12x - 14y = 19$

Find the value of the following 3×3 determinants by using Method 1 of this section.

41. $\begin{vmatrix} 1 & 2 & 0 \\ 0 & 2 & 1 \\ 1 & 1 & 1 \end{vmatrix}$

42. $\begin{vmatrix} -1 & 0 & 2 \\ 3 & 0 & 1 \\ 0 & 1 & 3 \end{vmatrix}$

43. $\begin{vmatrix} 1 & 2 & 3 \\ 3 & 2 & 1 \\ 1 & 1 & 1 \end{vmatrix}$

44. $\begin{vmatrix} -1 & 2 & 0 \\ 3 & -2 & 1 \\ 0 & 5 & 4 \end{vmatrix}$

Find the value of the following 3×3 determinants by using Method 2 and expanding across the first row.

45. $\begin{vmatrix} 0 & 1 & 2 \\ 1 & 0 & 1 \\ -1 & 2 & 0 \end{vmatrix}$

46. $\begin{vmatrix} 3 & -2 & 1 \\ 0 & -1 & 0 \\ 2 & 0 & 1 \end{vmatrix}$

47. $\begin{vmatrix} 3 & 0 & 2 \\ 0 & -1 & -1 \\ 4 & 0 & 0 \end{vmatrix}$

48. $\begin{vmatrix} 1 & 1 & 1 \\ 1 & -1 & 1 \\ 1 & 1 & -1 \end{vmatrix}$

Find the value of each of the following determinants by expanding across any row or down any column.

49. $\begin{vmatrix} 2 & -1 & 0 \\ 1 & 0 & -2 \\ 0 & 1 & 2 \end{vmatrix}$

50. $\begin{vmatrix} 5 & 0 & -4 \\ 0 & 1 & 3 \\ -1 & 2 & -1 \end{vmatrix}$

51. $\begin{vmatrix} 1 & 3 & 7 \\ -2 & 6 & 4 \\ 3 & 7 & -1 \end{vmatrix}$

52. $\begin{vmatrix} 2 & 1 & 5 \\ 6 & -3 & 4 \\ 8 & 9 & -2 \end{vmatrix}$

53. $\begin{vmatrix} -2 & 0 & 1 \\ 0 & 3 & 2 \\ 1 & 0 & -5 \end{vmatrix}$

54. $\begin{vmatrix} -1 & 1 & 1 \\ -2 & 2 & 2 \\ 5 & 7 & -4 \end{vmatrix}$

55. $\begin{vmatrix} -2 & 4 & -1 \\ 0 & 3 & 1 \\ -5 & -2 & 3 \end{vmatrix}$

56. $\begin{vmatrix} -3 & 2 & 4 \\ 1 & 2 & 3 \\ -1 & 1 & 5 \end{vmatrix}$

Solve each of the following systems using Cramer's rule.

57. $x + y + z = 4$
$x - y - z = 2$
$2x + 2y - z = 2$

58. $-x + y + 3z = 6$
$x + y + 2z = 7$
$2x + 3y + z = 4$

59. $x + y - z = 2$
$-x + y + z = 3$
$x + y + z = 4$

60. $-x - y + z = 1$
$x - y + z = 3$
$x + y - z = 4$

61. $3x - y + 2z = 4$
$6x - 2y + 4z = 8$
$x - 5y + 2z = 1$

62. $2x - 3y + z = 1$
$3x - y - z = 4$
$4x - 6y + 2z = 3$

63. $2x - y + 3z = 4$
$x - 5y - 2z = 1$
$-4x - 2y + z = 3$

64. $4x - y + 5z = 1$
$2x + 3y + 4z = 5$
$x + y + 3z = 2$

65. $x + 2y - z = 4$
$2x + 3y + 2z = 5$
$x - 3y + z = 6$

66. $3x + 2y + z = 6$
$2x + 3y - 2z = 4$
$x - 2y + 3z = 8$

67. $3x - 4y + 2z = 5$
$2x - 3y + 4z = 7$
$4x + 2y - 3z = 6$

68. $5x - 3y - 4z = 3$
$4x - 5y + 3z = 5$
$3x + 4y - 5z = -4$

69. $x - 3z = 1$
$y + 2z = 8$
$x + z = 10$

70. $x - 5y = -6$
$y - 4z = -5$
$2x + 3z = -6$

71. $-x - 7y = 1$
$x + 3z = 11$
$2y + z = 0$

72. $x + y = 2$
$-x + 3z = 0$
$2y + z = 3$

73. $x - y = 12$
$3x + z = 11$
$y - 2z = -3$

74. $4x + 5y = -1$
$2y + 3z = -5$
$x + 2z = -1$

Applying the Concepts

75. Slope-Intercept Form Show that the following determinant equation is another way to write the slope-intercept form of the equation of a line.

$$\begin{vmatrix} y & x \\ m & 1 \end{vmatrix} = b$$

76. Temperature Conversions Show that the following determinant equation is another way to write the equation $F = \frac{9}{5}C + 32$.

$$\begin{vmatrix} C & F & 1 \\ 5 & 41 & 1 \\ -10 & 14 & 1 \end{vmatrix} = 0$$

77. Amusement Park Income From 1986 to 1990, the annual income of amusement parks was linearly increasing, after which time it remained fairly constant. The annual income y, in billions of dollars, may be found for one of these years by evaluating the following determinant equation, in which x represents the number of years past January 1, 1986.

$$\begin{vmatrix} x & -1.7 \\ 2 & 0.3 \end{vmatrix} = y$$

  a. Write the determinant equation in slope-intercept form.
  b. Use the equation from part a to find the approximate income for amusement parks in the year 1988.

78. College Enrollment From 1981, the enrollment of women in the United States armed forces was linearly increasing until 1990, after which it declined. The approximate number of women, w, enrolled in the armed forces from 1981 to 1990 may be found by evaluating the following determinant equation, in which x represents the number of years past January 1, 1981.

$$\begin{vmatrix} 6,509 & -2 \\ 85,709 & x \end{vmatrix} = w$$

Use this equation to determine the number of women enrolled in the armed forces in 1985.

79. Per Capita Income From 1990 to 1998, the per capita income in California was linearly increasing, according to the following determinant equation

$$\begin{vmatrix} x & -3 \\ 7121 & 767.5 \end{vmatrix} = I$$

where I is income and x is the number of years since January 1, 1990 (U.S. Bureau of Economic Analysis, *Survey of Current Business,* May 1999 and unpublished data.).
  a. Write the determinant equation in slope-intercept form.
  b. Use the equation from part a to find the approximate personal income per capita in the year 1994.

80. **Median Income**   For the years 1990 through 1998, the U.S. median family income I, in dollars, can be estimated by the following determinant (x is the number of years since January 1, 1990) (U.S. Census Bureau).

$$\begin{vmatrix} x & 3535.3 \\ -10 & 1264.89 \end{vmatrix} = I$$

    a. Use the determinant equation to determine the median family income for 1994.

    b. Use the determinant equation to predict the median family income for 1999.

81. **School Enrollment**   Enrollment in higher education has been increasing from 1990 to 1999. The higher education enrollment E, in millions, may be found by evaluating the following determinant equation (U.S. Census Bureau). If x is the number of years since January 1, 1990, determine the higher education enrollment for 1996.

$$\begin{vmatrix} 0.1 & 6.9 \\ -2 & x \end{vmatrix} = y$$

82. **Earnings**   The median income for women I has increased throughout the years, according to the determinant equation below (x is the number of years since January 1, 1990) (Current Population Reports, U.S. Census Bureau.). Use the equation to find the median income for women in 2001.

$$\begin{vmatrix} 457.5 & -10 \\ 1007 & x \end{vmatrix} = I$$

83. **Organ Transplants**   The number of procedures for heart transplants H have increased during the years 1985 through 1994, according to the equation

$$H = 164.2x + 719$$

where x is the number of years since January 1, 1985 (*U.S. Department of Health and Human Services, Public Health Services, Division of Organ Transplantation and United Network of Organ Sharing*). Solving the system below for H will give the number of heart transplants in the year 1990. Solve this system for H using Cramer's rule.

$$-164.2x + H = 719$$
$$x = 5$$

84. **Automobile Air Bags**   The percent of automobiles with air bags P since 1990 can be modeled by the following equation.

$$P = 5.6x - 3.6$$

where x is the number of years since January 1, 1990 (*National Highway Traffic Safety Administration*). Solving the system below for x will allow you to find the year in which 80.4% of all automobiles will have air bags. Use Cramer's rule to solve this system for x.

$$5.6x - P = 3.6$$
$$P = 80.4$$

85. Break-Even Point If a company has fixed costs of $100 per week and each item it produces costs $10 to manufacture, then the total cost y per week to produce x items is

$$y = 10x + 100$$

If the company sells each item it manufactures for $12, then the total amount of money y the company brings in for selling x items is

$$y = 12x$$

Use Cramer's rule to solve the system

$$y = 10x + 100$$
$$y = 12x$$

for x to find the number of items the company must sell per week to break even.

86. Break-Even Point Suppose a company has fixed costs of $200 per week and each item it produces costs $20 to manufacture.
   a. Write an equation that gives the total cost per week y to manufacture x items.
   b. If each item sells for $25, write an equation that gives the total amount of money y the company brings in for selling x items.
   c. Use Cramer's rule to find the number of items the company must sell each week to break even.

87. Health Insurance For years between 1980 and 1991, the number (in millions) of U.S. residents without health insurance, y, may be approximated by the equation

$$y = 0.98x - 1,915.8$$

where x represents the year, and $1980 \le x \le 1991$. To determine the year in which 30 million U.S. residents were without health insurance, we solve the system of equations made up of the equation above and the equation $y = 30$. Solve this system using Cramer's rule. (When you obtain an answer, you will need to round it to the nearest year.)

88. Price Index From 1970 to 1990, the price index of dental care, d, may be closely approximated by the equation

$$d = 6x - 11,780$$

where x is the year, and $1970 \le x \le 1990$. Determine when the price index for dental care reached 120 by forming a system of equations using the equation above along with the equation $d = 120$. Solve this system using Cramer's rule.

Extending the Concepts

A 4 × 4 determinant can be evaluated only by using Method 2, expansion by minors; Method 1 will not work. Below is a 4 × 4 determinant and its associated sign array.

$$\begin{vmatrix} 2 & 0 & 1 & -3 \\ -1 & 2 & 0 & 1 \\ -3 & 0 & 1 & 0 \\ 1 & 1 & 0 & 0 \end{vmatrix} \qquad \begin{vmatrix} + & - & + & - \\ - & + & - & + \\ + & - & + & - \\ - & + & - & + \end{vmatrix}$$

4 × 4 determinant 4 × 4 sign array

89. Use expansion by minors to evaluate the preceding 4 × 4 determinant by expanding it across row 1.

90. Evaluate the preceding determinant by expanding it down column 4.

91. Use expansion by minors down column 3 to evaluate the preceding determinant.

92. Evaluate the preceding determinant by expanding it across row 4.

Find the value of the following determinants.

93. $\begin{vmatrix} 1 & 3 & 2 & -4 \\ 0 & 4 & 1 & 0 \\ -2 & 1 & 3 & 0 \\ 2 & 3 & 4 & -1 \end{vmatrix}$

94. $\begin{vmatrix} 2 & 4 & -2 & -3 \\ 1 & 2 & 0 & 2 \\ -1 & 2 & 3 & -2 \\ 3 & 2 & 1 & -3 \end{vmatrix}$

Use Cramer's rule to solve the following systems.

95. $x + 2y - z + 3w = 4$
$2x + y + 2z - 2w = 9$
$x - 3y + z - w = 1$
$-2x + y - z + 3w = -3$

96. $3x - 2y - z - w = -10$
$2x + y + 2z - 2w = -19$
$x - 3y + 3z + w = -9$
$-2x + 3y - z + 3w = 25$

97. $ax + y + z = 1$
$x + ay + z = 1$
$x + y + az = 1$

98. $ax + y + z = a$
$x + ay + z = a$
$x + y + az = a$

Getting Ready for the Next Section

Translate into symbols.

99. Two more than 3 times a number

100. One less than twice a number

Simplify.

101. $25 - \dfrac{385}{9}$

102. $0.30(12)$

103. $0.08(4,000)$

104. $500(1.5)$

Apply the distributive property, then simplify.

105. $10(0.2x + 0.5y)$

106. $100(0.09x + 0.08y)$

107. $x + (3x + 2) = 26$

108. $5x = 2,500$

Solve each system.

109. $3y + z = 17$
$\quad$ $5y + 20z = 65$

110. $x + y = 850$
$\quad$ $1.5x + y = 1,100$

Applications of Systems of Equations

© iStockphoto/Thomas_Vogel

Suppose a chemist needs to mix a 20% alcohol solution with a 50% alcohol solution to obtain 12 gallons of a 30% alcohol solution. In order to calculate how much of each solution the chemist must begin with, we will need to set up and solve a system of linear equations in two variables.

In this section you will practice solving application problems that involve linear systems of equations. Many times word problems involve more than one unknown quantity. If a problem is stated in terms of two unknowns, like the one above, and we represent each unknown quantity with a different variable, then we must write the relationships between the variables with two equations. The two equations written in terms of the two variables form a system of linear equations that we solve using the methods developed in this chapter. If we find a problem that relates three unknown quantities, then we need three equations to form a linear system we can solve.

Application Problems

Here is our Blueprint for Problem Solving, modified to fit the application problems that you will find in this section.

> **Note** When working an application problem, it is useful to draw a sketch or make a table to represent the knowns and the unknowns. This will help you better visualize how to solve the problem.

⟨Δ≠Σ⟩   *Using a System of Equations*

Step 1: *Read* the problem, and then mentally *list* the items that are known and the items that are unknown.

Step 2: *Assign variables* to each of the unknown items. That is, let $x =$ one of the unknown items and $y =$ the other unknown item (and $z =$ the third unknown item, if there is a third one). Then *translate* the other *information* in the problem to expressions involving the two (or three) variables.

Step 3: *Reread* the problem, and then *write a system of equations*, using the items and variables listed in steps 1 and 2, that describes the situation.

Step 4: *Solve the system* found in step 3.

Step 5: *Write your answers* using complete sentences.

Step 6: *Reread* the problem, and *check* your solution with the original words in the problem.

Video Examples

Section 3.7

Example 1   One number is 2 more than 3 times another. Their sum is 26. Find the two numbers.

SOLUTION   Applying the steps from our Blueprint, we have

Step 1: *Read and list.*
　　　　　We know that we have two numbers, whose sum is 26. One of them is 2 more than 3 times the other. The unknown quantities are the two numbers.

Step 2: *Assign variables and translate information.*
　　　　　Let x = one of the numbers and y = the other number.

Step 3: *Write a system of equations.*
　　　　　The first sentence in the problem translates into $y = 3x + 2$. The second sentence gives us a second equation $x + y = 26$. Together, these two equations give us the following system of equations:

$$x + y = 26$$
$$y = 3x + 2$$

Step 4: *Solve the system.*
　　　　　Substituting the expression for y from the second equation into the first and solving for x yields

$$x + (3x + 2) = 26$$
$$4x + 2 = 26$$
$$4x = 24$$
$$x = 6$$

　　　　　Using $x = 6$ in $y = 3x + 2$ gives the second number.

$$y = 3(6) + 2$$
$$y = 20$$

Step 5: *Write answers.*
　　　　　The two numbers are 6 and 20.

Step 6: *Reread and check.*
　　　　　The sum of 6 and 20 is 26, and 20 is 2 more than 3 times 6.

Example 2   Suppose 850 tickets were sold for a game for a total of $4,725. If adult tickets cost $7.00 and children's tickets cost $3.50, how many of each kind of ticket were sold?

SOLUTION

Step 1: *Read and list.*
　　　　　The total number of tickets sold is 850. The total income from tickets is $4,725. Adult tickets are $7.00 each. Children's tickets are $3.50 each. We don't know how many of each type of ticket have been sold.

Step 2: *Assign variables and translate information.*
　　　　　We let x = the number of adult tickets and y = the number of children's tickets.

Step 3: *Write a system of equations.*

The total number of tickets sold is 850, giving us our first equation.

$$x + y = 850$$

Because each adult ticket costs \$7.00, and each children's ticket costs \$3.50, and the total amount of money paid for tickets was \$4,725, a second equation is

$$7.00x + 3.50y = 4,725$$

The same information can also be obtained by summarizing the problem with a table. One such table follows. Notice that the two equations we obtained previously are given by the two rows of the table.

	Adult tickets	Children's tickets	Total
Number	x	y	850
Value	$7.00x$	$3.50y$	4,725

Whether we use a table to summarize the information in the problem or just talk our way through the problem, the system of equations that describes the situation is

$$x + y = 850$$
$$7.00x + 3.50y = 4,725$$

Step 4: *Solve the system.*

If we multiply the second equation by 10 to clear it of decimals, we have the system

$$x + y = 850$$
$$70x + 35y = 47,250$$

Multiplying the first equation by -35 and adding the result to the second equation eliminates the variable y from the system.

$$
\begin{array}{rcl}
-35x - 35y &=& -29,750 \\
70x + 35y &=& 47,250 \\
\hline
35x &=& 17,500 \\
x &=& 500
\end{array}
$$

The number of adult tickets sold was 500. To find the number of children's tickets, we substitute $x = 500$ into $x + y = 850$ to get

$$500 + y = 850$$
$$y = 350$$

Step 5: *Write answers.*

The number of children's tickets is 350, and the number of adult tickets
is 500.

Step 6: *Reread and check.*

The total number of tickets is $350 + 500 = 850$. The amount of money from selling the two types of tickets is

$$350 \text{ children's tickets at } \$3.50 \text{ each is } 350(3.50) = \$1,225$$
$$500 \text{ adult tickets at } \$7.00 \text{ each is } 500(7.00) = \$3,500$$

The total income from ticket sales is $4,725.

Example 3 Suppose a person has a total balance of $10,000 on two credit cards. One card has an 8% annual interest rate and the other has a 9% annual interest rate. If the total interest charged from both accounts in a year is $860, what was the balance of each card at the beginning of the year? (Assume this person did not make any payments or accrue any penalty fees during this year).

SOLUTION

Step 1: *Read and list.*

The total balance is $10,000 split between two accounts. One account charges 8% in interest annually, and the other charges 9% annually. The interest from both accounts is $860 in 1 year. We don't know how much is in each account.

Step 2: *Assign variables and translate information.*

We let x equal the amount at 9% and y be the amount at 8%.

Step 3: *Write a system of equations.*

Because the total balance is $10,000, one relationship between x and y can be written as

$$x + y = 10,000$$

The total interest charged from both accounts is $860. The amount of interest charged on x dollars at 9% is $0.09x$, while the amount of interest charged on y dollars at 8% is $0.08y$. This relationship is represented by the equation

$$0.09x + 0.08y = 860$$

The two equations we have just written can also be found by first summarizing the information from the problem in a table. Again, the two rows of the table yield the two equations just written. Here is the table:

	Dollars at 9%	Dollars at 8%	Total
Number	x	y	10,000
Interest	$0.09x$	$0.08y$	860

The system of equations that describes this situation is given by

$$x + y = 10,000$$
$$0.09x + 0.08y = 860$$

Step 4: *Solve the system.*

> *Note* Remember that most problems that involve percents require you to change each percent to a decimal (or fraction) before working with them, as you see in step 3 of Example 3.

Multiplying the second equation by 100 will clear it of decimals. The system that results after doing so is

$$x + y = 10{,}000$$

$$9x + 8y = 86{,}000$$

We can eliminate y from this system by multiplying the first equation by -8 and adding the result to the second equation.

$$-8x - 8y = -80{,}000$$
$$\underline{9x + 8y = 86{,}000}$$
$$x = 6{,}000$$

The amount of money on the card at 9% interest annually is $6,000. Because the total balance was $10,000, the amount on the card with 8% must be $4,000.

Step 5: *Write answers.*

The amount on the card with 8% interest is $4,000, and the amount on the card with 9% interest is $6,000.

Step 6: *Reread and check.*

The total balance is $4,000 + $6,000 = $10,000. The amount of interest charged from the two accounts is

In 1 year, $4,000 spent at 8% is charged $0.08(4{,}000) = \$320$
In 1 year, $6,000 spent at 9% is charged $0.09(6{,}000) = \$540$

The total interest from the two accounts is $860.

Example 4   Recall this application from the beginning of the section: how much 20% alcohol solution and 50% alcohol solution must be mixed to obtain 12 gallons of 30% alcohol solution?

SOLUTION   To solve this problem, we must first understand that a 20% alcohol solution is 20% alcohol and 80% water.

Step 1: *Read and list.*

We will mix two solutions to obtain 12 gallons of solution that is 30% alcohol. One of the solutions is 20% alcohol and the other 50% alcohol. We don't know how much of each solution we need.

Step 2: *Assign variables and translate information.*

Let x = the number of gallons of 20% alcohol solution needed, and y = the number of gallons of 50% alcohol solution needed.

Step 3: *Write a system of equations.*

Because we must end up with a total of 12 gallons of solution, one equation for the system is

$$x + y = 12$$

The amount of alcohol in the x gallons of 20% solution is $0.20x$, while the amount of alcohol in the y gallons of 50% solution is $0.50y$. Because the total amount of alcohol in the 20% and 50% solutions must add up to the amount of alcohol in the 12 gallons of 30% solution, the second equation in our system can be written as

$$0.20x + 0.50y = 0.30(12)$$

Again, let's make a table that summarizes the information we have to this point in the problem.

	20% Solution	50% Solution	Final Solution
Total number of gallons	x	y	12
Gallons of alcohol	$0.20x$	$0.50y$	$0.30(12)$

Our system of equations is

$$x + y = 12$$
$$0.20x + 0.50y = 0.30(12) = 3.6$$

Step 4: *Solve the system.*

Multiplying the second equation by 10 gives us an equivalent system.

$$x + y = 12$$
$$2x + 5y = 36$$

Multiplying the top equation by -2 to eliminate the x-variable, we have

$$
\begin{aligned}
-2x - 2y &= -24 \\
\underline{2x + 5y} &= \underline{\quad 36} \\
3y &= \quad 12 \\
y &= \quad 4
\end{aligned}
$$

Substituting $y = 4$ into $x + y = 12$, we solve for x.

$$x + 4 = 12$$
$$x = 8$$

Step 5: *Write answers.*

It takes 8 gallons of 20% alcohol solution and 4 gallons of 50% alcohol solution to produce 12 gallons of 30% alcohol solution.

Step 6: *Reread and check.*

If we mix 8 gallons of 20% solution and 4 gallons of 50% solution, we end up with a total of 12 gallons of solution. To check the percentages we look for the total amount of alcohol in the two initial solutions and in the final solution.

The amount of alcohol in 8 gallons of 20% solution is $0.20(8) = 1.6$ gallons
The amount of alcohol in 4 gallons of 50% solution is $0.50(4) = 2.0$ gallons

The total amount of alcohol in the initial solutions is 3.6 gallons.

The amount of alcohol in 12 gallons of 30% solution is $0.30(12) = 3.6$ gallons.

Example 5 It takes 2 hours for a boat to travel 28 miles downstream (with the current). The same boat can travel 18 miles upstream (against the current) in 3 hours. What is the speed of the boat in still water, and what is the speed of the current of the river?

SOLUTION

Step 1: *Read and list.*
A boat travels 18 miles upstream and 28 miles downstream. The trip upstream takes 3 hours. The trip downstream takes 2 hours. We don't know the speed of the boat or the speed of the current.

Step 2: *Assign variables and translate information.*
Let x = the speed of the boat in still water and let y = the speed of the current. The average speed (rate) of the boat upstream is $x - y$, because it is traveling against the current. The rate of the boat downstream is $x + y$, because the boat is traveling with the current.

Step 3: *Write a system of equations.*
Putting the information into a table, we have

	Distance d (miles)	Rate r (mph)	Time t (hours)
Upstream	18	$x - y$	3
Downstream	28	$x + y$	2

The formula for the relationship between distance d, rate r, and time t is $d = rt$ (the rate equation). Because $d = r \cdot t$, the system we need to solve the problem is

$$18 = (x - y) \cdot 3$$
$$28 = (x + y) \cdot 2$$

which is equivalent to

$$6 = x - y$$
$$14 = x + y$$

Step 4: *Solve the system.*
Adding the two equations, we have

$$20 = 2x$$
$$x = 10$$

Substituting $x = 10$ into $14 = x + y$, we see that
$$y = 4$$

Step 5: *Write answers.*
The speed of the boat in still water is 10 miles per hour; the speed of the current is 4 miles per hour.

Step 6: *Reread and check.*
The boat travels at $10 + 4 = 14$ miles per hour downstream, so in 2 hours it will travel $14 \cdot 2 = 28$ miles. The boat travels at $10 - 4 = 6$ miles per hour upstream, so in 3 hours it will travel $6 \cdot 3 = 18$ miles.

Example 6   A coin collection consists of 14 coins with a total value of $1.35. If the coins are nickels, dimes, and quarters, and the number of nickels is 3 less than twice the number of dimes, how many of each coin is there in the collection?

SOLUTION   This problem will require three variables and three equations.

Step 1: *Read and list.*

We have 14 coins with a total value of $1.35. The coins are nickels, dimes, and quarters. The number of nickels is 3 less than twice the number of dimes. We do not know how many of each coin we have.

Step 2: *Assign variables and translate information.*

Because we have three types of coins, we will have to use three variables. Let's let x = the number of nickels, y = the number of dimes, and z = the number of quarters.

Step 3: *Write a system of equations.*

Because the total number of coins is 14, our first equation is

$$x + y + z = 14$$

Because the number of nickels is 3 less than twice the number of dimes, a second equation is

$$x = 2y - 3 \qquad \text{which is equivalent to} \qquad x - 2y = -3$$

Our last equation is obtained by considering the value of each coin and the total value of the collection. Let's write the equation in terms of cents, so we won't have to clear it of decimals later.

$$5x + 10y + 25z = 135$$

Here is our system, with the equations numbered for reference:

$$
\begin{aligned}
x + y + z &= 14 & (1)\\
x - 2y &= -3 & (2)\\
5x + 10y + 25z &= 135 & (3)
\end{aligned}
$$

Note Writing our third equation in terms of cents is a helpful tip. Recall from the multiplication property of equality that doing so will not change the equation as long as we apply the same quantity to each term on both sides.

Step 4: *Solve the system.*

Let's begin by eliminating x from the first and second equations, and the first and third equations. Adding -1 times the second equation to the first equation gives us an equation in only y and z. We call this equation (4).

$$3y + z = 17 \qquad (4)$$

Adding -5 times equation (1) to equation (3) gives us

$$5y + 20z = 65 \qquad (5)$$

We can eliminate z from equations (4) and (5) by adding -20 times (4) to (5). Here is the result:

$$
\begin{aligned}
-55y &= -275\\
y &= 5
\end{aligned}
$$

Substituting $y = 5$ into equation (4) gives us $z = 2$. Substituting $y = 5$ and $z = 2$ into equation (1) gives us $x = 7$.

Step 5: *Write answers.*

The collection consists of 7 nickels, 5 dimes, and 2 quarters.

Step 6: *Reread and check.*

The total number of coins is $7 + 5 + 2 = 14$. The number of nickels, 7, is 3 less than twice the number of dimes, 5. To find the total value of the collection, we have

$$\text{The value of the 7 nickels is } 7(0.05) = \$0.35$$
$$\text{The value of the 5 dimes is } 5(0.10) = \$0.50$$
$$\text{The value of the 2 quarters is } 2(0.25) = \$0.50$$

$$\text{The total value of the collection is } \$1.35$$

If you go on to take a chemistry class, you may see the next example (or one much like it).

Example 7   In a chemistry lab, students record the temperature of water at room temperature and find that it is 77° on the Fahrenheit temperature scale and 25° on the Celsius temperature scale. The water is then heated until it boils. The temperature of the boiling water is 212°F and 100°C. Assume that the relationship between the two temperature scales is a linear one, then use the preceding data to find the formula that gives the Celsius temperature C in terms of the Fahrenheit temperature F.

SOLUTION   The data is summarized in the following table.

Corresponding Temperatures	
In Degrees Fahrenheit	In Degrees Celsius
77	25
212	100

If we assume the relationship is linear, then the formula that relates the two temperature scales can be written in slope-intercept form as

$$C = mF + b$$

Substituting $C = 25$ and $F = 77$ into this formula gives us

$$25 = 77m + b$$

Substituting $C = 100$ and $F = 212$ into the formula yields

$$100 = 212m + b$$

Together, the two equations form a system of equations, which we can solve using the elimination method.

$$25 = 77m + b \xrightarrow{\text{Multiply by } -1} -25 = -77m - b$$
$$100 = 212m + b \xrightarrow{\text{No Change}} \underline{100 = 212m + b}$$
$$75 = 135m$$

$$m = \frac{75}{135} = \frac{5}{9}$$

To find the value of b, we substitute $m = \frac{5}{9}$ into $25 = 77m + b$ and solve for b.

$$25 = 77\left(\frac{5}{9}\right) + b$$

$$25 = \frac{385}{9} + b$$

$$b = 25 - \frac{385}{9} = \frac{225}{9} - \frac{385}{9} = -\frac{160}{9}$$

The equation that gives C in terms of F is

$$C = \frac{5}{9}F - \frac{160}{9}$$

Getting Ready for Class

After reading through the preceding section, respond in your own words and in complete sentences.

A. To apply the Blueprint for Problem Solving to the examples in this section, what is the first step?

B. When would you write a system of equations while working a problem in this section using the Blueprint for Problem Solving?

C. When working application problems involving boats moving in rivers, how does the current of the river affect the speed of the boat?

D. Write an application problem for which the solution depends on solving the following system of equations:

$$x + y = 1{,}000$$
$$0.05x + 0.06y = 55$$

Problem Set 3.7

Number Problems

1. One number is 3 more than twice another. The sum of the numbers is 18. Find the two numbers.

2. The sum of two numbers is 32. One of the numbers is 4 less than 5 times the other. Find the two numbers.

3. The difference of two numbers is 6. Twice the smaller is 4 more than the larger. Find the two numbers.

4. The larger of two numbers is 5 more than twice the smaller. If the smaller is subtracted from the larger, the result is 12. Find the two numbers.

5. The sum of three numbers is 8. Twice the smallest is 2 less than the largest, while the sum of the largest and smallest is 5. Use a linear system in three variables to find the three numbers.

6. The sum of three numbers is 14. The largest is 4 times the smallest, while the sum of the smallest and twice the largest is 18. Use a linear system in three variables to find the three numbers.

7. One number is eight more than five times another; their sum is 26. Find the numbers.

8. One number is three less than four times another; their sum is 27. Find the numbers.

9. The difference of two positive numbers is nine. The larger number is six less than twice the smaller number. Find the numbers.

10. The difference of two positive numbers is 17. The larger number is one more than twice the smaller number. Find the numbers.

Ticket and Interest Problems

11. Linda sold 925 tickets for her choir's concert for a total of $6,000. If adult tickets sold for $8.00 and children's tickets sold for $6.00, how many of each kind of ticket did Linda sell?

12. Jarrett was selling tickets to ride the Ferris wheel at a local carnival. The tickets cost $2.00 for adults and $1.50 for children. How many of each kind of ticket did he sell if he sold a total of 300 tickets for $525?

13. Mr. Jones has $20,000 in credit on two credit cards. He charges part at 6% annual interest and the rest at 7%. If he accumulates $1,280 in interest on his balances after 1 year, how much did he initially charge at each rate? (Assume he makes no payments on either card during that year, nor does he accrue any fees.)

14. Noelle receives $17,000 in two loans. One loan charges 5% interest per year and the other 6.5%. If her total interest after 1 year is $970, how much was each loan?

15. Susan charges twice as much money on a credit card with a 7.5% annual interest rate as she does on a card with 6% interest. If her total interest after 1 year is $840, how much did she charge on each card? (Again, assume she does not make any payments or accrue any fees on her cards during the year.)

16. Katherine owes $1,350 in interest from two loan accounts in 1 year. If she has a balance that is three times as much at 7% interest as she does at 6%, how much does she have in each account?

17. William has withdrawn $2,200 from three loan accounts that charge 6%, 8%, and 9% in annual interest, respectively. He has three times as much from the account with 9% interest as he does from the account with 6%. If his total interest for the year is $178, how much was withdrawn from each account?

18. Mary has balances in three accounts that charge 5%, 7%, and 8% in annual interest. She has three times as much in the account with 8% as she does with 5%. If the total balance from all three accounts is $1,600 and her interest for the year comes to $115, how much was the loan for each account?

Mixture Problems

19. How many gallons of 20% alcohol solution and 50% alcohol solution must be mixed to get 9 gallons of 30% alcohol solution?

20. How many ounces of 30% hydrochloric acid solution and 80% hydrochloric acid solution must be mixed to get 10 ounces of 50% hydrochloric acid solution?

21. A mixture of 16% disinfectant solution is to be made from 20% and 14% disinfectant solutions. How much of each solution should be used if 15 gallons of the 16% solution are needed?

22. How much 25% antifreeze and 50% antifreeze should be combined to give 40 gallons of 30% antifreeze?

23. Paul mixes nuts worth $1.55 per pound with oats worth $1.35 per pound to get 25 pounds of trail mix worth $1.45 per pound. How many pounds of nuts and how many pounds of oats did he use?

24. A chemist has three different acid solutions. The first acid solution contains 20% acid, the second contains 40%, and the third contains 60%. He wants to use all three solutions to obtain a mixture of 60 liters containing 50% acid, using twice as much of the 60% solution as the 40% solution. How many liters of each solution should be used?

Rate Problems

25. It takes a boat 2 hours to travel 24 miles downstream and 3 hours to travel 18 miles upstream. What is the speed of the boat in still water? What is the speed of the current of the river?

26. A boat on a river travels 20 miles downstream in only 2 hours. It takes the same boat 6 hours to travel 12 miles upstream. What are the speed of the boat and the speed of the current?

27. Recall the airplane from the chapter introduction that flies from Denver International Airport to an airport 600 miles away in 2 hours with the wind and $2\frac{1}{2}$ hours against the wind. How fast is the plane and what is the speed of the wind?

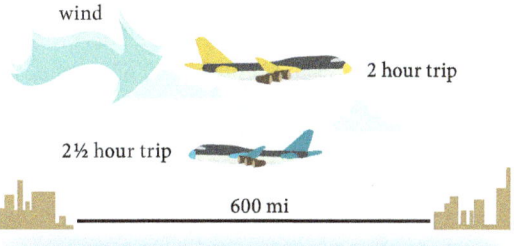

28. An airplane covers a distance of 1,500 miles in 3 hours when it flies with the wind and $3\frac{1}{3}$ hours when it flies against the wind. What is the speed of the plane in still air?

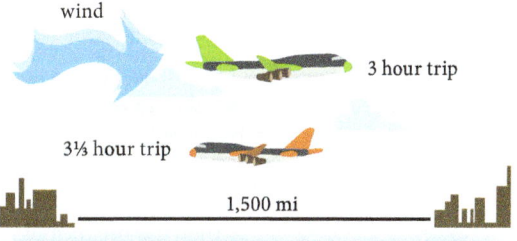

Coin Problems

29. Bob has 20 coins totaling $1.40. If he has only dimes and nickels, how many of each coin does he have?

30. If Amy has 15 coins totaling $2.70, and the coins are quarters and dimes, how many of each coin does she have?

31. A collection of nickels, dimes, and quarters consists of 9 coins with a total value of $1.20. If the number of dimes is equal to the number of nickels, find the number of each type of coin.

32. A coin collection consists of 12 coins with a total value of $1.20. If the collection consists only of nickels, dimes, and quarters, and the number of dimes is two more than twice the number of nickels, how many of each type of coin are in the collection?

33. Kaela has a collection of nickels, dimes, and quarters that amounts to $10.00. If there are 140 coins in all and there are twice as many dimes as there are quarters, find the number of nickels.

34. A cash register contains a total of 95 coins consisting of pennies, nickels, dimes, and quarters. There are only 5 pennies and the total value of the coins is $12.05. Also, there are 5 more quarters than dimes. How many of each coin is in the cash register?

35. John has $1.70 in nickels and dimes in his pocket. He has four more nickels than he does dimes. How many of each does he have?

36. Jamie has $2.65 in dimes and quarters in his pocket. He has two more dimes than she does quarters. How many of each does she have?

Additional Problems

37. Price and Demand A manufacturing company finds that they can sell 300 items if the price per item is $2.00, and 400 items if the price is $1.50 per item. If the relationship between the number of items sold x and the price per item p is a linear one, find a formula that gives x in terms of p. Then use the formula to find the number of items they will sell if the price per item is $3.00.

38. Price and Demand A company manufactures and sells bracelets. They have found from past experience that they can sell 300 bracelets each week if the price per bracelet is $2.00, but only 150 bracelets are sold if the price is $2.50 per bracelet. If the relationship between the number of bracelets sold x and the price per bracelet p is a linear one, find a formula that gives x in terms of p. Then use the formula to find the number of bracelets they will sell at $3.00 each.

39. The length of a rectangle is five inches more than three times the width. The perimeter is 58 inches. Find the length and width.

40. The length of a rectangle is three inches less than twice the width. The perimeter is 36 inches. Find the length and width.

41. Height of a Ball Lisa tosses a ball into the air. The height of the ball after 1, 3, and 5 seconds is as given in the following table.

t (sec)	h (ft)
1	128
3	128
5	0

h

If the relationship between the height of the ball h and the time t is quadratic, then the relationship can be written as

$$h = at^2 + bt + c$$

Use the information in the table to write a system of three equations in three variables a, b, and c. Solve the system to find the exact relationship between h and t.

42. **Height of a Ball** A ball is tossed into the air and its height above the ground after 1, 3, and 4 seconds is recorded as shown in the following table.

t (sec)	h (ft)
1	96
3	64
4	0

The relationship between the height of the ball h and the time t is quadratic and can be written as

$$h = at^2 + bt + c$$

Use the information in the table to write a system of three equations in three variables a, b, and c. Solve the system to find the exact relationship between the variables h and t.

43. **Relay Race** If 29 teams entered a relay race, and pre-registration costs $28 while on-site registration costs $38, find the amount of teams preregistered and on-site registered if the total fees paid were $922.

44. **Electric Current** In the following diagram of an electrical circuit, x, y, and z represent the amount of current (in amperes) flowing across the 20-ohm, 25-ohm, and 10-ohm resistors, respectively. (In circuit diagrams, resistors are represented by ─␣␣␣ and potential differences by ─┤├─.)

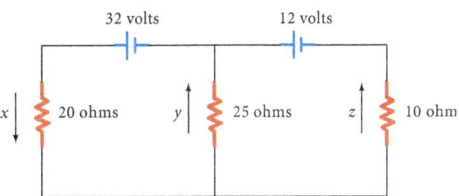

The system of equations used to find the three currents x, y, and z is

$$x - y - z = 0$$
$$20x - 25y = 32$$
$$25y - 10z = 12$$

Solve the system for all variables.

Maintaining Your Skills

45. Does the graph of $x + y < 4$ include the boundary line?

46. Does the graph of $-x + y \leq 3$ include the boundary line?

47. Where do the graphs of the lines $x + y = 4$ and $x - 2y = 4$ intersect?

48. Where do the graphs of the line $x = -1$ and $x - 2y = 4$ intersect?

Solve.

49. $20x + 9{,}300 > 18{,}000$

50. $20x + 4{,}800 > 18{,}000$

Systems of Linear Inequalities

Introduction

In Section 3.6, we graphed linear inequalities in two variables. To review, the solution set for a linear inequality is a *section of the coordinate plane*. The *boundary* for the section is found by replacing the inequality symbol with an equal sign and graphing the resulting equation. The boundary is included in the solution set (and is represented with a *solid line*) if the inequality symbol used originally is $\leq$ or $\geq$. The boundary is not included (and is represented with a *broken line*) if the original symbol is $<$ or $>$.

In the following example, we review the process for solving a single linear inequality in two variables.

Video Examples

Section 3.8

Example 1 Graph the solution set for $x + y \leq 4$.

SOLUTION The boundary for the graph is the graph of $x + y = 4$. The boundary is included in the solution set because the inequality symbol is $\leq$.
Figure 1 is the graph of the boundary:

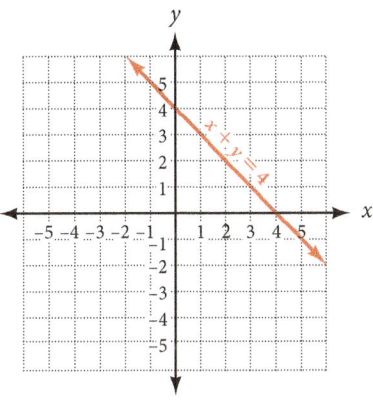

FIGURE 1

The boundary separates the coordinate plane into two regions: the region above the boundary and the region below it. The solution set for $x + y \leq 4$ is one of these two regions along with the boundary. To find the correct region, we simply choose any convenient point that is *not* on the boundary. We then substitute the coordinates of the point into the original inequality $x + y \leq 4$. If the point we choose satisfies the inequality, then it is a member of the solution set, and we can assume that all points on the same side of the boundary as the chosen point are also in the solution set. If the coordinates of our point do not satisfy the original inequality, then the solution set lies on the other side of the boundary.

In this example, a convenient point that is not on the boundary is the origin.

Substituting	$(0, 0)$	
into	$x + y \leq 4$	
gives us	$0 + 0 \leq 4$	
	$0 \leq 4$	A true statement

Because the origin is a solution to the inequality $x + y \le 4$ and the origin is below the boundary, all other points below the boundary are also solutions. We indicate this by shading the region below the boundary.

Figure 2 is the graph of $x + y \le 4$.

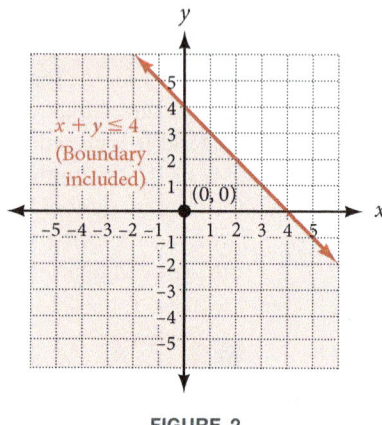

FIGURE 2

Systems of Linear Inequalities

Figure 3 shows the graph of the inequality $x + y < 4$. Note that the boundary is not included in the solution set, and is therefore drawn with a broken line. Figure 4 shows the graph of $-x + y \le 3$. Note that the boundary is drawn with a solid line, because it is part of the solution set.

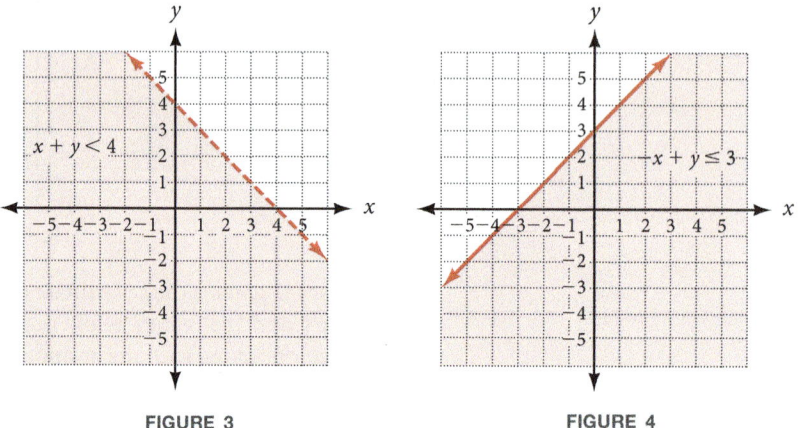

FIGURE 3   **FIGURE 4**

If we form a system of inequalities with the two inequalities, the solution set will be all the points common to both solution sets shown in the two figures above. It is the intersection of the two solution sets. Therefore, the solution set for the system of inequalities

$$x + y < 4$$
$$-x + y \le 3$$

is all the ordered pairs that satisfy both inequalities. It is the set of points that are below the line $x + y = 4$, and also below (and including) the line $-x + y = 3$. The graph of the solution set to this system is shown in Figure 5. We have written the system in Figure 5 with the word *and* just to remind you that the solution set to a system of equations or inequalities is all the points that satisfy both equations or inequalities.

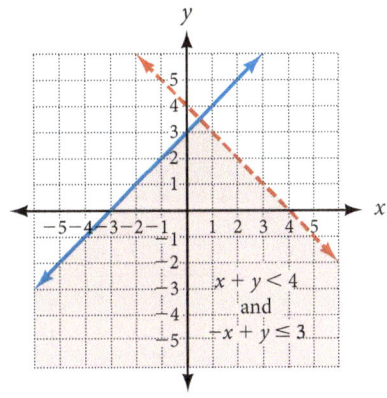

FIGURE 5

Example 2 Determine if each ordered pair is a solution to the system of linear inequalities.

$$x + y < 4$$
$$x - 2y \leq -2$$

a. $(3, 2)$ **b.** $(1, -1)$ **c.** $(-1, 3)$

SOLUTION We check each ordered pair to see if it satisfies both inequalities in the system.

a. Because $3 + 2 < 4$ is a false statement, $(3, 2)$ does not satisfy the first inequality. It cannot be a solution.

b. Substituting $x = 1$ and $y = -1$ we find

$$1 + (-1) < 4$$
$$0 < 4 \qquad \text{A true statement}$$
$$\text{and} \quad 1 - 2(-1) \leq -2$$
$$3 \leq -2 \qquad \text{A false statement}$$

Because $(1, -1)$ does not satisfy the second inequality, it is not a solution to the system.

c. Using $x = -1$ and $y = 3$ we obtain

$$-1 + 3 < 4$$
$$2 < 4 \qquad \text{A true statement}$$
$$\text{and} \quad -1 - 2(3) \leq -2$$
$$-7 \leq -2 \qquad \text{A true statement}$$

The pair $(-1, 3)$ is a solution because it satisfies both inequalities.

Example 3 Graph the solution set for the system of inequalities.

$$y < \frac{1}{2}x + 3$$

$$y \geq \frac{1}{2}x - 2$$

SOLUTION   Figures 6 and 7 show the solution set for each of the inequalities separately.

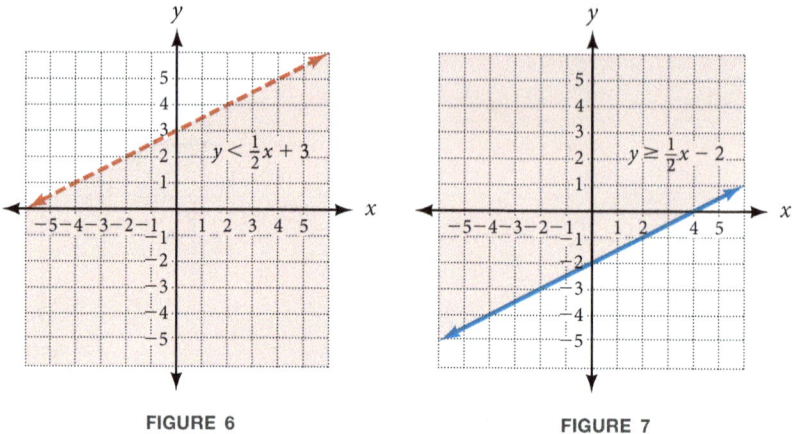

FIGURE 6   FIGURE 7

Figure 8 is the solution set to the system of inequalities. It is the region consisting of points whose coordinates satisfy both inequalities.

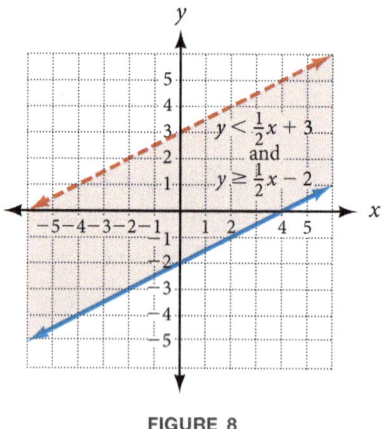

FIGURE 8

Example 4   Graph the solution set for the system of inequalities.

$$x + y < 4$$

$$x \geq 0$$

$$y \geq 0$$

SOLUTION   We graphed the first inequality, $x + y < 4$, in Figure 3 at the beginning of this section. The solution set to the inequality $x \geq 0$, shown in Figure 9, is all the points to the right of the y-axis; that is, all the points with x-coordinates that are greater than or equal to 0. Figure 10 shows the graph of $y \geq 0$. It consists of all points with y-coordinates greater than or equal to 0; that is, all points from the x-axis up.

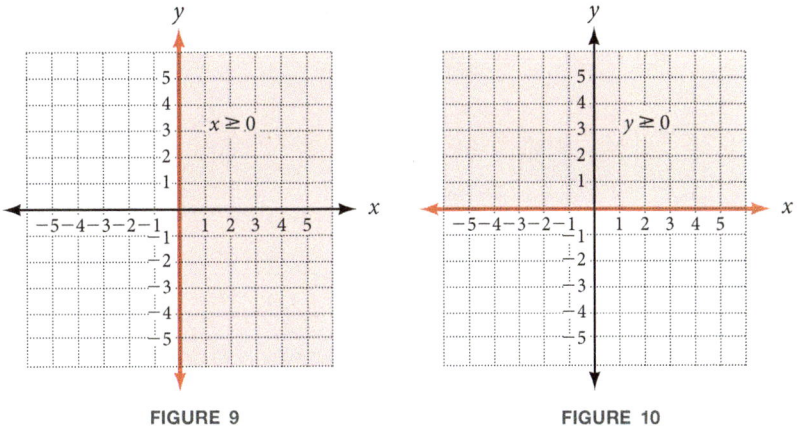

FIGURE 9   **FIGURE 10**

The regions shown in Figures 9 and 10 overlap in the first quadrant. Therefore, putting all three regions together we have the points in the first quadrant that are below the line $x + y = 4$. This region is shown in Figure 11, and it is the solution to our system of inequalities.

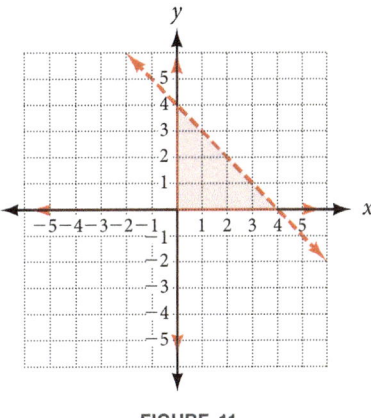

FIGURE 11

Example 5   Graph the solution set for the system of inequalities.

$$x \leq 4$$
$$y \geq -3$$

SOLUTION   The solution to this system will consist of all points to the left of and including the vertical line $x = 4$ that intersect with all points above and including the horizontal line $y = -3$. The solution set is shown in Figure 12.

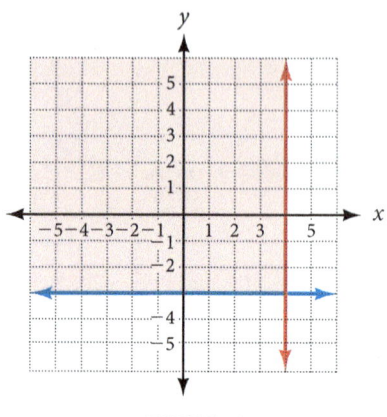

FIGURE 12

Example 6   Graph the solution set for the system of inequalities.

$$y \geq 2x + 3$$

$$2x - y > 2$$

SOLUTION   The solution set for the first inequality includes all points above and including the line $y = 2x + 3$ as shown in Figure 13. Figure 14 shows the solution set for the second inequality, which consists of all points below the line $2x - y = 2$.

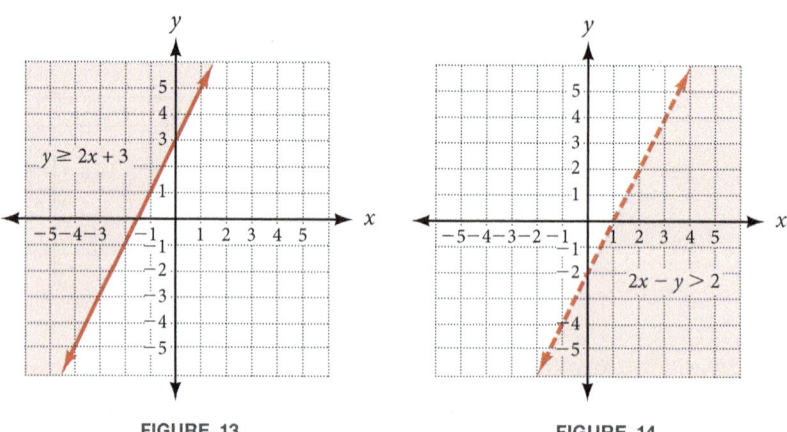

FIGURE 13   FIGURE 14

If we isolate y in the second inequality, we obtain $y < 2x - 2$. The lines in Figure 13 and Figure 14 have the same slope, and are therefore parallel. Looking at both graphs, it is evident the two shaded regions will never overlap. There are no ordered pairs that will satisfy both inequalities, so the system has no solution.

Example 7   Graph the solution set for the following system.

$$x - 2y \leq 4$$

$$x + y \leq 4$$

$$x \geq -1$$

SOLUTION   We have three linear inequalities, representing three sections of the coordinate plane. The graph of the solution set for this system will be the intersection of these three sections. The graph of $x - 2y \leq 4$ is the section above and including the boundary $x - 2y = 4$. The graph of $x + y \leq 4$ is the section below and including the boundary line $x + y = 4$. The graph of $x \geq -1$ is all the points to the right of, and including, the vertical line $x = -1$. The intersection of these three graphs is shown in Figure 15.

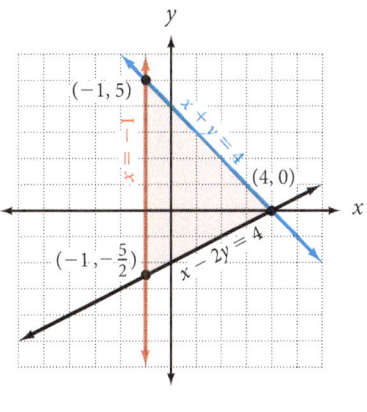

FIGURE 15

Example 8   A college basketball arena plans on charging $20 for certain seats and $15 for others. They want to bring in more than $18,000 from all ticket sales and have reserved at least 500 tickets at the $15 rate. Find a system of inequalities describing all possibilities and sketch the graph. If 620 tickets are sold for $15, at least how many tickets are sold for $20?

SOLUTION   Let $x =$ the number of $20 tickets and $y =$ the number of $15 tickets. We need to write a list of inequalities that describe this situation. That list will form our system of inequalities. First of all, we note that we cannot use negative numbers for either x or y. So, we have our first inequalities:

$$x \geq 0$$

$$y \geq 0$$

Next, we note that they are selling at least 500 tickets for $15, so we can replace our second inequality with $y \geq 500$. Now our system is

$$x \geq 0$$

$$y \geq 500$$

Now the amount of money brought in by selling $20 tickets is $20x$, and the amount of money brought in by selling $15 tickets is $15y$. If the total income from ticket sales is to be more than $18,000, then $20x + 15y$ must be greater than 18,000. This gives us our last inequality and completes our system.

$$20x + 15y > 18,000$$

$$x \geq 0$$

$$y \geq 500$$

We have used all the information in the problem to arrive at this system of inequalities. The solution set contains all the values of x and y that satisfy all the conditions given in the problem. Here is the graph of the solution set.

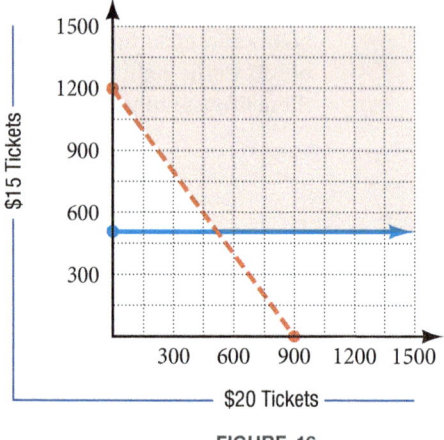

FIGURE 16

If 620 tickets are sold for $15, then we substitute 620 for y in our first inequality to obtain

$$20x + 15(620) > 18000 \qquad \text{Substitute 620 for } y$$
$$20x + 9300 > 18000 \qquad \text{Multiply}$$
$$20x > 8700 \qquad \text{Add } -9300 \text{ to each side}$$
$$x > 435 \qquad \text{Divide each side by 20}$$

If they sell 620 tickets for $15 each, then they need to sell more than 435 tickets at $20 each to bring in more than $18,000.

Getting Ready for Class

After reading through the preceding section, respond in your own words and in complete sentences.

A. What does it mean for an ordered pair to be a solution to a system of linear inequalities in two variables?

B. Explain the process of solving a system of linear inequalities in two variables.

C. What are the circumstances for which a system of linear inequalities in two variables will have no solution?

D. Is it possible for a system of linear inequalities in two variables to have a solution set consisting of the entire xy-plane? Explain why or why not.

Graph the solution set for each linear inequality.

1. $x + y < 5$ **2.** $x - y \geq -3$ **3.** $2x + 3y < 6$

4. $-x + 2y > -4$ **5.** $2x + y < 5$ **6.** $y < 2x - 1$

7. $3x - 4y < 12$ **8.** $-2x + 3y < 6$ **9.** $-5x + 2y \leq 10$

10. $4x - 2y \leq 8$

Determine if each ordered pair is a solution to the system of linear inequalities.

11. $x + y \leq -2$
$\quad x - y < \ 0$

   a. $(0, 0)$ **b.** $(-3, -1)$ **c.** $(1, -4)$ **d.** $(-2, 0)$

12. $3x - y > 3$
$\quad\quad y \leq 2$

   a. $(3, 2)$ **b.** $(0, -1)$ **c.** $(4, 3)$ **d.** $(1, -2)$

Graph the solution set for each system of linear inequalities.

13. $x + y < 5$ **14.** $x + y < 5$ **15.** $y < \dfrac{1}{3}x + 4$

$\quad\ 2x - y > 4$ $\quad\ 2x - y < 4$ $\quad y \geq \dfrac{1}{3}x - 3$

16. $y < 2x + 4$ **17.** $x \geq -3$ **18.** $x \leq 4$

$\quad\ y \geq 2x - 3$ $\quad\ y < -2$ $\quad\ y \geq -2$

19. $1 \leq x \leq 3$ **20.** $-4 \leq x \leq -2$ **21.** $x + 2y < \ 4$

$\quad\ 2 \leq y \leq 4$ $\quad\ 1 \leq y \leq \ 3$ $\quad\ x + 2y \leq -4$

22. $x \geq 3$ **23.** $y > 1$ **24.** $x - y \leq -3$

$\quad\ x > -2$ $\quad\ y < -3$ $\quad\ x - y \geq \ 1$

25. $x + y \leq 4$ **26.** $x - y \leq 2$ **27.** $x + \ y \leq \ 3$

$\quad\quad x \geq 0$ $\quad\quad x \geq 0$ $\quad\ x - 3y \leq \ 3$

$\quad\quad y \geq 0$ $\quad\quad y \leq 0$ $\quad\quad\quad x \geq -2$

28. $x - \ y \leq \ 4$ **29.** $x + y \leq \ 2$ **30.** $x - y \leq \ 3$

$\quad\ x + 2y \leq \ 4$ $\quad -x + y \leq \ 2$ $\quad -x - y \leq \ 3$

$\quad\quad\quad x \geq -1$ $\quad\quad\quad y \geq -2$ $\quad\quad\quad y \leq -1$

31. $x + y < 5$ **32.** $x + y < 5$ **33.** $2x + 3y \leq 6$

$\quad\quad y > x$ $\quad\quad y > x$ $\quad\quad x \geq 0$

$\quad\quad y \geq 0$ $\quad\quad x \geq 0$ $\quad\quad y \geq 0$

34. $x + 2y \leq 10$

$\quad\ 3x + 2y \leq 12$

$\quad\quad\quad x \geq 0$

$\quad\quad\quad y \geq 0$

For each figure below, find a system of inequalities that describes the shaded region.

35.

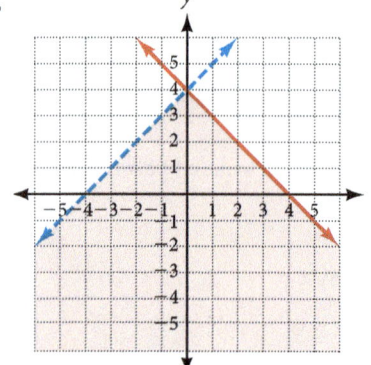

36.

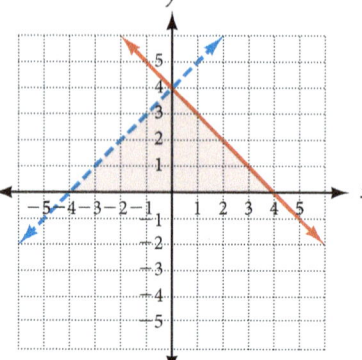

37.

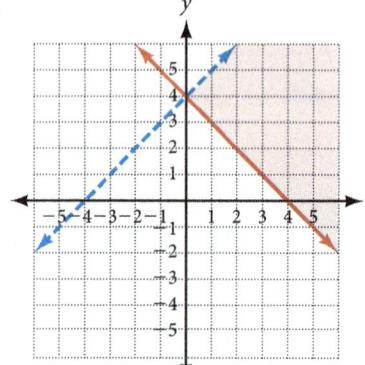

38.

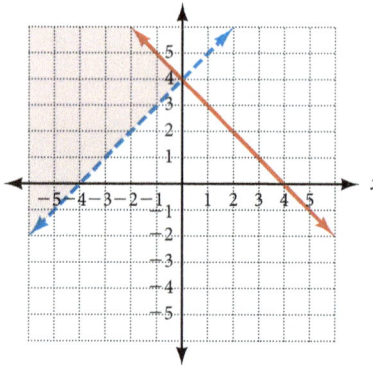

39.

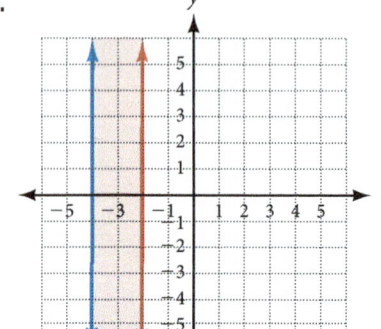

40.

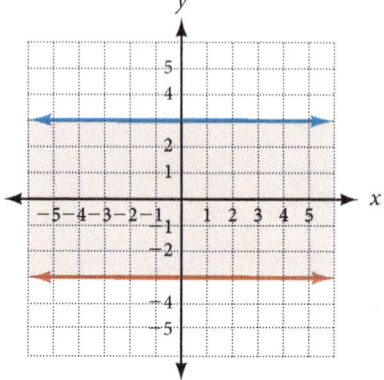

Applying the Concepts

41. Office Supplies An office worker wants to purchase some $0.55 postage stamps and also some $0.65 postage stamps totaling no more than $40. It is also desired to have at least twice as many $0.55 stamps and more than 15 $0.55 stamps.

    a. Find a system of inequalities describing all the possibilities and sketch the graph.

    b. If he purchases 20 $0.55 stamps, what is the maximum number of $0.65 stamps he can purchase?

42. **Inventory** A store sells two brands of DVD players. Customer demand indicates that it is necessary to stock at least twice as many DVD players of brand A as of brand B. At least 30 of brand A and 15 of brand B must be on hand. In the store, there is room for not more than 100 DVD players in the store.

a. Find a system of inequalities describing all possibilities, then sketch the graph.

b. If there are 35 DVD players of brand A, what is the most number of brand B DVD players on hand?

Learning Objectives Assessment

The following problems can be used to help assess if you have successfully met the learning objectives for this section.

43. **Which of the following ordered pairs is a solution to the given system of linear inequalities?**

$$x + 3y < 6$$

$$2x - y \geq 4$$

a. $(0, 0)$ **b.** $(4, 1)$ **c.** $(1, 3)$ **d.** $(3, -1)$

44. **Graph the solution set for the system of linear inequalities.**

$$x > y$$

$$x \leq 2$$

a.
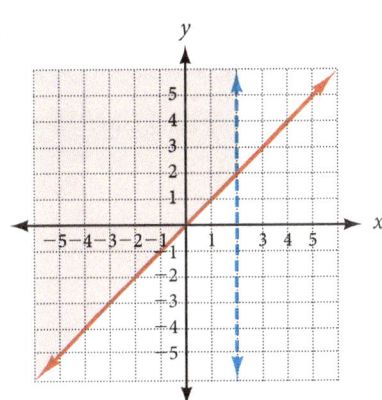

b.
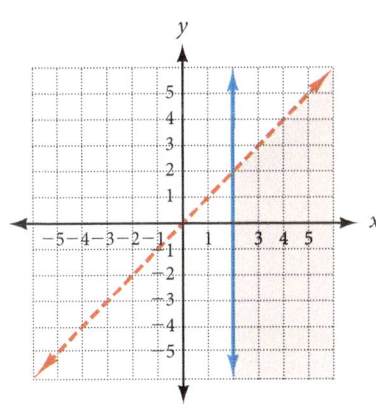

c.
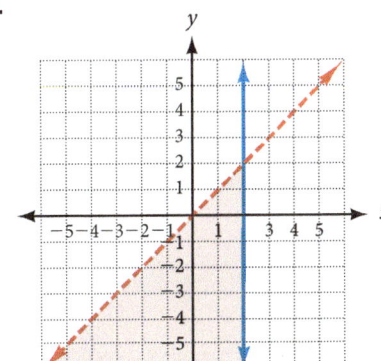

d.
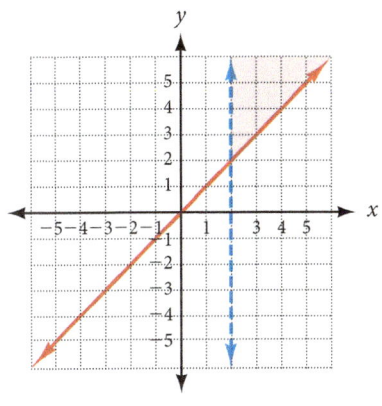

45. You need to purchase some cookies and cupcakes for an office party. Cookies cost $1.25 each and cupcakes cost $1.75 each. You can spend at most $100 and need at least twice as many cookies as cupcakes. Which system of linear inequalities describes all the possibilities?

a. $x + y \leq 100$

$\qquad 1.25x \geq 1.75y + 2$

$\qquad x \geq 0$

$\qquad y \geq 0$

b. $2x + y \leq 100$

$\qquad 1.25x \geq 1.75y$

$\qquad x \geq 0$

$\qquad y \geq 0$

c. $1.25x + 1.75y \leq 100$

$\qquad x \geq 2y$

$\qquad x \geq 0$

$\qquad y \geq 0$

d. $1.25x + 1.75y \leq 100$

$\qquad y \geq 2x$

$\qquad x \geq 0$

$\qquad y \geq 0$

Maintaining Your Skills

Solve each equation.

46. $5 - \dfrac{4}{7}a = -11$

47. $\dfrac{1}{5}x - \dfrac{1}{2} - \dfrac{1}{10}x + \dfrac{2}{5} = \dfrac{3}{10}x + \dfrac{1}{2}$

48. $5(x - 1) - 2(2x + 3) = 5x - 4$

49. $0.07 - 0.02(3x + 1) = -0.04x + 0.01$

Solve the following inequalities. Write the solution set using interval notation.

50. $-5t \leq 30$

51. $5 - \dfrac{3}{2}x > -1$

52. $1.6x - 2 < 0.8x + 2.8$

53. $3(2y + 4) \geq 5(y - 8)$

Solve the following equations.

54. $\left| \dfrac{1}{4}x - 1 \right| = \dfrac{1}{2}$

55. $\left| \dfrac{2}{3}a + 4 \right| = 6$

56. $|3 - 2x| + 5 = 2$

57. $5 = |3y + 6| - 4$

Definitions [3.1]

EXAMPLES

1. The solution to the system
$$x + 2y = 4$$
$$x - y = 1$$
is the ordered pair (2, 1). It is the only ordered pair that satisfies both equations.

1. A *system of linear equations*, as the term is used in this book, is two linear equations that each contain the same two variables.

2. The *solution set* for a system of equations is the set of all ordered pairs that satisfy *both* equations. The solution set to a system of linear equations will contain:

Case I   One ordered pair when the graphs of the two equations intersect at only one point (this is the most common situation)

Case II   No ordered pairs when the graphs of the two equations are parallel lines

Case III   An infinite number of ordered pairs when the graphs of the two equations coincide (are the same line)

Strategy for Solving a System by Graphing [3.1]

2. Solving the system in Example 1 by graphing looks like

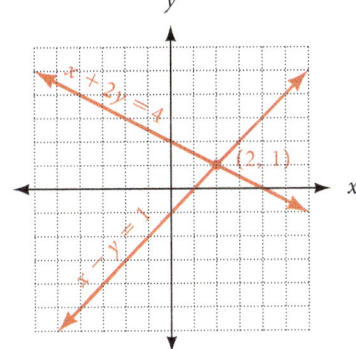

Step 1:   Graph the first equation.

Step 2:   Graph the second equation on the same set of axes.

Step 3:   Read the coordinates of the point where the graphs cross each other (the coordinates of the point of intersection).

Step 4:   Check the solution to see that it satisfies *both* equations.

Strategy for Solving a System by the Elimination Method [3.2]

3. We can eliminate the *y* variable from the system in Example 1 by multiplying both sides of the second equation by 2 and adding the result to the first equation

$$
\begin{array}{ll}
x + 2y = 4 & \quad x + 2y = 4 \\
x - y = 1 \xrightarrow{\text{Multiply by 2}} & \underline{2x - 2y = 2} \\
& \quad 3x \qquad = 6 \\
& \quad x \qquad = 2
\end{array}
$$

Substituting $x = 2$ into either of the original two equations gives $y = 1$. The solution is (2, 1).

Step 1:   Look the system over to decide which variable will be easier to eliminate.

Step 2:   Use the multiplication property of equality on each equation separately to ensure that the coefficients of the variable to be eliminated are opposites.

Step 3:   Add the left and right sides of the system produced in step 2, and solve the resulting equation.

Step 4:   Substitute the solution from step 3 back into any equation with both *x* and *y* variables, and solve.

Step 5:   Check your solution in both equations, if necessary.

Strategy for Solving a System by the Substitution Method [3.3]

4. We can apply the substitution method to the system in Example 1 by first solving the second equation for x to get $x = y + 1$. Substituting this expression for x into the first equation, we have

$$(y + 1) + 2y = 4$$
$$3y + 1 = 4$$
$$3y = 3$$
$$y = 1$$

Using $y = 1$ in either of the original equations gives $x = 2$.

Step 1: Solve either of the equations for one of the variables (this step is not necessary if one of the equations has the correct form already).

Step 2: Substitute the results of step 1 into the other equation, and solve.

Step 3: Substitute the results of step 2 into an equation with both x and y variables, and solve. (The equation produced in step 1 is usually a good one to use.)

Step 4: Check your solution, if necessary.

Special Cases [3.1, 3.2, 3.3]

In some cases, using the elimination or substitution method eliminates both variables. The situation is interpreted as follows.

1. If the resulting statement is *false*, then the lines are parallel and there is no solution to the system.

2. If the resulting statement is *true*, then the equations represent the same line (the lines coincide). In this case any ordered pair that satisfies either equation is a solution to the system.

> ### ⚠️ *Common Mistake*
>
> The most common mistake encountered in solving linear systems is the failure to complete the problem. Here is an example.
>
> $$x + y = 8$$
> $$x - y = 4$$
> $$2x = 12$$
> $$x = 6$$
>
> This is only half the solution. To find the other half, we must substitute the 6 back into one of the original equations and then solve for y.
>
> Remember, solutions to systems of linear equations always consist of ordered pairs. We need an x-coordinate and a y-coordinate; $x = 6$ can never be a solution to a system of linear equations.

Inconsistent and Dependent Equations [3.4]

5. If the two lines are parallel, then the system will be inconsistent and the solution is $\varnothing$. If the two lines coincide, then the equations are dependent.

A system of two linear equations that have no solutions in common is said to be an *inconsistent* system, whereas two linear equations that have all their solutions in common are said to be *dependent* equations.

Matrix Solutions [3.5]

A *matrix* is written as a rectangular array of $m \times n$ real numbers with m rows and n columns, and is used to display and solve a system of equations.

Determinants [3.6]

2×2 determinant: $\quad \begin{vmatrix} a & c \\ b & d \end{vmatrix} = ad - bc$

3×3 determinant: $\quad \begin{vmatrix} a_1 & b_1 & c_1 \\ a_2 & b_2 & c_2 \\ a_3 & b_3 & c_3 \end{vmatrix} = a_1 b_2 c_3 + a_3 b_1 c_2 + a_2 b_3 c_1$
$$- a_3 b_2 c_1 - a_1 b_3 c_2 - a_2 b_1 c_3$$

Applications [3.7]

Step 1: *Read* the problem, and then mentally *list* the items that are known and the items that are unknown.

Step 2: *Assign variables* to each of the unknown items. That is, let $x =$ one of the unknown items and $y =$ the other unknown item (and $z =$ the third unknown item, if there is a third one). Then *translate* the other *information* in the problem to expressions involving the two (or three) variables.

Step 3: *Reread* the problem, and then *write a system of equations*, using the items and variables listed in steps 1 and 2, that describes the situation.

Step 4: *Solve the system* found in step 3.

Step 5: *Write your answers* using complete sentences.

Step 6: *Reread* the problem, and *check* your solution with the original words in the problem.

Break-even Point $\quad R(x) = C(x) \quad$ [revenue = cost]

Equilibrium Point $\quad s(p) = d(p) \quad$ [supply = demand]

9. The graph of

$$x - y \leq 3$$

is

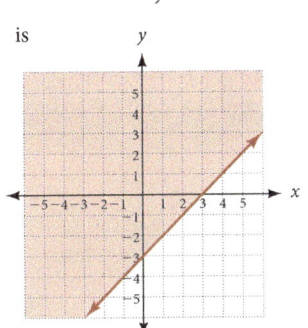

Linear Inequalities in Two Variables [3.8]

An inequality of the form $ax + by < c$ is a *linear inequality in two variables*. The equation for the boundary of the solution set is given by $ax + by = c$. (This equation is found by simply replacing the inequality symbol with an equal sign.)

To graph a linear inequality, first graph the boundary, using a solid line if the boundary is included in the solution set and a broken line if the boundary is not included in the solution set. Next, choose any point not on the boundary and substitute its coordinates into the original inequality. If the resulting statement is true, the graph lies on the same side of the boundary as the test point. A false statement indicates that the solution set lies on the other side of the boundary.

Systems of Linear Inequalities [3.8]

A system of linear inequalities is two or more linear inequalities considered at the same time. To find the solution set to the system, we graph each of the inequalities on the same coordinate system. The solution set is the region that is common to all the regions graphed.

 COMMON MISTAKE

A very common mistake in solving inequalities is to forget to reverse the direction of the inequality symbol when multiplying both sides by a negative number. When this mistake occurs, the graph of the solution set is always drawn on the wrong side of the endpoint.

Chapter 3 Test

1. Write the solution to the system which is graphed below. [3.1]

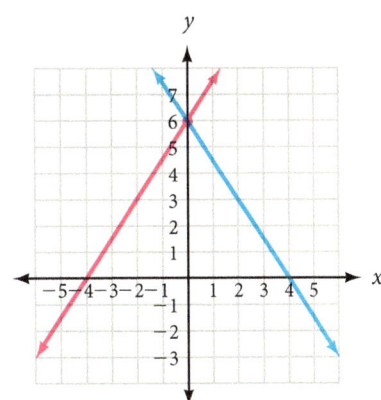

Solve each system by graphing. [3.1]

2. $4x - 2y = 8$
$y = \dfrac{2}{3}x$

3. $3x - 2y = 13$
$y = 4$

4. $2x - 2y = -12$
$-3x - y = 2$

Solve each system by the elimination method. [3.2]

5. $x - y = -9$
$2x + 3y = 7$

6. $3x - y = 1$
$5x - y = 3$

7. $2x + 3y = -3$
$x + 6y = 12$

8. $2x + 3y = 4$
$4x + 6y = 8$

Solve each system by the substitution method. [3.3]

9. $3x - y = 12$
$y = 2x - 8$

10. $3x + 6y = 3$
$x = 4y - 17$

11. $2x - 3y = -18$
$3x + y = -5$

12. $2x - 3y = 13$
$x - 4y = -1$

13. Solve the system using the elimination method. [3.4]
$x + 4y + 2z = 5$
$x - 2y - 4z = -3$
$4x - y - 2z = 2$

14. Solve the system using augmented matrices. [3.5]
$4x - y - 2z = -12$
$-3x - 6y + z = -5$
$-x + 5y + z = 13$

15. Find the determinant. [3.5]
$\begin{vmatrix} 3 & -5 \\ -2 & 4 \end{vmatrix}$

16. Find the determinant. [3.5]
$\begin{vmatrix} 1 & 2 & 3 \\ 4 & 5 & 6 \\ 7 & 8 & 9 \end{vmatrix}$

Solve the system using Cramer's rule. [3.6]

17. $4x - 2y = 5$
$3x + 5y = 11$

Solve each word problem. [3.7]

18. **Number Problem** A number is 2 more than half another. Their sum is 8. Find the two numbers.

19. **Investing** Ralph owes three times as much money on a credit card with a 17% annual interest rate as he does at 13%. If he owes a total of $768 in interest for 1 year, how much does he owe at each rate?

20. **Ticket Cost** There were 890 tickets sold for a baseball game for a total of $11,750. If adult tickets cost $15.00 and children's tickets cost $5.00, how many of each kind were sold?

21. **Speed of a Boat** A boat can travel 36 miles downstream in 4 hours. The same boat can travel 33 miles upstream in 11 hours. What is the speed of the boat in still water, and what is the speed of the current?

22. **Coin Problem** A collection of nickels, dimes, and quarters consists of 8 coins with a total value of $1.05. If the number of nickels is equal to the number of quarters and dimes together, how many of each coin are in the collection?

Graph the following linear inequalities. [8.8]

23. $3x - 4y < 12$

24. $y \le -x + 2$

Graph the solution set for each system of linear inequalities. [8.8]

25. $\quad x + 4y \le \quad 4$
$\quad -3x + 2y > -12$

26. $x + y \le -3$
$\quad y \ge \quad 2 - x$

27. $y < -\dfrac{1}{2}x + 4$
$\quad x \ge \quad 0$
$\quad y \ge \quad 0$

Exponents and Polynomials

4

iStockphoto.com © RomoloTavani

If you were given a penny on the first day of September, and then each day after that you were given twice the amount of money you received the day before, how much money would you receive on September 30th? To begin, Table 1 and Figure 1 show the amount of money you would receive on each of the first 10 days of the month. As you can see, on the tenth day of the month you would receive $5.12.

TABLE 1

Money That Doubles Each Day

Day	Money (in cents)
1	$1 = 2^0$
2	$2 = 2^1$
3	$4 = 2^2$
4	$8 = 2^3$
5	$16 = 2^4$
6	$32 = 2^5$
7	$64 = 2^6$
8	$128 = 2^7$
9	$256 = 2^8$
10	$512 = 2^9$

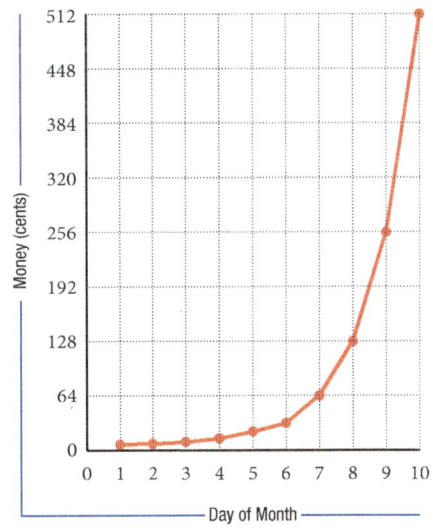

To find the amount of money on day 30, we could continue to double the amount on each of the next 20 days. Or, we could notice the pattern of exponents in the second column of the table and reason that the amount of money on day 30 would be 2^{29} cents, which is a very large number. In fact, 2^{29} cents is $5,368,709.12—a little less than $5.4 million. When you are finished with this chapter, you will have a good working knowledge of exponents.

Study Skills

The study skills for this chapter cover the way you approach new situations in mathematics. The first study skill is a point of view you hold about your natural instincts for what does and doesn't work in mathematics. The second study skill gives you a way of testing your instincts.

1. **Don't Let Your Intuition Fool You** As you become more experienced and more successful in mathematics you will be able to trust your mathematical intuition. For now, though, it can get in the way of your success. For example, if you ask some students to "subtract 3 from -5" they will answer -2 or 2. Both answers are incorrect, even though they may seem intuitively true. Likewise, some students will expand $(a + b)^2$ and arrive at $a^2 + b^2$, which is incorrect. In both cases, intuition leads directly to the wrong answer.

2. **Test Properties of Which You are Unsure** From time to time, you will be in a situation where you would like to apply a property or rule, but you are not sure it is true. You can always test a property or statement by substituting numbers for variables. For instance, I always have students that rewrite $(x + 3)^2$ as $x^2 + 9$, thinking that the two expressions are equivalent. The fact that the two expressions are not equivalent becomes obvious when we substitute 10 for x in each one.

   When $x = 10$, the expression $(x + 3)^2$ is $(10 + 3)^2 = 13^2 = 169$

   When $x = 10$, the expression $x^2 + 9 = 10^2 + 9 = 100 + 9 = 109$

When you test the equivalence of expressions by substituting numbers for the variable, make it easy on yourself by choosing numbers that are easy to work with, such as 10. Don't try to verify the equivalence of expressions by substituting 0, 1, or 2 for the variable, as using these numbers will occasionally give you false results.

It is not good practice to trust your intuition or instincts in every new situation in algebra. If you have any doubt about the generalizations you are making, test them by replacing variables with numbers and simplifying.

Multiplication with Exponents

Recall that an *exponent* is a number written just above and to the right of another number, which is called the *base*. In the expression 5^2, for example, the exponent is 2 and the base is 5. The expression 5^2 is read "5 to the second power" or "5 squared." The meaning of the expression is

$$5^2 = 5 \cdot 5 = 25$$

In the expression 5^3, the exponent is 3 and the base is 5. The expression 5^3 is read "5 to the third power" or "5 cubed." The meaning of the expression is

$$5^3 = 5 \cdot 5 \cdot 5 = 125$$

Here are some further examples.

Video Examples

Section 4.1

Example 1   Write each expression as a single number.

a. 4^3 **b.** -3^4 **c.** $(-2)^5$ **d.** $\left(-\dfrac{3}{4}\right)^2$

SOLUTION

a. $4^3 = 4 \cdot 4 \cdot 4 = 16 \cdot 4 = 64$ Exponent 3, base 4

b. $-3^4 = -3 \cdot 3 \cdot 3 \cdot 3 = -81$ Exponent 4, base 3

c. $(-2)^5 = (-2)(-2)(-2)(-2)(-2) = -32$ Exponent 5, base -2

d. $\left(-\dfrac{3}{4}\right)^2 = \left(-\dfrac{3}{4}\right)\left(-\dfrac{3}{4}\right) = \dfrac{9}{16}$ Exponent 2, base $-\dfrac{3}{4}$

Question: In what way are $(-5)^2$ and -5^2 different?

Answer: In the first case, the base is -5. In the second case, the base is 5. The answer to the first is 25. The answer to the second is -25. Can you tell why? Would there be a difference in the answers if the exponent in each case were changed to 3?

We can simplify our work with exponents by developing some properties of exponents. We want to list the things we know are true about exponents and then use these properties to simplify expressions that contain exponents.

The first property of exponents applies to products with the same base. We can use the definition of exponents, as indicating repeated multiplication, to simplify expressions like $7^4 \cdot 7^2$.

$$7^4 \cdot 7^2 = (7 \cdot 7 \cdot 7 \cdot 7)(7 \cdot 7)$$
$$= (7 \cdot 7 \cdot 7 \cdot 7 \cdot 7 \cdot 7)$$
$$= 7^6 \qquad \text{Notice: } 4 + 2 = 6$$

As you can see, multiplication with the same base resulted in addition of exponents. We can summarize this result with the following property.

> **Property 1 for Exponents**
>
> If a is any real number and r and s are integers, then
>
> $$a^r \cdot a^s = a^{r+s}$$
>
> *In words:*   To multiply two expressions with the same base, add exponents and use the common base.

Here is an example using Property 1.

Example 2   Use Property 1 to simplify the following expressions. Leave your answers in terms of exponents:

a. $5^3 \cdot 5^6$ **b.** $x^7 \cdot x^8$ **c.** $3^4 \cdot 3^8 \cdot 3^5$

SOLUTION

a. $5^3 \cdot 5^6 = 5^{3+6} = 5^9$

b. $x^7 \cdot x^8 = x^{7+8} = x^{15}$

c. $3^4 \cdot 3^8 \cdot 3^5 = 3^{4+8+5} = 3^{17}$

Note In Example 2, notice that in each case the base in the original problem is the same base that appears in the answer and that it is written only once in the answer. A very common mistake that people make when they first begin to use Property 1 is to write a 2 in front of the base in the answer. For example, people making this mistake would get $2x^{15}$ or $(2x)^{15}$ as the result in Example 2. To avoid this mistake, you must be sure you understand the meaning of Property 1 exactly as it is written.

Another common type of expression involving exponents is one in which an expression containing an exponent is raised to another power. The expression $(5^3)^2$ is an example:

$$(5^3)^2 = (5^3)(5^3)$$
$$= 5^{3+3}$$
$$= 5^6 \qquad \text{Notice: } 3 \cdot 2 = 6$$

This result offers justification for the second property of exponents.

$[\Delta \neq \Sigma]$ Property 2 for Exponents

If a is any real number and r and s are integers, then

$$(a^r)^s = a^{r \cdot s}$$

In words: A power raised to another power is the base raised to the product of the powers

---

Example 3   Simplify the following expressions:

a. $(4^5)^6$ **b.** $(x^3)^5$

SOLUTION

a. $(4^5)^6 = 4^{5 \cdot 6} = 4^{30}$

b. $(x^3)^5 = x^{3 \cdot 5} = x^{15}$

The third property of exponents applies to expressions in which the product of two or more numbers or variables is raised to a power. Let's look at how the expression $(2x)^3$ can be simplified:

$$(2x)^3 = (2x)(2x)(2x)$$
$$= (2 \cdot 2 \cdot 2)(x \cdot x \cdot x)$$
$$= 2^3 \cdot x^3 \qquad \text{Notice: The exponent 3 distributes}$$
$$\text{over the product } 2x$$
$$= 8x^3$$

We can generalize this result into a third property of exponents.

> ### ⟨Δ≠Σ⟩ *Property 3 for Exponents*
>
> If a and b are any two real numbers and r is an integer, then
>
> $$(ab)^r = a^r b^r$$
>
> *In words:* The power of a product is the product of the powers.

Here are some examples using Property 3 to simplify expressions.

Example 4 Simplify the following expressions:

a. $\left(-\dfrac{1}{4}x^2y^3\right)^2$ **b.** $(x^4)^3(x^2)^5$ **c.** $(2y)^3(3y^2)$ **d.** $(2x^2y^5)^3(3x^4y)^2$

SOLUTION

a. $\left(-\dfrac{1}{4}x^2y^3\right)^2 = \left(-\dfrac{1}{4}\right)^2(x^2)^2(y^3)^2$ *Property 3*

$\qquad\qquad = \dfrac{1}{16}x^4y^6$ *Property 2*

b. $(x^4)^3(x^2)^5 = x^{12} \cdot x^{10}$ *Property 2*

$\qquad\qquad = x^{22}$ *Property 1*

c. $(2y)^3(3y^2) = 2^3y^3(3y^2)$ *Property 3*

$\qquad\qquad = 8 \cdot 3(y^3 \cdot y^2)$ *Commutative and associative properties*

$\qquad\qquad = 24y^5$ *Property 1*

d. $(2x^2y^5)^3(3x^4y)^2 = 2^3(x^2)^3(y^5)^3 \cdot 3^2(x^4)^2y^2$ *Property 3*

$\qquad\qquad = 8x^6y^{15} \cdot 9x^8y^2$ *Property 2*

$\qquad\qquad = (8 \cdot 9)(x^6x^8)(y^{15}y^2)$ *Commutative and associative properties*

$\qquad\qquad = 72x^{14}y^{17}$ *Property 1*

> **Note** If we include units with the dimensions of the diagrams, then the units for the area will be square units and the units for volume will be cubic units. More specifically,
>
> If a square has a side 5 inches long, then its area will be
> $$A = (5 \text{ inches})^2 = 25 \text{ inches}^2$$
> where the unit inches² stands for square inches.
>
> If a cube has a single side 5 inches long, then its volume will be
> $$V = (5 \text{ inches})^3 = 125 \text{ inches}^3$$
> where the unit inches³ stands for cubic inches.
>
> If a rectangular solid has a length of 5 inches, a width of 4 inches, and a height of 3 inches, then its volume is
> $$V = (5 \text{ in.})(4 \text{ in.})(3 \text{ in.})$$
> $$= 60 \text{ inches}^3$$

⟨Ⓐ⟩ *Volume of a Rectangular Solid*

It is easy to see why the phrase "five squared" is associated with the expression 5^2. Simply find the area of the square shown in Figure 1 with a side of 5.

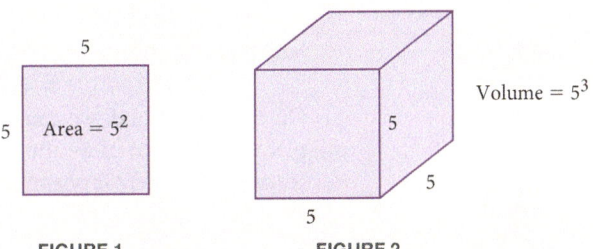

FIGURE 1   FIGURE 2

To see why the phrase "five cubed" is associated with the expression 5^3, we have to find the *volume* of a cube for which all three dimensions are 5 units long. The volume of a cube is a measure of the space occupied by the cube. To calculate the volume of the cube shown in Figure 2, we multiply the three dimensions together to get $5 \cdot 5 \cdot 5 = 5^3$.

The cube shown in Figure 2 is a special case of a general category of three dimensional geometric figures called *rectangular solids*. Rectangular solids have rectangles for sides, and all connecting sides meet at right angles. The three dimensions are length, width, and height. To find the volume of a rectangular solid, we find the product of the three dimensions.

Scientific Notation

Many branches of science require working with very large numbers. In astronomy, for example, distances commonly are given in light-years. A light-year is the distance light travels in a year. It is approximately

$$5{,}880{,}000{,}000{,}000 \text{ miles}$$

This number is difficult to use in calculations because of the number of zeros it contains. Scientific notation provides a way of writing very large numbers in a more manageable form.

> (děf'   *scientific notation*
>
> A number is in *scientific notation* when it is written as the product of a number between 1 and 10 and an integer power of 10. A number written in scientific notation has the form
>
> $$n \times 10^r$$
>
> where $1 \le n < 10$ and $r =$ an integer.

Example 5   Write 376,000 in scientific notation.

SOLUTION   We must rewrite 376,000 as the product of a number between 1 and 10 and a power of 10. To do so, we move the decimal point 5 places to the left so that it appears between the 3 and the 7. Then we multiply this number by 10^5. The number that results has the same value as our original number and is written in scientific notation:

$$376{,}000 = 3.76 \times 10^5$$

Moved 5 places.

Decimal point originally here.

Keeps track of the 5 places we moved the decimal point.

Example 6   Write 4.52×10^3 in expanded form.

SOLUTION   Since 10^3 is 1,000, we can think of this as simply a multiplication problem; that is,

$$4.52 \times 10^3 = 4.52 \times 1{,}000 = 4{,}520$$

On the other hand, we can think of the exponent 3 as indicating the number of places we need to move the decimal point to write our number in expanded form. Since our exponent is positive 3, we move the decimal point three places to the right:

$$4.52 \times 10^3 = 4{,}520$$

Getting Ready for Class

After reading through the preceding section, respond in your own words and in complete sentences.

A. Explain the difference between -5^2 and $(-5)2$.

B. How do you multiply two expressions containing exponents when they each have the same base?

C. What is Property 2 for exponents?

D. When is a number written in scientific notation?

Name the base and exponent in each of the following expressions. Then use the definition of exponents as repeated multiplication to simplify.

1. 4^2
2. 6^2
3. $(0.3)^2$
4. $(0.03)^2$
5. 4^3
6. 10^3

7. $(-5)^2$
8. -5^2
9. -2^3
10. $(-2)^3$
11. 3^4
12. $(-3)^4$

13. $\left(\dfrac{2}{3}\right)^2$
14. $\left(\dfrac{2}{3}\right)^3$
15. $\left(\dfrac{1}{2}\right)^4$
16. $\left(\dfrac{4}{5}\right)^2$

17. a. Complete the following table.

Number x	1	2	3	4	5	6	7
Square x^2							

  b. Using the results of part **a**, fill in the blank in the following statement: For numbers larger than 1, the square of the number is _____ than the number.

18. a. Complete the following table.

Number x	$\dfrac{1}{2}$	$\dfrac{1}{3}$	$\dfrac{1}{4}$	$\dfrac{1}{5}$	$\dfrac{1}{6}$	$\dfrac{1}{7}$	$\dfrac{1}{8}$
Square x^2							

  b. Using the results of part **a**, fill in the blank in the following statement: For numbers between 0 and 1, the square of the number is _____ than the number.

Use Property 1 to simplify the following expressions.

19. $x^4 \cdot x^5$
20. $x^7 \cdot x^3$
21. $y^{10} \cdot y^{20}$

22. $y^{30} \cdot y^{30}$
23. $2^5 \cdot 2^4 \cdot 2^3$
24. $4^2 \cdot 4^3 \cdot 4^4$

25. $x^4 \cdot x^6 \cdot x^8 \cdot x^{10}$
26. $x^{20} \cdot x^{18} \cdot x^{16} \cdot x^{14}$

Use Property 2 for exponents to write each of the following problems with a single exponent. (Assume all variables are positive numbers.)

27. $(x^2)^5$
28. $(x^5)^2$
29. $(5^4)^3$
30. $(5^3)^4$
31. $(y^3)^3$
32. $(y^2)^2$

33. $(2^5)^{10}$
34. $(10^5)^2$
35. $(a^3)^x$
36. $(a^5)^x$
37. $(b^x)^y$
38. $(b^r)^s$

Use Property 3 for exponents to simplify each of the following expressions.

39. $(4x)^2$
40. $(2x)^4$
41. $(2y)^5$
42. $(5y)^2$

43. $(-3x)^4$
44. $(-3x)^3$
45. $(0.5ab)^2$
46. $(0.4ab)^2$

47. $(4xyz)^3$
48. $(5xyz)^3$

Simplify the following expressions by using the properties of exponents.

49. $(2x^4)^3$
50. $(3x^5)^2$
51. $(4a^3)^2$
52. $(5a^2)^2$

53. $(x^2)^3(x^4)^2$
54. $(x^5)^2(x^3)^5$
55. $(a^3)^1(a^2)^4$
56. $(a^4)^1(a^1)^3$

57. $(2x)^3(2x)^4$ **58.** $(3x)^2(3x)^3$ **59.** $(3x^2)^3(2x)^4$ **60.** $(3x)^3(2x^3)^2$

61. $(4x^2y^3)^2$ **62.** $(9x^3y^5)^2$ **63.** $\left(\frac{2}{3}a^4b^5\right)^3$ **64.** $\left(\frac{3}{4}ab^7\right)^3$

65. Complete the following table, and then construct a line graph of the information in the table

Number x	−3	−2	−1	0	1	2	3
Square x^2							

66. Complete the table, and then construct a line graph of the information in the table.

Number x	−3	−2	−1	0	1	2	3
Cube x^3							

67. Complete the table. When you are finished, notice how the points in this table could be used to refine the line graph you created in Problem 65.

Number x	−2.5	−1.5	−0.5	0	0.5	1.5	2.5
Square x^2							

68. Complete the following table. When you are finished, notice that this table contains exactly the same entries as the table from Problem 67. This table uses fractions, whereas the table from Problem 67 uses decimals.

Number x	$-\frac{5}{2}$	$-\frac{3}{2}$	$-\frac{1}{2}$	0	$\frac{1}{2}$	$\frac{3}{2}$	$\frac{5}{2}$
Square x^2							

Write each number in scientific notation.

69. 43,200   **70.** 432,000   **71.** 570

72. 5,700   **73.** 238,000   **74.** 2,380,000

Write each number in expanded form.

75. 2.49×10^3 **76.** 2.49×10^4 **77.** 3.52×10^2

78. 3.52×10^5 **79.** 2.8×10^4 **80.** 2.8×10^3

Applying the Concepts

81. Volume of a Cube Find the volume of a cube if each side is 3 inches long.

82. Volume of a Cube Find the volume of a cube if each side is 3 feet long.

83. Volume of a Cube A bottle of perfume is packaged in a box that is in the shape of a cube. Find the volume of the box if each side is 2.5 inches long. Round to the nearest tenth.

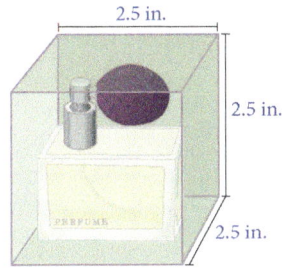

2.5 in.

2.5 in.

2.5 in.

84. Volume of a Cube A television set is packaged in a box that is in the shape of a cube. Find the volume of the box if each side is 18 inches long.

85. Volume of a Box A rented videotape is in a plastic container that has the shape of a rectangular solid. Find the volume of the container if the length is 8 inches, the width is 4.5 inches, and the height is 1 inch.

86. Volume of a Box Your textbook is in the shape of a rectangular solid. Find the volume in cubic inches.

87. Volume of a Box If a box has a volume of 42 cubic feet, is it possible for you to fit inside the box? Explain your answer.

88. Volume of a Box A box has a volume of 45 cubic inches. Will a can of soup fit inside the box? Explain your answer.

89. Age in seconds If you are 21 years old, you have been alive for more than 650,000,000 seconds. Write this last number in scientific notation.

90. Distance Around the Earth The distance around the Earth at the equator is more than 130,000,000 feet. Write this number in scientific notation.

91. Heart Beats per Year If your pulse is 72, then in one year your heart will beat at least 3.78×10^7 times. Write this last number in expanded form.

92. Investing If you put $1,000 into a savings account every year from the time you are 25 years old until you are 55 years old, you will have more than 1.8×10^5 dollars in the account when you reach 55 years of age (assuming 10% annual interest). Write 1.8×10^5 in expanded form.

93. Investing If you put $20 into a savings account every month from the time you are 20 years old until you are 30 years old, you will have more than 3.27×10^3 dollars in the account when you reach 30 years of age (assuming 6% annual interest compounded monthly). Write 3.27×10^3 in expanded form.

Displacement The displacement, in cubic inches, of a car engine is given by the formula

$$d = \pi \cdot s \cdot c \cdot \left(\frac{1}{2} \cdot b\right)^2$$

where s is the stroke and b is the bore, as shown in the figure, and c is the number of cylinders.

Calculate the engine displacement for each of the following cars. Use 3.14 to approximate π.

94. Ferrari Modena 8 cylinders, 3.35 inches of bore, 3.11 inches of stroke

95. Audi A8 8 cylinders, 3.32 inches of bore, 3.66 inches of stroke

96. Mitsubishi Eclipse 6 cylinders, 3.59 inches of bore, 2.99 inches of stroke

97. Porsche 911 GT3 6 cylinders, 3.94 inches of bore, 3.01 inches of stroke

Getting Ready for the Next Section

Subtract.

98. $4 - 7$

99. $-4 - 7$

100. $4 - (-7)$

101. $-4 - (-7)$

102. $15 - 20$

103. $15 - (-20)$

104. $-15 - (-20)$

105. $-15 - 20$

106. $2(3) - 4$

107. $5(3) - 10$

108. $4(3) - 3(2)$

109. $-8 - 2(3)$

110. $2(5 - 3)$

111. $2(3) - 4 - 3(-4)$

112. $5 + 4(-2) - 2(-3)$

113. $2(3) + 4(5) - 5(2)$

Division with Exponents

In Section 4.1 we found that multiplication with the same base results in addition of exponents; that is, $a^r \cdot a^s = a^{r+s}$. Since division is the inverse operation of multiplication, we can expect division with the same base to result in subtraction of exponents.

To develop the properties for exponents under division, we again apply the definition of exponents:

$$\frac{x^5}{x^3} = \frac{x \cdot x \cdot x \cdot x \cdot x}{x \cdot x \cdot x} \qquad \frac{2^4}{2^7} = \frac{2 \cdot 2 \cdot 2 \cdot 2}{2 \cdot 2 \cdot 2 \cdot 2 \cdot 2 \cdot 2 \cdot 2}$$

$$= \frac{x \cdot x \cdot x}{x \cdot x \cdot x}(x \cdot x) \qquad = \frac{2 \cdot 2 \cdot 2 \cdot 2}{2 \cdot 2 \cdot 2 \cdot 2} \cdot \frac{1}{2 \cdot 2 \cdot 2}$$

$$= 1(x \cdot x) \qquad\qquad = \frac{1}{2 \cdot 2 \cdot 2}$$

$$= x^2 \quad \text{Notice: } 5 - 3 = 2 \qquad = \frac{1}{2^3} \quad \text{Notice: } 7 - 4 = 3$$

In both cases division with the same base resulted in subtraction of the smaller exponent from the larger. The problem is deciding whether the answer is a fraction. The problem is resolved easily by the following definition.

> **(dĕf) _negative exponents_**
>
> If r is a positive integer, then $a^{-r} = \dfrac{1}{a^r} = \left(\dfrac{1}{a}\right)^r \qquad (a \neq 0)$

The following examples illustrate how we use this definition to simplify expressions that contain negative exponents.

Video Examples

Section 4.2

Example 1 Write each expression with a positive exponent and then simplify:

a. 2^{-3} **b.** 5^{-2} **c.** $3x^{-6}$

SOLUTION

a. $2^{-3} = \dfrac{1}{2^3} = \dfrac{1}{8}$ Notice: Negative exponents do not indicate negative numbers. They indicate reciprocals

b. $5^{-2} = \dfrac{1}{5^2} = \dfrac{1}{25}$

c. $3x^{-6} = 3 \cdot \dfrac{1}{x^6} = \dfrac{3}{x^6}$

Now let us look back to our original problem and try to work it again with the help of a negative exponent. We know that $\frac{2^4}{2^7} = \frac{1}{2^3}$. Let us decide now that with division of the same base, we will always subtract the exponent in the denominator from the exponent in the numerator and see if this conflicts with what we know is true.

$$\frac{2^4}{2^7} = 2^{4-7} \quad \text{Subtracting the bottom exponent from the top exponent}$$

$$= 2^{-3} \quad \text{Subtraction}$$

$$= \frac{1}{2^3} \quad \text{Definition of negative exponents}$$

Subtracting the exponent in the denominator from the exponent in the numerator and then using the definition of negative exponents gives us the same result we obtained previously. We can now continue the list of properties of exponents we started in Section 4.1.

⟨Δ≠Σ⟩   Property 4 for Exponents

If a is any real number and r and s are integers, then

$$\frac{a^r}{a^s} = a^{r-s} \qquad (a \neq 0)$$

In words: To divide with the same base, subtract the exponent in the denominator from the exponent in the numerator and raise the base to the exponent that results.

The following examples show how we use Property 4 and the definition for negative exponents to simplify expressions involving division.

Example 2   Simplify the following expressions:

a. $\dfrac{x^9}{x^6}$ **b.** $\dfrac{x^4}{x^{10}}$ **c.** $\dfrac{2^{15}}{2^{20}}$

SOLUTION

a. $\dfrac{x^9}{x^6} = x^{9-6} = x^3$

b. $\dfrac{x^4}{x^{10}} = x^{4-10} = x^{-6} = \dfrac{1}{x^6}$

c. $\dfrac{2^{15}}{2^{20}} = 2^{15-20} = 2^{-5} = \dfrac{1}{2^5} = \dfrac{1}{32}$ ■

Our final property of exponents is similar to Property 3 from Section 4.1, but it involves division instead of multiplication. After we have stated the property, we will give a proof of it. The proof shows why this property is true.

⟨Δ≠Σ⟩   Property 5 for Exponents

If a and b are any two real numbers ($b \neq 0$) and r is an integer, then

$$\left(\frac{a}{b}\right)^r = \frac{a^r}{b^r}$$

In words: A quotient raised to a power is the quotient of the powers.

Proof

$$\left(\frac{a}{b}\right)^r = \left(a \cdot \frac{1}{b}\right)^r \qquad \text{By the definition of division}$$

$$= a^r \cdot \left(\frac{1}{b}\right)^r \qquad \text{By Property 3}$$

$$= a^r \cdot b^{-r} \qquad \text{By the definition of negative exponents}$$

$$= a^r \cdot \frac{1}{b^r} \qquad \text{By the definition of negative exponents}$$

$$= \frac{a^r}{b^r} \qquad \text{By the definition of division}$$

Example 3   Simplify the following expressions.

a. $\left(\dfrac{x}{2}\right)^3$ **b.** $\left(\dfrac{5}{y}\right)^2$ **c.** $\left(\dfrac{2}{3}\right)^4$

SOLUTION

a. $\left(\dfrac{x}{2}\right)^3 = \dfrac{x^3}{2^3} = \dfrac{x^3}{8}$

b. $\left(\dfrac{5}{y}\right)^2 = \dfrac{5^2}{y^2} = \dfrac{25}{y^2}$

c. $\left(\dfrac{2}{3}\right)^4 = \dfrac{2^4}{3^4} = \dfrac{16}{81}$

Zero and One as Exponents

We have two special exponents left to deal with before our rules for exponents are complete: 0 and 1. To obtain an expression for x^1, we will solve a problem two different ways:

$$\left. \begin{array}{l} \dfrac{x^3}{x^2} = \dfrac{x \cdot x \cdot x}{x \cdot x} = x \\[2em] \dfrac{x^3}{x^2} = x^{3-2} = x^1 \end{array} \right\} \quad \text{Hence } x^1 = x$$

Stated generally, this rule says that $a^1 = a$. This seems reasonable and we will use it since it is consistent with our property of division using the same base.

We use the same procedure to obtain an expression for x^0:

$$\left. \begin{array}{l} \dfrac{5^2}{5^2} = \dfrac{25}{25} = 1 \\[2em] \dfrac{5^2}{5^2} = 5^{2-2} = 5^0 \end{array} \right\} \quad \text{Hence } 5^0 = 1$$

It seems, therefore, that the best definition of x^0 is 1 for all x except $x = 0$. In the case of $x = 0$, we have 0^0, which we will not define. This definition will probably seem awkward at first. Most people would like to define x^0 as 0 when they first encounter it. Remember, the zero in this expression is an exponent, so x^0 does not mean to multiply by zero. Thus, we can make the general statement that $a^0 = 1$ for all real numbers except $a = 0$.

Here are some examples involving the exponents 0 and 1.

Example 4   Simplify the following expressions:

a. 8^0 **b.** 8^1 **c.** $4^0 + 4^1$ **d.** $(2x^2 y)^0$

SOLUTION

a. $8^0 = 1$

b. $8^1 = 8$

c. $4^0 + 4^1 = 1 + 4 = 5$

d. $(2x^2 y)^0 = 1$

Here is a summary of the definitions and properties of exponents we have developed so far. For each definition or property in the list, a and b are real numbers, and r and s are integers.

Definitions	Properties
$a^{-r} = \dfrac{1}{a^r} = \left(\dfrac{1}{a}\right)^r \quad a \neq 0$	**1.** $a^r \cdot a^s = a^{r+s}$
$a^1 = a$	**2.** $(a^r)^s = a^{rs}$
$a^0 = 1 \quad a \neq 0$	**3.** $(ab)^r = a^r b^r$
	4. $\dfrac{a^r}{a^s} = a^{r-s} \quad a \neq 0$
	5. $\left(\dfrac{a}{b}\right)^r = \dfrac{a^r}{b^r} \quad b \neq 0$

Here are some additional examples. These examples use a combination of the preceding properties and definitions.

Examples   Simplify each expression. Write all answers with positive exponents only:

5. $\dfrac{(5x^3)^2}{x^4} = \dfrac{25x^6}{x^4}$ Properties 2 and 3

$\qquad\qquad = 25x^2$ Property 4

6. $\dfrac{x^{-8}}{(x^2)^3} = \dfrac{x^{-8}}{x^6}$ Property 2

$\qquad\qquad = x^{-8-6}$ Property 4

$\qquad\qquad = x^{-14}$ Subtraction

$\qquad\qquad = \dfrac{1}{x^{14}}$ Definition of negative exponents

7. $\left(\dfrac{y^5}{y^3}\right)^2 = \dfrac{(y^5)^2}{(y^3)^2}$ Property 5

$\qquad\qquad = \dfrac{y^{10}}{y^6}$ Property 2

$\qquad\qquad = y^4$ Property 4

Notice in Example 7 that we could have simplified inside the parentheses first and then raised the result to the second power:

$$\left(\dfrac{y^5}{y^3}\right)^2 = (y^2)^2 = y^4$$

8. $(3x^5)^{-2} = \dfrac{1}{(3x^5)^2}$ Definition of negative exponents

$\qquad\qquad = \dfrac{1}{9x^{10}}$ Properties 2 and 3

9. $x^{-8} \cdot x^5 = x^{-8+5}$ Property 1

$= x^{-3}$ Addition

$= \dfrac{1}{x^3}$ Definition of negative exponents

10. $\dfrac{(a^3)^2 a^{-4}}{(a^{-4})^3} = \dfrac{a^6 a^{-4}}{a^{-12}}$ Property 2

$= \dfrac{a^2}{a^{-12}}$ Property 1

$= a^{14}$ Property 4   ■

In the next two examples we use division to compare the area and volume of geometric figures.

■ **Example 11**   Suppose you have two squares, one of which is larger than the other. If the length of a side of the larger square is 3 times as long as the length of a side of the smaller square, how many of the smaller squares will it take to cover up the larger square?

SOLUTION   If we let x represent the length of a side of the smaller square, then the length of a side of the larger square is $3x$. The area of each square, along with a diagram of the situation, is given in Figure 1.

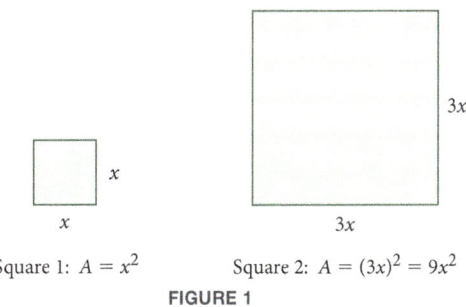

Square 1: $A = x^2$ Square 2: $A = (3x)^2 = 9x^2$

FIGURE 1

To find out how many smaller squares it will take to cover up the larger square, we divide the area of the larger square by the area of the smaller square.

$$\frac{\text{Area of square 2}}{\text{Area of square 1}} = \frac{9x^2}{x^2} = 9$$

It will take 9 of the smaller squares to cover the larger square.   ■

■ **Example 12**   Suppose you have two boxes, each of which is a cube. If the length of a side in the second box is 3 times as long as the length of a side of the first box, how many of the smaller boxes will fit inside the larger box?

SOLUTION   If we let x represent the length of a side of the smaller box, then the length of a side of the larger box is $3x$. The volume of each box, along with a diagram of the situation, is given in Figure 2.

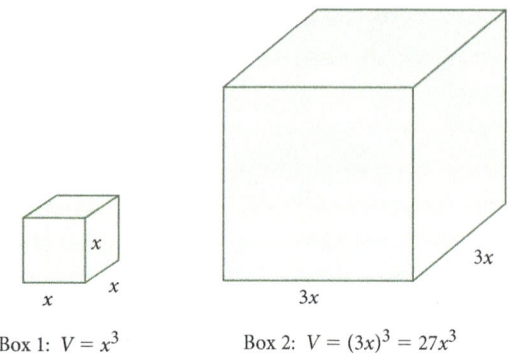

Box 1: $V = x^3$ Box 2: $V = (3x)^3 = 27x^3$

FIGURE 2

To find out how many smaller boxes will fit inside the larger box, we divide the volume of the larger box by the volume of the smaller box.

$$\frac{\text{Volume of box 2}}{\text{Volume of box 1}} = \frac{27x^3}{x^3} = 27$$

We can fit 27 of the smaller boxes inside the larger box.

More on Scientific Notation

Now that we have completed our list of definitions and properties of exponents, we can expand the work we did previously with scientific notation.

Recall that a number is in scientific notation when it is written in the form

$$n \times 10^r$$

where $1 \leq n < 10$ and r is an integer.

Since negative exponents give us reciprocals, we can use negative exponents to write very small numbers in scientific notation. For example, the number 0.00057, when written in scientific notation, is equivalent to 5.7×10^{-4}. Here's why:

$$5.7 \times 10^{-4} = 5.7 \times \frac{1}{10^4} = 5.7 \times \frac{1}{10,000} = \frac{5.7}{10,000} = 0.00057$$

The table below lists some other numbers in both scientific notation and expanded form.

Number Written the Long Way		Number Written Again in Scientific Notation
376,000	=	3.76×10^5
49,500	=	4.95×10^4
3,200	=	3.2×10^3
591	=	5.91×10^2
46	=	4.6×10^1
8	=	8×10^0
0.47	=	4.7×10^{-1}
0.093	=	9.3×10^{-2}
0.00688	=	6.88×10^{-3}
0.0002	=	2×10^{-4}
0.000098	=	9.8×10^{-5}

Notice that in each case, when the number is written in scientific notation, the decimal point in the first number is placed so that the number is between 1 and 10. The exponent on 10 in the second number keeps track of the number of places we moved the decimal point in the original number to get a number between 1 and 10:

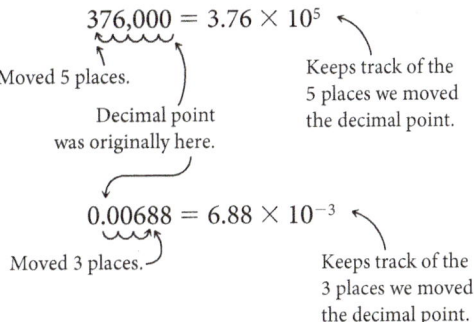

$$376,000 = 3.76 \times 10^5$$

Moved 5 places.

Decimal point was originally here.

Keeps track of the 5 places we moved the decimal point.

$$0.00688 = 6.88 \times 10^{-3}$$

Moved 3 places.

Keeps track of the 3 places we moved the decimal point.

Getting Ready for Class

After reading through the preceding section, respond in your own words and in complete sentences.

A. How do you divide two expressions containing exponents when they each have the same base?

B. Explain the difference between 3^2 and 3^{-2}.

C. If a positive base is raised to a negative exponent, can the result be a negative number?

D. Explain what happens when we use 0 as an exponent.

Problem Set 4.2

Simplify each expression.

1. 3^{-2} **2.** 3^{-3} **3.** 6^{-2} **4.** 2^{-6} **5.** 8^{-2} **6.** 3^{-4}

7. 5^{-3} **8.** 9^{-2} **9.** $2x^{-3}$ **10.** $5x^{-1}$ **11.** $(2x)^{-3}$ **12.** $(5x)^{-1}$

13. $(5y)^{-2}$ **14.** $5y^{-2}$ **15.** 10^{-2} **16.** 10^{-3}

17. Complete the following table.

Number x	Square x^2	Power of 2 2^x
-3		
-2		
-1		
0		
1		
2		
3		

18. Complete the following table.

Number x	Cube x^3	Power of 3 3^x
-3		
-2		
-1		
0		
1		
2		
3		

Use Property 4 to simplify each of the following expressions. Write all answers that contain exponents with positive exponents only.

19. $\dfrac{5^1}{5^3}$ **20.** $\dfrac{7^6}{7^8}$ **21.** $\dfrac{x^{10}}{x^4}$ **22.** $\dfrac{x^4}{x^{10}}$ **23.** $\dfrac{4^3}{4^0}$ **24.** $\dfrac{4^0}{4^3}$

25. $\dfrac{(2x)^7}{(2x)^4}$ **26.** $\dfrac{(2x)^4}{(2x)^7}$ **27.** $\dfrac{6^{11}}{6}$ **28.** $\dfrac{8^7}{8}$ **29.** $\dfrac{6}{6^{11}}$ **30.** $\dfrac{8}{8^7}$

31. $\dfrac{2^{-5}}{2^3}$ **32.** $\dfrac{2^{-5}}{2^{-3}}$ **33.** $\dfrac{2^5}{2^{-3}}$ **34.** $\dfrac{2^{-3}}{2^{-5}}$ **35.** $\dfrac{(3x)^{-5}}{(3x)^{-8}}$ **36.** $\dfrac{(2x)^{-10}}{(2x)^{-15}}$

Simplify the following expressions. Any answers that contain exponents should contain positive exponents only.

37. $(3xy)^4$ **38.** $(4xy)^3$ **39.** 10^0 **40.** 10^1

41. $(2a^2b)^1$ **42.** $(2a^2b)^0$ **43.** $(7y^3)^{-2}$ **44.** $(5y^4)^{-2}$

45. $x^{-3}x^{-5}$ **46.** $x^{-6} \cdot x^8$ **47.** $y^7 \cdot y^{-10}$ **48.** $y^{-4} \cdot y^{-6}$

49. $\dfrac{(x^2)^3}{x^4}$ **50.** $\dfrac{(x^5)^3}{x^{10}}$ **51.** $\dfrac{(a^4)^3}{(a^3)^2}$ **52.** $\dfrac{(a^5)^3}{(a^5)^2}$

53. $\dfrac{y^7}{(y^2)^8}$ **54.** $\dfrac{y^2}{(y^3)^4}$ **55.** $\left(\dfrac{y^7}{y^2}\right)^8$ **56.** $\left(\dfrac{y^2}{y^3}\right)^4$

57. $\dfrac{(x^{-2})^3}{x^{-5}}$ **58.** $\dfrac{(x^2)^{-3}}{x^{-5}}$ **59.** $\left(\dfrac{x^{-2}}{x^{-5}}\right)^3$ **60.** $\left(\dfrac{x^2}{x^{-5}}\right)^{-3}$

61. $\dfrac{(a^3)^2(a^4)^5}{(a^5)^2}$ **62.** $\dfrac{(a^4)^8(a^2)^5}{(a^3)^4}$ **63.** $\dfrac{(a^{-2})^3(a^4)^2}{(a^{-3})^{-2}}$ **64.** $\dfrac{(a^{-5})^{-3}(a^7)^{-1}}{(a^{-3})^5}$

65. Complete the following table, and then construct a line graph of the information in the table.

Number x	-3	-2 , -1	0	1	2	3
Power of 2 2^x						

66. Complete the following table, and then construct a line graph of the information in the table.

Number x	-3	-2	-1	0	1	2	3
Power of 3 3^x							

Write each of the following numbers in scientific notation.

67. 0.0048   **68.** 0.000048

69. 25   **70.** 35

71. 0.000009   **72.** 0.0009

73. Complete the following table.

Expanded Form	Scientific Notation $n \times 10^r$
0.000357	3.57×10^{-4}
0.00357	
0.0357	
0.357	
3.57	
35.7	
357	
3,570	
35,700	

74. Complete the following table.

	Scientific Notation
Expanded Form	$n \times 10^r$
0.000123	1.23×10^{-4}
	1.23×10^{-3}
	1.23×10^{-2}
	1.23×10^{-1}
	1.23×10^{0}
	1.23×10^{1}
	1.23×10^{2}
	1.23×10^{3}
	1.23×10^{4}

Write each of the following numbers in expanded form.

75. 4.23×10^{-3} **76.** 4.23×10^{3} **77.** 8×10^{-5}

78. 8×10^{5} **79.** 4.2×10^{0} **80.** 4.2×10^{1}

Applying the Concepts

Scientific Notation Problems

81. Some home computers can do a calculation in 2×10^{-3} seconds. Write this number in expanded form.

82. Some of the cells in the human body have a radius of 3×10^{-5} inches. Write this number in expanded form.

83. **Margin of Victory** Since 1993, the Nascar races with the smallest margin of victory are shown here.

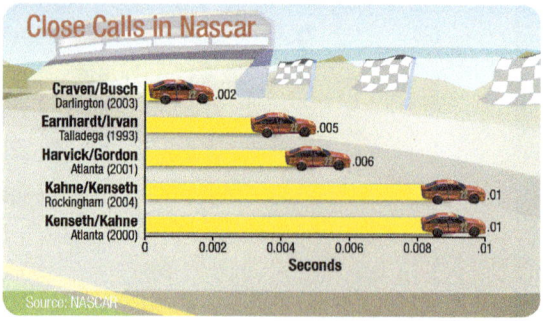

Write each number in scientific notation.

84. Some cameras used in scientific research can take one picture every 0.000000167 second. Write this number in scientific notation.

85. The number 25×10^{3} is not in scientific notation because 25 is larger than 10. Write 25×10^{3} in scientific notation.

86. The number 0.25×10^{3} is not in scientific notation because 0.25 is less than 1. Write 0.25×10^{3} in scientific notation.

87. The number 23.5×10^4 is not in scientific notation because 23.5 is not between 1 and 10. Rewrite 23.5×10^4 in scientific notation.

88. The number 375×10^3 is not in scientific notation because 375 is not between 1 and 10. Rewrite 375×10^3 in scientific notation.

89. The number 0.82×10^{-3} is not in scientific notation because 0.82 is not between 1 and 10. Rewrite 0.82×10^{-3} in scientific notation.

90. The number 0.93×10^{-2} is not in scientific notation because 0.93 is not between 1 and 10. Rewrite 0.93×10^{-2} in scientific notation.

Comparing Areas Suppose you have two squares, one of which is larger than the other. Suppose further that the side of the larger square is twice as long as the side of the smaller square.

91. If the length of the side of the smaller square is 10 inches, give the area of each square. Then find the number of smaller squares it will take to cover the larger square.

92. How many smaller squares will it take to cover the larger square if the length of the side of the smaller square is 1 foot?

93. If the length of the side of the smaller square is x, find the area of each square. Then find the number of smaller squares it will take to cover the larger square.

94. Suppose the length of the side of the larger square is 1 foot. How many smaller squares will it take to cover the larger square?

Comparing Volumes Suppose you have two boxes, each of which is a cube. Suppose further that the length of a side of the second box is twice as long as the length of a side of the first box.

95. If the length of a side of the first box is 6 inches, give the volume of each box. Then find the number of smaller boxes that will fit inside the larger box.

96. How many smaller boxes can be placed inside the larger box if the length of a side of the second box is 1 foot?

97. If the length of a side of the first box is x, find the volume of each box. Then find the number of smaller boxes that will fit inside the larger box.

98. Suppose the length of a side of the larger box is 12 inches. How many smaller boxes will fit inside the larger box?

Getting Ready for the Next Section

Simplify.

99. $3(4.5)$

100. $\dfrac{1}{2} \cdot \dfrac{5}{7}$

101. $\dfrac{4}{5}(10)$

102. $\dfrac{9.6}{3}$

103. $6.8(3.9)$

104. $9 - 20$

105. $-3 + 15$

106. $2x \cdot x \cdot \dfrac{1}{2}x$

107. $x^5 \cdot x^3$

108. $y^2 \cdot y$

109. $\dfrac{x^3}{(x^2)}$

110. $\dfrac{x^2}{x}$

111. $\dfrac{y^3}{y^5}$

112. $\dfrac{x^2}{x^5}$

Write in expanded form.

113. 3.4×10^2

114. 6.0×10^{-4}

Operations with Monomials

We have developed all the tools necessary to perform the four basic operations on the simplest of polynomials: monomials.

> **(dĕf** *monomial*
>
> A *monomial* is a one-term expression that is either a constant (number) or the product of a constant and one or more variables raised to whole number exponents.

The following are examples of monomials:

$$-3 \qquad 15x \qquad -23x^2y \qquad 49x^4y^2z^4 \qquad \frac{3}{4}a^2b^3$$

The numerical part of each monomial is called the **numerical coefficient**, or just *coefficient*. Monomials are also called **terms**.

Multiplication and Division of Monomials

There are two basic steps involved in the multiplication of monomials. First, we rewrite the products using the commutative and associative properties. Then, we simplify by multiplying coefficients and adding exponents of like bases.

Video Examples

Section 4.3

> **Example 1** Multiply:
>
> **a.** $(-3x^2)(4x^3)$ **b.** $\left(\frac{4}{5}x^5 \cdot y^2\right)(10x^3 \cdot y)$
>
> **SOLUTION**
>
> **a.** $(-3x^2)(4x^3) = (-3 \cdot 4)(x^2 \cdot x^3)$ *Commutative and associative properties*
>
> $\qquad\qquad\qquad = -12x^5$ *Multiply coefficients, add exponents*
>
> **b.** $\left(\frac{4}{5}x^5 \cdot y^2\right)(10x^3 \cdot y) = \left(\frac{4}{5} \cdot 10\right)(x^5 \cdot x^3)(y^2 \cdot y)$ *Commutative and associative properties*
>
> $\qquad\qquad\qquad\qquad = 8x^8y^3$ *Multiply coefficients, add exponents*

You can see that in each case the work was the same—multiply coefficients and add exponents of the same base. We can expect division of monomials to proceed in a similar way. Since our properties are consistent, division of monomials will result in division of coefficients and subtraction of exponents of like bases.

> **Example 2** Divide:
>
> **a.** $\dfrac{15x^3}{3x^2}$ **b.** $\dfrac{39x^2y^3}{3xy^5}$
>
> **SOLUTION**
>
> **a.** $\dfrac{15x^3}{3x^2} = \dfrac{15}{3} \cdot \dfrac{x^3}{x^2}$ *Write as separate fractions*
>
> $\qquad\qquad = 5x$ *Divide coefficients, subtract exponents*

b. $\dfrac{39x^2y^3}{3xy^5} = \dfrac{39}{3} \cdot \dfrac{x^2}{x} \cdot \dfrac{y^3}{y^5}$ *Write as separate fractions*

$= 13x \cdot \dfrac{1}{y^2}$ *Divide coefficients, subtract exponents*

$= \dfrac{13x}{y^2}$ *Write answer as a single fraction* ◼

In Example 2b, the expression $\frac{y^3}{y^5}$ simplifies to $\frac{1}{y^2}$ because of Property 4 for exponents and the definition of negative exponents. If we were to show all the work in this simplification process, it would look like this:

$$\dfrac{y^3}{y^5} = y^{3-5}$$ *Property 4 for exponents*

$$= y^{-2}$$ *Subtraction*

$$= \dfrac{1}{y^2}$$ *Definition of negative exponents*

The point of this explanation is this: Even though we may not show all the steps when simplifying an expression involving exponents, the result we obtain still can be justified using the properties of exponents. We have not introduced any new properties in Example 2; we have just not shown the details of each simplification.

Example 3   Divide $25a^5b^3$ by $50a^2b^7$.

SOLUTION

$$\dfrac{25a^5b^3}{50a^2b^7} = \dfrac{25}{50} \cdot \dfrac{a^5}{a^2} \cdot \dfrac{b^3}{b^7}$$ *Write as separate fractions*

$$= \dfrac{1}{2} \cdot a^3 \cdot \dfrac{1}{b^4}$$ *Divide coefficients, subtract exponents*

$$= \dfrac{a^3}{2b^4}$$ *Write answer as a single fraction* ◼

Notice in Example 3 that dividing 25 by 50 results in $\frac{1}{2}$. This is the same result we would obtain if we reduced the fraction $\frac{25}{50}$ to lowest terms, and there is no harm in thinking of it that way. Also, notice that the expression $\frac{b^3}{b^7}$ simplifies to $\frac{1}{b^4}$ by Property 4 for exponents and the definition of negative exponents, even though we have not shown the steps involved in doing so.

Multiplication and Division of Numbers Written in Scientific Notation

We multiply and divide numbers written in scientific notation using the same steps we used to multiply and divide monomials.

Example 4   Multiply $(4 \times 10^7)(2 \times 10^{-4})$.

SOLUTION   Since multiplication is commutative and associative, we can rearrange the order of these numbers and group them as follows:

$$(4 \times 10^7)(2 \times 10^{-4}) = (4 \times 2)(10^7 \times 10^{-4})$$

$$= 8 \times 10^3$$

Notice that we add exponents, $7 + (-4) = 3$, when we multiply with the same base.

◼

Example 5   Divide $\dfrac{9.6 \times 10^{12}}{3 \times 10^4}$.

SOLUTION   We group the numbers between 1 and 10 separately from the powers of 10 and proceed as we did in Example 4:

$$\frac{9.6 \times 10^{12}}{3 \times 10^4} = \frac{9.6}{3} \times \frac{10^{12}}{10^4}$$
$$= 3.2 \times 10^8$$

Notice that the procedure we used in both of these examples is very similar to multiplication and division of monomials, for which we multiplied or divided coefficients and added or subtracted exponents.

Addition and Subtraction of Monomials

Addition and subtraction of monomials will be almost identical since subtraction is defined as addition of the opposite. With multiplication and division of monomials, the key was rearranging the numbers and variables using the commutative and associative properties. With addition, the key is application of the distributive property. We sometimes use the phrase *combine monomials* to describe addition and subtraction of monomials.

> **def**   *similar terms*
>
> Two terms (monomials) with the same variable part (same variables raised to the same powers) are called *similar* (or *like*) *terms*.

You can add only similar terms. This is because the distributive property (which is the key to addition of monomials) cannot be applied to terms that are not similar.

Example 6   Combine the following monomials.

a. $-3x^2 + 15x^2$ **b.** $9x^2y - 20x^2y$ **c.** $5x^2 + 8y^2$

SOLUTION

a. $-3x^2 + 15x^2 = (-3 + 15)x^2$ Distributive property
$$= 12x^2 \qquad\qquad\quad \text{Add coefficients}$$

b. $9x^2y - 20x^2y = (9 - 20)x^2y$ Distributive property
$$= -11x^2y \qquad\qquad \text{Add coefficients}$$

c. $5x^2 + 8y^2$ In this case we cannot apply the distributive property, so we cannot add the monomials

The next examples show how we simplify expressions containing monomials when more than one operation is involved.

Example 7   Apply the distributive property.

a. $x^2\left(1 - \dfrac{6}{x}\right)$ **b.** $ab\left(\dfrac{1}{b} - \dfrac{1}{a}\right)$

SOLUTION

a. $x^2\left(1 - \dfrac{6}{x}\right) = x^2 \cdot 1 - x^2 \cdot \dfrac{6}{x} = x^2 - \dfrac{6x^2}{x} = x^2 - 6x$

b. $ab\left(\dfrac{1}{b} - \dfrac{1}{a}\right) = ab \cdot \dfrac{1}{b} - ab \cdot \dfrac{1}{a} = \dfrac{ab}{b} - \dfrac{ab}{a} = a - b$

Example 8   Simplify $\dfrac{(6x^4y)(3x^7y^5)}{9x^5y^2}$.

SOLUTION   We begin by multiplying the two monomials in the numerator:

$$\dfrac{(6x^4y)(3x^7y^5)}{9x^5y^2} = \dfrac{18x^{11}y^6}{9x^5y^2} \qquad \text{Simplify numerator}$$

$$= 2x^6y^4 \qquad \text{Divide}$$

Example 9   Simplify $\dfrac{(6.8 \times 10^5)(3.9 \times 10^{-7})}{7.8 \times 10^{-4}}$.

SOLUTION   We group the numbers between 1 and 10 separately from the powers of 10:

$$\dfrac{(6.8)(3.9)}{7.8} \times \dfrac{(10^5)(10^{-7})}{10^{-4}} = 3.4 \times 10^{5+(-7)-(-4)}$$

$$= 3.4 \times 10^2$$

Example 10   Simplify $\dfrac{14x^5}{2x^2} + \dfrac{15x^8}{3x^5}$.

SOLUTION   Simplifying each expression separately and then combining similar terms gives

$$\dfrac{14x^5}{2x^2} + \dfrac{15x^8}{3x^5} = 7x^3 + 5x^3 \qquad \text{Divide}$$

$$= 12x^3 \qquad \text{Add}$$

Example 11   A rectangular solid is twice as long as it is wide and one-half as high as it is wide. Write an expression for the volume.

SOLUTION   We begin by making a diagram of the object (Figure 1) with the dimensions labeled as given in the problem.

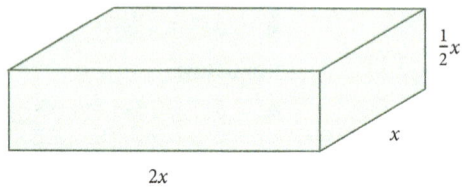

FIGURE 1

The volume is the product of the three dimensions:

$$V = 2x \cdot x \cdot \dfrac{1}{2}x = x^3$$

The box has the same volume as a cube with side x, as shown in Figure 2.

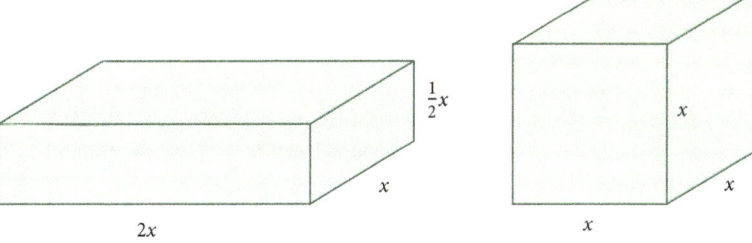

Equal Volumes

FIGURE 2

Getting Ready for Class

After reading through the preceding section, respond in your own words and in complete sentences.

A. What is a monomial?
B. Describe how you would multiply $3x^2$ and $5x^2$.
C. Describe how you would add $3x^2$ and $5x^2$.
D. Describe how you would multiply two numbers written in scientific notation.

Multiply.

1. $(3x^4)(4x^3)$ **2.** $(6x^5)(-2x^2)$ **3.** $(-2y^4)(8y^7)$

4. $(5y^{10})(2y^5)$ **5.** $(8x)(4x)$ **6.** $(7x)(5x)$

7. $(10a^3)(10a)(2a^2)$ **8.** $(5a^4)(10a)(10a^4)$ **9.** $(6ab^2)(-4a^2b)$

10. $(-5a^3b)(4ab^4)$ **11.** $(4x^2y)(3x^3y^3)(2xy^4)$ **12.** $(5x^6)(-10xy^4)(-2x^2y^6)$

Divide. Write all answers with positive exponents only.

13. $\dfrac{15x^3}{5x^2}$ **14.** $\dfrac{25x^5}{5x^4}$ **15.** $\dfrac{18y^9}{3y^{12}}$ **16.** $\dfrac{24y^4}{8y^7}$

17. $\dfrac{32a^3}{64a^4}$ **18.** $\dfrac{25a^5}{75a^6}$ **19.** $\dfrac{21a^2b^3}{-7ab^5}$ **20.** $\dfrac{32a^5b^6}{8ab^5}$

21. $\dfrac{3x^3y^2z}{27xy^2z^3}$ **22.** $\dfrac{5x^5y^4z}{30x^3yz^2}$

23. Fill in the table.

a	b	ab	$\dfrac{a}{b}$	$\dfrac{b}{a}$
10	$5x$			
$20x^3$	$6x^2$			
$25x^5$	$5x^4$			
$3x^{-2}$	$3x^2$			
$-2y^4$	$8y^7$			

24. Fill in the table.

a	b	ab	$\dfrac{a}{b}$	$\dfrac{b}{a}$
$10y$	$2y^2$			
$10y^2$	$2y$			
$5y^3$	15			
5	$15y^3$			
$4y^{-3}$	$4y^3$			

Find each product. Write all answers in scientific notation.

25. $(3 \times 10^3)(2 \times 10^5)$ **26.** $(4 \times 10^8)(1 \times 10^6)$

27. $(3.5 \times 10^4)(5 \times 10^{-6})$ **28.** $(7.1 \times 10^5)(2 \times 10^{-8})$

29. $(5.5 \times 10^{-3})(2.2 \times 10^{-4})$ **30.** $(3.4 \times 10^{-2})(4.5 \times 10^{-6})$

Find each quotient. Write all answers in scientific notation.

31. $\dfrac{8.4 \times 10^5}{2 \times 10^2}$ **32.** $\dfrac{9.6 \times 10^{20}}{3 \times 10^6}$ **33.** $\dfrac{6 \times 10^8}{2 \times 10^{-2}}$

34. $\dfrac{8 \times 10^{12}}{4 \times 10^{-3}}$ **35.** $\dfrac{2.5 \times 10^{-6}}{5 \times 10^{-4}}$ **36.** $\dfrac{4.5 \times 10^{-8}}{9 \times 10^{-4}}$

Combine by adding or subtracting as indicated.

37. $3x^2 + 5x^2$

38. $4x^3 + 8x^3$

39. $8x^5 - 19x^5$

40. $75x^6 - 50x^6$

41. $2a + a - 3a$

42. $5a + a - 6a$

43. $10x^3 - 8x^3 + 2x^3$

44. $7x^5 + 8x^5 - 12x^5$

45. $20ab^2 - 19ab^2 + 30ab^2$

46. $18a^3b^2 - 20a^3b^2 + 10a^3b^2$

47. Fill in the table.

a	b	ab	a + b
$5x$	$3x$		
$4x^2$	$2x^2$		
$3x^3$	$6x^3$		
$2x^4$	$-3x^4$		
x^5	$7x^5$		

48. Fill in the table.

a	b	ab	a − b
$2y$	$3y$		
$-2y$	$3y$		
$4y^2$	$5y^2$		
y^3	$-3y^3$		
$5y^4$	$7y^4$		

Simplify. Write all answers with positive exponents only.

49. $\dfrac{(3x^2)(8x^5)}{6x^4}$

50. $\dfrac{(7x^3)(6x^8)}{14x^5}$

51. $\dfrac{(9a^2b)(2a^3b^4)}{18a^5b^7}$

52. $\dfrac{(21a^5b)(2a^8b^4)}{14ab}$

53. $\dfrac{(4x^3y^2)(9x^4y^{10})}{(3x^5y)(2x^6y)}$

54. $\dfrac{(5x^4y^4)(10x^3y^3)}{(25xy^5)(2xy^7)}$

Apply the distributive property.

55. $xy\left(x + \dfrac{1}{y}\right)$

56. $xy\left(y + \dfrac{1}{x}\right)$

57. $xy\left(\dfrac{1}{y} + \dfrac{1}{x}\right)$

58. $xy\left(\dfrac{1}{x} - \dfrac{1}{y}\right)$

59. $x^2\left(1 - \dfrac{4}{x^2}\right)$

60. $x^2\left(1 - \dfrac{9}{x^2}\right)$

61. $x^2\left(1 - \dfrac{1}{x} - \dfrac{6}{x^2}\right)$

62. $x^2\left(1 - \dfrac{5}{x} + \dfrac{6}{x^2}\right)$

63. $x^2\left(1 - \dfrac{5}{x}\right)$

64. $x^2\left(1 - \dfrac{3}{x}\right)$

65. $x^2\left(1 - \dfrac{8}{x}\right)$

66. $x^2\left(1 - \dfrac{6}{x}\right)$

Simplify each expression, and write all answers in scientific notation.

67. $\dfrac{(6 \times 10^8)(3 \times 10^5)}{9 \times 10^7}$

68. $\dfrac{(8 \times 10^4)(5 \times 10^{10})}{2 \times 10^7}$

69. $\dfrac{(5 \times 10^3)(4 \times 10^{-5})}{2 \times 10^{-2}}$

70. $\dfrac{(7 \times 10^6)(4 \times 10^{-4})}{1.4 \times 10^{-3}}$

71. $\dfrac{(2.8 \times 10^{-7})(3.6 \times 10^4)}{2.4 \times 10^3}$

72. $\dfrac{(5.4 \times 10^2)(3.5 \times 10^{-9})}{4.5 \times 10^6}$

Simplify.

73. $\dfrac{18x^4}{3x} + \dfrac{21x^7}{7x^4}$

74. $\dfrac{24x^{10}}{6x^4} + \dfrac{32x^7}{8x}$

75. $\dfrac{45a^6}{9a^4} - \dfrac{50a^8}{2a^6}$

76. $\dfrac{16a^9}{4a} - \dfrac{28a^{12}}{4a^4}$

77. $\dfrac{6x^7y^4}{3x^2y^2} + \dfrac{8x^5y^8}{2y^6}$

78. $\dfrac{40x^{10}y^{10}}{8x^2y^5} + \dfrac{10x^8y^8}{5y^3}$

Getting Ready for the Next Section

Simplify.

79. $3 - 8$

80. $-5 + 7$

81. $-1 + 7$

82. $1 - 8$

83. $3(5)^2 + 1$

84. $3(-2)^2 - 5(-2) + 4$

85. $2x^2 + 4x^2$

86. $3x^2 - x^2$

87. $-5x + 7x$

88. $x - 2x$

89. $-(2x + 9)$

90. $-(4x^2 - 2x - 6)$

91. Find the value of $2x + 3$ when $x = 4$

92. Find the value of $(3x)^2$ when $x = 3$

Addition and Subtraction of Polynomials

In this section we will extend what we learned in Section 4.3 to expressions called polynomials. We begin this section with the definition of a polynomial.

> **(děf)** *polynomial*
>
> A *polynomial* is a finite sum of monomials (terms).

Here are some examples of polynomials:

$$3x^2 + 2x + 1 \qquad 15x^2y + 21xy^2 - y^2 \qquad 3a - 2b + 4c - 5d$$

Polynomials can be further classified by the number of terms they contain. A polynomial with two terms is called a binomial. If it has three terms, it is a trinomial. As stated before, a monomial has only one term.

> **(děf)** *degree*
>
> The *degree* of a polynomial in one variable is the highest power to which the variable is raised.

Various degrees of polynomials:

$3x^5 + 2x^3 + 1$	A trinomial of degree 5
$2x + 1$	A binomial of degree 1
$3x^2 + 2x + 1$	A trinomial of degree 2
$3x^5$	A monomial of degree 5
-9	A monomial of degree 0

There are no new rules for adding one or more polynomials. We rely only on our previous knowledge. Here are some examples.

Video Examples

Section 4.4

■ **Example 1**   Add $(2x^2 - 5x + 3) + (4x^2 + 7x - 8)$.

SOLUTION   We use the commutative and associative properties to group similar terms together and then apply the distributive property to add

$$(2x^2 - 5x + 3) + (4x^2 + 7x - 8)$$

$$= (2x^2 + 4x^2) + (-5x + 7x) + (3 - 8) \qquad \text{Commutative and associative properties}$$

$$= (2 + 4)x^2 + (-5 + 7)x + (3 - 8) \qquad \text{Distributive property}$$

$$= 6x^2 + 2x - 5 \qquad \text{Addition}$$

The results here indicate that to add two polynomials, we add coefficients of similar terms ■

Example 2   Add $x^2 + 3x + 2x + 6$.

SOLUTION   The only similar terms here are the two middle terms. We combine them as usual to get

$$x^2 + 3x + 2x + 6 = x^2 + 5x + 6$$

You will recall from Chapter 1 the definition of subtraction: $a - b = a + (-b)$. To subtract one expression from another, we simply add its opposite. The letters a and b in the definition can each represent polynomials. The opposite of a polynomial is the opposite of each of its terms. When you subtract one polynomial from another you subtract each of its terms.

Example 3   Subtract $(3x^2 + x + 4) - (x^2 + 2x + 3)$.

SOLUTION   To subtract $x^2 + 2x + 3$, we change the sign of each of its terms and add. If you are having trouble remembering why we do this, remember that we can think of $-(x^2 + 2x + 3)$ as $-1(x^2 + 2x + 3)$. If we distribute the -1 across $x^2 + 2x + 3$, we get $-x^2 - 2x - 3$:

$$(3x^2 + x + 4) - (x^2 + 2x + 3)$$
$$= 3x^2 + x + 4 - x^2 - 2x - 3 \qquad \text{Take the opposite of each}$$
$$\text{term in the second polynomial}$$
$$= (3x^2 - x^2) + (x - 2x) + (4 - 3)$$
$$= 2x^2 - x + 1$$

Example 4   Subtract $-4x^2 + 5x - 7$ from $x^2 - x - 1$.

SOLUTION   The polynomial $x^2 - x - 1$ comes first, then the subtraction sign, and finally the polynomial $-4x^2 + 5x - 7$ in parentheses.

$$(x^2 - x - 1) - (-4x^2 + 5x - 7)$$
$$= x^2 - x - 1 + 4x^2 - 5x + 7 \qquad \text{Take the opposite of each term}$$
$$\text{in the second polynomial}$$
$$= (x^2 + 4x^2) + (-x - 5x) + (-1 + 7)$$
$$= 5x^2 - 6x + 6$$

The last topic we want to consider in this section is finding the value of a polynomial for a given value of the variable.

To find the value of the polynomial $3x^2 + 1$ when x is 5, we replace x with 5 and simplify the result:

$$\text{When} \qquad x = 5$$
$$\text{the polynomial} \qquad 3x^2 + 1$$
$$\text{becomes} \qquad 3(5)^2 + 1 = 3(25) + 1$$
$$= 75 + 1$$
$$= 76$$

■ **Example 5**   Find the value of $3x^2 - 5x + 4$ when $x = -2$.

SOLUTION

When $x = -2$

the polynomial $3x^2 - 5x + 4$

becomes $3(-2)^2 - 5(-2) + 4 = 3(4) + 10 + 4$

$$= 12 + 10 + 4$$

$$= 26$$

Getting Ready for Class

After reading through the preceding section, respond in your own words and in complete sentences.

A. What are similar terms?

B. What is the degree of a polynomial?

C. Describe how you would subtract one polynomial from another.

D. How you would find the value of $3x^2 - 5x + 4$ when x is -2?

Problem Set 4.4

Identify each of the following polynomials as a trinomial, binomial, or monomial, and give the degree in each case.

1. $2x^3 - 3x^2 + 1$

2. $4x^2 - 4x + 1$

3. $5 + 8a - 9a^3$

4. $6 + 12x^3 + x^4$

5. $2x - 1$

6. $4 + 7x$

7. $45x^2 - 1$

8. $3a^3 + 8$

9. $7a^2$

10. $90x$

11. -4

12. 56

Perform the following additions and subtractions.

13. $(2x^2 + 3x + 4) + (3x^2 + 2x + 5)$

14. $(x^2 + 5x + 6) + (x^2 + 3x + 4)$

15. $(3a^2 - 4a + 1) + (2a^2 - 5a + 6)$

16. $(5a^2 - 2a + 7) + (4a^2 - 3a + 2)$

17. $x^2 + 4x + 2x + 8$

18. $x^2 + 5x - 3x - 15$

19. $6x^2 - 3x - 10x + 5$

20. $10x^2 + 30x - 2x - 6$

21. $x^2 - 3x + 3x - 9$

22. $x^2 - 5x + 5x - 25$

23. $3y^2 - 5y - 6y + 10$

24. $y^2 - 18y + 2y - 12$

25. $(6x^3 - 4x^2 + 2x) + (9x^2 - 6x + 3)$

26. $(5x^3 + 2x^2 + 3x) + (2x^2 + 5x + 1)$

27. $\left(\dfrac{2}{3}x^2 - \dfrac{1}{5}x - \dfrac{3}{4}\right) + \left(\dfrac{4}{3}x^2 - \dfrac{4}{5}x + \dfrac{7}{4}\right)$

28. $\left(\dfrac{3}{8}x^3 - \dfrac{5}{7}x^2 - \dfrac{2}{5}\right) + \left(\dfrac{5}{8}x^3 - \dfrac{2}{7}x^2 + \dfrac{7}{5}\right)$

29. $(a^2 - a - 1) - (-a^2 + a + 1)$

30. $(5a^2 - a - 6) - (-3a^2 - 2a + 4)$

31. $\left(\dfrac{5}{9}x^3 + \dfrac{1}{3}x^2 - 2x + 1\right) - \left(\dfrac{2}{3}x^3 + x^2 + \dfrac{1}{2}x - \dfrac{3}{4}\right)$

32. $\left(4x^3 - \dfrac{2}{5}x^2 + \dfrac{3}{8}x - 1\right) - \left(\dfrac{9}{2}x^3 + \dfrac{1}{4}x^2 - x + \dfrac{5}{6}\right)$

33. $(4y^2 - 3y + 2) + (5y^2 + 12y - 4) - (13y^2 - 6y + 20)$

34. $(2y^2 - 7y - 8) - (6y^2 + 6y - 8) + (4y^2 - 2y + 3)$

35. Subtract $10x^2 + 23x - 50$ from $11x^2 - 10x + 13$.

36. Subtract $2x^2 - 3x + 5$ from $4x^2 - 5x + 10$.

37. Subtract $3y^2 + 7y - 15$ from $11y^2 + 11y + 11$.

38. Subtract $15y^2 - 8y - 2$ from $3y^2 - 3y + 2$.

39. Add $50x^2 - 100x - 150$ to $25x^2 - 50x + 75$.

40. Add $7x^2 - 8x + 10$ to $-8x^2 + 2x - 12$.

41. Subtract $2x + 1$ from the sum of $3x - 2$ and $11x + 5$.

42. Subtract $3x - 5$ from the sum of $5x + 2$ and $9x - 1$.

43. Find the value of the polynomial $x^2 - 2x + 1$ when x is 3.

44. Find the value of the polynomial $(x - 1)^2$ when x is 3.

Applying the Concepts

45. Packaging A crystal ball with a diameter of 6 inches is being packaged for shipment. If the crystal ball is placed inside a circular cylinder with radius 3 inches and height 6 inches, how much volume will need to be filled with padding? (The volume of a sphere with radius r is $\frac{4}{3}\pi r^3$, and the volume of a right circular cylinder with radius r and height h is $\pi r^2 h$.) Use 3.14 to approximate π.

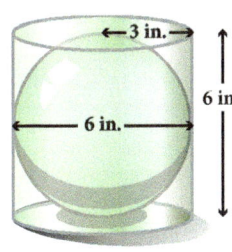

46. Packaging Suppose the circular cylinder of Problem 45 has a radius of 4 inches and a height of 7 inches. How much volume will need to be filled with padding?

Getting Ready for the Next Section

Simplify.

47. $(-5)(-1)$

48. $3(-4)$

49. $(-1)(6)$

50. $(-7) \cdot 8$

51. $(5x)(-4x)$

52. $(3x)(2x)$

53. $3x(-7)$

54. $3x(-1)$

55. $5x + (-3x)$

56. $-3x - 10x$

57. $3(2x - 6)$

58. $-4x(x + 5)$

SPOTLIGHT ON SUCCESS   *Instructor Edwin*

> *You never fail until you stop trying.*
> —Albert Einstein

Coming to the United States at the age of 10 and not knowing how to speak English was a very difficult hurdle to overcome. However, with hard work and dedication I was able to rise above those obstacles. When I came to the U.S. our school did not have a strong English development program as it was known at that time, English as a Second Language (ESL). The approach back then was "sink or swim." When my self-esteem was low, my mom and my three older sisters were always there for me and they would always encourage me to do well. My mom was a single parent, and her number one priority was that we would receive a good education. My mother's perseverance is what has made me the person I am today. At a young age I was able to see that she had overcome more than what my situation was, and I would always tell myself, "if Mom can do it, I could also do it." Not only did she not have an education, but she also saved us from a civil war that was happening in my home country of El Salvador.

When things in school got hard, I would always reflect on all the hard work, sacrifice and effort of mother. I would just tell myself that I should not have any excuses and that I needed to keep going. If my mother, who worked as a housekeeper, could could send all four of her kids to college doesn't motivate you, I don't know what does. It definitely motivated me. The day everything began to change for me was when I was in eighth grade. I was sitting in my biology class not paying attention to the teacher because I was really focusing on a piece of paper on the wall. It said, "You never fail until you stop trying." I read it over and over, trying to digest what the quote meant. With my limited English I was doing my best to translate what it meant in my native language. It finally clicked! I was able to figure out what those seven words meant. I memorized the quote and began to apply it to my academics and to real-life situations. I began to really focus in my studies. I wanted to do well in school, and most important I wanted to improve my English. To this day I always reflect to that quote when I feel I can't do something.

I was able to finish junior high successfully. Going to high school was a lot easier and I ended up with very good grades and eventually I was accepted to an excellent college. I was never the smartest student on campus, but I always did well because I never quit. I earned my college degree and now I teach at a dual immersion elementary school. I have that same quote in my classroom and I constantly remind my students to never stop trying.

Multiplication with Polynomials

We begin our discussion of multiplication of polynomials by finding the product of a monomial and a trinomial.

Video Examples

Section 4.5

Example 1   Multiply $3x^2(2x^2 + 4x + 5)$.

SOLUTION   Applying the distributive property gives us

$$3x^2(2x^2 + 4x + 5) = 3x^2(2x^2) + 3x^2(4x) + 3x^2(5) \qquad \text{Distributive property}$$

$$= 6x^4 + 12x^3 + 15x^2 \qquad \text{Multiplication}$$

The distributive property is the key to multiplication of polynomials. We can use it to find the product of any two polynomials. There are some shortcuts we can use in certain situations, however. Let's look at an example that involves the product of two binomials.

Example 2   Multiply $(3x - 5)(2x - 1)$.

SOLUTION $(3x - 5)(2x - 1) = 3x(2x - 1) - 5(2x - 1)$

$$= 3x(2x) + 3x(-1) + (-5)(2x) + (-5)(-1)$$

$$= 6x^2 - 3x - 10x + 5$$

$$= 6x^2 - 13x + 5$$

If we look closely at the second and third lines of work in this example, we can see that the terms in the answer come from all possible products of terms in the first binomial with terms in the second binomial. This result is generalized as follows.

> **⌈Δ≠Σ   Rule**
>
> To multiply any two polynomials, multiply each term in the first with each term in the second.

There are two ways we can put this rule to work.

FOIL Method

If we look at the original problem in Example 2 and then to the answer, we see that the first term in the answer came from multiplying the first terms in each binomial:

$$3x \cdot 2x = 6x^2 \qquad \text{First}$$

The middle term in the answer came from adding the products of the two outside terms with the two inside terms in each binomial:

$$3x(-1) = -3x \qquad \text{Outside}$$
$$\underline{-5(2x) = -10x} \qquad \text{Inside}$$
$$= -13x$$

The last term in the answer came from multiplying the two last terms:

$$-5(-1) = 5 \qquad \text{Last}$$

To summarize the FOIL method, we will multiply another two binomials.

Example 3   Multiply $(2x + 3)(5x - 4)$.

SOLUTION $(2x + 3)(5x - 4) = \underline{2x(5x)} + \underline{2x(-4)} + \underline{3(5x)} + \underline{3(-4)}$

First   Outside   Inside   Last

$$= 10x^2 - 8x + 15x - 12$$

$$= 10x^2 + 7x - 12$$

With practice $-8x + 15x = 7x$ can be done mentally.

COLUMN Method

The FOIL method can be applied only when multiplying two binomials. To find products of polynomials with more than two terms, we use what is called the COLUMN method.

The COLUMN method of multiplying two polynomials is very similar to long multiplication with whole numbers. It is just another way of finding all possible products of terms in one polynomial with terms in another polynomial.

Example 4   Multiply $(2x + 3)(3x^2 - 2x + 1)$.

SOLUTION
$$
\begin{array}{r}
3x^2 - 2x + 1 \\
2x + 3 \\
\hline
6x^3 - 4x^2 + 2x \\
9x^2 - 6x + 3 \\
\hline
6x^3 + 5x^2 - 4x + 3
\end{array}
$$
$\leftarrow 2x(3x^2 - 2x + 1)$
$\leftarrow 3(3x^2 - 2x + 1)$
$\leftarrow$ Add similar terms

It will be to your advantage to become very fast and accurate at multiplying polynomials. You should be comfortable using either method. The following examples illustrate two types of multiplication.

Example 5   Multiply:

a. $4a^2(2a^2 - 3a + 5) = 4a^2(2a^2) + 4a^2(-3a) + 4a^2(5)$
$$= 8a^4 - 12a^3 + 20a^2$$

b. $(x - 2)(y + 3) = x(y) + x(3) + (-2)(y) + (-2)(3)$
$$\qquad\qquad\qquad F \qquad O \qquad I \qquad L$$
$$= xy + 3x - 2y - 6$$

c. $(x + y)(a - b) = x(a) + x(-b) + y(a) + y(-b)$
$$\qquad\qquad\qquad F \qquad O \qquad I \qquad L$$
$$= xa - xb + ya - yb$$

d. $(5x - 1)(2x + 6) = 5x(2x) + 5x(6) + (-1)(2x) + (-1)(6)$
$$\qquad\qquad\qquad\qquad F \qquad O \qquad I \qquad L$$
$$= 10x^2 + 30x + (-2x) + (-6)$$
$$= 10x^2 + 28x - 6$$

Example 6 The length of a rectangle is 3 more than twice the width. Write an expression for the area of the rectangle.

SOLUTION We begin by drawing a rectangle and labeling the width with x. Since the length is 3 more than twice the width, we label the length with $2x + 3$.

$$2x + 3$$

$$x$$

Since the area A of a rectangle is the product of the length and width, we write our formula for the area of this rectangle as

$$A = x(2x + 3)$$

$$A = 2x^2 + 3x \qquad \text{Multiply}$$

Revenue

Suppose that a store sells x items at p dollars per item. The total amount of money obtained by selling the items is called the *revenue*. It can be found by multiplying the number of items sold, x, by the price per item, p. For example, if 100 items are sold for \$6 each, the revenue is $100(6) = \$600$. Similarly, if 500 items are sold for \$8 each, the total revenue is $500(8) = \$4,000$. If we denote the revenue with the letter R, then the formula that relates R, x, and p is

$$\text{Revenue} = (\text{number of items sold})(\text{price of each item})$$

In symbols: $R = xp$.

Example 7 A store selling USB drives for home computers knows from past experience that it can sell x 8GB USB drives each day at a price of p dollars per drive, according to the equation $x = 800 - 100p$. Write a formula for the daily revenue that involves only the variables R and p.

SOLUTION From our previous discussion we know that the revenue R is given by the formula

$$R = xp$$

But, since $x = 800 - 100p$, we can substitute $800 - 100p$ for x in the revenue equation to obtain

$$R = (800 - 100p)p$$

$$R = 800p - 100p^2$$

This last formula gives the revenue, R, in terms of the price, p.

Getting Ready for Class

After reading through the preceding section, respond in your own words and in complete sentences.

A. How do we multiply two polynomials?

B. Describe how the distributive property is used to multiply a monomial and a polynomial.

C. Describe how you would use the foil method to multiply two binomials.

D. Show how the product of two binomials can be a trinomial.

Problem Set 4.5

Multiply the following by applying the distributive property.

1. $2x(3x + 1)$

2. $4x(2x - 3)$

3. $2x^2(3x^2 - 2x + 1)$

4. $5x(4x^3 - 5x^2 + x)$

5. $2ab(a^2 - ab + 1)$

6. $3a^2b(a^3 + a^2b^2 + b^3)$

7. $y^2(3y^2 + 9y + 12)$

8. $5y(2y^2 - 3y + 5)$

9. $4x^2y(2x^3y + 3x^2y^2 + 8y^3)$

10. $6xy^3(2x^2 + 5xy + 12y^2)$

Multiply the following binomials. You should do about half the problems using the FOIL method and the other half using the COLUMN method. Remember, you want to be comfortable using both methods.

11. $(x + 3)(x + 4)$　　**12.** $(x + 2)(x + 5)$　　**13.** $(x + 6)(x + 1)$

14. $(x + 1)(x + 4)$　　**15.** $\left(x + \dfrac{1}{2}\right)\left(x + \dfrac{3}{2}\right)$　　**16.** $\left(x + \dfrac{3}{5}\right)\left(x + \dfrac{2}{5}\right)$

17. $(a + 5)(a - 3)$　　**18.** $(a - 8)(a + 2)$　　**19.** $(x - a)(y + b)$

20. $(x + a)(y - b)$　　**21.** $(x + 6)(x - 6)$　　**22.** $(x + 3)(x - 3)$

23. $\left(y + \dfrac{5}{6}\right)\left(y - \dfrac{5}{6}\right)$　　**24.** $\left(y - \dfrac{4}{7}\right)\left(y + \dfrac{4}{7}\right)$　　**25.** $(2x - 3)(x - 4)$

26. $(3x - 5)(x - 2)$　　**27.** $(a + 2)(2a - 1)$　　**28.** $(a - 6)(3a + 2)$

29. $(2x - 5)(3x - 2)$　　**30.** $(3x + 6)(2x - 1)$　　**31.** $(2x + 3)(a + 4)$

32. $(2x - 3)(a - 4)$　　**33.** $(5x - 4)(5x + 4)$　　**34.** $(6x + 5)(6x - 5)$

35. $\left(2x - \dfrac{1}{2}\right)\left(x + \dfrac{3}{2}\right)$　　**36.** $\left(4x - \dfrac{3}{2}\right)\left(x + \dfrac{1}{2}\right)$　　**37.** $(1 - 2a)(3 - 4a)$

38. $(1 - 3a)(3 + 2a)$

For each of the following problems, fill in the area of each small rectangle and square, and then add the results together to find the indicated product.

39. $(x + 2)(x + 3)$

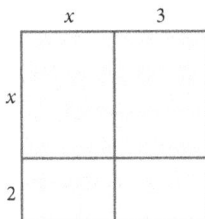

40. $(x + 4)(x + 5)$

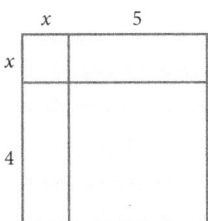

41. $(x + 1)(2x + 2)$

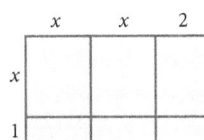

42. $(2x + 1)(2x + 2)$

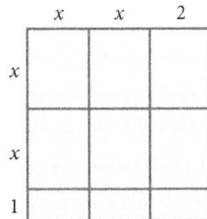

449

Multiply the following.

43. $(a - 3)(a^2 - 3a + 2)$

44. $(a + 5)(a^2 + 2a + 3)$

45. $(x + 2)(x^2 - 2x + 4)$

46. $(x + 3)(x^2 - 3x + 9)$

47. $(2x + 1)(x^2 + 8x + 9)$

48. $(3x - 2)(x^2 - 7x + 8)$

49. $(5x^2 + 2x + 1)(x^2 - 3x + 5)$

50. $(2x^2 + x + 1)(x^2 - 4x + 3)$

51. $(x^2 + 3)(2x^2 - 5)$

52. $(4x^3 - 8)(5x^3 + 4)$

53. $(3a^4 + 2)(2a^2 + 5)$

54. $(7a^4 - 8)(4a^3 - 6)$

55. $(x + 3)(x + 4)(x + 5)$

56. $(x - 3)(x - 4)(x - 5)$

Simplify.

57. $(x - 3)(x - 2) + 2$

58. $(2x - 5)(3x + 2) - 4$

59. $(2x - 3)(4x + 3) + 4$

60. $(3x + 8)(5x - 7) + 52$

61. $(x + 4)(x - 5) + (-5)(2)$

62. $(x + 3)(x - 4) + (-4)(2)$

63. $2(x - 3) + x(x + 2)$

64. $5(x + 3) + 1(x + 4)$

65. $3x(x + 1) - 2x(x - 5)$

66. $4x(x - 2) - 3x(x - 4)$

67. $x(x + 2) - 3$

68. $2x(x - 4) + 6$

69. $a(a - 3) + 6$

70. $a(a - 4) + 8$

Applying the Concepts

71. Area The length of a rectangle is 5 units more than twice the width. Write an expression for the area of the rectangle.

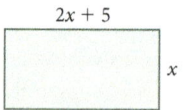

72. Area The length of a rectangle is 2 more than three times the width. Write an expression for the area of the rectangle

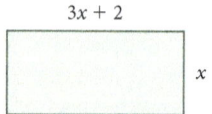

73. Area The width and length of a rectangle are given by two consecutive integers. Write an expression for the area of the rectangle.

74. Area The width and length of a rectangle are given by two consecutive even integers. Write an expression for the area of the rectangle.

Getting Ready for the Next Section

Simplify.

75. $13 \cdot 13$

76. $3x \cdot 3x$

77. $2(x)(-5)$

78. $2(2x)(-3)$

79. $6x + (-6x)$

80. $3x + (-3x)$

81. $(2x)(-3) + (2x)(3)$

82. $(2x)(-5y) + (2x)(5y)$

Multiply.

83. $-4(3x - 4)$

84. $-2x(2x + 7)$

85. $(x - 1)(x + 2)$

86. $(x + 5)(x - 6)$

87. $(x + 3)(x + 3)$

88. $(3x - 2)(3x - 2)$

Binomial Squares and Other Special Products

In this section we will combine the results of the last section with our definition of exponents to find some special products.

Video Examples

Section 4.6

Example 1   Find the square of $(3x - 2)$.

SOLUTION   To square $(3x - 2)$, we multiply it by itself:

$$(3x - 2)^2 = (3x - 2)(3x - 2) \qquad \text{Definition of exponents}$$
$$= 9x^2 - 6x - 6x + 4 \qquad \text{FOIL method}$$
$$= 9x^2 - 12x + 4 \qquad \text{Combine similar terms}$$

Notice that the first and last terms in the answer are the square of the first and last terms in the original problem and that the middle term is twice the product of the two terms in the original binomial.

Example 2   Expand and multiply.

a. $(a + b)^2$ **b.** $(a - b)^2$

SOLUTION

a. $(a + b)^2 = (a + b)(a + b)$
$$= a^2 + 2ab + b^2$$

b. $(a - b)^2 = (a - b)(a - b)$
$$= a^2 - 2ab + b^2$$

> **Note**   A very common mistake when squaring binomials is to write
>
> $$(a + b)^2 = a^2 + b^2$$
>
> which just isn't true. The mistake becomes obvious when we substitute 2 for a and 3 for b:
>
> $$(2 + 3)^2 \neq 2^2 + 3^2$$
>
> $$25 \neq 13$$
>
> Exponents do not distribute over addition or subtraction.

Binomial squares having the form of Example 2 occur very frequently in algebra. It will be to your advantage to memorize the following rule for squaring a binomial.

> **⌈Δ≠Σ⌉   Rule**
>
> The square of a binomial is the sum of the square of the first term, the square of the last term, and twice the product of the two original terms. In symbols this rule is written as follows:
>
> $$(x + y)^2 = \underset{\text{Square of first term}}{x^2} + \underset{\text{Twice product of the two terms}}{2xy} + \underset{\text{Square of last term}}{y^2}$$

Examples   Multiply using the preceding rule:

	First term squared		Twice their product		Last term squared		Answer
3. $(x - 5)^2 =$	x^2	$+$	$2(x)(-5)$	$+$	25	$=$	$x^2 - 10x + 25$
4. $(x + 2)^2 =$	x^2	$+$	$2(x)(2)$	$+$	4	$=$	$x^2 + 4x + 4$
5. $(2x - 3)^2 =$	$4x^2$	$+$	$2(2x)(-3)$	$+$	9	$=$	$4x^2 - 12x + 9$
6. $(5x - 4)^2 =$	$25x^2$	$+$	$2(5x)(-4)$	$+$	16	$=$	$25x^2 - 40x + 16$

Another special product that occurs frequently is $(a + b)(a - b)$. The only difference in the two binomials is the sign between the two terms. The interesting thing about this type of product is that the middle term is always zero. Here are some examples.

| Examples | Multiply using the FOIL method:

7. $(2x - 3)(2x + 3) = 4x^2 + 6x - 6x - 9$ *Foil method*

$= 4x^2 - 9$

8. $(x - 5)(x + 5) = x^2 + 5x - 5x - 25$ *Foil method*

$= x^2 - 25$

9. $(3x - 1)(3x + 1) = 9x^2 + 3x - 3x - 1$ *Foil method*

$= 9x^2 - 1$

Notice that in each case the middle term is zero and therefore doesn't appear in the answer. The answers all turn out to be the difference of two squares. Here is a rule to help you memorize the result.

⎰Δ≠Σ   ***Rule***

When multiplying two binomials that differ only in the sign between their terms, subtract the square of the last term from the square of the first term.

$$(a - b)(a + b) = a^2 - b^2$$

Here are some problems that result in the difference of two squares.

| Examples | Multiply using the preceding rule:

10. $(x + 3)(x - 3) = x^2 - 9$

11. $(a + 2)(a - 2) = a^2 - 4$

12. $(9a + 1)(9a - 1) = 81a^2 - 1$

13. $(2x - 5y)(2x + 5y) = 4x^2 - 25y^2$

14. $(3a - 7b)(3a + 7b) = 9a^2 - 49b^2$

Although all the problems in this section can be worked correctly using the methods in the previous section, they can be done much faster if the two rules are *memorized*. Here is a summary of the two rules:

$$(a + b)^2 = (a + b)(a + b) = a^2 + 2ab + b^2$$
$$(a - b)^2 = (a - b)(a - b) = a^2 - 2ab + b^2$$
$$(a - b)(a + b) = a^2 - b^2$$

Example 15   Write an expression in symbols for the sum of the squares of three consecutive even integers. Then, simplify that expression.

SOLUTION   If we let $x =$ the first of the even integers, then $x + 2$ is the next consecutive even integer, and $x + 4$ is the one after that. An expression for the sum of their squares is

$$x^2 + (x + 2)^2 + (x + 4)^2 \qquad \text{Sum of squares}$$
$$= x^2 + (x^2 + 4x + 4) + (x^2 + 8x + 16) \qquad \text{Expand squares}$$
$$= 3x^2 + 12x + 20 \qquad \text{Add similar terms}$$

Getting Ready for Class

After reading through the preceding section, respond in your own words and in complete sentences.

A. Explain why $(x + 3)^2$ cannot be $x^2 + 9$.

B. What kind of products result in the difference of two squares?

C. When multiplied out, how will $(x + 3)^2$ and $(x - 3)^2$ differ?

Problem Set 4.6

Perform the indicated operations.

1. $(x - 2)^2$

2. $(x + 2)^2$

3. $(a + 3)^2$

4. $(a - 3)^2$

5. $(x - 5)^2$

6. $(x - 4)^2$

7. $\left(a - \dfrac{1}{2}\right)^2$

8. $\left(a + \dfrac{1}{2}\right)^2$

9. $(x + 10)^2$

10. $(x - 10)^2$

11. $(a + 0.8)^2$

12. $(a - 0.4)^2$

13. $(2x - 1)^2$

14. $(3x + 2)^2$

15. $(4a + 5)^2$

16. $(4a - 5)^2$

17. $(3x - 2)^2$

18. $(2x - 3)^2$

19. $(3a + 5b)^2$

20. $(5a - 3b)^2$

21. $(4x - 5y)^2$

22. $(5x + 4y)^2$

23. $(7m + 2n)^2$

24. $(2m - 7n)^2$

25. $(6x - 10y)^2$

26. $(10x + 6y)^2$

27. $(x^2 + 5)^2$

28. $(x^2 + 3)^2$

29. $(a^2 + 1)^2$

30. $(a^2 - 2)^2$

Comparing Expressions Fill in each table.

31.

x	$(x + 3)^2$	$x^2 + 9$	$x^2 + 6x + 9$
1			
2			
3			
4			

32.

x	$(x - 5)^2$	$x^2 + 25$	$x^2 - 10x + 25$
1			
2			
3			
4			

33.

a	1	3	3	4
b	1	5	4	5
$(a + b)^2$				
$a^2 + b^2$				
$a^2 + ab + b^2$				
$a^2 + 2ab + b^2$				

34.

a	2	5	2	4
b	1	2	5	3
$(a - b)^2$				
$a^2 - b^2$				
$a^2 - 2ab + b^2$				

Multiply.

35. $(a + 5)(a - 5)$ **36.** $(a - 6)(a + 6)$ **37.** $(y - 1)(y + 1)$

38. $(y - 2)(y + 2)$ **39.** $(9 + x)(9 - x)$ **40.** $(10 - x)(10 + x)$

41. $(2x + 5)(2x - 5)$ **42.** $(3x + 5)(3x - 5)$ **43.** $\left(4x + \dfrac{1}{3}\right)\left(4x - \dfrac{1}{3}\right)$

44. $\left(6x + \dfrac{1}{4}\right)\left(6x - \dfrac{1}{4}\right)$ **45.** $(2a + 7)(2a - 7)$ **46.** $(3a + 10)(3a - 10)$

47. $(6 - 7x)(6 + 7x)$ **48.** $(7 - 6x)(7 + 6x)$ **49.** $(x^2 + 3)(x^2 - 3)$

50. $(x^2 + 2)(x^2 - 2)$ **51.** $(a^2 + 4)(a^2 - 4)$ **52.** $(a^2 + 9)(a^2 - 9)$

53. $(5y^4 - 8)(5y^4 + 8)$ **54.** $(7y^5 + 6)(7y^5 - 6)$

Multiply and simplify.

55. $(x + 3)(x - 3) + (x - 5)(x + 5)$ **56.** $(x - 7)(x + 7) + (x - 4)(x + 4)$

57. $(2x + 3)^2 - (4x - 1)^2$ **58.** $(3x - 5)^2 - (2x + 3)^2$

59. $(a + 1)^2 - (a + 2)^2 + (a + 3)^2$ **60.** $(a - 1)^2 + (a - 2)^2 - (a - 3)^2$

61. $(2x + 3)^3$ **62.** $(3x - 2)^3$

Applying the Concepts

63. Shortcut The formula for the difference of two squares can be used as a shortcut to multiplying certain whole numbers if they have the correct form. Use the difference of two squares formula to multiply 49(51) by first writing 49 as $(50 - 1)$ and 51 as $(50 + 1)$.

64. Shortcut Use the difference of two squares formula to multiply 101(99) by first writing 101 as $(100 + 1)$ and 99 as $(100 - 1)$.

65. Comparing Expressions Evaluate the expression $(x + 3)^2$ and the expression $x^2 + 6x + 9$ for $x = 2$.

66. Comparing Expressions Evaluate the expression $x^2 - 25$ and the expression $(x - 5)(x + 5)$ for $x = 6$.

67. Number Problem Write an expression for the sum of the squares of two consecutive integers. Then, simplify that expression.

68. Number Problem Write an expression for the sum of the squares of two consecutive odd integers. Then, simplify that expression.

69. Number Problem Write an expression for the sum of the squares of three consecutive integers. Then, simplify that expression.

70. Number Problem Write an expression for the sum of the squares of three consecutive odd integers. Then, simplify that expression.

71. Area We can use the concept of area to further justify our rule for squaring a binomial. The length of each side of the square shown in the figure is $a + b$. (The longer line segment has length a and the shorter line segment has length b.) The area of the whole square is $(a + b)^2$. However, the whole area is the sum of the areas of the two smaller squares and the two smaller rectangles that make it up. Write the area of the two smaller squares and the two smaller rectangles and then add them together to verify the formula $(a + b)^2 = a^2 + 2ab + b^2$.

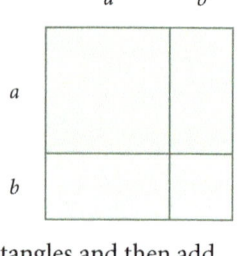

72. Area The length of each side of the large square shown in the figure is $x + 5$. Therefore, its area is $(x + 5)^2$. Find the area of the two smaller squares and the two smaller rectangles that make up the large square, then add them together to verify the formula $(x + 5)^2 = x^2 + 10x + 25$.

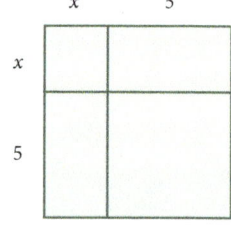

For each problem, fill in the area of each small rectangle and square, and then add the results together to find the indicated product.

Getting Ready for the Next Section

Simplify.

73. $\dfrac{10x^3}{5x}$ **74.** $\dfrac{15x^2}{5x}$ **75.** $\dfrac{3x^2}{3}$ **76.** $\dfrac{4x^2}{2}$

77. $\dfrac{9x^2}{3x}$ **78.** $\dfrac{3x^4}{3x^2}$ **79.** $\dfrac{24x^3y^2}{8x^2y}$ **80.** $\dfrac{4x^2y^3}{8x^2y}$

Dividing a Polynomial by a Monomial

To divide a polynomial by a monomial, we will use the definition of division and apply the distributive property. Follow the steps in this example closely.

Video Examples

Section 4.7

Example 1 Divide $10x^3 - 15x^2$ by $5x$.

SOLUTION

$$\frac{10x^3 - 15x^2}{5x} = (10x^3 - 15x^2)\frac{1}{5x}$$ Division by $5x$ is the same as multiplication by $\frac{1}{5x}$

$$= 10x^3\left(\frac{1}{5x}\right) - 15x^2\left(\frac{1}{5x}\right)$$ Distribute $\frac{1}{5x}$ to both terms

$$= \frac{10x^3}{5x} - \frac{15x^2}{5x}$$ Multiplication by $\frac{1}{5x}$ is the same as division by $5x$

$$= 2x^2 - 3x$$ Division of monomials as done in Section 4.3

If we were to leave out the first steps, the problem would look like this:

$$\frac{10x^3 - 15x^2}{5x} = \frac{10x^3}{5x} - \frac{15x^2}{5x}$$

$$= 2x^2 - 3x$$

The problem is much shorter and clearer this way. You may leave out the first two steps from Example 1 when working problems in this section. They are part of Example 1 only to help show you why the following rule is true.

> ⎡Δ≠Σ **Rule**
>
> To divide a polynomial by a monomial, simply divide each term in the polynomial by the monomial.

Here are some further examples using our rule for division of a polynomial by a monomial.

Example 2 Divide $\frac{3x^2 - 6}{3}$.

SOLUTION We begin by writing the 3 in the denominator under each term in the numerator. Then we simplify the result:

$$\frac{3x^2 - 6}{3} = \frac{3x^2}{3} - \frac{6}{3}$$ Divide each term in the numerator by 3

$$= x^2 - 2$$ Simplify

Example 3 Divide $\frac{4x^2 - 2}{2}$.

SOLUTION Dividing each term in the numerator by 2, we have

$$\frac{4x^2 - 2}{2} = \frac{4x^2}{2} - \frac{2}{2}$$ Divide each term in the numerator by 2

$$= 2x^2 - 1$$ Simplify

■ **Example 4**   Find the quotient of $27x^3 - 9x^2$ and $3x$.

SOLUTION   We again are asked to divide the first polynomial by the second one:

$$\frac{27x^3 - 9x^2}{3x} = \frac{27x^3}{3x} - \frac{9x^2}{3x} \qquad \text{Divide each term by } 3x$$

$$= 9x^2 - 3x \qquad \text{Simplify}$$

■

■ **Example 5**   Divide $(15x^2y - 21xy^2) \div (-3xy)$.

SOLUTION   This is the same type of problem we have shown in the first four examples; it is just worded a little differently. Note that when we divide each term in the first polynomial by $-3xy$, the negative sign must be taken into account:

$$\frac{15x^2y - 21xy^2}{-3xy} = \frac{15x^2y}{-3xy} - \frac{21xy^2}{-3xy} \qquad \text{Divide each term by } -3xy$$

$$= -5x - (-7y) \qquad \text{Simplify}$$

$$= -5x + 7y \qquad \text{Simplify}$$

■

■ **Example 6**   Divide $\dfrac{24x^3y^2 + 16x^2y^2 - 4x^2y^3}{8x^2y}$

SOLUTION   Writing $8x^2y$ under each term in the numerator and then simplifying, we have

$$\frac{24x^3y^2 + 16x^2y^2 - 4x^2y^3}{8x^2y} = \frac{24x^3y^2}{8x^2y} + \frac{16x^2y^2}{8x^2y} - \frac{4x^2y^3}{8x^2y}$$

$$= 3xy + 2y - \frac{y^2}{2}.$$

■

⚠ **Common Mistake**

From the examples in this section, it is clear that to divide a polynomial by a monomial, we must divide each term in the polynomial by the monomial. Often, students taking algebra for the first time will make the following mistake:

$$\frac{x + 2}{2} = x + 1 \qquad \text{Mistake}$$

The mistake here is in not dividing both terms in the numerator by 2. The correct way to divide $x + 2$ by 2 looks like this:

$$\frac{x + 2}{2} = \frac{x}{2} + \frac{2}{2} = \frac{x}{2} + 1 \qquad \text{Correct}$$

Getting Ready for Class

After reading through the preceding section, respond in your own words and in complete sentences.

A. What property of real numbers is the key to dividing a polynomial by a monomial?

B. Describe how you would divide a polynomial by $5x$.

C. Why is our answer to Example 6 not a polynomial?

Problem Set 4.7

Divide the following polynomials by $5x$.

1. $5x^2 - 10x$ **2.** $10x^3 - 15x$

3. $15x - 10x^3$ **4.** $50x^3 - 20x^2$

5. $25x^2y - 10xy$ **6.** $15xy^2 + 20x^2y$

7. $35x^5 - 30x^4 + 25x^3$ **8.** $40x^4 - 30x^3 + 20x^2$

9. $50x^5 - 25x^3 + 5x$ **10.** $75x^6 + 50x^3 - 25x$

Divide the following by $-2a$.

11. $8a^2 - 4a$ **12.** $a^3 - 6a^2$

13. $16a^5 + 24a^4$ **14.** $30a^6 + 20a^3$

15. $8ab + 10a^2$ **16.** $6a^2b - 10ab^2$

17. $12a^3b - 6a^2b^2 + 14ab^3$ **18.** $4ab^3 - 16a^2b^2 - 22a^3b$

19. $a^2 + 2ab + b^2$ **20.** $a^2b - 2ab^2 + b^3$

Perform the following divisions (find the following quotients).

21. $\dfrac{6x + 8y}{2}$ **22.** $\dfrac{9x - 3y}{3}$

23. $\dfrac{7y - 21}{-7}$ **24.** $\dfrac{14y - 12}{2}$

25. $\dfrac{10xy - 8x}{2x}$ **26.** $\dfrac{12xy^2 - 18x}{-6x}$

27. $\dfrac{x^2y - x^3y^2}{x}$ **28.** $\dfrac{x^2y - x^3y^2}{x^2}$

29. $\dfrac{x^2y - x^3y^2}{-x^2y}$ **30.** $\dfrac{ab + a^2b^2}{ab}$

31. $\dfrac{a^2b^2 - ab^2}{-ab^2}$ **32.** $\dfrac{a^2b^2c - ab^2c^2}{abc}$

33. $\dfrac{x^3 - 3x^2y + xy^2}{x}$ **34.** $\dfrac{x^2 - 3xy^2 + xy^3}{x}$

35. $\dfrac{10a^2 - 15a^2b + 25a^2b^2}{5a^2}$ **36.** $\dfrac{11a^2b^2 - 33ab}{-11ab}$

37. $\dfrac{26x^2y^2 - 13xy}{-13xy}$ **38.** $\dfrac{6x^2y^2 - 3xy}{6xy}$

39. $\dfrac{4x^2y^2 - 2xy}{4xy}$ **40.** $\dfrac{6x^2a + 12x^2b - 6x^2c}{36x^2}$

41. $\dfrac{5a^2x - 10ax^2 + 15a^2x^2}{20a^2x^2}$ **42.** $\dfrac{12ax - 9bx + 18cx}{6x^2}$

43. $\dfrac{16x^5 + 8x^2 + 12x}{12x^3}$ **44.** $\dfrac{27x^2 - 9x^3 - 18x^4}{-18x^3}$

Divide. Assume all variables represent positive numbers.

45. $\dfrac{9a^{5m} - 27a^{3m}}{3a^{2m}}$ **46.** $\dfrac{26a^{3m} - 39a^{5m}}{13a^{3m}}$

47. $\dfrac{10x^{5m} - 25x^{3m} + 35x^m}{5x^m}$ **48.** $\dfrac{18x^{2m} + 24x^{4m} - 30x^{6m}}{6x^{2m}}$

Simplify each numerator, and then divide.

49. $\dfrac{2x^3(3x + 2) - 3x^2(2x - 4)}{2x^2}$

50. $\dfrac{5x^2(6x - 3) + 6x^3(3x - 1)}{3x}$

51. $\dfrac{(x + 2)^2 - (x - 2)^2}{2x}$

52. $\dfrac{(x - 3)^2 - (x + 3)^2}{3x}$

53. $\dfrac{(x + 5)^2 + (x + 5)(x - 5)}{2x}$

54. $\dfrac{(x - 4)^2 + (x + 4)(x - 4)}{2x}$

55. Comparing Expressions Evaluate the expression $\dfrac{10x + 15}{5}$ and the expression $2x + 3$ when $x = 2$.

56. Comparing Expressions Evaluate the expression $\dfrac{6x^2 + 4x}{2x}$ and the expression $3x + 2$ when $x = 5$.

57. Comparing Expressions Show that the expression $\dfrac{3x + 8}{2}$ is not the same as the expression $3x + 4$ by replacing x with 10 in both expressions and simplifying the results.

58. Comparing Expressions Show that the expression $\dfrac{x + 10}{x}$ is not equal to 10 by replacing x with 5 and simplifying.

Getting Ready for the Next Section

Divide.

59. $27\overline{)3{,}962}$

60. $13\overline{)18{,}780}$

61. $\dfrac{2x^2 + 5x}{x}$

62. $\dfrac{7x^5 + 9x^3 + 3x^7}{x^3}$

Multiply.

63. $(x - 3)x$

64. $(x - 3)(-2)$

65. $2x^2(x - 5)$

66. $10x(x - 5)$

Subtract.

67. $(x^2 - 5x) - (x^2 - 3x)$

68. $(2x^3 + 0x^2) - (2x^3 - 10x^2)$

69. $(-2x + 8) - (-2x + 6)$

70. $(4x - 14) - (4x - 10)$

Dividing a Polynomial by a Polynomial

4.8

Since long division for polynomials is very similar to long division with whole numbers, we will begin by reviewing a division problem with whole numbers. You may realize when looking at Example 1 that you don't have a very good idea why you proceed as you do with long division. What you do know is that the process always works. We are going to approach the explanations in this section in much the same manner; that is, we won't always be sure why the steps we will use are important, only that they always produce the correct result.

Example 1 Divide $27\overline{)3{,}962}$.

SOLUTION

$$\begin{array}{r} 1 \\ 27\overline{)3{,}962} \\ 2\ 7 \\ \hline 1\ 2 \end{array}$$

← Estimate 27 into 39
← Multiply 1 × 27 = 27
← Subtract 39 − 27 = 12

$$\begin{array}{r} 1 \\ 27\overline{)3{,}962} \\ 2\ 7\!\downarrow \\ \hline 1\ 26 \end{array}$$

← Bring down the 6

These are the four basic steps in long division. Estimate, multiply, subtract, and bring down the next term. To finish the problem, we simply perform the same four steps again:

$$\begin{array}{r} 14 \\ 27\overline{)3{,}962} \\ 2\ 7\!\downarrow \\ \hline 1\ 26 \\ 1\ 08 \\ \hline 182 \end{array}$$

← 4 is the estimate

← Multiply to get 108
← Subtract to get 18, then bring down the 2

One more time.

$$\begin{array}{r} 146 \\ 27\overline{)3{,}962} \\ 2\ 7 \\ \hline 1\ 26 \\ 1\ 08 \\ \hline 182 \\ 162 \\ \hline 20 \end{array}$$

← 6 is the estimate

← Multiply to get 162
← Subtract to get 20

Since there is nothing left to bring down, we have our answer.

$$\frac{3{,}962}{27} = 146 + \frac{20}{27} \qquad \text{or} \qquad 146\frac{20}{27}$$

Here is how it works with polynomials.

Example 2 Divide $\dfrac{x^2 - 5x + 8}{x - 3}$

SOLUTION

$$
\begin{array}{r}
x \\
x - 3 \overline{)\; x^2 - 5x + 8\;} \\
\end{array}
$$
$\quad\leftarrow$ Estimate $x^2 \div x = x$

$\not{+}\, x^2 \not{+}\, 3x \qquad\leftarrow$ Multiply $x(x - 3) = x^2 - 3x$

$\quad\; -2x \qquad\qquad\leftarrow$ Subtract $(x^2 - 5x) - (x^2 - 3x) = -2x$

$$
\begin{array}{r}
x \\
x - 3 \overline{)\; x^2 - 5x + 8\;} \\
\end{array}
$$

$\not{+}\; x^2 \not{+}\, 3x$

$\quad\; -2x + 8 \quad\leftarrow$ Bring down the 8

Notice that to subtract one polynomial from another, we add its opposite. That is why we change the signs on $x^2 - 3x$ and add what we get to $x^2 - 5x$. (To subtract the second polynomial, simply change the signs and add.)

We perform the same four steps again:

$$
\begin{array}{r}
x - 2 \\
x - 3 \overline{)\; x^2 - 5x + 8\;} \\
\end{array}
$$
$\leftarrow -2$ is the estimate $(-2x \div x = -2)$

$\not{+}\, x^2 \not{+}\, 3x \qquad\downarrow$

$\quad\; -2x + 8$

$\not{+}\, 2x \not{+}\, 6 \qquad\leftarrow$ Multiply $-2(x - 3) = -2x + 6$.

$\qquad\quad 2 \quad\leftarrow$ Subtract $(-2x + 8) - (-2x + 6) = 2$

Since there is nothing left to bring down, we have our answer:

$$
\frac{x^2 - 5x + 8}{x - 3} = x - 2 + \frac{2}{x - 3}
$$

To check our answer, we multiply $(x - 3)(x - 2)$ to get $x^2 - 5x + 6$. Then, adding on the remainder, 2, we have $x^2 - 5x + 8$. ∎

Example 3 Divide $\dfrac{6x^2 - 11x - 14}{2x - 5}$.

SOLUTION

$$
\begin{array}{r}
3x + 2 \\
2x - 5 \overline{)\; 6x^2 - 11x - 14\;} \\
\end{array}
$$

$\not{+}\, 6x^2 \not{+}\, 15x \qquad\downarrow$

$\quad\; +\; 4x - 14$

$\not{+}\quad 4x \not{+}\, 10$

$\qquad\quad -4$

$$
\frac{6x^2 - 11x - 14}{2x - 5} = 3x + 2 + \frac{-4}{2x - 5}
$$
∎

One last step is sometimes necessary. The two polynomials in a division problem must both be in descending powers of the variable and cannot skip any powers from the highest power down to the constant term.

Example 4 Divide $\dfrac{2x^3 - 3x + 2}{x - 5}$.

SOLUTION The problem will be much less confusing if we write $2x^3 - 3x + 2$ as $2x^3 + 0x^2 - 3x + 2$. Adding $0x^2$ does not change our original problem.

$$
\begin{array}{r}
2x^2 \qquad\qquad\qquad \\
x - 5 \overline{)\ 2x^3 + \ 0x^2 - 3x + 2} \\
\mp 2x^3 \mp 10x^2 \qquad\quad \\
+\ 10x^2 - 3x
\end{array}
$$

← Estimate $2x^3 \div x = 2x^2$

← Multiply $2x^2(x - 5) = 2x^3 - 10x^2$

← Subtract:
$\quad (2x^3 + 0x^2) - (2x^3 - 10x^2) = 10x^2$

Bring down the next term

Adding the term $0x^2$ gives us a column in which to write $10x^2$. (Remember, you can add and subtract only similar terms.)

Here is the completed problem:

$$
\begin{array}{r}
2x^2 + 10x + \ 47 \\
x - 5 \overline{)\ 2x^3 + \ 0x^2 - \ 3x + \ 2} \\
\mp 2x^3 \mp 10x^2 \qquad\qquad \\
+\ 10x^2 - \ 3x \qquad \\
\mp 10x^2 \mp 50x \qquad \\
+\ 47x + \ 2 \\
\mp 47x \mp 235 \\
237
\end{array}
$$

Our answer is $\dfrac{2x^3 - 3x + 2}{x - 5} = 2x^2 + 10x + 47 + \dfrac{237}{x - 5}$.

As you can see, long division with polynomials is a mechanical process. Once you have done it correctly a couple of times, it becomes very easy to produce the correct answer.

Getting Ready for Class

After reading through the preceding section, respond in your own words and in complete sentences.

A. What are the four steps used in long division with whole numbers?

B. How is division of two polynomials similar to long division with whole numbers?

C. What are the four steps used in long division with polynomials?

D. How do we use 0 when dividing the polynomial $2x^3 - 3x + 2$ by $x - 5$?

Problem Set 4.8

Divide.

1. $\dfrac{x^2 - 5x + 6}{x - 3}$

2. $\dfrac{x^2 - 5x + 6}{x - 2}$

3. $\dfrac{a^2 + 9a + 20}{a + 5}$

4. $\dfrac{a^2 + 9a + 20}{a + 4}$

5. $\dfrac{x^2 - 6x + 9}{x - 3}$

6. $\dfrac{x^2 + 10x + 25}{x + 5}$

7. $\dfrac{2x^2 + 5x - 3}{2x - 1}$

8. $\dfrac{4x^2 + 4x - 3}{2x - 1}$

9. $\dfrac{2a^2 - 9a - 5}{2a + 1}$

10. $\dfrac{4a^2 - 8a - 5}{2a + 1}$

11. $\dfrac{x^2 + 5x + 8}{x + 3}$

12. $\dfrac{x^2 + 5x + 4}{x + 3}$

13. $\dfrac{a^2 + 3a + 2}{a + 5}$

14. $\dfrac{a^2 + 4a + 3}{a + 5}$

15. $\dfrac{x^2 + 2x + 1}{x - 2}$

16. $\dfrac{x^2 + 6x + 9}{x - 3}$

17. $\dfrac{x^2 + 5x - 6}{x + 1}$

18. $\dfrac{x^2 - x - 6}{x + 1}$

19. $\dfrac{a^2 + 3a + 1}{a + 2}$

20. $\dfrac{a^2 - a + 3}{a + 1}$

21. $\dfrac{2x^2 - 2x + 5}{2x + 4}$

22. $\dfrac{15x^2 + 19x - 4}{3x + 8}$

23. $\dfrac{6a^2 + 5a + 1}{2a + 3}$

24. $\dfrac{4a^2 + 4a + 3}{2a + 1}$

25. $\dfrac{6a^3 - 13a^2 - 4a + 15}{3a - 5}$

26. $\dfrac{2a^3 - a^2 + 3a + 2}{2a + 1}$

Fill in the missing terms in the numerator, and then use long division to find the quotients (see Example 4).

27. $\dfrac{x^3 + 4x + 5}{x + 1}$

28. $\dfrac{x^3 + 4x^2 - 8}{x + 2}$

29. $\dfrac{x^3 - 1}{x - 1}$

30. $\dfrac{x^3 + 1}{x + 1}$

31. $\dfrac{x^3 - 8}{x - 2}$

32. $\dfrac{x^3 + 27}{x + 3}$

Long Division Use the information in the table to find the monthly payment for auto insurance for the cities below. Round to the nearest cent.

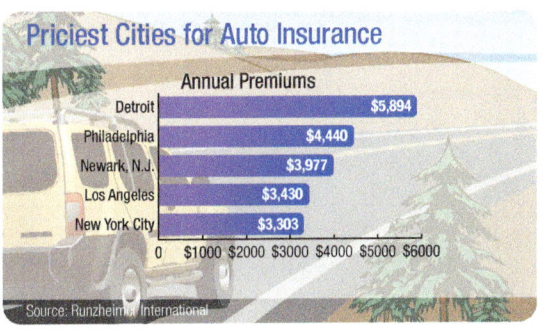

33. Detroit   **34.** Philadelphia   **35.** Newark, N.J.   **36.** Los Angeles

Maintaining Your Skills

Simplify.

37. $6(3 + 4) + 5$

38. $[(1 + 2)(2 + 3)] + (4 \div 2)$

39. $1^2 + 2^2 + 3^2$

40. $(1 + 2 + 3)^2$

41. $5(6 + 3 \cdot 2) + 4 + 3 \cdot 2$

42. $(1 + 2)^3 + [(2 \cdot 3) + (4 \cdot 5)]$

43. $(1^3 + 2^3) + [(2 \cdot 3) + (4 \cdot 5)]$

44. $[2(3 + 4 + 5)] \div 3$

45. $(2 \cdot 3 + 4 + 5) \div 3$

46. $10^4 + 10^3 + 10^2 + 10^1$

47. $6 \cdot 10^3 + 5 \cdot 10^2 + 4 \cdot 10^1$

48. $5 \cdot 10^3 + 2 \cdot 10^2 + 8 \cdot 10^1$

49. $1 \cdot 10^3 + 7 \cdot 10^2 + 6 \cdot 10^1$

50. $4(2 - 1) + 5(3 - 2)$

51. $4 \cdot 2 - 1 + 5 \cdot 3 - 2$

52. $2^3 + 3^2 \cdot 4 - 5$

53. $(2^3 + 3^2) \cdot 4 - 5$

54. $4^2 - 2^4 + (2 \cdot 2)^2$

55. $2(2^2 + 3^2) + 3(3^2)$

56. $2 \cdot 2^2 + 3^2 + 3 \cdot 3^2$

Chapter 4 Summary

Exponents: Definition and Properties [4.1, 4.2]

EXAMPLES

Integer exponents indicate repeated multiplications.

1. a. $2^3 = 2 \cdot 2 \cdot 2 = 8$

$a^r \cdot a^s = a^{r+s}$ *To multiply with the same base, you add exponents*

b. $x^5 \cdot x^3 = x^{5+3} = x^8$

c. $\frac{x^5}{x^3} = x^{5-3} = x^2$

$\frac{a^r}{a^s} = a^{r-s}$ *To divide with the same base, you subtract exponents*

d. $(3x)^2 = 3^2 \cdot x^2 = 9x^2$

$(ab)^r = a^r \cdot b^r$ *Exponents distribute over multiplication*

e. $\left(\frac{2}{3}\right)_3 = \frac{2^3}{3^3} = \frac{8}{27}$

$\left(\frac{a}{b}\right)_r = \frac{a^r}{b^r}$ *Exponents distribute over division*

f. $(x^5)^3 = x^{5\cdot3} = x^{15}$

$(a^r)^s = a^{r \cdot s}$ *A power of a power is the product of the powers*

g. $3^{-2} = \frac{1}{3^2} = \frac{1}{9}$

$a^{-r} = \frac{1}{a^r}$ *Negative exponents imply reciprocals*

Multiplication of Monomials [4.3]

To multiply two monomials, multiply coefficients and add exponents.

2. $(5x^2)(3x^4) = 15x^6$

Division of Monomials [4.3]

To divide two monomials, divide coefficients and subtract exponents.

3. $\frac{12x^9}{4x^5} = 3x^4$

Scientific Notation [4.1, 4.2, 4.3]

A number is in scientific notation when it is written as the product of a number between 1 and 10 and an integer power of 10.

4. $768,000 = 7.68 \times 10^5$
$0.00039 = 3.9 \times 10^{-4}$

Addition of Polynomials [4.4]

To add two polynomials, add coefficients of similar terms.

5. $(3x^2 - 2x + 1) + (2x^2 + 7x - 3)$
$= 5x^2 + 5x - 2$

Subtraction of Polynomials [4.4]

To subtract one polynomial from another, add the opposite of the second to the first.

6. $(3x + 5) - (4x - 3)$
$= 3x + 5 - 4x + 3$
$= -x + 8$

7. a. $2a^2(5a^2 + 3a - 2)$
$= 10a^4 + 6a^3 - 4a^2$

b. $(x + 2)(3x - 1)$
$= 3x^2 - x + 6x - 2$
$= 3x^2 + 5x - 2$

c.
$$
\begin{array}{r}
2x^2 - 3x + 4 \\
3x - 2 \\
\hline
6x^3 - 9x^2 + 12x \\
- 4x^2 + 6x - 8 \\
\hline
6x^3 - 13x^2 + 18x - 8
\end{array}
$$

Multiplication of Polynomials [4.5]

To multiply a polynomial by a monomial, we apply the distributive property. To multiply two binomials we use the FOIL method. In other situations we use the COLUMN method. Each method achieves the same result: To multiply any two polynomials, we multiply each term in the first polynomial by each term in the second polynomial.

Special Products [4.6]

8. $(x + 3)^2 = x^2 + 6x + 9$
$(x - 3)^2 = x^2 - 6x + 9$
$(x + 3)(x - 3) = x^2 - 9$

$\left. \begin{array}{l} (a + b)^2 = a^2 + 2ab + b^2 \\ \\ (a - b)^2 = a^2 - 2ab + b^2 \end{array} \right\}$ Binomial squares

$(a + b)(a - b) = a^2 - b^2$ Difference of two squares

Dividing a Polynomial by a Monomial [4.7]

9. $\frac{12x^3 - 18x^2}{6x} = 2x^2 - 3x$

To divide a polynomial by a monomial, divide each term in the polynomial by the monomial.

Long Division with Polynomials [4.8]

10.
$$
\begin{array}{r}
x - 2 \\
x - 3 \overline{)\; x^2 - 5x + 8} \\
\underline{\mp x^2 \mp 3x } \downarrow \\
- 2x + 8 \\
\underline{\pm 2x \mp 6} \\
2
\end{array}
$$

Division with polynomials is similar to long division with whole numbers. The steps in the process are estimate, multiply, subtract, and bring down the next term. The divisors in all the long-division problems in this chapter were binomials.

Chapter 4 Test

Simplify each of the following expressions. [4.1]

1. $(-2)^5$

2. $\left(\dfrac{2}{3}\right)^3$

3. $(4x^2)^2(2x^3)^3$

Simplify each expression. Write all answers with positive exponents only. [4.2]

4. 4^{-2}

5. $(4a^5b^3)^0$

6. $\dfrac{x^{-4}}{x^{-7}}$

7. $\dfrac{(x^{-3})^2(x^{-5})^{-3}}{(x^{-3})^{-4}}$

8. Write 0.04307 in scientific notation. [4.2]

9. Write 7.63×10^6 in expanded form. [4.1]

Simplify. Write all answers with positive exponents only. [4.3]

10. $\dfrac{17x^2y^5z^3}{51x^4y^2z}$

11. $\dfrac{(3a^3b)(4a^2b^5)}{24a^2b^4}$

12. $\dfrac{28x^4}{4x} + \dfrac{30x^7}{6x^4}$

13. $\dfrac{(1.1 \times 10^5)(3 \times 10^{-2})}{4.4 \times 10^{-5}}$

Add or subtract as indicated. [4.4]

14. $9x^2 - 2x + 7x + 4$

15. $(4x^2 + 5x - 6) - (2x^2 - x - 4)$

16. Subtract $2x + 7$ from $7x + 3$. [4.4]

17. Find the value of $3a^2 + 4a + 6$ when a is -3. [4.4]

Multiply. [4.5]

18. $3x^2(5x^2 - 2x + 4)$

19. $\left(x + \dfrac{1}{4}\right)\left(x - \dfrac{1}{3}\right)$

20. $(2x - 3)(5x + 6)$

21. $(x + 4)(x^2 - 4x + 16)$

Multiply. [4.6]

22. $(x - 6)^2$

23. $(2a + 4b)^2$

24. $(3x - 6)(3x + 6)$

25. $(x^2 - 4)(x^2 + 4)$

26. Divide $18x^3 - 36x^2 + 6x$ by $6x$. [4.7]

Divide. [4.8]

27. $\dfrac{9x^2 - 6x - 4}{3x - 1}$

28. $\dfrac{4x^2 - 5x + 6}{x - 4}$

29. **Volume** Find the volume of a cube if the length of a side is 3.2 inches. [4.1]

30. **Volume** Find the volume of a rectangular solid if the length is three times the width, and the height is one third the width. [4.3]

Factoring

iStockphoto.com © miflippo

I f you watch professional football on television, you will hear the announcers refer to "hang time" when the punter punts the ball. Hang time is the amount of time the ball is in the air, and it depends on only one thing—the initial vertical velocity imparted to the ball by the kicker's foot. We can find the hang time of a football by solving equations. Table 1 shows the equations to solve for hang time, given various initial vertical velocities. Figure 1 is a visual representation of some equations associated with the ones in Table 1. In Figure 1, you can find hang time on the horizontal axis.

TABLE 1

Hang Time for a Football

Intial Vertical Velocity	Equation in factored form	Hang Time
16	$16t(1 - t) = 0$	1
32	$16t(2 - t) = 0$	2
48	$16t(3 - t) = 0$	3
64	$16t(4 - t) = 0$	4
80	$16t(5 - t) = 0$	5

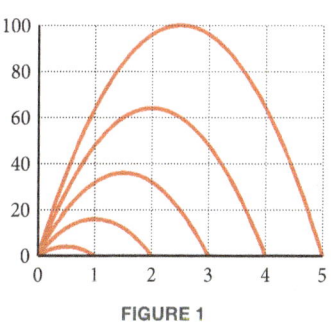

FIGURE 1

The equations in the second column of the table are in what is called "factored form." Once the equation is in factored form, hang time can be read from the second factor. In this chapter we develop techniques that allow us to factor a variety of polynomials. Factoring is the key to solving equations like the ones in Table 1.

Study Skills

This is the last chapter in which we will mention study skills. You know by now what works best for you and what you have to do to achieve your goals for this course. From now on, it is simply a matter of sticking with the things that work for you and avoiding the things that do not. It seems simple, but as with anything that takes effort, it is up to you to see that you maintain the skills that get you where you want to be in the course.

If you intend to take more classes in mathematics and want to ensure your success in those classes, then you can work toward this goal: *Become the type of student who can learn mathematics on his or her own.* Most people who have degrees in mathematics were students who could learn mathematics on their own. This doesn't mean that you have to learn it all on your own; it simply means that if you have to, you can learn it on your own. Attaining this goal gives you independence and puts you in control of your success in any math class you take.

The Greatest Common Factor and Factoring by Grouping

In Chapter 0 we used the following diagram to illustrate the relationship between multiplication and factoring.

$$\text{Factors} \rightarrow \quad 3 \cdot 5 = 15 \leftarrow \text{Product}$$

Multiplication (above), Factoring (below)

A similar relationship holds for multiplication of polynomials. Reading the following diagram from left to right, we say the product of the binomials $x + 2$ and $x + 3$ is the trinomial $x^2 + 5x + 6$. However, if we read in the other direction, we can say that $x^2 + 5x + 6$ factors into the product of $x + 2$ and $x + 3$.

$$\text{Factors} \rightarrow (x + 2)(x + 3) = x^2 + 5x + 6 \leftarrow \text{Product}$$

Multiplication (above), Factoring (below)

In this chapter we develop a systematic method of factoring polynomials.

In this section we will apply the distributive property to polynomials to factor from them what is called the greatest common factor.

> **(děf′) Definition**
>
> The *greatest common factor* for a polynomial is the largest monomial that divides (is a factor of) each term of the polynomial.

We use the term *largest monomial* to mean the monomial with the greatest coefficient and highest power of the variable.

Video Examples

Section 5.1

Example 1   Find the greatest common factor for the polynomial:

$$3x^5 + 12x^2$$

SOLUTION   The terms of the polynomial are $3x^5$ and $12x^2$. The largest number that divides the coefficients is 3, and the highest power of x that is a factor of x^5 and x^2 is x^2. Therefore, the greatest common factor for $3x^5 + 12x^2$ is $3x^2$; that is, $3x^2$ is the largest monomial that divides each term of $3x^5 + 12x^2$.

Example 2   Find the greatest common factor for:

$$8a^3b^2 + 16a^2b^3 + 20a^3b^3$$

SOLUTION   The largest number that divides each of the coefficients is 4. The highest power of the variable that is a factor of a^3b^2, a^2b^3, and a^3b^3 is a^2b^2. The greatest common factor for $8a^3b^2 + 16a^2b^3 + 20a^3b^3$ is $4a^2b^2$. It is the largest monomial that is a factor of each term.

Once we have recognized the greatest common factor of a polynomial, we can apply the distributive property and factor it out of each term. We rewrite the polynomial as the product of its greatest common factor with the polynomial that remains after the greatest common factor has been factored from each term in the original polynomial.

Example 3   Factor the greatest common factor from $3x - 15$.

SOLUTION   The greatest common factor for the terms $3x$ and 15 is 3. We can rewrite both $3x$ and 15 so that the greatest common factor 3 is showing in each term. It is important to realize that $3x$ means $3 \cdot x$. The 3 and the x are not "stuck" together:

$$3x - 15 = 3 \cdot x - 3 \cdot 5$$

Now, applying the distributive property, we have:

$$3 \cdot x - 3 \cdot 5 = 3(x - 5)$$

To check a factoring problem like this, we can multiply 3 and $x - 5$ to get $3x - 15$, which is what we started with. Factoring is simply a procedure by which we change sums and differences into products. In this case we changed the difference $3x - 15$ into the product $3(x - 5)$. Note, however, that we have not changed the meaning or value of the expression. The expression we end up with is equivalent to the expression we started with.

Example 4   Factor the greatest common factor from:

$$5x^3 - 15x^2$$

SOLUTION   The greatest common factor is $5x^2$. We rewrite the polynomial as:

$$5x^3 - 15x^2 = 5x^2 \cdot x - 5x^2 \cdot 3$$

Then we apply the distributive property to get:

$$5x^2 \cdot x - 5x^2 \cdot 3 = 5x^2(x - 3)$$

To check our work, we simply multiply $5x^2$ and $(x - 3)$ to get $5x^3 - 15x^2$, which is our original polynomial.

Example 5   Factor the greatest common factor from:

$$16x^5 - 20x^4 + 8x^3$$

SOLUTION   The greatest common factor is $4x^3$. We rewrite the polynomial so we can see the greatest common factor $4x^3$ in each term; then we apply the distributive property to factor it out.

$$16x^5 - 20x^4 + 8x^3 = 4x^3 \cdot 4x^2 - 4x^3 \cdot 5x + 4x^3 \cdot 2$$
$$= 4x^3(4x^2 - 5x + 2)$$

■ **Example 6**   Factor the greatest common factor from:

$$6x^3y - 18x^2y^2 + 12xy^3$$

SOLUTION   The greatest common factor is $6xy$. We rewrite the polynomial in terms of $6xy$ and then apply the distributive property as follows:

$$6x^3y - 18x^2y^2 + 12xy^3 = 6xy \cdot x^2 - 6xy \cdot 3xy + 6xy \cdot 2y^2$$
$$= 6xy(x^2 - 3xy + 2y^2)$$

■ **Example 7**   Factor the greatest common factor from:

$$3a^2b - 6a^3b^2 + 9a^3b^3$$

SOLUTION   The greatest common factor is $3a^2b$:

$$3a^2b - 6a^3b^2 + 9a^3b^3 = 3a^2b(1) - 3a^2b(2ab) + 3a^2b(3ab^2)$$
$$= 3a^2b(1 - 2ab + 3ab^2)$$

Factoring by Grouping

To develop our next method of factoring, called *factoring by grouping*, we start by examining the polynomial $xc + yc$. The greatest common factor for the two terms is c. Factoring c from each term we have:

$$xc + yc = c(x + y)$$

But suppose that c itself was a more complicated expression, such as $a + b$, so that the expression we were trying to factor was $x(a + b) + y(a + b)$, instead of $xc + yc$. The greatest common factor for $x(a + b) + y(a + b)$ is $(a + b)$. Factoring this common factor from each term looks like this:

$$x(a + b) + y(a + b) = (a + b)(x + y)$$

To see how all of this applies to factoring polynomials, consider the polynomial

$$xy + 3x + 2y + 6$$

There is no greatest common factor other than the number 1. However, if we group the terms together two at a time, we can factor an x from the first two terms and a 2 from the last two terms:

$$xy + 3x + 2y + 6 = x(y + 3) + 2(y + 3)$$

The expression on the right can be thought of as having two terms: $x(y + 3)$ and $2(y + 3)$. Each of these expressions contains the common factor $y + 3$, which can be factored out using the distributive property:

$$x(y + 3) + 2(y + 3) = (y + 3)(x + 2)$$

This last expression is in factored form. The process we used to obtain it is called factoring by grouping. Here are some additional examples.

Example 8   Factor $ax + bx + ay + by$.

SOLUTION   We begin by factoring x from the first two terms and y from the last two terms:

$$ax + bx + ay + by = x(a + b) + y(a + b)$$
$$= (a + b)(x + y)$$

To convince yourself that this is factored correctly, multiply the two factors $(a + b)$ and $(x + y)$. ∎

Example 9   Factor by grouping: $3ax - 2a + 15x - 10$.

SOLUTION   First, we factor a from the first two terms and 5 from the last two terms. Then, we factor $3x - 2$ from the remaining two expressions:

$$3ax - 2a + 15x - 10 = a(3x - 2) + 5(3x - 2)$$
$$= (3x - 2)(a + 5)$$

Again, multiplying $(3x - 2)$ and $(a + 5)$ will convince you that these are the correct factors. ∎

Example 10   Factor $2x^2 + 5ax - 2xy - 5ay$.

SOLUTION   From the first two terms we factor x. From the second two terms we must factor $-y$ so that the binomial that remains after we do so matches the binomial produced by the first two terms:

$$2x^2 + 5ax - 2xy - 5ay = x(2x + 5a) - y(2x + 5a)$$
$$= (2x + 5a)(x - y)$$

Another way to accomplish the same result is to use the commutative property to interchange the middle two terms, and then factor by grouping:

$$2x^2 + 5ax - 2xy - 5ay = 2x^2 - 2xy + 5ax - 5ay \qquad \textcolor{green}{\textit{Commutative property}}$$
$$= 2x(x - y) + 5a(x - y)$$
$$= (x - y)(2x + 5a)$$

This is the same result we obtained previously. ∎

Getting Ready for Class

After reading through the preceding section, respond in your own words and in complete sentences.

A. What is the greatest common factor for a polynomial?
B. After factoring a polynomial, how can you check your result?
C. When would you try to factor by grouping?
D. What is the relationship between multiplication and factoring?

Problem Set 5.1

Factor the following by taking out the greatest common factor.

1. $15x + 25$

2. $14x + 21$

3. $6a + 9$

4. $8a + 10$

5. $4x - 8y$

6. $9x - 12y$

7. $3x^2 - 6x - 9$

8. $2x^2 + 6x + 4$

9. $3a^2 - 3a - 60$

10. $2a^2 - 18a + 28$

11. $24y^2 - 52y + 24$

12. $18y^2 + 48y + 32$

13. $9x^2 - 8x^3$

14. $7x^3 - 4x^2$

15. $13a^2 - 26a^3$

16. $5a^2 - 10a^3$

17. $21x^2y - 28xy^2$

18. $30xy^2 - 25x^2y$

19. $22a^2b^2 - 11ab^2$

20. $15x^3 - 25x^2 + 30x$

21. $7x^3 + 21x^2 - 28x$

22. $16x^4 - 20x^2 - 16x$

23. $121y^4 - 11x^4$

24. $25a^4 - 5b^4$

25. $100x^4 - 50x^3 + 25x^2$

26. $36x^5 + 72x^3 - 81x^2$

27. $8a^2 + 16b^2 + 32c^2$

28. $9a^2 - 18b^2 - 27c^2$

29. $4a^2b - 16ab^2 + 32a^2b^2$

30. $5ab^2 + 10a^2b^2 + 15a^2b$

31. $121a^3b^2 - 22a^2b^3 + 33a^3b^3$

32. $20a^4b^3 - 18a^3b^4 + 22a^4b^4$

33. $12x^2y^3 - 72x^5y^3 - 36x^4y^4$

34. $49xy - 21x^2y^2 + 35x^3y^3$

Factor by grouping.

35. $xy + 5x + 3y + 15$ **36.** $xy + 2x + 4y + 8$ **37.** $xy + 6x + 2y + 12$

38. $xy + 2y + 6x + 12$ **39.** $ab + 7a - 3b - 21$ **40.** $ab + 3b - 7a - 21$

41. $ax - bx + ay - by$ **42.** $ax - ay + bx - by$ **43.** $2ax + 6x - 5a - 15$

44. $3ax + 21x - a - 7$ **45.** $3xb - 4b - 6x + 8$ **46.** $3xb - 4b - 15x + 20$

47. $x^2 + ax + 2x + 2a$ **48.** $x^2 + ax + 3x + 3a$ **49.** $x^2 - ax - bx + ab$

50. $x^2 + ax - bx - ab$

Factor by grouping. You can group the terms together two at a time or three at a time. Either way will produce the same result.

51. $ax + ay + bx + by + cx + cy$ **52.** $ax + bx + cx + ay + by + cy$

Factor the following polynomials by grouping the terms together two at a time.

53. $6x^2 + 9x + 4x + 6$ **54.** $6x^2 - 9x - 4x + 6$

55. $20x^2 - 2x + 50x - 5$ **56.** $20x^2 + 25x + 4x + 5$

57. $20x^2 + 4x + 25x + 5$ **58.** $20x^2 + 4x - 25x - 5$

59. $x^3 + 2x^2 + 3x + 6$ **60.** $x^3 - 5x^2 - 4x + 20$

61. $6x^3 - 4x^2 + 15x - 10$ **62.** $8x^3 - 12x^2 + 14x - 21$

63. The greatest common factor of the binomial $3x + 6$ is 3. The greatest common factor of the binomial $2x + 4$ is 2. What is the greatest common factor of their product $(3x + 6)(2x + 4)$ when it has been multiplied out?

64. The greatest common factors of the binomials $4x + 2$ and $5x + 10$ are 2 and 5, respectively. What is the greatest common factor of their product $(4x + 2)(5x + 10)$ when it has been multiplied out?

65. The following factorization is incorrect. Find the mistake, and correct the right-hand side:

$$12x^2 + 6x + 3 = 3(4x^2 + 2x)$$

66. Find the mistake in the following factorization, and then rewrite the right-hand side correctly:

$$10x^2 + 2x + 6 = 2(5x^2 + 3)$$

Applying the Concepts

67. **Investing** If you invest $1,000 in an account with an annual interest rate of r compounded annually, the amount of money you have in the account after one year is:

$$A = 1,000 + 1,000r$$

Write this formula again with the right side in factored form. Then, find the amount of money in this account at the end of one year if the interest rate is 12%.

68. **Investing** If you invest P dollars in an account with an annual interest rate of 8% compounded annually, then the amount of money in that account after one year is given by the formula:

$$A = P + 0.08P$$

Rewrite this formula with the right side in factored form, and then find the amount of money in the account at the end of one year if $500 was the initial investment.

69. **Biological Growth** If 1,000,000 bacteria are placed in a petri dish and the bacteria have a growth rate of r (a percent expressed as a decimal) per hour, then 1 hour later the amount of bacteria will be $A = 1,000,000 + 1,000,000r$ bacteria.

   a. Factor the right side of the equation.

   b. If $r = 30\%$, find the number of bacteria present after one hour.

70. Biological Growth If there are B E. coli bacteria present initially in a petri dish and their growth rate is r (a percent expressed as a decimal) per hour, then after one hour there will be $A = B + Br$ bacteria present.

   a. Factor the right side of this equation.

   b. The following bar graph shows the number of E. coli bacteria present initially and the number of bacteria present hours later. Use the bar chart to find B and A in the preceding equation.

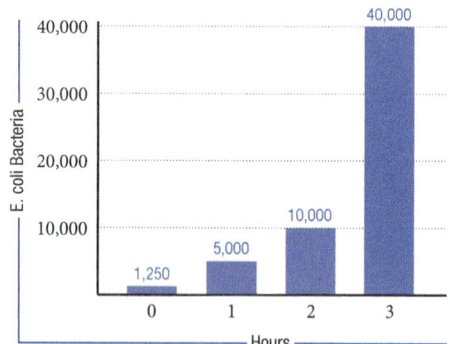

Getting Ready for the Next Section

Multiply.

71. $(x - 7)(x + 2)$ **72.** $(x - 7)(x - 2)$

73. $(x - 3)(x + 2)$ **74.** $(x + 3)(x - 2)$

75. $(x + 3)(x^2 - 3x + 9)$ **76.** $(x - 2)(x^2 + 2x + 4)$

77. $(2x + 1)(x^2 + 4x - 3)$ **78.** $(3x + 2)(x^2 - 2x - 4)$

79. $3x^4(6x^3 - 4x^2 + 2x)$ **80.** $2x^4(5x^3 + 4x^2 - 3x)$

81. $\left(x + \dfrac{1}{3}\right)\left(x + \dfrac{2}{3}\right)$ **82.** $\left(x + \dfrac{1}{4}\right)\left(x + \dfrac{3}{4}\right)$

83. $(6x + 4y)(2x - 3y)$ **84.** $(8a - 3b)(4a - 5b)$

85. $(9a + 1)(9a - 1)$ **86.** $(7b + 1)(7b + 1)$

87. $(x - 9)(x - 9)$ **88.** $(x - 8)(x - 8)$

89. $(x + 2)(x^2 - 2x + 4)$ **90.** $(x - 3)(x^2 + 3x + 9)$

Factoring Trinomials

In this section we will factor trinomials in which the coefficient of the squared term is 1. The more familiar we are with multiplication of binomials the easier factoring trinomials will be.

Recall multiplication of binomials from Chapter 4:

$$(x + 3)(x + 4) = x^2 + 7x + 12$$
$$(x - 5)(x + 2) = x^2 - 3x - 10$$

The first term in the answer is the product of the first terms in each binomial. The last term in the answer is the product of the last terms in each binomial. The middle term in the answer comes from adding the product of the outside terms to the product of the inside terms.

Let's have a and b represent real numbers and look at the product of $(x + a)$ and $(x + b)$:

$$(x + a)(x + b) = x^2 + ax + bx + ab$$
$$= x^2 + (a + b)x + ab$$

The coefficient of the middle term is the sum of a and b. The last term is the product of a and b. Writing this as a factoring problem, we have:

$$x^2 + \underset{\text{Sum}}{(a + b)}x + \underset{\text{Product}}{ab} = (x + a)(x + b)$$

To factor a trinomial in which the coefficient of x^2 is 1, we need only find the numbers a and b whose sum is the coefficient of the middle term and whose product is the constant term (last term).

Video Examples

Section 5.2

Example 1 Factor $x^2 + 8x + 12$.

SOLUTION The coefficient of x^2 is 1. We need two numbers whose sum is 8 and whose product is 12. The numbers are 6 and 2:

$$x^2 + 8x + 12 = (x + 6)(x + 2)$$

We can easily check our work by multiplying $(x + 6)$ and $(x + 2)$

$$\text{Check:} \quad (x + 6)(x + 2) = x^2 + 6x + 2x + 12$$
$$= x^2 + 8x + 12$$

Example 2 Factor $x^2 - 2x - 15$.

SOLUTION The coefficient of x^2 is again 1. We need to find a pair of numbers whose sum is -2 and whose product is -15. Here are all the possibilities for products that are -15.

Products	Sums
$-1(15) = -15$	$-1 + 15 = 14$
$1(-15) = -15$	$1 + (-15) = -14$
$-5(3) = -15$	$-5 + 3 = -2$
$5(-3) = -15$	$5 + (-3) = 2$

The third line gives us what we want. The factors of $x^2 - 2x - 15$ are $(x - 5)$ and $(x + 3)$:

$$x^2 - 2x - 15 = (x - 5)(x + 3)$$

■ **Example 3**   Factor $2x^2 + 10x - 28$.

SOLUTION   The coefficient of x^2 is 2. We begin by factoring out the greatest common factor, which is 2:

$$2x^2 + 10x - 28 = 2(x^2 + 5x - 14)$$

Now, we factor the remaining trinomial by finding a pair of numbers whose sum is 5 and whose product is -14. Here are the possibilities:

Products	Sums
$-1(14) = -14$	$-1 + 14 = 13$
$1(-14) = -14$	$1 + (-14) = -13$
$-7(2) = -14$	$-7 + 2 = -5$
$7(-2) = -14$	$7 + (-2) = 5$

> *Note*   In Example 3 we began by factoring out the greatest common factor. The first step in factoring any trinomial is to look for the greatest common factor. If the trinomial in question has a greatest common factor other than 1, we factor it out first and then try to factor the trinomial that remains.

From the last line we see that the factors of $x^2 + 5x - 14$ are $(x + 7)$ and $(x - 2)$. Here is the complete problem:

$$2x^2 + 10x - 28 = 2(x^2 + 5x - 14)$$
$$= 2(x + 7)(x - 2)$$ ■

■ **Example 4**   Factor $3x^3 - 3x^2 - 18x$.

SOLUTION   We begin by factoring out the greatest common factor, which is $3x$. Then we factor the remaining trinomial. Without showing the table of products and sums as we did in Examples 2 and 3, here is the complete problem:

$$3x^3 - 3x^2 - 18x = 3x(x^2 - x - 6)$$
$$= 3x(x - 3)(x + 2)$$ ■

■ **Example 5**   Factor $x^2 + 8xy + 12y^2$.

SOLUTION   This time we need two expressions whose product is $12y^2$ and whose sum is $8y$. The two expressions are $6y$ and $2y$ (see Example 1 in this section):

$$x^2 + 8xy + 12y^2 = (x + 6y)(x + 2y)$$

You should convince yourself that these factors are correct by finding their product.   ■

> *Note*   Trinomials in which the coefficient of the second-degree term is 1 are the easiest to factor. Success in factoring any type of polynomial is directly related to the amount of time spent working the problems. The more we practice, the more accomplished we become at factoring.

Getting Ready for Class

After reading through the preceding section, respond in your own words and in complete sentences.

A. When the leading coefficient of a trinomial is 1, what is the relationship between the other two coefficients and the factors of the trinomial?

B. When factoring polynomials, what should you look for first?

C. How can you check to see that you have factored a trinomial correctly?

D. Describe how you would find the factors of $x^2 + 8x + 12$.

Factor the following trinomials.

1. $x^2 + 7x + 12$
2. $x^2 + 7x + 10$
3. $x^2 + 3x + 2$
4. $x^2 + 7x + 6$
5. $a^2 + 10a + 21$
6. $a^2 - 7a + 12$
7. $x^2 - 7x + 10$
8. $x^2 - 3x + 2$
9. $y^2 - 10y + 21$
10. $y^2 - 7y + 6$
11. $x^2 - x - 12$
12. $x^2 - 4x - 5$
13. $y^2 + y - 12$
14. $y^2 + 3y - 18$
15. $x^2 + 5x - 14$
16. $x^2 - 5x - 24$
17. $r^2 - 8r - 9$
18. $r^2 - r - 2$
19. $x^2 - x - 30$
20. $x^2 + 8x + 12$
21. $a^2 + 15a + 56$
22. $a^2 - 9a + 20$
23. $y^2 - y - 42$
24. $y^2 + y - 42$
25. $x^2 + 13x + 42$
26. $x^2 - 13x + 42$

Factor the following problems completely. First, factor out the greatest common factor, and then factor the remaining trinomial.

27. $2x^2 + 6x + 4$
28. $3x^2 - 6x - 9$
29. $3a^2 - 3a - 60$
30. $2a^2 - 18a + 28$
31. $100x^2 - 500x + 600$
32. $100x^2 - 900x + 2,000$
33. $100p^2 - 1,300p + 4,000$
34. $100p^2 - 1,200p + 3,200$
35. $x^4 - x^3 - 12x^2$
36. $x^4 - 11x^3 + 24x^2$
37. $2r^3 + 4r^2 - 30r$
38. $5r^3 + 45r^2 + 100r$
39. $2y^4 - 6y^3 - 8y^2$
40. $3r^3 - 3r^2 - 6r$
41. $x^5 + 4x^4 + 4x^3$
42. $x^5 + 13x^4 + 42x^3$
43. $3y^4 - 12y^3 - 15y^2$
44. $5y^4 - 10y^3 + 5y^2$
45. $4x^4 - 52x^3 + 144x^2$
46. $3x^3 - 3x^2 - 18x$

Factor the following trinomials.

47. $x^2 + 5xy + 6y^2$
48. $x^2 - 5xy + 6y^2$
49. $x^2 - 9xy + 20y^2$
50. $x^2 + 9xy + 20y^2$
51. $a^2 + 2ab - 8b^2$
52. $a^2 - 2ab - 8b^2$
53. $a^2 - 10ab + 25b^2$
54. $a^2 + 6ab + 9b^2$
55. $a^2 + 10ab + 25b^2$
56. $a^2 - 6ab + 9b^2$
57. $x^2 + 2xa - 48a^2$
58. $x^2 - 3xa - 10a^2$
59. $x^2 - 5xb - 36b^2$
60. $x^2 - 13xb + 36b^2$

Factor completely.

61. $x^4 - 5x^2 + 6$

62. $x^6 - 2x^3 - 15$

63. $x^2 - 80x - 2{,}000$

64. $x^2 - 190x - 2{,}000$

65. $x^2 - x + \dfrac{1}{4}$

66. $x^2 - \dfrac{2}{3}x + \dfrac{1}{9}$

67. $x^2 + 0.6x + 0.08$

68. $x^2 + 0.8x + 0.15$

69. If one of the factors of $x^2 + 24x + 128$ is $x + 8$, what is the other factor?

70. If one factor of $x^2 + 260x + 2{,}500$ is $x + 10$, what is the other factor?

71. What polynomial, when factored, gives $(4x + 3)(x - 1)$?

72. What polynomial factors to $(4x - 3)(x + 1)$?

Getting Ready for the Next Section

Multiply using the FOIL method.

73. $(6a + 1)(a + 2)$

74. $(6a - 1)(a - 2)$

75. $(3a + 2)(2a + 1)$

76. $(3a - 2)(2a - 1)$

77. $(6a + 2)(a + 1)$

78. $(3a + 1)(2a + 2)$

We will now consider trinomials whose greatest common factor is 1 and whose leading coefficient (the coefficient of the squared term) is a number other than 1.

Suppose we want to factor the trinomial $2x^2 - 5x - 3$. We know the factors (if they exist) will be a pair of binomials. The product of their first terms is $2x^2$ and the product of their last term is -3. Let us list all the possible factors along with the trinomial that would result if we were to multiply them together. Remember, the middle term comes from the product of the inside terms plus the product of the outside terms.

Binomial Factors	First Term	Middle Term	Last Term
$(2x - 3)(x + 1)$	$2x^2$	$-x$	-3
$(2x + 3)(x - 1)$	$2x^2$	$+x$	-3
$(2x - 1)(x + 3)$	$2x^2$	$+5x$	-3
$(2x + 1)(x - 3)$	$2x^2$	$-5x$	-3

We can see from the last line that the factors of $2x^2 - 5x - 3$ are $(2x + 1)$ and $(x - 3)$. There is no straightforward way, as there was in the previous section, to find the factors, other than by trial and error or by simply listing all the possibilities. We look for possible factors that, when multiplied, will give the correct first and last terms, and then we see if we can adjust them to give the correct middle term.

Video Examples

Section 5.3

Note Remember, we can always check our results by multiplying the factors we have and comparing that product with our original polynomial.

Example 1 Factor $6a^2 + 7a + 2$.

SOLUTION We list all the possible pairs of factors that, when multiplied together, give a trinomial whose first term is $6a^2$ and whose last term is $+2$.

Binomial Factors	First Term	Middle Term	Last Term
$(6a + 1)(a + 2)$	$6a^2$	$+13a$	$+2$
$(6a - 1)(a - 2)$	$6a^2$	$-13a$	$+2$
$(3a + 2)(2a + 1)$	$6a^2$	$+7a$	$+2$
$(3a - 2)(2a - 1)$	$6a^2$	$-7a$	$+2$

The factors of $6a^2 + 7a + 2$ are $(3a + 2)$ and $(2a + 1)$.

Check: $(3a + 2)(2a + 1) = 6a^2 + 7a + 2$

Notice that in the preceding list we did not include the factors $(6a + 2)$ and $(a + 1)$. We do not need to try these since the first factor has a 2 common to each term and so could be factored again, giving $2(3a + 1)(a + 1)$. Since our original trinomial, $6a^2 + 7a + 2$, did *not* have a greatest common factor of 2, neither of its factors will.

Example 2   Factor $4x^2 - x - 3$.

SOLUTION We list all the possible factors that, when multiplied, give a trinomial whose first term is $4x^2$ and whose last term is -3.

Binomial Factors	First Term	Middle Term	Last Term
$(4x + 1)(x - 3)$	$4x^2$	$-11x$	-3
$(4x - 1)(x + 3)$	$4x^2$	$+11x$	-3
$(4x + 3)(x - 1)$	$4x^2$	$-x$	-3
$(4x - 3)(x + 1)$	$4x^2$	$+x$	-3
$(2x + 1)(2x - 3)$	$4x^2$	$-4x$	-3
$(2x - 1)(2x + 3)$	$4x^2$	$+4x$	-3

The third line shows that the factors are $(4x + 3)$ and $(x - 1)$.

$$\text{Check:}\quad (4x + 3)(x - 1) = 4x^2 - x - 3$$

You will find that the more practice you have at factoring this type of trinomial, the faster you will get the correct factors. You will pick up some shortcuts along the way, or you may come across a system of eliminating some factors as possibilities. Whatever works best for you is the method you should use. Factoring is a very important tool, and you must be good at it.

Example 3   Factor $12y^3 + 10y^2 - 12y$.

SOLUTION We begin by factoring out the greatest common factor, $2y$:

$$12y^3 + 10y^2 - 12y = 2y(6y^2 + 5y - 6)$$

We now list all possible factors of a trinomial with the first term $6y^2$ and last term -6, along with the associated middle terms.

> **Note** Once again, the first step in any factoring problem is to factor out the greatest common factor if it is other than 1.

Possible Factors	Middle Term When Multiplied
$(3y + 2)(2y - 3)$	$-5y$
$(3y - 2)(2y + 3)$	$+5y$
$(6y + 1)(y - 6)$	$-35y$
$(6y - 1)(y + 6)$	$+35y$

The second line gives the correct factors. The complete problem is:

$$12y^3 + 10y^2 - 12y = 2y(6y^2 + 5y - 6)$$
$$= 2y(3y - 2)(2y + 3)$$

Example 4   Factor $30x^2y - 5xy^2 - 10y^3$.

SOLUTION The greatest common factor is $5y$:

$$30x^2y - 5xy^2 - 10y^3 = 5y(6x^2 - xy - 2y^2)$$
$$= 5y(2x + y)(3x - 2y)$$

Example 5   A ball is tossed into the air with an upward velocity of 16 feet per second from the top of a building 32 feet high. The equation that gives the height of the ball above the ground at any time t is

$$h = 32 + 16t - 16t^2$$

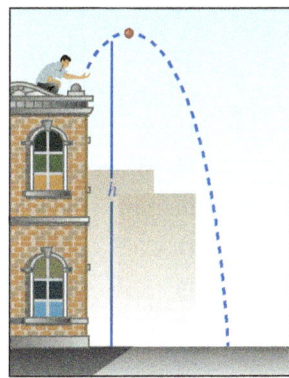

Factor the right side of this equation and then find h when t is 2.

SOLUTION   We begin by factoring out the greatest common factor, 16. Then, we factor the trinomial that remains:

$$h = 32 + 16t - 16t^2$$
$$h = 16(2 + t - t^2)$$
$$h = 16(2 - t)(1 + t) \qquad \text{Letting } t = 2 \text{ in the equation, we have}$$
$$h = 16(0)(3) = 0$$

When t is 2, h is 0.

Getting Ready for Class

After reading through the preceding section, respond in your own words and in complete sentences.

A. What is the first step in factoring a trinomial?

B. Describe the criteria you would use to set up a table of possible factors of a trinomial.

C. What does it mean if you factor a trinomial and one of your factors has a greatest common factor of 3?

D. Describe how you would look for possible factors of $6a^2 + 7a + 2$.

Factor the following trinomials.

1. $2x^2 + 7x + 3$
2. $2x^2 + 5x + 3$
3. $2a^2 - a - 3$
4. $2a^2 + a - 3$
5. $3x^2 + 2x - 5$
6. $3x^2 - 2x - 5$
7. $3y^2 - 14y - 5$
8. $3y^2 + 14y - 5$
9. $6x^2 + 13x + 6$
10. $6x^2 - 13x + 6$
11. $4x^2 - 12xy + 9y^2$
12. $4x^2 + 12xy + 9y^2$
13. $4y^2 - 11y - 3$
14. $4y^2 + y - 3$
15. $20x^2 - 41x + 20$
16. $20x^2 + 9x - 20$
17. $20a^2 + 48ab - 5b^2$
18. $20a^2 + 29ab + 5b^2$
19. $20x^2 - 21x - 5$
20. $20x^2 - 48x - 5$
21. $12m^2 + 16m - 3$
22. $12m^2 + 20m + 3$
23. $20x^2 + 37x + 15$
24. $20x^2 + 13x - 15$
25. $12a^2 - 25ab + 12b^2$
26. $12a^2 + 7ab - 12b^2$
27. $3x^2 - xy - 14y^2$
28. $3x^2 + 19xy - 14y^2$
29. $14x^2 + 29x - 15$
30. $14x^2 + 11x - 15$
31. $6x^2 - 43x + 55$
32. $6x^2 - 7x - 55$
33. $15t^2 - 67t + 38$
34. $15t^2 - 79t - 34$

Factor each of the following completely. Look first for the greatest common factor.

35. $4x^2 + 2x - 6$
36. $6x^2 - 51x + 63$
37. $24a^2 - 50a + 24$
38. $18a^2 + 48a + 32$
39. $10x^3 - 23x^2 + 12x$
40. $10x^4 + 7x^3 - 12x^2$
41. $6x^4 - 11x^3 - 10x^2$
42. $6x^3 + 19x^2 + 10x$
43. $10a^3 - 6a^2 - 4a$
44. $6a^3 + 15a^2 + 9a$
45. $15x^3 - 102x^2 - 21x$
46. $2x^4 - 24x^3 + 64x^2$
47. $35y^3 - 60y^2 - 20y$
48. $14y^4 - 32y^3 + 8y^2$
49. $15a^4 - 2a^3 - a^2$
50. $10a^5 - 17a^4 + 3a^3$
51. $24x^2y - 6xy - 45y$
52. $8x^2y^2 + 26xy^2 + 15y^2$
53. $12x^2y - 34xy^2 + 14y^3$
54. $12x^2y - 46xy^2 + 14y^3$

55. Evaluate the expression $2x^2 + 7x + 3$ and the expression $(2x + 1)(x + 3)$ for $x = 2$.

56. Evaluate the expression $2a^2 - a - 3$ and the expression $(2a - 3)(a + 1)$ for $a = 5$.

57. What polynomial factors to $(2x + 3)(2x - 3)$?

58. What polynomial factors to $(5x + 4)(5x - 4)$?

59. What polynomial factors to $(x + 3)(x - 3)(x^2 + 9)$?

60. What polynomial factors to $(x + 2)(x - 2)(x^2 + 4)$?

Applying the Concepts

61. Archery Margaret shoots an arrow into the air. The equation for the height (in feet) of the tip of the arrow is:

$$h = 8 + 62t - 16t^2$$

Factor the right side of this equation. Then fill in the table for various heights of the arrow, using the factored form of the equation.

Time t (seconds)	0	1	2	3	4
Height h (feet)					

62. Coin Toss At the beginning of every football game, the referee flips a coin to see who will kick off. The equation that gives the height (in feet) of the coin tossed in the air is:

$$h = 6 + 29t - 16t^2$$

a. Factor this equation.

b. Use the factored form of the equation to find the height of the quarter after 0 seconds, 1 second, and 2 seconds.

63. Constructing a Box Yesterday I was experimenting with how to cut and fold a certain piece of cardboard to make a box with different volumes. Unfortunately, today I have lost both the cardboard and most of my notes. I remember that I made the box by cutting equal squares from the corners then folding up the side flaps:

I don't remember how big the cardboard was, and I can only find the last page of notes, which says that if x is the length of a side of a small square (in inches), then the volume is $V = 99x - 40x^2 + 4x^3$.

a. Factor the right side of this expression completely.

b. What were the dimensions of the original piece of cardboard?

64. Constructing a Box Repeat Problem 63 if the remaining formula is $V = 15x - 16x^2 + 4x^3$.

Getting Ready for the Next Section

Multiply each of the following.

65. $(x + 3)(x - 3)$

66. $(x - 4)(x + 4)$

67. $(x + 5)(x - 5)$

68. $(x - 6)(x + 6)$

69. $(x + 7)(x - 7)$

70. $(x - 8)(x + 8)$

71. $(x + 9)(x - 9)$

72. $(x - 10)(x + 10)$

73. $(2x - 3y)(2x + 3y)$

74. $(5x - 6y)(5x + 6y)$

75. $(x^2 + 4)(x + 2)(x - 2)$

76. $(x^2 + 9)(x + 3)(x - 3)$

77. $(x + 3)^2$

78. $(x - 4)^2$

79. $(x + 5)^2$

80. $(x - 6)^2$

81. $(x + 7)^2$

82. $(x - 8)^2$

83. $(x + 9)^2$

84. $(x - 10)^2$

85. $(2x + 3)^2$

86. $(3x - y)^2$

87. $(4x - 2y)^2$

88. $(5x - 6y)^2$

Perfect Square Trinomials and the Difference of Two Squares

In Chapter 4 we listed the following three special products:

$$(a + b)^2 = (a + b)(a + b) = a^2 + 2ab + b^2$$
$$(a - b)^2 = (a - b)(a - b) = a^2 - 2ab + b^2$$
$$(a + b)(a - b) = a^2 - b^2$$

Since factoring is the reverse of multiplication, we can also consider the three special products as three special factorings:

$$a^2 + 2ab + b^2 = (a + b)^2$$
$$a^2 - 2ab + b^2 = (a - b)^2$$
$$a^2 - b^2 = (a + b)(a - b)$$

Any trinomial of the form $a^2 + 2ab + b^2$ or $a^2 - 2ab + b^2$ can be factored by the methods of Section 4.6. The last line is the factoring to obtain the difference of two squares. The difference of two squares always factors in this way. Again, these are patterns you must be able to recognize on sight.

Video Examples

Section 5.4

Example 1 Factor $16x^2 - 25$.

SOLUTION We can see that the first term is a perfect square, and the last term is also. This fact becomes even more obvious if we rewrite the problem as:

$$16x^2 - 25 = (4x)^2 - (5)^2$$

The first term is the square of the quantity $4x$, and the last term is the square of 5. The completed problem looks like this:

$$16x^2 - 25 = (4x)^2 - (5)^2$$
$$= (4x + 5)(4x - 5)$$

To check our results, we multiply:

$$(4x + 5)(4x - 5) = 16x^2 + 20x - 20x - 25$$
$$= 16x^2 - 25$$

Example 2 Factor $36a^2 - 1$.

SOLUTION We rewrite the two terms to show they are perfect squares and then factor. Remember, 1 is its own square, $1^2 = 1$.

$$36a^2 - 1 = (6a)^2 - (1)^2$$
$$= (6a + 1)(6a - 1)$$

To check our results, we multiply:

$$(6a + 1)(6a - 1) = 36a^2 + 6a - 6a - 1$$
$$= 36a^2 - 1$$

Example 3   Factor $x^4 - y^4$.

SOLUTION x^4 is the perfect square $(x^2)^2$, and y^4 is $(y^2)^2$:

$$x^4 - y^4 = (x^2)^2 - (y^2)^2$$
$$= (x^2 - y^2)(x^2 + y^2)$$

The factor $(x^2 - y^2)$ is itself the difference of two squares and therefore can be factored again. The factor $(x^2 + y^2)$ is the *sum* of two squares and cannot be factored again. The complete problem is this:

$$x^4 - y^4 = (x^2)^2 - (y^2)^2$$
$$= (x^2 - y^2)(x^2 + y^2)$$
$$= (x + y)(x - y)(x^2 + y^2)$$

> *Note*   If you think the sum of two squares $x^2 + y^2$ factors, you should try it. Write down the factors you think it has, and then multiply them using the foil method. You won't get $x^2 + y^2$.

Example 4   Factor $25x^2 - 60x + 36$.

SOLUTION   Although this trinomial can be factored by the method we used in Section 5.3, we notice that the first and last terms are the perfect squares $(5x)^2$ and $(6)^2$. Before going through the method for factoring trinomials by listing all possible factors, we can check to see if $25x^2 - 60x + 36$ factors to $(5x - 6)^2$. We need only multiply to check:

$$(5x - 6)^2 = (5x - 6)(5x - 6)$$
$$= 25x^2 - 30x - 30x + 36$$
$$= 25x^2 - 60x + 36$$

The trinomial $25x^2 - 60x + 36$ factors to $(5x - 6)(5x - 6) = (5x - 6)^2$.

> *Note*   As we have indicated before, perfect square trinomials like the ones in Examples 4 and 5 can be factored by the methods developed in previous sections. Recognizing that they factor to binomial squares simply saves time in factoring.

Example 5   Factor $5x^2 + 30x + 45$.

SOLUTION   We begin by factoring out the greatest common factor, which is 5. Then we notice that the trinomial that remains is a perfect square trinomial:

$$5x^2 + 30x + 45 = 5(x^2 + 6x + 9)$$
$$= 5(x + 3)^2$$

Example 6   Factor $(x - 3)^2 - 25$.

SOLUTION   This example has the form $a^2 - b^2$, where a is $x - 3$ and b is 5. We factor it according to the formula for the difference of two squares:

$$(x - 3)^2 - 25 = (x - 3)^2 - 5^2 \qquad \text{Write 25 as } 5^2$$
$$= [(x - 3) - 5][(x - 3) + 5] \qquad \text{Factor}$$
$$= (x - 8)(x + 2) \qquad \text{Simplify}$$

Notice in this example we could have expanded $(x - 3)^2$, subtracted 25, and then factored to obtain the same result:

$$(x - 3)^2 - 25 = x^2 - 6x + 9 - 25 \qquad \text{Expand } (x \cdot 3)^2$$
$$= x^2 - 6x - 16 \qquad \text{Simplify}$$
$$= (x - 8)(x + 2) \qquad \text{Factor}$$

Getting Ready for Class

After reading through the preceding section, respond in your own words and in complete sentences.

A. Describe how you factor the difference of two squares.

B. What is a perfect square trinomial?

C. How do you know when you've factored completely?

D. Describe how you would factor $25x^2 - 60x + 36$.

SPOTLIGHT ON SUCCESS   *Student Instructor Stefanie*

> *Never confuse a single defeat with a final defeat.*
> —F. Scott Fitzgerald

The idea that has worked best for my success in college, and more specifically in my math courses, is to stay positive and be resilient. I have learned that a 'bad' grade doesn't make me a failure; if anything it makes me strive to do better. That is why I never let a bad grade on a test or even in a class get in the way of my overall success.

By sticking with this positive attitude, I have been able to achieve my goals. My grades have never represented how well I know the material. This is because I have struggled with test anxiety and it has consistently lowered my test scores in a number of courses. However, I have not let it defeat me. When I applied to graduate school, I did not meet the grade requirements for my top two schools, but that did not stop me from applying.

One school asked that I convince them that my knowledge of mathematics was more than my grades indicated. If I had let my grades stand in the way of my goals, I wouldn't have been accepted to both of my top two schools, and will be attending one of them in the Fall, on my way to becoming a mathematics teacher.

Problem Set 5.4

Factor the following.

1. $x^2 - 9$ **2.** $x^2 - 25$ **3.** $a^2 - 36$ **4.** $a^2 - 64$

5. $x^2 - 49$ **6.** $x^2 - 121$ **7.** $4a^2 - 16$ **8.** $4a^2 + 16$

9. $9x^2 + 25$ **10.** $16x^2 - 36$ **11.** $25x^2 - 169$ **12.** $x^2 - y^2$

13. $9a^2 - 16b^2$ **14.** $49a^2 - 25b^2$ **15.** $9 - m^2$ **16.** $16 - m^2$

17. $25 - 4x^2$ **18.** $36 - 49y^2$ **19.** $2x^2 - 18$ **20.** $3x^2 - 27$

21. $32a^2 - 128$ **22.** $3a^3 - 48a$ **23.** $8x^2y - 18y$ **24.** $50a^2b - 72b$

25. $a^4 - b^4$ **26.** $a^4 - 16$ **27.** $16m^4 - 81$ **28.** $81 - m^4$

29. $3x^3y - 75xy^3$ **30.** $2xy^3 - 8x^3y$

Factor the following.

31. $x^2 - 2x + 1$ **32.** $x^2 - 6x + 9$

33. $x^2 + 2x + 1$ **34.** $x^2 + 6x + 9$

35. $a^2 - 10a + 25$ **36.** $a^2 + 10a + 25$

37. $y^2 + 4y + 4$ **38.** $y^2 - 8y + 16$

39. $x^2 - 4x + 4$ **40.** $x^2 + 8x + 16$

41. $m^2 - 12m + 36$ **42.** $m^2 + 12m + 36$

43. $4a^2 + 12a + 9$ **44.** $9a^2 - 12a + 4$

45. $49x^2 - 14x + 1$

46. $64x^2 - 16x + 1$

47. $9y^2 - 30y + 25$

48. $25y^2 + 30y + 9$

49. $x^2 + 10xy + 25y^2$

50. $25x^2 + 10xy + y^2$

51. $9a^2 + 6ab + b^2$

52. $9a^2 - 6ab + b^2$

Factor the following by first factoring out the greatest common factor.

53. $3a^2 + 18a + 27$

54. $4a^2 - 16a + 16$

55. $2x^2 + 20xy + 50y^2$

56. $3x^2 + 30xy + 75y^2$

57. $5x^3 + 30x^2y + 45xy^2$

58. $12x^2y - 36xy^2 + 27y^3$

Factor by grouping the first three terms together.

59. $x^2 + 6x + 9 - y^2$

60. $x^2 + 10x + 25 - y^2$

61. $x^2 + 2xy + y^2 - 9$

62. $a^2 + 2ab + b^2 - 25$

63. Find a value for b so that the polynomial $x^2 + bx + 49$ factors to $(x + 7)^2$.

64. Find a value of b so that the polynomial $x^2 + bx + 81$ factors to $(x + 9)^2$.

65. Find the value of c for which the polynomial $x^2 + 10x + c$ factors to $(x + 5)^2$.

66. Find the value of a for which the polynomial $ax^2 + 12x + 9$ factors to $(2x + 3)^2$.

Applying the Concepts

67. Area

   a. What is the area of the following figure?

   b. Factor the answer from part **a.**

   c. Find a way to cut the figure into two pieces and put them back together to show that the factorization in part **b.** is correct.

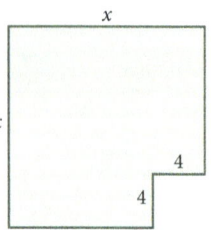

68. Area

   a. What is the area of the following figure?

   b. Factor the expression from part **a.**

   c. Cut and rearrange the figure to show that the factorization is correct.

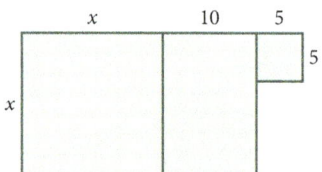

Find the area for the shaded regions; then write your result in factored form.

69.

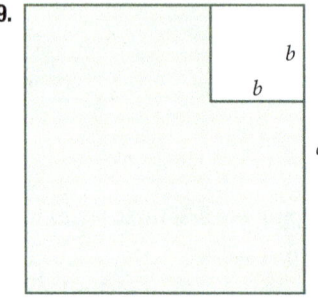

70.

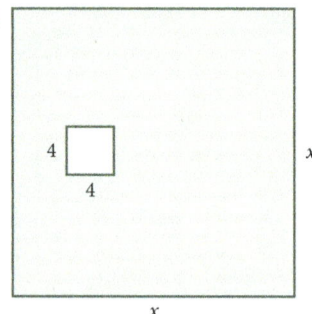

Getting Ready for the Next Section

Multiply each of the following.

71. a. 1^3 **b.** 2^3 **c.** 3^3 **d.** 4^3 **e.** 5^3

72. a. $(-1)^3$ **b.** $(-2)^3$ **c.** $(-3)^3$ **d.** $(-4)^3$ **e.** $(-5)^3$

73. a. $x(x^2 - x + 1)$ **b.** $1(x^2 - x + 1)$ **c.** $(x + 1)(x^2 - x + 1)$

74. a. $x(x^2 + x + 1)$ **b.** $-1(x^2 + x + 1)$ **c.** $(x - 1)(x^2 + x + 1)$

75. a. $x(x^2 - 2x + 4)$ **b.** $2(x^2 - 2x + 4)$ **c.** $(x + 2)(x^2 - 2x + 4)$

76. a. $x(x^2 + 2x + 4)$ **b.** $-2(x^2 + 2x + 4)$ **c.** $(x - 2)(x^2 + 2x + 4)$

77. a. $x(x^2 - 3x + 9)$ **b.** $3(x^2 - 3x + 9)$ **c.** $(x + 3)(x^2 - 3x + 9)$

78. a. $x(x^2 + 3x + 9)$ **b.** $-3(x^2 + 3x + 9)$ **c.** $(x - 3)(x^2 + 3x + 9)$

Previously, we factored a variety of polynomials. Among the polynomials we factored were polynomials that were the difference of two squares. The formula we used to factor the difference of two squares looks like this:

$$a^2 - b^2 = (a + b)(a - b)$$

If we ran across a binomial that had the form of the difference of two squares, we factored it by applying this formula. For example, to factor $x^2 - 25$, we simply notice that it can be written in the form $x^2 - 5^2$, which looks like the difference of two squares. According to the formula above, this binomial factors into $(x + 5)$ $(x - 5)$.

In this section we want to use two new formulas that will allow us to factor the sum and difference of two cubes. For example, we want to factor the binomial $x^3 - 8$, which is the difference of two cubes. (To see that it is the differrence of two cubes, notice that it can be written $x^3 - 2^3$.) We also want to factor $y^3 + 27$, which is the sum of two cubes. (To see this, notice that $y^3 + 27$ can be written as $y^3 + 3^3$.)

The formulas that allow us to factor the sum of two cubes and the difference of two cubes are not as simple as the formula for factoring the difference of two squares. Here is what they look like:

$$a^3 + b^3 = (a + b)(a^2 - ab + b^2)$$

$$a^3 - b^3 = (a - b)(a^2 + ab + b^2)$$

Let's begin our work with these two formulas by showing that they are true. To do so, we multiply out the right side of each formula.

Video Examples

Section 5.5

Example 1 Verify the two formulas.

SOLUTION We verify the formulas by multiplying the right sides and comparing the results with the left sides:

$$
\begin{array}{r}
a^2 - ab + b^2 \\
a + b \\
\hline
a^3 - a^2b + ab^2 \\
a^2b - ab^2 + b^3 \\
\hline
a^3 \qquad\qquad + b^3
\end{array}
\qquad\qquad
\begin{array}{r}
a^2 + ab + b^2 \\
a - b \\
\hline
a^3 + a^2b + ab^2 \\
- a^2b - ab^2 - b^3 \\
\hline
a^3 \qquad\qquad - b^3
\end{array}
$$

The first formula is correct.   The second formula is correct.

Here are some examples that use the formulas for factoring the sum and difference of two cubes.

Example 2 Factor $x^3 - 8$.

SOLUTION Since the two terms are prefect cubes, we write them as such and apply the formula:

$$x^3 - 8 = x^3 - 2^3$$
$$= (x - 2)(x^2 + 2x + 2^2)$$
$$= (x - 2)(x^2 + 2x + 4)$$

Example 3   Factor $y^3 + 27$.

SOLUTION   Proceeding as we did in Example 2, we first write 27 as 3^3. Then, we apply the formula for factoring the sum of two cubes, which is $a^3 + b^3 = (a + b)(a^2 - ab + b^2)$:

$$y^3 + 27 = y^3 + 3^3$$
$$= (y + 3)(y^2 - 3y + 3^2)$$
$$= (y + 3)(y^2 - 3y + 9)$$

Here are some examples using the formulas for factoring the sum and difference of two cubes.

Example 4   Factor $64 + t^3$.

SOLUTION   The first term is the cube of 4 and the second term is the cube of t. Therefore,

$$64 + t^3 = 4^3 + t^3$$
$$= (4 + t)(16 - 4t + t^2)$$

Example 5   Factor $27x^3 + 125y^3$.

SOLUTION   Writing both terms as perfect cubes, we have

$$27x^3 + 125y^3 = (3x)^3 + (5y)^3$$
$$= (3x + 5y)(9x^2 - 15xy + 25y^2)$$

Example 6   Factor $a^3 - \dfrac{1}{8}$.

SOLUTION   The first term is the cube of a, whereas the second term is the cube of $\frac{1}{2}$:

$$a^3 - \frac{1}{8} = a^3 - \left(\frac{1}{2}\right)^3$$
$$= \left(a - \frac{1}{2}\right)\left(a^2 + \frac{1}{2}a + \frac{1}{4}\right)$$

Example 7   Factor $x^6 - y^6$.

SOLUTION   We have a choice of how we want to write the two terms to begin. We can write the expression as the difference of two squares, $(x^3)^2 - (y^3)^2$, or as the difference of two cubes, $(x^2)^3 - (y^2)^3$. It is better to use the difference of two squares if we have a choice:

$$x^6 - y^6 = (x^3)^2 - (y^3)^2$$
$$= (x^3 - y^3)(x^3 + y^3)$$
$$= (x - y)(x^2 + xy + y^2)(x + y)(x^2 - xy + y^2)$$

Getting Ready for Class

After reading through the preceding section, respond in your own words and in complete sentences.

A. How can you check your work when factoring?

B. Why are the numbers 8, 27, 64, and 125 used so frequently in this section?

C. List the cubes of the numbers 1 through 10.

D. How are you going to remember that the sum of two cubes factors, while the sum of two squares is prime?

Factor each of the following.

1. $x^3 - y^3$ **2.** $x^3 + y^3$ **3.** $a^3 + 8$

4. $a^3 - 8$ **5.** $27 + x^3$ **6.** $27 - x^3$

7. $y^3 - 1$ **8.** $y^3 + 1$ **9.** $y^3 - 64$

10. $y^3 + 64$ **11.** $125h^3 - t^3$ **12.** $t^3 + 125h^3$

13. $x^3 - 216$ **14.** $216 + x^3$ **15.** $2y^3 - 54$

16. $81 + 3y^3$ **17.** $2a^3 - 128b^3$ **18.** $128a^3 + 2b^3$

19. $2x^3 + 432y^3$ **20.** $432x^3 - 2y^3$ **21.** $10a^3 - 640b^3$

22. $640a^3 + 10b^3$ **23.** $10r^3 - 1{,}250$ **24.** $10r^3 + 1{,}250$

25. $64 + 27a^3$ **26.** $27 - 64a^3$ **27.** $8x^3 - 27y^3$

28. $27x^3 - 8y^3$ **29.** $t^3 + \dfrac{1}{27}$ **30.** $t^3 - \dfrac{1}{27}$

31. $27x^3 - \dfrac{1}{27}$ **32.** $8x^3 + \dfrac{1}{8}$ **33.** $64a^3 + 125b^3$

34. $125a^3 - 27b^3$ **35.** $\dfrac{1}{8}x^3 - \dfrac{1}{27}y^3$ **36.** $\dfrac{1}{27}x^3 + \dfrac{1}{8}y^3$

37. $a^6 - b^6$ **38.** $x^6 - 64y^6$ **39.** $64x^6 - y^6$

40. $x^6 - (3y)^6$ **41.** $x^6 - (5y)^6$ **42.** $(4x)^6 - (7y)^6$

Getting Ready for the Next Section

Multiply each of the following.

43. $2x^3(x + 2)(x - 2)$ **44.** $3x^2(x + 3)(x - 3)$

45. $3x^2(x - 3)^2$ **46.** $2x^2(x + 5)^2$

47. $y(y^2 + 25)$ **48.** $y^3(y^2 + 36)$

49. $(5a - 2)(3a + 1)$ **50.** $(3a - 4)(2a - 1)$

51. $4x^2(x - 5)(x + 2)$ **52.** $6x(x - 4)(x + 2)$

53. $2ab^3(b^2 - 4b + 1)$ **54.** $2a^3b(a^2 + 3a + 1)$

In this section we will review the different methods of factoring that we presented in the previous sections of the chapter. This section is important because it will give you an opportunity to factor a variety of polynomials. Prior to this section, the polynomials you worked with were grouped together according to the method used to factor them; that is, in Section 5.4 all the polynomials you factored were either the difference of two squares or perfect square trinomials. What usually happens in a situation like this is that you become proficient at factoring the kind of polynomial you are working with at the time but have trouble when given a variety of polynomials to factor.

We begin this section with a checklist that can be used in factoring polynomials of any type. When you have finished this section and the problem set that follows, you want to be proficient enough at factoring that the checklist is second nature to you.

> **⟨Δ≠Σ⟩   *How to Factor a Polynomial***
>
> **Step 1:** If the polynomial has a greatest common factor other than 1, then factor out the greatest common factor.
> **Step 2:** If the polynomial has two terms (it is a binomial), then see if it is the difference of two squares or the sum or difference of two cubes, and then factor accordingly. Remember, if it is the sum of two squares, it will not factor.
> **Step 3:** If the polynomial has three terms (a trinomial), then either it is a perfect square trinomial, which will factor into the square of a binomial, or it is not a perfect square trinomial, in which case you use the trial and error method developed in Section 5.3.
> **Step 4:** If the polynomial has more than three terms, try to factor it by grouping.
> **Step 5:** As a final check, see if any of the factors you have written can be factored further. If you have overlooked a common factor, you can catch it here.

Here are some examples illustrating how we use the checklist.

Example 1   Factor $2x^5 - 8x^3$.

SOLUTION   First, we check to see if the greatest common factor is other than 1. Since the greatest common factor is $2x^3$, we begin by factoring it out. Once we have done so, we notice that the binomial that remains is the difference of two squares:

$$2x^5 - 8x^3 = 2x^3(x^2 - 4) \qquad \text{\textcolor{green}{Factor out the greatest common factor, } } 2x^3$$

$$= 2x^3(x + 2)(x - 2) \qquad \text{\textcolor{green}{Factor the difference of two squares}}$$

Note that the greatest common factor $2x^3$ that we factored from each term in the first step of Example 1 remains as part of the answer to the problem; that is because it is one of the factors of the original binomial. Remember, the expression we end up with when factoring must be equal to the expression we start with. We can't just drop a factor and expect the resulting expression to equal the original expression.

Example 2   Factor $3x^4 - 18x^3 + 27x^2$.

SOLUTION   Step 1 is to factor out the greatest common factor, $3x^2$. After we have done so, we notice that the trinomial that remains is a perfect square trinomial, which will factor as the square of a binomial:

$$3x^4 - 18x^3 + 27x^2 = 3x^2(x^2 - 6x + 9) \qquad \text{Factor out } 3x^2$$
$$= 3x^2(x - 3)^2 \qquad \qquad x^2 - 6x + 9 \text{ is the}$$
$$\text{square of } x - 3$$

Example 3   Factor $y^3 + 25y$.

SOLUTION   We begin by factoring out the y that is common to both terms. The binomial that remains after we have done so is the sum of two squares, which does not factor, so after the first step we are finished:

$$y^3 + 25y = y(y^2 + 25) \qquad \text{Factor out the greatest common factor, } y;$$
$$\text{then notice that } y^2 + 25 \text{ cannot}$$
$$\text{factored further}$$

Example 4   Factor $6a^2 - 11a + 4$.

SOLUTION   Here we have a trinomial that does not have a greatest common factor other than 1. Since it is not a perfect square trinomial, we factor it by trial and error; that is, we look for binomial factors of the product whose first terms is $6a^2$ and of the product whose last terms is 4. Then we look for the combination of these types of binomials whose product gives us a middle term of $-11a$. Without showing all the different possibilities, here is the answer:

$$6a^2 - 11a + 4 = (3a - 4)(2a - 1)$$

Example 5   Factor $6x^3 - 12x^2 - 48x$.

SOLUTION   This trinomial has a greatest common factor of $6x$. The trinomial that remains after the $6x$ has been factored from each term must be factored by trial and error:

$$6x^3 - 12x^2 - 48x = 6x(x^2 - 2x - 8)$$
$$= 6x(x - 4)(x + 2)$$

Example 6   Factor $2ab^5 + 8ab^4 + 2ab^3$.

SOLUTION   The greatest common factor is $2ab^3$. We begin by factoring it from each term. After that we find the trinomial that remains cannot be factored further:

$$2ab^5 + 8ab^4 + 2ab^3 = 2ab^3(b^2 + 4b + 1)$$

Example 7   Factor $xy + 8x + 3y + 24$.

SOLUTION   Since our polynomial has four terms, we try factoring by grouping:

$$xy + 8x + 3y + 24 = x(y + 8) + 3(y + 8)$$
$$= (y + 8)(x + 3)$$

Example 8   Factor $125 + t^3$.

SOLUTION   The first term is the cube of 4 and the second term is the cube of t. Therefore,

$$125 + t^3 = 5^3 + t^3$$
$$= (5 + t)(25 - 5t + t^2)$$ ◼

Example 9   Factor $a^3 - \dfrac{1}{27}$.

SOLUTION   The first term is the cube of a, whereas the second term is the cube of $\frac{1}{2}$:

$$a^3 - \frac{1}{27} = a^3 - \left(\frac{1}{3}\right)^3$$
$$= \left(a - \frac{1}{3}\right)\left(a^2 + \frac{1}{3}a + \frac{1}{9}\right)$$ ◼

Getting Ready for Class

After reading through the preceding section, respond in your own words and in complete sentences.

A. What is the first step in factoring any polynomial?

B. If a polynomial has four terms, what method of factoring should you try?

C. If a polynomial has two terms, what method of factoring should you try?

D. What is the last step in factoring any polynomial?

Factor each of the following polynomials completely; that is, once you are finished factoring, none of the factors you obtain should be factorable. Also, note that the even-numbered problems are not necessarily similar to the odd-numbered problems that precede them in this problem set.

1. $x^2 - 81$ **2.** $x^2 - 18x + 81$ **3.** $x^2 + 2x - 15$

4. $15x^2 + 11x - 6$ **5.** $x^2 + 6x + 9$ **6.** $12x^2 - 11x + 2$

7. $y^2 - 10y + 25$ **8.** $21y^2 - 25y - 4$ **9.** $2a^3b + 6a^2b + 2ab$

10. $6a^2 - ab - 15b^2$ **11.** $x^2 + x + 1$ **12.** $2x^2 - 4x + 2$

13. $12a^2 - 75$ **14.** $18a^2 - 50$ **15.** $9x^2 - 12xy + 4y^2$

16. $x^3 - x^2$ **17.** $4x^3 + 16xy^2$ **18.** $16x^2 + 49y^2$

19. $2y^3 + 20y^2 + 50y$ **20.** $3y^2 - 9y - 30$

21. $a^6 + 4a^4b^2$ **22.** $5a^2 - 45b^2$

23. $xy + 3x + 4y + 12$ **24.** $xy + 7x + 6y + 42$

25. $x^4 - 16$ **26.** $x^4 - 81$

27. $xy - 5x + 2y - 10$ **28.** $xy - 7x + 3y - 21$

29. $5a^2 + 10ab + 5b^2$ **30.** $3a^3b^2 + 15a^2b^2 + 3ab^2$

31. $x^2 + 49$ **32.** $16 - x^4$

33. $3x^2 + 15xy + 18y^2$ **34.** $3x^2 + 27xy + 54y^2$

35. $2x^2 + 15x - 38$ **36.** $2x^2 + 7x - 85$

37. $100x^2 - 300x + 200$ **38.** $100x^2 - 400x + 300$

39. $x^2 - 64$ **40.** $9x^2 - 4$

41. $x^2 + 3x + ax + 3a$ **42.** $x^2 + 4x + bx + 4b$

43. $49a^7 - 9a^5$ **44.** $a^4 - 1$

45. $49x^2 + 9y^2$ **46.** $12x^4 - 62x^3 + 70x^2$

47. $25a^3 + 20a^2 + 3a$ **48.** $36a^4 - 100a^2$

49. $xa - xb + ay - by$ **50.** $xy - bx + ay - ab$

51. $48a^4b - 3a^2b$ **52.** $18a^4b^2 - 12a^3b^3 + 8a^2b^4$

53. $20x^4 - 45x^2$ **54.** $16x^3 + 16x^2 + 3x$

55. $3x^2 + 35xy - 82y^2$ **56.** $3x^2 + 37xy - 86y^2$

57. $16x^5 - 44x^4 + 30x^3$ **58.** $16x^2 + 16x - 1$

59. $2x^2 + 2ax + 3x + 3a$ **60.** $2x^2 + 2ax + 5x + 5a$

61. $y^4 - 1$ **62.** $25y^7 - 16y^5$

63. $12x^4y^2 + 36x^3y^3 + 27x^2y^4$ **64.** $16x^3y^2 - 4xy^2$

Getting Ready for the Next Section

Solve each equation.

65. $3x - 6 = 9$ **66.** $5x - 1 = 14$ **67.** $2x + 3 = 0$

68. $4x - 5 = 0$ **69.** $4x + 3 = 0$ **70.** $3x - 1 = 0$

Solving Equations by Factoring

In this section we will use the methods of factoring developed in previous sections, along with a special property of 0, to solve quadratic equations.

> **(děf)** **quadratic equation**
>
> Any equation that can be put in the form $ax^2 + bx + c = 0$, where a, b, and c are real numbers ($a \neq 0$), is called a **quadratic equation.** The equation $ax^2 + bx + c = 0$ is called **standard form** for a quadratic equation:
>
> $$\underset{\text{an } x^2 \text{ term}}{a(\text{variable})^2} + \underset{\text{an } x \text{ term}}{b(\text{variable})} + \underset{\text{and a constant term}}{c(\text{absence of the variable})} = 0$$

The number 0 has a special property. If we multiply two numbers and the product is 0, then one or both of the original two numbers must be 0. In symbols, this property looks like this.

> **[Δ≠Σ]** **Zero-Factor Property**
>
> Let a and b represent real numbers. If $a \cdot b = 0$, then $a = 0$ or $b = 0$.

Suppose we want to solve the quadratic equation $x^2 + 5x + 6 = 0$. We can factor the left side into $(x + 2)(x + 3)$. Then we have:

$$x^2 + 5x + 6 = 0$$
$$(x + 2)(x + 3) = 0$$

Now, $(x + 2)$ and $(x + 3)$ both represent real numbers. Their product is 0; therefore, either $(x + 3)$ is 0 or $(x + 2)$ is 0. Either way we have a solution to our equation. We use the property of 0 stated to finish the problem:

$$x^2 + 5x + 6 = 0$$
$$(x + 2)(x + 3) = 0$$
$$x + 2 = 0 \quad \text{or} \quad x + 3 = 0$$
$$x = -2 \quad \text{or} \quad x = -3$$

Our solution set is $\{-2, -3\}$. Our equation has two solutions. To check our solutions we have to check each one separately to see that they both produce a true statement when used in place of the variable:

When $\qquad\qquad\qquad\qquad\qquad x = -3$

the equation $\qquad\qquad\qquad x^2 + 5x + 6 = 0$

becomes $\qquad\qquad (-3)^2 + 5(-3) + 6 \overset{?}{=} 0$

$$9 + (-15) + 6 = 0$$
$$0 = 0$$

$$\text{When} \qquad\qquad\qquad x = -2$$

$$\text{the equation} \qquad\qquad x^2 + 5x + 6 = 0$$

$$\text{becomes} \qquad\qquad (-2)^2 + 5(-2) + 6 \overset{?}{=} 0$$

$$4 + (-10) + 6 = 0$$

$$0 = 0$$

We have solved a quadratic equation by replacing it with two linear equations in one variable.

⟨Δ≠Σ⟩   *How to Solve a Quadratic Equation by Factoring*

Step 1: Put the equation in standard form; that is, 0 on one side and decreasing powers of the variable on the other.
Step 2: Factor completely.
Step 3: Use the zero-factor property to set each variable factor from step 2 to 0.
Step 4: Solve each equation produced in step 3.
Step 5: Check each solution, if necessary.

Video Examples

Section 5.7

Example 1   Solve the equation $2x^2 - 5x = 12$.

SOLUTION

Step 1: Begin by adding -12 to both sides, so the equation is in standard form:

$$2x^2 - 5x = 12$$

$$2x^2 - 5x - 12 = 0$$

Step 2: Factor the left side completely:

$$(2x + 3)(x - 4) = 0$$

Step 3: Set each factor to 0:

$$2x + 3 = 0 \qquad \text{or} \qquad x - 4 = 0$$

Step 4: Solve each of the equations from step 3:

$$2x + 3 = 0 \qquad\qquad x - 4 = 0$$

$$2x = -3 \qquad\qquad\quad x = 4$$

$$x = -\frac{3}{2}$$

Step 5: Substitute each solution into $2x^2 - 5x = 12$ to check:

$$\text{Check: } -\frac{3}{2} \qquad\qquad\qquad \text{Check: } 4$$

$$2\left(-\frac{3}{2}\right)^2 - 5\left(-\frac{3}{2}\right) \overset{?}{=} 12 \qquad\qquad 2(4)^2 - 5(4) \overset{?}{=} 12$$

$$2\left(\frac{9}{4}\right) + 5\left(\frac{3}{2}\right) = 12 \qquad\qquad 2(16) - 20 = 12$$

$$\frac{9}{2} + \frac{15}{2} = 12 \qquad\qquad\qquad 32 - 20 = 12$$

$$\frac{24}{2} = 12 \qquad\qquad\qquad\qquad 12 = 12$$

$$12 = 12$$

Example 2   Solve for a: $16a^2 - 25 = 0$.

SOLUTION   The equation is already in standard form:

$$16a^2 - 25 = 0$$

$$(4a - 5)(4a + 5) = 0 \qquad \text{Factor the left side}$$

$$4a - 5 = 0 \quad \text{or} \quad 4a + 5 = 0 \qquad \text{Set each factor to 0}$$

$$4a = 5 \qquad\qquad 4a = -5 \qquad \text{Solve the resulting equations}$$

$$a = \frac{5}{4} \qquad\qquad a = -\frac{5}{4}$$

The solutions are $\frac{5}{4}$ and $-\frac{5}{4}$. ■

Example 3   Solve $4x^2 = 8x$.

SOLUTION   We begin by adding $-8x$ to each side of the equation to put it in standard form. Then we factor the left side of the equation by factoring out the greatest common factor.

$$4x^2 = 8x$$

$$4x^2 - 8x = 0 \qquad \text{Add } -8x \text{ to each side}$$

$$4x(x - 2) = 0 \qquad \text{Factor the left side}$$

$$4x = 0 \quad \text{or} \quad x - 2 = 0 \qquad \text{Set each factor to 0}$$

$$x = 0 \quad \text{or} \quad x = 2 \qquad \text{Solve the resulting equations}$$

The solutions are 0 and 2. ■

Example 4   Solve $x(2x + 3) = 44$.

SOLUTION   We must multiply out the left side first and then put the equation in standard form:

$$x(2x + 3) = 44$$

$$2x^2 + 3x = 44 \qquad \text{Multiply out the left side}$$

$$2x^2 + 3x - 44 = 0 \qquad \text{Add } -44 \text{ to each side}$$

$$(2x + 11)(x - 4) = 0 \qquad \text{Factor the left side}$$

$$2x + 11 = 0 \quad \text{or} \quad x - 4 = 0 \qquad \text{Set each factor to 0}$$

$$2x = -11 \quad \text{or} \quad x = 4 \qquad \text{Solve the resulting equations}$$

$$x = -\frac{11}{2}$$

The two solutions are $-\frac{11}{2}$ and 4. ■

Example 5   Solve for x: $5^2 = x^2 + (x + 1)^2$.

SOLUTION   Before we can put this equation in standard form we must square the binomial. Remember, to square a binomial, we use the formula $(a + b)^2 = a^2 + 2ab + b^2$:

$$5^2 = x^2 + (x + 1)^2$$
$$25 = x^2 + x^2 + 2x + 1 \qquad \text{Expand } 5^2 \text{ and } (x + 1)^2$$
$$25 = 2x^2 + 2x + 1 \qquad \text{Simplify the right side}$$
$$0 = 2x^2 + 2x - 24 \qquad \text{Add } -25 \text{ to each side}$$
$$0 = 2(x^2 + x - 12) \qquad \text{Begin factoring}$$
$$0 = 2(x + 4)(x - 3) \qquad \text{Factor completely}$$
$$x + 4 = 0 \quad \text{or} \quad x - 3 = 0 \qquad \text{Set each variable factor to 0}$$
$$x = -4 \quad \text{or} \qquad x = 3$$

Note, in the second to the last line, that we do not set 2 equal to 0. That is because 2 can never be 0. It is always 2. We only use the zero-factor property to set variable factors to 0 because they are the only factors that can possibly be 0.

   Also notice that it makes no difference which side of the equation is 0 when we write the equation in standard form.

Although the equation in the next example is not a quadratic equation, it can be solved by the method shown in the first five examples.

Example 6   Solve $24x^3 = -10x^2 + 6x$ for x.

SOLUTION   First, we write the equation in standard form:

$$24x^3 + 10x^2 - 6x = 0 \qquad \text{Standard form}$$
$$2x(12x^2 + 5x - 3) = 0 \qquad \text{Factor out } 2x$$
$$2x(3x - 1)(4x + 3) = 0 \qquad \text{Factor remaining trinomial}$$
$$2x = 0 \quad \text{or} \quad 3x - 1 = 0 \quad \text{or} \quad 4x + 3 = 0 \qquad \text{Set factors to 0}$$
$$x = 0 \quad \text{or} \qquad x = \frac{1}{3} \quad \text{or} \qquad x = -\frac{3}{4} \qquad \text{Solutions}$$

Getting Ready for Class

After reading through the preceding section, respond in your own words and in complete sentences.

A. When is an equation in standard form?
B. What is the first step in solving an equation by factoring?
C. Describe the zero-factor property in your own words.
D. Describe how you would solve the equation $2x^2 - 5x = 12$.

Problem Set 5.7

The following equations are already in factored form. Use the special zero factor property to set the factors to 0 and solve.

1. $(x + 2)(x - 1) = 0$ **2.** $(x + 3)(x + 2) = 0$

3. $(a - 4)(a - 5) = 0$ **4.** $(a + 6)(a - 1) = 0$

5. $x(x + 1)(x - 3) = 0$ **6.** $x(2x + 1)(x - 5) = 0$

7. $(3x + 2)(2x + 3) = 0$ **8.** $(4x - 5)(x - 6) = 0$

9. $m(3m + 4)(3m - 4) = 0$ **10.** $m(2m - 5)(3m - 1) = 0$

11. $2y(3y + 1)(5y + 3) = 0$ **12.** $3y(2y - 3)(3y - 4) = 0$

Solve the following equations.

13. $x^2 + 3x + 2 = 0$ **14.** $x^2 - x - 6 = 0$

15. $x^2 - 9x + 20 = 0$ **16.** $x^2 + 2x - 3 = 0$

17. $a^2 - 2a - 24 = 0$ **18.** $a^2 - 11a + 30 = 0$

19. $100x^2 - 500x + 600 = 0$ **20.** $100x^2 - 300x + 200 = 0$

21. $x^2 = -6x - 9$ **22.** $x^2 = 10x - 25$

23. $a^2 - 16 = 0$ **24.** $a^2 - 36 = 0$

25. $2x^2 + 5x - 12 = 0$ **26.** $3x^2 + 14x - 5 = 0$

27. $9x^2 + 12x + 4 = 0$ **28.** $12x^2 - 24x + 9 = 0$

29. $a^2 + 25 = 10a$ **30.** $a^2 + 16 = 8a$

31. $2x^2 = 3x + 20$ **32.** $6x^2 = x + 2$

33. $3m^2 = 20 - 7m$ **34.** $2m^2 = -18 + 15m$

35. $4x^2 - 49 = 0$ **36.** $16x^2 - 25 = 0$

37. $x^2 + 6x = 0$ **38.** $x^2 - 8x = 0$

39. $x^2 - 3x = 0$ **40.** $x^2 + 5x = 0$

41. $2x^2 = 8x$ **42.** $2x^2 = 10x$

43. $3x^2 = 15x$ **44.** $5x^2 = 15x$

45. $1,400 = 400 + 700x - 100x^2$ **46.** $2,700 = 700 + 900x - 100x^2$

47. $6x^2 = -5x + 4$ **48.** $9x^2 = 12x - 4$

49. $x(2x - 3) = 20$ **50.** $x(3x - 5) = 12$

51. $t(t + 2) = 80$ **52.** $t(t + 2) = 99$

53. $4,000 = (1,300 - 100p)p$ **54.** $3,200 = (1,200 - 100p)p$

55. $x(14 - x) = 48$ **56.** $x(12 - x) = 32$

57. $(x + 5)^2 = 2x + 9$ **58.** $(x + 7)^2 = 2x + 13$

59. $(y - 6)^2 = y - 4$ **60.** $(y + 4)^2 = y + 6$

61. $10^2 = (x + 2)^2 + x^2$ **62.** $15^2 = (x + 3)^2 + x^2$

63. $2x^3 + 11x^2 + 12x = 0$ **64.** $3x^3 + 17x^2 + 10x = 0$

65. $4y^3 - 2y^2 - 30y = 0$ **66.** $9y^3 + 6y^2 - 24y = 0$

67. $8x^3 + 16x^2 = 10x$ **68.** $24x^3 - 22x^2 = -4x$

69. $20a^3 = -18a^2 + 18a$ **70.** $12a^3 = -2a^2 + 10a$

71. $16t^2 - 32t + 12 = 0$ **72.** $16t^2 - 64t + 48 = 0$

Simplify each side as much as possible, then solve the equation.

73. $(a - 5)(a + 4) = -2a$

74. $(a + 2)(a - 3) = -2a$

75. $3x(x + 1) - 2x(x - 5) = -42$

76. $4x(x - 2) - 3x(x - 4) = -3$

77. $2x(x + 3) = x(x + 2) - 3$

78. $3x(x - 3) = 2x(x - 4) + 6$

79. $a(a - 3) + 6 = 2a$

80. $a(a - 4) + 8 = 2a$

81. $15(x + 20) + 15x = 2x(x + 20)$

82. $15(x + 8) + 15x = 2x(x + 8)$

83. $15 = a(a + 2)$

84. $6 = a(a - 5)$

Use factoring by grouping to solve the following equations.

85. $x^3 + 3x^2 - 4x - 12 = 0$

86. $x^3 + 5x^2 - 9x - 45 = 0$

87. $x^3 + x^2 - 16x - 16 = 0$

88. $4x^3 + 12x^2 - 9x - 27 = 0$

89. Paying Attention to Instructions Work each problem according to the instructions given.

    a. Factor $x^2 - x - 2$.   **b.** Solve $x^2 - x - 2 = 0$ **c.** Solve $x^2 - x - 2 = 4$

90. Paying Attention to Instructions Work each problem according to the instructions given.

    a. Factor $x^2 - 2x - 8$.   **b.** Solve $x^2 - 2x - 8 = 0$ **c.** Solve $x^2 - 2x - 8 = 7$

Getting Ready for the Next Section

Write each sentence as an algebraic equation.

91. The product of two consecutive integers is 72.

92. The product of two consecutive even integers is 80.

93. The product of two consecutive odd integers is 99.

94. The product of two consecutive odd integers is 63.

95. The product of two consecutive even integers is 10 less than 5 times their sum.

96. The product of two consecutive odd integers is 1 less than 4 times their sum.

The following word problems are taken from the book *Academic Algebra*, written by William J. Milne and published by the American Book Company in 1901. Solve each problem.

97. Cost of a Bicycle and a Suit A bicycle and a suit cost $90. How much did each cost, if the bicycle cost 5 times as much as the suit?

98. Cost of a Cow and a Calf A man bought a cow and a calf for $36, paying 8 times as much for the cow as for the calf. What was the cost of each?

99. Cost of a House and a Lot A house and a lot cost $3,000. If the house cost 4 times as much as the lot, what was the cost of each?

100. Daily Wages A plumber and two helpers together earned $7.50 per day. How much did each earn per day, if the plumber earned 4 times as much as each helper?

Applications

In this section we will look at some application problems, the solutions to which require solving a quadratic equation. We will also introduce the Pythagorean theorem, one of the oldest theorems in the history of mathematics. The person whose name we associate with the theorem, Pythagoras (of Samos), was a Greek philosopher and mathematician who lived from about 560 B.C. to 480 B.C. According to the British philosopher Bertrand Russell, Pythagoras was "intellectually one of the most important men that ever lived."

Also in this section, the solutions to the examples show only the essential steps from our Blueprint for Problem Solving. Recall that step 1 is done mentally; we read the problem and mentally list the items that are known and the items that are unknown. This is an essential part of problem solving. However, now that you have had experience with application problems, you are doing step 1 automatically.

Number Problems

Video Examples

Section 5.8

Example 1 The product of two consecutive odd integers is 63. Find the integers.

SOLUTION Let x = the first odd integer; then $x + 2$ = the second odd integer. An equation that describes the situation is:

$$x(x + 2) = 63 \qquad \text{\textit{Their product is 63}}$$

We solve the equation:

$$x(x + 2) = 63$$
$$x^2 + 2x = 63$$
$$x^2 + 2x - 63 = 0$$
$$(x - 7)(x + 9) = 0$$
$$x - 7 = 0 \quad \text{or} \quad x + 9 = 0$$
$$x = 7 \quad \text{or} \quad x = -9$$

If the first odd integer is 7, the next odd integer is $7 + 2 = 9$. If the first odd integer is -9, the next consecutive odd integer is $-9 + 2 = -7$. We have two pairs of consecutive odd integers that are solutions. They are 7, 9 and $-9, -7$.

We check to see that their products are 63:

$$7(9) = 63$$
$$-7(-9) = 63$$

Suppose we know that the sum of two numbers is 50. We want to find a way to represent each number using only one variable. If we let x represent one of the two numbers, how can we represent the other? Let's suppose for a moment that x turns out to be 30. Then the other number will be 20, because their sum is 50; that is, if two numbers add up to 50 and one of them is 30, then the other must be $50 - 30 = 20$. Generalizing this to any number x, we see that if two numbers have a sum of 50 and one of the numbers is x, then the other must be $50 - x$. The table that follows shows some additional examples.

If two numbers have a sum of	and one of them is	then the other must be
50	x	$50 - x$
100	x	$100 - x$
10	y	$10 - y$
12	n	$12 - n$

Now, let's look at an example that uses this idea.

Example 2   The sum of two numbers is 13. Their product is 40. Find the numbers.

SOLUTION   If we let x represent one of the numbers, then $13 - x$ must be the other number because their sum is 13. Since their product is 40, we can write:

$$x(13 - x) = 40 \qquad \text{\small The product of the two numbers is 40}$$

$$13x - x^2 = 40 \qquad \text{\small Multiply the left side}$$

$$x^2 - 13x = -40 \qquad \text{\small Multiply both sides by } -1 \text{ and reverse the order of the terms on the left side}$$

$$x^2 - 13x + 40 = 0 \qquad \text{\small Add 40 to each side}$$

$$(x - 8)(x - 5) = 0 \qquad \text{\small Factor the left side}$$

$$x - 8 = 0 \quad \text{or} \quad x - 5 = 0$$

$$x = 8 \quad \text{or} \qquad x = 5$$

The two solutions are 8 and 5. If x is 8, then the other number is $13 - x = 13 - 8 = 5$. Likewise, if x is 5, the other number is $13 - x = 13 - 5 = 8$. Therefore, the two numbers we are looking for are 8 and 5. Their sum is 13 and their product is 40.

Geometry Problems

Many word problems dealing with area can best be described algebraically by quadratic equations.

Example 3   The length of a rectangle is 3 more than twice the width. The area is 44 square inches. Find the dimensions (find the length and width).

SOLUTION   As shown in Figure 1, let x = the width of the rectangle. Then $2x + 3$ = the length of the rectangle because the length is three more than twice the width.

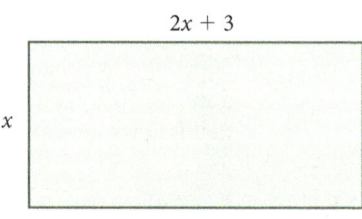

FIGURE 1

Since the area is 44 square inches, an equation that describes the situation is

$$x(2x + 3) = 44 \qquad \text{Length} \cdot \text{width} = \text{area}$$

We now solve the equation:

$$x(2x + 3) = 44$$
$$2x^2 + 3x = 44$$
$$2x^2 + 3x - 44 = 0$$
$$(2x + 11)(x - 4) = 0$$
$$2x + 11 = 0 \qquad \text{or} \quad x - 4 = 0$$
$$x = -\frac{11}{2} \quad \text{or} \qquad x = 4$$

The solution $x = -\frac{11}{2}$ cannot be used since length and width are always given in positive units. The width is 4. The length is 3 more than twice the width or $2(4) + 3 = 11$.

$$\text{Width} = 4 \text{ inches}$$

$$\text{Length} = 11 \text{ inches}$$

The solutions check in the original problem since $4(11) = 44$.

Example 4   The numerical value of the area of a square is twice its perimeter. What is the length of its side?

SOLUTION   As shown in Figure 2, let $x =$ the length of its side. Then $x^2 =$ the area of the square and $4x =$ the perimeter of the square:

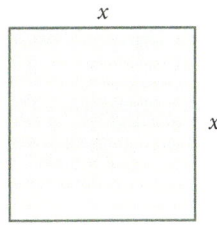

x

x

FIGURE 2

An equation that describes the situation is

$$x^2 = 2(4x) \qquad \textit{The area is 2 times the perimeter}$$
$$x^2 = 8x$$
$$x^2 - 8x = 0$$
$$x(x - 8) = 0$$
$$x = 0 \quad \text{or} \quad x = 8$$

Since $x = 0$ does not make sense in our original problem, we use $x = 8$. If the side has length 8, then the perimeter is $4(8) = 32$ and the area is $8^2 = 64$. Since 64 is twice 32, our solution is correct.

The Pythagorean Theorem

Next, we will work some problems involving the Pythagorean theorem, which we mentioned in the introduction to this section. It may interest you to know that Pythagoras formed a secret society around the year 540 B.C. Known as the Pythagoreans, members kept no written record of their work; everything was handed down by spoken word. They influenced not only mathematics, but religion, science, medicine, and music as well. Among other things, they discovered the correlation between musical notes and the reciprocals of counting numbers, $\frac{1}{2}, \frac{1}{3}, \frac{1}{4}$, and so on. In their daily lives, they followed strict dietary and moral rules to achieve a higher rank in future lives.

Pythagorean Theorem

In any right triangle (Figure 3), the square of the longer side (called the hypotenuse) is equal to the sum of the squares of the other two sides (called legs).

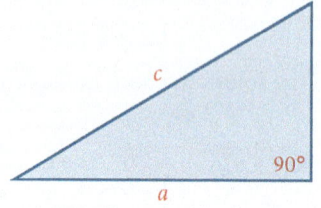

$$c^2 = a^2 + b^2$$

FIGURE 3

Example 5   The three sides of a right triangle are three consecutive integers. Find the lengths of the three sides.

SOLUTION   Let $x =$ the first integer (shortest side)

then $x + 1 =$ the next consecutive integer

and $x + 2 =$ the last consecutive integer (longest side)

A diagram of the triangle is shown in Figure 4.

The Pythagorean theorem tells us that the square of the longest side $(x + 2)^2$ is equal to the sum of the squares of the two shorter sides, $(x + 1)^2 + x^2$. Here is the equation:

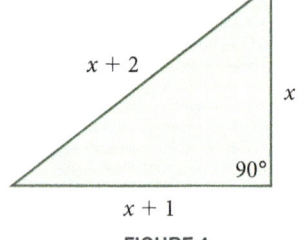

FIGURE 4

$$(x + 2)^2 = (x + 1)^2 + x^2$$

$$x^2 + 4x + 4 = x^2 + 2x + 1 + x^2 \qquad \text{Expand squares}$$

$$x^2 - 2x - 3 = 0 \qquad \text{Standard form}$$

$$(x - 3)(x + 1) = 0 \qquad \text{Factor}$$

$$x - 3 = 0 \quad \text{or} \quad x + 1 = 0 \qquad \text{Set factors to 0}$$

$$x = 3 \quad \text{or} \quad x = -1$$

Since a triangle cannot have a side with a negative number for its length, we must not use -1 for a solution to our original problem; therefore, the shortest side is 3. The other two sides are the next two consecutive integers, 4 and 5.

Example 6   The hypotenuse of a right triangle is 5 inches, and the lengths of the two legs (the other two sides) are given by two consecutive integers. Find the lengths of the two legs.

SOLUTION   If we let x = the length of the shortest side, then the other side must be $x + 1$. A diagram of the triangle is shown in Figure 5.

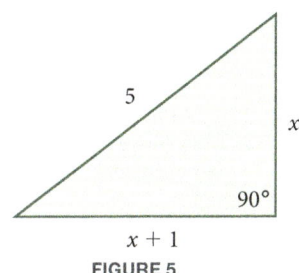

FIGURE 5

The Pythagorean theorem tells us that the square of the longest side, 5^2, is equal to the sum of the squares of the two shorter sides, $x^2 + (x + 1)^2$. Here is the equation:

$5^2 = x^2 + (x + 1)^2$	Pythagorean theorem
$25 = x^2 + x^2 + 2x + 1$	Expand 5^2 and $(x + 1)^2$
$25 = 2x^2 + 2x + 1$	Simplify the right side
$0 = 2x^2 + 2x - 24$	Add -25 to each side
$0 = 2(x^2 + x - 12)$	Begin factoring
$0 = 2(x + 4)(x - 3)$	Factor completely
$x + 4 = 0$ or $x - 3 = 0$	Set variable factors to 0
$x = -4$ or $x = 3$	

Since a triangle cannot have a side with a negative number for its length, we cannot use -4; therefore, the shortest side must be 3 inches. The next side is $x + 1 = 3 + 1 = 4$ inches. Since the hypotenuse is 5, we can check our solutions with the Pythagorean theorem as shown in Figure 6.

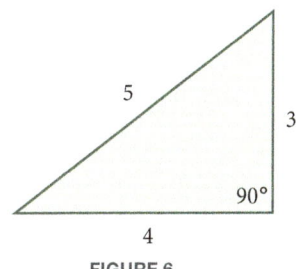

FIGURE 6

Example 7   A company can manufacture x hundred items for a total cost of $C = 300 + 500x - 100x^2$. How many items were manufactured if the total cost is \$900?

SOLUTION   We are looking for x when C is 900. We begin by substituting 900 for C in the cost equation. Then we solve for x:

When	$C = 900$
the equation	$C = 300 + 500x - 100x^2$
becomes	$900 = 300 + 500x - 100x^2$

We can write this equation in standard form by adding -300, $-500x$, and $100x^2$ to each side. The result looks like this:

$$100x^2 - 500x + 600 = 0$$

$$100(x^2 - 5x + 6) = 0 \qquad \text{\textit{Begin factoring}}$$

$$100(x - 2)(x - 3) = 0 \qquad \text{\textit{Factor completely}}$$

$$x - 2 = 0 \quad \text{or} \quad x - 3 = 0 \qquad \text{\textit{Set variable factors to 0}}$$

$$x = 2 \quad \text{or} \qquad x = 3$$

Our solutions are 2 and 3, which means that the company can manufacture 2 hundred items or 3 hundred items for a total cost of \$900. ■

Example 8   A manufacturer of small portable radios knows that the number of radios she can sell each week is related to the price of the radios by the equation $x = 1{,}300 - 100p$ (x is the number of radios and p is the price per radio). What price should she charge for the radios to have a weekly revenue of \$4,000?

SOLUTION   First, we must find the revenue equation. The equation for total revenue is $R = xp$, where x is the number of units sold and p is the price per unit. Since we want R in terms of p, we substitute $1{,}300 - 100p$ for x in the equation $R = xp$:

If	$R = xp$
and	$x = 1{,}300 - 100p$
then	$R = (1{,}300 - 100p)p$

We want to find p when R is 4,000. Substituting 4,000 for R in the equation gives us:

$$4{,}000 = (1{,}300 - 100p)p$$

If we multiply out the right side, we have:

$$4{,}000 = 1{,}300p - 100p^2$$

To write this equation in standard form, we add $100p^2$ and $-1{,}300p$ to each side:

$$100p^2 - 1{,}300p + 4{,}000 = 0 \qquad \text{\textit{Add } } 100p^2 \text{ \textit{and} } -1{,}300p$$

$$100(p^2 - 13p + 40) = 0 \qquad \text{\textit{Begin factoring}}$$

$$100(p - 5)(p - 8) = 0 \qquad \text{\textit{Factor completely}}$$

$$p - 5 = 0 \quad \text{or} \quad p - 8 = 0 \qquad \text{\textit{Set variable factors to 0}}$$

$$p = 5 \quad \text{or} \qquad p = 8$$

If she sells the radios for \$5 each or for \$8 each, she will have a weekly revenue of \$4,000. ■

Getting Ready for Class

After reading through the preceding section, respond in your own words and in complete sentences.

A. What are consecutive integers?

B. Explain the Pythagorean theorem in words.

C. Write an application problem for which the solution depends on solving the equation $x(x + 1) = 12$.

D. Write an application problem for which the solution depends on solving the equation $x(2x - 3) = 40$.

SPOTLIGHT ON SUCCESS   *Student Instructor Aaron*

Sometimes you have to take a step back in order to get a running start forward.
—Anonymous

As a high school senior I was encouraged to go to college immediately after graduating. I earned good grades in high school and I knew that I would have a pretty good group of schools to pick from. Even though I felt like "more school" was not quite what I wanted, the counselors had so much faith and had done this process so many times that it was almost too easy to get the applications out. I sent out applications to schools I knew I could get into and a "dream school."

One night in my email inbox there was a letter of acceptance from my dream school. There was just one problem with getting into this school. It was going to be difficult and I still had senioritis. Going into my first quarter of college was as exciting and difficult as I knew it would be. But after my first quarter I could see that this was not the time for me to be here. I was interested in the subject matter but I could not find my motivating purpose like I had in high school. Instead of dropping out completely, I decided a community college would be a good way for me to stay on track. Without necessarily knowing my direction, I could take the general education classes and get those out of the way while figuring out exactly what and where I felt a good place for me to be.

Now I know what I want to go to school for and the next time I walk onto a four year campus it will be on my terms with my reasons for being there driving me to succeed. I encourage everyone to continue school after high school, even if you have no clue as to what you want to study. There are always stepping stones, like community colleges, that can help you get a clearer picture of what you want to strive for.

Solve the following word problems. Be sure to show the equation used.

Number Problems

1. The product of two consecutive even integers is 80. Find the two integers.
2. The product of two consecutive integers is 72. Find the two integers.
3. The product of two consecutive odd integers is 99. Find the two integers.
4. The product of two consecutive integers is 132. Find the two integers.
5. The product of two consecutive even integers is 10 less than 5 times their sum. Find the two integers.
6. The product of two consecutive odd integers is 1 less than 4 times their sum. Find the two integers.
7. The sum of two numbers is 14. Their product is 48. Find the numbers.
8. The sum of two numbers is 12. Their product is 32. Find the numbers.
9. One number is 2 more than 5 times another. Their product is 24. Find the numbers.
10. One number is 1 more than twice another. Their product is 55. Find the numbers.
11. One number is 4 times another. Their product is 4 times their sum. Find the numbers.
12. One number is 2 more than twice another. Their product is 2 more than twice their sum. Find the numbers.

Geometry Problems

13. The length of a rectangle is 1 more than the width. The area is 12 square inches. Find the dimensions.
14. The length of a rectangle is 3 more than twice the width. The area is 44 square inches. Find the dimensions.
15. The height of a triangle is twice the base. The area is 9 square inches. Find the base.
16. The height of a triangle is 2 more than twice the base. The area is 20 square feet. Find the base.
17. The hypotenuse of a right triangle is 10 inches. The lengths of the two legs are given by two consecutive even integers. Find the lengths of the two legs.
18. The hypotenuse of a right triangle is 15 inches. One of the legs is 3 inches more than the other. Find the lengths of the two legs.
19. The shorter leg of a right triangle is 5 meters. The hypotenuse is 1 meter longer than the longer leg. Find the length of the longer leg.
20. The shorter leg of a right triangle is 12 yards. If the hypotenuse is 20 yards, how long is the other leg?

Business Problems

21. A company can manufacture x hundred items for a total cost of $C = 400 + 700x - 100x^2$. Find x if the total cost is \$1,400.

22. If the total cost C of manufacturing x hundred items is given by the equation $C = 700 + 900x - 100x^2$, find x when C is \$2,700.

23. The relationship between the number of calculators a company sells per week, x, and the price p of each calculator is given by the equation $x = 1,700 - 100p$. At what price should the calculators be sold if the weekly revenue is to be \$7,000?

24. The relationship between the number of pencil sharpeners a company can sell each week, x, and the price p of each sharpener is given by the equation $x = 1,800 - 100p$. At what price should the sharpeners be sold if the weekly revenue is to be \$7,200?

25. Pythagorean Theorem A 13-foot ladder is placed so that it reaches to a point on the wall that is 2 feet higher than twice the distance from the base of the wall to the base of the ladder.

   a. How far from the wall is the base of the ladder?

   b. How high does the ladder reach?

26. Constructing a Box I have a piece of cardboard that is twice as long as it is wide. If I cut a 2-inch by 2-inch square from each corner and fold up the resulting flaps, I get a box with a volume of 32 cubic inches. What are the dimensions of the cardboard.

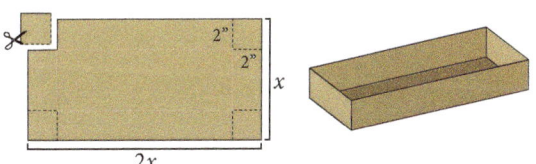

27. Projectile Motion A gun fires a bullet almost straight up from the edge of a 100-foot cliff. If the bullet leaves the gun with a speed of 396 feet per second, its height at time t is given by $h(t) = -16t^2 + 396t + 100$, measured from the ground below the cliff.

   a. When will the bullet land on the ground below the cliff? (*Hint:* What is its height when it lands? Remember that we are measuring from the ground below, not from the cliff.)

   b. Make a table showing the bullet's height every five seconds, from the time it is fired ($t = 0$) to the time it lands. (*Note:* It is faster to substitute into the factored form.)

28. Height of a Projectile If a rocket is fired vertically into the air with a speed of 240 feet per second, its height at time t seconds is given by $h(t) = -16t^2 + 240t$.

At what time(s) will the rocket be the following number of feet above the ground?

a. 704 feet

b. 896 feet

c. Why do parts **a.** and **b.** each have two answers?

d. How long will the rocket be in the air? (*Hint:* How high is it when it hits the ground?)

e. When the equation for part **d.** is solved, one of the answers is $t = 0$ seconds. What does this represent?

Maintaining Your Skills

Simplify each expression. (Write all answers with positive exponents only.)

29. $(5x^3)^2(2x^6)^3$

30. 2^{-3}

31. $\dfrac{x^4}{x^{-3}}$

32. $\dfrac{(20x^2y^3)(5x^4y)}{(2xy^5)(10x^2y^3)}$

33. $(2 \times 10^{-4})(4 \times 10^5)$

34. $\dfrac{9 \times 10^{-3}}{3 \times 10^{-2}}$

35. $20ab^2 - 16ab^2 + 6ab^2$

36. Subtract $6x^2 - 5x - 7$ from $9x^2 + 3x - 2$.

Multiply.

37. $2x^2(3x^2 + 3x - 1)$

38. $(2x + 3)(5x - 2)$

39. $(3y - 5)^2$

40. $(a - 4)(a^2 + 4a + 16)$

41. $(2a^2 + 7)(2a^2 - 7)$

42. Divide $15x^{10} - 10x^8 + 25x^6$ by $5x^6$.

Chapter 5 Summary

Greatest Common Factor [5.1]

1. $8x^4 - 10x^3 + 6x^2$
$= 2x^2 \cdot 4x^2 - 2x^2 \cdot 5x + 2x^2 \cdot 3$
$= 2x^2(4x^2 - 5x + 3)$

The largest monomial that divides each term of a polynomial is called the greatest common factor for that polynomial. We begin all factoring by factoring out the greatest common factor.

Factoring Trinomials [5.2, 5.3]

2. $x^2 + 5x + 6 = (x + 2)(x + 3)$
$x^2 - 5x + 6 = (x - 2)(x - 3)$
$6x^2 - x - 2 = (2x + 1)(3x - 2)$
$6x^2 + 7x + 2 = (2x + 1)(3x + 2)$

One method of factoring a trinomial is to list all pairs of binomials whose product of the first terms gives the first term of the trinomial and whose product of the last terms gives the last term of the trinomial. We then choose the pair that gives the correct middle term for the original trinomial.

Special Factoring [5.4]

3. $x^2 + 10x + 25 = (x + 5)^2$
$x^2 - 10x + 25 = (x - 5)^2$
$x^2 - 25 = (x + 5)(x - 5)$

$$a^2 + 2ab + b^2 = (a + b)^2$$
$$a^2 - 2ab + b^2 = (a - b)^2$$
$$a^2 - b^2 = (a + b)(a - b)$$

Sum and Difference of Two Cubes [5.5]

4. $x^3 - 27 = (x - 3)(x^2 + 3x + 9)$
$x^3 + 27 = (x + 3)(x^2 - 3x + 9)$

$$a^3 - b^3 = (a - b)(a^2 + ab + b^2) \quad \text{Difference of two cubes}$$
$$a^3 + b^3 = (a + b)(a^2 - ab + b^2) \quad \text{Sum of two cubes}$$

Strategy for Factoring a Polynomial [5.6]

5. a. $2x^5 - 8x^3 = 2x^3(x^2 - 4)$
$\qquad\qquad\quad = 2x^3(x + 2)(x - 2)$

b. $3x^4 - 18x^3 + 27x^2$
$\quad = 3x^2(x^2 - 6x + 9)$
$\quad = 3x^2(x - 3)^2$

c. $6x^3 - 12x^2 - 48x$
$\quad = 6x(x^2 - 2x - 8)$
$\quad = 6x(x - 4)(x + 2)$

d. $x^2 + ax + bx + ab$
$\quad = x(x + a) + b(x + a)$
$\quad = (x + a)(x + b)$

Step 1: If the polynomial has a greatest common factor other than 1, then factor out the greatest common factor.

Step 2: If the polynomial has two terms (it is a binomial), then see if it is the difference of two squares or the sum or difference of two cubes, and then factor accordingly. Remember, if it is the sum of two squares, it will not factor.

Step 3: If the polynomial has three terms (a trinomial), then it is either a perfect square trinomial that will factor into the square of a binomial, or it is not a perfect square trinomial, in which case you use the trial and error method developed in Section 5.3.

Step 4: If the polynomial has more than three terms, then try to factor it by grouping.

Step 5: As a final check, see if any of the factors you have written can be factored further. If you have overlooked a common factor, you can catch it here.

Strategy for Solving a Quadratic Equation [5.7]

6. Solve $x^2 - 6x = -8$.
$$x^2 - 6x + 8 = 0$$
$$(x - 4)(x - 2) = 0$$
$$x - 4 = 0 \quad \text{or} \quad x - 2 = 0$$
$$x = 4 \quad \text{or} \quad x = 2$$
Both solutions check.

Step 1: Write the equation in standard form $ax^2 + bx + c = 0$

Step 2: Factor completely.

Step 3: Set each variable factor equal to 0.

Step 4: Solve the equations found in step 3.

Step 5: Check solutions, if necessary.

The Pythagorean Theorem [5.8]

7. The hypotenuse of a right triangle is 5 inches, and the lengths of the two legs (the other two sides) are given by two consecutive integers. Find the lengths of the two legs.

In any right triangle, the square of the longest side (called the hypotenuse) is equal to the sum of the squares of the other two sides (called legs).

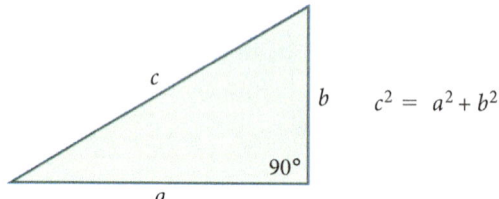

If we let $x =$ the length of the shortest side, then the other side must be $x + 1$. The Pythagorean theorem tells us that
$$5^2 = x^2 + (x + 1)^2$$
$$25 = x^2 + x^2 + 2x + 1$$
$$25 = 2x^2 + 2x + 1$$
$$0 = 2x^2 + 2x - 24$$
$$0 = 2(x^2 + x - 12)$$
$$0 = 2(x + 4)(x - 3)$$
$$x + 4 = 0 \quad \text{or} \quad x - 3 = 0$$
$$x = -4 \quad \text{or} \quad x = 3$$
Since a triangle cannot have a side with a negative number for its length, we cannot use -4. One leg is $x = 3$ and the other leg is $x + 1 = 3 + 1 = 4$.

⚠ *Common Mistake*

It is a mistake to apply the zero-factor property to numbers other than zero. For example, consider the equation $(x - 3)(x + 4) = 18$. A fairly common mistake is to attempt to solve it with the following steps:
$$(x - 3)(x + 4) = 18$$
$$x - 3 = 18 \quad \text{or} \quad x + 4 = 18 \leftarrow \text{Mistake}$$
$$x = 21 \quad \text{or} \quad x = 14$$

These are obviously not solutions, as a quick check will verify:

$$\text{Check: } x = 21 \qquad\qquad \text{Check: } x = 14$$
$$(21 - 3)(21 + 4) \overset{?}{=} 18 \qquad (14 - 3)(14 + 4) \overset{?}{=} 18$$
$$18 \cdot 25 = 18 \qquad\qquad 11 \cdot 18 = 18$$
$$450 = 18 \quad \xleftarrow{\text{false statements}} \quad 198 = 18$$

The mistake is in setting each factor equal to 18. It is not necessarily true that when the product of two numbers is 18, either one of them is itself 18. The correct solution looks like this:
$$(x - 3)(x + 4) = 18$$
$$x^2 + x - 12 = 18$$
$$x^2 + x - 30 = 0$$
$$(x + 6)(x - 5) = 0$$
$$x + 6 = 0 \quad\quad \text{or} \quad x - 5 = 0$$
$$x = -6 \quad\quad \text{or} \quad x = 5$$

To avoid this mistake, remember that before you factor a quadratic equation, you must write it in standard form. It is in standard form only when 0 is on one side and decreasing powers of the variable are on the other.

Chapter 5 Test

Factor out the greatest common factor. [5.1]

1. $6x + 18$

2. $12a^2b - 24ab + 8ab^2$

Factor by grouping. [5.1]

3. $x^2 + 3ax - 2bx - 6ab$

4. $15y - 5xy - 12 + 4x$

Factor the following completely. [5.2–5.6]

5. $x^2 + x - 12$

6. $x^2 - 4x - 21$

7. $x^2 - 25$

8. $x^4 - 16$

9. $x^2 + 36$

10. $18x^2 - 32y^2$

11. $x^3 + 4x^2 - 3x - 12$

12. $x^2 + bx - 3x - 3b$

13. $4x^2 - 6x - 10$

14. $4n^2 + 13n - 12$

15. $12c^2 + c - 6$

16. $12x^3 + 12x^2 - 9x$

17. $x^3 + 125y^3$

18. $54b^3 - 128$

Solve the following equations. [5.7]

19. $x^2 - 2x - 15 = 0$

20. $x^2 - 7x + 12 = 0$

21. $x^2 - 25 = 0$

22. $x^2 = 5x + 14$

23. $x^2 + x = 30$

24. $y^3 = 9y$

25. $2x^2 = -5x + 12$

26. $15x^3 - 65x^2 - 150x = 0$

Solve the following word problems. Be sure to show the system of equations used. [5.8]

27. **Number Problem** Two numbers have a sum of 18. Their product is 72. Find the numbers.

28. **Consecutive Integers** The product of two consecutive even integers is 14 more than their sum. Find the integers.

29. **Geometry** The length of a rectangle is 1 foot more than 3 times the width. The area is 52 square feet. Find the dimensions.

30. **Geometry** One leg of a right triangle is 2 feet more than the other. The hypotenuse is 10 feet. Find the lengths of the two legs.

31. **Production Cost** A company can manufacture x hundred items for a total cost C, given the equation $C = 100 + 500x - 100x^2$. How many items can be manufactured if the total cost is to be $700?

32. **Price and Revenue** A manufacturer knows that the number of items he can sell each week, x, is related to the price p of each item by the equation $x = 800 - 100p$. What price should he charge for each item to have a weekly revenue of $1,500? (*Remember: $R = xp$.*)

Functions and Function Notation

Chapter Outline

A student is heating water in a chemistry lab. As the water heats, she records the temperature readings from two thermometers, one giving temperature in degrees Fahrenheit and the other in degrees Celsius. The table below shows some of the data she collects. The scatter diagram that gives a visual representation of the data in the table.

Corresponding Temperatures

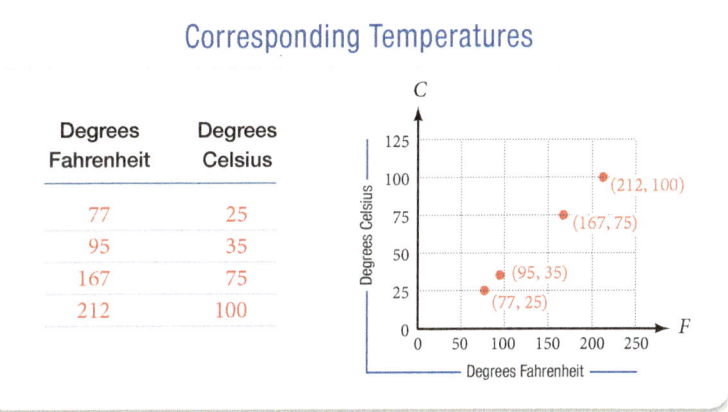

Degrees Fahrenheit	Degrees Celsius
77	25
95	35
167	75
212	100

The exact relationship between the Fahrenheit and Celsius temperature scales is given by the formula

$$C = \frac{5}{9}(F - 32)$$

We have three ways to describe the relationship between the two temperature scales: a table, a graph, and an equation. But, most important to us, we don't need to accept this formula on faith. Later, you will derive the formula from the data in the table above.

If you have made it this far, then you have the study skills necessary to be successful in this course. Success skills are more general in nature and will help you with all your classes and ensure your success in college as well.

Let's start with a question:

Question: What quality is most important for success in any college course?

Answer: Independence. You want to become an independent learner.

We all know people like this. They are generally happy. They don't worry about getting the right instructor, or whether or not things work out every time. They have a confidence that comes from knowing that they are responsible for their success or failure in the goals they set for themselves.

Here are some of the qualities of an independent learner:

- Intends to succeed.
- Doesn't let setbacks deter them.
- Knows their resources.
  - Instructor's office hours
  - Math lab
  - Student Solutions Manual
  - Group study
  - Internet
- Doesn't mistake activity for achievement.
- Has a positive attitude.

There are other traits as well. The first step in becoming an independent learner is doing a little self-evaluation and then making of list of traits that you would like to acquire. What skills do you have that align with those of an independent learner? What attributes do you have that keep you from being an independent learner? What qualities would you like to obtain that you don't have now?

Introduction to Functions

The ad shown here appeared in the Help Wanted section of the local newspaper the day I was writing this section of the book. If you held the job described in the ad, you would earn $7.50 for every hour you worked. The amount of money you make in one week depends on the number of hours you work that week. In mathematics, we say that your weekly earnings are a *function* of the number of hours you work.

HELP WANTED

YARD PERSON   **NEV**

Full time 40 hrs. with weekend   Full tim
work required. Cleaning &   with we
loading trucks. $7.50/hr.   Delivery
                                      $8.50/h
Valid CDL with clean record &
drug screen required.   Valid CD
                                      drug sc
Submit current MVR to KCI,   Call (80
225 Suburban Rd., SLO 93405
(805) 555-3304.
                                      COM
BABY SITTER

An Informal Look at Functions

Suppose you have a job that pays $7.50 per hour and that you work anywhere from 0 to 40 hours per week. If we let the variable x represent hours and the variable y represent the money you make, then the relationship between x and y can be written as

$$y = 7.5x \quad \text{for} \quad 0 \leq x \leq 40$$

Video Examples

Section 6.1

Example 1   Construct a table and graph for the function

$$y = 7.5x \quad \text{for} \quad 0 \leq x \leq 40$$

SOLUTION   Table 1 gives some of the paired data that satisfy the equation $y = 7.5x$. Figure 1 is the graph of the equation with the restriction $0 \leq x \leq 40$.

TABLE 1   Weekly Wages

Hours Worked	Rule	Pay
x	$y = 7.5x$	y
0	$y = 7.5(0)$	0
10	$y = 7.5(10)$	75
20	$y = 7.5(20)$	150
30	$y = 7.5(30)$	225
40	$y = 7.5(40)$	300

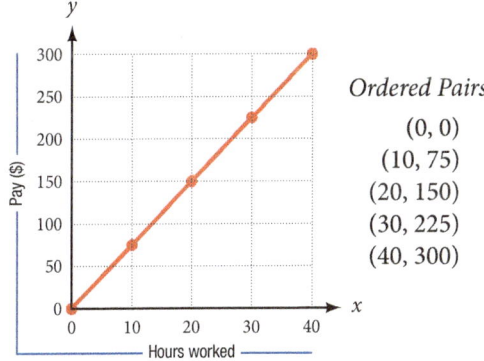

Ordered Pairs

(0, 0)
(10, 75)
(20, 150)
(30, 225)
(40, 300)

FIGURE 1 *Weekly wages at $7.50 per hour*

The equation $y = 7.5x$ with the restriction $0 \leq x \leq 40$, Table 1, and Figure 1 are three ways to describe the same relationship between the number of hours you work in one week and your gross pay for that week. In all three, we **input** values of x, and then use the function rule to **output** values of y.

Domain and Range of a Function

We began this discussion by saying that the number of hours worked during the week was from 0 to 40, so these are the values that x can assume. From the line graph in Figure 1, we see that the values of y range from 0 to 300. We call the complete set of values that x can assume the *domain* of the function. The values that are assigned to y are called the *range* of the function.

Domain: The set of all inputs   The Function Rule   Range: The set of all outputs

Example 2   State the domain and range for the function

$$y = 7.5x, \quad 0 \le x \le 40$$

SOLUTION   From the previous discussion, we have

Domain $= \{x \mid 0 \le x \le 40\}$

Range $= \{y \mid 0 \le y \le 300\}$

Function Maps

Another way to visualize the relationship between x and y is with the diagram in Figure 2, which we call a *function map*.

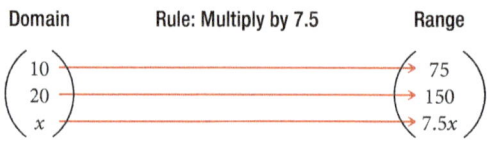

Domain   Rule: Multiply by 7.5   Range

10 → 75
20 → 150
x → $7.5x$

FIGURE 2 *A function map*

Although Figure 2 does not show all the values that x and y can assume, it does give us a visual description of how x and y are related. It shows that values of y in the range come from values of x in the domain according to a specific rule (multiply by 7.5 each time).

A Formal Look at Functions

We are now ready for the formal definition of a function.

> (dĕf′   *function*
>
> A *function* is a rule that pairs each element in one set, called the *domain,* with exactly one element from a second set, called the *range.*

In other words, a function is a rule for which each input is paired with exactly one output.

Example 3   Kendra tosses a softball into the air with an underhand motion. The distance of the ball above her hand is given by the function

$$h = 32t - 16t^2 \qquad \text{for} \qquad 0 \leq t \leq 2$$

where h is the height of the ball in feet and t is the time in seconds. Construct a table that gives the height of the ball at quarter-second intervals, starting with $t = 0$ and ending with $t = 2$, then graph the function.

SOLUTION   We construct Table 2 using the following values of t: $0, \frac{1}{4}, \frac{1}{2}, \frac{3}{4}, 1, \frac{5}{4}, \frac{3}{2}, \frac{7}{4}, 2$. Then we construct the graph in Figure 3 from the table. The graph appears only in the first quadrant because neither t nor h can be negative.

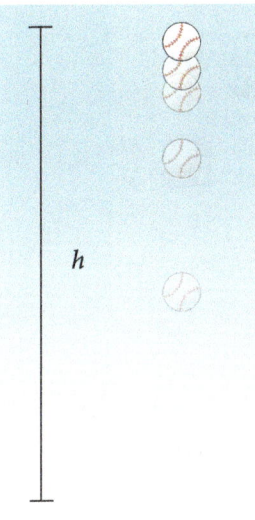

h

TABLE 2 Tossing a Softball into the Air		
Input		Output
Time (sec) t	Function Rule $h = 32t - 16t^2$	Distance (ft) h
0	$h = 32(0) - 16(0)^2 = 0 - 0 = 0$	0
$\frac{1}{4}$	$h = 32\left(\frac{1}{4}\right) - 16\left(\frac{1}{4}\right)^2 = 8 - 1 = 7$	7
$\frac{1}{2}$	$h = 32\left(\frac{1}{2}\right) - 16\left(\frac{1}{2}\right)^2 = 16 - 4 = 12$	12
$\frac{3}{4}$	$h = 32\left(\frac{3}{4}\right) - 16\left(\frac{3}{4}\right)^2 = 24 - 9 = 15$	15
1	$h = 32(1) - 16(1)^2 = 32 - 16 = 16$	16
$\frac{5}{4}$	$h = 32\left(\frac{5}{4}\right) - 16\left(\frac{5}{4}\right)^2 = 40 - 25 = 15$	15
$\frac{3}{2}$	$h = 32\left(\frac{3}{2}\right) - 16\left(\frac{3}{2}\right)^2 = 48 - 36 = 12$	12
$\frac{7}{4}$	$h = 32\left(\frac{7}{4}\right) - 16\left(\frac{7}{4}\right)^2 = 56 - 49 = 7$	7
2	$h = 32(2) - 16(2)^2 = 64 - 64 = 0$	0

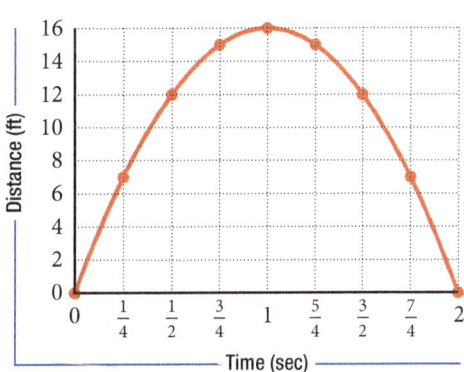

FIGURE 3

Here is a summary of what we know about functions as it applies to this example: We input values of t and output values of h according to the function rule

$$h = 32t - 16t^2 \qquad \text{for} \qquad 0 \leq t \leq 2$$

The domain is given by the inequality that follows the equation; it is

$$\text{Domain} = \{t \mid 0 \leq t \leq 2\}$$

The range is the set of all outputs that are possible by substituting the values of t from the domain into the equation. From our table and graph, it seems that the range is

$$Range = \{h \mid 0 \le h \le 16\}$$

More About Example 3

Most graphing calculators can easily produce the information in Table 2. Simply set Y_1 equal to $32X - 16X^2$. Then set up the table so it starts at 0 and increases by an increment of 0.25 each time. (On a TI-82/83, use the [TBLSET] key to set up the table.)

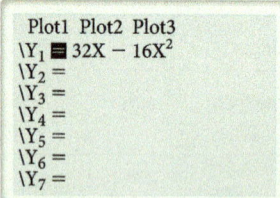

Plot1 Plot2 Plot3
$\backslash Y_1 = 32X - 16X^2$
$\backslash Y_2 =$
$\backslash Y_3 =$
$\backslash Y_4 =$
$\backslash Y_5 =$
$\backslash Y_6 =$
$\backslash Y_7 =$

TABLE SETUP
TblStart = 0
ΔTbl = .25
Indpnt: **Auto** Ask
Depend: **Auto** Ask

The table will look like this:

X	Y_1
0	0
.25	7
.5	12
.75	15
1	16
1.25	15
1.5	12

Graph each equation and build a table as indicated.

1. $y = 64t - 16t^2$ TblStart = 0 ΔTbl = 1
2. $y = \frac{1}{2}x - 4$ TblStart = -5 ΔTbl = 1
3. $y = \frac{12}{x}$ TblStart = 0.5 ΔTbl = 0.5

Functions as Ordered Pairs

As you can see from the examples we have done to this point, the function rule produces ordered pairs of numbers. We use this result to write an alternative definition for a function.

(děf) function (alternate definition)

A *function* is a set of ordered pairs in which no two different ordered pairs have the same first coordinate. The set of all first coordinates is called the *domain* of the function. The set of all second coordinates is called the *range* of the function.

The restriction on first coordinates in the alternative definition keeps us from assigning a number in the domain to more than one number in the range.

A Relationship That is Not a Function

You may be wondering if any sets of paired data fail to qualify as functions. The answer is yes, as the next example reveals.

■ **Example 4**   Table 3 shows the prices of used Ford Mustangs that were listed in the local newspaper. The diagram in Figure 4 is called a *scatter diagram*. It gives a visual representation of the data in Table 3. Why is this data not a function?

TABLE 3   Used Mustang Prices

Year x	Price ($) y
1997	13,925
1997	11,850
1997	9,995
1996	10,200
1996	9,600
1995	9,525
1994	8,675
1994	7,900
1993	6,975

Used Mustang Prices

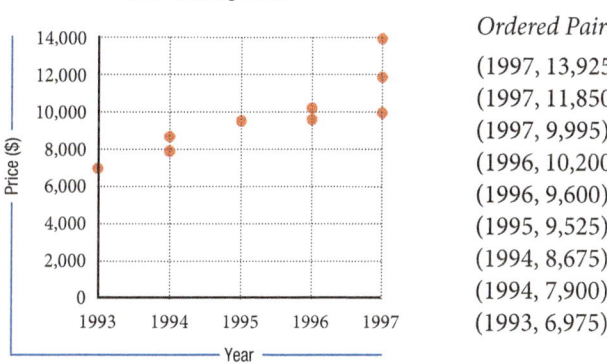

Ordered Pairs

(1997, 13,925)
(1997, 11,850)
(1997, 9,995)
(1996, 10,200)
(1996, 9,600)
(1995, 9,525)
(1994, 8,675)
(1994, 7,900)
(1993, 6,975)

FIGURE 4   *Scatter diagram of data in Table 3*

SOLUTION   In Table 3, the year 1997 is paired with three different prices: $13,925, $11,850, and $9,995. That is enough to disqualify the data from belonging to a function. For a set of paired data to be considered a function, each number in the domain must be paired with exactly one number in the range.   ■

Still, there is a relationship between the first coordinates and second coordinates in the used car data. It is not a function relationship, but it is a relationship. To classify all relationships specified by ordered pairs, whether they are functions or not, we include the following two definitions.

> (dĕf) **relation**
>
> A *relation* is a rule that pairs each element in one set, called the domain, with *one or more elements* from a second set, called the *range*.

> (dĕf) **relation (alternate definition)**
>
> A *relation* is a set of ordered pairs. The set of all first coordinates is the *domain* of the relation. The set of all second coordinates is the *range* of the relation.

Here are some facts that will help clarify the distinction between relations and functions:

1. Any rule that assigns numbers from one set to numbers in another set is a relation. If that rule makes the assignment so no input has more than one output, then it is also a function.
2. Any set of ordered pairs is a relation. If none of the first coordinates of those ordered pairs is repeated, the set of ordered pairs is also a function.
3. Every function is a relation.
4. Not every relation is a function.

Example 5   Sketch the graph of $x = y^2$.

SOLUTION Without going into much detail, we graph the equation $x = y^2$ by finding a number of ordered pairs that satisfy the equation, plotting these points, then drawing a smooth curve that connects them. A table of values for x and y that satisfy the equation follows, along with the graph of $x = y^2$ shown in Figure 5.

x	y
0	0
1	1
1	-1
4	2
4	-2
9	3
9	-3

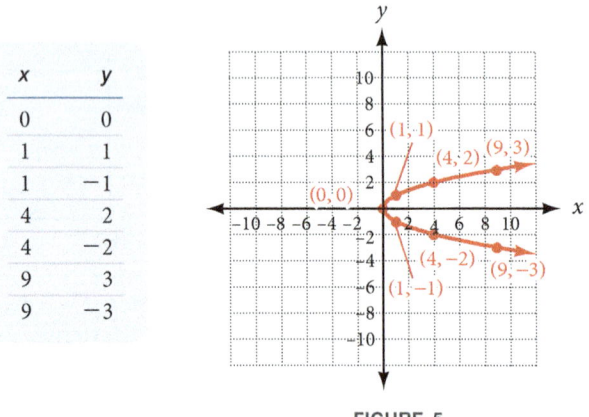

FIGURE 5

As you can see from looking at the table and the graph in Figure 5, several ordered pairs whose graphs lie on the curve have repeated first coordinates, for instance $(1, 1)$ and $(1, -1)$, $(4, 2)$ and $(4, -2)$, as well as $(9, 3)$ and $(9, -3)$. The graph is therefore not the graph of a function.

Vertical Line Test

Look back at the scatter diagram for used Mustang prices shown in Figure 4. Notice that some of the points on the diagram lie above and below each other along vertical lines. This is an indication that the data do not constitute a function. Two data points that lie on the same vertical line must have come from two ordered pairs with the same first coordinates.

Now, look at the graph shown in Figure 5. The reason this graph is the graph of a relation, but not of a function, is that some points on the graph have the same first coordinates, for example, the points $(4, 2)$ and $(4, -2)$. Furthermore, any time two points on a graph have the same first coordinates, those points must lie on a vertical line. [To convince yourself, connect the points $(4, 2)$ and $(4, -2)$ with a straight line. You will see that it must be a vertical line.] This allows us to write the following test that uses the graph to determine whether a relation is also a function.

> ### [Δ≠Σ]   *Vertical Line Test*
>
> If a vertical line crosses the graph of a relation in more than one place, the relation cannot be a function. If no vertical line can be found that crosses a graph in more than one place, then the graph represents a function.

If we look back to the graph of $h = 32t - 16t^2$ as shown in Figure 3, we see that no vertical line can be found that crosses this graph in more than one place. The graph shown in Figure 3 is therefore the graph of a function.

Example 6   Match each relation with its graph, then indicate which relations are functions

a. $y = |x| - 4$ **b.** $y = x^2 - 4$ **c.** $y = 2x + 2$

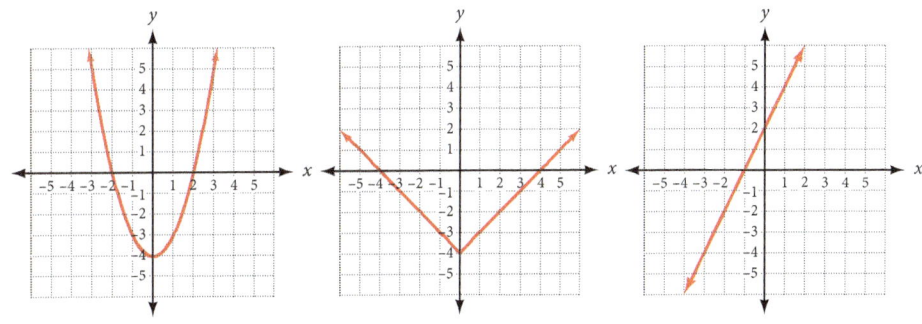

FIGURE 6   FIGURE 7   FIGURE 8

SOLUTION   Using the basic graphs for a guide along with our knowledge of translations, we have the following:

a. Figure 7   **b.** Figure 6   **c.** Figure 8

And, since all graphs pass the vertical line test, all are functions.

Getting Ready for Class

After reading through the preceding section, respond in your own words and in complete sentences.

A. What is a function?

B. What is the vertical line test?

C. Is every line the graph of a function? Explain.

D. Which variable is usually associated with the domain of a function?

SPOTLIGHT ON SUCCESS   *Student Instructor CJ*

> *We are what we repeatedly do. Excellence, then, is not an act, but a habit.*
> —Aristotle

Something that has worked for me in college, in addition to completing the assigned homework, is working on some extra problems from each section. Working on these extra problems is a great habit to get into because it helps further your understanding of the material, and you see the many different types of problems that can arise. If you have completed every problem that your book offers, and you still don't feel confident that you have a full grasp of the material, look for more problems. Many problems can be found online or in other books. Your professors may even have some problems that they would suggest doing for extra practice. The biggest benefit to working all the problems in the course's assigned textbook is that often teachers will choose problems either straight from the book or ones similar to problems that were not assigned for tests. Doing this will ensure that you do your best in all your classes.

For each of the following relations, give the domain and range, and indicate which are also functions.

1. (1, 2), (3, 4), (5, 6), (7, 8)

2. (2, 1), (4, 3), (6, 5), (8, 7)

3. (2, 5), (3, 4), (1, 4), (0, 6)

4. (0, 4), (1, 6), (2, 4), (1, 5)

5. $(a, 3), (b, 4), (c, 3), (d, 5)$

6. $(a, 5), (b, 5), (c, 4), (d, 5)$

7. $(a, 1), (a, 2), (a, 3), (a, 4)$

8. $(a, 1), (b, 1), (c, 1), (d, 1)$

State whether each of the following graphs represents a function.

9.
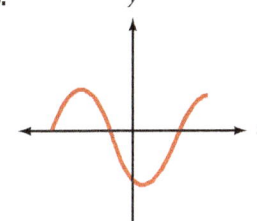

10.
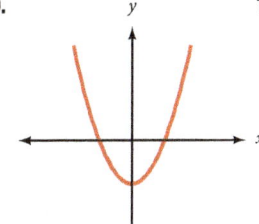

11.
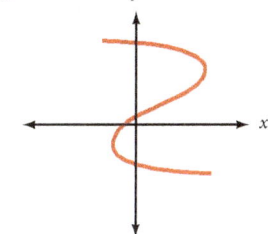

12.
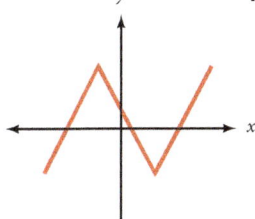

13.
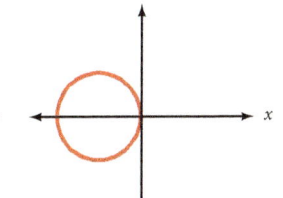

14.
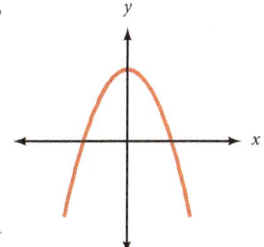

15.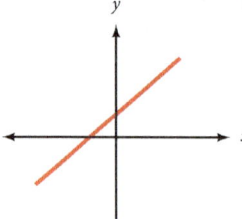

16.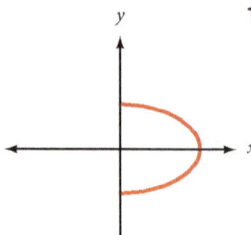

17.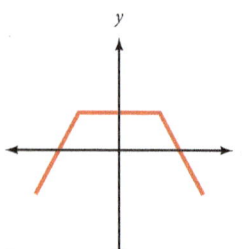

18.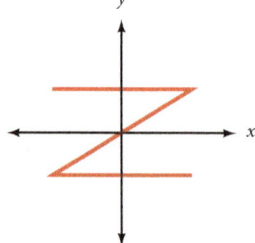

Determine the domain and range of the following functions. Assume the *entire* function is shown.

19.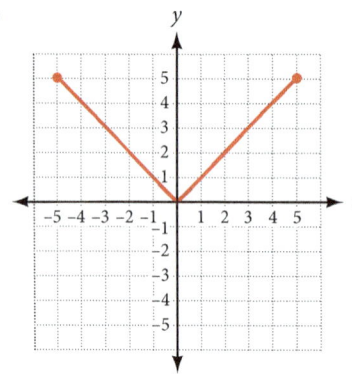

20.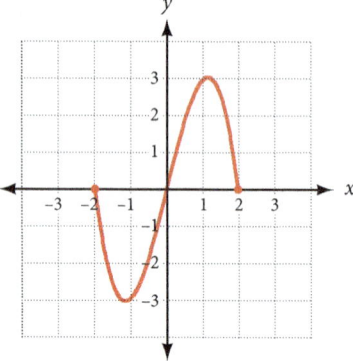

21.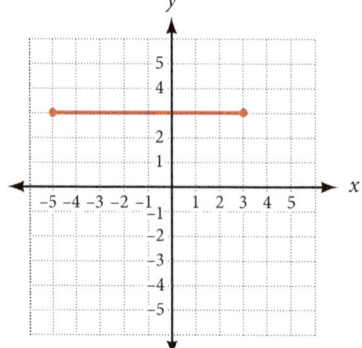

22.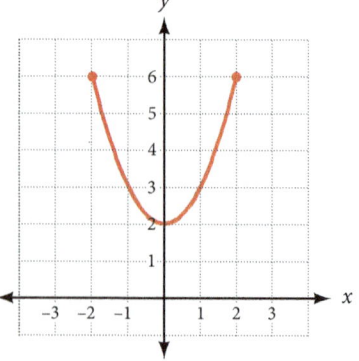

Graph each of the following relations. In each case, use the graph to find the domain and range, and indicate whether the graph is the graph of a function.

23. $y = x^2 - 1$ **24.** $y = x^2 + 1$ **25.** $y = x^2 + 4$ **26.** $y = x^2 - 9$

27. $x = y^2 - 1$ **28.** $x = y^2 + 1$ **29.** $y = (x + 2)^2$ **30.** $y = (x - 3)^2$

31. $x = (y + 1)^2$ **32.** $x = 3 - y^2$

33. Suppose you have a job that pays $8.50 per hour and you work anywhere from 10 to 40 hours per week.

 a. Write an equation, with a restriction on the variable x, that gives the amount of money, y, you will earn for working x hours in one week.

 b. Use the function rule you have written in part **a.** to complete Table 4.

TABLE 4   Weekly Wages

Hours Worked	Function Rule	Gross Pay ($)
x		y
10		
20		
30		
40		

 c. Construct a line graph from the information in Table 4.

 d. State the domain and range of this function.

 e. What is the minimum amount you can earn in a week with this job? What is the maximum amount?

34. The ad shown here was in the local newspaper. Suppose you are hired for the job described in the ad.

312 HELP WANTED

ESPRESSO BAR OPERATOR

Must be dependable, honest, serivce-oriented. Coffee exp desired. 15-30 hrs per wk. $5.25/hour. Start 5/31. Apply in person:

Espresso Yourself
Central Coast Mall
Deadline 5/23

a. If x is the number of hours you work per week and y is your weekly gross pay, write the equation for y. (Be sure to include any restrictions on the variable x that are given in the ad.)

b. Use the function rule you have written in part **a.** to complete Table 5.

TABLE 5   Weekly Wages

Hours Worked	Function Rule	Gross Pay ($)
x		y
15		
20		
25		
30		

c. Construct a line graph from the information in Table 5.

d. State the domain and range of this function.

e. What is the minimum amount you can earn in a week with this job? What is the maximum amount?

35. Android vs. iOS Phones The chart shows the number of Apple iOS and Google Android OS phones sold from 2009 to 2015. Using the chart, list all the values in the domain and range for the total phones sales.

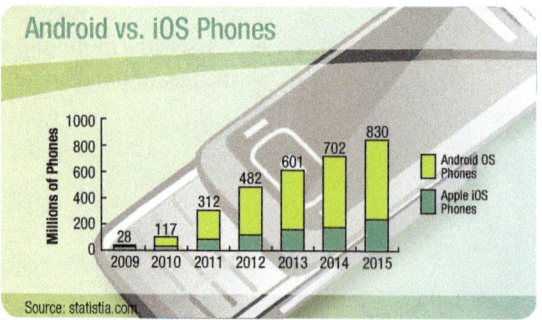

36. **Light Bulbs** The chart shows a comparison of power usage between incandescent and energy efficient light bulbs. Use the chart to state the domain and range of the function for an energy efficient bulb.

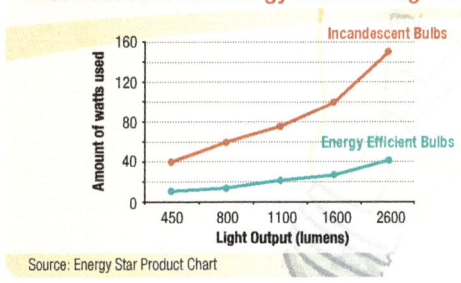

Incandescent vs. Energy Efficient Light Bulbs

Source: Energy Star Product Chart

37. **Profits** Match each of the following statements to the appropriate graph indicated by labels I–IV.
    a. Sarah works 25 hours to earn $250.
    b. Justin works 35 hours to earn $560.
    c. Rosemary works 30 hours to earn $360.
    d. Marcus works 40 hours to earn $320.

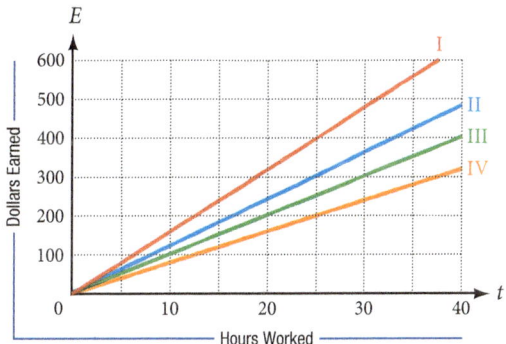

38. Find an equation for each of the functions shown in the graph. Show dollars earned, E, as a function of hours worked, t. Then, indicate the domain and range of each function.

   a. Graph I: $E =$ _____   Domain $= \{t \mid$ _____ $\}$ Range $= \{E \mid$ _____ $\}$

   b. Graph II: $E =$ _____   Domain $= \{t \mid$ _____ $\}$ Range $= \{E \mid$ _____ $\}$

   c. Graph III: $E =$ _____   Domain $= \{t \mid$ _____ $\}$ Range $= \{E \mid$ _____ $\}$

   d. Graph IV: $E =$ _____   Domain $= \{t \mid$ _____ $\}$ Range $= \{E \mid$ _____ $\}$

Getting Ready for the Next Section

Simplify. Round to the nearest whole number if necessary.

39. $4(3.14)(9)$

40. $\frac{4}{3}(3.14) \cdot 3^3$

41. $4(-2) - 1$

42. $3(3)^2 + 2(3) - 1$

43. If $s = \dfrac{60}{t}$, find s when

    a. $t = 10$ **b.** $t = 8$

44. If $y = 3x^2 + 2x - 1$, find y when

    a. $x = 0$ **b.** $x = -2$

45. Find the value of $x^2 + 2$ for

    a. $x = 5$ **b.** $x = -2$

46. Find the value of $125 \cdot 2^t$ for

    a. $t = 0$ **b.** $t = 1$

For the equation $y = x^2 - 3$:

47. Find y if x is 2.

48. Find y if x is -2.

49. Find y if x is 0.

50. Find y if x is -4.

The problems that follow review some of the more important skills you have learned in previous sections and chapters.

51. If $x - 2y = 4$, and $x = \dfrac{8}{5}$ find y.

52. If $\dfrac{x^2}{25} + \dfrac{y^2}{9} = 1$, find y when x is -4.

53. Let $x = 0$ and $y = 0$ in $y = a(x - 8)^2 + 70$ and solve for a.

54. Find R if $p = 2.5$ and $R = (900 - 300p)p$.

Let's return to the discussion that introduced us to functions. If a job pays $7.50 per hour for working from 0 to 40 hours a week, then the amount of money y earned in one week is a function of the number of hours worked x. The exact relationship between x and y is written

$$y = 7.5x \quad \text{for} \quad 0 \le x \le 40$$

Because the amount of money earned y depends on the number of hours worked x, we call y the *dependent variable* and x the *independent variable*. Furthermore, if we let f represent all the ordered pairs produced by the equation, then we can write

$$f = \{(x, y) \mid y = 7.5x \quad \text{and} \quad 0 \le x \le 40\}$$

Once we have named a function with a letter, we can use an alternative notation to represent the dependent variable y. The alternative notation for y is $f(x)$. It is read "f of x" and can be used instead of the variable y when working with functions. The notation y and the notation $f(x)$ are equivalent. That is,

$$y = 7.5x \Leftrightarrow f(x) = 7.5x$$

When we use the notation $f(x)$ we are using *function notation*. The benefit of using function notation is that we can write more information with fewer symbols than we can by using just the variable y. For example, asking how much money a person will make for working 20 hours is simply a matter of asking for $f(20)$. Without function notation, we would have to say, "Find the value of y that corresponds to a value of $x = 20$." To illustrate further, using the variable y, we can say "y is 150 when x is 20." Using the notation $f(x)$, we simply say "$f(20) = 150$." Each expression indicates that you will earn $150 for working 20 hours.

Video Examples

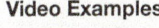

Section 6.2

Note Some students like to think of functions as machines. Values of x are put into the machine, which transforms them into values of $f(x)$, which are then output by the machine.

■ **Example 1**   If $f(x) = 7.5x$, find $f(0)$, $f(10)$, and $f(20)$.

SOLUTION   To find $f(0)$, we substitute 0 for x in the expression $7.5x$ and simplify. We find $f(10)$ and $f(20)$ in a similar manner — by substitution.

$$\text{If} \qquad f(x) = 7.5x$$
$$\text{then} \qquad f(0) = 7.5(0) = 0$$
$$f(10) = 7.5(10) = 75$$
$$f(20) = 7.5(20) = 150$$

■

If we changed the example in the discussion that opened this section so the hourly wage was $6.50 per hour, we would have a new equation to work with, namely,

$$y = 6.5x \qquad \text{for} \qquad 0 \le x \le 40$$

Suppose we name this new function with the letter g. Then

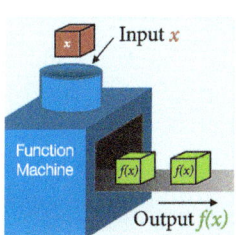

$$g = \{(x, y) \mid y = 6.5x \quad \text{and} \quad 0 \le x \le 40\}$$

and

$$g(x) = 6.5x$$

If we want to talk about both functions in the same discussion, having two different letters, f and g, makes it easy to distinguish between them. For example, since

$f(x) = 7.5x$ and $g(x) = 6.5x$, asking how much money a person makes for working 20 hours is simply a matter of asking for $f(20)$ or $g(20)$, avoiding any confusion over which hourly wage we are talking about.

> **Note** The symbol $\in$ means "is a member of".

The diagrams shown in Figure 1 further illustrate the similarities and differences between the two functions we have been discussing.

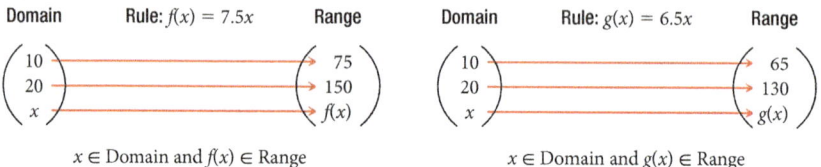

FIGURE 1 *Function maps*

Function Notation and Graphs

We can visualize the relationship between x and $f(x)$ on the graph of the function. Figure 2 shows the graph of $f(x) = 7.5x$ along with two additional line segments. The horizontal line segment corresponds to $x = 20$, and the vertical line segment corresponds to $f(20)$. (Note that the domain is restricted to $0 \leq x \leq 40$.)

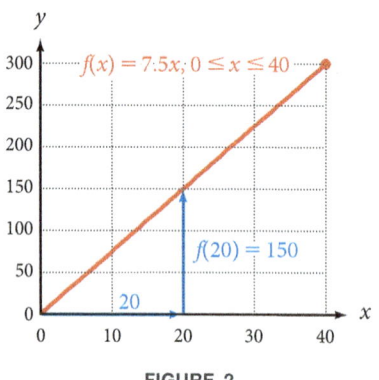

FIGURE 2

We can use functions and function notation to talk about numbers in the chart on gasoline prices. Let's let x represent one of the years in the chart.

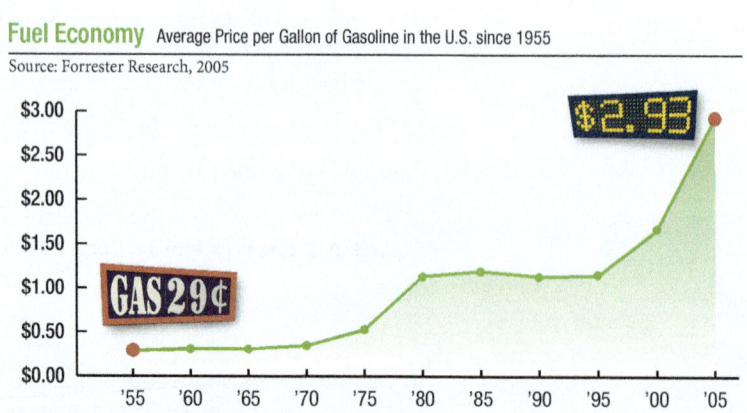

Fuel Economy Average Price per Gallon of Gasoline in the U.S. since 1955

Source: Forrester Research, 2005

If the function f pairs each year in the chart with the average price of regular gasoline for that year, then each statement below is true:

$$f(1955) = \$0.29$$

The domain of $f =$
$$\{1955, 1960, 1965, 1970, 1975, 1980, 1985, 1990, 1995, 2000, 2005\}$$

In general, when we refer to the function f we are referring to the domain, the range, and the rule that takes elements in the domain and outputs elements in the range. When we talk about $f(x)$ we are talking about the rule itself, or an element in the range, or the variable y.

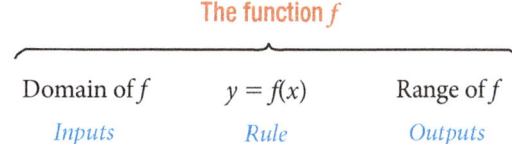

Using Function Notation

The remaining examples in this section show a variety of ways to use and interpret function notation.

Example 2   If it takes Lorena t minutes to run a mile, then her average speed s, in miles per hour, is given by the formula

$$s(t) = \frac{60}{t} \qquad \text{for} \qquad t > 0$$

Find $s(10)$ and $s(8)$, and then explain what they mean.

SOLUTION   To find $s(10)$, we substitute 10 for t in the equation and simplify:

$$s(10) = \frac{60}{10} = 6$$

In words: When Lorena runs a mile in 10 minutes, her average speed is 6 miles per hour.
  We calculate $s(8)$ by substituting 8 for t in the equation. Doing so gives us

$$s(8) = \frac{60}{8} = 7.5$$

In words: Running a mile in 8 minutes is running at a rate of 7.5 miles per hour.

Example 3   A painting is purchased as an investment for \$125. If its value increases continuously so that it doubles every 5 years, then its value is given by the function

$$V(t) = 125 \cdot 2^{t/5} \qquad \text{for} \qquad t \geq 0$$

where t is the number of years since the painting was purchased, and V is its value (in dollars) at time t. Find $V(5)$ and $V(10)$, and explain what they mean.

SOLUTION The expression $V(5)$ is the value of the painting when $t = 5$ (5 years after it is purchased). We calculate $V(5)$ by substituting 5 for t in the equation $V(t) = 125 \cdot 2^{t/5}$. Here is our work:

$$V(5) = 125 \cdot 2^{5/5} = 125 \cdot 2^1 = 125 \cdot 2 = 250$$

In words: After 5 years, the painting is worth $250.

The expression $V(10)$ is the value of the painting after 10 years. To find this number, we substitute 10 for t in the equation:

$$V(10) = 125 \cdot 2^{10/5} = 125 \cdot 2^2 = 125 \cdot 4 = 500$$

In words: The value of the painting 10 years after it is purchased is $500.

Example 4   A balloon has the shape of a sphere with a radius of 3 inches. Use the following formulas to find the volume and surface area of the balloon.

$$V(r) = \frac{4}{3}\pi r^3 \qquad S(r) = 4\pi r^2$$

SOLUTION As you can see, we have used function notation to write the formulas for volume and surface area, because each quantity is a function of the radius. To find these quantities when the radius is 3 inches, we evaluate $V(3)$ and $S(3)$:

$$V(3) = \frac{4}{3}\pi \cdot 3^3 = \frac{4}{3}\pi \cdot 27$$

$$= 36\pi \text{ cubic inches, or } 113 \text{ cubic inches}$$
$$\text{(to the nearest whole number)}$$

$$S(3) = 4\pi \cdot 3^2$$

$$= 36\pi \text{ square inches, or } 113 \text{ square inches}$$
$$\text{(to the nearest whole number)}$$

The fact that $V(3) = 36\pi$ means that the ordered pair $(3, 36\pi)$ belongs to the function V. Likewise, the fact that $S(3) = 36\pi$ tells us that the ordered pair $(3, 36\pi)$ is a member of function S.

We can generalize the discussion at the end of Example 4 this way:

$$(a, b) \in f \qquad \text{if and only if} \qquad f(a) = b$$

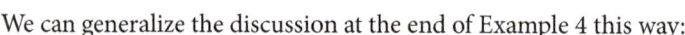

More About Example 4

If we look at Example 4, we see that when the radius of a sphere is 3, the numerical values of the volume and surface area are equal. How unusual is this? Are there other values of r for which $V(r)$ and $S(r)$ are equal? We can answer this question by looking at the graphs of both V and S.

To graph the function $V(r) = \frac{4}{3}\pi r^3$, set $Y_1 = 4\pi X^3/3$. To graph $S(r) = 4\pi r^2$, set $Y_2 = 4\pi X^2$. Graph the two functions in each of the following windows:

> Window 1:   X from -4 to 4, Y from -2 to 10
>
> Window 2:   X from 0 to 4, Y from 0 to 50
>
> Window 3:   X from 0 to 4, Y from 0 to 150

Then use the Trace and Zoom features of your calculator to locate the point in the first quadrant where the two graphs intersect. How do the coordinates of this point compare with the results in Example 4?

Example 5 If $f(x) = 3x^2 + 2x - 1$, find $f(0)$, $f(3)$, and $f(-2)$.

SOLUTION Since $f(x) = 3x^2 + 2x - 1$, we have

$$f(0) = 3(0)^2 + 2(0) - 1 = 0 - 1 = -1$$

$$f(3) = 3(3)^2 + 2(3) - 1 = 27 + 6 - 1 = 32$$

$$f(-2) = 3(-2)^2 + 2(-2) - 1 = 12 - 4 - 1 = 7$$

In Example 5, the function f is defined by the equation $f(x) = 3x^2 + 2x - 1$. We could just as easily have said $y = 3x^2 + 2x - 1$. That is, $y = f(x)$. Saying $f(-2) = 7$ is exactly the same as saying y is 7 when x is -2.

Example 6 If $f(x) = 4x - 1$ and $g(x) = x^2 + 2$, then

$$f(5) = 4(5) - 1 = 19 \quad \text{and} \quad g(5) = 5^2 + 2 = 27$$

$$f(-2) = 4(-2) - 1 = -9 \quad \text{and} \quad g(-2) = (-2)^2 + 2 = 6$$

$$f(0) = 4(0) - 1 = -1 \quad \text{and} \quad g(0) = 0^2 + 2 = 2$$

$$f(z) = 4z - 1 \quad \text{and} \quad g(z) = z^2 + 2$$

$$f(a) = 4a - 1 \quad \text{and} \quad g(a) = a^2 + 2$$

$$f(a + 3) = 4(a + 3) - 1 \qquad g(a + 3) = (a + 3)^2 + 2$$

$$= 4a + 12 - 1 \qquad\qquad = (a^2 + 6a + 9) + 2$$

$$= 4a + 11 \qquad\qquad\quad = a^2 + 6a + 11$$

More About Example 6

Most graphing calculators can use tables to evaluate functions. To work Example 6 using a graphing calculator table, set Y_1 equal to $4X - 1$ and Y_2 equal to $X^2 + 2$. Then set the independent variable in the table to Ask instead of Auto. Go to your table and input 5, -2, and 0. Under Y_1 in the table, you will find $f(5)$, $f(-2)$, and $f(0)$. Under Y_2, you will find $g(5)$, $g(-2)$, and $g(0)$.

Plot1 Plot2 Plot3
\Y₁ ▆ 4X − 1
\Y₂ ▆ X² + 2
\Y₃ =
\Y₄ =
\Y₅ =
\Y₆ =
\Y₇ =

TABLE SETUP
TblStart = 0
ΔTbl = 1
Indpnt: Auto **Ask**
Depend: Auto **Ask**

The table will look like this:

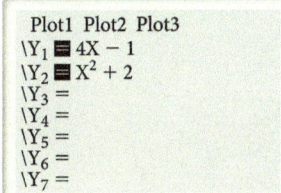

X	Y_1	Y_2
5	19	27
−2	−9	6
0	−1	2

Although the calculator asks us for a table increment, the increment doesn't matter because we are inputting the X values ourselves.

Example 7   If the function f is given by

$$f = \{(-2, 0), (3, -1), (2, 4), (7, 5)\}$$

then $f(-2) = 0$, $f(3) = -1$, $f(2) = 4$, and $f(7) = 5$.

Example 8   If $f(x) = 2x^2$ and $g(x) = 3x - 1$, find

a. $f[g(2)]$ **b.** $g[f(2)]$

SOLUTION   The expression $f[g(2)]$ is read "f of g of 2."

a. Because $g(2) = 3(2) - 1 = 5$,

$$f[g(2)] = f(5) = 2(5)^2 = 50$$

b. Because $f(2) = 2(2)^2 = 8$,

$$g[f(2)] = g(8) = 3(8) - 1 = 23$$

Getting Ready for Class

After reading through the preceding section, respond in your own words and in complete sentences.

A. Explain what you are calculating when you find $f(2)$ for a given function f.

B. If $s(t) = \frac{60}{t}$ how do you find $s(10)$?

C. If $f(2) = 3$ for a function f, what is the relationship between the numbers 2 and 3 and the graph of f?

D. If $f(6) = 0$ for a particular function f, then you can immediately graph one of the intercepts. Explain.

Let $f(x) = 2x - 5$ and $g(x) = x^2 + 3x + 4$. Evaluate the following.

1. $f(2)$ **2.** $f(3)$ **3.** $f(-3)$ **4.** $g(-2)$

5. $g(-1)$ **6.** $f(-4)$ **7.** $g(-3)$ **8.** $g(2)$

9. $g(a)$ **10.** $f(a)$ **11.** $f(a + 6)$ **12.** $g(a + 6)$

Let $f(x) = 3x^2 - 4x + 1$ and $g(x) = 2x - 1$. Evaluate the following.

13. $f(0)$ **14.** $g(0)$ **15.** $g(-4)$ **16.** $f(1)$

17. $f(-1)$ **18.** $g(-1)$ **19.** $g\left(\dfrac{1}{2}\right)$ **20.** $g\left(\dfrac{1}{4}\right)$

21. $f(a)$ **22.** $g(a)$ **23.** $f(a + 2)$ **24.** $g(a + 2)$

If $f = \left\{ (1, 4), (-2, 0), \left(3, \tfrac{1}{2}\right), (\pi, 0) \right\}$ and $g = \left\{ (1, 1), (-2, 2), \left(\tfrac{1}{2}, 0\right) \right\}$, find each of the following values of f and g.

25. $f(1)$ **26.** $g(1)$ **27.** $g\left(\dfrac{1}{2}\right)$ **28.** $f(3)$

29. $g(-2)$ **30.** $f(\pi)$

Let $f(x) = x^2 - 2x$ and $g(x) = 5x - 4$. Evaluate the following.

31. $f(-4)$ **32.** $g(-3)$ **33.** $f(-2) + g(-1)$

34. $f(-1) + g(-2)$ **35.** $2f(x) - 3g(x)$ **36.** $f(x) - g(x^2)$

37. $f[g(3)]$ **38.** $g[f(3)]$

Let $f(x) = \dfrac{1}{x + 3}$ and $g(x) = \dfrac{1}{x} + 1$. Evaluate the following.

39. $f\left(\dfrac{1}{3}\right)$ **40.** $g\left(\dfrac{1}{3}\right)$ **41.** $f\left(-\dfrac{1}{2}\right)$ **42.** $g\left(-\dfrac{1}{2}\right)$

43. $f(-3)$ **44.** $g(0)$

45. For the function $f(x) = x^2 - 4$, evaluate each of the following expressions.

   a. $f(a) - 3$ **b.** $f(a - 3)$ **c.** $f(x) + 2$

   d. $f(x + 2)$ **e.** $f(a + b)$ **f.** $f(x + h)$

46. For the function $f(x) = 3x^2$, evaluate each of the following expressions.

   a. $f(a) - 2$ **b.** $f(a - 2)$ **c.** $f(x) + 5$

   d. $f(x + 5)$ **e.** $f(a + b)$ **f.** $f(x + h)$

47. Graph the function $f(x) = \dfrac{1}{2}x + 2$. Then draw and label the line segments that represent $x = 4$ and $f(4)$.

48. Graph the function $f(x) = -\dfrac{1}{2}x + 6$. Then draw and label the line segments that represent $x = 4$ and $f(4)$.

49. For the function $f(x) = \frac{1}{2}x + 2$, find the value of x for which $f(x) = x$.

50. For the function $f(x) = -\frac{1}{2}x + 6$, find the value of x for which $f(x) = x$.

51. Graph the function $f(x) = x^2$. Then draw and label the line segments that represent $x = 1$ and $f(1)$, $x = 2$ and $f(2)$ and, finally, $x = 3$ and $f(3)$.

52. Graph the function $f(x) = x^2 - 2$. Then draw and label the line segments that represent $x = 2$ and $f(2)$ and the line segments corresponding to $x = 3$ and $f(3)$.

Applying the Concepts

53. **Investing in Art** A painting is purchased as an investment for \$150. If its value increases continuously so that it doubles every 3 years, then its value is given by the function

$$V(t) = 150 \cdot 2^{t/3} \qquad \text{for} \qquad t \geq 0$$

where t is the number of years since the painting was purchased, and $V(t)$ is its value (in dollars) at time t. Find $V(3)$ and $V(6)$, and then explain what they mean.

54. **Average Speed** If it takes Minke t minutes to run a mile, then her average speed $s(t)$, in miles per hour, is given by the formula

$$s(t) = \frac{60}{t} \qquad \text{for} \qquad t > 0$$

Find $s(4)$ and $s(5)$, and then explain what they mean.

55. **Antidepressant Sales** Suppose x represents one of the years in the chart. Suppose further that we have three functions f, g, and h that do the following:

f pairs each year with the total sales of Zoloft in billions of dollars for that year.
g pairs each year with the total sales of Effexor in billions of dollars for that year.
h pairs each year with the total sales of Wellbutrin in billions of dollars for that year.

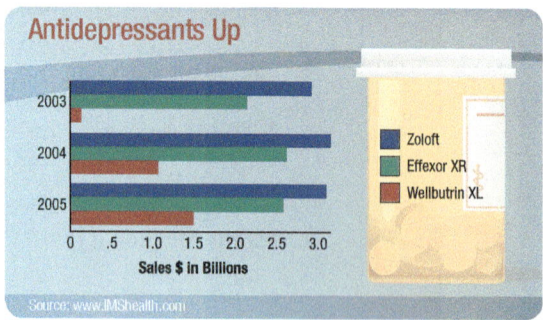

For each statement below, indicate whether the statement is true or false.
a. The domain of g is {2003, 2004, 2005}
b. The domain of g is $\{x \mid 2003 \leq x \leq 2005\}$
c. $f(2004) > g(2004)$
d. $h(2005) > 1.5$
e. $h(2005) > h(2004) > h(2003)$

56. **Mobile Phone Sales** Suppose x represents one of the years in the chart. Suppose further that we have three functions f, g, and h that do the following:

f pairs each year with the number of iOS phones sold that year.
g pairs each year with the number of Android phones sold that year.
h is such that $h(x) = f(x) + g(x)$.

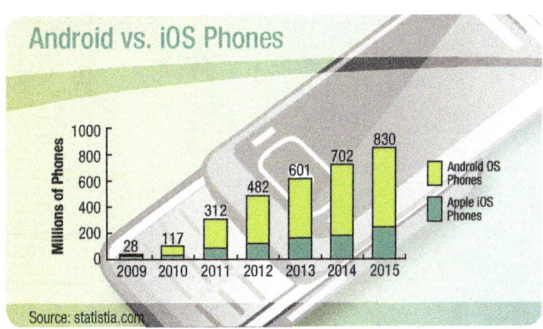

Android vs. iOS Phones

For each statement below, indicate whether the statement is true or false.

   a. The domain of f is {2009, 2010, 2011, 2012, 2013, 2014, 2015}

   b. $h(2010) = 127,000,000$

   c. $f(2009) > g(2009)$

   d. $f(2014) < f(2015)$

   e. $h(2014) > h(2013) > h(2012)$

Straight-Line Depreciation Straight-line depreciation is an accounting method used to help spread the cost of new equipment over a number of years. It takes into account both the cost when new and the salvage value, which is the value of the equipment at the time it gets replaced.

57. **Value of a Copy Machine** The function $V(t) = -3,300t + 18,000$, where V is value and t is time in years, can be used to find the value of a large copy machine during the first 5 years of use.

   a. What is the value of the copier after 3 years and 9 months?

   b. What is the salvage value of this copier if it is replaced after 5 years?

   c. State the domain of this function.

   d. Sketch the graph of this function.

   e. What is the range of this function?

   f. After how many years will the copier be worth only $10,000?

58. Step Function Figure 3 shows the graph of the step function C that was used to calculate the first-class postage on a letter weighing x ounces in 2006. Use this graph to answer questions **a.** through **d.**

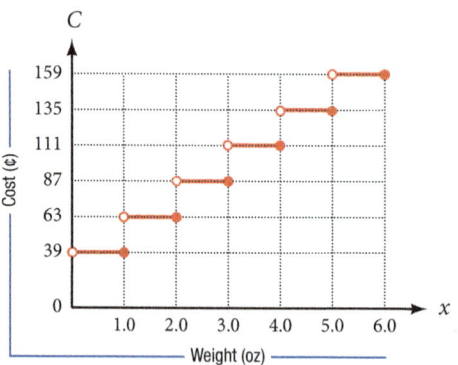

FIGURE 3 *The graph of C(x)*

a. Fill in the following table:

Weight (ounces)	0.6	1.0	1.1	2.5	3.0	4.8	5.0	5.3
Cost (cents)								

b. If a letter cost 87 cents to mail, how much does it weigh? State your answer in words. State your answer as an inequality.

c. If the entire function is shown in Figure 3, state the domain.

d. State the range of the function shown in Figure 3.

Getting Ready for the Next Section

Simplify.

59. $16(3.5)^2$ **60.** $\dfrac{2{,}400}{100}$ **61.** $\dfrac{180}{45}$ **62.** $4(2)(4)^2$

63. $\dfrac{0.0005(200)}{(0.25)^2}$ **64.** $\dfrac{0.2(0.5)^2}{100}$

65. If $y = Kx$, find K if $x = 5$ and $y = 15$.

66. If $d = Kt^2$, find K if $t = 2$ and $d = 64$.

67. If $P = \dfrac{K}{V}$, find K if $P = 48$ and $V = 50$.

68. If $y = Kxz^2$, find K if $x = 5$, $z = 3$, and $y = 180$.

Variation

If you are a runner and you average t minutes for every mile you run during one of your workouts, then your speed s in miles per hour is given by the equation and graph shown here. The graph (Figure 1) is shown in the first quadrant only because both t and s are positive.

$$s = \frac{60}{t}$$

Input	Output
t	s
4	15
6	10
8	7.5
10	6
12	5
14	4.3

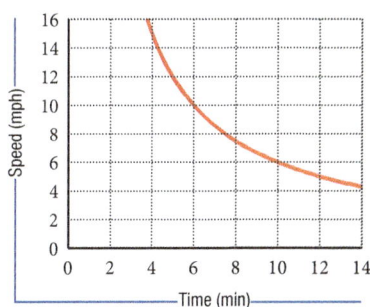

FIGURE 1

You know intuitively that as your average time per mile t increases, your speed s decreases. Likewise, lowering your time per mile will increase your speed. The equation and Figure 1 also show this to be true: Increasing t decreases s, and decreasing t increases s. Quantities that are connected in this way are said to *vary inversely* with each other. Inverse variation is one of the topics we will study in this section.

There are two main types of variation: **direct variation** and **inverse variation**. Variation problems are most common in the sciences, particularly in chemistry and physics.

Direct Variation

When we say the variable y *varies directly* with the variable x, we mean that the relationship can be written in symbols as $y = Kx$, where K is a nonzero constant called the **constant of variation** (or *proportionality constant*).

Another way of saying y varies directly with x is to say y is **directly proportional** to x.

Study the following list. It gives the mathematical equivalent of some direct variation statements.

Verbal Phrase	Algebraic Equation
y varies directly with x.	$y = Kx$
s varies directly with the square of t.	$s = Kt^2$
y is directly proportional to the cube of z.	$y = Kz^3$
u is directly proportional to the square root of v.	$u = K\sqrt{v}$

Video Examples

Section 6.3

■ **Example 1**   *y* varies directly with *x*. If *y* is 15 when *x* is 5, find *y* when *x* is 7.

SOLUTION   The first sentence gives us the general relationship between *x* and *y*. The equation equivalent to the statement "*y* varies directly with *x*" is

$$y = Kx$$

The first part of the second sentence in our example gives us the information necessary to evaluate the constant *K*:

When	$y = 15$
and	$x = 5$
the equation	$y = Kx$
becomes	$15 = K \cdot 5$
or	$K = 3$

The equation can now be written specifically as

$$y = 3x$$

Letting $x = 7$, we have

$$y = 3 \cdot 7$$
$$y = 21$$

■

■ **Example 2**   A skydiver jumps from a plane. Like any object that falls toward earth, the distance the skydiver falls is directly proportional to the square of the time he has been falling, until he reaches his terminal velocity. If the skydiver falls 64 feet in the first 2 seconds of the jump, then

a. How far will he have fallen after 3.5 seconds?
b. Graph the relationship between distance and time.
c. How long will it take him to fall 256 feet?

SOLUTION   We let *t* represent the time the skydiver has been falling, then we can let $d(t)$ represent the distance he has fallen.

a. Since $d(t)$ is directly proportional to the square of *t*, we have the general function that describes this situation:

$$d(t) = Kt^2$$

Next, we use the fact that $d(2) = 64$ to find *K*.

$$64 = K(2)^2$$
$$K = 16$$

The specific equation that describes this situation is

$$d(t) = 16t^2$$

To find how far a skydiver will fall after 3.5 seconds, we find $d(3.5)$,

$$d(3.5) = 16(3.5)^2$$
$$d(3.5) = 196$$

A skydiver will fall 196 feet after 3.5 seconds.

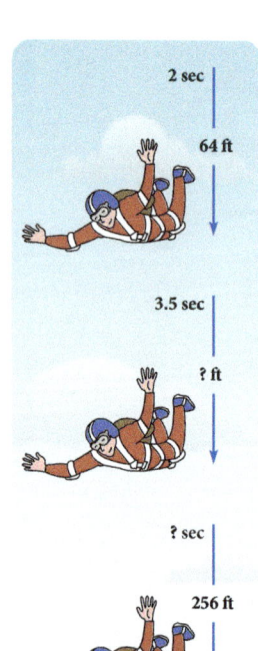

2 sec

64 ft

3.5 sec

? ft

? sec

256 ft

b. To graph this equation, we use a table:

Input	Output
t	$d(t)$
0	0
1	16
2	64
3	144
4	256
5	400

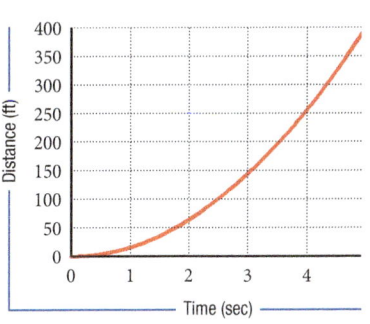

FIGURE 2

c. From the table or the graph (Figure 2), we see that it will take 4 seconds for the skydiver to fall 256 feet.

Inverse Variation

Running

From the introduction to this section, we know that the relationship between the number of minutes t it takes a person to run a mile and his or her average speed in miles per hour s can be described with the following equation and table, and with Figure 3.

$$s = \frac{60}{t}$$

Input	Output
t	s
4	15
6	10
8	7.5
10	6
12	5
14	4.3

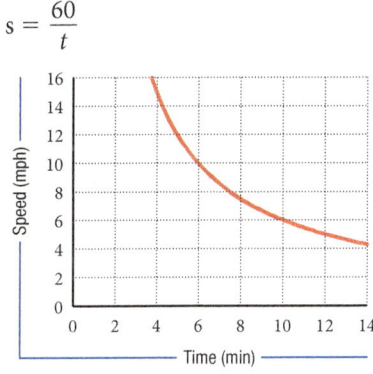

FIGURE 3

If t decreases, then s will increase, and if t increases, then s will decrease. The variable s is **inversely proportional** to the variable t. In this case, the *constant of proportionality* is 60.

Photography

If you are familiar with the terminology and mechanics associated with photography, you know that the f-stop for a particular lens will increase as the aperture (the maximum diameter of the opening of the lens) decreases. In mathematics, we say that f-stop and aperture vary inversely with each other. The following diagram illustrates this relationship.

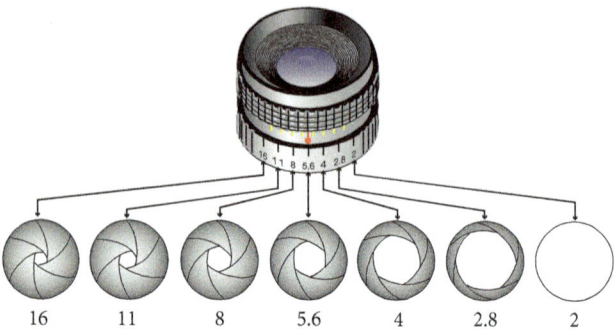

| 16 | 11 | 8 | 5.6 | 4 | 2.8 | 2 |

If *f* is the *f*-stop and *d* is the aperture, then their relationship can be written

$$f = \frac{K}{d}$$

In this case, *K* is the constant of proportionality. (Those of you familiar with photography know that *K* is also the focal length of the camera lens.)

In General
We generalize this discussion of inverse variation as follows: If *y* varies inversely with *x*, then

$$y = K\frac{1}{x} \qquad \text{or} \qquad y = \frac{K}{x}$$

We can also say *y* is inversely proportional to *x*. The constant *K* is again called the constant of variation or proportionality constant.

Verbal Phrase	Algebraic Equation
y is inversely proportional to *x*.	$y = \dfrac{K}{x}$
s varies inversely with the square of *t*.	$s = \dfrac{K}{t^2}$
y is inversely proportional to x^4.	$y = \dfrac{K}{x^4}$
z varies inversely with the cube root of *t*.	$z = \dfrac{K}{\sqrt[3]{t}}$

Example 3   The volume of a gas is inversely proportional to the pressure of the gas on its container. If a pressure of 48 pounds per square inch corresponds to a volume of 50 cubic feet, what pressure is needed to produce a volume of 100 cubic feet?

SOLUTION   We can represent volume with *V* and pressure with *P*:

$$V = \frac{K}{P}$$

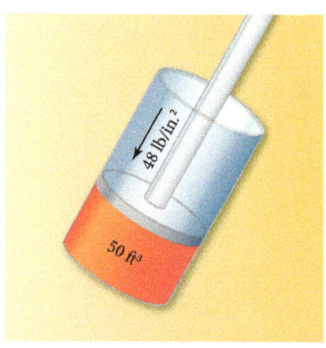

Using $P = 48$ and $V = 50$, we have

$$50 = \frac{K}{48}$$

$$K = 50(48)$$

$$K = 2,400$$

The equation that describes the relationship between P and V is

$$V = \frac{2,400}{P}$$

Here is a graph of this relationship.

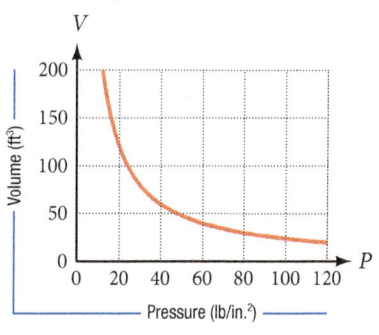

FIGURE 4

Note The relationship between pressure and volume as given in this example is known as Boyle's law and applies to situations such as those encountered in a piston-cylinder arrangement. It was Robert Boyle (1627–1691) who, in 1662, published the results of some of his experiments that showed, among other things, that the volume of a gas decreases as the pressure increases. This is an example of inverse variation.

Substituting $V = 100$ into our last equation, we get

$$100 = \frac{2,400}{P}$$

$$100P = 2,400$$

$$P = \frac{2,400}{100}$$

$$P = 24$$

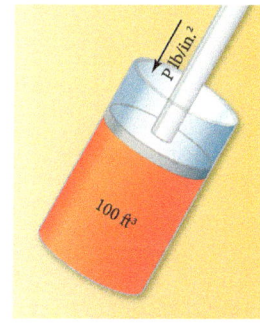

A volume of 100 cubic feet is produced by a pressure of 24 pounds per square inch.

Joint Variation and Other Variation Combinations

Many times relationships among different quantities are described in terms of more than two variables. If the variable y varies directly with *two* other variables, say x and z, then we say y varies *jointly* with x and z. In addition to *joint variation*, there are many other combinations of direct and inverse variation involving more than two variables. The following table is a list of some variation statements and their equivalent mathematical forms:

Verbal Phrase	Algebraic Equation
y varies jointly with x and z.	$y = Kxz$
z varies jointly with r and the square of s.	$z = Krs^2$
V is directly proportional to T and inversely proportional to P.	$V = \frac{KT}{P}$
F varies jointly with m_1 and m_2 and inversely with the square of r.	$F = \frac{Km_1 m_2}{r^2}$

Example 4 y varies jointly with x and the square of z. When x is 5 and z is 3, y is 180. Find y when x is 2 and z is 4.

SOLUTION   The general equation is given by

$$y = Kxz^2$$

Substituting $x = 5$, $z = 3$, and $y = 180$, we have

$$180 = K(5)(3)^2$$

$$180 = 45K$$

$$K = 4$$

The specific equation is

$$y = 4xz^2$$

When $x = 2$ and $z = 4$, the last equation becomes

$$y = 4(2)(4)^2$$

$$y = 128$$

Example 5   In electricity, the resistance of a cable is directly proportional to its length and inversely proportional to the square of the diameter. If a 100-foot cable 0.5 inch in diameter has a resistance of 0.2 ohm, what will be the resistance of a cable made from the same material if it is 200 feet long with a diameter of 0.25 inch?

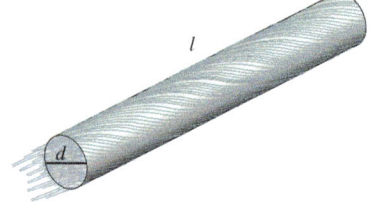

SOLUTION   Let R = resistance, l = length, and d = diameter. The equation is

$$R = \frac{Kl}{d^2}$$

When $R = 0.2$, $l = 100$, and $d = 0.5$, the equation becomes

$$0.2 = \frac{K(100)}{(0.5)^2}$$

or

$$K = 0.0005$$

Using this value of K in our original equation, the result is

$$R = \frac{0.0005l}{d^2}$$

When $l = 200$ and $d = 0.25$, the equation becomes

$$R = \frac{0.0005(200)}{(0.25)^2}$$

$$R = 1.6 \text{ ohms}$$

Getting Ready for Class

After reading through the preceding section, respond in your own words and in complete sentences.

A. Give an example of a direct variation statement, and then translate it into symbols.

B. Translate the equation $y = \frac{K}{X}$ into words.

C. For the inverse variation equation $y = \frac{3}{x}$ what happens to the values of y as x gets larger?

D. How are direct variation statements and linear equations in two variables related?

Problem Set 6.3

For the following problems, y varies directly with x.

1. If y is 10 when x is 2, find y when x is 6.

2. If y is -32 when x is 4, find x when y is -40.

For the following problems, r is inversely proportional to s.

3. If r is -3 when s is 4, find r when s is 2.

4. If r is 8 when s is 3, find s when r is 48.

For the following problems, d varies directly with the square of r.

5. If $d = 10$ when $r = 5$, find d when $r = 10$.

6. If $d = 12$ when $r = 6$, find d when $r = 9$.

For the following problems, y varies inversely with the square of x.

7. If $y = 45$ when $x = 3$, find y when x is 5.

8. If $y = 12$ when $x = 2$, find y when x is 6.

For the following problems, z varies jointly with x and the square of y.

9. If z is 54 when x and y are 3, find z when $x = 2$ and $y = 4$.

10. If z is 27 when $x = 6$ and $y = 3$, find x when $z = 50$ and $y = 4$.

For the following problems, I varies inversely with the cube of w.

11. If $I = 32$ when $w = \dfrac{1}{2}$, find I when $w = \dfrac{1}{3}$.

12. If $I = \dfrac{1}{25}$ when $w = 5$, find I when $w = 10$.

For the following problems, z varies jointly with y and the square of x.

13. If $z = 72$ when $x = 3$ and $y = 2$, find z when $x = 5$ and $y = 3$.

14. If $z = 240$ when $x = 4$ and $y = 5$, find z when $x = 6$ and $y = 3$.

15. If $x = 1$ when $z = 25$ and $y = 5$, find x when $z = 160$ and $y = 8$.

16. If $x = 4$ when $z = 96$ and $y = 2$, find x when $z = 108$ and $y = 1$.

For the following problems, F varies directly with m and inversely with the square of d.

17. If $F = 150$ when $m = 240$ and $d = 8$, find F when $m = 360$ and $d = 3$.

18. If $F = 72$ when $m = 50$ and $d = 5$, find F when $m = 80$ and $d = 6$.

19. If $d = 5$ when $F = 24$ and $m = 20$, find d when $F = 18.75$ and $m = 40$.

20. If $d = 4$ when $F = 75$ and $m = 20$, find d when $F = 200$ and $m = 120$.

Applying the Concepts

21. **Length of a Spring** The length a spring stretches is directly proportional to the force applied. If a force of 5 pounds stretches a spring 3 inches, how much force is necessary to stretch the same spring 10 inches?

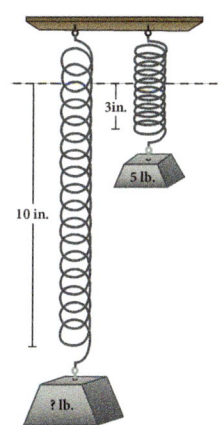

22. **Weight and Surface Area** The weight of a certain material varies directly with the surface area of that material. If 8 square feet weighs half a pound, how much will 10 square feet weigh?

23. **Pressure and Temperature** The temperature of a gas varies directly with its pressure. A temperature of 200 K produces a pressure of 50 pounds per square inch.

    a. Find the equation that relates pressure and temperature.
    b. Graph the equation from part **a.** in the first quadrant only.
    c. What pressure will the gas have at 280 K?

24. **Circumference and Diameter** The circumference of a wheel is directly proportional to its diameter. A wheel has a circumference of 8.5 feet and a diameter of 2.7 feet.

    a. Find the equation that relates circumference and diameter.
    b. Graph the equation from part **a.** in the first quadrant only.
    c. What is the circumference of a wheel that has a diameter of 11.3 feet?

25. **Volume and Pressure** The volume of a gas is inversely proportional to the pressure. If a pressure of 36 pounds per square inch corresponds to a volume of 25 cubic feet, what pressure is needed to produce a volume of 75 cubic feet?

26. **Wave Frequency** The frequency of an electromagnetic wave varies inversely with the wavelength. If a wavelength of 200 meters has a frequency of 800 kilocycles per second, what frequency will be associated with a wavelength of 500 meters?

27. **f-Stop and Aperture Diameter** The relative aperture, or *f*-stop, for a camera lens is inversely proportional to the diameter of the aperture. An *f*-stop of 2 corresponds to an aperture diameter of 40 millimeters for the lens on an automatic camera.

    a. Find the equation that relates *f*-stop and diameter.
    b. Graph the equation from part **a.** in the first quadrant only.
    c. What is the *f*-stop of this camera when the aperture diameter is 10 millimeters?

28. **f-Stop and Aperture Diameter** The relative aperture, or f-stop, for a camera lens is inversely proportional to the diameter of the aperture. An f-stop of 2.8 corresponds to an aperture diameter of 75 millimeters for a certain telephoto lens.

    a. Find the equation that relates f-stop and diameter.

    b. Graph the equation from part a. in the first quadrant only.

    c. What aperture diameter corresponds to an f-stop of 5.6?

29. **Surface Area of a Cylinder** The surface area of a hollow cylinder varies jointly with the height and radius of the cylinder. If a cylinder with radius 3 inches and height 5 inches has a surface area of 94 square inches, what is the surface area of a cylinder with radius 2 inches and height 8 inches?

30. **Capacity of a Cylinder** The capacity of a cylinder varies jointly with its height and the square of its radius. If a cylinder with a radius of 3 centimeters and a height of 6 centimeters has a capacity of 169.56 cubic centimeters, what will be the capacity of a cylinder with radius 4 centimeters and height 9 centimeters?

31. **Electrical Resistance** The resistance of a wire varies directly with its length and inversely with the square of its diameter. If 100 feet of wire with diameter 0.01 inch has a resistance of 10 ohms, what is the resistance of 60 feet of the same type of wire if its diameter is 0.02 inch?

32. **Volume and Temperature** The volume of a gas varies directly with its temperature and inversely with the pressure. If the volume of a certain gas is 30 cubic feet at a temperature of 300 K and a pressure of 20 pounds per square inch, what is the volume of the same gas at 340 K when the pressure is 30 pounds per square inch?

33. **Period of a Pendulum** The time it takes for a pendulum to complete one period varies directly with the square root of the length of the pendulum. A 100-centimeter pendulum takes 2.1 seconds to complete one period.

    a. Find the equation that relates period and pendulum length.

    b. Graph the equation from part **a.** in quadrant I only.

    c. How long does it take to complete one period if the pendulum hangs 225 centimeters?

Getting Ready for the Next Section

Multiply.

34. $x(35 - 0.1x)$

35. $0.6(M - 70)$

36. $(4x - 3)(x - 1)$

37. $(4x - 3)(4x^2 - 7x + 3)$

Simplify.

38. $(35x - 0.1x^2) - (8x + 500)$

39. $(4x - 3) + (4x^2 - 7x + 3)$

40. $(4x^2 + 3x + 2) - (2x^2 - 5x - 6)$

41. $(4x^2 + 3x + 2) + (2x^2 - 5x - 6)$

42. $4(2)^2 - 3(2)$

43. $4(-1)^2 - 7(-1)$

Algebra and Composition with Functions

A company produces and sells copies of an accounting program for home computers. The price they charge for the program is related to the number of copies sold by the demand function

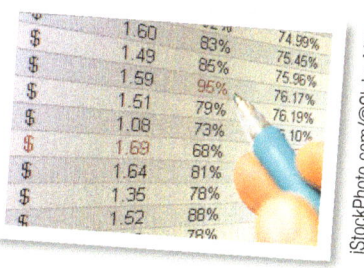

$$p(x) = 35 - 0.1x$$

We find the revenue for this business by multiplying the number of items sold by the price per item. When we do so, we are forming a new function by combining two existing functions. That is, if $n(x) = x$ is the number of items sold and $p(x) = 35 - 0.1x$ is the price per item, then revenue is

$$R(x) = n(x) \cdot p(x) = x(35 - 0.1x) = 35x - 0.1x^2$$

In this case, the revenue function is the product of two functions. When we combine functions in this manner, we are applying our rules for algebra to functions.

To carry this situation further, we know the profit function is the difference between two functions. If the cost function for producing x copies of the accounting program is $C(x) = 8x + 500$, then the profit function is

$$P(x) = R(x) - C(x) = (35x - 0.1x^2) - (8x + 500) = -500 + 27x - 0.1x^2$$

The relationship between these last three functions is represented visually in Figure 1.

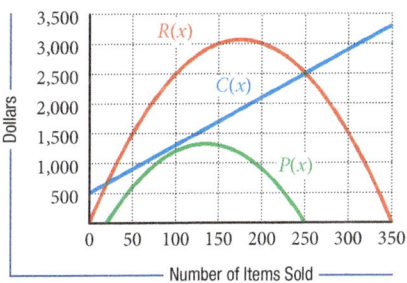

FIGURE 1

Algebra with Functions

Again, when we combine functions in the manner shown, we are applying our rules for algebra to functions. To begin this section, we take a formal look at addition, subtraction, multiplication, and division with functions.

If we are given two functions f and g with a common domain, we can define four other functions as follows.

> ### (dĕf) *Definition*
>
> $(f + g)(x) = f(x) + g(x)$ The function $f + g$ is the sum of the functions f and g.
>
> $(f - g)(x) = f(x) - g(x)$ The function $f - g$ is the difference of the functions f and g.
>
> $(fg)(x) = f(x)g(x)$ The function fg is the product of the functions f and g.
>
> $\left(\dfrac{f}{g}\right)(x) = \dfrac{f(x)}{g(x)}$ The function $\dfrac{f}{g}$ is the quotient of the functions f and g, where $g(x) \neq 0$.

Video Examples

Section 6.4

Example 1   If $f(x) = 4x^2 + 3x + 2$ and $g(x) = 2x^2 - 5x - 6$, write the formulas for the functions $f + g$, $f - g$, fg, and f/g.

SOLUTION   The function $f + g$ is defined by

$$(f + g)(x) = f(x) + g(x)$$
$$= (4x^2 + 3x + 2) + (2x^2 - 5x - 6)$$
$$= 6x^2 - 2x - 4$$

The function $f - g$ is defined by

$$(f - g)(x) = f(x) - g(x)$$
$$= (4x^2 + 3x + 2) - (2x^2 - 5x - 6)$$
$$= 4x^2 + 3x + 2 - 2x^2 + 5x + 6$$
$$= 2x^2 + 8x + 8$$

The function fg is defined by

$$(fg)(x) = f(x)g(x)$$
$$= (4x^2 + 3x + 2)(2x^2 - 5x - 6)$$
$$= 8x^4 - 20x^3 - 24x^2 + 6x^3 - 15x^2 - 18x + 4x^2 - 10x - 12$$
$$= 8x^4 - 14x^3 - 35x^2 - 28x - 12$$

The function f/g is defined by

$$\left(\frac{f}{g}\right)(x) = \frac{f(x)}{g(x)}$$
$$= \frac{4x^2 + 3x + 2}{2x^2 - 5x - 6}$$

Example 2   Let $f(x) = 4x - 3$, $g(x) = 4x^2 - 7x + 3$, and $h(x) = x - 1$. Find $f + g$, fh, fg and $\dfrac{g}{f}$.

SOLUTION   The function $f + g$, the sum of functions f and g, is defined by

$$(f + g)(x) = f(x) + g(x)$$
$$= (4x - 3) + (4x^2 - 7x + 3)$$
$$= 4x^2 - 3x$$

The function fh, the product of functions f and h, is defined by

$$(fh)(x) = f(x)h(x)$$
$$= (4x - 3)(x - 1)$$
$$= 4x^2 - 7x + 3$$
$$= g(x)$$

The function fg, the product of the functions f and g, is defined by

$$(fg)(x) = f(x)g(x)$$
$$= (4x - 3)(4x^2 - 7x + 3)$$
$$= 16x^3 - 28x^2 + 12x - 12x^2 + 21x - 9$$
$$= 16x^3 - 40x^2 + 33x - 9$$

The function $\frac{g}{f}$, the quotient of the functions g and f, is defined by

$$\left(\frac{g}{f}\right)(x) = \frac{g(x)}{f(x)}$$
$$= \frac{4x^2 - 7x + 3}{4x - 3}$$

Factoring the numerator, we can reduce to lowest terms:

$$\left(\frac{g}{f}\right)(x) = \frac{(4x - 3)(x - 1)}{4x - 3}$$
$$= x - 1$$
$$= h(x)$$

Example 3   If f, g, and h are the same functions defined in Example 2, evaluate $(f + g)(2)$, $(fh)(-1)$, $(fg)(0)$, and $\left(\frac{g}{f}\right)(5)$.

SOLUTION   We use the formulas for $f + g$, fh, fg and $\frac{g}{f}$ found in Example 2:

$$(f + g)(2) = 4(2)^2 - 3(2)$$
$$= 16 - 6$$
$$= 10$$

$$(fh)(-1) = 4(-1)^2 - 7(-1) + 3$$
$$= 4 + 7 + 3$$
$$= 14$$

$$(fg)(0) = 16(0)^3 - 40(0)^2 + 33(0) - 9$$
$$= 0 - 0 + 0 - 9$$
$$= -9$$

$$\left(\frac{g}{f}\right)(5) = 5 - 1$$
$$= 4$$

Composition of Functions

In addition to the four operations used to combine functions shown so far in this section, there is a fifth way to combine two functions to obtain a new function. It is called *composition of functions.* To illustrate the concept, recall from Chapter 2 the definition of training heart rate: training heart rate, in beats per minute, is resting heart rate plus 60% of the difference between maximum heart rate and resting heart rate. If your resting heart rate is 70 beats per minute, then your training heart rate is a function of your maximum heart rate M.

$$T(M) = 70 + 0.6(M - 70) = 70 + 0.6M - 42 = 28 + 0.6M$$

But your maximum heart rate is found by subtracting your age in years from 220. So, if x represents your age in years, then your maximum heart rate is

$$M(x) = 220 - x$$

Therefore, if your resting heart rate is 70 beats per minute and your age in years is x, then your training heart rate can be written as a function of x.

$$T(x) = 28 + 0.6(220 - x)$$

This last line is the composition of functions T and M. We input x into function M, which outputs $M(x)$. Then, we input $M(x)$ into function T, which outputs $T(M(x))$, which is the training heart rate as a function of age x. Here is a diagram, called a function map, of the situation:

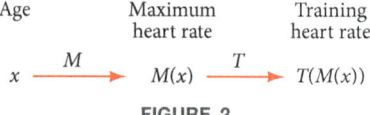

FIGURE 2

Now let's generalize the preceding ideas into a formal development of composition of functions. To find the composition of two functions f and g, we first require that the range of g have numbers in common with the domain of f. Then the composition of f with g, is defined this way:

$$(f \circ g)(x) = f(g(x))$$

To understand this new function, we begin with a number x, and we operate on it with g, giving us $g(x)$. Then we take $g(x)$ and operate on it with f, giving us $f(g(x))$. The only numbers we can use for the domain of the composition of f with g are numbers x in the domain of g, for which $g(x)$ is in the domain of f. The diagrams in Figure 3 illustrate the composition of f with g.

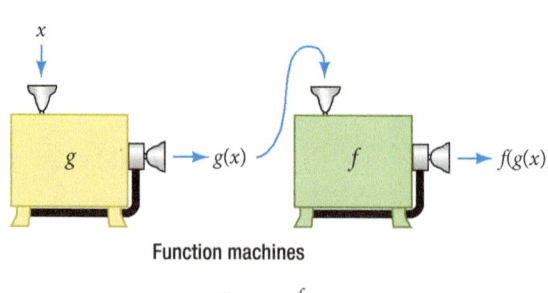

Function machines

$$x \xrightarrow{g} g(x) \xrightarrow{f} f(g(x))$$

FIGURE 3

Composition of functions is not commutative. The composition of f with g, $f \circ g$, may therefore be different from the composition of g with f, $g \circ f$.

$$(g \circ f)(x) = g(f(x))$$

Again, the only numbers we can use for the domain of the composition of g with f are numbers in the domain of f, for which $f(x)$ is in the domain of g. The diagrams in Figure 4 illustrate the composition of g with f.

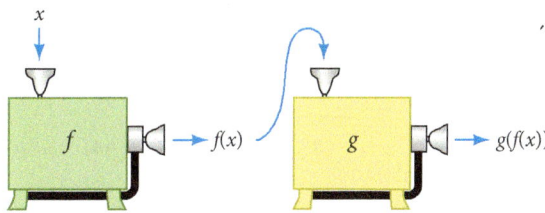

Function machines

$$x \xrightarrow{f} f(x) \xrightarrow{g} g(f(x))$$

FIGURE 4

Example 4   If $f(x) = x + 5$ and $g(x) = x^2 - 2x$, find $(f \circ g)(x)$ and $(g \circ f)(x)$.

SOLUTION   The composition of f with g is

$$(f \circ g)(x) = f(g(x))$$
$$= f(x^2 - 2x)$$
$$= (x^2 - 2x) + 5$$
$$= x^2 - 2x + 5$$

The composition of g with f is

$$(g \circ f)(x) = g(f(x))$$
$$= g(x + 5)$$
$$= (x + 5)^2 - 2(x + 5)$$
$$= (x^2 + 10x + 25) - 2x - 10$$
$$= x^2 + 8x + 15$$

Getting Ready for Class

After reading through the preceding section, respond in your own words and in complete sentences.

A. How are profit, revenue, and cost related?

B. How do you find maximum heart rate?

C. For functions f and g, how do you find the composition of f with g?

D. For functions f and g, how do you find the composition of g with f?

Problem Set 6.4

Let $f(x) = 4x - 3$ and $g(x) = 2x + 5$. Write a formula for each of the following functions.

1. $f + g$ **2.** $f - g$ **3.** $g - f$ **4.** $g + f$

5. fg **6.** $\dfrac{f}{g}$ **7.** $\dfrac{g}{f}$ **8.** ff

If the functions f, g, and h are defined by $f(x) = 3x - 5$, $g(x) = x - 2$ and $h(x) = 3x^2 - 11x + 10$, write a formula for each of the following functions.

9. $g + f$ **10.** $f + h$ **11.** $g + h$ **12.** $f - g$

13. $g - f$ **14.** $h - g$ **15.** fg **16.** gf

17. fh **18.** gh **19.** $\dfrac{h}{f}$ **20.** $\dfrac{h}{g}$

21. $\dfrac{f}{h}$ **22.** $\dfrac{g}{h}$ **23.** $f + g + h$ **24.** $h - g + f$

25. $h + fg$ **26.** $h - fg$

Let $f(x) = 2x + 1$, $g(x) = 4x + 2$, and $h(x) = 4x^2 + 4x + 1$, and find the following.

27. $(f + g)(2)$ **28.** $(f - g)(-1)$ **29.** $(fg)(3)$ **30.** $(f/g)(-3)$

31. $(h/g)(1)$ **32.** $(hg)(1)$ **33.** $(fh)(0)$ **34.** $(h - g)(-4)$

35. $(f + g + h)(2)$ **36.** $(h - f + g)(0)$ **37.** $(h + fg)(3)$ **38.** $(h - fg)(5)$

39. Let $f(x) = x^2$ and $g(x) = x + 4$, and find

     a. $(f \circ g)(5)$ **b.** $(g \circ f)(5)$ **c.** $(f \circ g)(x)$ **d.** $(g \circ f)(x)$

40. Let $f(x) = 3 - x$ and $g(x) = x^3 - 1$, and find

     a. $(f \circ g)(0)$ **b.** $(g \circ f)(0)$ **c.** $(f \circ g)(x)$ **d.** $(g \circ f)(x)$

41. Let $f(x) = x^2 + 3x$ and $g(x) = 4x - 1$, and find

     a. $(f \circ g)(0)$ **b.** $(g \circ f)(0)$ **c.** $(f \circ g)(x)$ **d.** $(g \circ f)(x)$

42. Let $f(x) = (x - 2)^2$ and $g(x) = x + 1$, and find the following

     a. $(f \circ g)(-1)$ **b.** $(g \circ f)(-1)$ **c.** $(f \circ g)(x)$ **d.** $(g \circ f)(x)$

For each of the following pairs of functions f and g, show that $(f \circ g)(x) = (g \circ f)(x) = x$.

43. $f(x) = 5x - 4$ and $g(x) = \dfrac{x + 4}{5}$ **44.** $f(x) = \dfrac{x}{6} - 2$ and $g(x) = 6x + 12$

Applying the Concepts

45. **Profit, Revenue, and Cost** A company manufactures and sells Blu-Ray Discs. Here are the equations they use in connection with their business.

Number of Blu-Rays sold each day: $n(x) = x$
Selling price for each Blu-Rays: $p(x) = 11.5 - 0.05x$
Daily fixed costs: $f(x) = 200$
Daily variable costs: $v(x) = 2x$
Find the following functions.

a. Revenue $= R(x) =$ the product of the number of Blu-Rays sold each day and the selling price of each Blu-Ray.

b. Cost $= C(x) =$ the sum of the fixed costs and the variable costs.

c. Profit $= P(x) =$ the difference between revenue and cost.

d. Average cost $= \overline{C}(x) =$ the quotient of cost and the number of Blu-Rays sold each day.

46. **Profit, Revenue, and Cost** A company manufactures and sells CDs for home computers. Here are the equations they use in connection with their business.

Number of CDs sold each day: $n(x) = x$
Selling price for each CDs: $p(x) = 3 - \dfrac{1}{300}x$
Daily fixed costs: $f(x) = 200$
Daily variable costs: $v(x) = 2x$
Find the following functions.

a. Revenue $= R(x) =$ the product of the number of CDs sold each day and the selling price of each diskette.

b. Cost $= C(x) =$ the sum of the fixed costs and the variable costs.

c. Profit $= P(x) =$ the difference between revenue and cost.

d. Average cost $= \overline{C}(x) =$ the quotient of cost and the number of CDs sold each day.

47. **Training Heart Rate** Find the training heart rate function, $T(M)$ for a person with a resting heart rate of 62 beats per minute, then find the following.

a. Find the maximum heart rate function, $M(x)$, for a person x years of age.

b. What is the maximum heart rate for a 24-year-old person?

c. What is the training heart rate for a 24-year-old person with a resting heart rate of 62 beats per minute?

d. What is the training heart rate for a 36-year-old person with a resting heart rate of 62 beats per minute?

e. What is the training heart rate for a 48-year-old person with a resting heart rate of 62 beats per minute?

48. Training Heart Rate Find the training heart rate function, $T(M)$ for a person with a resting heart rate of 72 beats per minute, then find the following to the nearest whole number.

   a. Find the maximum heart rate function, $M(x)$, for a person x years of age.

   b. What is the maximum heart rate for a 20-year-old person?

   c. What is the training heart rate for a 20-year-old person with a resting heart rate of 72 beats per minute?

   d. What is the training heart rate for a 30-year-old person with a resting heart rate of 72 beats per minute?

   e. What is the training heart rate for a 40-year-old person with a resting heart rate of 72 beats per minute?

Getting Ready for the Next Section

Solve for y.

49. $y - 2.74 = 0.055(x - 2010)$ **50.** $y - 1.32 = 0.0137(x - 221)$

51. $y - 180{,}000 = -3{,}400(x - 10)$

Simplify.

52. $\dfrac{2.74 - 1.10}{2010 - 1980}$ **53.** $\dfrac{64.7 - 1.32}{4860 - 221}$

54. $\dfrac{95{,}000 - 180{,}000}{35 - 10}$

Chapter 6 Summary

Relations and Functions [6.1]

1. The relation

$$\{(8, 1), (6, 1), (-3, 0)\}$$

is also a function because no ordered pairs have the same first coordinates. The domain is $\{8, 6, -3\}$ and the range is $\{1, 0\}$.

A *function* is a rule that pairs each element in one set, called the *domain*, with exactly one element from a second set, called the *range*.

A *relation* is any set of ordered pairs. The set of all first coordinates is called the *domain* of the relation, and the set of all second coordinates is the *range* of the relation. A function is a relation in which no two different ordered pairs have the same first coordinates.

Vertical Line Test [6.1]

2. The graph of $x = y^2$ shown in Figure 5 in Section 3.5 fails the vertical line test. It is not the graph of a function.

If a vertical line crosses the graph of a relation in more than one place, the relation cannot be a function. If no vertical line can be found that crosses the graph in more than one place, the relation must be a function.

Function Notation [6.2]

3. If $f(x) = 5x - 3$ then
$$f(0) = 5(0) - 3$$
$$= -3$$
$$f(1) = 5(1) - 3$$
$$= 2$$
$$f(-2) = 5(-2) - 3$$
$$= -13$$
$$f(a) = 5a - 3$$

The alternative notation for y is $f(x)$. It is read "f of x" and can be used instead of the variable y when working with functions. The notation y and the notation $f(x)$ are equivalent; that is, $y = f(x)$.

Variation [6.3]

If y *varies directly* with x (y is directly proportional to x), then

$$y = Kx$$

If y *varies inversely* with x (y is inversely proportional to x), then

$$y = \frac{K}{x}$$

If z *varies jointly* with x and y (z is directly proportional to both x and y), then

$$z = Kxy$$

In each case, K is called the *constant of variation*.

Algebra with Functions [6.4]

If f and g are any two functions with a common domain, then:

$(f + g)(x) = f(x) + g(x)$ The function $f + g$ is the sum of the functions f and g.

$(f - g)(x) = f(x) - g(x)$ The function $f - g$ is the difference of the functions f and g.

$(fg)(x) = f(x)g(x)$ The function fg is the product of the functions f and g.

$\dfrac{f}{g}(x) = \dfrac{f(x)}{g(x)}$ The function $\dfrac{f}{g}$ is the quotient of the functions f and g, where $g(x) \neq 0$

Composition of Functions [6.4]

If f and g are two functions for which the range of each has numbers in common with the domain of the other, then we have the following definitions:

The composition of f with g: $(f \circ g)(x) = f[g(x)]$

The composition of g with f: $(g \circ f)(x) = g[f(x)]$

Chapter 6 Test

State the domain and range for the following relations, and indicate which relations are also functions. [6.1]

1. $\{(-2, 0), (-3, 0), (-2, 1)\}$

2. $y = x^2 - 9$

Let $f(x) = x - 2$, $g(x) = 3x + 4$ and $h(x) = 3x^2 - 2x - 8$, and find the following. [6.2, 6.3]

3. $f(3) + g(2)$

4. $h(0) + g(0)$

5. $(f \circ g)(2)$

6. $(g \circ f)(2)$

Solve the following variation problems. [6.4]

7. Direct Variation Quantity y varies directly with the square of x. If y is 50 when x is 5, find y when x is 3.

8. Joint Variation Quantity z varies jointly with x and the cube of y. If z is 15 when x is 5 and y is 2, find z when x is 2 and y is 3.

9. Maximum Load The maximum load (L) a horizontal beam can safely hold varies jointly with the width (w) and the square of the depth (d) and inversely with the length (l). If a 10-foot beam with width 3 feet and depth 4 feet will safely hold up to 800 pounds, how many pounds will a 12-foot beam with width 3 feet and depth 4 feet hold?

Rational Expressions and Rational Functions

7

Chapter Outline

iStockphoto.com © Davizro

If you have ever put yourself on a weight loss diet, you know that you lose more weight at the beginning of the diet than you do later. If we let $W(x)$ represent a person's weight after x weeks on the diet, then the rational function

$$W(x) = \frac{80(2x + 15)}{x + 6}$$

is a mathematical model of the person's weekly progress on a diet intended to take them from 200 pounds to about 160 pounds. Rational functions are good models for quantities that fall off rapidly to begin with, and then level off over time. The table shows some values for this function, along with the graph of this function.

Weekly Weight Loss

Weeks Since Starting Diet	Weight (Nearest Pound)
0	200
4	184
8	177
12	173
16	171
20	169
24	168

As you progress through this chapter, you will acquire an intuitive feel for these types of functions, and as a result, you will see why they are good models for situations such as dieting.

Never mistake activity for achievement.

— John Wooden, legendary UCLA basketball coach

You may think that the John Wooden quote above has to do with being productive and efficient, or using your time wisely, but it is really about being honest with yourself. I have had students come to me after failing a test saying, "I can't understand why I got such a low grade after I put so much time in studying." One student even had help from a tutor and felt she understood everything that we covered. After asking her a few questions, it became clear that she spent all her time studying with a tutor and the tutor was doing most of the work. The tutor can work all the homework problems, but the student cannot. She has mistaken activity for achievement.

Can you think of situations in your life when you are mistaking activity for achievement?

How would you describe someone who is mistaking activity for achievement in the way they study for their math class?

Which of the following best describes the idea behind the John Wooden quote?

- ▸ Always be efficient.
- ▸ Don't kid yourself.
- ▸ Take responsibility for your own success.
- ▸ Study with purpose.

We will begin this section with the definition of a rational expression. We will then state the two basic properties associated with rational expressions and go on to apply one of the properties to reduce rational expressions to lowest terms.

Recall from Chapter 1 that a *rational number* is any number that can be expressed as the ratio of two integers:

$$\text{Rational numbers} = \left\{ \frac{a}{b} \mid a \text{ and } b \text{ are integers, } b \neq 0 \right\}$$

A *rational expression* is defined similarly as any expression that can be written as the ratio of two polynomials:

$$\text{Rational expressions} = \left\{ \frac{P}{Q} \mid P \text{ and } Q \text{ are polynominals, } Q \neq 0 \right\}$$

Some examples of rational expressions are

$$\frac{2x - 3}{x + 5} \qquad \frac{x^2 - 5x - 6}{x^2 - 1} \qquad \frac{a - b}{b - a}$$

Basic Properties

For rational expressions, multiplying the numerator and denominator by the same nonzero expression may change the form of the rational expression, but it will always produce an expression equivalent to the original one. The same is true when dividing the numerator and denominator by the same nonzero quantity.

⟨Δ≠Σ⟩   *Properties of Rational Expressions*

If P, Q, and K are polynomials with $Q \neq 0$ and $K \neq 0$, then

$$\frac{P}{Q} = \frac{PK}{QK} \qquad \text{and} \qquad \frac{P}{Q} = \frac{\frac{P}{K}}{\frac{Q}{K}}$$

Reducing to Lowest Terms

The fraction $\frac{6}{8}$ can be written in lowest terms as $\frac{3}{4}$. The process is shown here:

$$\frac{6}{8} = \frac{3 \cdot 2}{4 \cdot 2} = \frac{3}{4}$$

Reducing $\frac{6}{8}$ to $\frac{3}{4}$ involves dividing the numerator and denominator by 2, the factor they have in common. Before dividing out the common factor 2, we must notice that the common factor *is* 2. (This may not be obvious because we are very familiar with the numbers 6 and 8 and therefore do not have to put much thought into finding what number divides both of them.)

We reduce rational expressions to lowest terms by first factoring the numerator and denominator and then dividing both numerator and denominator by any factors they have in common.

Video Examples

Section 7.1

Note The lines drawn through the $(x-3)$ in the numerator and denominator indicate that we have divided through by $(x-3)$. As the problems become more involved, these lines will help keep track of which factors have been divided out and which have not.

Example 1 Reduce $\dfrac{x^2 - 9}{x - 3}$ to lowest terms.

SOLUTION Factoring, we have

$$\frac{x^2 - 9}{x - 3} = \frac{(x + 3)(x - 3)}{x - 3}$$

The numerator and denominator have the factor $x - 3$ in common. Dividing the numerator and denominator by $x - 3$, we have

$$\frac{(x + 3)\cancel{(x - 3)}}{\cancel{x - 3}} = \frac{x + 3}{1} = x + 3$$

For the problem in Example 1, there is an implied restriction on the variable x: It cannot be 3. If x were 3, the expression $\frac{(x^2 - 9)}{(x - 3)}$ would become $\frac{0}{0}$, an expression that we cannot associate with a real number. For all problems involving rational expressions, we restrict the variable to only those values that result in a nonzero denominator. When we state the relationship

$$\frac{x^2 - 9}{x - 3} = x + 3$$

we are assuming that it is true for all values of x except $x = 3$.

Here are some other examples of reducing rational expressions to lowest terms.

Example 2 Reduce $\dfrac{y^2 - 5y - 6}{y^2 - 1}$ to lowest terms.

SOLUTION

$$\frac{y^2 - 5y - 6}{y^2 - 1} = \frac{(y - 6)(y + 1)}{(y - 1)(y + 1)}$$

$$= \frac{y - 6}{y - 1}$$

Example 3 Reduce $\dfrac{2a^3 - 16}{4a^2 - 12a + 8}$ to lowest terms.

SOLUTION

$$\frac{2a^3 - 16}{4a^2 - 12a + 8} = \frac{2(a^3 - 8)}{4(a^2 - 3a + 2)}$$

$$= \frac{2(a - 2)(a^2 + 2a + 4)}{4(a - 2)(a - 1)}$$

$$= \frac{a^2 + 2a + 4}{2(a - 1)}$$

Example 4 Reduce $\dfrac{x^2 - 3x + ax - 3a}{x^2 - ax - 3x + 3a}$ to lowest terms.

SOLUTION

$$\frac{x^2 - 3x + ax - 3a}{x^2 - ax - 3x + 3a} = \frac{x(x - 3) + a(x - 3)}{x(x - a) - 3(x - a)}$$

$$= \frac{(x - 3)(x + a)}{(x - a)(x - 3)}$$

$$= \frac{x + a}{x - a}$$

The answer to Example 4 cannot be reduced further. It is a fairly common mistake to attempt to divide out an x or an a in this last expression. Remember, we can divide out only the factors common to the numerator and denominator of a rational expression.

The next example involves what we call a trick. The trick is to reverse the order of the terms in a difference by factoring -1 from each term in either the numerator or the denominator. The next examples illustrate how this is done.

Example 5   Reduce to lowest terms: $\dfrac{a - b}{b - a}$

SOLUTION   The relationship between $a - b$ and $b - a$ is that they are opposites. We can show this fact by factoring -1 from each term in the numerator:

$$\frac{a - b}{b - a} = \frac{-1(-a + b)}{b - a} \qquad \text{Factor } -1 \text{ from each term in the numerator}$$

$$= \frac{-1(b - a)}{b - a} \qquad \text{Reverse the order of the terms in the numerator}$$

$$= -1 \qquad \text{Divide out common factor } b - a$$

Example 6   Reduce to lowest terms: $\dfrac{x^2 - 25}{5 - x}$

SOLUTION   We begin by factoring the numerator:

$$\frac{x^2 - 25}{5 - x} = \frac{(x - 5)(x + 5)}{5 - x}$$

The factors $x - 5$ and $5 - x$ are similar but are not exactly the same. We can reverse the order of either by factoring -1 from it.

That is: $5 - x = -1(-5 + x) = -1(x - 5)$.

$$\frac{(x - 5)(x + 5)}{5 - x} = \frac{(x - 5)(x + 5)}{-1(x - 5)}$$

$$= \frac{x + 5}{-1}$$

$$= -(x + 5)$$

Rational Functions

We can extend our knowledge of rational expressions to rational functions with the following definition:

> **def**   *rational function*
>
> A *rational function* is any function that can be written in the form
>
> $$f(x) = \frac{P(x)}{Q(x)}$$
>
> where $P(x)$ and $Q(x)$ are polynomials and $Q(x) \neq 0$.

Example 7   For the rational function $f(x) = \dfrac{x-4}{x-2}$, find $f(0), f(-4), f(4),$
$f(-2),$ and $f(2).$

SOLUTION   To find these function values, we substitute the given value of x into
the rational expression, and then simplify if possible.

$$f(0) = \frac{0-4}{0-2} = \frac{-4}{-2} = 2$$

$$f(-4) = \frac{-4-4}{-4-2} = \frac{-8}{-6} = \frac{4}{3}$$

$$f(4) = \frac{4-4}{4-2} = \frac{0}{2} = 0$$

$$f(-2) = \frac{-2-4}{-2-2} = \frac{-6}{-4} = \frac{3}{2}$$

$$f(2) = \frac{2-4}{2-2} = \frac{-2}{0} \quad \text{Undefined}$$

Because the rational function in Example 7 is not defined when x is 2, the domain
of that function does not include 2. We have more to say about the domain of a
rational function next.

The Domain of a Rational Function

If the domain of a rational function is not specified, it is assumed to be all real
numbers for which the function is defined. That is, the domain of the rational
function

$$f(x) = \frac{P(x)}{Q(x)}$$

is all x for which $Q(x)$ is nonzero.

Example 8   Find the domain for each function.

a. $f(x) = \dfrac{x-4}{x-2}$ **b.** $g(x) = \dfrac{x^2+5}{x+1}$ **c.** $h(x) = \dfrac{x}{x^2-9}$

SOLUTION

a. The domain for $f(x) = \dfrac{x-4}{x-2}$ is $\{x \mid x \neq 2\}$.

b. The domain for $g(x) = \dfrac{x^2+5}{x+1}$ is $\{x \mid x \neq -1\}$.

c. The domain for $h(x) = \dfrac{x}{x^2-9}$ is $\{x \mid x \neq -3, x \neq 3\}$.

Notice that, for these functions, $f(2), g(-1), h(-3),$ and $h(3)$ are all undefined, and
that is why the domains are written as shown.

Difference Quotients

The diagram in Figure 1 is an important diagram from calculus. Although it may look complicated, the point of it is simple: The slope of the line passing through the points P and Q is given by the formula

$$\text{Slope of line through } PQ = m = \frac{f(x) - f(a)}{x - a}$$

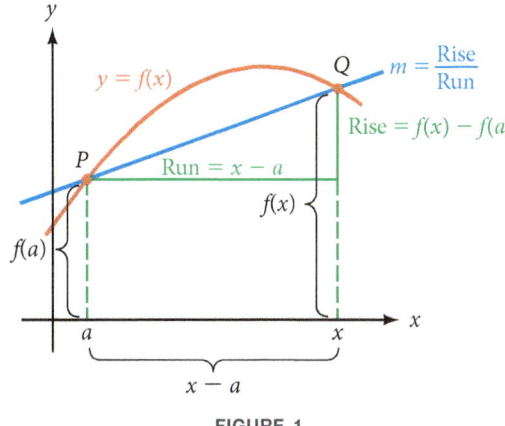

FIGURE 1

The expression $\frac{f(x) - f(a)}{x - a}$ is called a *difference quotient*. When $f(x)$ is a polynomial, it will be a rational expression.

Example 9 If $f(x) = 3x - 5$, find $\dfrac{f(x) - f(a)}{x - a}$.

SOLUTION

$$\begin{aligned}
\frac{f(x) - f(a)}{x - a} &= \frac{(3x - 5) - (3a - 5)}{x - a} \\
&= \frac{3x - 3a}{x - a} \\
&= \frac{3(x - a)}{x - a} \\
&= 3
\end{aligned}$$

Example 10 If $f(x) = x^2 - 4$, find $\dfrac{f(x) - f(a)}{x - a}$ and simplify.

SOLUTION Because $f(x) = x^2 - 4$ and $f(a) = a^2 - 4$, we have

$$\begin{aligned}
\frac{f(x) - f(a)}{x - a} &= \frac{(x^2 - 4) - (a^2 - 4)}{x - a} \\
&= \frac{x^2 - 4 - a^2 + 4}{x - a} \\
&= \frac{x^2 - a^2}{x - a} \\
&= \frac{(x + a)(x - a)}{x - a} \qquad \text{Factor and divide out common factor} \\
&= x + a
\end{aligned}$$

The diagram in Figure 2 is similar to the one in Figure 1. The main difference is in how we label the points. From Figure 2, we can see another difference quotient that gives us the slope of the line through the points P and Q.

$$\text{Slope of line through } PQ = m = \frac{f(x+h)-f(x)}{h}$$

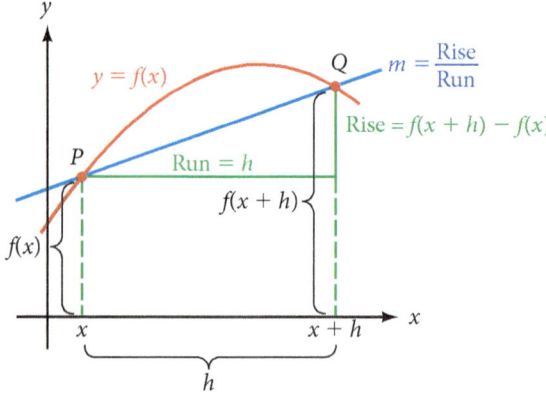

FIGURE 2

Examples 11 and 12 use the same functions used in Examples 9 and 10, but this time the new difference quotient is used.

Example 11   If $f(x) = 3x - 5$, find $\dfrac{f(x+h)-f(x)}{h}$.

SOLUTION   The expression $f(x + h)$ is given by

$$f(x+h) = 3(x+h) - 5$$
$$= 3x + 3h - 5$$

Using this result gives us

$$\frac{f(x+h)-f(x)}{h} = \frac{(3x+3h-5)-(3x-5)}{h}$$
$$= \frac{3h}{h}$$
$$= 3$$

Example 12   If $f(x) = x^2 - 4$, find $\dfrac{f(x+h)-f(x)}{h}$.

SOLUTION   The expression $f(x + h)$ is given by

$$f(x+h) = (x+h)^2 - 4$$
$$= x^2 + 2xh + h^2 - 4$$

Using this result gives us

$$\frac{f(x+h)-f(x)}{h} = \frac{(x^2+2xh+h^2-4)-(x^2-4)}{h}$$
$$= \frac{2xh+h^2}{h}$$
$$= \frac{h(2x+h)}{h}$$
$$= 2x + h$$

Getting Ready for Class

After reading through the preceding section, respond in your own words and in complete sentences.

A. What is a rational expression?

B. Explain how to determine if a rational expression is in "lowest terms."

C. When is a rational expression undefined?

D. Explain the process we use to reduce a rational expression or a fraction to lowest terms.

Problem Set 7.1

1. If $g(x) = \frac{x+3}{x-1}$, find $g(0)$, $g(-3)$, $g(3)$, $g(-1)$, and $g(1)$, if possible.

2. If $g(x) = \frac{x-2}{x-1}$, find $g(0)$, $g(-2)$, $g(2)$, $g(-1)$, and $g(1)$, if possible.

3. If $h(t) = \frac{t-3}{t+1}$, find $h(0)$, $h(-3)$, $h(3)$, $h(-1)$, and $h(1)$, if possible.

4. If $h(t) = \frac{t-2}{t+1}$, find $h(0)$, $h(-2)$, $h(2)$, $h(-1)$, and $h(1)$, if possible.

State the domain for each rational function.

5. $f(x) = \dfrac{x-3}{x-1}$

6. $f(x) = \dfrac{x+4}{x-2}$

7. $g(x) = \dfrac{x^2-4}{x-2}$

8. $g(x) = \dfrac{x^2-9}{x-3}$

9. $h(t) = \dfrac{t-4}{t^2-16}$

10. $h(t) = \dfrac{t-5}{t^2-25}$

Reduce each rational expression to lowest terms.

11. $\dfrac{x^2-16}{6x+24}$

12. $\dfrac{12x-9y}{3x^2+3xy}$

13. $\dfrac{a^4-81}{a-3}$

14. $\dfrac{a^2-4a-12}{a^2+8a+12}$

15. $\dfrac{20y^2-45}{10y^2-5y-15}$

16. $\dfrac{20x^2-93x+34}{4x^2-9x-34}$

17. $\dfrac{12y-2xy-2x^2y}{6y-4xy-2x^2y}$

18. $\dfrac{250a+100ax+10ax^2}{50a-2ax^2}$

19. $\dfrac{(x-3)^2(x+2)}{(x+2)^2(x-3)}$

20. $\dfrac{(x-4)^3(x+3)}{(x+3)^2(x-4)}$

21. $\dfrac{x^3+1}{x^2-1}$

22. $\dfrac{x^3-1}{x^2-1}$

23. $\dfrac{4am-4an}{3n-3m}$

24. $\dfrac{ad-ad^2}{d-1}$

25. $\dfrac{ab-a+b-1}{ab+a+b+1}$

26. $\dfrac{6cd-4c-9d+6}{6d^2-13d+6}$

27. $\dfrac{21x^2-23x+6}{21x^2+x-10}$

28. $\dfrac{36x^2-11x-12}{20x^2-39x+18}$

29. $\dfrac{8x^2-6x-9}{8x^2-18x+9}$

30. $\dfrac{42x^2+23x-10}{14x^2+45x-14}$

31. $\dfrac{4x^2+29x+45}{8x^2-10x-63}$

32. $\dfrac{30x^2-61x+30}{60x^2+22x-60}$

33. $\dfrac{a^3+b^3}{a^2-b^2}$

34. $\dfrac{a^2-b^2}{a^3-b^3}$

35. $\dfrac{8x^4-8x}{4x^4+4x^3+4x^2}$

36. $\dfrac{6x^5-48x^3}{12x^3+24x^2+48x}$

37. $\dfrac{ax+2x+3a+6}{ay+2y-4a-8}$

38. $\dfrac{x^2-3ax-2x+6a}{x^2-3ax+2x-6a}$

39. $\dfrac{x^3+3x^2-4x-12}{x^2+x-6}$

40. $\dfrac{x^3+5x^2-4x-20}{x^2+7x+10}$

41. $\dfrac{x^3-8}{x^2-4}$

42. $\dfrac{y^2-9}{y^3+27}$

43. $\dfrac{8x^3-27}{4x^2-9}$

44. $\dfrac{25y^2-4}{125y^3+8}$

Refer to Examples 5 and 6 in this section, and reduce the following to lowest terms.

45. $\dfrac{x-4}{4-x}$

46. $\dfrac{6-x}{x-6}$

47. $\dfrac{y^2-36}{6-y}$

48. $\dfrac{1-y}{y^2-1}$

49. $\dfrac{1-9a^2}{9a^2-6a+1}$

50. $\dfrac{1-a^2}{a^2-2a+1}$

Simplify each expression.

51. $\dfrac{(3x-5)-(3a-5)}{x-a}$

52. $\dfrac{(2x+3)-(2a+3)}{x-a}$

53. $\dfrac{(x^2-4)-(a^2-4)}{x-a}$

54. $\dfrac{(x^2-1)-(a^2-1)}{x-a}$

For the functions below, evaluate

a. $\dfrac{f(x)-f(a)}{x-a}$

b. $\dfrac{f(x+h)-f(x)}{h}$

55. $f(x)=4x$

56. $f(x)=-3x$

57. $f(x)=5x+3$

58. $f(x)=6x-5$

59. $f(x)=x^2$

60. $f(x)=3x^2$

61. $f(x)=x^2+1$

62. $f(x)=x^2-3$

63. $f(x)=x^2-3x+4$

64. $f(x)=x^2+4x-7$

The graphs of two rational functions are given in Figures 3 and 4. Use the graphs to find the following.

65.   **a.** $f(2)$ **b.** $f(-1)$ **c.** $f(0)$ **d.** $g(3)$

66.   **a.** $g(6)$ **b.** $g(-1)$ **c.** $f(g(6))$ **d.** $g(f(-2))$

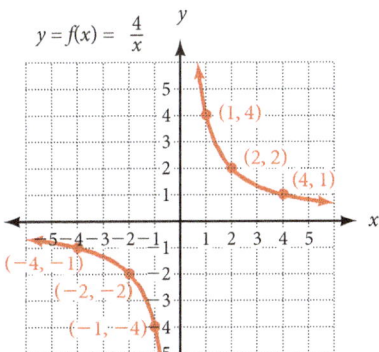

FIGURE 3

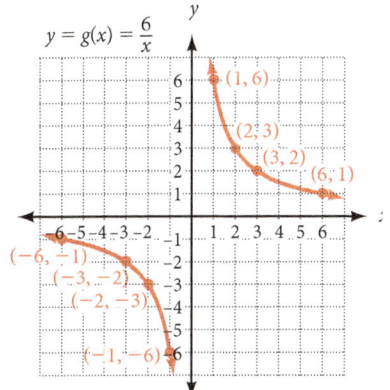

FIGURE 4

Applying the Concepts

67. Diet The following rational function is the one we mentioned in the introduction to this chapter. The quantity $W(x)$ is the weight (in pounds) of the person after x weeks of dieting. Use the function to fill in the table. Then compare your results with the graph in the chapter introduction.

$$W(x) = \frac{80(2x + 15)}{x + 6}$$

Weeks	Weight (lb)
x	$W(x)$
0	
1	
4	
12	
24	

68. Drag Racing The following rational function gives the speed $V(x)$, in miles per hour, of a dragster at each second x during a quarter-mile race.

Use the function to fill in the table.

$$V(x) = \frac{340x}{x + 3}$$

Time (sec)	Speed (mi/hr)
x	$V(x)$
0	
1	
2	
3	
4	
5	
6	

Getting Ready for the Next Section

Multiply or divide, as indicated.

69. $\dfrac{6}{7} \cdot \dfrac{14}{18}$ **70.** $\dfrac{6}{8} \div \dfrac{3}{5}$ **71.** $5y^2 \cdot 4x^2$

72. $4y^3 \cdot 3x^2$ **73.** $9x^4 \cdot 8y^5$ **74.** $6x^4 \cdot 12y^5$

Factor.

75. $x^2 - 4$ **76.** $x^2 - 6x + 9$ **77.** $x^3 - x^2y$

78. $a^2 - 5a + 6$ **79.** $2y^2 - 2$ **80.** $xa + xb + ya + yb$

Multiplication and Division of Rational Expressions

If you have ever taken a home videotape to be transferred to DVD, you know the amount you pay for the transfer depends on the number of copies you have made: The more copies you have made, the lower the charge per copy. The following demand function gives the price (in dollars) per tape $p(x)$ a company charges for making x DVDs. As you can see, it is a rational function.

$$p(x) = \frac{2(x + 60)}{x + 5}$$

The graph in Figure 1 shows this function from $x = 0$ to $x = 100$. As you can see, the more copies that are made, the lower the price per copy.

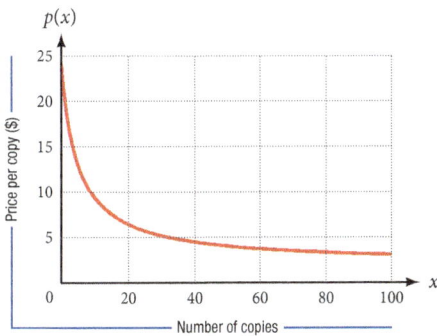

FIGURE 1

If we were interested in finding the revenue function for this situation, we would multiply the number of copies made x by the price per copy $p(x)$. This involves multiplication with a rational expression, which is one of the topics we cover in this section.

In Section 7.1, we found the process of reducing rational expressions to lowest terms to be the same process used in reducing fractions to lowest terms. The similarity also holds for the process of multiplication or division of rational expressions.

Multiplication with fractions is the simplest of the four basic operations. To multiply two fractions, we simply multiply numerators and multiply denominators. That is, if a, b, c, and d are real numbers, with $b \neq 0$ and $d \neq 0$, then

$$\frac{a}{b} \cdot \frac{c}{d} = \frac{ac}{bd}$$

Video Examples

Section 7.2

Example 1 Multiply $\dfrac{6}{7} \cdot \dfrac{14}{18}$.

SOLUTION

$$\frac{6}{7} \cdot \frac{14}{18} = \frac{6(14)}{7(18)} \qquad \text{Multiply numerators and denominators}$$

$$= \frac{2 \cdot 3(2 \cdot 7)}{7(2 \cdot 3 \cdot 3)} \qquad \text{Factor}$$

$$= \frac{2}{3} \qquad \text{Divide out common factors}$$

Our next example is similar to some of the problems we worked in Chapter 0. We multiply fractions whose numerators and denominators are monomials by multiplying numerators and multiplying denominators and then reducing to lowest terms. Here is how it looks.

Example 2   Multiply $\dfrac{8x^3}{27y^8} \cdot \dfrac{9y^3}{12x^2}$.

SOLUTION   We multiply numerators and denominators without actually carrying out the multiplication:

$$\frac{8x^3}{27y^8} \cdot \frac{9y^3}{12x^2} = \frac{8 \cdot 9x^3y^3}{27 \cdot 12x^2y^8} \qquad \text{Multiply Numerators}$$
$$\text{Multiply Denominators}$$

$$= \frac{4 \cdot 2 \cdot 9x^3y^3}{9 \cdot 3 \cdot 4 \cdot 3x^2y^8} \qquad \text{Factor coefficients}$$

$$= \frac{2x}{9y^5} \qquad \text{Divide out common factors} \qquad ■$$

The product of two rational expressions is the product of their numerators over the product of their denominators.

Once again, we should mention that the little slashes we have drawn through the factors are simply used to denote the factors we have divided out of the numerator and denominator.

Example 3   Multiply $\dfrac{x-3}{x^2-4} \cdot \dfrac{x+2}{x^2-6x+9}$.

SOLUTION   We begin by multiplying numerators and denominators. We then factor all polynomials and divide out factors common to the numerator and denominator:

$$\frac{x-3}{x^2-4} \cdot \frac{x+2}{x^2-6x+9} = \frac{(x-3)(x+2)}{(x^2-4)(x^2-6x+9)} \qquad \text{Multiply}$$

$$= \frac{(x-3)(x+2)}{(x+2)(x-2)(x-3)(x-3)} \qquad \text{Factor}$$

$$= \frac{1}{(x-2)(x-3)} \qquad ■$$

The first two steps can be combined to save time. We can perform the multiplication and factoring steps together.

Example 4   Multiply $\dfrac{2y^2-4y}{2y^2-2} \cdot \dfrac{y^2-2y-3}{y^2-5y+6}$.

SOLUTION

$$\frac{2y^2-4y}{2y^2-2} \cdot \frac{y^2-2y-3}{y^2-5y+6} = \frac{2y(y-2)(y-3)(y+1)}{2(y+1)(y-1)(y-3)(y-2)}$$

$$= \frac{y}{y-1} \qquad ■$$

Notice in both of the preceding examples that we did not actually multiply the polynomials as we did in Chapter 4.5. It would be senseless to do that because we would then have to factor each of the resulting products to reduce them to lowest terms.

The quotient of two rational expressions is the product of the first and the reciprocal of the second. That is, we find the quotient of two rational expressions the same way we find the quotient of two fractions. Here is an example that reviews division with fractions.

Example 5   Divide $\dfrac{6}{8} \div \dfrac{3}{5}$.

SOLUTION

$$\dfrac{6}{8} \div \dfrac{3}{5} = \dfrac{6}{8} \cdot \dfrac{5}{3} \qquad \text{Write division in terms of multiplication}$$

$$= \dfrac{6(5)}{8(3)} \qquad \text{Multiply numerators and denominators}$$

$$= \dfrac{2 \cdot 3(5)}{2 \cdot 2 \cdot 2(3)} \qquad \text{Factor}$$

$$= \dfrac{5}{4} \qquad \text{Divide out common factors} \qquad \blacksquare$$

To divide one rational expression by another, we use the definition of division to multiply by the reciprocal of the expression that follows the division symbol.

Example 6   Divide $\dfrac{8x^3}{5y^2} \div \dfrac{4x^2}{10y^6}$.

SOLUTION   First, we rewrite the problem in terms of multiplication. Then we multiply.

$$\dfrac{8x^3}{5y^2} \div \dfrac{4x^2}{10y^6} = \dfrac{8x^3}{5y^2} \cdot \dfrac{10y^6}{4x^2}$$

$$= \dfrac{\overset{2}{8} \cdot \overset{2}{10}x^3 y^6}{4 \cdot 5 x^2 y^2}$$

$$= 4xy^4 \qquad \blacksquare$$

Example 7   Divide $\dfrac{x^2 - y^2}{x^2 - 2xy + y^2} \div \dfrac{x^3 + y^3}{x^3 - x^2 y}$.

SOLUTION   We begin by writing the problem as the product of the first and the reciprocal of the second and then proceed as in the previous two examples:

$$\dfrac{x^2 - y^2}{x^2 - 2xy + y^2} \div \dfrac{x^3 + y^3}{x^3 - x^2 y} \qquad \text{Multiply by the reciprocal of the divisor}$$

$$= \dfrac{x^2 - y^2}{x^2 - 2xy + y^2} \cdot \dfrac{x^3 - x^2 y}{x^3 + y^3}$$

$$= \dfrac{(x - y)(x + y)(x^2)(x - y)}{(x - y)(x - y)(x + y)(x^2 - xy + y^2)} \qquad \text{Factor and multiply}$$

$$= \dfrac{x^2}{x^2 - xy + y^2} \qquad \text{Divide out common factors} \qquad \blacksquare$$

Here are some more examples of multiplication and division with rational expressions.

Example 8 Perform the indicated operations.

$$\frac{a^2 - 8a + 15}{a + 4} \cdot \frac{a + 2}{a^2 - 5a + 6} \div \frac{a^2 - 3a - 10}{a^2 + 2a - 8}$$

SOLUTION First, we rewrite the division as multiplication by the reciprocal. Then we proceed as usual.

$$\frac{a^2 - 8a + 15}{a + 4} \cdot \frac{a + 2}{a^2 - 5a + 6} \div \frac{a^2 - 3a - 10}{a^2 + 2a - 8}$$ *Change division to multiplication by the reciprocal*

$$= \frac{(a^2 - 8a + 15)(a + 2)(a^2 + 2a - 8)}{(a + 4)(a^2 - 5a + 6)(a^2 - 3a - 10)}$$ *Factor*

$$= \frac{(a - 5)(a - 3)(a + 2)(a + 4)(a - 2)}{(a + 4)(a - 3)(a - 2)(a - 5)(a + 2)}$$ *Divide out common factors*

$$= 1$$

Our next example involves factoring by grouping. As you may have noticed, working the problems in this chapter gives you a very detailed review of factoring.

Example 9 Multiply $\dfrac{xa + xb + ya + yb}{xa - xb - ya + yb} \cdot \dfrac{xa + xb - ya - yb}{xa - xb + ya - yb}$.

SOLUTION We will factor each polynomial by grouping, which takes two steps.

$$\frac{xa + xb + ya + yb}{xa - xb - ya + yb} \cdot \frac{xa + xb - ya - yb}{xa - xb + ya - yb}$$

$$= \frac{x(a + b) + y(a + b)}{x(a - b) - y(a - b)} \cdot \frac{x(a + b) - y(a + b)}{x(a - b) + y(a - b)}$$ *Factor by grouping*

$$= \frac{(a + b)(x + y)(a + b)(x - y)}{(a - b)(x - y)(a - b)(x + y)}$$

$$= \frac{(a + b)^2}{(a - b)^2}$$

Example 10 Multiply $(4x^2 - 36) \cdot \dfrac{12}{4x + 12}$.

SOLUTION We can think of $4x^2 - 36$ as having a denominator of 1. Thinking of it in this way allows us to proceed as we did in the previous examples.

$$(4x^2 - 36) \cdot \frac{12}{4x + 12}$$

$$= \frac{4x^2 - 36}{1} \cdot \frac{12}{4x + 12}$$ *Write $4x^2 - 36$ with denominator 1*

$$= \frac{4(x - 3)(x + 3)12}{4(x + 3)}$$ *Factor*

$$= 12(x - 3)$$ *Divide out common factors*

Example 11 Multiply $3(x - 2)(x - 1) \cdot \dfrac{5}{x^2 - 3x + 2}$.

SOLUTION This problem is very similar to the problem in Example 10. Writing the first rational expression with a denominator of 1, we have

$$\frac{3(x - 2)(x - 1)}{1} \cdot \frac{5}{x^2 - 3x + 2} = \frac{3(x - 2)(x - 1)5}{(x - 2)(x - 1)}$$

$$= 3 \cdot 5$$

$$= 15$$

Getting Ready for Class

After reading through the preceding section, respond in your own words and in complete sentences.

A. Summarize the steps used to multiply fractions.

B. What is the first step in multiplying two rational expressions?

C. Why is factoring important when multiplying and dividing rational expressions?

D. How is division with rational expressions different than multiplication of rational expressions?

Perform the indicated operations.

1. $\dfrac{2}{9} \cdot \dfrac{3}{4}$

2. $\dfrac{5}{6} \cdot \dfrac{7}{8}$

3. $\dfrac{3}{4} \div \dfrac{1}{3}$

4. $\dfrac{3}{8} \div \dfrac{5}{4}$

5. $\dfrac{3}{7} \cdot \dfrac{14}{24} \div \dfrac{1}{2}$

6. $\dfrac{6}{5} \cdot \dfrac{10}{36} \div \dfrac{3}{4}$

7. $\dfrac{10x^2}{5y^2} \cdot \dfrac{15y^3}{2x^4}$

8. $\dfrac{8x^3}{7y^4} \cdot \dfrac{14y^6}{16x^2}$

9. $\dfrac{11a^2b}{5ab^2} \div \dfrac{22a^3b^2}{10ab^4}$

10. $\dfrac{8ab^3}{9a^2b} \div \dfrac{16a^2b^2}{18ab^3}$

11. $\dfrac{6x^2}{5y^3} \cdot \dfrac{11z^2}{2x^2} \div \dfrac{33z^5}{10y^8}$

12. $\dfrac{4x^3}{7y^2} \cdot \dfrac{6z^5}{5x^6} \div \dfrac{24z^2}{35x^6}$

Perform the indicated operations. Be sure to write all answers in lowest terms.

13. $\dfrac{x^2 - 9}{x^2 - 4} \cdot \dfrac{x - 2}{x - 3}$

14. $\dfrac{x^2 - 16}{x^2 - 25} \cdot \dfrac{x - 5}{x - 4}$

15. $\dfrac{y^2 - 1}{y + 2} \cdot \dfrac{y^2 + 5y + 6}{y^2 + 2y - 3}$

16. $\dfrac{y - 1}{y^2 - y - 6} \cdot \dfrac{y^2 + 5y + 6}{y^2 - 1}$

17. $\dfrac{3x - 12}{x^2 - 4} \cdot \dfrac{x^2 + 6x + 8}{x - 4}$

18. $\dfrac{x^2 + 5x + 1}{4x - 4} \cdot \dfrac{x - 1}{x^2 + 5x + 1}$

19. $\dfrac{xy}{xy + 1} \div \dfrac{x}{y}$

20. $\dfrac{y}{x} \div \dfrac{xy}{xy - 1}$

21. $\dfrac{1}{x^2 - 9} \div \dfrac{1}{x^2 + 9}$

22. $\dfrac{1}{x^2 - 9} \div \dfrac{1}{(x - 3)^2}$

23. $\dfrac{y - 3}{y^2 - 6y + 9} \cdot \dfrac{y - 3}{4}$

24. $\dfrac{y - 3}{y^2 - 6y + 9} \div \dfrac{y - 3}{4}$

25. $\dfrac{5x + 2y}{25x^2 - 5xy - 6y^2} \cdot \dfrac{20x^2 - 7xy - 3y^2}{4x + y}$

26. $\dfrac{7x + 3y}{42x^2 - 17xy - 15y^2} \cdot \dfrac{12x^2 - 4xy - 5y^2}{2x + y}$

27. $\dfrac{a^2 - 5a + 6}{a^2 - 2a - 3} \div \dfrac{a - 5}{a^2 + 3a + 2}$

28. $\dfrac{a^2 + 7a + 12}{a - 5} \div \dfrac{a^2 + 9a + 18}{a^2 - 7a + 10}$

29. $\dfrac{4t^2 - 1}{6t^2 + t - 2} \div \dfrac{8t^3 + 1}{27t^3 + 8}$

30. $\dfrac{9t^2 - 1}{6t^2 + 7t - 3} \div \dfrac{27t^3 + 1}{8t^3 + 27}$

31. $\dfrac{2x^2 - 5x - 12}{4x^2 + 8x + 3} \div \dfrac{x^2 - 16}{2x^2 + 7x + 3}$

32. $\dfrac{x^2 - 2x + 1}{3x^2 + 7x - 20} \div \dfrac{x^2 + 3x - 4}{3x^2 - 2x - 5}$

33. $\dfrac{2a^2 - 21ab - 36b^2}{a^2 - 11ab - 12b^2} \div \dfrac{10a + 15b}{a^2 - b^2}$

34. $\dfrac{3a^2 + 7ab - 20b^2}{a^2 + 5ab + 4b^2} \div \dfrac{3a^2 - 17ab + 20b^2}{3a - 12b}$

35. $\dfrac{6c^2 - c - 15}{9c^2 - 25} \cdot \dfrac{15c^2 + 22c - 5}{6c^2 + 5c - 6}$

36. $\dfrac{m^2 + 4m - 21}{m^2 - 12m + 27} \cdot \dfrac{m^2 - 7m + 12}{m^2 + 3m - 28}$

37. $\dfrac{6a^2b + 2ab^2 - 20b^3}{4a^2b - 16b^3} \cdot \dfrac{10a^2 - 22ab + 4b^2}{27a^3 - 125b^3}$

38. $\dfrac{12a^2b - 3ab^2 - 42b^3}{9a^2 - 36b^2} \cdot \dfrac{6a^2 - 15ab + 6b^2}{8a^3b - b^4}$

39. $\dfrac{360x^3 - 490x}{36x^2 + 84x + 49} \cdot \dfrac{30x^2 + 83x + 56}{150x^3 + 65x^2 - 280x}$

40. $\dfrac{490x^2 - 640}{49x^2 - 112x + 64} \cdot \dfrac{28x^2 - 95x + 72}{56x^3 - 62x^2 - 144x}$

41. $\dfrac{x^5 - x^2}{5x^2 - 5x} \cdot \dfrac{10x^4 - 10x^2}{2x^4 + 2x^3 + 2x^2}$ **42.** $\dfrac{2x^4 - 16x}{3x^6 - 48x^2} \cdot \dfrac{6x^5 + 24x^3}{4x^4 + 8x^3 + 16x^2}$

43. $\dfrac{a^2 - 16b^2}{a^2 - 8ab + 16b^2} \cdot \dfrac{a^2 - 9ab + 20b^2}{a^2 - 7ab + 12b^2} \div \dfrac{a^2 - 25b^2}{a^2 - 6ab + 9b^2}$

44. $\dfrac{a^2 - 6ab + 9b^2}{a^2 - 4b^2} \cdot \dfrac{a^2 - 5ab + 6b^2}{(a - 3b)^2} \div \dfrac{a^2 - 9b^2}{a^2 - ab - 6b^2}$

45. $\dfrac{2y^2 - 7y - 15}{42y^2 - 29y - 5} \cdot \dfrac{12y^2 - 16y + 5}{7y^2 - 36y + 5} \div \dfrac{4y^2 - 9}{49y^2 - 1}$

46. $\dfrac{8y^2 + 18y - 5}{21y^2 - 16y + 3} \cdot \dfrac{35y^2 - 22y + 3}{6y^2 + 17y + 5} \div \dfrac{16y^2 - 1}{9y^2 - 1}$

47. $\dfrac{xy - 2x + 3y - 6}{xy + 2x - 4y - 8} \cdot \dfrac{xy + x - 4y - 4}{xy - x + 3y - 3}$

48. $\dfrac{ax + bx + 2a + 2b}{ax - 3a + bx - 3b} \cdot \dfrac{ax - bx - 3a + 3b}{ax - bx - 2a + 2b}$

49. $\dfrac{xy^2 - y^2 + 4xy - 4y}{xy - 3y + 4x - 12} \div \dfrac{xy^3 + 2xy^2 + y^3 + 2y^2}{xy^2 - 3y^2 + 2xy - 6y}$

50. $\dfrac{4xb - 8b + 12x - 24}{xb^2 + 3b^2 + 3xb + 9b} \div \dfrac{4xb - 8b - 8x + 16}{xb^2 + 3b^2 - 2xb - 6b}$

51. $\dfrac{2x^3 + 10x^2 - 8x - 40}{x^3 + 4x^2 - 9x - 36} \cdot \dfrac{x^2 + x - 12}{2x^2 + 14x + 20}$

52. $\dfrac{x^3 + 2x^2 - 9x - 18}{x^4 + 3x^3 - 4x^2 - 12x} \cdot \dfrac{x^3 + 5x^2 + 6x}{x^2 - x - 6}$

53. $\dfrac{w^3 - w^2x}{wy - w} \div \left(\dfrac{w - x}{y - 1} \right)^2$ **54.** $\dfrac{a^3 - a^2b}{ac - a} \div \left(\dfrac{a - b}{c - 1} \right)^2$

55. $\dfrac{mx + my + 2x + 2y}{6x^2 - 5xy - 4y^2} \div \dfrac{2mx - 4x + my - 2y}{3mx - 6x - 4my + 8y}$

56. $\dfrac{ax - 2a + 2xy - 4y}{ax + 2a - 2xy - 4y} \div \dfrac{ax + 2a + 2xy + 4y}{ax - 2a - 2xy + 4y}$

57. $(3x - 6) \cdot \dfrac{x}{x - 2}$ **58.** $(4x + 8) \cdot \dfrac{x}{x + 2}$

59. $(x^2 - 25) \cdot \dfrac{2}{x - 5}$ **60.** $(x^2 - 49) \cdot \dfrac{5}{x + 7}$

61. $(x^2 - 3x + 2) \cdot \dfrac{3}{3x - 3}$ **62.** $(x^2 - 3x + 2) \cdot \dfrac{-1}{x - 2}$

63. $(y - 3)(y - 4)(y + 3) \cdot \dfrac{-1}{y^2 - 9}$ **64.** $(y + 1)(y + 4)(y - 1) \cdot \dfrac{3}{y^2 - 1}$

65. $a(a + 5)(a - 5) \cdot \dfrac{a + 1}{a^2 + 5a}$ **66.** $a(a + 3)(a - 3) \cdot \dfrac{a - 1}{a^2 - 3a}$

67. Paying Attention to Instructions Work each problem according to the instructions given..

a. Simplify: $\dfrac{16 - 1}{64 - 1}$

b. Reduce: $\dfrac{25x^2 - 9}{125x^3 - 27}$

c. Multiply: $\dfrac{25x^2 - 9}{125x^3 - 27} \cdot \dfrac{5x - 3}{5x + 3}$

d. Divide: $\dfrac{25x^2 - 9}{125x^3 - 27} \div \dfrac{5x - 3}{25x^2 + 15x + 9}$

68. Paying Attention to Instructions Work each problem according to the instructions given..

a. Simplify: $\dfrac{64 - 49}{64 + 112 + 49}$

b. Reduce: $\dfrac{9x^2 - 49}{9x^2 + 42x + 49}$

c. Multiply: $\dfrac{9x^2 - 49}{9x^2 + 42x + 49} \cdot \dfrac{3x + 7}{3x - 7}$

d. Divide: $\dfrac{9x^2 - 49}{9x^2 + 42x + 49} \div \dfrac{3x + 7}{3x - 7}$

Getting Ready for the Next Section

Combine.

69. $\dfrac{4}{9} + \dfrac{2}{9}$ **70.** $\dfrac{3}{8} + \dfrac{1}{8}$ **71.** $\dfrac{3}{14} + \dfrac{7}{30}$ **72.** $\dfrac{3}{10} + \dfrac{11}{42}$

Multiply.

73. $-1(7 - x)$ **74.** $-1(3 - x)$

Factor.

75. $x^2 - 1$ **76.** $x^2 - 2x - 3$ **77.** $2x + 10$

78. $x^2 + 4x + 3$ **79.** $a^3 - b^3$ **80.** $8y^3 - 27$

This section is concerned with addition and subtraction of rational expressions. In the first part of this section, we will look at addition of expressions that have the same denominator. In the second part of this section, we will look at addition of expressions that have different denominators.

Addition and Subtraction with the Same Denominator

To add two expressions that have the same denominator, we simply add numerators and put the sum over the common denominator. Because the process we use to add and subtract rational expressions is the same process used to add and subtract fractions, we will begin with an example involving fractions.

Video Examples

Section 7.3

■ **Example 1**   Add $\dfrac{4}{9} + \dfrac{2}{9}$.

SOLUTION   We add fractions with the same denominator by using the distributive property. Here is a detailed look at the steps involved.

$$\frac{4}{9} + \frac{2}{9} = 4\left(\frac{1}{9}\right) + 2\left(\frac{1}{9}\right)$$

$$= (4 + 2)\left(\frac{1}{9}\right) \qquad \text{Distributive property}$$

$$= 6\left(\frac{1}{9}\right)$$

$$= \frac{6}{9}$$

$$= \frac{2}{3} \qquad \text{Divide numerator and denominator by common factor 3}$$

Note that the important thing about the fractions in this example is that they each have a denominator of 9. If they did not have the same denominator, we could not have written them as two terms with a factor of $\frac{1}{9}$ in common. Without the $\frac{1}{9}$ common to each term, we couldn't apply the distributive property. Without the distributive property, we would not have been able to add the two fractions in this form.   ■

In the following examples, we will not show all the steps we showed in Example 1. The steps are shown in Example 1 so you will see why both fractions must have the same denominator before we can add them. In practice, we simply add numerators and place the result over the common denominator.

We add and subtract rational expressions with the same denominator by combining numerators and writing the result over the common denominator. Then we reduce the result to lowest terms, if possible. Example 2 shows this process in detail. If you see the similarities between operations on rational numbers and operations on rational expressions, this chapter will look like an extension of rational numbers rather than a completely new set of topics.

Example 2 Add $\dfrac{x}{x^2-1} + \dfrac{1}{x^2-1}$.

SOLUTION Because the denominators are the same, we simply add numerators:

$$\frac{x}{x^2-1} + \frac{1}{x^2-1} = \frac{x+1}{x^2-1} \qquad \text{Add numerators}$$

$$= \frac{x+1}{(x-1)(x+1)} \qquad \text{Factor denominator}$$

$$= \frac{1}{x-1} \qquad \text{Divide out common factor } x+1$$

Our next example involves subtraction of rational expressions. Pay careful attention to what happens to the signs of the terms in the numerator of the second expression when we subtract it from the first expression.

Example 3 Subtract $\dfrac{2x-5}{x-2} - \dfrac{x-3}{x-2}$.

SOLUTION Because each expression has the same denominator, we simply subtract the numerator in the second expression from the numerator in the first expression and write the difference over the common denominator $x-2$. We must be careful, however, that we subtract both terms in the second numerator. To ensure that we do, we will enclose that numerator in parentheses.

$$\frac{2x-5}{x-2} - \frac{x-3}{x-2} = \frac{2x-5-(x-3)}{x-2} \qquad \text{Subtract numerators}$$

$$= \frac{2x-5-x+3}{x-2} \qquad \text{Remove parentheses}$$

$$= \frac{x-2}{x-2} \qquad \text{Combine similar terms in the numerator}$$

$$= 1 \qquad \text{Reduce (or divide)}$$

Note the $+3$ in the numerator of the second step. It is a common mistake to write this as -3, by forgetting to subtract both terms in the numerator of the second expression. Whenever the expression we are subtracting has two or more terms in its numerator, we have to watch for this mistake.

Next we consider addition and subtraction of fractions and rational expressions that have different denominators.

Addition and Subtraction With Different Denominators

Before we look at an example of addition of fractions with different denominators, we need to review the definition for the least common denominator (LCD).

> (dĕf' *least common denominator*
>
> The *least common denominator* for a set of denominators is the smallest expression that is divisible by each of the denominators.

The first step in combining two fractions is to find the LCD. Once we have the common denominator, we rewrite each fraction as an equivalent fraction with the common denominator. After that, we simply add or subtract as we did in our first three examples.

Example 4 is a review of the step-by-step procedure used to add two fractions with different denominators.

Example 4   Add $\dfrac{3}{14} + \dfrac{7}{30}$.

SOLUTION

Step 1: *Find the LCD.*

To do this, we first factor both denominators into prime factors.

Factor 14: $14 = 2 \cdot 7$

Factor 30: $30 = 2 \cdot 3 \cdot 5$

Because the LCD must be divisible by 14, it must have factors of 2 and 7. It must also be divisible by 30 and, therefore, have factors of 2, 3, and 5. We do not need to repeat the 2 that appears in both the factors of 14 and those of 30. Therefore,

$$LCD = 2 \cdot 3 \cdot 5 \cdot 7 = 210$$

Step 2: *Change to equivalent fractions.*

Because we want each fraction to have a denominator of 210 and at the same time keep its original value, we multiply each by 1 in the appropriate form.

Change $\frac{3}{14}$ to a fraction with denominator 210:

$$\frac{3}{14} \cdot \frac{15}{15} = \frac{45}{210}$$

Change $\frac{7}{30}$ to a fraction with denominator 210:

$$\frac{7}{30} \cdot \frac{7}{7} = \frac{49}{210}$$

Step 3: *Add numerators of equivalent fractions found in step 2:*

$$\frac{45}{210} + \frac{49}{210} = \frac{94}{210}$$

Step 4: *Reduce to lowest terms, if necessary:*

$$\frac{94}{210} = \frac{47}{105}$$

The main idea in adding fractions is to write each fraction again with the LCD for a denominator. In doing so, we must be sure not to change the value of either of the original fractions.

Example 5   Add $\dfrac{-2}{x^2 - 2x - 3} + \dfrac{3}{x^2 - 9}$.

SOLUTION

Step 1: *Factor each denominator and build the LCD from the factors:*

$$x^2 - 2x - 3 = (x - 3)(x + 1)$$
$$x^2 - 9 \quad = (x - 3)(x + 3) \qquad LCD = (x - 3)(x + 3)(x + 1)$$

Step 2: *Change each rational expression to an equivalent expression that has the LCD for a denominator:*

$$\frac{-2}{x^2 - 2x - 3} = \frac{-2}{(x - 3)(x + 1)} \cdot \frac{(x + 3)}{(x + 3)} = \frac{-2x - 6}{(x - 3)(x + 3)(x + 1)}$$

$$\frac{3}{x^2 - 9} = \frac{3}{(x - 3)(x + 3)} \cdot \frac{(x + 1)}{(x + 1)} = \frac{3x + 3}{(x - 3)(x + 3)(x + 1)}$$

Step 3: *Add numerators of the rational expressions found in step 2:*

$$\frac{-2x - 6}{(x - 3)(x + 3)(x + 1)} + \frac{3x + 3}{(x - 3)(x + 3)(x + 1)} = \frac{x - 3}{(x - 3)(x + 3)(x + 1)}$$

Step 4: *Reduce to lowest terms by dividing out the common factor $x - 3$:*

$$\frac{x - 3}{(x - 3)(x + 3)(x + 1)} = \frac{1}{(x + 3)(x + 1)}$$

Example 6   Subtract $\dfrac{x + 4}{2x + 10} - \dfrac{5}{x^2 - 25}$.

SOLUTION   We begin by factoring each denominator:

$$\frac{x + 4}{2x + 10} - \frac{5}{x^2 - 25} = \frac{x + 4}{2(x + 5)} - \frac{5}{(x + 5)(x - 5)}$$

The LCD is $2(x + 5)(x - 5)$. Completing the problem, we have

$$= \frac{x + 4}{2(x + 5)} \cdot \frac{(x - 5)}{(x - 5)} - \frac{5}{(x + 5)(x - 5)} \cdot \frac{2}{2}$$

$$= \frac{x^2 - x - 20}{2(x + 5)(x - 5)} - \frac{10}{2(x + 5)(x - 5)}$$

$$= \frac{x^2 - x - 30}{2(x + 5)(x - 5)}$$

To see if this expression will reduce, we factor the numerator into $(x - 6)(x + 5)$.

$$= \frac{(x - 6)(x + 5)}{2(x + 5)(x - 5)}$$

$$= \frac{x - 6}{2(x - 5)}$$

Example 7   Subtract $\dfrac{2x-2}{x^2+4x+3} - \dfrac{x-1}{x^2+5x+6}$.

SOLUTION   We factor each denominator and build the LCD from those factors:

$$\frac{2x-2}{x^2+4x+3} - \frac{x-1}{x^2+5x+6}$$

$$= \frac{2x-2}{(x+3)(x+1)} - \frac{x-1}{(x+3)(x+2)}$$

$$= \frac{2x-2}{(x+3)(x+1)} \cdot \frac{(x+2)}{(x+2)} - \frac{x-1}{(x+3)(x+2)} \cdot \frac{(x+1)}{(x+1)} \qquad \text{The LCD is } (x+1)(x+2)(x+3)$$

$$= \frac{2x^2+2x-4}{(x+1)(x+2)(x+3)} - \frac{x^2-1}{(x+1)(x+2)(x+3)} \qquad \text{Multiply out each numerator}$$

$$= \frac{(2x^2+2x-4)-(x^2-1)}{(x+1)(x+2)(x+3)} \qquad \text{Subtract numerators}$$

$$= \frac{x^2+2x-3}{(x+1)(x+2)(x+3)} \qquad \text{Factor numerator to see if we can rdeuce}$$

$$= \frac{(x+3)(x-1)}{(x+1)(x+2)(x+3)} \qquad \text{Reduce}$$

$$= \frac{x-1}{(x+1)(x+2)}$$

■

Example 8   Add $\dfrac{x^2}{x-7} + \dfrac{6x+7}{7-x}$.

SOLUTION   In Section 7.1, we were able to reverse the terms in a factor such as $7-x$ by factoring -1 from each term. In a problem like this, the same result can be obtained by multiplying the numerator and denominator by -1:

$$\frac{x^2}{x-7} + \frac{6x+7}{7-x} \cdot \frac{-1}{-1} = \frac{x^2}{x-7} + \frac{-6x-7}{x-7}$$

$$= \frac{x^2-6x-7}{x-7} \qquad \text{Add numerators}$$

$$= \frac{(x-7)(x+1)}{(x-7)} \qquad \text{Factor numerator}$$

$$= x+1 \qquad \text{Divide out } x-7 \quad ■$$

For our next example, we will look at a problem in which we combine a whole number and a rational expression.

Example 9 Subtract $2 - \dfrac{9}{3x + 1}$.

SOLUTION To subtract these two expressions, we think of 2 as a rational expression with a denominator of 1.

$$2 - \frac{9}{3x + 1} = \frac{2}{1} - \frac{9}{3x + 1}$$

The LCD is $3x + 1$. Multiplying the numerator and denominator of the first expression by $3x + 1$ gives us a rational expression equivalent to 2, but with a denominator of $3x + 1$.

$$\frac{2}{1} \cdot \frac{(3x + 1)}{(3x + 1)} - \frac{9}{3x + 1} = \frac{6x + 2 - 9}{3x + 1}$$

$$= \frac{6x - 7}{3x + 1}$$

The numerator and denominator of this last expression do not have any factors in common other than 1, so the expression is in lowest terms. ∎

Example 10 Write an expression for the sum of a number and twice its reciprocal. Then, simplify that expression.

SOLUTION If x is the number, then its reciprocal is $\frac{1}{x}$. Twice its reciprocal is $\frac{2}{x}$. The sum of the number and twice its reciprocal is

$$x + \frac{2}{x}$$

To combine these two expressions, we think of the first term x as a rational expression with a denominator of 1. The LCD is x:

$$x + \frac{2}{x} = \frac{x}{1} + \frac{2}{x}$$

$$= \frac{x}{1} \cdot \frac{x}{x} + \frac{2}{x}$$

$$= \frac{x^2 + 2}{x}$$

∎

Getting Ready for Class

After reading through the preceding section, respond in your own words and in complete sentences.

A. Briefly describe how you would add two rational expressions that have the same denominator.

B. Why is factoring important in finding a least common denominator?

C. What is the last step in adding or subtracting two rational expressions?

D. Explain how you would change the fraction $\dfrac{5}{x - 3}$ to an equivalent fraction with denominator $x^2 - 9$.

Problem Set 7.3

Combine the following fractions.

1. $\dfrac{3}{4} + \dfrac{1}{2}$ **2.** $\dfrac{5}{6} + \dfrac{1}{3}$ **3.** $\dfrac{2}{5} - \dfrac{1}{15}$ **4.** $\dfrac{5}{8} - \dfrac{1}{4}$

5. $\dfrac{5}{6} + \dfrac{7}{8}$ **6.** $\dfrac{3}{4} + \dfrac{2}{3}$ **7.** $\dfrac{9}{48} - \dfrac{3}{54}$ **8.** $\dfrac{6}{28} - \dfrac{5}{42}$

9. $\dfrac{3}{4} - \dfrac{1}{8} + \dfrac{2}{3}$ **10.** $\dfrac{1}{3} - \dfrac{5}{6} + \dfrac{5}{12}$

Combine the following rational expressions. Reduce all answers to lowest terms.

11. $\dfrac{x}{x+3} + \dfrac{3}{x+3}$ **12.** $\dfrac{5x}{5x+2} + \dfrac{2}{5x+2}$ **13.** $\dfrac{4}{y-4} - \dfrac{y}{y-4}$

14. $\dfrac{8}{y+8} + \dfrac{y}{y+8}$ **15.** $\dfrac{x}{x^2-y^2} - \dfrac{y}{x^2-y^2}$ **16.** $\dfrac{x}{x^2-y^2} + \dfrac{y}{x^2-y^2}$

17. $\dfrac{2x-3}{x-2} - \dfrac{x-1}{x-2}$ **18.** $\dfrac{2x-4}{x+2} - \dfrac{x-6}{x+2}$ **19.** $\dfrac{1}{a} + \dfrac{2}{a^2} - \dfrac{3}{a^3}$

20. $\dfrac{3}{a} + \dfrac{2}{a^2} - \dfrac{1}{a^3}$ **21.** $\dfrac{7x-2}{2x+1} - \dfrac{5x-3}{2x+1}$ **22.** $\dfrac{7x-1}{3x+2} - \dfrac{4x-3}{3x+2}$

23. Paying Attention to Instructions Work each problem according to the instructions given..

    a. Multiply: $\dfrac{3}{8} \cdot \dfrac{1}{6}$ **b.** Divide: $\dfrac{3}{8} \div \dfrac{1}{6}$

    c. Add: $\dfrac{3}{8} + \dfrac{1}{6}$ **d.** Multiply: $\dfrac{x+3}{x-3} \cdot \dfrac{5x+15}{x^2-9}$

    e. Divide: $\dfrac{x+3}{x-3} \div \dfrac{5x+15}{x^2-9}$ **f.** Subtract: $\dfrac{x+3}{x-3} - \dfrac{5x+15}{x^2-9}$

24. Paying Attention to Instructions Work each problem according to the instructions given..

    a. Multiply: $\dfrac{16}{49} \cdot \dfrac{1}{28}$ **b.** Divide: $\dfrac{16}{49} \div \dfrac{1}{28}$

    c. Subtract: $\dfrac{16}{49} - \dfrac{1}{28}$ **d.** Multiply: $\dfrac{3x-2}{3x+2} \cdot \dfrac{15x+6}{9x^2-4}$

    e. Divide: $\dfrac{3x-2}{3x+2} \div \dfrac{15x+6}{9x^2-4}$ **f.** Subtract: $\dfrac{3x+2}{3x-2} - \dfrac{15x+6}{9x^2-4}$

Combine the following rational expressions. Reduce all answers to lowest terms.

25. $\dfrac{3x+1}{2x-6} - \dfrac{x+2}{x-3}$

26. $\dfrac{x+1}{x-2} - \dfrac{4x+7}{5x-10}$

27. $\dfrac{6x+5}{5x-25} - \dfrac{x+2}{x-5}$

28. $\dfrac{4x+2}{3x+12} - \dfrac{x-2}{x+4}$

29. $\dfrac{x+1}{2x-2} - \dfrac{2}{x^2-1}$

30. $\dfrac{x+7}{2x+12} + \dfrac{6}{x^2-36}$

31. $\dfrac{1}{a-b} - \dfrac{3ab}{a^3-b^3}$

32. $\dfrac{1}{a+b} + \dfrac{3ab}{a^3+b^3}$

33. $\dfrac{1}{2y-3} - \dfrac{18y}{8y^3-27}$

34. $\dfrac{1}{3y-2} - \dfrac{18y}{27y^3-8}$

35. $\dfrac{x}{x^2-5x+6} - \dfrac{3}{3-x}$

36. $\dfrac{x}{x^2+4x+4} - \dfrac{2}{2+x}$

37. $\dfrac{2}{4t-5} + \dfrac{9}{8t^2-38t+35}$

38. $\dfrac{3}{2t-5} + \dfrac{21}{8t^2-14t-15}$

39. $\dfrac{1}{a^2-5a+6} + \dfrac{3}{a^2-a-2}$

40. $\dfrac{-3}{a^2+a-2} + \dfrac{5}{a^2-a-6}$

41. $\dfrac{1}{8x^3-1} - \dfrac{1}{4x^2-1}$

42. $\dfrac{1}{27x^3-1} - \dfrac{1}{9x^2-1}$

43. $\dfrac{4}{4x^2-9} - \dfrac{6}{8x^2-6x-9}$

44. $\dfrac{9}{9x^2+6x-8} - \dfrac{6}{9x^2-4}$

45. $\dfrac{4a}{a^2+6a+5} - \dfrac{3a}{a^2+5a+4}$

46. $\dfrac{3a}{a^2+7a+10} - \dfrac{2a}{a^2+6a+8}$

47. $\dfrac{2x-1}{x^2+x-6} - \dfrac{x+2}{x^2+5x+6}$

48. $\dfrac{4x+1}{x^2+5x+4} - \dfrac{x+3}{x^2+4x+3}$

49. $\dfrac{2x-8}{3x^2+8x+4} + \dfrac{x+3}{3x^2+5x+2}$

50. $\dfrac{5x+3}{2x^2+5x+3} - \dfrac{3x+9}{2x^2+7x+6}$

51. $\dfrac{2}{x^2 + 5x + 6} - \dfrac{4}{x^2 + 4x + 3} + \dfrac{3}{x^2 + 3x + 2}$

52. $\dfrac{-5}{x^2 + 3x - 4} + \dfrac{5}{x^2 + 2x - 3} + \dfrac{1}{x^2 + 7x + 12}$

53. $\dfrac{2x + 8}{x^2 + 5x + 6} - \dfrac{x + 5}{x^2 + 4x + 3} - \dfrac{x - 1}{x^2 + 3x + 2}$

54. $\dfrac{2x + 11}{x^2 + 9x + 20} - \dfrac{x + 1}{x^2 + 7x + 12} - \dfrac{x + 6}{x^2 + 8x + 15}$

55. $2 + \dfrac{3}{2x + 1}$ 　　　　　　　 **56.** $3 - \dfrac{2}{2x + 3}$

57. $5 + \dfrac{2}{4 - t}$ 　　　　　　　 **58.** $7 + \dfrac{3}{5 - t}$

59. $x - \dfrac{4}{2x + 3}$ 　　　　　　　 **60.** $x - \dfrac{5}{3x + 4} + 1$

61. $\dfrac{x}{x + 2} + \dfrac{1}{2x + 4} - \dfrac{3}{x^2 + 2x}$ 　　 **62.** $\dfrac{x}{x + 3} + \dfrac{7}{3x + 9} - \dfrac{2}{x^2 + 3x}$

63. $\dfrac{1}{x} + \dfrac{x}{2x + 4} - \dfrac{2}{x^2 + 2x}$ 　　 **64.** $\dfrac{1}{x} + \dfrac{x}{3x + 9} - \dfrac{3}{x^2 + 3x}$

65. Let $f(x) = \dfrac{2}{x + 4}$ and $g(x) = \dfrac{x - 1}{x^2 + 3x - 4}$; find $f(x) + g(x)$

66. Let $f(t) = \dfrac{5}{3t - 2}$ and $g(t) = \dfrac{t - 3}{3t^2 + 7t - 6}$; find $f(t) - g(t)$

67. Let $f(x) = \dfrac{2x}{x^2 - x - 2}$ and $g(x) = \dfrac{5}{x^2 + x - 6}$; find $f(x) + g(x)$

68. Let $f(x) = \dfrac{7}{x^2 - x - 12}$ and $g(x) = \dfrac{5}{x^2 + x - 6}$; find $f(x) - g(x)$

Applying the Concepts

69. Optometry The formula

$$P = \frac{1}{a} + \frac{1}{b}$$

is used by optometrists to help determine how strong to make the lenses for a pair of eyeglasses. If a is 10 and b is 0.2, find the corresponding value of P.

70. Quadratic Formula Later in the book we will work with the quadratic formula. The derivation of the formula requires that you can add the fractions below. Add the fractions.

$$\frac{-c}{a} + \frac{b^2}{(2a)^2}$$

71. Number Problem Write an expression for the sum of a number and 4 times its reciprocal. Then, simplify that expression.

72. Number Problem Write an expression for the sum of a number and 3 times its reciprocal. Then, simplify that expression.

73. Number Problem Write an expression for the sum of the reciprocals of two consecutive integers. Then, simplify that expression.

74. Number Problem Write an expression for the sum of the reciprocals of two consecutive even integers. Then, simplify that expression.

Getting Ready for the Next Section

Divide.

75. $\dfrac{3}{4} \div \dfrac{5}{8}$

76. $\dfrac{2}{3} \div \dfrac{5}{6}$

Multiply.

77. $x\left(1 + \dfrac{2}{x}\right)$ **78.** $3\left(x + \dfrac{1}{3}\right)$ **79.** $3x\left(\dfrac{1}{x} - \dfrac{1}{3}\right)$ **80.** $3x\left(\dfrac{1}{x} + \dfrac{1}{3}\right)$

Factor.

81. $x^2 - 4$

82. $x^2 - x - 6$

Complex Fractions

The quotient of two fractions or two rational expressions is called a *complex fraction*. This section is concerned with the simplification of complex fractions.

Video Examples

Section 7.4

Example 1 Simplify $\dfrac{\frac{3}{4}}{\frac{5}{8}}$.

SOLUTION There are generally two methods that can be used to simplify complex fractions.

Method 1 We can multiply the numerator and denominator of the complex fractions by the LCD for both of the fractions, which in this case is 8.

$$\frac{\frac{3}{4}}{\frac{5}{8}} = \frac{\frac{3}{4} \cdot 8}{\frac{5}{8} \cdot 8} = \frac{6}{5}$$

Method 2 Instead of dividing by $\frac{5}{8}$ we can multiply by $\frac{8}{5}$.

$$\frac{\frac{3}{4}}{\frac{5}{8}} = \frac{3}{4} \cdot \frac{8}{5} = \frac{24}{20} = \frac{6}{5}$$

Here are some examples of complex fractions involving rational expressions. Most can be solved using either of the two methods shown in Example 1.

Example 2 Simplify $\dfrac{\frac{1}{x} + \frac{1}{y}}{\frac{1}{x} - \frac{1}{y}}$.

SOLUTION This problem is most easily solved using Method 1. We begin by multiplying both the numerator and denominator by the quantity xy, which is the LCD for all the fractions:

$$\frac{\frac{1}{x} + \frac{1}{y}}{\frac{1}{x} - \frac{1}{y}} = \frac{\left(\frac{1}{x} + \frac{1}{y}\right) \cdot xy}{\left(\frac{1}{x} - \frac{1}{y}\right) \cdot xy}$$

$$= \frac{\frac{1}{x}(xy) + \frac{1}{y}(xy)}{\frac{1}{x}(xy) - \frac{1}{y}(xy)}$$

Apply the distributive property to distribute xy over both terms in the numerator and denominator.

$$= \frac{y + x}{y - x}$$

Example 3   Simplify $\dfrac{\frac{x-2}{x^2-9}}{\frac{x^2-4}{x+3}}$.

SOLUTION   Applying Method 2, we have

$$\frac{\frac{x-2}{x^2-9}}{\frac{x^2-4}{x+3}} = \frac{x-2}{x^2-9} \cdot \frac{x+3}{x^2-4}$$

$$= \frac{(x-2)(x+3)}{(x+3)(x-3)(x+2)(x-2)}$$

$$= \frac{1}{(x-3)(x+2)}$$

Example 4   Simplify $\dfrac{1-\frac{4}{x^2}}{1-\frac{1}{x}-\frac{6}{x^2}}$.

SOLUTION   The simplest way to simplify this complex fraction is to multiply the numerator and denominator by the LCD, x^2:

$$\frac{1-\frac{4}{x^2}}{1-\frac{1}{x}-\frac{6}{x^2}} = \frac{x^2\left(1-\frac{4}{x^2}\right)}{x^2\left(1-\frac{1}{x}-\frac{6}{x^2}\right)}$$ Multiply numerator and denominator by x^2

$$= \frac{x^2 \cdot 1 - x^2 \cdot \frac{4}{x^2}}{x^2 \cdot 1 - x^2 \cdot \frac{1}{x} - x^2 \cdot \frac{6}{x^2}}$$ Distributive property

$$= \frac{x^2-4}{x^2-x-6}$$ Simplify

$$= \frac{(x-2)(x+2)}{(x-3)(x+2)}$$ Factor

$$= \frac{x-2}{x-3}$$ Reduce

Example 5   Simplify $2 - \dfrac{3}{x+\frac{1}{3}}$.

SOLUTION   First, we simplify the expression that follows the subtraction sign.

$$2 - \frac{3}{x+\frac{1}{3}} = 2 - \frac{3 \cdot 3}{3\left(x+\frac{1}{3}\right)} = 2 - \frac{9}{3x+1}$$

Now we subtract by rewriting the first term, 2, with the LCD, $3x+1$.

$$2 - \frac{9}{3x+1} = \frac{2}{1} \cdot \frac{3x+1}{3x+1} - \frac{9}{3x+1}$$

$$= \frac{6x+2-9}{3x+1} = \frac{6x-7}{3x+1}$$

Getting Ready for Class

After reading through the preceding section, respond in your own words and in complete sentences.

A. What is a complex fraction?

B. Explain how a least common denominator can be used to simplify a complex fraction.

C. Explain how some complex fractions can be converted to division problems. When is it more efficient to convert a complex fraction to a division problem of rational expressions?

D. Which method of simplifying complex fractions do you prefer? Why?

Simplify each of the following as much as possible.

1. $\dfrac{\dfrac{3}{4}}{\dfrac{2}{3}}$

2. $\dfrac{\dfrac{5}{9}}{\dfrac{7}{12}}$

3. $\dfrac{\dfrac{1}{3} - \dfrac{1}{4}}{\dfrac{1}{2} + \dfrac{1}{8}}$

4. $\dfrac{\dfrac{1}{6} - \dfrac{1}{3}}{\dfrac{1}{4} - \dfrac{1}{8}}$

5. $\dfrac{3 + \dfrac{2}{5}}{1 - \dfrac{3}{7}}$

6. $\dfrac{2 + \dfrac{5}{6}}{1 - \dfrac{7}{8}}$

7. $\dfrac{\dfrac{1}{x}}{1 + \dfrac{1}{x}}$

8. $\dfrac{1 - \dfrac{1}{x}}{\dfrac{1}{x}}$

9. $\dfrac{1 + \dfrac{1}{a}}{1 - \dfrac{1}{a}}$

10. $\dfrac{1 - \dfrac{2}{a}}{1 - \dfrac{3}{a}}$

11. $\dfrac{\dfrac{1}{x} - \dfrac{1}{y}}{\dfrac{1}{x} + \dfrac{1}{y}}$

12. $\dfrac{\dfrac{1}{x} + \dfrac{2}{y}}{\dfrac{2}{x} + \dfrac{1}{y}}$

13. $\dfrac{\dfrac{x - 5}{x^2 - 4}}{\dfrac{x^2 - 25}{x + 2}}$

14. $\dfrac{\dfrac{3x + 1}{x^2 - 49}}{\dfrac{9x^2 - 1}{x - 7}}$

15. $\dfrac{\dfrac{4a}{2a^3 + 2}}{\dfrac{8a}{4a + 4}}$

16. $\dfrac{\dfrac{2a}{3a^3 - 3}}{\dfrac{4a}{6a - 6}}$

17. $\dfrac{1 - \dfrac{9}{x^2}}{1 - \dfrac{1}{x} - \dfrac{6}{x^2}}$

18. $\dfrac{4 - \dfrac{1}{x^2}}{4 + \dfrac{4}{x} + \dfrac{1}{x^2}}$

19. $\dfrac{2 + \dfrac{5}{a} - \dfrac{3}{a^2}}{2 - \dfrac{5}{a} + \dfrac{2}{a^2}}$

20. $\dfrac{3 + \dfrac{5}{a} - \dfrac{2}{a^2}}{3 - \dfrac{10}{a} + \dfrac{3}{a^2}}$

21. $\dfrac{2 + \dfrac{3}{x} - \dfrac{18}{x^2} - \dfrac{27}{x^3}}{2 + \dfrac{9}{x} + \dfrac{9}{x^2}}$

22. $\dfrac{3 + \dfrac{5}{x} - \dfrac{12}{x^2} - \dfrac{20}{x^3}}{3 + \dfrac{11}{x} + \dfrac{10}{x^2}}$

23. $\dfrac{1 + \dfrac{1}{x + 3}}{1 - \dfrac{1}{x + 3}}$

24. $\dfrac{1 + \dfrac{1}{x - 2}}{1 - \dfrac{1}{x - 2}}$

25. $\dfrac{1 + \dfrac{1}{x + 3}}{1 + \dfrac{7}{x - 3}}$

26. $\dfrac{1 + \dfrac{1}{x - 2}}{1 - \dfrac{3}{x + 2}}$

27. $\dfrac{1 - \dfrac{1}{a + 1}}{1 + \dfrac{1}{a - 1}}$

28. $\dfrac{\dfrac{1}{a - 1} + 1}{\dfrac{1}{a + 1} - 1}$

29. $\dfrac{\dfrac{1}{x + 3} + \dfrac{1}{x - 3}}{\dfrac{1}{x + 3} - \dfrac{1}{x - 3}}$

30. $\dfrac{\dfrac{1}{x + a} + \dfrac{1}{x - a}}{\dfrac{1}{x + a} - \dfrac{1}{x - a}}$

31. $\dfrac{\dfrac{y+1}{y-1}+\dfrac{y-1}{y+1}}{\dfrac{y+1}{y-1}-\dfrac{y-1}{y+1}}$

32. $\dfrac{\dfrac{y-1}{y+1}-\dfrac{y+1}{y-1}}{\dfrac{y-1}{y+1}+\dfrac{y+1}{y-1}}$

33. $1-\dfrac{x}{1-\dfrac{1}{x}}$

34. $x-\dfrac{1}{x-\dfrac{1}{2}}$

35. $1+\dfrac{1}{1+\dfrac{1}{1+1}}$

36. $1-\dfrac{1}{1-\dfrac{1}{1-\dfrac{1}{2}}}$

37. $\dfrac{1-\dfrac{1}{x+\dfrac{1}{2}}}{1+\dfrac{1}{x+\dfrac{1}{2}}}$

38. $\dfrac{2+\dfrac{1}{x-\dfrac{1}{3}}}{2-\dfrac{1}{x-\dfrac{1}{3}}}$

39. $\dfrac{\dfrac{1}{x+h}-\dfrac{1}{x}}{h}$

40. $\dfrac{\dfrac{1}{(x+h)^2}-\dfrac{1}{x^2}}{h}$

41. $\dfrac{\dfrac{3}{ab}+\dfrac{4}{bc}-\dfrac{2}{ac}}{\dfrac{5}{abc}}$

42. $\dfrac{\dfrac{x}{yz}-\dfrac{y}{xz}+\dfrac{z}{xy}}{\dfrac{1}{x^2y^2}-\dfrac{1}{x^2z^2}+\dfrac{1}{y^2z^2}}$

43. $\dfrac{\dfrac{t^2-2t-8}{t^2+7t+6}}{\dfrac{t^2-t-6}{t^2+2t+1}}$

44. $\dfrac{\dfrac{y^2-5y-14}{y^2+3y-10}}{\dfrac{y^2-8y+7}{y^2+6y+5}}$

45. $\dfrac{5+\dfrac{4}{b-1}}{\dfrac{7}{b+5}-\dfrac{3}{b-1}}$

46. $\dfrac{\dfrac{6}{x+5}-7}{\dfrac{8}{x+5}-\dfrac{9}{x+3}}$

47. $\dfrac{\dfrac{3}{x^2-x-6}}{\dfrac{2}{x+2}-\dfrac{4}{x-3}}$

48. $\dfrac{\dfrac{9}{a-7}+\dfrac{8}{2a+3}}{\dfrac{10}{2a^2-11a-21}}$

49. $\dfrac{\dfrac{1}{m-4}+\dfrac{1}{m-5}}{\dfrac{1}{m^2-9m+20}}$

50. $\dfrac{\dfrac{1}{k^2-7k+12}}{\dfrac{1}{k-3}+\dfrac{1}{k-4}}$

Applying the Concepts

51. **Difference Quotient** For each rational function below, find the difference quotient

$$\frac{f(x)-f(a)}{x-a}$$

a. $f(x)=\dfrac{4}{x}$

b. $f(x)=\dfrac{1}{x+1}$

c. $f(x)=\dfrac{1}{x^2}$

52. **Difference Quotient** For each rational function below, find the difference quotient

$$\frac{f(x+h)-f(x)}{h}$$

a. $f(x)=\dfrac{4}{x}$

b. $f(x)=\dfrac{1}{x+1}$

c. $f(x)=\dfrac{1}{x^2}$

53. **Doppler Effect** The change in the pitch of a sound (such as a train whistle) as an object passes is called the Doppler effect, named after C. J. Doppler (1803–1853). A person will *hear* a sound with a frequency, *h*, according to the formula

$$h = \frac{f}{1 + \dfrac{v}{s}}$$

where *f* is the actual frequency of the sound being produced, *s* is the speed of sound (about 740 miles per hour), and *v* is the velocity of the moving object.

a. Examine this fraction, and then explain why *h* and *f* approach the same value as *v* becomes smaller and smaller.

b. Solve this formula for *v*.

54. **Work Problem** A water storage tank has two drains. It can be shown that the time it takes to empty the tank if both drains are open is given by the formula

$$\frac{1}{\dfrac{1}{a} + \dfrac{1}{b}}$$

where *a* = time it takes for the first drain to empty the tank, and *b* = time for the second drain to empty the tank.

a. Simplify this complex fraction.

b. Find the amount of time needed to empty the tank using both drains if, used alone, the first drain empties the tank in 4 hours and the second drain can empty the tank in 3 hours.

Getting Ready for the Next Section

Multiply.

55. $x(y - 2)$

56. $x(y - 1)$

57. $6\left(\dfrac{x}{2} - 3\right)$

58. $6\left(\dfrac{x}{3} + 1\right)$

59. $xab \cdot \dfrac{1}{x}$

60. $xab\left(\dfrac{1}{b} + \dfrac{1}{a}\right)$

Factor.

61. $y^2 - 25$

62. $x^2 - 3x + 2$

63. $xa + xb$

64. $xy - y$

Solve.

65. $5x - 4 = 6$

66. $y^2 + y - 20 = 2y$

Equations With Rational Expressions

7.5

The first step in solving an equation that contains one or more rational expressions is to find the LCD for all denominators in the equation. We then multiply both sides of the equation by the LCD to clear the equation of all fractions. That is, after we have multiplied through by the LCD, each term in the resulting equation will have a denominator of 1.

Video Examples

Section 7.5

Example 1   Solve $\dfrac{x}{2} - 3 = \dfrac{2}{3}$.

SOLUTION   The LCD for 2 and 3 is 6. Multiplying both sides by 6, we have

$$6\left(\frac{x}{2} - 3\right) = 6\left(\frac{2}{3}\right)$$

$$6\left(\frac{x}{2}\right) - 6(3) = 6\left(\frac{2}{3}\right)$$

$$3x - 18 = 4$$

$$3x = 22$$

$$x = \frac{22}{3}$$

Multiplying both sides of an equation by the LCD clears the equation of fractions because the LCD has the property that all the denominators divide it evenly.

Example 2   Solve $\dfrac{6}{a - 4} = \dfrac{3}{8}$.

SOLUTION   The LCD for $a - 4$ and 8 is $8(a - 4)$. Multiplying both sides by this quantity yields

$$8(a - 4) \cdot \frac{6}{a - 4} = 8(a - 4) \cdot \frac{3}{8}$$

$$48 = (a - 4) \cdot 3$$

$$48 = 3a - 12$$

$$60 = 3a$$

$$20 = a$$

The solution set is 20, which checks in the original equation.

When we multiply both sides of an equation by an expression containing the variable, we must be sure to check our solutions. The multiplication property of equality does not allow multiplication by 0. If the expression we multiply by contains the variable, then it has the possibility of being 0. In the last example, we multiplied both sides by $8(a - 4)$. This gives a restriction $a \neq 4$ for any solution we come up with.

Example 3 Solve $\dfrac{x}{x-2} + \dfrac{2}{3} = \dfrac{2}{x-2}$.

SOLUTION The LCD is $3(x-2)$. We are assuming $x \neq 2$ when we multiply both sides of the equation by $3(x-2)$:

$$3(x-2) \cdot \left(\dfrac{x}{x-2} + \dfrac{2}{3} \right) = 3(x-2) \cdot \dfrac{2}{x-2}$$

$$3x + (x-2) \cdot 2 = 3 \cdot 2$$

$$3x + 2x - 4 = 6$$

$$5x - 4 = 6$$

$$5x = 10$$

$$x = 2$$

> **Note** In the process of solving the equation, we multiplied both sides by $3(x-2)$, solved for x, and got $x = 2$ for our solution. But when x is 2, the quantity $3(x-2) = 3(2-2) = 3(0) = 0$, which means we multiplied both sides of our equation by 0, which is not allowed under the multiplication property of equality.

The only possible solution is $x = 2$. Checking this value back in the original equation gives

$$\dfrac{2}{2-2} + \dfrac{2}{3} \overset{?}{=} \dfrac{2}{2-2}$$

$$\dfrac{2}{0} + \dfrac{2}{3} \overset{?}{=} \dfrac{2}{0}$$

The first and last terms are undefined. The proposed solution, $x = 2$, does not check in the original equation. The solution set is the empty set. There is no solution to the original equation.

When the proposed solution to an equation is not actually a solution, it is called an *extraneous* solution. In the last example, $x = 2$ is an extraneous solution.

Example 4 Solve $\dfrac{5}{x^2 - 3x + 2} - \dfrac{1}{x-2} = \dfrac{1}{3x-3}$.

SOLUTION Writing the equation again with the denominators in factored form, we have

$$\dfrac{5}{(x-2)(x-1)} - \dfrac{1}{x-2} = \dfrac{1}{3(x-1)}$$

> **Note** We can check the proposed solution in any of the equations obtained before multiplying through by the LCD. We cannot check the proposed solution in an equation obtained after multiplying through by the LCD because, if we have multiplied by 0, the resulting equations will not be equivalent to the original one.

The LCD is $3(x-2)(x-1)$. Multiplying through by the LCD, we have

$$3(x-2)(x-1) \dfrac{5}{(x-2)(x-1)} - 3(x-2)(x-1) \cdot \dfrac{1}{(x-2)}$$

$$= 3(x-2)(x-1) \cdot \dfrac{1}{3(x-1)}$$

$$3 \cdot 5 - 3(x-1) \cdot 1 = (x-2) \cdot 1$$

$$15 - 3x + 3 = x - 2$$

$$-3x + 18 = x - 2$$

$$-4x + 18 = -2$$

$$-4x = -20$$

$$x = 5$$

Checking the proposed solution $x = 5$ in the original equation yields a true statement. Try it and see.

Example 5   Solve $3 + \dfrac{1}{x} = \dfrac{10}{x^2}$.

SOLUTION   To clear the equation of denominators, we multiply both sides by x^2:

$$x^2\left(3 + \frac{1}{x}\right) = x^2\left(\frac{10}{x^2}\right)$$

$$3(x^2) + \left(\frac{1}{x}\right)(x^2) = \left(\frac{10}{x^2}\right)(x^2)$$

$$3x^2 + x = 10$$

Rewrite in standard form, and solve:

$$3x^2 + x - 10 = 0$$

$$(3x - 5)(x + 2) = 0$$

$$3x - 5 = 0 \qquad \text{or} \qquad x + 2 = 0$$

$$x = \frac{5}{3} \qquad \text{or} \qquad x = -2$$

The solution set is $\left[-2, \frac{5}{3}\right]$. Both solutions check in the original equation. Remember: We have to check all solutions any time we multiply both sides of the equation by an expression that contains the variable, just to be sure we haven't multiplied by 0.   ■

Example 6   Solve $\dfrac{y - 4}{y^2 - 5y} = \dfrac{2}{y^2 - 25}$.

SOLUTION   Factoring each denominator, we find the LCD is $y(y - 5)(y + 5)$. Multiplying each side of the equation by the LCD clears the equation of denominators and leads us to our possible solutions:

$$y(y - 5)(y + 5) \cdot \frac{y - 4}{y(y - 5)} = \frac{2}{(y - 5)(y + 5)} \cdot y(y - 5)(y + 5)$$

$$(y + 5)(y - 4) = 2y$$

$$y^2 + y - 20 = 2y \qquad \text{\color{green}Multiply out the left side}$$

$$y^2 - y - 20 = 0 \qquad \text{\color{green}Add $-2y$ to each side}$$

$$(y - 5)(y + 4) = 0$$

$$y - 5 = 0 \qquad \text{or} \qquad y + 4 = 0$$

$$y = 5 \qquad \text{or} \qquad y = -4$$

The two possible solutions are 5 and -4. If we substitute -4 for y in the original equation, we find that it leads to a true statement. It is therefore a solution. On the other hand, if we substitute 5 for y in the original equation, we find that both sides of the equation are undefined. The only solution to our original equation is $y = -4$. The other possible solution $y = 5$ is extraneous.   ■

Example 7 Solve for y: $x = \dfrac{y-4}{y-2}$

SOLUTION To solve for y, we first multiply each side by $y-2$ to obtain

$$x(y-2) = y-4$$

$$xy - 2x = y - 4 \qquad \text{Distributive property}$$

$$xy - y = 2x - 4 \qquad \text{Collect all terms containing } y \text{ on the left side}$$

$$y(x-1) = 2x - 4 \qquad \text{Factor } y \text{ from each term on the left side}$$

$$y = \frac{2x-4}{x-1} \qquad \text{Divide each side by } x-1$$

Example 8 Solve the formula $\dfrac{1}{x} = \dfrac{1}{b} + \dfrac{1}{a}$ for x.

SOLUTION We begin by multiplying both sides by the least common denominator xab. As you can see from our previous examples, multiplying both sides of an equation by the LCD is equivalent to multiplying each term of both sides by the LCD:

$$xab \cdot \frac{1}{x} = \frac{1}{b} \cdot xab + \frac{1}{a} \cdot xab$$

$$ab = xa + xb$$

$$ab = (a+b)x \qquad \text{Factor } x \text{ from the right side}$$

$$\frac{ab}{a+b} = x$$

We know we are finished because the variable we were solving for is alone on one side of the equation and does not appear on the other side.

Graphing Rational Functions

In our next example, we investigate the graph of a rational function.

Example 9 Graph the rational function $f(x) = \dfrac{6}{x-2}$.

SOLUTION To find the y-intercept, we let x equal 0.

$$\text{When } x = 0: \qquad y = \frac{6}{0-2} = \frac{6}{-2} = -3 \qquad y\text{-intercept}$$

The graph will not cross the x-axis. If it did, we would have a solution to the equation

$$0 = \frac{6}{x-2}$$

which has no solution because there is no number to divide 6 by to obtain 0.

The graph of our equation is shown in Figure 1 along with a table giving values of x and y that satisfy the equation. Notice that y is undefined when x is 2. This means that the graph will not cross the vertical line $x = 2$. (If it did, there would be a value of y for $x = 2$.) The line $x = 2$ is called a *vertical asymptote* of the graph. The graph will get very close to the vertical asymptote, but will never touch or cross it.

x	y
−4	−1
−1	−2
0	−3
1	−6
2	Undefined
3	6
4	3
5	2

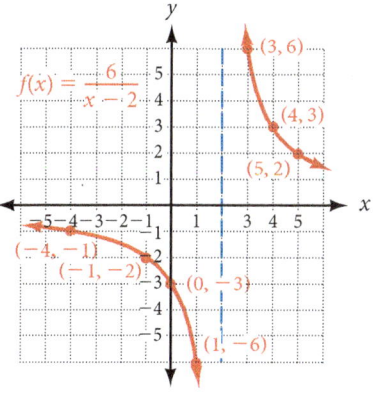

FIGURE 1 *The graph of* $f(x) = \dfrac{6}{x-2}$

If you were to graph $y = \dfrac{6}{x}$ on the coordinate system in Figure 1, you would see that the graph of $y = \dfrac{6}{x-2}$ is the graph of $y = \dfrac{6}{x}$ with all points shifted 2 units to the right.

More About Example 9

We know the graph of $f(x) = \dfrac{6}{x-2}$ will not cross the vertical asymptote $x = 2$ because replacing x with 2 in the equation gives us an undefined expression, meaning there is no value of y to associate with $x = 2$. We can use a graphing calculator to explore the behavior of this function when x gets closer and closer to 2 by using the table function on the calculator. We want to put our own values for X into the table, so we set the independent variable to Ask. (On a TI-82/83, use the TBLSET key to set up the table.) To see how the function behaves as x gets close to 2, we let X take on values of 1.9, 1.99, and 1.999. Then we move to the other side of 2 and let X become 2.1, 2.01, and 2.001.

```
TABLE SETUP
  TblStart = 0
  ΔTbl = 1
Indpnt:  Auto  Ask
Depend:  Auto  Ask
```

```
Plot1  Plot2  Plot3
\Y₁ ■ 6/(X − 2)
\Y₂ =
\Y₃ =
\Y₄ =
\Y₅ =
\Y₆ =
\Y₇ =
```

The table will look like this:

X	Y₁
1.9	−60
1.99	−600
1.999	−6000
2.1	60
2.01	600
2.001	6000

Again, the calculator asks us for a table increment. Because we are inputting the x values ourselves, the increment value does not matter.

As you can see, the values in the table support the shape of the curve in Figure 1 around the vertical asymptote $x = 2$.

Example 10   Graph: $g(x) = \dfrac{6}{x + 2}$

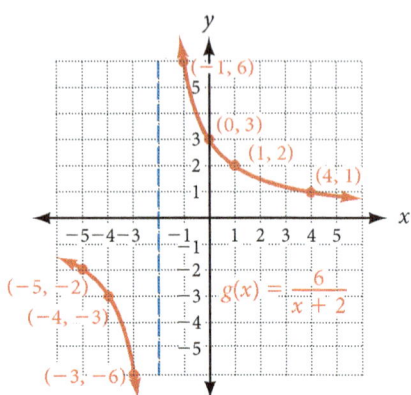

FIGURE 2 *The graph of $g(x) = \dfrac{6}{x + 2}$*

SOLUTION   The only difference between this equation and the equation in Example 9 is in the denominator. This graph will have the same shape as the graph in Example 9, but the vertical asymptote will be $x = -2$ instead of $x = 2$. Figure 2 shows the graph.

Notice that the graphs shown in Figures 1 and 2 are both graphs of functions because no vertical line will cross either graph in more than one place. Notice the similarities and differences in our two functions,

$$f(x) = \frac{6}{x - 2} \qquad \text{and} \qquad g(x) = \frac{6}{x + 2}$$

and their graphs. The vertical asymptotes shown in Figures 1 and 2 correspond to the fact that both $f(2)$ and $g(-2)$ are undefined. The domain for the function f is all real numbers except $x = 2$, while the domain for g is all real numbers except $x = -2$.

Getting Ready for Class

After reading through the preceding section, respond in your own words and in complete sentences.

A. Explain how a least common denominator can be used to simplify an equation.

B. What is an extraneous solution?

C. How does the location of the vertical asymptote in the graph of a rational function relate to the equation of the function?

D. What is the last step in solving an equation that contains rational expressions?

Problem Set 7.5

Solve each of the following equations.

1. $\dfrac{x}{5} + 4 = \dfrac{5}{3}$

2. $\dfrac{x}{5} = \dfrac{x}{2} - 9$

3. $\dfrac{a}{3} + 2 = \dfrac{4}{5}$

4. $\dfrac{a}{4} + \dfrac{1}{2} = \dfrac{2}{3}$

5. $\dfrac{y}{2} + \dfrac{y}{4} + \dfrac{y}{6} = 3$

6. $\dfrac{y}{3} - \dfrac{y}{6} + \dfrac{y}{2} = 1$

7. $\dfrac{5}{2x} = \dfrac{1}{x} + \dfrac{3}{4}$

8. $\dfrac{1}{2a} = \dfrac{2}{a} - \dfrac{3}{8}$

9. $\dfrac{1}{x} = \dfrac{1}{3} - \dfrac{2}{3x}$

10. $\dfrac{5}{2x} = \dfrac{2}{x} - \dfrac{1}{12}$

11. $\dfrac{2x}{x-3} + 2 = \dfrac{2}{x-3}$

12. $\dfrac{2}{x+5} = \dfrac{2}{5} - \dfrac{x}{x+5}$

13. $1 - \dfrac{1}{x} = \dfrac{12}{x^2}$

14. $2 + \dfrac{5}{x} = \dfrac{3}{x^2}$

15. $y - \dfrac{4}{3y} = -\dfrac{1}{3}$

16. $\dfrac{y}{2} - \dfrac{4}{y} = -\dfrac{7}{2}$

17. $\dfrac{x+2}{x+1} = \dfrac{1}{x+1} + 2$

18. $\dfrac{x+6}{x+3} = \dfrac{3}{x+3} + 2$

19. $\dfrac{3}{a-2} = \dfrac{2}{a-3}$

20. $\dfrac{5}{a+1} = \dfrac{4}{a+2}$

21. $6 - \dfrac{5}{x^2} = \dfrac{7}{x}$

22. $10 - \dfrac{3}{x^2} = -\dfrac{1}{x}$

23. $\dfrac{1}{x-1} - \dfrac{1}{x+1} = \dfrac{3x}{x^2-1}$

24. $\dfrac{5}{x-1} + \dfrac{2}{x-1} = \dfrac{4}{x+1}$

25. $\dfrac{2}{x-3} + \dfrac{x}{x^2-9} = \dfrac{4}{x+3}$

26. $\dfrac{2}{x+5} + \dfrac{3}{x+4} = \dfrac{2x}{x^2+9x+20}$

27. $\dfrac{3}{2} - \dfrac{1}{x-4} = \dfrac{-2}{2x-8}$

28. $\dfrac{2}{x} - \dfrac{1}{x+1} = \dfrac{-2}{5x+5}$

29. $\dfrac{t-4}{t^2-3t} = \dfrac{-2}{t^2-9}$

30. $\dfrac{t+3}{t^2-2t} = \dfrac{10}{t^2-4}$

31. $\dfrac{3}{y-4} - \dfrac{2}{y+1} = \dfrac{5}{y^2-3y-4}$

32. $\dfrac{1}{y+2} - \dfrac{2}{y-3} = \dfrac{-2y}{y^2-y-6}$

33. $\dfrac{2}{1+a} = \dfrac{3}{1-a} + \dfrac{5}{a}$

34. $\dfrac{1}{a+3} - \dfrac{a}{a^2-9} = \dfrac{2}{3-a}$

35. $\dfrac{3}{2x-6} - \dfrac{x+1}{4x-12} = 4$

36. $\dfrac{2x-3}{5x+10} + \dfrac{3x-2}{4x+8} = 1$

37. $\dfrac{y+2}{y^2-y} - \dfrac{6}{y^2-1} = 0$

38. $\dfrac{y+3}{y^2-y} - \dfrac{8}{y^2-1} = 0$

39. $\dfrac{4}{2x-6} - \dfrac{12}{4x+12} = \dfrac{12}{x^2-9}$

40. $\dfrac{1}{x+2} + \dfrac{1}{x-2} = \dfrac{4}{x^2-4}$

41. $\dfrac{2}{y^2-7y+12} - \dfrac{1}{y^2-9} = \dfrac{4}{y^2-y-12}$

42. $\dfrac{1}{y^2+5y+4} + \dfrac{3}{y^2-1} = \dfrac{-1}{y^2+3y-4}$

43. Let $f(x) = \dfrac{1}{x-3}$ and $g(x) = \dfrac{1}{x+3}$ and find x if

   a. $f(x) + g(x) = \dfrac{5}{8}$ **b.** $\dfrac{f(x)}{g(x)} = 5$ **c.** $f(x) = g(x)$

44. Let $f(x) = \dfrac{4}{x+2}$ and $g(x) = \dfrac{4}{x-2}$ and find x if

   a. $f(x) - g(x) = -\dfrac{4}{3}$ **b.** $\dfrac{g(x)}{f(x)} = -7$ **c.** $f(x) = -g(x)$

45. Solve each equation.

   a. $6x - 2 = 0$ **b.** $\dfrac{6}{x} - 2 = 0$ **c.** $\dfrac{x}{6} - 2 = -\dfrac{1}{2}$

   d. $\dfrac{6}{x} - 2 = -\dfrac{1}{2}$ **e.** $\dfrac{6}{x^2} + 6 = \dfrac{20}{x}$

46. Solve each equation.

   a. $5x - 2 = 0$ **b.** $5 - \dfrac{2}{x} = 0$ **c.** $\dfrac{x}{2} - 5 = -\dfrac{3}{4}$

   d. $\dfrac{2}{x} - 5 = -\dfrac{3}{4}$ **e.** $-\dfrac{3}{x} + \dfrac{2}{x^2} = 5$

47. Paying Attention to Instructions Work each problem according to the instructions given..

   a. Divide: $\dfrac{6}{x^2 - 2x - 8} \div \dfrac{x+3}{x+2}$

   b. Add: $\dfrac{6}{x^2 - 2x - 8} + \dfrac{x+3}{x+2}$

   c. Solve: $\dfrac{6}{x^2 - 2x - 8} + \dfrac{x+3}{x+2} = 2$

48. Paying Attention to Instructions Work each problem according to the instructions given..

   a. Divide: $\dfrac{-10}{x^2 - 25} \div \dfrac{x-4}{x-5}$

   b. Add: $\dfrac{-10}{x^2 - 25} + \dfrac{x-4}{x-5}$

   c. Solve: $\dfrac{-10}{x^2 - 25} + \dfrac{x-4}{x-5} = \dfrac{4}{5}$

49. Solve $\dfrac{1}{x} = \dfrac{1}{b} - \dfrac{1}{a}$ for x.   **50.** Solve $\dfrac{1}{x} = \dfrac{1}{a} - \dfrac{1}{b}$ for x.

Solve for y.

51. $x = \dfrac{y-3}{y-1}$ **52.** $x = \dfrac{y-2}{y-3}$ **53.** $x = \dfrac{2y+1}{3y+1}$ **54.** $x = \dfrac{3y+2}{5y+1}$

Graph each function. Show the vertical asymptote.

55. $f(x) = \dfrac{1}{x-3}$ **56.** $f(x) = \dfrac{1}{x+3}$ **57.** $f(x) = \dfrac{4}{x+2}$ **58.** $f(x) = \dfrac{4}{x-2}$

59. $g(x) = \dfrac{2}{x-4}$ **60.** $g(x) = \dfrac{2}{x+4}$ **61.** $g(x) = \dfrac{6}{x+1}$ **62.** $g(x) = \dfrac{6}{x-1}$

Applying the Concepts

63. Geometry From plane geometry and the principle of similar triangles, the relationship between y_1, y_2, and h shown in Figure 3 can be expressed as

$$\frac{1}{h} = \frac{1}{y_1} + \frac{1}{y_2}$$

Two poles are 12 feet high and 8 feet high. If a cable is attached to the top of each one and stretched to the bottom of the other, what is the height above the ground at which the two wires will meet?

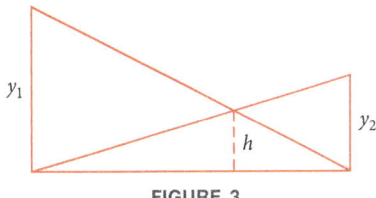

FIGURE 3

64. Kayak Race In a kayak race, the participants must paddle a kayak 450 meters down a river and then return 450 meters up the river to the starting point (Figure 4). Susan has correctly deduced that the total time t (in seconds) depends on the speed c (in meters per second) of the water according to the following expression:

$$t = \frac{450}{v + c} + \frac{450}{v - c}$$

where v is the speed of the kayak relative to the water (the speed of the kayak in still water).

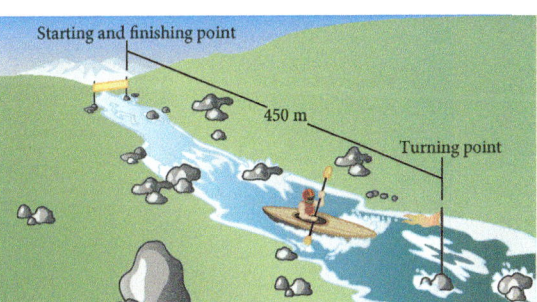

FIGURE 4

a. Fill in the following table.

Time	Speed of Kayak Relative to the Water	Current of the River
t(sec)	v(m/sec)	c(m/sec)
240		1
300		2
	4	3
	3	1
540	3	
	3	3

  b. If the kayak race were conducted in the still waters of a lake, do you think that the total time of a given participant would be greater than, equal to, or smaller than the time in the river? Justify your answer.

  c. Suppose Peter can drive his kayak at 4.1 meters per second and that the speed of the current is 4.1 meters per second. What will happen when Peter makes the turn and tries to come back up the river? How does this situation show up in the equation for total time?

Getting Ready for the Next Section

Multiply.

65. $39.3 \cdot 60$

66. $1{,}100 \cdot 60 \cdot 60$

Divide. Round to the nearest tenth, if necessary.

67. $65{,}000 \div 5{,}280$

68. $3{,}960{,}000 \div 5{,}280$

Multiply.

69. $2x\left(\dfrac{1}{x} + \dfrac{1}{2x}\right)$

70. $3x\left(\dfrac{1}{x} + \dfrac{1}{3x}\right)$

Solve.

71. $12(x + 3) + 12(x - 3) = 3(x^2 - 9)$ **72.** $40 + 2x = 60 - 3x$

73. $\dfrac{1}{10} - \dfrac{1}{12} = \dfrac{1}{x}$

74. $\dfrac{1}{x} + \dfrac{1}{2x} = 2$

Applications

We begin this section with some application problems, the solutions to which involve equations that contain rational expressions. As you will see, the solutions to the examples show only the essential steps from our Blueprint for Problem Solving on page 133. Recall that step 1 was done mentally; we read the problem and mentally list the items that are known and the items that are unknown. This is an essential part of problem solving. Now that you have had experience with application problems, however, you are doing step 1 automatically.

Video Examples

Section 7.6

Example 1   One number is twice another. The sum of their reciprocals is 2. Find the numbers.

SOLUTION   Let x = the smaller number. The larger number is $2x$. Their reciprocals are $\frac{1}{x}$ and $\frac{1}{2x}$. The equation that describes the situation is

$$\frac{1}{x} + \frac{1}{2x} = 2$$

Multiplying both sides by the LCD $2x$, we have

$$2x \cdot \frac{1}{x} + 2x \cdot \frac{1}{2x} = 2x(2)$$

$$2 + 1 = 4x$$

$$3 = 4x$$

$$x = \frac{3}{4}$$

The smaller number is $\frac{3}{4}$. The larger is $2\left(\frac{3}{4}\right) = \frac{6}{4} = \frac{3}{2}$. Adding their reciprocals, we have

$$\frac{4}{3} + \frac{2}{3} = \frac{6}{3} = 2$$

The sum of the reciprocals of $\frac{3}{4}$ and $\frac{3}{2}$ is 2.

Example 2   Two families from the same neighborhood plan a ski trip together. The first family is driving a newer vehicle and makes the 455-mile trip at a speed 5 miles per hour faster than the second family who is traveling in an older vehicle. The second family takes a half-hour longer to make the trip. What are the speeds of the two families?

SOLUTION   The following table will be helpful in finding the equation necessary to solve this problem.

	d(distance)	r(rate)	t(time)
First Family			
Second Family			

If we let x be the speed of the second family, then the speed of the first family will be $x + 5$. Both families travel the same distance of 455 miles. Putting this information into the table we have

	d	r	t
First Family	455	$x + 5$	
Second Family	455	x	

To fill in the last two spaces in the table, we use the relationship $d = r \cdot t$. Since the last column of the table is the time, we solve the equation $d = r \cdot t$ for t and get

$$t = \frac{d}{r}$$

Taking the distance and dividing by the rate (speed) for each family, we complete the table.

	d	r	t
First Family	455	$x + 5$	$\dfrac{455}{x + 5}$
Second Family	455	x	$\dfrac{455}{x}$

Reading the problem again, we find that the time for the second family is longer than the time for the first family by one-half hour. In other words, the time for the second family can be found by adding one-half hour to the time for the first family, or

$$\frac{455}{x + 5} + \frac{1}{2} = \frac{455}{x}$$

Multiplying both sides by the LCD of $2x(x + 5)$ gives

$$2x \cdot (455) + x(x + 5) \cdot 1 = 455 \cdot 2(x + 5)$$

$$910x + x^2 + 5x = 910x + 4550$$

$$x^2 + 5x - 4550 = 0$$

$$(x + 70)(x - 65) = 0$$

$$x = -70 \quad \text{or} \quad x = 65$$

Since we cannot have a negative speed, the only solution is $x = 65$. Then

$$x + 5 = 65 + 5 = 70$$

The speed of the first family is 70 miles per hour, and the speed of the second family is 65 miles per hour.

Example 3   The current of a river is 3 miles per hour. It takes a motorboat a total of 3 hours to travel 12 miles upstream and return 12 miles downstream. What is the speed of the boat in still water?

SOLUTION   This time we let $x =$ the speed of the boat in still water. Then, we fill in as much of the table as possible using the information given in the problem. For instance, because we let $x =$ the speed of the boat in still water, the rate upstream (against the current) must be $x - 3$. The rate downstream (with the current) is $x + 3$.

	d	r	t
Upstream	12	$x - 3$	
Downstream	12	$x + 3$	

The last two boxes can be filled in using the relationship

$$t = \frac{d}{r}$$

	d	r	t
Upstream	12	$x - 3$	$\frac{12}{x - 3}$
Downstream	12	$x + 3$	$\frac{12}{x + 3}$

The total time for the trip up and back is 3 hours:

Time upstream + Time downstream = Total time

$$\frac{12}{x - 3} \quad + \quad \frac{12}{x + 3} \quad = \quad 3$$

Multiplying both sides by $(x - 3)(x + 3)$, we have

$$12(x + 3) + 12(x - 3) = 3(x^2 - 9)$$
$$12x + 36 + 12x - 36 = 3x^2 - 27$$
$$3x^2 - 24x - 27 = 0$$
$$x^2 - 8x - 9 = 0 \qquad \text{Divide both sides by 3}$$
$$(x - 9)(x + 1) = 0$$
$$x = 9 \quad \text{or} \quad x = -1$$

The speed of the motorboat in still water is 9 miles per hour. (We don't use $x = -1$ because the speed of the motorboat cannot be a negative number.)

Example 4 An inlet pipe can fill a pool in 10 hours, while the drain can empty it in 12 hours. If the pool is empty and both the inlet pipe and drain are open, how long will it take to fill the pool?

10 hours to fill pool

12 hours to empty pool

SOLUTION It is helpful to think in terms of how much work is done by each pipe in 1 hour.

Let x = the time it takes to fill the pool with both pipes open.

If the inlet pipe can fill the pool in 10 hours, then in 1 hour it is $\frac{1}{10}$ full. If the outlet pipe empties the pool in 12 hours, then in 1 hour it is $\frac{1}{12}$ empty. If the pool can be filled in x hours with both the inlet pipe and the drain open, then in 1 hour it is $\frac{1}{x}$ full when both pipes are open.

Here is the equation:

In 1 hour

$$\begin{bmatrix} \text{Amount filled} \\ \text{by inlet pipe} \end{bmatrix} - \begin{bmatrix} \text{Amount emptied} \\ \text{by the drain} \end{bmatrix} = \begin{bmatrix} \text{Fraction of pool} \\ \text{filled with both pipes} \end{bmatrix}$$

$$\frac{1}{10} \quad - \quad \frac{1}{12} \quad = \quad \frac{1}{x}$$

Multiplying through by $60x$, we have

$$60x \cdot \frac{1}{10} - 60x \cdot \frac{1}{12} = 60x \cdot \frac{1}{x}$$

$$6x - 5x = 60$$

$$x = 60$$

It takes 60 hours to fill the pool if both the inlet pipe and the drain are open.

More About Graphing Rational Functions

We continue our investigation of the graphs of rational functions by considering the graph of a rational function with binomials in the numerator and denominator.

Example 5   Graph the rational function $y = \dfrac{x-4}{x-2}$.

SOLUTION   In addition to making a table to find some points on the graph, we can analyze the graph as follows:

1. The graph will have a y-intercept of 2, because when $x = 0$, $y = \dfrac{-4}{-2} = 2$.

2. To find the x-intercept, we let $y = 0$ to get

$$0 = \frac{x-4}{x-2}$$

   The only way this expression can be 0 is if the numerator is 0, which happens when $x = 4$. (If you want to solve this equation, multiply both sides by $x - 2$. You will get the same solution, $x = 4$.)

3. The graph will have a vertical asymptote at $x = 2$, because $x = 2$ will make the denominator of the function 0, meaning y is undefined when x is 2.

4. The graph will have a *horizontal asymptote* at $y = 1$ because for very large values of x, $\frac{x-4}{x-2}$ is very close to 1. The larger x is, the closer $\frac{x-4}{x-2}$ is to 1. The same is true for very small values of x, such as $-1{,}000$ and $-10{,}000$.

Putting this information together with the ordered pairs in the table next to the figure, we have the graph shown in Figure 1.

x	y
-1	$\frac{5}{3}$
0	2
1	3
2	Undefined
3	-1
4	0
5	$\frac{1}{3}$

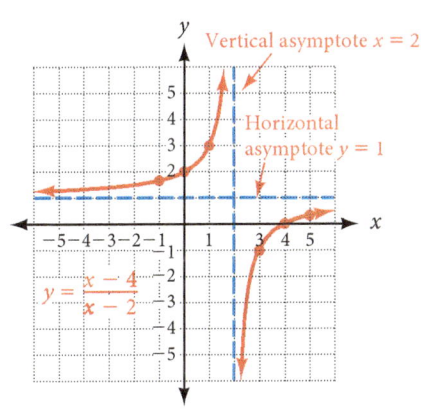

FIGURE 1

More About Example 5

In the previous section, we used technology to explore the graph of a rational function around a vertical asymptote. This time, we are going to explore the graph near the horizontal asymptote. In Figure 1, the horizontal asymptote is at $y = 1$. To show that the graph approaches this line as x becomes very large, we use the table function on our graphing calculator, with X taking values of 100, 1,000, and 10,000. To show that the graph approaches the line $y = 1$ on the left side of the coordinate system, we let X become -100, $-1,000$ and $-10,000$.

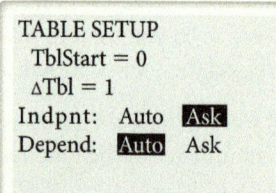

TABLE SETUP
TblStart = 0
ΔTbl = 1
Indpnt: Auto **Ask**
Depend: **Auto** Ask

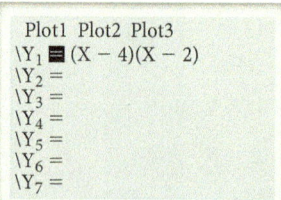

Plot1 Plot2 Plot3
\Y₁ ■ (X − 4)(X − 2)
\Y₂ =
\Y₃ =
\Y₄ =
\Y₅ =
\Y₆ =
\Y₇ =

The table will look like this:

X	Y_1	
100	.97959	
1000	.998	
10000	.9998	
−100	1.0196	
−1000	1.002	
−100000	1.0002	

As you can see, as x becomes very large in the positive direction, the graph approaches the line $y = 1$ from below. As x becomes very small in the negative direction, the graph approaches the line $y = 1$ from above.

Getting Ready for Class

After reading through the preceding section, respond in your own words and in complete sentences.

A. Briefly list the steps in the Blueprint for Problem Solving that you have used previously to solve application problems.

B. Write an application problem for which the solution depends on solving the equation $\frac{1}{2} + \frac{1}{3} = \frac{1}{x}$.

C. One number is twice another, write an expression for the sum of their reciprocals.

D. Write a formula for the relationship between distance, rate, and time.

Problem Set 7.6

Solve the following word problems. Be sure to show the equation in each case.

Number Problems

1. One number is 3 times another. The sum of their reciprocals is $\frac{20}{3}$. Find the numbers.

2. One number is 3 times another. The sum of their reciprocals is $\frac{4}{9}$. Find the numbers.

3. The sum of a number and its reciprocal is $\frac{10}{3}$. Find the number.

4. The sum of a number and twice its reciprocal is $\frac{27}{5}$. Find the number.

5. The sum of the reciprocals of two consecutive integers is $\frac{7}{12}$. Find the two integers.

6. Find two consecutive even integers, the sum of whose reciprocals is $\frac{3}{4}$.

7. If a certain number is added to the numerator and denominator of $\frac{7}{9}$, the result is $\frac{5}{6}$. Find the number.

8. Find the number you would add to both the numerator and denominator of $\frac{8}{11}$ so that the result would be $\frac{6}{7}$.

9. The speed of a boat in still water is 5 miles per hour. If the boat travels 3 miles downstream in the same amount of time it takes to travel 1.5 miles upstream, what is the speed of the current?

   a. Let x be the speed of the current. Complete the distance and rate columns in the table.

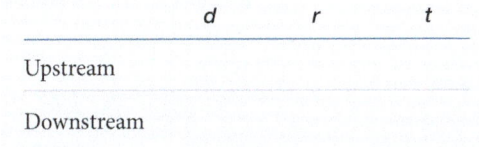

	d	r	t
Upstream			
Downstream			

   b. Now use the distance and rate information to complete the time column.
   c. What does the problem tell us about the two times? Use this fact to write an equation involving the two expressions for time.
   d. Solve the equation. Write your answer as a complete sentence.

10. A boat, which moves at 18 miles per hour in still water, travels 14 miles downstream in the same amount of time it takes to travel 10 miles upstream. Find the speed of the current.

    a. Let x be the speed of the current. Complete the distance and rate columns in the table.

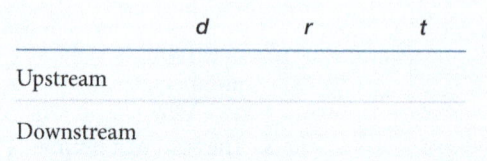

	d	r	t
Upstream			
Downstream			

    b. Now use the distance and rate information to complete the time column.

    c. What does the problem tell us about the two times? Use this fact to write an equation involving the two expressions for time.

    d. Solve the equation. Write your answer as a complete sentence.

Rate Problems

11. The current of a river is 2 miles per hour. A boat travels to a point 8 miles upstream and back again in 3 hours. What is the speed of the boat in still water?

12. A motorboat travels at 4 miles per hour in still water. It goes 12 miles upstream and 12 miles back again in a total of 8 hours. Find the speed of the current of the river.

13. Train A has a speed 15 miles per hour greater than that of train B. If train A travels 150 miles in the same time train B travels 120 miles, what are the speeds of the two trains?

    a. Let x be the speed of the train B. Complete the distance and rate columns in the table.

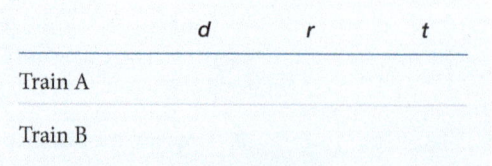

	d	r	t
Train A			
Train B			

    b. Now use the distance and rate information to complete the time column.

    c. What does the problem tell us about the two times? Use this fact to write an equation involving the two expressions for time.

    d. Solve the equation. Write your answer as a complete sentence.

14. A train travels 30 miles per hour faster than a car. If the train covers 120 miles in the same time the car covers 80 miles, what are the speeds of each of them?

  a. Let x be the speed of the car. Complete the distance and rate columns in the table.

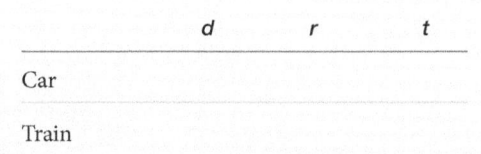

	d	r	t
Car			
Train			

  b. Now use the distance and rate information to complete the time column.

  c. What does the problem tell us about the two times? Use this fact to write an equation involving the two expressions for time.

  d. Solve the equation. Write your answer as a complete sentence.

15. A small airplane flies 810 miles from Los Angeles to Portland, OR, with an average speed of 270 miles per hour. An hour and a half after the plane leaves, a Boeing 747 leaves Los Angeles for Portland. Both planes arrive in Portland at the same time. What was the average speed of the 747?

16. Lou leaves for a cross-country excursion on a bicycle traveling at 20 miles per hour. His friends are driving the trip and will meet him at several rest stops along the way. The first stop is scheduled 30 miles from the original starting point. If the people driving leave 15 minutes after Lou from the same place, how fast will they have to drive to reach the first rest stop at the same time as Lou?

17. A tour bus leaves Sacramento every Friday evening at 5:00 P.M. for a 270-mile trip to Las Vegas. This week, however, the bus leaves at 5:30 P.M. To arrive in Las Vegas on time, the driver drives 6 miles per hour faster than usual. What is the bus' usual speed?

18. A bakery delivery truck leaves the bakery at 5:00 A.M. each morning on its 140-mile route. One day the driver gets a late start and does not leave the bakery until 5:30 A.M. To finish her route on time the driver drives 5 miles per hour faster than usual. At what speed does she usually drive?

Work Problems

19. A water tank can be filled by an inlet pipe in 8 hours. It takes twice that long for the outlet pipe to empty the tank. How long will it take to fill the tank if both pipes are open?

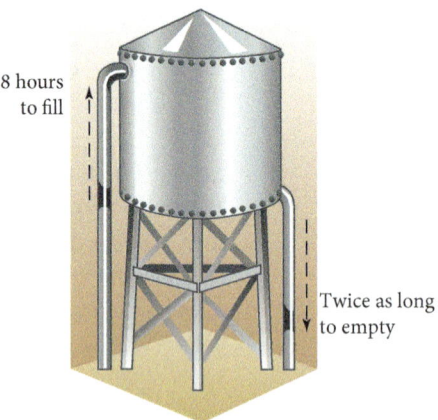

8 hours to fill

Twice as long to empty

20. A sink can be filled from the faucet in 5 minutes. It takes only 3 minutes to empty the sink when the drain is open. If the sink is full and both the faucet and the drain are open, how long will it take to empty the sink?

21. It takes 10 hours to fill a pool with the inlet pipe. It can be emptied in 15 hours with the outlet pipe. If the pool is half full to begin with, how long will it take to fill it from there if both pipes are open?

10 hours to fill pool

15 hours to empty pool

22. A sink is one-quarter full when both the faucet and the drain are opened. The faucet alone can fill the sink in 6 minutes, while it takes 8 minutes to empty it with the drain. How long will it take to fill the remaining three quarters of the sink?

23. A sink has two faucets: one for hot water and one for cold water. The sink can be filled by a cold water faucet in 3.5 minutes. If both faucets are open, the sink is filled in 2.1 minutes. How long does it take to fill the sink with just the hot water faucet open?

24. A water tank is being filled by two inlet pipes. Pipe A can fill the tank in $4\frac{1}{2}$ hours, but both pipes together can fill the tank in 2 hours. How long does it take to fill the tank using only pipe B?

Miscellaneous Problems

25. Rhind Papyrus Nearly 4,000 years ago, Egyptians worked mathematical exercises involving reciprocals. The *Rhind Papyrus* contains a wealth of such problems, and one of them is as follows:

> "A quantity and its two thirds are added together, one third of this is added, then one third of the sum is taken, and the result is 10."

Write an equation and solve this exercise.

26. Photography For clear photographs, a camera must be properly focused. Professional photographers use a mathematical relationship relating the distance from the camera lens to the object being photographed, *a*; the distance from the lens to the film, *b*; and the focal length of the lens, *f*. These quantities, *a*, *b*, and *f*, are related by the equation

$$\frac{1}{a} + \frac{1}{b} = \frac{1}{f}$$

A camera has a focal length of 3 inches. If the lens is 5 inches from the film, how far should the lens be placed from the object being photographed for the camera to be perfectly focused?

The Periodic Table If you take a chemistry class, you will work with the Periodic Table of Elements. Figure 3 shows three of the elements listed in the periodic table. As you can see, the bottom number in each figure is the molecular weight of the element. In chemistry, a mole is the amount of a substance that will give the weight in grams equal to the molecular weight. For example, 1 mole of lead is 207.2 grams.

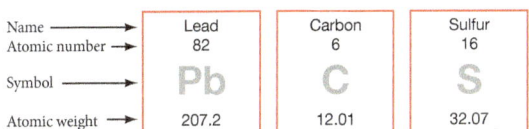

FIGURE 3

27. Chemistry For the element carbon, 1 mole = 12.01 grams.

a. To the nearest gram, how many grams of carbon are in 2.5 moles of carbon?

b. How many moles of carbon are in 39 grams of carbon? Round to the nearest hundredth.

28. Chemistry For the element sulfur, 1 mole = 32.07 grams.

a. How many grams of sulfur are in 3 moles of sulfur?

b. How many moles of sulfur are found in 80.2 grams of sulfur?

Graph each rational function. In each case, show the vertical asymptote, the horizontal asymptote, and any intercepts that exist.

29. $f(x) = \dfrac{x-3}{x-1}$

30. $f(x) = \dfrac{x+4}{x-2}$

31. $f(x) = \dfrac{x+3}{x-1}$

32. $f(x) = \dfrac{x-2}{x-1}$

33. $g(x) = \dfrac{x-3}{x+1}$

34. $g(x) = \dfrac{x-2}{x+1}$

Getting Ready for the Next Section

Divide.

35. $\dfrac{10x^2}{5x^2}$

36. $\dfrac{-15x^4}{5x^2}$

37. $\dfrac{4x^4y^3}{-2x^2y}$

38. $\dfrac{10a^4b^2}{4a^2b^2}$

39. $4{,}628 \div 25$

40. $7{,}546 \div 35$

Multiply.

41. $2x^2(2x - 4)$

42. $3x^2(x - 2)$

43. $(2x - 4)(2x^2 + 4x + 5)$

44. $(x - 2)(3x^2 + 6x + 15)$

Subtract.

45. $(2x^2 - 7x + 9) - (2x^2 - 4x)$

46. $(x^2 - 6xy - 7y^2) - (x^2 + xy)$

Factor.

47. $x^2 - a^2$

48. $x^2 - 1$

49. $x^2 - 6xy - 7y^2$

50. $2x^2 - 5xy + 3y^2$

Division of Polynomials

First Bank of San Luis Obispo charges $2.00 per month and $0.15 per check for a regular checking account. So, if you write x checks in one month, the total monthly cost of the checking account will be $C(x) = 2.00 + 0.15x$. From this formula, we see that the more checks we write in a month, the more we pay for the account. But it is also true that the more checks we write in a month, the lower the cost per check. To find the cost per check, we use the *average cost* function. To find the average cost function, we divide the total cost by the number of checks written.

$$\text{Average Cost} = \overline{C}(x) = \frac{C(x)}{x} = \frac{2.00 + 0.15x}{x}$$

This last expression gives us the average cost per check for each of the x checks written. To work with this last expression, we need to know something about division with polynomials, and that is what we will cover in this section.

We begin this section by considering division of a polynomial by a monomial. This is the simplest kind of polynomial division. The rest of the section is devoted to division of a polynomial by a polynomial. This kind of division is similar to long division with whole numbers.

Dividing a Polynomial by a Monomial

To divide a polynomial by a monomial, we use the definition of division and apply the distributive property. The following example illustrates the procedure.

Video Examples

Section 7.7

Example 1 Divide $\dfrac{10x^5 - 15x^4 + 20x^3}{5x^2}$.

SOLUTION

$$= (10x^5 - 15x^4 + 20x^3) \cdot \frac{1}{5x^2}$$

Dividing by $5x^2$ is the same as multiplying by $\frac{1}{5x^2}$

$$= 10x^5 \cdot \frac{1}{5x^2} - 15x^4 \cdot \frac{1}{5x^2} + 20x^3 \cdot \frac{1}{5x^2}$$

Distributive property

$$= \frac{10x^5}{5x^2} - \frac{15x^4}{5x^2} + \frac{20x^3}{5x^2}$$

Multiplying by $\frac{1}{5x^2}$ is the same as dividing by $5x^2$

$$= 2x^3 - 3x^2 + 4x$$

Notice that division of a polynomial by a monomial is accomplished by dividing each term of the polynomial by the monomial. The first two steps are usually not shown in a problem like this. They are part of Example 1 to justify distributing $5x^2$ under all three terms of the polynomial $10x^5 - 15x^4 + 20x^3$.

Here are some more examples of this kind of division.

Example 2 Divide $\dfrac{8x^3y^5 - 16x^2y^2 + 4x^4y^3}{-2x^2y}$. Write the result with positive exponents.

SOLUTION

$$\frac{8x^3y^5 - 16x^2y^2 + 4x^4y^3}{-2x^2y} = \frac{8x^3y^5}{-2x^2y} + \frac{-16x^2y^2}{-2x^2y} + \frac{4x^4y^3}{-2x^2y}$$

$$= -4xy^4 + 8y - 2x^2y^2$$

Example 3   Divide $\dfrac{10a^4b^2 + 8ab^3 - 12a^3b + 6ab}{4a^2b^2}$. Write the result with positive exponents.

SOLUTION

$$\frac{10a^4b^2 + 8ab^3 - 12a^3b + 6ab}{4a^2b^2} = \frac{10a^4b^2}{4a^2b^2} + \frac{8ab^3}{4a^2b^2} - \frac{12a^3b}{4a^2b^2} + \frac{6ab}{4a^2b^2}$$

$$= \frac{5a^2}{2} + \frac{2b}{a} - \frac{3a}{b} + \frac{3}{2ab}$$

Notice in Example 3 that the result is not a polynomial because of the last three terms. If we were to write each as a product, some of the variables would have negative exponents. For example, the second term would be

$$\frac{2b}{a} = 2a^{-1}b$$

The divisor in each of the preceding examples was a monomial. We now want to turn our attention to division of polynomials in which the divisor has two or more terms.

Dividing a Polynomial by a Polynomial

Example 4   Divide: $\dfrac{x^2 - 6xy - 7y^2}{x + y}$

SOLUTION   In this case, we can factor the numerator and perform division by simply dividing out common factors, just like we did in previous sections:

$$\frac{x^2 - 6xy - 7y^2}{x + y} = \frac{(x + y)(x - 7y)}{x + y}$$

$$= x - 7y$$

Long Division

For the type of division shown in Example 4, the denominator must be a factor of the numerator. When the denominator is not a factor of the numerator, or in the case where we can't factor the numerator, the method used in Example 4 won't work. We need to develop a new method for these cases. Because this new method is very similar to *long division* with whole numbers, we will review the method of long division here.

Example 5   Divide $25\overline{)4{,}628}$.

SOLUTION

$$
\begin{array}{r}
1 \\
25\overline{)4{,}628} \\
\underline{25} \\
21
\end{array}
$$
     Estimate 25 into 46.

     Multiply 1 × 25 = 25

     Subtract 46 − 25 = 21

$$
\begin{array}{r}
1 \\
25\overline{)4{,}628} \\
\underline{25\downarrow} \\
212
\end{array}
$$
     Bring down the 2.

These are the four basic steps in long division: estimate, multiply, subtract, and bring down the next term. To complete the problem, we simply perform the same four steps:

$$
\begin{array}{r}
18 \\
25\overline{)4{,}628} \\
25 \\
\hline
2\,12 \\
2\,00\downarrow \\
\hline
128
\end{array}
$$

8 is the estimate

Multiply to get 200
Subtract to get 12, then bring down the 8

One more time:

$$
\begin{array}{r}
185 \\
25\overline{)4{,}628} \\
25 \\
\hline
2\,12 \\
2\,00\downarrow \\
\hline
128 \\
125 \\
\hline
3
\end{array}
$$

5 is the estimate

Multiply to get 125
Subtract to get 3

Because 3 is less than 25 and we have no more terms to bring down, we have our answer:

$$\frac{4{,}628}{25} = 185 + \frac{3}{25}$$

To check our answer, we multiply 185 by 25 and then add 3 to the result:

$$25(185) + 3 = 4{,}625 + 3 = 4{,}628$$

Long division with polynomials is similar to long division with whole numbers. Both use the same four basic steps: estimate, multiply, subtract, and bring down the next term. We use long division with polynomials when the denominator has two or more terms and is not a factor of the numerator. Here is an example.

Example 6   Divide $\dfrac{2x^2 - 7x + 9}{x - 2}$.

SOLUTION

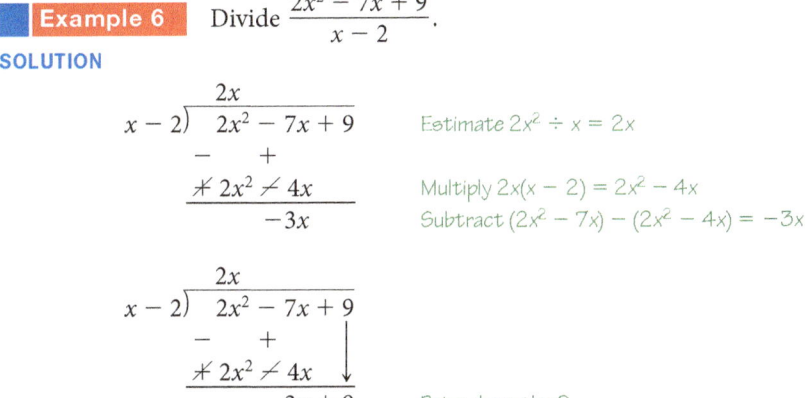

Notice we change the signs on $2x^2 - 4x$ and add in the subtraction step. Subtracting a polynomial is equivalent to adding its opposite.

We repeat the four steps.

$$
\begin{array}{r}
2x - 3 \\
x - 2 \overline{\smash{)}\; 2x^2 - 7x + 9} \\
\end{array}
$$

−3 is the estimate: −3x ÷ x = −3

$$
\begin{array}{r}
\underline{\;\;-\;\;\;\;\;\;+\;\;\;\;} \\
\cancel{2x^2}\; \cancel{4x} \\
\underline{-3x + 9} \\
\underline{\;\;+\;\;\;\;\;\;-\;\;} \\
\cancel{3x}\;\cancel{6} \\
3
\end{array}
$$

Multiply −3(x − 2) = −3x + 6
Subtract (−3x + 9) − (−3x + 6) = 3

Because we have no other term to bring down, we have our answer:

$$\frac{2x^2 - 7x + 9}{x - 2} = 2x - 3 + \frac{3}{x - 2}$$

To check, we multiply $(2x - 3)(x - 2)$ to get $2x^2 - 7x + 6$; then, adding the remainder 3 to this result, we have $2x^2 - 7x + 9$.

In setting up a division problem involving two polynomials, we must remember two things: (1) Both polynomials should be in decreasing powers of the variable, and (2) neither should skip any powers from the highest power down to the constant term. If there are any missing terms, they can be filled in using a coefficient of 0.

Example 7   Divide $2x - 4 \overline{\smash{)}\; 4x^3 - 6x - 11}$.

SOLUTION   Because the trinomial is missing a term in x^2, we can fill it in with $0x^2$:
$$4x^3 - 6x - 11 = 4x^3 + 0x^2 - 6x - 11$$

Adding $0x^2$ does not change our original problem.

> *Note*   Adding the $0x^2$ term gives us a column in which to write $-8x^2$.

$$
\begin{array}{r}
2x^2 + 4x + \;\;\;5 \\
2x - 4 \overline{\smash{)}\; 4x^3 + 0x^2 - \;\;\;6x - 11} \\
\underline{\;\;-\;\;\;\;\;\;\;\;+\;\;\;\;\;\;\;\;\;\;} \\
\cancel{4x^3}\;\cancel{8x^2} \\
\underline{+ 8x^2 - \;\;\;6x} \\
\underline{\;\;-\;\;\;\;\;\;\;+\;\;\;\;\;} \\
\cancel{8x^2}\;\cancel{16x} \\
\underline{+ 10x - 11} \\
\underline{\;\;-\;\;\;\;\;\;\;+\;\;} \\
\cancel{10x}\;\cancel{20} \\
+ \;\;9
\end{array}
$$

$$\frac{4x^3 - 6x - 11}{2x - 4} = 2x^2 + 4x + 5 + \frac{9}{2x - 4}$$

To check this result, we multiply $2x - 4$ and $2x^2 + 4x + 5$:

$$
\begin{array}{r}
2x^2 + 4x + \;\;5 \\
\times \;\;\;\;\;\;2x - \;\;4 \\
\hline
4x^3 + 8x^2 + 10x \\
\underline{+ \;\;\;- 8x^2 - 16x - 20} \\
4x^3 \;\;\;\;\;\;\;\;\;\;\;- 6x - 20
\end{array}
$$

Adding 9 (the remainder) to this result gives us the polynomial $4x^3 - 6x - 11$. Our answer checks.

For our next example, let's do Example 4 again, but this time use long division.

Example 8 Divide $\dfrac{x^2 - 6xy - 7y^2}{x + y}$.

SOLUTION

$$
\begin{array}{r}
x \;\; - 7y \\
x + y \overline{)\; x^2 - 6xy - 7y^2} \\
\underline{\cancel{+}\, x^2 \,\cancel{+}\; xy} \\
- 7xy - 7y^2 \\
\underline{+ \qquad +} \\
- 7xy - 7y^2 \\
0
\end{array}
$$

In this case, the remainder is 0, and we have

$$
\frac{x^2 - 6xy - 7y^2}{x + y} = x - 7y
$$

which is easy to check because

$$
(x + y)(x - 7y) = x^2 - 6xy - 7y^2
$$

Example 9 Factor $x^3 + 9x^2 + 26x + 24$ completely if $x + 2$ is one of its factors.

SOLUTION Because $x + 2$ is one of the factors of the polynomial we are trying to factor, it must divide that polynomial evenly — that is, without a remainder. Therefore, we begin by dividing the polynomial by $x + 2$:

$$
\begin{array}{r}
x^2 + 7x \; + 12 \\
x + 2 \overline{)\; x^3 + 9x^2 + 26x + 24} \\
\underline{\cancel{+}\, x^3 \,\cancel{+}\, 2x^2} \\
+ 7x^2 + 26x \\
\underline{\cancel{+}\, 7x^2 \,\cancel{+}\, 14x} \\
+ 12x + 24 \\
\underline{\cancel{+}\, 12x \,\cancel{+}\, 24} \\
0
\end{array}
$$

Now we know that the polynomial we are trying to factor is equal to the product of $x + 2$ *and* $x^2 + 7x + 12$. To factor completely, we simply factor $x^2 + 7x + 12$:

$$
x^3 + 9x^2 + 26x + 24 = (x + 2)(x^2 + 7x + 12)
$$

$$
= (x + 2)(x + 3)(x + 4)
$$

Getting Ready for Class

After reading through the preceding section, respond in your own words and in complete sentences.

A. What are the four steps used in long division with polynomials?

B. What does it mean to have a remainder of 0?

C. When must long division be performed, and when can factoring be used to divide polynomials?

D. What property of real numbers is the key to dividing a polynomial by a monomial?

Find the following quotients.

1. $\dfrac{4x^3 - 8x^2 + 6x}{2x}$

2. $\dfrac{6x^3 + 12x^2 - 9x}{3x}$

3. $\dfrac{10x^4 + 15x^3 - 20x^2}{-5x^2}$

4. $\dfrac{12x^5 - 18x^4 - 6x^3}{6x^3}$

5. $\dfrac{8y^5 + 10y^3 - 6y}{4y^3}$

6. $\dfrac{6y^4 - 3y^3 + 18y^2}{9y^2}$

7. $\dfrac{5x^3 - 8x^2 - 6x}{-2x^2}$

8. $\dfrac{-9x^5 + 10x^3 - 12x}{-6x^4}$

9. $\dfrac{28a^3b^5 + 42a^4b^3}{7a^2b^2}$

10. $\dfrac{a^2b + ab^2}{ab}$

11. $\dfrac{10x^3y^2 - 20x^2y^3 - 30x^3y^3}{-10x^2y}$

12. $\dfrac{9x^4y^4 + 18x^3y^4 - 27x^2y^4}{-9xy^3}$

Divide by factoring numerators and then dividing out common factors.

13. $\dfrac{x^2 - x - 6}{x - 3}$

14. $\dfrac{x^2 - x - 6}{x + 2}$

15. $\dfrac{2a^2 - 3a - 9}{2a + 3}$

16. $\dfrac{2a^2 + 3a - 9}{2a - 3}$

17. $\dfrac{5x^2 - 14xy - 24y^2}{x - 4y}$

18. $\dfrac{5x^2 - 26xy - 24y^2}{5x + 4y}$

19. $\dfrac{x^3 - y^3}{x - y}$

20. $\dfrac{x^3 + 8}{x + 2}$

21. $\dfrac{y^4 - 16}{y - 2}$

22. $\dfrac{y^4 - 81}{y - 3}$

23. $\dfrac{x^3 + 2x^2 - 25x - 50}{x - 5}$

24. $\dfrac{x^3 + 2x^2 - 25x - 50}{x + 5}$

25. $\dfrac{4x^3 + 12x^2 - 9x - 27}{x + 3}$

26. $\dfrac{9x^3 + 18x^2 - 4x - 8}{x + 2}$

Divide using the long division method.

27. $\dfrac{x^2 - 5x - 7}{x + 2}$

28. $\dfrac{x^2 + 4x - 8}{x - 3}$

29. $\dfrac{6x^2 + 7x - 18}{3x - 4}$

30. $\dfrac{8x^2 - 26x - 9}{2x - 7}$

31. $\dfrac{2x^3 - 3x^2 - 4x + 5}{x + 1}$

32. $\dfrac{3x^3 - 5x^2 + 2x - 1}{x - 2}$

33. $\dfrac{2y^3 - 9y^2 - 17y + 39}{2y - 3}$

34. $\dfrac{3y^3 - 19y^2 + 17y + 4}{3y - 4}$

35. $\dfrac{2x^3 - 9x^2 + 11x - 6}{2x^2 - 3x + 2}$

36. $\dfrac{6x^3 + 7x^2 - x + 3}{3x^2 - x + 1}$

37. $\dfrac{6y^3 - 8y + 5}{2y - 4}$

38. $\dfrac{9y^3 - 6y^2 + 8}{3y - 3}$

39. $\dfrac{a^4 - 2a + 5}{a - 2}$

40. $\dfrac{a^4 + a^3 - 1}{a + 2}$

41. $\dfrac{y^4 - 16}{y - 2}$

42. $\dfrac{y^4 - 81}{y - 3}$

43. $\dfrac{x^4 + x^3 - 3x^2 - x + 2}{x^2 + 3x + 2}$

44. $\dfrac{2x^4 + x^3 + 4x - 3}{2x^2 - x + 3}$

45. Factor $x^3 + 6x^2 + 11x + 6$ completely if one of its factors is $x + 3$.

46. Factor $x^3 + 10x^2 + 29x + 20$ completely if one of its factors is $x + 4$.

47. Factor $x^3 + 5x^2 - 2x - 24$ completely if one of its factors is $x + 3$.

48. Factor $x^3 + 3x^2 - 10x - 24$ completely if one of its factors is $x + 2$.

49. Problems 21 and 41 are the same problem. Are the two answers you obtained equivalent?

50. Problems 22 and 42 are the same problem. Are the two answers you obtained equivalent?

51. Find $P(-2)$ if $P(x) = x^2 - 5x - 7$. Compare it with the remainder in Problem 27.

52. Find $P(3)$ if $P(x) = x^2 + 4x - 8$. Compare it with the remainder in Problem 28.

Applying the Concepts

53. The Factor Theorem The factor theorem of algebra states that if $x - a$ is a factor of a polynomial, $P(x)$, then $P(a) = 0$. Verify the following.
   a. That $x - 2$ is a factor of $P(x) = x^3 - 3x^2 + 5x - 6$, and that $P(2) = 0$
   b. That $x - 5$ is a factor of $P(x) = x^4 - 5x^3 - x^2 + 6x - 5$, and that $P(5) = 0$

54. The Remainder Theorem The remainder theorem of algebra states that if a polynomial, $P(x)$, is divided by $x - a$, then the remainder is $P(a)$. Verify the remainder theorem by showing that when $P(x) = x^2 - x + 3$ is divided by $x - 2$ the remainder is 5, and that $P(2) = 5$.

55. Checking Account First Bank of San Luis Obispo charges $2.00 per month and $0.15 per check for a regular checking account. As we mentioned in the introduction to this section, the total monthly cost of this account is $C(x) = 2.00 + 0.15x$. To find the average cost of each of the x checks, we divide the total cost by the number of checks written. That is,

$$\overline{C}(x) = \frac{C(x)}{x}$$

   a. Use the total cost function to fill in the following table.

x	1	5	10	15	20
$C(x)$					

   b. Find the formula for the average cost function, $\overline{C}(x)$.
   c. Use the average cost function to fill in the following table.

x	1	5	10	15	20
$\overline{C}(x)$					

   d. What happens to the average cost as more checks are written?
   e. Give the domain and range of each of the functions.

56. **Average Cost** A company that manufactures computer diskettes uses the function $C(x) = 200 + 2x$ to represent the daily cost of producing x diskettes.

a. Find the average cost function, $\overline{C}(x)$.

b. Use the average cost function to fill in the following table:

x	1	5	10	15	20
$\overline{C}(x)$					

c. What happens to the average cost as more items are produced?

d. Graph the function $y = \overline{C}(x)$ for $x > 0$.

e. What is the domain of this function?

f. What is the range of this function?

57. **Average Cost** For long distance service, a particular phone company charges a monthly fee of $4.95 plus $0.07 per minute of calling time used. The relationship between the number of minutes of calling time used, m, and the amount of the monthly phone bill $T(m)$ is given by the function $T(m) = 4.95 + 0.07m$.

a. Find the total cost when 100, 400, and 500 minutes of calling time is used in 1 month.

b. Find a formula for the average cost per minute function $\overline{T}(m)$.

c. Find the average cost per minute of calling time used when 100, 400, and 500 minutes are used in 1 month.

58. **Average Cost** A company manufactures electric pencil sharpeners. Each month they have fixed costs of $40,000 and variable costs of $8.50 per sharpener. Therefore, the total monthly cost to manufacture x sharpeners is given by the function $C(x) = 40,000 + 8.5x$.

a. Find the total cost to manufacture 1,000, 5,000, and 10,000 sharpeners a month.

b. Write an expression for the average cost per sharpener function $\overline{C}(x)$.

c. Find the average cost per sharpener to manufacture 1,000, 5,000, and 10,000 sharpeners per month.

Maintaining Your Skills

Reviewing these problems will help clarify the different methods we have used in this chapter.

Perform the indicated operations.

59. $\dfrac{2a + 10}{a^3} \cdot \dfrac{a^2}{3a + 15}$

60. $\dfrac{4a + 8}{a^2 - a - 6} \div \dfrac{a^2 + 7a + 12}{a^2 - 9}$

61. $(x^2 - 9)\left(\dfrac{x + 2}{x + 3}\right)$

62. $\dfrac{1}{x + 4} + \dfrac{8}{x^2 - 16}$

63. $\dfrac{2x - 7}{x - 2} - \dfrac{x - 5}{x - 2}$

64. $2 + \dfrac{25}{5x - 1}$

Simplify each expression.

65. $\dfrac{\dfrac{1}{x} - \dfrac{1}{3}}{\dfrac{1}{x} + \dfrac{1}{3}}$

66. $\dfrac{1 - \dfrac{9}{x^2}}{1 - \dfrac{1}{x} - \dfrac{6}{x^2}}$

Solve each equation.

67. $\dfrac{x}{x - 3} + \dfrac{3}{2} = \dfrac{3}{x - 3}$

68. $1 - \dfrac{3}{x} = \dfrac{-2}{x^2}$

Chapter 7 Summary

Rational Numbers and Expressions [7.1]

1. $\frac{3}{4}$ is a rational number. $\frac{x-3}{x^2-9}$ is a rational expression.

A *rational number* is any number that can be expressed as the ratio of two integers:

$$\text{Rational numbers} = \left\{ \frac{a}{b} \,\middle|\, a \text{ and } b \text{ are integers, } b \neq 0 \right\}$$

A *rational expression* is any quantity that can be expressed as the ratio of two polynomials:

$$\text{Rational expressions} = \left\{ \frac{P}{Q} \,\middle|\, P \text{ and } Q \text{ are polynomials, } Q \neq 0 \right\}$$

Properties of Rational Expressions [7.1]

If P, Q, and K are polynomials with $Q \neq 0$ and $K \neq 0$, then

$$\frac{P}{Q} = \frac{PK}{QK} \qquad \text{and} \qquad \frac{P}{Q} = \frac{\frac{P}{K}}{\frac{Q}{K}}$$

which is to say that multiplying or dividing the numerator and denominator of a rational expression by the same nonzero quantity always produces an equivalent rational expression.

Reducing to Lowest Terms [7.1]

2. $\dfrac{x-3}{x^2-9} = \dfrac{x-3}{(x-3)(x+3)}$

$\qquad = \dfrac{1}{x+3}$

To reduce a rational expression to lowest terms, we first factor the numerator and denominator and then divide the numerator and denominator by any factors they have in common.

Multiplication [7.2]

3. $\dfrac{x+1}{x^2-4} \cdot \dfrac{x+2}{3x+3}$

$\qquad = \dfrac{(x+1)(x+2)}{(x-2)(x+2)(3)(x+1)}$

$\qquad = \dfrac{1}{3(x-2)}$

To multiply two rational numbers or rational expressions, multiply numerators and multiply denominators. In symbols,

$$\frac{P}{Q} \cdot \frac{R}{S} = \frac{PR}{QS} \qquad (Q \neq 0 \text{ and } S \neq 0)$$

In practice, we don't really multiply, but rather, we factor and then divide out common factors.

Division [7.2]

4. $\dfrac{x^2-y^2}{x^3+y^3} \div \dfrac{x-y}{x^2-xy+y^2}$

$\qquad = \dfrac{x^2-y^2}{x^3+y^3} \cdot \dfrac{x^2-xy+y^2}{x-y}$

$\qquad = \dfrac{(x+y)(x-y)(x^2-xy+y^2)}{(x+y)(x^2-xy+y^2)(x-y)}$

$\qquad = 1$

To divide one rational expression by another, we use the definition of division to rewrite our division problem as an equivalent multiplication problem. To divide by a rational expression we multiply by its reciprocal. In symbols,

$$\frac{P}{Q} \div \frac{R}{S} = \frac{P}{Q} \cdot \frac{S}{R} = \frac{PS}{QR} \qquad (Q \neq 0, S \neq 0, R \neq 0)$$

Least Common Denominator [7.3]

5. The LCD for $\frac{2}{x-3}$ and $\frac{3}{5}$ is $5(x-3)$.

The *least common denominator*, LCD, for a set of denominators is the smallest quantity divisible by each of the denominators.

Addition and Subtraction [7.3]

6. $\dfrac{2}{x-3} + \dfrac{3}{5}$

$= \dfrac{2}{x-3} \cdot \dfrac{5}{5} + \dfrac{3}{5} \cdot \dfrac{x-3}{x-3}$

$= \dfrac{3x+1}{5(x-3)}$

If P, Q, and R represent polynomials, $R \neq 0$, then

$$\frac{P}{R} + \frac{Q}{R} = \frac{P+Q}{R} \quad \text{and} \quad \frac{P}{R} - \frac{Q}{R} = \frac{P-Q}{R}$$

When adding or subtracting rational expressions with different denominators, we must find the LCD for all denominators and change each rational expression to an equivalent expression that has the LCD.

Complex Fractions [7.4]

7. $\dfrac{\frac{1}{x} + \frac{1}{y}}{\frac{1}{x} - \frac{1}{y}} = \dfrac{xy\left(\frac{1}{x} + \frac{1}{y}\right)}{xy\left(\frac{1}{x} - \frac{1}{y}\right)}$

$= \dfrac{y+x}{y-x}$

A rational expression that contains, in its numerator or denominator, other rational expressions is called a *complex fraction*. One method of simplifying a complex fraction is to multiply the numerator and denominator by the LCD for all denominators.

Equations Involving Rational Expressions [7.5]

8. Solve $\dfrac{x}{2} + 3 = \dfrac{1}{3}$.

$6\left(\dfrac{x}{2}\right) + 6 \cdot 3 = 6 \cdot \dfrac{1}{3}$

$3x + 18 = 2$

$x = -\dfrac{16}{3}$

To solve an equation involving rational expressions, we first find the LCD for all denominators appearing on either side of the equation. We then multiply both sides by the LCD to clear the equation of all fractions and solve as usual.

Dividing a Polynomial by a Monomial [7.7]

9. $\dfrac{15x^3 - 20x^2 + 10x}{5x}$

$= 3x^2 - 4x + 2$

To divide a polynomial by a monomial, divide each term of the polynomial by the monomial.

Long Division with Polynomials [7.7]

10.
$$
\begin{array}{r}
x - 2 \\
x - 3 \overline{)\, x^2 - 5x + 8} \\
\cancel{+}x^2 \cancel{+} 3x \\
\hline
-2x + 8 \\
\cancel{+}2x \cancel{-} 6 \\
\hline
2
\end{array}
$$

If division with polynomials cannot be accomplished by dividing out factors common to the numerator and denominator, then we use a process similar to long division with whole numbers. The steps in the process are estimate, multiply, subtract, and bring down the next term.

⚠️ **Common Mistakes**

1. Attempting to divide the numerator and denominator of a rational expression by a quantity that is not a factor of both. Like this:

$$\frac{x^2 - \overset{3}{\cancel{9x}} + \overset{2}{\cancel{20}}}{x^2 - \underset{1}{\cancel{3x}} - \underset{1}{\cancel{10}}} \qquad \textit{Mistake}$$

This makes no sense at all. The numerator and denominator must be factored completely before any factors they have in common can be recognized:

$$\frac{x^2 - 9x + 20}{x^2 - 3x - 10} = \frac{\cancel{(x - 5)}(x - 4)}{\cancel{(x - 5)}(x + 2)}$$

$$= \frac{x - 4}{x + 2}$$

2. Forgetting to check solutions to equations involving rational expressions. When we multiply both sides of an equation by a quantity containing the variable, we must be sure to check for extraneous solutions.

Chapter 7 Test

Reduce to lowest terms. [7.1]

1. $\dfrac{x^2 - y^2}{x - y}$

2. $\dfrac{2x^2 - 5x + 3}{2x^2 - x - 3}$

Multiply and divide as indicated. [7.2]

3. $\dfrac{a^2 - 16}{5a - 15} \cdot \dfrac{10(a - 3)^2}{a^2 - 7a + 12}$

4. $\dfrac{a^4 - 81}{a^2 + 9} \div \dfrac{a^2 - 8a + 15}{4a - 20}$

5. $\dfrac{x^3 - 8}{2x^2 - 9x + 10} \div \dfrac{x^2 + 2x + 4}{2x^2 + x - 15}$

Add and subtract as indicated. [7.3]

6. $\dfrac{4}{21} + \dfrac{6}{35}$

7. $\dfrac{3}{4} - \dfrac{1}{2} + \dfrac{5}{8}$

8. $\dfrac{a}{a^2 - 9} + \dfrac{3}{a^2 - 9}$

9. $\dfrac{1}{x} + \dfrac{2}{x - 3}$

10. $\dfrac{4x}{x^2 + 6x + 5} - \dfrac{3x}{x^2 + 5x + 4}$

11. $\dfrac{2x + 8}{x^2 + 4x + 3} - \dfrac{x + 4}{x^2 + 5x + 6}$

Simplify each complex fraction. [7.4]

12. $\dfrac{3 - \dfrac{1}{a + 3}}{3 + \dfrac{1}{a + 3}}$

13. $\dfrac{1 - \dfrac{9}{x^2}}{1 + \dfrac{1}{x} - \dfrac{6}{x^2}}$

Solve each of the following equations. [7.5]

14. $\dfrac{1}{x} + 3 = \dfrac{4}{3}$

15. $\dfrac{x}{x - 3} + 3 = \dfrac{3}{x - 3}$

16. $\dfrac{y + 3}{2y} + \dfrac{5}{y - 1} = \dfrac{1}{2}$

17. $1 - \dfrac{1}{x} = \dfrac{6}{x^2}$

18. Graph $f(x) = \dfrac{x + 4}{x - 1}$.

Solve the following applications. Be sure to show the equation in each case. [7.6]

19. **Number Problem** What number must be subtracted from the denominator of $\frac{10}{23}$ to make the result $\frac{1}{3}$?

20. **Speed of a Boat** The current of a river is 2 miles per hour. It takes a motorboat a total of 3 hours to travel 8 miles upstream and return 8 miles downstream. What is the speed of the boat in still water?

21. **Filling a Pool** An inlet pipe can fill a pool in 10 hours, and the drain can empty it in 15 hours. If the pool is half full and both the inlet pipe and the drain are left open, how long will it take to fill the pool the rest of the way?

22. **Unit Analysis** The top of Mount Whitney, the highest point in California, is 14,494 feet above sea level. Give this height in miles to the nearest tenth of a mile.

23. **Unit Analysis** A bullet fired from a gun travels a distance of 4,750 feet in 3.2 seconds. Find the average speed of the bullet in miles per hour. Round to the nearest whole number.

Divide. [7.7]

24. $\dfrac{24x^3y + 12x^2y^2 - 16xy^3}{4xy}$

25. $\dfrac{2x^3 - 9x^2 + 10}{2x - 1}$

Rational Exponents and Roots

iStockphoto.com © greenaperature

Ecology and conservation are topics that interest most college students. If our rivers and oceans are to be preserved for future generations, we need to work to eliminate pollution from our waters. If a river is flowing at 1 meter per second and a pollutant is entering the river at a constant rate, the shape of the pollution plume can often be modeled by the simple equation

$$y = \sqrt{x}$$

The following table and graph were produced from the equation.

Width of a Pollutant Plume

Distance from Source (meters)	Width of Plume (meters)
x	y
0	0
1	1
4	2
9	3
16	4

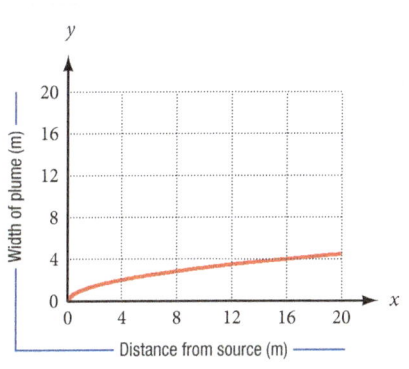

To visualize how the graph models the pollutant plume, imagine that the river is flowing from left to right, parallel to the x-axis, with the x-axis as one of its banks. The pollutant is entering the river from the bank at (0, 0).

By modeling pollution with mathematics, we can use our knowledge of mathematics to help control and eliminate pollution.

iStockphoto.com © Rawpixel Ltd

Think about the most successful people you have met or heard about. What are the qualities they tend to have in common? One of these qualities usually involves making a resolute commitment. If you are not firmly committed to something, then you will tend to give less than your full effort. Consider this quote from Faust by Johann Wolfgang Von Goethe:

Until one is committed, there is hesitancy, the chance to draw back, always ineffectiveness. Concerning all acts of initiative and creation, there is one elementary truth the ignorance of which kills countless ideas and splendid plans: that the moment one definitely commits oneself, then providence moves too. All sorts of things occur to help one that would never otherwise have occurred. A whole stream of events issues from the decision, raising in one's favor all manner of unforeseen incidents, meetings and material assistance which no man could have dreamed would have come his way. Whatever you can do or dream you can, begin it. Boldness has genius, power and magic in it.

Successful people do not give up easily. They forge ahead, even when confronted by difficulties or when the odds seem stacked against them.

Take a moment to reflect on your own life experiences. When have you been the most successful? Can you think of a time when providence has moved in your favor, perhaps unexpectedly?

Rational Exponents

Figure 1 shows a square in which each of the four sides is 1 inch long. To find the square of the length of the diagonal c, we apply the Pythagorean theorem:

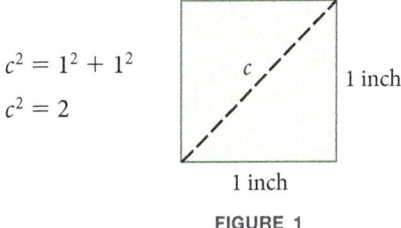

$$c^2 = 1^2 + 1^2$$
$$c^2 = 2$$

1 inch

1 inch

FIGURE 1

Because we know that c is positive and that its square is 2, we call c the **positive square root** of 2, and we write $c = \sqrt{2}$. Associating numbers, such as $\sqrt{2}$, with the diagonal of a square or rectangle allows us to analyze some interesting items from geometry. One particularly interesting geometric object that we will study in this section is shown in Figure 2. It is constructed from a right triangle, and the length of the diagonal is found from the Pythagorean theorem. We will come back to this figure at the end of this section.

The Golden Rectangle

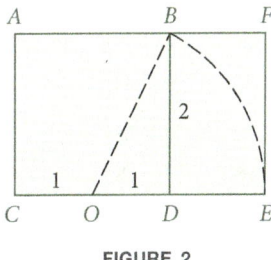

FIGURE 2

In Chapter 1, we developed notation (exponents) to give us the square, cube, or any other power of a number. For instance, if we wanted the square of 3, we wrote $3^2 = 9$. If we wanted the cube of 3, we wrote $3^3 = 27$. In this section, we will develop notation that will take us in the reverse direction, that is, from the square of a number, say 25, back to the original number, 5.

(dĕf′ positive square root

If x is a nonnegative real number, then the expression $\sqrt{x}$ is called the **positive square root** of x and is such that

$$(\sqrt{x})^2 = x$$

In words: $\sqrt{x}$ is the positive number we square to get x.

The negative square root of x, $-\sqrt{x}$, is defined in a similar manner.

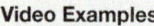

Note It is a common mistake to assume that an expression like $\sqrt{25}$ indicates both square roots, 5 and -5. The expression $\sqrt{25}$ indicates only the positive square root of 25, which is 5. If we want the negative square root, we must use a negative sign: $-\sqrt{25} = -5$.

Note We have restricted the even roots in this definition to nonnegative numbers. Even roots of negative numbers exist, but are not represented by real numbers. That is, $\sqrt{-4}$ is not a real number because there is no real number whose square is -4.

Example 1 The positive square root of 64 is 8 because 8 is the positive number with the property $8^2 = 64$. The negative square root of 64 is -8 because -8 is the negative number whose square is 64. We can summarize both these facts by saying

$$\sqrt{64} = 8 \qquad \text{and} \qquad -\sqrt{64} = -8$$

The higher roots, cube roots, fourth roots, and so on, are defined by definitions similar to that of square roots.

(děf Definition

If x is a real number and n is a positive integer, then

Positive square root of x, $\sqrt{x}$, is such that $(\sqrt{x})^2 = x$ $\qquad x \geq 0$

Cube root of x, $\sqrt[3]{x}$, is such that $(\sqrt[3]{x})^3 = x$

Positive fourth root of x, $\sqrt[4]{x}$, is such that $(\sqrt[4]{x})^4 = x$ $\qquad x \geq 0$

Fifth root of x, $\sqrt[5]{x}$, is such that $(\sqrt[5]{x})^5 = x$

$\qquad\qquad\qquad .\qquad\qquad .\quad .$

$\qquad\qquad\qquad .\qquad\qquad .\quad .$

$\qquad\qquad\qquad .\qquad\qquad .\quad .$

The nth root of x, $\sqrt[n]{x}$, is such that $(\sqrt[n]{x})^n = x$ $\qquad x \geq 0$ if n is even

---

The following is a table of the most common roots used in this book. Any of the roots that are unfamiliar should be memorized.

Square Roots		Cube Roots	Fourth Roots
$\sqrt{0} = 0$	$\sqrt{49} = 7$	$\sqrt[3]{0} = 0$	$\sqrt[4]{0} = 0$
$\sqrt{1} = 1$	$\sqrt{64} = 8$	$\sqrt[3]{1} = 1$	$\sqrt[4]{1} = 1$
$\sqrt{4} = 2$	$\sqrt{81} = 9$	$\sqrt[3]{8} = 2$	$\sqrt[4]{16} = 2$
$\sqrt{9} = 3$	$\sqrt{100} = 10$	$\sqrt[3]{27} = 3$	$\sqrt[4]{81} = 3$
$\sqrt{16} = 4$	$\sqrt{121} = 11$	$\sqrt[3]{64} = 4$	
$\sqrt{25} = 5$	$\sqrt{144} = 12$	$\sqrt[3]{125} = 5$	
$\sqrt{36} = 6$	$\sqrt{169} = 13$		

Notation An expression like $\sqrt[3]{8}$ that involves a root is called a *radical expression*. In the expression $\sqrt[3]{8}$, the ^{3} is called the *index*, the $\sqrt{}$ is the *radical sign*, and 8 is called the *radicand*. The index of a radical must be a positive integer greater than 1. If no index is written, it is assumed to be 2.

Roots and Negative Numbers

When dealing with negative numbers and radicals, the only restriction concerns negative numbers under even roots. We can have negative signs in front of radicals and negative numbers under odd roots and still obtain real numbers. Here are some examples to help clarify this. In the last section of this chapter, we will see how to deal with even roots of negative numbers.

| Examples | Simplify each expression, if possible.

2. $\sqrt[3]{-8} = -2$ because $(-2)^3 = -8$.

3. $\sqrt{-4}$ is not a real number because there is no real number whose square is -4.

4. $-\sqrt{25} = -5$, because -5 is the negative square root of 25.

5. $\sqrt[5]{-32} = -2$ because $(-2)^5 = -32$.

6. $\sqrt[4]{-81}$ is not a real number because there is no real number we can raise to the fourth power and obtain -81. ∎

Variables Under a Radical

From the preceding examples, it is clear that we must be careful that we do not try to take an even root of a negative number. For this reason, we will assume that all variables appearing under a radical sign represent nonnegative numbers.

| Examples | Assume all variables represent nonnegative numbers, and simplify each expression as much as possible.

7. $\sqrt{25a^4b^6} = 5a^2b^3$ because $(5a^2b^3)^2 = 25a^4b^6$.

8. $\sqrt[3]{x^6y^{12}} = x^2y^4$ because $(x^2y^4)^3 = x^6y^{12}$.

9. $\sqrt[4]{81r^8s^{20}} = 3r^2s^5$ because $(3r^2s^5)^4 = 81r^8s^{20}$. ∎

Rational Numbers as Exponents

We will now develop a second kind of notation involving exponents that will allow us to designate square roots, cube roots, and so on in another way.

Consider the equation $x = 8^{1/3}$. Although we have not encountered fractional exponents before, let's assume that all the properties of exponents hold in this case. Cubing both sides of the equation, we have

$$x^3 = (8^{1/3})^3$$
$$x^3 = 8^{(1/3)(3)}$$
$$x^3 = 8^1$$
$$x^3 = 8$$

The last line tells us that x is the number whose cube is 8. It must be true, then, that x is the cube root of 8, $x = \sqrt[3]{8}$. Because we started with $x = 8^{1/3}$, it follows that

$$8^{1/3} = \sqrt[3]{8}$$

It seems reasonable, then, to define fractional exponents as indicating roots. Here is the formal definition.

> (děf) **Definition**
>
> If x is a real number and n is a positive integer greater than 1, then
>
> $$x^{1/n} = \sqrt[n]{x} \qquad (x \geq 0 \text{ when } n \text{ is even})$$
>
> *In words:* The quantity $x^{1/n}$ is the nth root of x.

With this definition, we have a way of representing roots with exponents. Here are some examples.

■■ **Examples**   Write each expression as a root and then simplify, if possible.

10. $8^{1/3} = \sqrt[3]{8} = 2$

11. $36^{1/2} = \sqrt{36} = 6$

12. $-25^{1/2} = -\sqrt{25} = -5$

13. $(-25)^{1/2} = \sqrt{-25}$, which is not a real number

14. $\left(\dfrac{4}{9}\right)^{1/2} = \sqrt{\dfrac{4}{9}} = \dfrac{2}{3}$ ■

The properties of exponents developed in Chapter 4 were applied to integer exponents only. We will now extend these properties to include rational exponents also. We do so without proof.

> ⌈Δ≠Σ⌉   *Properties of Exponents*
>
> If a and b are real numbers and r and s are rational numbers, and a and b are nonnegative whenever r and s indicate even roots, then
>
> **1.** $a^r \cdot a^s = a^{r+s}$ **4.** $a^{-r} = \dfrac{1}{a^r}$ $(a \neq 0)$
>
> **2.** $(a^r)^s = a^{rs}$ **5.** $\left(\dfrac{a}{b}\right)^r = \dfrac{a^r}{b^r}$ $(b \neq 0)$
>
> **3.** $(ab)^r = a^r b^r$ **6.** $\dfrac{a^r}{a^s} = a^{r-s}$ $(a \neq 0)$

Sometimes rational exponents can simplify our work with radicals. Here are Examples 8 and 9 again, but this time we will work them using rational exponents.

■■ **Examples**   Write each radical with a rational exponent, then simplify.

15. $\sqrt[3]{x^6 y^{12}} = (x^6 y^{12})^{1/3}$

$\qquad = (x^6)^{1/3}(y^{12})^{1/3}$

$\qquad = x^2 y^4$

16. $\sqrt[4]{81 r^8 s^{20}} = (81 r^8 s^{20})^{1/4}$

$\qquad = 81^{1/4}(r^8)^{1/4}(s^{20})^{1/4}$

$\qquad = 3 r^2 s^5$ ■

So far, the numerators of all the rational exponents we have encountered have been 1. The next theorem extends the work we can do with rational exponents to rational exponents with numerators other than 1.

We can extend our properties of exponents with the following theorem.

> **⟨Δ≠Σ⟩ Rational Exponent Theorem**
>
> If a is a nonnegative real number, m is an integer, and n is a positive integer, then
> $$a^{m/n} = (a^{1/n})^m = (a^m)^{1/n}$$

Proof   We can prove this theorem using the properties of exponents. Because $m/n = m(1/n)$, we have

$$a^{m/n} = a^{m(1/n)} \qquad a^{m/n} = a^{(1/n)(m)}$$
$$= (a^m)^{1/n} \qquad = (a^{1/n})^m$$

Here are some examples that illustrate how we use this theorem.

Examples   Simplify as much as possible.

Note On a scientific calculator, Example 17 would look like this:

8 $\boxed{y^x}$ $\boxed{(}$ 2 $\boxed{\div}$ 3 $\boxed{)}$ $\boxed{=}$

17. $8^{2/3} = (8^{1/3})^2$ Rational Exponent Theorem

       $= 2^2$ Definition of fractional exponents

       $= 4$ The square of 2 is 4.

18. $25^{(3/2)} = (25^{1/2})^3$ Rational Exponent Theorem

       $= 5^3$ Definition of fractional exponents

       $= 125$ The cube of 5 is 125.

19. $9^{-3/2} = (9^{1/2})^{-3}$ Rational Exponent Theorem

       $= 3^{-3}$ Definition of fractional exponents

       $= \dfrac{1}{3^3}$ Property 4 for exponents

       $= \dfrac{1}{27}$ The cube of 3 is 27

20. $\left(\dfrac{27}{8}\right)^{-4/3} = \left[\left(\dfrac{27}{8}\right)^{1/3}\right]^{-4}$ Rational Exponent Theorem

       $= \left(\dfrac{3}{2}\right)^{-4}$ Definition of fractional exponents

       $= \left(\dfrac{2}{3}\right)^{4}$ Property 4 for exponents

       $= \dfrac{16}{81}$ The fourth power of $\frac{2}{3}$ is $\frac{16}{81}$

The following examples show the application of the properties of exponents to rational exponents.

Examples   Assume all variables represent positive quantities, and simplify as much as possible.

21. $x^{1/3} \cdot x^{5/6} = x^{1/3 + 5/6}$ Property 1

       $= x^{2/6 + 5/6}$ LCD is 6

       $= x^{7/6}$ Add fractions

22. $(y^{2/3})^{3/4} = y^{(2/3)(3/4)}$ Property 2

$\qquad\qquad\quad = y^{1/2}$ Multiply fractions: $\frac{2}{3} \cdot \frac{3}{4} = \frac{6}{12} = \frac{1}{2}$

23. $\dfrac{z^{1/3}}{z^{1/4}} = z^{1/3 - 1/4}$ Property 6

$\qquad\quad = z^{4/12 - 3/12}$ LCD is 12

$\qquad\quad = z^{1/12}$ Subtract fractions

24. $\left(\dfrac{a^{-1/3}}{b^{1/2}}\right)^6 = \dfrac{(a^{-1/3})^6}{(b^{1/2})^6}$ Property 5

$\qquad\qquad = \dfrac{a^{-2}}{b^3}$ Property 2

$\qquad\qquad = \dfrac{1}{a^2 b^3}$ Property 4

25. $\dfrac{(x^{-3} y^{1/2})^4}{x^{10} y^{3/2}} = \dfrac{(x^{-3})^4 (y^{1/2})^4}{x^{10} y^{3/2}}$ Property 3

$\qquad\qquad = \dfrac{x^{-12} y^2}{x^{10} y^{3/2}}$ Property 2

$\qquad\qquad = x^{-22} y^{1/2}$ Property 6

$\qquad\qquad = \dfrac{y^{1/2}}{x^{22}}$ Property 4

The Pythagorean Theorem (Again) and the Golden Rectangle

Now that we have had some experience working with square roots, we can rewrite the Pythagorean theorem using a square root. If triangle *ABC* is a right triangle with $C = 90°$, then the length of the longest side is the *positive square root* of the sum of the squares of the other two sides (see Figure 3).

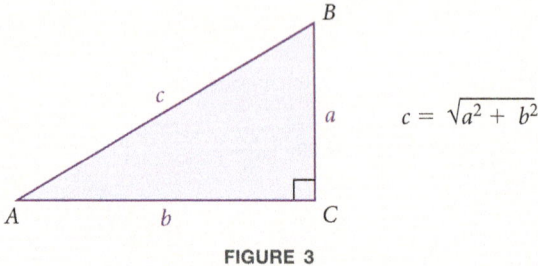

$$c = \sqrt{a^2 + b^2}$$

FIGURE 3

In the introduction to this chapter, we mentioned the golden rectangle. Its origins can be traced back over 2,000 years to the Greek civilization that produced Pythagoras, Socrates, Plato, Aristotle, and Euclid. The most important mathematical work to come from that Greek civilization was Euclid's *Elements,* an elegantly written summary of all that was known about geometry at that time in history. Euclid's *Elements,* according to Howard Eves, an authority on the history of mathematics, exercised a greater influence on scientific thinking than any other work. Here is how we construct a golden rectangle from a square of side 2, using the same method that Euclid used in his *Elements.*

Constructing a Golden Rectangle
From a Square of Side 2

Step 1: Draw a square with a side of length 2. Connect the midpoint of side *CD* to corner *B*. (Note that we have labeled the midpoint of segment *CD* with the letter *O*.)

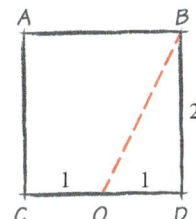

Step 2: Drop the diagonal from step 1 down so it aligns with side *CD*.

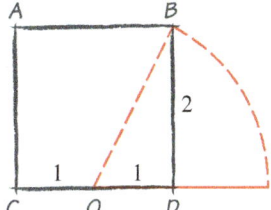

Step 3: Form rectangle *ACEF*. This is a golden rectangle.

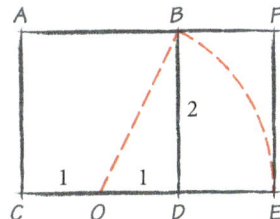

All golden rectangles are constructed from squares. Every golden rectangle, no matter how large or small it is, will have the same shape. To associate a number with the shape of the golden rectangle, we use the ratio of its length to its width. This ratio is called the *golden ratio*. To calculate the golden ratio, we must first find the length of the diagonal we used to construct the golden rectangle. Figure 4 shows the golden rectangle we constructed from a square of side 2. The length of the diagonal *OB* is found by applying the Pythagorean theorem to triangle *OBD*.

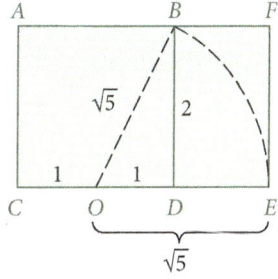

FIGURE 4

The length of segment OE is equal to the length of diagonal OB; both are $\sqrt{5}$. Because the distance from C to O is 1, the length CE of the golden rectangle is $1 + \sqrt{5}$. Now we can find the golden ratio:

$$\text{Golden ratio} = \frac{\text{length}}{\text{width}} = \frac{CE}{EF} = \frac{1 + \sqrt{5}}{2}$$

Graphing Calculators—A Word of Caution

Some graphing calculators give surprising results when evaluating expressions such as $(-8)^{2/3}$. As you know from reading this section, the expression $(-8)^{2/3}$ simplifies to 4, either by taking the cube root first and then squaring the result, or by squaring the base first and then taking the cube root of the result. Here are three different ways to evaluate this expression on your calculator:

1. $(-8)\wedge(2/3)$ To evaluate $(-8)^{2/3}$
2. $((-8)\wedge2)\wedge(1/3)$ To evaluate $((-8)^2)^{1/3}$
3. $((-8)\wedge(1/3))\wedge2$ To evaluate $((-8)^{1/3})^2$

Note any differences in the results.

   Next, graph each of the following functions, one at a time.

1. $Y_1 = X^{2/3}$ 2. $Y_2 = (X^2)^{1/3}$ 3. $Y_3 = (X^{1/3})^2$

The correct graph is shown in Figure 5. Note which of your graphs match the correct graph.

   Different calculators evaluate exponential expressions in different ways. You should use the method (or methods) that gave you the correct graph.

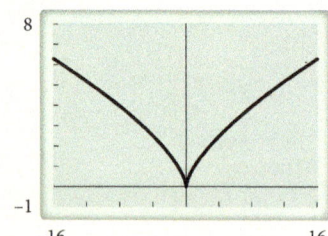

FIGURE 5

Getting Ready for Class

After reading through the preceding section, respond in your own words and in complete sentences.

A. Every real number has two square roots. Explain the notation we use to tell them apart. Use the square roots of 3 for examples.

B. Explain why a square root of -4 is not a real number.

C. We use the notation $\sqrt{2}$ to represent the positive square root of 2. Explain why there isn't a simpler way to express the positive square root of 2.

D. For the expression $a^{m/n}$, explain the significance of the numerator m and the significance of the denominator n in the exponent.

Problem Set 8.1

Find each of the following roots, if possible.

1. $\sqrt{144}$ **2.** $-\sqrt{144}$ **3.** $\sqrt{-144}$ **4.** $\sqrt{-49}$

5. $-\sqrt{49}$ **6.** $\sqrt{49}$ **7.** $\sqrt[3]{-27}$ **8.** $-\sqrt[3]{27}$

9. $\sqrt[4]{16}$ **10.** $-\sqrt[4]{16}$ **11.** $\sqrt[4]{-16}$ **12.** $-\sqrt[4]{-16}$

13. $\sqrt{0.04}$ **14.** $\sqrt{0.81}$ **15.** $\sqrt[3]{0.008}$ **16.** $\sqrt[3]{0.125}$

Simplify each expression. Assume all variables represent nonnegative numbers.

17. $\sqrt{36a^8}$ **18.** $\sqrt{49a^{10}}$ **19.** $\sqrt[3]{27a^{12}}$ **20.** $\sqrt[3]{8a^{15}}$

21. $\sqrt[3]{x^3y^6}$ **22.** $\sqrt[3]{x^6y^3}$ **23.** $\sqrt[5]{32x^{10}y^5}$ **24.** $\sqrt[5]{32x^5y^{10}}$

25. $\sqrt[4]{16a^{12}b^{20}}$ **26.** $\sqrt[4]{81a^{24}b^8}$

Use the definition of rational exponents to write each of the following with the appropriate root. Then simplify.

27. $36^{1/2}$ **28.** $49^{1/2}$ **29.** $-9^{1/2}$ **30.** $-16^{1/2}$

31. $8^{1/3}$ **32.** $-8^{1/3}$ **33.** $(-8)^{1/3}$ **34.** $-27^{1/3}$

35. $32^{1/5}$ **36.** $81^{1/4}$ **37.** $\left(\dfrac{81}{25}\right)^{1/2}$ **38.** $\left(\dfrac{9}{16}\right)^{1/2}$

39. $\left(\dfrac{64}{125}\right)^{1/3}$ **40.** $\left(\dfrac{8}{27}\right)^{1/3}$

Use Theorem 8.1 to simplify each of the following as much as possible.

41. $27^{2/3}$ **42.** $8^{4/3}$ **43.** $25^{3/2}$ **44.** $9^{3/2}$

45. $16^{3/4}$ **46.** $81^{3/4}$

Simplify each expression. Remember, negative exponents give reciprocals.

47. $27^{-1/3}$ **48.** $9^{-1/2}$ **49.** $81^{-3/4}$ **50.** $4^{-3/2}$

51. $\left(\dfrac{25}{36}\right)^{-1/2}$ **52.** $\left(\dfrac{16}{49}\right)^{-1/2}$ **53.** $\left(\dfrac{81}{16}\right)^{-3/4}$ **54.** $\left(\dfrac{27}{8}\right)^{-2/3}$

55. $16^{1/2} + 27^{1/3}$ **56.** $25^{1/2} + 100^{1/2}$ **57.** $8^{-2/3} + 4^{-1/2}$ **58.** $49^{-1/2} + 25^{-1/2}$

Use the properties of exponents to simplify each of the following as much as possible. Assume all bases are positive.

59. $x^{3/5} \cdot x^{1/5}$ **60.** $x^{3/4} \cdot x^{5/4}$ **61.** $(a^{3/4})^{4/3}$ **62.** $(a^{2/3})^{3/4}$

63. $\dfrac{x^{1/5}}{x^{3/5}}$ **64.** $\dfrac{x^{2/7}}{x^{5/7}}$ **65.** $\dfrac{x^{5/6}}{x^{2/3}}$ **66.** $\dfrac{x^{7/8}}{x^{8/7}}$

67. $(x^{3/5}y^{5/6}z^{1/3})^{3/5}$ **68.** $(x^{3/4}y^{1/8}z^{5/6})^{4/5}$ **69.** $\dfrac{a^{3/4}b^2}{a^{7/8}b^{1/4}}$ **70.** $\dfrac{a^{1/3}b^4}{a^{3/5}b^{1/3}}$

71. $\dfrac{(y^{2/3})^{3/4}}{(y^{1/3})^{3/5}}$ **72.** $\dfrac{(y^{5/4})^{2/5}}{(y^{1/4})^{4/3}}$ **73.** $\left(\dfrac{a^{-1/4}}{b^{1/2}}\right)^8$ **74.** $\left(\dfrac{a^{-1/5}}{b^{1/3}}\right)^{15}$

Simplify. (Assume all variables are nonnegative.)

75. **a.** $\sqrt{25}$ **b.** $\sqrt{0.25}$ **c.** $\sqrt{2500}$ **d.** $\sqrt{0.0025}$

76. **a.** $\sqrt[3]{8}$ **b.** $\sqrt[3]{0.008}$ **c.** $\sqrt[3]{8{,}000}$ **d.** $\sqrt[3]{8 \times 10^{-6}}$

77. **a.** $\sqrt{16a^4b^8}$ **b.** $\sqrt[3]{16a^4b^8}$ **c.** $\sqrt[4]{16a^4b^8}$

78. **a.** $\sqrt{64x^5y^{10}}$ **b.** $\sqrt[3]{64x^5y^{10}}$ **c.** $\sqrt[4]{64x^5y^{10}}$

79. Show that the expression $(a^{1/2} + b^{1/2})^2$ is not equal to $a + b$ by replacing a with 9 and b with 4 in both expressions and then simplifying each.

80. Show that the statement $(a^2 + b^2)^{1/2} = a + b$ is not, in general, true by replacing a with 3 and b with 4 and then simplifying both sides.

81. You may have noticed, if you have been using a calculator to find roots, that you can find the fourth root of a number by pressing the square root button twice. Written in symbols, this fact looks like this:

$$\sqrt{\sqrt{a}} = \sqrt[4]{a} \qquad (a \geq 0)$$

Show that this statement is true by rewriting each side with exponents instead of radical notation and then simplifying the left side.

82. Show that the statement is true by rewriting each side with exponents instead of radical notation and then simplifying the left side.

$$\sqrt[3]{\sqrt{a}} = \sqrt[6]{a} \qquad (a \geq 0)$$

Applying the Concepts

83. Maximum Speed The maximum speed (v) that an automobile can travel around a curve of radius r without skidding is given by the equation

$$v = \left(\frac{5r}{2}\right)^{1/2}$$

where v is in miles per hour and r is measured in feet. What is the maximum speed a car can travel around a curve with a radius of 250 feet without skidding?

84. Relativity The equation

$$L = \left(1 - \frac{v^2}{c^2}\right)^{1/2}$$

gives the relativistic length of a 1-foot ruler traveling with velocity v. Find L if

$$\frac{v}{c} = \frac{3}{5}$$

85. Golden Ratio The golden ratio is the ratio of the length to the width in any golden rectangle. The exact value of this number is $\frac{1+\sqrt{5}}{2}$. Use a calculator to find a decimal approximation to this number and round it to the nearest thousandth.

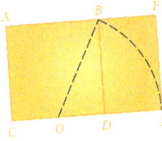

86. Golden Ratio The reciprocal of the golden ratio is $\frac{2}{1+\sqrt{5}}$. Find a decimal approximation to this number that is accurate to the nearest thousandth.

87. Sequences Find the next term in the following sequence. Then explain how this sequence is related to the Fibonacci sequence.

$$\frac{3}{2}, \frac{5}{3}, \frac{8}{5}, \cdots$$

88. Sequences Write the first 10 terms in the sequence shown in Problem 87. Then find a decimal approximation to each of the 10 terms, rounding each to the nearest thousandth.

89. Chemistry Figure 6 shows part of a model of a magnesium oxide (MgO) crystal. Each corner of the square is at the center of one oxygen ion (O^{2-}), and the center of the middle ion is at the center of the square. The radius for each oxygen ion is 60 picometers (pm), and the radius for each magnesium ion (Mg^{2+}) is 150 picometers.

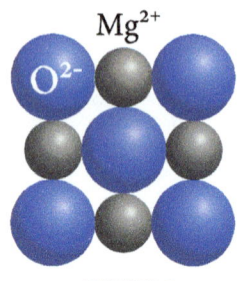

FIGURE 6

   a. Find the length of the side of the square. Write your answer in picometers.

   b. Find the length of the diagonal of the square. Write your answer in picometers.

   c. If 1 meter is 10^{12} picometers, give the length of the diagonal of the square in meters.

90. Geometry The length of each side of the cube shown in Figure 7 is 1 inch.

   a. Find the length of the diagonal CH.

   b. Find the length of the diagonal CF.

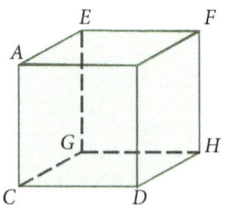

FIGURE 7

Getting Ready for the Next Section

Simplify. Assume all variable are positive real numbers.

91. $\sqrt{25}$ **92.** $\sqrt{4}$ **93.** $\sqrt{6^2}$ **94.** $\sqrt{3^2}$

95. $\sqrt{16x^4y^2}$ **96.** $\sqrt{4x^6y^8}$ **97.** $\sqrt{(5y)^2}$ **98.** $\sqrt{(8x^3)^2}$

99. $\sqrt[3]{27}$ **100.** $\sqrt[3]{-8}$ **101.** $\sqrt[3]{2^3}$ **102.** $\sqrt[3]{(-5)^3}$

103. $\sqrt[3]{8a^3b^3}$ **104.** $\sqrt[3]{64a^6b^3}$

Fill in the blank.

105. $50 = \underline{\hspace{1cm}} \cdot 2$ **106.** $12 = \underline{\hspace{1cm}} \cdot 3$

107. $48x^4y^3 = \underline{\hspace{1cm}} \cdot y$ **108.** $40a^5b^4 = \underline{\hspace{1cm}} \cdot 5a^2b$

109. $12x^7y^6 = \underline{\hspace{1cm}} \cdot 3x$ **110.** $54a^6b^2c^4 = \underline{\hspace{1cm}} \cdot 2b^2c$

Simplified Form for Radicals

Earlier in this chapter, we showed how the Pythagorean theorem can be used to construct a golden rectangle. In a similar manner, the Pythagorean theorem can be used to contruct the attractive spiral shown here.

The Spiral of Roots

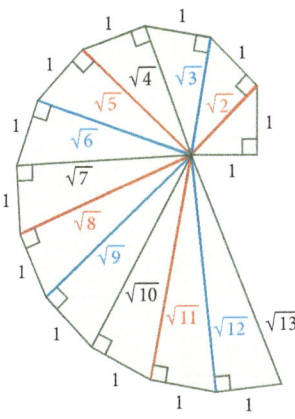

This spiral is called the Spiral of Roots because each of the diagonals is the positive square root of one of the positive integers. At the end of this section, we will use the Pythagorean theorem and some of the material in this section to construct this spiral.

In this section, we will use radical notation instead of rational exponents. We will begin by stating two properties of radicals. Following this, we will give a definition for simplified form for radical expressions. The examples in this section show how we use the properties of radicals to write radical expresions in simplified form.

Here are the first two properties of radicals. For these two properties, we will assume a and b are nonnegative real numbers whenever n is an even number.

> **Note** There is not a property for radicals that says the nth root of a sum is the sum of the nth roots. That is,
>
> $$\sqrt[n]{a+b} \neq \sqrt[n]{a} + \sqrt[n]{b}$$

Property 1 for Radicals

$$\sqrt[n]{ab} = \sqrt[n]{a}\sqrt[n]{b}$$

In words: The nth root of a product is the product of the nth roots.

Proof of Property 1

$$\sqrt[n]{ab} = (ab)^{1/n} \qquad \text{Definition of fractional exponents}$$

$$= a^{1/n}b^{1/n} \qquad \text{Exponents distribute over products}$$

$$= \sqrt[n]{a}\sqrt[n]{b} \qquad \text{Definition of fractional exponents}$$

Property 2 for Radicals

$$\sqrt[n]{\frac{a}{b}} = \frac{\sqrt[n]{a}}{\sqrt[n]{b}} = \qquad (b \neq 0)$$

In words: The nth root of a quotient is the quotient of the nth roots.

The proof of Property 2 is similar to the proof of Property 1.

These two properties of radicals allow us to change the form of and simplify radical expressions without changing their value.

> $\boxed{\Delta\neq\Sigma}$ *Simplified Form for Radical Expressions*
>
> A radical expression is in *simplified form* if
>
> 1. None of the factors of the radicand (the quantity under the radical sign) can be written as powers greater than or equal to the index—that is, no perfect squares can be factors of the quantity under a square root sign, no perfect cubes can be factors of what is under a cube root sign, and so forth.
> 2. There are no fractions under the radical sign.
> 3. There are no radicals in the denominator.

Satisfying the first condition for simplified form actually amounts to taking as much out from under the radical sign as possible. The following examples illustrate the first condition for simplified form.

Video Examples

Section 8.2

Example 1   Write $\sqrt{50}$ in simplified form.

SOLUTION   The largest perfect square that divides 50 is 25. We write 50 as $25 \cdot 2$ and apply Property 1 for radicals:

$$\sqrt{50} = \sqrt{25 \cdot 2} \qquad 50 = 25 \cdot 2$$
$$= \sqrt{25}\sqrt{2} \qquad \text{Property 1}$$
$$= 5\sqrt{2} \qquad \sqrt{25} = 5$$

We have taken as much as possible out from under the radical sign—in this case, factoring 25 from 50 and then writing $\sqrt{25}$ as 5.

As we progress through this chapter you will see more and more expressions that involve the product of a number and a radical. Here are some examples:

$$3\sqrt{2} \qquad \frac{1}{2}\sqrt{5} \qquad 5\sqrt{7} \qquad 3x\sqrt{2x} \qquad 2ab\sqrt{5a}$$

All of these are products. The first expression $3\sqrt{2}$ is the product of 3 and $\sqrt{2}$. That is,

$$3\sqrt{2} = 3 \cdot \sqrt{2}$$

The 3 and the $\sqrt{2}$ are not stuck together is some mysterious way. The expression $3\sqrt{2}$ is simply the product of two numbers, one of which is rational, and the other is irrational.

Example 2   Write in simplified form: $\sqrt{48x^4y^3}$, where $x, y \geq 0$

SOLUTION   The largest perfect square that is a factor of the radicand is $16x^4y^2$. Applying Property 1, we have

$$\sqrt{48x^4y^3} = \sqrt{16x^4y^2 \cdot 3y}$$
$$= \sqrt{16x^4y^2}\sqrt{3y}$$
$$= 4x^2y\sqrt{3y}$$

Example 3   Write $\sqrt[3]{40a^5b^4}$ in simplified form.

SOLUTION   We now want to factor the largest perfect cube from the radicand. We write $40a^5b^4$ as $8a^3b^3 \cdot 5a^2b$ and proceed as we did in Examples 1 and 2.

$$\sqrt[3]{40a^5b^4} = \sqrt[3]{8a^3b^3 \cdot 5a^2b}$$
$$= \sqrt[3]{8a^3b^3}\sqrt[3]{5a^2b}$$
$$= 2ab\sqrt[3]{5a^2b}$$

Our next examples involve fractions and simplified form for radicals.

Example 4   Simplify each expression.

a. $\dfrac{\sqrt{12}}{6}$ **b.** $\dfrac{5\sqrt{18}}{15}$ **c.** $\dfrac{6 + \sqrt{8}}{2}$ **d.** $\dfrac{-1 + \sqrt{45}}{2}$

SOLUTION   In each case, we simplify the radical first, then we factor and reduce to lowest terms.

a.
$$\frac{\sqrt{12}}{6} = \frac{2\sqrt{3}}{6} \qquad \text{Simplify the radical } \sqrt{12} = \sqrt{4\cdot3} = \sqrt{4}\sqrt{3} = 2\sqrt{3}$$
$$= \frac{2\sqrt{3}}{2 \cdot 3} \qquad \text{Factor denominator}$$
$$= \frac{\sqrt{3}}{3} \qquad \text{Divide out common factors}$$

b.
$$\frac{5\sqrt{18}}{15} = \frac{5 \cdot 3\sqrt{2}}{15} \qquad \sqrt{18} = \sqrt{9\cdot2} = \sqrt{9}\sqrt{2} = 3\sqrt{2}$$
$$= \frac{5 \cdot 3\sqrt{2}}{3 \cdot 5} \qquad \text{Factor denominator}$$
$$= \sqrt{2} \qquad \text{Divide out common factors}$$

c.
$$\frac{6 + \sqrt{8}}{2} = \frac{6 + 2\sqrt{2}}{2} \qquad \sqrt{8} = \sqrt{4\cdot2} = \sqrt{4}\sqrt{2} = 2\sqrt{2}$$
$$= \frac{2(3 + \sqrt{2})}{2} \qquad \text{Factor numerator}$$
$$= 3 + \sqrt{2} \qquad \text{Divide out common factors}$$

d.
$$\frac{-1 + \sqrt{45}}{2} = \frac{-1 + 3\sqrt{5}}{2} \qquad \sqrt{45} = \sqrt{9\cdot5} = \sqrt{9}\sqrt{5} = 3\sqrt{5}$$

This expression cannot be simplified further because $-1 + 3\sqrt{5}$ and 2 have no factors in common.

Rationalizing the Denominator

Example 5   Simplify $\sqrt{\dfrac{3}{4}}$.

SOLUTION   Applying Property 2 for radicals, we have

$$\sqrt{\frac{3}{4}} = \frac{\sqrt{3}}{\sqrt{4}} \qquad \text{Property 2}$$
$$= \frac{\sqrt{3}}{2} \qquad \sqrt{4} = 2$$

The last expression is in simplified form because it satisfies all three conditions for simplified form.

Example 6 Write $\sqrt{\dfrac{5}{6}}$ in simplified form.

SOLUTION Proceeding as in Example 5, we have

$$\sqrt{\frac{5}{6}} = \frac{\sqrt{5}}{\sqrt{6}}$$

The resulting expression satisfies the second condition for simplified form because neither radical contains a fraction. It does, however, violate Condition 3 because it has a radical in the denominator. Getting rid of the radical in the denominator is called *rationalizing the denominator* and is accomplished, in this case, by multiplying the numerator and denominator by $\sqrt{6}$:

$$\frac{\sqrt{5}}{\sqrt{6}} = \frac{\sqrt{5}}{\sqrt{6}} \cdot \frac{\sqrt{6}}{\sqrt{6}}$$

$$= \frac{\sqrt{30}}{\sqrt{6^2}}$$

$$= \frac{\sqrt{30}}{6}$$

Examples Rationalize the denominator.

7. $\dfrac{4}{\sqrt{3}} = \dfrac{4}{\sqrt{3}} \cdot \dfrac{\sqrt{3}}{\sqrt{3}}$

$$= \frac{4\sqrt{3}}{\sqrt{3^2}}$$

$$= \frac{4\sqrt{3}}{3}$$

8. $\dfrac{2\sqrt{3x}}{\sqrt{5y}} = \dfrac{2\sqrt{3x}}{\sqrt{5y}} \cdot \dfrac{\sqrt{5y}}{\sqrt{5y}}$

$$= \frac{2\sqrt{15xy}}{\sqrt{(5y)^2}}$$

$$= \frac{2\sqrt{15xy}}{5y}$$

When the denominator involves a cube root, we must multiply by a radical that will produce a perfect cube under the cube root sign in the denominator, as Example 9 illustrates.

Example 9 Rationalize the denominator in $\dfrac{7}{\sqrt[3]{4}}$.

SOLUTION Because $4 = 2^2$, we can multiply both numerator and denominator by $\sqrt[3]{2}$ and obtain $\sqrt[3]{2^3}$ in the denominator.

$$\frac{7}{\sqrt[3]{4}} = \frac{7}{\sqrt[3]{2^2}}$$

$$= \frac{7}{\sqrt[3]{2^2}} \cdot \frac{\sqrt[3]{2}}{\sqrt[3]{2}}$$

$$= \frac{7\sqrt[3]{2}}{\sqrt[3]{2^3}}$$

$$= \frac{7\sqrt[3]{2}}{2}$$

Example 10 Simplify $\sqrt{\dfrac{12x^5y^3}{5z}}$.

SOLUTION We use Property 2 to write the numerator and denominator as two separate radicals:

$$\sqrt{\frac{12x^5y^3}{5z}} = \frac{\sqrt{12x^5y^3}}{\sqrt{5z}}$$

Simplifying the numerator, we have

$$\frac{\sqrt{12x^5y^3}}{\sqrt{5z}} = \frac{\sqrt{4x^4y^2}\sqrt{3xy}}{\sqrt{5z}}$$

$$= \frac{2x^2y\sqrt{3xy}}{\sqrt{5z}}$$

To rationalize the denominator, we multiply the numerator and denominator by $\sqrt{5z}$:

$$\frac{2x^2y\sqrt{3xy}}{\sqrt{5z}} \cdot \frac{\sqrt{5z}}{\sqrt{5z}} = \frac{2x^2y\sqrt{15xyz}}{\sqrt{(5z)^2}}$$

$$= \frac{2x^2y\sqrt{15xyz}}{5z}$$

Square Root of a Perfect Square

So far in this chapter, we have assumed that all our variables are nonnegative when they appear under a square root symbol. There are times, however, when this is not the case.

Consider the following two statements:

$$\sqrt{3^2} = \sqrt{9} = 3 \qquad \text{and} \qquad \sqrt{(-3)^2} = \sqrt{9} = 3$$

Whether we operate on 3 or -3, the result is the same: Both expressions simplify to 3. The other operation we have worked with in the past that produces the same result is absolute value. That is,

$$|3| = 3 \qquad \text{and} \qquad |-3| = 3$$

This leads us to the next property of radicals.

> **[Δ≠Σ] Property 3 for Radicals**
>
> If a is a real number, then $\sqrt{a^2} = |a|$.

The result of this discussion and Property 3 is simply this:

If we know a is positive, then $\sqrt{a^2} = a$.

If we know a is negative, then $\sqrt{a^2} = |a|$.

If we don't know if a is positive or negative, then $\sqrt{a^2} = |a|$.

Examples Simplify each expression. Do *not* assume the variables represent positive numbers.

11. $\sqrt{9x^2} = 3|x|$

12. $\sqrt{x^3} = |x|\sqrt{x}$

13. $\sqrt{x^2 - 6x + 9} = \sqrt{(x - 3)^2} = |x - 3|$

14. $\sqrt{x^3 - 5x^2} = \sqrt{x^2(x - 5)} = |x|\sqrt{x - 5}$

As you can see, we must use absolute value symbols when we take a square root of a perfect square, unless we know the base of the perfect square is a positive number. The same idea holds for higher even roots, but not for odd roots. With odd roots, no absolute value symbols are necessary.

Examples   Simplify each expression.

15 $\sqrt[3]{(-2)^3} = \sqrt[3]{-8} = -2$

16. $\sqrt[3]{(-5)^3} = \sqrt[3]{-125} = -5$

We can extend this discussion to all roots as follows:

> **⌈Δ≠Σ⌋   *Extending Property 3 for Radicals***
>
> If a is a real number, then
>
> $$\sqrt[n]{a^n} = |a| \quad \text{if} \quad n \text{ is even}$$
>
> $$\sqrt[n]{a^n} = a \quad \text{if} \quad n \text{ is odd}$$

The Spiral of Roots

To visualize the square roots of the positive integers, we can construct the spiral of roots that we mentioned in the introduction to this section. To begin, we draw two line segments, each of length 1, at right angles to each other. Then we use the Pythagorean theorem to find the length of the diagonal. Figure 1 illustrates this procedure.

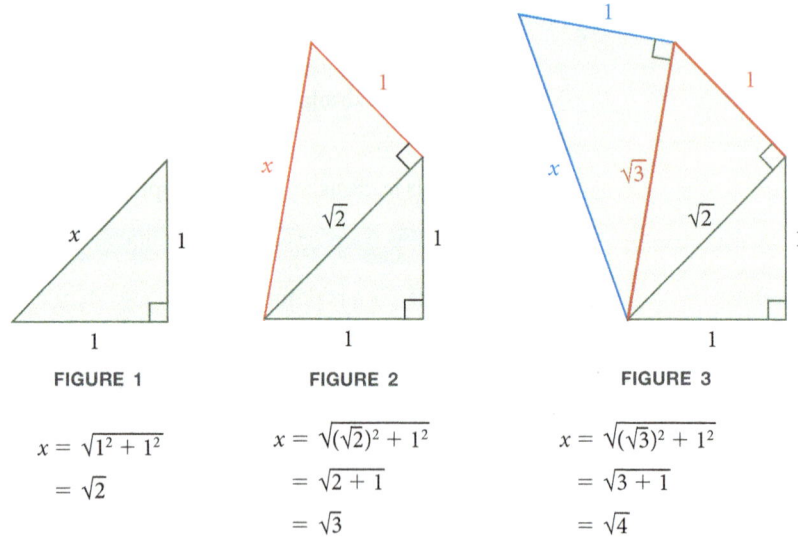

FIGURE 1	FIGURE 2	FIGURE 3

$$x = \sqrt{1^2 + 1^2}$$
$$= \sqrt{2}$$

$$x = \sqrt{(\sqrt{2})^2 + 1^2}$$
$$= \sqrt{2 + 1}$$
$$= \sqrt{3}$$

$$x = \sqrt{(\sqrt{3})^2 + 1^2}$$
$$= \sqrt{3 + 1}$$
$$= \sqrt{4}$$

Next, we construct a second triangle by connecting a line segment of length 1 to the end of the first diagonal so that the angle formed is a right angle. We find the length of the second diagonal using the Pythagorean theorem. Figure 2 illustrates this procedure. Continuing to draw new triangles by connecting line segments of length 1 to the end of each new diagonal, so that the angle formed is a right angle, the spiral of roots begins to appear (Figure 3).

The Spiral of Roots and Function Notation

Looking over the diagrams and calculations in the preceding discússion, we see that each diagonal in the spiral of roots is found by using the length of the previous diagonal.

First diagonal: $\sqrt{1^2 + 1^2} = \sqrt{2}$

Second diagonal: $\sqrt{(\sqrt{2})^2 + 1^2} = \sqrt{3}$

Third diagonal: $\sqrt{(\sqrt{3})^2 + 1^2} = \sqrt{4}$

Fourth diagonal: $\sqrt{(\sqrt{4})^2 + 1^2} = \sqrt{5}$

A process like this one, in which the answer to one calculation is used to find the answer to the next calculation, is called a *recursive* process. In this particular case, we can use function notation to model the process. If we let x represent the length of any diagonal, then the length of the next diagonal is given by

$$f(x) = \sqrt{x^2 + 1}$$

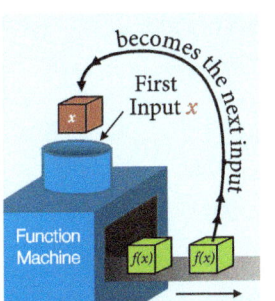

becomes the next input

First Input x

Function Machine

$f(x)$ $f(x)$

Output $f(x)$

To begin the process of finding the diagonals, we let $x = 1$:

$$f(1) = \sqrt{1^2 + 1} = \sqrt{2}$$

To find the next diagonal, we substitue $\sqrt{2}$ for x to obtain

$$f[f(1)] = f(\sqrt{2}) = \sqrt{(\sqrt{2})^2 + 1} = \sqrt{3}$$

$$f(f[f(1)]) = f(\sqrt{3}) = \sqrt{(\sqrt{3})^2 + 1} = \sqrt{4}$$

We can describe this process of finding the diagonals of the spiral of roots very concisely this way:

$$f(1), f[f(1)], f(f[f(1)]), \ldots \qquad \text{where } f(x) = \sqrt{x^2 + 1}$$

This sequence of function values is a special case of a general category of similar sequences that are closely connected to *fractals* and *chaos,* two topics in mathematics that are currently receiving a good deal of attention.

Using Technology

As our preceding discussion indicates, the length of each diagonal in the spiral of roots is used to calculate the length of the next diagonal. The ANS key on a graphing calculator can be used effectively in a situation like this. To begin, we store the number 1 in the variable ANS. Next, we key in the fomula used to produce each diagonal using ANS for the variable. After that, it is simply a matter of pressing ENTER, as many times as we like, to produce the lengths of as many diagonals as we like. Here is a summary of what we do:

Enter This	*Display Shows*
1 ENTER	1.000
$\sqrt{}$ (ANS² + 1) ENTER	1.414
ENTER	1.732
ENTER	2.000
ENTER	2.236

If you continue to press the ENTER key, you will produce decimal approximations for as many of the diagonals in the spiral of roots as you like.

Getting Ready for Class

After reading through the preceding section, respond in your own words and in complete sentences.

A. Explain why this statement is false: "The square root of a sum is the sum of the square roots."

B. What is simplified form for an expression that contains a square root?

C. Why is it not necessarily true that $\sqrt{a^2} = a$?

D. What does it mean to rationalize the denominator in an expression?

Problem Set 8.2

Use Property 1 for radicals to write each of the following expressions in simplified form. (Assume all variables are nonnegative through Problem 70.)

1. $\sqrt{8}$ **2.** $\sqrt{32}$ **3.** $\sqrt{98}$ **4.** $\sqrt{75}$

5. $\sqrt{288}$ **6.** $\sqrt{128}$ **7.** $\sqrt{80}$ **8.** $\sqrt{200}$

9. $\sqrt{48}$ **10.** $\sqrt{27}$ **11.** $\sqrt{675}$ **12.** $\sqrt{972}$

13. $\sqrt[3]{54}$ **14.** $\sqrt[3]{24}$ **15.** $\sqrt[3]{128}$ **16.** $\sqrt[3]{162}$

17. $\sqrt[3]{432}$ **18.** $\sqrt[3]{1,536}$ **19.** $\sqrt[5]{64}$ **20.** $\sqrt[4]{48}$

21. $\sqrt{18x^3}$ **22.** $\sqrt{27x^5}$ **23.** $\sqrt[4]{32y^7}$ **24.** $\sqrt[5]{32y^7}$

25. $\sqrt[3]{40x^4y^7}$ **26.** $\sqrt[3]{128x^6y^2}$ **27.** $\sqrt{48a^2b^3c^4}$ **28.** $\sqrt{72a^4b^3c^2}$

29. $\sqrt[3]{48a^2b^3c^4}$ **30.** $\sqrt[3]{72a^4b^3c^2}$ **31.** $\sqrt[5]{64x^8y^{12}}$ **32.** $\sqrt[4]{32x^9y^{10}}$

33. $\sqrt[5]{243x^7y^{10}z^5}$ **34.** $\sqrt[5]{64x^8y^4z^{11}}$

Substitute the given numbers into the expression $\sqrt{b^2 - 4ac}$, and then simplify.

35. $a = 2, b = -6, c = 3$ **36.** $a = 6, b = 7, c = -5$

37. $a = 1, b = 2, c = 6$ **38.** $a = 2, b = 5, c = 3$

39. $a = \dfrac{1}{2}, b = -\dfrac{1}{2}, c = -\dfrac{5}{4}$ **40.** $a = \dfrac{7}{4}, b = -\dfrac{3}{4}, c = -2$

41. Simplify each expression.

     a. $\dfrac{\sqrt{20}}{4}$ **b.** $\dfrac{3\sqrt{20}}{15}$ **c.** $\dfrac{4 + \sqrt{12}}{2}$ **d.** $\dfrac{2 + \sqrt{9}}{5}$

42. Simplify each expression.

     a. $\dfrac{\sqrt{12}}{4}$ **b.** $\dfrac{2\sqrt{32}}{8}$ **c.** $\dfrac{9 + \sqrt{27}}{3}$ **d.** $\dfrac{-6 - \sqrt{64}}{2}$

43. Simplify each expression.

a. $\dfrac{10 + \sqrt{75}}{5}$
b. $\dfrac{-6 + \sqrt{45}}{3}$
c. $\dfrac{-2 - \sqrt{27}}{6}$

44. Simplify each expression.

a. $\dfrac{12 - \sqrt{12}}{6}$
b. $\dfrac{-4 - \sqrt{8}}{2}$
c. $\dfrac{6 - \sqrt{48}}{8}$

Rationalize the denominator in each of the following expressions.

45. $\dfrac{2}{\sqrt{3}}$

46. $\dfrac{3}{\sqrt{2}}$

47. $\dfrac{5}{\sqrt{6}}$

48. $\dfrac{7}{\sqrt{5}}$

49. $\sqrt{\dfrac{1}{2}}$

50. $\sqrt{\dfrac{1}{3}}$

51. $\sqrt{\dfrac{1}{5}}$

52. $\sqrt{\dfrac{1}{6}}$

53. $\dfrac{4}{\sqrt[3]{2}}$

54. $\dfrac{5}{\sqrt[3]{3}}$

55. $\dfrac{2}{\sqrt[3]{9}}$

56. $\dfrac{3}{\sqrt[3]{4}}$

57. $\sqrt[4]{\dfrac{3}{2x^2}}$

58. $\sqrt[4]{\dfrac{5}{3x^2}}$

59. $\sqrt[4]{\dfrac{8}{y}}$

60. $\sqrt[4]{\dfrac{27}{y}}$

61. $\sqrt[3]{\dfrac{4x}{3y}}$

62. $\sqrt[3]{\dfrac{7x}{6y}}$

63. $\sqrt[3]{\dfrac{2x}{9y}}$

64. $\sqrt[3]{\dfrac{5x}{4y}}$

Write each of the following in simplified form.

65. $\sqrt{\dfrac{27x^3}{5y}}$

66. $\sqrt{\dfrac{12x^5}{7y}}$

67. $\sqrt{\dfrac{75x^3y^2}{2z}}$

68. $\sqrt{\dfrac{50x^2y^3}{3z}}$

Rationalize the denominator.

69. a. $\dfrac{1}{\sqrt{2}}$
b. $\dfrac{1}{\sqrt[3]{2}}$
c. $\dfrac{1}{\sqrt[4]{2}}$

70. a. $\dfrac{1}{\sqrt{3}}$
b. $\dfrac{1}{\sqrt[3]{9}}$
c. $\dfrac{1}{\sqrt[4]{27}}$

Simplify each expression. Do *not* assume the variables represent positive numbers.

71. $\sqrt{25x^2}$

72. $\sqrt{49x^2}$

73. $\sqrt{27x^3y^2}$

74. $\sqrt{40x^3y^2}$

75. $\sqrt{x^2 - 10x + 25}$

76. $\sqrt{x^2 - 16x + 64}$

77. $\sqrt{4x^2 + 12x + 9}$

78. $\sqrt{16x^2 + 40x + 25}$

79. $\sqrt{4a^4 + 16a^3 + 16a^2}$

80. $\sqrt{9a^4 + 18a^3 + 9a^2}$

81. $\sqrt{4x^3 - 8x^2}$

82. $\sqrt{18x^3 - 9x^2}$

83. Show that the statement $\sqrt{a + b} = \sqrt{a} + \sqrt{b}$ is not true by replacing a with 9 and b with 16 and simplifying both sides.

84. Find a pair of values for a and b that will make the statement $\sqrt{a + b} = \sqrt{a} + \sqrt{b}$ true.

Applying the Concepts

85. Diagonal Distance The distance d between opposite corners of a rectangular room with length l and width w is given by

$$d = \sqrt{l^2 + w^2}$$

How far is it between opposite corners of a living room that measures 10 by 15 feet?

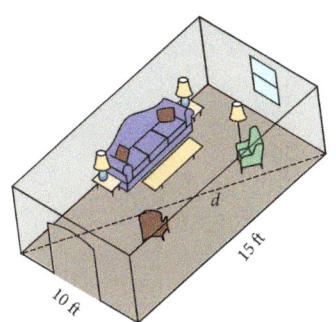

86. Radius of a Sphere The radius r of a sphere with volume V can be found by using the formula

$$r = \sqrt[3]{\frac{3V}{4\pi}}$$

Find the radius of a sphere with volume 9 cubic feet. Write your answer in simplified form. (Use $\frac{22}{7}$ for π.)

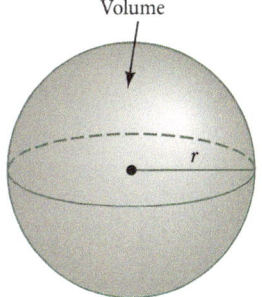

Volume

87. Distance to the Horizon If you are at a point k miles above the surface of the Earth, the distance you can see, in miles, is approximated by the equation $d = \sqrt{8000k + k^2}$.

    a. How far can you see from a point that is 1 mile above the surface of the Earth?

    b. How far can you see from a point that is 2 miles above the surface of the Earth?

    c. How far can you see from a point that is 3 miles above the surface of the Earth?

88. Investing If you invest P dollars and you want the investment to grow to A dollars in t years, the interest rate that must be earned if interest is compounded annually is given by the formula

$$r = \sqrt[t]{\frac{A}{P}} - 1.$$

If you invest $4,000 and want to have $7,000 in 8 years, what interest rate must be earned?

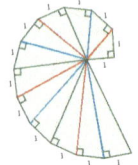

89. Spiral of Roots Construct your own spiral of roots by using a ruler. Draw the first triangle by using two 1-inch lines. The first diagonal will have a length of $\sqrt{2}$ inches. Each new triangle will be formed by drawing a 1-inch line segment at the end of the previous diagonal so the angle formed is 90°.

90. Spiral of Roots Construct a spiral of roots by using line segments of length 2 inches. The length of the first diagonal will be $2\sqrt{2}$ inches. The length of the second diagonal will be $2\sqrt{3}$ inches.

91. Spiral of Roots If $f(x) = \sqrt{x^2 + 1}$, find the first six terms in the following sequence. Use your results to predict the value of the 10th term and the 100th term.

$$f(1), f[f(1)], f(f[f(1)]), \ldots$$

92. Spiral of Roots If $f(x) = \sqrt{x^2 + 4}$, find the first six terms in the following sequence. Use your results to predict the value of the 10th term and the 100th term. (The numbers in this sequence are the lengths of the diagonals of the spiral you drew in Problem 90.)

$$f(2), f[f(2)], f(f[f(2)]), \ldots$$

Getting Ready for the Next Section

Simplify the following.

93. $5x - 4x + 6x$ **94.** $12x + 8x - 7x$

95. $35xy^2 - 8xy^2$ **96.** $20a^2b + 33a^2b$

97. $\dfrac{1}{2}x + \dfrac{1}{3}x$ **98.** $\dfrac{2}{3}x + \dfrac{5}{8}x$

Write in simplified form for radicals.

99. $\sqrt{18}$ **100.** $\sqrt{8}$

101. $\sqrt{75xy^3}$ **102.** $\sqrt{12xy}$

103. $\sqrt[3]{8a^4b^2}$ **104.** $\sqrt[3]{27ab^2}$

Addition and Subtraction of Radical Expressions

In Chapter 4, we found we could add similar terms when combining polynomials. The same idea applies to addition and subtraction of radical expressions.

> **(děf) *similar radicals***
>
> Two radicals are said to be *similar radicals* if they have the same index and the same radicand.

The expressions $5\sqrt[3]{7}$ and $-8\sqrt[3]{7}$ are similar since the index is 3 in both cases and the radicands are 7. The expressions $3\sqrt[4]{5}$ and $7\sqrt[3]{5}$ are not similar because they have different indices, and the expressions $2\sqrt[5]{8}$ and $3\sqrt[5]{9}$ are not similar because the radicands are not the same.

We add and subtract radical expressions in the same way we add and subtract polynomials — by combining similar terms under the distributive property.

Video Examples

Section 8.3

Example 1   Combine $5\sqrt{3} - 4\sqrt{3} + 6\sqrt{3}$.

SOLUTION   All three radicals are similar. We apply the distributive property to get

$$5\sqrt{3} - 4\sqrt{3} + 6\sqrt{3} = (5 - 4 + 6)\sqrt{3}$$
$$= 7\sqrt{3}$$

Example 2   Combine $3\sqrt{8} + 5\sqrt{18}$.

SOLUTION   The two radicals do not seem to be similar. We must write each in simplified form before applying the distributive property.

$$3\sqrt{8} + 5\sqrt{18} = 3\sqrt{4 \cdot 2} + 5\sqrt{9 \cdot 2}$$
$$= 3\sqrt{4}\,\sqrt{2} + 5\sqrt{9}\,\sqrt{2}$$
$$= 3 \cdot 2\,\sqrt{2} + 5 \cdot 3\,\sqrt{2}$$
$$= 6\,\sqrt{2} + 15\,\sqrt{2}$$
$$= (6 + 15)\,\sqrt{2}$$
$$= 21\,\sqrt{2}$$

The result of Example 2 can be generalized to the following rule for sums and differences of radical expressions.

> **(Δ≠Σ) *Rule***
>
> To add or subtract radical expressions, put each in simplified form and apply the distributive property, if possible. We can add only similar radicals. We must write each expression in simplified form for radicals before we can tell if the radicals are similar.

Example 3   Combine $7\sqrt{75xy^3} - 4y\sqrt{12xy}$, where $x, y \geq 0$.

SOLUTION   We write each expression in simplified form and combine similar radicals:

$$7\sqrt{75xy^3} - 4y\sqrt{12xy} = 7\sqrt{25y^2}\,\sqrt{3xy} - 4y\sqrt{4}\,\sqrt{3xy}$$

$$= 35y\sqrt{3xy} - 8y\sqrt{3xy}$$

$$= (35y - 8y)\sqrt{3xy}$$

$$= 27y\sqrt{3xy}$$

Example 4   Combine $10\sqrt[3]{8a^4b^2} + 11a\sqrt[3]{27ab^2}$.

SOLUTION   Writing each radical in simplified form and combining similar terms, we have

$$10\sqrt[3]{8a^4b^2} + 11a\sqrt[3]{27ab^2} = 10\sqrt[3]{8a^3}\,\sqrt[3]{ab^2} + 11a\sqrt[3]{27}\,\sqrt[3]{ab^2}$$

$$= 20a\sqrt[3]{ab^2} + 33a\sqrt[3]{ab^2}$$

$$= 53a\sqrt[3]{ab^2}$$

Example 5   Combine $\dfrac{\sqrt{3}}{2} + \dfrac{1}{\sqrt{3}}$.

SOLUTION   We begin by writing the second term in simplified form.

$$\frac{\sqrt{3}}{2} + \frac{1}{\sqrt{3}} = \frac{\sqrt{3}}{2} + \frac{1}{\sqrt{3}} \cdot \frac{\sqrt{3}}{\sqrt{3}}$$

$$= \frac{\sqrt{3}}{2} + \frac{\sqrt{3}}{3}$$

$$= \frac{1}{2}\sqrt{3} + \frac{1}{3}\sqrt{3}$$

$$= \left(\frac{1}{2} + \frac{1}{3}\right)\sqrt{3}$$

$$= \frac{5}{6}\sqrt{3} = \frac{5\sqrt{3}}{6}$$

Example 6   Construct a golden rectangle from a square of side 4. Then show that the ratio of the length to the width is the golden ratio $\frac{1+\sqrt{5}}{2}$.

SOLUTION   Figure 1 shows the golden rectangle constructed from a square of side 4. The length of the diagonal OB is found from the Pythagorean theorem.

$$OB = \sqrt{2^2 + 4^2} = \sqrt{4 + 16} = \sqrt{20} = 2\sqrt{5}$$

The ratio of the length to the width for the rectangle is the golden ratio.

$$\text{Golden ratio} = \frac{CE}{EF} = \frac{2 + 2\sqrt{5}}{4} = \frac{2(1 + \sqrt{5})}{2 \cdot 2} = \frac{1 + \sqrt{5}}{2}$$

As you can see, showing that the ratio of length to width in this rectangle is the golden ratio depends on our ability to write $\sqrt{20}$ as $2\sqrt{5}$ and our ability to reduce to lowest terms by factoring and then dividing out the common factor 2 from the numerator and denominator.

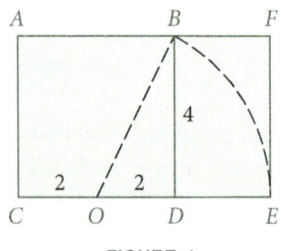

FIGURE 1

Getting Ready for Class

After reading through the preceding section, respond in your own words and in complete sentences.

A. What are similar radicals?

B. When can we add two radical expressions?

C. What is the first step when adding or subtracting expressions containing radicals?

D. What is the golden ratio, and where does it come from?

Combine the following expressions. (Assume any variables under an even root are nonnegative.)

1. $3\sqrt{5} + 4\sqrt{5}$

2. $6\sqrt{3} - 5\sqrt{3}$

3. $3x\sqrt{7} - 4x\sqrt{7}$

4. $6y\sqrt{a} + 7y\sqrt{a}$

5. $5\sqrt[3]{10} - 4\sqrt[3]{10}$

6. $6\sqrt[4]{2} + 9\sqrt[4]{2}$

7. $8\sqrt[5]{6} - 2\sqrt[5]{6} + 3\sqrt[5]{6}$

8. $7\sqrt[6]{7} - \sqrt[6]{7} + 4\sqrt[6]{7}$

9. $3x\sqrt{2} - 4x\sqrt{2} + x\sqrt{2}$

10. $5x\sqrt{6} - 3x\sqrt{6} - 2x\sqrt{6}$

11. $\sqrt{20} - \sqrt{80} + \sqrt{45}$

12. $\sqrt{8} - \sqrt{32} - \sqrt{18}$

13. $4\sqrt{8} - 2\sqrt{50} - 5\sqrt{72}$

14. $\sqrt{48} - 3\sqrt{27} + 2\sqrt{75}$

15. $5x\sqrt{8} + 3\sqrt{32x^2} - 5\sqrt{50x^2}$

16. $2\sqrt{50x^2} - 8x\sqrt{18} - 3\sqrt{72x^2}$

17. $5\sqrt[3]{16} - 4\sqrt[3]{54}$

18. $\sqrt[3]{81} + 3\sqrt[3]{24}$

19. $\sqrt[3]{x^4y^2} + 7x\sqrt[3]{xy^2}$

20. $2\sqrt[3]{x^8y^6} - 3y^2\sqrt[3]{8x^8}$

21. $5a^2\sqrt{27ab^3} - 6b\sqrt{12a^5b}$

22. $9a\sqrt{20a^3b^2} + 7b\sqrt{45a^5}$

23. $b\sqrt[3]{24a^5b} + 3a\sqrt[3]{81a^2b^4}$

24. $7\sqrt[3]{a^4b^3c^2} - 6ab\sqrt[3]{ac^2}$

25. $5x\sqrt[4]{3y^5} + y\sqrt[4]{243x^4y} + \sqrt[4]{48x^4y^5}$

26. $x\sqrt[4]{5xy^8} + y\sqrt[4]{405x^5y^4} + y^2\sqrt[4]{80x^5}$

27. $\dfrac{\sqrt{2}}{2} + \dfrac{1}{\sqrt{2}}$

28. $\dfrac{\sqrt{3}}{3} + \dfrac{1}{\sqrt{3}}$

29. $\dfrac{\sqrt{5}}{3} + \dfrac{1}{\sqrt{5}}$

30. $\dfrac{\sqrt{6}}{2} + \dfrac{1}{\sqrt{6}}$

31. $\sqrt{x} - \dfrac{1}{\sqrt{x}}$

32. $\sqrt{x} + \dfrac{1}{\sqrt{x}}$

33. $\dfrac{\sqrt{18}}{6} + \sqrt{\dfrac{1}{2}} + \dfrac{\sqrt{2}}{2}$

34. $\dfrac{\sqrt{12}}{6} + \sqrt{\dfrac{1}{3}} + \dfrac{\sqrt{3}}{3}$

35. $\sqrt{6} - \sqrt{\dfrac{2}{3}} + \sqrt{\dfrac{1}{6}}$

36. $\sqrt{15} - \sqrt{\dfrac{3}{5}} + \sqrt{\dfrac{5}{3}}$

37. $\sqrt[3]{25} + \dfrac{3}{\sqrt[3]{5}}$

38. $\sqrt[4]{8} + \dfrac{1}{\sqrt[4]{2}}$

39. Use a calculator to find a decimal approximation for $\sqrt{12}$ and for $2\sqrt{3}$.

40. Use a calculator to find decimal approximations for $\sqrt{50}$ and $5\sqrt{2}$.

41. Use a calculator to find a decimal approximation for $\sqrt{8} + \sqrt{18}$. Is it equal to the decimal approximation for $\sqrt{26}$ or $\sqrt{50}$?

42. Use a calculator to find a decimal approximation for $\sqrt{3} + \sqrt{12}$. Is it equal to the decimal approximation for $\sqrt{15}$ or $\sqrt{27}$?

Each of the following statements is false. Correct the right side of each one to make the statement true.

43. $3\sqrt{2x} + 5\sqrt{2x} = 8\sqrt{4x}$

44. $5\sqrt{3} - 7\sqrt{3} = -2\sqrt{9}$

45. $\sqrt{9 + 16} = 3 + 4$

46. $\sqrt{36 + 64} = 6 + 8$

Applying the Concepts

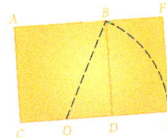

47. Golden Rectangle Construct a golden rectangle from a square of side 8. Then show that the ratio of the length to the width is the golden ratio $\frac{1+\sqrt{5}}{2}$.

48. Golden Rectangle Construct a golden rectangle from a square of side 10. Then show that the ratio of the length to the width is the golden ratio $\frac{1+\sqrt{5}}{2}$.

49. Golden Rectangle Use a ruler to construct a golden rectangle from a square of side 1 inch. Then show that the ratio of the length to the width is the golden ratio.

50. Golden Rectangle Use a ruler to construct a golden rectangle from a square of side $\frac{2}{3}$ inch. Then show that the ratio of the length to the width is the golden ratio.

51. Golden Rectangle To show that all golden rectangles have the same ratio of length to width, construct a golden rectangle from a square of side $2x$. Then show that the ratio of the length to the width is the golden ratio.

52. Golden Rectangle To show that all golden rectangles have the same ratio of length to width, construct a golden rectangle from a square of side x. Then show that the ratio of the length to the width is the golden ratio.

53. Isosceles Right Triangles A triangle is isosceles if it has two equal sides, and a triangle is a right triangle if it has a right angle in it. Sketch an isosceles right triangle, and find the ratio of the hypotenuse to a leg.

54. Equilateral Triangles A triangle is equilateral if it has three equal sides. The triangle in the figure is equilateral with each side of length $2x$. Find the ratio of the height to a side.

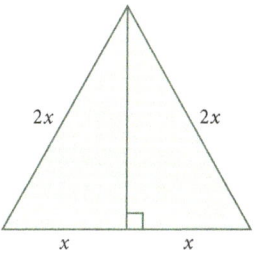

55. Pyramids The following solid is called a regular square pyramid because its base is a square and all eight edges are the same length, 5. It is also true that the vertex, V, is directly above the center of the base.

a. Find the ratio of a diagonal of the base to the length of a side.

b. Find the ratio of the area of the base to the diagonal of the base.

c. Find the ratio of the area of the base to the perimeter of the base.

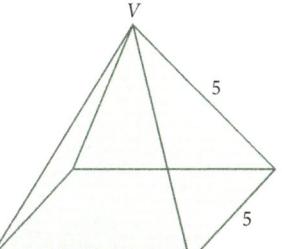

56. Pyramids Refer to this diagram of a square pyramid. Find the ratio of the height h of the pyramid to the altitude a.

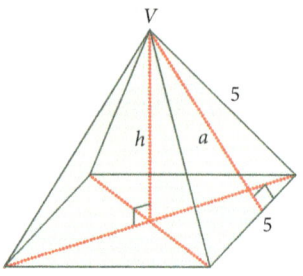

Getting Ready for the Next Section

Simplify the following.

57. $3 \cdot 2$

58. $5 \cdot 7$

59. $(x + y)(4x - y)$

60. $(2x + y)(x - y)$

61. $(x + 3)^2$

62. $(3x - 2y)^2$

63. $(x - 2)(x + 2)$

64. $(2x + 5)(2x - 5)$

Simplify the following expressions.

65. $2\sqrt{18}$

66. $5\sqrt{36}$

67. $(\sqrt{6})^2$

68. $(\sqrt{2})^2$

69. $(3\sqrt{x})^2$

70. $(2\sqrt{y})^2$

Rationalize the denominator.

71. $\dfrac{\sqrt{3}}{\sqrt{2}}$

72. $\dfrac{\sqrt{5}}{\sqrt{6}}$

Multiplication and Division of Radical Expressions

We have worked with the golden rectangle more than once in this chapter. The following is one such golden rectangle.

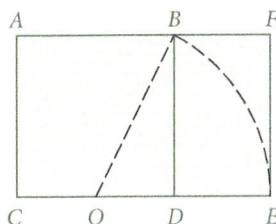

By now you know that, in any golden rectangle constructed from a square (of any size), the ratio of the length to the width will be

$$\frac{1 + \sqrt{5}}{2}$$

which we call the golden ratio. What is interesting is that the smaller rectangle on the right, *BFED*, is also a golden rectangle. We will use the mathematics developed in this section to confirm this fact.

In this section, we will look at multiplication and division of expressions that contain radicals. As you will see, multiplication of expressions that contain radicals is very similar to multiplication of polynomials. The division problems in this section are just an extension of the work we did previously when we rationalized denominators.

Video Examples

Section 8.4

Example 1   Multiply $(3\sqrt{5})(2\sqrt{7})$.

SOLUTION   We can rearrange the order and grouping of the numbers in this product by applying the commutative and associative properties. Following this, we apply Property 1 for radicals and multiply:

$$(3\sqrt{5})(2\sqrt{7}) = (3 \cdot 2)(\sqrt{5}\sqrt{7}) \qquad \text{Communicative and associative properties}$$

$$= (3 \cdot 2)(\sqrt{5 \cdot 7}) \qquad \text{Property 1 for radicals}$$

$$= 6\sqrt{35} \qquad \text{Multiplication}$$

In practice, it is not necessary to show the first two steps.

Example 2   Multiply $\sqrt{3}(2\sqrt{6} - 5\sqrt{12})$.

SOLUTION   Applying the distributive property, we have

$$\sqrt{3}(2\sqrt{6} - 5\sqrt{12}) = \sqrt{3} \cdot 2\sqrt{6} - \sqrt{3} \cdot 5\sqrt{12}$$

$$= 2\sqrt{18} - 5\sqrt{36}$$

Writing each radical in simplified form gives

$$2\sqrt{18} - 5\sqrt{36} = 2\sqrt{9}\sqrt{2} - 5\sqrt{36}$$

$$= 6\sqrt{2} - 30$$

Example 3　Multiply $(\sqrt{3} + \sqrt{5})(4\sqrt{3} - \sqrt{5})$.

SOLUTION　The same principle that applies when multiplying two binomials applies to this product. We must multiply each term in the first expression by each term in the second one. Any convenient method can be used. Let's use the FOIL method.

$$(\sqrt{3} + \sqrt{5})(4\sqrt{3} - \sqrt{5}) = \overset{F}{\sqrt{3} \cdot 4\sqrt{3}} - \overset{O}{\sqrt{3} \cdot \sqrt{5}} + \overset{I}{\sqrt{5} \cdot 4\sqrt{3}} - \overset{L}{\sqrt{5} \cdot \sqrt{5}}$$

$$= 4 \cdot 3 - \sqrt{15} + 4\sqrt{15} - 5$$

$$= 12 + 3\sqrt{15} - 5$$

$$= 7 + 3\sqrt{15}$$

Example 4　Expand and simplify $(\sqrt{x} + 3)^2$.

SOLUTION 1　We can write this problem as a multiplication problem and proceed as we did in Example 3:

$$(\sqrt{x} + 3)^2 = (\sqrt{x} + 3)(\sqrt{x} + 3)$$

$$= \overset{F}{\sqrt{x} \cdot \sqrt{x}} + \overset{O}{3\sqrt{x}} + \overset{I}{3\sqrt{x}} + \overset{L}{3 \cdot 3}$$

$$= x + 3\sqrt{x} + 3\sqrt{x} + 9$$

$$= x + 6\sqrt{x} + 9$$

SOLUTION 2　We can obtain the same result by applying the formula for the square of a sum: $(a + b)^2 = a^2 + 2ab + b^2$.

$$(\sqrt{x} + 3)^2 = (\sqrt{x})^2 + 2(\sqrt{x})(3) + 3^2$$

$$= x + 6\sqrt{x} + 9$$

Example 5　Expand $(3\sqrt{x} - 2\sqrt{y})^2$ and simplify the result.

SOLUTION　Let's apply the formula for the square of a difference, $(a - b)^2 = a^2 - 2ab + b^2$.

$$(3\sqrt{x} - 2\sqrt{y})^2 = (3\sqrt{x})^2 - 2(3\sqrt{x})(2\sqrt{y}) + (2\sqrt{y})^2$$

$$= 9x - 12\sqrt{xy} + 4y$$

Example 6　Expand and simplify $(\sqrt{x + 2} - 1)^2$.

SOLUTION　Applying the formula $(a - b)^2 = a^2 - 2ab + b^2$, we have

$$(\sqrt{x + 2} - 1)^2 = (\sqrt{x + 2})^2 - 2\sqrt{x + 2}(1) + 1^2$$

$$= x + 2 - 2\sqrt{x + 2} + 1$$

$$= x + 3 - 2\sqrt{x + 2}$$

Example 7   Multiply $(\sqrt{6} + \sqrt{2})(\sqrt{6} - \sqrt{2})$.

SOLUTION   We notice the product is of the form $(a + b)(a - b)$, which always gives the difference of two squares, $a^2 - b^2$:

$$(\sqrt{6} + \sqrt{2})(\sqrt{6} - \sqrt{2}) = (\sqrt{6})^2 - (\sqrt{2})^2$$
$$= 6 - 2$$
$$= 4$$

In Example 7, the two expressions $(\sqrt{6} + \sqrt{2})$ and $(\sqrt{6} - \sqrt{2})$ are called *conjugates*. In general, the conjugate of $\sqrt{a} + \sqrt{b}$ is $\sqrt{a} - \sqrt{b}$. If a and b are integers, multiplying conjugates of this form always produces a rational number. That is, if a and b are positive integers, then

$$(\sqrt{a} + \sqrt{b})(\sqrt{a} - \sqrt{b}) = \sqrt{a}\sqrt{a} - \sqrt{a}\sqrt{b} + \sqrt{a}\sqrt{b} - \sqrt{b}\sqrt{b}$$
$$= a - \sqrt{ab} + \sqrt{ab} - b$$
$$= a - b$$

and is rational if a and b are rational.

Division with radical expressions is the same as rationalizing the denominator. In Section 8.2, we were able to divide $\sqrt{3}$ by $\sqrt{2}$ by rationalizing the denominator:

$$\frac{\sqrt{3}}{\sqrt{2}} = \frac{\sqrt{3}}{\sqrt{2}} \cdot \frac{\sqrt{2}}{\sqrt{2}} = \frac{\sqrt{6}}{2}$$

We can accomplish the same result with expressions such as

$$\frac{6}{\sqrt{5} - \sqrt{3}}$$

by multiplying the numerator and denominator by the conjugate of the denominator.

Example 8   Divide $\dfrac{6}{\sqrt{5} - \sqrt{3}}$. (Rationalize the denominator.)

SOLUTION   Because the product of two conjugates is a rational number, we multiply the numerator and denominator by the conjugate of the denominator.

$$\frac{6}{\sqrt{5} - \sqrt{3}} = \frac{6}{\sqrt{5} - \sqrt{3}} \cdot \frac{(\sqrt{5} + \sqrt{3})}{(\sqrt{5} + \sqrt{3})}$$
$$= \frac{6\sqrt{5} + 6\sqrt{3}}{(\sqrt{5})^2 - (\sqrt{3})^2}$$
$$= \frac{6\sqrt{5} + 6\sqrt{3}}{5 - 3}$$
$$= \frac{6\sqrt{5} + 6\sqrt{3}}{2}$$

The numerator and denominator of this last expression have a factor of 2 in common. We can reduce to lowest terms by factoring 2 from the numerator and then dividing both the numerator and denominator by 2:

$$= \frac{2(3\sqrt{5} + 3\sqrt{3})}{2}$$
$$= 3\sqrt{5} + 3\sqrt{3}$$

Example 9   Rationalize the denominator $\dfrac{\sqrt{5} - 2}{\sqrt{5} + 2}$.

SOLUTION   To rationalize the denominator, we multiply the numerator and denominator by the conjugate of the denominator:

$$\frac{\sqrt{5} - 2}{\sqrt{5} + 2} = \frac{\sqrt{5} - 2}{\sqrt{5} + 2} \cdot \frac{(\sqrt{5} - 2)}{(\sqrt{5} - 2)}$$

$$= \frac{5 - 2\sqrt{5} - 2\sqrt{5} + 4}{(\sqrt{5})^2 - 2^2}$$

$$= \frac{9 - 4\sqrt{5}}{5 - 4}$$

$$= \frac{9 - 4\sqrt{5}}{1}$$

$$= 9 - 4\sqrt{5}$$

Example 10   A golden rectangle constructed from a square of side 2 is shown in Figure 1. Show that the smaller rectangle *BDEF* is also a golden rectangle by finding the ratio of its length to its width.

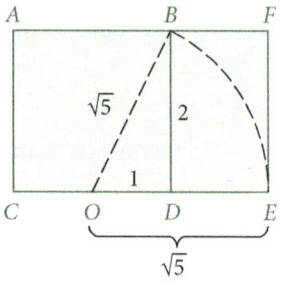

FIGURE 1

SOLUTION   First, find expressions for the length and width of the smaller rectangle.

$$\text{Length} = EF = 2$$

$$\text{Width} = DE = \sqrt{5} - 1$$

Next, we find the ratio of length to width.

$$\text{Ratio of length to width} = \frac{EF}{DE} = \frac{2}{\sqrt{5} - 1}$$

To show that the small rectangle is a golden rectangle, we must show that the ratio of length to width is the golden ratio. We do so by rationalizing the denominator.

$$\frac{2}{\sqrt{5} - 1} = \frac{2}{\sqrt{5} - 1} \cdot \frac{\sqrt{5} + 1}{\sqrt{5} + 1}$$

$$= \frac{2(\sqrt{5} + 1)}{5 - 1}$$

$$= \frac{2(\sqrt{5} + 1)}{4}$$

$$= \frac{\sqrt{5} + 1}{2} \qquad \text{Divide out common factor 2}$$

Because addition is commutative, this last expression is the golden ratio. Therefore, the small rectangle in Figure 1 is a golden rectangle.

Getting Ready for Class

After reading through the preceding section, respond in your own words and in complete sentences.

A. Explain why $(\sqrt{5} + \sqrt{2})^2 \neq 5 + 2$.

B. Explain in words how you would rationalize the denominator in the expression $\frac{\sqrt{3}}{\sqrt{5} - \sqrt{2}}$.

C. What are conjugates?

D. What result is guaranteed when multiplying radical expressions that are conjugates?

Problem Set 8.4

Multiply. (Assume all expressions appearing under a square root symbol represent nonnegative numbers throughout this problem set.)

1. $\sqrt{6}\sqrt{3}$

2. $\sqrt{6}\sqrt{2}$

3. $(2\sqrt{3})(5\sqrt{7})$

4. $(3\sqrt{5})(2\sqrt{7})$

5. $(4\sqrt{6})(2\sqrt{15})(3\sqrt{10})$

6. $(4\sqrt{35})(2\sqrt{21})(5\sqrt{15})$

7. $(3\sqrt[3]{3})(6\sqrt[3]{9})$

8. $(2\sqrt[3]{2})(6\sqrt[3]{4})$

9. $\sqrt{3}(\sqrt{2} - 3\sqrt{3})$

10. $\sqrt{2}(5\sqrt{3} + 4\sqrt{2})$

11. $6\sqrt[3]{4}(2\sqrt[3]{2} + 1)$

12. $7\sqrt[3]{5}(3\sqrt[3]{25} - 2)$

13. $(\sqrt{3} + \sqrt{2})(3\sqrt{3} - \sqrt{2})$

14. $(\sqrt{5} - \sqrt{2})(3\sqrt{5} + 2\sqrt{2})$

15. $(\sqrt{x} + 5)(\sqrt{x} - 3)$

16. $(\sqrt{x} + 4)(\sqrt{x} + 2)$

17. $(3\sqrt{6} + 4\sqrt{2})(\sqrt{6} + 2\sqrt{2})$

18. $(\sqrt{7} - 3\sqrt{3})(2\sqrt{7} - 4\sqrt{3})$

19. $(\sqrt{3} + 4)^2$

20. $(\sqrt{5} - 2)^2$

21. $(\sqrt{x} - 3)^2$

22. $(\sqrt{x} + 4)^2$

23. $(2\sqrt{a} - 3\sqrt{b})^2$

24. $(5\sqrt{a} - 2\sqrt{b})^2$

25. $(\sqrt{x - 4} + 2)^2$

26. $(\sqrt{x - 3} + 2)^2$

27. $(\sqrt{x - 5} - 3)^2$

28. $(\sqrt{x - 3} - 4)^2$

29. $(\sqrt{3} - \sqrt{2})(\sqrt{3} + \sqrt{2})$

30. $(\sqrt{5} - \sqrt{2})(\sqrt{5} + \sqrt{2})$

31. $(\sqrt{a} + 7)(\sqrt{a} - 7)$

32. $(\sqrt{a} + 5)(\sqrt{a} - 5)$

33. $(5 - \sqrt{x})(5 + \sqrt{x})$

34. $(3 - \sqrt{x})(3 + \sqrt{x})$

35. $(\sqrt{x - 4} + 2)(\sqrt{x - 4} - 2)$

36. $(\sqrt{x + 3} + 5)(\sqrt{x + 3} - 5)$

37. $(\sqrt{3} + 1)^3$

38. $(\sqrt{5} - 2)^3$

Rationalize the denominator in each of the following.

39. $\dfrac{\sqrt{2}}{\sqrt{6} - \sqrt{2}}$

40. $\dfrac{\sqrt{5}}{\sqrt{5} + \sqrt{3}}$

41. $\dfrac{\sqrt{5}}{\sqrt{5} + 1}$

42. $\dfrac{\sqrt{7}}{\sqrt{7} - 1}$

43. $\dfrac{\sqrt{x}}{\sqrt{x} - 3}$

44. $\dfrac{\sqrt{x}}{\sqrt{x} + 2}$

45. $\dfrac{\sqrt{5}}{2\sqrt{5} - 3}$

46. $\dfrac{\sqrt{7}}{3\sqrt{7} - 2}$

47. $\dfrac{3}{\sqrt{x} - \sqrt{y}}$

48. $\dfrac{2}{\sqrt{x} + \sqrt{y}}$

49. $\dfrac{\sqrt{6} + \sqrt{2}}{\sqrt{6} - \sqrt{2}}$

50. $\dfrac{\sqrt{5} - \sqrt{3}}{\sqrt{5} + \sqrt{3}}$

51. $\dfrac{\sqrt{7} - 2}{\sqrt{7} + 2}$

52. $\dfrac{\sqrt{11} + 3}{\sqrt{11} - 3}$

53. Work each problem according to the instructions given.

    a. Add: $(\sqrt{x} + 2) + (\sqrt{x} - 2)$

    b. Multiply: $(\sqrt{x} + 2)(\sqrt{x} - 2)$

    c. Square: $(\sqrt{x} + 2)^2$

    d. Divide: $\dfrac{\sqrt{x} + 2}{\sqrt{x} - 2}$

54. Work each problem according to the instructions given.

    a. Add: $(\sqrt{x} - 3) + (\sqrt{x} + 3)$

    b. Multiply: $(\sqrt{x} - 3)(\sqrt{x} + 3)$

    c. Square: $(\sqrt{x} + 3)^2$

    d. Divide: $\dfrac{\sqrt{x} + 3}{\sqrt{x} - 3}$

55. Paying Attention to Instructions Work each problem according to the instructions given..

  a. Add: $(5 + \sqrt{2}) + (5 - \sqrt{2})$ **b.** Multiply: $(5 + \sqrt{2})(5 - \sqrt{2})$

  c. Square: $(5 + \sqrt{2})^2$ **d.** Divide: $\dfrac{5 + \sqrt{2}}{5 - \sqrt{2}}$

56. Paying Attention to Instructions Work each problem according to the instructions given..

  a. Add: $(2 + \sqrt{3}) + (2 - \sqrt{3})$ **b.** Multiply: $(2 + \sqrt{3})(2 - \sqrt{3})$

  c. Square: $(2 + \sqrt{3})^2$ **d.** Divide: $\dfrac{2 + \sqrt{3}}{2 - \sqrt{3}}$

57. Paying Attention to Instructions Work each problem according to the instructions given..

  a. Add: $\sqrt{2} + (\sqrt{6} + \sqrt{2})$ **b.** Multiply: $\sqrt{2}(\sqrt{6} + \sqrt{2})$

  c. Divide: $\dfrac{\sqrt{6} + \sqrt{2}}{\sqrt{2}}$ **d.** Divide: $\dfrac{\sqrt{2}}{\sqrt{6} + \sqrt{2}}$

58. Paying Attention to Instructions Work each problem according to the instructions given..

  a. Add: $\sqrt{5} + (\sqrt{5} + \sqrt{10})$ **b.** Multiply: $\sqrt{5}(\sqrt{5} + \sqrt{10})$

  c. Divide: $\dfrac{\sqrt{5} + \sqrt{10}}{\sqrt{5}}$ **d.** Divide: $\dfrac{\sqrt{5}}{\sqrt{5} + \sqrt{10}}$

59. Paying Attention to Instructions Work each problem according to the instructions given..

  a. Add: $\left(\dfrac{1 + \sqrt{5}}{2}\right) + \left(\dfrac{1 - \sqrt{5}}{2}\right)$ **b.** $\left(\dfrac{1 + \sqrt{5}}{2}\right)\left(\dfrac{1 - \sqrt{5}}{2}\right)$

60. Paying Attention to Instructions Work each problem according to the instructions given..

  a. Add: $\left(\dfrac{1 + \sqrt{3}}{2}\right) + \left(\dfrac{1 - \sqrt{3}}{2}\right)$ **b.** Multiply: $\left(\dfrac{1 + \sqrt{3}}{2}\right)\left(\dfrac{1 - \sqrt{3}}{2}\right)$

61. Show that the product below is 5:
$$(\sqrt[3]{2} + \sqrt[3]{3})(\sqrt[3]{4} - \sqrt[3]{6} + \sqrt[3]{9})$$

62. Show that the product below is $x + 8$:
$$(\sqrt[3]{x} + 2)(\sqrt[3]{x^2} - 2\sqrt[3]{x} + 4)$$

Each of the following statements below is false. Correct the right side of each one to make it true.

63. $5(2\sqrt{3}) = 10\sqrt{15}$ **64.** $3(2\sqrt{x}) = 6\sqrt{3x}$ **65.** $(\sqrt{x} + 3)^2 = x + 9$

66. $(\sqrt{x} - 7)^2 = x - 49$ **67.** $(5\sqrt{3})^2 = 15$ **68.** $(3\sqrt{5})^2 = 15$

Applying the Concepts

69. Gravity If an object is dropped from the top of a 100-foot building, the amount of time t (in seconds) that it takes for the object to be h feet from the ground is given by the formula

$$t = \frac{\sqrt{100 - h}}{4}$$

How long does it take before the object is 50 feet from the ground? How long does it take to reach the ground? (When it is on the ground, h is 0.)

70. Gravity Use the formula given in Problem 69 to determine h if t is 1.25 seconds.

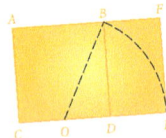

71. Golden Rectangle Rectangle $ACEF$ in Figure 2 is a golden rectangle. If side AC is 6 inches, show that the smaller rectangle $BDEF$ is also a golden rectangle.

72. Golden Rectangle Rectangle $ACEF$ in Figure 2 is a golden rectangle. If side AC is 1 inch, show that the smaller rectangle $BDEF$ is also a golden rectangle.

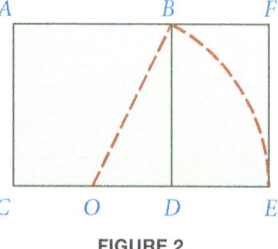

FIGURE 2

73. Golden Rectangle If side AC in Figure 2 is $2x$, show that rectangle $BDEF$ is a golden rectangle.

74. Golden Rectangle If side AC in Figure 2 is x, show that rectangle $BDEF$ is a golden rectangle.

Getting Ready for the Next Section

Simplify.

75. $(t + 5)^2$ **76.** $(x - 4)^2$ **77.** $\sqrt{x} \cdot \sqrt{x}$ **78.** $\sqrt{3x} \cdot \sqrt{3x}$

Solve.

79. $3x + 4 = 5^2$ **80.** $4x - 7 = 3^2$

81. $t^2 + 7t + 12 = 0$ **82.** $x^2 - 3x - 10 = 0$

83. $t^2 + 10t + 25 = t + 7$ **84.** $x^2 - 4x + 4 = x - 2$

85. $(x + 4)^2 = x + 6$ **86.** $(x - 6)^2 = x - 4$

87. Is $x = 7$ a solution to $\sqrt{3x + 4} = 5$?

88. Is $x = 4$ a solution to $\sqrt{4x - 7} = -3$?

89. Is $t = -6$ a solution to $t + 5 = \sqrt{t + 7}$?

90. Is $t = -3$ a solution to $t + 5 = \sqrt{t + 7}$?

Equations Involving Radicals

This section is concerned with solving equations that involve one or more radicals. The first step in solving an equation that contains a radical is to eliminate the radical from the equation. To do so, we need an additional property.

> **Squaring Property of Equality**
>
> If both sides of an equation are squared, the solutions to the original equation are solutions to the resulting equation.

We will never lose solutions to our equations by squaring both sides. We may, however, introduce *extraneous solutions*. Extraneous solutions satisfy the equation obtained by squaring both sides of the original equation, but do not satisfy the original equation.

We know that if two real numbers a and b are equal, then so are their squares:

$$\text{If} \quad a = b$$
$$\text{then} \quad a^2 = b^2$$

On the other hand, extraneous solutions are introduced when we square opposites. That is, even though opposites are not equal, their squares are. For example,

$$5 = -5 \qquad \textit{A false statement}$$
$$(5)^2 = (-5)^2 \qquad \textit{Square both sides}$$
$$25 = 25 \qquad \textit{A true statement}$$

We are free to square both sides of an equation any time it is convenient. We must be aware, however, that doing so may introduce extraneous solutions. We must, therefore, check all our solutions in the original equation if at any time we square both sides of the original equation.

Video Examples

Section 8.5

Example 1   Solve for x: $\sqrt{3x + 4} = 5$.

SOLUTION   We square both sides and proceed as usual:

$$\sqrt{3x + 4} = 5$$
$$(\sqrt{3x + 4})^2 = 5^2$$
$$3x + 4 = 25$$
$$3x = 21$$
$$x = 7$$

Checking $x = 7$ in the original equation, we have

$$\sqrt{3(7) + 4} \overset{?}{=} 5$$
$$\sqrt{21 + 4} \overset{?}{=} 5$$
$$\sqrt{25} \overset{?}{=} 5$$
$$5 = 5$$

The solution $x = 7$ satisfies the original equation.

Example 2   Solve $\sqrt{4x - 7} = -3$.

SOLUTION   Squaring both sides, we have

$$\sqrt{4x - 7} = -3$$
$$(\sqrt{4x - 7})^2 = (-3)^2$$
$$4x - 7 = 9$$
$$4x = 16$$
$$x = 4$$

Checking $x = 4$ in the original equation gives

$$\sqrt{4(4) - 7} \overset{?}{=} -3$$
$$\sqrt{16 - 7} \overset{?}{=} -3$$
$$\sqrt{9} \overset{?}{=} -3$$
$$3 = -3 \qquad \text{A false statement}$$

> *Note*   The fact that there is no solution to the equation in Example 2 was obvious to begin with. Notice that the left side of the equation is the positive square root of $4x - 7$, which must be a positive number or 0. The right side of the equation is -3. Because we cannot have a number that is either positive or zero equal to a negative number, there is no solution to the equation.

The solution $x = 4$ produces a false statement when checked in the original equation. Because $x = 4$ was the only possible solution, there is no solution to the original equation. The possible solution $x = 4$ is an extraneous solution. It satisfies the equation obtained by squaring both sides of the original equation, but does not satisfy the original equation.

Example 3   Solve $\sqrt{5x - 1} + 3 = 7$.

SOLUTION   We must isolate the radical on the left side of the equation. If we attempt to square both sides without doing so, the resulting equation will also contain a radical. Adding -3 to both sides, we have

$$\sqrt{5x - 1} + 3 = 7$$
$$\sqrt{5x - 1} = 4$$

We can now square both sides and proceed as usual:

$$(\sqrt{5x - 1})^2 = 4^2$$
$$5x - 1 = 16$$
$$5x = 17$$
$$x = \frac{17}{5}$$

Checking $x = \frac{17}{5}$, we have

$$\sqrt{5\left(\frac{17}{5}\right) - 1} + 3 \overset{?}{=} 7$$
$$\sqrt{17 - 1} + 3 \overset{?}{=} 7$$
$$\sqrt{16} + 3 \overset{?}{=} 7$$
$$4 + 3 \overset{?}{=} 7$$
$$7 = 7$$

Example 4   Solve $t + 5 = \sqrt{t + 7}$.

SOLUTION   This time, squaring both sides of the equation results in a quadratic equation:

$$(t + 5)^2 = (\sqrt{t + 7})^2 \qquad \text{Square both sides}$$

$$t^2 + 10t + 25 = t + 7$$

$$t^2 + 9t + 18 = 0 \qquad \text{Standard form}$$

$$(t + 3)(t + 6) = 0 \qquad \text{Factor the left side}$$

$$t + 3 = 0 \quad \text{or} \quad t + 6 = 0 \qquad \text{Set factors equal to 0}$$

$$t = -3 \quad \text{or} \qquad t = -6$$

We must check each solution in the original equation:

Check $t = -3$ Check $t = -6$

$-3 + 5 \overset{?}{=} \sqrt{-3 + 7}$ $-6 + 5 \overset{?}{=} \sqrt{-6 + 7}$

$2 \overset{?}{=} \sqrt{4}$ $-1 \overset{?}{=} \sqrt{1}$

$2 = 2$ A true statement $-1 = 1$ A false statement

Because $t = -6$ does not check, our only solution is $t = -3$.   ■

Example 5   Solve $\sqrt{x - 3} = \sqrt{x} - 3$.

SOLUTION   We begin by squaring both sides. Note carefully what happens when we square the right side of the equation, and compare the square of the right side with the square of the left side. You must convince yourself that these results are correct. (The note in the margin will help if you are having trouble convincing yourself that what is written below is true.)

$$(\sqrt{x - 3})^2 = (\sqrt{x} - 3)^2$$

$$x - 3 = x - 6\sqrt{x} + 9$$

Now we still have a radical in our equation, so we will have to square both sides again. Before we do, though, let's isolate the remaining radical.

$$x - 3 = x - 6\sqrt{x} + 9$$

$$-3 = -6\sqrt{x} + 9 \qquad \text{Add } -x \text{ to each side}$$

$$-12 = -6\sqrt{x} \qquad \text{Add } -9 \text{ to each side}$$

$$2 = \sqrt{x} \qquad \text{Divide each side by } -6$$

$$4 = x \qquad \text{Square each side}$$

Our only possible solution is $x = 4$, which we check in our original equation as follows:

$$\sqrt{4 - 3} \overset{?}{=} \sqrt{4} - 3$$

$$\sqrt{1} \overset{?}{=} 2 - 3$$

$$1 = -1 \qquad \text{A false statement}$$

Substituting 4 for x in the original equation yields a false statement. Because 4 was our only possible solution, there is no solution to our equation.   ■

Note   It is very important that you realize that the square of $(\sqrt{x} - 3)$ is not $x + 9$. Remember, when we square a difference with two terms, we use the formula

$$(a - b)^2 = a^2 - 2ab + b^2$$

Applying this formula to $(\sqrt{x} - 3)^2$ we have

$$(\sqrt{x} - 3)^2 =$$
$$(\sqrt{x})^2 - 2(\sqrt{x})(3) + 3^2$$
$$= x - 6\sqrt{x} + 9$$

Here is another example of an equation for which we must apply our squaring property twice before all radicals are eliminated.

Example 6   Solve $\sqrt{x+1} = 1 - \sqrt{2x}$.

SOLUTION   This equation has two separate terms involving radical signs.
   Squaring both sides gives

$$x + 1 = 1 - 2\sqrt{2x} + 2x$$

$$-x = -2\sqrt{2x} \qquad \text{Add } -2x \text{ and } -1 \text{ to both sides}$$

$$x^2 = 4(2x) \qquad \text{Square both sides}$$

$$x^2 - 8x = 0 \qquad \text{Standard form}$$

Our equation is a quadratic equation in standard form. To solve for x, we factor the left side and set each factor equal to 0:

$$x(x - 8) = 0 \qquad \text{Factor left side}$$

$$x = 0 \quad \text{or} \quad x - 8 = 0$$

$$x = 8 \qquad \text{Set factors equal to 0}$$

Because we squared both sides of our equation, we have the possibility that one or both of the solutions are extraneous. We must check each one in the original equation:

Check $x = 8$ Check $x = 0$

$$\sqrt{8+1} \overset{?}{=} 1 - \sqrt{2 \cdot 8} \qquad\qquad \sqrt{0+1} \overset{?}{=} 1 - \sqrt{2 \cdot 0}$$

$$\sqrt{9} \overset{?}{=} 1 - \sqrt{16} \qquad\qquad\qquad \sqrt{1} \overset{?}{=} 1 - \sqrt{0}$$

$$3 \overset{?}{=} 1 - 4 \qquad\qquad\qquad\qquad 1 \overset{?}{=} 1 - 0$$

$$3 = -3 \quad \text{A false statement} \qquad 1 = 1 \quad \text{A true statement}$$

Because $x = 8$ does not check, it is an extraneous solution. Our only solution is $x = 0$.

Example 7   Solve $\sqrt{x+1} = \sqrt{x+2} - 1$.

SOLUTION   Squaring both sides we have

$$(\sqrt{x+1})^2 = (\sqrt{x+2} - 1)^2$$

$$x + 1 = x + 2 - 2\sqrt{x+2} + 1$$

Once again, we are left with a radical in our equation. Before we square each side again, we must isolate the radical on the right side of the equation.

$$x + 1 = x + 3 - 2\sqrt{x+2} \qquad \text{Simplify the right side}$$

$$1 = 3 - 2\sqrt{x+2} \qquad \text{Add } -x \text{ to each side}$$

$$-2 = -2\sqrt{x+2} \qquad \text{Add } -3 \text{ to each side}$$

$$1 = \sqrt{x+2} \qquad \text{Divide each side by } -2$$

$$1 = x + 2 \qquad \text{Square both sides}$$

$$-1 = x \qquad \text{Add } -2 \text{ to each side}$$

Checking our only possible solution, $x = -1$, in our original equation, we have

$$\sqrt{-1 + 1} \stackrel{?}{=} \sqrt{-1 + 2} - 1$$

$$\sqrt{0} \stackrel{?}{=} \sqrt{1} - 1$$

$$0 \stackrel{?}{=} 1 - 1$$

$$0 = 0 \qquad \text{A true statement}$$

Our solution checks.

It is also possible to raise both sides of an equation to powers greater than 2. We only need to check for extraneous solutions when we raise both sides of an equation to an even power. Raising both sides of an equation to an odd power will not produce extraneous solutions.

Example 8   Solve $\sqrt[3]{4x + 5} = 3$.

SOLUTION   Cubing both sides, we have

$$(\sqrt[3]{4x + 5})^3 = 3^3$$

$$4x + 5 = 27$$

$$4x = 22$$

$$x = \frac{22}{4}$$

$$x = \frac{11}{2}$$

We do not need to check $x = \frac{11}{2}$ because we raised both sides to an odd power.

We end this section by looking at graphs of some equations that contain radicals.

Example 9   Graph $y = \sqrt{x}$ and $y = \sqrt[3]{x}$.

SOLUTION   The graphs are shown in Figures 1 and 2. Notice that the graph of $y = \sqrt{x}$ appears in the first quadrant only, because in the equation $y = \sqrt{x}$, x and y cannot be negative.

The graph of $y = \sqrt[3]{x}$ appears in Quadrants 1 and 3 because the cube root of a positive number is also a positive number, and the cube root of a negative number is a negative number. That is, when x is positive, y will be positive, and when x is negative, y will be negative.

The graphs of both equations will contain the origin, because $y = 0$ when $x = 0$ in both equations.

x	y
-4	Undefined
-1	Undefined
0	0
1	1
4	2
9	3
16	4

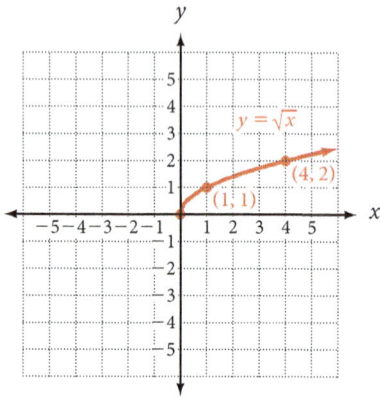

FIGURE 1

x	y
-27	-3
-8	-2
-1	-1
0	0
1	1
8	2
27	3

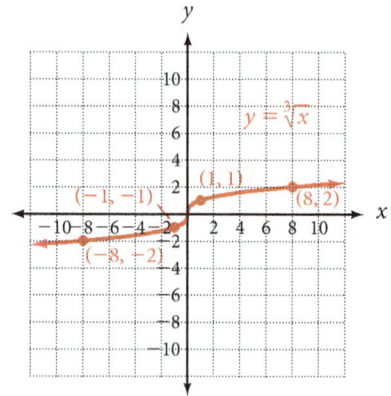

FIGURE 2

If we were looking at these two equations in terms of functions, then the domain for the function $f(x) = \sqrt{x}$ would be $\{x \mid x \geq 0\}$. The domain for the function $f(x) = \sqrt[3]{x}$ would be $\{x \mid x \text{ is any real number}\}$.

Getting Ready for Class

After reading through the preceding section, respond in your own words and in complete sentences.

A. What is the squaring property of equality?

B. Under what conditions do we obtain extraneous solutions to equations that contain radical expressions?

C. If we have raised both sides of an equation to a power, when is it not necessary to check for extraneous solutions?

D. When will you need to apply the squaring property of equality twice in the process of solving an equation containing radicals?

Problem Set 8.5

Solve each of the following equations.

1. $\sqrt{2x+1} = 3$

2. $\sqrt{3x+1} = 4$

3. $\sqrt{4x+1} = -5$

4. $\sqrt{6x+1} = -5$

5. $\sqrt{2y-1} = 3$

6. $\sqrt{3y-1} = 2$

7. $\sqrt{5x-7} = -1$

8. $\sqrt{8x+3} = -6$

9. $\sqrt{2x-3} - 2 = 4$

10. $\sqrt{3x+1} - 4 = 1$

11. $\sqrt{4a+1} + 3 = 2$

12. $\sqrt{5a-3} + 6 = 2$

13. $\sqrt[4]{3x+1} = 2$

14. $\sqrt[4]{4x+1} = 3$

15. $\sqrt[3]{2x-5} = 1$

16. $\sqrt[3]{5x+7} = 2$

17. $\sqrt[3]{3a+5} = -3$

18. $\sqrt[3]{2a+7} = -2$

19. $\sqrt{y-3} = y - 3$

20. $\sqrt{y+3} = y - 3$

21. $\sqrt{a+2} = a + 2$

22. $\sqrt{a+10} = a - 2$

23. $\sqrt{2x+4} = \sqrt{1-x}$

24. $\sqrt{3x+4} = -\sqrt{2x+3}$

25. $\sqrt{4a+7} = -\sqrt{a+2}$

26. $\sqrt{7a-1} = \sqrt{2a+4}$

27. $\sqrt[4]{5x-8} = \sqrt[4]{4x-1}$

28. $\sqrt[4]{6x+7} = \sqrt[4]{x+2}$

29. $x + 1 = \sqrt{5x+1}$

30. $x - 1 = \sqrt{6x+1}$

31. $t + 5 = \sqrt{2t+9}$

32. $t + 7 = \sqrt{2t+13}$

33. $\sqrt{y-8} = \sqrt{8-y}$

34. $\sqrt{2y+5} = \sqrt{5y+2}$

35. $\sqrt[3]{3x+5} = \sqrt[3]{5-2x}$

36. $\sqrt[3]{4x+9} = \sqrt[3]{3-2x}$

The following equations will require that you square both sides twice before all the radicals are eliminated. Solve each equation using the methods shown in Examples 5, 6, and 7.

37. $\sqrt{x-8} = \sqrt{x} - 2$

38. $\sqrt{x+3} = \sqrt{x} - 3$

39. $\sqrt{x+1} = \sqrt{x} + 1$

40. $\sqrt{x-1} = \sqrt{x} - 1$

41. $\sqrt{x+8} = \sqrt{x-4} + 2$

42. $\sqrt{x+5} = \sqrt{x-3} + 2$

43. $\sqrt{x-5} - 3 = \sqrt{x-8}$

44. $\sqrt{x-3} - 4 = \sqrt{x-3}$

45. Solve each equation.

   a. $\sqrt{y} - 4 = 6$

   b. $\sqrt{y-4} = 6$

   c. $\sqrt{y-4} = -6$

   d. $\sqrt{y-4} = y - 6$

46. Solve each equation.

   a. $\sqrt{2y} + 15 = 7$

   b. $\sqrt{2y+15} = 7$

   c. $\sqrt{2y+15} = y$

   d. $\sqrt{2y+15} = y + 6$

47. Solve each equation.

   a. $x - 3 = 0$

   b. $\sqrt{x} - 3 = 0$

   c. $\sqrt{x-3} = 0$

   d. $\sqrt{x+3} = 0$

   e. $\sqrt{x+3} = 5$

   f. $\sqrt{x+3} = -5$

   g. $x - 3 = \sqrt{5-x}$

48. Solve each equation.

   a. $x - 2 = 0$

   b. $\sqrt{x} - 2 = 0$

   c. $\sqrt{x} + 2 = 0$

   d. $\sqrt{x+2} = 0$

   e. $\sqrt{x+2} = 7$

   f. $x - 2 = \sqrt{2x-1}$

Applying the Concepts

49. Solving a Formula Solve the following formula for h:

$$t = \frac{\sqrt{100 - h}}{4}$$

50. Solving a Formula Solve the following formula for h:

$$t = \sqrt{\frac{2h - 40t}{g}}$$

51. Pendulum Clock The length of time (T) in seconds it takes the pendulum of a clock to swing through one complete cycle is given by the formula

$$T = 2\pi\sqrt{\frac{L}{32}}$$

where L is the length, in feet, of the pendulum, and π is approximately $\frac{22}{7}$. How long must the pendulum be if one complete cycle takes 2 seconds?

52. Pollution A long straight river, 100 meters wide, is flowing at 1 meter per second. A pollutant is entering the river at a constant rate from one of its banks. As the pollutant disperses in the water, it forms a plume that is modeled by the equation $y = \sqrt{x}$. Use this information to answer the following questions.

a. How wide is the plume 25 meters down river from the source of the pollution?

b. How wide is the plume 100 meters down river from the source of the pollution?

c. How far down river from the source of the pollution does the plume reach halfway across the river?

d. How far down the river from the source of the pollution does the plume reach the other side of the river?

Graph each equation.

53. $y = 2\sqrt{x}$ **54.** $y = -2\sqrt{x}$ **55.** $y = \sqrt{x} - 2$ **56.** $y = \sqrt{x} + 2$

57. $y = \sqrt{x - 2}$ **58.** $y = \sqrt{x + 2}$ **59.** $y = 3\sqrt[3]{x}$ **60.** $y = -3\sqrt[3]{x}$

61. $y = \sqrt[3]{x} + 3$ **62.** $y = \sqrt[3]{x} - 3$ **63.** $y = \sqrt[3]{x + 3}$ **64.** $y = \sqrt[3]{x - 3}$

Getting Ready for the Next Section

Simplify.

65. $\sqrt{25}$ **66.** $\sqrt{49}$ **67.** $\sqrt{12}$ **68.** $\sqrt{50}$

69. $(-1)^{15}$ **70.** $(-1)^{20}$ **71.** $(-1)^{50}$ **72.** $(-1)^5$

Solve.

73. $3x = 12$ **74.** $4 = 8y$ **75.** $4x - 3 = 5$ **76.** $7 = 2y - 1$

Perform the indicated operation.

77. $(3 + 4x) + (7 - 6x)$ **78.** $(2 - 5x) + (-1 + 7x)$

79. $(7 + 3x) - (5 + 6x)$ **80.** $(5 - 2x) - (9 - 4x)$

81. $(3 - 4x)(2 + 5x)$ **82.** $(8 + x)(7 - 3x)$

83. $2x(4 - 6x)$ **84.** $3x(7 + 2x)$

85. $(2 + 3x)^2$ **86.** $(3 + 5x)^2$

87. $(2 - 3x)(2 + 3x)$ **88.** $(4 - 5x)(4 + 5x)$

Complex Numbers

The equation $x^2 = -9$ has no real number solutions because the square of a real number is always positive. We have been unable to work with square roots of negative numbers like $\sqrt{-25}$ and $\sqrt{-16}$ for the same reason. Complex numbers allow us to expand our work with radicals to include square roots of negative numbers and to solve equations like $x^2 = -9$ and $x^2 = -64$. Our work with complex numbers is based on the following definition.

> **(děf′ the number i**
>
> The **number i** is such that $i = \sqrt{-1}$ (which is the same as saying $i^2 = -1$).

The number i, as we have defined it here, is not a real number. Because of the way we have defined i, we can use it to simplify square roots of negative numbers.

> **⟨Δ≠Σ Square Roots of Negative Numbers**
>
> If a is a positive number, then $\sqrt{-a}$ can always be written as $i\sqrt{a}$. That is,
>
> $$\sqrt{-a} = i\sqrt{a} \qquad \text{if } a \text{ is a positive number}$$

To justify our rule, we simply square the quantity $i\sqrt{a}$ to obtain $-a$. Here is what it looks like when we do so:

$$(i\sqrt{a})^2 = i^2 \cdot (\sqrt{a})^2$$
$$= -1 \cdot a$$
$$= -a$$

Here are some examples that illustrate the use of our new rule.

Video Examples

Section 8.6

Examples Write each square root in terms of the number i.

1. $\sqrt{-25} = i\sqrt{25} = i \cdot 5 = 5i$ **2.** $\sqrt{-49} = i\sqrt{49} = i \cdot 7 = 7i$

3. $\sqrt{-12} = i\sqrt{12} = i \cdot 2\sqrt{3} = 2i\sqrt{3}$ **4.** $\sqrt{-17} = i\sqrt{17}$

Note In Examples 3 and 4, we wrote i before the radical simply to avoid confusion. If we were to write the answer to 3 as $2\sqrt{3}i$, some people would think the i was under the radical sign, but it is not.

If we assume all the properties of exponents hold when the base is i, we can write any power of i as i, -1, $-i$, or 1. Using the fact that $i^2 = -1$, we have

$$i^1 = i$$
$$i^2 = -1$$
$$i^3 = i^2 \cdot i = -1(i) = -i$$
$$i^4 = i^2 \cdot i^2 = -1(-1) = 1$$

Because $i^4 = 1$, i^5 will simplify to i, and we will begin repeating the sequence i, -1, $-i$, 1 as we simplify higher powers of i: Any power of i simplifies to i, -1, $-i$, or 1. The easiest way to simplify higher powers of i is to write them in terms of i^2. For instance, to simplify i^{21}, we would write it as

$$(i^2)^{10} \cdot i \qquad \text{because} \qquad 2 \cdot 10 + 1 = 21$$

Then, because $i^2 = -1$, we have

$$(-1)^{10} \cdot i = 1 \cdot i = i$$

Examples   Simplify as much as possible.

5. $i^{30} = (i^2)^{15} = (-1)^{15} = -1$

6. $i^{11} = (i^2)^5 \cdot i = (-1)^5 \cdot i = (-1)i = -i$

7. $i^{40} = (i^2)^{20} = (-1)^{20} = 1$

(děf′   *complex number*

A *complex number* is any number that can be put in the form

$$a + bi$$

where a and b are real numbers and $i = \sqrt{-1}$. The form $a + bi$ is called *standard form* for complex numbers. The number a is called the *real part* of the complex number. The number b is called the *imaginary part* of the complex number.

Every real number is a complex number. For example, 8 can be written as $8 + 0i$. Likewise, $-\frac{1}{2}, \pi, \sqrt{3}$, and 29 are complex numbers because they can all be written in the form $a + bi$:

$$-\frac{1}{2} = -\frac{1}{2} + 0i \qquad \pi = \pi + 0i \qquad \sqrt{3} = \sqrt{3} + 0i \qquad -9 = -9 + 0i$$

The rest of the complex numbers that are not real numbers, are divided into two additional categories; *compound numbers* and *pure imaginary numbers*. The diagram below shows all three subsets of the complex numbers, along with examples of the type of numbers that fall into those subsets.

Subsets of the Complex Numbers

All numbers of the form $a + bi$ fall into one of the following categories. Each category is a subset of the complex numbers.

Real Numbers	Compound Numbers	Pure Imaginary Numbers
When $a \neq 0$ and $b = 0$	When neither a nor b is 0	When $a = 0$ and $b \neq 0$
Examples include:	Examples include:	Examples include:
$-10, 0, 1, \sqrt{3}, \frac{5}{8}, \pi$	$5 + 4i, \frac{1}{3} + 4i, \sqrt{5} - i,$ $-6 + i\sqrt{5}$	$-4i, i\sqrt{3}, -5i\sqrt{7}, \frac{3}{4}i$

©2009 James Robert Metz

Note   See Section 0.8 for a review of the subsets of real numbers.

Note: The definition for compound numbers is from Jim Metz of Kapiolani Community College in Hawaii. Some textbooks use the phrase *imaginary numbers* to represent both the compound numbers and the pure imaginary numbers. In those books, the pure imaginary numbers are a subset of the imaginary numbers. We like the definition from Mr. Metz because it keeps the three subsets from overlapping.

Equality for Complex Numbers

Two complex numbers are equal if and only if their real parts are equal and their imaginary parts are equal. That is, for real numbers a, b, c, and d,

$$a + bi = c + di \qquad \text{if and only if} \qquad a = c \qquad \text{and} \qquad b = d$$

Example 8   Find x and y if $3x + 4i = 12 - 8yi$.

SOLUTION   Because the two complex numbers are equal, their real parts are equal and their imaginary parts are equal:

$$3x = 12 \quad \text{and} \quad 4 = -8y$$
$$x = 4 \qquad\qquad y = -\frac{1}{2}$$

Example 9   Find x and y if $(4x - 3) + 7i = 5 + (2y - 1)i$.

SOLUTION   The real parts are $4x - 3$ and 5. The imaginary parts are 7 and $2y - 1$:

$$4x - 3 = 5 \quad \text{and} \quad 7 = 2y - 1$$
$$4x = 8 \qquad\qquad 8 = 2y$$
$$x = 2 \qquad\qquad y = 4$$

Addition and Subtraction of Complex Numbers

To add two complex numbers, add their real parts and their imaginary parts. That is, if a, b, c, and d are real numbers, then

$$(a + bi) + (c + di) = (a + c) + (b + d)i$$

If we assume that the commutative, associative, and distributive properties hold for the number i, then the definition of addition is simply an extension of these properties.

We define subtraction in a similar manner. If a, b, c, and d are real numbers, then

$$(a + bi) - (c + di) = (a - c) + (b - d)i$$

Examples   Add or subtract as indicated.

10. $(3 + 4i) + (7 - 6i) = (3 + 7) + (4 - 6)i = 10 - 2i$

11. $(7 + 3i) - (5 + 6i) = (7 - 5) + (3 - 6)i = 2 - 3i$

12. $(5 - 2i) - (9 - 4i) = (5 - 9) + (-2 + 4)i = -4 + 2i$

Multiplication of Complex Numbers

Because complex numbers have the same form as binomials, we find the product of two complex numbers the same way we find the product of two binomials.

Example 13   Multiply $(3 - 4i)(2 + 5i)$.

SOLUTION   Multiplying each term in the second complex number by each term in the first, we have

$$(3 - 4i)(2 + 5i) = \overset{F}{3 \cdot 2} + \overset{O}{3 \cdot 5i} - \overset{I}{2 \cdot 4i} - \overset{L}{4i(5i)}$$
$$= 6 + 15i - 8i - 20i^2$$

Combining similar terms and using the fact that $i^2 = -1$, we can simplify as follows:

$$6 + 15i - 8i - 20i^2 = 6 + 7i - 20(-1)$$
$$= 6 + 7i + 20$$
$$= 26 + 7i$$

The product of the complex numbers $3 - 4i$ and $2 + 5i$ is the complex number $26 + 7i$. ∎

Example 14 Multiply $2i(4 - 6i)$.

SOLUTION Applying the distributive property gives us

$$2i(4 - 6i) = 2i \cdot 4 - 2i \cdot 6i$$
$$= 8i - 12i^2$$
$$= 12 + 8i$$

Example 15 Expand $(3 + 5i)^2$.

SOLUTION We treat this like the square of a binomial. Remember, $(a + b)^2 = a^2 + 2ab + b^2$:

$$(3 + 5i)^2 = 3^2 + 2(3)(5i) + (5i)^2$$
$$= 9 + 30i + 25i^2$$
$$= 9 + 30i - 25$$
$$= -16 + 30i$$

Example 16 Multiply $(2 - 3i)(2 + 3i)$.

SOLUTION This product has the form $(a - b)(a + b)$, which we know results in the difference of two squares, $a^2 - b^2$:

$$(2 - 3i)(2 + 3i) = 2^2 - (3i)^2$$
$$= 4 - 9i^2$$
$$= 4 + 9$$
$$= 13$$

The product of the two complex numbers $2 - 3i$ and $2 + 3i$ is the real number 13. The two complex numbers $2 - 3i$ and $2 + 3i$ are called complex conjugates. The fact that their product is a real number is very useful.

(dĕf′) complex conjugates

The complex numbers $a + bi$ and $a - bi$ are called **complex conjugates**. One important property they have is that their product is the real number $a^2 + b^2$. Here's why :

$$(a + bi)(a - bi) = a^2 - (bi)^2$$
$$= a^2 - b^2i^2$$
$$= a^2 - b^2(-1)$$
$$= a^2 + b^2$$

Division With Complex Numbers

The fact that the product of two complex conjugates is a real number is the key to division with complex numbers.

Example 17 Divide $\dfrac{2 + i}{3 - 2i}$.

SOLUTION We want a complex number in standard form that is equivalent to the quotient $\frac{2+i}{3-2i}$. We need to eliminate i from the denominator. Multiplying the numerator and denominator by $3 + 2i$ will give us what we want:

$$\frac{2 + i}{3 - 2i} = \frac{2 + i}{3 - 2i} \cdot \frac{(3 + 2i)}{(3 + 2i)}$$

$$= \frac{6 + 4i + 3i + 2i^2}{9 - 4i^2}$$

$$= \frac{6 + 7i - 2}{9 + 4}$$

$$= \frac{4 + 7i}{13}$$

$$= \frac{4}{13} + \frac{7}{13}i$$

Dividing the complex number $2 + i$ by $3 - 2i$ gives the complex number $\frac{4}{13} + \frac{7}{13}i$.

Example 18 Divide $\dfrac{7 - 4i}{i}$.

SOLUTION The conjugate of the denominator is $-i$. Multiplying numerator and denominator by this number, we have

$$\frac{7 - 4i}{i} = \frac{7 - 4i}{i} \cdot \frac{-i}{-i}$$

$$= \frac{-7i + 4i^2}{-i^2}$$

$$= \frac{-7i + 4(-1)}{-(-1)}$$

$$= -4 - 7i$$

Getting Ready for Class

After reading through the preceding section, respond in your own words and in complete sentences.

A. What is the number i?

B. What is a complex number?

C. What kind of number will always result when we multiply complex conjugates?

D. Explain how to divide complex numbers.

Problem Set 8.6

Write the following in terms of i, and simplify as much as possible.

1. $\sqrt{-36}$ **2.** $\sqrt{-49}$ **3.** $-\sqrt{-25}$ **4.** $-\sqrt{-81}$

5. $\sqrt{-72}$ **6.** $\sqrt{-48}$ **7.** $-\sqrt{-12}$ **8.** $-\sqrt{-75}$

Write each of the following as i, -1, $-i$, or 1.

9. i^{28} **10.** i^{31} **11.** i^{26} **12.** i^{37}

13. i^{75} **14.** i^{42}

Find x and y so each of the following equations is true.

15. $2x + 3yi = 6 - 3i$ **16.** $4x - 2yi = 4 + 8i$

17. $2 - 5i = -x + 10yi$ **18.** $4 + 7i = 6x - 14yi$

19. $2x + 10i = -16 - 2yi$ **20.** $4x - 5i = -2 + 3yi$

21. $(2x - 4) - 3i = 10 - 6yi$ **22.** $(4x - 3) - 2i = 8 + yi$

23. $(7x - 1) + 4i = 2 + (5y + 2)i$ **24.** $(5x + 2) - 7i = 4 + (2y + 1)i$

Combine the following complex numbers.

25. $(2 + 3i) + (3 + 6i)$ **26.** $(4 + i) + (3 + 2i)$

27. $(3 - 5i) + (2 + 4i)$ **28.** $(7 + 2i) + (3 - 4i)$

29. $(5 + 2i) - (3 + 6i)$ **30.** $(6 + 7i) - (4 + i)$

31. $(3 - 5i) - (2 + i)$ **32.** $(7 - 3i) - (4 + 10i)$

33. $[(3 + 2i) - (6 + i)] + (5 + i)$ **34.** $[(4 - 5i) - (2 + i)] + (2 + 5i)$

35. $[(7 - i) - (2 + 4i)] - (6 + 2i)$ **36.** $[(3 - i) - (4 + 7i)] - (3 - 4i)$

37. $(3 + 2i) - [(3 - 4i) - (6 + 2i)]$ **38.** $(7 - 4i) - [(-2 + i) - (3 + 7i)]$

39. $(4 - 9i) + [(2 - 7i) - (4 + 8i)]$ **40.** $(10 - 2i) - [(2 + i) - (3 - i)]$

Find the following products.

41. $3i(4 + 5i)$

42. $2i(3 + 4i)$

43. $6i(4 - 3i)$

44. $11i(2 - i)$

45. $(3 + 2i)(4 + i)$

46. $(2 - 4i)(3 + i)$

47. $(4 + 9i)(3 - i)$

48. $(5 - 2i)(1 + i)$

49. $(1 + i)^3$

50. $(1 - i)^3$

51. $(2 - i)^3$

52. $(2 + i)^3$

53. $(2 + 5i)^2$

54. $(3 + 2i)^2$

55. $(1 - i)^2$

56. $(1 + i)^2$

57. $(3 - 4i)^2$

58. $(6 - 5i)^2$

59. $(2 + i)(2 - i)$

60. $(3 + i)(3 - i)$

61. $(6 - 2i)(6 + 2i)$

62. $(5 + 4i)(5 - 4i)$

63. $(2 + 3i)(2 - 3i)$

64. $(2 - 7i)(2 + 7i)$

65. $(10 + 8i)(10 - 8i)$

66. $(11 - 7i)(11 + 7i)$

Find the following quotients. Write all answers in standard form for complex numbers.

67. $\dfrac{2 - 3i}{i}$

68. $\dfrac{3 + 4i}{i}$

69. $\dfrac{5 + 2i}{-i}$

70. $\dfrac{4 - 3i}{-i}$

71. $\dfrac{4}{2 - 3i}$

72. $\dfrac{3}{4 - 5i}$

73. $\dfrac{6}{-3 + 2i}$

74. $\dfrac{-1}{-2 - 5i}$

75. $\dfrac{2 + 3i}{2 - 3i}$

76. $\dfrac{4 - 7i}{4 + 7i}$

77. $\dfrac{5 + 4i}{3 + 6i}$

78. $\dfrac{2 + i}{5 - 6i}$

Applying the Concepts

79. Electric Circuits Complex numbers may be applied to electrical circuits. Electrical engineers use the fact that resistance R to electrical flow of the electrical current I and the voltage V are related by the formula $V = RI$. (Voltage is measured in volts, resistance in ohms, and current in amperes.) Find the resistance to electrical flow in a circuit that has a voltage $V = (80 + 20i)$ volts and current $I = (-6 + 2i)$ amps.

80. Electric Circuits Refer to the information about electrical circuits in Problem 79, and find the current in a circuit that has a resistance of $(4 + 10i)$ ohms and a voltage of $(5 - 7i)$ volts.

Maintaining Your Skills

The following problems review material we covered in Sections 5.5 and 5.6.

Solve each equation. [5.5]

81. $\dfrac{t}{3} - \dfrac{1}{2} = -1$

82. $\dfrac{x}{x-2} + \dfrac{2}{3} = \dfrac{2}{x-2}$

83. $2 + \dfrac{5}{y} = \dfrac{3}{y^2}$

84. $1 - \dfrac{1}{y} = \dfrac{12}{y^2}$

Solve each application problem. [5.6]

85. The sum of a number and its reciprocal is $\dfrac{41}{20}$. Find the number.

86. It takes an inlet pipe 8 hours to fill a tank. The drain can empty the tank in 6 hours. If the tank is full and both the inlet pipe and drain are open, how long will it take to drain the tank?

Chapter 8 Summary

The numbers in brackets refer to the section(s) in which the topic can be found.

Square Roots [8.1]

1. The number 49 has two square roots, 7 and -7. They are written like this:

$$\sqrt{49} = 7 \qquad -\sqrt{49} = -7$$

Every positive real number x has two square roots. The ***positive square root*** of x is written $\sqrt{x}$, and the ***negative square root*** of x is written $-\sqrt{x}$. Both the positive and the negative square roots of x are numbers we square to get x; that is,

$$\left. \begin{array}{l} (\sqrt{x})^2 = x \\ \text{and} \qquad (-\sqrt{x})^2 = x \end{array} \right\} \text{ for } x \geq 0$$

Higher Roots [8.1]

2. $\sqrt[3]{8} = 2$

$\sqrt[3]{-27} = -3$

In the expression $\sqrt[n]{a}$, n is the ***index***, a is the ***radicand***, and $\sqrt{}$ is the ***radical sign***. The expression $\sqrt[n]{a}$ is such that

$$(\sqrt[n]{a})^n = a \qquad a \geq 0 \text{ when } n \text{ is even}$$

Rational Exponents [8.1]

3. $25^{1/2} = \sqrt{25} = 5$

$8^{2/3} = (\sqrt[3]{8})^2 = 2^2 = 4$

$9^{3/2} = (\sqrt{9})^3 = 3^3 = 27$

Rational exponents are used to indicate roots. The relationship between rational exponents and roots is as follows:

$$a^{1/n} = \sqrt[n]{a} \qquad \text{and} \qquad a^{m/n} = (a^{1/n})^m = (a^m)^{1/n}$$

$$a \geq 0 \text{ when } n \text{ is even}$$

Properties of Radicals [8.2]

4. $\sqrt{4 \cdot 5} = \sqrt{4}\,\sqrt{5} = 2\sqrt{5}$

$\sqrt{\dfrac{7}{9}} = \dfrac{\sqrt{7}}{\sqrt{9}} = \dfrac{\sqrt{7}}{3}$

If a and b are nonnegative real numbers whenever n is even, then

1. $\sqrt[n]{ab} = \sqrt[n]{a}\,\sqrt[n]{b}$

2. $\sqrt[n]{\dfrac{a}{b}} = \dfrac{\sqrt[n]{a}}{\sqrt[n]{b}} \qquad (b \neq 0)$

Simplified Form for Radicals [8.2]

5. $\sqrt{\dfrac{4}{5}} = \dfrac{\sqrt{4}}{\sqrt{5}}$

$= \dfrac{2}{\sqrt{5}} \cdot \dfrac{\sqrt{5}}{\sqrt{5}}$

$= \dfrac{2\sqrt{5}}{5}$

A radical expression is said to be in ***simplified form***

1. If there is no factor of the radicand that can be written as a power greater than or equal to the index;

2. If there are no fractions under the radical sign; and

3. If there are no radicals in the denominator.

6. $5\sqrt{3} - 7\sqrt{3} = (5 - 7)\sqrt{3}$
$= -2\sqrt{3}$

$\sqrt{20} + \sqrt{45} = 2\sqrt{5} + 3\sqrt{5}$
$= (2 + 3)\sqrt{5}$
$= 5\sqrt{5}$

Addition and Subtraction of Radical Expressions [8.3]

We add and subtract radical expressions by using the distributive property to combine similar radicals. Similar radicals are radicals with the same index and the same radicand.

Multiplication of Radical Expressions [8.4]

7. $(\sqrt{x} + 2)(\sqrt{x} + 3)$
$= \sqrt{x}\,\sqrt{x} + 3\sqrt{x} + 2\sqrt{x} + 2 \cdot 3$
$= x + 5\sqrt{x} + 6$

We multiply radical expressions in the same way that we multiply polynomials. We can use the distributive property and the FOIL method.

Rationalizing the Denominator [8.2, 8.4]

8. $\dfrac{3}{\sqrt{2}} = \dfrac{3}{\sqrt{2}} \cdot \dfrac{\sqrt{2}}{\sqrt{2}} = \dfrac{3\sqrt{2}}{2}$

$\dfrac{3}{\sqrt{5} - \sqrt{3}} = \dfrac{3}{\sqrt{5} - \sqrt{3}} \cdot \dfrac{\sqrt{5} + \sqrt{3}}{\sqrt{5} + \sqrt{3}}$

$= \dfrac{3\sqrt{5} + 3\sqrt{3}}{5 - 3}$

$= \dfrac{3\sqrt{5} + 3\sqrt{3}}{2}$

When a fraction contains a square root in the denominator, we rationalize the denominator by multiplying numerator and denominator by

1. The square root itself if there is only one term in the denominator, or

2. The conjugate of the denominator if there are two terms in the denominator.

Rationalizing the denominator is also called division of radical expressions.

Squaring Property of Equality [8.5]

9. $\sqrt{2x + 1} = 3$
$(\sqrt{2x + 1})^2 = 3^2$
$2x + 1 = 9$
$x = 4$

We may square both sides of an equation any time it is convenient to do so, as long as we check all resulting solutions in the original equation.

Complex Numbers [8.6]

10. $3 + 4i$ is a complex number.

Addition
$(3 + 4i) + (2 - 5i) = 5 - i$

Multiplication
$(3 + 4i)(2 - 5i)$
$= 6 - 15i + 8i - 20i^2$
$= 6 - 7i + 20$
$= 26 - 7i$

Division
$\dfrac{2}{3 + 4i} = \dfrac{2}{3 + 4i} \cdot \dfrac{3 - 4i}{3 - 4i}$

$= \dfrac{6 - 8i}{9 + 16}$

$= \dfrac{6}{25} - \dfrac{8}{25}i$

A *complex number* is any number that can be put in the form

$$a + bi$$

where a and b are real numbers and $i = \sqrt{-1}$. The *real part* of the complex number is a, and b is the *imaginary part*.

If a, b, c, and d are real numbers, then we have the following definitions associated with complex numbers:

1. Equality

$$a + bi = c + di \quad \text{if and only if} \quad a = c \text{ and } b = d$$

2. Addition and subtraction

$$(a + bi) + (c + di) = (a + c) + (b + d)i$$
$$(a + bi) - (c + di) = (a - c) + (b - d)i$$

3. Multiplication

$$(a + bi)(c + di) = (ac - bd) + (ad + bc)i$$

4. Division is similar to rationalizing the denominator.

Chapter 8 Test

Simplify each of the following. (Assume all variable bases are positive integers and all variable exponents are positive real numbers throughout this test.) [8.1]

1. $27^{-2/3}$

2. $\left(\dfrac{25}{49}\right)^{-1/2}$

3. $a^{3/4} \cdot a^{-1/3}$

4. $\dfrac{(x^{2/3}y^{-3})^{1/2}}{(x^{3/4}y^{1/2})^{-1}}$

5. $\sqrt{49x^8y^{10}}$

6. $\sqrt[5]{32x^{10}y^{20}}$

7. $\dfrac{(36a^8b^4)^{1/2}}{(27a^9b^6)^{1/3}}$

8. $\dfrac{(x^n y^{1/n})^n}{(x^{1/n}y^n)^{n^2}}$

Multiply. [8.1]

9. $2a^{1/2}(3a^{3/2} - 5a^{1/2})$

10. $(4a^{3/2} - 5)^2$

Factor. [8.1]

11. $3x^{2/3} + 5x^{1/3} - 2$

12. $9x^{2/3} - 49$

Combine. [8.3]

13. $\dfrac{4}{x^{1/2}} + x^{1/2}$

14. $\dfrac{x^2}{(x^2 - 3)^{1/2}} - (x^2 - 3)^{1/2}$

Write in simplified form. [8.2]

15. $\sqrt{125x^3y^5}$

16. $\sqrt[3]{40x^7y^8}$

17. $\sqrt{\dfrac{2}{3}}$

18. $\sqrt{\dfrac{12a^4b^3}{5c}}$

Combine. [8.3]

19. $3\sqrt{12} - 4\sqrt{27}$

20. $\sqrt[3]{24a^3b^3} - 5a\sqrt[3]{3b^3}$

Multiply. [8.4]

21. $(\sqrt{x} + 7)(\sqrt{x} - 4)$

22. $(3\sqrt{2} - \sqrt{3})^2$

Rationalize the denominator. [8.4]

23. $\dfrac{5}{\sqrt{3} - 1}$

24. $\dfrac{\sqrt{x} - \sqrt{2}}{\sqrt{x} + \sqrt{2}}$

Solve for x. [8.5]

25. $\sqrt{3x + 1} = x - 3$

26. $\sqrt[3]{2x + 7} = -1$

27. $\sqrt{x + 3} = \sqrt{x + 4} - 1$

Graph. [8.5]

28. $y = \sqrt{x - 2}$

29. $y = \sqrt[3]{x} + 3$

30. Solve for x and y so that the following equation is true [8.6]:

$$(2x + 5) - 4i = 6 - (y - 3)i$$

Perform the indicated operations. [8.6]

31. $(3 + 2i) - [(7 - i) - (4 + 3i)]$

32. $(2 - 3i)(4 + 3i)$

33. $(5 - 4i)^2$

34. $\dfrac{2 - 3i}{2 + 3i}$

35. Show that i^{38} can be written as -1. [8.6}

Quadratic Equations

Fir0002/Flagstaffotos
http://commons.wikimedia.org/wiki/Commons:GNU_Free_Documentation_License,_version_1.2

I f you have been to the circus or the county fair recently, you may have witnessed one of the more spectacular acts, the human cannonball. The human cannonball shown in the photograph will reach a height of 70 feet, and travel a distance of 160 feet, before landing in a safety net. In this chapter, we use this information to derive the equation

$$f(x) = -\frac{7}{640}(x - 80)^2 + 70 \quad \text{for } 0 \le x \le 160$$

which describes the path flown by this particular cannonball. The table and graph below were constructed from this equation.

Path of a Human Cannonball

x (feet)	f(x) (nearest foot)
0	0
40	53
80	70
120	53
160	0

All objects that are projected into the air, whether they are basketballs, bullets, arrows, or coins, follow parabolic paths like the one shown in the graph. Studying the material in this chapter will give you a more mathematical hold on the world around you.

Success Skills

Dear Student,

Now that you are close to finishing this course, I want to pass on a couple of things that have helped me a great deal with my career. I'll introduce each one with a quote:

Do something for the person you will be 5 years from now.

I have always made sure that I arranged my life so that I was doing something for the person I would be 5 years later. For example, when I was 20 years old, I was in college. I imagined that the person I would be as a 25-year-old, would want to have a college degree, so I made sure I stayed in school. That's all there is to this. It is not a hard, rigid philosophy. It is a soft, behind the scenes, foundation. It does not include ideas such as "Five years from now I'm going to graduate at the top of my class from the best college in the country." Instead, you think, "five years from now I will have a college degree, or I will still be in school working towards it."

This philosophy led to a community college teaching job, writing textbooks, doing videos with the textbooks, then to MathTV and the book you are reading right now. Along the way there were many other options and directions that I didn't take, but all the choices I made were due to keeping the person I would be in 5 years in mind.

It's easier to ride a horse in the direction it is going.

I started my college career thinking that I would become a dentist. I enrolled in all the courses that were required for dental school. When I completed the courses, I applied to a number of dental schools, but wasn't accepted. I kept going to school, and applied again the next year, again, without success. My life was not going in the direction of dental school, even though I had worked hard to put it in that direction. So I did a little inventory of the classes I had taken and the grades I earned, and realized that I was doing well in mathematics. My life was actually going in that direction so I decided to see where that would take me. It was a good decision.

It is a good idea to work hard toward your goals, but it is also a good idea to take inventory every now and then to be sure you are headed in the direction that is best for you.

I wish you good luck with the rest of your college years, and with whatever you decide you want to do as a career.

Pat McKeague
Fall 2010

Completing the Square

Table 1 is taken from the trail map given to skiers at the Northstar at Tahoe Ski Resort in Lake Tahoe, California. The table gives the length of each chair lift at Northstar, along with the change in elevation from the beginning of the lift to the end of the lift.

Right triangles are good mathematical models for chair lifts. In this section, we will use our knowledge of right triangles, along with the new material developed in the section, to solve problems involving chair lifts and a variety of other examples.

TABLE 1   From the Trail Map for the Northstar at Tahoe Ski Resort

Lift	Vertical Rise (feet)	Length (feet)
Big Springs Gondola	480	4,100
Bear Paw Double	120	790
Echo Triple	710	4,890
Aspen Express Quad	900	5,100
Forest Double	1,170	5,750
Lookout Double	960	4,330
Comstock Express Quad	1,250	5,900
Rendezvous Triple	650	2,900
Schaffer Camp Triple	1,860	6,150
Chipmunk Tow Lift	28	280
Bear Cub Tow Lift	120	750

In this section, we will develop the first of our new methods of solving quadratic equations. The new method is called *completing the square*. Completing the square on a quadratic equation allows us to obtain solutions, regardless of whether the equation can be factored. Before we solve equations by completing the square, we need to learn how to solve equations by taking square roots of both sides.

Consider the equation

$$x^2 = 16$$

We could solve it by writing it in standard form, factoring the left side, and proceeding as we did in Chapter 5. We can shorten our work considerably, however, if we simply notice that x must be either the positive square root of 16 or the negative square root of 16. That is,

If $x^2 = 16$

Then $x = \sqrt{16}$ or $x = -\sqrt{16}$

        $x = 4$ or $x = -4$

We can generalize this result as follows.

> **⟨Δ≠Σ⟩** **Square Root Property for Equality**
>
> If $a^2 = b$, where b is a real number, then $a = \sqrt{b}$ or $a = -\sqrt{b}$.

Notation   The expression $a = \sqrt{b}$ or $a = -\sqrt{b}$ can be written in shorthand form as $a = \pm\sqrt{b}$. The symbol $\pm$ is read "plus or minus."

We can apply the Square Root Property for Equations to some fairly complicated quadratic equations.

Video Examples

Section 9.1

■ **Example 1**   Solve $(2x - 3)^2 = 25$.

SOLUTION

$$(2x - 3)^2 = 25$$

$$2x - 3 = \pm\sqrt{25} \qquad \text{Square Root Property for Equations}$$

$$2x - 3 = \pm 5 \qquad \sqrt{25} = 5$$

$$2x = 3 \pm 5 \qquad \text{Add 3 to both sides}$$

$$x = \frac{3 \pm 5}{2} \qquad \text{Divide both sides by 2}$$

The last equation can be written as two separate statements:

$$x = \frac{3 + 5}{2} \quad \text{or} \quad x = \frac{3 - 5}{2}$$

$$= \frac{8}{2} \qquad\qquad = \frac{-2}{2}$$

$$= 4 \qquad \text{or} \qquad = -1$$

The solution set is $4, -1$.   ■

Notice that we could have solved the equation in Example 1 by expanding the left side, writing the resulting equation in standard form, and then factoring. The problem would look like this:

$$(2x - 3)^2 = 25 \qquad \text{Original equation}$$

$$4x^2 - 12x + 9 = 25 \qquad \text{Expand the left side}$$

$$4x^2 - 12x - 16 = 0 \qquad \text{Add } -25 \text{ to each side}$$

$$4(x^2 - 3x - 4) = 0 \qquad \text{Begin factoring}$$

$$4(x - 4)(x + 1) = 0 \qquad \text{Factor completely}$$

$$x - 4 = 0 \quad \text{or} \quad x + 1 = 0 \qquad \text{Set variable factors equal to 0}$$

$$x = 4 \quad \text{or} \qquad x = -1$$

As you can see, solving the equation by factoring leads to the same two solutions.

Example 2   Solve for x: $(3x - 1)^2 = -12$

SOLUTION

$$(3x - 1)^2 = -12$$
$$3x - 1 = \pm\sqrt{-12} \qquad \text{Square Root Property for Equations}$$
$$3x - 1 = \pm 2i\sqrt{3} \qquad \sqrt{-12} = 2i\sqrt{3}$$
$$3x = 1 \pm 2i\sqrt{3} \qquad \text{Add 1 to both sides}$$
$$x = \frac{1 \pm 2i\sqrt{3}}{3} \qquad \text{Divide both sides by 3}$$

The solution set is $\left\{ \dfrac{1 + 2i\sqrt{3}}{3}, \dfrac{1 - 2i\sqrt{3}}{3} \right\}$.

Both solutions are complex. Here is a check of the first solution:

When $\qquad\qquad\qquad\qquad\qquad\qquad\qquad x = \dfrac{1 + 2i\sqrt{3}}{3}$

the equation $\qquad\qquad\qquad\qquad\qquad (3x - 1)^2 = -12$

becomes $\qquad\qquad\qquad\qquad \left(3 \cdot \dfrac{1 + 2i\sqrt{3}}{3} - 1 \right)^2 \overset{?}{=} -12$

or $\qquad\qquad\qquad\qquad\qquad (1 + 2i\sqrt{3} - 1)^2 \overset{?}{=} -12$

$\qquad\qquad\qquad\qquad\qquad\qquad\qquad (2i\sqrt{3})^2 \overset{?}{=} -12$

$\qquad\qquad\qquad\qquad\qquad\qquad\quad 4 \cdot i^2 \cdot 3 \overset{?}{=} -12$

$\qquad\qquad\qquad\qquad\qquad\qquad\quad 12(-1) \overset{?}{=} -12$

$\qquad\qquad\qquad\qquad\qquad\qquad\qquad -12 = -12$

> *Note* We cannot solve the equation in Example 2 by factoring. If we expand the left side and write the resulting equation in standard form, we are left with a quadratic equation that does not factor:
>
> $(3x - 1)^2 = -12$
>
> Equation from Example 2
>
> $9x^2 - 6x + 1 = -12$
>
> Expand the left side.
>
> $9x^2 - 6x + 13 = 0$
>
> Standard form, but not factorable

Example 3   Solve $x^2 + 6x + 9 = 12$.

SOLUTION   We can solve this equation as we have the equations in Examples 1 and 2 if we first write the left side as $(x + 3)^2$.

$$x^2 + 6x + 9 = 12 \qquad \text{Original equation}$$
$$(x + 3)^2 = 12 \qquad \text{Write } x^2 + 6x + 9 \text{ as } (x + 3)^2$$
$$x + 3 = \pm 2\sqrt{3} \qquad \text{Square Root Property for Equations}$$
$$x = -3 \pm 2\sqrt{3} \qquad \text{Add } -3 \text{ to each side}$$

We have two irrational solutions: $-3 + 2\sqrt{3}$ and $-3 - 2\sqrt{3}$. What is important about this problem, however, is the fact that the equation was easy to solve because the left side was a perfect square trinomial.

Method of Completing the Square

The method of completing the square is simply a way of transforming any quadratic equation into an equation of the form found in the preceding three examples. The key to understanding the method of completing the square lies in recognizing the relationship between the last two terms of any perfect square trinomial whose leading coefficient is 1.

Consider the following list of perfect square trinomials and their corresponding binomial squares:

$$x^2 - 6x + 9 = (x - 3)^2$$
$$x^2 + 8x + 16 = (x + 4)^2$$
$$x^2 - 10x + 25 = (x - 5)^2$$
$$x^2 + 12x + 36 = (x + 6)^2$$

In each case, the leading coefficient is 1. A more important observation comes from noticing the relationship between the linear and constant terms (middle and last terms) in each trinomial. Observe that the constant term in each case is the square of half the coefficient of x in the middle term. For example, in the last expression, the constant term 36 is the square of half of 12, where 12 is the coefficient of x in the middle term. (Notice also that the second terms in all the binomials on the right side are half the coefficients of the middle terms of the trinomials on the left side.) We can use these observations to build our own perfect square trinomials and, in doing so, solve some quadratic equations.

■ **Example 4**   Solve $x^2 - 6x + 5 = 0$ by completing the square.

SOLUTION   We begin by adding -5 to both sides of the equation. We want just $x^2 - 6x$ on the left side so that we can add on our own final term to get a perfect square trinomial:

$$x^2 - 6x + 5 = 0$$
$$x^2 - 6x \qquad = -5 \qquad \text{Add } -5 \text{ to both sides}$$

Now we can add 9 to both sides and the left side will be a perfect square:

$$x^2 - 6x + 9 = -5 + 9$$
$$(x - 3)^2 = 4$$

The final line is in the form of the equations we solved previously:

$$x - 3 = \pm 2$$
$$x = 3 \pm 2 \qquad \text{Add 3 to both sides}$$
$$x = 3 + 2 \quad \text{or} \quad x = 3 - 2$$
$$x = 5 \qquad \text{or} \quad x = 1$$

The two solutions are 5 and 1.   ■

> *Note*   The equation in Example 4 can be solved quickly by factoring:
> $$x^2 - 6x + 5 = 0$$
> $$(x - 5)(x - 1) = 0$$
> $$x - 5 = 0 \quad \text{or} \quad x - 1 = 0$$
> $$x = 5 \quad \text{or} \qquad x = 1$$
> The reason we didn't solve it by factoring is we want to practice completing the square on some simple equations.

■ **Example 5**   Solve by completing the square: $x^2 + 5x - 2 = 0$

SOLUTION   We must begin by adding 2 to both sides. (The left side of the equation, as it is, is not a perfect square, because it does not have the correct constant term. We will simply "move" that term to the other side and use our own constant term.)

$$x^2 + 5x = 2 \qquad \text{Add 2 to each side}$$

We complete the square by adding the square of half the coefficient of the linear term to both sides:

$$x^2 + 5x + \frac{25}{4} = 2 + \frac{25}{4}$$

Half of 5 is $\frac{5}{2}$, the square of which is $\frac{25}{4}$

$$\left(x + \frac{5}{2}\right)^2 = \frac{33}{4}$$

$2 + \frac{25}{4} = \frac{8}{4} + \frac{25}{4} = \frac{33}{4}$

$$x + \frac{5}{2} = \pm\sqrt{\frac{33}{4}}$$

Square Root Property for Equations

$$x + \frac{5}{2} = \pm\frac{\sqrt{33}}{2}$$

Simplify the radical

$$x = -\frac{5}{2} \pm \frac{\sqrt{33}}{2}$$

Add $-\frac{5}{2}$ to both sides

$$x = \frac{-5 \pm \sqrt{33}}{2}$$

The solution set is $\left\{ \dfrac{-5 + \sqrt{33}}{2}, \dfrac{-5 - \sqrt{33}}{2} \right\}$.

We can use a calculator to get decimal approximations to these solutions. If $\sqrt{33} \approx 5.74$, then

$$\frac{-5 + 5.74}{2} = 0.37$$

$$\frac{-5 - 5.74}{2} = -5.37$$

Example 6   Solve for x: $3x^2 - 8x + 7 = 0$

SOLUTION

$$3x^2 - 8x + 7 = 0$$

$$3x^2 - 8x = -7$$ Add -7 to both sides

We cannot complete the square on the left side because the leading coefficient is not 1. We take an extra step and divide both sides by 3:

$$\frac{3x^2}{3} - \frac{8x}{3} = -\frac{7}{3}$$

$$x^2 - \frac{8}{3}x = -\frac{7}{3}$$

Half of $\frac{8}{3}$ is $\frac{4}{3}$, the square of which is $\frac{16}{9}$:

$$x^2 - \frac{8}{3}x + \frac{16}{9} = -\frac{7}{3} + \frac{16}{9}$$

Add $\frac{16}{9}$ to both sides

$$\left(x - \frac{4}{3}\right)^2 = -\frac{5}{9}$$

Simplify right side

$$x - \frac{4}{3} = \pm\sqrt{-\frac{5}{9}}$$

Square Root Property for Equations

$$x - \frac{4}{3} = \pm\frac{i\sqrt{5}}{3}$$

$\sqrt{-\frac{5}{9}} = \frac{\sqrt{-5}}{3} = \frac{i\sqrt{5}}{3}$

$$x = \frac{4}{3} \pm \frac{i\sqrt{5}}{3}$$

Add $\frac{4}{3}$ to both sides

$$x = \frac{4 \pm i\sqrt{5}}{3}$$

The solution set is $\left\{ \dfrac{4 + i\sqrt{5}}{3}, \dfrac{4 - i\sqrt{5}}{3} \right\}$.

$\triangle \neq \Sigma$ *How To Solve a Quadratic Equation by Completing the Square*

To summarize the method used in the preceding two examples, we list the following steps:

Step 1: Write the equation in the form $ax^2 + bx = c$.

Step 2: If the leading coefficient is not 1, divide both sides by the coefficient so that the resulting equation has a leading coefficient of 1. That is, if $a \neq 1$, then divide both sides by a.

Step 3: Add the square of half the coefficient of the linear term to both sides of the equation.

Step 4: Write the left side of the equation as the square of a binomial, and simplify the right side if possible.

Step 5: Apply the Square Root Property for Equations, and solve as usual.

More Special Triangles

The triangles shown in Figures 1 and 2 occur frequently in mathematics.

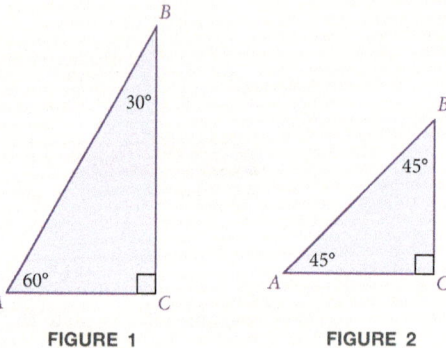

FIGURE 1   FIGURE 2

Note that both of the triangles are right triangles. We refer to the triangle in Figure 1 as a $30°-60°-90°$ triangle, and the triangle in Figure 2 as a $45°-45°-90°$ triangle.

Example 7   If the shortest side in a 30°–60°–90° triangle is 1 inch, find the lengths of the other two sides.

SOLUTION   In Figure 3, triangle ABC is a $30° - 60° - 90°$ triangle in which the shortest side AC is 1 inch long. Triangle DBC is also a $30° - 60° - 90°$ triangle in which the shortest side DC is 1 inch long.

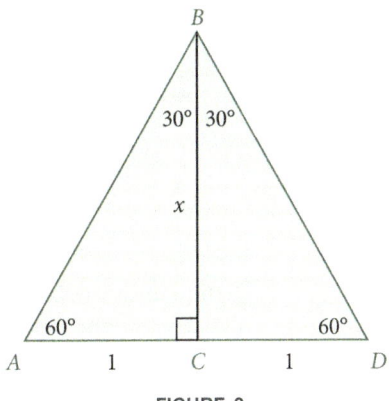

FIGURE 3

Notice that the large triangle ABD is an equilateral triangle because each of its interior angles is 60°. Each side of triangle ABD is 2 inches long. Side AB in triangle ABC is therefore 2 inches. To find the length of side BC, we use the Pythagorean theorem.

$$BC^2 + AC^2 = AB^2$$
$$x^2 + 1^2 = 2^2$$
$$x^2 + 1 = 4$$
$$x^2 = 3$$
$$x = \sqrt{3} \text{ inches}$$

Note that we write only the positive square root because x is the length of a side in a triangle and is therefore a positive number.

Example 8   Table 1 in the introduction to this section gives the vertical rise of the Forest Double chair lift as 1,170 feet and the length of the chair lift as 5,750 feet. To the nearest foot, find the horizontal distance covered by a person riding this lift.

SOLUTION   Figure 4 is a model of the Forest Double chair lift. A rider gets on the lift at point A and exits at point B. The length of the lift is AB.

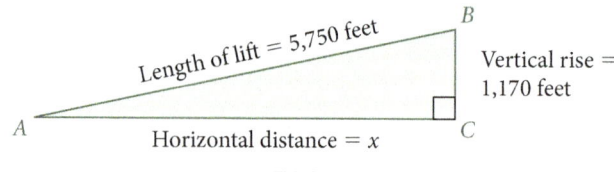

B
Vertical rise = 1,170 feet

A
Horizontal distance = x C

FIGURE 4

To find the horizontal distance covered by a person riding the chair lift, we use the Pythagorean theorem.

$$5,750^2 = x^2 + 1,170^2 \qquad \text{Pythagorean theorem}$$

$$33,062,500 = x^2 + 1,368,900 \qquad \text{Simplify squares}$$

$$x^2 = 33,062,500 - 1,368,900 \qquad \text{Solve for } x^2$$

$$x^2 = 31,693,600 \qquad \text{Simplify the right side}$$

$$x = \sqrt{31,693,600} \qquad \text{Square Root Property for Equations}$$

$$= 5,630 \text{ feet} \qquad \text{to the nearest foot}$$

A rider getting on the lift at point A and riding to point B will cover a horizontal distance of approximately 5,630 feet.

Getting Ready for Class

After reading through the preceding section, respond in your own words and in complete sentences.

A. What kind of equation do we solve using the method of completing the square?

B. Explain in words how you would complete the square on $x^2 - 16x = 4$.

C. What is the relationship between the shortest side and the longest side in a 30°–60°–90° triangle?

D. What two expressions together are equivalent to $x = \pm 4$?

Solve the following equations.

1. $x^2 = 25$ **2.** $x^2 = 16$ **3.** $a^2 = -9$ **4.** $a^2 = -49$

5. $y^2 = \dfrac{3}{4}$ **6.** $y^2 = \dfrac{5}{9}$ **7.** $x^2 + 12 = 0$ **8.** $x^2 + 8 = 0$

9. $4a^2 - 45 = 0$ **10.** $9a^2 - 20 = 0$ **11.** $(2y - 1)^2 = 25$ **12.** $(3y + 7)^2 = 1$

13. $(2a + 3)^2 = -9$ **14.** $(3a - 5)^2 = -49$

15. $(5x + 2)^2 = -8$ **16.** $(6x - 7)^2 = -75$

17. $x^2 + 8x + 16 = -27$ **18.** $x^2 - 12x + 36 = -8$

19. $4a^2 - 12a + 9 = -4$ **20.** $9a^2 - 12a + 4 = -9$

Copy each of the following, and fill in the blanks so the left side of each is a perfect square trinomial. That is, complete the square.

21. $x^2 + 12x + \underline{} = (x + \underline{})^2$ **22.** $x^2 + 6x + \underline{} = (x + \underline{})^2$

23. $x^2 - 4x + \underline{} = (x - \underline{})^2$ **24.** $x^2 - 2x + \underline{} = (x - \underline{})^2$

25. $a^2 - 10a + \underline{} = (a - \underline{})^2$ **26.** $a^2 - 8a + \underline{} = (a - \underline{})^2$

27. $x^2 + 5x + \underline{} = (x + \underline{})^2$ **28.** $x^2 + 3x + \underline{} = (x + \underline{})^2$

29. $y^2 - 7y + \underline{} = (y - \underline{})^2$ **30.** $y^2 - y + \underline{} = (y - \underline{})^2$

31. $x^2 + \dfrac{1}{2}x + \underline{} = (x + \underline{})^2$ **32.** $x^2 - \dfrac{3}{4}x + \underline{} = (x - \underline{})^2$

33. $x^2 + \dfrac{2}{3}x + \underline{} = (x + \underline{})^2$ **34.** $x^2 - \dfrac{4}{5}x + \underline{} = (x - \underline{})^2$

Solve each of the following quadratic equations by completing the square.

35. $x^2 + 4x = 12$ **36.** $x^2 - 2x = 8$ **37.** $x^2 + 12x = -27$

38. $x^2 - 6x = 16$ **39.** $a^2 - 2a + 5 = 0$ **40.** $a^2 + 10a + 22 = 0$

41. $y^2 - 8y + 1 = 0$ **42.** $y^2 + 6y - 1 = 0$ **43.** $x^2 - 5x - 3 = 0$

44. $x^2 - 5x - 2 = 0$ **45.** $2x^2 - 4x - 8 = 0$ **46.** $3x^2 - 9x - 12 = 0$

47. $3t^2 - 8t + 1 = 0$ **48.** $5t^2 + 12t - 1 = 0$ **49.** $4x^2 - 3x + 5 = 0$

50. $7x^2 - 5x + 2 = 0$ **51.** $3x^2 + 4x - 1 = 0$ **52.** $2x^2 + 6x - 1 = 0$

53. $2x^2 - 10x = 11$ **54.** $25x^2 - 20x = 1$ **55.** $4x^2 - 10x + 11 = 0$

56. $4x^2 - 6x + 1 = 0$

57. For the equation $x^2 = -9$
    a. Can it be solved by factoring? **b.** Solve it.

58. For the equation $x^2 - 10x + 18 = 0$
    a. Can it be solved by factoring? **b.** Solve it.

59. Solve the equation $x^2 - 6x = 0$
    a. by factoring **b.** by completing the square

60. Solve the equation $x^2 + ax = 0$
    a. by factoring **b.** by completing the square

61. Solve the equation $x^2 + 2x = 35$
    a. by factoring **b.** by completing the square

62. Solve the equation $8x^2 - 10x - 25 = 0$
    a. by factoring **b.** by completing the square

63. Is $x = -3 + \sqrt{2}$ a solution to $x^2 - 6x = 7$?

64. Is $x = 2 - \sqrt{5}$ a solution to $x^2 - 4x = 1$?

65. Solve each equation.

a. $5x - 7 = 0$ **b.** $5x - 7 = 8$ **c.** $(5x - 7)^2 = 8$

d. $\sqrt{5x - 7} = 8$ **e.** $\dfrac{5}{2} - \dfrac{7}{2x} = \dfrac{4}{x}$

66. Solve each equation.

a. $5x + 11 = 0$ **b.** $5x + 11 = 9$ **c.** $(5x + 11)^2 = 9$

d. $\sqrt{5x + 11} = 9$ **e.** $\dfrac{5}{3} - \dfrac{11}{3x} = \dfrac{3}{x}$

Applying the Concepts

67. Geometry If the shortest side in a $30° - 60° - 90°$ triangle is $\frac{1}{2}$ inch long, find the lengths of the other two sides.

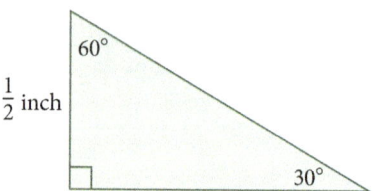

68. Geometry If the length of the longest side of a $30° - 60° - 90°$ triangle is x, find the lengths of the other two sides in terms of x.

69. Geometry If the length of the shorter sides of a $45° - 45° - 90°$ triangle is 1 inch, find the length of the hypotenuse.

70. Geometry If the length of the shorter sides of a $45° - 45° - 90°$ triangle is x, find the length of the hypotenuse, in terms of x.

71. Chair Lift Use Table 1 from the introduction to this section to find the horizontal distance covered by a person riding the Bear Paw Double chair lift. Round your answer to the nearest foot.

72. Fermat's Last Theorem As mentioned in a previous chapter, the postage stamp shows Fermat's last theorem, which states that if n is an integer greater than 2, then there are no positive integers x, y, and z that will make the formula $x^n + y^n = z^n$ true. Use the formula $x^n + y^n = z^n$ to

a. find z if $n = 2$, $x = 6$, and $y = 8$.   **b.** find y if $n = 2$, $x = 5$, and $z = 13$.

73. **Interest Rate** Suppose a deposit of $3,000 in a savings account that paid an annual interest rate r (compounded yearly) is worth $3,456 after 2 years. Using the formula $A = P(1 + r)^t$, we have

$$3,456 = 3,000(1 + r)^2$$

Solve for r to find the annual interest rate.

74. **Special Triangles** In Figure 5, triangle ABC has angles 45° and 30°, and height x. Find the lengths of sides AB, BC, and AC, in terms of x.

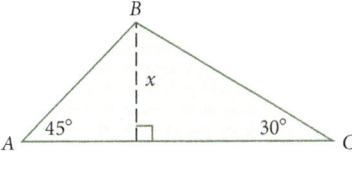

FIGURE 5

75. **Length of an Escalator** An escalator in a department store is made to carry people a vertical distance of 20 feet between floors. How long is the escalator if it makes an angle of 45° with the ground? (See Figure 6.)

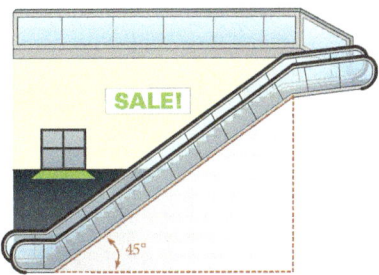

FIGURE 6

76. **Dimensions of a Tent** A two-person tent is to be made so the height at the center is 4 feet. If the sides of the tent are to meet the ground at an angle of 60° and the tent is to be 6 feet in length, how many square feet of material will be needed to make the tent? (Figure 7; assume that the tent has a floor and is closed at both ends.) Give your answer to the nearest tenth of a square foot.

FIGURE 7

Getting Ready for the Next Section

Simplify.

77. $49 - 4(6)(-5)$

78. $49 - 4(6)(2)$

79. $(-27)^2 - 4(0.1)(1,700)$

80. $25 - 4(4)(-10)$

81. $-7 + \dfrac{169}{12}$

82. $-7 - \dfrac{169}{12}$

Factor.

83. $27t^3 - 8$

84. $125t^3 + 1$

The Quadratic Formula

If you go on to take a business course or an economics course, you will find yourself spending lots of time with the three expressions that form the mathematical foundation of business: profit, revenue, and cost. Many times these expressions are given as polynomials, the topic of this section. The relationship between the three equations is known as the profit equation:

$$\text{Profit} = \text{Revenue} - \text{Cost}$$

$$P(x) = R(x) - C(x)$$

The table and graphs below were produced on a graphing calculator. They give numerical and graphical descriptions of revenue, profit, and cost for a company that manufactures and sells prerecorded videotapes according to the equations

$$R(x) = 11.5x - 0.05x^2 \qquad \text{and} \qquad C(x) = 200 + 2x$$

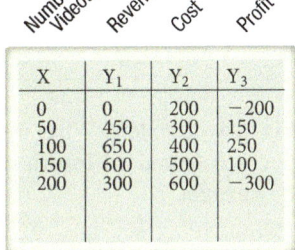

X	Y_1	Y_2	Y_3
0	0	200	−200
50	450	300	150
100	650	400	250
150	600	500	100
200	300	600	−300

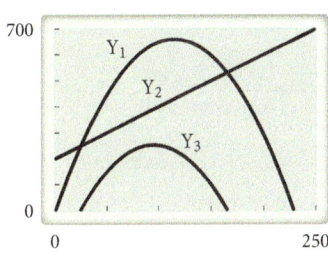

FIGURE 1

By studying the material in this section, you will get a more thorough look at the equations and relationships that are emphasized in business and economics.

In this section, we will use the method of completing the square from the preceding section to derive the quadratic formula. The *quadratic formula* is a very useful tool in mathematics. It allows us to solve all types of quadratic equations.

> ⌈Δ≠Σ⌉ *The Quadratic Theorem*
>
> For any quadratic equation in the form $ax^2 + bx + c = 0$, $a \neq 0$, the two solutions are
>
> $$x = \frac{-b + \sqrt{b^2 - 4ac}}{2a} \qquad \text{and} \qquad x = \frac{-b - \sqrt{b^2 - 4ac}}{2a}$$

Proof We will prove the quadratic theorem by completing the square on $ax^2 + bx + c = 0$:

$$ax^2 + bx + c = 0$$

$$ax^2 + bx = -c \qquad \text{Add } -c \text{ to both sides}$$

$$x^2 + \frac{b}{a}x = -\frac{c}{a} \qquad \text{Divide both sides by } a$$

To complete the square on the left side, we add the square of $\frac{1}{2}$ of $\frac{b}{a}$ to both sides $\left(\frac{1}{2} \text{ of } \frac{b}{a} \text{ is } \frac{b}{2a}\right)$.

$$x^2 + \frac{b}{a}x + \left(\frac{b}{2a}\right)^2 = -\frac{c}{a} + \left(\frac{b}{2a}\right)^2$$

We now simplify the right side as a separate step. We combine the two terms by writing each with the least common denominator $4a^2$:

$$-\frac{c}{a} + \left(\frac{b}{2a}\right)^2 = -\frac{c}{a} + \frac{b^2}{4a^2} = \frac{4a}{4a}\left(\frac{-c}{a}\right) + \frac{b^2}{4a^2} = \frac{-4ac + b^2}{4a^2}$$

It is convenient to write this last expression as

$$\frac{b^2 - 4ac}{4a^2}$$

Continuing with the proof, we have

$$x^2 + \frac{b}{a}x + \left(\frac{b}{2a}\right)^2 = \frac{b^2 - 4ac}{4a^2}$$

$$\left(x + \frac{b}{2a}\right)^2 = \frac{b^2 - 4ac}{4a^2} \qquad \text{\color{green}Write left side as a binomial square}$$

$$x + \frac{b}{2a} = \pm\frac{\sqrt{b^2 - 4ac}}{2a} \qquad \text{\color{green}Square Root Property for Equations}$$

$$x = -\frac{b}{2a} \pm \frac{\sqrt{b^2 - 4ac}}{2a} \qquad \text{\color{green}Add $-\frac{b}{2a}$ to both sides}$$

$$= \frac{-b \pm \sqrt{b^2 - 4ac}}{2a}$$

Our proof is now complete. What we have is this: If our equation is in the form $ax^2 + bx + c = 0$ (standard form), where $a \neq 0$, the two solutions are always given by the formula

$$x = \frac{-b \pm \sqrt{b^2 - 4ac}}{2a}$$

This formula is known as the **quadratic formula**. If we substitute the coefficients a, b, and c of any quadratic equation in standard form into the formula, we need only perform some basic arithmetic to arrive at the solution set.

Video Examples

Section 9.2

Note Whenever the solutions to our quadratic equations turn out to be rational numbers, as in Example 1, it means the original equation could have been solved by factoring. (We didn't solve the equation in Example 1 by factoring because we were trying to get some practice with the quadratic formula.)

Example 1   Solve $x^2 - 5x - 6 = 0$ by using the quadratic formula.

SOLUTION   To use the quadratic formula, we must make sure the equation is in standard form; identify a, b, and c; substitute them into the formula; and work out the arithmetic.

For the equation $x^2 - 5x - 6 = 0$, $a = 1$, $b = -5$, and $c = -6$:

$$x = \frac{-b \pm \sqrt{b^2 - 4ac}}{2a}$$

$$= \frac{-(-5) \pm \sqrt{(-5)^2 - 4(1)(-6)}}{2(1)}$$

$$= \frac{5 \pm \sqrt{49}}{2}$$

$$= \frac{5 \pm 7}{2}$$

$$x = \frac{5 + 7}{2} \quad \text{or} \quad x = \frac{5 - 7}{2}$$

$$x = \frac{12}{2} \qquad\qquad x = -\frac{2}{2}$$

$$x = 6 \qquad\qquad x = -1$$

The two solutions are 6 and -1.

Example 2   Solve for x: $2x^2 = -4x + 3$.

SOLUTION   Before we can identify a, b, and c, we must write the equation in standard form. To do so, we add $4x$ and -3 to each side of the equation:

$$2x^2 = -4x + 3$$

$$2x^2 + 4x - 3 = 0 \qquad \text{\textit{\color{green}{Add 4x and} } -3 \text{ \textit{\color{green}{to each side}}}}$$

Now that the equation is in standard form, we see that $a = 2$, $b = 4$, and $c = -3$. Using the quadratic formula we have:

$$x = \frac{-b \pm \sqrt{b^2 - 4ac}}{2a}$$

$$= \frac{-4 \pm \sqrt{4^2 - 4(2)(-3)}}{2(2)}$$

$$= \frac{-4 \pm \sqrt{40}}{4}$$

$$= \frac{-4 \pm 2\sqrt{10}}{4}$$

We can reduce the final expression in the preceding equation to lowest terms by factoring 2 from the numerator and denominator and then dividing it out:

$$x = \frac{2(-2 \pm \sqrt{10})}{2 \cdot 2}$$

$$= \frac{-2 \pm \sqrt{10}}{2}$$

Our two solutions are $\dfrac{-2 + \sqrt{10}}{2}$ and $\dfrac{-2 - \sqrt{10}}{2}$

Example 3   Solve $x^2 - 6x = -7$.

SOLUTION   We begin by writing the equation in standard form:

$$x^2 - 6x = -7$$

$$x^2 - 6x + 7 = 0 \qquad \text{\textit{\color{green}{Add 7 to each side}}}$$

Using $a = 1$, $b = -6$, and $c = 7$ in the quadratic formula

$$x = \frac{-b \pm \sqrt{b^2 - 4ac}}{2a}$$

we have:

$$x = \frac{-(-6) \pm \sqrt{(-6)^2 - 4(1)(7)}}{2(1)}$$

$$= \frac{6 \pm \sqrt{36 - 28}}{2}$$

$$= \frac{6 \pm \sqrt{8}}{2}$$

$$= \frac{6 \pm 2\sqrt{2}}{2}$$

The two terms in the numerator have a 2 in common. We reduce to lowest terms by factoring the 2 from the numerator and then dividing numerator and denominator by 2:

$$= \frac{2(3 \pm \sqrt{2})}{2}$$

$$= 3 \pm \sqrt{2}$$

The two solutions are $3 + \sqrt{2}$ and $3 - \sqrt{2}$. This time, let's check our solutions in the original equation $x^2 - 6x = -7$.

Checking $x = 3 + \sqrt{2}$, we have:

$$(3 + \sqrt{2})^2 - 6(3 + \sqrt{2}) \overset{?}{=} -7$$

$$9 + 6\sqrt{2} + 2 - 18 - 6\sqrt{2} = -7 \qquad \text{Multiply}$$

$$11 - 18 + 6\sqrt{2} - 6\sqrt{2} = -7 \qquad \text{Add 9 and 2}$$

$$-7 + 0 = -7 \qquad \text{Subtraction}$$

$$-7 = -7 \qquad \text{A true statement}$$

Checking $x = 3 - \sqrt{2}$, we have:

$$(3 - \sqrt{2})^2 - 6(3 - \sqrt{2}) \overset{?}{=} -7$$

$$9 - 6\sqrt{2} + 2 - 18 + 6\sqrt{2} = -7 \qquad \text{Multiply}$$

$$11 - 18 - 6\sqrt{2} + 6\sqrt{2} = -7 \qquad \text{Add 9 and 2}$$

$$-7 + 0 = -7 \qquad \text{Subtraction}$$

$$-7 = -7 \qquad \text{A true statement}$$

As you can see, both solutions yield true statements when used in place of the variable in the original equation.

Example 4   Solve for x: $\dfrac{1}{10}x^2 - \dfrac{1}{5}x = -\dfrac{1}{2}$.

SOLUTION   It will be easier to apply the quadratic formula if we clear the equation of fractions. Multiplying both sides of the equation by the LCD 10 gives us:

$$x^2 - 2x = -5$$

Next, we add 5 to both sides to put the equation into standard form:

$$x^2 - 2x + 5 = 0 \qquad \text{Add 5 to both sides}$$

Applying the quadratic formula with $a = 1$, $b = -2$, and $c = 5$, we have:

$$x = \frac{-(-2) \pm \sqrt{(-2)^2 - 4(1)(5)}}{2(1)} = \frac{2 \pm \sqrt{-16}}{2} = \frac{2 \pm 4i}{2}$$

Dividing the numerator and denominator by 2, we have the two solutions:

$$x = 1 \pm 2i$$

The two solutions are $1 + 2i$ and $1 - 2i$.

Example 5   Solve $(2x - 3)(2x - 1) = -4$.

SOLUTION   We multiply the binomials on the left side and then add 4 to each side to write the equation in standard form. From there we identify a, b, and c and apply the quadratic formula:

$$(2x - 3)(2x - 1) = -4$$

$$4x^2 - 8x + 3 = -4 \qquad \text{Multiply binomials on left side}$$

$$4x^2 - 8x + 7 = 0 \qquad \text{Add 4 to each side}$$

Placing $a = 4$, $b = -8$, and $c = 7$ in the quadratic formula we have:

$$x = \frac{-(-8) \pm \sqrt{(-8)^2 - 4(4)(7)}}{2(4)}$$

$$= \frac{8 \pm \sqrt{64 - 112}}{8}$$

$$= \frac{8 \pm \sqrt{-48}}{8}$$

$$= \frac{8 \pm 4i\sqrt{3}}{8} \qquad\qquad \sqrt{-48} = i\sqrt{48} = i\sqrt{16}\sqrt{3} = 4i\sqrt{3}$$

> **Note**   It would be a mistake to try to reduce this final expression further. Sometimes first-year algebra students will try to divide the 2 in the denominator into the 2 in the numerator, which is a mistake. Remember, when we reduce to lowest terms, we do so by dividing the numerator and denominator by any factors they have in common. In this case 2 is not a factor of the numerator. This expression is in lowest terms.

To reduce this final expression to lowest terms, we factor a 4 from the numerator and then divide the numerator and denominator by 4:

$$= \frac{4(2 \pm i\sqrt{3})}{4 \cdot 2}$$

$$= \frac{2 \pm i\sqrt{3}}{2} \qquad\qquad\qquad\qquad ∎$$

Although the equation in our next example is not a quadratic equation, we solve it by using both factoring and the quadratic formula.

Example 6   Solve $27t^3 - 8 = 0$.

SOLUTION   It would be a mistake to add 8 to each side of this equation and then take the cube root of each side because we would lose two of our solutions. Instead, we factor the left side, and then set the factors equal to 0:

$$27t^3 - 8 = 0 \qquad\qquad \text{Equation in standard form}$$

$$(3t - 2)(9t^2 + 6t + 4) = 0 \qquad\qquad \text{Factor as the difference of two cubes.}$$

$$3t - 2 = 0 \quad \text{or} \quad 9t^2 + 6t + 4 = 0 \qquad \text{Set each factor equal to 0}$$

The first equation leads to a solution of $t = \frac{2}{3}$. The second equation does not factor, so we use the quadratic formula with $a = 9$, $b = 6$, and $c = 4$:

$$t = \frac{-6 \pm \sqrt{36 - 4(9)(4)}}{2(9)}$$

$$= \frac{-6 \pm \sqrt{36 - 144}}{18}$$

$$= \frac{-6 \pm \sqrt{-108}}{18}$$

$$= \frac{-6 \pm 6i\sqrt{3}}{18} \qquad\qquad \sqrt{-108} = i\sqrt{36 \cdot 3} = 6i\sqrt{3}$$

$$= \frac{6(-1 \pm i\sqrt{3})}{6 \cdot 3} \qquad\qquad \text{Factor 6 from the numerator and denominator}$$

$$= \frac{-1 \pm i\sqrt{3}}{3} \qquad\qquad \text{Divide out common factor 6}$$

The three solutions to our original equation are

$$\frac{2}{3}, \qquad \frac{-1 + i\sqrt{3}}{3}, \qquad \text{and} \qquad \frac{-1 - i\sqrt{3}}{3} \qquad\qquad ∎$$

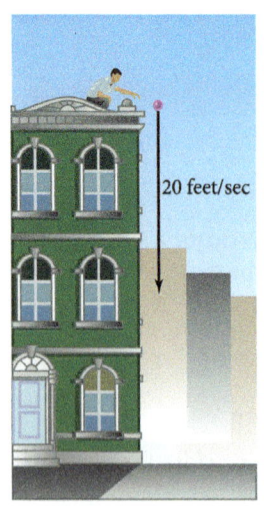

20 feet/sec

■ **Example 7**   If an object is thrown downward with an initial velocity of 20 feet per second, the distance $s(t)$, in feet, it travels in t seconds is given by the function $s(t) = 20t + 16t^2$. How long does it take the object to fall 40 feet?

SOLUTION   We let $s(t) = 40$, and solve for t:

When $s(t) = 40$

the function $s(t) = 20t + 16t^2$

becomes $40 = 20t + 16t^2$

or $16t^2 + 20t - 40 = 0$

                  $4t^2 + 5t - 10 = 0$ Divide by 4

Using the quadratic formula, we have

$$t = \frac{-5 \pm \sqrt{25 - 4(4)(-10)}}{2(4)}$$

$$= \frac{-5 \pm \sqrt{185}}{8}$$

$$= \frac{-5 + \sqrt{185}}{8} \quad \text{or} \quad t = \frac{-5 - \sqrt{185}}{8}$$

The second solution is impossible because it is a negative number and time t must be positive. It takes

$$t = \frac{-5 + \sqrt{185}}{8} \quad \text{or approximately} \quad \frac{-5 + 13.60}{8} \approx 1.08 \text{ seconds}$$

for the object to fall 40 feet.   ■

The relationship between profit, revenue, and cost is given by the formula

$$P(x) = R(x) - C(x)$$

where $P(x)$ is the profit, $R(x)$ is the total revenue, and $C(x)$ is the total cost of producing and selling x items.

■ **Example 8**   A company produces and sells copies of an accounting program for home computers. The total weekly cost (in dollars) to produce x copies of the program is $C(x) = 8x + 500$, and the weekly revenue for selling all x copies of the program is $R(x) = 35x - 0.1x^2$. How many programs must be sold each week for the weekly profit to be $1,200?

SOLUTION   Substituting the given expressions for $R(x)$ and $C(x)$ in the equation $P(x) = R(x) - C(x)$, we have a polynomial in x that represents the weekly profit $P(x)$:

$$P(x) = R(x) - C(x)$$

$$= 35x - 0.1x^2 - (8x + 500)$$

$$= 35x - 0.1x^2 - 8x - 500$$

$$= -500 + 27x - 0.1x^2$$

Setting this expression equal to 1,200, we have a quadratic equation to solve that gives us the number of programs x that need to be sold each week to bring in a profit of $1,200:

$$1,200 = -500 + 27x - 0.1x^2$$

We can write this equation in standard form by adding the opposite of each term on the right side of the equation to both sides of the equation. Doing so produces the following equation:

$$0.1x^2 - 27x + 1,700 = 0$$

Applying the quadratic formula to this equation with $a = 0.1$, $b = -27$, and $c = 1,700$, we have

$$x = \frac{27 \pm \sqrt{(-27)^2 - 4(0.1)(1,700)}}{2(0.1)}$$

$$= \frac{27 \pm \sqrt{729 - 680}}{0.2}$$

$$= \frac{27 \pm \sqrt{49}}{0.2}$$

$$= \frac{27 \pm 7}{0.2}$$

Writing this last expression as two separate expressions, we have our two solutions:

$$x = \frac{27 + 7}{0.2} \quad \text{or} \quad x = \frac{27 - 7}{0.2}$$

$$= \frac{34}{0.2} \qquad\qquad = \frac{20}{0.2}$$

$$= 170 \qquad\qquad = 100$$

The weekly profit will be $1,200 if the company produces and sells 100 programs or 170 programs.

What is interesting about this last example is that it has rational solutions, meaning it could have been solved by factoring. But looking back at the equation, factoring does not seem like a reasonable method of solution because the coefficients are either very large or very small. So, there are times when using the quadratic formula is a faster method of solution, even though the equation you are solving is factorable.

Graphing Calculator

More About Example 7

We can solve the problem discussed in Example 7 by graphing the function $Y_1 = 20X + 16X^2$ in a window with X from 0 to 2 (because X is taking the place of t and we know t is a positive quantity) and Y from 0 to 50 (because we are looking for X when Y_1 is 40).
Graphing Y_1 gives a graph similar to the graph in Figure 2. Using the Zoom and Trace features at $Y_1 = 40$ gives us $X = 1.08$ to the nearest hundredth, matching the results we obtained by solving the original equation algebraically.

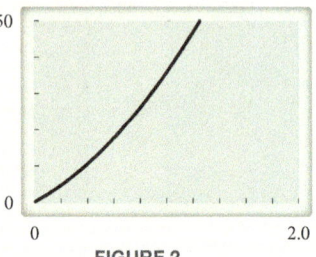

FIGURE 2

More About Example 8

To visualize the functions in Example 8, we set up our calculator this way:

$$Y_1 = 35X - .1X^2 \qquad \text{Revenue function}$$

$$Y_2 = 8X + 500 \qquad \text{Cost function}$$

$$Y_3 = Y_1 - Y_2 \qquad \text{Profit function}$$

Window: X from 0 to 350, Y from 0 to 3,500

Graphing these functions produces graphs similar to the ones shown in Figure 3. The lowest graph is the graph of the profit function. Using the Zoom and Trace features on the lowest graph at $Y_3 = 1,200$ produces two corresponding values of X, 170 and 100, which match the results in Example 8.

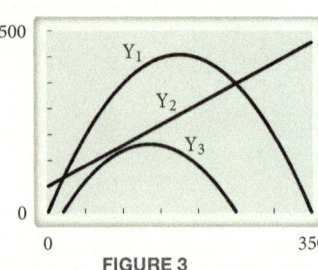

FIGURE 3

We will continue this discussion of the relationship between graphs of functions and solutions to equations in the Using Technology material in the next section.

Getting Ready for Class

After reading through the preceding section, respond in your own words and in complete sentences.

A. What is the quadratic formula?
B. Under what circumstances should the quadratic formula be applied?
C. When would the quadratic formula result in complex solutions?
D. When will the quadratic formula result in only one solution?

Solve each equation. Use factoring or the quadratic formula, whichever is appropriate. (Try factoring first. If you have any difficulty factoring, then go right to the quadratic formula.)

1. $x^2 + 5x + 6 = 0$

2. $x^2 + 5x - 6 = 0$

3. $a^2 - 4a + 1 = 0$

4. $a^2 + 4a + 1 = 0$

5. $\frac{1}{6}x^2 - \frac{1}{2}x + \frac{1}{3} = 0$

6. $\frac{1}{6}x^2 + \frac{1}{2}x + \frac{1}{3} = 0$

7. $\frac{x^2}{2} + 1 = \frac{2x}{3}$

8. $\frac{x^2}{2} + \frac{2}{3} = -\frac{2x}{3}$

9. $y^2 - 5y = 0$

10. $2y^2 + 10y = 0$

11. $30x^2 + 40x = 0$

12. $50x^2 - 20x = 0$

13. $\frac{2t^2}{3} - t = -\frac{1}{6}$

14. $\frac{t^2}{3} - \frac{t}{2} = -\frac{3}{2}$

15. $0.01x^2 + 0.06x - 0.08 = 0$

16. $0.02x^2 - 0.03x + 0.05 = 0$

17. $2x + 3 = -2x^2$

18. $2x - 3 = 3x^2$

19. $100x^2 - 200x + 100 = 0$

20. $100x^2 - 600x + 900 = 0$

21. $\frac{1}{2}r^2 = \frac{1}{6}r - \frac{2}{3}$

22. $\frac{1}{4}r^2 = \frac{2}{5}r + \frac{1}{10}$

23. $(x - 3)(x - 5) = 1$

24. $(x - 3)(x + 1) = -6$

25. $(x + 3)^2 + (x - 8)(x - 1) = 16$

26. $(x - 4)^2 + (x + 2)(x + 1) = 9$

27. $\frac{x^2}{3} - \frac{5x}{6} = \frac{1}{2}$

28. $\frac{x^2}{6} + \frac{5}{6} = -\frac{x}{3}$

Multiply both sides of each equation by its LCD. Then solve the resulting equation.

29. $\frac{1}{x + 1} - \frac{1}{x} = \frac{1}{2}$

30. $\frac{1}{x + 1} + \frac{1}{x} = \frac{1}{3}$

31. $\frac{1}{y - 1} + \frac{1}{y + 1} = 1$

32. $\frac{2}{y + 2} + \frac{3}{y - 2} = 1$

33. $\frac{1}{x + 2} + \frac{1}{x + 3} = 1$

34. $\frac{1}{x + 3} + \frac{1}{x + 4} = 1$

35. $\frac{6}{r^2 - 1} - \frac{1}{2} = \frac{1}{r + 1}$

36. $2 + \frac{5}{r - 1} = \frac{12}{(r - 1)^2}$

Solve each equation. In each case you will have three solutions.

37. $x^3 - 8 = 0$

38. $x^3 - 27 = 0$

39. $8a^3 + 27 = 0$

40. $27a^3 + 8 = 0$

41. $125t^3 - 1 = 0$

42. $64t^3 + 1 = 0$

Each of the following equations has three solutions. Look for the greatest common factor; then use the quadratic formula to find all solutions.

43. $2x^3 + 2x^2 + 3x = 0$

44. $6x^3 - 4x^2 + 6x = 0$

45. $3y^4 = 6y^3 - 6y^2$

46. $4y^4 = 16y^3 - 20y^2$

47. $6t^5 + 4t^4 = -2t^3$

48. $8t^5 + 2t^4 = -10t^3$

49. Which two of the expressions below are equivalent?

   a. $\dfrac{6 + 2\sqrt{3}}{4}$
   b. $\dfrac{3 + \sqrt{3}}{2}$
   c. $6 + \dfrac{\sqrt{3}}{2}$

50. Which two of the expressions below are equivalent?

   a. $\dfrac{8 - 4\sqrt{2}}{4}$
   b. $2 - 4\sqrt{3}$
   c. $2 - \sqrt{2}$

51. Solve $3x^2 - 5x = 0$

    a. by factoring   **b.** by the quadratic formula

52. Solve $3x^2 + 23x - 70 = 0$

    a. by factoring   **b.** by the quadratic formula

53. Can the equation $x^2 - 4x + 7 = 0$ be solved by factoring? Solve it.

54. Can the equation $x^2 = 5$ be solved by factoring? Solve it.

55. Is $x = -1 + i$ a solution to $x^2 + 2x = -2$.

56. Is $x = 2 + 2i$ a solution to $(x - 2)^2 = -4$.

Applying the Concepts

57. Falling Object An object is thrown downward with an initial velocity of 5 feet per second. The relationship between the distance s it travels and time t is given by $s = 5t + 16t^2$. How long does it take the object to fall 74 feet?

58. Coin Toss A coin is tossed upward with an initial velocity of 32 feet per second from a height of 16 feet above the ground. The equation giving the object's height h at any time t is $h = 16 + 32t - 16t^2$. Does the object ever reach a height of 32 feet?

59. Profit The total cost (in dollars) for a company to manufacture and sell x items per week is $C = 60x + 300$, whereas the revenue brought in by selling all x items is $R = 100x - 0.5x^2$. How many items must be sold to obtain a weekly profit of $300?

60. Profit Suppose a company manufactures and sells x picture frames each month with a total cost of $C = 1,200 + 3.5x$ dollars. If the revenue obtained by selling x frames is $R = 9x - 0.002x^2$, find the number of frames it must sell each month if its monthly profit is to be $2,300.

Getting Ready for the Next Section

Find the value of $b^2 - 4ac$ when

61. $a = 1, b = -3, c = -40$ **62.** $a = 2, b = 3, c = 4$

63. $a = 4, b = 12, c = 9$ **64.** $a = -3, b = 8, c = -1$

Solve.

65. $k^2 - 144 = 0$ **66.** $36 - 20k = 0$

Multiply.

67. $(x - 3)(x + 2)$ **68.** $(t - 5)(t + 5)$

69. $(x - 3)(x - 3)(x + 2)$ **70.** $(t - 5)(t + 5)(t - 3)$

More Equations

We are now in a position to put our knowledge of quadratic equations to work to solve a variety of equations.

Video Examples

Section 9.3

Example 1   Solve $(x + 3)^2 - 2(x + 3) - 8 = 0$.

SOLUTION   We can see that this equation is quadratic in form by replacing $x + 3$ with another variable, say, y. Replacing $x + 3$ with y we have

$$y^2 - 2y - 8 = 0$$

We can solve this equation by factoring the left side and then setting each factor equal to 0.

$$y^2 - 2y - 8 = 0$$
$$(y - 4)(y + 2) = 0 \qquad \text{Factor}$$
$$y - 4 = 0 \quad \text{or} \quad y + 2 = 0 \qquad \text{Set factors to 0}$$
$$y = 4 \quad \text{or} \quad y = -2$$

Because our original equation was written in terms of the variable x, we want our solutions in terms of x also. Replacing y with $x + 3$ and then solving for x, we have

$$x + 3 = 4 \quad \text{or} \quad x + 3 = -2$$
$$x = 1 \quad \text{or} \quad x = -5$$

The solutions to our original equation are 1 and -5.

The method we have just shown lends itself well to other types of equations that are quadratic in form, as we will see. In this example, however, there is another method that works just as well. Let's solve our original equation again, but this time, let's begin by expanding $(x + 3)^2$ and $2(x + 3)$.

$$(x + 3)^2 - 2(x + 3) - 8 = 0$$
$$x^2 + 6x + 9 - 2x - 6 - 8 = 0 \qquad \text{Multiply}$$
$$x^2 + 4x - 5 = 0 \qquad \text{Combine similar terms}$$
$$(x - 1)(x + 5) = 0 \qquad \text{Factor}$$
$$x - 1 = 0 \quad \text{or} \quad x + 5 = 0 \qquad \text{Set factors to 0}$$
$$x = 1 \quad \text{or} \quad x = -5$$

As you can see, either method produces the same result.

Example 2   Solve $4x^4 + 7x^2 = 2$.

SOLUTION   This equation is quadratic in x^2. We can make it easier to look at by using the substitution $y = x^2$. (The choice of the letter y is arbitrary. We could just as easily use the substitution $m = x^2$.) Making the substitution $y = x^2$ and then solving the resulting equation we have

$$4y^2 + 7y = 2$$
$$4y^2 + 7y - 2 = 0 \qquad \text{Standard form}$$
$$(4y - 1)(y + 2) = 0 \qquad \text{Factor}$$
$$4y - 1 = 0 \quad \text{or} \quad y + 2 = 0 \qquad \text{Set factors to 0}$$
$$y = \frac{1}{4} \quad \text{or} \quad y = -2$$

Now we replace y with x^2 to solve for x:

$$x^2 = \frac{1}{4} \quad \text{or} \quad x^2 = -2$$

$$x = \pm\sqrt{\frac{1}{4}} \quad \text{or} \quad x = \pm\sqrt{-2} \qquad \textcolor{green}{\text{Square Root Property for Equations}}$$

$$x = \pm\frac{1}{2} \quad \text{or} \quad = \pm i\sqrt{2}$$

The solution set is $\left\{ \frac{1}{2}, -\frac{1}{2}, i\sqrt{2}, -i\sqrt{2} \right\}$.

Example 3   Solve for x: $x + \sqrt{x} - 6 = 0$

SOLUTION   To see that this equation is quadratic in form, we have to notice that $(\sqrt{x})^2 = x$. That is, the equation can be rewritten as

$$(\sqrt{x})^2 + \sqrt{x} - 6 = 0$$

Replacing $\sqrt{x}$ with y and solving as usual, we have

$$y^2 + y - 6 = 0$$
$$(y + 3)(y - 2) = 0$$
$$y + 3 = 0 \quad \text{or} \quad y - 2 = 0$$
$$y = -3 \quad \text{or} \quad y = 2$$

Again, to find x, we replace y with x and solve:

$$\sqrt{x} = -3 \quad \text{or} \quad \sqrt{x} = 2$$
$$x = 9 \quad \text{or} \quad x = 4 \qquad \textcolor{green}{\text{Square both sides of each equation}}$$

Because we squared both sides of each equation, we have the possibility of obtaining extraneous solutions. We have to check both solutions in our original equation.

When $x = 9$ the equation becomes
$$x + \sqrt{x} - 6 = 0$$
$$9 + \sqrt{9} - 6 \stackrel{?}{=} 0$$
$$9 + 3 - 6 \stackrel{?}{=} 0$$
$$6 \neq 0$$

$\textcolor{green}{\text{This means 9 is extraneous}}$

When $x = 4$ the equation becomes
$$x + \sqrt{x} - 6 = 0$$
$$4 + \sqrt{4} - 6 \stackrel{?}{=} 0$$
$$4 + 2 - 6 \stackrel{?}{=} 0$$
$$0 = 0$$

$\textcolor{green}{\text{This means 4 is a solution}}$

The only solution to the equation $x + \sqrt{x} - 6 = 0$ is $x = 4$.

We should note here that the two possible solutions, 9 and 4, to the equation in Example 3 can be obtained by another method. Instead of substituting for x, we can isolate it on one side of the equation and then square both sides to clear the equation of radicals.

$$x + \sqrt{x} - 6 = 0$$

$$\sqrt{x} = -x + 6 \qquad \text{Isolate } \sqrt{x}$$

$$x = x^2 - 12x + 36 \qquad \text{Square both sides}$$

$$0 = x^2 - 13x + 36 \qquad \text{Add } -x \text{ to both sides}$$

$$0 = (x - 4)(x - 9) \qquad \text{Factor}$$

$$x - 4 = 0 \quad \text{or} \quad x - 9 = 0$$

$$x = 4 \qquad\qquad x = 9$$

We obtain the same two possible solutions. Because we squared both sides of the equation to find them, we would have to check each one in the original equation. As was the case in Example 3, only $x = 4$ is a solution; $x = 9$ is extraneous.

Example 4 If an object is tossed into the air with an upward velocity of 12 feet per second from the top of a building h feet high, the time it takes for the object to hit the ground below is given by the formula

$$16t^2 - 12t - h = 0$$

Solve this formula for t.

SOLUTION The formula is in standard form and is quadratic in t. The coefficients a, b, and c that we need to apply to the quadratic formula are $a = 16$, $b = -12$, and $c = -h$. Substituting these quantities into the quadratic formula, we have

$$t = \frac{12 \pm \sqrt{144 - 4(16)(-h)}}{2(16)}$$

$$= \frac{12 \pm \sqrt{144 + 64h}}{32}$$

We can factor the perfect square 16 from the two terms under the radical and simplify our radical somewhat:

$$t = \frac{12 \pm \sqrt{16(9 + 4h)}}{32}$$

$$= \frac{12 \pm 4\sqrt{9 + 4h}}{32}$$

Now we can reduce to lowest terms by factoring a 4 from the numerator and denominator:

$$t = \frac{4(3 \pm \sqrt{9 + 4h})}{4 \cdot 8}$$

$$= \frac{3 \pm \sqrt{9 + 4h}}{8}$$

If we were given a value of h, we would find that one of the solutions to this last formula would be a negative number. Because time is always measured in positive units, we wouldn't use that solution.

More About Example 1

As we mentioned before, algebraic expressions entered into a graphing calculator do not have to be simplified to be evaluated. This fact also applies to equations. We can graph the equation $y = (x + 3)^2 - 2(x + 3) - 8$ to assist us in solving the equation in Example 1. The graph is shown in Figure 1. Using the Zoom and Trace features at the x-intercepts gives us $x = 1$ and $x = -5$ as the solutions to the equation $0 = (x + 3)^2 - 2(x + 3) - 8$.

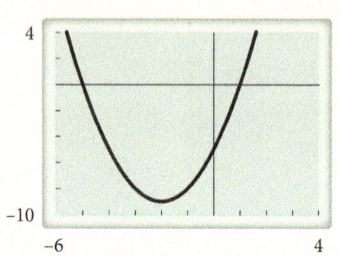

FIGURE 1

More About Example 2

Figure 2 shows the graph of $y = 4x^4 + 7x^2 - 2$. As we expect, the x-intercepts give the real number solutions to the equation $0 = 4x^4 + 7x^2 - 2$. The complex solutions do not appear on the graph.

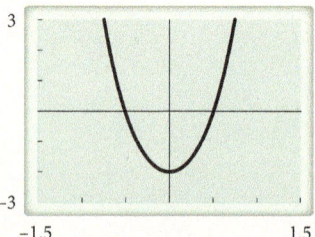

FIGURE 2

More About Example 3

In solving the equation in Example 3, we found that one of the possible solutions was an extraneous solution. If we solve the equation $x + \sqrt{x} - 6 = 0$ by graphing the function $y = x + \sqrt{x} - 6$, we find that the extraneous solution, 9, is not an x-intercept. Figure 3 shows that the only solution to the equation occurs at the x-intercept 4.

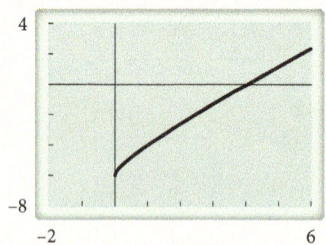

FIGURE 3

Getting Ready for Class

After reading through the preceding section, respond in your own words and in complete sentences.

A. What does it mean for an equation to be quadratic in form?

B. What are all the circumstances in solving equations (that we have studied) in which it is necessary to check for extraneous solutions?

C. How would you start to solve the equation $x + \sqrt{x} - 6 = 0$?

D. Is 9 a solution to $x + \sqrt{x} - 6 = 0$?

Problem Set 9.3

Solve each equation.

1. $(x - 3)^2 + 3(x - 3) + 2 = 0$

2. $(x + 4)^2 - (x + 4) - 6 = 0$

3. $2(x + 4)^2 + 5(x + 4) - 12 = 0$

4. $3(x - 5)^2 + 14(x - 5) - 5 = 0$

5. $x^4 - 6x^2 - 27 = 0$

6. $x^4 + 2x^2 - 8 = 0$

7. $x^4 + 9x^2 = -20$

8. $x^4 - 11x^2 = -30$

9. $(2a - 3)^2 - 9(2a - 3) = -20$

10. $(3a - 2)^2 + 2(3a - 2) = 3$

11. $2(4a + 2)^2 = 3(4a + 2) + 20$

12. $6(2a + 4)^2 = (2a + 4) + 2$

13. $6t^4 = -t^2 + 5$

14. $3t^4 = -2t^2 + 8$

15. $9x^4 - 49 = 0$

16. $25x^4 - 9 = 0$

Solve each of the following equations. Remember, if you square both sides of an equation in the process of solving it, you have to check all solutions in the original equation.

17. $x - 7\sqrt{x} + 10 = 0$

18. $x - 6\sqrt{x} + 8 = 0$

19. $t - 2\sqrt{t} - 15 = 0$

20. $t - 3\sqrt{t} - 10 = 0$

21. $6x + 11\sqrt{x} = 35$

22. $2x + \sqrt{x} = 15$

23. $(a - 2) - 11\sqrt{a - 2} + 30 = 0$

24. $(a - 3) - 9\sqrt{a - 3} + 20 = 0$

25. $(2x + 1) - 8\sqrt{2x + 1} + 15 = 0$

26. $(2x - 3) - 7\sqrt{2x - 3} + 12 = 0$

27. Solve the formula $16t^2 - vt - h = 0$ for t.

28. Solve the formula $16t^2 + vt + h = 0$ for t.

29. Solve the formula $kx^2 + 8x + 4 = 0$ for x.

30. Solve the formula $k^2x^2 + kx + 4 = 0$ for x.

31. Solve $x^2 + 2xy + y^2 = 0$ for x by using the quadratic formula with $a = 1$, $b = 2y$, and $c = y^2$.

32. Solve $x^2 - 2xy + y^2 = 0$ for x by using the quadratic formula, with $a = 1$, $b = -2y$, $c = y^2$.

Applying the Concepts

For Problems 33 and 34, t is in seconds.

33. Falling Object   An object is tossed into the air with an upward velocity of 8 feet per second from the top of a building h feet high. The time it takes for the object to hit the ground below is given by the formula $16t^2 - 8t - h = 0$. Solve this formula for t.

34. Falling Object   An object is tossed into the air with an upward velocity of 6 feet per second from the top of a building h feet high. The time it takes for the object to hit the ground below is given by the formula $16t^2 - 6t - h = 0$. Solve this formula for t.

35. Saint Louis Arch   The shape of the famous "Gateway to the West" arch in Saint Louis can be modeled by a parabola. The equation for one such parabola is:

$$y = -\frac{1}{150}x^2 + \frac{21}{5}x$$

a. Sketch the graph of the arch's equation on a coordinate axis.

b. Approximately how far do you have to walk to get from one side of the arch to the other?

36. Area In the following diagram, $ABCD$ is a rectangle with diagonal AC. Find its area.

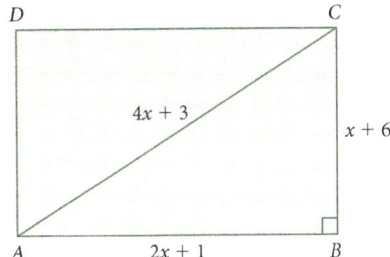

37. Area and Perimeter A total of 160 yards of fencing is to be used to enclose part of a lot that borders on a river. This situation is shown in the following diagram.

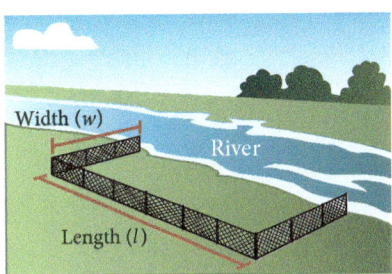

a. Write an equation that gives the relationship between the length and width and the 160 yards of fencing.

b. The formula for the area that is enclosed by the fencing and the river is $A = lw$. Solve the equation in part **a** for l, and then use the result to write the area in terms of w only.

c. Make a table that gives at least five possible values of w and associated area A.

d. From the pattern in your table shown in part **c**, what is the largest area that can be enclosed by the 160 yards of fencing? (Try some other table values if necessary.)

38. Area and Perimeter Rework all four parts of the preceding problem if it is desired to have an opening 2 yards wide in one of the shorter sides, as shown in the diagram.

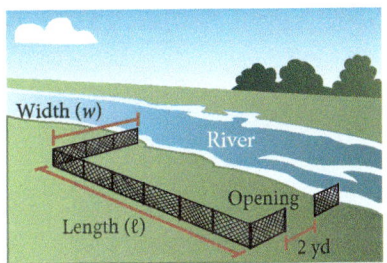

Getting Ready for the Next Section

39. Evaluate $y = 3x^2 - 6x + 1$ for $x = 1$

40. Evaluate $y = -2x^2 + 6x - 5$ for $x = \dfrac{3}{2}$.

41. Let $P(x) = -0.1x^2 + 27x - 500$ and find $P(135)$.

42. Let $P(x) = -0.1x^2 + 12x - 400$ and find $P(600)$.

Solve.

43. $0 = a(80)^2 + 70$

44. $0 = a(80)^2 + 90$

45. $x^2 - 6x + 5 = 0$

46. $x^2 - 3x - 4 = 0$

47. $-x^2 - 2x + 3 = 0$

48. $-x^2 + 4x + 12 = 0$

49. $2x^2 - 6x + 5 = 0$

50. $x^2 - 4x + 5 = 0$

Fill in the blanks to complete the square.

51. $x^2 - 6x + \square = (x - \square)^2$

52. $x^2 - 10x + \square = (x - \square)^2$

53. $y^2 + 2y + \square = (y + \square)^2$

54. $y^2 - 12y + \square = (x - \square)^2$

Graphing Parabolas

The solution set to the equation

$$y = x^2 - 3$$

consists of ordered pairs. One method of graphing the solution set is to find a number of ordered pairs that satisfy the equation and to graph them. We can obtain some ordered pairs that are solutions to $y = x^2 - 3$ by use of a table as follows:

x	$y = x^2 - 3$	y	Solutions
-3	$y = (-3)^2 - 3 = 9 - 3 = 6$	6	$(-3, 6)$
-2	$y = (-2)^2 - 3 = 4 - 3 = 1$	1	$(-2, 1)$
-1	$y = (-1)^2 - 3 = 1 - 3 = -2$	-2	$(-1, -2)$
0	$y = 0^2 - 3 = 0 - 3 = -3$	-3	$(0, -3)$
1	$y = 1^2 - 3 = 1 - 3 = -2$	-2	$(1, -2)$
2	$y = 2^2 - 3 = 4 - 3 = 1$	1	$(2, 1)$
3	$y = 3^2 - 3 = 9 - 3 = 6$	6	$(3, 6)$

Graphing these solutions and then connecting them with a smooth curve, we have the graph of $y = x^2 - 3$. (See Figure 1.)

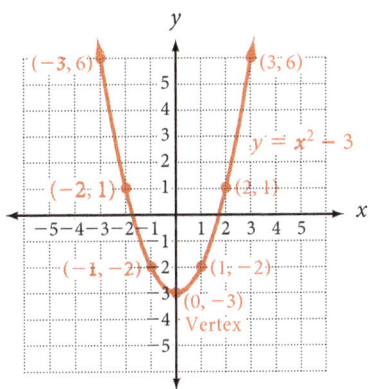

FIGURE 1

This graph is an example of a ***parabola***. All equations of the form $y = ax^2 + bx + c$, $a \neq 0$, have parabolas for graphs.

   Although it is always possible to graph parabolas by making a table of values of x and y that satisfy the equation, there are other methods that are faster and, in some cases, more accurate.

   The important points associated with the graph of a parabola are the highest (or lowest) point on the graph and the x-intercepts. The y-intercepts can also be useful.

Intercepts for Parabolas

The graph of the equation $y = ax^2 + bx + c$ crosses the y-axis at $y = c$, because substituting $x = 0$ into $y = ax^2 + bx + c$ yields $y = c$.

Because the graph crosses the x-axis when $y = 0$, the x-intercepts are those values of x that are solutions to the quadratic equation $0 = ax^2 + bx + c$.

The Vertex of a Parabola

The highest or lowest point on a parabola is called the *vertex*. The vertex for the graph of $y = ax^2 + bx + c$ will always occur when

$$x = \frac{-b}{2a}$$

To see this, we must transform the right side of $y = ax^2 + bx + c$ into an expression that contains x in just one of its terms. This is accomplished by completing the square on the first two terms. Here is what it looks like:

$$y = ax^2 + bx + c$$

$$= a\left(x^2 + \frac{b}{a}x\right) + c$$

$$= a\left[x^2 + \frac{b}{a}x + \left(\frac{b}{2a}\right)^2\right] + c - a\left(\frac{b}{2a}\right)^2$$

$$= a\left(x + \frac{b}{2a}\right)^2 + \frac{4ac - b^2}{4a}$$

It may not look like it, but this last line indicates that the vertex of the graph of $y = ax^2 + bx + c$ has an x-coordinate of $\frac{-b}{2a}$. Because a, b, and c are constants, the only quantity that is varying in the last expression is the x in $\left(x + \frac{b}{2a}\right)^2$. Because the quantity $\left(x + \frac{b}{2a}\right)^2$ is the square of $x + \frac{b}{2a}$, the smallest it will ever be is 0, and that will happen when $x = \frac{-b}{2a}$.

We can use the vertex point along with the x- and y-intercepts to sketch the graph of any equation of the form $y = ax^2 + bx + c$. Here is a summary of the preceding information.

⌈Δ≠Σ⌉   *Graphing Parabolas in Standard Form*

The graph of $y = ax^2 + bx + c$, $a \neq 0$, will be a parabola with
1. A y-intercept at $y = c$
2. x-intercepts (if they exist) at

$$x = \frac{-b \pm \sqrt{b^2 - 4ac}}{2a}$$

3. A vertex when $x = \dfrac{-b}{2a}$

Video Examples

Section 9.4

Example 1   Sketch the graph of $y = x^2 - 6x + 5$.

SOLUTION   To find the x-intercepts, we let $y = 0$ and solve for x:

$$0 = x^2 - 6x + 5$$

$$0 = (x - 5)(x - 1)$$

$$x = 5 \quad \text{or} \quad x = 1$$

To find the coordinates of the vertex, we first find

$$x = \frac{-b}{2a} = \frac{-(-6)}{2(1)} = 3$$

The x-coordinate of the vertex is 3. To find the y-coordinate, we substitute 3 for x in our original equation:

$$y = 3^2 - 6(3) + 5 = 9 - 18 + 5 = -4$$

The graph crosses the x-axis at 1 and 5 and has its vertex at $(3, -4)$. Plotting these points and connecting them with a smooth curve, we have the graph shown in Figure 2.

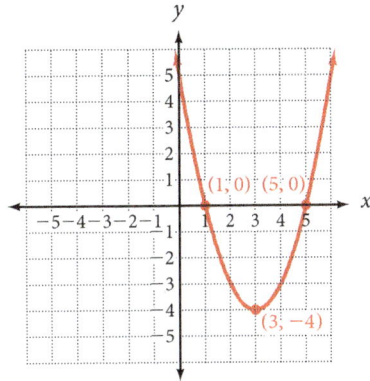

FIGURE 2

The graph is a parabola that opens up, so we say the graph is *concave up*. The vertex is the lowest point on the graph. (Note that the graph crosses the y-axis at 5, which is the value of y we obtain when we let $x = 0$.)

Finding the Vertex by Completing the Square

Another way to locate the vertex of the parabola in Example 1 is by completing the square on the first two terms on the right side of the equation $y = x^2 - 6x + 5$. In this case, we would do so by adding 9 to and subtracting 9 from the right side of the equation. This amounts to adding 0 to the equation, so we know we haven't changed its solutions. This is what it looks like:

$$y = (x^2 - 6x \quad) + 5$$
$$= (x^2 - 6x + 9) + 5 - 9$$
$$= (x - 3)^2 - 4$$

You may have to look at this last equation awhile to see this, but when $x = 3$, then $y = (x - 3)^2 - 4 = 0^2 - 4 = -4$ is the smallest y will ever be. That is why the vertex is at $(3, -4)$. As a matter of fact, this is the same kind of reasoning we used when we derived the formula $x = -\frac{b}{2a}$ for the x-coordinate of the vertex.

Example 2   Graph $y = -x^2 - 2x + 3$.

SOLUTION   To find the x-intercepts, we let $y = 0$:

$$0 = -x^2 - 2x + 3$$
$$0 = x^2 + 2x - 3 \qquad \textcolor{green}{\text{Multiply each side by } -1}$$
$$0 = (x + 3)(x - 1)$$
$$x = -3 \quad \text{or} \quad x = 1$$

The x-coordinate of the vertex is given by

$$x = \frac{-b}{2a} = \frac{-(-2)}{2(-1)} = \frac{2}{-2} = -1$$

To find the y-coordinate of the vertex, we substitute -1 for x in our original equation to get

$$y = -(-1)^2 - 2(-1) + 3 = -1 + 2 + 3 = 4$$

Our parabola has x-intercepts at -3 and 1, and a vertex at $(-1, 4)$. Figure 3 shows the graph.

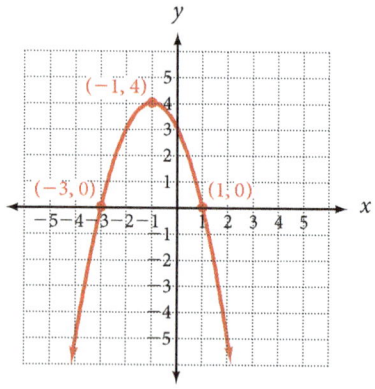

FIGURE 3

We say the graph is *concave down* because it opens downward. Again, we could have obtained the coordinates of the vertex by completing the square on the first two terms on the right side of our equation. To do so, we must first factor -1 from the first two terms. (Remember, the leading coefficient must be 1 to complete the square.) When we complete the square, we add 1 inside the parentheses, which actually decreases the right side of the equation by -1 because everything in the parentheses is multiplied by -1. To make up for it, we add 1 outside the parentheses.

$$y = -1(x^2 + 2x \qquad) + 3$$
$$= -1(x^2 + 2x + 1) + 3 + 1$$
$$= -1(x + 1)^2 + 4$$

The last line tells us that the *largest* value of y will be 4, and that will occur when $x = -1$. ∎

Example 3   Graph $y = 3x^2 - 6x + 1$.

SOLUTION   To find the x-intercepts, we let $y = 0$ and solve for x:

$$0 = 3x^2 - 6x + 1$$

Because the right side of this equation does not factor, we can look at the discrim-inant to see what kind of solutions are possible. The discriminant for this equation is

$$b^2 - 4ac = 36 - 4(3)(1) = 24$$

Because the discriminant is a positive number but not a perfect square, the equation will have irrational solutions. This means that the x-intercepts are irratio-nal numbers and will have to be approximated with decimals using the quadratic formula. Rather than use the quadratic formula, we will find some other points on the graph, but first let's find the vertex.

Here are both methods of finding the vertex:

Using the formula that gives us the x-coordinate of the vertex, we have:

$$x = \frac{-b}{2a} = \frac{-(-6)}{2(3)} = 1$$

Substituting 1 for x in the equation gives us the y-coordinate of the vertex:

$$y = 3 \cdot 1^2 - 6 \cdot 1 + 1 = -2$$

To complete the square on the right side of the equation, we factor 3 from the first two terms, add 1 inside the parentheses, and add -3 outside the parentheses (this amounts to adding 0 to the right side):

$$y = 3(x^2 - 2x \quad) + 1$$
$$= 3(x^2 - 2x + 1) + 1 - 3$$
$$= 3(x - 1)^2 - 2$$

In either case, the vertex is $(1, -2)$.

If we can find two points, one on each side of the vertex, we can sketch the graph. Let's let $x = 0$ and $x = 2$, because each of these numbers is the same distance from $x = 1$, and $x = 0$ will give us the y-intercept.

When $x = 0$

$$y = 3(0)^2 - 6(0) + 1$$
$$= 0 - 0 + 1$$
$$= 1$$

When $x = 2$

$$y = 3(2)^2 - 6(2) + 1$$
$$= 12 - 12 + 1$$
$$= 1$$

The two points just found are $(0, 1)$ and $(2, 1)$. Plotting these two points along with the vertex $(1, -2)$, we have the graph shown in Figure 4.

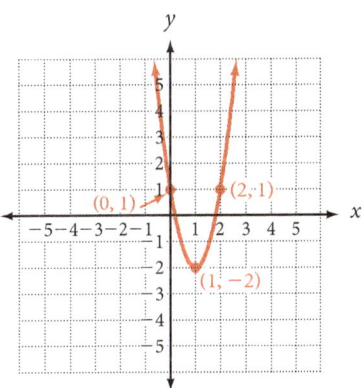

FIGURE 4

Example 4 Graph $y = -2x^2 + 6x - 5$.

SOLUTION Letting $y = 0$, we have

$$0 = -2x^2 + 6x - 5$$

Again, the right side of this equation does not factor. The discriminant is $b^2 - 4ac = 36 - 4(-2)(-5) = -4$, which indicates that the solutions are complex numbers. This means that our original equation does not have x-intercepts. The graph does not cross the x-axis.

Let's find the vertex.

Using our formula for the x-coordinate of the vertex, we have

$$x = \frac{-b}{2a} = \frac{-6}{2(-2)} = \frac{6}{4} = \frac{3}{2}$$

To find the y-coordinate, we let $x = \frac{3}{2}$:

$$y = -2\left(\frac{3}{2}\right)^2 + 6\left(\frac{3}{2}\right) - 5$$

$$= \frac{-18}{4} + \frac{18}{2} - 5$$

$$= \frac{-18 + 36 - 20}{4}$$

$$= -\frac{1}{2}$$

Finding the vertex by completing the square is a more complicated matter. To make the coefficient of x^2 a 1, we must factor -2 from the first two terms. To complete the square inside the parentheses, we add $\frac{9}{4}$. Since each term inside the parentheses is multiplied by -2, we add $\frac{9}{2}$ outside the parentheses so that the net result is the same as adding 0 to the right side:

$$y = -2(x^2 - 3x \qquad) - 5$$

$$= -2\left(x^2 - 3x + \frac{9}{4}\right) - 5 + \frac{9}{2}$$

$$= -2\left(x - \frac{3}{2}\right)^2 - \frac{1}{2}$$

The vertex is $\left(\frac{3}{2}, -\frac{1}{2}\right)$. Because this is the only point we have so far, we must find two others. Let's let $x = 3$ and $x = 0$, because each point is the same distance from $x = \frac{3}{2}$ and on either side:

When $x = 3$

$$y = -2(3)^2 + 6(3) - 5$$

$$= -18 + 18 - 5$$

$$= -5$$

When $x = 0$

$$y = -2(0)^2 + 6(0) - 5$$

$$= 0 + 0 - 5$$

$$= -5$$

The two additional points on the graph are $(3, -5)$ and $(0, -5)$. Figure 5 shows the graph.

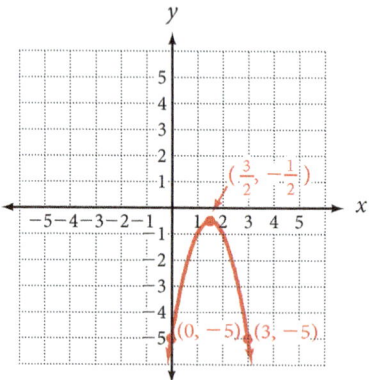

FIGURE 5

The graph is concave down. The vertex is the highest point on the graph. ■

By looking at the equations and graphs in Examples 1 through 4, we can conclude that the graph of $y = ax^2 + bx + c$ will be concave up when a is positive, and concave down when a is negative. Taking this even further, if $a > 0$, then the vertex is the lowest point on the graph, and if $a < 0$, the vertex is the highest point on the graph. Finally, if we complete the square on x in the equation $y = ax^2 + bx + c$, $a \neq 0$, we can rewrite the equation of our parabola as $y = a(x - h)^2 + k$. When the equation is in this form, the vertex is at the point (h, k). Here is a summary:

> $\lceil \Delta \neq \Sigma$ *Graphing Parabolas in Vertex Form*
>
> The graph of
>
> $$y = a(x - h)^2 + k, a \neq 0$$
>
> will be a parabola with a vertex at (h, k). The vertex will be the highest point on the graph when $a < 0$, and the lowest point on the graph when $a > 0$.

Example 5   A company selling copies of an accounting program for home computers finds that it will make a weekly profit of P dollars from selling x copies of the program, according to the equation

$$P(x) = -0.1x^2 + 27x - 500$$

How many copies of the program should it sell to make the largest possible profit, and what is the largest possible profit?

SOLUTION   Because the coefficient of x^2 is negative, we know the graph of this parabola will be concave down, meaning that the vertex is the highest point of the curve. We find the vertex by first finding its x-coordinate:

$$x = \frac{-b}{2a} = \frac{-27}{2(-0.1)} = \frac{27}{0.2} = 135$$

This represents the number of programs the company needs to sell each week to make a maximum profit. To find the maximum profit, we substitute 135 for x in the original equation. (A calculator is helpful for these kinds of calculations.)

$$P(135) = -0.1(135)^2 + 27(135) - 500$$

$$= -0.1(18,225) + 3,645 - 500$$

$$= -1,822.5 + 3,645 - 500$$

$$= 1,322.5$$

The maximum weekly profit is $1,322.50 and is obtained by selling 135 programs a week.

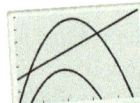

Example 6   An art supply store finds that they can sell x sketch pads each week at p dollars each, according to the equation $x = 900 - 300p$. Graph the revenue equation $R = xp$. Then use the graph to find the price p that will bring in the maximum revenue. Finally, find the maximum revenue.

SOLUTION   As it stands, the revenue equation contains three variables. Because we are asked to find the value of p that gives us the maximum value of R, we rewrite the equation using just the variables R and p. Because $x = 900 - 300p$, we have

$$R = xp = (900 - 300p)p$$

The graph of this equation is shown in Figure 6. The graph appears in the first quadrant only, because R and p are both positive quantities.

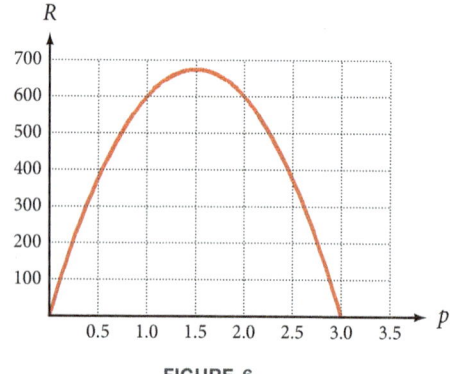

FIGURE 6

From the graph, we see that the maximum value of R occurs when $p = \$1.50$. We can calculate the maximum value of R from the equation:

When $p = 1.5$

the equation $R = (900 - 300p)p$

becomes $R = (900 - 300 \cdot 1.5)1.5$

$$= (900 - 450)1.5$$

$$= 450 \cdot 1.5$$

$$= 675$$

The maximum revenue is $\$675$. It is obtained by setting the price of each sketch pad at $p = \$1.50$.   ■

Graphing Calculators

If you have been using a graphing calculator for some of the material in this course, you are well aware that your calculator can draw all the graphs in this section very easily. It is important, however, that you be able to recognize and sketch the graph of any parabola by hand. It is a skill that all successful intermediate algebra students should possess, even if they are proficient in the use of a graphing calculator. My suggestion is that you work the problems in this section and problem set without your calculator. Then use your calculator to check your results.

Finding the Equation from the Graph

Example 7   At the 1997 Washington County Fair in Oregon, David Smith, Jr., The Bullet, was shot from a cannon. As a human cannonball, he reached a height of 70 feet before landing in a net 160 feet from the cannon. Sketch the graph of his path, and then find the equation of the graph.

SOLUTION   We assume that the path taken by the human cannonball is a parabola. If the origin of the coordinate system is at the opening of the cannon, then the net that catches him will be at 160 on the x-axis. Figure 7 shows the graph.

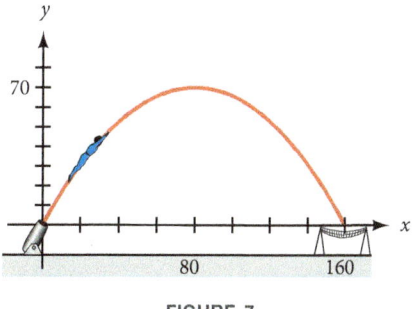

FIGURE 7

Because the curve is a parabola, we know the equation will have the form

$$y = a(x - h)^2 + k$$

Because the vertex of the parabola is at (80, 70), we can fill in two of the three constants in our equation, giving us

$$y = a(x - 80)^2 + 70$$

To find a, we note that the landing point will be (160, 0). Substituting the coordinates of this point into the equation, we solve for a:

$$0 = a(160 - 80)^2 + 70$$

$$0 = a(80)^2 + 70$$

$$0 = 6{,}400a + 70$$

$$a = -\frac{70}{6{,}400} = -\frac{7}{640}$$

The equation that describes the path of the human cannonball is

$$y = -\frac{7}{640}(x - 80)^2 + 70 \quad \text{for} \quad 0 \le x \le 160$$

Graphing Calculators

Graph the equation found in Example 7 on a graphing calculator using the window shown here. (We will use this graph later in the book to find the angle between the cannon and the horizontal.)

> Window: X from 0 to 180, increment 20
> Y from 0 to 80, increment 10

On the TI-83, an increment of 20 for X means Xscl = 20.

Getting Ready for Class

After reading through the preceding section, respond in your own words and in complete sentences.

A. What is a parabola?

B. What part of the equation of a parabola determines whether the graph is concave up or concave down?

C. Suppose $f(x) = ax^2 + bx + c$ is the equation of a parabola. Explain how $f(4) = 1$ relates to the graph of the parabola.

D. A line can be graphed with two points. How many points are necessary to get a reasonable sketch of a parabola? Explain.

Problem Set 9.4

For each of the following equations, give the x-intercepts and the coordinates of the vertex, and sketch the graph.

1. $y = x^2 + 2x - 3$ **2.** $y = x^2 - 2x - 3$ **3.** $y = -x^2 - 4x + 5$

4. $y = x^2 + 4x - 5$ **5.** $y = x^2 - 1$ **6.** $y = x^2 - 4$

7. $y = -x^2 + 9$ **8.** $y = -x^2 + 1$ **9.** $y = 2x^2 - 4x - 6$

10. $y = 2x^2 + 4x - 6$ **11.** $y = x^2 - 2x - 4$ **12.** $y = x^2 - 2x - 2$

Graph each parabola. Label the vertex and any intercepts that exist.

13. $y = 2(x - 1)^2 + 3$ **14.** $y = 2(x + 1)^2 - 3$

15. $f(x) = -(x + 2)^2 + 4$ **16.** $f(x) = -(x - 3)^2 + 1$

17. $g(x) = \frac{1}{2}(x - 2)^2 - 4$ **18.** $g(x) = \frac{1}{3}(x - 3)^2 - 3$

19. $f(x) = -2(x - 4)^2 - 1$ **20.** $f(x) = -4(x - 1)^2 + 4$

Find the vertex and any two convenient points to sketch the graphs of the following equations.

21. $y = x^2 - 4x - 4$ **22.** $y = x^2 - 2x + 3$ **23.** $y = -x^2 + 2x - 5$

24. $y = -x^2 + 4x - 2$ **25.** $f(x) = x^2 + 1$ **26.** $f(x) = x^2 + 4$

27. $y = -x^2 - 3$ **28.** $y = -x^2 - 2$ **29.** $g(x) = 3x^2 + 4x + 1$

30. $g(x) = 2x^2 + 4x + 3$

For each of the following equations, find the coordinates of the vertex, and indicate whether the vertex is the highest point on the graph or the lowest point on the graph. (Do not graph.)

31. $y = x^2 - 6x + 5$ **32.** $y = -x^2 + 6x - 5$ **33.** $y = -x^2 + 2x + 8$

34. $y = x^2 - 2x - 8$ **35.** $y = 12 + 4x - x^2$ **36.** $y = -12 - 4x + x^2$

37. $y = -x^2 - 8x$ **38.** $y = x^2 + 8x$

Applying the Concepts

39. Maximum Profit A company finds that it can make a profit of P dollars each month by selling x patterns, according to the formula $P(x) = -0.002x^2 + 3.5x - 800$. How many patterns must it sell each month to have a maximum profit? What is the maximum profit?

40. Maximum Profit A company selling picture frames finds that it can make a profit of P dollars each month by selling x frames, according to the formula $P(x) = -0.002x^2 + 5.5x - 1,200$. How many frames must it sell each month to have a maximum profit? What is the maximum profit?

41. Maximum Height Chaudra is tossing a softball into the air with an underhand motion. The distance of the ball above her hand at any time is given by the function

$$h(t) = 32t - 16t^2 \quad \text{for} \quad 0 \le t \le 2$$

where $h(t)$ is the height of the ball (in feet) and t is the time (in seconds). Find the times at which the ball is in her hand, and the maximum height of the ball.

42. Maximum Area Justin wants to fence three sides of a rectangular exercise yard for his dog. The fourth side of the exercise yard will be a side of the house. He has 80 feet of fencing available. Find the dimensions of the exercise yard that will enclose the maximum area.

43. **Maximum Revenue** A company that manufactures typewriter ribbons knows that the number of ribbons x it can sell each week is related to the price p of each ribbon by the equation $x = 1{,}200 - 100p$. Graph the revenue equation $R = xp$. Then use the graph to find the price p that will bring in the maximum revenue. Finally, find the maximum revenue.

44. **Maximum Revenue** A company that manufactures diskettes for home computers finds that it can sell x diskettes each day at p dollars per diskette, according to the equation $x = 800 - 100p$. Graph the revenue equation $R = xp$. Then use the graph to find the price p that will bring in the maximum revenue. Finally, find the maximum revenue.

45. **Maximum Revenue** The relationship between the number of calculators x a company sells each day and the price p of each calculator is given by the equation $x = 1{,}700 - 100p$. Graph the revenue equation $R = xp$, and use the graph to find the price p that will bring in the maximum revenue. Then find the maximum revenue.

46. **Maximum Revenue** The relationship between the number x of pencil sharpeners a company sells each week and the price p of each sharpener is given by the equation $x = 1{,}800 - 100p$. Graph the revenue equation $R = xp$, and use the graph to find the price p that will bring in the maximum revenue. Then find the maximum revenue.

47. **Human Cannonball** A human cannonball is shot from a cannon at the county fair. He reaches a height of 60 feet before landing in a net 180 feet from the cannon. Sketch the graph of his path, and then find the equation of the graph.

48. Interpreting Graphs The graph below shows the different paths taken by the human cannonball when his velocity out of the cannon is 50 miles/hour, and his cannon is inclined at varying angles.

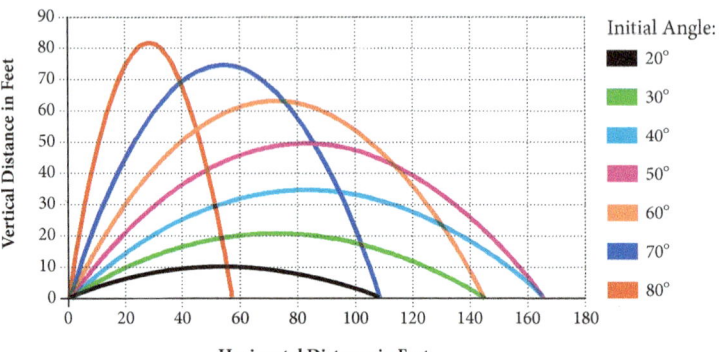

Initial Velocity: 50 miles per hour
Angle: 20°, 30°, 40°, 50°, 60°, 70°, 80°

a. If his landing net is placed 104 feet from the cannon, at what angle should the cannon be inclined so that he lands in the net?
b. Approximately where do you think he would land if the cannon was inclined at 45°?
c. If the cannon was inclined at 45°, approximately what height do you think he would attain?
d. Do you think there is another angle for which he would travel the same distance he travels at 80°? Give an estimate of that angle.
e. The fact that every landing point can come from two different paths makes us think that the equations that give us the landing points must be what type of equations?

Getting Ready for the Next Section

Solve.

49. $x^2 - 2x - 8 = 0$ **50.** $x^2 - x - 12 = 0$

51. $6x^2 - x = 2$ **52.** $3x^2 - 5x = 2$

53. $x^2 - 6x + 9 = 0$ **54.** $x^2 + 8x + 16 = 0$

Quadratic Inequalities

Quadratic inequalities in one variable are inequalities of the form

$$ax^2 + bx + c < 0 \qquad ax^2 + bx + c > 0$$
$$ax^2 + bx + c \leq 0 \qquad ax^2 + bx + c \geq 0$$

where a, b, and c are constants, with $a \neq 0$. The technique we will use to solve inequalities of this type involves graphing. Suppose, for example, we want to find the solution set for the inequality $x^2 - x - 6 > 0$. We begin by factoring the left side to obtain

$$(x - 3)(x + 2) > 0$$

We have two real numbers $x - 3$ and $x + 2$ whose product $(x - 3)(x + 2)$ is greater than zero. That is, their product is positive. The only way the product can be positive is either if both factors, $(x - 3)$ and $(x + 2)$, are positive or if they are both negative. To help visualize where $x - 3$ is positive and where it is negative, we draw a real number line and label it accordingly:

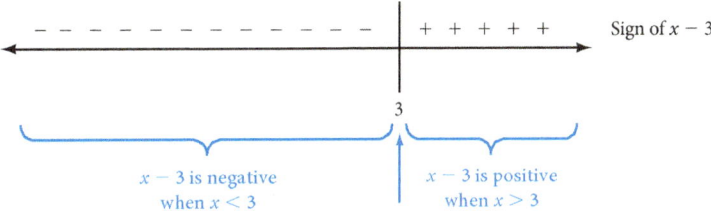

Here is a similar diagram showing where the factor $x + 2$ is positive and where it is negative:

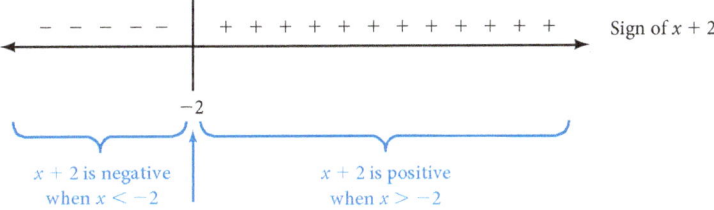

Drawing the two number lines together and eliminating the unnecessary numbers, we have

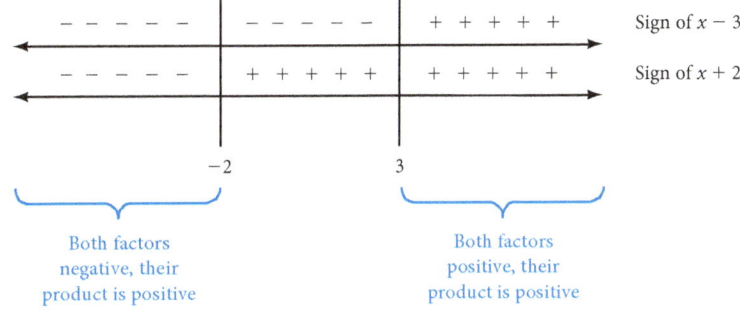

We can see from the preceding diagram that the graph of the solution to $x^2 - x - 6 > 0$ is

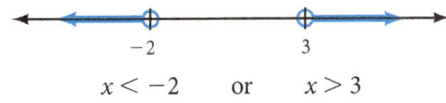

$$x < -2 \qquad \text{or} \qquad x > 3$$

Graphical Solutions to Quadratic Inequalities

We can solve the preceding problem by using a graphing calculator to visualize where the product $(x - 3)(x + 2)$ is positive. First, we graph the function $y = (x - 3)(x + 2)$ as shown in Figure 1.

Next, we observe where the graph is above the x-axis. As you can see, the graph is above the x-axis to the right of 3 and to the left of -2, as shown in Figure 2.

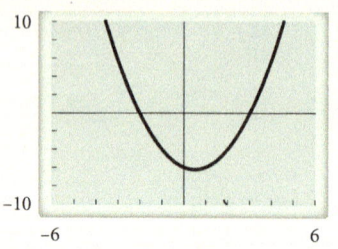

FIGURE 1

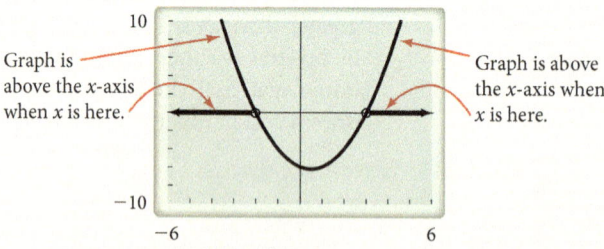

Graph is above the x-axis when x is here.

Graph is above the x-axis when x is here.

FIGURE 2

When the graph is above the x-axis, we have points whose y-coordinates are positive. Because these y-coordinates are the same as the expression $(x - 3)(x + 2)$, the values of x for which the graph of $y = (x - 3)(x + 2)$ is above the x-axis are the values of x for which the inequality $(x - 3)(x + 2) > 0$ is true. Our solution set is therefore

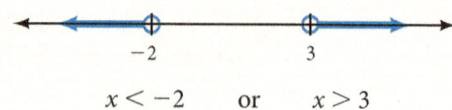

$$x < -2 \quad \text{or} \quad x > 3$$

Video Examples

Section 9.5

Example 1 Solve for x: $x^2 - 2x - 8 \leq 0$

ALGEBRAIC SOLUTION We begin by factoring:

$$x^2 - 2x - 8 \leq 0$$

$$(x - 4)(x + 2) \leq 0$$

The product $(x - 4)(x + 2)$ is negative or zero. The factors must have opposite signs. We draw a diagram showing where each factor is positive and where each factor is negative:

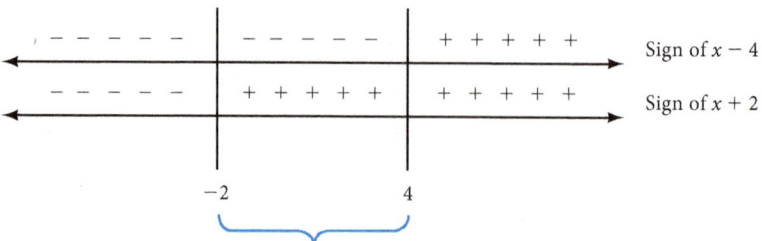

From the diagram, we have the graph of the solution set:

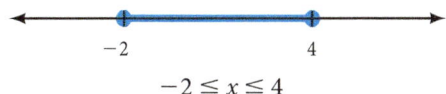

$$-2 \leq x \leq 4$$

GRAPHICAL SOLUTION To solve this inequality with a graphing calculator, we graph the function $y = (x - 4)(x + 2)$ and observe where the graph is below the x-axis. These points have negative y-coordinates, which means that the product $(x - 4)(x + 2)$ is negative for these points. Figure 3 shows the graph of $y = (x - 4)(x + 2)$, along with the region on the x-axis where the graph contains points with negative y-coordinates.

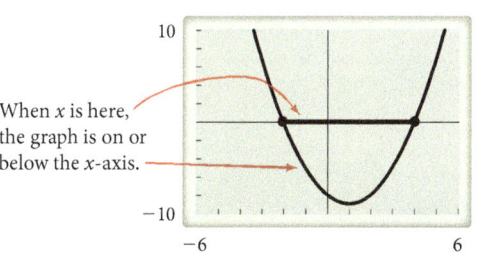

When x is here, the graph is on or below the x-axis.

FIGURE 3

As you can see, the graph is below the x-axis when x is between -2 and 4. Because our original inequality includes the possibility that $(x - 4)(x + 2)$ is 0, we include the endpoints, -2 and 4, with our solution set.

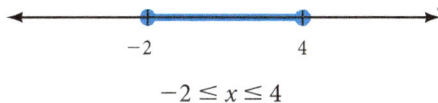

$$-2 \leq x \leq 4$$

Example 2 Solve for x: $6x^2 - x \geq 2$

ALGEBRAIC SOLUTION

$$6x^2 - x \geq 2$$
$$6x^2 - x - 2 \geq 0 \quad \leftarrow \text{Standard form}$$
$$(3x - 2)(2x + 1) \geq 0$$

The product is positive or zero, so the factors must agree in sign. Here is the diagram showing where that occurs:

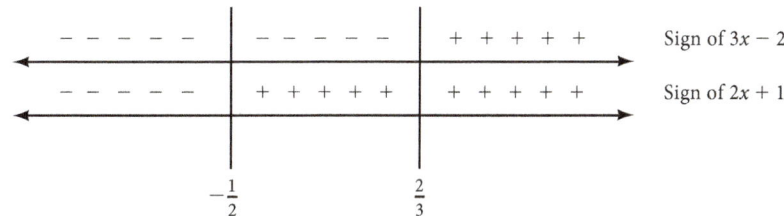

Because the factors agree in sign below $-\frac{1}{2}$ and above $\frac{2}{3}$, the graph of the solution set is

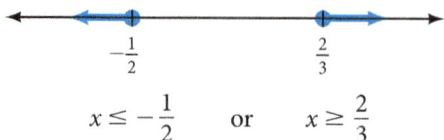

$$x \le -\frac{1}{2} \qquad \text{or} \qquad x \ge \frac{2}{3}$$

GRAPHICAL SOLUTION   To solve this inequality with a graphing calculator, we graph the function $y = (3x - 2)(2x + 1)$ and observe where the graph is above the x-axis. These are the points that have positive y-coordinates, which means that the product $(3x - 2)(2x + 1)$ is positive for these points. Figure 4 shows the graph of $y = (3x - 2)(2x + 1)$, along with the regions on the x-axis where the graph is on or above the x-axis.

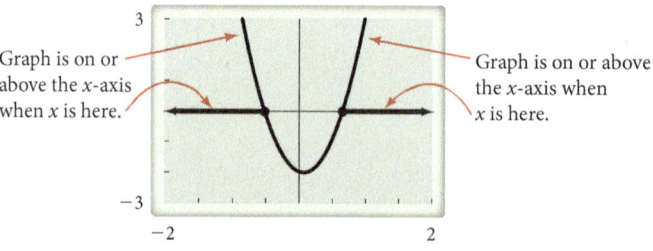

Graph is on or above the x-axis when x is here.

Graph is on or above the x-axis when x is here.

FIGURE 4

To find the points where the graph crosses the x-axis, we need to use either the Trace and Zoom features to zoom in on each point, or the calculator function that finds the intercepts automatically (on the TI-82/83 this is the root/zero function under the CALC key). Whichever method we use, we will obtain the following result:

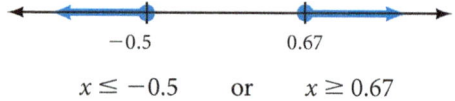

$$x \le -0.5 \qquad \text{or} \qquad x \ge 0.67$$

Example 3   Solve $x^2 - 6x + 9 \ge 0$.

ALGEBRAIC SOLUTION

$$x^2 - 6x + 9 \ge 0$$

$$(x - 3)^2 \ge 0$$

This is a special case in which both factors are the same. Because $(x - 3)^2$ is always positive or zero, the solution set is all real numbers. That is, any real number that is used in place of x in the original inequality will produce a true statement.

GRAPHICAL SOLUTION   The graph of $y = (x - 3)^2$ is shown in Figure 5.

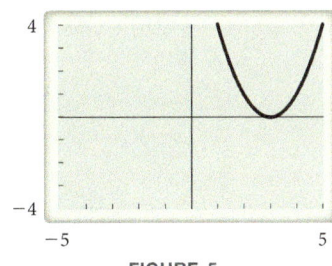

FIGURE 5

Notice that it touches the x-axis at 3 and is above the x-axis everywhere else. This means that every point on the graph has a y-coordinate greater than or equal to 0, no matter what the value of x. The conclusion that we draw from the graph is that the inequality $(x - 3)^2 \geq 0$ is true for all values of x. ∎

Our next two examples involve inequalities that contain rational expressions.

Example 4   Solve: $\dfrac{x - 4}{x + 1} \leq 0$

SOLUTION   The inequality indicates that the quotient of $(x - 4)$ and $(x + 1)$ is negative or 0 (less than or equal to 0). We can use the same reasoning we used to solve the first three examples, because quotients are positive or negative under the same conditions that products are positive or negative. Here is the diagram that shows where each factor is positive and where each factor is negative:

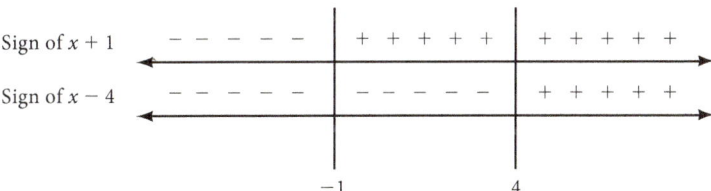

Between -1 and 4 the factors have opposite signs, making the quotient negative. Thus, the region between -1 and 4 is where the solutions lie, because the original inequality indicates the quotient $\frac{x - 4}{x + 1}$ is negative. The solution set and its graph are shown here:

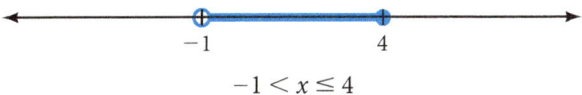

$$-1 < x \leq 4$$

Notice that the left endpoint is open—that is, it is not included in the solution set—because $x = -1$ would make the denominator in the original inequality 0. It is important to check all endpoints of solution sets to inequalities that involve rational expressions. ∎

Example 5　Solve: $\dfrac{3}{x-2} - \dfrac{2}{x-3} > 0$

SOLUTION　We begin by adding the two rational expressions on the left side. The common denominator is $(x-2)(x-3)$:

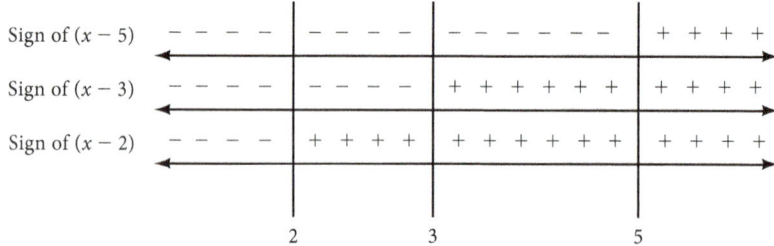

$$\frac{3}{x-2} \cdot \frac{(x-3)}{(x-3)} - \frac{2}{x-3} \cdot \frac{(x-2)}{(x-2)} > 0$$

$$\frac{3x-9-2x+4}{(x-2)(x-3)} > 0$$

$$\frac{x-5}{(x-2)(x-3)} > 0$$

This time the quotient involves three factors. Here is the diagram that shows the signs of the three factors:

```
Sign of (x − 5)   − − − −  | − − − −  | − − − − − −  | + + + +
Sign of (x − 3)   − − − −  | − − − −  | + + + + + +  | + + + +
Sign of (x − 2)   − − − −  | + + + +  | + + + + + +  | + + + +
                           2          3              5
```

The original inequality indicates that the quotient is positive. For this to happen, either all three factors must be positive, or exactly two factors must be negative. Looking back at the diagram, we see the regions that satisfy these conditions are between 2 and 3 or above 5. Here is our solution set:

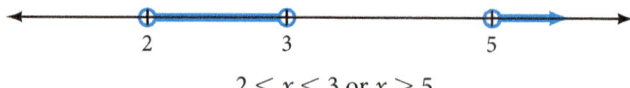

$$2 < x < 3 \text{ or } x > 5$$

Getting Ready for Class

After reading through the preceding section, respond in your own words and in complete sentences.

A. What is the first step in solving a quadratic inequality?

B. How do you show that the endpoint of a line segment is not part of the graph of a quadratic inequality?

C. How would you use the graph of $y = ax^2 + bx + c$ to help you find the graph of $ax^2 + bx + c < 0$?

D. Can a quadratic inequality have exactly one solution? Give an example.

Solve each of the following inequalities, and graph the solution set.

1. $x^2 + x - 6 > 0$ **2.** $x^2 + x - 6 < 0$ **3.** $x^2 - x - 12 \leq 0$

4. $x^2 - x - 12 \geq 0$ **5.** $x^2 + 5x \geq -6$ **6.** $x^2 - 5x > 6$

7. $6x^2 < 5x - 1$ **8.** $4x^2 \geq -5x + 6$ **9.** $x^2 - 9 < 0$

10. $x^2 - 16 \geq 0$ **11.** $4x^2 - 9 \geq 0$ **12.** $9x^2 - 4 < 0$

13. $2x^2 - x - 3 < 0$ **14.** $3x^2 + x - 10 \geq 0$ **15.** $x^2 - 4x + 4 \geq 0$

16. $x^2 - 4x + 4 < 0$ **17.** $x^2 - 10x + 25 < 0$ **18.** $x^2 - 10x + 25 > 0$

19. $(x - 2)(x - 3)(x - 4) > 0$ **20.** $(x - 2)(x - 3)(x - 4) < 0$

21. $(x + 1)(x + 2)(x + 3) \leq 0$ **22.** $(x + 1)(x + 2)(x + 3) \geq 0$

23. $\dfrac{x - 1}{x + 4} \leq 0$ **24.** $\dfrac{x + 4}{x - 1} \leq 0$

25. $\dfrac{3x}{x + 6} - \dfrac{8}{x + 6} < 0$ **26.** $\dfrac{5x}{x + 1} - \dfrac{3}{x + 1} < 0$

27. $\dfrac{4}{x - 6} + 1 > 0$ **28.** $\dfrac{2}{x - 3} + 1 \geq 0$

29. $\dfrac{x - 2}{(x + 3)(x - 4)} < 0$ **30.** $\dfrac{x - 1}{(x + 2)(x - 5)} < 0$

31. $\dfrac{2}{x - 4} - \dfrac{1}{x - 3} > 0$ **32.** $\dfrac{4}{x + 3} - \dfrac{3}{x + 2} > 0$

33. $\dfrac{x + 7}{2x + 12} + \dfrac{6}{x^2 - 36} \leq 0$ **34.** $\dfrac{x + 1}{2x - 2} - \dfrac{2}{x^2 - 1} \leq 0$

35. The graph of $y = x^2 - 4$ is shown in Figure 6. Use the graph to write the solution set for each of the following:

a. $x^2 - 4 < 0$ **b.** $x^2 - 4 > 0$ **c.** $x^2 - 4 = 0$

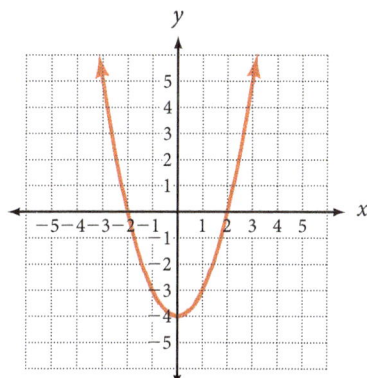

FIGURE 6

36. The graph of $y = 4 - x^2$ is shown in Figure 7. Use the graph to write the solution set for each of the following:

a. $4 - x^2 < 0$ **b.** $4 - x^2 > 0$ **c.** $4 - x^2 = 0$

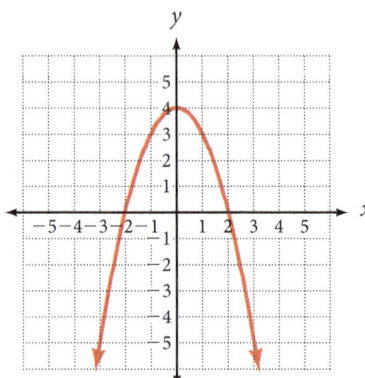

FIGURE 7

37. The graph of $y = x^2 - 3x - 10$ is shown in Figure 8. Use the graph to write the solution set for each of the following:

a. $x^2 - 3x - 10 < 0$ **b.** $x^2 - 3x - 10 > 0$ **c.** $x^2 - 3x - 10 = 0$

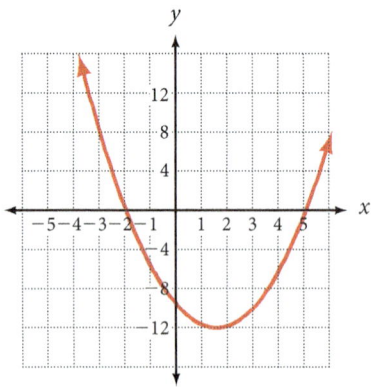

FIGURE 8

38. The graph of $y = x^2 + x - 12$ is shown in Figure 9. Use the graph to write the solution set for each of the following:

a. $x^2 + x - 12 < 0$ **b.** $x^2 + x - 12 > 0$ **c.** $x^2 + x - 12 = 0$

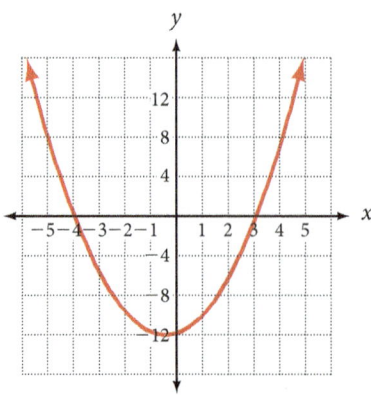

FIGURE 9

39. The graph of $y = x^3 - 3x^2 - x + 3$ is shown in Figure 10. Use the graph to write the solution set for each of the following:

a. $x^3 - 3x^2 - x + 3 < 0$ b. $x^3 - 3x^2 - x + 3 > 0$

c. $x^3 - 3x^2 - x + 3 = 0$

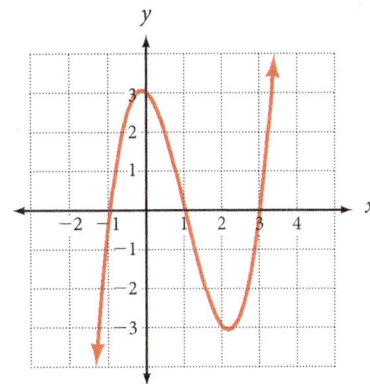

FIGURE 10

40. The graph of $y = x^3 + 4x^2 - 4x - 16$ is shown in Figure 11. Use the graph to write the solution set for each of the following:

a. $x^3 + 4x^2 - 4x - 16 < 0$ b. $x^3 + 4x^2 - 4x - 16 > 0$

c. $x^3 + 4x^2 - 4x - 16 = 0$

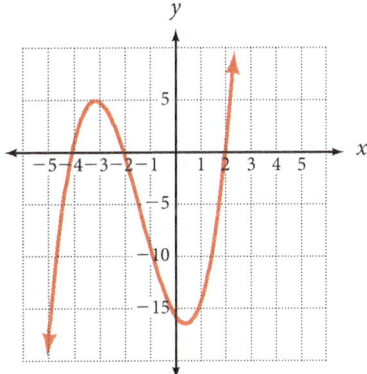

FIGURE 11

Applying the Concepts

41. **Dimensions of a Rectangle** The length of a rectangle is 3 inches more than twice the width. If the area is to be at least 44 square inches, what are the possibilities for the width?

42. **Dimensions of a Rectangle** The length of a rectangle is 5 inches less than three times the width. If the area is to be less than 12 square inches, what are the possibilities for the width?

43. Revenue A manufacturer of portable radios knows that the weekly revenue produced by selling x radios is given by the equation $R = 1{,}300p - 100p^2$, where p is the price of each radio (in dollars). What price should be charged for each radio if the weekly revenue is to be at least $4,000?

44. Revenue A manufacturer of small calculators knows that the weekly revenue produced by selling x calculators is given by the equation $R = 1{,}700p - 100p^2$, where p is the price of each calculator (in dollars). What price should be charged for each calculator if the revenue is to be at least $7,000 each week?

45. Union Dues A labor union has 10,000 members. For every $10 increase in union dues, membership is decreased by 200 people. If the current dues are $100, what should be the new dues (to the nearest multiple of $10) so income from dues is greatest, and what is that income? *Hint:* Because Income = (membership)(dues), we can let x = the number of $10 increases in dues, and then this will give us income of $y = (10{,}000 - 200x)(100 + 10x)$.

46. Bookstore Receipts The owner of a used book store charges $2 for quality paperbacks and usually sells 40 per day. For every 10-cent increase in the price of these paperbacks, he thinks that he will sell two fewer per day. What is the price he should charge (to the nearest 10 cents) for these books to maximize his income, and what would be that income? *Hint:* Let x = the number of 10-cent increases in price.

47. Jiffy-Lube The owner of a quick oil-change business charges $20 per oil change and has 40 customers per day. If each increase of $2 results in 2 fewer daily customers, what price should the owner charge (to the nearest $2) for an oil change if the income from this business is to be as great as possible?

48. Computer Sales A computer manufacturer charges $2,200 for its basic model and sells 1,500 computers per month at this price. For every $200 increase in price, it is believed that 75 fewer computers will be sold. What price should the company place on its basic model of computer (to the nearest $100) to have the greatest income?

Maintaining Your Skills

Use a calculator to evaluate, give answers to 4 decimal places

49. $\dfrac{50{,}000}{32{,}000}$ **50.** $\dfrac{2.4362}{1.9758} - 1$ **51.** $\dfrac{1}{2}\left(\dfrac{4.5926}{1.3876} - 2\right)$ **52.** $1 + \dfrac{0.06}{12}$

Solve each equation

53. $2\sqrt{3t - 1} = 2$ **54.** $\sqrt{4t + 5} + 7 = 3$

55. $\sqrt{x + 3} = x - 3$ **56.** $\sqrt{x + 3} = \sqrt{x} - 3$

Graph each equation

57. $y = \sqrt[3]{x - 1}$ **58.** $y = \sqrt[3]{x} - 1$

Chapter 9 Summary

The Square Root Property for Equations [9.1]

1. If $(x - 3)^2 = 25$
then $x - 3 = \pm 5$
$x = 3 \pm 5$
$x = 8$ or $x = -2$

If $a^2 = b$, where b is a real number, then

$$a = \sqrt{b} \quad \text{or} \quad a = -\sqrt{b}$$

which can be written as $a = \pm\sqrt{b}$.

To Solve a Quadratic Equation by Completing the Square [9.1]

2. Solve $x^2 - 6x - 6 = 0$
$x^2 - 6x = 6$
$x^2 - 6x + 9 = 6 + 9$
$(x - 3)^2 = 15$
$x - 3 = \pm\sqrt{15}$
$x = 3 \pm \sqrt{15}$

Step 1: Write the equation in the form $ax^2 + bx = c$.
Step 2: If $a \neq 1$, divide through by the constant a so the coefficient of x^2 is 1.
Step 3: Complete the square on the left side by adding the square of $\frac{1}{2}$ the coefficient of x to both sides.
Step 4: Write the left side of the equation as the square of a binomial. Simplify the right side if possible.
Step 5: Apply the square root property for equations, and solve as usual.

The Quadratic Theorem [9.2]

3. If $2x^2 + 3x - 4 = 0$, then

$$x = \frac{-3 \pm \sqrt{9 - 4(2)(-4)}}{2(2)}$$

$$= \frac{-3 \pm \sqrt{41}}{4}$$

For any quadratic equation in the form $ax^2 + bx + c = 0$, $a \neq 0$, the two solutions are

$$x = \frac{-b \pm \sqrt{b^2 - 4ac}}{2a}$$

This last equation is known as the **Quadratic Formula**.

Equations Quadratic in Form [9.3]

4. The equation $x^4 - x^2 - 12 = 0$ is quadratic in x^2. Letting $y = x^2$ we have
$y^2 - y - 12 = 0$
$(y - 4)(y + 3) = 0$
$y = 4$ or $y = -3$

Resubstituting x^2 for y, we have
$x^2 = 4$ or $x^2 = -3$
$x = \pm 2$ or $x = \pm i\sqrt{3}$

There are a variety of equations whose form is quadratic. We solve most of them by making a substitution so the equation becomes quadratic, and then solving the equation by factoring or the quadratic formula. For example,

The equation	is quadratic in
$(2x - 3)^2 + 5(2x - 3) - 6 = 0$	$2x - 3$
$4x^4 - 7x^2 - 2 = 0$	x^2
$2x - 7\sqrt{x} + 3 = 0$	$\sqrt{x}$

Quadratic Inequalities [9.4]

5. Solve $x^2 - 2x - 8 > 0$. We factor and draw the sign diagram:
$$(x - 4)(x + 2) > 0$$

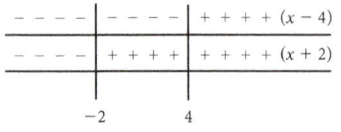

The solution is $x < -2$ or $x > 4$.

We solve quadratic inequalities by manipulating the inequality to get 0 on the right side and then factoring the left side. We then make a diagram that indicates where the factors are positive and where they are negative. From this sign diagram and the original inequality we graph the appropriate solution set.

Chapter 9 Test

Solve each equation. [9.1, 9.2]

1. $(2x + 4)^2 = 25$ **2.** $(2x - 6)^2 = -8$ **3.** $y^2 - 10y + 25 = -4$

4. $(y + 1)(y - 3) = -6$ **5.** $8t^3 - 125 = 0$ **6.** $\dfrac{1}{a + 2} - \dfrac{1}{3} = \dfrac{1}{a}$

7. Solve the formula $64(1 + r)^2 = A$ for r. [9.1]

8. Solve $x^2 - 4x = -2$ by completing the square. [9.1]

9. Projectile Motion An object projected upward with an initial velocity of 32 feet per second will rise and fall according to the equation $s(t) = 32t - 16t^2$, where s is its distance above the ground at time t. At what times will the object be 12 feet above the ground? [9.2]

10. Revenue The total weekly cost for a company to make x ceramic coffee cups is given by the formula $C(x) = 2x + 100$. If the weekly revenue from selling all x cups is $R(x) = 25x - 0.2x^2$, how many cups must it sell a week to make a profit of $200 a week? [9.2]

Solve each equation. [9.4]

11. $4x^4 - 7x^2 - 2 = 0$ **12.** $(2t + 1)^2 - 5(2t + 1) + 6 = 0$

13. $2t - 7\sqrt{t} + 3 = 0$

14. Projectile Motion An object is tossed into the air with an upward velocity of 14 feet per second from the top of a building h feet high. The time it takes for the object to hit the ground below is given by the formula $16t^2 - 14t - h = 0$. Solve this formula for t. [9.4]

Sketch the graph of each of the following equations. Give the coordinates of the vertex in each case. [9.5]

15. $y = x^2 - 2x - 3$ **16.** $y = -x^2 + 2x + 8$

Graph each of the following inequalities. [9.6]

17. $x^2 - x - 6 \le 0$ **18.** $2x^2 + 5x > 3$

19. Profit Find the maximum weekly profit for a company with weekly costs of $C = 5x + 100$ and weekly revenue of $R = 25x - 0.1x^2$. [9.6]

Absolute Value and Set Theory

iStockphoto.com © Andresr

Martina is an international student who is planning on taking some of her college courses here in the U.S. Because her country uses the Celsius scale, she is not familiar with temperatures measured in degrees Fahrenheit. The formula

$$F = \frac{9}{5}C + 32$$

gives the relationship between the Celsius and Fahrenheit temperature scales. Using this formula, we can construct a table that shows the Fahrenheit values for a variety of temperatures measured in degrees Celsius.

Degrees Celsius	Degrees Fahrenheit
20°	68°
25°	77°
30°	86°
35°	95°
40°	104°

In this chapter we will see how Martina could use a linear equation or compound inequality to find the Celsius values for temperatures given in degrees Fahrenheit.

Although the examples and problems in this section may not be review for you, you have in fact been recognizing patterns and relationships among numbers since you started your work in mathematics. What we are doing in this section is giving structure to the pattern recognition that accompanies the study of mathematics. Let's begin by giving a name to the type of reasoning we use when we recognize a pattern in a group of numbers.

Inductive Reasoning

Much of what we do in mathematics is concerned with classifying groups of numbers that share a common characteristic. For instance, suppose you were asked to give the next number in this sequence:

$$3, 5, 7, \ldots$$

Looking for a pattern, you may observe that each number is 2 more than the number preceding it. That being the case, the next number in the sequence will be 9 because 9 is 2 more than 7. Reasoning in this manner is called *inductive reasoning*. In mathematics, we use inductive reasoning when we notice a pattern to a sequence of numbers and then extend the sequence using the pattern.

Video Examples

Section 10.1

Example 1   Use inductive reasoning to find the next term in each sequence.

a. $5, 8, 11, 14, \ldots$ **b.** $\triangle, \triangleright, \triangledown, \triangleleft, \ldots$ **c.** $1, 4, 9, 16, \ldots$

SOLUTION   In each case, we use the pattern we observe in the first few terms to write the next term.

a. Each term comes from the previous term by adding 3. Therefore, the next term would be 17.

b. The triangles rotate a quarter turn to the right each time. The next term would be a triangle that points up, $\triangle$.

c. This looks like the sequence of squares, $1^2, 2^2, 3^2, 4^2, \ldots$ The next term is $5^2 = 25$.

Now that we have an intuitive idea of inductive reasoning, here is a formal definition.

> **(def   Inductive reasoning**
>
> ***Inductive reasoning*** is reasoning in which a conclusion is drawn based on evidence and observations that support that conclusion. In mathematics, this usually involves noticing that a few items in a group have a trait or characteristic in common, and then concluding that all items in the group have that same trait.

Arithmetic Sequences

We can extend our work with sequences by classifying sequences that share a common characteristic. Our first classification is for sequences that are constructed by adding the same number each time.

> (dĕf'   *Arithmetic sequence*
>
> An **arithmetic sequence** is a sequence of numbers in which each number (after the first number) comes from adding the same amount to the number before it.

The sequence

$$4, 7, 10, 13, \ldots$$

is an example of an arithmetic sequence because each term is obtained from the preceding term by adding 3 each time. The number we add each time—in this case, 3 —is the *common difference* because it can be obtained by subtraction.

Example 2   Each sequence shown here is an arithmetic sequence. Find the next two numbers in each sequence.

a. $10, 16, 22, \ldots$

b. $\frac{1}{2}, 1, \frac{3}{2}, \ldots$

c. $5, 0, -5, \ldots$

SOLUTION   Because we know that each sequence is arithmetic, we know how to look for the number that is added to each term to produce the next consecutive term.

a. $10, 16, 22, \ldots$: Each term is found by adding 6 to the term before it. Therefore, the next two terms will be 28 and 34.

b. $\frac{1}{2}, 1, \frac{3}{2}, \ldots$: Each term comes from the term before it by adding $\frac{1}{2}$. The fourth term will be $\frac{3}{2} + \frac{1}{2} = 2$, while the fifth term will be $2 + \frac{1}{2} = \frac{5}{2}$.

c. $5, 0, -5, \ldots$: Each term comes from adding -5 to the term before it. Therefore, the next two terms will be $-5 + (-5) = -10$, and $-10 + (-5) = -15$.   ■

Deductive Reasoning

The day after my daughter Amy turned 17, she and her friend Jenny had the following conversation with me.

AMY: Dad, now that I'm 17, can my curfew be extended?

ME: To how late?

AMY: One o'clock.

ME: No.

AMY: Dad, everyone else gets to stay out as long as they want. It's not fair that I have to be in by midnight.

ME: There is nothing to do here after midnight, except get in trouble.

AMY: Okay then, can I spend the night at Jenny's?

There are messages within this conversation, some explicit and some implied, that mathematics, and the forms of reasoning on which mathematics is built, can clarify. For instance, one fact begins to emerge from this conversation:

If I don't give Amy permission to stay out late, then she will anyway.

In this section, we cover the kind of reasoning I would use to understand the conversation with my daughter. You may be surprised to find that it is the same kind of reasoning that accompanies most topics in mathematics.

Consider the two statements below:

Statement 1: If I study, then I will get good grades.
Statement 2: If x is a negative number, then $-x$ is a positive number.

In Statement 1, if we let A represent the phrase "I study" and B represent the phrase "I will get good grades," then Statement 1 has the form

If A, then B.

Likewise, in Statement 2, if A is the phrase "x is a negative number" and B is "$-x$ is a positive number," then Statement 2 has the form

If A, then B.

Each statement has the same form: If A, then B. We call this the "if/then" form, and any statement that has this form is called a *conditional statement*. For every conditional statement, the first phrase, A, is called the *hypothesis*, and the second phrase, B, is called the *conclusion*. All conditional statements can be written in the form

If *hypothesis,* then *conclusion.*

$\lceil \Delta \neq \Sigma \rceil$ Notation

A shorthand way to write an "if/then" statement is with the implies symbol

$$A \Rightarrow B$$

This statement is read "A implies B." It is equivalent to saying "If A, then B."

Example 3 Identify the hypothesis and conclusion in each statement.

a. If a and b are positive numbers, then $-a(-b) = ab$.

b. If it is raining, then the streets are wet.

c. $C = 90° \Rightarrow c^2 = a^2 + b^2$

SOLUTION

a. *Hypothesis:* a and b are positive numbers.
   Conclusion: $-a(-b) = ab$

b. *Hypothesis:* It is raining.
   Conclusion: The streets are wet.

c. *Hypothesis:* $C = 90°$
   Conclusion: $c^2 = a^2 + b^2$

For each conditional statement $A \Rightarrow B$, we can find three related statements that may or may not be true depending on whether the original conditional statement is true.

(dĕf Definition

For every conditional statement $A \Rightarrow B$, there exist the following associated statements.

The converse:	$B \Rightarrow A$	If B, then A.
The inverse:	not $A \Rightarrow$ not B	If not A, then not B.
The contrapostive:	not $B \Rightarrow$ not A	If not B, then not A.

Example 4 For the statement below, write the converse, the inverse, and the contrapositive.

If it is raining, then the streets are wet.

SOLUTION   It is sometimes easier to work a problem like this if we write out the phrases A, B, not A, and not B.

Let $A =$ it is raining; then not $A =$ it is not raining.
Let $B =$ the streets are wet; then not $B =$ the streets are not wet.

Here are the three associated statements:

The converse: (If B, then A.) If the streets are wet, then it is raining.
The inverse: (If not A, then not B.) If it is not raining, then the streets are not wet.
The contrapositive: (If not B, then not A.) If the streets are not wet, then it is not raining.

True or False?

Next, we want to answer this question: "If a conditional statement is true, which, if any, of the associated statements are true also?" Consider the statement below.

If it is a square, then it has four sides.

We know from our experience with squares that this is a true statement. Now, is the converse necessarily true? Here is the converse:

If it has four sides, then it is a square.

Obviously, the converse is *not* true because there are many four-sided figures that are not squares—rectangles, parallelograms, and trapezoids, to mention a few. So, the converse of a true conditional statement is not necessarily true itself.

Next, we consider the inverse of our original statement.

If it is not a square, then it does not have four sides.

Again, the inverse is not true because there are many nonsquare figures that do have four sides. For example, a 3-inch by 5-inch rectangle fits that description.

Finally, we consider the contrapositive:

If it does not have four sides, then it is not a square.

As you can see, the contrapositive is true. That is, if something doesn't have four sides, it can't possibly be a square.

The preceding discussion leads us to the following theorem.

Theorem

If a conditional statement is true, then so is its contrapositive. That is, the two statements

If A, then B and   If not B, then not A

are equivalent; one can't be true without the other being true also. That is, they are either both true or both false.

The theorem doesn't mention the inverse and the converse because they are true or false independent of the original statement. That is, knowing that a conditional statement is true tells us that the contrapositive is also true—but the truth of the inverse and the converse does not follow from the truth of the original statement.

The next two examples are intended to clarify the preceding discussion and our theorem. As you read through them, be careful not to let your intuition, experience, or opinion get in the way.

Example 5   If the statement "If you are guilty, then you will be convicted" is true, give another statement that must also be true.

SOLUTION   From our theorem, and the discussion preceding it, we know that the contrapositive of a true conditional statement is also true. Here is the contrapositive of our original statement:

> If you are not convicted, then you are not guilty.

Remember, we are not asking for your opinion; we are simply asking for another conditional statement that must be true if the original statement is true. The answer is *always* the contrapositive. Now, you may be wondering about the converse:

> If you are convicted, then you must be guilty.

It may be that the converse is actually true. But if it is, it is not because of the original conditional statement. That is, the truth of the converse *does not follow* from the truth of the original statement.

Example 6   If the following statement is true, what other conditional statement must also be true?

$$\text{If } a = b, \text{ then } a^2 = b^2.$$

SOLUTION   Again, every true conditional statement has a true contrapositive. Therefore, the statement below is also true:

$$\text{If } a^2 \neq b^2, \text{ then } a \neq b.$$

In this case, we know from experience that the original statement is true; that is, if two numbers are equal, then so are their squares. We also know from experience that the contrapositive is true; if the squares of two numbers are not equal, then the numbers themselves can't be equal. Do you think the inverse and converse are true also? Here is the converse:

$$\text{If } a^2 = b^2, \text{ then } a = b.$$

The converse is not true. If a is -3 and b is 3, then a^2 and b^2 are equal, but a and b are not. This same kind of reasoning will show that the inverse is not necessarily true. This example, then gives further evidence that our therom is true: A true conditional statement has a true contrapositive. No conclusion can be drawn about the inverse or the converse.

Everyday Language

In everyday life, we don't always use the "if/then" form exactly as we have illustrated it here. Many times we use shortened, reversed, or otherwise altered forms of "if/then" statements. For instance, each of the following statements is a variation of the "if/then" form, and each carries the same meaning.

If it is raining, then the streets are wet.

If it is raining, the streets are wet.

When it rains, the streets get wet.

The streets are wet if it is raining.

The streets are wet because it is raining.

Rain will make the streets wet.

Example 7   Write the following statement in "if/then" form.

Romeo loves Juliet.

SOLUTION   We must be careful that we do not change the meaning of the statement when we write it in "if/then" form. Here is an "if/then" form that has the same meaning as the original statement:

If he is Romeo, then he loves Juliet.

We can see that it would be incorrect to rewrite the original statement as

If she is Juliet, then she loves Romeo

because the original statement is Romeo loves Juliet, not Juliet loves Romeo. It would also be incorrect to rewrite our statement as either

If he is not Romeo, then he does not love Juliet

or

If he loves Juliet, then he is Romeo

because people other than Romeo may also love Juliet. (The preceding statements are actually the inverse and converse, respectively, of the original statement.) Finally, another statement that has the same meaning as our original statement is

If he does not love Juliet, then he is not Romeo

because this is the contrapositive of our original statement, and we know that the contrapositive is always true when the original statement is true.

For each conditional statement, state the hypothesis and the conclusion.

1. If you argue for your limitations, then they are yours.

2. If you think you can, then you can.

3. If x is an even number, then x is divisible by 2.

4. If x is an odd number, then x is not divisible by 2.

5. If a triangle is equilateral, then all of its angles are equal.

6. If a triangle is isosceles, then two of its angles are equal.

7. If $x + 5 = -2$, then $x = -7$.

8. If $x - 5 = -2$, then $x = 3$.

For each of the following conditional statements, give the converse, the inverse, and the contrapositive.

9. If $a = 8$, then $a^2 = 64$.

10. If $x = y$, then $x^2 = y^2$.

11. If $\dfrac{a}{b} = 1$, then $a = b$.

12. If $a + b = 0$, then $a = -b$.

13. If it is a square, then it is a rectangle.

14. If you live in a glass house, then you shouldn't throw stones.

15. If better is possible, then good is not enough.

16. If a and b are positive, then ab is positive.

For each statement below, write an equivalent statement in "if/then" form.

17. $E \Rightarrow F$

18. $a^3 = b^3 \Rightarrow a = b$

19. Misery loves company.

20. Rollerblading is not a crime,

21. The squeaky wheel gets the grease.

22. The girl who can't dance says the band can't play.

Extending the Concepts

23. **Contrapositive of the Contrapositive.** You have learned that the opposite of a negative number is a positive number. In the same way, the contrapositive of a statement's contrapositive is the statement itself. Illustrate this idea with the following statement: "If you are sleeping, then your eyes are closed."

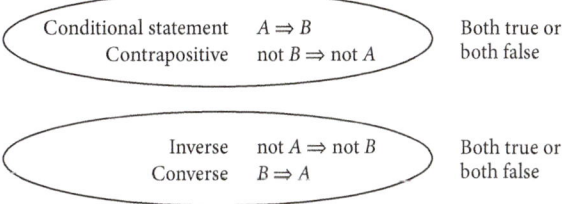

24. **True Statements Come in Pairs** The theorem in this section states that a conditional statement and its contrapositive are either both true or both false. However, it is also true that any conditional statement's inverse and converse are both true or both false. Explain why this second relationship is also true.

25. **Truth Table** Using the information from the preceding exercise, fill in the blank spaces in the following truth table with true or false. (One part of this exercise contains a contradiction and is impossible.)

	Statement	Inverse	Converse	Contrapositive
(a)	True	True	?	?
(b)	?	True	?	False
(c)	?	?	False	True
(d)	False	?	True	?
(e)	?	False	True	?

26. **Logic** Modern mathematicians who use the rules of logic developed in this section are called logicians, and include such notables as *George Boole, Alfred North Whitehead,* and *Bertrand Russell.* Logicians divide conditional statements into two types, deductive and inductive. The conclusion of a deductive statement must follow from its hypothesis, while the conclusion of an inductive statement will probably follow from the hypothesis. The statement "If $x = 2$, then $x + 7 = 9$" is a deductive statement because the conclusion, $x + 7 = 9$, must follow from the hypothesis, $x = 2$. On the other hand, the statement "If I study, then I will earn an A" is an inductive statement because the conclusion (earning an A) will probably (but not necessarily) follow from studying.

    Write three conditional statements that are also deductive statements, and three conditional statements that are also inductive statements.

27. **More About Amy** Suppose after reading the introduction to this section you decide that the following statement is true:

    If I don't extend her curfew,
    Amy will stay out late anyway.

    Write another statement that must also be true if this statement is true. Now, if the preceding statement is true, and I want Amy to be home at her regular time, what should I tell her when she asks if she can have her curfew extended?

28. **Critical Thinking and Subway Tokens** Pat and Tom visit New York City for a week. At the beginning of the trip, they each buy ten subway tokens. Even though they each pay the same amount for their tokens, Tom can ride the subway for half price because he is a senior. Here is how it happens: Each time Tom uses a token to ride the subway, he shows his driver's license to prove he is a senior and then he is given a pass he can use instead of a token for his next subway ride. So, one token gets Tom a ride on the subway and a pass for another ride. After 2 days of riding the subway together, Pat has four tokens left, and Tom has seven tokens left. Has Tom lost a token, or is everything the way it should be? Explain your answer.

Introduction

This chapter marks the transition from introductory algebra to intermediate algebra. Some of the material here is a review of material we covered earlier, and some of the material here is new. If you cover all the sections in this chapter, you will review all the important points contained in the first six chapters of the book. So, it is a good idea to put some extra time and effort into this chapter to ensure that you get a good start with the rest of the course. Let's begin by reviewing the methods we use to solve equations.

iStockPhoto.com/©zorani

Video Examples

Section 10.2

Linear Equations in One Variable

A *linear equation in one variable* is any equation that can be put in the form

$$ax + b = c$$

where a, b, and c are constants and $a \neq 0$. For example, each of the equations

$$5x + 3 = 2 \qquad 2x = 7 \qquad 2x + 5 = 0$$

is linear because it can be put in the form $ax + b = c$. In the first equation, $5x$, 3, and 2 are called *terms* of the equation: $5x$ is a variable term; 3 and 2 are constant terms.

> **(dĕf′** | *solution set*
>
> The *solution set* for an equation is the set of all numbers that, when used in place of the variable, make the equation a true statement.

> **(dĕf′** | *equivalent equations*
>
> Two or more equations with the same solution set are called *equivalent equations.*

The equations $2x - 5 = 9$, $x - 1 = 6$, and $x = 7$ are all equivalent equations because the solution set for each is {7}.

Properties of Equality

The first property of equality states that adding the same quantity to both sides of an equation preserves equality. Or, more importantly, adding the same amount to both sides of an equation *never changes* the solution set. This property is called the *addition property of equality* and is stated in symbols as follows:

> **⟨Δ≠Σ** | *Addition Property of Equality*
>
> For any three algebraic expressions A, B, and C,
>
> $$\text{if} \qquad A = B$$
> $$\text{then} \qquad A + C = B + C$$
>
> *In words:* Adding the same quantity to both sides of an equation will not change the solution set.

Note Because subtraction is defined in terms of addition and division is defined in terms of multiplication, we do not need to introduce separate properties for subtraction and division. The solution set for an equation will never be changed by subtracting the same amount from both sides or by dividing both sides by the same nonzero quantity.

Our second property is called the ***multiplication property of equality*** and is stated as follows:

> ⌈Δ≠Σ⌉ **Multiplication Property of Equality**
>
> For any three algebraic expressions A, B, and C, where $C \neq 0$,
>
> $$\text{if} \qquad A = B$$
> $$\text{then} \qquad AC = BC$$
>
> *In words:* Multiplying both sides of an equation by the same nonzero quantity will not change the solution set.

Example 1   Find the solution set for $3a - 5 = -6a + 1$.

SOLUTION   To solve for a, we must isolate it on one side of the equation. Let's decide to isolate a on the left side. We start by adding $6a$ to both sides of the equation.

$$3a - 5 = -6a + 1$$

$$3a + 6a - 5 = -6a + 6a + 1 \qquad \text{Add } 6a \text{ to both sides}$$

$$9a - 5 = 1$$

$$9a - 5 + 5 = 1 + 5 \qquad \text{Add 5 to both sides}$$

$$9a = 6$$

$$\frac{1}{9}(9a) = \frac{1}{9}(6) \qquad \text{Multiply both sides by } \frac{1}{9}$$

$$a = \frac{2}{3} \qquad \frac{1}{9}(6) = \frac{6}{9} = \frac{2}{3}$$

The solution set is $\left\{ \dfrac{2}{3} \right\}$.

> *Note* We know that multiplication by a number and division by its reciprocal always produce the same result. Because of this fact, instead of multiplying each side of our equation by $\frac{1}{9}$, we could just as easily divide each side by 9. If we did so, the last two lines in our solution would look like this:
>
> $$\frac{9a}{9} = \frac{6}{9}$$
>
> $$a = \frac{2}{3}$$

The next example involves fractions. The least common denominator, which is the smallest expression that is divisible by each of the denominators, can be used with the multiplication property of equality to simplify equations containing fractions.

Example 2   Solve $\dfrac{2}{3}x + \dfrac{1}{2} = -\dfrac{3}{8}$.

SOLUTION   We can solve this equation by applying our properties and working with fractions, or we can begin by eliminating the fractions. Let's work the problem using both methods.

Method 1: *Working with the fractions*

$$\frac{2}{3}x + \frac{1}{2} + \left(-\frac{1}{2}\right) = -\frac{3}{8} + \left(-\frac{1}{2}\right) \qquad \text{Add } -\frac{1}{2} \text{ to each side.}$$

$$\frac{2}{3}x = -\frac{7}{8} \qquad -\frac{3}{8} + \left(-\frac{1}{2}\right) = -\frac{3}{8} + \left(-\frac{4}{8}\right)$$

$$\frac{3}{2}\left(\frac{2}{3}x\right) = \frac{3}{2}\left(-\frac{7}{8}\right) \qquad \text{Multiply each side by } \frac{3}{2}$$

$$x = -\frac{21}{16}$$

Method 2: *Eliminating the fractions in the beginning*
Our original equation has denominators of 3, 2, and 8. The least common denominator, abbreviated LCD, for these three denominators is 24, and it has the property that all three denominators will divide it evenly. Therefore, if we multiply both sides of our equation by 24, each denominator will divide into 24, and we will be left with an equation that does not contain any denominators other than 1.

$$24\left(\frac{2}{3}x + \frac{1}{2}\right) = 24\left(-\frac{3}{8}\right) \quad \text{Multiply each side by the LCD 24}$$

$$24\left(\frac{2}{3}x\right) + 24\left(\frac{1}{2}\right) = 24\left(-\frac{3}{8}\right) \quad \text{Distributive property on the left side}$$

$$16x + 12 = -9 \quad \text{Multiply}$$

$$16x = -21 \quad \text{Add} -12 \text{ to each side}$$

$$x = -\frac{21}{16} \quad \text{Multiply each side by } \frac{1}{16}$$

As the third line above indicates, multiplying each side of the equation by the LCD eliminates all the fractions from the equation. Both methods yield the same solution.

Example 3 Solve the equation $0.06x + 0.05(10{,}000 - x) = 560$.

SOLUTION We can solve the equation in its original form by working with the decimals, or we can eliminate the decimals first by using the multiplication property of equality and solve the resulting equation. Here are both methods.

Method 1: *Working with the decimals*

$$0.06x + 0.05(10{,}000 - x) = 560 \quad \text{Original equation}$$

$$0.06x + 0.05(10{,}000) - 0.05x = 560 \quad \text{Distributive property}$$

$$0.01x + 500 = 560 \quad \text{Simplify the left side}$$

$$0.01x + 500 + (-500) = 560 + (-500) \quad \text{Add} -500 \text{ to each side}$$

$$0.01x = 60$$

$$\frac{0.01x}{0.01} = \frac{60}{0.01} \quad \text{Divide each side by 0.01}$$

$$x = 6{,}000$$

Method 2: *Eliminating the decimals in the beginning*
To move the decimal point two places to the right in $0.06x$ and 0.05, we multiply each side of the equation by 100.

$$0.06x + 0.05(10{,}000 - x) = 560 \quad \text{Original equation}$$

$$0.06x + 500 - 0.05x = 560 \quad \text{Distributive property}$$

$$100(0.06x) + 100(500) - 100(0.05x) = 100(560) \quad \text{Multiply each side by 100}$$

$$6x + 50{,}000 - 5x = 56{,}000 \quad \text{Multiply}$$

$$x + 50{,}000 = 56{,}000 \quad \text{Simplify the left side}$$

$$x = 6{,}000 \quad \text{Add} -50{,}000 \text{ to each side}$$

Using either method, the solution to our equation is 6,000. We check our work (to be sure we have not made a mistake in applying the properties or an arithmetic mistake) by substituting 6,000 into our original equation and simplifying each side of the result separately.

Note We are placing question marks over the equal signs because we don't know yet if the expressions on the left will be equal to the expressions on the right.

Check: Substituting 6,000 for x in the original equation, we have

$$0.06(6,000) + 0.05(10,000 - 6,000) \overset{?}{=} 560$$

$$0.06(6,000) + 0.05(4,000) \overset{?}{=} 560$$

$$360 + 200 \overset{?}{=} 560$$

$$560 = 560 \qquad \textit{A true statement} \quad ■$$

Here is a list of steps to use as a guideline for solving linear equations in one variable.

△≠Σ   *How To: Solve Linear Equations in One Variable*

Step 1a: Use the distributive property to separate terms, if necessary.

1b: If fractions are present, consider multiplying both sides by the LCD to eliminate the fractions. If decimals are present, consider multiplying both sides by a power of 10 to clear the equation of decimals.

1c: Combine similar terms on each side of the equation.

Step 2: Use the addition property of equality to get all variable terms on one side of the equation and all constant terms on the other side. A variable term is a term that contains the variable. A constant term is a term that does not contain the variable (the number 3, for example).

Step 3: Use the multiplication property of equality to get the variable by itself on one side of the equation.

Step 4: Check your solution in the original equation to be sure that you have not made a mistake in the solution process.

As you work through the problems in the problem set, you will see that it is not always necessary to use all four steps when solving equations. The number of steps used depends on the equation. In Example 4, there are no fractions or decimals in the original equation, so step 1b will not be used.

■ Example 4   Solve the equation $8 - 3(4x - 2) + 5x = 35$.

SOLUTION We must begin by distributing the -3 across the quantity $4x - 2$. (It would be a mistake to subtract 3 from 8 first, because the rule for order of operations indicates we are to do multiplication before subtraction.) After we have simplified the left side of our equation, we apply the addition property and the multiplication property. In this example, we will show only the results:

$$8 - 3(4x - 2) + 5x = 35 \qquad \textit{Original equation}$$

Step 1a:
$$8 - 12x + 6 + 5x = 35 \qquad \textit{Distributive property}$$

Step 1c:
$$-7x + 14 = 35 \qquad \textit{Simplify}$$

Step 2:
$$-7x = 21 \qquad \textit{Add } -14 \textit{ to each side}$$

Step 3:
$$x = -3 \qquad \textit{Multiply by } -\tfrac{1}{7}$$

Step 4: When x is replaced by -3 in the original equation, a true statement results. Therefore, -3 is the solution to our equation. ■

Solving Equations by Factoring

Next we will use our knowledge of factoring to solve equations. Most of the equations we will see are *quadratic equations*.

> **(dĕf´   quadratic equations**
>
> Any equation that can be written in the form
>
> $$ax^2 + bx + c = 0$$
>
> where a, b, and c are constants and a is not 0 ($a \neq 0$), is called a *quadratic equation.* The form $ax^2 + bx + c = 0$ is called *standard form* for quadratic equations.

> *Note* For a quadratic equation written in standard form, the first term ax^2 is called the *quadratic term*, the second term bx is the *linear term,* and the last term c is called the *constant term.*

Each of the following is a quadratic equation:

$$2x^2 = 5x + 3 \qquad 5x^2 = 75 \qquad 4x^2 - 3x + 2 = 0$$

The number 0 is a special number, and is the key to solving quadratic equations. If we multiply two expressions and get 0, then one, or both, of the expressions must have been 0. In other words, the only way to multiply and get 0 for an answer is to multiply by 0. This fact allows us to solve certain quadratic equations. We state this fact as follows:

> **[Δ≠Σ   Zero-Factor Property**
>
> For all real numbers r and s,
>
> $$r \cdot s = 0 \qquad \text{if and only if} \qquad r = 0 \qquad \text{or} \qquad s = 0 \qquad \text{(or both)}$$

Example 5   Solve $x^2 - 2x - 24 = 0$.

SOLUTION   We begin by factoring the left side as $(x - 6)(x + 4)$ and get

$$(x - 6)(x + 4) = 0$$

Now both $(x - 6)$ and $(x + 4)$ represent real numbers. We notice that their product is 0. By the zero-factor property, one or both of them must be 0:

$$x - 6 = 0 \qquad \text{or} \qquad x + 4 = 0$$

We have used factoring and the zero-factor property to rewrite our original second-degree equation as two first-degree equations connected by the word *or.* Completing the solution, we solve the two first-degree equations:

$$x - 6 = 0 \qquad \text{or} \qquad x + 4 = 0$$
$$x = 6 \qquad \text{or} \qquad x = -4$$

We check our solutions in the original equation as follows:

Check $x = 6$	Check $x = -4$
$6^2 - 2(6) - 24 \stackrel{?}{=} 0$	$(-4)^2 - 2(-4) - 24 \stackrel{?}{=} 0$
$36 - 12 - 24 \stackrel{?}{=} 0$	$16 + 8 - 24 \stackrel{?}{=} 0$
$0 = 0$	$0 = 0$

In both cases the result is a true statement, which means that both 6 and -4 are solutions to the original equation.

To generalize, here are the steps used in solving a quadratic equation by factoring.

$\lceil \Delta \neq \Sigma$ *How To: Solve an Equation by Factoring*

Step 1: Write the equation in standard form.
Step 2: Factor the left side.
Step 3: Use the zero-factor property to set each factor equal to 0.
Step 4: Solve the resulting linear equations.
Step 5: Check the solutions in the original equation.

Example 6   Solve $100x^2 = 300x$.

SOLUTION   We begin by writing the equation in standard form and factoring:

$$100x^2 = 300x$$

$$100x^2 - 300x = 0 \qquad \text{Standard form}$$

$$100x(x - 3) = 0 \qquad \text{Factor}$$

Using the zero-factor property to set each factor to 0, we have:

$$100x = 0 \quad \text{or} \quad x - 3 = 0$$

$$x = 0 \quad \text{or} \quad x = 3$$

The two solutions are 0 and 3.

Example 7   Solve $(x - 2)(x + 1) = 4$.

SOLUTION   We begin by multiplying the two factors on the left side. (Notice that it would be incorrect to set each of the factors on the left side equal to 4. The fact that the product is 4 does not imply that either of the factors must be 4.)

$$(x - 2)(x + 1) = 4$$

$$x^2 - x - 2 = 4 \qquad \text{Multiply the left side}$$

$$x^2 - x - 6 = 0 \qquad \text{Standard form}$$

$$(x - 3)(x + 2) = 0 \qquad \text{Factor}$$

$$x - 3 = 0 \quad \text{or} \quad x + 2 = 0 \qquad \text{Zero-factor property}$$

$$x = 3 \quad \text{or} \quad x = -2$$

We can use factoring to solve other types of equations that contain polynomial expressions, as illustrated in the next two examples.

Example 8   Solve $2x^3 = 5x^2 + 3x$.

SOLUTION   First we add $-5x^2$ and $-3x$ to each side so the right side will become 0.

$$2x^3 - 5x^2 - 3x = 0 \qquad \text{Standard Form}$$

We factor the left side and then use the zero-factor property to set each factor to 0.

$$x(2x^2 - 5x - 3) = 0 \qquad \text{Factor out the greatest common factor}$$

$$x(2x + 1)(x - 3) = 0 \qquad \text{Continue factoring}$$

$$x = 0 \quad \text{or} \quad 2x + 1 = 0 \quad \text{or} \quad x - 3 = 0 \qquad \text{Zero-factor property}$$

Solving each of the resulting equations, we have

$$x = 0 \quad \text{or} \quad x = -\frac{1}{2} \quad \text{or} \quad x = 3$$

Example 9   Solve for x: $x^3 + 2x^2 - 9x - 18 = 0$

SOLUTION   We start with factoring by grouping.

$$x^3 + 2x^2 - 9x - 18 = 0$$

$$x^2(x + 2) - 9(x + 2) = 0$$

$$(x + 2)(x^2 - 9) = 0$$

$$(x + 2)(x - 3)(x + 3) = 0 \quad \textit{The difference of two squares}$$

$$x + 2 = 0 \quad \text{or} \quad x - 3 = 0 \quad \text{or} \quad x + 3 = 0$$

$$x = -2 \quad \text{or} \quad x = 3 \quad \text{or} \quad x = -3$$

We have three solutions: -2, 3, and -3.

Identities and Equations with No Solution

There are two special cases associated with solving linear equations in one variable, which are illustrated in the following examples.

Example 10   Solve for x: $2(3x - 4) = 3 + 6x$

SOLUTION   Applying the distributive property to the left side gives us

$$6x - 8 = 3 + 6x \qquad \textit{Distributive property}$$

Now, if we add $-6x$ to each side, we are left with

$$-8 = 3$$

which is a false statement. This means that there is no solution to our equation. Any number we substitute for x in the original equation will lead to a similar false statement. We call this type of equation a *contradiction*.

Example 11   Solve for x: $-15 + 3x = 3(x - 5)$

SOLUTION   We start by applying the distributive property to the right side.

$$-15 + 3x = 3x - 15 \qquad \textit{Distributive property}$$

If we add $-3x$ to each side, we are left with the true statement

$$-15 = -15$$

In this case, our result tells us that any number we use in place of x in the original equation will lead to a true statement. Therefore, all real numbers are solutions to our equation. We say the original equation is an *identity* because the left side is always identically equal to the right side.

Applications

Example 12   In the chapter opener we mentioned that the relationship between temperature in degrees Fahrenheit, F, and degrees Celsius, C, is given by the formula

$$F = \frac{9}{5}C + 32$$

Solve the following equation to find the temperature in degrees Celsius if it is 77 degrees Fahrenheit.

$$77 = \frac{9}{5}C + 32$$

SOLUTION   First, we multiply both sides of the equation by the LCD, which is 5, to eliminate fractions. Then we isolate C.

$$5(77) = 5\left(\frac{9}{5}C + 32\right)$$ *Multiply each side by the LCD 5*

$$5(77) = 5\left(\frac{9}{5}C\right) + 5(32)$$ *Distributive property on the right side*

$$385 = 9C + 160$$ *Multiply*

$$225 = 9C$$ *Add* -160 *to each side*

$$25 = C$$ *Multiply each side by* $\frac{1}{9}$

A temperature of 77°F corresponds to 25°C.

Getting Ready for Class

After reading through the preceding section, respond in your own words and in complete sentences.

A. Name the constant terms in the equation $5x + 3 = 2$.
B. What is the first step in solving the equation $100x^2 = 300x$?
C. How do you use the zero-factor property to help solve a quadratic equation by factoring?
D. Explain how to recognize a contradiction or an identity.

Problem Set 10.2

Each odd/even pair of problems below is matched to an example in the text. If you have any trouble with any of these problems, go to the example that is matched with that problem.

Solve each of the following equations.

1. $7y - 4 = 2y + 11$

2. $5 - 2x = 3x + 1$

3. $-\dfrac{2}{5}x + \dfrac{2}{15} = \dfrac{2}{3}$

4. $\dfrac{1}{2}x + \dfrac{1}{4} = \dfrac{1}{3}x + \dfrac{5}{4}$

5. $0.14x + 0.08(10{,}000 - x) = 1220$

6. $-0.3y + 0.1 = 0.5$

7. $5(y + 2) - 4(y + 1) = 3$

8. $6(y - 3) - 5(y + 2) = 8$

9. $x^2 - 5x - 6 = 0$

10. $x^2 - x - 12 = 0$

11. $9a^3 = 16a$

12. $-100x = 10x^2$

13. $(x + 6)(x - 2) = -7$

14. $(x - 7)(x + 5) = -20$

15. $2y^3 - 9y = -3y^2$

16. $3y^2 + 10y = 17y^2$

17. $4x^3 + 12x^2 - 9x - 27 = 0$

18. $2x^3 + x^2 - 18x - 9 = 0$

19. Paying Attention to Instructions Work each problem according to the instructions given.

  a. Solve: $8x - 5 = 0$

  b. Add: $(8x - 5) + (2x - 3)$

  c. Multiply: $(8x - 5)(2x - 3)$

  d. Solve: $16x^2 - 34x + 15 = 0$

20. Paying Attention to Instructions Work each problem according to the instructions given.

  a. Subtract: $(3x + 5) - (7x - 4)$

  b. Solve: $3x + 5 = 7x - 4$

  c. Multiply: $(3x + 5)(7x - 4)$

  d. Solve: $21x^2 + 23x - 20 = 0$

21. Solve each equation.

  a. $9x - 25 = 0$

  b. $9x^2 - 25 = 0$

  c. $9x^2 - 25 = 56$

  d. $9x^2 - 25 = 30x - 50$

22. Solve each equation.

  a. $5x - 6 = 0$

  b. $(5x - 6)^2 = 0$

  c. $25x^2 - 36 = 0$

  d. $25x^2 - 36 = 28$

Now that you have practiced solving a variety of equations, we can turn our attention to the types of equations you will see as you progress through the book. Each equation appears later in the book exactly as you see it below.

Solve each equation.

23. $-3 - 4x = 15$

24. $-\dfrac{3}{5}a + 2 = 8$

25. $x^3 - 5x^2 + 6x = 0$

26. $x^3 + 3x^2 - 4x - 12 = 0$

27. $0 = 6400a + 70$

28. $.07x = 1.4$

29. $5(2x + 1) = 12$

30. $50 = \dfrac{K}{48}$

31. $100P = 2,400$

32. $2x - 3(3x - 5) = -6$

33. $5\left(-\dfrac{19}{15}\right) + 5y = 9$

34. $2\left(-\dfrac{29}{22}\right) - 3y = 4$

35. $3x^2 + x = 10$

36. $12(x + 3) + 12(x - 3) = 3(x^2 - 9)$

37. $(y + 3)^2 + y^2 = 9$

38. $3x + (x - 2) \cdot 2 = 6$

39. $15 - 3(x - 1) = x - 2$

40. $2(2x - 3) + 2x = 45$

41. $2(20 + x) = 3(20 - x)$

42. $2x + 1.5(75 - x) = 127.5$

43. $0.08x + 0.09(9,000 - x) = 750$

44. $0.12x + 0.10(15,000 - x) = 1,600$

45. $(x + 3)^2 + 1^2 = 2$

46. $(x + 2)(x) = 2^3$

Solve each equation, if possible.

47. $3x - 6 = 3(x + 4)$

48. $4y + 2 - 3y + 5 = 3 + y + 4$

49. $2(4t - 1) + 3 = 5t + 4 + 3t$

50. $7x - 3(x - 2) = -4(5 - x)$

51. $7(x + 2) - 4(2x - 1) = 18 - x$

52. $2x^2 + x - 1 = (2x + 3)(x - 1)$

Applying the Concepts

53. **Temperature and Altitude** As an airplane gains altitude, the temperature outside the plane decreases. The relationship between temperature T (in degrees) and altitude A (in feet) can be described with the formula

$$T = -0.0035A + 70$$

when the temperature on the ground is 70°F. Solve the equation below to find the altitude at which the temperature outside the plane is -35°F.

$$-35 = -0.0035A + 70$$

54. **Revenue** A company manufactures and sells DVDs. The revenue obtained by selling x DVDs is given by the formula

$$R = 11.5x - 0.05x^2$$

Solve the equation below to find the number of DVDs they must sell to receive $650 in revenue.

$$650 = 11.5x - 0.05x^2$$

Learning Objectives Assessment

The following problems can be used to help assess if you have successfully met the learning objectives for this section.

55. Solve: $11 + 4x = 2x - 3$

    a. 4   **b.** -4 **c.** 7   **d.** -7

56. Which of the following is an identity?

    a. $2x + 3 = 2(x + 1) + 1$ **b.** $2x + 3 = 2(x + 1) - 1$

    c. $2x + 3 = 2(x + 1) + x$ **d.** $2x + 3 = 2(x + 1) - x$

57. Solve: $x^2 - x - 12 = 0$.

    a. $-3, 4$ **b.** $3, -4$ **c.** $2, -6$ **d.** $-2, 6$

58. Solve: $2x^3 + x^2 - 18x - 9 = 0$.

    a. $-\dfrac{1}{2}$ **b.** $-3, \dfrac{1}{2}$ **c.** $-3, -\dfrac{1}{2}, 3$ **d.** $3, \dfrac{1}{2}$

Getting Ready for the Next Section

To understand all of the explanations and examples in the next section you must be able to work the problems below.

Solve each equation.

59. $2a - 1 = -7$ 60. $3x - 6 = 9$ 61. $\dfrac{2}{3}x - 3 = 7$

62. $\dfrac{2}{3}x - 3 = -7$ 63. $x - 5 = x - 7$ 64. $x + 3 = x + 8$

65. $x - 5 = -x + 7$ 66. $x + 3 = -x - 8$

Reviewing Elementary Algebra

As you progress through this chapter, you will find a set of review problems at the end of each problem set. These problems review material from the first seven chapters of the book. If you are starting the course in this chapter, these problems will help you get ready for the rest of the course.

Simplify each expression.

67. $|-3|$ 68. $-|-3|$ 69. $-|3|$ 70. $-(-3)$

71. Give a definition for the absolute value of x that involves the number line. (This is the geometric definition.)

72. Give a definition of the absolute value of x that does not involve the number line. (This is the algebraic definition.)

73. $-|-5|$

74. $\left(-\dfrac{2}{3}\right)^3$

75. $-3 - 4(-2)$

76. $2^4 + 3^3 \div 9 - 4^2$

77. $5|3 - 8| - 6|2 - 5|$

78. $7 - 3(2 - 6)$

79. $5 - 2[-3(5 - 7) - 8]$ **80.** $\dfrac{5 + 3(7 - 2)}{2(-3) - 4}$

81. Find the difference of -3 and -9.

82. If you add -4 to the product of -3 and 5, what number results?

83. Apply the distributive property to $\dfrac{1}{2}(4x - 6)$.

84. Use the associative property to simplify $-6\left(\dfrac{1}{3}x\right)$.

For the set $\left\{-3, -\dfrac{4}{5}, 0, \dfrac{5}{8}, 2, \sqrt{5}\right\}$, which numbers are

85. Integers

86. Rational numbers

Equations with Absolute Value

iStockPhoto.com/©Rob Vomund

At one time, Amtrak's annual passenger revenue could be modeled approximately by the formula

$$R = -60|x - 11| + 962$$

where R is the annual revenue in millions of dollars and x is the number of years after 1980 (Association of American Railroads, Washington, DC, *Railroad Facts, Statistics of Railroads of Class 1*, annual). Notice the absolute symbols in the equation.

Equations Containing Absolute Value

You may recall that the *absolute value* of x, $|x|$, is the distance between x and 0 on the number line. The absolute value of a number measures its distance from 0.

Video Examples

Section 10.3

Example 1 Solve for x: $|x| = 5$.

SOLUTION Using the definition of absolute value, we can read the equation as, "The distance between x and 0 on the number line is 5." If x is 5 units from 0, then x can be 5 or -5:

$$\text{If } |x| = 5 \quad \text{then} \quad x = 5 \quad \text{or} \quad x = -5$$

In general, then, we can see that any equation of the form $|x| = b$ is equivalent to the equations $x = b$ or $x = -b$, as long as $b > 0$. We generalize this result with the following property.

> **⟨Δ≠Σ⟩ *Absolute Value Equations***
>
> For any algebraic expression A and positive constant b,
>
> $$\text{If} \quad |A| = b$$
> $$\text{then} \quad A = b \quad \text{or} \quad A = -b$$

Example 2 Solve $|2a - 1| = 7$.

SOLUTION We can read this question as "$2a - 1$ is 7 units from 0 on the number line." The quantity $2a - 1$ must be equal to 7 or -7:

$$|2a - 1| = 7$$
$$2a - 1 = 7 \quad \text{or} \quad 2a - 1 = -7$$

We have transformed our absolute value equation into two equations that do not involve absolute value. We can solve each equation using the method in Section 8.1:

$$2a - 1 = 7 \quad \text{or} \quad 2a - 1 = -7$$
$$2a = 8 \quad \text{or} \quad 2a = -6 \qquad \text{Add 1 to both sides}$$
$$a = 4 \quad \text{or} \quad a = -3 \qquad \text{Multiply by } \tfrac{1}{2}$$

Our solution set is $\{-3, 4\}$.

To check our solutions, we put them into the original absolute value equation:

When $a = 4$ When $a = -3$

the equation $|2a - 1| \overset{?}{=} 7$ the equation $|2a - 1| \overset{?}{=} 7$

becomes $|2(4) - 1| \overset{?}{=} 7$ becomes $|2(-3) - 1| \overset{?}{=} 7$

$|7| \overset{?}{=} 7$ $|-7| \overset{?}{=} 7$

$7 = 7$ $7 = 7$

⟨Δ≠Σ⟩ *How To: Solve an Absolute Value Equation*

Step 1: Isolate the absolute value on one side of the equation.
Step 2: If the constant term on the other side of the equation is positive, proceed to Step 3. If it is zero or negative, treat the problem as a special case.
Step 3: Use the property of absolute value equations to write two equations that do not involve an absolute value.
Step 4: Solve for the variable in the resulting two equations.
Step 5: Check the solutions in the original equation.

Example 3   Solve: $\left|\dfrac{2}{3}x - 3\right| + 5 = 12$.

SOLUTION   To use the property of absolute value equations to solve this problem, we must isolate the absolute value on the left side of the equal sign. To do so, we add -5 to both sides of the equation to obtain

$$\left|\frac{2}{3}x - 3\right| = 7$$

Now that the equation is in the correct form, we can write

$$\frac{2}{3}x - 3 = 7 \quad \text{or} \quad \frac{2}{3}x - 3 = -7$$

$$\frac{2}{3}x = 10 \quad \text{or} \quad \frac{2}{3}x = -4 \qquad \textit{Add 3 to both sides}$$

$$x = 15 \quad \text{or} \quad x = -6 \qquad \textit{Multiply by } \tfrac{3}{2}$$

The solution set is $\{-6, 15\}$.

The next two examples illustrate the special cases where the constant term is zero or negative after the absolute value is isolated.

Example 4   Solve: $|3a - 6| + 4 = 0$.

SOLUTION   First, we isolate the absolute value by adding -4 to both sides of the equation to obtain

$$|3a - 6| = -4$$

The solution set is $\varnothing$ because the right side is negative but the left side cannot be negative. No matter what we try to substitute for the variable a, the quantity $|3a - 6|$ will always be positive or zero. It can never be -4.

> **Note** Recall that $\varnothing$ is the symbol we use to denote the empty set. When we use it to indicate the solutions to an equation, then we are saying the equation has no solution.

Example 5   Solve: $|2 - 5x| = 0$.

SOLUTION   The absolute value is already isolated, but we have 0 on the right side, which makes this a special case. Because there is no difference between 0 and -0, the property of absolute value equations results in the following single equation:

$$2 - 5x = 0$$

$$-5x = -2$$

$$x = \frac{2}{5}$$

The solution set is $\left\{ \frac{2}{5} \right\}$. Notice that we get a single solution in this case. ■

Consider the statement $|a| = |b|$. What can we say about a and b? We know they are equal in absolute value. By the definition of absolute value, they are the same distance from 0 on the number line. They must be equal to each other or opposites of each other. In symbols, we write:

$$|a| = |b| \quad \Leftrightarrow \quad a = b \quad \text{or} \quad a = -b$$

↑   ↑   or   ↑
Equal in   Equals   Opposites
absolute value

> **Note** ⇔ means "if and only if" and "is equivalent to"

Example 6   Solve $|3a + 2| = |2a + 3|$.

SOLUTION   The quantities $3a + 2$ and $2a + 3$ have equal absolute values. They are, therefore, the same distance from 0 on the number line. They must be equals or opposites:

$$|3a + 2| = |2a + 3|$$

Equals		Opposites
$3a + 2 = 2a + 3$	or	$3a + 2 = -(2a + 3)$
$a + 2 = 3$		$3a + 2 = -2a - 3$
$a = 1$		$5a + 2 = -3$
		$5a = -5$
		$a = -1$

The solution set is $\{1, -1\}$.

It makes no difference in the outcome of the problem if we take the opposite of the first or second expression. It is very important, once we have decided which one to take the opposite of, that we take the opposite of both its terms and not just the first term. That is, the opposite of $2a + 3$ is $-(2a + 3)$, which we can think of as $-1(2a + 3)$. Distributing the -1 across *both* terms, we have

$$-1(2a + 3) = -2a - 3$$ ■

Example 7   Solve $|x - 5| = |x - 7|$.

SOLUTION   As was the case in Example 6, the quantities $x - 5$ and $x - 7$ must be equal or they must be opposites, because their absolute values are equal:

Equals		Opposites
$x - 5 = x - 7$	or	$x - 5 = -(x - 7)$
$-5 = -7$		$x - 5 = -x + 7$
↑		$2x - 5 = 7$
No solution here		$2x = 12$
		$x = 6$

Because the first equation leads to a false statement, it will not give us a solution. (If either of the two equations were to reduce to a true statement, it would mean all real numbers would satisfy the original equation.) In this case, our only solution is $x = 6$. ∎

Getting Ready for Class

After reading through the preceding section, respond in your own words and in complete sentences.

A. Why do some of the equations in this section have two solutions instead of one?

B. Translate $|x| = 6$ into words using the definition of absolute value.

C. Explain in words what the equation $|x - 3| = 4$ means with respect to distance on the number line.

D. In your own words, describe the process for solving an equation that contains two absolute value expressions.

Problem Set 10.3

Use the property of absolute value equations to solve each of the following problems.

1. $|x| = 4$

2. $|x| = 7$

3. $2 = |a|$

4. $5 = |a|$

5. $|x| = -3$

6. $|x| = -4$

7. $|a| + 2 = 3$

8. $|a| - 5 = 2$

9. $|y| + 4 = 3$

10. $|y| + 3 = 1$

11. $|a - 4| = \dfrac{5}{3}$

12. $|a + 2| = \dfrac{7}{5}$

13. $\left|\dfrac{3}{5}a + \dfrac{1}{2}\right| = 1$

14. $\left|\dfrac{2}{7}a + \dfrac{3}{4}\right| = 1$

15. $60 = |20x - 40|$

16. $800 = |400x - 200|$

17. $|2x + 1| = -3$

18. $|2x - 5| = -7$

19. $\left|\dfrac{3}{4}x - 6\right| = 9$

20. $\left|\dfrac{4}{5}x - 5\right| = 15$

21. $\left|1 - \dfrac{1}{2}a\right| = 3$

22. $\left|2 - \dfrac{1}{3}a\right| = 10$

23. $|2x - 5| = 3$

24. $|3x + 1| = 4$

25. $|4 - 7x| = 5$

26. $|9 - 4x| = 1$

27. $\left|3 - \dfrac{2}{3}y\right| = 5$

28. $\left|-2 - \dfrac{3}{4}y\right| = 6$

29. $|3x + 12| = 0$

30. $|8 - 6x| = 0$

Solve each equation.

31. $|3x + 4| + 1 = 7$

32. $|5x - 3| - 4 = 3$

33. $|3 - 2y| + 4 = 3$

34. $|8 - 7y| + 9 = 1$

35. $3 + |4t - 1| = 8$

36. $2 + |2t - 6| = 10$

37. $5 + |3a + 2| = 5$

38. $|6a - 5| - 11 = -11$

39. $\left|9 - \dfrac{3}{5}x\right| + 6 = 12$

40. $\left|4 - \dfrac{2}{7}x\right| + 2 = 14$

41. $5 = \left|\dfrac{2}{7}x + \dfrac{4}{7}\right| - 3$

42. $7 = \left|\dfrac{3}{5}x + \dfrac{1}{5}\right| + 2$

43. $2 = -8 + \left|4 - \dfrac{1}{2}y\right|$

44. $1 = -3 + \left|2 - \dfrac{1}{4}y\right|$

45. $|3(x + 1)| - 4 = -1$

46. $|2(2x + 3)| - 5 = -1$

47. $|1 + 3(2x - 1)| = 5$

48. $|3 + 4(3x + 1)| = 7$

49. $3 = -2 + \left|5 - \dfrac{2}{3}a\right|$

50. $4 = -1 + \left|6 - \dfrac{4}{5}a\right|$

51. $6 = |7(k + 3) - 4|$

52. $5 = |6(k - 2) + 1|$

53. $|3a + 1| = |2a - 4|$

54. $|5a + 2| = |4a + 7|$

55. $\left|x - \dfrac{1}{3}\right| = \left|\dfrac{1}{2}x + \dfrac{1}{6}\right|$

56. $\left|\dfrac{1}{10}x - \dfrac{1}{2}\right| = \left|\dfrac{1}{5}x + \dfrac{1}{10}\right|$

57. $|y - 2| = |y + 3|$

58. $|y - 5| = |y - 4|$

59. $|3x - 1| = |3x + 1|$

60. $|5x - 8| = |5x + 8|$

61. $|0.03 - 0.01x| = |0.04 + 0.05x|$

62. $|0.07 - 0.01x| = |0.08 - 0.02x|$

63. $|x - 2| = |2 - x|$

64. $|x - 4| = |4 - x|$

65. $\left|\dfrac{x}{5} - 1\right| = \left|1 - \dfrac{x}{5}\right|$

66. $\left|\dfrac{x}{3} - 1\right| = \left|1 - \dfrac{x}{3}\right|$

67. $\left|\dfrac{2}{3}b - \dfrac{1}{4}\right| = \left|\dfrac{1}{6}b + \dfrac{1}{2}\right|$

68. $\left|-\dfrac{1}{4}x + 1\right| = \left|\dfrac{1}{2}x - \dfrac{1}{3}\right|$

69. $|0.1a - 0.04| = |0.3a + 0.08|$

70. $|-0.4a + 0.6| = |1.3 - 0.2a|$

71. Paying Attention to Instructions Work each problem according to the instructions given.

    a. Solve: $4x - 5 = 0$ **b.** Solve: $|4x - 5| = 0$

    c. Solve: $4x - 5 = 3$ **d.** Solve: $|4x - 5| = 3$

    e. Solve: $|4x - 5| = |2x + 3|$

72. Paying Attention to Instructions Work each problem according to the instructions given.

    a. Solve: $3x + 6 = 0$ **b.** Solve: $|3x + 6| = 0$

    c. Solve: $3x + 6 = 4$ **d.** Solve: $|3x + 6| = 4$

    e. Solve: $|3x + 6| = |7x + 4|$

Applying the Concepts

73. Amtrak Amtrak's annual passenger revenue for the years 1985–1995 is modeled approximately by the formula

$$R = -60|x - 11| + 962$$

where R is the annual revenue in millions of dollars and x is the number of years after 1980 (Association of American Railroads, Washington, DC, *Railroad Facts, Statistics of Railroads of Class 1*, annual). In what years was the passenger revenue $722 million?

74. Corporate Profits The corporate profits for various U.S. industries vary from year to year. An approximate model for profits of U.S. "communications companies" during a given year between 1990 and 1997 is given by

$$P = -3{,}400|x - 5.5| + 36{,}000$$

where P is the annual profits (in millions of dollars) and x is the number of years after 1990 (U.S. Bureau of Economic Analysis, Income and Product Accounts of the U.S. (1929–1994), *Survey of Current Business*, September 1998). Use the model to determine the years in which profits of "communications companies" were $31.5 billion ($31,500 million).

Learning Objectives Assessment

The following problems can be used to help assess if you have successfully met the learning objectives for this section.

75. Solve: $|x + 9| - 3 = 5$.

a. $\{-1, -11\}$ **b.** $\{-1, -17\}$ **c.** $\{-1\}$ **d.** $\varnothing$

76. Solve: $8 + |3x + 7| = 5$.

a. $\left\{-\dfrac{4}{3}, -\dfrac{10}{3}\right\}$ **b.** $\left\{-\dfrac{20}{3}, -\dfrac{10}{3}\right\}$ **c.** $\varnothing$ **d.** $\left\{-\dfrac{10}{3}\right\}$

77. Solve: $|2a + 3| = |a - 4|$.

a. $\{-7\}$ **b.** $\left\{-7, -\dfrac{7}{3}\right\}$ **c.** $\left\{-7, \dfrac{1}{3}\right\}$ **d.** $\varnothing$

Getting Ready for the Next Section

To understand all of the explanations and examples in the next section you must be able to work the problems below.

Graph each interval on a number line.

78. $(-\infty, 4)$ **79.** $[-1, \infty)$ **80.** $[-2, \infty)$ **81.** $(-\infty, -1)$

Graph the solution set for each inequality on a number line.

82. $x \geq -2$ **83.** $x > 3$ **84.** $x < 2$ **85.** $x \leq -\dfrac{11}{3}$

Solve each inequality.

86. $3(1 - 4x) \leq 27$ **87.** $5x - 9 > 2x + 3$

88. $3x + 7 \geq 4$ **89.** $3x + 7 \leq -4$

90. $-3 \leq 2x - 5$ **91.** $2x - 5 \leq 3$

Reviewing Elementary Algebra

Simplify each expression. Assume all variables represent nonzero real numbers, and write your answer with positive exponents only.

92. 3^{-2}

93. $\dfrac{x^6}{x^{-4}}$

94. $\dfrac{15x^3y^8}{5xy^{10}}$

95. $(2a^{-3}b^4)^2$

96. $\dfrac{(3x^{-3}y^5)^{-2}}{(9xy^{-2})^{-1}}$

97. $(3x^4y)^2(5x^3y^4)^3$

Write each number in scientific notation.

98. 54,000

99. 0.0359

Write each number in expanded form.

100. 6.44×10^3

101. 2.5×10^{-2}

Simplify each expression as much as possible. Write all answers in scientific notation.

102. $(3 \times 10^8)(4 \times 10^{-5})$

103. $\dfrac{8 \times 10^5}{2 \times 10^{-8}}$

Interval Notation and Compound Inequalities

Introduction

A company is about to introduce a new product. Their revenue is given by the formula $R = 15x$ and their cost by the formula $C = 400 + 3x$, where x is the number of units produced and sold each month. To be successful, the company needs a monthly revenue of at least \$12,000, but they must keep their monthly costs to no more than \$5,500. As a result, the company must determine how many units of their product, x, to produce so that

$$15x \geq 12,000 \quad \text{and} \quad 400 + 3x \leq 5,500$$

Solving both inequalities gives us $x \geq 800$ and $x \leq 1,700$. The company can produce between 800 and 1,700 units per month, inclusive, to remain successful. This scenario leads us to the concept of a *compound inequality*. But before we can address compound inequalities, we must first introduce some new notation and then extend our work with sets.

Interval Notation and Graphing

As we saw in Section 2.8, the solution set to a linear inequality in one variable is typically a subset of the real numbers, which can be represented graphically by an entire portion of the number line. A continuous segment of the number line is called an *interval*, and we can describe an interval using *interval notation*. In doing so, we always work from left to right on the number line, indicating where the interval begins on the left, followed by where it ends on the right. In general, if an interval begins at a and ends at b, then the notation will look like this:

$$(a, b) \quad [a, b) \quad (a, b] \quad [a, b]$$

An endpoint is included in the interval if a bracket is used.
An endpoint is not included in the interval if a parenthesis is used.

If the interval extends indefinitely to the left, the symbol $-\infty$ is used for the left endpoint a. If the interval extends indefinitely to the right, the symbol ∞ is used for the right endpoint b. If the values a and b are included in the solution set, then brackets are used. Otherwise parentheses are used. A parenthesis is always used with $-\infty$ or ∞.

Using interval notation, the solution set $x \geq 800$ would be expressed as $[800, \infty)$, indicating that the solution set is all real numbers beginning with 800 and continuing indefinitely.

The following table shows the connection between set-builder notation, interval notation, and number line graphs. We have included the graphs with open and closed circles for those of you who have used this type of graph previously. In this book, we will continue to show our graphs using the parentheses/brackets method.

Note The English mathematician John Wallis (1616–1703) was the first person to use the ∞ symbol to represent infinity. When we encounter the interval $[800, \infty)$, we read it as "the interval from 800 to infinity," and we mean the set of real numbers that are greater than or equal to 800. Likewise, the interval $(-\infty, 1,700]$ is read "the interval from negative infinity to 1,700," which is all real numbers less than or equal to 1,700.

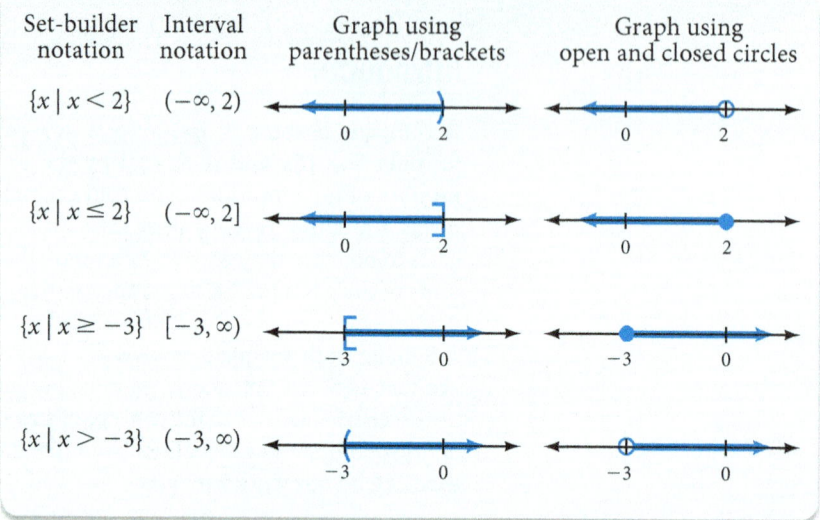

Video Examples

Section 10.4

Note Because we always describe an interval from left to right on the number line, the notation $[7, -\infty)$ would be incorrect for the solution set to $x \le 7$.

Example 1   For each inequality, describe the solution set in words. Then write the solution set using set-builder and interval notation, and graph the solution set on the number line.

a. $x \le 7$ **b.** $x > 0$

SOLUTION

a. The solution set is all real numbers up to and including 7.

Set-builder notation	Interval notation	Graph using parentheses/brackets	Graph using open and closed circles
$\{x \mid x \le 7\}$	$(-\infty, 7]$		

b. The solution set is all real numbers to the right of, but not including, 0.

Set-builder notation	Interval notation	Graph using parentheses/brackets	Graph using open and closed circles
$\{x \mid x > 0\}$	$(0, \infty)$		

Union and Intersection

> (dĕf′   *union*
>
> The union of two sets A and B is the set of all elements that are in either A or B, and is denoted by $A \cup B$.

The idea behind the union is to merge the two sets into a single set. Everything in A should appear in the union and everything in B should also appear in the union. The word *or* is the key word in the definition.

> **(děf'** *intersection*
>
> The intersection of two sets A and B is the set of all elements contained in both A and B, and is denoted by $A \cap B$.

With the intersection, we are looking for the things that are common to both sets, or where the two sets overlap. Everything in the intersection must appear in A and also in B. The key word in the definition is *and*.

Example 2   If $A = \{2, 4, 6, 8\}$ and $B = \{6, 7, 8, 9\}$, find $A \cup B$ and $A \cap B$.

SOLUTION   For the union, we combine the two sets into a single set.

$$A \cup B = \{2, 4, 6, 7, 8, 9\}$$

Notice that we only list the elements 6 and 8 once.

The intersection contains the common elements, which are 6 and 8.

$$A \cap B = \{6, 8\}$$

Because intervals are sets of real numbers, we can also find the union and intersection of two intervals. We illustrate this in the next couple of examples.

Example 3   If $A = (-\infty, 4)$ and $B = [-1, \infty)$, find $A \cup B$ and $A \cap B$.

SOLUTION   With intervals, it is helpful to graph both intervals on a single number line. We have done this below using different colors for A and B.

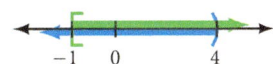

For the union, we identify the portion of the number line that is covered by either color. In this case, the whole number line is covered by either blue or green, so

$$A \cup B = (-\infty, \infty)$$

To find the intersection, we look for the overlap of the two colors; that is, the portion of the number line that is covered by both blue and green. We see that

$$A \cap B = [-1, 4)$$

The endpoint -1 is included in the intersection because of the bracket. It is a value contained in both intervals. However, because of the parenthesis, 4 is not an element of set A, and therefore not included in the intersection.

Example 4   If $A = [-2, \infty)$ and $B = [3, \infty)$, find $A \cup B$ and $A \cap B$.

SOLUTION   We begin by graphing both intervals on a common number line.

The portion of the number line covered by either color begins at -2, so

$$A \cup B = [-2, \infty)$$

The portion of the number line covered by both colors (the overlap) begins at 3. Therefore,

$$A \cap B = [3, \infty)$$

Example 5   If $A = (-\infty, -1)$ and $B = (1, \infty)$, find $A \cup B$ and $A \cap B$.

SOLUTION   The graph of the two intervals is shown below.

We see that

$$A \cup B = (-\infty, -1) \cup (1, \infty)$$

and

$$A \cap B = \varnothing$$

Because the union consists of two separate segments of the number line, it cannot be expressed as a single interval. Also, since the two intervals never overlap, the intersection is the empty set.

Compound Inequalities

We can use the concepts of union and intersection, together with our methods of graphing inequalities, to graph some *compound inequalities*. Compound inequalities are expressions containing two inequalities together with the word *and* or *or*.

Example 6   Solve: $x \geq -2$ or $x > 3$. Graph the solution set.

SOLUTION   We begin by graphing each inequality on a single number line:

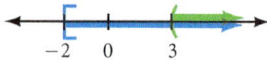

The two inequalities are connected by the word *or*, which indicates a union. The compound inequality will be true for any value of x that satisfies either inequality. So the solution set for the compound inequality is the union of the two intervals we have graphed. In interval notation, the union is

$$[-2, \infty)$$

and the graph of the union is

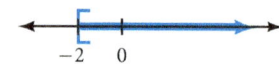

Example 7   Solve: $x > -1$ and $x < 2$. Graph the solution set.

SOLUTION   We first graph each inequality on a single number line:

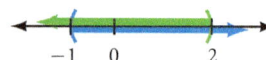

Because the two inequalities are connected by the word *and*, an intersection is indicated. The compound inequality will be true for any value of x that satisfies both inequalities. Thus, the solution set is the intersection of the two intervals we have graphed. Using interval notation, we have

$$(-1, 2)$$

The graph of the solution set is shown below:

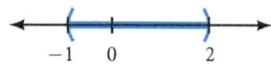

Here is a summary of the general process for solving a compound inequality.

> **How To: Solve a Compound Inequality**
>
> **Step 1:** Solve the individual inequalities appearing in the compound inequality.
> **Step 2:** Graph the solution sets of the individual inequalities on a common number line.
> **Step 3:** If the word *or* is used in the compound inequality, find the union of the two solution sets. If the word *and* is used, find the intersection of the two solution sets.
> **Step 4:** Write your answer using interval notation and graph it on a number line.

The next examples illustrate this process.

Example 8 Solve: $3t + 7 \le -4$ or $3t + 7 \ge 4$. Graph the solution set.

SOLUTION First, we solve each individual inequality separately by isolating the variable.

$$
\begin{array}{llll}
3t + 7 \le -4 & \text{or} & 3t + 7 \ge 4 & \\
3t \le -11 & \text{or} & 3t \ge -3 & \text{Add } -7 \\
t \le -\dfrac{11}{3} & \text{or} & t \ge -1 & \text{Multiply by } \tfrac{1}{3}
\end{array}
$$

Now we graph the two solution sets as intervals on a number line.

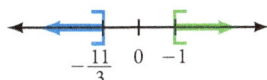

The word *or* indicates a union. We write the union using interval notation and graph it on a number line.

Interval Notation   Number Line Graph

$$\left(-\infty, -\frac{11}{3}\right] \cup [-1, \infty)$$

Example 9 Solve: $3(1 - 4x) \le 27$ and $5x - 9 > 2x + 3$. Graph the solution set.

SOLUTION We begin by solving the two individual inequalities.

$$
\begin{array}{lll}
3(1 - 4x) \le 27 & \text{and} & 5x - 9 > 2x + 3 \\
3 - 12x \le 27 & \text{and} & 3x - 9 > 3 \\
-12x \le 24 & \text{and} & 3x > 12 \\
\end{array}
$$

$$
\begin{array}{lll}
x \ge -2 & \text{and} & x > 4
\end{array}
$$

The graphs of the individual solution sets are shown below.

The word *and* indicates an intersection. From the graph, we see that the intersection of these intervals is all real numbers greater than 4. The interval notation and number line graph of the solution set for the compound inequality is

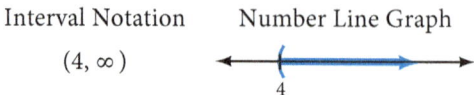

Interval Notation   Number Line Graph

$(4, \infty)$

Continued Inequalities

Sometimes compound inequalities that use the word *and* as the connecting word can be written in a shorter form. For example, the compound inequality $-3 \le x$ and $x \le 4$ can be written $-3 \le x \le 4$. The word *and* does not appear when an inequality is written in this form. It is implied. Inequalities of the form $-3 \le x \le 4$ are called *continued inequalities.* This new notation is useful because writing it takes fewer symbols. The graph of $-3 \le x \le 4$ is

The table below shows the connection between set-builder notation, interval notation, and number line graphs for a variety of continued inequalities. Again, we have included the graphs with open and closed circles for those of you who have used this type of graph previously. Remember, however, that in this book we will be using the parentheses/brackets method of graphing.

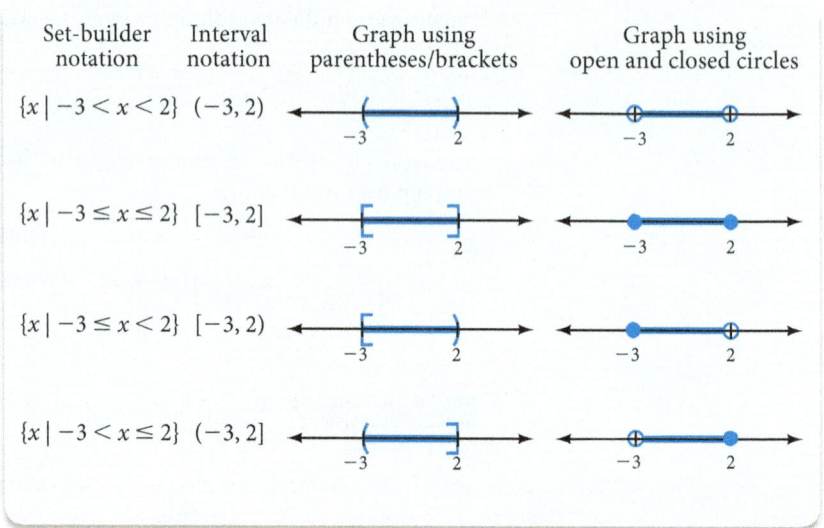

Set-builder notation	Interval notation	Graph using parentheses/brackets	Graph using open and closed circles
$\{x \mid -3 < x < 2\}$	$(-3, 2)$		
$\{x \mid -3 \le x \le 2\}$	$[-3, 2]$		
$\{x \mid -3 \le x < 2\}$	$[-3, 2)$		
$\{x \mid -3 < x \le 2\}$	$(-3, 2]$		

Example 10   Solve $-3 \le 2x - 5 \le 3$ and graph the solution set.

SOLUTION   The continued inequality is equivalent to the compound inequality

$$-3 \le 2x - 5 \quad \text{and} \quad 2x - 5 \le 3$$

We could solve this compound inequality using the process we have illustrated in the previous examples. However, with continued inequalities it is much simpler to solve using the original format and not rewriting the problem as a compound inequality.

We can extend our properties for addition and multiplication to cover this situation. If we add a number to the middle expression, we must add the same number to the outside expressions. If we multiply the center expression by a number, we must do the same to the outside expressions, remembering to reverse the direction of the inequality symbols if we multiply by a negative number. We begin by adding 5 to all three parts of the inequality:

$$-3 \le 2x - 5 \le 3$$

$$2 \le \quad 2x \quad \le 8 \qquad \text{Add 5 to all three members}$$

$$1 \le \quad x \quad \le 4 \qquad \text{Multiply through by } \tfrac{1}{2}$$

The solution set is all real numbers between 1 and 4, inclusive. The interval notation and graph are shown below.

Interval Notation | Number Line Graph

$$[1, 4]$$

Notice that we did not need to graph individual solution sets or find an intersection. By isolating x in the continued inequality we are led directly to the solution set of the equivalent compound inequality.

Example 11 In the chapter opener, we introduced the formula $F = \tfrac{9}{5}C + 32$, which gives the relationship between the Celsius and Fahrenheit temperature scales. If the temperature range on a certain day is 86° to 104° Fahrenheit, what is the temperature range in degrees Celsius?

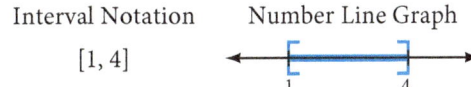

SOLUTION From the given information, we can write $86 \le F \le 104$. However, because F is equal to $\tfrac{9}{5}C + 32$, we can also write:

$$86 \le \frac{9}{5}C + 32 \le 104$$

$$54 \le \quad \frac{9}{5}C \quad \le 72 \qquad \text{Add } -32 \text{ to each number}$$

$$\frac{5}{9}(54) \le \frac{5}{9}\left(\frac{9}{5}C\right) \le \frac{5}{9}(72) \qquad \text{Multiply each number by } \tfrac{5}{9}$$

$$30 \le \quad C \quad \le 40$$

A temperature range of 86° to 104° Fahrenheit corresponds to a temperature range of 30° to 40° Celsius.

Getting Ready for Class

After reading through the preceding section, respond in your own words and in complete sentences.

A. What is the difference between the union and the intersection of two sets?

B. How do we solve a compound inequality containing the word *or*?

C. If a compound inequality contained the word *and*, how would your answer to B be different?

D. In your own words, explain how to solve a continued inequality.

For each of the following inequalities, write the solution set in set-builder and interval notation, and graph the solution set on a number line.

1. $x < 6$ **2.** $x \leq -2$ **3.** $x \geq -1$ **4.** $x > 0$

5. $x > \dfrac{3}{2}$ **6.** $x \geq \dfrac{13}{3}$ **7.** $x \leq -\dfrac{5}{4}$ **8.** $x < -\dfrac{7}{6}$

For each of the following graphs, express the interval shown using interval notation.

9.

10.

11.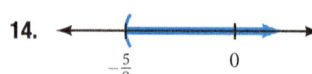

12.

13.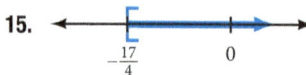

14.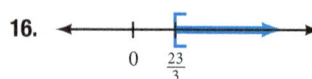

15.

16.

Find the union, $A \cup B$, for each of the following pairs of sets.

17. $A = \{1, 2, 3\}, B = \{4, 5, 6\}$

18. $A = \{5, 10, 15, 20\}, B = \{10, 20\}$

19. $A = \{5, 6, 7, 8\}, B = \{2, 4, 6, 8\}$

20. $A = \{3, 13, 23\}, B = \varnothing$

21. $A = (1, \infty), B = (6, \infty)$

22. $A = [-5, \infty), B = [2, \infty)$

23. $A = (-\infty, -3], B = (-\infty, -4)$

24. $A = (-\infty, 0), B = \left(-\infty, \dfrac{3}{2}\right]$

25. $A = (-\infty, -7), B = (7, \infty)$

26. $A = \left(-\infty, -\dfrac{1}{4}\right], B = \left[\dfrac{1}{4}, \infty\right)$

27. $A = \left(-\infty, \dfrac{3}{5}\right], B = (-2, \infty)$

28. $A = (-\infty, 9), B = \left(\dfrac{7}{3}, \infty\right)$

Find the intersection, $A \cap B$, for each of the following pairs of sets.

29. $A = \{1, 2, 3\}, B = \{4, 5, 6\}$

30. $A = \{5, 10, 15, 20\}, B = \{10, 20\}$

31. $A = \{5, 6, 7, 8\}, B = \{2, 4, 6, 8\}$

32. $A = \{3, 13, 23\}, B = \varnothing$

33. $A = (1, \infty), B = (6, \infty)$

34. $A = [-5, \infty), B = [2, \infty)$

35. $A = (-\infty, -3], B = (-\infty, -4)$

36. $A = (-\infty, 0), B = \left(-\infty, \dfrac{3}{2}\right]$

37. $A = (-\infty, -7), B = (7, \infty)$ **38.** $A = \left(-\infty, -\dfrac{1}{4}\right], B = \left[\dfrac{1}{4}, \infty\right)$

39. $A = \left(-\infty, \dfrac{3}{5}\right], B = (-2, \infty)$ **40.** $A = (-\infty, 9), B = \left(\dfrac{7}{3}, \infty\right)$

Solve the following compound inequalities. Write the solution set using interval notation and graph it on a number line (when possible).

41. $x < 4$ or $x > 1$ **42.** $x < -1$ or $x > -5$

43. $x \geq -9$ or $x \geq -2$ **44.** $x \leq -3$ or $x \leq 6$

45. $2x - 9 < 5$ or $5x + 1 \leq 6$ **46.** $3x + 4 > 13$ or $6x - 2 \geq -8$

47. $10 - x \leq 15$ or $7 + x \geq 4$ **48.** $3 + x < 12$ or $3 - x > 4$

49. $x + 5 \leq -2$ or $x + 5 \geq 2$ **50.** $3x + 2 < -3$ or $3x + 2 > 3$

51. $5y + 1 \leq -4$ or $5y + 1 \geq 4$ **52.** $7y - 5 \leq -2$ or $7y - 5 \geq 2$

53. $5 - 3x > 3x$ or $8x + 1 \geq 2x$ **54.** $3 - 5x \leq x$ or $4x < x + 2$

55. $2x + 5 < 3x - 1$ or $x - 4 < 2x + 6$

56. $3x - 1 > 2x + 4$ or $5x - 2 > 3x + 4$

57. $2(3y + 1) \geq 3(y - 4)$ or $7(2y + 3) \geq 4(3y - 1)$

58. $5(2y - 1) \leq 4(y + 3)$ or $6(y - 2) \geq 2(4y + 3)$

59. $\dfrac{1}{2} \geq -\dfrac{1}{6} - \dfrac{2}{9}x$ or $4 - \dfrac{1}{2}x < \dfrac{2}{3}x - 5$

60. $\dfrac{9}{5} < -\dfrac{1}{5} - \dfrac{1}{2}x$ or $5 - \dfrac{1}{3}x > \dfrac{1}{4}x + 2$

Solve the following compound inequalities. Write the solution set using interval notation and graph it on a number line (when possible).

61. $x < 3$ and $x > 1$ **62.** $x \leq -2$ and $x \geq -6$

63. $x \geq -8$ and $x \geq -3$ **64.** $x < -4$ and $x < 5$

65. $3x - 4 > 2$ and $6x + 2 > -10$ **66.** $2x + 9 < 1$ and $5x - 1 < 14$

67. $3x + 1 < -8$ and $-2x + 1 \leq -3$ **68.** $2x - 5 \leq -1$ and $-3x - 6 < -15$

69. $x + 3 \geq -1$ and $x + 3 \leq 1$ **70.** $2x - 5 > -3$ and $2x - 5 < 3$

71. $4y - 1 > -2$ and $4y - 1 < 2$ **72.** $5y + 7 \geq -4$ and $5y + 7 \leq 4$

73. $4 - 2x \leq x$ and $7x > x - 5$ **74.** $3x + 5 > 4x$ and $1 - 8x \geq 5x$

75. $3(y - 5) < 4(2y + 3)$ and $2(5y + 1) < 9(y + 2)$

76. $6(y + 1) > 5(3y - 2)$ and $3(4y - 5) > 4(y - 8)$

77. $\dfrac{1}{2} - \dfrac{x}{12} \leq \dfrac{7}{12}$ and $3 - \dfrac{x}{5} < 5 - \dfrac{x}{4}$

78. $\dfrac{1}{2} - \dfrac{x}{10} < -\dfrac{1}{5}$ and $-2 + \dfrac{x}{3} \geq \dfrac{x}{2} - 5$

Solve the following continued inequalities. Use interval notation to write each solution set.

79. $-2 \leq m - 5 \leq 2$ **80.** $-3 \leq m + 1 \leq 3$

81. $-60 < 20a + 20 < 60$ **82.** $-60 < 50a - 40 < 60$

83. $0.5 \leq 0.3a - 0.7 \leq 1.1$ **84.** $0.1 \leq 0.4a + 0.1 \leq 0.3$

85. $3 < \dfrac{1}{2}x + 5 < 6$ **86.** $5 < \dfrac{1}{4}x + 1 < 9$

87. $4 < 6 + \dfrac{2}{3}x < 8$ **88.** $3 < 7 + \dfrac{4}{5}x < 15$

Translate each of the following phrases into an equivalent inequality statement.

89. x is greater than -2 and at most 4   **90.** x is less than 9 and at least -3

91. x is less than -4 or at least 1   **92.** x is at most 1 or more than 6

Applying the Concepts

93. Temperature Range Each of the following temperature ranges is in degrees Fahrenheit. Use the formula $F = \dfrac{9}{5}C + 32$ to find the corresponding temperature range in degrees Celsius.

    a. $95°$ to $113°$ **b.** $68°$ to $86°$ **c.** $-13°$ to $14°$ **d.** $-4°$ to $23°$

94. **Survival Rates for 'Apapane** Here is what the United States Geological Survey has to say about the survival rates of the 'Apapane, one of the endemic birds of Hawaii.

> *Annual survival rates based on 1,584 recaptures of 429 banded individuals 0.72 ± 0.11 for adults and 0.13 ± 0.07 for juveniles.*

Write the survival rates using inequalities. Then give the survival rates in terms of percent.

95. **Survival Rates for Sea Gulls** Here is part of a report concerning the survival rates of Western Gulls that appeared on the web site of Cornell University.

> *Survival of eggs to hatching is 70%–80%; of hatched chicks to fledglings 50%–70%; of fledglings to age of first breeding <50%.*

Write the survival rates using inequalities without percent.

Learning Objectives Assessment

The following problems can be used to help assess if you have successfully met the learning objectives for this section.

96. Find the union of $[-2, \infty)$ and $(3, \infty)$.
    a. $[-2, 3)$ b. $(-\infty, \infty)$ c. $(3, \infty)$ d. $[-2, \infty)$

97. Find the intersection of $[-2, \infty)$ and $(3, \infty)$.
    a. $[-2, 3)$ b. $\varnothing$ c. $(3, \infty)$ d. $[-2, \infty)$

98. Solve the compound inequality $2x + 5 \leq 3$ or $4 - x \leq 9$.
    a. $[-5, -1]$ b. $(-\infty, -5] \cup [-1, \infty)$
    c. $(-\infty, \infty)$ d. $\varnothing$

99. Solve the compound inequality $5x - 3 > 2$ and $x + 9 < 4$.
    a. $(-5, 1)$ b. $(-\infty, -5) \cup (1, \infty)$
    c. $(-\infty, \infty)$ d. $\varnothing$

Getting Ready for the Next Section

To understand all of the explanations and examples in the next section you must be able to work the problems below.

Solve each inequality. Do not graph the solution set.

100. $2x - 5 < 3$ 101. $-3 < 2x - 5$ 102. $-4 \leq 3a + 7$

103. $3a + 2 \leq 4$ 104. $4t - 3 \leq -9$ 105. $4t - 3 \geq 9$

Reviewing Elementary Algebra

For each of the following straight lines, identify the x-intercept, y-intercept, and slope, and sketch the graph.

106. $2x + y = 6$ **107.** $y = \dfrac{3}{2}x + 4$ **108.** $x = -2$

Find the equation for each line.

109. Give the equation of the line through $(-1, 3)$ that has slope $m = 2$.

110. Give the equation of the line through $(-3, 2)$ and $(4, -1)$.

111. Line l contains the point $(5, -3)$ and has a graph parallel to the graph of $2x - 5y = 10$. Find the equation for l.

112. Give the equation of the vertical line through $(4, -7)$.

Introduction

iStockPhoto.com/©bluestocking

In a student survey conducted by the University of Minnesota, it was found that 30% of students were solely responsible for their finances. The survey was reported to have a margin of error plus or minus 3.74%. This means that the difference between the sample estimate of 30% and the actual percent of students who are responsible for their own finances is most likely less than 3.74%. We can write this as an inequality:

$$|x - 0.30| \leq 0.0374$$

where x represents the true percent of students who are responsible for their own finances.

In this section, we will apply the definition of absolute value to solve inequalities involving absolute value. Again, the absolute value of x, which is denoted $|x|$, represents the distance that x is from 0 on the number line. We will begin by considering three absolute value expressions and their verbal translations:

Expression	In Words
$|x| = 5$	x is exactly 5 units from 0 on the number line.
$|a| < 5$	a is less than 5 units from 0 on the number line.
$|y| > 5$	y is greater than 5 units from 0 on the number line.

Once we have translated the expression into words, we can use the translation to graph the original equation or inequality. The graph is then used to write a final equation or inequality that does not involve absolute value.

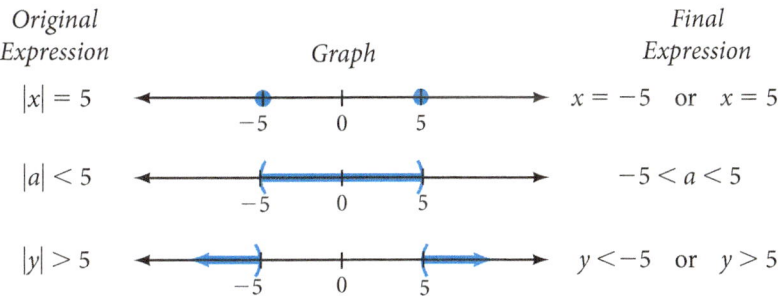

Original Expression	Graph	Final Expression
$|x| = 5$		$x = -5$ or $x = 5$
$|a| < 5$		$-5 < a < 5$
$|y| > 5$		$y < -5$ or $y > 5$

Although we will not always write out the verbal translation of an absolute value inequality, it is important that we understand the translation. Our second expression, $|a| < 5$, means a is within 5 units of 0 on the number line. That is, a must lie *between* the values -5 and 5, as expressed by the continued inequality $-5 < a < 5$. With the third expression, $|y| > 5$, notice that y must lie *outside* the values -5 and 5. That is, y must lie further to the left of -5 or further to the right of 5. The compound inequality $y < -5$ or $y > 5$ expresses this fact.

Absolute Value Inequalities

We can follow this same kind of reasoning to solve more complicated absolute value inequalities by generalizing these results as follows:

> **(dĕf'**   *Absolute Value Inequalities*
>
> For any algebraic expression A and positive constant b,
>
> $$\text{if } |A| < b \text{ then } -b < A < b \quad (A \text{ is between } -b \text{ and } b.)$$
>
> and
>
> $$\text{if } |A| > b \text{ then } A < -b \text{ or } A > b \quad (A \text{ is outside } -b \text{ and } b.)$$
>
> These properties also hold if the strict inequalities are replaced with appropriate inclusive inequality symbols $\leq$ and $\geq$.

Video Examples

Section 10.5

Example 1   Graph the solution set: $|2x - 5| < 3$

SOLUTION   The absolute value of $2x - 5$ is the distance that $2x - 5$ is from 0 on the number line. We can translate the inequality as, "$2x - 5$ is less than 3 units from 0 on the number line." That is, $2x - 5$ must appear between -3 and 3 on the number line.

A picture of this relationship is

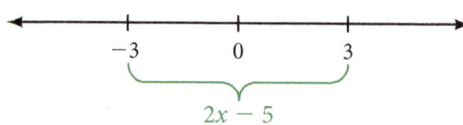

Using the picture, we can write an inequality without absolute value that describes the situation. The value of $2x - 5$ must lie between -3 and 3:

$$-3 < 2x - 5 < 3$$

Next, we solve the continued inequality by first adding 5 to all three members and then multiplying all three by $\frac{1}{2}$.

$$-3 < 2x - 5 < 3$$
$$2 < 2x < 8 \qquad \text{\small\color{green}Add 5 to all three expressions}$$
$$1 < x < 4 \qquad \text{\small\color{green}Multiply each expression by } \tfrac{1}{2}$$

We can express the solution set in three ways:

Set-Builder Notation	Number Line Graph	Interval Notation
$\{x \mid 1 < x < 4\}$	(graph: open circles at 1 and 4)	$(1, 4)$

We can see from the solution that for the quantity $2x - 5$ to be within 3 units of 0 on the number line, x must be between 1 and 4.

Example 2   Solve $|x - 3| > 5$, and graph the solution set.

SOLUTION   We interpret the absolute value inequality to mean that $x - 3$ is more than 5 units from 0 on the number line. The values of $x - 3$ must lie outside -5 and 5; that is, to the left of -5 or to the right of 5. Here is a picture of the relationship:

An inequality without absolute value that also describes this situation is

$$x - 3 < -5 \quad \text{or} \quad x - 3 > 5$$

Adding 3 to both sides of each inequality we have

$$x < -2 \quad \text{or} \quad x > 8$$

Here are three ways to write our result:

Set-Builder Notation	Number Line Graph	Interval Notation
$\{x \mid x < -2 \text{ or } x > 8\}$		$(-\infty, -2) \cup (8, \infty)$

We can see from Examples 1 and 2 that to solve an inequality involving absolute value, we must be able to write an equivalent expression that does not involve absolute value.

⎡Δ≠Σ⎤   *How To: Solve an Absolute Value Inequality*

Step 1: Isolate the absolute value on one side of the inequality.

Step 2: If the constant term on the other side of the inequality is positive, proceed to Step 3. If it is zero or negative, treat the problem as a special case.

Step 3: Use the property of absolute value inequalities to write an equivalent expression that does not involve an absolute value.

Step 4: Solve for the variable in the resulting expression.

Step 5: Write the solution set using set-builder or interval notation, and graph it on a number line.

Example 3   Solve and graph the solution set for $|3a + 7| + 6 \leq 10$.

SOLUTION   First, we isolate the absolute value by adding -6 to both sides.

$$|3a + 7| \leq 4$$

We can read the resulting inequality as, "The distance between $3a + 7$ and 0 is less than or equal to 4." Or, "$3a + 7$ is within 4 units of 0 on the number line." The value of $3a + 7$ must lie between -4 and 4, inclusive. This relationship can be written without absolute value as:

$$-4 \leq 3a + 7 \leq 4$$

Solving as usual, we have

$$-4 \leq 3a + 7 \leq 4$$
$$-11 \leq \quad 3a \quad \leq -3 \qquad \text{Add } -7 \text{ to all three members}$$
$$-\frac{11}{3} \leq \quad a \quad \leq -1 \qquad \text{Multiply each expression by } \tfrac{1}{3}$$

We can now express the solution set in three ways:

Set-Builder Notation	Number Line Graph	Interval Notation
$\left\{a \mid -\frac{11}{3} \leq a \leq -1\right\}$		$\left[-\frac{11}{3}, -1\right]$

Example 4   Graph the solution set: $2|4t - 3| \geq 18$.

SOLUTION   We must first isolate the absolute value by multiplying both sides of the inequality by $\frac{1}{2}$.

$$|4t - 3| \geq 9$$

The quantity $4t - 3$ is greater than or equal to 9 units from 0. The value of $4t - 3$ must equal -9 or 9, or lie outside of these numbers; that is, to the left of -9 or to the right of 9.

$4t - 3 \leq -9$	or	$4t - 3 \geq 9$
$4t \leq -6$	or	$4t \geq 12$ Add 3
$t \leq -\dfrac{6}{4}$	or	$t \geq \dfrac{12}{4}$ Multiply by $\frac{1}{4}$
$t \leq -\dfrac{3}{2}$	or	$t \geq 3$

Here are three ways to write the solution:

Set-Builder Notation   Number Line Graph   Interval Notation

$\{t \mid t \leq -\frac{3}{2} \text{ or } t \geq 3\}$ $\left(-\infty,\ -\frac{3}{2}\right] \cup [3, \infty)$

$-\frac{3}{2}$ 3

Example 5   Solve and graph the solution set for $|4 - 2t| > 2$.

SOLUTION   Because the absolute value is already isolated, we can use the property of absolute value inequalities to write an equivalent expression without absolute value symbols as

$4 - 2t < -2$	or	$4 - 2t > 2$

To solve these inequalities we begin by adding -4 to each side.

$4 + (-4) - 2t < -2 + (-4)$	or	$4 + (-4) - 2t > 2 + (-4)$
$-2t < -6$	or	$-2t > -2$

Next we must multiply both sides of each inequality by $-\frac{1}{2}$. When we do so, we must also reverse the direction of each inequality symbol.

$-2t < -6$	or	$-2t > -2$
$-\dfrac{1}{2}(-2t) > -\dfrac{1}{2}(-6)$	or	$-\dfrac{1}{2}(-2t) < -\dfrac{1}{2}(-2)$
$t > 3$	or	$t < 1$

Although in situations like this we are used to seeing the "less than" symbol written first, the meaning of the solution is clear. We want all real numbers that are either greater than 3 or less than 1. Here are three ways to express this:

Set-Builder Notation   Number Line Graph   Interval Notation

$\{t \mid t < 1 \text{ or } t > 3\}$ $(-\infty, 1) \cup (3, \infty)$

1   3

We can use the results of our first few examples and the material in the previous section to summarize the information we have related to absolute value equations and inequalities.

(děf **Rewriting Absolute Value Equations and Inequalities**

If c is a positive real number, then each of the following statements on the left is equivalent to the corresponding statement on the right.

With Absolute Value	Without Absolute Value
$\lvert x \rvert = c$	$x = -c$ or $x = c$
$\lvert x \rvert < c$	$-c < x < c$
$\lvert x \rvert > c$	$x < -c$ or $x > c$
$\lvert ax + b \rvert = c$	$ax + b = -c$ or $ax + b = c$
$\lvert ax + b \rvert < c$	$-c < ax + b < c$
$\lvert ax + b \rvert > c$	$ax + b < -c$ or $ax + b > c$

Special Cases

Because absolute value always results in a nonnegative quantity, we sometimes come across special cases when a negative number or zero appears on the right side of an absolute value inequality after the absolute value has been isolated.

Example 6   Solve: $\lvert 7y - 1 \rvert < -2$.

SOLUTION   The *left* side is never negative because it is an absolute value. The *right* side is negative. We have a positive quantity (or zero) less than a negative quantity, which is impossible. The solution set is the empty set, $\varnothing$. There is no real number to substitute for y to make this inequality a true statement.

Example 7   Solve: $\lvert 6x + 2 \rvert \geq -5$.

SOLUTION   This is the opposite case from that in Example 6. No matter what real number we use for x on the *left* side, the result will always be positive, or zero. The *right* side is negative. We have a positive quantity (or zero) greater than or equal to a negative quantity. Every real number we choose for x gives us a true statement. The absolute value will never *equal* -5, but it will always be *greater than* -5. Therefore, the solution set is the set of all real numbers.

Example 8   Solve: $|3 - 4a| \leq 0$.

SOLUTION   For any value of a, it is not possible for the absolute value on the left side to be *less than* zero, but it is possible for the absolute value to *equal* zero. Therefore, we must solve the equation

$$|3 - 4a| = 0$$
$$3 - 4a = 0 \qquad \text{\textit{Special case}}$$
$$-4a = -3 \qquad \text{\textit{Add} -3 \textit{to both sides}}$$
$$a = \frac{3}{4} \qquad \text{\textit{Divide both sides by} -4}$$

The solution set is a single value, $\left\{ \frac{3}{4} \right\}$.

Getting Ready for Class

After reading through the preceding section, respond in your own words and in complete sentences.

A. Write an inequality containing absolute value, the solution to which is all the numbers between -5 and 5 on the number line.

B. Translate $|x| \geq 3$ into words using the definition of absolute value.

C. Explain in words what the inequality $|x - 5| < 2$ means with respect to distance on the number line.

D. Why is there no solution to the inequality $|2x - 3| < 0$?

Problem Set 10.5

Solve each of the following inequalities using the definition of absolute value. Write your answer using interval notation (when possible), and graph the solution set in each case.

1. $|x| < 3$ **2.** $|x| \le 7$ **3.** $|x| \ge 2$ **4.** $|x| > 4$

5. $|x| + 2 < 5$ **6.** $|x| - 3 < -1$ **7.** $|t| - 3 > 4$ **8.** $|t| + 5 > 8$

9. $|y| < -5$ **10.** $|y| > -3$ **11.** $|x| \ge -2$ **12.** $|x| \le -4$

13. $|x - 3| < 7$ **14.** $|x + 4| < 2$ **15.** $|a + 5| \ge 4$ **16.** $|a - 6| \ge 3$

17. $|b + 1| < 0$ **18.** $|b - 9| \le 0$ **19.** $|b - 2| \ge 0$ **20.** $|b + 8| > 0$

Solve each inequality and graph the solution set.

21. $|a - 1| < -3$ **22.** $|a + 2| \ge -5$ **23.** $|2x - 4| < 6$

24. $|2x + 6| < 2$ **25.** $|3y + 9| \ge 6$ **26.** $|5y - 1| \ge 4$

27. $|2k + 3| \ge 7$ **28.** $|2k - 5| \ge 3$ **29.** $|x - 3| + 2 < 6$

30. $|x + 4| - 3 < -1$ **31.** $|2a + 1| + 4 \ge 7$ **32.** $|2a - 6| - 1 \ge 2$

33. $|3x + 5| - 8 < 5$ **34.** $|6x - 1| - 4 \le 2$

35. $9 + |5y - 6| < 4$ **36.** $15 + |3y + 7| \ge 1$

Solve each inequality and write your answer using interval notation. Keep in mind that if you multiply or divide both sides of an inequality by a negative number you must reverse the sense of the inequality.

37. $|x - 3| \le 5$ **38.** $|a + 4| < 6$ **39.** $|3y + 1| < 5$

40. $|2x - 5| \le 3$ **41.** $|a + 4| \ge 1$ **42.** $|y - 3| > 6$

43. $|2x + 5| > 2$ **44.** $|-3x + 1| \ge 7$ **45.** $|-5x + 3| \le 8$

46. $|-3x + 4| \le 7$ **47.** $|-3x + 7| < 2$ **48.** $|-4x + 2| < 6$

Solve each inequality and graph the solution set.

49. $|5 - x| > 3$ **50.** $|7 - x| > 2$ **51.** $\left|3 - \frac{2}{3}x\right| \ge 5$

52. $\left|3 - \frac{3}{4}x\right| \ge 9$ **53.** $\left|2 - \frac{1}{2}x\right| > 1$ **54.** $\left|3 - \frac{1}{3}x\right| > 1$

Solve each inequality.

55. $|x - 1| < 0.01$ **56.** $|x + 1| < 0.01$ **57.** $|2x + 1| \ge \frac{1}{5}$

58. $|2x - 1| \geq \dfrac{1}{8}$ **59.** $|3x - 2| \leq \dfrac{1}{3}$ **60.** $|2x + 5| < \dfrac{1}{2}$

61. $\left|\dfrac{3x + 1}{2}\right| > \dfrac{1}{2}$ **62.** $\left|\dfrac{2x - 5}{3}\right| \geq \dfrac{1}{6}$ **63.** $\left|\dfrac{4 - 3x}{2}\right| \geq 1$

64. $\left|\dfrac{2x - 3}{4}\right| < 0.35$ **65.** $\left|\dfrac{3x - 2}{5}\right| \leq \dfrac{1}{2}$ **66.** $\left|\dfrac{4x - 3}{2}\right| \leq \dfrac{1}{3}$

67. $\left|2x - \dfrac{1}{5}\right| < 0.3$ **68.** $\left|3x - \dfrac{3}{5}\right| < 0.2$

69. Write the continued inequality $-4 \leq x \leq 4$ as a single inequality involving absolute value.

70. Write the continued inequality $-8 \leq x \leq 8$ as a single inequality involving absolute value.

71. Write $-1 \leq x - 5 \leq 1$ as a single inequality involving absolute value.

72. Write $-3 \leq x + 2 \leq 3$ as a single inequality involving absolute value.

73. Paying Attention to Instructions Work each problem according to the instructions given.
   a. Evaluate when $x = 0$: $|5x + 3|$ **b.** Solve: $|5x + 3| = 7$
   c. Is 0 a solution to $|5x + 3| > 7$ **d.** Solve: $|5x + 3| > 7$

74. Paying Attention to Instructions Work each problem according to the instructions given.
   a. Evaluate when $x = 0$: $|-2x - 5|$ **b.** Solve: $|-2x - 5| = 1$
   c. Is 0 a solution to $|-2x - 5| > 1$ **d.** Solve: $|-2x - 5| > 1$

Applying the Concepts

75. Speed Limits The interstate speed limit for cars is 75 miles per hour in Nebraska, Nevada, New Mexico, Oklahoma, South Dakota, Utah, and Wyoming and is the highest in the United States. To discourage passing, minimum speeds are also posted, so that the difference between the fastest and slowest moving traffic is no more than 20 miles per hour. Write an absolute value inequality that describes the relationship between the minimum allowable speed and a maximum speed of 75 miles per hour.

76. Wavelengths of Light When white light from the sun passes through a prism, it is broken down into bands of light that form colors. The wavelength, v, (in nanometers) of some common colors are:

Blue:	$424 < v < 491$
Green:	$491 < v < 575$
Yellow:	$575 < v < 585$
Orange:	$585 < v < 647$
Red:	$647 < v < 700$

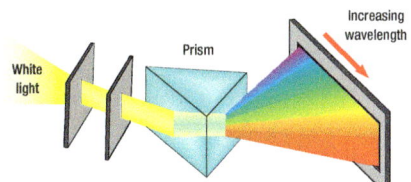

When a fireworks display made of copper is burned, it lets out light with wavelengths, v, that satisfy the relationship $|v - 455| < 23$. Write this inequality without absolute values, find the range of possible values for v, and then using the preceding list of wavelengths, determine the color of that copper fireworks display.

Learning Objectives Assessment

The following problems can be used to help assess if you have successfully met the learning objectives for this section.

77. Solve: $|x - 9| + 5 \leq 10$.

   a. $(-\infty, 14]$ **b.** $[-6, 14]$ **c.** $(-\infty, 4] \cup [14, \infty)$ **d.** $[4, 14]$

78. Solve: $|x + 4| > 2$.

   a. $(-2, \infty)$ **b.** $(-6, \infty)$ **c.** $(-\infty, -6) \cup (-2, \infty)$ **d.** $(-6, 2)$

79. Solve: $|5 - y| < -7$.

   a. $\varnothing$ **b.** $(12, \infty)$
   c. $(-\infty, -2) \cup (12, \infty)$ **d.** All real numbers

80. Solve: $|2y + 8| + 11 \geq 9$.

   a. $[-5, \infty)$ **b.** $(-\infty, -5] \cup [-3, \infty)$
   c. $\varnothing$ **d.** All real numbers

Getting Ready for the Next Section

Simplify each expression.

81. $(4x + 3y) - (6x + 3y)$ **82.** $2x - 3(3x - 5)$

83. Solve $x - 2y = 6$ for x.   **84.** Solve $2x - y = 9$ for y.

85. Solve $2x + y = 4$ for y if $x = 1$.   **86.** Solve $2x - 3y = 1$ for x if $y = 7$.

Determine which ordered pair satisfies the equation.

87. $4x + 3y = 10$, $(-1, 5)$ or $(1, 2)$ **88.** $2x - 3y = -6$, $(3, 4)$ or $(2, 3)$

Reviewing Elementary Algebra

Multiply.

89. $(x + 7)(-5x + 4)$

90. $(3x - 2)(2x^2 + 6x - 5)$

91. $(3a^4 - 7)^2$

92. $(2x + 3)(2x - 3)$

93. $x(x - 7)(3x + 4)$

94. $\left(2x - \dfrac{1}{7}\right)\left(7x + \dfrac{1}{2}\right)$

Divide.

95. $\dfrac{24x^3y + 12x^2y^2 - 16xy^3}{4xy}$

96. $\dfrac{2x^3 - 9x^2 + 10}{2x - 1}$

Factor the following expressions.

97. $x^2 - 6x + 5$

98. $15x^4 + 33x^2 - 36$

99. $81x^4 - 16y^4$

100. $6ax - ay + 18b^2x - 3b^2y$

101. $y^3 - \dfrac{1}{27}$

102. $3x^4y^4 + 15x^3y^5 - 72x^2y^6$

Inductive Reasoning [10.1]

Inductive reasoning is reasoning in which a conclusion is drawn based on evidence and observations that support that conclusion. In mathematics, this usually involves noticing that a few items in a group have a trait or characteristic in common, and then concluding that all items in the group have that same trait.

An *arithmetic sequence* is a sequence of numbers in which each number (after the first number) comes from adding the same amount to the number before it.

Deductive Reasoning [10.1]

For every conditional statement $A \Rightarrow B$, there exist the following associated statements.

The converse:	$B \Rightarrow A$	If B, then A.
The inverse:	not $A \Rightarrow$ not B	If not A, then not B.
The contrapostive:	not $B \Rightarrow$ not A	If not B, then not A.

Strategy for Solving Linear Equations in One Variable [10.2]

EXAMPLES

1. Solve: $3(2x - 1) = 9$.

$$3(2x - 1) = 9$$
$$6x - 3 = 9$$
$$6x - 3 + 3 = 9 + 3$$
$$6x = 12$$
$$\frac{1}{6}(6x) = \frac{1}{6}(12)$$
$$x = 2$$

Step 1:   **a.** Use the distributive property to separate terms, if necessary.

        b. If fractions are present, consider multiplying both sides by the LCD to eliminate the fractions. If decimals are present, consider multiplying both sides by a power of 10 to clear the equation of decimals.

        c. Combine similar terms on each side of the equation.

Step 2: Use the addition property of equality to get all variable terms on one side of the equation and all constant terms on the other side. A variable term is a term that contains the variable (for example, $5x$). A constant term is a term that does not contain the variable (the number 3, for example).

Step 3: Use the multiplication property of equality to get the variable by itself on one side of the equation.

Step 4: Check your solution in the original equation to be sure that you have not made a mistake in the solution process.

Absolute Value Equations [10.3]

2. To solve

$$|2x - 1| + 2 = 7$$

we first isolate the absolute value on the left side by adding -2 to each side to obtain

$$|2x - 1| = 5$$

$$
\begin{array}{lll}
2x - 1 = 5 & \text{or} & 2x - 1 = -5 \\
2x = 6 & \text{or} & 2x = -4 \\
x = 3 & \text{or} & x = -2
\end{array}
$$

To solve an equation that involves absolute value, we isolate the absolute value on one side of the equation and then rewrite the absolute value equation as two separate equations that do not involve absolute value. In general, if b is a positive real number, then

$$|A| = b \quad \text{is equivalent to} \quad A = b \quad \text{or} \quad A = -b$$

Compound Inequalities [10.4]

3. Solve: $3x - 1 \le 5$ and $x + 4 > 1$.

$$
\begin{array}{lll}
3x - 1 \le 5 & \text{and} & x + 4 > 1 \\
3x \le 6 & \text{and} & x > -3 \\
x \le 2 & &
\end{array}
$$

The intersection of $x \le 2$ and $x > -3$ is $-3 < x \le 2$, or $(-3, 2]$ using interval notation.

To solve a compound inequality that contains the word "and," solve the two inequalities separately and then find the intersection of the two solution sets.

To solve a compound inequality that contains the word "or," solve the two inequalities separately and then find the union of the two solution sets.

Absolute Value Inequalities [10.5]

4. To solve

$$|x - 3| + 2 < 6$$

we first add -2 to both sides to obtain

$$|x - 3| < 4$$

which is equivalent to

$$
\begin{array}{c}
-4 < x - 3 < 4 \\
-1 < x < 7
\end{array}
$$

To solve an inequality that involves absolute value, we first isolate the absolute value on the left side of the inequality symbol. Then we rewrite the absolute value inequality as an equivalent continued or compound inequality that does not contain absolute value symbols. In general, if b is a positive real number, then

$$|A| < b \quad \text{is equivalent to} \quad -b < A < b$$

and

$$|A| > b \quad \text{is equivalent to} \quad A < -b \quad \text{or} \quad A > b$$

Chapter 10 Test

Solve the following equations. [10.3]

1. $5 - \frac{4}{7}a = -11$

2. $\frac{1}{5}x - \frac{1}{2} - \frac{1}{10}x + \frac{2}{5} = \frac{3}{10}x + \frac{1}{2}$

3. $5(x - 1) - 2(2x + 3) = 5x - 4$

4. $0.07 - 0.02(3x + 1) = -0.04x + 0.01$

Solve each equation. [10.3]

5. $\frac{1}{4}x^2 = -\frac{21}{8}x - \frac{5}{4}$

6. $243x^3 = 81x^4$

7. $(x + 5)(x - 2) = 8$

8. $x^3 + 5x^2 - 9x - 45 = 0$

Solve the following equations. [10.4]

9. $|x + 6| - 3 = 1$

10. $\left|\frac{1}{4}x - 1\right| = \frac{1}{2}$

11. $|3 - 2x| + 5 = 2$

12. $|x - 1| = |5x + 2|$

Find the union. [10.5]

13. $\{1, 2, 3\} \cup \{2, 4, 6\}$

14. $(-\infty, -1) \cup (-\infty, 4]$

Find the intersection. [10.5]

15. $\{1, 2, 3\} \cap \{2, 4, 6\}$

16. $(-\infty, -1) \cap (-\infty, 4]$

Solve the compound inequality. [10.5]

17. $x + 5 \le 9$ or $x - 2 > -8$

18. $5x - 3 < 7$ and $4 - x > 7$

Solve the following inequalities and graph the solution sets. [10.6]

19. $|6x - 1| > 7$

20. $|3x - 5| - 4 \le 3$

21. $|5 - 4x| \ge -7$

22. $|4t - 1| < -3$

Introduction to Trigonometry

© Nathan Watkins Photography/iStockPhoto

The first Ferris wheel was designed and built by American engineer George Ferris in 1893 for the World's Columbian Exposition in Chicago, Illinois. The diameter of this wheel was 250 feet. It had 36 cars, each of which held 60 passengers. The top of the wheel was 264 feet above ground. It took 20 minutes to complete two revolutions.

As you will see as we progress through this chapter, trigonometric functions can be used to model the motion of a rider on a Ferris wheel. The model can be used to give information about the position of the rider at any time during the ride.

I have always been fascinated by the extent to which trigonometry can be applied to other fields. Trigonometry has applications in almost every branch of science and mathematics, including physics, chemistry, and biology, as well as engineering, surveying, and navigation.

Degrees, Radians, and Special Triangles

Angles in General

An angle is formed when two rays have a common endpoint. The common endpoint is called the **vertex** of the angle, and the rays are called the **sides** of the angle (Figure 1).

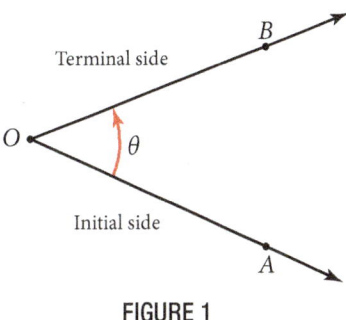

FIGURE 1

We can think of θ as having been formed by rotating $\overline{OA}$ about the vertex to side $\overline{OB}$. In this case, we call side $\overline{OA}$ the **initial side** of θ and side $\overline{OB}$ the **terminal side** of θ.

When the rotation from the initial side to the terminal side takes place in a counterclockwise direction, the angle formed is considered a **positive angle**. If the rotation is in a clockwise direction, the angle formed is a **negative angle** (Figure 2).

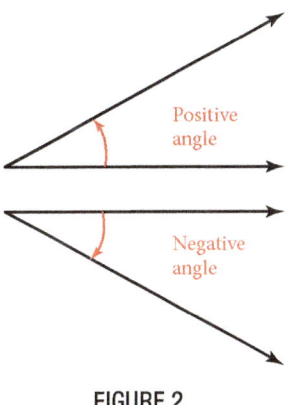

FIGURE 2

Degree Measure Recall that the angle formed by rotating a ray through one complete revolution has a measure of 360 degrees, written 360° (Figure 3).

Angles that measure between 0° and 90° are called **acute angles**, while angles that measure between 90° and 180° are called **obtuse angles**.

If two angles have a sum of 90°, then they are called **complementary angles**, and we say each is the **complement** of the other. Two angles with a sum of 180° are called **supplementary angles**.

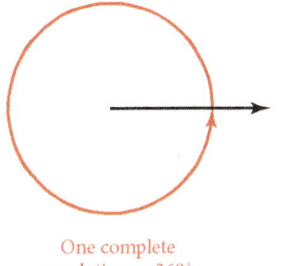

One complete
revolution = 360°

FIGURE 3

Example 1	Give the complement and the supplement of each angle.

a. $40°$ **b.** $110°$ **c.** θ

SOLUTION

a. The complement of $40°$ is $50°$ since $40° + 50° = 90°$.
The supplement of $40°$ is $140°$ since $40° + 140° = 180°$.

b. The complement of $110°$ is $-20°$ since $110° + (-20°) = 90°$.
The supplement of $110°$ is $70°$ since $110° + 70° = 180°$.

c. The complement of θ is $(90° - \theta)$ since $\theta + (90° - \theta) = 90°$.
The supplement of θ is $(180° - \theta)$ since $\theta + (180° - \theta) = 180°$.

Radian Measure

Another way to specify the measure of an angle is with **radian measure**. To understand the definition for radian measure, we have to recall from geometry that a **central angle** is an angle with its vertex at the center of a circle.

Note It is common practice to omit the word *radian* when using radian measure. If no units are showing, an angle is understood to be measured in radians; with degree measure, the degree symbol ° must be written.

$\theta = 2$ means the measure of θ is 2 radians

$\theta = 2°$ means the measure of θ is 2 degrees

> **(dĕf´**   *central angle*
>
> In a circle, a **central angle** that cuts off an arc equal in length to the radius of the circle has a measure of 1 radian. That is, in a circle of radius r, a central angle that measures 1 radian will cut off an arc of length r (Figure 4).
>
>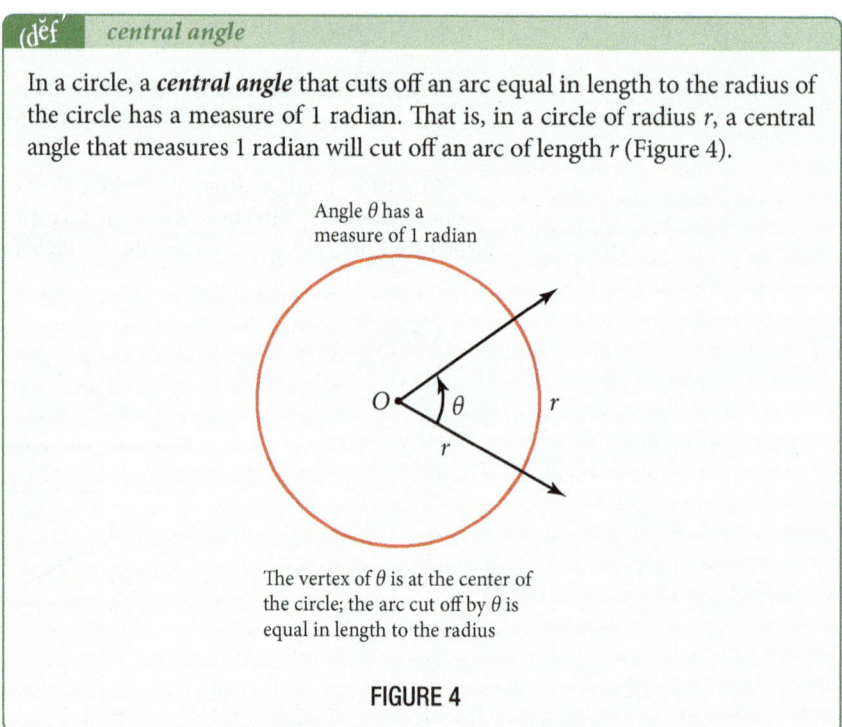
>
> Angle θ has a measure of 1 radian
>
> The vertex of θ is at the center of the circle; the arc cut off by θ is equal in length to the radius
>
> **FIGURE 4**

To find the radian of *any* central angle, we must find how many radii there are in the arc it cuts off. To do so, we divide the arc length by radius. If the radius is 2 centimeters and the arc cut off by central angle θ is 6 centimeters, then the radian measures of θ is $\frac{6}{2} = 3$ radians. Here is the formal definition:

(děf' *measure of θ in radians*

If a central angle θ in a circle of radius r cuts off an arc of length s, then the **measure of θ in radians** is given by $\frac{s}{r}$. (See Figure 5.)

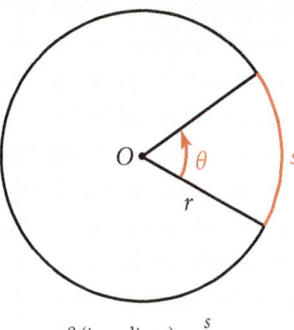

$$\theta \text{ (in radians)} = \frac{s}{r}$$

FIGURE 5

Comparing Degrees and Radians

To see the relationship between degrees and radians, we can compare the number of degrees and the number of radians in one full rotation.

The angle formed by one full rotation about the center of a circle of radius r will cut off an arc equal to the circumference of the circle (Figure 6). Since the circumference of a circle of radius r is $2\pi r$, we have

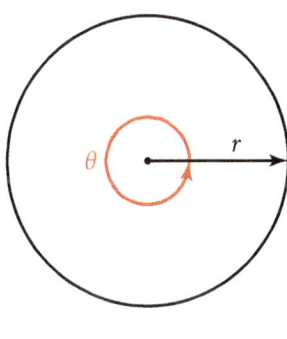

FIGURE 6

θ measures one full rotation. $\qquad \theta = \dfrac{2\pi r}{r} = 2\pi \qquad$ The measure of θ in radians is 2π.

Since one full rotation in degrees is 360°, we have the following relationship between radians and degrees:

$$360° = 2\pi \text{ radians}$$

Dividing both sides by 2, we have

$$180° = \pi \text{ radians}$$

To obtain conversion factors that will allow us to change back and forth between degrees and radians, we divide both sides of this last equation alternately by 180 and by π:

Divide both sides by 180. $\qquad$ — $180° = \pi$ radians — $\qquad$ Divide both sides by π.

$$1° = \frac{\pi}{180} \text{ radians} \qquad \left(\frac{180}{\pi}\right)° = 1 \text{ radian}$$

To gain some insight into the relationship between degrees and radians, we can approximate π as 3.14 to obtain the approximate number of degrees in 1 radian:

$$1 \text{ radian} = 1\left(\frac{180}{\pi}\right)°$$

$$\approx 1\left(\frac{180}{3.14}\right)°$$

$$\approx 57.3°$$

We see that 1 radian is approximately 57°. A radian is much larger than a degree. Figure 7 illustrates the relationship between 20° and 20 radians.

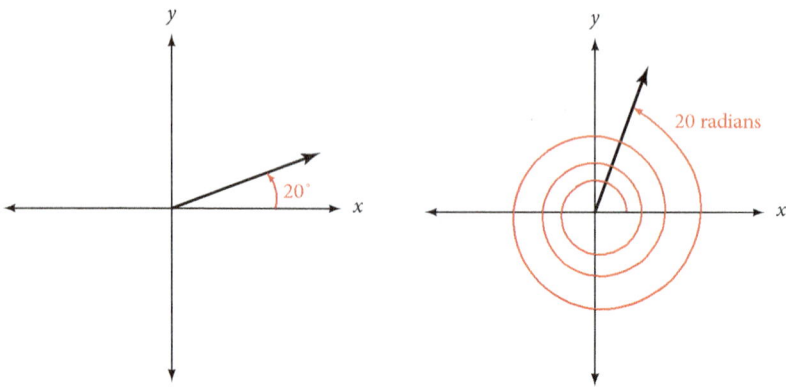

FIGURE 7

Here are some further conversions between degrees and radians.

Converting from Degrees to Radians

Example 2   Convert 45° to radians.

SOLUTION Since $1° = \frac{\pi}{180}$ radians, and 45° is the same as 45(1°), we have

$45° = 45\left(\frac{\pi}{180}\right)$ radians $= \frac{\pi}{4}$ radians as illustrated in Figure 8.

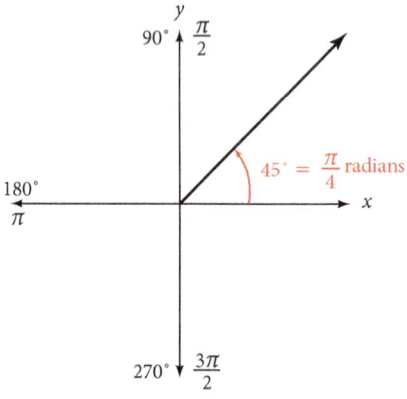

FIGURE 8

When we leave our answer in terms of π, as in $\frac{\pi}{4}$, we are writing an exact value. If we wanted a decimal approximation, we would substitute 3.14 for π.

$$\text{Exact value} \quad \frac{\pi}{4} \approx \frac{3.14}{4} = 0.785 \quad \text{Approximate value}$$

Note also that if we wanted the radian equivalent of 90°, we could simply multiply $\frac{\pi}{4}$ by 2, since $90° = 2 \times 45°$:

$$90° = 2 \times 45° = 3 \times \frac{\pi}{4} = \frac{\pi}{2}$$

Example 3 Convert 450° to radians.

SOLUTION Multiplying by $\frac{\pi}{180}$, we have $450° = 450\left(\frac{\pi}{180}\right) = \frac{5\pi}{2}$ radians. (See Figure 9.)

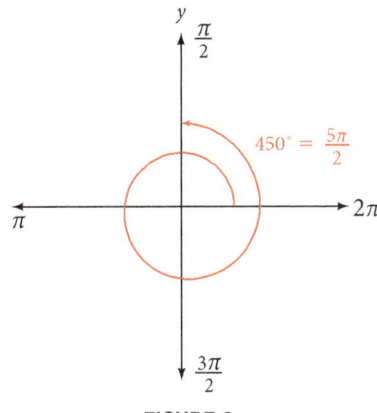

FIGURE 9

Again, $\frac{5\pi}{2}$ is the exact value. If we wanted a decimal approximation, we would substitute 3.14 for π.

$$\text{Exact value} \quad \frac{5\pi}{2} \approx \frac{5(3.14)}{2} = 7.85 \quad \text{Approximate value}$$

Converting from Radians to Degrees

Example 4 Convert $\frac{\pi}{6}$ to degrees.

SOLUTION To convert from radians to degrees, we multiply by $\frac{180}{\pi}$.

$$\frac{\pi}{6} \text{ (radians)} = \frac{\pi}{6}\left(\frac{180}{\pi}\right)°$$

$$= 30°$$

Note that 60° is twice 30°, so $2\left(\frac{\pi}{6}\right) = \frac{\pi}{3}$ must be the radian equivalent of 60°. Figure 10 illustrates this.

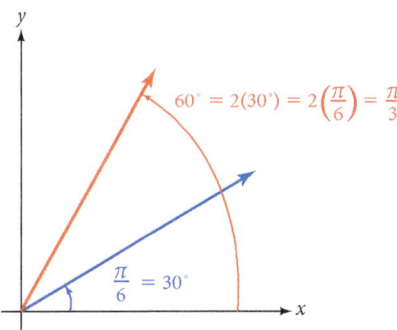

FIGURE 10

Example 5   Convert $\frac{4\pi}{3}$ degrees.

SOLUTION Multiplying by $\frac{180}{\pi}$, we have

$$\frac{4\pi}{3} \text{ (radians)} = \frac{4\pi}{3}\left(\frac{180}{\pi}\right)^{\circ}$$
$$= 240^{\circ}$$

See Figure 11.

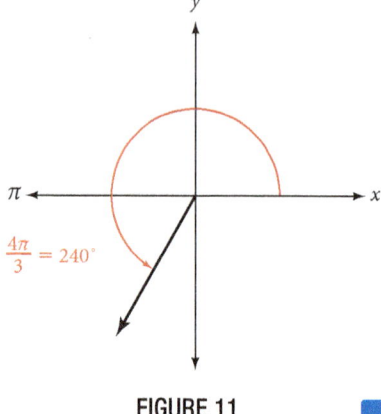

FIGURE 11

As is apparent from the preceding examples, changing from degrees to radians and from radians to degrees is simply a matter of multiplying by the appropriate conversion factors.

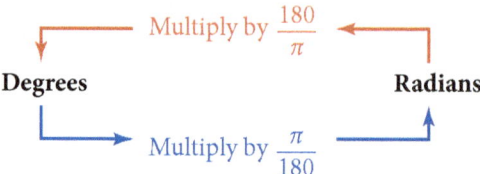

Figure 12 shows the most common angles written in both degrees and radians. Table 1 gives approximations to some of the exact radian measures, accurate to the nearest hundredth of a radian.

Radians	
Exact Values	**Approximations**
0	0
$\frac{\pi}{6}$	0.52
$\frac{\pi}{4}$	0.79
$\frac{\pi}{3}$	1.05
$\frac{\pi}{2}$	1.57
π	3.14
$\frac{3\pi}{2}$	4.71
2π	6.28

FIGURE 12

Special Triangles

Recall that a right triangle is a triangle in which one of the angles is a right angle. Recall also that the Pythagorean Theorem is an important theorem about right triangles.

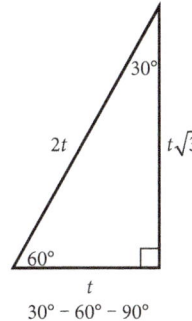

30° − 60° − 90°

FIGURE 13

> ### The 30°-60°-90° Triangle
> In any right triangle which the two acute angles are 30° and 60°, the longest side (the hypotenuse) is always twice the shortest side(the side opposite the 30° angle), and the side of medium length (the side opposite the 60° angle) is always $\sqrt{3}$ times the shortest side (Figure 13).

Note that the shortest side, t, is opposite the smallest angle, 30°. The longest side, $2t$, is opposite the largest angle, 90°. To verify the relationship between the sides in this triangle we draw an **equilateral triangle** (one in which all three sides are equal) and label half the base with t (Figure 14).

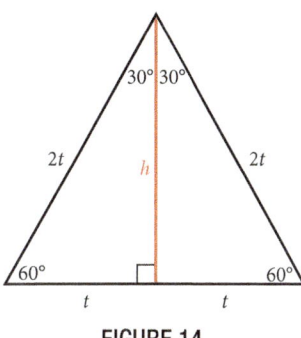

FIGURE 14

The altitude h (shown in red) bisects the base. We have two 30°– 60°– 90° triangles. The longest side in each is $2t$. We find that h is $t\sqrt{3}$ by applying the Pythagorean Theorem:

$$t^2 + h^2 = (2t)^2$$

$$h = \sqrt{4t^2 - t^2}$$

$$= \sqrt{3t^2}$$

$$= t\sqrt{3}$$

Example 6   If the shortest side of a 30°– 60°– 90° triangle is 5, find the other two sides.

SOLUTION   The longest side is 10 (twice the shortest side), and the side opposite the 60° angle is $5\sqrt{3}$ (Figure 15).

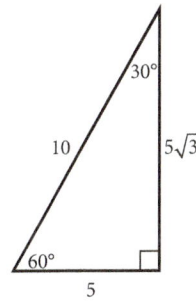

FIGURE 15

Example 7   A ladder is leaning against a wall. The top of the ladder is 4 feet above the ground, and the bottom of the ladder makes an angle of 60° with the ground. How long is the ladder, and how far from the wall is the bottom of the ladder?

SOLUTION The triangle formed by the ladder, the wall, and the ground is a 30°–60°–90° triangle. If we let x represent the distance from the bottom of the ladder to the wall, then the length of the ladder can be represented by $2x$ (Figure 16). The distance from the top of the ladder to the ground is $x\sqrt{3}$, since it is opposite the 60° angle. Therefore,

$$x\sqrt{3} = 4$$

$$x = \frac{4}{\sqrt{3}}$$

$$= \frac{4\sqrt{3}}{3}$$

Rationalize the denominator by multiplying the numerator and denominator by $\sqrt{3}$

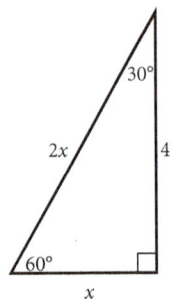

FIGURE 16

The distance from the bottom of the ladder to the wall, x, is $\frac{4\sqrt{3}}{3}$ feet, so the length of the ladder, $2x$, must be $\frac{8\sqrt{3}}{3}$ feet. Note that these lengths are given in exact values. If we want a decimal approximation for them, we can replace $\sqrt{3}$ with 1.732 to obtain

$$\frac{4\sqrt{3}}{3} \approx \frac{4(1.732)}{3} \approx 2.309 \text{ feet}$$

$$\frac{8\sqrt{3}}{3} \approx \frac{8(1.732)}{3} \approx 4.619 \text{ feet}$$

The other special right triangle is the 45°–45°–90° triangle.

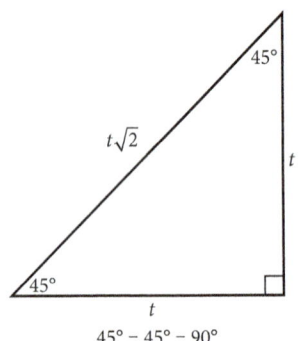

FIGURE 17

> **The 45°-45°-90° Triangle**
> If the two acute angles in a right triangle are both 45°, then the two shorter sides (the legs) are equal, and the longest side (the hypotenuse) is $\sqrt{2}$ times as long as the shorter sides. That is, if the shorter sides are of length t, then the longest side has length $t\sqrt{2}$ (Figure 17).

To verify this relationship, we simply note that if the two acute angles are equal, then the sides opposite them are also equal. We apply the Pythagorean Theorem to them to find the length of the hypotenuse:

$$\text{Hypotenuse} = \sqrt{t^2 + t^2}$$

$$= \sqrt{2t^2}$$

$$= t\sqrt{2}$$

Example 8   A 10-foot rope connects the top of a tent pole to the ground. If the rope makes an angle of 45° with the ground, find the length of the tent pole.

SOLUTION Assuming that the tent pole forms an angle of 90° with the ground, the triangle formed by rope, tent pole, and the ground is a 45°– 45°– 90° triangle. (See Figure 18.)

If we let x represent the length of the tent pole, then the length of the rope, in terms of x, is $x\sqrt{2}$. It is also given as 10 feet. Therefore,

$$x\sqrt{2} = 10$$

$$x = \frac{10}{\sqrt{2}}$$

$$= 5\sqrt{2}$$

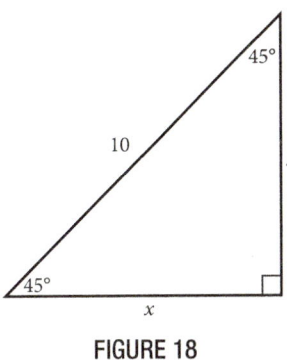

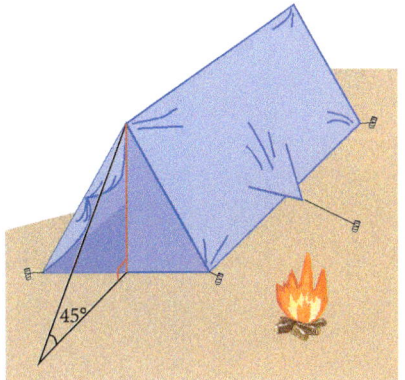

FIGURE 18

The length of the tent pole is $5\sqrt{2}$ feet. Again, $5\sqrt{2}$ is the exact value of the length of the tent pole. To find a decimal approximation, we replace $\sqrt{2}$ with 1.414 to obtain

$$5\sqrt{2} \approx 5(1.414) = 7.07 \text{ feet}$$

Getting Ready for Class

After reading through the preceding section, respond in your own words and in complete sentences.

A. Approximately how many degrees are in an angle of 1 radian?
B. Explain how we convert from degrees to radians.
C. How many degrees are in an angle that measures π radians?
D. How many radians are in an angle that measures 240°?

Problem Set 11.1

Indicate which of the angles below are acute angles and which are obtuse angles. Then give the complement and the supplement of each angle.

1. $10°$ **2.** $50°$ **3.** $45°$ **4.** $90°$

5. $120°$ **6.** $160°$ **7.** x **8.** y

Convert each of the following from degree measure to radian measure.

9. $30°$ **10.** $60°$ **11.** $90°$ **12.** $270°$

13. $120°$ **14.** $-240°$ **15.** $-225°$ **16.** $135°$

17. $-150°$ **18.** $-210°$ **19.** $420°$ **20.** $390°$

Convert each of the following from radian measure to degree measure.

21. $\dfrac{\pi}{3}$ **22.** $\dfrac{\pi}{4}$ **23.** $\dfrac{2\pi}{3}$ **24.** $\dfrac{3\pi}{4}$

25. $-\dfrac{7\pi}{6}$ **26.** $-\dfrac{5\pi}{6}$ **27.** $-\dfrac{3\pi}{2}$ **28.** $-\dfrac{5\pi}{3}$

29. $\dfrac{11\pi}{6}$ **30.** $\dfrac{7\pi}{4}$ **31.** 4π **32.** 3π

33. What acute positive angle does the line $y = x$ make with the positive x-axis?

34. What obtuse positive angle does the line $y = -x$ make with the positive x-axis?

35. Through how many degrees does the hour hand of a clock move in 4 hours?

36. Through how many degrees does the minute hand of a clock move in 40 minutes?

37. It takes the earth 24 hours to make one complete revolution on its axis. Through how many degrees does the earth turn in 12 hours?

38. Through how many degrees does the earth turn in 6 hours?

Each of the following problems refers to a right triangle ABC with $C = 90°$.

39. If $a = 4$ and $b = 3$, find c.

40. If $a = 1$ and $b = 2$, find c.

41. If $a = 7$ and $c = 25$, find b.

42. If $a = 2$ and $c = 6$, find b.

43. If $b = 12$ and $c = 13$, find a

44. If $b = 6$ and $c = 10$, find a.

Find the remaining sides of a 30°–60°–90° triangle if:

45. The shortest side is 1.

46. The shortest side is 3.

47. The longest side is 8.

48. The longest side is 5.

49. The longest side is $\frac{2}{3}$.

50. The longest side is 24.

51. The medium side is $3\sqrt{3}$.

52. The medium side is $2\sqrt{3}$.

53. The medium side is 6.

54. The medium side is 4.

Find the remaining sides of a 45°–45°–90° triangle if:

55. The shorter sides are each 1.

56. The shorter sides are each 5.

57. The shorter sides are each $\frac{4}{5}$.

58. The shorter sides are each $\frac{1}{2}$.

59. The longest side is $8\sqrt{2}$.

60. The longest side is $5\sqrt{2}$.

61. The longest side is 4.

62. The longest side is 12.

Getting Ready for the Next Section

Find the distance between the given point and the origin.

63. $(-2, 3)$ **64.** $(1, 1)$ **65.** $(-\sqrt{3}, 1)$ **66.** $(-12, -5)$

Rationalize the denominator

67. $\dfrac{1}{\sqrt{2}}$ **68.** $\dfrac{2}{\sqrt{3}}$ **69.** $\dfrac{3}{\sqrt{13}}$ **70.** $-\dfrac{2}{\sqrt{13}}$

Trigonometric Functions and Calculators

Until now, we have been able to determine trigonometric functions only for angles for which we could find a point on the terminal side or angles that were part of special triangles. We can find decimal approximations for trigonometric functions of any acute angle by using a calculator with keys for sine, cosine, and tangent.

Video Examples

Section 11.2

Note We will give answers accurate to four places past the decimal point. You can set your calculator to four-place fixed-point mode, and it will show you the same result without you having to round your answers mentally.

Example 1 Use a calculator to find cos 37.8°.

SOLUTION First, be sure your calculator is in degree mode. Then, depending on the type of calculator you have, press the indicated keys.

Scientific Calculator	**Graphing Calculator**
37.8 $\boxed{\cos}$	$\boxed{\cos}$ 37.8 $\boxed{\text{ENTER}}$

Your calculator will display a number that rounds to 0.7902. The number 0.7902 is just an approximation of cos 37.8°, which is actually an irrational number, as are the trigonometric functions of most angles.

Example 2 Find sin 58.75°.

SOLUTION This time we use the $\boxed{\sin}$ key.

Scientific Calculator	**Graphing Calculator**
58.75 $\boxed{\sin}$	$\boxed{\sin}$ 58.75 $\boxed{\text{ENTER}}$

Example 3 Find sec 78°.

SOLUTION Standard calculators rarely have a secant functions, so we use the reciprocal of the cosine.

Since sec 78° = 1/cos 78°, the calculator sequence is:

Scientific Calculator

78 $\boxed{\cos}$ $\boxed{1/x}$

or

1 $\boxed{\div}$ 78 $\boxed{\cos}$ $\boxed{=}$

Graphing Calculator

1 $\boxed{\div}$ $\boxed{\cos}$ 78 $\boxed{\text{ENTER}}$

or

$\boxed{\cos}$ 78 $\boxed{\text{ENTER}}$ $\boxed{x^{-1}}$ $\boxed{\text{ENTER}}$

Rounding to four digits past the decimal point, we have

$$\sec 78° \approx 4.8097$$

Next we want to use a calculator to find an angle, given the value of one of the trigonometric functions of the angle. This process is somewhat like going in the opposite direction from that shown in the examples above.

Example 4   Find the acute angle θ for which $\tan \theta = 3.152$. Round your answer to the nearest tenth of a degree.

SOLUTION We are looking for the angle whose tangent is 3.152. To find this angle on a calculator, we must use the $\tan^{-1}$ or arctan function. This is usually accomplished by pressing the key labeled $\boxed{\text{inv}}$, $\boxed{\text{arc}}$, or $\boxed{\text{2nd}}$, and then the $\boxed{\tan}$ key. (Check your manual to see how your calculator does this. In the index, look under inverse trigonometric functions.) In this book we use the following sequences. (Your calculator may require a different sequence.)

Scientific Calculator	Graphing Calculator
$3.152\,\boxed{\tan^{-1}}$	$\boxed{\tan^{-1}}3.152\,\boxed{\text{ENTER}}$

To the nearest tenth of a degree the answer 72.4°. That is, if $\tan \theta = 3.152$, then $\theta \approx 72.4°$.

Example 5   Find the acute angle A for which $\sin A = 0.3733$. Round your answer to the nearest tenth of a degree.

SOLUTION The sequences are:

Scientific Calculator	Graphing Calculator
$0.3733\,\boxed{\sin^{-1}}$	$\boxed{\sin^{-1}}0.3733\,\boxed{\text{ENTER}}$

The result is $A \approx 21.9°$.

Example 6   To the nearest hundredth of a degree, find the acute angle B for which $\sec B = 1.0768$.

SOLUTION Since we do not have a secant key on the calculator, we must use a reciprocal to first see how we can convert this problem into a problem involving $\cos B$ (as in Example 3).
    If $\sec B = 1.0768$, then

$$\frac{1}{\sec B} = \frac{1}{1.0768} \qquad \textit{Take the reciprocal of each side.}$$

$$\cos B = \frac{1}{1.0768} \qquad \textit{Since the cosine is the reciprocal of the secant.}$$

From the last line we see that the keys to press are:

Scientific Calculator	Graphing Calculator
$1.0768\,\boxed{1/x}\,\boxed{\cos^{-1}}$	$\boxed{\cos^{-1}}\boxed{(}1.0768\,\boxed{x^{-1}}\boxed{)}\boxed{\text{ENTER}}$

To the nearest hundredth of a degree our answer is $B \approx 21.77°$.

Example 7 Find the acute angle C for which $\cot C = 0.0975$. Round to the nearest degree.

SOLUTION First, we rewrite the problem in terms of $\tan C$.

If $\cot C = 0.0975$, then

$$\frac{1}{\cot C} = \frac{1}{0.0975} \qquad \text{Take the reciprocal of each side.}$$

$$\tan C = \frac{1}{0.0975} \qquad \text{Since the tangent is the reciprocal of the cotangent}$$

From this last line we see that the keys to press are:

Scientific Calculator	**Graphing Calculator**
0.0975 $\boxed{1/x}$ $\boxed{\tan^{-1}}$	$\boxed{\tan^{-1}}$ $\boxed{(}$ 0.0975 $\boxed{x^{-1}}$ $\boxed{)}$ $\boxed{\text{ENTER}}$

To the nearest degree our answer is $C \approx 84°$.

Reference Angle

In Section 11.2, we found exact values for trigonometric functions of certain angles between $0°$ and $90°$ (acute angles). Table 1 is a summary of those results.

Table 1 Exact Values

θ	$\sin \theta$	$\cos \theta$	$\tan \theta$
$30°$	$\dfrac{1}{2}$	$\dfrac{\sqrt{3}}{2}$	$\dfrac{1}{\sqrt{3}}$
$45°$	$\dfrac{1}{\sqrt{2}}$	$\dfrac{1}{\sqrt{2}}$	1
$60°$	$\dfrac{\sqrt{3}}{2}$	$\dfrac{1}{2}$	$\sqrt{3}$

We can expand our table of exact values to include angles outside the interval $0°$ to $90°$ by using what are called **reference angles**. Here is the definition:

> (děf) *reference angle*
>
> The **reference angle** (sometimes called **related angle**) for any angle θ in standard position is the positive acute angle between the terminal side of θ and the x-axis. In this book, we will denote the reference angle for θ by $\hat{\theta}$.

Note that, for this definition, $\hat{\theta}$ is always positive and always between $0°$ and $90°$. That is, a reference angle is always an acute angle.

Example 8 Name the reference angle for each of the following angles:

a. $30°$ **b.** $135°$ **c.** $240°$ **d.** $330°$

SOLUTION We draw each angle in standard position. The reference angle is the positive acute angle formed by the terminal side of the angle in question and the x-axis.

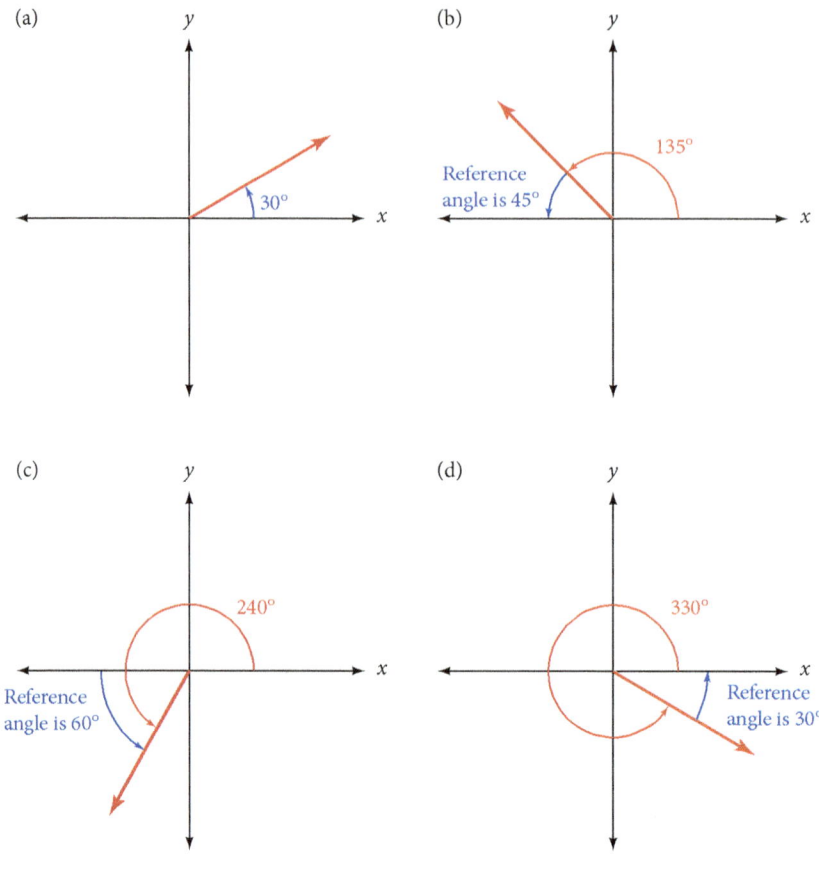

We can generalize the results of Example 8 as follows: If θ is a positive angle between 0° and 360°, then:

If $\theta \in$ QI,   then $\hat{\theta} = \theta$

If $\theta \in$ QII,   then $\hat{\theta} = 180° - \theta$

If $\theta \in$ QIII,   then $\hat{\theta} = \theta - 180°$

If $\theta \in$ QIV,   then $\hat{\theta} = 360° - \theta$

We can use out information on reference angles and the signs of the trigonometric functions to write the following theorem.

> **⌈Δ≠Σ⌉   *Reference Angle Theorem***
>
> A trigonometric function of an angle and its reference angle differ at most in sign.

We will not give a detailed proof of this theorem but, rather, justify it by example. Let's look at the sines of all the angles between 0° and 360° that have a reference angle of 30°. These angles are 30°, 150°, 210°, and 330°.

From Figure 1 we have the following:

$$\sin 150° = \sin 30° = \frac{1}{2}$$

$$\sin 210° = \sin 330° = -\frac{1}{2}$$

They differ in sign only.

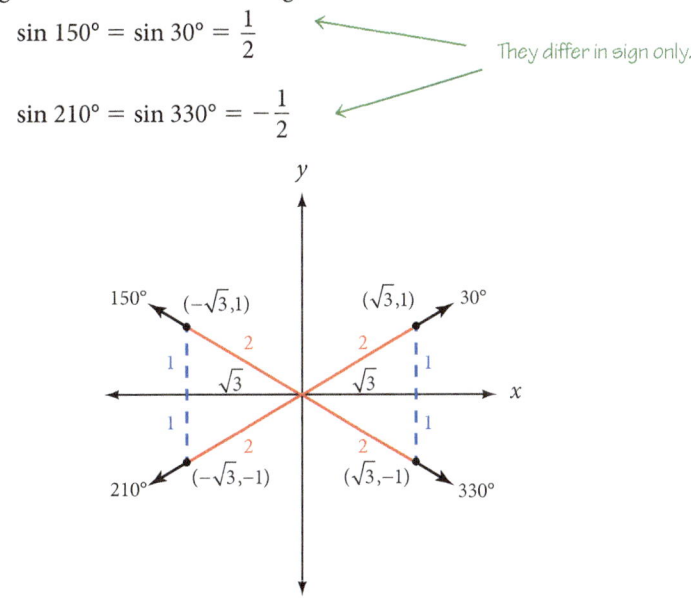

FIGURE 1

As you can see, any angle with a reference angle of 30° will have a sine of $\frac{1}{2}$ or $-\frac{1}{2}$. The sign, $+$ or $-$, will depend on the quadrant in which the angle terminates. Using this discussion as justification, we write the following steps used to find trigonometric functions of angles between 0° and 360°.

Step 1: Find $\hat{\theta}$, the reference angle.

Step 2: Determine the sign of the trigonometric function based on the quadrant in which θ terminates.

Step 3: Write the original trigonometric function of θ in terms of the same trigonometric function of $\hat{\theta}$.

Step 4: Find the trigonometric function of $\hat{\theta}$.

Example 9   For the exact value of sin 240°.

SOLUTION For this first example, we will list the steps given on the preceding page as we use them. Figure 2 is a diagram of the situation.

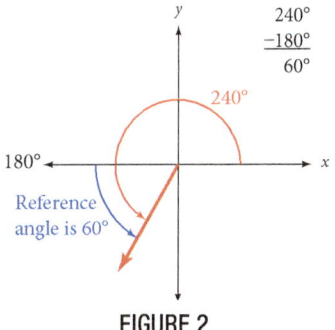

$$\begin{array}{r} 240° \\ -180° \\ \hline 60° \end{array}$$

Reference angle is 60°

FIGURE 2

Step 1: We find $\hat{\theta}$ by subtracting 180° from θ.

$$240° - 180° = 60°$$

Step 2: Since θ terminates in quadrant III, and the sine function is negative in quadrant III, our answer will be negative. That is, in this case, $\sin \theta = -\sin \hat{\theta}$.

Step 3: Using the results of Steps 1 and 2, we write

$$\sin 240° = -\sin 60°$$

Step 4: We finish by finding $\sin 60°$:

$$\sin 240° = -\sin 60° = -\frac{\sqrt{3}}{2}$$ ■

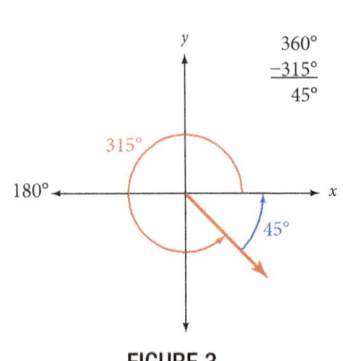

FIGURE 3

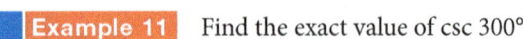 **Example 10**   Find the exact value of tan 315°.

SOLUTION The reference angle is $360° - 315° = 45°$ (see Figure 3). Since 315° terminates in quadrant IV, its tangent will be negative.

$$\tan 315° = -\tan 45° \qquad \textit{Because tangent is now negative in QIV}$$

$$= -1$$ ■

Example 11   Find the exact value of csc 300°.

SOLUTION The reference angle is $360° - 300° = 60°$ (see Figure 4). To find the exact value of csc 60°, we use the fact that cosecant and sine are reciprocals.

$$\csc 300° = -\csc 60° \qquad \textit{Because cosecant is negative in QIV}$$

$$= -\frac{1}{\sin 60°}$$

$$= -\frac{1}{\sqrt{3}/2}$$

$$= -\frac{2}{\sqrt{3}}$$ ■

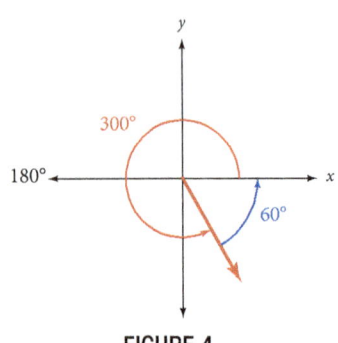

FIGURE 4

> (děf)   *coterminal angles*
>
> Two angles with the same terminal side are called **coterminal angles**.

Coterminal angles always differ from each other by multiples of 360°. For example, 10° and 370° are coterminal, as are −45° and 315° (Figure 5).

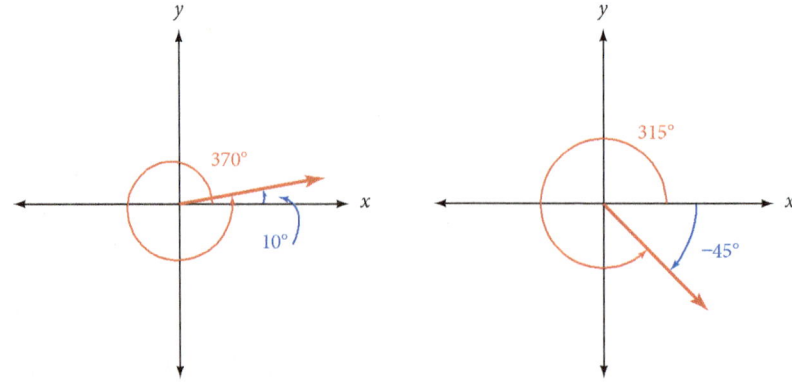

FIGURE 5

The trigonometric functions of an angle and any angle coterminal with it are always equal. For sine and cosine, we can write this in symbols as follows:

> **⌠Δ≠Σ**
>
> For any integer k,
>
> $$\sin(\theta + 360°k) = \sin\theta \quad \text{and} \quad \cos(\theta + 360°k) = \cos\theta$$

To find values of trigonometric functions for an angle larger than 360° or smaller than 0°, we simply find an angle between 0° and 360° that is coterminal with it, and then use the steps outlines in Examples 9–11.

Example 12   Find the exact value of cos 495°.

SOLUTION   By subtracting 360° from 495°, we obtain 135°, which is coterminal with 495°. The reference angle for 135° is 45° (see Figure 6). Since 495° terminates in quadrant II, its cosine is negative.

$$\cos 495° = \cos 135° \qquad \text{\color{green}495° and 135° are coterminal.}$$

$$= -\cos 45° \qquad \text{\color{green}In QII } \cos\theta = -\cos\hat{\theta}.$$

$$= -\frac{1}{\sqrt{2}} \qquad \text{\color{green}Exact value}$$

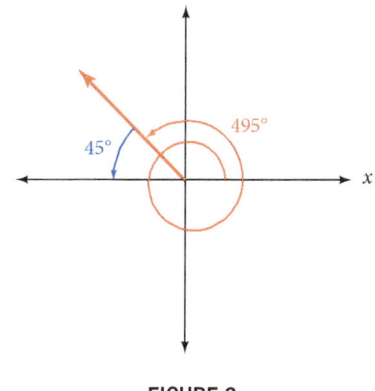

FIGURE 6

Approximations

To find trigonometric functions of angles that do not lend themselves to exact values, we use a calculator. To find an approximation for sin θ, cos θ, or tan θ, we press the appropriate keys on the calculator. Check to see that you can obtain the following values for sine, cosine, and tangent of 250° and $-160°$ in your calculator. (These answers are rounded to the nearest ten thousandth.)

$$\sin 250° \approx -0.9397 \qquad \sin(-160°) \approx -0.3420$$
$$\cos 250° \approx -0.3420 \qquad \cos(-160°) \approx -0.9397$$
$$\tan 250° \approx 2.7475 \qquad \tan(-160°) \approx 0.3640$$

To find csc 250°, sec 250°, and cot 250°, we must use the reciprocals of sin 250°, cos 250°, and tan 250°.

	Scientific Calculator	Graphing Calculator
$\csc 250° = \dfrac{1}{\sin 250°} \approx -1.0642$	250 $\boxed{\sin}$ $\boxed{1/x}$	1 $\boxed{\div}$ $\boxed{\sin}$ 250 $\boxed{\text{ENTER}}$
$\sec 250° = \dfrac{1}{\cos 250°} \approx -2.9238$	250 $\boxed{\cos}$ $\boxed{1/x}$	1 $\boxed{\div}$ $\boxed{\cos}$ 250 $\boxed{\text{ENTER}}$
$\cot 250° = \dfrac{1}{\tan 250°} \approx 0.3640$	250 $\boxed{\tan}$ $\boxed{1/x}$	1 $\boxed{\div}$ $\boxed{\tan}$ 250 $\boxed{\text{ENTER}}$

Next we use a calculator to find an approximation for θ, given one of the trigonometric functions of θ and the quadrant in which θ terminates.

Example 13   Find θ if $\sin \theta = -0.5592$ and θ terminates in QIII with $0° < \theta < 360°$.

SOLUTION   In this example, we must use a calculator in the reverse direction from the way we used it in the discussion above. Using the $\boxed{\sin^{-1}}$ key, we find that 34° is the angle whose sine is 0.5592. That is,

$$\hat{\theta} \approx 34°$$

This is our reference angle, $\hat{\theta}$. The angle in quadrant III whose reference angle is 34° is $\theta = 180° + 34° = 214°$ (see Figue 7).

Calculator Note   If you were to try Example 13 on your calculator by using -0.5592 and the $\boxed{\sin^{-1}}$ key, you would not obtain 214° for your answer. Instead you would get approximately $-34°$ for the answer, which is wrong. To see why this happen, you will have to wait until we cover inverse trigonometric functions. In the meantime, to use a calculator on this kind of problem, use it to find the reference angle and then proceed as we did in Example 13.

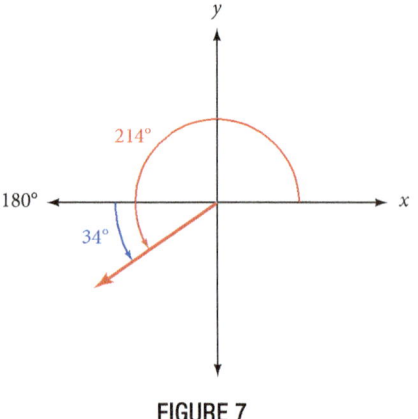

FIGURE 7

If $\sin \theta = -0.5592$ and θ terminates in QIII, then

$$\theta = 180° + 34°$$

$$= 214°$$

If we wanted to list *all* the angles that terminate in quadrant III and have a sine of -0.5592, we would write

$$\theta = 214° + 360°k$$

where $k =$ an integer. This gives us all angles coterminal with 214°.

Example 14   Find θ to the nearest tenth of a degree if $\tan \theta = -0.8541$ and θ terminates in QIV with $0° < \theta < 360°$.

SOLUTION Using 0.8541 and the $\boxed{\tan^{-1}}$ key gives the reference angle as $\hat{\theta} = 40.5°$. The angle in QIV with a reference angle of 40.5° is

$$\theta = 360° - 40.5° = 319.5°$$

Again, if we wanted to list all angles in the quadrant IV with a tangent of -0.8541, we would write

$$\theta = 319.5° + 360°k \qquad \textit{k = an integer}$$

to include not only 319.5° but all angles coterminal with it.

Example 15   Find θ if $\sin \theta = -\frac{1}{2}$ with θ in QIII and $0° < \theta < 360°$.

SOLUTION From the table of exact values, we find that the angle whose sine is $\frac{1}{2}$ is 30°. This is the reference angle. The angle in quadrant III with a reference angle of 30° is $180° + 30° = 210°$.

Notation   The notation $\sin^2 \theta$ means $(\sin \theta)^2 = \sin \theta \cdot \sin \theta$. Raising trigonometric ratios to integer exponents is something that occurs frequently in trigonometry. The expression $\sin^2 \theta$ is the square of the sine of θ. That is, we find the sine of θ first and then square the result.

Example 16   Use exact values to simplify:

$$\sin^2 60° - \cos^2 60° + \cos^3 60°$$

SOLUTION From Table 1 we have,

$$\sin 60° = \frac{\sqrt{3}}{2} \quad \text{and} \quad \cos 60° = \frac{1}{2}$$

Substituting these values into the original expression, we have

$$\sin^2 60° - \cos^2 60° + \cos^3 60° = \left(\frac{\sqrt{3}}{2}\right)^2 - \left(\frac{1}{2}\right)^2 + \left(\frac{1}{2}\right)^3$$

$$= \frac{3}{4} - \frac{1}{4} + \frac{1}{8}$$

$$= \frac{6}{8} - \frac{2}{8} + \frac{1}{8}$$

$$= \frac{5}{8}$$

Getting Ready for Class

After reading through the preceding section, respond in your own words and in complete sentences.

A. Explain how you would find sec 78° on your calculator.
B. How do you find the reference angle for 135°?
C. What are coterminal angles?
D. How do you find the exact value of tan 315°?

Problem Set 11.2

Use a calculator to find each of the following. Round all answers to four places past the decimal point.

1. $\sin 27.2°$ **2.** $\cos 82.9°$ **3.** $\cos 18°$

4. $\sin 42°$ **5.** $\tan 87.32°$ **6.** $\tan 81.43°$

7. $\cot 31°$ **8.** $\cot 24°$ **9.** $\sec 48.2°$

10. $\sec 71.8°$ **11.** $\csc 14.15°$ **12.** $\csc 12.21°$

Find θ if θ is between 0° and 90°. Round your answer to the nearest tenth of a degree.

13. $\cos \theta = 0.9770$ **14.** $\sin \theta = 0.3971$ **15.** $\tan \theta = 0.6873$

16. $\cos \theta = 0.5490$ **17.** $\sin \theta = 0.9813$ **18.** $\tan \theta = 0.6273$

19. $\sin \theta = 0.7038$ **20.** $\cos \theta = 0.9153$ **21.** $\cos \theta = 0.4112$

22. $\sin \theta = 0.9954$ **23.** $\tan \theta = 1.1953$ **24.** $\tan \theta = 1.7391$

25. $\csc \theta = 3.9451$ **26.** $\sec \theta = 2.1609$ **27.** $\cot \theta = 5.5764$

28. $\cot \theta = 4.6252$ **29.** $\sec \theta = 1.0129$ **30.** $\csc \theta = 7.0683$

Draw each of the following angles in standard position and then name the reference angle.

31. 210° **32.** 150°

33. 143.4° **34.** 253.8°

35. −30° **36.** −45°

37. −300° **38.** −330°

39. −120° **40.** −150°

Find the exact value of each of the following:

41. cos 225°

42. cos 135°

43. sin 120°

44. sin 210°

45. tan 135°

46. tan 315°

47. cos $\dfrac{4\pi}{3}$

48. cos $\dfrac{5\pi}{6}$

49. csc 330°

50. sec 330°

51. sec 300°

52. csc 300°

53. sin 390°

54. cos 420°

55. cot 480°

56. cot 510°

Use a calculator to find θ, to the nearest tenth of a degree, is $0° < \theta < 360°$ and:

57. sin $\theta = -0.3090$ with θ in QIII

58. sin $\theta = -0.3090$ with θ in QIV

59. cos $\theta = -0.7660$ with θ in QII

60. cos $\theta = -0.7660$ with θ in QIII

61. tan $\theta = 0.5890$ with θ in QIII

62. tan $\theta = 0.5890$ with θ in QI

63. cos $\theta = 0.2644$ with θ in QI

64. cos $\theta = 0.2644$ with θ in QIV

65. sin $\theta = 0.9652$ with θ in QII

66. sin $\theta = 0.9652$ with θ in QI

Find θ if $0° < \theta < 360°$ and:

67. sin $\theta = -\dfrac{\sqrt{3}}{2}$ and θ in QIII

68. sin $\theta = -\dfrac{1}{\sqrt{2}}$ and θ in QIII

69. cos $\theta = -\dfrac{1}{\sqrt{2}}$ and θ in QII

70. cos $\theta = -\dfrac{\sqrt{3}}{2}$ and θ in QIII

71. $\sin \theta = -\dfrac{\sqrt{3}}{2}$ and θ in QIV

72. $\sin \theta = \dfrac{1}{\sqrt{2}}$ and θ in QII

73. $\tan \theta = \sqrt{3}$ and θ in QIII

74. $\tan \theta = \dfrac{1}{\sqrt{3}}$ and θ in QIII

Use exact values to simplify each expression.

75. $\cos^2 30°$

76. $\sin^2 30°$

77. $\tan^4 60°$

78. $\tan^3 60°$

79. $\sin^2 45° + \cos^2 45°$

80. $(\sin 45° + \cos 45°)^2$

81. $\sin^2 60° + \cos^2 60°$

82. $(\sin 60° + \cos 60°)^2$

Getting Ready for the Next Section

Give the reciprocal of each number.

83. $\dfrac{1}{2}$

84. $\dfrac{3}{5}$

85. $\dfrac{\sqrt{3}}{2}$

86. $\dfrac{1}{\sqrt{2}}$

Simplify.

87. $\sqrt{1 - \left(\dfrac{3}{5}\right)^2}$

88. $\sqrt{1 - \left(\dfrac{1}{2}\right)^2}$

Sine and Cosine Graphs

The Sine Graph

To graph the equation $y = \sin x$ we begin by making a table of values of x and y that satisfy the equation, and then use the information in the table to sketch the graph. To make it easy on ourselves, we will let x take on values that are multiples of $\frac{\pi}{4}$. As an aid in sketching the graphs, we will approximate $\frac{1}{\sqrt{2}}$ with 0.7.

Table 1

x	$y = \sin x$	(x, y)
0	$y = \sin 0 = 0$	$(0, 0)$
$\dfrac{\pi}{4}$	$y = \sin \dfrac{\pi}{4} = \dfrac{1}{\sqrt{2}} = 0.7$	$\left(\dfrac{\pi}{4}, 0.7\right)$
$\dfrac{\pi}{2}$	$y = \sin \dfrac{\pi}{2} = 1$	$\left(\dfrac{\pi}{2}, 1\right)$
$\dfrac{3\pi}{4}$	$y = \sin \dfrac{3\pi}{4} = \dfrac{1}{\sqrt{2}} = 0.7$	$\left(\dfrac{3\pi}{4}, 0.7\right)$
π	$y = \sin \pi = 0$	$(\pi, 0)$
$\dfrac{5\pi}{4}$	$y = \sin \dfrac{5\pi}{4} = -\dfrac{1}{\sqrt{2}} = -0.7$	$\left(\dfrac{5\pi}{4}, -0.7\right)$
$\dfrac{3\pi}{2}$	$y = \sin \dfrac{3\pi}{2} = -1$	$\left(\dfrac{3\pi}{2}, -1\right)$
$\dfrac{7\pi}{4}$	$y = \sin \dfrac{7\pi}{4} = -\dfrac{1}{\sqrt{2}} = -0.7$	$\left(\dfrac{7\pi}{4}, -0.7\right)$
2π	$y = \sin 2\pi = 0$	$(2\pi, 0)$

Graphing each ordered pair and then connecting them with a smooth curve, we obtain the following graph:

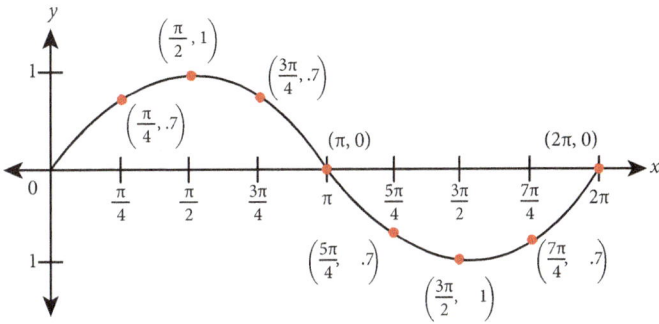

FIGURE 1

To further justify the graph in Figure 1, we could find additional ordered pairs that satisfy the equation. For example, we could continue our table by letting x take on multiples of $\frac{\pi}{6}$ and $\frac{\pi}{3}$. If we were to do so, we would find that any new ordered pair that satisfied the equation $y = \sin x$ would be such that its graph would lie on the curve in Figure 1. Figure 2 shows the curve in Figure 1 again, but this time with all the ordered pairs with x-coordinates that are multiples of $\frac{\pi}{6}$ or $\frac{\pi}{3}$ and the corresponding y-coordinates that satisfy the equation $y = \sin x$.

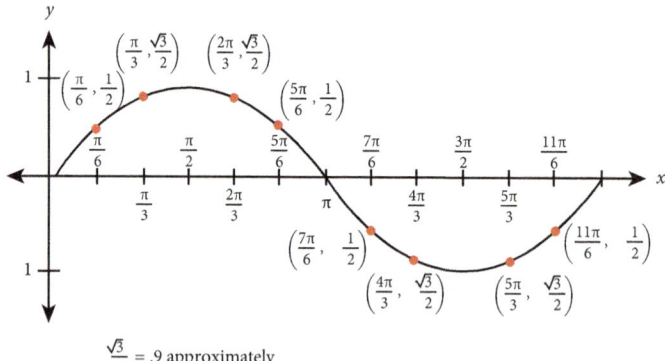

$\frac{\sqrt{3}}{2} = .9$ approximately

FIGURE 2

Video Examples

Section 11.3

■ **Example 1**   Use the graph of $y = \sin x$ in Figure 2 to find all values of x between 0 and 2π for which $\sin x = \frac{1}{2}$.

SOLUTION   We locate $\frac{1}{2}$ on the y-axis and draw a horizontal line through it. We follow this line to the points where it intersects the graph of $y = \sin x$. The values of x just below these points of intersection are the values of x for which $\sin x = \frac{1}{2}$. As Figure 3 indicates, they are $\frac{\pi}{6}$ and $\frac{5\pi}{6}$.

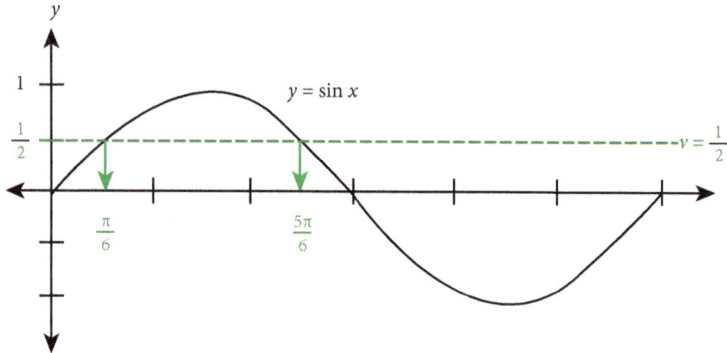

FIGURE 3

The Cosine Curve

The graph of $y = \cos x$ has the same general shape as the graph of $y = \sin x$.

Example 2   Sketch the graph of $y = \cos x$.

SOLUTION   We can arrive at the graph by making a table of convenient values of x and y.

Table 2

x	$y = \cos x$	(x, y)
0	$y = \cos 0 = 1$	$(0, 1)$
$\dfrac{\pi}{4}$	$y = \cos \dfrac{\pi}{4} = -\dfrac{1}{\sqrt{2}}$	$\left(\dfrac{\pi}{4}, \dfrac{1}{\sqrt{2}}\right)$
$\dfrac{\pi}{2}$	$y = \cos \dfrac{\pi}{2} = 0$	$\left(\dfrac{\pi}{2}, 0\right)$
$\dfrac{3\pi}{4}$	$y = \cos \dfrac{3\pi}{4} = \dfrac{1}{\sqrt{2}}$	$\left(\dfrac{3\pi}{4}, -\dfrac{1}{\sqrt{2}}\right)$
π	$y = \cos \pi = -1$	$(\pi, -1)$
$\dfrac{5\pi}{4}$	$y = \cos \dfrac{5\pi}{4} = -\dfrac{1}{\sqrt{2}}$	$\left(\dfrac{5\pi}{4}, -\dfrac{1}{\sqrt{2}}\right)$
$\dfrac{3\pi}{2}$	$y = \cos \dfrac{3\pi}{2} = 0$	$\left(\dfrac{3\pi}{2}, 0\right)$
$\dfrac{7\pi}{4}$	$y = \cos \dfrac{7\pi}{4} = \dfrac{1}{\sqrt{2}}$	$\left(\dfrac{7\pi}{4}, \dfrac{1}{\sqrt{2}}\right)$
2π	$y = \cos 2\pi = 1$	$(2\pi, 1)$

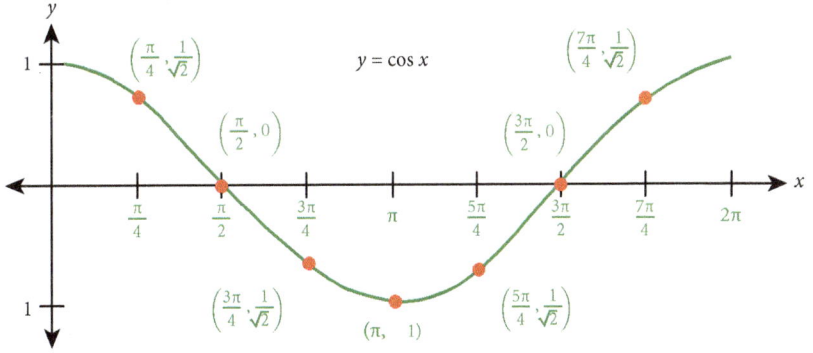

FIGURE 4

Example 3   Find all values of x for which $\cos x = -1$.

SOLUTION   We draw a horizontal line through $y = -1$ and notice where it intersects the graph of $y = \cos x$. The x-coordinates of those points are solutions to $\cos x = -1$. (Figure 5 is the graph of $y = \cos x$ extended beyond the interval from $x = 0$ to $x = 2\pi$.)

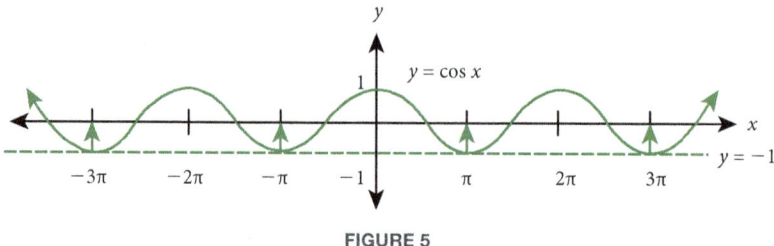

FIGURE 5

Figure 5 indicates that all solutions to $\cos x = -1$ are

$$x = \ldots -3\pi,\ -\pi,\ \pi,\ 3\pi, \ldots$$

Since each pair of consecutive solutions differ by 2π, we can write the solutions in a more compact form as

$$x = \pi + 2k\pi \quad \text{where } k \text{ is an integer}$$

Make a table of values for the function using multiples of $\frac{\pi}{4}$ for x. Then use the entries in the table to sketch the graph of each function for x between 0 and 2π.

1. $y = \cos x$ **2.** $y = \sin x$

Use the graphs you found in Problems 1 and 2 to find all values of x between 0 and 2π for which each of the following is true:

3. $\cos x = \dfrac{1}{2}$ **4.** $\sin x = \dfrac{1}{2}$ **5.** $\cos x = \dfrac{-1}{\sqrt{2}}$

6. $\sin x = \dfrac{-\sqrt{3}}{2}$ **7.** $\cos x = \dfrac{\sqrt{3}}{2}$ **8.** $\sin x = \dfrac{1}{\sqrt{2}}$

Sketch the graphs of each of the following between $x = -4\pi$ and $x = 4\pi$ by extending the graphs you made in Problems 1 and 2:

9. $y = \sin x$ **10.** $y = \cos x$ **11.** $y = \sec x$

Use the graphs you found in Problems 9 through 11 to find all values of x between $x = 0$ and $x = 4\pi$ for which each of the following is true:

12. $\sin x = \dfrac{\sqrt{3}}{2}$ **13.** $\cos x = \dfrac{1}{\sqrt{2}}$ **14.** $\sin x = \dfrac{-1}{2}$

15. $\cos x = \dfrac{-1}{2}$ **16.** $\sin x = \dfrac{1}{\sqrt{2}}$ **17.** $\cos x = \dfrac{-\sqrt{3}}{2}$

Find all values of x for which the following are true:

18. $\sin x = 0$ **19.** $\sin x = 1$

Give the amplitude and period of each of the following graphs:

20.

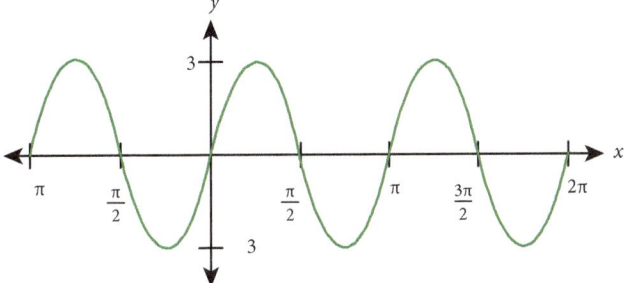

Angles [11.1]

An angle is formed when two rays have a common endpoint. The common endpoint is called the *vertex* of the angle, and the rays are called the *sides* of the angle.

Angles that measure between 0° and 90° are called *acute angles*, while angles that measure between 90° and 180° are called *obtuse angles*.

If two angles have a sum of 90°, then they are called *complementary angles*, and we say each is the *complement* of the other. Two angles with a sum of 180° are called *supplementary angles*.

Radian Measure [11.1]

In a circle, a *central angle* that cuts off an arc equal in length to the radius of the circle has a measure of 1 radian. That is, in a circle of radius r, a central angle that measures 1 radian will cut off an arc of length r (Figure 4).

If a central angle θ in a circle of radius r cuts off an arc of length s, then the *measure of θ in radians* is given by $\frac{s}{r}$.

Special Triangles [11.1]

The 30°-60°-90° Triangle   In any right triangle which the two acute angles are 30° and 60°, the longest side (the hypotenuse) is always twice the shortest side(the side opposite the 30° angle), and the side of medium length (the side opposite the 60° angle) is always $\sqrt{3}$ times the shortest side.

The 45°-45°-90° Triangle   If the two acute angles in a right triangle are both 45°, then the two shorter sides (the legs) are equal, and the longest side (the hypotenuse) is $\sqrt{2}$ times as long as the shorter sides. That is, if the shorter sides are of length t, then the longest side has length $t\sqrt{2}$.

Reference and Coterminal Angles [11.2]

The *reference angle* (sometimes called *related angle*) for any angle θ in standard position is the positive acute angle between the terminal side of θ and the x-axis.

Two angles with the same terminal side are called *coterminal angles*. For any interval k, $\sin(\theta + 360°k) = \sin\theta$ and $\cos(\theta + 360°k) = \cos\theta$.

Sine Graph [11.3]

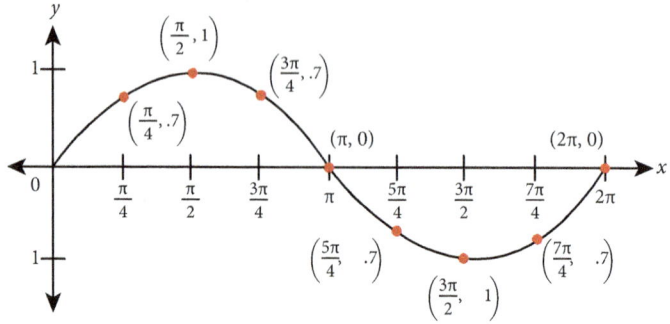

Cosine Graph [11.3]

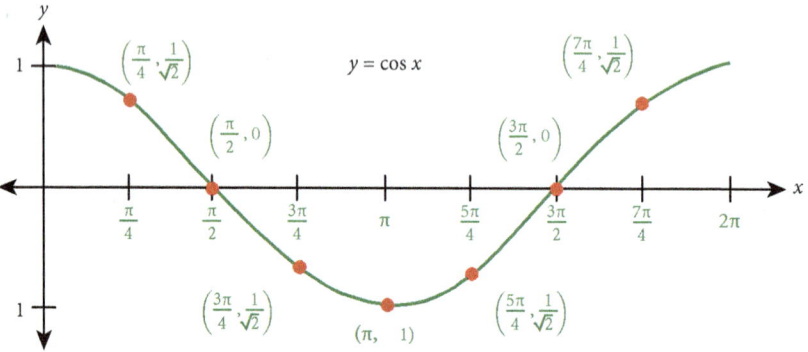

Chapter 11 Test

Convert each angle to radian measure. [11.1]

1. 75°   **2.** 120°

Convert to degree measure. [11.1]

3. $\dfrac{10\pi}{9}$ **4.** $\dfrac{11\pi}{6}$

5. Find the other two sides of a 30°–60°–90° triangle if the shortest side is 5. [11.1]

6. Find the other two sides of a 45°–45°–90° triangle if the longest side is 12. [11.1]

7. Find the six trigonometric functions of θ if the point $(4, -3)$ is on the terminal side of θ. [11.2]

8. In which quadrant must θ lie if $\sin \theta < 0$ and $\tan \theta > 0$? [11.2]

9. Find the remaining trigonometric functions of θ if $\sin \theta = \frac{1}{2}$ and θ terminates in QII. [11.2]

Exponential and Logarithmic Functions

12

Chapter Outline

iStockphoto.com © Uberimages

If you have had any problems with or had testing done on your thyroid gland, then you may have come in contact with radioactive iodine-131. Like all radioactive elements, iodine-131 decays naturally. The half-life of iodine-131 is 8 days, which means that every 8 days a sample of iodine-131 will decrease to half of its original amount. The following table and graph show what happens to a 1,600-microgram sample of iodine-131 over time.

Iodine-131 as a Function of Time

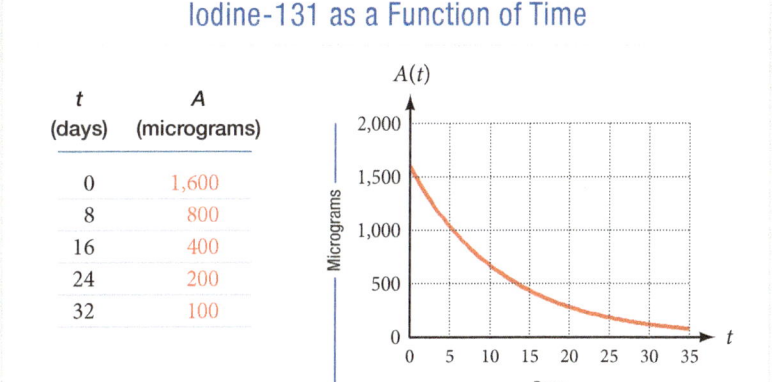

t (days)	A (micrograms)
0	1,600
8	800
16	400
24	200
32	100

The function represented by the information in the table and graph is

$$A(t) = 1,600 \cdot 2^{-t/8}$$

It is one of the types of functions we will study in this chapter.

Exponential Functions

To obtain an intuitive idea of how exponential functions behave, we can consider the heights attained by a bouncing ball. When a ball used in the game of racquetball is dropped from any height, the first bounce will reach a height that is $\frac{2}{3}$ of the original height. The second bounce will reach $\frac{2}{3}$ of the height of the first bounce, and so on, as shown in Figure 1.

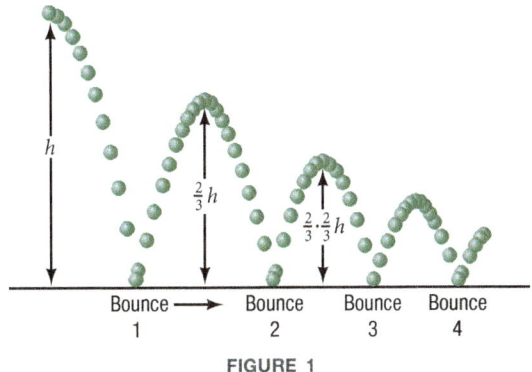

FIGURE 1

If the ball is initially dropped from a height of 1 meter, then during the first bounce it will reach a height of $\frac{2}{3}$ meter. The height of the second bounce will reach $\frac{2}{3}$ of the height reached on the first bounce. The maximum height of any bounce is $\frac{2}{3}$ of the height of the previous bounce.

Initial height: $h = 1$

Bounce 1: $\quad h = \frac{2}{3}(1) = \frac{2}{3}$

Bounce 2: $\quad h = \frac{2}{3}\left(\frac{2}{3}\right) = \left(\frac{2}{3}\right)^2$

Bounce 3: $\quad h = \frac{2}{3}\left(\frac{2}{3}\right)^2 = \left(\frac{2}{3}\right)^3$

Bounce 4: $\quad h = \frac{2}{3}\left(\frac{2}{3}\right)^3 = \left(\frac{2}{3}\right)^4$

$\qquad \vdots \qquad\qquad\qquad \vdots$

Bounce n: $\quad h = \frac{2}{3}\left(\frac{2}{3}\right)^{n-1} = \left(\frac{2}{3}\right)^n$

This last equation is exponential in form. We classify all exponential functions together with the following definition.

> **(dĕf´) exponential function**
>
> An **exponential function** is any function that can be written in the form
> $$f(x) = b^x$$
> where b is a positive real number other than 1.

Each of the following is an exponential function:

$$f(x) = 2^x \qquad y = 3^x \qquad f(x) = \left(\frac{1}{4}\right)^x$$

The first step in becoming familiar with exponential functions is to find some values for specific exponential functions.

Example 1   If the exponential functions f and g are defined by

$$f(x) = 2^x \quad \text{and} \quad g(x) = 3^x$$

then

$f(0) = 2^0 = 1$	$g(0) = 3^0 = 1$
$f(1) = 2^1 = 2$	$g(1) = 3^1 = 3$
$f(2) = 2^2 = 4$	$g(2) = 3^2 = 9$
$f(3) = 2^3 = 8$	$g(3) = 3^3 = 27$
$f(-2) = 2^{-2} = \dfrac{1}{2^2} = \dfrac{1}{4}$	$g(-2) = 3^{-2} = \dfrac{1}{3^2} = \dfrac{1}{9}$
$f(-3) = 2^{-3} = \dfrac{1}{2^3} = \dfrac{1}{8}$	$g(-3) = 3^{-3} = \dfrac{1}{3^3} = \dfrac{1}{27}$

In the introduction to this chapter, we indicated that the half-life of iodine-131 is 8 days, which means that every 8 days a sample of iodine-131 will decrease to half of its original amount. If we start with A_0 micrograms of iodine-131, then after t days the sample will contain

$$A(t) = A_0 \cdot 2^{-t/8}$$

micrograms of iodine-131.

Example 2   A patient is administered a 1,200-microgram dose of iodine-131. How much iodine-131 will be in the patient's system after 10 days, and after 16 days?

SOLUTION   The initial amount of iodine-131 is $A_0 = 1,200$, so the function that gives the amount left in the patient's system after t days is

$$A(t) = 1,200 \cdot 2^{-t/8}$$

After 10 days, the amount left in the patient's system is

$$A(10) = 1,200 \cdot 2^{-10/8} = 1,200 \cdot 2^{-1.25} \approx 504.5 \text{ micrograms}$$

After 16 days, the amount left in the patient's system is

$$A(16) = 1,200 \cdot 2^{-16/8} = 1,200 \cdot 2^{-2} = 300 \text{ micrograms}$$

Note Recall that the symbol $\approx$ is read "is approximately equal to".

We will now turn our attention to the graphs of exponential functions. Because the notation y is easier to use when graphing, and $y = f(x)$, for convenience we will write the exponential functions as

$$y = b^x$$

Example 3 Sketch the graph of the exponential function $y = 2^x$.

SOLUTION Using the results of Example 1, we produce the following table. Graphing the ordered pairs given in the table and connecting them with a smooth curve, we have the graph of $y = 2^x$ shown in Figure 2.

x	y
-3	$\frac{1}{8}$
-2	$\frac{1}{4}$
0	1
1	2
2	4
3	8

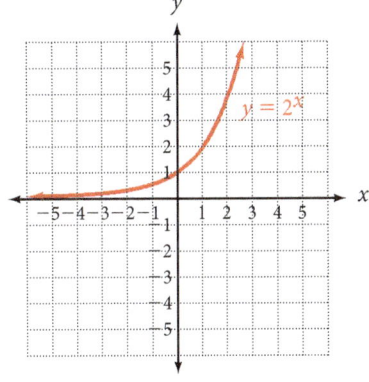

FIGURE 2

Notice that the graph does not cross the x-axis. It *approaches* the x-axis — in fact, we can get it as close to the x-axis as we want without it actually intersecting the x-axis. For the graph of $y = 2^x$ to intersect the x-axis, we would have to find a value of x that would make $2^x = 0$. Because no such value of x exists, the graph of $y = 2^x$ cannot intersect the x-axis.

Example 4 Sketch the graph of $y = \left(\frac{1}{3}\right)^x$.

SOLUTION The table beside Figure 3 gives some ordered pairs that satisfy the equation. Using the ordered pairs from the table, we have the graph shown in Figure 3.

x	y
23	27
22	9
-1	3
0	1
1	$\frac{1}{3}$
2	$\frac{1}{9}$
3	$\frac{1}{27}$

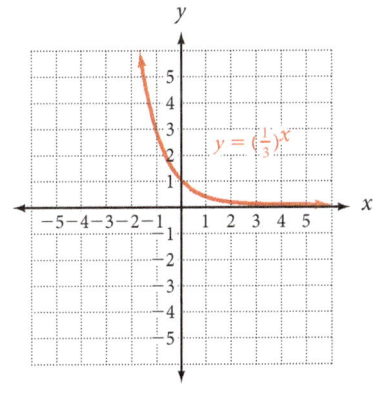

FIGURE 3

The graphs of all exponential functions have two things in common: (1) Each crosses the y-axis at $(0, 1)$ because $b^0 = 1$; and (2) none can cross the x-axis because $b^x = 0$ is impossible due to the restrictions on b.

Figures 4 and 5 show some families of exponential curves to help you become more familiar with them on an intuitive level.

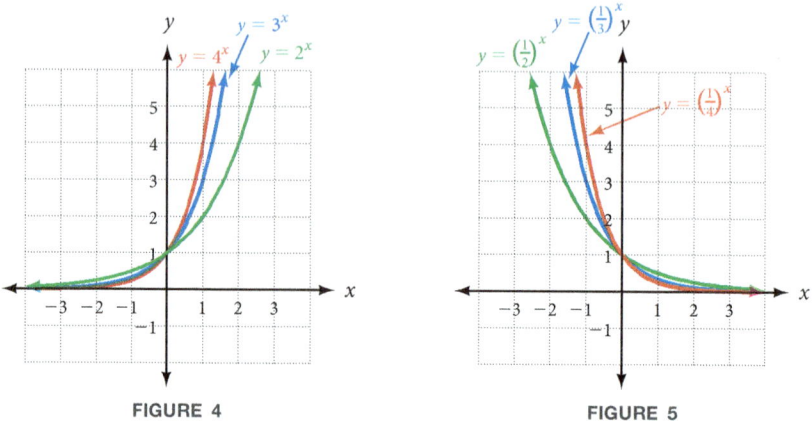

FIGURE 4   FIGURE 5

Among the many applications of exponential functions are the applications having to do with interest-bearing accounts. Here are the details.

Compound Interest   If P dollars are deposited in an account with annual interest rate r, compounded n times per year, then the amount of money in the account after t years is given by the formula

$$A(t) = P\left(1 + \frac{r}{n}\right)^{nt}$$

Example 5   Suppose you deposit $500 in an account with an annual interest rate of 8% compounded quarterly. Find an equation that gives the amount of money in the account after t years. Then find

a. The amount of money in the account after 5 years.

b. The number of years it will take for the account to contain $1,000.

SOLUTION   First, we note that $P = 500$ and $r = 0.08$. Interest that is compounded quarterly is compounded four times a year, giving us $n = 4$. Substituting these numbers into the preceding formula, we have our function

$$A(t) = 500\left(1 + \frac{0.08}{4}\right)^{4t} = 500(1.02)^{4t}$$

a. To find the amount after 5 years, we let $t = 5$:

$$A(5) = 500(1.02)^{4 \cdot 5} = 500(1.02)^{20} \approx \$742.97$$

Our answer is found on a calculator, and then rounded to the nearest cent.

b. To see how long it will take for this account to total $1,000, we graph the equation $Y_1 = 500(1.02)^{4X}$ on a graphing calculator, and then look to see where it intersects the line $Y_2 = 1,000$. The two graphs are shown in Figure 6.

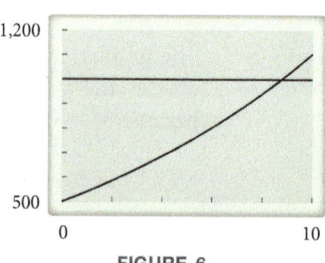

FIGURE 6

Using Zoom and Trace, or the Intersect function on the graphing calculator, we find that the two curves intersect at X ≈ 8.75 and Y = 1,000. This means that our account will contain $1,000 after the money has been on deposit for 8.75 years.

The Natural Exponential Function

A commonly occurring exponential function is based on a special number we denote with the letter e. The number e is a number like π. It is irrational and occurs in many formulas that describe the world around us. Like π, it can be approximated with a decimal number. Whereas π is approximately 3.1416, e is approximately 2.7183. (If you have a calculator with a key labeled e^x, you can use it to find e^1 to find a more accurate approximation to e.) We cannot give a more precise definition of the *number e* without using some of the topics taught in calculus. For the work we are going to do with the number e, we only need to know that it is an irrational number that is approximately 2.7183.

Here are a table and graph (Figure 7) for the natural exponential function

$$y = f(x) = e^x$$

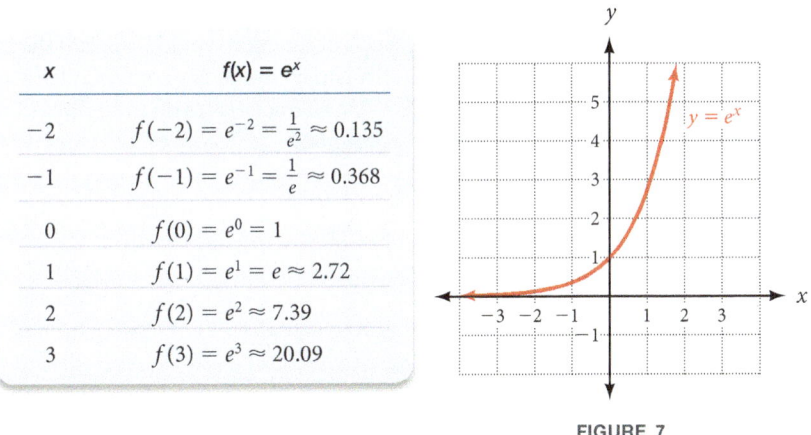

x	$f(x) = e^x$
-2	$f(-2) = e^{-2} = \frac{1}{e^2} \approx 0.135$
-1	$f(-1) = e^{-1} = \frac{1}{e} \approx 0.368$
0	$f(0) = e^0 = 1$
1	$f(1) = e^1 = e \approx 2.72$
2	$f(2) = e^2 \approx 7.39$
3	$f(3) = e^3 \approx 20.09$

FIGURE 7

One common application of natural exponential functions is with interest-bearing accounts. In Example 5, we worked with the formula

$$A(t) = P\left(1 + \frac{r}{n}\right)^{nt}$$

that gives the amount of money in an account if P dollars are deposited for t years at annual interest rate r, compounded n times per year. In Example 5, the number of compounding periods was four. What would happen if we let the number of compounding periods become larger and larger, so that we compounded the interest every day, then every hour, then every second, and so on? If we take this as far as it can go, we end up compounding the interest every moment. When this happens, we have an account with interest that is compounded continuously, and the amount of money in such an account depends on the number e. Here are the details.

Continuously Compounded Interest   If P dollars are deposited in an account with annual interest rate r, compounded continuously, then the amount of money in the account after t years is given by the formula

$$A(t) = Pe^{rt}$$

Example 6   Suppose you deposit $500 in an account with an annual interest rate of 8% compounded continuously. Find an equation that gives the amount of money in the account after t years. Then find the amount of money in the account after 5 years.

SOLUTION   Because the interest is compounded continuously, we use the formula $A(t) = Pe^{rt}$. Substituting $P = 500$ and $r = 0.08$ into this formula, we have

$$A(t) = 500e^{0.08t}$$

After 5 years, this account will contain

$$A(5) = 500e^{0.08 \cdot 5} = 500e^{0.4} \approx \$745.91$$

to the nearest cent. Compare this result with the answer to Example 5a.

Getting Ready for Class

After reading through the preceding section, respond in your own words and in complete sentences.

A. What is an exponential function?

B. In an exponential function, explain why the base b cannot equal 1. (What kind of function would you get if the base was equal to 1?)

C. Explain continuously compounded interest.

D. What characteristics do the graphs of $y = 2^x$ and $y = \left(\frac{1}{2}\right)^x$ have in common?

Let $f(x) = 3^x$ and $g(x) = \left(\dfrac{1}{2}\right)^x$, and evaluate each of the following.

1. $g(0)$ **2.** $f(0)$ **3.** $g(-1)$ **4.** $g(-4)$

5. $f(-3)$ **6.** $f(-1)$ **7.** $f(2) + g(-2)$ **8.** $f(2) - g(-2)$

Let $f(x) = 4^x$ and $g(x) = \left(\dfrac{1}{3}\right)^x$. Evaluate each of the following.

9. $f(-1) + g(1)$ **10.** $f(2) + g(-2)$ **11.** $\dfrac{f(-2)}{g(1)}$ **12.** $f(3) - f(2)$

Graph each of the following functions.

13. $y = 4^x$ **14.** $y = 2^{-x}$ **15.** $y = 3^{-x}$ **16.** $y = \left(\dfrac{1}{3}\right)^{-x}$

17. $y = 2^{x+1}$ **18.** $y = 2^{x-3}$ **19.** $y = e^x$ **20.** $y = e^{-x}$

21. $y = \left(\dfrac{1}{3}\right)^x$ **22.** $y = \left(\dfrac{1}{2}\right)^{-x}$ **23.** $y = 3^{x+2}$ **24.** $y = 2 \cdot 3^{-x}$

Graph each of the following functions on the same coordinate system for positive values of x only.

25. $y = 2x, y = x^2, y = 2^x$ **26.** $y = 3x, y = x^3, y = 3^x$

27. On a graphing calculator, graph the family of curves $y = b^x$, $b = 2, 4, 6, 8$.

28. On a graphing calculator, graph the family of curves $y = b^x$, $b = \dfrac{1}{2}, \dfrac{1}{4}, \dfrac{1}{6}, \dfrac{1}{8}$.

Applying the Concepts

29. Bouncing Ball Suppose the ball mentioned in the introduction to this section is dropped from a height of 6 feet above the ground. Find an exponential equation that gives the height h the ball will attain during the nth bounce. How high will it bounce on the fifth bounce?

30. Bouncing Ball A golf ball is manufactured so that if it is dropped from A feet above the ground onto a hard surface, the maximum height of each bounce will be one half of the height of the previous bounce. Find an exponential equation that gives the height h the ball will attain during the nth bounce. If the ball is dropped from 10 feet above the ground onto a hard surface, how high will it bounce on the eighth bounce?

31. Exponential Decay Twinkies on the shelf of a convenience store lose their fresh tastiness over time. We say that the taste quality is 1 when the Twinkies are first put on the shelf at the store, and that the quality of tastiness declines according to the function $Q(t) = 0.85^t$ (t in days). Graph this function on a graphing calculator, and determine when the taste quality will be one half of its original value.

32. Exponential Growth Automobiles built before 1993 use Freon in their air conditioners. The federal government now prohibits the manufacture of Freon. Because the supply of Freon is decreasing, the price per pound is increasing exponentially. Current estimates put the formula for the price per pound of Freon at $p(t) = 1.89(1.25)^t$, where t is the number of years since 1990. Find the price of Freon in 1995 and 1990. How much will Freon cost in the year 2010?

33. **Compound Interest** Suppose you deposit $1,200 in an account with an annual interest rate of 6% compounded quarterly.

   a. Find an equation that gives the amount of money in the account after t years.

   b. Find the amount of money in the account after 8 years.

   c. How many years will it take for the account to contain $2,400?

   d. If the interest were compounded continuously, how much money would the account contain after 8 years?

34. **Compound Interest** Suppose you deposit $500 in an account with an annual interest rate of 8% compounded monthly.

   a. Find an equation that gives the amount of money in the account after t years.

   b. Find the amount of money in the account after 5 years.

   c. How many years will it take for the account to contain $1,000?

   d. If the interest were compounded continuously, how much money would the account contain after 5 years?

Declining-Balance Depreciation The declining-balance method of depreciation is an accounting method businesses use to deduct most of the cost of new equipment during the first few years of purchase. Unlike other methods, the declining-balance formula does not consider salvage value.

35. **Value of a Crane** The function

$$V(t) = 450,000 \, (1 - 0.30)^t,$$

   where V is value and t is time in years, can be used to find the value of a crane for the first 6 years of use.

   a. What is the value of the crane after 3 years and 6 months?

   b. State the domain of this function.

   c. Sketch the graph of this function.

   d. State the range of this function.

   e. After how many years will the crane be worth only $85,000?

36. **Value of a Printing Press** The function $V(t) = 375,000(1 - 0.25)^t$, where V is value and t is time in years, can be used to find the value of a printing press during the first 7 years of use.

   a. What is the value of the printing press after 4 years and 9 months?

   b. State the domain of this function.

   c. Sketch the graph of this function.

   d. State the range of this function.

   e. After how many years will the printing press be worth only $65,000?

37. **Bacteria Growth** Suppose it takes 12 hours for a certain strain of bacteria to reproduce by dividing in half. If 50 bacteria are present to begin with, then the total number present after x days will be $f(x) = 50 \cdot 4^x$. Find the total number present after 1 day, 2 days, and 3 days.

38. **Bacteria Growth** Suppose it takes 1 day for a certain strain of bacteria to reproduce by dividing in half. If 100 bacteria are present to begin with, then the total number present after x days will be $f(x) = 100 \cdot 2^x$. Find the total number present after 1 day, 2 days, 3 days, and 4 days. How many days must elapse before over 100,000 bacteria are present?

39. **Value of a Painting** A painting is purchased as an investment for $150. If the painting's value doubles every 3 years, then its value is given by the function

$$V(t) = 150 \cdot 2^{t/3} \text{ for } t \geq 0$$

where t is the number of years since it was purchased, and $V(t)$ is its value (in dollars) at that time. Graph this function.

40. **Value of a Painting** A painting is purchased as an investment for $125. If the painting's value doubles every 5 years, then its value is given by the function

$$V(t) = 125 \cdot 2^{t/5} \text{ for } t \geq 0$$

where t is the number of years since it was purchased, and $V(t)$ is its value (in dollars) at that time. Graph this function.

41. **Cost Increase** The cost of a can of Coca Cola in 1960 was $0.10. The exponential function that models the cost of a Coca Cola by year is given below, where t is the number of years since 1960.

$$C(t) = 0.10e^{0.0576t}$$

   a. What was the expected cost of a can of Coca Cola in 1985?

   b. What was the expected cost of a can of Coca Cola in 2000?

   c. What was the expected cost of a can of Coca Cola in 2010?

   d. What is the expected cost of a can of Coca Cola in 2050?

42. **Airline Travel** The number of airline passengers in 1990 was 466 million. The number of passengers traveling by airplane each year has increased exponentially according to the model, $P(t) = 466 \cdot 1.035^t$, where t is the number of years since 1990 (U.S. Census Bureau).

   a. How many passengers traveled in 1997?

   b. How many passengers were expected to travel in 2015?

43. **Bankruptcy Model** In 1997, there were a total of 1,316,999 bankruptcies filed under the Bankruptcy Reform Act (Administrative Office of the U.S. Courts, Statistical Tables for the Federal Judiciary). The model for the number of bankruptcies filed is $B(t) = 0.798 \cdot 1.164^t$, where t is the number of years since 1994 and B is the number of bankruptcies filed in terms of millions. How close was the model in predicting the actual number of bankruptcies filed in 1997?

44. **Value of a Car** As a car ages, its value decreases. The value of a particular car with an original purchase price of $25,600 is modeled by the following function, where c is the value at time t (Kelly Blue Book).

$$c(t) = 25,600(1 - 0.22)^t$$

   a. What is the value of the car when it is 3 years old?

   b. What is the total depreciation amount after 4 years?

45. **Bacteria Decay** You are conducting a biology experiment and begin with 5,000,000 cells, but some of those cells are dying each minute. The rate of death of the cells is modeled by the function $A(t) = A_0 \cdot e^{-0.598t}$, where A_0 is the original number of cells, t is time in minutes, and A is the number of cells remaining after t minutes.

   a. How may cells remain after 5 minutes?

   b. How many cells remain after 10 minutes?

   c. How many cells remain after 20 minutes?

46. Health Care In 1990, \$699 billion were spent on health care expenditures. The amount of money, E, in billions spent on health care expenditures can be estimated using the function $E(t) = 78.16(1.11)^t$, where t is time in years since 1970 (U.S. Census Bureau).

  a. How close was the estimate determined by the function in estimating the actual amount of money spent on health care expenditures in 1990?

  b. What are the expected health care expenditures in 2008, 2009, and 2010?

Getting Ready for the Next Section

Solve each equation for y.

47. $x = 2y - 3$

48. $x = \dfrac{y + 7}{5}$

49. $x = y^2 - 3$

50. $x = (y + 4)^3$

51. $x = \dfrac{y - 4}{y - 2}$

52. $x = \dfrac{y + 5}{y - 3}$

53. $x = \sqrt{y - 3}$

54. $x = \sqrt{y} + 5$

The Inverse of a Function

The following diagram (Figure 1) shows the route Justin takes to school. He leaves his home and drives 3 miles east, and then turns left and drives 2 miles north. When he leaves school to drive home, he drives the same two segments, but in the reverse order and the opposite direction; that is, he drives 2 miles south, turns right, and drives 3 miles west. When he arrives home from school, he is right where he started. His route home "undoes" his route to school, leaving him where he began.

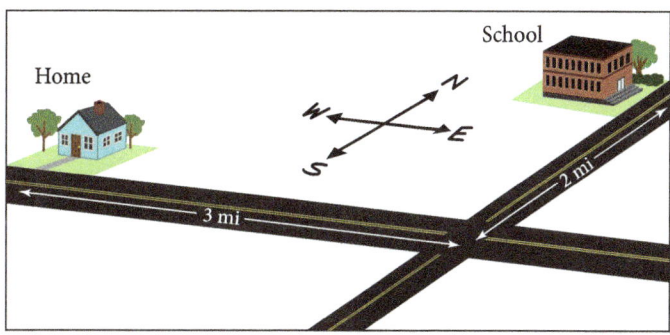

FIGURE 1

As you will see, the relationship between a function and its inverse function is similar to the relationship between Justin's route from home to school and his route from school to home.

Suppose the function f is given by

$$f = (1, 4), (2, 5), (3, 6), (4, 7)$$

The inverse of f is obtained by reversing the order of the coordinates in each ordered pair in f. The inverse of f is the relation given by

$$g = (4, 1), (5, 2), (6, 3), (7, 4)$$

It is obvious that the domain of f is now the range of g, and the range of f is now the domain of g. Every function (or relation) has an inverse that is obtained from the original function by interchanging the components of each ordered pair.

Suppose a function f is defined with an equation instead of a list of ordered pairs. We can obtain the equation of the inverse of f by interchanging the role of x and y in the equation for f.

Video Examples

Section 12.2

Example 1   If the function f is defined by $f(x) = 2x - 3$, find the equation that represents the inverse of f.

SOLUTION   Because the inverse of f is obtained by interchanging the components of all the ordered pairs belonging to f, and each ordered pair in f satisfies the equation $y = 2x - 3$, we simply exchange x and y in the equation $y = 2x - 3$ to get the formula for the inverse of f:

$$x = 2y - 3$$

We now solve this equation for y in terms of x:

$$x + 3 = 2y$$
$$\frac{x + 3}{2} = y$$
$$y = \frac{x + 3}{2}$$

The last line gives the equation that defines the inverse of f. Let's compare the graphs of f and its inverse as given here. (See Figure 2.)

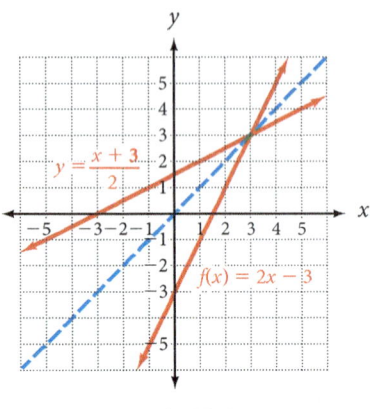

FIGURE 2

The graphs of f and its inverse have symmetry about the line $y = x$. This is a reasonable result since the one function was obtained from the other by interchanging x and y in the equation. The ordered pairs (a, b) and (b, a) always have symmetry about the line $y = x$.

Example 2   Graph the function $y = x^2 - 2$ and its inverse. Give the equation for the inverse.

SOLUTION   We can obtain the graph of the inverse of $y = x^2 - 2$ by graphing $y = x^2 - 2$ by the usual methods, and then reflecting the graph about the line $y = x$.

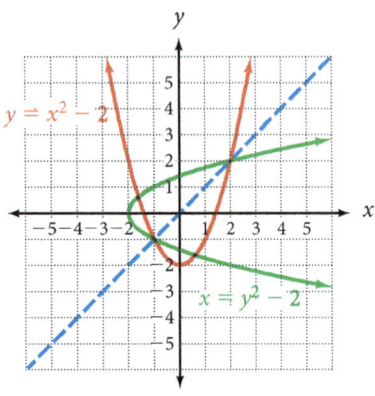

FIGURE 3

The equation that corresponds to the inverse of $y = x^2 - 2$ is obtained by interchanging x and y to get $x = y^2 - 2$.

We can solve the equation $x = y^2 - 2$ for y in terms of x as follows:

$$x = y^2 - 2$$
$$x + 2 = y^2$$
$$y = \pm\sqrt{x + 2}$$

Comparing the graphs from Examples 1 and 2, we observe that the inverse of a function is not always a function. In Example 1, both f and its inverse have graphs that are nonvertical straight lines and therefore both represent functions. In Example 2, the inverse of function f is not a function, since a vertical line crosses it in more than one place.

One-to-One Functions

We can distinguish between those functions with inverses that are also functions and those functions with inverses that are not functions with the following definition.

> (dĕf′   *one-to-one functions*
>
> A function is a *one-to-one function* if every element in the range comes from exactly one element in the domain.

This definition indicates that a one-to-one function will yield a set of ordered pairs in which no two different ordered pairs have the same second coordinates. For example, the function

$$f = \{(2, 3), (-1, 3), (5, 8)\}$$

is not one-to-one because the element 3 in the range comes from both 2 and -1 in the domain. On the other hand, the function

$$g = \{(5, 7), (3, -1), (4, 2)\}$$

is a one-to-one function because every element in the range comes from only one element in the domain.

Horizontal Line Test

If we have the graph of a function, we can determine if the function is one-to-one with the following test. If a horizontal line crosses the graph of a function in more than one place, then the function is not a one-to-one function because the points at which the horizontal line crosses the graph will be points with the same y-coordinates, but different x-coordinates. Therefore, the function will have an element in the range (the y-coordinate) that comes from more than one element in the domain (the x-coordinates).

Of the functions we have covered previously, all the linear functions and exponential functions are one-to-one functions because no horizontal lines can be found that will cross their graphs in more than one place.

Functions Whose Inverses Are Also Functions

Because one-to-one functions do not repeat second coordinates, when we reverse the order of the ordered pairs in a one-to-one function, we obtain a relation in which no two ordered pairs have the same first coordinate — by definition, this relation must be a function. In other words, every one-to-one function has an inverse that is itself a function. Because of this, we can use function notation to represent that inverse.

> (Δ≠Σ   *Inverse Function Notation*
>
> If $y = f(x)$ is a one-to-one function, then the inverse of f is also a function and can be denoted by $y = f^{-1}(x)$.

Note The notation f^{-1} does not represent the reciprocal of f. That is, the -1 in this notation is not an exponent. The notation f^{-1} is defined as representing the inverse function for a one-to-one function.

To illustrate, in Example 1 we found that the inverse of $f(x) = 2x - 3$ was the function $y = \frac{x+3}{2}$. We can write this inverse function with inverse function notation as

$$f^{-1}(x) = \frac{x+3}{2}$$

On the other hand, the inverse of the function in Example 2 is not itself a function, so we do not use the notation $f^{-1}(x)$ to represent it.

Example 3   Find the inverse of $g(x) = \dfrac{x-4}{x-2}$.

SOLUTION   To find the inverse for g, we begin by replacing $g(x)$ with y to obtain

$$y = \frac{x-4}{x-2} \qquad \text{\color{green}{The original function}}$$

To find an equation for the inverse, we exchange x and y.

$$x = \frac{y-4}{y-2} \qquad \text{\color{green}{The inverse of the original function}}$$

To solve for y, we first multiply each side by $y - 2$ to obtain

$$
\begin{aligned}
x(y - 2) &= y - 4 \\
xy - 2x &= y - 4 && \text{\color{green}{Distributive property}} \\
xy - y &= 2x - 4 && \text{\color{green}{Collect all terms containing y on the left side}} \\
y(x - 1) &= 2x - 4 && \text{\color{green}{Factor y from each term on the left side}} \\
y &= \frac{2x - 4}{x - 1} && \text{\color{green}{Divide each side by $x-1$}}
\end{aligned}
$$

Because our original function is one-to-one, as verified by the graph in Figure 4, its inverse is also a function. Therefore, we can use inverse function notation to write

$$g^{-1}(x) = \frac{2x-4}{x-1}$$

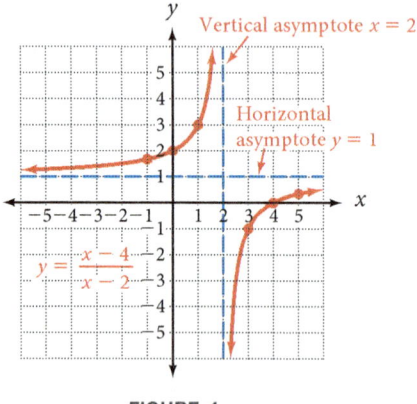

FIGURE 4

Example 4   Graph the function $y = 2^x$ and its inverse $x = 2^y$.

SOLUTION   We graphed $y = 2^x$ in the preceding section. We simply reflect its graph about the line $y = x$ to obtain the graph of its inverse $x = 2^y$.

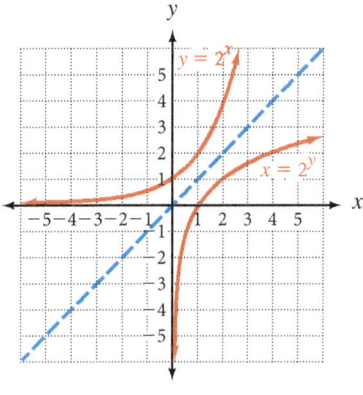

FIGURE 5

As you can see from the graph, $x = 2^y$ is a function. We do not have the mathematical tools to solve this equation for y, however. Therefore, we are unable to use the inverse function notation to represent this function. In the next section, we will give a definition that solves this problem. For now, we simply leave the equation as $x = 2^y$.

Functions, Relations, and Inverses—A Summary

Here is a summary of some of the things we know about functions, relations, and their inverses:

1. Every function is a relation, but not every relation is a function.

2. Every function has an inverse, but only one-to-one functions have inverses that are also functions.

3. The domain of a function is the range of its inverse, and the range of a function is the domain of its inverse.

4. If $y = f(x)$ is a one-to-one function, then we can use the notation $y = f^{-1}(x)$ to represent its inverse function.

5. The graph of a function and its inverse have symmetry about the line $y = x$.

6. If (a, b) belongs to the function f, then the point (b, a) belongs to its inverse.

Getting Ready for Class

After reading through the preceding section, respond in your own words and in complete sentences.

A. What is the inverse of a function?

B. What is the relationship between the graph of a function and the graph of its inverse?

C. Explain why only one-to-one functions have inverses that are also functions.

D. Describe the vertical line test, and explain the difference between the vertical line test and the horizontal line test.

Problem Set 12.2

For each of the following one-to-one functions, find the equation of the inverse. Write the inverse using the notation $f^{-1}(x)$.

1. $f(x) = 3x - 1$ **2.** $f(x) = 2x - 5$ **3.** $f(x) = x^3$

4. $f(x) = x^3 - 2$ **5.** $f(x) = \dfrac{x-3}{x-1}$ **6.** $f(x) = \dfrac{x-2}{x-3}$

7. $f(x) = \dfrac{x-3}{4}$ **8.** $f(x) = \dfrac{x+7}{2}$ **9.** $f(x) = \dfrac{1}{2}x - 3$

10. $f(x) = \dfrac{1}{3}x + 1$ **11.** $f(x) = \dfrac{2}{3}x - 3$ **12.** $f(x) = -\dfrac{1}{2}x + 4$

13. $f(x) = x^3 - 4$ **14.** $f(x) = -3x^3 + 2$ **15.** $f(x) = \dfrac{4x-3}{2x+1}$

16. $f(x) = \dfrac{3x-5}{4x+3}$ **17.** $f(x) = \dfrac{2x+1}{3x+1}$ **18.** $f(x) = \dfrac{3x+2}{5x+1}$

For each of the following relations, sketch the graph of the relation and its inverse, and write an equation for the inverse.

19. $y = 2x - 1$ **20.** $y = 3x + 1$ **21.** $y = x^2 - 3$ **22.** $y = x^2 + 1$

23. $y = x^2 - 2x - 3$ **24.** $y = x^2 + 2x - 3$

25. $y = 3^x$ **26.** $y = \left(\dfrac{1}{2}\right)^x$ **27.** $y = 4$ **28.** $y = -2$

29. $y = \dfrac{1}{2}x^3$ **30.** $y = x^3 - 2$ **31.** $y = \dfrac{1}{2}x + 2$ **32.** $y = \dfrac{1}{3}x - 1$

33. $y = \sqrt{x+2}$ **34.** $y = \sqrt{x} + 2$

35. Determine if the following functions are one-to-one.

a.

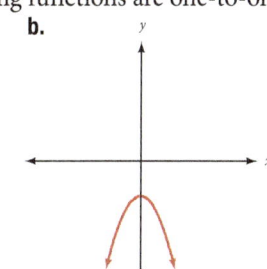

b.

c.

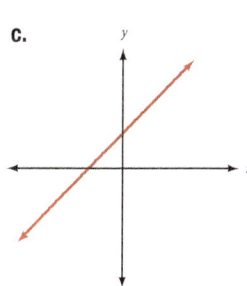

36. Could the following tables of values represent ordered pairs from one-to-one functions? Explain your answer.

a.

x	y
−2	5
−1	4
0	3
1	4
2	5

b.

x	y
1.5	0.1
2.0	0.2
2.5	0.3
3.0	0.4
3.5	0.5

37. If $f(x) = 3x - 2$, then $f^{-1}(x) = \dfrac{x + 2}{3}$. Use these two functions to find

  a. $f(2)$ **b.** $f^{-1}(2)$ **c.** $f[f^{-1}(2)]$ **d.** $f^{-1}[f(2)]$

38. If $f(x) = \dfrac{1}{2}x + 5$, then $f^{-1}(x) = 2x - 10$. Use these two functions to find

  a. $f(-4)$ **b.** $f^{-1}(-4)$ **c.** $f[f^{-1}(-4)]$ **d.** $f^{-1}[f(-4)]$

39. Let $f(x) = \dfrac{1}{x}$, and find $f^{-1}(x)$.

40. Let $f(x) = \dfrac{a}{x}$, and find $f^{-1}(x)$. (a is a real number constant.)

Applying the Concepts

41. Inverse Functions in Words Inverses may also be found by *inverse reasoning*. For example, to find the inverse of $f(x) = 3x + 2$, first list, in order, the operations done to variable x:

  a. Multiply by 3.   **b.** Add 2.

Then, to find the inverse, simply apply the inverse operations, in reverse order, to the variable x. That is:

  c. Subtract 2.   **d.** Divide by 3.

The inverse function then becomes $f^{-1}(x) = \frac{x-2}{3}$. Use this method of "inverse reasoning" to find the inverse of the function $f(x) = \frac{x}{7} - 2$.

42. **Inverse Functions in Words** Refer to the method of *inverse reasoning* explained in Problem 41. Use *inverse reasoning* to find the following inverses:

    a. $f(x) = 2x + 7$ **b.** $f(x) = \sqrt{x} - 9$ **c.** $f(x) = x^3 - 4$ **d.** $f(x) = \sqrt{x^3 - 4}$

43. **Reading Tables** Evaluate each of the following functions using the functions defined by Tables 1 and 2.

    a. $f[g(-3)]$ **b.** $g[f(-6)]$ **c.** $g[f(2)]$

    d. $f[g(3)]$ **e.** $f[g(-2)]$ **f.** $g[f(3)]$

    g. What can you conclude about the relationship between functions f and g?

TABLE 1	
x	$f(x)$
-6	3
2	-3
3	-2
6	4

TABLE 2	
x	$g(x)$
-3	2
-2	3
3	-6
4	6

44. **Reading Tables** Use the functions defined in Tables 1 and 2 in Problem 43 to answer the following questions.

    a. What are the domain and range of f?

    b. What are the domain and range of g?

    c. How are the domain and range of f related to the domain and range of g?

    d. Is f a one-to-one function?

    e. Is g a one-to-one function?

45. **Social Security** A function that models the billions of dollars of Social Security payment (as shown in the chart) per year is $s(t) = 16t + 249.4$, where t is time in years since 1990 (U.S. Census Bureau).

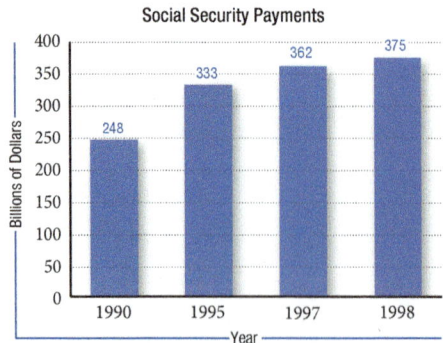

Social Security Payments

    a. Use the model to estimate the amount of Social Security payments to be paid in 2005.

    b. Write the inverse of the function.

    c. Using the inverse function, estimate the year in which payments will reach $507 billion.

46. Families The function for the percentage of one-parent families (as shown in the following chart) is $f(x) = 0.417x + 24$, when x is the time in years since 1990 (U.S. Census Bureau).

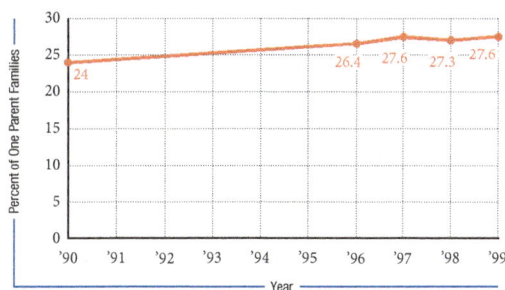

a. Use the function to predict the percentage of families with one parent in the year 2010.

b. Determine the inverse of the function, and estimate the year in which approximately 29% of the families are one-parent families.

47. Speed The fastest type of plane, a rocket plane, can travel at a speed of 4,520 miles per hour. The function $f(m) = \frac{22m}{15}$ converts miles per hour, m, to feet per second (World Book Encyclopedia).

a. Use the function to convert the speed of the rocket plane to feet per second.

b. Write the inverse of the function.

c. Using the inverse function, convert 2 feet per second to miles per hour.

48. Speed A Lockheed SR-71A airplane set a world record (as reported by Air Force Armament Museum in 1996) with an absolute speed record of 2,193.167 miles per hour. The function $s(h) = 0.4468424h$ converts miles per hour, h, to meters per second, s (Air Force Armament Museum).

a. What is the absolute speed of the Lockheed SR-71A in meters per second?

b. What is the inverse of this function?

c. Using the inverse function, determine the speed of an airplane in miles per hour that flies 150 meters per second.

Getting Ready for the Next Section

Simplify.

49. 3^{-2}

50. 2^3

Solve.

51. $2 = 3x$ **52.** $3 = 5x$ **53.** $4 = x^3$ **54.** $12 = x^2$

Fill in the boxes to make each statement true.

55. $8 = 2^{\square}$

56. $27 = 3^{\square}$

57. $10{,}000 = 10^{\square}$

58. $1{,}000 = 10^{\square}$

59. $81 = 3^{\square}$

60. $81 = 9^{\square}$

61. $6 = 6^{\square}$

62. $1 = 5^{\square}$

Logarithms are Exponents

In January 1999, ABC News reported that an earthquake had occurred in Colombia, causing massive destruction. They reported the strength of the quake by indicating that it measured 6.0 on the Richter scale. For comparison, Table 1 gives the Richter magnitude of a number of other earthquakes.

Although the size of the numbers in the table do not seem to be very different, the intensity of the earthquakes they measure can be very different. For example, the 1989 San Francisco earthquake was more than 10 times stronger than the 1999 earthquake in Colombia. The reason behind this is that the Richter scale is a *logarithmic scale*.

José Gomez/©Reuters

TABLE 1   Earthquakes

Year	Earthquake	Richter Magnitude
1971	Los Angeles	6.6
1985	Mexico City	8.1
1989	San Francisco	7.1
1992	Kobe, Japan	7.2
1994	Northridge	6.6
1999	Armenia, Colombia	6.0

In this section, we start our work with logarithms, which will give you an understanding of the Richter scale. Let's begin.

As you know from your work in the previous sections, equations of the form

$$y = b^x \quad b > 0, b \neq 1$$

are called exponential functions. Because the equation of the inverse of a function can be obtained by exchanging x and y in the equation of the original function, the inverse of an exponential function must have the form

$$x = b^y \quad b > 0, b \neq 1$$

Now, this last equation is actually the equation of a logarithmic function, as the following definition indicates:

> (dĕf´ **Definition**
>
> The expression $y = \log_b x$ is read "y is the logarithm to the base b of x" and is equivalent to the expression
>
> $$x = b^y \qquad b > 0, b \neq 1$$
>
> In words, we say "y is the number we raise b to in order to get x."

Notation   When an expression is in the form $x = b^y$, it is said to be in exponential form. On the other hand, if an expression is in the form $y = \log_b x$, it is said to be in logarithmic form.

Here are some equivalent statements written in both forms.

Exponential Form		Logarithmic Form
$8 = 2^3$	$\Leftrightarrow$	$\log_2 8 = 3$
$25 = 5^2$	$\Leftrightarrow$	$\log_5 25 = 2$
$0.1 = 10^{-1}$	$\Leftrightarrow$	$\log_{10} 0.1 = -1$
$\frac{1}{8} = 2^{-3}$	$\Leftrightarrow$	$\log_2 \frac{1}{8} = -3$
$r = z^s$	$\Leftrightarrow$	$\log_z r = s$

Video Examples

Section 12.3

Example 1   Solve for x: $\log_3 x = -2$

SOLUTION   In exponential form, the equation looks like this:

$$x = 3^{-2}$$

or

$$x = \frac{1}{9}$$

The solution is $\frac{1}{9}$.

Example 2   Solve $\log_x 4 = 3$.

SOLUTION   Again, we use the definition of logarithms to write the expression in exponential form:

$$4 = x^3$$

Taking the cube root of both sides, we have

$$\sqrt[3]{4} = \sqrt[3]{x^3}$$

$$x = \sqrt[3]{4}$$

The solution set is $\{\sqrt[3]{4}\}$.

Example 3   Solve $\log_8 4 = x$.

SOLUTION   We write the expression again in exponential form:

$$4 = 8^x$$

Because both 4 and 8 can be written as powers of 2, we write them in terms of powers of 2:

$$2^2 = (2^3)^x$$

$$2^2 = 2^{3x}$$

The only way the left and right sides of this last line can be equal is if the exponents are equal — that is, if

$$2 = 3x$$

or

$$x = \frac{2}{3}$$

The solution is $\frac{2}{3}$. We check as follows:

$$\log_8 4 = \frac{2}{3} \Leftrightarrow 4 = 8^{2/3}$$
$$4 = (\sqrt[3]{8})^2$$
$$4 = 2^2$$
$$4 = 4$$

The solution checks when used in the original equation.

Graphing Logarithmic Functions

Graphing logarithmic functions can be done using the graphs of exponential functions and the fact that the graphs of inverse functions have symmetry about the line $y = x$. Here's an example to illustrate.

Example 4   Graph the equation $y = \log_2 x$.

SOLUTION   The equation $y = \log_2 x$ is, by definition, equivalent to the exponential equation

$$x = 2^y$$

which is the equation of the inverse of the function

$$y = 2^x$$

The graph of $y = 2^x$ was given in Figure 2 of Section 8.1. We simply reflect the graph of $y = 2^x$ about the line $y = x$ to get the graph of $x = 2^y$, which is also the graph of $y = \log_2 x$. (See Figure 1.)

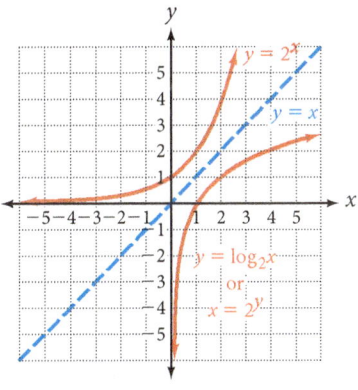

FIGURE 1

It is apparent from the graph that $y = \log_2 x$ is a function, because no vertical line will cross its graph in more than one place. The same is true for all logarithmic equations of the form $y = \log_b x$, where b is a positive number other than 1. Note also that the graph of $y = \log_b x$ will always appear to the right of the y-axis, meaning that x will always be positive in the expression $y = \log_b x$.

Two Special Identities

If b is a positive real number other than 1, then each of the following is a consequence of the definition of a logarithm:

$$(1)\ b^{\log_b x} = x \qquad \text{and} \qquad (2)\ \log_b b^x = x$$

The justifications for these identities are similar. Let's consider only the first one. Consider the expression

$$y = \log_b x$$

By definition, it is equivalent to

$$x = b^y$$

Substituting $\log_b x$ for y in the last line gives us

$$x = b^{\log_b x}$$

The next examples in this section show how these two special properties can be used to simplify expressions involving logarithms.

Example 5   Simplify the following logarithmic expressions.

a. $\log_2 8$ 　　　　　　**b.** $\log_{10} 10,000$ 　　　　**c.** $\log_b b$

d. $\log_b 1$ 　　　　　　**e.** $\log_4 (\log_5 5)$

SOLUTION

a. Substitute 2^3 for 8:

$$\log_2 8 = \log_2 2^3$$
$$= 3$$

b. 10,000 can be written as 10^4:

$$\log_{10} 10,000 = \log_{10} 10^4$$
$$= 4$$

c. Because $b^1 = b$, we have

$$\log_b b = \log_b b^1$$
$$= 1$$

d. Because $1 = b^0$, we have

$$\log_b 1 = \log_b b^0$$
$$= 0$$

e. Because $\log_5 5 = 1$,

$$\log_4(\log_5 5) = \log_4 1$$
$$= 0$$

Application

As we mentioned in the introduction to this section, one application of logarithms is in measuring the magnitude of an earthquake. If an earthquake has a shock wave T times greater than the smallest shock wave that can be measured on a seismograph, then the magnitude M of the earthquake, as measured on the Richter scale, is given by the formula

$$M = \log_{10} T$$

(When we talk about the size of a shock wave, we are talking about its amplitude. The amplitude of a wave is half the difference between its highest point and its lowest point.)

To illustrate the discussion, an earthquake that produces a shock wave that is 10,000 times greater than the smallest shock wave measurable on a seismograph will have a magnitude M on the Richter scale of

$$M = \log_{10} 10,000 = 4$$

Example 6   If an earthquake has a magnitude of $M = 5$ on the Richter scale, what can you say about the size of its shock wave?

SOLUTION   To answer this question, we put $M = 5$ into the formula $M = \log_{10} T$ to obtain

$$5 = \log_{10} T$$

Writing this expression in exponential form, we have

$$T = 10^5 = 100,000$$

We can say that an earthquake that measures 5 on the Richter scale has a shock wave 100,000 times greater than the smallest shock wave measurable on a seismograph.

From Example 6 and the discussion that preceded it, we find that an earthquake of magnitude 5 has a shock wave that is 10 times greater than an earthquake of magnitude 4, because 100,000 is 10 times 10,000.

Getting Ready for Class

After reading through the preceding section, respond in your own words and in complete sentences.

A. What is a logarithm?

B. What is the relationship between $y = 2^x$ and $y = \log_2 x$? How are their graphs related?

C. Will the graph of $y = \log_b x$ ever appear in the second or third quadrants? Explain why or why not.

D. Explain why $\log_2 0 = x$ has no solution for x.

Write each of the following expressions in logarithmic form.

1. $2^4 = 16$ **2.** $3^2 = 9$ **3.** $125 = 5^3$ **4.** $16 = 4^2$

5. $0.01 = 10^{-2}$ **6.** $0.001 = 10^{-3}$ **7.** $2^{-5} = \dfrac{1}{32}$ **8.** $4^{-2} = \dfrac{1}{16}$

9. $\left(\dfrac{1}{2}\right)^{-3} = 8$ **10.** $\left(\dfrac{1}{3}\right)^{-2} = 9$ **11.** $27 = 3^3$ **12.** $81 = 3^4$

Write each of the following expressions in exponential form.

13. $\log_{10} 100 = 2$ **14.** $\log_2 8 = 3$ **15.** $\log_2 64 = 6$

16. $\log_2 32 = 5$ **17.** $\log_8 1 = 0$ **18.** $\log_9 9 = 1$

19. $\log_{10} 0.001 = -3$ **20.** $\log_{10} 0.0001 = -4$ **21.** $\log_6 36 = 2$

22. $\log_7 49 = 2$ **23.** $\log_5 \dfrac{1}{25} = -2$ **24.** $\log_3 \dfrac{1}{81} = -4$

Solve each of the following equations for x.

25. $\log_3 x = 2$ **26.** $\log_4 x = 3$ **27.** $\log_5 x = -3$ **28.** $\log_2 x = -4$

29. $\log_2 16 = x$ **30.** $\log_3 27 = x$ **31.** $\log_8 2 = x$ **32.** $\log_{25} 5 = x$

33. $\log_x 4 = 2$ **34.** $\log_x 16 = 4$ **35.** $\log_x 5 = 3$ **36.** $\log_x 8 = 2$

37. $\log_5 25 = x$ **38.** $\log_5 x = -2$ **39.** $\log_x 36 = 2$ **40.** $\log_x \dfrac{1}{25} = 2$

41. $\log_8 4 = x$ **42.** $\log_{16} 8 = x$ **43.** $\log_9 \dfrac{1}{3} = x$ **44.** $\log_{27} 9 = x$

45. $\log_8 x = -2$ **46.** $\log_{36} \dfrac{1}{6} = x$

Sketch the graph of each of the following logarithmic equations.

47. $y = \log_3 x$ **48.** $y = \log_{1/2} x$ **49.** $y = \log_{1/3} x$ **50.** $y = \log_4 x$

51. $y = \log_5 x$ **52.** $y = \log_{1/5} x$ **53.** $y = \log_{10} x$ **54.** $y = \log_{1/4} x$

Each of the following graphs has an equation of the form $y = b^x$ or $y = \log_b x$. Find the equation for each graph.

55.

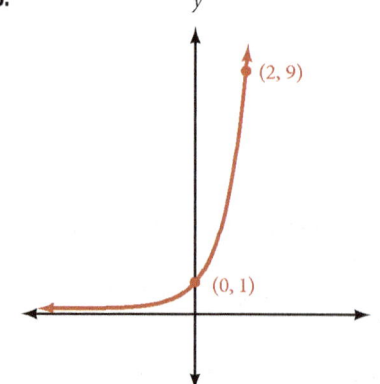

56.

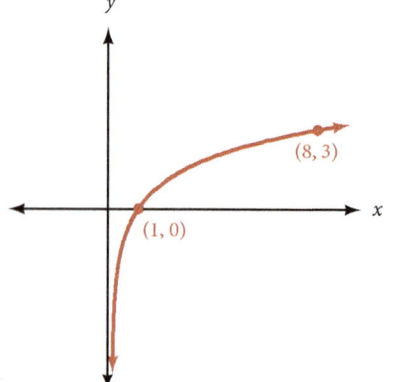

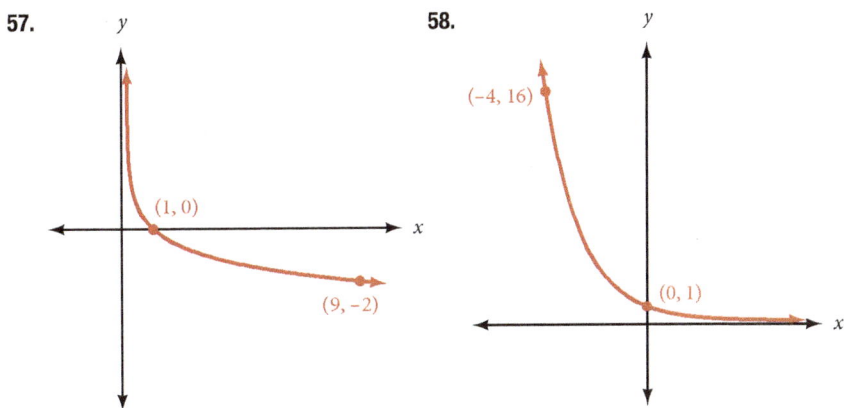

Simplify each of the following.

59. $\log_2 16$ **60.** $\log_3 9$ **61.** $\log_{25} 125$ **62.** $\log_9 27$

63. $\log_{10} 1{,}000$ **64.** $\log_{10} 10{,}000$ **65.** $\log_3 3$ **66.** $\log_4 4$

67. $\log_5 1$ **68.** $\log_{10} 1$ **69.** $\log_{17} 1$ **70.** $\log_4 8$

71. $\log_{16} 4$ **72.** $\log_{10} 0.0001$ **73.** $\log_{100} 1000$ **74.** $\log_{32} 16$

75. $\log_3 (\log_2 8)$ **76.** $\log_5 (\log_{32} 2)$ **77.** $\log_{1/2} (\log_3 81)$ **78.** $\log_9 (\log_8 2)$

79. $\log_3 (\log_6 6)$ **80.** $\log_5 (\log_3 3)$ **81.** $\log_4 [\log_2(\log_2 16)]$

82. $\log_4 [\log_3(\log_2 8)]$

Applying the Concepts

83. **Metric System** The metric system uses logical and systematic prefixes for multiplication. For instance, to multiply a unit by 100, the prefix "hecto" is applied, so a hectometer is equal to 100 meters. For each of the prefixes in the following table find the logarithm, base 10, of the multiplying factor.

Prefix	Multiplying Factor	$\log_{10}$ (Multiplying Factor)
Nano	0.000 000 001	
Micro	0.000 001	
Deci	0.1	
Giga	1,000,000,000	
Peta	1,000,000,000,000,000	

84. **Domain and Range** Use the graphs of $y = 2^x$ and $y = \log_2 x$ shown in Figure 1 of this section to find the domain and range for each function. Explain how the domain and range found for $y = 2^x$ relate to the domain and range found for $y = \log_2 x$.

85. **Magnitude of an Earthquake** Find the magnitude M of an earthquake with a shock wave that measures $T = 100$ on a seismograph.

86. Magnitude of an Earthquake Find the magnitude M of an earthquake with a shock wave that measures T = 100,000 on a seismograph.

87. Shock Wave If an earthquake has a magnitude of 8 on the Richter scale, how many times greater is its shock wave than the smallest shock wave measurable on a seismograph?

88. Shock Wave If the 1999 Colombia earthquake had a magnitude of 6 on the Richter scale, how many times greater was its shock wave than the smallest shock wave measurable on a seismograph?

Earthquake The table below categorizes earthquake by the magnitude and identifies the average annual occurrence.

Earthquakes		
Descriptor	Magnitude	Average Annual Occurrence
Great	≥8.0	1
Major	7–7.9	18
Strong	6–6.9	120
Moderate	5–5.9	800
Light	4–4.9	6,200
Minor	3–3.9	49,000
Very Minor	2–2.9	1,000 per day
Very Minor	1–1.9	8,000 per day

SOURCE: *USGS National Earthquake Information.*

89. What is the average number of earthquakes that occur per year when the number of times the associated shockwave is greater than the smallest measurable shockwave, T, is 1,000,000?

90. What is the average number of earthquakes that occur per year when T = 1,000,000 or greater?

Getting Ready for the Next Section

Simplify.

91. $8^{2/3}$

92. $27^{2/3}$

Solve.

93. $(x + 2)(x) = 2^3$

94. $(x + 3)(x) = 2^2$

95. $\dfrac{x - 2}{x + 1} = 9$

96. $\dfrac{x + 1}{x - 4} = 25$

Write in exponential form.

97. $\log_2 [(x + 2)(x)] = 3$

98. $\log_4 [x(x - 6)] = 2$

99. $\log_3 \left(\dfrac{x - 2}{x + 1}\right) = 4$

100. $\log_3 \left(\dfrac{x - 1}{x - 4}\right) = 2$

Properties of Logarithms

If we search for a definition of the word *decibel*, we find the following: A unit used to express relative difference in power or intensity, usually between two acoustic or electric signals, equal to ten times the common logarithm of the ratio of the two levels.

Decibels	Comparable to
10	A light whisper
20	Quiet conversation
30	Normal conversation
40	Light traffic
50	Typewriter, loud conversation
60	Noisy office
70	Normal traffic, quiet train
80	Rock music, subway
90	Heavy traffic, thunder
100	Jet plane at takeoff

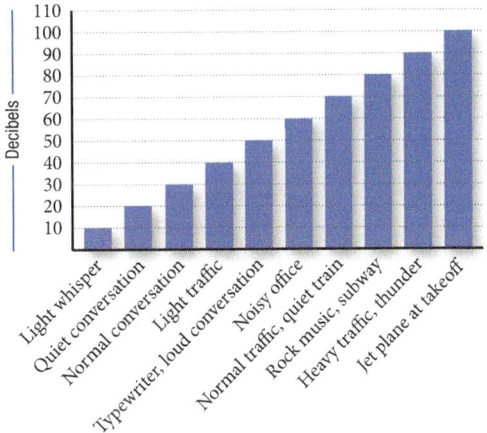

The precise definition for a *decibel* is

$$D = 10 \log_{10}\left(\frac{I}{I_0}\right)$$

where I is the intensity of the sound being measured, and I_0 is the intensity of the least audible sound. (Sound intensity is related to the amplitude of the sound wave that models the sound and is given in units of watts per meter^2.) In this section, we will see that the preceding formula can also be written as

$$D = 10(\log_{10} I - \log_{10} I_0)$$

The rules we use to rewrite expressions containing logarithms are called the *properties of logarithms*. There are three of them.

For the following three properties, x, y, and b are all positive real numbers, $b \neq 1$, and r is any real number.

⌠Δ≠Σ   *Property 1*

$$\log_b(xy) = \log_b x + \log_b y$$

In words: The logarithm of a **product** is the **sum** of the logarithms.

⌠Δ≠Σ   *Property 2*

$$\log_b\left(\frac{x}{y}\right) = \log_b x - \log_b y$$

In words: The logarithm of a **quotient** is the **difference** of the logarithms.

⌠Δ≠Σ   *Property 3*

$$\log_b x^r = r \log_b x$$

In words: The logarithm of a number raised to a **power** is the **product** of the power and the logarithm of the number.

Proof of Property 1   To prove Property 1, we simply apply the first identity for logarithms given in the preceding section:

$$b^{\log_b xy} = xy = (b^{\log_b x})(b^{\log_b y}) = b^{\log_b x + \log_b y}$$

Because the first and last expressions are equal and the bases are the same, the exponents $\log_b xy$ and $\log_b x + \log_b y$ must be equal. Therefore,

$$\log_b xy = \log_b x + \log_b y$$

The proofs of Properties 2 and 3 proceed in much the same manner, so we will omit them here. The examples that follow show how the three properties can be used.

Video Examples

Section 12.4

Example 1   Expand, using the properties of logarithms: $\log_5 \dfrac{3xy}{z}$

SOLUTION   Applying Property 2, we can write the quotient of $3xy$ and z in terms of a difference:

$$\log_5 \frac{3xy}{z} = \log_5 3xy - \log_5 z$$

Applying Property 1 to the product $3xy$, we write it in terms of addition:

$$\log_5 \frac{3xy}{z} = \log_5 3 + \log_5 x + \log_5 y - \log_5 z$$

Example 2   Expand, using the properties of logarithms:

$$\log_2 \frac{x^4}{\sqrt{y} \cdot z^3}$$

SOLUTION   We write $\sqrt{y}$ as $y^{1/2}$ and apply the properties:

$$\log_2 \frac{x^4}{\sqrt{y} \cdot z^3} = \log_2 \frac{x^4}{y^{1/2}z^3} \qquad \textcolor{green}{\sqrt{y} = y^{1/2}}$$

$$= \log_2 x^4 - \log_2(y^{1/2} \cdot z^3) \qquad \textcolor{green}{\text{Property 2}}$$

$$= \log_2 x^4 - (\log_2 y^{1/2} + \log_2 z^3) \qquad \textcolor{green}{\text{Property 1}}$$

$$= \log_2 x^4 - \log_2 y^{1/2} - \log_2 z^3 \qquad \textit{Remove parentheses and distribute} - 1$$

$$= 4 \log_2 x - \frac{1}{2} \log_2 y - 3 \log_2 z \qquad \textit{Property 3}$$

We can also use the three properties to write an expression in expanded form as just one logarithm.

Example 3   Write as a single logarithm:

$$2 \log_{10} a + 3 \log_{10} b - \frac{1}{3} \log_{10} c$$

SOLUTION   We begin by applying Property 3:

$$2 \log_{10} a + 3 \log_{10} b - \frac{1}{3} \log_{10} c = \log_{10} a^2 + \log_{10} b^3 - \log_{10} c^{1/3} \qquad \textit{Property 3}$$

$$= \log_{10} (a^2 \cdot b^3) - \log_{10} c^{1/3} \qquad \textit{Property 1}$$

$$= \log_{10} \frac{a^2 b^3}{c^{1/3}} \qquad \textit{Property 2}$$

$$= \log_{10} \frac{a^2 b^3}{\sqrt[3]{c}} \qquad c^{1/3} = \sqrt[3]{c}$$

The properties of logarithms along with the definition of logarithms are useful in solving equations that involve logarithms.

Example 4   Solve for x: $\log_2(x + 2) + \log_2 x = 3$

SOLUTION   Applying Property 1 to the left side of the equation allows us to write it as a single logarithm:

$$\log_2(x + 2) + \log_2 x = 3$$

$$\log_2[(x + 2)(x)] = 3$$

The last line can be written in exponential form using the definition of logarithms:

$$(x + 2)(x) = 2^3$$

Solve as usual:

$$x^2 + 2x = 8$$

$$x^2 + 2x - 8 = 0$$

$$(x + 4)(x - 2) = 0$$

$$x + 4 = 0 \quad \text{or} \quad x - 2 = 0$$

$$x = -4 \quad \text{or} \quad x = 2$$

In the previous section, we noted the fact that x in the expression $y = \log_b x$ cannot be a negative number. Because substitution of $x = -4$ into the original equation gives

$$\log_2(-2) + \log_2(-4) = 3$$

which contains logarithms of negative numbers, we cannot use -4 as a solution. The solution set is 2.

Getting Ready for Class

After reading through the preceding section, respond in your own words and in complete sentences.

A. Explain why the following statement is false: "The logarithm of a product is the product of the logarithms."

B. Explain why the following statement is false: "The logarithm of a quotient is the quotient of the logarithms."

C. Explain the difference between $\log_b m + \log_b n$ and $\log_b(m + n)$. Are they equivalent?

D. Explain the difference between $\log_b(mn)$ and $(\log_b m)(\log_b n)$ Are they equivalent?

Problem Set 12.4

Use the three properties of logarithms given in this section to expand each expression as much as possible.

1. $\log_3 4x$

2. $\log_2 5x$

3. $\log_6 \dfrac{5}{x}$

4. $\log_3 \dfrac{x}{5}$

5. $\log_2 y^5$

6. $\log_7 y^3$

7. $\log_9 \sqrt[3]{z}$

8. $\log_8 \sqrt{z}$

9. $\log_6 x^2 y^4$

10. $\log_{10} x^2 y^4$

11. $\log_5 \sqrt{x} \cdot y^4$

12. $\log_8 \sqrt[3]{xy^6}$

13. $\log_b \dfrac{xy}{z}$

14. $\log_b \dfrac{3x}{y}$

15. $\log_{10} \dfrac{4}{xy}$

16. $\log_{10} \dfrac{5}{4y}$

17. $\log_{10} \dfrac{x^2 y}{\sqrt{z}}$

18. $\log_{10} \dfrac{\sqrt{x} \cdot y}{z^3}$

19. $\log_{10} \dfrac{x^3 \sqrt{y}}{z^4}$

20. $\log_{10} \dfrac{x^4 \sqrt[3]{y}}{\sqrt{z}}$

21. $\log_b \sqrt[3]{\dfrac{x^2 y}{z^4}}$

22. $\log_b \sqrt[4]{\dfrac{x^4 y^3}{z^5}}$

23. $\log_3 \sqrt[3]{\dfrac{x^2 y}{z^6}}$

24. $\log_8 \sqrt[4]{\dfrac{x^5 y^6}{z^3}}$

25. $\log_a \dfrac{4x^5}{9a^2}$

26. $\log_b \dfrac{16b^2}{25y^3}$

Write each expression as a single logarithm.

27. $\log_b x + \log_b z$

28. $\log_b x - \log_b z$

29. $2 \log_3 x - 3 \log_3 y$

30. $4 \log_2 x + 5 \log_2 y$

31. $\dfrac{1}{2} \log_{10} x + \dfrac{1}{3} \log_{10} y$

32. $\dfrac{1}{3} \log_{10} x - \dfrac{1}{4} \log_{10} y$

33. $3 \log_2 x + \dfrac{1}{2} \log_2 y - \log_2 z$

34. $2 \log_3 x + 3 \log_3 y - \log_3 z$

35. $\dfrac{1}{2} \log_2 x - 3 \log_2 y - 4 \log_2 z$

36. $3 \log_{10} x - \log_{10} y - \log_{10} z$

37. $\dfrac{3}{2} \log_{10} x - \dfrac{3}{4} \log_{10} y - \dfrac{4}{5} \log_{10} z$

38. $3 \log_{10} x - \dfrac{4}{3} \log_{10} y - 5 \log_{10} z$

39. $\dfrac{1}{2} \log_5 x + \dfrac{2}{3} \log_5 y - 4 \log_5 z$

40. $\dfrac{1}{4} \log_7 x + 5 \log_7 y - \dfrac{1}{3} \log_7 z$

41. $\log_3(x^2 - 16) - 2 \log_3(x + 4)$

42. $\log_4(x^2 - x - 6) - \log_4(x^2 - 9)$

Solve each of the following equations.

43. $\log_2 x + \log_2 3 = 1$

44. $\log_3 x + \log_3 3 = 1$

45. $\log_3 x - \log_3 2 = 2$

46. $\log_3 x + \log_3 2 = 2$

47. $\log_3 x + \log_3(x - 2) = 1$

48. $\log_6 x + \log_6(x - 1) = 1$

49. $\log_3(x + 3) - \log_3(x - 1) = 1$

50. $\log_4(x - 2) - \log_4(x + 1) = 1$

51. $\log_2 x + \log_2(x - 2) = 3$

52. $\log_4 x + \log_4(x + 6) = 2$

53. $\log_8 x + \log_8(x - 3) = \dfrac{2}{3}$

54. $\log_{27} x + \log_{27}(x + 8) = \dfrac{2}{3}$

55. $\log_3(x + 2) - \log_3 x = 1$

56. $\log_2(x + 3) - \log_2(x - 3) = 2$

57. $\log_2(x + 1) + \log_2(x + 2) = 1$

58. $\log_3 x + \log_3(x + 6) = 3$

59. $\log_9 \sqrt{x} + \log_9 \sqrt{2x + 3} = \dfrac{1}{2}$

60. $\log_8 \sqrt{x} + \log_8 \sqrt{5x + 2} = \dfrac{2}{3}$

61. $4 \log_3 x - \log_3 x^2 = 6$

62. $9 \log_4 x - \log_4 x^3 = 12$

63. $\log_5 \sqrt{x} + \log_5 \sqrt{6x + 5} = 1$

64. $\log_2 \sqrt{x} + \log_2 \sqrt{6x + 5} = 1$

Applying the Concepts

65. Decibel Formula Use the properties of logarithms to rewrite the decibel formula $D = 10 \log_{10}\left(\dfrac{I}{I_0}\right)$ as

$$D = 10(\log_{10} I - \log_{10} I_0).$$

66. Decibel Formula In the decibel formula $D = 10 \log_{10}\left(\dfrac{I}{I_0}\right)$, the threshold of hearing, I_0, is

$$I_0 = 10^{-12} \text{ watts/meter}^2$$

Substitute 10^{-12} for I_0 in the decibel formula, then show that it simplifies to

$$D = 10(\log_{10} I + 12)$$

67. **Finding Logarithms** If $\log_{10} 8 = 0.903$ and $\log_{10} 5 = 0.699$, find the following without using a calculator.

   a. $\log_{10} 40$ **b.** $\log_{10} 320$ **c.** $\log_{10} 1,600$

68. **Matching** Match each expression in the first column with an equivalent expression in the second column:

   a. $\log_2(ab)$ **i.** b

   b. $\log_2\left(\dfrac{a}{b}\right)$ **ii.** 2

   c. $\log_5 a^b$ **iii.** $\log_2 a + \log_2 b$

   d. $\log_a b^a$ **iv.** $\log_2 a - \log_2 b$

   e. $\log_a a^b$ **v.** $a \log_a b$

   f. $\log_3 9$ **vi.** $b \log_5 a$

69. **Henderson–Hasselbalch Formula** Doctors use the Henderson–Hasselbalch formula to calculate the pH of a person's blood. pH is a measure of the acidity and/or the alkalinity of a solution. This formula is represented as

$$\text{pH} = 6.1 + \log_{10}\left(\frac{x}{y}\right)$$

where x is the base concentration and y is the acidic concentration. Rewrite the Henderson–Hasselbalch formula so that the logarithm of a quotient is not involved.

70. **Henderson–Hasselbalch Formula** Refer to the information in the preceding problem about the Henderson–Hasselbalch formula. If most people have a blood pH of 7.4, use the Henderson–Hasselbalch formula to find the ratio of $\frac{x}{y}$ for an average person.

71. **Food Processing** The formula $M = 0.21(\log_{10} a - \log_{10} b)$ is used in the food processing industry to find the number of minutes M of heat processing a certain food should undergo at 250°F to reduce the probability of survival of *Clostridium botulinum* spores. The letter a represents the number of spores per can before heating, and b represents the number of spores per can after heating. Find M if $a = 1$ and $b = 10^{-12}$. Then find M using the same values for a and b in the formula $M = 0.21 \log_{10} \frac{a}{b}$.

72. **Acoustic Powers** The formula $N = \log_{10} \frac{P_1}{P_2}$ is used in radio electronics to find the ratio of the acoustic powers of two electric circuits in terms of their electric powers. Find N if P_1 is 100 and P_2 is 1. Then use the same two values of P_1 and P_2 to find N in the formula $N = \log_{10} P_1 - \log_{10} P_2$.

Getting Ready for the Next Section

Simplify.

73. 5^0

74. 4^1

75. $\log_3 3$

76. $\log_5 5$

77. $\log_b b^4$

78. $\log_a a^k$

Use a calculator to find each of the following. Write your answer in scientific notation with the first number in each answer rounded to the nearest tenth.

79. $10^{-5.6}$

80. $10^{-4.1}$

Divide and round to the nearest whole number

81. $\dfrac{2.00 \times 10^8}{3.96 \times 10^6}$

82. $\dfrac{3.25 \times 10^{12}}{1.72 \times 10^{10}}$

Common Logarithms and Natural Logarithms

Acid rain was first discovered in the 1960s by Gene Likens and his research team who studied the damage caused by acid rain to Hubbard Brook in New Hampshire. Acid rain is rain with a pH of 5.6 and below. As you will see as you work your way through this section, pH is defined in terms of common logarithms — one of the topics we present in this section. So, when you are finished with this section, you will have a more detailed knowledge of pH and acid rain.

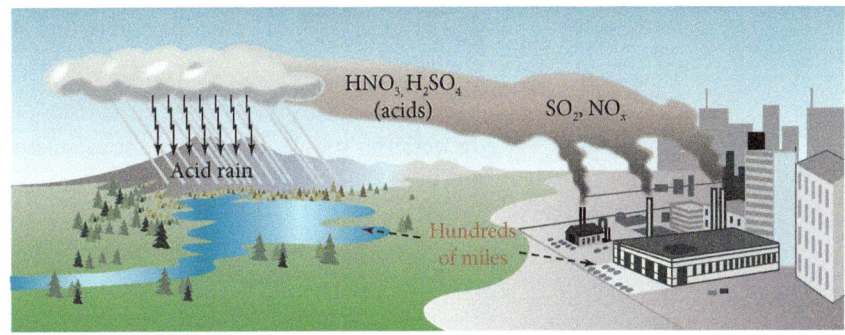

Two kinds of logarithms occur more frequently than other logarithms. Logarithms with a base of 10 are very common because our number system is a base-10 number system. For this reason, we call base-10 logarithms *common logarithms*.

> **(dĕf′   *common logarithms***
>
> A *common logarithm* is a logarithm with a base of 10. Because common logarithms are used so frequently, it is customary, in order to save time, to omit notating the base. That is,
>
> $$\log_{10} x = \log x$$
>
> When the base is not shown, it is assumed to be 10.

Common Logarithms

Common logarithms of powers of 10 are simple to evaluate. We need only recognize that $\log 10 = \log_{10} 10 = 1$ and apply the third property of logarithms: $\log_b x^r = r \log_b x$.

$$\log 1{,}000 = \log 10^3 \ = \ 3 \log 10 = \ 3(1) = \ 3$$
$$\log 100 \ = \log 10^2 \ = \ 2 \log 10 = \ 2(1) = \ 2$$
$$\log 10 \ \ = \log 10^1 \ = \ 1 \log 10 = \ 1(1) = \ 1$$
$$\log 1 \ \ \ = \log 10^0 \ = \ 0 \log 10 = \ 0(1) = \ 0$$
$$\log 0.1 \ \ = \log 10^{-1} = -1 \log 10 = -1(1) = -1$$
$$\log 0.01 \ \ = \log 10^{-2} = -2 \log 10 = -2(1) = -2$$
$$\log 0.001 = \log 10^{-3} = -3 \log 10 = -3(1) = -3$$

To find common logarithms of numbers that are not powers of 10, we use a calculator with a log key.

Check the following logarithms to be sure you know how to use your calculator. (These answers have been rounded to the nearest ten-thousandth.)

$$\log 7.02 \approx 0.8463$$

$$\log 1.39 \approx 0.1430$$

$$\log 6.00 \approx 0.7782$$

$$\log 9.99 \approx 0.9996$$

Video Examples

Section 12.5

Example 1   Use a calculator to find log 2,760.

SOLUTION

$$\log 2{,}760 \approx 3.4409$$

To work this problem on a scientific calculator, we simply enter the number 2,760 and press the key labeled $\log$ . On a graphing calculator we press the $\log$ key first, then 2,760.

The 3 in the answer is called the *characteristic*, and the decimal part of the logarithm is called the *mantissa*.

Example 2   Find log 0.0391.

SOLUTION $\log 0.0391 \approx -1.4078$

Example 3   Find log 0.00523.

SOLUTION $\log 0.00523 \approx -2.2815$

Example 4   Find x if $\log x = 3.8774$.

SOLUTION   We are looking for the number whose logarithm is 3.8774. On a scientific calculator, we enter 3.8774 and press the key labeled 10^x. On a graphing calculator we press 10^x first, then 3.8774. The result is 7,540 to four significant digits. Here's why:

If $\log x = 3.8774$

then $x = 10^{3.8774}$

$$\approx 7{,}540$$

The number 7,540 is called the *antilogarithm* or just *antilog* of 3.8774. That is, 7,540 is the number whose logarithm is 3.8774.

Example 5   Find x if $\log x = -2.4179$.

SOLUTION   Using the 10^x key, the result is 0.00382.

If $\log x = -2.4179$

then $x = 10^{-2.4179}$

$$\approx 0.00382$$

The antilog of -2.4179 is 0.00382. That is, the logarithm of 0.00382 is -2.4179.

In Section 12.3, we found that the magnitude M of an earthquake that produces a shock wave T times larger than the smallest shock wave that can be measured on a seismograph is given by the formula

$$M = \log_{10} T$$

We can rewrite this formula using our shorthand notation for common logarithms as

$$M = \log T$$

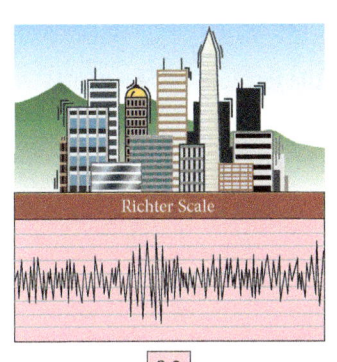
8.3

Example 6   The San Francisco earthquake of 1906 is estimated to have measured 8.3 on the Richter scale. The San Fernando earthquake of 1971 measured 6.6 on the Richter scale. Find T for each earthquake, and then give some indication of how much stronger the 1906 earthquake was than the 1971 earthquake.

SOLUTION   For the 1906 earthquake:

If $\log T = 8.3$, then $T = 2.00 \times 10^8$.

For the 1971 earthquake:

If $\log T = 6.6$, then $T = 3.98 \times 10^6$.

Dividing the two values of T and rounding our answer to the nearest whole number, we have

$$\frac{2.00 \times 10^8}{3.98 \times 10^6} \approx 50$$

The shock wave for the 1906 earthquake was approximately 50 times larger than the shock wave for the 1971 earthquake.

In chemistry, the pH of a solution is the measure of the acidity of the solution. The definition for pH involves common logarithms. Here it is:

$$\text{pH} = -\log[\text{H}^+]$$

where $[\text{H}^+]$ is the concentration of the hydrogen ion in moles per liter. The range for pH is from 0 to 14. Pure water, a neutral solution, has a pH of 7. An acidic solution, such as vinegar, will have a pH less than 7, and an alkaline solution, such as ammonia, has a pH above 7.

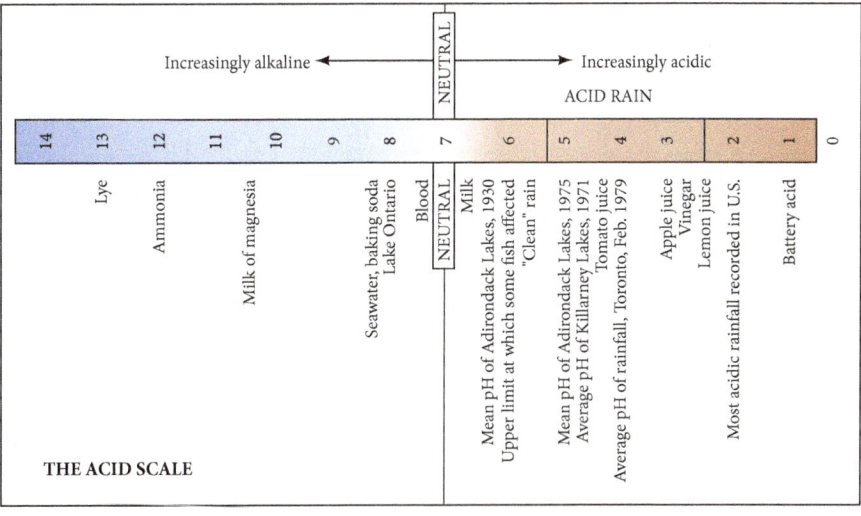

Example 7   Normal rainwater has a pH of 5.6. What is the concentration of the hydrogen ion in normal rainwater?

SOLUTION   Substituting 5.6 for pH in the formula $pH = -\log[H^+]$, we have

$$5.6 = -\log[H^+] \qquad \text{\textit{Substitution}}$$
$$\log[H^+] = -5.6 \qquad \text{\textit{Isolate the logarithm}}$$
$$[H^+] = 10^{-5.6} \qquad \text{\textit{Write in exponential form}}$$
$$\approx 2.5 \times 10^{-6} \text{ moles per liter} \qquad \text{\textit{Answer in scientific notation}}$$

Example 8   The concentration of the hydrogen ion in a sample of acid rain known to kill fish is 3.2×10^{-5} mole per liter. Find the pH of this acid rain to the nearest tenth.

SOLUTION   Substituting 3.2×10^{-5} for $[H^+]$ in the formula $pH = -\log[H^+]$, we have

$$pH = -\log[3.2 \times 10^{-5}] \qquad \text{\textit{Substitution}}$$
$$\approx -(-4.5) \qquad \text{\textit{Evaluate the logarithm}}$$
$$\approx 4.5 \qquad \text{\textit{Simplify}}$$

Natural Logarithms

> **(dĕf'   *natural logarithms***
>
> A *natural logarithm* is a logarithm with a base of e. The natural logarithm of x is denoted by $\ln x$. That is,
>
> $$\ln x = \log_e x$$

We can assume that all our properties of exponents and logarithms hold for expressions with a base of e, because e is a real number. Here are some examples intended to make you more familiar with the number e and natural logarithms.

Example 9   Simplify each of the following expressions.

a. $e^0 = 1$

b. $e^1 = e$

c. $\ln e = 1$ *In exponential form, $e^1 = e$*

d. $\ln 1 = 0$ *In exponential form, $e^0 = 1$*

e. $\ln e^3 = 3$

f. $\ln e^{-4} = -4$

g. $\ln e^t = t$

Example 10 Use the properties of logarithms to expand the expression ln Ae^{5t}.

SOLUTION Because the properties of logarithms hold for natural logarithms, we have

$$\ln Ae^{5t} = \ln A + \ln e^{5t}$$

$$= \ln A + 5t \ln e$$

$$= \ln A + 5t \qquad \text{Because } \ln e = 1$$

Example 11 If ln 2 = 0.6931 and ln 3 = 1.0986, find

a. ln 6   **b.** ln 0.5   **c.** ln 8

SOLUTION

a. Because $6 = 2 \cdot 3$, we have

$$\ln 6 = \ln 2 \cdot 3$$

$$= \ln 2 + \ln 3$$

$$= 0.6931 + 1.0986$$

$$= 1.7917$$

b. Writing 0.5 as $\frac{1}{2}$ and applying Property 2 for logarithms gives us

$$\ln 0.5 = \ln \frac{1}{2}$$

$$= \ln 1 - \ln 2$$

$$= 0 - 0.6931$$

$$= -0.6931$$

c. Writing 8 as 2^3 and applying Property 3 for logarithms, we have

$$\ln 8 = \ln 2^3$$

$$= 3 \ln 2$$

$$= 3(0.6931)$$

$$= 2.0793$$

Getting Ready for Class

After reading through the preceding section, respond in your own words and in complete sentences.

A. What is a common logarithm?
B. What is a natural logarithm?
C. Is e a rational number? Explain.
D. Find ln e, and explain how you arrived at your answer.

Problem Set 12.5

Find the following logarithms.

1. $\log 378$ **2.** $\log 426$ **3.** $\log 37.8$ **4.** $\log 42{,}600$

5. $\log 3{,}780$ **6.** $\log 0.4260$ **7.** $\log 0.0378$ **8.** $\log 0.0426$

9. $\log 37{,}800$ **10.** $\log 4{,}900$ **11.** $\log 600$ **12.** $\log 900$

13. $\log 2{,}010$ **14.** $\log 10{,}200$ **15.** $\log 0.00971$ **16.** $\log 0.0312$

17. $\log 0.0314$ **18.** $\log 0.00052$ **19.** $\log 0.399$ **20.** $\log 0.111$

Find x in the following equations.

21. $\log x = 2.8802$ **22.** $\log x = 4.8802$ **23.** $\log x = -2.1198$

24. $\log x = -3.1198$ **25.** $\log x = 3.1553$ **26.** $\log x = 5.5911$

27. $\log x = -5.3497$ **28.** $\log x = -1.5670$ **29.** $\log x = -7.0372$

30. $\log x = -4.2000$ **31.** $\log x = 10$ **32.** $\log x = -1$

33. $\log x = -10$ **34.** $\log x = 1$ **35.** $\log x = 20$

36. $\log x = -20$ **37.** $\log x = -2$ **38.** $\log x = 4$

39. $\log x = \log_2 8$ **40.** $\log x = \log_3 9$ **41.** $\ln x = -1$

42. $\ln x = 4$ **43.** $\log x = 2 \log 5$ **44.** $\log x = -\log 4$

45. $\ln x = -3 \ln 2$ **46.** $\ln x = 5 \ln 3$

Simplify each of the following expressions.

47. $\ln e$

48. $\ln 1$

49. $\ln e^5$

50. $\ln e^{-3}$

51. $\ln e^x$

52. $\ln e^y$

53. $\log 10,000$

54. $\log 0.001$

55. $\ln \dfrac{1}{e^3}$

56. $\ln \sqrt{e}$

57. $\log \sqrt{1000}$

58. $\log \sqrt[3]{10,000}$

Use the properties of logarithms to expand each of the following expressions.

59. $\ln 10e^{3t}$

60. $\ln 10e^{4t}$

61. $\ln Ae^{-2t}$

62. $\ln Ae^{-3t}$

63. $\log [100(1.01)^{3t}]$

64. $\log \left[\dfrac{1}{10} (1.5)^{t+2} \right]$

65. $\ln (Pe^{rt})$

66. $\ln \left(\dfrac{1}{2} e^{-kt} \right)$

67. $-\log (4.2 \times 10^{-3})$

68. $-\log (5.7 \times 10^{-10})$

If $\ln 2 = 0.6931$, $\ln 3 = 1.0986$, and $\ln 5 = 1.6094$, find each of the following.

69. $\ln 15$

70. $\ln 10$

71. $\ln \dfrac{1}{3}$

72. $\ln \dfrac{1}{5}$

73. $\ln 9$

74. $\ln 25$

75. $\ln 16$

76. $\ln 81$

Applying the Concepts

77. Atomic Bomb Tests The formula for determining the magnitude, M, of an earthquake on the Richter Scale is $M = \log_{10} T$, where T is the number of times the shockwave is greater than the smallest measurable shockwave. The Bikini Atoll in the Pacific Ocean was used as a location for atomic bomb tests by the United States government in the 1950s. One such test resulted in an earthquake measurement of 5.0 on the Richter scale. Compare the 1906 San Francisco earthquake of estimated magnitude 8.3 on the Richter scale to this atomic bomb test. Use the shock wave T for purposes of comparison.

78. Atomic Bomb Tests Today's nuclear weapons are 1,000 times more powerful than the atomic bombs tested in the Bikini Atoll mentioned in Problem 77. Use the shock wave T to determine the Richter scale measurement of a nuclear test today.

79. Getting Close to *e* Use a calculator to complete the following table.

x	$(1 + x)^{1/x}$
1	
0.5	
0.1	
0.01	
0.001	
0.0001	
0.00001	

What number does the expression $(1 + x)^{1/x}$ seem to approach as x gets closer and closer to zero?

80. Getting Close to *e* Use a calculator to complete the following table.

x	$\left(1 + \frac{1}{x}\right)^x$
1	
10	
50	
100	
500	
1,000	
10,000	
1,000,000	

What number does the expression $\left(1 + \frac{1}{x}\right)^x$ seem to approach as x gets larger and larger?

81. University Enrollment The percentage of students enrolled in a university who are between the ages of 25 and 34 can be modeled by the formula $s = 5 \ln x$, where s is the percentage of students and x is the number of years since 1989. Predict the year in which approximately 15% of students enrolled in a university are between the ages of 25 and 34.

82. Memory A class of students take a test on the mathematics concept of solving quadratic equations. That class agrees to take a similar form of the test each month for the next 6 months to test their memory of the topic since instruction. The function of the average score earned each month on the test is $m(x) = 75 - 5 \ln(x + 1)$, where x represents time in months. Complete the table to indicate the average score earned by the class at each month.

Time, x	Score, m
0	
1	
2	
3	
4	
5	
6	

Use the following figure to solve Problems 83 – 86.

pH Scale

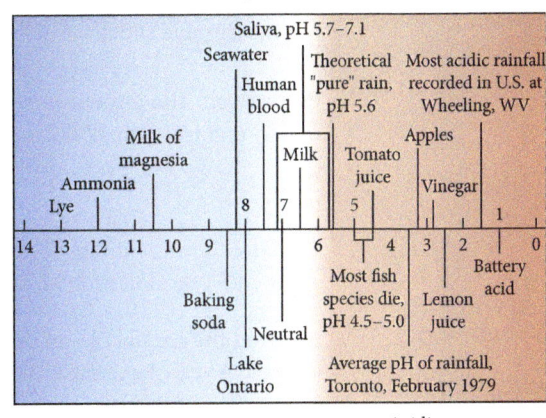

83. **pH** Find the pH of orange juice if the concentration of the hydrogen ion in the juice is $[H^+] = 6.50 \times 10^{-4}$.

84. **pH** Find the pH of milk if the concentration of the hydrogen ions in milk is $[H^+] = 1.88 \times 10^{-6}$.

85. **pH** Find the concentration of hydrogen ions in a glass of wine if the pH is 4.75.

86. **pH** Find the concentration of hydrogen ions in a bottle of vinegar if the pH is 5.75.

The Richter Scale Find the relative size T of the shock wave of earthquakes with the following magnitudes, as measured on the Richter scale.

87. 5.5   88. 6.6   89. 8.3   90. 8.7

91. **Earthquake** The chart below is a partial listing of earthquakes that were recorded in Canada during one year. Complete the chart by computing the magnitude on the Richter Scale, M, or the number of times the associated shockwave is larger than the smallest measurable shockwave, T.

Location	Date	Magnitude M	Shockwave T
Moresby Island	Jan. 23	4.0	
Vancouver Island	Apr. 30		1.99×10^5
Quebec City	June 29	3.2	
Mould Bay	Nov. 13	5.2	
St. Lawrence	Dec. 14		5.01×10^3

SOURCE: *National Resources Canada, National Earthquake Hazards Program.*

92. Earthquake On January 6, 2001, an earthquake with a magnitude of 7.7 on the Richter Scale hit southern India (*National Earthquake Information Center*). By what factor was this earthquake's shockwave greater than the smallest measurable shockwave?

Depreciation The annual rate of depreciation r on a car that is purchased for P dollars and is worth W dollars t years later can be found from the formula.

$$\log(1 - r) = \frac{1}{t} \log \frac{W}{P}$$

93. Find the annual rate of depreciation on a car that is purchased for \$9,000 and sold 5 years later for \$4,500.

94. Find the annual rate of depreciation on a car that is purchased for \$9,000 and sold 4 years later for \$3,000.

Two cars depreciate in value according to the following depreciation tables. In each case, find the annual rate of depreciation.

95.

Age in Years	Value in Dollars
New	7,550
5	5,750

96.

Age in Years	Value in Dollars
New	7,550
3	5,750

Getting Ready for the Next Section

Solve.

97. $5(2x + 1) = 12$

98. $4(3x - 2) = 21$

Use a calculator to evaluate, give answers to 4 decimal places.

99. $\dfrac{100,000}{32,000}$

100. $\dfrac{1.4982}{6.5681} + 3$

101. $\dfrac{1}{2}\left(\dfrac{-0.6931}{1.4289} + 3\right)$

102. $1 + \dfrac{0.04}{52}$

Use the power rule to rewrite the following logarithms.

103. $\log 1.05^t$

104. $\log 1.033^t$

Use identities to simplify.

105. $\ln e^{0.05t}$

106. $\ln e^{-0.000121t}$

Exponential Equations and Change of Base

For items involved in exponential growth, the time it takes for a quantity to double is called the *doubling time*. For example, if you invest $5,000 in an account that pays 5% annual interest, compounded quarterly, you may want to know how long it will take for your money to double in value. You can find this doubling time if you can solve the equation

$$10{,}000 = 5{,}000 \, (1.0125)^{4t}$$

As you will see as you progress through this section, logarithms are the key to solving equations of this type.

Logarithms are very important in solving equations in which the variable appears as an exponent. The equation

$$5^x = 12$$

is an example of one such equation. Equations of this form are called *exponential equations*. Because the quantities 5^x and 12 are equal, so are their common logarithms. We begin our solution by taking the logarithm of both sides:

$$\log 5^x = \log 12$$

We now apply Property 3 for logarithms, $\log x^r = r \log x$, to turn x from an exponent into a coefficient:

$$x \log 5 = \log 12$$

Dividing both sides by $\log 5$ gives us

$$x = \frac{\log 12}{\log 5}$$

If we want a decimal approximation to the solution, we can find $\log 12$ and $\log 5$ on a calculator and divide:

$$x \approx \frac{1.0792}{0.6990}$$

$$\approx 1.5439$$

The complete problem looks like this:

$$5^x = 12$$

$$\log 5^x = \log 12$$

$$x \log 5 = \log 12$$

$$x = \frac{\log 12}{\log 5}$$

$$\approx \frac{1.0792}{0.6990}$$

$$\approx 1.5439$$

Here is another example of solving an exponential equation using logarithms.

Video Examples

Section 12.6

Example 1   Solve for x: $25^{2x+1} = 15$

SOLUTION   Taking the logarithm of both sides and then writing the exponent $(2x + 1)$ as a coefficient, we proceed as follows:

$$25^{2x+1} = 15$$

$$\log 25^{2x+1} = \log 15 \qquad \text{Take the log of both sides}$$

$$(2x + 1)\log 25 = \log 15 \qquad \text{Property 3}$$

$$2x + 1 = \frac{\log 15}{\log 25} \qquad \text{Divide by log 25}$$

$$2x = \frac{\log 15}{\log 25} - 1 \qquad \text{Add } -1 \text{ to both sides}$$

$$x = \frac{1}{2}\left(\frac{\log 15}{\log 25} - 1\right) \qquad \text{Multiply both sides by } \tfrac{1}{2}$$

Using a calculator, we can write a decimal approximation to the answer:

$$x \approx \frac{1}{2}\left(\frac{1.1761}{1.3979} - 1\right)$$

$$\approx \frac{1}{2}(0.8413 - 1)$$

$$\approx \frac{1}{2}(-0.1587)$$

$$\approx -0.079$$

If you invest P dollars in an account with an annual interest rate r that is compounded n times a year, then t years later the amount of money in that account will be

$$A = P\left(1 + \frac{r}{n}\right)^{nt}$$

Example 2   How long does it take for \$5,000 to double if it is deposited in an account that yields 5% interest compounded once a year?

SOLUTION   Substituting $P = 5{,}000$, $r = 0.05$, $n = 1$, and $A = 10{,}000$ into our formula, we have

$$10{,}000 = 5{,}000(1 + 0.05)^t$$

$$10{,}000 = 5{,}000(1.05)^t$$

$$2 = (1.05)^t \qquad \text{Divide by 5,000}$$

This is an exponential equation. We solve by taking the logarithm of both sides:

$$\log 2 = \log(1.05)^t$$

$$= t \log 1.05$$

Dividing both sides by $\log 1.05$, we have

$$t = \frac{\log 2}{\log 1.05}$$

$$\approx 14.2$$

It takes a little over 14 years for \$5,000 to double if it earns 5% interest per year, compounded once a year.

There is a fourth property of logarithms we have not yet considered. This last property allows us to change from one base to another and is therefore called the *change-of-base property.*

> ⎧△≠∑⎫   **Property 4 (Change of Base)**
>
> If a and b are both positive numbers other than 1, and if $x > 0$, then
>
> $$\log_a x = \frac{\log_b x}{\log_b a}$$
>
>   ↑   ↑
>   Base a   Base b

The logarithm on the left side has a base of a, and both logarithms on the right side have a base of b. This allows us to change from base a to any other base b that is a positive number other than 1. Here is a proof of Property 4 for logarithms.

Proof   We begin by writing the identity

$$a^{\log_a x} = x$$

Taking the logarithm base b of both sides and writing the exponent $\log_a x$ as a coefficient, we have

$$\log_b a^{\log_a x} = \log_b x$$

$$\log_a x \log_b a = \log_b x$$

Dividing both sides by $\log_b a$, we have the desired result:

$$\frac{\log_a x \log_b a}{\log_b a} = \frac{\log_b x}{\log_b a}$$

$$\log_a x = \frac{\log_b x}{\log_b a}$$

We can use this property to find logarithms we could not otherwise compute on our calculators — that is, logarithms with bases other than 10 or e. The next example illustrates the use of this property.

■ **Example 3**   Find $\log_8 24$.

SOLUTION   Because we do not have base-8 logarithms on our calculators, we can change this expression to an equivalent expression that contains only base-10 logarithms:

$$\log_8 24 = \frac{\log 24}{\log 8} \qquad \text{Property 4}$$

Don't be confused. We did not just drop the base, we changed to base 10. We could have written the last line like this:

$$\log_8 24 = \frac{\log_{10} 24}{\log_{10} 8}$$

From our calculators, we write

$$\log_8 24 \approx \frac{1.3802}{0.9031}$$

$$\approx 1.5283$$

■

Application

Example 4   Suppose that the population in a small city is 32,000 in the beginning of 2010 and that the city council assumes that the population size t years later can be estimated by the equation

$$P = 32,000e^{0.05t}$$

Approximately when will the city have a population of 50,000?

SOLUTION   We substitute 50,000 for P in the equation and solve for t:

$$50,000 = 32,000e^{0.05t}$$

$$1.5625 = e^{0.05t} \qquad \frac{50,000}{32,000} = 1.5625$$

To solve this equation for t, we can take the natural logarithm of each side:

$$\ln 1.5625 = \ln e^{0.05t}$$

$$= 0.05t \ln e \qquad \text{Property 3 for logarithms}$$

$$= 0.05t \qquad \text{Because } \ln e = 1$$

$$t = \frac{\ln 1.5625}{0.05} \qquad \text{Divide each side by 0.05}$$

$$\approx 8.93 \text{ years}$$

We can estimate that the population will reach 50,000 toward the end of 2018. ■

Using Technology

We can evaluate many logarithmic expressions on a graphing calculator by using the fact that logarithmic functions and exponential functions are inverses.

Example 5   Evaluate the logarithmic expression $\log_3 7$ from the graph of an exponential function.

SOLUTION   First, we let $\log_3 7 = x$. Next, we write this expression in exponential form as $3^x = 7$. We can solve this equation graphically by finding the intersection of the graphs $Y_1 = 3^x$ and $Y_2 = 7$, as shown in Figure 1.

Using the calculator, we find the two graphs intersect at $(1.77, 7)$. Therefore, $\log_3 7 = 1.77$ to the nearest hundredth. We can check our work by evaluating the expression $3^{1.77}$ on our calculator with the key strokes

$$3 \ \wedge \ 1.77 \ \text{ENTER}$$

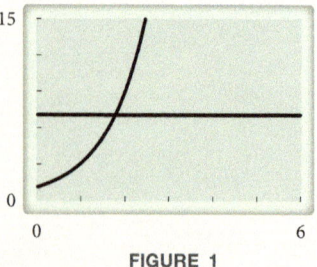
FIGURE 1

The result is 6.99 to the nearest hundredth, which seems reasonable since 1.77 is accurate to the nearest hundredth. To get a result closer to 7, we would need to find the intersection of the two graphs more accurately. ■

Getting Ready for Class

After reading through the preceding section, respond in your own words and in complete sentences.

A. What is an exponential equation?

B. How do logarithms help you solve exponential equations?

C. What is the change-of-base property?

D. Write an application modeled by the equation
$A = 10,000\left(1 + \frac{0.08}{2}\right)^{2 \cdot 5}$.

Solve each exponential equation. Use a calculator to write the answer in decimal form.

1. $3^x = 5$ **2.** $4^x = 3$ **3.** $5^x = 3$ **4.** $3^x = 4$

5. $5^{-x} = 12$ **6.** $7^{-x} = 8$ **7.** $12^{-x} = 5$ **8.** $8^{-x} = 7$

9. $8^{x+1} = 4$ **10.** $9^{x+1} = 3$ **11.** $4^{x-1} = 4$ **12.** $3^{x-1} = 9$

13. $3^{2x+1} = 2$ **14.** $2^{2x+1} = 3$ **15.** $3^{1-2x} = 2$ **16.** $2^{1-2x} = 3$

17. $15^{3x-4} = 10$ **18.** $10^{3x-4} = 15$ **19.** $6^{5-2x} = 4$ **20.** $9^{7-3x} = 5$

21. $3^{-4x} = 81$ **22.** $2^{5x} = \dfrac{1}{16}$ **23.** $5^{3x-2} = 15$ **24.** $7^{4x+3} = 200$

25. $100e^{3t} = 250$ **26.** $150e^{0.065t} = 400$

27. $1200\left(1 + \dfrac{0.072}{4}\right)^{4t} = 25000$ **28.** $2700\left(1 + \dfrac{0.086}{12}\right)^{12t} = 10000$

29. $50e^{-0.0742t} = 32$ **30.** $19e^{-0.000243t} = 12$

Use the change-of-base property and a calculator to find a decimal approximation to each of the following logarithms.

31. $\log_8 16$ **32.** $\log_9 27$ **33.** $\log_{16} 8$ **34.** $\log_{27} 9$

35. $\log_7 15$ **36.** $\log_3 12$ **37.** $\log_{15} 7$ **38.** $\log_{12} 3$

39. $\log_8 240$ **40.** $\log_6 180$ **41.** $\log_4 321$ **42.** $\log_5 462$

Find a decimal approximation to each of the following natural logarithms.

43. $\ln 345$ **44.** $\ln 3,450$ **45.** $\ln 0.345$ **46.** $\ln 0.0345$

47. $\ln 10$ **48.** $\ln 100$ **49.** $\ln 45,000$ **50.** $\ln 450,000$

Applying the Concepts

51. Compound Interest How long will it take for $500 to double if it is invested at 6% annual interest compounded 2 times a year?

52. Compound Interest How long will it take for $500 to double if it is invested at 6% annual interest compounded 12 times a year?

53. Compound Interest How long will it take for $1,000 to triple if it is invested at 12% annual interest compounded 6 times a year?

54. Compound Interest How long will it take for $1,000 to become $4,000 if it is invested at 12% annual interest compounded 6 times a year?

55. Doubling Time How long does it take for an amount of money P to double itself if it is invested at 8% interest compounded 4 times a year?

56. Tripling Time How long does it take for an amount of money P to triple itself if it is invested at 8% interest compounded 4 times a year?

57. Tripling Time If a $25 investment is worth $75 today, how long ago must that $25 have been invested at 6% interest compounded twice a year?

58. Doubling Time If a $25 investment is worth $50 today, how long ago must that $25 have been invested at 6% interest compounded twice a year?

Recall from Section 8.1 that if P dollars are invested in an account with annual interest rate r, compounded continuously, then the amount of money in the account after t years is given by the formula

$$A(t) = Pe^{rt}$$

59. **Continuously Compounded Interest** Repeat Problem 51 if the interest is compounded continuously.

60. **Continuously Compounded Interest** Repeat Problem 54 if the interest is compounded continuously.

61. **Continuously Compounded Interest** How long will it take $500 to triple if it is invested at 6% annual interest, compounded continuously?

62. **Continuously Compounded Interest** How long will it take $500 to triple if it is invested at 12% annual interest, compounded continuously?

63. **Continuously Compounded Interest** How long will it take for $1,000 to be worth $2,500 at 8% interest, compounded continuously?

64. **Continuously Compounded Interest** How long will it take for $1,000 to be worth $5,000 at 8% interest, compounded continuously?

65. **Exponential Growth** Suppose that the population in a small city is 32,000 at the beginning of 2005 and that the city council assumes that the population size t years later can be estimated by the equation

$$P(t) = 32{,}000e^{0.05t}$$

Approximately when will the city have a population of 64,000?

66. **Exponential Growth** Suppose the population of a city is given by the equation

$$P(t) = 100{,}000e^{0.05t}$$

where t is the number of years from the present time. How large is the population now? (*Now* corresponds to a certain value of t. Once you realize what that value of t is, the problem becomes very simple.)

67. **Airline Travel** The number of airline passengers in 1990 was 466 million. The number of passengers traveling by airplane each year has increased exponentially according to the model, $P(t) = 466 \cdot 1.035^t$, where t is the number of years since 1990 (U.S. Census Bureau). In what year is it predicted that 900 million passengers will travel by airline?

68. **Bankruptcy Model** In 1997, there were a total of 1,316,999 bankruptcies filed under the Bankruptcy Reform Act. The model for the number of bankruptcies filed is $B(t) = 0.798 \cdot 1.164^t$, where t is the number of years since 1994 and B is the number of bankruptcies filed in terms of millions (Administrative Office of the U.S. Courts, *Statistical Tables for the Federal Judiciary*). In what year is it predicted that 12 million bankruptcies will be filed?

69. **Health Care** In 1990, $699 billion was spent on health care expenditures. The amount of money, E, in billions spent on health care expenditures can be estimated using the function $E(t) = 78.16(1.11)^t$, where t is time in years since 1970 (*U.S. Census Bureau*). In what year was it estimated that $800 billion will be spent on health care expenditures?

70. Value of a Car As a car ages, its value decreases. The value of a particular car with an original purchase price of $25,600 is modeled by the function $c(t) = 25{,}600(1 - 0.22)^t$, where c is the value at time t (Kelly Blue Book). How old is the car when its value is $10,000?

71. Compound Interest In 1986, the average cost of attending a public university through graduation was $16,552 (U.S. Department of Education, National Center for Educational Statistics). If John's parents deposited that amount in an account in 1986 at an interest rate of 7% compounded semi-annually, how long will it take for the money to double?

72. Carbon Dating Scientists use Carbon-14 dating to find the age of fossils and other artifacts. The amount of Carbon-14 in an organism will yield information concerning its age. A formula used in Carbon-14 dating is $A(t) = A_0 \cdot 2^{-t/5600}$, where A_0 is the amount of carbon originally in the organism, t is time in years, and A is the amount of carbon remaining after t years. Determine the number of years since an organism died if it originally contained 1,000 gram of Carbon-14 and it currently contains 600 gram of Carbon-14.

73. Cost Increase The cost of a can of Coca Cola in 1960 was $0.10. The function that models the cost of a Coca Cola by year is $C(t) = 0.10e^{0.0576t}$, where t is the number of years since 1960. In what year is it expected that a can of Coca Cola will cost $1.00?

74. Online Banking Use The number of households using online banking services has increased from 754,000 in 1995 to 12,980,000 in 2000. The formula $H(t) = 0.76e^{0.55t}$ models the number of households, H, in millions when time is t years since 1995 according to the Home Banking Report. In what year is it estimated that 50,000,000 households will use online banking services?

Maintaining Your Skills

The following problems review material we covered in Section 9.5.

Find the vertex for each of the following parabolas, and then indicate if it is the highest or lowest point on the graph.

75. $y = 2x^2 + 8x - 15$

76. $y = 3x^2 - 9x - 10$

77. $y = 12x - 4x^2$

78. $y = 18x - 6x^2$

79. Maximum Height An object is projected into the air with an initial upward velocity of 64 feet per second. Its height h at any time t is given by the formula $h = 64t - 16t^2$. Find the time at which the object reaches its maximum height. Then, find the maximum height.

80. Maximum Height An object is projected into the air with an initial upward velocity of 64 feet per second from the top of a building 40 feet high. If the height h of the object t seconds after it is projected into the air is $h = 40 + 64t - 16t^2$, find the time at which the object reaches its maximum height. Then, find the maximum height it attains.

Chapter 12 Summary

Exponential Functions [12.1]

1. For the exponential function
$f(x) = 2^x$,
$$f(0) = 2^0 = 1$$
$$f(1) = 2^1 = 2$$
$$f(2) = 2^2 = 4$$
$$f(3) = 2^3 = 8$$

Any function of the form
$$f(x) = b^x$$
where $b > 0$ and $b \neq 1$, is an **exponential function**.

One-to-One Functions [12.2]

2. The function $f(x) = x^2$ is not one-to-one because 9, which is in the range, comes from both 3 and -3 in the domain.

A function is a **one-to-one function** if every element in the range comes from exactly one element in the domain.

Inverse Functions [12.2]

3. The inverse of $f(x) = 2x - 3$ is
$$f^{-1}(x) = \frac{x + 3}{2}$$

The **inverse** of a function is obtained by reversing the order of the coordinates of the ordered pairs belonging to the function. Only one-to-one functions have inverses that are also functions.

Definition of Logarithms [12.3]

4. The definition allows us to write expressions like
$$y = \log_3 27$$
equivalently in exponential form as
$$3^y = 27$$
which makes it apparent that y is 3.

If b is a positive number not equal to 1, then the expression
$$y = \log_b x$$
is equivalent to $x = b^y$; that is, in the expression $y = \log_b x$, y is the number to which we raise b in order to get x. Expressions written in the form $y = \log_b x$ are said to be in **logarithmic form**. Expressions like $x = b^y$ are in **exponential form**.

Two Special Identities [12.3]

5. Examples of the two special identities are
$$5^{\log_5 12} = 12$$
and
$$\log_8 8^3 = 3$$

For $b > 0$, $b \neq 1$, the following two expressions hold for all positive real numbers x:

(1) $b^{\log_b x} = x$

(2) $\log_b b^x = x$

Properties of Logarithms [12.4]

6. We can rewrite the expression
$$\log_{10} \frac{45^6}{273}$$
using the properties of logarithms, as
$$6 \log_{10} 45 - \log_{10} 273$$

If x, y, and b are positive real numbers, $b \neq 1$, and r is any real number, then:

1. $\log_b(xy) = \log_b x + \log_b y$

2. $\log_b \left(\dfrac{x}{y} \right) = \log_b x - \log_b y$

3. $\log_b x^r = r \log_b x$

Common Logarithms [12.5]

7. $\log_{10} 10{,}000 = \log 10{,}000$
$= \log 10^4$
$= 4$

Common logarithms are logarithms with a base of 10. To save time in writing, we omit the base when working with common logarithms; that is,

$$\log x = \log_{10} x$$

Natural Logarithms [12.5]

8. $\ln e = 1$
$\ln 1 = 0$

Natural logarithms, written *ln x*, are logarithms with a base of *e*, where the number *e* is an irrational number (like the number π). A decimal approximation for *e* is 2.7183. All the properties of exponents and logarithms hold when the base is *e*.

Change of Base [12.6]

9. $\log_6 475 = \dfrac{\log 475}{\log 6}$

$\approx \dfrac{2.6767}{0.7782}$

≈ 3.44

If *x*, *a*, and *b* are positive real numbers, $a \neq 1$ and $b \neq 1$, then

$$\log_a x = \frac{\log_b x}{\log_b a}$$

> ⚠️ **Common Mistake**
>
> The most common mistakes that occur with logarithms come from trying to apply the three properties of logarithms to situations in which they don't apply. For example, a very common mistake looks like this:
>
> $$\frac{\log 3}{\log 2} = \log 3 - \log 2 \qquad \text{Mistake}$$
>
> This is not a property of logarithms. To write the equation $\log 3 - \log 2$, we would have to start with
>
> $$\log \frac{3}{2} \qquad NOT \qquad \frac{\log 3}{\log 2}$$
>
> There is a difference.

Chapter 12 Test

Graph each exponential function. [12.1]

1. $f(x) = 2^x$

2. $g(x) = 3^{-x}$

Sketch the graph of each function and its inverse. Find $f^{-1}(x)$ for Problem 3. [12.2]

3. $f(x) = 2x - 3$

4. $f(x) = x^2 - 4$

Solve for x. [12.3]

5. $\log_4 x = 3$

6. $\log_x 5 = 2$

Graph each of the following [12.3]

7. $y = \log_2 x$

8. $y = \log_{1/2} x$

Evaluate each of the following. [12.3, 12.4, 12.5]

9. $\log_8 4$ **10.** $\log_7 21$ **11.** $\log 23{,}400$ **12.** $\log 0.0123$

13. $\ln 46.2$ **14.** $\ln 0.0462$

Use the properties of logarithms to expand each expression. [12.4]

15. $\log_2 \dfrac{8x^2}{y}$

16. $\log \dfrac{\sqrt{x}}{(y^4)\sqrt[5]{z}}$

Write each expression as a single logarithm. [12.4]

17. $2 \log_3 x - \dfrac{1}{2} \log_3 y$

18. $\dfrac{1}{3} \log x - \log y - 2 \log z$

Use a calculator to find x. [12.5]

19. $\log x = 4.8476$

20. $\log x = -2.6478$

Solve for x. [12.4, 12.6]

21. $5 = 3^x$

22. $4^{2x-1} = 8$

23. $\log_5 x - \log_5 3 = 1$

24. $\log_2 x + \log_2(x - 7) = 3$

25. **pH** Find the pH of a solution in which $[H^+] = 6.6 \times 10^{-7}$. [12.5]

26. **Compound Interest** If $400 is deposited in an account that earns 10% annual interest compounded twice a year, how much money will be in the account after 5 years? [12.1]

27. **Compound Interest** How long will it take $600 to become $1,800 if the $600 is deposited in an account that earns 8% annual interest compounded 4 times a year? [12.6]

28. **Depreciation** If a car depreciates in value 20% per year for the first 5 years after it is purchased for P_0 dollars, then its value after t years will be $V(t) = P_0(1 - r)^t$ for $0 \le t \le 5$. To the nearest dollar, find the value of a car 4 years after it is purchased for $18,000. [12.1]

Answers to Odd-Numbered Problems

Chapter 0

PROBLEM SET 0.1

1. $x + 5 = 14$ **3.** $5y < 30$ **5.** $5y \geq y - 16$ **7.** $\frac{x}{3} = x + 2$ **9.** 9 **11.** 49 **13.** 8 **15.** 64 **17.** 16 **19.** 100 **21.** 121

23. 11 **25.** 16 **27.** 17 **29.** 42 **31.** 30 **33.** 30 **35.** 24 **37.** 80 **39.** 27 **41.** 35 **43.** 13 **45.** 4 **47.** 37 **49.** 37 **51.** 16

53. 16 **55.** 81 **57.** 41 **59.** 345 **61.** 2,345 **63.** 2 **65.** 148 **67.** 36 **69.** 36 **71.** 58 **73.** 62 **75.** 100 **77.** 9 **79.** 18

81. 8 **83.** 12 **85.** 18 **87.** 42 **89.** 53 **91.** 10 **93.** 420 **95.** About 224 chips **97.** 95g **99. a.** 600 mg **b.** 231 mg

101.

Calories Burned by 150-Pound Person	
Activity	Calories Burned in 1 Hour
Bicycling	374
Bowling	265
Handball	680
Jogging	680
Skiing	544

103. 5 **105.** 10 **107.** 25 **109.** 10

PROBLEM SET 0.2

1–7.

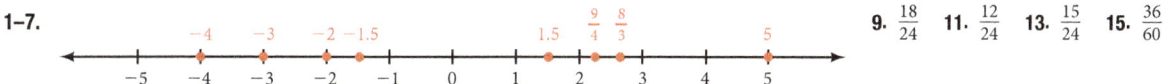

9. $\frac{18}{24}$ **11.** $\frac{12}{24}$ **13.** $\frac{15}{24}$ **15.** $\frac{36}{60}$

17. $\frac{22}{60}$ **19.** $-10, \frac{1}{10}, 10$ **21.** $-\frac{3}{4}, \frac{4}{3}, \frac{3}{4}$ **23.** $-\frac{11}{2}, \frac{2}{11}, \frac{11}{2}$ **25.** $3, -\frac{1}{3}, 3$ **27.** $\frac{2}{5}, -\frac{5}{2}, \frac{2}{5}$ **29.** $-x, \frac{1}{x}, |x|$

31. $<$ **33.** $>$ **35.** $>$ **37.** $>$ **39.** $<$ **41.** $<$ **43.** 6 **45.** 22 **47.** 3 **49.** 7 **51.** 3 **53.** $\frac{8}{15}$ **55.** $\frac{3}{2}$ **57.** $\frac{5}{4}$ **59.** 1 **61.** 1

63. 1 **65.** $\frac{9}{16}$ **67.** $\frac{8}{27}$ **69.** $\frac{1}{10,000}$ **71.** $\frac{1}{9}$ **73.** $\frac{1}{25}$ **75.** 4 inches; 1 square inch **77.** 4.5 inches; 1.125 square inches

79. 10.25 centimeters; 5 square centimeters **81.** $-8, -2$ **83.** $-64°F; -54°F$ **85.** $-15°F$ **87.** -100 feet; -105 feet

89. 93.5 square inches, 39 inches **91.** 1,387 calories **93.** 654 more calories **95. a.** 93 **b.** False **c.** True

PROBLEM SET 0.3

1. $3 + 5 = 8, 3 + (-5) = -2, -3 + 5 = 2, -3 + (-5) = -8$

3. $15 + 20 = 35, 15 + (-20) = -5, -15 + 20 = 5, -15 + (-20) = -35$ **5.** 3 **7.** -7 **9.** -14 **11.** -3 **13.** -25

15. -12 **17.** -19 **19.** -25 **21.** -8 **23.** -4 **25.** 6 **27.** 6 **29.** 8 **31.** -4 **33.** -14 **35.** -17 **37.** 4 **39.** 3 **41.** 15

43. -8 **45.** 12 **47.** 23, 28 **49.** 30, 35 **51.** 0, -5 **53.** $-12, -18$ **55.** $-4, -8$ **57.** Yes **59.** $5 + 9 = 14$

61. $[-7 + (-5)] + 4 = -8$ **63.** $[-2 + (-3)] + 10 = 5$ **65.** 3 **67.** -3 **69.** $-12 + 4$ **71.** $10 + (-6) + (-8) = -\$4$

73. $-30 + 40 = 10$ **75.** \$2,000 **77.** 2013, \$500

PROBLEM SET 0.4

1. -3 **3.** -6 **5.** 0 **7.** -10 **9.** -16 **11.** -12 **13.** -7 **15.** 35 **17.** 0 **19.** -4 **21.** 4 **23.** -24 **25.** -28 **27.** 25

29. 4 **31.** 7 **33.** 17 **35.** 8 **37.** 4 **39.** 18 **41.** 10 **43.** 17 **45.** 1 **47.** 1 **49.** 27 **51.** -26 **53.** -2 **55.** 68

57. $-7 - 4 = -11$ **59.** $12 - (-8) = 20$ **61.** $-5 - (-7) = 2$ **63.** $[4 + (-5)] - 17 = -18$ **65.** $8 - 5 = 3$

67. $-8 - 5 = -13$ **69.** $8 - (-5) = 13$ **71.** 10 **73.** -2 **75.** $1,500 - 730$ **77.** $-35 + 15 - 20 = -\$40$

79. $73 + 10 - 8, 75°F$ **81.** \$4,500, \$3,950, \$3,400, \$2,850, \$2,300; yes **83.** 35° **85.** 60°

Answers to Odd-Numbered Problems

87. a.

Day	Plant Height (inches)
0	0
2	1
4	3
6	6
8	13
10	23

b. 12 inches   **89. a.** Yes, the hundreds place   **b.** 8,400   **c.** 29,800

PROBLEM SET 0.5

1. Commutative   **3.** Multiplicative inverse   **5.** Commutative   **7.** Distributive   **9.** Commutative, associative

11. Commutative, associative   **13.** Commutative   **15.** Commutative, associative   **17.** Commutative   **19.** Additive inverse

21. $3x + 6$ **23.** $9a + 9b$ **25.** 0   **27.** 0   **29.** 10   **31.** $(4 + 2) + x = 6 + x$ **33.** $x + (2 + 7) = x + 9$

35. $(3 \cdot 5)x = 15x$ **37.** $(9 \cdot 6)y = 54y$ **39.** $\left(\frac{1}{2} \cdot 3\right)a = \frac{3}{2}a$ **41.** $\left(\frac{1}{3} \cdot 3\right)x = x$ **43.** $\left(\frac{1}{2} \cdot 2\right)y = y$ **45.** $\left(\frac{3}{4} \cdot \frac{4}{3}\right)x = x$

47. $\left(\frac{6}{5} \cdot \frac{5}{6}\right)a = a$ **49.** $8x + 16$ **51.** $8x - 16$ **53.** $4y + 4$ **55.** $18x + 15$ **57.** $6a + 14$ **59.** $54y - 72$ **61.** $x + 2$

63. $12x + 18y$ **65.** $12a - 8b$ **67.** $3x + 2y$ **69.** $4a + 25$ **71.** $6x + 12$ **73.** $14x + 38$ **75.** $2x + 1$ **77.** $6x - 3$ **79.** $5x + 10$

81. $6x + 5$ **83.** $5x + 6$ **85.** $6m - 5$ **87.** $7 + 3x$ **89.** $3x - 2y$ **91.** $0.09x + 180$ **93.** $0.12x + 60$ **95.** $a + 1$ **97.** $1 - a$

99. No   **101.** Answers will vary; $8 \div 4 \neq 4 \div 8$ **103.** $4(2 + 3) = 20, (4 \cdot 2) + (4 \cdot 3) = 20$

PROBLEM SET 0.6

1. -42 **3.** -16 **5.** 3   **7.** 121   **9.** 6   **11.** -60 **13.** 24   **15.** 49   **17.** -27 **19.** 6   **21.** 10   **23.** 9   **25.** 45   **27.** 14   **29.** -2

31. 216   **33.** -2 **35.** -18 **37.** 29   **39.** 38   **41.** -5 **43.** 37   **45.** 80   **47.** $-\frac{10}{21}$ **49.** -4 **51.** 1   **53.** $\frac{9}{16}$ **55.** $-8x$

57. $42x$ **59.** x **61.** $-4a - 8$ **63.** $-\frac{3}{2}x + 3$ **65.** $-6x + 8$ **67.** $-15x - 30$ **69.** -25 **71.** $2(-4x) = -8x$ **73.** -26 **75.** 8

77. -80 **79.** $\frac{1}{8}$ **81.** -24 **83.** $3x - 11$ **85.** 14   **87.** 81   **89.** $\frac{9}{4}$ **91.** $\frac{2}{3}x - 2$ **93.** $-2x + y$ **95.** 1°F   **97.** 465 calories

PROBLEM SET 0.7

1. -2 **3.** -3 **5.** $-\frac{1}{3}$ **7.** 3   **9.** $\frac{1}{7}$ **11.** 0   **13.** 9   **15.** -15 **17.** -36 **19.** $-\frac{1}{4}$ **21.** $\frac{16}{15}$ **23.** $\frac{4}{3}$ **25.** $-\frac{8}{13}$ **27.** -1

29. 1   **31.** $\frac{3}{5}$ **33.** $-\frac{5}{3}$ **35.** -2 **37.** -3 **39.** Undefined   **41.** Undefined   **43.** 5   **45.** $-\frac{7}{3}$ **47.** -1 **49.** -7 **51.** $\frac{15}{17}$

53. $-\frac{32}{17}$ **55.** $\frac{1}{3}$ **57.** 1   **59.** 1   **61.** -2 **63.** $\frac{9}{7}$ **65.** $\frac{16}{11}$ **67.** -1 **69. a.** 25   **b.** -25 **c.** -25 **d.** -25 **e.** 25

71. a. 10   **b.** 0   **c.** -100 **d.** -20 **73.** $5x + 6$ **75.** $3x + 20$ **77.** $3 + x$ **79.** $3x - 7y$ **81.** 1   **83.** 3   **85.** -10 **87.** -3

89. -8 **91.** 350 **93.** Drops 3.5°F each hour   **95.** 14 blankets   **97.** 48 bags   **99.** 6 eighth-teaspoons

101. 28 half-pint cartons

103. a. $20,000   **b.** $50,000   **c.** Yes, the projected revenue for 5,000 email addresses is $10,000, which is $5,000 more than the list costs.

PROBLEM SET 0.8

1. 0, 1   **3.** $-3, -2.5, 0, 1, \frac{3}{2}$ **5.** All   **7.** $-10, -8, -2, 9$ **9.** π **11.** T   **13.** F   **15.** F   **17.** T   **19.** Composite, $2^4 \cdot 3$

21. Prime   **23.** Composite, $3 \cdot 11 \cdot 31$ **25.** $2^4 \cdot 3^2$ **27.** $2 \cdot 19$ **29.** $3 \cdot 5 \cdot 7$ **31.** $2^2 \cdot 3^2 \cdot 5$ **33.** $5 \cdot 7 \cdot 11$ **35.** 11^2

37. $2^2 \cdot 3 \cdot 5 \cdot 7$ **39.** $2^2 \cdot 5 \cdot 31$ **41.** $\frac{7}{11}$ **43.** $\frac{5}{7}$ **45.** $\frac{11}{13}$ **47.** $\frac{14}{15}$ **49.** $\frac{5}{9}$ **51.** $\frac{5}{8}$ **53.** $2^3 \cdot 3^3$

55. $2^8 \cdot 3^8$ **57.** $2^2 \cdot 3 \cdot 5$ **59.** Irrational numbers   **61.** 8, 21, 34

PROBLEM SET 0.9

1. $\frac{2}{3}$ **3.** $-\frac{1}{4}$ **5.** $\frac{1}{2}$ **7.** $\frac{x - 1}{3}$ **9.** $\frac{3}{2}$ **11.** $\frac{x + 6}{2}$ **13.** $-\frac{3}{5}$ **15.** $\frac{10}{a}$

17.

First Number a	Second Number b	The Sum of a and b $a + b$
$\frac{1}{2}$	$\frac{1}{3}$	$\frac{5}{6}$
$\frac{1}{3}$	$\frac{1}{4}$	$\frac{7}{12}$
$\frac{1}{4}$	$\frac{1}{5}$	$\frac{9}{20}$
$\frac{1}{5}$	$\frac{1}{6}$	$\frac{11}{30}$

19.

First Number a	Second Number b	The Sum of a and b $a + b$
$\frac{1}{12}$	$\frac{1}{2}$	$\frac{7}{12}$
$\frac{1}{12}$	$\frac{1}{3}$	$\frac{5}{12}$
$\frac{1}{12}$	$\frac{1}{4}$	$\frac{1}{3}$
$\frac{1}{12}$	$\frac{1}{6}$	$\frac{1}{4}$

21. $\frac{7}{9}$ **23.** $\frac{7}{3}$ **25.** $\frac{1}{4}$ **27.** $\frac{7}{6}$

29. $\frac{19}{24}$ **31.** $\frac{13}{60}$ **33.** $\frac{29}{35}$ **35.** $\frac{949}{1,260}$ **37.** $\frac{13}{420}$ **39.** $\frac{41}{24}$ **41.** $\frac{5}{4}$ **43.** $-\frac{3}{2}$ **45.** $\frac{3}{2}$ **47.** $\frac{160}{63}$ **49.** $\frac{5}{8}$ **51.** $-\frac{2}{3}$ **53.** $\frac{7}{3}$ **55.** $\frac{1}{125}$

57. $\frac{3}{2}$ ft $= 1\frac{1}{2}$ ft **59.** $\frac{11}{5}$ cm $= 2\frac{1}{5}$ cm **61.** $\frac{9}{2}$ pints $= 4\frac{1}{2}$ pints **63.** \$1,325 **65.** $\frac{2}{5}$

67.

Grade	Number of Students	Fraction of Students
A	5	$\frac{1}{8}$
B	8	$\frac{1}{5}$
C	20	$\frac{1}{2}$
below C	7	$\frac{7}{40}$
Total	40	1

69. 10 lots

PROBLEM SET 0.10

Vocabulary Review **1.** percent **2.** ratio **3.** left **4.** right **5.** % symbol **6.** decimal

Problems **1.** $\frac{20}{100}$ **3.** $\frac{60}{100}$ **5.** $\frac{24}{100}$ **7.** $\frac{65}{100}$ **9.** 0.23 **11.** 1.92 **13.** 0.09 **15.** 0.034 **17.** 0.00087

19. 0.009 **21.** 23% **23.** 92.3% **25.** 45% **27.** 3% **29.** 60% **31.** 0.8% **33.** 2700% **35.** 123%

37. $\frac{3}{5}$ **39.** $\frac{3}{4}$ **41.** $\frac{1}{25}$ **43.** $2\frac{13}{20}$ **45.** $\frac{7,187}{10,000}$ **47.** $\frac{3}{400}$ **49.** $\frac{1}{16}$ **51.** $\frac{1}{3}$ **53.** 50% **55.** 75%

57. $33\frac{1}{3}$% **59.** 80% **61.** 87.5% **63.** 14% **65.** 325% **67.** 150% **69.** 48.8% **71.** 0.50; 0.75

73. a. Nokia: $\frac{1}{50}$; Android: $\frac{3}{100}$; BlackBerry: $\frac{3}{50}$; Other: $\frac{3}{25}$; iPhone: $\frac{77}{100}$ **b.** Nokia: 0.02; Android: 0.03; BlackBerry: 0.06; Other: 0.12; iPhone: 0.77 **c.** About 2 times as likely.

75. 20% **77.** Liberal Arts: 15%, Science & Math: 15%, Engineering: 27.78%, Business: 11.11%, Architecture & Environmental Design: 11.11%, Agriculture: 22.22% **79.** 78.4% **81.** 11.8%

83. 72.2% **85.** 8.3%; 0.2% **87.** 18.5 **89.** 10.875 **91.** 0.5 **93.** 62.5 **95.** $n = 0.5$

Find the Mistake **1.** Writing 0.4% as a decimal gives us .004. **2.** To write 3.21 as a percent, multiply the number by 100; that is, move the decimal two places to the right. **3.** Writing 25% as a fraction in lowest terms gives us $\frac{1}{4}$. **4.** To change $\frac{5}{8}$ to a percent, we change $\frac{5}{8}$ to 0.625 and then move the decimal two places to the right to get 62.5%.

PROBLEM SET 0.11

Vocabulary Review **1.** equals sign **2.** multiply **3.** variable **4.** decimal **5.** fraction

Problems **1.** 8 **3.** 24 **5.** 20.52 **7.** 7.37 **9.** 50% **11.** 10% **13.** 25% **15.** 75% **17.** 64 **19.** 50

21. 925 **23.** 400 **25.** 17.4 **27.** 120 **29.** 13.72 **31.** 22.5 **33.** 50% **35.** 942.684 **37.** 97.8

39. What number is 25% of 350? **41.** What percent of 24 is 16? **43.** 46 is 75% of what number?

45. 11.3% calories from fat; healthy **47.** 56.9% calories from fat; not healthy **49.** 0.80 **51.** 0.76 **53.** 48

55. Fewer than 175 to 280 gulls of breeding age

Answers to Odd-Numbered Problems

Find the Mistake   **1.** The question, "What number is 28.5% of 30?" translates to $n = 0.285 \cdot 30$.   **2.** Asking "75 is 30% of what number?" gives us 250.   **3.** To answer the question, "What number is 45% of 90?", we can solve the proportion $\frac{x}{90} = \frac{45}{100}$.
4. Using a proportion to answer the question, "What percent of 65 is 26?" will give us $n = 40\%$.

Landmark Review   **1.** $\frac{15}{100}$ **2.** $\frac{27}{100}$ **3.** $\frac{14}{100}$ **4.** $\frac{89}{100}$ **5.** 0.17   **6.** 0.28   **7.** 0.05   **8.** 0.0637   **9.** 38%

10. 98%   **11.** 9%   **12.** 487%   **13.** 10%   **14.** 33.3%   **15.** 14.3%   **16.** 320%   **17.** 5.25   **18.** 62.35%

19. 237.84

PROBLEM SET 0.12

Vocabulary Review   **1.** What number is $y\%$ of x?   **2.** What percent of x is z?   **3.** z is $y\%$ of what number?

Problems   **1.** 70%   **3.** 40mL   **5.** 45 mL   **7.** 18.2 acres for farming; 9.8 acres are not available for farming

9. 3,000 students   **11.** 400 students   **13.** 1,664 female students   **15.** 31.25%   **17.** 50%   **19.** 1,267 students

21. 33   **23.** 8,685   **25.** 136   **27.** 0.05   **29.** 15,300   **31.** 0.15   **33.** 36.7%, to the nearest tenth of a percent

35. 158 hits   **37.** 19 hits

Find the Mistake   **1.** On a test with 110 questions, a student answered 98 questions correctly. The percentage of questions the student answered correctly is 89.1%.   **2.** A school track team consists of 12 boys and 10 girls. The total number of girls makes up 45.5% percent of the whole team.   **3.** Suppose 39 students in a college class of 130 students received a B on their tests. To find what percent of students earned a B, solve the proportion $\frac{39}{130} = \frac{x}{100}$.   **4.** Suppose a basketball player made 120 out of 150 free throws attempted. To find what percent of free throws the player made, solve the proportion $\frac{120}{150} = \frac{x}{100}$.

PROBLEM SET 0.13

Vocabulary Review   **1.** D   **2.** P   **3.** P   **4.** D

Problems   **1.** $52.50   **3.** $2.70; $47.70   **5.** $150; $156   **7.** 5%   **9.** $2,820   **11.** $200   **13.** 14%   **15.** $11.93

17. 4.5%   **19.** $3,995   **21.** 1,100   **23.** 75   **25.** 0.16   **27.** 4   **29.** 396   **31.** 415.8

33. Sales tax = $3,180; luxury tax = $2,300   **35.** $1,846   **37.** You saved $1,600 on the sticker price and $150 in luxury tax. If you lived in a state with a 6% sales tax rate, you saved an additional 0.06($1600) = $96.

Find the Mistake   **1.** Suppose the sales tax rate on a new computer is 8%. If the computer cost $650, then the total price of purchase would be $702.   **2.** If a new shirt that costs $32 has sales tax equal to $1.92, then the sales tax rate is 6%.   **3.** A car salesman's commission rate is 7%. To find his commission on a $15,000 sale of a Ford truck, we would solve $15,000 \cdot 0.07 = n$.   **4.** A saleswoman makes a commission of $6.80 on a sale of $85 worth of clothing. To find the woman's commission rate, solve the equation $85n = 6.80$.

PROBLEM SET 0.14

Vocabulary Review   **1.** b   **2.** d   **3.** a   **4.** c

Problems   **1.** $24,610   **3.** $3,510   **5.** $13,200   **7.** 10%   **9.** 20%   **11.** 61%   **13.** $45; $255   **15.** $381.60

17. $46,595.88   **19. a.** 51.9% **b.** 7.8%   **21.** 140   **23.** 4   **25.** 152.25   **27.** 3,434.7   **29.** 10,150   **31.** 10,456.78

33. 2,140   **35.** 3,210

Find the Mistake   **1.** If a new model of a car increases 12% from and old model's price of $24,000, then the new selling price is $26,880.   **2.** A lawnmower goes on sale from $98 to $63.70. The percent decrease of the lawnmower's price is 35%.   **3.** A backpack that normally sells for $75 is on sale. The new price of $45 shows a percent decrease of 40%.   **4.** A designer pair of sunglasses is on sale from $125 for 20% off. If the sales tax is 6% of the sale price, then the total bill for the glasses would be $106.

CHAPTER 0 TEST

1. $15 - x = 12$ **2.** $6a = 30$ **3.** 2   **4.** 10   **5.** d   **6.** e   **7.** a   **8.** c   **9.** -13 **10.** -10 **11.** -7 **12.** 62   **13.** 2   **14.** -6

15. $3x + 12$ **16.** $-15y$ **17.** $-10x + 15$ **18.** $2x + 4$ **19.** $-3, 2$ **20.** $-3, -\frac{1}{2}, 2$ **21.** $2^2 \cdot 3 \cdot 5 \cdot 11$ **22.** $3^3 \cdot 5^2 \cdot 7$ **23.** $\frac{11}{24}$

24. $\frac{5+6}{y} = \frac{11}{y}$ **25.** $6 + (-9) = -3$ **26.** $-5 - (-12) = 7$ **27.** $6 \cdot (-7) = -42$ **28.** $32 \div -8 = -4$ **29.** 13   **30.** 1

31. 0.27   **32.** 0.06   **33.** 0.009   **34.** 64%   **35.** 30%   **36.** 149%   **37.** $\frac{9}{20}$ **38.** $1\frac{9}{25}$ **39.** $\frac{9}{125}$ **40.** 65%

41. 87.5%   **42.** 225%   **43.** 12   **44.** 35%   **45.** 75   **46.** 96%   **47.** $900   **48.** $145; 20% off   **49.** $135.32

50. $866.40

Chapter 1

PROBLEM SET 1.1

1. $-3x$ **3.** $-a$ **5.** $12x$ **7.** $6a$ **9.** $6x - 3$ **11.** $7a + 5$ **13.** $5x - 5$ **15.** $4a + 2$ **17.** $-9x - 2$ **19.** $12a + 3$ **21.** $10x - 1$

23. $21y + 6$ **25.** $-6x + 8$ **27.** $-2a + 3$ **29.** $-4x + 26$ **31.** $4y - 16$ **33.** $-6x - 1$ **35.** $2x - 12$ **37.** $10a + 33$

39. $4x - 9$ **41.** $7y - 39$ **43.** $-19x - 14$ **45.** 5 **47.** -9 **49.** 4 **51.** 4 **53.** -37 **55.** -41 **57.** 64 **59.** 64 **61.** 144

63. 144 **65.** 3 **67.** 0 **69.** 15 **71.** 6 **73. a.**

n	1	2	3	4
$3n$	3	6	9	12

b.

n	1	2	3	4
n^3	1	8	27	64

75. 1, 4, 7, 10, an arithmetic sequence **77.** 0, 1, 4, 9, . . . a sequence of squares **79.** $-6y + 4$ **81.** $0.17x$ **83.** $2x$

85. $5x - 4$ **87.** $7x - 5$ **89.** $-2x - 9$ **91.** $7x + 2$ **93.** $-7x + 6$ **95.** $7x$ **97.** $-y$ **99.** $10y$ **101.** $0.17x + 180$

103. $0.22x + 60$ **105.** 49 **107.** 40 **109. a.** $42°F$ **b.** $28°F$ **c.** $-14°F$ **111. a.** \$45 **b.** \$55 **c.** \$75 **113.** 12

115. -3 **117.** -9.7 **119.** $-\frac{5}{4}$ **121.** 53 **123.** $a - 12$ **125.** 7

PROBLEM SET 1.2

1. 11 **3.** 4 **5.** $-\frac{3}{4}$ **7.** -5.8 **9.** -17 **11.** $-\frac{1}{8}$ **13.** -4 **15.** -3.6 **17.** 1 **19.** $-\frac{7}{45}$ **21.** 3 **23.** $\frac{11}{8}$ **25.** 21 **27.** 7

29. 3.5 **31.** 22 **33.** -2 **35.** -16 **37.** -3 **39.** 10 **41.** -12 **43.** 4 **45.** 2 **47.** -5 **49.** -1 **51.** -3 **53.** 8 **55.** -8

57. 2 **59.** 11 **61.** -5.8 **63. a.** 6% **b.** 5% **c.** 2% **d.** 75% **65.** y **67.** x **69.** 6 **71.** 6 **73.** -9 **75.** $-\frac{15}{8}$ **77.** 8

79. $-\frac{5}{4}$ **81.** $3x$

PROBLEM SET 1.3

1. 2 **3.** 4 **5.** $-\frac{1}{2}$ **7.** -2 **9.** 3 **11.** 4 **13.** 0 **15.** 0 **17.** 6 **19.** -50 **21.** $\frac{3}{2}$ **23.** 12 **25.** -3 **27.** 32 **29.** -8 **31.** $\frac{1}{2}$

33. 4 **35.** 8 **37.** -4 **39.** 4 **41.** -15 **43.** $-\frac{1}{2}$ **45.** 3 **47.** 1 **49.** $\frac{1}{4}$ **51.** -3 **53.** 3 **55.** 2 **57.** $-\frac{3}{2}$ **59.** $-\frac{3}{2}$ **61.** 1

63. 1 **65.** -2 **67. a.** $\frac{3}{2}$ **b.** 1 **c.** $-\frac{3}{2}$ **d.** -4 **e.** $\frac{8}{5}$ **69.** 200 tickets **71.** \$1,390.85 per month **73.** 2 **75.** 6 **77.** 3,000

79. $3x - 11$ **81.** $0.09x + 180$ **83.** $-6y + 4$ **85.** $4x - 11$ **87.** $5x$ **89.** $0.17x$

PROBLEM SET 1.4

1. 3 **3.** -2 **5.** -1 **7.** 2 **9.** -4 **11.** -2 **13.** 0 **15.** 1 **17.** $\frac{1}{2}$ **19.** 7 **21.** 8 **23.** $-\frac{1}{3}$ **25.** $\frac{3}{4}$ **27.** 75 **29.** 2 **31.** 6

33. 8 **35.** 0 **37.** $\frac{3}{7}$ **39.** 1 **41.** 1 **43.** -1 **45.** 6 **47.** $\frac{3}{4}$ **49.** 3 **51.** $\frac{3}{4}$ **53.** 8 **55.** 6 **57.** -2 **59.** -2 **61.** 2 **63.** -6

65. 2 **67.** 20 **69.** 4,000 **71.** 700 **73.** 11 **75.** 7 **77.** No solution **79.** No solution.

81. a. $\frac{5}{4} = 1.25$ **b.** $\frac{15}{2} = 7.5$ **c.** $6x + 20$ **d.** 15 **e.** $4x - 20$ **f.** $\frac{45}{2} = 22.5$ **83.** 14 **85.** -3 **87.** $\frac{1}{4}$ **89.** $\frac{1}{3}$ **91.** $-\frac{3}{2}x + 3$

PROBLEM SET 1.5

1. 100 feet **3.** 0 **5.** 2 **7.** 15 **9.** 10 **11.** -2 **13.** 1 **15. a.** 2 **b.** 4 **17. a.** 5 **b.** 18 **19.** $l = \frac{A}{w}$ **21.** $h = \frac{V}{lw}$

23. $a = P - b - c$ **25.** $x = 3y - 1$ **27.** $y = 3x + 6$ **29.** $y = -\frac{2}{3}x + 2$ **31.** $y = -2x - 5$ **33.** $y = -\frac{2}{3}x + 1$

35. $w = \frac{P - 2l}{2}$ **37.** $v = \frac{h - 16t^2}{t}$ **39.** $h = \frac{A - \pi r^2}{2\pi r}$ **41. a.** $y = \frac{3}{5}x + 1$ **b.** $y = \frac{1}{2}x + 2$ **c.** $y = 4x + 3$

43. $y = \frac{3}{7}x - 3$ **45.** $y = 2x + 8$ **47.** $60°; 150°$ **49.** $45°; 135°$ **51.** 10 **53.** 240 **55.** 25% **57.** 35% **59.** 64 **61.** 2,000

63. $100°C$; yes **65.** $20°C$; yes **67.** $C = \frac{5}{9}(F - 32)$ **69.** $4°F$ over **71.** 7 meters **73.** $\frac{3}{2}$ or 1.5 inches **75.** 132 feet

77. $\frac{2}{9}$ centimeters **79.** 60% **81.** 26.5% **83.** The sum of 4 and 1 is 5. **85.** The difference of 6 and 2 is 4.

87. The difference of a number and 5 is -12. **89.** The sum of a number and 3 is four times the difference of that number and 3.

91. $2(6 + 3) = 18$ **93.** $2(5) + 3 = 13$ **95.** $x + 5 = 13$ **97.** $5(x + 7) = 30$

PROBLEM SET 1.6

1. 8 **3.** 5 **5.** -1 **7.** 3 and 5 **9.** 6 and 14 **11.** Shelly is 39; Michele is 36 **13.** Evan is 11; Cody is 22

15. Barney is 27; Fred is 31 **17.** Lacy is 16; Jack is 32 **19.** Patrick is 18; Pat is 38 **21.** $s = 9$ inches **23.** $s = 15$ feet

25. 11 feet, 18 feet, 33 feet **27.** 26 feet, 13 feet, 14 feet **29.** $l = 11$ inches; $w = 6$ inches **31.** $l = 25$ inches; $w = 9$ inches

33. $l = 15$ feet; $w = 3$ feet **35.** 9 dimes; 14 quarters **37.** 12 quarters; 27 nickels **39.** 8 nickels; 17 dimes

41. 7 nickels; 10 dimes; 12 quarters   **43.** 3 nickels; 9 dimes; 6 quarters   **45.** $5x$ **47.** $1.075x$ **49.** $0.09x + 180$ **51.** 6,000   **53.** 30

PROBLEM SET 1.7

1. 5 and 6   **3.** -4 and -5 **5.** 13 and 15   **7.** 52 and 54   **9.** -14 and -16 **11.** 17, 19, and 21   **13.** 42, 44, and 46

15. $4,000 invested at 8%, $6,000 invested at 9%   **17.** $700 invested at 10%, $1,200 invested at 12%

19. $500 at 8%, $1,000 at 9%, $1,500 at 10%   **21.** 45°, 45°, 90°   **23.** 22.5°, 45°, 112.5°   **25.** 53°, 90°   **27.** 80°, 60°, 40°

29. 16 adult and 22 children's tickets   **31.** 16 minutes   **33.** 39 hours   **35.** They are in offices 7329 and 7331.

37. Kendra is 8 years old and Marissa is 10 years old.   **39.** Jeff   **41.** $10.38   **43.** $l = 12$ meters; $w = 10$ meters   **45.** 59°, 60°, 61°

47. $54.00   **49.** Yes   **51. a.** 9   **b.** 3   **c.** -9 **d.** -3 **53. a.** -8 **b.** 8   **c.** 8   **d.** -8 **55.** -2.3125 **57.** $\frac{10}{3}$

PROBLEM SET 1.8

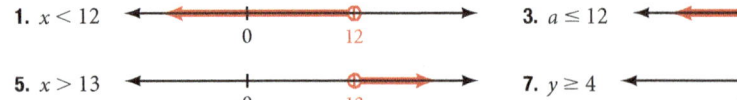

1. $x < 12$ **3.** $a \le 12$

5. $x > 13$ **7.** $y \ge 4$

9. $x > 9$ **11.** $x < 2$

13. $a \le 5$ **15.** $x > 15$

17. $x < -3$ **19.** $x \le 6$

21. $x \ge -50$ **23.** $y < -6$

25. $x < 6$ **27.** $y \ge -5$

29. $x < 3$ **31.** $x \le 18$

33. $a < -20$ **35.** $y < 25$

37. $a \le 3$ **39.** $x \ge \frac{15}{2}$

41. $x < -1$ **43.** $y \ge -2$

45. $x < -1$ **47.** $m \le -6$

49. $x \le -5$ **51.** $y < -\frac{3}{2}x + 3$ **53.** $y < \frac{2}{5}x - 2$ **55.** $y \le \frac{3}{7}x + 3$ **57.** $y \le \frac{1}{2}x + 1$

59. a. 3   **b.** 2   **c.** No   **d.** $x > 2$ **61.** $x < 3$ **63.** $x \le 3$ **65.** At least 291   **67.** $x < 2$ **69.** $x > -\frac{8}{3}$ **71.** $x \ge 6$; the width is at least 6 meters.   **73.** $x > 6$; the shortest side is even and greater than 6 inches.   **75.** $x \ge 2$ **77.** $x < 4$ **79.** $x < -1$

PROBLEM SET 1.9

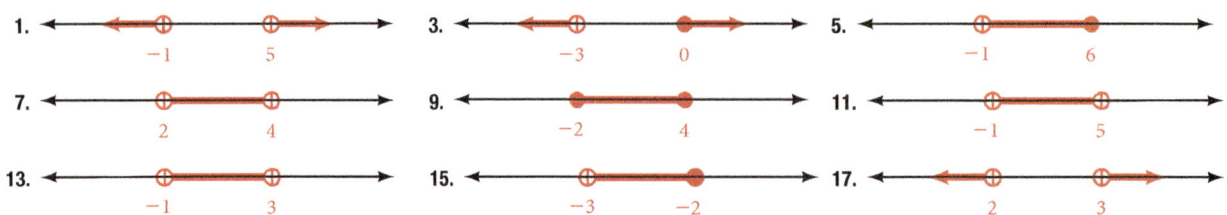

1.   **3.**   **5.**

7.   **9.**   **11.**

13.   **15.**   **17.**

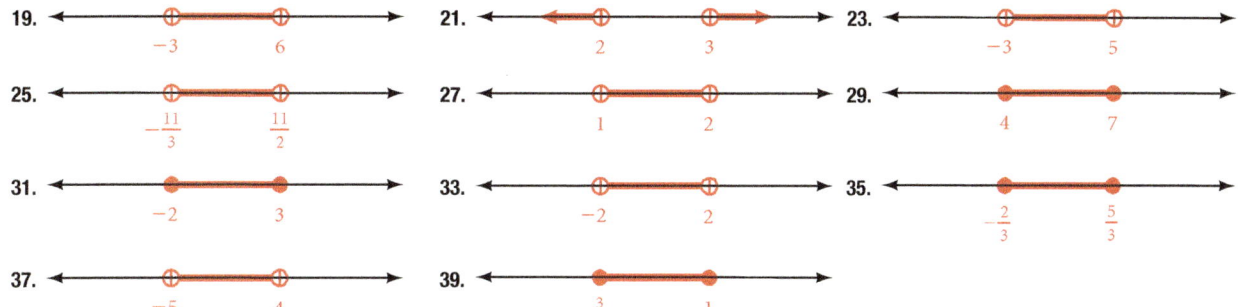

19. number line with open circles at -3 and 6

21. number line with open circles at 2 and 3, shaded outward

23. number line with open circles at -3 and 5

25. number line with open circles at $-\frac{11}{3}$ and $\frac{11}{2}$

27. number line with open circles at 1 and 2

29. number line with closed circles at 4 and 7

31. number line with closed circles at -2 and 3

33. number line with open circles at -2 and 2

35. number line with closed circles at $-\frac{2}{3}$ and $\frac{5}{3}$

37. number line with open circles at -5 and 4

39. number line with closed circles at $-\frac{3}{2}$ and 1

41. $-2 < x < 3$ **43.** $x \le -2$ or $x \ge 3$ **45.** **a.** $2x + x > 10; x + 10 > 2x; 2x + 10 > x$ **b.** $\frac{10}{3} < x < 10$

47. number line with closed circles at 50 and 266 **49.** $4 < x < 5$ **51.** **a.** $20 < P < 30$ **b.** $3 < w < \frac{11}{2}$ **c.** $7 < l \le \frac{19}{2}$

53. 8 **55.** 24 **57.** 25% **59.** 10% **61.** 80 **63.** 400 **65.** -5 **67.** 5 **69.** 7 **71.** 9 **73.** 6 **75.** $2x - 3$ **77.** $-3, 0, 2$

CHAPTER 1 TEST

1. $-y + 1$ **2.** $4x - 1$ **3.** $4 - 2y$ **4.** $x - 22$ **5.** -3 **6.** -4 **7.** **a.**

n	$(n + 2)^2$
1	9
2	16
3	25
4	36

b.

n	$n^2 + 2$
1	3
2	6
3	11
4	18

8. $x = 3$ **9.** $y = -5$ **10.** $x = -3$ **11.** $x = 4$ **12.** $x = 1$ **13.** 55 **14.** $t = -3$ **15.** $x = \frac{10}{4}$ **16.** $x = (.40)(56)$

17. $720 = 0.24x$ **18.** -1 **19.** 8 **20.** $y = 2 - \frac{1}{3x}$ **21.** $a = \frac{x^2 - v^2}{2d}$ **22.** $18, 36$ **23.** 20 cm, 55 cm **24.** 6 nickles, 14 dimes

25. \$700, \$1,200 **26.** $x > 10$ number line with open circle at 10 shaded right, marks at 0, 10 **27.** $y \ge -4$ number line with closed circle at -4 shaded right, marks at -4, 0

28. $x > -4$ number line with open circle at -4 shaded right, marks at -4, 0 **29.** $n \le -2$ number line with closed circle at -2 shaded left, marks at -2, 0

30. $1 > x$ or $x > 3$ number line with open circles at 1 and 3 **31.** $2 \le x \le 8$ number line with closed circles at 2 and 8

Chapter 2

PROBLEM SET 2.1

1–17.

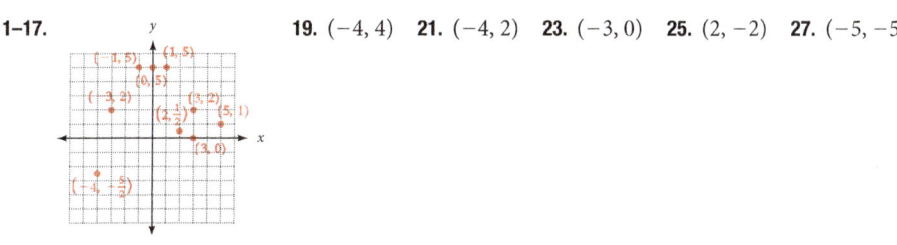

19. $(-4, 4)$ **21.** $(-4, 2)$ **23.** $(-3, 0)$ **25.** $(2, -2)$ **27.** $(-5, -5)$

29. Yes **31.** No **33.** Yes **35.** No

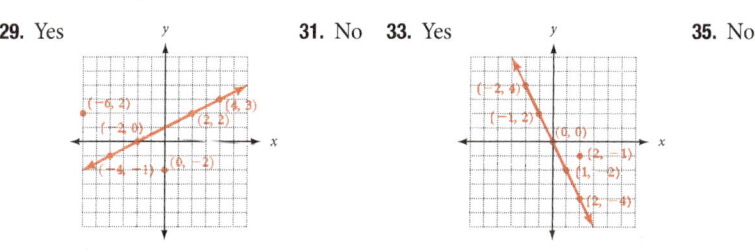

37. Yes

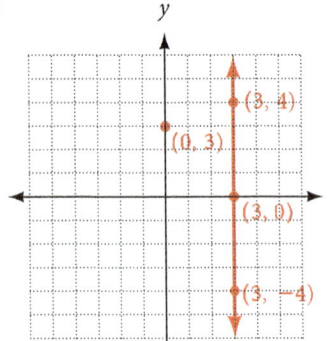

39. No **41.** No

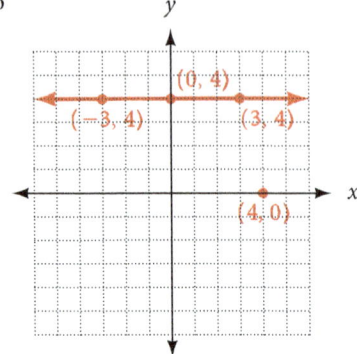

43. No

45. a. (5, 40), (10, 80), (20, 160), Answers may vary **b.** $320 **c.** 30 hours **d.** No, if she works 35 hours, she should be paid $280.

47.

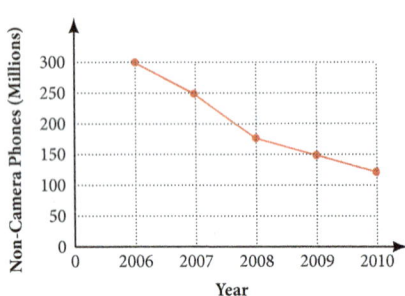

49. (1985, 20.2), (1990, 34.4), (1995, 44.8), (2000, 65.4), (2005, 104)

51. $A = (1, 2), B = (6, 7)$ **53.** $A = (2, 2), B = (2, 5), C = (7, 5)$

55. a. -3 **b.** 6 **c.** 0 **d.** -4 **57. a.** 4 **b.** 2 **c.** -1 **d.** 9

PROBLEM SET 2.2

1. $(0, 6), (3, 0), (6, -6)$ **3.** $(0, 3), (4, 0), (-4, 6)$ **5.** $(1, 1), \left(\frac{3}{4}, 0\right), (5, 17)$ **7.** $(2, 13), (1, 6), (0, -1)$ **9.** $(-5, 4), (-5, -3), (-5, 0)$

11.

x	y
1	3
-3	-9
4	12
6	18

13.

x	y
0	0
$-\frac{1}{2}$	-2
-3	-12
3	12

15.

x	y
2	3
3	2
5	0
9	-4

17.

x	y
2	0
3	2
1	-2
-3	-10

19.

x	y
0	-1
-1	-7
-3	-19
$\frac{3}{2}$	8

21. $(0, -2)$

23. $(1, 5), (0, -2),$ and $(-2, -16)$ **25.** $(1, 6),$ and $(0, 0)$ **27.** $(2, -2)$ **29.** $(3, 0)$ and $(3, -3)$ **31.** 12 inches

33. a. Yes **b.** No, she should earn $108 for working 9 hours. **c.** No, she should earn $84 for working 7 hours. **d.** Yes

35. a. $375,000 **b.** At the end of 6 years. **c.** No, the crane will be worth $195,000 after 9 years. **d.** $600,000

37. -3 **39.** 2 **41.** 0 **43.** $y = -5x + 4$ **45.** $y = \frac{3}{2}x - 3$

PROBLEM SET 2.3

1. $(0, 4), (2, 2), (4, 0)$

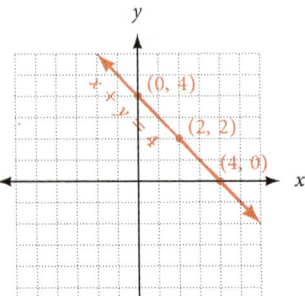

3. $(0, 3), (2, 1), (4, -1)$

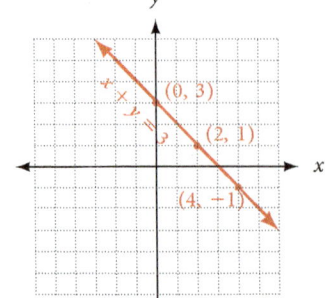

5. $(0, 0), (-2, -4), (2, 4)$

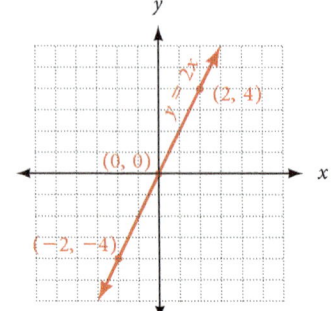

7. $(-3, -1), (0, 0), (3, 1)$

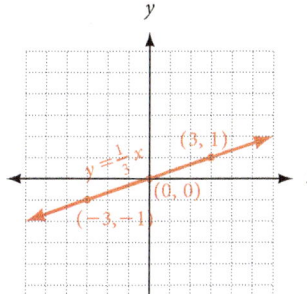

9. $(0, 1), (-1, -1), (1, 3)$

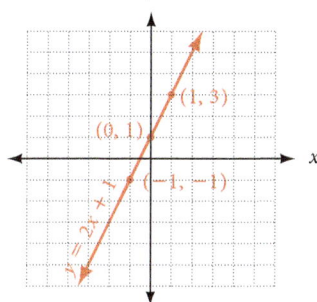

11. $(0, 4), (-1, 4), (2, 4)$

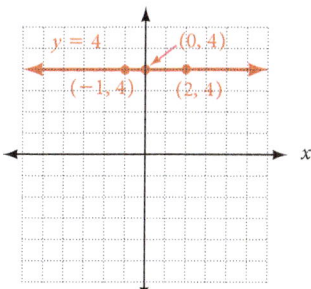

13. $(-2, 2), (0, 3), (2, 4)$

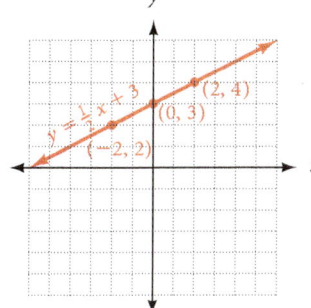

15. $(-3, 3), (0, 1), (3, -1)$

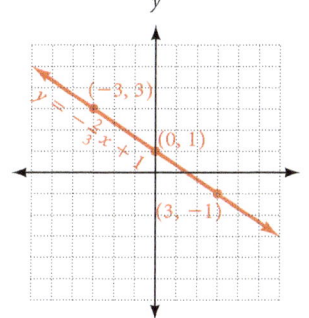

17. $(-1, 5), (0, 3), (1, 1)$

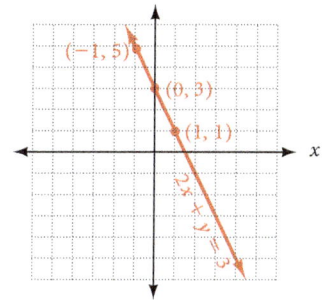

19. $(0, 3), (2, 0), (4, -3)$

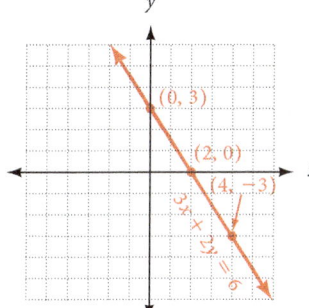

21. $(-2, 2), (0, 3), (2, 4)$

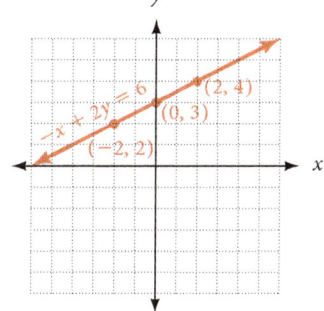

23.

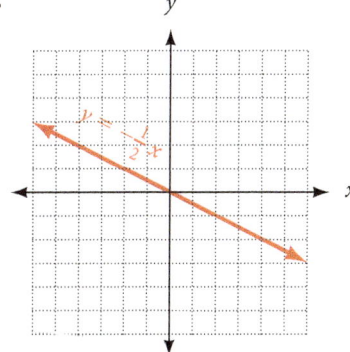

25.

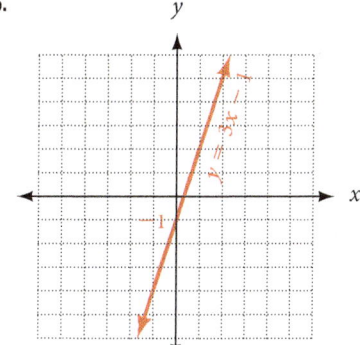

27.

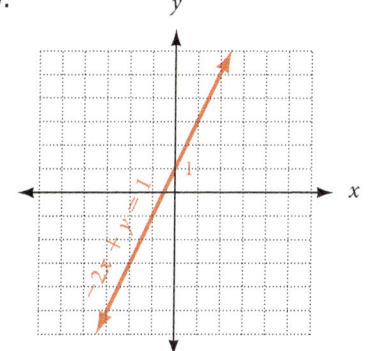

29.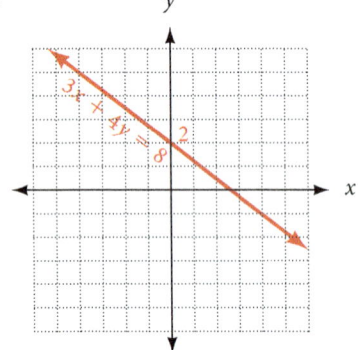

31.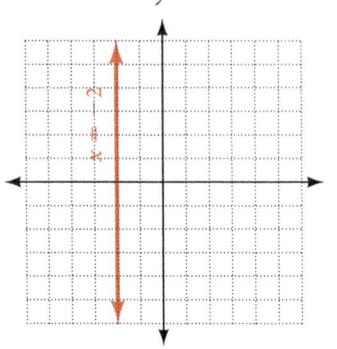

33.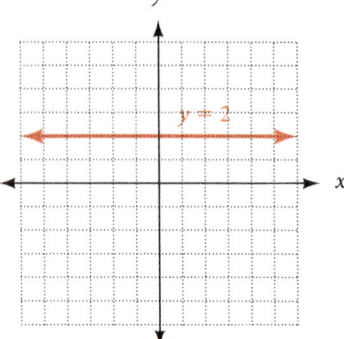

35.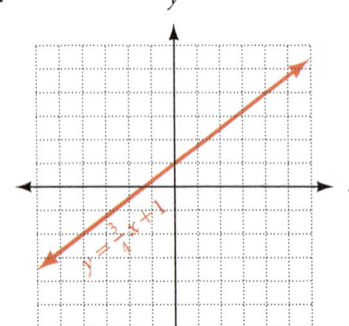

37.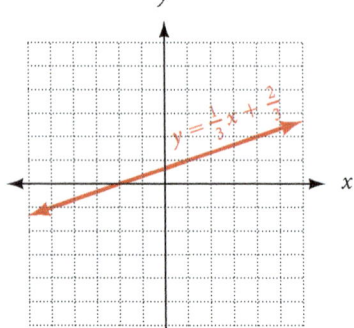

39.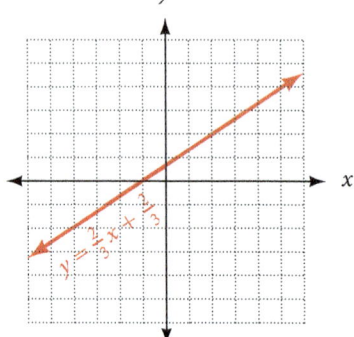

41.

Equation	H, V, and/or O
$x = 3$	V
$y = 3$	H
$y = 3x$	O
$y = 0$	O, H

43.

Equation	H, V, and/or O
$x = -\frac{3}{5}$	V
$y = -\frac{3}{5}$	H
$y = -\frac{3}{5}x$	O
$x = 0$	O, V

45.

x	y
-4	-3
-2	-2
0	-1
2	0
6	2

47. **a.** $\frac{5}{2}$ **b.** 5 **c.** 2 **d.**

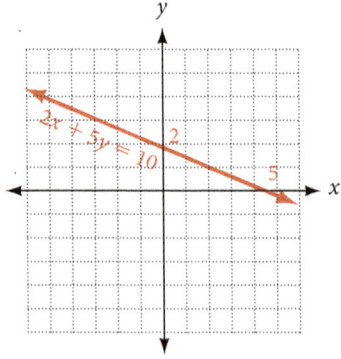

e. $y = -\frac{2}{5}x + 2$

49. **a.** 2 **b.** 3 **51.** **a.** -4 **b.** 2 **53.** **a.** 6 **b.** 2

PROBLEM SET 2.4

1.
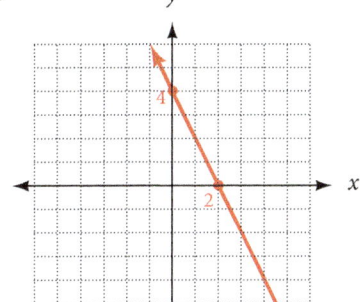

3.
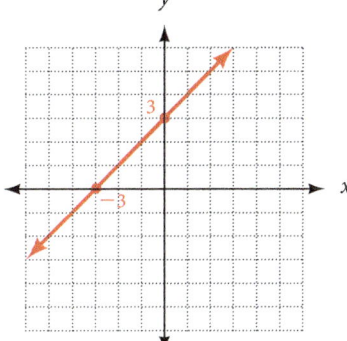

5.
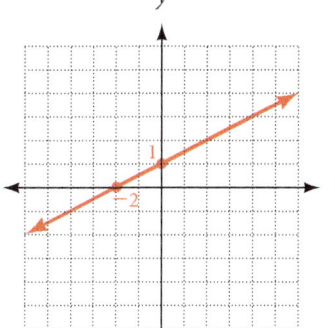

7.
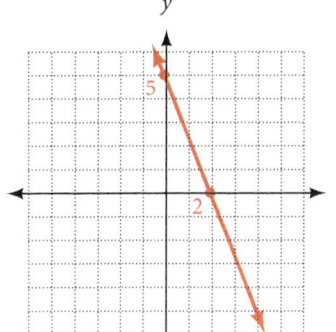

9.
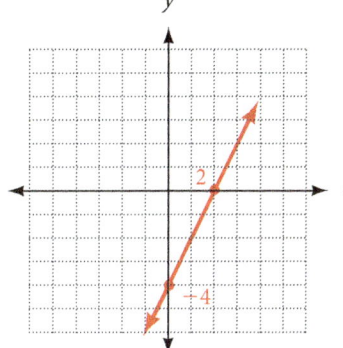

11.
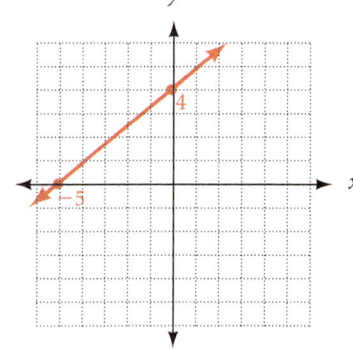

13.
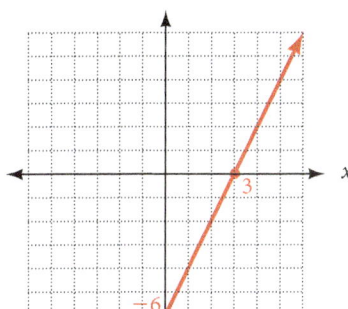

15.
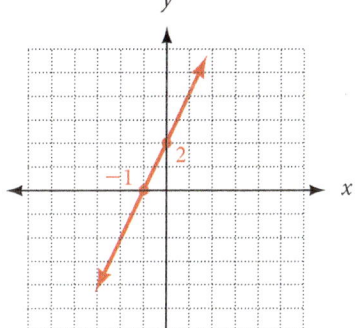

17.
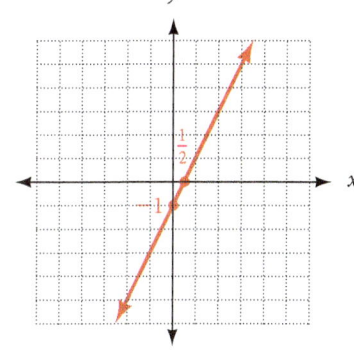

19.
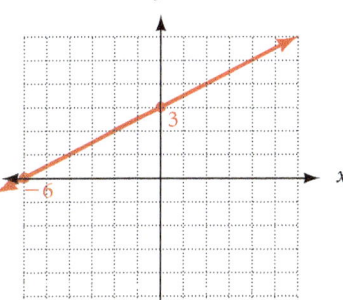

21.
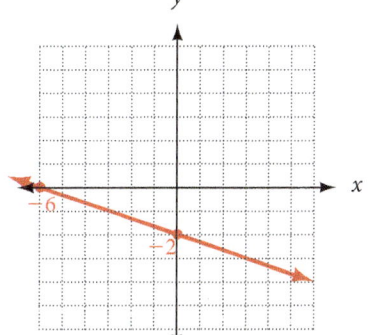

23.
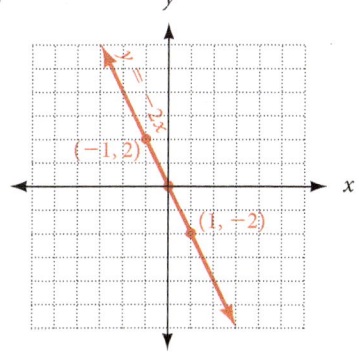

25.

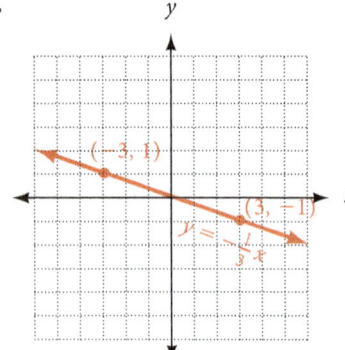

27.

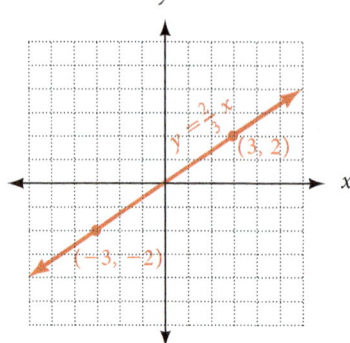

29.

Equation	x-intercept	y-intercept
$3x + 4y = 12$	4	3
$3x + 4y = 4$	$\frac{4}{3}$	1
$3x + 4y = 3$	1	$\frac{3}{4}$
$3x + 4y = 2$	$\frac{2}{3}$	$\frac{1}{2}$

31.

Equation	x-intercept	y-intercept
$x - 3y = 2$	2	$-\frac{2}{3}$
$y = \frac{1}{3}x - \frac{2}{3}$	2	$-\frac{2}{3}$
$x - 3y = 0$	0	0
$y = \frac{1}{3}x$	0	0

33. a. 0 **b.** $-\frac{3}{2}$ **c.** 1 **d.**

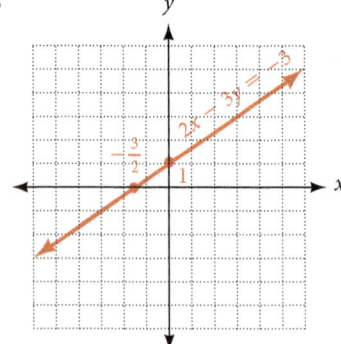

e. $y = \frac{2}{3}x + 1$

35. x-intercept = 3; y-intercept = 5 **37.** x-intercept = -1; y-intercept = -3

39.

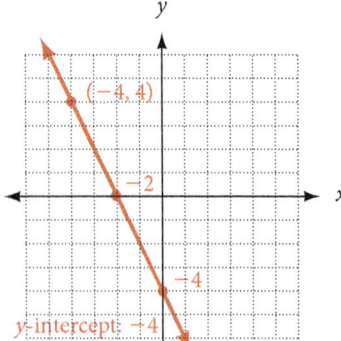

41.

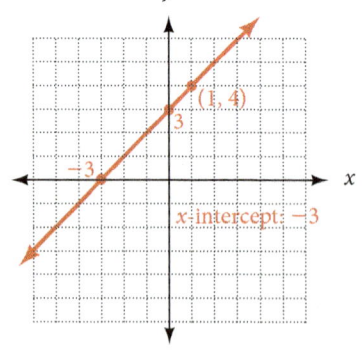

43.

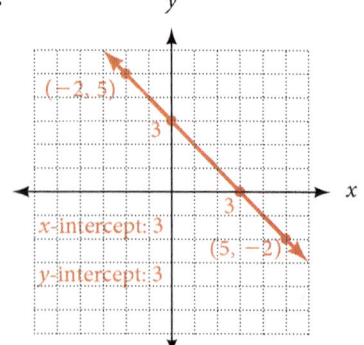

45.

x	y
−2	1
0	−1
−1	0
1	−2

47.

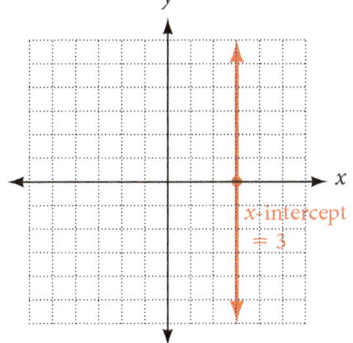

49.

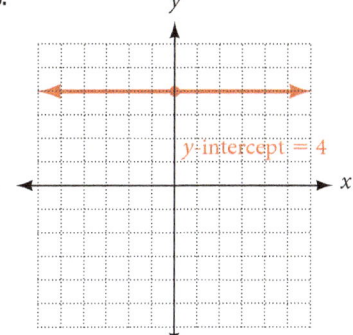

51.

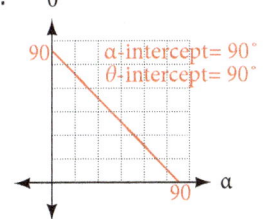

53. a. $\frac{3}{2}$ b. $\frac{3}{2}$ **55.** a. $\frac{3}{2}$ b. $\frac{3}{2}$

PROBLEM SET 2.5

1.

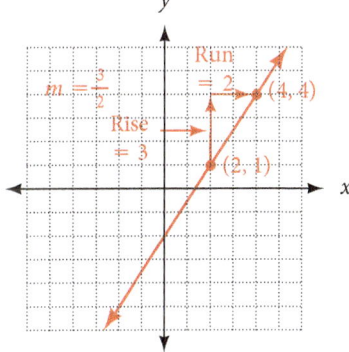

3.

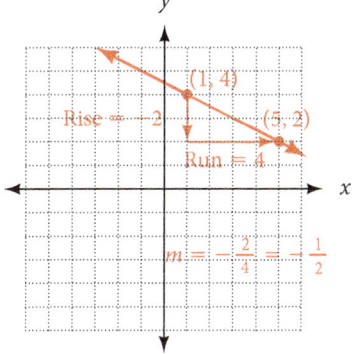

5.

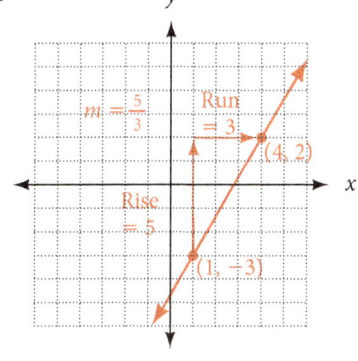

7.

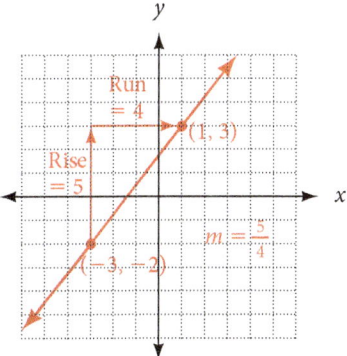

9.

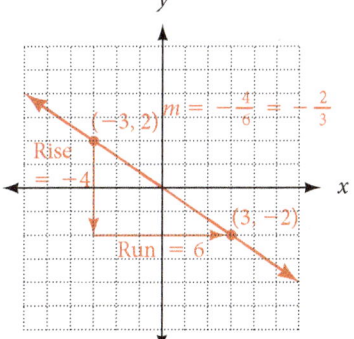

11.

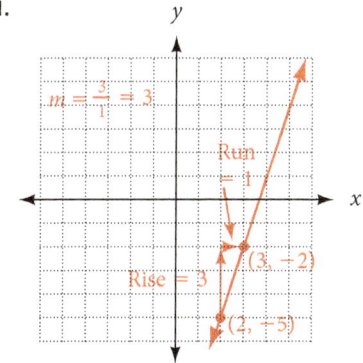

13.

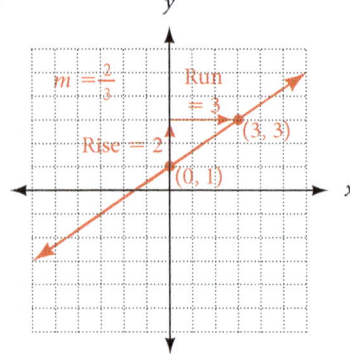

15.

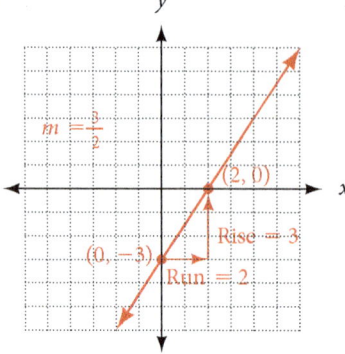

17.

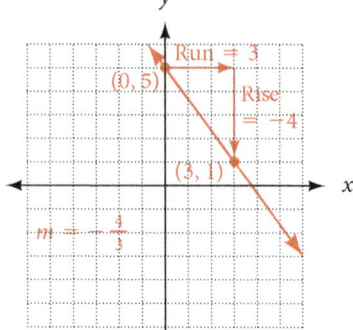

19.

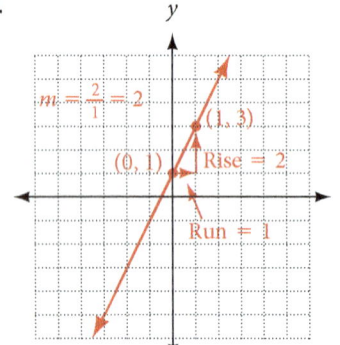

21.

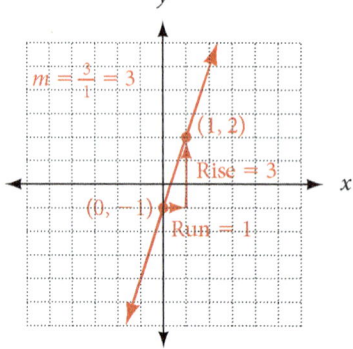

23. Slope = 3; y-intercept = 2   **25.** Slope = 2; y-intercept = -2

27.

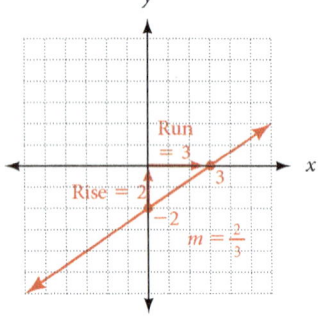

29.

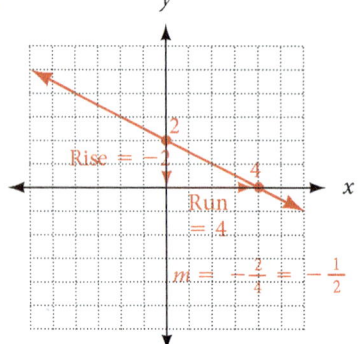

31.

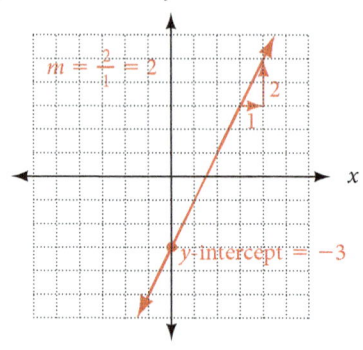

33.

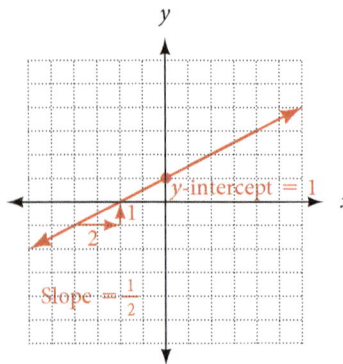

35. 6   **37.**

Equation	Slope
$x = 3$	no slope
$y = 3$	0
$y = 3x$	3

39.

Equation	Slope
$y = -\frac{2}{3}$	0
$x = -\frac{2}{3}$	no slope
$y = -\frac{2}{3}x$	$-\frac{2}{3}$

41. $3a + 6$ **43.** $11y$ **45.** $3x + 7y$ **47.** $6x + 7y$ **49.** Slopes: A, 3.3; B, 3.1; C, 5.3; D, 1.9   **51.** Slopes: A, -50; B, -75; C, -25

53. $y = 2x + 4$ **55.** $y = -2x + 3$ **57.** $y = \frac{4}{5}x - 4$ **59.** $y = 2x + 5$ **61.** $y = \frac{2}{3}x - 1$ **63.** $y = -\frac{3}{2}x + 1$

Answers to Odd-Numbered Problems

PROBLEM SET 2.6

1. $y = \frac{2}{3}x + 1$ **3.** $y = \frac{3}{2}x - 1$ **5.** $y = -\frac{2}{3}x + 3$ **7.** $y = 2x - 4$

9. $m = 2; b = 4$  **11.** $m = -3; b = 3$ **13.** $m = -\frac{3}{2}; b = 3$

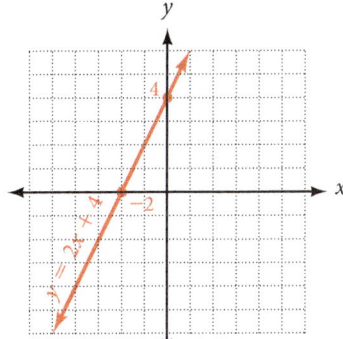 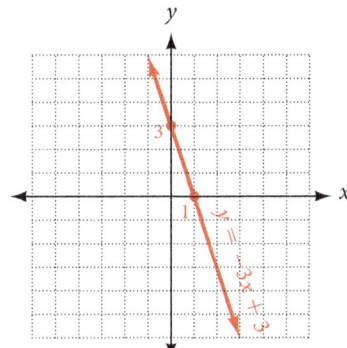 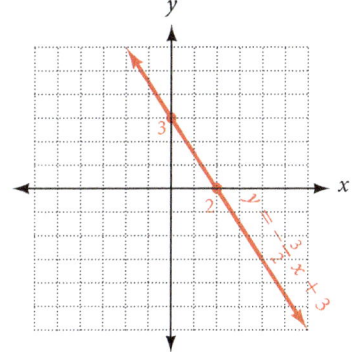

15. $m = \frac{4}{5}; b = -4$ **17.** $m = -\frac{2}{5}; b = -2$

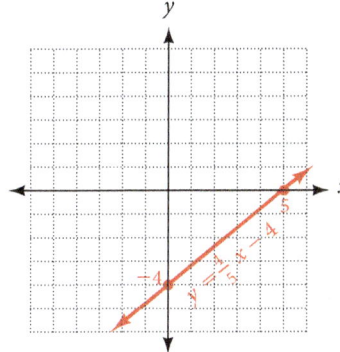 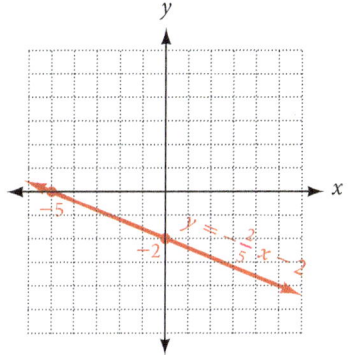

19. $y = 2x - 1$ **21.** $y = -\frac{1}{2}x - 1$ **23.** $y = \frac{3}{2}x - 6$ **25.** $y = -3x + 1$ **27.** $y = x - 2$ **29.** $y = 2x - 3$ **31.** $y = \frac{4}{3}x + 2$

33. $y = -\frac{2}{3}x - 3$ **35.** $m = 3, b = 3, y = 3x + 3$ **37.** $m = \frac{1}{4}, b = -1, y = \frac{1}{4}x - 1$

39. a. $-\frac{5}{2}$ **b.** $y = 2x + 6$ **c.** 6 **d.** 2 **e.** 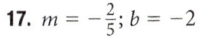 **41.** $y = -\frac{2}{3}x + 2$ **43.** $y = -\frac{5}{2}x - 5$

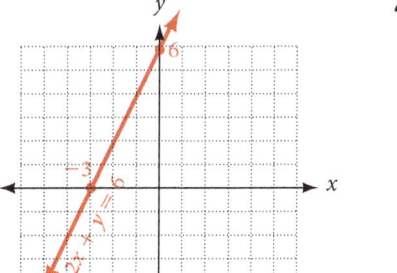

45. $x = 3$ **47.** $2a^2 - 2a - 2$ **49.** $x^3 + 6x^2 + 12x + 8$ **51. a.** 2 **b.** 1 **c.** 3

47. a. \$6,000 **b.** 3 years **c.** slope $= -3,000$ **d.** \$3,000 **e.** $V = -3,000t + 21,000$

49. 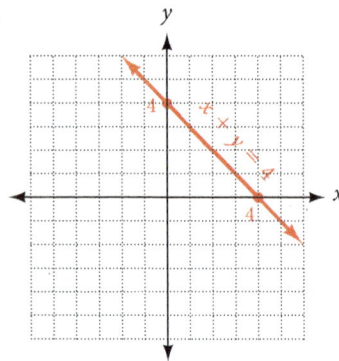   **51.** 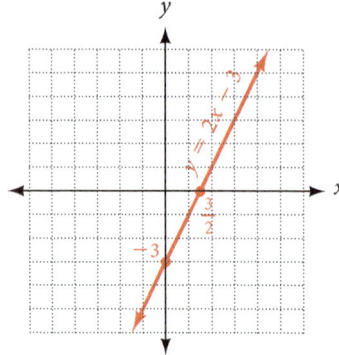   **53.**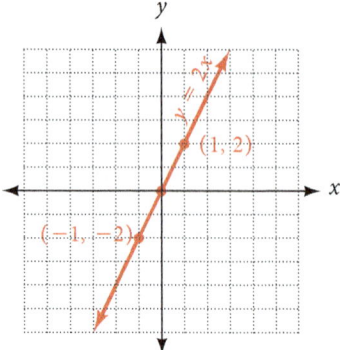

PROBLEM SET 2.7

Vocabulary Review **1.** average   **2.** mean   **3.** median   **4.** mode   **5.** range   **6.** variance   **7.** standard deviation

Problems 1. 3   **3.** 6   **5.** 16,194   **7.** 7.5   **9.** 11   **11.** 50   **13.** 900   **15.** 3.2   **17.** 18   **19.** 87   **21.** 1   **23.** 22

25. 2.9   **27.** 38   **29.** 11.67   **31.** 51.67   **33.** $\sqrt{14}$ **35.** $3\sqrt{2}$ **37.** Mean = 79.5, median = 83

39. *Both are $31,000*   **41. a.** 78.5 **b.** 76 **c.** 76   **43.** Mean = $6,868.83; median = $6,993

45. Mean = $19,985, median = $19,788   **47.** 47   **49.** $3,190   **51.** $1,530   **53. a.** 3,055 **b.** Mean   **55.** 7

Find the Mistake   1. Based on the list, the mean cost of lunch is $3.35.   2. You would find the median by putting the list in order of shortest to longest, then finding half the sum of 2.7 and 3.0, which is 2.85 inches.   3. The mode for the following list of numbers is 12.   4. Suppose a basketball team scored 80 points during their highest scoring game, and 42 points during their lowest scoring game. The range of points scored is $80 - 42 = 38$.

PROBLEM SET 2.8

1. Answers may vary   **3. a.** No **b.** Answers may vary

5. a. No **b.** Answers may vary **c.** The more games played, the higher the hitting ratio per game.   **7.** Answers may vary.

9. $y = 0.5226x + 2.7782$ **11.** $y = 2.8685x - 0.4701$

13. a. $y = 0.4963x + 17.7339$ **c.** $22.20 **d.** $28.16 **e.** $r = 0.9914$

15. 12   **17.** 28   **19.** $-\frac{7}{4}$ **21.** $w = \frac{P - 2\ell}{2}$ **23.** $[-6, \infty)$ ⟵━━━━[━━━━⟶
    −6

25. $(-\infty, 6)$ ⟵━━━━━━)━━⟶   **27.** 6, 2   **29.** $\varnothing$
                          6

PROBLEM SET 2.9

1. 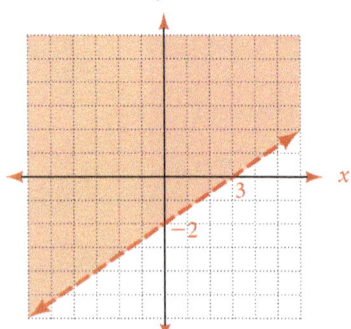   **3.** 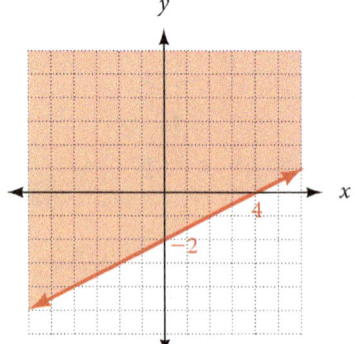   **5.**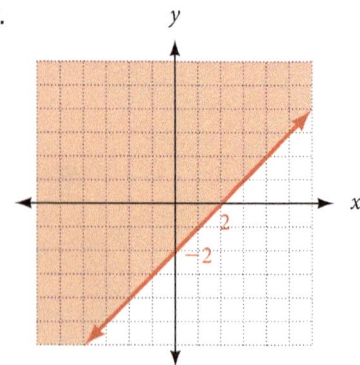

7.

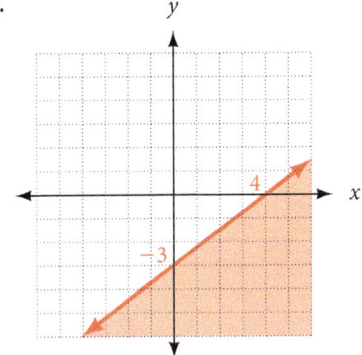

9.

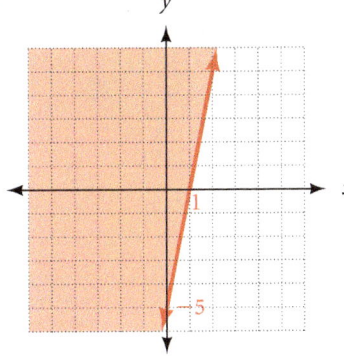

11.

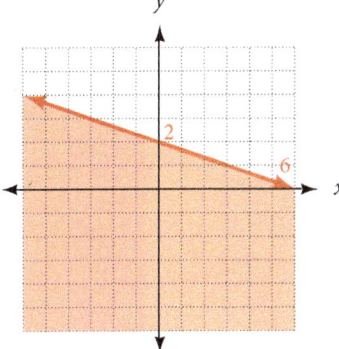

13.

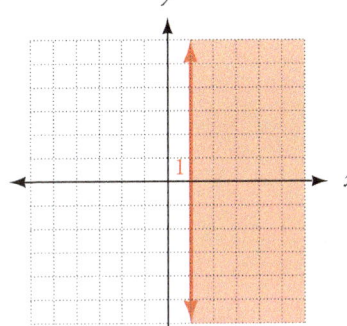

15.

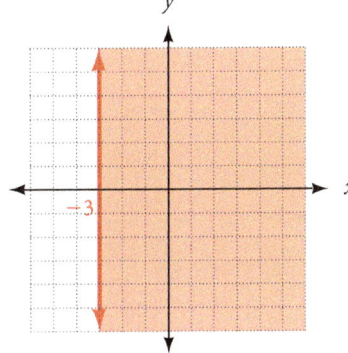

17.

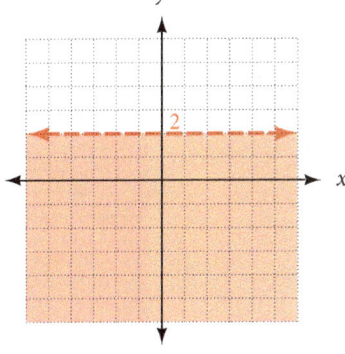

19.

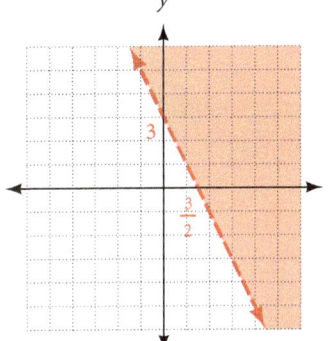

21.

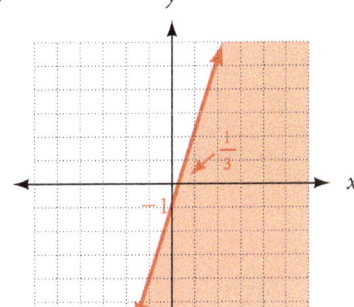

23.

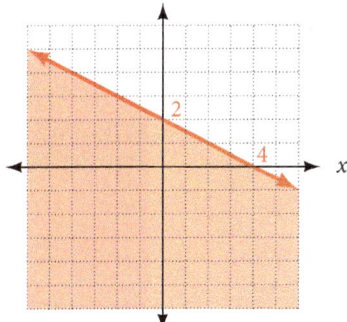

25. **a.** $y < \frac{8}{3}$ **b.** $y > -\frac{8}{3}$ **c.** $y = -\frac{4}{3}x + 4$ **d.**

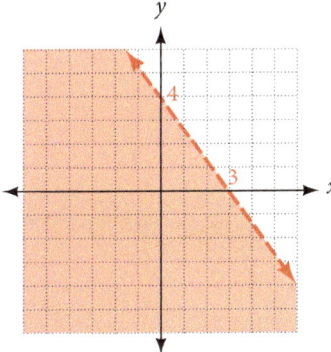

27. **a.** $y = \frac{2}{5}x + 2$ **b.** $y < \frac{2}{5}x + 2$ **c.** $y > \frac{2}{5}x + 2$ **29.** $-6x + 11$ **31.** -8 **33.** -4 **35.** $w = \frac{P - 2l}{2}$

37.

39. $y \geq \frac{3}{2}x - 6$ **41.** Width 2 inches, length 11 inches

CHAPTER 2 TEST

1.-4.

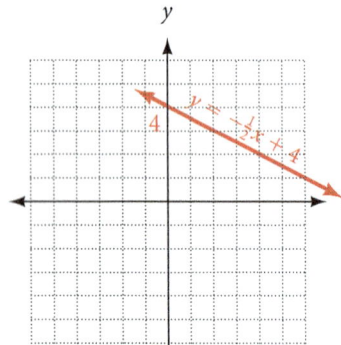

5. $(0, -3), (2, 0), (4, 3), (-2, -6)$ **6.** $(0, 7), (4, -5)$

7.

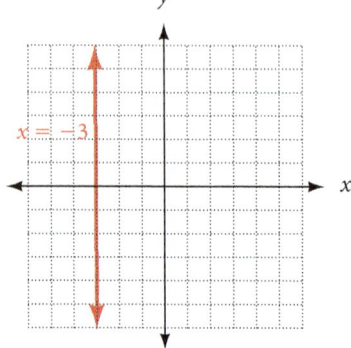

8.

9. $(2, 0), (0, -4)$ **10.** $(-4, 0), (0, 6)$ **11.** No x-intercept. $(0, 3)$ **12.** $-\frac{1}{2}$ **13.** $-\frac{8}{7}$ **14.** -3 **15.** Undefined **16.** 0

17. $y = -\frac{1}{2}x + 3$ **18.** $y = 3x - 5$ **19.** $y = -\frac{2}{3}x - 2$ **20.** $y = -\frac{6}{5}x + \frac{18}{5}$

21. mean = 23, mode = 26, median = 26, range = 14 **22.** mean = 13, mode = none, median = 13.5, range = 12

23. mean = 27, variance = 60, std dev ≈ 7.75 **24.** mean = 22, variance = 36.5, std dev ≈ 5.87

25.

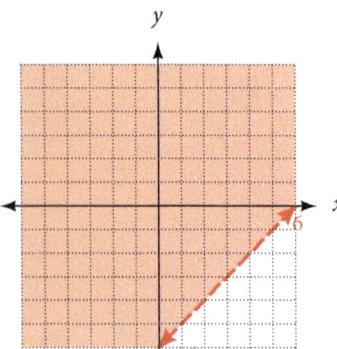

26.

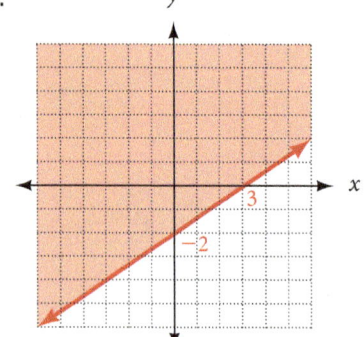

10. a.

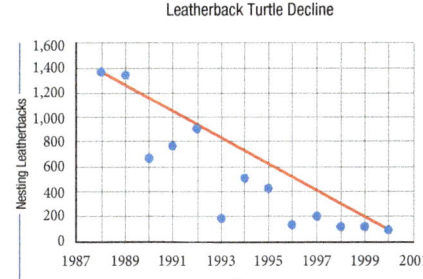

b. $-\dfrac{1,279}{12}$ **c.** $y = -\dfrac{1,279}{12}x + \dfrac{17,683}{12}$ **d.** No

e.

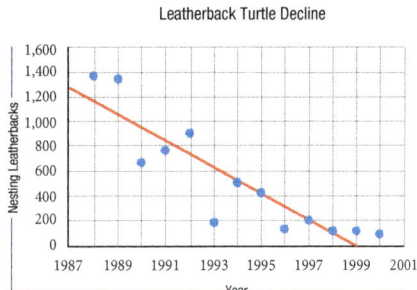

Chapter 3

PROBLEM SET 3.1

1.

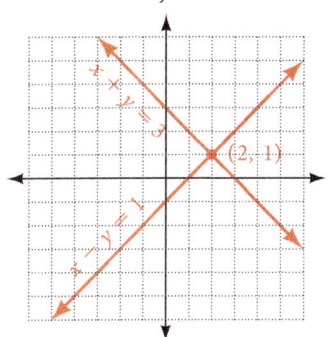

3.

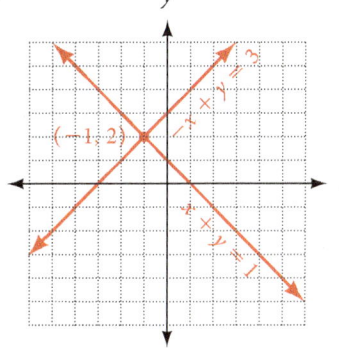

5.

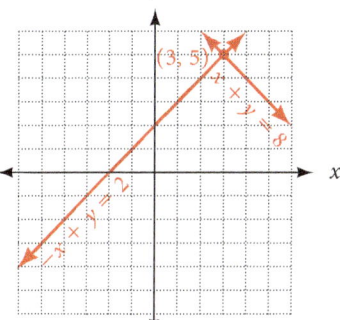

7.

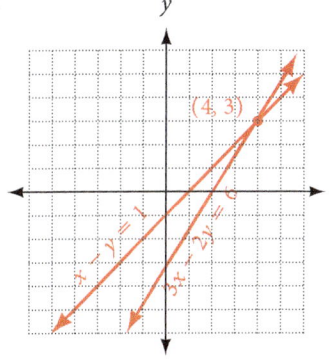

9.

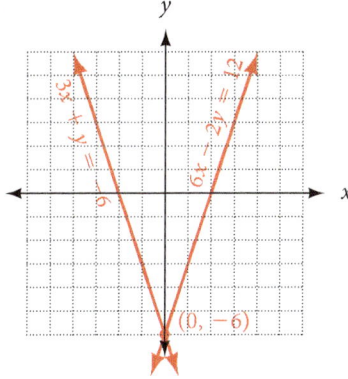

11.

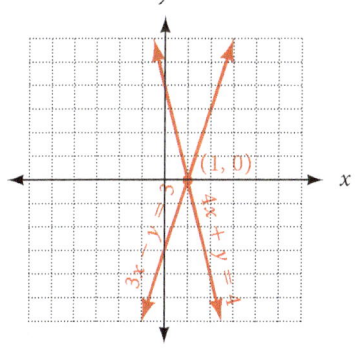

13.

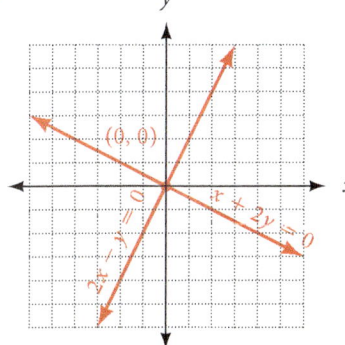

15.

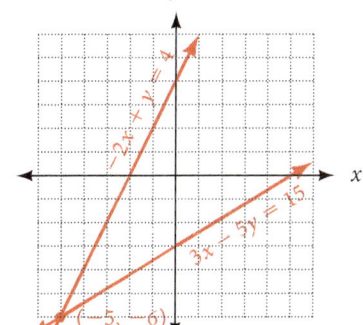

17.

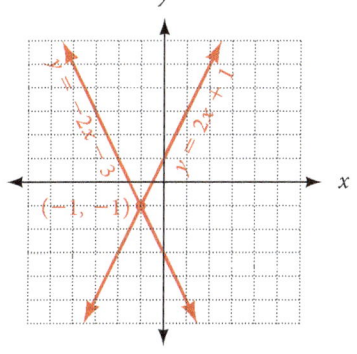

Answers to Odd-Numbered Problems

19.
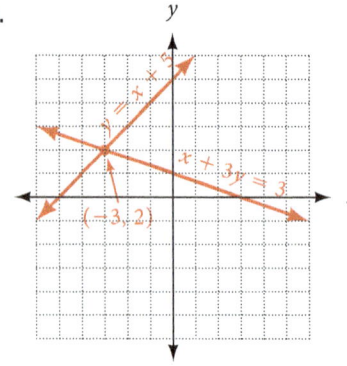

21.
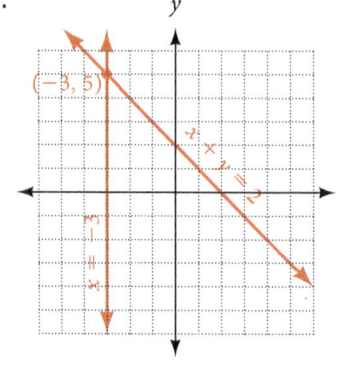

23.
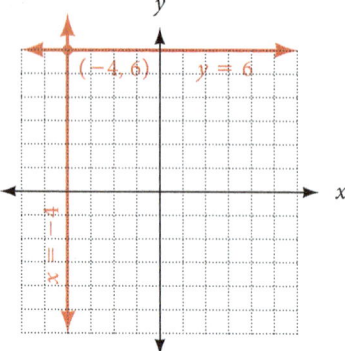

25. $\varnothing$
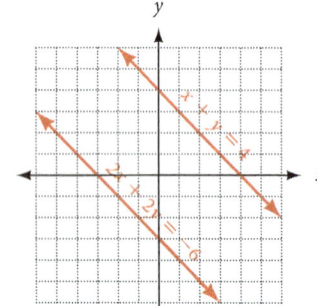

27. Any point on the line
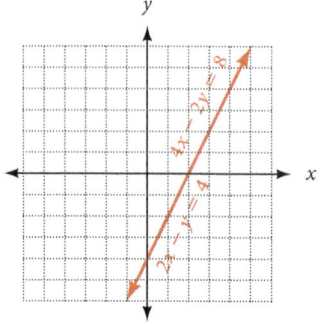

29.
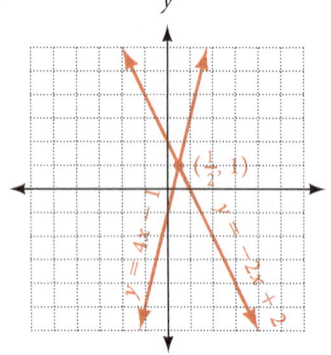

31.
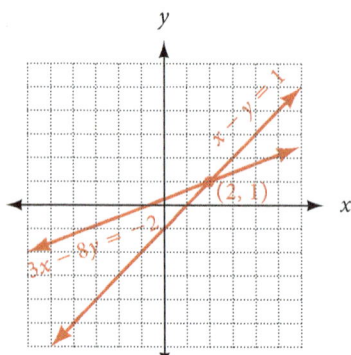

33. **a.** 25 hours **b.** Gigi's **c.** Marcy's

35. $2x$ **37.** $7x$ **39.** $13x$ **41.** $3x - 2y$ **43.** 1 **45.** 0 **47.** -5

PROBLEM SET 3.2

1. $(2, 1)$ **3.** $(3, 7)$ **5.** $(2, -5)$ **7.** $(-1, 0)$ **9.** Lines coincide. **11.** $(4, 8)$ **13.** $\left(\frac{1}{5}, 1\right)$ **15.** $(1, 0)$ **17.** $(-1, -2)$

19. $\left(-5, \frac{3}{4}\right)$ **21.** $(-4, 5)$ **23.** $(-3, -10)$ **25.** $(3, 2)$ **27.** $\left(5, \frac{1}{3}\right)$ **29.** $\left(-2, \frac{2}{3}\right)$ **31.** $(2, 2)$ **33.** Lines are parallel. $\varnothing$

35. $(1, 1)$ **37.** Lines are parallel. $\varnothing$ **39.** $(10, 12)$ **41.** 1 **43.** 2 **45.** All real numbers. **47.** $x = 3y - 1$ **49.** 1 **51.** 5

53. 34.5 **55.** 33.95

PROBLEM SET 3.3

1. $(4, 7)$ **3.** $(3, 17)$ **5.** $\left(\frac{3}{2}, 2\right)$ **7.** $(2, 4)$ **9.** $(0, 4)$ **11.** $(-1, 3)$ **13.** $(1, 1)$ **15.** $(2, -3)$ **17.** $\left(-2, \frac{3}{5}\right)$ **19.** $(-3, 5)$

21. Lines are parallel. $\varnothing$ **23.** $(3, 1)$ **25.** $\left(\frac{1}{2}, \frac{3}{4}\right)$ **27.** $(2, 6)$ **29.** $(4, 4)$ **31.** $(5, -2)$ **33.** $(18, 10)$ **35.** Lines coincide.

37. $(10, 12)$ **39.** **a.** 1,000 miles **b.** Car **c.** Truck **d.** We are only working with positive numbers. **41.** 3 and 23

43. 15 and 24 **45.** Length = 23 in.; width = 6 in. **47.** 14 nickels and 10 dimes

PROBLEM SET 3.4

1. $(1, 2, 1)$ **3.** $(2, 1, 3)$ **5.** $(2, 0, 1)$ **7.** $\left(\frac{1}{2}, \frac{2}{3}, -\frac{1}{2}\right)$ **9.** Inconsistent (no solution) **11.** $(4, -3, -5)$

13. Dependent (parallel planes)   **15.** $(4, -5, -3)$ **17.** Dependent (parallel planes)   **19.** $\left(\frac{1}{2}, 1, 2\right)$ **21.** $\left(\frac{1}{2}, \frac{1}{3}, \frac{1}{4}\right)$

23. $\left(\frac{10}{3}, -\frac{5}{3}, -\frac{1}{3}\right)$ **25.** $\left(\frac{1}{4}, -\frac{1}{3}, \frac{1}{8}\right)$ **27.** $(6, 8, 12)$ **29.** $(-141, -210, -104)$ **31.** 4 amp, 3 amp, 1 amp   **33.** $3x + 2$

35. $2x + 5y$ **37.** 6   **39.** $(-1, 5)$ **41.** $3, 7, 10$ **43.** 3 ft, 6 ft, 11 ft

PROBLEM SET 3.5

1. $(2, 3)$ **3.** $(-1, -2)$ **5.** $(7, 1)$ **7.** $(-3, 4)$ **9.** $(0, -9)$ **11.** $(-4, 3)$ **13.** $(-5, 7)$ **15.** $(0, -8)$

17. $(8, 4)$ **19.** $(1, 2, 1)$ **21.** $(2, 0, 1)$ **23.** $(0, 1, -2)$ **25.** $(0, -2, 4)$ **27.** $(2, 1, 1)$ **29.** $(1, 1, 2)$ **31.** $(4, 1, 5)$

33. $(1, 3, 1)$ **35.** $(-4, 3, 5)$**37.** $(0, 3, -1)$ **39.** $(1, 3, -4)$ **41.** $\left(4, \frac{10}{3}\right)$ **43.** $(6, 4)$

49.

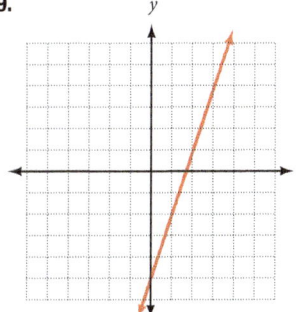

51.

PROBLEM SET 3.6

1. 3   **3.** 5   **5.** -2 **7.** -1 **9.** 0   **11.** 10   **13.** 2   **15.** -3 **17.** -2 **19.** -3 **21.** -2 **23.** $-2, 5$

25. $-8, 4$ **27.** $-3, 3$ **29.** $(3, 1)$ **31.** inconsistent system; $\varnothing$ **33.** $\left(-\frac{15}{43}, -\frac{27}{43}\right)$ **35.** $\left(\frac{60}{43}, \frac{46}{43}\right)$ **37.** $(2, 0)$

39. $\left(\frac{474}{323}, \frac{40}{323}\right)$ **41.** 3   **43.** 0   **45.** 3   **47.** 8   **49.** 6   **51.** -228 **53.** 27   **55.** -57 **57.** $(3, -1, 2)$

59. $\left(\frac{1}{2}, \frac{5}{2}, 1\right)$ **61.** No unique solution   **63.** $\left(-\frac{10}{91}, -\frac{9}{13}, \frac{107}{91}\right)$ **65.** $\left(\frac{83}{18}, -\frac{7}{9}, -\frac{17}{18}\right)$ **67.** $\left(\frac{111}{53}, \frac{57}{53}, \frac{80}{53}\right)$

69. $\left(\frac{31}{4}, \frac{7}{2}, \frac{9}{4}\right)$ **71.** $\left(\frac{71}{13}, -\frac{12}{13}, \frac{24}{13}\right)$ **73.** $(3, 1, 2)$ **75.** $y - mx = b; y = mx + b$

77. a. $y = 0.3x + 3.4$ **b.** $y = 0.3(2) + 3.4; 4$ billion   **79. a.** $I = 767.5x + 21,363$ **b.** $I = 767.5(4) + 21,363; \$24,433$

81. 14.4 million   **83.** 1,540 heart transplants   **85.** $x = 50$ items   **87.** 1986   **89.** 4   **91.** 4   **93.** 171

95. $(2, 1, 3, 1)$ **97.** $\left(\frac{1}{a+2}, \frac{1}{a+2}, \frac{1}{a+2}\right)$ **99.** $3x + 2$ **101.** $-\frac{160}{9}$ **103.** 320   **105.** $2x + 5y$ **107.** 6

109. $y = 5, z = 2$

PROBLEM SET 3.7

1. 5, 13   **3.** 10, 16   **5.** 1, 3, 4   **7.** 3 and 23   **9.** 15 and 24   **11.** 225 adult and 700 children's tickets

13. \$12,000 at 6%, \$8,000 at 7%   **15.** \$4,000 at 6%, \$8,000 at 7.5%   **17.** \$200 at 6%, \$1,400 at 8%, \$600 at 9%

19. 6 gallons of 20%, 3 gallons of 50%   **21.** 5 gallons of 20%, 10 gallons of 14%   **23.** 12.5 lbs of oats, 12.5 lbs of nuts

25. Speed of boat: 9 miles/hour, speed of current: 3 miles/hour   **27.** Airplane: 270 miles per hour, wind: 30 miles per hour

29. 12 nickels, 8 dimes   **31.** 3 of each   **33.** 110 nickels   **35.** 14 nickels and 10 dimes

37. $x = -200p + 700$; when $p = \$3, x = 100$ items   **39.** Length = 23 inches; Width = 6 inches;

41. $h = -16t^2 + 64t + 80$ **43.** 18 Preregistered, 11 on-site   **45.** No   **47.** $(4, 0)$ **49.** $x > 435$

Answers to Odd-Numbered Problems

1.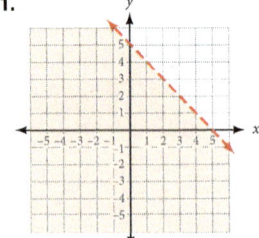

3.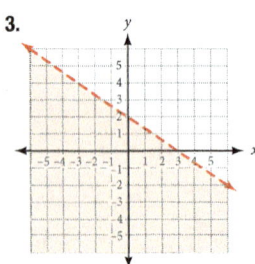

5.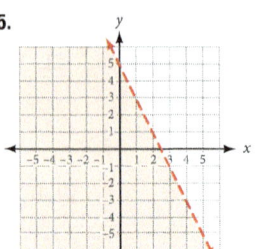

7.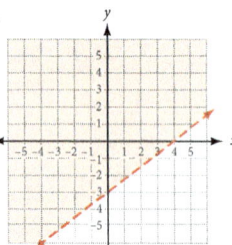

9.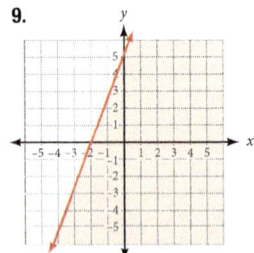

11. a. No **b.** Yes **c.** No **d.** Yes

13.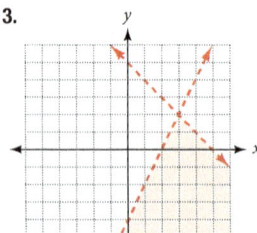

15.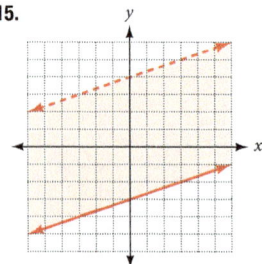

17.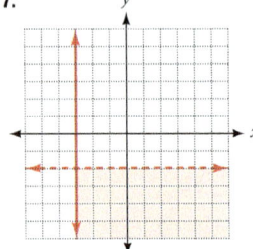

19.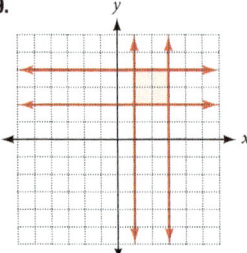

21.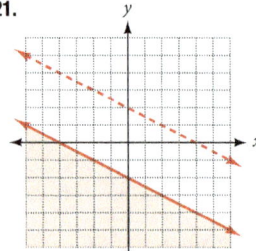

23. No solution

25.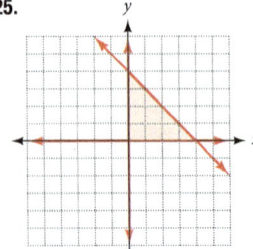

27.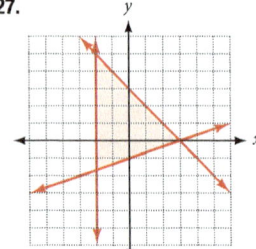

29.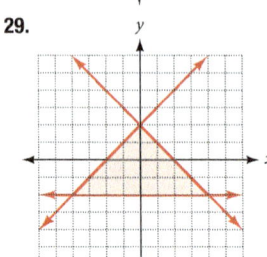

31.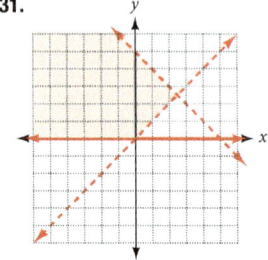

33.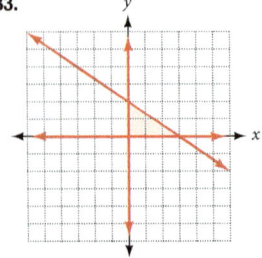

35. $x + y \leq 4; -x + y < 4$

37. $x + y \geq 4; -x + y < 4$

39. $x \geq -4; x \leq -2$

41. a. $0.55x + 0.65y \leq 40; x \geq 2y; x > 15; y \geq 0$ **b.** 10 65-cent stamps

43. d **45.** c **47.** 3 **49.** 2 **51.** $(-\infty, 4)$

53. $[-52, \infty)$ **55.** 3, 15 **57.** 5, 1

CHAPTER 3 TEST

1. $(0, 6)$ **2.**

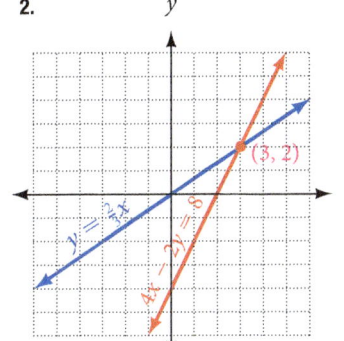

3.

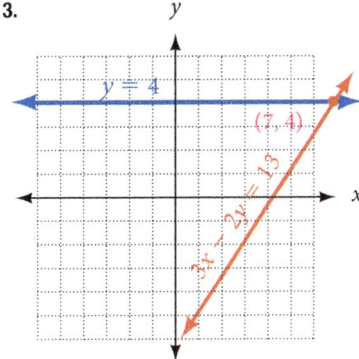

4.

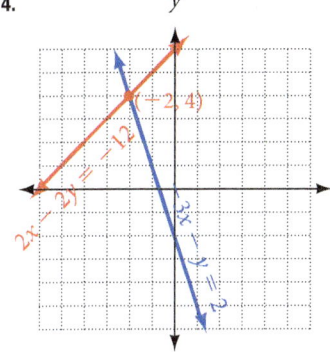

5. $(-4, 5)$ **6.** $(1, 2)$ **7.** $(-6, 3)$ **8.** Lines coincide **9.** $(4, 0)$ **10.** $(19, 9)$ **11.** $(-3, 4)$ **12.** $(11, 3)$ **13.** $\left(1, \frac{2}{3}, \frac{2}{3}\right)$

14. $(-2, 2, 1)$ **15.** 2 **16.** 0 **17.** $\left(\frac{47}{26}, \frac{29}{26}\right)$ **18.** $4, 4$ **19.** \$1,200 at 13%, \$3,600 at 17%

20. 730 adult tickets, 160 children's tickets **21.** Boat: 6 mph; Current: 3 mph **22.** 3 quarters, 1 dime, 4 nickels

23.

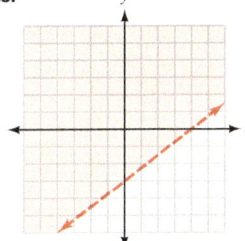

24.

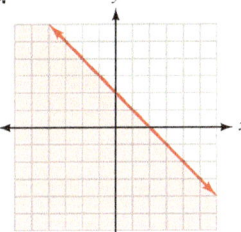

25.

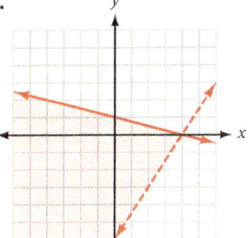

26. No solution

27.

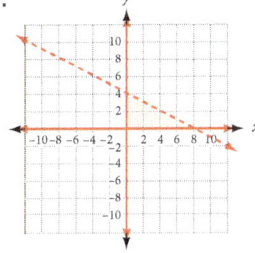

Chapter 4

PROBLEM SET 4.1

1. Base = 4, exponent = 2, 16 **3.** Base = .3, exponent = 2, 0.09 **5.** Base = 4, exponent = 3, 64

7. Base = -5, exponent = 2, 25 **9.** Base = 2, exponent = 3, -8 **11.** Base = 3, exponent = 4, 81

13. Base = $\frac{2}{3}$, exponent = 2, $\frac{4}{9}$ **15.** Base = $\frac{1}{2}$, exponent = 4, $\frac{1}{16}$

17. a.

Number x	1	2	3	4	5	6	7
Square x^2	1	4	9	16	25	36	49

b. Either *larger* or *greater* will work. **19.** x^9 **21.** y^{30} **23.** 2^{12}

25. x^{28} **27.** x^{10} **29.** 5^{12} **31.** y^9 **33.** 2^{50} **35.** a^{3x} **37.** b^{xy} **39.** $16x^2$ **41.** $32y^5$ **43.** $81x^4$ **45.** $0.25a^2b^2$ **47.** $64x^3y^3z^3$ **49.** $8x^{12}$

51. $16a^6$ **53.** x^{14} **55.** a^{11} **57.** $128x^7$ **59.** $432x^{10}$ **61.** $16x^4y^6$ **63.** $\frac{8}{27}a^{12}b^{15}$

65.

Number x	−3	−2	−1	0	1	2	3
Square x²	9	4	1	0	1	4	9

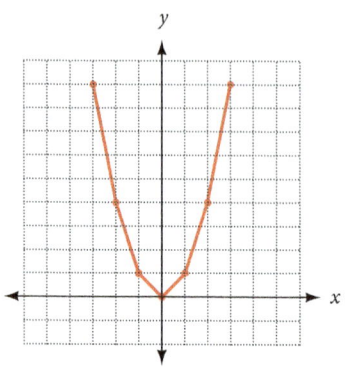

67.

Number x	−2.5	−1.5	−0.5	0	0.5	1.5	2.5
Square x²	6.25	2.25	0.25	0	0.25	2.25	6.25

69. 4.32×10^4 **71.** 5.7×10^2 **73.** 2.38×10^5 **75.** 2,490 **77.** 352 **79.** 28,000 **81.** 27 inches³ **83.** 15.6 inches³ **85.** 36 inches³

87. answers will vary **89.** 6.5×10^8 seconds **91.** \$740,000 **93.** \$180,000 **95.** 253 inches³ **97.** 220 inches³ **99.** −11

101. 3 **103.** 35 **105.** −35 **107.** 5 **109.** −14 **111.** 14 **113.** 16

PROBLEM SET 4.2

1. $\frac{1}{9}$ **3.** $\frac{1}{36}$ **5.** $\frac{1}{64}$ **7.** $\frac{1}{125}$ **9.** $\frac{2}{x^3}$ **11.** $\frac{1}{8x^3}$ **13.** $\frac{1}{25y^2}$ **15.** $\frac{1}{100}$ **17.**

19. $\frac{1}{25}$ **21.** x^6 **23.** 64 **25.** $8x^3$ **27.** 6^{10} **29.** $\frac{1}{6^{10}}$ **31.** $\frac{1}{2^8}$ **33.** 2^8

35. $27x^3$ **37.** $81x^4y^4$ **39.** 1 **41.** $2a^2b$ **43.** $\frac{1}{49y^6}$ **45.** $\frac{1}{x^8}$ **47.** $\frac{1}{y^3}$

49. x^2 **51.** a^6 **53.** $\frac{1}{y^9}$ **55.** y^{40} **57.** $\frac{1}{x}$ **59.** x^9 **61.** a^{16} **63.** $\frac{1}{a^4}$

65.

Number x	−3	−2	−1	0	1	2	3
Power of 2 2^x	$\frac{1}{8}$	$\frac{1}{4}$	$\frac{1}{2}$	1	2	4	8

17.

Number x	Square x²	Power of 2 2^x
−3	9	$\frac{1}{8}$
−2	4	$\frac{1}{4}$
−1	1	$\frac{1}{2}$
0	0	1
1	1	2
2	4	4
3	9	8

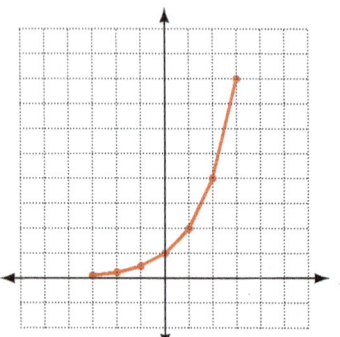

67. 4.8×10^{-3} **69.** 2.5×10^1 **71.** 9×10^{-6} **73.** *shown below*

Expanded Form	Scientific Notation $n \times 10^r$
0.000357	3.57×10^{-4}
0.00357	3.57×10^{-3}
0.0357	3.57×10^{-2}
0.357	3.57×10^{-1}
3.57	3.57×10^0
35.7	3.57×10^1
357	3.57×10^2
3,570	3.57×10^3
35,700	3.57×10^4

75. 0.00423 **77.** 0.00008 **79.** 4.2 **81.** 0.002 **83.** Craven/Bush 2×10^{-3}, Earnhardt/Irvan 5×10^{-3}, Harvick/Gordon 6×10^{-3}, Kahne/Kenseth 1×10^{-2}, Kenseth/Kahne 1×10^{-2}

85. 2.5×10^4 **87.** 2.35×10^5 **89.** 8.2×10^{-4} **91.** 100 inches², 400 inches²; 4 **93.** x^2; $4x^2$; 4

95. 216 inches³; 1,728 inches³; 8 **97.** x^3; $8x^3$; 8 **99.** 13.5 **101.** 8 **103.** 26.52 **105.** 12 **107.** x^8 **109.** x **111.** $\frac{1}{y^2}$ **113.** 340

Answers to Odd-Numbered Problems

PROBLEM SET 4.3

1. $12x^7$ **3.** $-16y^{11}$ **5.** $32x^2$ **7.** $200a^6$ **9.** $-24a^3b^3$ **11.** $24x^6y^8$ **13.** $3x$ **15.** $\frac{6}{y^3}$ **17.** $\frac{1}{2a}$ **19.** $-\frac{3a}{b^2}$ **21.** $\frac{x^2}{9z^2}$

23.

a	b	ab	$\frac{a}{b}$	$\frac{b}{a}$
10	$5x$	$50x$	$\frac{2}{x}$	$\frac{x}{2}$
$20x^3$	$6x^2$	$120x^5$	$\frac{10x}{3}$	$\frac{3}{10x}$
$25x^5$	$5x^4$	$125x^9$	$5x$	$\frac{1}{5x}$
$3x^{-2}$	$3x^2$	9	$\frac{1}{x^4}$	x^4
$-2y^4$	$8y^7$	$-16y^{11}$	$-\frac{1}{4y^3}$	$-4y^3$

25. 6×10^8 **27.** 1.75×10^{-1} **29.** 1.21×10^{-6} **31.** 4.2×10^3
33. 3×10^{10} **35.** 5×10^{-3} **37.** $8x^2$ **39.** $-11x^5$ **41.** 0 **43.** $4x^3$
45. $31ab^2$ **47.**

a	b	ab	$a + b$
$5x$	$3x$	$15x^2$	$8x$
$4x^2$	$2x^2$	$8x^4$	$6x^2$
$3x^3$	$6x^3$	$18x^6$	$9x^3$
$2x^4$	$-3x^4$	$-6x^8$	$-x^4$
x^5	$7x^5$	$7x^{10}$	$8x^5$

49. $4x^3$ **51.** $\frac{1}{b^2}$ **53.** $\frac{6y^{10}}{x^4}$ **55.** $x^2y + x$ **57.** $x + y$ **59.** $x^2 - 4$ **61.** $x^2 - x - 6$ **63.** $x^2 - 5x$ **65.** $x^2 - 8x$ **67.** 2×10^6
69. 1×10^1 **71.** 4.2×10^{-6} **73.** $9x^3$ **75.** $-20a^2$ **77.** $6x^5y^2$ **79.** -5 **81.** 6 **83.** 76 **85.** $6x^2$ **87.** $2x$ **89.** $-2x - 9$ **91.** 11

PROBLEM SET 4.4

1. Trinomial, 3 **3.** Trinomial, 3 **5.** Binomial, 1 **7.** Binomial, 2 **9.** Monomial, 2 **11.** Monomial, 0 **13.** $5x^2 + 5x + 9$
15. $5a^2 - 9a + 7$ **17.** $x^2 + 6x + 8$ **19.** $6x^2 - 13x + 5$ **21.** $x^2 - 9$ **23.** $3y^2 - 11y + 10$ **25.** $6x^3 + 5x^2 - 4x + 3$
27. $2x^2 - x + 1$ **29.** $2a^2 - 2a - 2$ **31.** $-\frac{1}{9}x^3 - \frac{2}{3}x^2 - \frac{5}{2}x + \frac{7}{4}$ **33.** $-4y^2 + 15y - 22$ **35.** $x^2 - 33x + 63$
37. $8y^2 + 4y + 26$ **39.** $75x^2 - 150x - 75$ **41.** $12x + 2$ **43.** 4 **45.** 56.52 in^3 **47.** 5 **49.** -6 **51.** $-20x^2$ **53.** $-21x$
55. $2x$ **57.** $6x - 18$

PROBLEM SET 4.5

1. $6x^2 + 2x$ **3.** $6x^4 - 4x^3 + 2x^2$ **5.** $2a^3b - 2a^2b^2 + 2ab$ **7.** $3y^4 + 9y^3 + 12y^2$ **9.** $8x^5y^2 + 12x^4y^3 + 32x^2y^4$ **11.** $x^2 + 7x + 12$
13. $x^2 + 7x + 6$ **15.** $x^2 + 2x + \frac{3}{4}$ **17.** $a^2 + 2a - 15$ **19.** $xy + bx - ay - ab$ **21.** $x^2 - 36$ **23.** $y^2 - \frac{25}{36}$ **25.** $2x^2 - 11x + 12$
27. $2a^2 + 3a - 2$ **29.** $6x^2 - 19x + 10$ **31.** $2ax + 8x + 3a + 12$ **33.** $25x^2 - 16$ **35.** $2x^2 + \frac{5}{2}x - \frac{3}{4}$ **37.** $3 - 10a + 8a^2$
39. $(x + 2)(x + 3) = x^2 + 2x + 3x + 6 = x^2 + 5x + 6$ **41.** $(x + 1)(2x + 2) = 2x^2 + 4x + 2$

43. $a^3 - 6a^2 + 11a - 6$ **45.** $x^3 + 8$ **47.** $2x^3 + 17x^2 + 26x + 9$ **49.** $5x^4 - 13x^3 + 20x^2 + 7x + 5$ **51.** $2x^4 + x^2 - 15$
53. $6a^6 + 15a^4 + 4a^2 + 10$ **55.** $x^3 + 12x^2 + 47x + 60$ **57.** $x^2 - 5x + 8$ **59.** $8x^2 - 6x - 5$ **61.** $x^2 - x - 30$ **63.** $x^2 + 4x - 6$
65. $x^2 + 13x$ **67.** $x^2 + 2x - 3$ **69.** $a^2 - 3a + 6$ **71.** $A = x(2x + 5) = 2x^2 + 5x$ **73.** $A = x(x + 1) = x^2 + x$ **75.** 169
77. $-10x$ **79.** 0 **81.** 0 **83.** $-12x + 16$ **85.** $x^2 + x - 2$ **87.** $x^2 + 6x + 9$

PROBLEM SET 4.6

1. $x^2 - 4x + 4$ **3.** $a^2 + 6a + 9$ **5.** $x^2 - 10x + 25$ **7.** $a^2 - a + \frac{1}{4}$ **9.** $x^2 + 20x + 100$ **11.** $a^2 + 1.6a + 0.64$
13. $4x^2 - 4x + 1$ **15.** $16a^2 + 40a + 25$ **17.** $9x^2 - 12x + 4$ **19.** $9a^2 + 30ab + 25b^2$ **21.** $16x^2 - 40xy + 25y^2$
23. $49m^2 + 28mn + 4n^2$ **25.** $36x^2 - 120xy + 100y^2$ **27.** $x^4 + 10x^2 + 25$ **29.** $a^4 + 2a^2 + 1$

31.

x	$(x + 3)^2$	$x^2 + 9$	$x^2 + 6x + 9$
1	16	10	16
2	25	13	25
3	36	18	36
4	49	25	49

33.

a	1	3	3	4
b	1	5	4	5
$(a + b)^2$	4	64	49	81
$a^2 + b^2$	2	34	25	41
$a^2 + ab + b^2$	3	49	37	61
$a^2 + 2ab + b^2$	4	64	49	81

35. $a^2 - 25$ **37.** $y^2 - 1$ **39.** $81 - x^2$ **41.** $4x^2 - 25$ **43.** $16x^2 - \frac{1}{9}$ **45.** $4a^2 - 49$ **47.** $36 - 49x^2$ **49.** $x^4 - 9$ **51.** $a^4 - 16$

53. $25y^8 - 64$ **55.** $2x^2 - 34$ **57.** $-12x^2 + 20x + 8$ **59.** $a^2 + 4a + 6$ **61.** $8x^3 + 36x^2 + 54x + 27$

63. $(50 - 1)(50 + 1) = 2500 - 1 = 2499$ **65.** Both equal 25. **67.** $x^2 + (x + 1)^2 = 2x^2 + 2x + 1$

69. $x^2 + (x + 1)^2 + (x + 2)^2 = 3x^2 + 6x + 5$

71.

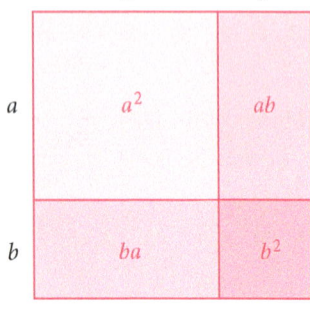

$a^2 + ab + ba + b^2 = a^2 + 2ab + b^2$ **73.** $2x^2$ **75.** x^2 **77.** $3x$ **79.** $3xy$

PROBLEM SET 4.7

1. $x - 2$ **3.** $3 - 2x^2$ **5.** $5xy - 2y$ **7.** $7x^4 - 6x^3 + 5x^2$ **9.** $10x^4 - 5x^2 + 1$ **11.** $-4a + 2$ **13.** $-8a^4 - 12a^3$ **15.** $-4b - 5a$

17. $-6a^2b + 3ab^2 - 7b^3$ **19.** $-\frac{a}{2} - b - \frac{b^2}{2a}$ **21.** $3x + 4y$ **23.** $-y + 3$ **25.** $5y - 4$ **27.** $xy - x^2y^2$ **29.** $-1 + xy$

31. $-a + 1$ **33.** $x^2 - 3xy + y^2$ **35.** $2 - 3b + 5b^2$ **37.** $-2xy + 1$ **39.** $xy - \frac{1}{2}$ **41.** $\frac{1}{4x} - \frac{1}{2a} + \frac{3}{4}$ **43.** $\frac{4x^2}{3} + \frac{2}{3x} + \frac{1}{x^2}$

45. $3a^{3m} - 9a^m$ **47.** $2x^{4m} - 5x^{2m} + 7$ **49.** $3x^2 - x + 6$ **51.** 4 **53.** $x + 5$ **55.** Both equal 7.

57. $\frac{3(10) + 8}{2} = 19; 3(10) + 4 = 34$ **59.** $146\frac{20}{27}$ **61.** $2x + 5$ **63.** $x^2 - 3x$ **65.** $2x^3 - 10x^2$ **67.** $-2x$ **69.** 2

PROBLEM SET 4.8

1. $x - 2$ **3.** $a + 4$ **5.** $x - 3$ **7.** $x + 3$ **9.** $a - 5$ **11.** $x + 2 + \frac{2}{x + 3}$ **13.** $a - 2 + \frac{12}{a + 5}$ **15.** $x + 4 + \frac{9}{x - 2}$

17. $x + 4 + \frac{-10}{x + 1}$ **19.** $a + 1 + \frac{-1}{a + 2}$ **21.** $x - 3 + \frac{17}{2x + 4}$ **23.** $3a - 2 + \frac{7}{2a + 3}$ **25.** $2a^2 - a - 3$ **27.** $x^2 - x + 5$

29. $x^2 + x + 1$ **31.** $x^2 + 2x + 4$ **33.** $491.17 **35.** $331.42 **37.** 47 **39.** 14 **41.** 70 **43.** 35 **45.** 5 **47.** 6,540 **49.** 1,760

51. 20 **53.** 63 **55.** 53

CHAPTER 4 TEST

1. -32 **2.** $\frac{8}{27}$ **3.** $128x^{13}$ **4.** $\frac{1}{16}$ **5.** 1 **6.** x^3 **7.** $\frac{1}{x^3}$ **8.** 4.307×10^{-2} **9.** 7,630,000 **10.** $\frac{y^3z^2}{3x^2}$ **11.** $\frac{a^3b^2}{2}$ **12.** $12x^3$

13. 7.5×10^7 **14.** $9x^2 + 5x + 4$ **15.** $2x^2 + 6x - 2$ **16.** $5x - 4$ **17.** 21 **18.** $15x^4 - 6x^3 + 12x^2$ **19.** $x^2 - \frac{1}{12}x - \frac{1}{12}$

20. $10x^2 - 3x - 18$ **21.** $x^3 + 64$ **22.** $x^2 - 12x + 36$ **23.** $4a^2 + 16ab + 16b^2$ **24.** $9x^2 - 36$ **25.** $x^4 - 16$ **26.** $3x^2 - 6x + 1$

27. $3x - 1 + \frac{-5}{3x - 1}$ **28.** $4x + 11 + \frac{50}{x - 4}$ **29.** 32.77 in^3 **30.** $V = w^3$

Answers to Odd-Numbered Problems

Chapter 5

PROBLEM SET 5.1

1. $5(3x + 5)$ **3.** $3(2a + 3)$ **5.** $4(x - 2y)$ **7.** $3(x^2 - 2x - 3)$ **9.** $3(a^2 - a - 20)$ **11.** $4(6y^2 - 13y + 6)$ **13.** $x^2(9 - 8x)$

15. $13a^2(1 - 2a)$ **17.** $7xy(3x - 4y)$ **19.** $11ab^2(2a - 1)$ **21.** $7x(x^2 + 3x - 4)$ **23.** $11(11y^4 - x^4)$ **25.** $25x^2(4x^2 - 2x + 1)$

27. $8(a^2 + 2b^2 + 4c^2)$ **29.** $4ab(a - 4b + 8ab)$ **31.** $11a^2b^2(11a - 2b + 3ab)$ **33.** $12x^2y^3(1 - 6x^3 - 3x^2y)$

35. $(x + 3)(y + 5)$ **37.** $(x + 2)(y + 6)$ **39.** $(a - 3)(b + 7)$ **41.** $(a - b)(x + y)$ **43.** $(2x - 5)(a + 3)$ **45.** $(b - 2)(3x - 4)$

47. $(x + 2)(x + a)$ **49.** $(x - b)(x - a)$ **51.** $(x + y)(a + b + c)$ **53.** $(3x + 2)(2x + 3)$ **55.** $(10x - 1)(2x + 5)$

57. $(4x + 5)(5x + 1)$ **59.** $(x + 2)(x^2 + 3)$ **61.** $(3x - 2)(2x^2 + 5)$ **63.** 6 **65.** $3(4x^2 + 2x + 1)$

67. $A = 1,000(1 + r)$; $1120.00   **69.** **a.** $A = 1,000,000(1 + r)$ **b.** $1,300,000   **71.** $x^2 - 5x - 14$ **73.** $x^2 - x - 6$

75. $x^3 + 27$ **77.** $2x^3 + 9x^2 - 2x - 3$ **79.** $18x^7 - 12x^6 + 6x^5$ **81.** $x^2 + x + \frac{2}{9}$ **83.** $12x^2 - 10xy - 12y^2$ **85.** $81a^2 - 1$

87. $x^2 - 18x + 81$ **89.** $x^3 + 8$

PROBLEM SET 5.2

1. $(x + 3)(x + 4)$ **3.** $(x + 1)(x + 2)$ **5.** $(a + 3)(a + 7)$ **7.** $(x - 2)(x - 5)$ **9.** $(y - 3)(y - 7)$ **11.** $(x - 4)(x + 3)$

13. $(y + 4)(y - 3)$ **15.** $(x + 7)(x - 2)$ **17.** $(r - 9)(r + 1)$ **19.** $(x - 6)(x + 5)$ **21.** $(a + 7)(a + 8)$ **23.** $(y + 6)(y - 7)$

25. $(x + 6)(x + 7)$ **27.** $2(x + 1)(x + 2)$ **29.** $3(a + 4)(a - 5)$ **31.** $100(x - 2)(x - 3)$ **33.** $100(p - 5)(p - 8)$

35. $x^2(x + 3)(x - 4)$ **37.** $2r(r + 5)(r - 3)$ **39.** $2y^2(y + 1)(y - 4)$ **41.** $x^3(x + 2)^2$ **43.** $3y^2(y + 1)(y - 5)$

45. $4x^2(x - 4)(x - 9)$ **47.** $(x + 2y)(x + 3y)$ **49.** $(x - 4y)(x - 5y)$ **51.** $(a + 4b)(a - 2b)$ **53.** $(a - 5b)^2$

55. $(a + 5b)^2$ **57.** $(x - 6a)(x + 8a)$ **59.** $(x + 4b)(x - 9b)$ **61.** $(x^2 - 3)(x^2 - 2)$ **63.** $(x - 100)(x + 20)$

65. $\left(x - \frac{1}{2}\right)^2$ **67.** $(x + 0.2)(x + 0.4)$ **69.** $x + 16$ **71.** $4x^2 - x - 3$ **73.** $6a^2 + 13a + 2$ **75.** $6a^2 + 7a + 2$

77. $6a^2 + 8a + 2$

PROBLEM SET 5.3

1. $(2x + 1)(x + 3)$ **3.** $(2a - 3)(a + 1)$ **5.** $(3x + 5)(x - 1)$ **7.** $(3y + 1)(y - 5)$ **9.** $(2x + 3)(3x + 2)$

11. $(2x - 3y)^2$ **13.** $(4y + 1)(y - 3)$ **15.** $(4x - 5)(5x - 4)$ **17.** $(10a - b)(2a + 5b)$ **19.** $(4x - 5)(5x + 1)$

21. $(6m - 1)(2m + 3)$ **23.** $(4x + 5)(5x + 3)$ **25.** $(3a - 4b)(4a - 3b)$ **27.** $(3x - 7y)(x + 2y)$ **29.** $(2x + 5)(7x - 3)$

31. $(3x - 5)(2x - 11)$ **33.** $(5t - 19)(3t - 2)$ **35.** $2(2x + 3)(x - 1)$ **37.** $2(4a - 3)(3a - 4)$ **39.** $x(5x - 4)(2x - 3)$

41. $x^2(3x + 2)(2x - 5)$ **43.** $2a(5a + 2)(a - 1)$ **45.** $3x(5x + 1)(x - 7)$ **47.** $5y(7y + 2)(y - 2)$ **49.** $a^2(5a + 1)(3a - 1)$

51. $3y(2x - 3)(4x + 5)$ **53.** $2y(2x - y)(3x - 7y)$ **55.** Both equal 25.   **57.** $4x^2 - 9$ **59.** $x^4 - 81$

61. $h = 2(4 - t)(1 + 8t)$

63. **a.** $V = x \cdot (11 - 2x)(9 - 2x)$ **b.** 11 inch $\times$ 9 inch

Time t (seconds)	Height h (feet)
0	8
1	54
2	68
3	50
4	0

65. $x^2 - 9$ **67.** $x^2 - 25$ **69.** $x^2 - 49$ **71.** $x^2 - 81$ **73.** $4x^2 - 9y^2$ **75.** $x^4 - 16$ **77.** $x^2 + 6x + 9$ **79.** $x^2 + 10x + 25$

81. $x^2 + 14x + 49$ **83.** $x^2 + 18x + 81$ **85.** $4x^2 + 12x + 9$ **87.** $16x^2 - 16xy + 4y^2$

PROBLEM SET 5.4

1. $(x + 3)(x - 3)$ **3.** $(a + 6)(a - 6)$ **5.** $(x + 7)(x - 7)$ **7.** $4(a + 2)(a - 2)$ **9.** Cannot be factored.

11. $(5x + 13)(5x - 13)$ **13.** $(3a + 4b)(3a - 4b)$ **15.** $(3 + m)(3 - m)$ **17.** $(5 + 2x)(5 - 2x)$ **19.** $2(x + 3)(x - 3)$

21. $32(a + 2)(a - 2)$ **23.** $2y(2x + 3)(2x - 3)$ **25.** $(a^2 + b^2)(a + b)(a - b)$ **27.** $(4m^2 + 9)(2m + 3)(2m - 3)$

29. $3xy(x + 5y)(x - 5y)$ **31.** $(x - 1)^2$ **33.** $(x + 1)^2$ **35.** $(a - 5)^2$ **37.** $(y + 2)^2$ **39.** $(x - 2)^2$ **41.** $(m - 6)^2$ **43.** $(2a + 3)^2$

45. $(7x - 1)^2$ **47.** $(3y - 5)^2$ **49.** $(x + 5y)^2$ **51.** $(3a + b)^2$ **53.** $3(a + 3)^2$ **55.** $2(x + 5y)^2$ **57.** $5x(x + 3y)^2$

59. $(x + 3 + y)(x + 3 - y)$ **61.** $(x + y + 3)(x + y - 3)$ **63.** 14 **65.** 25

67. a. $x^2 - 16$ **b.** $(x + 4)(x - 4)$ **c.**

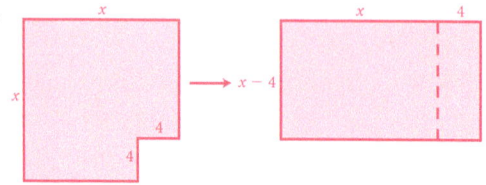

69. $a^2 - b^2 = (a + b)(a - b)$ **71. a.** 1 **b.** 8 **c.** 27 **d.** 64 **e.** 125

73. a. $x^3 - x^2 + x$ **b.** $x^2 - x + 1$ **c.** $x^3 + 1$ **75. a.** $x^3 - 2x^2 + 4x$ **b.** $2x^2 - 4x + 8$ **c.** $x^3 + 8$

77. a. $x^3 - 3x^2 + 9x$ **b.** $3x^2 - 9x + 27$ **c.** $x^3 + 27$

PROBLEM SET 5.5

1. $(x - y)(x^2 + xy + y^2)$ **3.** $(a + 2)(a^2 - 2a + 4)$ **5.** $(3 + x)(9 - 3x + x^2)$ **7.** $(y - 1)(y^2 + y + 1)$

9. $(y - 4)(y^2 + 4y + 16)$ **11.** $(5h - t)(25h^2 + 5ht + t^2)$ **13.** $(x - 6)(x^2 + 6x + 36)$ **15.** $2(y - 3)(y^2 + 3y + 9)$

17. $2(a - 4b)(a^2 + 4ab + 16b^2)$ **19.** $2(x + 6y)(x^2 - 6xy + 36y^2)$ **21.** $10(a - 4b)(a^2 + 4ab + 16b^2)$

23. $10(r - 5)(r^2 + 5r + 25)$ **25.** $(4 + 3a)(16 - 12a + 9a^2)$ **27.** $(2x - 3y)(4x^2 + 6xy + 9y^2)$ **29.** $\left(t + \frac{1}{3}\right)\left(t^2 - \frac{1}{3}t + \frac{1}{9}\right)$

31. $\left(3x - \frac{1}{3}\right)\left(9x^2 + x + \frac{1}{9}\right)$ **33.** $(4a + 5b)(16a^2 - 20ab + 25b^2)$ **35.** $\left(\frac{1}{2}x - \frac{1}{3}y\right)\left(\frac{1}{4}x^2 + \frac{1}{6}xy + \frac{1}{9}y^2\right)$

37. $(a - b)(a^2 + ab + b^2)(a + b)(a^2 - ab + b^2)$ **39.** $(2x - y)(4x^2 + 2xy + y^2)(2x + y)(4x^2 - 2xy + y^2)$

41. $(x - 5y)(x^2 + 5xy + 25y^2)(x + 5y)(x^2 - 5xy + 25y^2)$ **43.** $2x^5 - 8x^3$ **45.** $3x^4 - 18x^3 + 27x^2$ **47.** $y^3 + 25y$

49. $15a^2 - a - 2$ **51.** $4x^4 - 12x^3 - 40x^2$ **53.** $2ab^5 - 8ab^4 + 2ab^3$

PROBLEM SET 5.6

1. $(x + 9)(x - 9)$ **3.** $(x + 5)(x - 3)$ **5.** $(x + 3)^2$ **7.** $(y - 5)^2$ **9.** $2ab(a^2 + 3a + 1)$ **11.** Cannot be factored.

13. $3(2a + 5)(2a - 5)$ **15.** $(3x - 2y)^2$ **17.** $4x(x^2 + 4y^2)$ **19.** $2y(y + 5)^2$ **21.** $a^4(a^2 + 4b^2)$ **23.** $(x + 4)(y + 3)$

25. $(x^2 + 4)(x + 2)(x - 2)$ **27.** $(x + 2)(y - 5)$ **29.** $5(a + b)^2$ **31.** Cannot be factored. **33.** $3(x + 2y)(x + 3y)$

35. $(2x + 19)(x - 2)$ **37.** $100(x - 2)(x - 1)$ **39.** $(x + 8)(x - 8)$ **41.** $(x + a)(x + 3)$ **43.** $a^5(7a + 3)(7a - 3)$

45. Cannot be factored. **47.** $a(5a + 1)(5a + 3)$ **49.** $(x + y)(a - b)$ **51.** $3a^2b(4a + 1)(4a - 1)$ **53.** $5x^2(2x + 3)(2x - 3)$

55. $(3x + 41y)(x - 2y)$ **57.** $2x^3(2x - 3)(4x - 5)$ **59.** $(2x + 3)(x + a)$ **61.** $(y^2 + 1)(y + 1)(y - 1)$ **63.** $3x^2y^2(2x + 3y)^2$

65. 5 **67.** $-\frac{3}{2}$ **69.** $-\frac{3}{4}$

PROBLEM SET 5.7

1. $-2, 1$ **3.** $4, 5$ **5.** $0, -1, 3$ **7.** $-\frac{2}{3}, -\frac{3}{2}$ **9.** $0, -\frac{4}{3}, \frac{4}{3}$ **11.** $0, -\frac{1}{3}, -\frac{3}{5}$ **13.** $-1, -2$ **15.** $4, 5$ **17.** $6, -4$ **19.** $2, 3$

21. -3 **23.** $4, -4$ **25.** $\frac{3}{2}, -4$ **27.** $-\frac{2}{3}$ **29.** 5 **31.** $4, -\frac{5}{2}$ **33.** $\frac{5}{3}, -4$ **35.** $\frac{7}{2}, -\frac{7}{2}$ **37.** $0, -6$ **39.** $0, 3$ **41.** $0, 4$ **43.** $0, 5$

45. $2, 5$ **47.** $\frac{1}{2}, -\frac{4}{3}$ **49.** $4, -\frac{5}{2}$ **51.** $8, -10$ **53.** $5, 8$ **55.** $6, 8$ **57.** -4 **59.** $5, 8$ **61.** $6, -8$ **63.** $0, -\frac{3}{2}, -4$ **65.** $0, 3, -\frac{5}{2}$

67. $0, \frac{1}{2}, -\frac{5}{2}$ **69.** $0, \frac{3}{5}, -\frac{3}{2}$ **71.** $\frac{1}{2}, \frac{3}{2}$ **73.** $-5, 4$ **75.** $-7, -6$ **77.** $-3, -1$ **79.** $2, 3$ **81.** $-15, 10$ **83.** $-5, 3$

85. $-3, -2, 2$ **87.** $-4, -1, 4$ **89. a.** $(x - 2)(x + 1)$ **b.** $-1, 2$ **c.** $-2, 3$ **91.** $x(x + 1) = 72$ **93.** $x(x + 2) = 99$

95. $x(x + 2) = 5[x + (x + 2)] - 10$ **97.** Bicycle $75, suit $15 **99.** House $2,400, lot $600

PROBLEM SET 5.8

1. 8, 10 and $-10, -8$ **3.** 9, 11 and $-11, -9$ **5.** 8, 10 and 0, 2 **7.** 8, 6 **9.** 2, 12 and $-\frac{12}{5}, -10$ **11.** 5, 20 and 0, 0

13. Width 3 inches, length 4 inches **15.** Base 3 inches **17.** 6 inches and 8 inches **19.** 12 meters

21. 2 hundred items or 5 hundred items **23.** $7 or $10 **25. a.** 5 feet **b.** 12 feet

27. a. 25 seconds later **b.**

t	h
0	100
5	1680
10	2460
15	2440
20	1620
25	0

29. $200x^{24}$ **31.** x^7 **33.** 8×10^1 **35.** $10ab^2$

37. $6x^4 + 6x^3 - 2x^2$ **39.** $9y^2 - 30y + 25$ **41.** $4a^4 - 49$

CHAPTER 5 TEST

1. $6(x + 3)$ **2.** $4ab(3a - 6 + 2b)$ **3.** $(x - 2b)(x + 3a)$ **4.** $(5y - 4)(3 - x)$ **5.** $(x + 4)(x - 3)$ **6.** $(x - 7)(x + 3)$

7. $(x + 5)(x - 5)$ **8.** $(x^2 + 4)(x + 2)(x - 2)$ **9.** Cannot be factored. **10.** $2(3x + 4y)(3y - 4y)$ **11.** $(x^2 - 3)(x + 4)$

12. $(x - 3)(x + b)$ **13.** $2(2x - 5)(x + 1)$ **14.** $(4n - 3)(n + 4)$ **15.** $(3c - 2)(4c + 3)$ **16.** $3x(2x - 1)(2x + 3)$

17. $(x + 5y)(x^2 - 5xy + 25y^2)$ **18.** $2(3b - 4)(9b^2 + 12b + 16)$ **19.** $5, -3$ **20.** $3, 4$ **21.** $5, -5$ **22.** $-2, 7$ **23.** $5, -6$

24. $0, 3, -3$ **25.** $\frac{3}{2}, -4$ **26.** $0, -\frac{5}{3}, 6$ **27.** $6, 12$ **28.** $\{4, 6\}, \{-4, -2\}$ **29.** width $= 4$ ft, length $= 13$ ft **30.** 6 ft, 8 ft

31. 200 items or 300 items **32.** $3, $5

Chapter 6

PROBLEM SET 6.1

1. Domain $= \{1, 3, 5, 7\}$, Range $= \{2, 4, 6, 8\}$; a function **3.** Domain $= \{0, 1, 2, 3\}$, Range $= \{4, 5, 6\}$; a function

5. Domain $= \{a, b, c, d\}$; Range $= \{3, 4, 5\}$; a function **7.** Domain $= \{a\}$; Range $= \{1, 2, 3, 4\}$; not a function **9.** Yes **11.** No

13. No **15.** Yes **17.** Yes **19.** Domain $= \{x \mid -5 \leq x \leq 5\}$, Range $= \{y \mid 0 \leq y \leq 5\}$

21. Domain $= \{x \mid -5 \leq x \leq 3\}$, Range $= \{y \mid y = 3\}$ **23.** Domain $=$ All real numbers, Range $= \{y \mid y \geq -1\}$, A function

25. Domain $=$ All real numbers, Range $= \{y \mid y \geq 4\}$, A function

27. Domain $= \{x \mid x \geq -1\}$, Range $=$ All real numbers, Not a function

29. Domain $=$ All real numbers, Range $= \{y \mid y \geq 0\}$; a function

31. Domain $= \{x \mid x \geq 0\}$, Range $=$ All real numbers; not a function

33. a. $y = 8.5x$ for $10 \leq x \leq 40$ **b.**

c.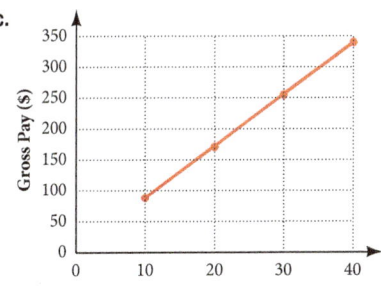

TABLE 4 Weekly Wages

Hours Worked	Function Rule	Gross Pay ($)
x	$y = 8.5x$	y
10	$y = 8.5(10)$	85
20	$y = 8.5(20)$	170
30	$y = 8.5(30)$	255
40	$y = 8.5(40)$	340

d. Domain $= \{x \mid 10 \leq x \leq 40\}$; Range $= \{y \mid 85 \leq y \leq 340\}$ **e.** Minimum $= \$85$; Maximum $= \$340$

35. Domain $= \{2009, 2010, 2011, 2012, 2013, 2014, 2015\}$, Range $= \{28, 117, 312, 482, 601, 702, 830\}$

37. a. III **b.** I **c.** II **d.** IV **39.** 113 **41.** -9 **43. a.** 6 **b.** 7.5 **45. a.** 27 **b.** 6 **47.** 1 **49.** -3 **51.** $-\frac{6}{5}$ **53.** $-\frac{35}{32}$

PROBLEM SET 6.2

1. -1 **3.** -11 **5.** 2 **7.** 4 **9.** $a^2 + 3a + 4$ **11.** $2a + 7$ **13.** 1 **15.** -9 **17.** 8 **19.** 0 **21.** $3a^2 - 4a + 1$

23. $3a^2 + 8a + 5$ **25.** 4 **27.** 0 **29.** 2 **31.** 24 **33.** -1 **35.** $2x^2 - 19x + 12$ **37.** 99 **39.** $\frac{3}{10}$ **41.** $\frac{2}{5}$ **43.** undefined

45. **a.** $a^2 - 7$ **b.** $a^2 - 6a + 5$ **c.** $x^2 - 2$ **d.** $x^2 + 4x$ **e.** $a^2 + 2ab + b^2 - 4$ **f.** $x^2 + 2xh + h^2 - 4$

47.

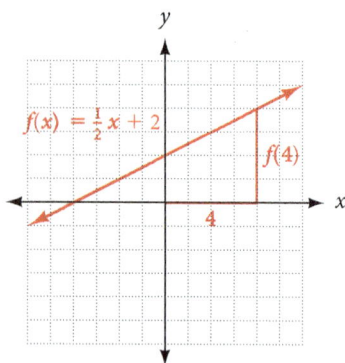

49. $x = 4$ **51.**

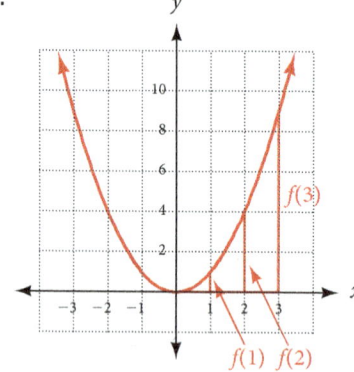

53. $V(3) = 300$, the painting is worth \$300 in 3 years; $V(6) = 600$, the painting is worth \$600 in 6 years.

55. **a.** True **b.** False **c.** True **d.** False **e.** True

57. **a.** \$5,625 **b.** \$1,500 **c.** $\{t \mid 0 \le t \le 5\}$ **d.**

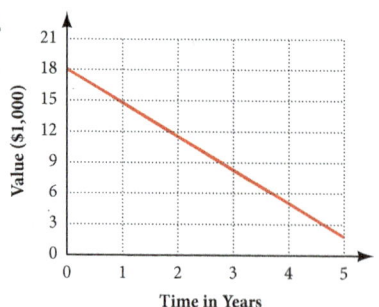

e. $\{V(t) \mid 1,500 \le V(t) \le 18,000\}$

f. About 2.42 years

59. 196 **61.** 4 **63.** 1.6 **65.** 3 **67.** 2,400

PROBLEM SET 6.3

1. 30 **3.** -6 **5.** 40 **7.** $\frac{81}{5}$ **9.** 64 **11.** 108 **13.** 300 **15.** ± 2 **17.** 1600 **19.** ± 8 **21.** $\frac{50}{3}$ pounds

23. **a.** $T = 4P$ **b.** T **c.** 70 pounds per square inch

Answers to Odd-Numbered Problems

25. 12 pounds per square inch   **27.   a.** $f = \frac{80}{d}$ **b.**   **c.** An f-stop of 8

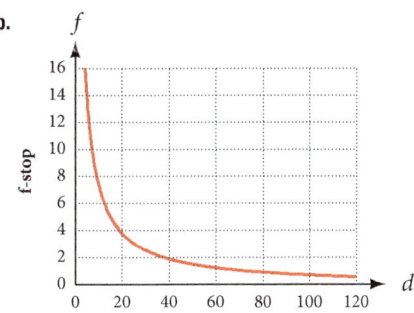

Aperture Diameter (mm)

29. $\frac{1504}{15}$ square inches   **31.** 1.5 ohms   **33.   a.** $P = 0.21\sqrt{L}$ **b.**   **c.** 3.15

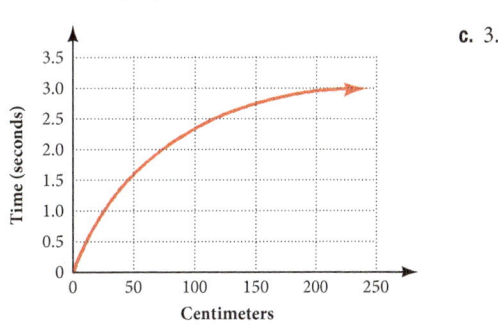

Centimeters

35. $.6M - 42$ **37.** $16x^3 - 40x^2 + 33x - 9$ **39.** $4x^2 - 3x$ **41.** $6x^2 - 2x - 4$ **43.** 11

PROBLEM SET 6.4

1. $6x + 2$ **3.** $-2x + 8$ **5.** $8x^2 + 14x - 15$ **7.** $\frac{2x + 5}{4x - 3}$ **9.** $4x - 7$ **11.** $3x^2 - 10x + 8$ **13.** $-2x + 3$ **15.** $3x^2 - 11x + 10$

17. $9x^3 - 48x^2 + 85x - 50$ **19.** $x - 2$ **21.** $\frac{1}{x - 2}$ **23.** $3x^2 - 7x + 3$ **25.** $6x^2 - 22x + 20$ **27.** 15   **29.** 98   **31.** $\frac{3}{2}$ **33.** 1

35. 40   **37.** 147   **39.   a.** 81   **b.** 29   **c.** $(x + 4)^2$ **d.** $x^2 + 4$ **41.   a.** -2 **b.** -1 **c.** $16x^2 + 4x - 2$ **d.** $4x^2 + 12x - 1$

43. $(f \circ g)(x) = 5\left[\frac{x + 4}{5}\right] - 4 = x + 4 - 4 = x,\ (g \circ f)(x) = \frac{(5x - 4) + 4}{5} = \frac{5x}{5} = x$

45.   a. $R(x) = 11.5x - 0.05x^2$ **b.** $C(x) = 2x + 200$ **c.** $P(x) = -0.05x^2 + 9.5x - 200$ **d.** $\overline{C}(x) = 2 + \frac{200}{x}$

47.   a. $M(x) = 220 - x$ **b.** $M(24) = 196$ **c.** 142   **d.** 135   **e.** 128   **49.** $y = 0.055x - 107.81$ **51.** $y = -3,400x - 214,000$

53. ≈ 0.0137

CHAPTER 6 TEST

1. domain $= \{-3, -2\}$, range $= \{0, 1\}$, not a function   **2.** domain $=$ all real numbers, range $= \{y | y \geq -9\}$, is a function

3. 11   **4.** -4 **5** 8   **6.** 4   **7.** 18   **8.** $\frac{81}{4}$ **9.** $\frac{2000}{3}$ pounds

Chapter 7

PROBLEM SET 7.1

1. $g(0) = -3, g(-3) = 0, g(3) = 3, g(-1) = -1, g(1) =$ undefined

3. $h(0) = -3, h(-3) = 3, h(3) = 0, h(-1)$ is undefined, $h(1) = -1$ **5.** $\{x \mid x \neq 1\}$ **7.** $\{x \mid x \neq 2\}$ **9.** $\{t \mid t \neq 4, t \neq -4\}$

11. $\frac{x - 4}{6}$ **13.** $(a^2 + 9)(a + 3)$ **15.** $\frac{2y + 3}{y + 1}$ **17.** $\frac{x - 2}{x - 1}$ **19.** $\frac{x - 3}{x + 2}$ **21.** $\frac{x^2 - x + 1}{x - 1}$ **23.** $-\frac{4a}{3}$ **25.** $\frac{b - 1}{b + 1}$ **27.** $\frac{7x - 3}{7x + 5}$

29. $\frac{4x + 3}{4x - 3}$ **31.** $\frac{x + 5}{2x - 7}$ **33.** $\frac{a^2 - ab + b^2}{a - b}$ **35.** $\frac{2x - 2}{x}$ **37.** $\frac{x + 3}{y - 4}$ **39.** $x + 2$ **41.** $\frac{x^2 + 2x + 4}{x + 2}$ **43.** $\frac{4x^2 + 6x + 9}{2x + 3}$ **45.** -1

47. $-(y + 6)$ **49.** $-\frac{3a + 1}{3a - 1}$ **51.** 3   **53.** $x + a$ **55.   a.** 4   **b.** 4   **57.   a.** 5   **b.** 5   **59.   a.** $x + a$ **b.** $2x + h$

61.   a. $x + a$ **b.** $2x + h$ **63.   a.** $x + a - 3$ **b.** $2x + h - 3$ **65.   a.** 2   **b.** -4 **c.** Undefined   **d.** 2

Answers to Odd-Numbered Problems

67.

Weeks	Weight (lb)
x	$W(x)$
0	200
1	194
4	184
12	173
24	168

69. $\frac{2}{3}$ **71.** $20x^2y^2$ **73.** $72x^4y^5$ **75.** $(x+2)(x-2)$ **77.** $x^2(x-y)$ **79.** $2(y+1)(y-1)$

PROBLEM SET 7.2

1. $\frac{1}{6}$ **3.** $\frac{9}{4}$ **5.** $\frac{1}{2}$ **7.** $\frac{15y}{x^2}$ **9.** $\frac{b}{a}$ **11.** $\frac{2y^5}{z^3}$ **13.** $\frac{x+3}{x+2}$ **15.** $y+1$ **17.** $\frac{3(x+4)}{x-2}$ **19.** $\frac{y^2}{xy+1}$ **21.** $\frac{x^2+9}{x^2-9}$ **23.** $\frac{1}{4}$ **25.** 1

27. $\frac{(a-2)(a+2)}{a-5}$ **29.** $\frac{9t^2-6t+4}{4t^2-2t+1}$ **31.** $\frac{x+3}{x+4}$ **33.** $\frac{a-b}{5}$ **35.** $\frac{5c-1}{3c-2}$ **37.** $\frac{5a-b}{9a^2+15ab+25b^2}$ **39.** 2 **41.** $x(x-1)(x+1)$

43. $\frac{(a+4b)(a-3b)}{(a-4b)(a+5b)}$ **45.** $\frac{2y-1}{2y-3}$ **47.** $\frac{(y-2)(y+1)}{(y+2)(y-1)}$ **49.** $\frac{x-1}{x+1}$ **51.** $\frac{x-2}{x+3}$ **53.** $\frac{w(y-1)}{w-x}$ **55.** $\frac{(m+2)(x+y)}{(2x+y)^2}$

57. $3x$ **59.** $2(x+5)$ **61.** $x-2$ **63.** $-(y-4)$ or $4-y$ **65.** $(a-5)(a+1)$

67. a. $\frac{5}{21}$ **b.** $\frac{5x+3}{25x^2+15x+9}$ **c.** $\frac{5x-3}{25x^2+15x+9}$ **d.** $\frac{5x+3}{5x-3}$ **69.** $\frac{2}{3}$ **71.** $\frac{47}{105}$ **73.** $x-7$ **75.** $(x+1)(x-1)$ **77.** $2(x+5)$

79. $(a-b)(a^2+ab+b^2)$

PROBLEM SET 7.3

1. $\frac{5}{4}$ **3.** $\frac{1}{3}$ **5.** $\frac{41}{24}$ **7.** $\frac{19}{144}$ **9.** $\frac{31}{24}$ **11.** 1 **13.** -1 **15.** $\frac{1}{x+y}$ **17.** 1 **19.** $\frac{a^2+2a-3}{a^3}$ **21.** 1

23. a. $\frac{1}{16}$ **b.** $\frac{9}{4}$ **c.** $\frac{13}{24}$ **d.** $\frac{5x+15}{(x-3)^2}$ **e.** $\frac{x+3}{5}$ **f.** $\frac{x-2}{x-3}$ **25.** $\frac{1}{2}$ **27.** $\frac{1}{5}$ **29.** $\frac{x+3}{2(x+1)}$ **31.** $\frac{a-b}{a^2+ab+b^2}$ **33.** $\frac{2y-3}{4y^2+6y+9}$

35. $\frac{2(2x-3)}{(x-3)(x-2)}$ **37.** $\frac{1}{2t-7}$ **39.** $\frac{4}{(a-3)(a+1)}$ **41.** $\frac{-4x^2}{(2x+1)(2x-1)(4x^2+2x+1)}$ **43.** $\frac{2}{(2x+3)(4x+3)}$ **45.** $\frac{a}{(a+4)(a+5)}$

47. $\frac{x+1}{(x-2)(x+3)}$ **49.** $\frac{x-1}{(x+1)(x+2)}$ **51.** $\frac{1}{(x+2)(x+1)}$ **53.** $\frac{1}{(x+2)(x+3)}$ **55.** $\frac{4x+5}{2x+1}$ **57.** $\frac{22-5t}{4-t}$ **59.** $\frac{2x^2+3x-4}{2x+3}$

61. $\frac{2x-3}{2x}$ **63.** $\frac{1}{2}$ **65.** $\frac{3}{x+4}$ **67.** $\frac{(2x+1)(x+5)}{(x-2)(x+1)(x+3)}$ **69.** $\frac{51}{10} = 5.1$ **71.** $x + \frac{4}{x} = \frac{x^2+4}{x}$ **73.** $\frac{1}{x} + \frac{1}{x+1} = \frac{2x+1}{x(x+1)}$

75. $\frac{6}{5}$ **77.** $x+2$ **79.** $3-x$ **81.** $(x+2)(x-2)$

PROBLEM SET 7.4

1. $\frac{9}{8}$ **3.** $\frac{2}{15}$ **5.** $\frac{119}{20}$ **7.** $\frac{1}{x+1}$ **9.** $\frac{a+1}{a-1}$ **11.** $\frac{y-x}{y+x}$ **13.** $\frac{1}{(x+5)(x-2)}$ **15.** $\frac{1}{a^2-a+1}$ **17.** $\frac{x+3}{x+2}$ **19.** $\frac{a+3}{a-2}$ **21.** $\frac{x-3}{x}$

23. $\frac{x+4}{x+2}$ **25.** $\frac{x-3}{x+3}$ **27.** $\frac{a-1}{a+1}$ **29.** $-\frac{x}{3}$ **31.** $\frac{y^2+1}{2y}$ **33.** $\frac{-x^2+x-1}{x-1}$ **35.** $\frac{5}{3}$ **37.** $\frac{2x-1}{2x+3}$ **39.** $-\frac{1}{x(x+h)}$ **41.** $\frac{3c+4a-2b}{5}$

43. $\frac{(t-4)(t+1)}{(t+6)(t-3)}$ **45.** $\frac{(5b-1)(b+5)}{2(2b-11)}$ **47.** $-\frac{3}{2x+14}$ **49.** $2m-9$ **51. a.** $\frac{-4}{ax}$ **b.** $\frac{-1}{(x+1)(a+1)}$ **c.** $-\frac{a+x}{a^2x^2}$

53. a. As v approaches 0, the denominator approaches 1 **b.** $v = \frac{fs}{h} - s$ **55.** $xy - 2x$ **57.** $3x - 18$ **59.** ab

61. $(y+5)(y-5)$ **63.** $x(a+b)$ **65.** 2

PROBLEM SET 7.5

1. $-\frac{35}{3}$ **3.** $-\frac{18}{5}$ **5.** $\frac{36}{11}$ **7.** 2 **9.** 5 **11.** 2 **13.** $-3, 4$ **15.** $1, -\frac{4}{3}$ **17.** Possible solution -1, which does not check; $\varnothing$

19. 5 **21.** $-\frac{1}{2}, \frac{5}{3}$ **23.** $\frac{2}{3}$ **25.** 18 **27.** Possible solution 4, which does not check; $\varnothing$

29. Possible solutions 3 and -4; only -4 checks; -4 **31.** -6 **33.** -5 **35.** $\frac{53}{17}$

37. Possible solutions 1 and 2; only 2 checks; 2 **39.** Possible solution 3, which does not check; $\varnothing$ **41.** $\frac{22}{3}$

43. a. $-\frac{9}{5}, 5$ **b.** $\frac{9}{2}$ **c.** no solution **45. a.** $\frac{1}{3}$ **b.** 3 **c.** 9 **d.** 4 **e.** $\frac{1}{3}, 3$ **47. a.** $\frac{6}{(x-4)(x+3)}$ **b.** $\frac{x-3}{x-4}$ **c.** 5

49. $x = \frac{ab}{a-b}$ **51.** $y = \frac{x-3}{x-1}$ **53.** $y = \frac{1-x}{3x-2}$

55.

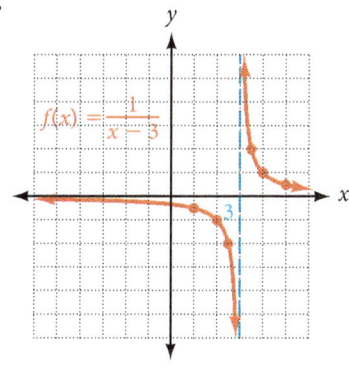

57.

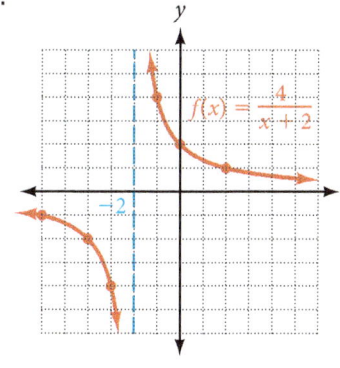

59.

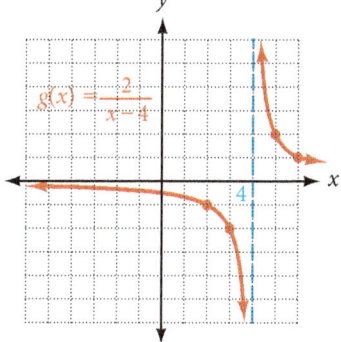

61.

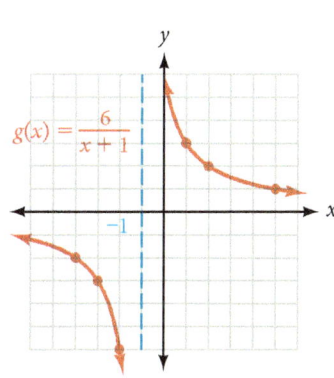

63. $\frac{24}{5}$ feet **65.** 2,358 **67.** 12.3 **69.** 3 **71.** 9, -1 **73.** 60

PROBLEM SET 7.6

1. $\frac{1}{x} + \frac{1}{3x} = \frac{20}{3}$; $\frac{1}{5}$ and $\frac{3}{5}$ **3.** $x + \frac{1}{x} = \frac{10}{3}$; 3 or $\frac{1}{3}$ **5.** $\frac{1}{x} + \frac{1}{x+1} = \frac{7}{12}$; 3, 4 **7.** $\frac{7+x}{9+x} = \frac{5}{6}$; 3

9. **a.** and **b.**

c. They are the same. $\frac{1.5}{5-x} = \frac{3}{5+x}$

d. The speed of the current is 1.7 mph

	d	r	t
Upstream	1.5	$5 - c$	$\frac{1.5}{5-c}$
Downstream	3	$5 + c$	$\frac{3}{5+c}$

11. $\frac{8}{x+2} + \frac{8}{x-2} = 3$; 6 mph **13.** **a.** and **b.**

	d	r	t
Train A	150	$x + 15$	$\frac{150}{x+15}$
Train B	120	x	$\frac{120}{x}$

c. They are the same, $\frac{150}{x+5} = \frac{120}{x}$ **d.** The speed of the train A is 75 mph, train B is 60 mph

15. 540 mph **17.** 54 mph **19.** 16 hours **21.** 15 hours **23.** 5.25 minutes **25.** $10 = \frac{1}{3}\left[\left(x + \frac{2}{3}x\right) + \frac{1}{3}\left(x + \frac{2}{3}x\right)\right]$; $x = \frac{27}{2}$

27. **a.** 30 grams **b.** 3.25 moles

Answers to Odd-Numbered Problems

29.

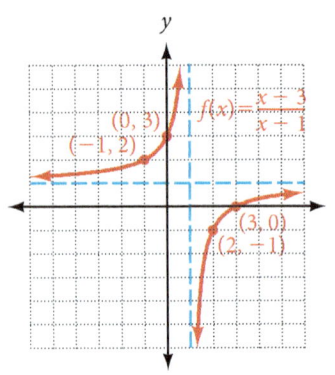

31.

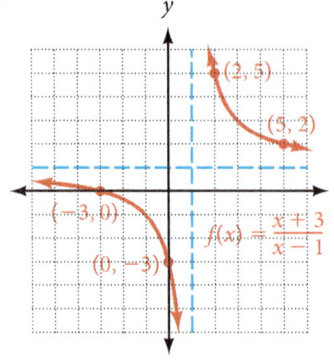

33.

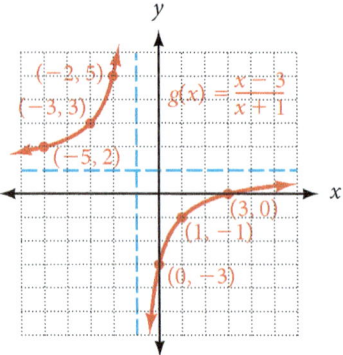

35. 2   **37.** $-2x^2y^2$ **39.** 185.12   **41.** $4x^3 - 8x^2$ **43.** $4x^3 - 6x - 20$ **45.** $-3x + 9$ **47.** $(x + a)(x - a)$ **49.** $(x - 7y)(x + y)$

PROBLEM SET 7.7

1. $2x^2 - 4x + 3$ **3.** $-2x^2 - 3x + 4$ **5.** $2y^2 + \frac{5}{2} - \frac{3}{2y^2}$ **7.** $-\frac{5}{2}x + 4 + \frac{3}{x}$ **9.** $4ab^3 + 6a^2b$ **11.** $-xy + 2y^2 + 3xy^2$

13. $x + 2$ **15.** $a - 3$ **17.** $5x + 6y$ **19.** $x^2 + xy + y^2$ **21.** $(y^2 + 4)(y + 2)$ **23.** $(x + 2)(x + 5)$ **25.** $(2x + 3)(2x - 3)$

27. $x - 7 + \frac{7}{x + 2}$ **29.** $2x + 5 + \frac{2}{3x - 4}$ **31.** $2x^2 - 5x + 1 + \frac{4}{x + 1}$ **33.** $y^2 - 3y - 13$ **35.** $x - 3$ **37.** $3y^2 + 6y + 8 + \frac{37}{2y - 4}$

39. $a^3 + 2a^2 + 4a + 6 + \frac{17}{a - 2}$ **41.** $y^3 + 2y^2 + 4y + 8$ **43.** $x^2 - 2x + 1$ **45.** $(x + 3)(x + 2)(x + 1)$

47. $(x + 3)(x + 4)(x - 2)$ **49.** yes   **51.** same   **53. a.** $(x - 2)(x^2 - x + 3)$ **b.** $(x - 5)(x^3 - x + 1)$

55. a.

x	1	5	10	15	20
$C(x)$	2.15	2.75	3.50	4.25	5.00

b. $\overline{C}(x) = \frac{2 + 0.15}{x}$ **c.**

x	1	5	10	15	20
$\overline{C}(x)$	2.15	0.55	0.35	0.28	0.25

d. It decreases.

e. $y = C(x)$: domain $= \{x | 1 \le x \le 20\}$; range $= \{y | 2.15 \le y \le 5.00\}$
$y = \overline{C}(x)$: domain $= \{x | 1 \le x \le 20\}$; range $= \{y | 0.25 \le y \le 2.15\}$

57. a. $T(100) = \$11.95$, $T(400) = \$32.95$, $T(500) = \$39.95$ **b.** $\overline{T}(m) = \frac{4.95 + .07}{m}$ **c.** $\overline{T}(100) = \$0.1195$, $\overline{T}(400) = \$0.0824$, $\overline{T}(500) = \$0.0799$

59. $\frac{2}{3a}$ **61.** $(x - 3)(x + 2)$ **63.** 1   **65.** $\frac{3 - x}{x + 3}$ **67.** no solution

CHAPTER 7 TEST

1. $x + y$ **2.** $\frac{x - 1}{x + 1}$ **3.** $2(a + 4)$ **4.** $4(a + 3)$ **5.** $x + 3$ **6.** $\frac{38}{105}$ **7.** $\frac{7}{8}$ **8.** $\frac{1}{a - 3}$ **9.** $\frac{3(x - 1)}{x(x - 3)}$ **10.** $\frac{x}{(x + 4)(x + 5)}$

11. $\frac{x + 4}{(x + 1)(x + 2)}$ **12.** $\frac{3a + 8}{3a + 10}$ **13.** $\frac{x - 3}{x - 2}$ **14.** $-\frac{3}{5}$ **15.** no solution (3 does not check)   **16.** $\frac{3}{13}$ **17.** $-2, 3$

18.

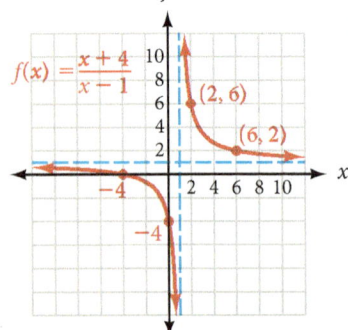

19. -7 **20.** 6 mph   **21.** 15 hours   **22.** 2.7 miles   **23.** 1,012 mph

24. $6x^2 + 3xy - 4y^2$ **25.** $x^2 - 4x - 2 + \frac{8}{2x - 1}$

Chapter 8

PROBLEM SET 8.1

1. 12 **3.** Not a real number **5.** -7 **7.** -3 **9.** 2 **11.** Not a real number **13.** 0.2 **15.** 0.2 **17.** $6a^4$ **19.** $3a^4$ **21.** xy^2

23. $2x^2y$ **25.** $2a^3b^5$ **27.** 6 **29.** -3 **31.** 2 **33.** -2 **35.** 2 **37.** $\frac{9}{5}$ **39.** $\frac{4}{5}$ **41.** 9 **43.** 125 **45.** 8 **47.** $\frac{1}{3}$ **49.** $\frac{1}{27}$

51. $\frac{6}{5}$ **53.** $\frac{8}{27}$ **55.** 7 **57.** $\frac{3}{4}$ **59.** $x^{4/5}$ **61.** a **63.** $\frac{1}{x^{2/5}}$ **65.** $x^{1/6}$ **67.** $x^{9/25}y^{1/2}z^{1/5}$ **69.** $\frac{b^{7/4}}{a^{1/8}}$ **71.** $y^{3/10}$ **73.** $\frac{1}{a^2b^4}$

75. a. 5 **b.** 0.5 **c.** 50 **d.** 0.05 **77. a.** $4a^2b^4$ **b.** $2ab^2\sqrt[3]{2ab^2}$ **79.** $(\sqrt{9}+\sqrt{4})^2 \overset{?}{=} 9 + 4; (3 + 4)^2 \overset{?}{=} 13; 7^2 \overset{?}{=} 13; 49 \neq 13$

81. $(a^{1/2})^{1/2} = a^{1/4}; a^{1/2 \cdot 1/2} = a^{1/4}; a^{1/4} = a^{1/4}$ **83.** 25 mph **85.** 1.618

87. $\frac{13}{8}$. The denominator is the sum of the 2 previous denominators, and the numerator is the sum of the 2 previous numerators.

89. a. 420 picometers **b.** 594 picometers **c.** 5.94×10^{-10} meters **91.** 5 **93.** 6 **95.** $4x^2y$ **97.** $5y$ **99.** 3 **101.** 2

103. $2ab$ **105.** 25 **107.** $48x^4y^2$ **109.** $4x^6y^6$

PROBLEM SET 8.2

1. $2\sqrt{2}$ **3.** $7\sqrt{2}$ **5.** $12\sqrt{2}$ **7.** $4\sqrt{5}$ **9.** $4\sqrt{3}$ **11.** $15\sqrt{3}$ **13.** $3\sqrt[3]{2}$ **15.** $4\sqrt[3]{2}$ **17.** $6\sqrt[3]{2}$ **19.** $2\sqrt[5]{2}$ **21.** $3x\sqrt{2x}$

23. $2y\sqrt[4]{2y^3}$ **25.** $2xy^2\sqrt[3]{5xy}$ **27.** $4abc^2\sqrt{3b}$ **29.** $2bc\sqrt[3]{6a^2c}$ **31.** $2xy^2\sqrt[5]{2x^3y^2}$ **33.** $3xy^2z\sqrt[5]{x^2}$ **35.** $2\sqrt{3}$

37. $\sqrt{-20}$; not real number **39.** $\frac{\sqrt{11}}{2}$ **41. a.** $\frac{\sqrt{5}}{2}$ **b.** $\frac{2\sqrt{5}}{5}$ **c.** $2 + \sqrt{3}$ **d.** 1

43. a. $2 + \sqrt{3}$ **b.** $-2 + \sqrt{5}$ **c.** $\frac{-2 - 3\sqrt{3}}{6}$ **45.** $\frac{2\sqrt{3}}{3}$ **47.** $\frac{5\sqrt{6}}{6}$ **49.** $\frac{\sqrt{2}}{2}$ **51.** $\frac{\sqrt{5}}{5}$ **53.** $2\sqrt[3]{4}$ **55.** $\frac{2\sqrt[3]{3}}{3}$ **57.** $\frac{\sqrt[4]{24x^2}}{2x}$

59. $\frac{\sqrt[4]{8y^3}}{y}$ **61.** $\frac{\sqrt[3]{36xy^2}}{3y}$ **63.** $\frac{\sqrt[3]{6xy^2}}{3y}$ **65.** $\frac{3x\sqrt{15xy}}{5y}$ **67.** $\frac{5xy\sqrt{6xz}}{2z}$ **69. a.** $\frac{\sqrt{2}}{2}$ **b.** $\frac{\sqrt[3]{4}}{2}$ **c.** $\frac{\sqrt[4]{8}}{2}$ **71.** $5|x|$ **73.** $3|xy|$

75. $|x - 5|$ **77.** $|2x + 3|$ **79.** $2|a(a + 2)|$ **81.** $2|x|\sqrt{x - 2}$ **83.** $\sqrt{9 + 16} \overset{?}{=} \sqrt{9} + \sqrt{16}$
$\sqrt{25} \overset{?}{=} 3 + 4$
$5 \neq 7$

85. $5\sqrt{13}$ feet **87. a.** ≈ 89.4 miles **b.** ≈ 126.5 miles **c.** ≈ 154.9 miles

91. $\sqrt{2}, \sqrt{3}, 2, \sqrt{5}, \sqrt{6}, \sqrt{7}; a_{10} = \sqrt{11}; a_{100} = \sqrt{101}$ **93.** $7x$ **95.** $27xy^2$ **97.** $\frac{5}{6}x$ **99.** $3\sqrt{2}$ **101.** $5y\sqrt{3xy}$

103. $2a\sqrt[3]{ab^2}$

PROBLEM SET 8.3

1. $7\sqrt{5}$ **3.** $-x\sqrt{7}$ **5.** $\sqrt[3]{10}$ **7.** $9\sqrt[5]{6}$ **9.** 0 **11.** $\sqrt{5}$ **13.** $-32\sqrt{2}$ **15.** $-3x\sqrt{2}$ **17.** $-2\sqrt[3]{2}$ **19.** $8x\sqrt[3]{xy^2}$

21. $3a^2b\sqrt{3ab}$ **23.** $11ab\sqrt[3]{3a^2b}$ **25.** $10xy\sqrt[4]{3y}$ **27.** $\sqrt{2}$ **29.** $\frac{8\sqrt{5}}{15}$ **31.** $\frac{(x - 1)\sqrt{x}}{x}$ **33.** $\frac{3\sqrt{2}}{2}$ **35.** $\frac{5\sqrt{6}}{6}$ **37.** $\frac{8\sqrt[3]{25}}{5}$

39. $\sqrt{12} \approx 3.464; 2\sqrt{3} \approx 2(1.732) = 3.464$ **41.** $\sqrt{8} + \sqrt{18} \approx 2.828 + 4.243 = 7.071; \sqrt{50} \approx 7.071; \sqrt{26} \approx 5.099$

43. $8\sqrt{2x}$ **45.** 5 **53.** $\sqrt{2}:1$ **55. a.** $\sqrt{2}:1 \approx 1.414:1$ **b.** $5:\sqrt{2}$ **c.** $5:4$ **57.** 6 **59.** $4x^2 + 3xy - y^2$ **61.** $x^2 + 6x + 9$

63. $x^2 - 4$ **65.** $6\sqrt{2}$ **67.** 6 **69.** $9x$ **71.** $\frac{\sqrt{6}}{2}$

PROBLEM SET 8.4

1. $3\sqrt{2}$ **3.** $10\sqrt{21}$ **5.** 720 **7.** 54 **9.** $\sqrt{6} - 9$ **11.** $24 + 6\sqrt[3]{4}$ **13.** $7 + 2\sqrt{6}$ **15.** $x + 2\sqrt{x} - 15$ **17.** $34 + 20\sqrt{3}$

19. $19 + 8\sqrt{3}$ **21.** $x - 6\sqrt{x} + 9$ **23.** $4a - 12\sqrt{ab} + 9b$ **25.** $x + 4\sqrt{x - 4}$ **27.** $x - 6\sqrt{x - 5} + 4$ **29.** 1 **31.** $a - 49$

33. $25 - x$ **35.** $x - 8$ **37.** $10 + 6\sqrt{3}$ **39.** $\frac{1 + \sqrt{3}}{2}$ **41.** $\frac{5 - \sqrt{5}}{4}$ **43.** $\frac{x + 3\sqrt{x}}{x - 9}$ **45.** $\frac{10 + 3\sqrt{5}}{11}$ **47.** $\frac{3\sqrt{x} + 3\sqrt{y}}{x - y}$

49. $2 + \sqrt{3}$ **51.** $\frac{11 - 4\sqrt{7}}{3}$ **53. a.** $2\sqrt{x}$ **b.** $x - 4$ **c.** $x + 4\sqrt{x} + 4$ **d.** $\frac{x + 4\sqrt{x} + 4}{x - 4}$

55. a. 10 **b.** 23 **c.** $27 + 10\sqrt{2}$ **d.** $\frac{27 + 10\sqrt{2}}{23}$ **57. a.** $2\sqrt{2} + \sqrt{6}$ **b.** $2\sqrt{3} + 2$ **c.** $\sqrt{3} + 1$ **d.** $\frac{-1 + \sqrt{3}}{2}$

59. a. 1 **b.** -1 **61.** $(\sqrt[3]{2} + \sqrt[3]{3})(\sqrt[3]{4} - \sqrt[3]{6} + \sqrt[3]{9}) = \sqrt[3]{8} - \sqrt[3]{12} + \sqrt[3]{18} + \sqrt[3]{12} - \sqrt[3]{18} + \sqrt[3]{27} = 2 + 3 = 5$

63. $10\sqrt{3}$ **65.** $x + 6\sqrt{x} + 9$ **67.** 75 **69.** $\frac{5\sqrt{2}}{4}$ second; $\frac{5}{2}$ second **75.** $t^2 + 10t + 25$ **77.** x **79.** 7 **81.** $-4, -3$

83. $-6, -3$ **85.** $-5, -2$ **87.** Yes **89.** No

PROBLEM SET 8.5

1. 4   **3.** ∅   **5.** 5   **7.** ∅   **9.** $\frac{39}{2}$ **11.** ∅   **13.** 5   **15.** 3   **17.** $-\frac{32}{3}$ **19.** 3, 4   **21.** $-1, -2$ **23.** -1 **25.** ∅   **27.** 7   **29.** 0, 3

31. -4 **33.** 8   **35.** 0   **37.** 9   **39.** 0   **41.** 8   **43.** Possible solution 9, which does not check; ∅

45. a. 100   **b.** 40   **c.** ∅   **d.** Possible solutions 5, 8; only 8 checks

47. a. 3   **b.** 9   **c.** 3   **d.** ∅   **e.** 4.   **f.** ∅   **g.** Possible solutions 1,4; only 4 checks   **49.** $h = 100 - 16t^2$ **51.** $\frac{392}{121} \approx 3.24$ feet

53.

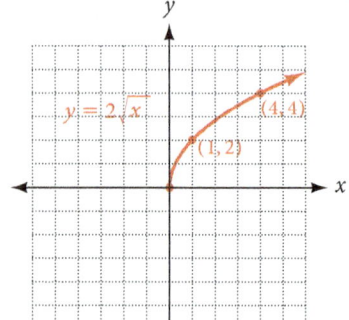

55.

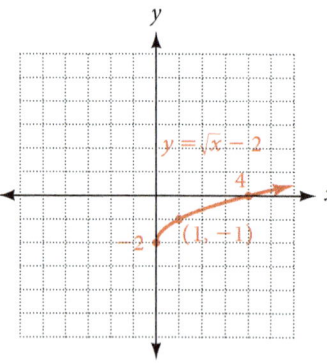

57.

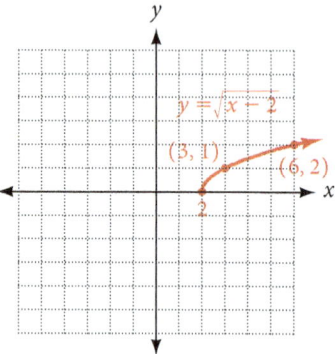

59.

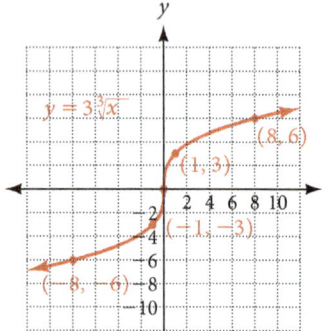

61.

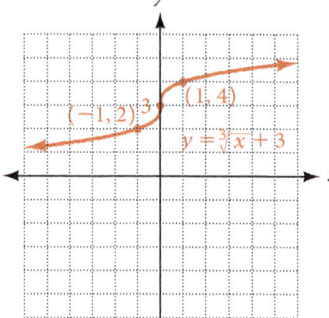

63.

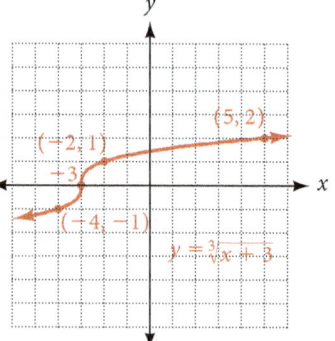

65. 5   **67.** $2\sqrt{3}$ **69.** -1 **71.** 1   **73.** 4   **75.** 2   **77.** $10 - 2x$ **79.** $2 - 3x$ **81.** $6 + 7x - 20x^2$ **83.** $8x - 12x^2$

85. $4 + 12x + 9x^2$ **87.** $4 - 9x^2$

PROBLEM SET 8.6

1. $6i$ **3.** $-5i$ **5.** $6i\sqrt{2}$ **7.** $-2i\sqrt{3}$ **9.** 1   **11.** -1 **13.** $-i$ **15.** $x = 3, y = -1$ **17.** $x = -2, y = -\frac{1}{2}$

19. $x = -8, y = -5$ **21.** $x = 7, y = \frac{1}{2}$ **23.** $x = \frac{3}{7}, y = \frac{2}{5}$ **25.** $5 + 9i$ **27.** $5 - i$ **29.** $2 - 4i$ **31.** $1 - 6i$ **33.** $2 + 2i$
35. $-1 - 7i$ **37.** $6 + 8i$ **39.** $2 - 24i$ **41.** $-15 + 12i$ **43.** $18 + 24i$ **45.** $10 + 11i$ **47.** $21 + 23i$ **49.** $-2 + 2i$ **51.** $2 - 11i$
53. $-21 + 20i$ **55.** $-2i$ **57.** $-7 - 24i$ **59.** 5   **61.** 40   **63.** 13   **65.** 164   **67.** $-3 - 2i$ **69.** $-2 + 5i$ **71.** $\frac{8}{13} + \frac{12}{13}i$
73. $-\frac{18}{13} - \frac{12}{13}i$ **75.** $-\frac{5}{13} + \frac{12}{13}i$ **77.** $\frac{13}{15} - \frac{2}{5}i$ **79.** $R = -11 - 7i$ ohms   **81.** $-\frac{3}{2}$ **83.** $-3, \frac{1}{2}$ **85.** $\frac{5}{4}$ or $\frac{4}{5}$

CHAPTER 8 TEST

1. $\frac{1}{9}$ **2.** $\frac{7}{5}$ **3.** $a^{5/12}$ **4.** $\frac{x^{13/12}}{y}$ **5.** $7x^4y^5$ **6.** $2x^2y^4$ **7.** $2a$ **8.** $x^{n^2-n}y^{1-n^3}$ **9.** $6a^2 - 10a$ **10.** $16a^3 - 40a^{3/2} + 25$

11. $(3x^{1/3} - 1)(x^{1/3} + 2)$ **12.** $(3x^{1/3} - 7)(3x^{1/3} + 7)$ **13.** $\frac{x+4}{x^{1/2}}$ **14.** $\frac{3}{(x^2-3)^{1/2}}$ **15.** $5xy^2\sqrt{5xy}$ **16.** $2x^2y^2\sqrt[3]{5xy^2}$ **17.** $\frac{\sqrt{6}}{3}$

18. $\frac{2a^2b\sqrt{15bc}}{5c}$ **19.** $-6\sqrt{3}$ **20.** $-3ab\sqrt[3]{3}$ **21.** $x + 3\sqrt{x} - 28$ **22.** $21 - 6\sqrt{6}$ **23.** $\frac{5+5\sqrt{3}}{2}$ **24.** $\frac{x - 2\sqrt{2x} + 2}{x - 2}$

25. 8 (1 does not check)   **26.** -4 **27.** -3

28.

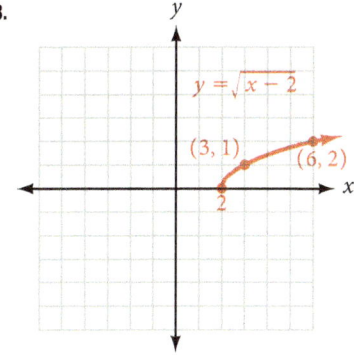

$y = \sqrt{x - 2}$

$(3, 1)$

$(6, 2)$

29.

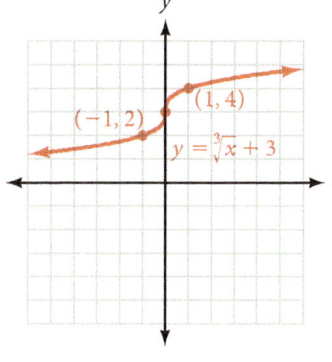

$(-1, 2)$

$(1, 4)$

$y = \sqrt[3]{x} + 3$

30. $x = \frac{1}{2}, y = 7$ **31.** $6i$ **32.** $17 - 6i$

33. $9 - 40i$ **34.** $-\frac{5}{13} - \frac{12}{13}i$

35. $i^{38} = (i^2)^{19} = (-1)^{19} = -1$

Chapter 9

PROBLEM SET 9.1

1. ± 5 **3.** $\pm 3i$ **5.** $\pm \frac{\sqrt{3}}{2}$ **7.** $\pm 2i\sqrt{3}$ **9.** $\pm \frac{3\sqrt{5}}{2}$ **11.** $-2, 3$ **13.** $\frac{-3 \pm 3i}{2}$ **15.** $\frac{-2 \pm 2i\sqrt{2}}{5}$ **17.** $-4 \pm 3i\sqrt{3}$ **19.** $\frac{3 \pm 2i}{2}$

21. $36, 6$ **23.** $4, 2$ **25.** $25, 5$ **27.** $\frac{25}{4}, \frac{5}{2}$ **29.** $\frac{49}{4}, \frac{7}{2}$ **31.** $\frac{1}{16}, \frac{1}{4}$ **33.** $\frac{1}{9}, \frac{1}{3}$ **35.** $-6, 2$ **37.** $-3, -9$ **39.** $1 \pm 2i$ **41.** $4 \pm \sqrt{15}$

43. $\frac{5 \pm \sqrt{37}}{2}$ **45.** $1 \pm \sqrt{5}$ **47.** $\frac{4 \pm \sqrt{13}}{3}$ **49.** $\frac{3 \pm i\sqrt{71}}{8}$ **51.** $\frac{-2 \pm \sqrt{7}}{3}$ **53.** $\frac{5 \pm \sqrt{47}}{2}$ **55.** $\frac{5 \pm i\sqrt{19}}{4}$ **57. a.** No **b.** $\pm 3i$

59. a. $0, 6$ **b.** $0, 6$ **61. a.** $-7, 5$ **b.** $-7, 5$ **63.** No **65. a.** $\frac{7}{5}$ **b.** 3 **c.** $\frac{7 \pm 2\sqrt{2}}{5}$ **d.** $\frac{71}{5}$ **e.** 3 **67.** $\frac{\sqrt{3}}{2}$ inch, 1 inch

69. $\sqrt{2}$ inches **71.** 781 feet **73.** 7.3% to the nearest tenth **75.** $20\sqrt{2} \approx 28$ feet **77.** 169 **79.** 49 **81.** $\frac{85}{12}$

83. $(3t - 2)(9t^2 + 6t + 4)$

PROBLEM SET 9.2

1. $-3, -2$ **3.** $2 \pm \sqrt{3}$ **5.** $1, 2$ **7.** $\frac{2 \pm i\sqrt{14}}{3}$ **9.** $0, 5$ **11.** $0, -\frac{4}{3}$ **13.** $\frac{3 \pm \sqrt{5}}{4}$ **15.** $-3 \pm \sqrt{17}$ **17.** $\frac{-1 \pm i\sqrt{5}}{2}$ **19.** 1

21. $\frac{1 \pm i\sqrt{47}}{6}$ **23.** $4 \pm \sqrt{2}$ **25.** $\frac{1}{2}, 1$ **27.** $-\frac{1}{2}, 3$ **29.** $\frac{-1 \pm i\sqrt{7}}{2}$ **31.** $1 \pm \sqrt{2}$ **33.** $\frac{-3 \pm \sqrt{5}}{2}$ **35.** $3, -5$

37. $2, -1 \pm i\sqrt{3}$ **39.** $-\frac{3}{2}, \frac{3 \pm 3i\sqrt{3}}{4}$ **41.** $\frac{1}{5}, \frac{-1 \pm i\sqrt{3}}{10}$ **43.** $0, \frac{-1 \pm i\sqrt{5}}{2}$ **45.** $0, 1 \pm i$ **47.** $0, \frac{-1 \pm i\sqrt{2}}{3}$ **49.** a and b

51. a. $\frac{5}{3}, 0$ **b.** $\frac{5}{3}, 0$ **53.** No, $2 \pm i\sqrt{3}$ **55.** Yes **57.** 2 seconds **59.** 20 or 60 items **61.** 169 **63.** 0 **65.** ± 12

67. $x^2 - x - 6$ **69.** $x^3 - 4x^2 - 3x + 18$

PROBLEM SET 9.3

1. $1, 2$ **3.** $-8, -\frac{5}{2}$ **5.** $\pm 3, \pm i\sqrt{3}$ **7.** $\pm 2i, \pm i\sqrt{5}$ **9.** $\frac{7}{2}, 4$ **11.** $-\frac{9}{8}, \frac{1}{2}$ **13.** $\pm \frac{\sqrt{30}}{6}, \pm i$ **15.** $\pm \frac{\sqrt{21}}{3}, \pm \frac{i\sqrt{21}}{3}$ **17.** $4, 25$

19. only 25 checks **21.** only $\frac{25}{9}$ checks **23.** 27, 38 **25.** 4, 12 **27.** $t = \frac{v \pm \sqrt{v^2 + 64h}}{32}$ **29.** $x = \frac{-4 \pm 2\sqrt{4 - k}}{k}$ **31.** $x = -y$

33. $t = \frac{1 \pm \sqrt{1 + h}}{4}$ **35. a.** y **b.** 630 ft.

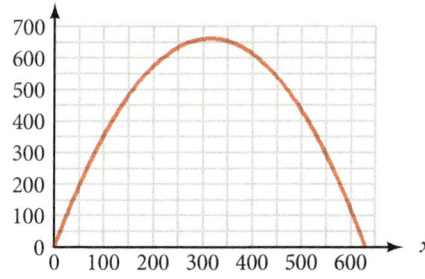

37. **a.** $l + 2w = 160$ **b.** $A = -2w^2 + 160w$ **c.**   **d.** 3,200 square yards

w	l	A
50	60	3,000
45	70	3,150
40	80	3,200
35	90	3,150
30	100	3,000

39. -2 **41.** $1,322.5$ **43.** $-\dfrac{7}{640}$ **45.** $1, 5$ **47.** $-3, 1$ **49.** $\dfrac{3}{2} \pm \dfrac{1}{2}i$ **51.** $9, 3$ **53.** $1, 1$

PROBLEM SET 9.4

1. x-intercepts $= -3, 1$; vertex $= (-1, -4)$ **3.** x-intercepts $= -5, 1$; vertex $= (-2, 9)$

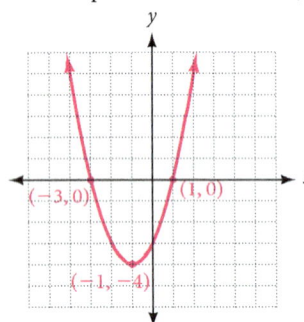
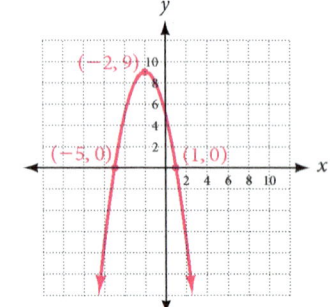

5. x-intercepts $= -1, 1$; vertex $= (0, -1)$ **7.** x-intercepts $= -3, 3$; vertex $= (0, 9)$

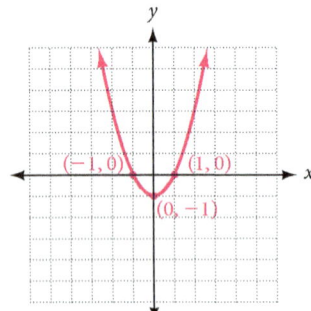
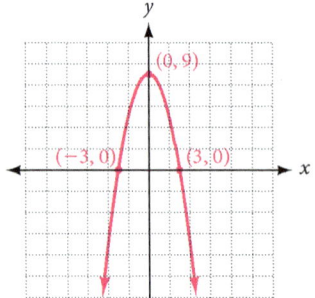

9. x-intercepts $= -1, 3$; vertex $= (1, -8)$ **11.** x-intercepts $= 1 - \sqrt{5}, 1 + \sqrt{5}$; vertex $= (1, -5)$

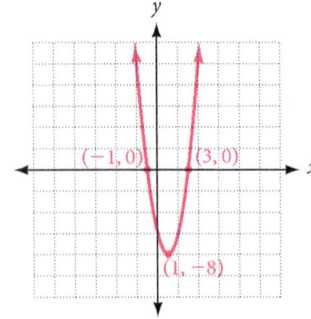
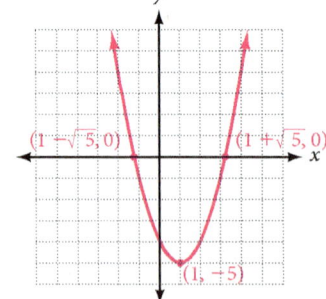

Answers to Odd-Numbered Problems

13.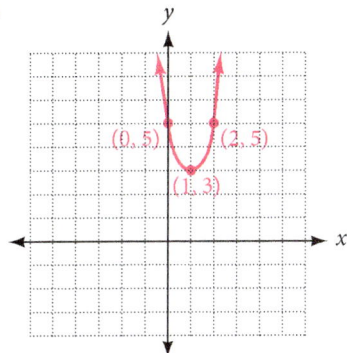

15.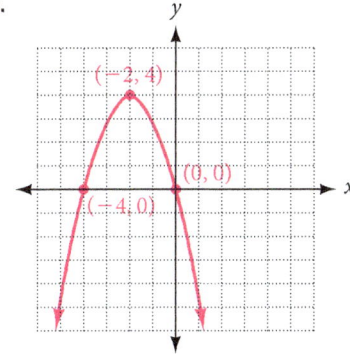

17.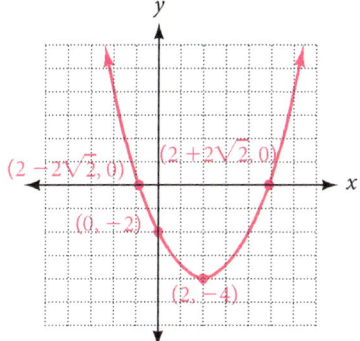

19.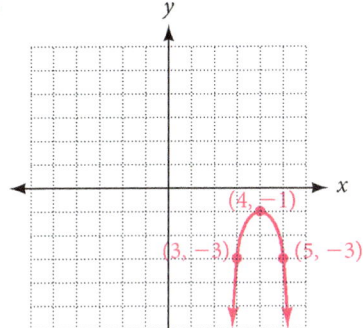

21. vertex $= (2, -8)$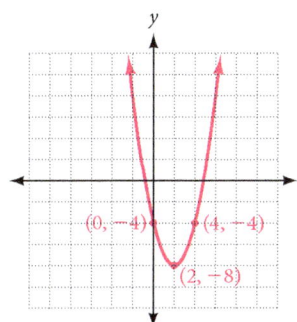

23. vertex $= (1, -4)$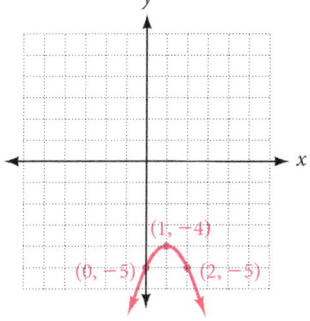

25. vertex $= (0, 1)$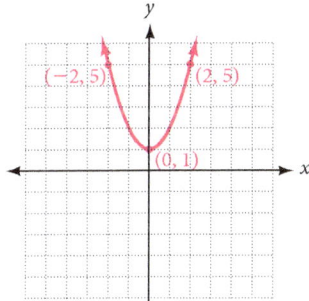

27. vertex $= (0, -3)$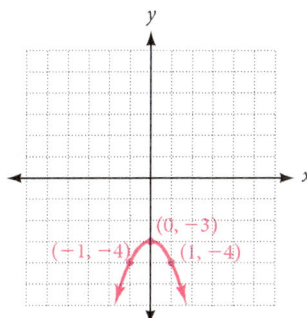

29. vertex $= \left(-\dfrac{2}{3}, -\dfrac{1}{3}\right)$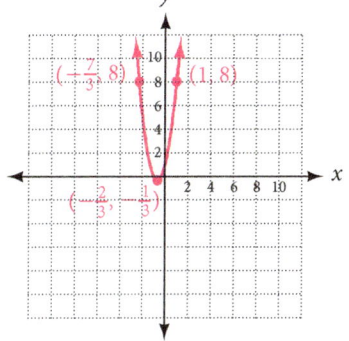

31. $(3, -4)$ lowest **33.** $(1, 9)$ highest **35.** $(2, 16)$ highest **37.** $(-4, 16)$ highest **39.** 875 patterns; maximum profit $731.25

41. The ball is in her hand when $h(t) = 0$, which means $t = 0$ or $t = 2$ seconds. Maximum height is $h(1) = 16$ feet.

43. Maximum $R = \$3,600$ when $p = \$6.00$ **45.** Maximum $R = \$7,225$ when $p = \$8.50$ **47.** $y = -\dfrac{1}{135}(x - 90)^2 + 60$

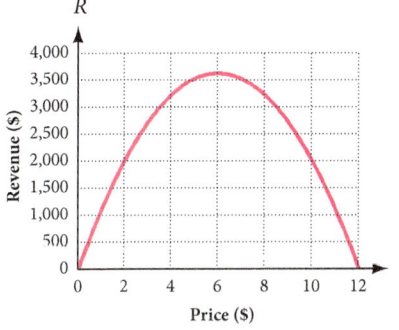

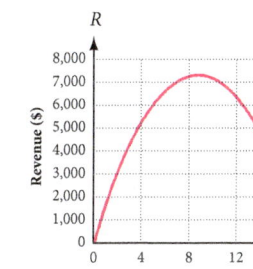

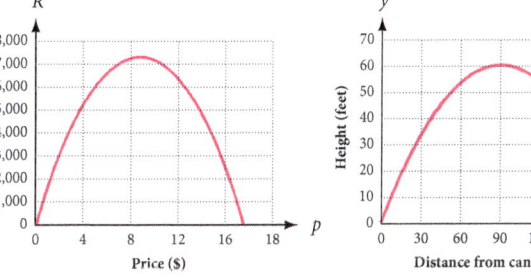

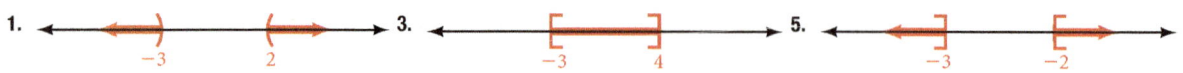

PROBLEM SET 9.5

1. (graph: open at -3 and 2) **3.** (graph: bracket at -3 and 4) **5.** (graph: bracket at -3 and -2)

7. (graph: open at $\frac{1}{3}$ and $\frac{1}{2}$) **9.** (graph: open at -3 and 3) **11.** (graph: bracket at $-\frac{3}{2}$ and $\frac{3}{2}$)

13. (graph: open at -1 and $\frac{3}{2}$) **15.** All real numbers **17.** $\varnothing$

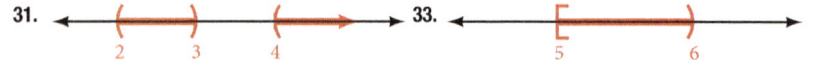

19. (graph: open at 2, 3, 4) **21.** (graph: bracket at -3, -2, -1) **23.** (graph: bracket at -4 and 1)

25. (graph: open at -6 and $\frac{8}{3}$) **27.** (graph: open at 2 and 6) **29.** (graph: open at -3, 2, 4)

31. (graph: open at 2, 3, 4) **33.** (graph: bracket at 5 and open at 6)

35. **a.** $-2 < x < 2$ **b.** $x < -2$ or $x > 2$ **c.** $x = -2$ or $x = 2$ **37.** **a.** $-2 < x < 5$ **b.** $x < -2$ or $x > 5$ **c.** $x = -2$ or $x = 5$

39. **a.** $x < -1$ or $1 < x < 3$ **b.** $-1 < x < 1$ or $x > 3$ **c.** $x = -1$ or $x = 1$ or $x = 3$ **41.** $x \geq 4$; the width is at least 4 inches

43. $5 \leq p \leq 8$; she should charge at least \$5 but no more than \$8 for each radio **45.** \$300, \$1,800,000 **47.** \$30

49. 1.5625 **51.** 0.6549 **53.** $\frac{2}{3}$ **55.** Possible solutions 1 and 6; only 6 checks; 6 **57.**

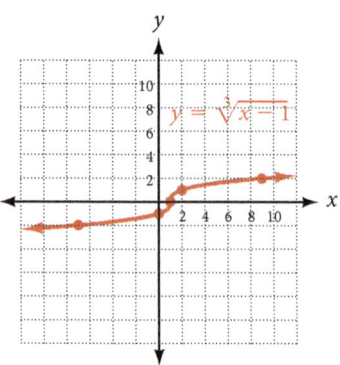

CHAPTER 9 TEST

1. $-\frac{9}{2}, \frac{1}{2}$ **2.** $3 \pm i\sqrt{2}$ **3.** $5 \pm 2i$ **4.** $1 \pm i\sqrt{2}$ **5.** $\frac{5}{2}, \frac{-5 \pm 5i\sqrt{3}}{4}$ **6.** $-1 \pm i\sqrt{5}$ **7.** $r = \pm\frac{\sqrt{A}}{8} - 1$ **8.** $2 \pm \sqrt{2}$

9. $\frac{1}{2}$ or $\frac{3}{2}$ sec **10.** 15 or 100 cups **11.** $\pm\sqrt{2}, \pm\frac{1}{2}i$ **12.** $\frac{1}{2}, 1$ **13.** $\frac{1}{4}, 9$ **14.** $t = \frac{7 + \sqrt{49 + 16h}}{16}$

15. vertex: $(1, -4)$ **16.** vertex: $(1, 9)$

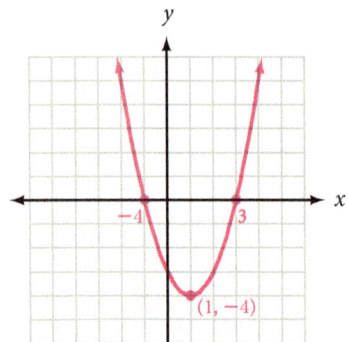

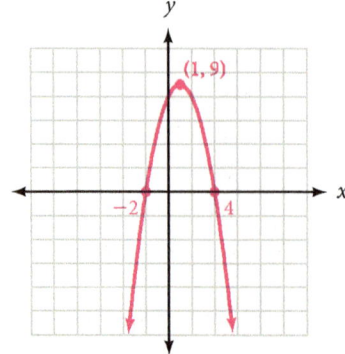

17. $-2 \le x \le 3$

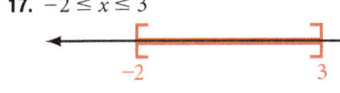

18. $x < -3$ or $x > \frac{1}{2}$

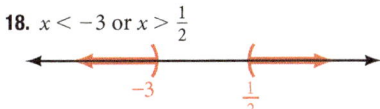

19. profit = \$900

Chapter 10

PROBLEM SET 10.1

1. hypothesis: you argue for your limitations; conclusion: they are yours

3. hypothesis: x is an even number; conclusion: x is divisible by 2

5. hypothesis: a triangle is equilateral; conclusion: all of its angles are equal

7. hypothesis: $x + 5 = -2$; conclusion: $x = -7$

9. converse: If $a^2 = 64$, then $a = 8$; inverse: If $a \ne 8$, then $a^2 \ne 64$; contrapositive: If $a^2 \ne 64$, then $a \ne 8$.

11. converse: If $a = b$, then $\frac{a}{b} = 1$; inverse: If $\frac{a}{b} \ne 1$, then $a \ne b$; contrapositive: If $a \ne b$, then $\frac{a}{b} \ne 1$.

13. converse: If it is a rectangle, then it is a square; inverse: If it is not a square, then it is not a rectangle; contrapositive: If it is not a rectangle, then it is not a square.

15. converse: If good is not enough, then better is possible; inverse: If better is not possible, then good is enough; contrapositive: If good is enough, then better is not possible.

17. If E, then F.   **19.** If it is misery, then it loves company.   **21.** If the wheel is squeaky, then it gets the grease.

23. contrapositive: If your eyes are not closed, then you are not sleeping; contrapositive of contrapositive: If you are sleeping, then your eyes are closed.

25.

	Statement	Inverse	Converse	Contrapositive
(a)	True	True	True	True
(b)	False	True	True	False
(c)	True	False	False	True
(d)	False	True	True	False
(e)	?	False	True	?

27. If Amy does not stay out late, then I'll extend her curfew.; Yes, extend her curfew.

PROBLEM SET 10.2

1. 3   **3.** $-\frac{4}{3}$ **5.** 7,000   **7.** -3 **9.** $-1, 6$ **11.** $-\frac{4}{3}, 0, \frac{4}{3}$ **13.** $-5, 1$ **15.** $0, -3, \frac{3}{2}$ **17.** $-3, -\frac{3}{2}, \frac{3}{2}$

19. a. $\frac{5}{8}$ **b.** $10x - 8$ **c.** $16x^2 - 34x + 15$ **d.** $\frac{3}{2}, \frac{5}{8}$ **21. a.** $\frac{25}{9}$ **b.** $-\frac{5}{3}, \frac{5}{3}$ **c.** $-3, 3$ **d.** $\frac{5}{3}$ **23.** $-\frac{9}{2}$

25. $0, 2, 3$ **27.** $-\frac{7}{640}$ **29.** $\frac{7}{10}$ **31.** 24 **33.** $\frac{46}{15}$ **35.** $-2, \frac{5}{3}$ **37.** $-3, 0$ **39.** 5 **41.** 4 **43.** $6,000$

45. $-4, -2$ **47.** No solution   **49.** No solution   **51.** All real numbers   **53.** $30,000$ **55.** d   **57.** a

59. -3 **61.** 15 **63.** No solution   **65.** 6 **67.** 3 **69.** -3 **71.** The distance between x and 0 on the number line.

73. -5 **75.** 5 **77.** 7 **79.** 9 **81.** 6 **83.** $2x - 3$ **85.** $-3, 0, 2$

PROBLEM SET 10.3

1. $-4, 4$ **3.** $-2, 2$ **5.** $\varnothing$ **7.** $-1, 1$ **9.** $\varnothing$ **11.** $\frac{17}{3}, \frac{7}{3}$ **13.** $-\frac{5}{2}, \frac{5}{6}$ **15.** $-1, 5$ **17.** $\varnothing$

19. $-4, 20$ **21.** $-4, 8$ **23.** $1, 4$ **25.** $-\frac{1}{7}, \frac{9}{7}$ **27.** $-3, 12$ **29.** -4 **31.** $\frac{2}{3}, -\frac{10}{3}$ **33.** $\varnothing$

35. $\frac{3}{2}, -1$ **37.** $-\frac{2}{3}$ **39.** $5, 25$ **41.** $-30, 26$ **43.** $-12, 28$ **45.** $-2, 0$ **47.** $-\frac{1}{2}, \frac{7}{6}$ **49.** $0, 15$

51. $-\frac{23}{7}, -\frac{11}{7}$ **53.** $-5, \frac{3}{5}$ **55.** $1, \frac{1}{9}$ **57.** $-\frac{1}{2}$ **59.** 0 **61.** $-\frac{1}{6}, -\frac{7}{4}$ **63.** All real numbers

65. All real numbers   **67.** $-\frac{3}{10}, \frac{3}{2}$ **69.** $-\frac{1}{10}, -\frac{3}{5}$ **71. a.** $\frac{5}{4} = 1.25$ **b.** $\frac{5}{4} = 1.25$ **c.** 2 **d.** $\frac{1}{2}, 2$ **e.** $\frac{1}{3}, 4$

73. 1987 and 1995   **75.** b   **77.** c   **79.** ![]   **81.** ![]   **83.** ![]

85. ![]   **87.** $x > 4$ **89.** $x \le -\frac{11}{3}$ **91.** $x \le 4$ **93.** x^{10} **95.** $\frac{4b^8}{a^0}$ **97.** $1125x^{17}y^{14}$ **99.** 3.59×10^{-2}

101. 0.025 **103.** 4×10^{13}

Answers to Odd-Numbered Problems

PROBLEM SET 10.4

1. $\{x \mid x < 6\}, (-\infty, 6)$ **3.** $\{x \mid x \geq -1\}, [-1, \infty)$

5. $\left\{x \mid x > \frac{3}{2}\right\}, \left(\frac{3}{2}, \infty\right)$ **7.** $\left\{x \mid x \leq -\frac{5}{4}\right\}, \left(-\infty, -\frac{5}{4}\right]$

9. $(-\infty, -3]$ **11.** $(20, \infty)$ **13.** $\left(-\infty, \frac{1}{2}\right)$ **15.** $\left[-\frac{17}{4}, \infty\right)$ **17.** $\{1, 2, 3, 4, 5, 6\}$ **19.** $\{2, 4, 5, 6, 7, 8\}$ **21.** $(1, \infty)$

23. $(-\infty, -3]$ **25.** $(-\infty, -7) \cup (7, \infty)$ **27.** $(-\infty, \infty)$ **29.** $\varnothing$ **31.** $\{6, 8\}$ **32.** $\varnothing$ **33.** $(6, \infty)$

35. $(-\infty, -4)$ **37.** $\varnothing$ **39.** $\left(-2, \frac{3}{5}\right]$ **41.** $(-\infty, \infty)$ **43.** $[-9, \infty)$

45. $(-\infty, 7)$ **47.** $[-5, \infty)$

49. $(-\infty, -7] \cup [-3, \infty)$ **51.** $(-\infty, -1] \cup \left[\frac{3}{5}, \infty\right)$

53. $(-\infty, \infty)$ **55.** $(-10, \infty)$ **57.** $\left[-\frac{25}{2}, \infty\right)$

59. $[-3, \infty)$ **61.** $(1, 3)$ **63.** $[-3, \infty)$

65. $(2, \infty)$ **67.** $\varnothing$ **69.** $[-4, -2]$

71. $\left(-\frac{1}{4}, \frac{3}{4}\right)$ **73.** $\left[\frac{4}{3}, \infty\right)$ **75.** $\left(-\frac{27}{5}, 16\right)$

77. $[-1, 40)$ **79.** $[3, 7]$ **81.** $(-4, 2)$ **83.** $[4, 6]$ **85.** $(-4, 2)$ **87.** $(-3, 3)$ **89.** $-2 < x \leq 4$

91. $x < -4$ or $x \geq 1$ **93. a.** $35° \leq C \leq 45°$ **b.** $20° \leq C \leq 30°$ **c.** $-25° \leq C \leq -10°$ **d.** $-20° \leq C \leq -5°$

95. Eggs to hatching: $0.7 \leq r \leq 0.8$; Hatching to fledgling: $0.5 \leq r \leq 0.7$; Fledglings to first breeding: $r < 0.5$

97. c   **99.** d   **101.** $1 < x$ **103.** $a \leq \frac{2}{3}$ **105.** $t \geq 3$ **107.** x-intercept $= -\frac{8}{3}$; y-intercept $= 4$; slope $= \frac{3}{2}$

109. $y = 2x + 5$ **111.** $y = \frac{2}{5}x - 5$

PROBLEM SET 10.5

1. $(-3, 3)$ **3.** $(-\infty, -2] \cup [2, \infty)$ **5.** $(-3, 3)$ **7.** $(-\infty, -7) \cup (7, \infty)$ **9.** $\varnothing$

11. All real numbers, $(-\infty, \infty)$ **13.** $(-4, 10)$ **15.** $(-\infty, -9] \cup [-1, \infty)$ **17.** $\varnothing$

19. All real numbers, $(-\infty, \infty)$ **21.** $\varnothing$

23. $-1 < x < 5$ **25.** $y \leq -5$ or $y \geq -1$

27. $k \leq -5$ or $k \geq 2$ **29.** $-1 < x < 7$

31. $a \leq -2$ or $a \geq 1$ **33.** $-6 < x < \frac{8}{3}$

35. $\varnothing$ **37.** $[-2, 8]$ **39.** $\left(-2, \frac{4}{3}\right)$ **41.** $(-\infty, -5] \cup [-3, \infty)$ **43.** $\left(-\infty, -\frac{7}{2}\right) \cup \left(-\frac{3}{2}, \infty\right)$

45. $\left[-1, \frac{11}{5}\right]$ **47.** $\left(\frac{5}{3}, 3\right)$ **49.** $x < 2$ or $x > 8$

51. $x \leq -3$ or $x \geq 12$

53. $x < 2$ or $x > 6$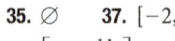

55. $0.99 < x < 1.01$ **57.** $x \leq -\frac{3}{5}$ or $x \geq -\frac{2}{5}$ **59.** $\frac{5}{9} \leq x \leq \frac{7}{9}$ **61.** $x < -\frac{2}{3}$ or $x > 0$ **63.** $x \leq \frac{2}{3}$ or $x \geq 2$

65. $-\frac{1}{6} \le x \le \frac{3}{2}$ **67.** $-0.05 < x < 0.25$ **69.** $|x| \le 4$ **71.** $|x - 5| \le 1$

73. a. 3   **b.** $\left\{ -2, \frac{4}{5} \right\}$ **c.** no   **d.** $x < -2$ or $x > \frac{4}{5}$ **75.** $|x - 65| \le 10$ **77.** d   **79.** a   **81.** $-2x$

83. $x = 2y + 6$ **85.** 2   **87.** $(1, 2)$ **89.** $-5x^2 - 31x + 28$ **91.** $9a^8 - 42a^4 + 49$ **93.** $3x^3 - 17x^2 - 28x$

95. $6x^2 + 3xy - 4y^2$ **97.** $(x - 1)(x - 5)$ **99.** $(3x + 2y)(3x - 2y)(9x^2 + 4y^2)$ **101.** $\left(y - \frac{1}{3} \right)\left(y^2 + \frac{1}{3}y + \frac{1}{9} \right)$

CHAPTER 10 TEST

1. 28   **2.** -3 **3.** $-\frac{7}{4}$ **4.** 2   **5.** $-10, -\frac{1}{2}$ **6.** $0, 3$ **7.** $-6, 3$ **8.** $-5, -3, 3$ **9.** $\{-10, -2\}$

10. $\{2, 6\}$ **11.** $\varnothing$ **12.** $\left\{ -\frac{3}{4}, -\frac{1}{6} \right\}$ **13.** $\{1, 2, 3, 4, 6\}$ **14.** $(-\infty, 4]$ **15.** $\{2\}$ **16.** $(-\infty, -1)$

17. All real numbers   **18.** $(-\infty, -3)$ **19.** $x < -1$ or $x > \frac{4}{3}$
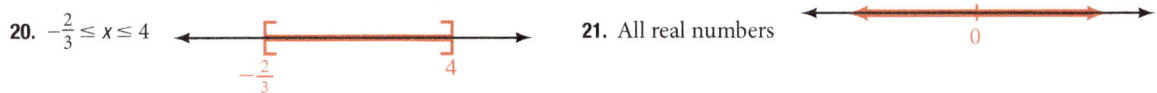

20. $-\frac{2}{3} \le x \le 4$ **21.** All real numbers

22. $\varnothing$

Chapter 11

PROBLEM SET 11.1

1. Acute; complement = 80°, supplement = 170°   **3.** Acute; complement = 45°, supplement = 135°

5. Obtuse; complement = −30°, supplement = 60°   **7.** Complement = 90° − x, supplement = 180° − x

9. $\frac{\pi}{6}$ **11.** $\frac{\pi}{2}$ **13.** $\frac{2\pi}{3}$ **15.** $-\frac{5\pi}{4}$ **17.** $-\frac{5\pi}{6}$ **19.** $\frac{7\pi}{3}$ **21.** 60°   **23.** 120°   **25.** −210°

27. −270°   **29.** 330°   **31.** 720°   **33.** 45° or $\frac{\pi}{4}$ **35.** 120°   **37.** 180°   **39.** 5   **41.** 24   **43.** 5

45. $\sqrt{3}, 2$ **47.** $4, 4\sqrt{3}$ **49.** $\frac{1}{3}, \frac{\sqrt{3}}{3}$ **51.** $3, 6$ **53.** $2\sqrt{3}, 4\sqrt{3}$ **55.** $\sqrt{2}$ **57.** $\frac{4\sqrt{2}}{5}$ **59.** $8, 8$

61. $2\sqrt{2}, 2\sqrt{2}$ **63.** $\sqrt{13}$ **65.** 2   **67.** $\frac{\sqrt{2}}{2}$ **69.** $\frac{3\sqrt{13}}{13}$

PROBLEM SET 11.2

1. 0.4571   **3.** 0.9511   **5.** 21.3634   **7.** 1.6643   **9.** 1.5003   **11.** 4.0906   **13.** 12.3°   **15.** 34.5°   **17.** 78.9°

19. 44.7°   **21.** 65.7°   **23.** 50.1°   **25.** 14.7°   **27.** 10.2°   **29.** 9.2°   **31.** 30°   **33.** 36.6°   **35.** 30°   **37.** 60°

39. 60°   **41.** $-\frac{1}{\sqrt{2}}$ **43.** $\frac{\sqrt{3}}{2}$ **45.** -1 **47.** $-\frac{1}{2}$ **49.** -2 **51.** 2   **53.** $\frac{1}{2}$ **54.**   **55.** $-\frac{1}{\sqrt{3}}$ **57.** 198.0°

59. 140.0°   **61.** 210.5°   **63.** 74.7°   **65.** 105.2°   **67.** 240°   **69.** 135°   **71.** 300°   **73.** 240°   **75.** $\frac{3}{4}$ **77.** 9

79. 1   **81.** 1   **83.** 2   **85.** $\frac{2}{\sqrt{3}}$ **87.** $\frac{4}{5}$

PROBLEM SET 11.3

If you want your graphs to match the ones here, use graph paper on which each square is $\frac{1}{4}$ inch on each side. Then let two squares equal one unit. This way you can let the number π be approximately 6 units. Here is an example:

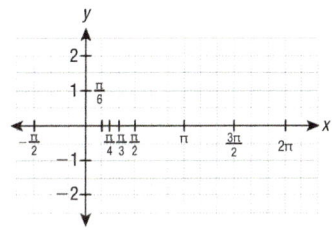

Answers to Odd-Numbered Problems

1.

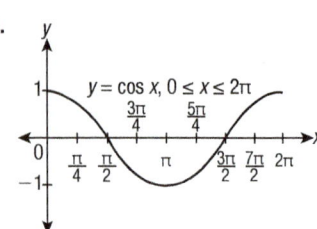

3. $\dfrac{\pi}{3}, \dfrac{5\pi}{3}$ **5.** $\dfrac{3\pi}{4}, \dfrac{5\pi}{4}$ **7.** $\dfrac{\pi}{6}, \dfrac{11\pi}{6}$

9.

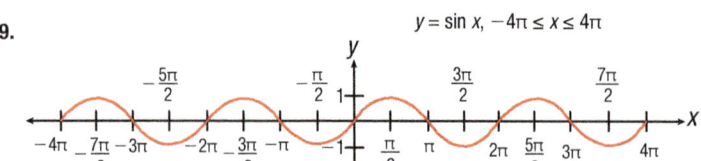

11.

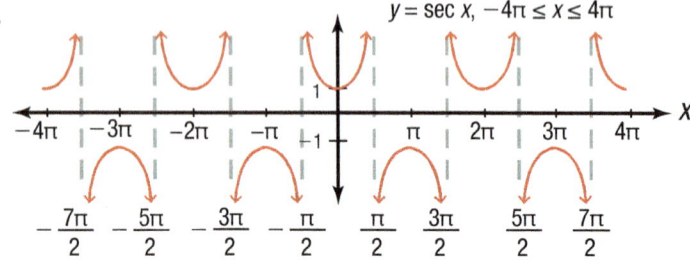

12. $\dfrac{\pi}{3}, \dfrac{2\pi}{3}, \dfrac{7\pi}{3}, \dfrac{8\pi}{3}$

14. $\dfrac{7\pi}{6}, \dfrac{11\pi}{6}, \dfrac{19\pi}{6}, \dfrac{23\pi}{6}$ **16.** $\dfrac{\pi}{4}, \dfrac{3\pi}{4}, \dfrac{9\pi}{4}, \dfrac{11\pi}{4}$ **19.** $\dfrac{\pi}{2} + 2k\pi$ **20.** Amplitude = 3, period = π

CHAPTER 11 TEST

1. $\dfrac{5\pi}{12}$ **2.** $\dfrac{2\pi}{3}$ **3.** $200°$ **4.** $330°$ **5.** $5\sqrt{3}, 10$ **6.** $6\sqrt{2}, 6\sqrt{2}$

7. $\sin\theta = -\dfrac{3}{5}, \cos\theta = \dfrac{4}{5}, \tan\theta = -\dfrac{3}{4}, \cot\theta = -\dfrac{4}{3} \sec\theta = \dfrac{5}{4}, \csc\theta = -\dfrac{5}{3}$ **8.** QIII

9. $\cos\theta = -\dfrac{\sqrt{3}}{2}, \tan\theta = -\dfrac{1}{\sqrt{3}}, \cot\theta = -\sqrt{3}, \sec\theta = -\dfrac{2}{\sqrt{3}}, \csc\theta = 2$

Chapter 12

PROBLEM SET 12.1

1. 1 **3.** 2 **5.** $\dfrac{1}{27}$ **7.** 13 **9.** $\dfrac{7}{12}$ **11.** $\dfrac{3}{16}$ **13.**

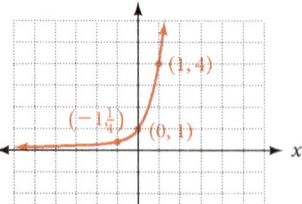

15.

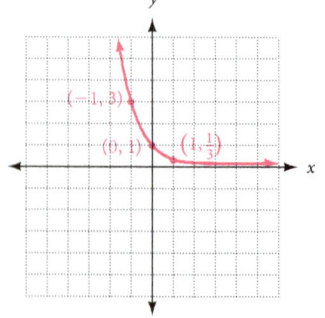

17.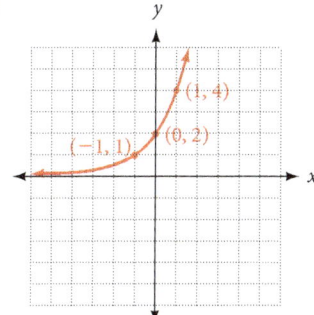

19.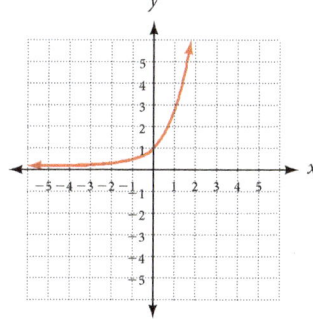

21.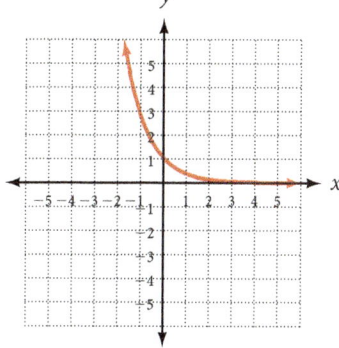

23.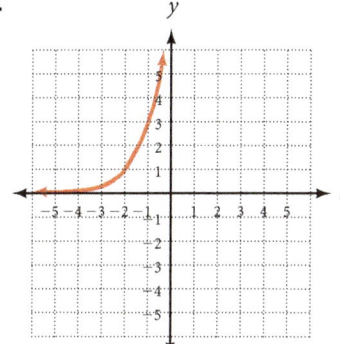

25.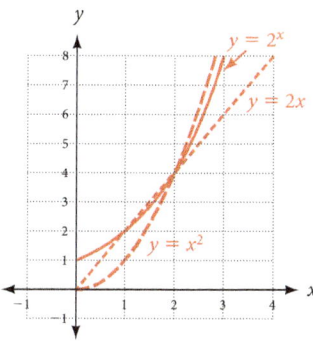

27.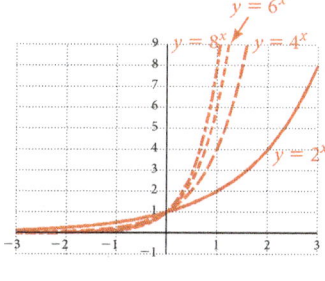

29. $h = 6 \cdot \left(\frac{2}{3}\right)^n$; 5th bounce: $6\left(\frac{2}{3}\right)^5 \approx 0.79$ feet   **31.** 4.27 days

33. **a.** $A(t) = 1,200\left(1 + \frac{.06}{4}\right)^{4t}$ **b.** \$1,932.39   **c.** About 11.64 years   **d.** \$1,939.29   **35.** **a.** \$129,138.48   **b.** $\{t \mid 0 \le t \le 6\}$

d. $\{V(t) \mid 52,942.05 \le V(t) \le 450,000\}$ **e.** After approximately 4 years and 8 months

c.

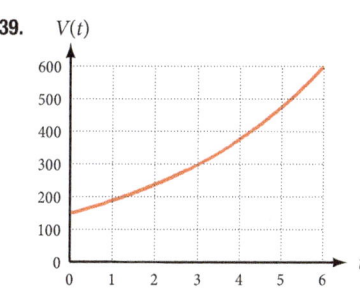

37. $f(1) = 200, f(2) = 800, f(3) = 3,200$

39. $V(t)$

41. **a.** \$0.42   **b.** \$1.00   **c.** \$1.78   **d.** \$17.84

43. 1,258,525 bankruptcies, which is 58,474 less than the actual number.   **45.** **a.** 251,437 cells   **b.** 12,644 cells   **c.** 32 cells

47. $y = \frac{x + 3}{2}$ **49.** $y = \pm\sqrt{x + 3}$ **51.** $y = \frac{2x - 4}{x - 1}$ **53.** $y = x^2 + 3$

Answers to Odd-Numbered Problems

PROBLEM SET 12.2

1. $f^{-1}(x) = \frac{x+1}{3}$ **3.** $f^{-1}(x) = \sqrt[3]{x}$ **5.** $f^{-1}(x) = \frac{x-3}{x-1}$ **7.** $f^{-1}(x) = 4x + 3$ **9.** $f^{-1}(x) = 2(x+3) = 2x + 6$

11. $f^{-1}(x) = \frac{3}{2}(x+3) = \frac{3}{2}x + \frac{9}{2}$ **13.** $f^{-1}(x) = \sqrt[3]{x+4}$ **15.** $f^{-1}(x) = \frac{x+3}{4-2x}$ **17.** $f^{-1}(x) = \frac{1-x}{3x-2}$

19.

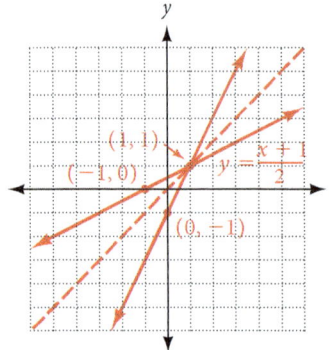

21.

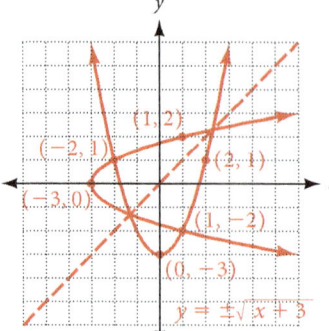

23.

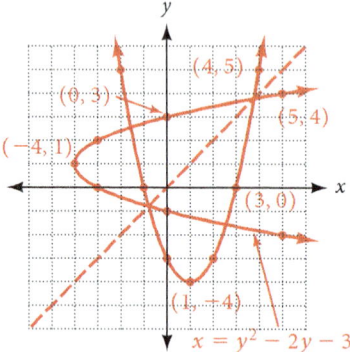

25.

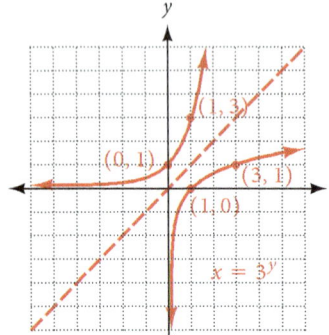

27.

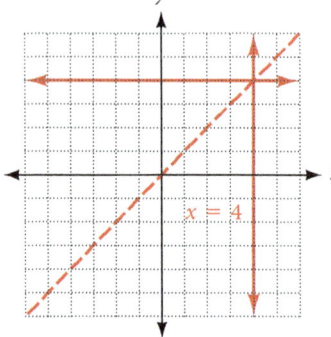

29.

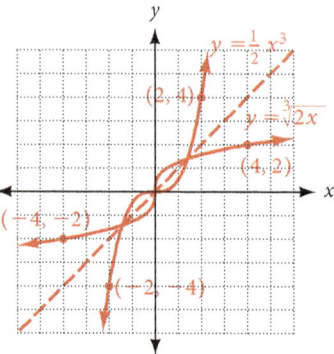

31.

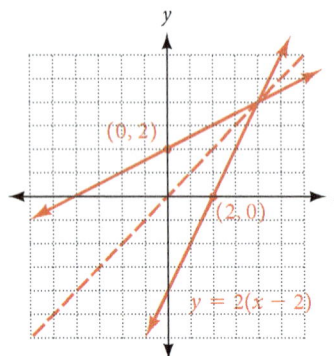

33.

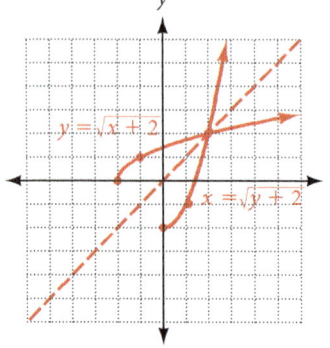

35. **a.** Yes   **b.** No   **c.** Yes

37. **a.** 4   **b.** $\frac{4}{3}$ **c.** 2   **d.** 2   **39.** $f^{-1}(x) = \frac{1}{x}$ **41.** $f^{-1}(x) = 7(x+2) = 7x + 14$

43. **a.** -3 **b.** -6 **c.** 2   **d.** 3   **e.** -2 **f.** 3   **g.** inverses   **45.** **a.** 489.4   **b.** $s^{-1}(t) = \frac{t - 249.4}{16}$ **c.** 2006

47. **a.** 6629.33 ft/s   **b.** $f^{-1}(m) = \frac{15m}{22}$ **c.** 1.36 mph   **49.** $\frac{1}{9}$ **51.** $\frac{2}{3}$ **53.** $\sqrt[3]{4}$ **55.** 3   **57.** 4   **59.** 4   **61.** 1

PROBLEM SET 12.3

1. $\log_2 16 = 4$ **3.** $\log_5 125 = 3$ **5.** $\log_{10} 0.01 = -2$ **7.** $\log_2 \frac{1}{32} = -5$ **9.** $\log_{1/2} 8 = -3$ **11.** $\log_3 27 = 3$ **13.** $10^2 = 100$

15. $2^6 = 64$ **17.** $8^0 = 1$ **19.** $10^{-3} = 0.001$ **21.** $6^2 = 36$ **23.** $5^{-2} = \frac{1}{25}$ **25.** 9   **27.** $\frac{1}{125}$ **29.** 4   **31.** $\frac{1}{3}$ **33.** 2   **35.** $\sqrt[3]{5}$

37. 2   **39.** 6   **41.** $\frac{2}{3}$ **43.** $-\frac{1}{2}$ **45.** $\frac{1}{64}$

47.

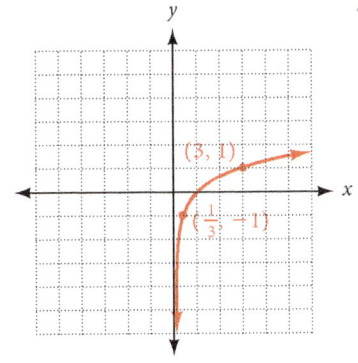

49.

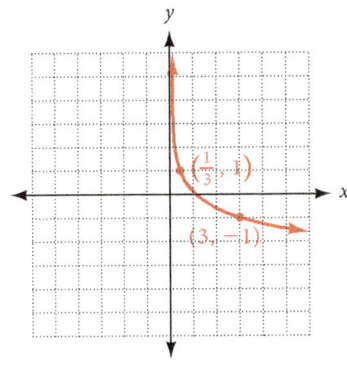

51.

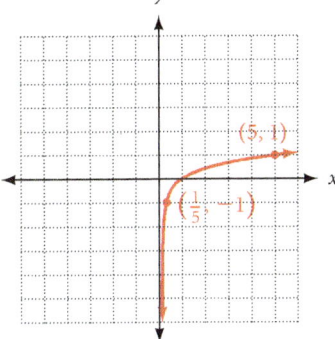

53.

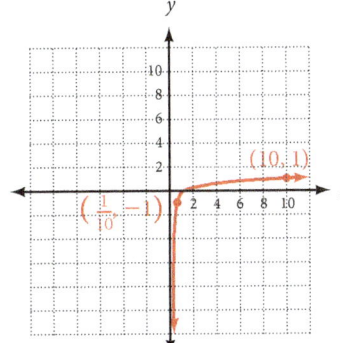

55. $y = 3^x$ **57.** $y = \log_{1/3} x$ **59.** 4 **61.** $\frac{3}{2}$ **63.** 3 **65.** 1 **67.** 0 **69.** 0 **71.** $\frac{1}{2}$

73. $\frac{3}{2}$ **75.** 1 **77.** -2 **79.** 0 **81.** $\frac{1}{2}$

83.

Prefix	Multiplying Factor	$\log_{10}$ (Multiplying Factor)
Nano	0.000 000 001	-9
Micro	0.000 001	-6
Deci	0.1	-1
Giga	1,000,000,000	9
Peta	1,000,000,000,000,000	15

85. 2 **87.** 10^8 times as large **89.** 120 **91.** 4 **93.** $-4, 2$ **95.** $-\frac{11}{8}$ **97.** $2^3 = (x + 2)(x)$ **99.** $3^4 = \frac{x - 2}{x + 1}$

PROBLEM SET 12.4

1. $\log_3 4 + \log_3 x$ **3.** $\log_6 5 - \log_6 x$ **5.** $5 \log_2 y$ **7.** $\frac{1}{3} \log_9 z$ **9.** $2 \log_6 x + 4 \log_6 y$ **11.** $\frac{1}{2} \log_5 x + 4 \log_5 y$

13. $\log_b x + \log_b y - \log_b z$ **15.** $\log_{10} 4 - \log_{10} x - \log_{10} y$ **17.** $2 \log_{10} x + \log_{10} y - \frac{1}{2} \log_{10} z$

19. $3 \log_{10} x + \frac{1}{2} \log_{10} y - 4 \log_{10} z$ **21.** $\frac{2}{3} \log_b x + \frac{1}{3} \log_b y - \frac{4}{3} \log_b z$ **23.** $\frac{2}{3} \log_3 x + \frac{1}{3} \log_3 y - 2 \log_3 z$

25. $2 \log_a 2 + 5 \log_a x - 2 \log_a 3 - 2$ **27.** $\log_b xz$ **29.** $\log_3 \frac{x^2}{y^3}$ **31.** $\log_{10} \sqrt{x} \sqrt[3]{y}$ **33.** $\log_2 \frac{x^3 \sqrt{y}}{z}$ **35.** $\log_2 \frac{\sqrt{x}}{y^3 z^4}$

37. $\log_{10} \frac{x^{3/2}}{y^{3/4} z^{4/5}}$ **39.** $\log_5 \frac{\sqrt{x} \cdot \sqrt[3]{y^2}}{z^4}$ **41.** $\log_3 \frac{x - 4}{x + 4}$ **43.** $\frac{2}{3}$ **45.** 18 **47.** 3 **49.** 3 **51.** 4 **53.** 4 **55.** 1 **57.** 0 **59.** $\frac{3}{2}$

61. 27 **63.** $\frac{5}{3}$ **67. a.** 1.602 **b.** 2.505 **c.** 3.204 **69.** $\text{pH} = 6.1 + \log_{10} x - \log_{10} y$ **71.** 2.52 **73.** 1 **75.** 1 **77.** 4

79. 2.5×10^{-6} **81.** 51

PROBLEM SET 12.5

1. 2.5775 **3.** 1.5775 **5.** 3.5775 **7.** -1.4225 **9.** 4.5775 **11.** 2.7782 **13.** 3.3032 **15.** -2.0128 **17.** -1.5031 **19.** -0.3990

21. 759 **23.** 0.00759 **25.** 1,430 **27.** 0.00000447 **29.** 0.0000000918 **31.** 10^{10} **33.** 10^{-10} **35.** 10^{20} **37.** $\frac{1}{100}$ **39.** 1,000

41. $\frac{1}{e}$ **43.** 25 **45.** $\frac{1}{8}$ **47.** 1 **49.** 5 **51.** x **53.** 4 **55.** -3 **57.** $\frac{3}{2}$ **59.** $\ln 10 + 3t$ **61.** $\ln A - 2t$ **63.** $2 + 3t \log 1.01$

65. $rt + \ln P$ **67.** $3 - \log 4.2$ **69.** 2.7080 **71.** -1.0986 **73.** 2.1972 **75.** 2.7724

77. San Francisco was approx. 2,000 times greater.   **79.**

x	$(1 + x)^{1/x}$
1	2
0.5	2.25
0.1	2.5937
0.01	2.7048
0.001	2.7169
0.0001	2.7181
0.00001	2.7183

81. 2009   **83.** Approximately 3.19

85. 1.78×10^{-5} **87.** 3.16×10^5 **89.** 2.00×10^8 **91.**

Location	Date	Magnitude M	Shockwave T
Moresby Island	Jan. 23	4.0	1.00×10^4
Vancouver Island	Apr. 30	5.3	1.99×10^5
Quebec City	June 29	3.2	1.58×10^3
Mould Bay	Nov. 13	5.2	1.58×10^5
St. Lawrence	Dec. 14	3.7	5.01×10^3

SOURCE: *National Resources Canada, National Earthquake Hazards Program.*

93. 12.9%   **95.** 5.3%   **97.** $\frac{7}{10}$ **99.** 3.1250   **101.** 1.2575   **103.** $t\log 1.05$ **105.** $0.05t$

PROBLEM SET 12.6

1. 1.4650   **3.** 0.6826   **5.** -1.5440 **7.** -0.6477 **9.** -0.3333 **11.** 2   **13.** -0.1845 **15.** 0.1845   **17.** 1.6168   **19.** 2.1131

21. -1 **23.** 1.2275   **25.** 0.3054   **27.** 42.5528   **29.** 6.0147   **31.** 1.333   **33.** 0.75   **35.** 1.3917   **37.** 0.7186   **39.** 2.6356

41. 4.1632   **43.** 5.8435   **45.** -1.0642 **47.** 2.3026   **49.** 10.7144   **51.** 11.72 years   **53.** 9.25 years   **55.** 8.75 years

57. 18.58 years   **59.** 11.55 years   **61.** 18.31 years   **63.** 11.45 years   **65.** October 2018   **67.** 2009   **69.** 1992   **71.** 10.07 years

73. 2000   **75.** $(-2, -23)$, lowest   **77.** $\left(\frac{3}{2}, 9\right)$, highest   **79.** 2 seconds, 64 feet

CHAPTER 12 TEST

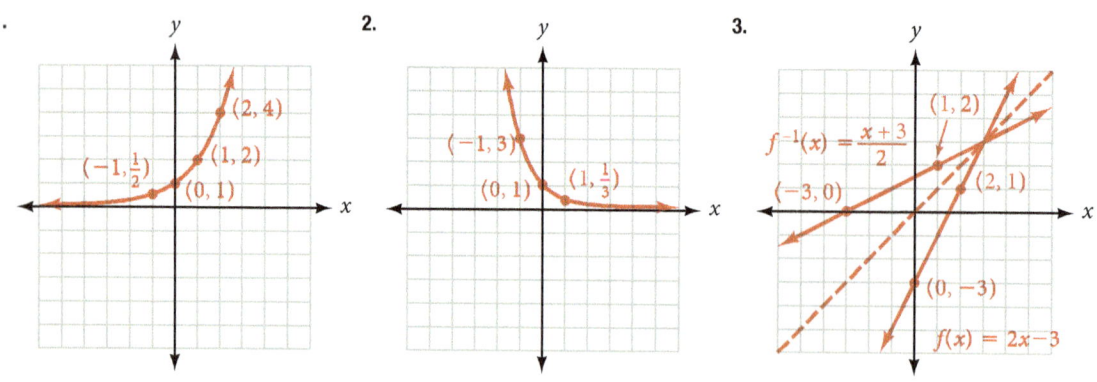

4.

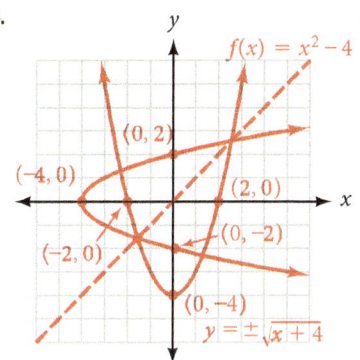

5. 64   **6.** $\sqrt{5}$ **7.**

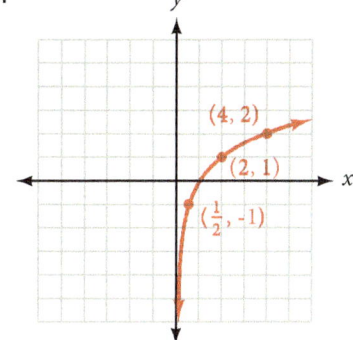

8.

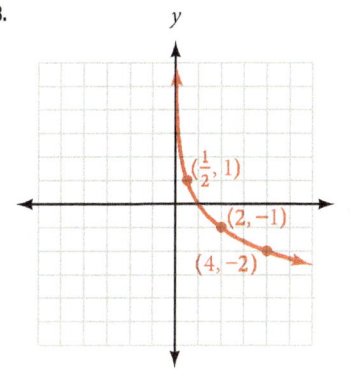

9. $\frac{2}{3}$ **10.** 1.5646   **11.** 4.3692   **12.** -1.9101 **13.** 3.8330   **14.** -3.0748

15. $3 + 2\log_2 x - \log_2 y$ **16.** $\frac{1}{2}\log x - 4\log y - \frac{1}{5}\log z$ **17.** $\log_3 \frac{x^2}{\sqrt{y}}$

18. $\log \frac{\sqrt[3]{x}}{yz^2}$ **19.** 70,404   **20.** 0.00225   **21.** 1.4650   **22.** $\frac{5}{4}$ **23.** 15

24. 8 (-1 does not check)   **25.** 6.18   **26.** \$651.56   **27.** 13.87 years   **28.** \$7,373

Index